W9-CFA-401

(Continued on back endpapers)

FINANCIAL
ACCOUNTING

An Introduction to Decision Making

Henry Dauderis

Concordia University

Holt, Rinehart and Winston of Canada, Limited, Toronto

Canadian Cataloguing in Publication Data

Dauderis, Henry, 1941–
    Financial accounting : an introduction to
decision making

Includes bibliographical references and index.
ISBN 0-03-921809-0

1. Accounting. I. Title.

HF5635.D38 1987   657'.044   C86-094299-6

Acquisitions Editor: Michael Roche
Editorial Co-ordinator: Edie Franks
Production Co-ordinator: Karen Eakin
Copy Editor: Susan Quirk
Cover Design: Peter Maher
Interior Design: Blair Kerrigan
Cover Photo: Pete Turner/The Image Bank Canada
Typesetting and Assembly: Compeer Typographic Services Limited

Printed in Canada

    2 3 4 5   91 90 89 88 87

To Anne and Mary

CONTENTS IN BRIEF: ACCOUNTING CYCLES

The above Contents in Brief groups chapters by individual cycle. Manufacturing Operations, for example, is part of the conversion cycle; however, for pedagogical reasons it is discussed out of the cycle sequence in this text. Likewise, Business Combinations is part of the investment cycle but is also covered later in the text.

CONTENTS

Financial Accounting: An Introduction to Decision Making is a text designed for use in the first financial accounting course. It is intended for students who require an understanding of issues that face users of financial statements, such as the big picture, accounting and accountants, the social responsibilities of the accountant, and the rules of the game. Business administration and commerce majors will find that the "cycles" orientation that the text adopts facilitates the application of their accounting knowledge to other courses, such as finance, marketing, management, quantitative methods, and M.I.S., they have or will study. After completion of their first accounting course, accounting majors will find themselves at the cutting-edge for such courses as computer-based information systems, electronic data processing, and auditing. Students majoring in other academic disciplines, but enrolled in a beginning financial accounting course, will have become accounting literate by having been exposed to the issues with which accounting as the language of business is involved.

The Big Picture

Canadian professional accountants are creatures of their environment. This environment includes, but is not limited to, the nature of the economy, and the political orientation of the provincial and federal governments. Accountants collect, analyze, evaluate, interpret, and report on the myriad of transactions occurring among individuals, corporations, and institutions of this environment. The challenge to professional and academic accountants, as well as to managers and other readers of financial statements is to become sufficiently familiar with the language of business to be able to identify financial diarrhea whenever it occurs and to make decisions on the basis of fact, and not fiction.

As you read and study this text, a number of non-accounting situations will challenge you. One of these will be the national debt. A large part of Canada's national income is required to service its national debt, a legacy of past governments, and, in effect, a mortgage that you and future generations will have to deal with. To put it in perspective, one-half of all monies received by the federal government in 1987 will go toward financing the national debt. This increased national debt, if coupled with classical inflation, could lead to a collapsed economy. Similarly, the current controversy about increasing or decreasing contributions to unemployment insurance payments, implementing universal medicare, indexing old age pensions, and augmenting the amount of welfare payments requested by recipients could have ramifications for the health of the national debt. The paths that governments take for these issues, such as lowering or raising taxes, and/or changing the method by which they collect monies, could lead to economic and social prosperity, or to economic collapse.

Following along the same lines is the case for the reliance on debt within an accounting entity which could lead to prosperity and growth for that entity or to economic failure and bankruptcy. The recent collapse of two chartered banks and the high failure rate of small businesses in Canada are examples of debt reliance that have lead to economic failure. Whichever course of action is undertaken by an entity, the accountant will be faced with the challenge of collecting, analyzing, evaluating, and interpreting the financial events that occur. The user of financial statements can appreciate the nature of the challenge only if he or she is accounting literate. This is why the big picture and the topics interwoven throughout this text are important and should be incorporated into the first accounting course in accordance with curriculum requirements.

It is no secret that technology is revolutionizing the management process and, in particular, the information-collection and dissemination system which is at the heart of the accounting process. For example, the widespread use of computers is causing frightening social and emotional problems. Students learning financial accounting should learn to look beyond the numbers contained in the financial statements and should become aware of the social responsibility of the entity. The social responsibility of the accountant is explored in Conceptual Issue 1-1 contributed by Robert Anderson of the University of Regina.

The Rules of the Game

This text recognizes that professional accountants belong to a self-regulating profession that establishes its own rules. These rules, referred to as generally accepted accounting principles (GAAP), are codified in the *CICA Handbook* and have a quasi-legal status in Canada. Accordingly, as professionals, accountants agree to follow a code of ethical conduct. This conduct, however, must recognize the public interest and the changing environment. There is therefore the necessity of understanding, designing, and applying GAAP to protect the public interest, and to adapt the current environment.

In addition to the role of the *CICA Handbook*, the Canadian Academic Accounting Association and its publication, *Contemporary Accounting Research*, edited by Haim Falk of McMaster University, also contribute to the design and application of GAAP by accounting professionals. An article such as "Auditors and Deceptive Financial Statements: Assigning Responsibility and Blame" by J.C. Gaa and C.H. Smith (C.A.R. Vol. 1/No. 2/Spring 1985), is an excellent example of how the environment within which the professional accountant operates is changing, and of how the profession is and should be reacting to these changes.

Lyman MacInnis, FCA, president of the CICA, described the situation as follows:

> We are in the middle of an era of tremendous change. The very underpinnings of our economy are changing. We are no longer a manufacturing economy: we are now a service and communications based economy. And those are our products: service and communication. Information travels faster and is disseminated more broadly than ever before in history. And information is primarily what we deal in." (From *Dialogue*, published by the CICA, November 1986, p. 1.)

You Can't Tell the Actors Without a Program

A unique feature of this text is its organization around cycles occurring naturally within an entity. Not only does this structure organize topics into a relevant and meaningful format, but it also integrates with the structure of other courses which delve further into one or more of these cycles. Part One of this text introduces the accounting process and gives an overview of the conceptual foundations that underly the study of financial accounting. Part Two describes the revenue-expenditure cycle, and introduces accounting systems. Part Three deals with the conversion cycle. Chapter 18, which describes accounting for manufacturing operations, can be covered with chapters 8 and 9 to highlight the focus on cycles. Part Four discusses the financing cycle that is critical in the evaluation of an entity. The debt to equity ratio, for example, is one situation that will challenge you as you study this text. Part Five describes the investment cycle and includes a chapter on business combinations. Part Six concludes the introductory financial accounting course with a discussion of disclosure and the financial reporting issues facing the reader of financial statements. An overview of the cycles approach of this text is outlined in the Contents in Brief on page v.

Text Orientation

The introductory financial accounting course is continuously evolving. The last decade saw a debate among accounting faculties about course content and the purpose of an accounting course. In Canada, there was also the desire to reflect on the various segments of Canadian business that financial accounting serves. My intention for writing *Financial Accounting: An Introduction to Decision Making* was to satisfy the different needs of instructors and students. One of my focuses was to make the text clear and readable, and the material understandable to students. This, I believed, would allow instructors more class time to concentrate on the concepts and their applications. One of the most compelling reasons for writing an original Canadian text instead of adapting a U.S. text was the different environment represented in texts originating in other countries. Accordingly, a solely Canadian text permitted me to tailor its contents to the needs of Canadian accounting students and instructors. Hence, the Real Life Examples, Conceptual Issues, and Discussion Cases included in the text offer a range of settings found solely in the Canadian business environment.

This text is designed to be user friendly. The following are some of its features.

1. Student Orientation

The chapter material is clear and readable. Much attention has been paid to text layout, explanatory notes, figures, and the boxed high-interest examples.

2. Teaching Flexibility

Each chapter contains sub-sections that allow the instructor great flexibility in course design. Individual sections can be omitted without compromising continuity. Because of the detailed attention spent on the development of this text, I feel that it can be understood by the student thus allowing the instructor greater flexibility for teaching more interesting and challenging topics. Furthermore, this text has been divided into sections that I feel allows its eighteen chapters to fit into a comprehensible whole. Instructors may wish to teach a chapter or chapters out of order to emphasize certain topics.

3. Assignment Material

The assignment material included in the text is the most complete and varied available. Eight types of assignment material are available to instructors at the end of the chapters, including different levels of directed and non-directed requirements. The Assignment Material consists of: Discussion Questions, Discussion Cases, Comprehension Problems, Problems, Alternate Problems, Decision Problems, Supplementary Problems, and Review Problems. The Assignment Material has been designed to be flexible and to allow instructors to assign the material at the levels and depths of their students' analytical abilities.

4. Accelerated Coverage

This text has been designed to allow maximum flexibility early in the course. The first four chapters, therefore, allow for accelerated coverage.

5. Computer Compatibility

The same terminology and chart of accounts is used throughout the text thus eliminating unlearning and confusion. The general ledger package available with this text is also identical to this chart of accounts. I would like to thank Brenda Mallouk of the University of Toronto who tested *PC General Ledger* in class and provided me with a detailed list of the problems that she encountered in using a general ledger system in the introductory financial accounting course. It is my hope that the manual that accompanies this package will minimize many of the problems associated with integrating the computer into the first accounting course.

6. Impact of Inflation

The impact of inflation is discussed wherever appropriate throughout the text. However, this material is optional and can easily be omitted. A complete section in Chapter 15, however, has been added on the effects of changing prices and can be incorporated into an earlier coverage of this topic.

7. Real Life Examples

Numerous Real Life Examples are used to emphasize the concepts and issues discussed. The Real Life Examples have been boxed to allow instructors to skip over some of them and to facilitate student review. A sample of a Real Life Example that might interest an instructor of accounting follows:

Real Life Example

Drexel exams: No more blue books

Drexel University accounting students are taking their final exam on Apple Computer Inc.'s Macintosh personal computer. In addition, students in Accounting B101 are doing their homework on "Macs." As at many engineering and technical schools, all incoming freshmen are required to buy computers. "It takes more time to assign all the homework and put tests on the Mac, but I think it's worth it," says Professor Henry Dauderis. In the two-hour final exam, students are required to prepare and print out a worksheet, an income statement for a merchandising firm and closing entries. One benefit: less cheating since "it's harder to see something off someone else's monitor," says Dauderis.

Source   Computerline: A Quick Read on Trends in Personal Computing, *USA Today*, April 17, 1986.

---

8. Conceptual Issues

Several individuals have contributed to the Conceptual Issues in the text. Their contributions have allowed for greater exploration of the issues not normally covered in introductory texts. It is my hope that the Real Life Examples and the Conceptual Issues will motivate students, and will dissuade the view that accounting is only "number crunching."

9. Running Glossary

All technical terms are defined in the page margin when they are first introduced. This eliminates the tendency that many students have of guess reading. By defining the term where it appears the students will easily see what the definition is, and will not substitute what they think it means. Two examples of terms that an introductory student will encounter are **entity concept** and **generally accepted accounting principles**.

10. Supplementary Materials

The ancillary package that accompanies *Financial Accounting: An Introduction to Decision Making* is among the most complete available. A description follows of the carefully developed student and instructor supplements.

For the Student

Self Study Guide

Authored by Esther Deutsch of Ryerson Polytechnical Institute, this study guide identifies Learning Objectives, contains Chapter Overviews, True-False Questions, and Multiple Choice Questions, and has Practice Problems with complete and detailed solutions.

Working Papers

Prepared by Steve Martin of John Abbott College, this complete set of working papers is provided in order to minimize the formatting aspects of accounting assignments.

Practice Set

Authored by Joe Figueredo of Vanier College, this practice set provides students with an opportunity to apply accounting concepts and procedures to a merchandising concern. The Practice Set can be solved manually or can be assigned with the use of an IBM-PC computer package — The Freelance Accounting System.

For the Instructor

Computer Disks

The IBM *PC General Ledger* Package which includes the Chart of Accounts for the Bluebeard Computer Corporation, the fictitious in-text entity, is available free of charge to adopters of the text. As well, several problems from the text have been adapted for use in conjunction with *Lotus 1-2-3* by Steve Spector. Contact your local Holt representative for information regarding the *PC General Ledger* Package and the *Lotus 1-2-3* templates.

Solutions Manual

This manual provides suggested solutions to all assignment material from the text. Special care has been taken to provide full and complete solutions with explanations. The solutions were prepared by Vittoria Fortunato of the University of Toronto and myself.

Instructor's Manual

The instructor's manual identifies learning objectives and the key terms introduced in the chapters. The manual includes Lecture Outlines, Lecture Topics, and a summary of the Assignment Material for each chapter. Also included is the material on the computer disks (both the *PC General Ledger Package* and the *Lotus 1-2-3* disks), and the solutions to the *Practice Set* that accompanies the text.

Transparencies

The transparencies of the solutions to all the Problems, Alternate Problems, Supplementary Problems, and Review Problems are available upon adoption of the text.

ACKNOWLEDGEMENTS

This text would not have been possible without the suggestions and advice of colleagues, students, and others. Especially helpful were the comments, support, and suggestions, of the following individuals:

T. Anderson	University of Ottawa
R.L. Benke Jr.	James Madison University
M.R. Bates	University of Guelph
T. Beechy	York University
L. Branchaud	Ordre des comptables agréés du Québec
D. Charron	Concordia University
P.E. Dascher	Drexel University
E. Deutsch	Ryerson Polytechnical Institute
D. Ferries	Algonquin College
V. Fortunato	University of Toronto
M. Gibbins	University of Alberta
G. Hirtle	Northern Alberta Institute of Technology
M.W. Hopkins	University of Southern California
R. Kapoor	Concordia University
H.V.V. Rao	Drexel University
P. Salomon	McGill University
C.A. Srinivasan	Drexel University
B. Trenholm	University of New Brunswick

Special thanks go to Esther Deutsch of Ryerson who authored the *Study Guide*, Steve Martin of John Abbott College who prepared the *Working Papers*, and Vittoria Fortunato of the University of Toronto who prepared some of the solutions and reviewed them all. I am indebted to the faculty members and students at both Concordia University and Drexel University. I had the opportunity to integrate the computer into the introductory financial accounting course, including the first examinations taken by students using a spreadsheet program and a microcomputer. Without the stimulating environments that these schools provided this text would not have been possible.

Special thanks go to Michael Roche who delayed this text one and a half years and made it better. Michael had the foresight and the willingness to put in long hours to ensure that the text would become a standard by which other accounting texts would be measured. I would also like to thank Ron Munro, Vice-President of the Holt, Rinehart and Winston College Division, for always being there and being supportive, Richard Kitowski, the publisher, and Louis Tetu, the local sales representative in Montreal. I also appreciate the work contributed to the project by Susan Quirk, the copy editor, and by Anna Kress, Publishing Services Manager, Karen Eakin, Production Co-ordinator, Edie Franks, Editorial Co-ordinator, and Franca Cesario, Editorial Assistant, at Holt Rinehart and Winston. They were able to understand the difficulties that are encountered in writing an accounting text, and were able to accommodate all of the peculiar demands that an accounting text presented.

Henry Danders

Montreal, Quebec

Whatever your motivation for taking the course for which this text is being used, you are about to begin the study of accounting. This prologue outlines the importance of financial accounting in Canadian business. In Canada, transactions are completed in terms of Canadian dollars. These dollars constitute numerical units that accountants have accepted as being the most appropriate method of recording transactions and communicating them to interested parties who use the reported amounts to evaluate business organizations, whether profit-oriented or not.

The term *accounting process* is applied to the way in which the dollar amount of transactions is transformed into financial statement information for communication purposes. This process consists of three steps, as shown in Figure 1.

Step 1: Transactions are analyzed and recorded

Transactions are first analyzed and then recorded in a manner that has gradually evolved for this purpose. This recording process is often referred to as *bookkeeping*, and those involved in this work are usually called *bookkeepers*. The increased use of computers has greatly reduced the manual work required.

Step 2: Transactions are summarized

This step is usually referred to as *classifying accounting information*. Accounting information is accumulated for the entity and a total calculated for each related group

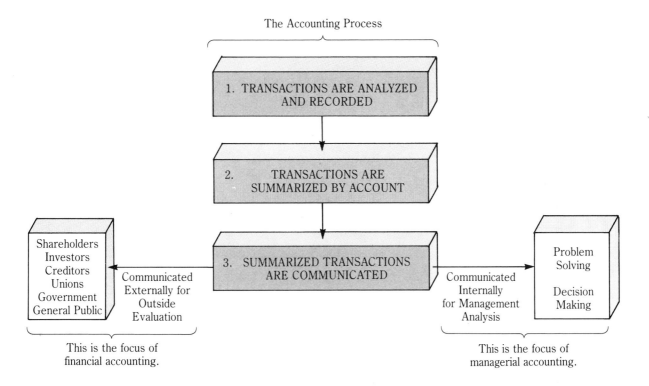

Figure 1   The accounting process and its uses

of transactions at the end of a time period, so that the financial information can be communicated.

Step 3: *Transactions are communicated*
The summarized transactions are communicated through the preparation and distribution of financial statements at regular time intervals. These statements satisfy external reporting requirements and also management's need for information on which to base decisions and problem solving.

The focus of financial accounting is the communication of information generated through the accounting process; this information is communicated externally for analysis and evaluation through the publication of financial statements. Financial accounting is inter-related with management accounting, which is accounting that focuses on the internal use of financial data for analysis and evaluation of future courses of action.

Information generated by the accounting process is also used by management in analyzing the entity's operations and evaluating future courses of action. The financial results of future courses of action are subsequently reported through the preparation of financial statements; financial statement users can then evaluate the results.

As you read through the chapters of this text, you should gain an appreciation of accounting that will serve you well in your career. Note that the numbers that appear in this and any other accounting text appear to be artificial; in fact, marketing, management, and external economic factors such as inflation directly influence the results generated by accountants. The contents of this text should bridge this gap and provide you with a true appreciation of the role of financial accounting in the business world.

PART ONE

The Accounting Process

Accountants must be familiar with the accounting process in order to understand the methods underlying the accumulation of financial information and to direct the efforts of bookkeepers responsible for the recording and summarizing of this information. Familiarity with accounting methods is also required for making sound interpretations of the information communicated in the financial statements and for adjusting recorded information as necessary. The techniques for adjusting financial information to meet the requirements of generally accepted accounting principles are explained and illustrated in chapters 1 to 4.

Financial Statements and the Accounting Model

Accountants communicate financial information to interested users for decision-making purposes. The answers to the following questions are discussed in Chapter 1.

1. What is a financial transaction from the accountant's point of view?
2. In what way do financial transactions constitute one of the boundaries of accounting?
3. What specialized vocabulary is used to condense transactions?
4. How are financial transactions completed in Canada?
5. How do accountants communicate financial information to interested parties?
6. What is the entity concept, and how is it also one of the boundaries of accounting?
7. What are the advantages and disadvantages of different forms of business organization?
8. Which accounting report measures profitability? financial position?
9. In what way does financial accounting differ from managerial accounting?
10. What was Luca Pacioli's role in establishing the accounting model?
11. Accountants view financial transactions as economic events that change components within the accounting equation. What are these components and how do they change?
12. How does the accounting process transform transactions into financial statement data?
13. How do shareholders participate in day-to-day management?
14. What is the distinction between a calendar year-end and a fiscal year-end?
15. What impact does the periodicity concept have on the reporting of financial information?

A. Financial Statements

Accounting
The process of recording, classifying, and accumulating financial transactions of an entity; the reporting of these transactions to interested individuals through the preparation of financial statements; the interpretation of these financial statements.

Asset
Anything of value that is owned; often referred to as an *economic resource.*

Liability
An obligation to pay an asset or to provide a service or goods in the future.

Transaction
An exchange of assets, obligations, services, or goods.

Financial transaction
The financial aspect of a transaction; expressed in terms of dollars in Canada.

Financial accounting
A method of accounting that focuses on the analysis of financial transactions, in order to provide financial information to interested parties.

Entity
A unit of accountability that exists separately from its owners; the term *legal entity* is used when referring to a corporation, which has a legal existence separate from its owners.

Accounting is often called the language of business. Like any language, **accounting** is used to communicate information, in this case, financial information. Like any language, too, accounting has its own special vocabulary. Two commonly used terms are *assets* and *liabilities*. **Assets** consist of anything that has value and is owned. **Liabilities** are obligations to pay an asset at some time in the future, or to perform a service or provide goods at a later date.

Assets are continually being exchanged, as are obligations; each exchange is referred to as a **transaction**. Any exchange of an asset for another asset is also a transaction. Acceptance of an obligation in return for an asset is also a transaction. Because exchanges usually involve dollar amounts, they are called **financial transactions**. Understanding **financial accounting** is essentially a matter of understanding financial transactions.

For example, a financial transaction occurs when the Hudson's Bay Company exchanges a cash asset for land and buildings assets. Or, instead of paying cash, the company may incur a liability in the form of a mortgage. The mortgage is an obligation to pay an asset at a later date.

The Entity Concept

There are always two or more parties to each transaction. Accountants view each party as a separate financial unit — that is, as a separate entity. An **entity** can be thought of as a unit of accountability that exists separately from other units of accountability and also exists separately from those who own the entity. The accountant for the entity focuses only on the transactions of the business, which he/she translates into accounting information.

1. Business transactions are translated into accounting information.
2. In selecting transactions to be translated into accounting information, the accountant is only interested in those affecting the unit of accountability, or entity.

In Canada, entities seek to use their assets in activities that will not only increase the value of the assets but will also increase the total assets of the entity. For example, the Hudson's Bay Company operates a chain of department stores where assets, in the form of merchandise, are exchanged for customers' assets, usually in the form of cash but sometimes in the form of credit. Similarly, Petro-Canada uses its assets in the exploration of oil, so that the oil can be exchanged for other assets of its customers. Both of these entities provide goods in exchange for assets belonging to others. Other entities provide services that they exchange for assets belonging to others. The emphasis in chapters 1 to 4 is on a company that provides a service. In Chapter 5, the focus is on companies that provide goods, commonly referred to as merchandising. In Chapter 18, accounting for manufacturing operations is introduced.

Some entities are more successful than other entities in the performance of the activities for which they were formed; accounting information is necessary to measure the progress of each entity and to conform with legal requirements. This information is reported in terms of dollars, and the accounting reports that communicate this information are commonly referred to as *financial statements*. Financial accounting is the process of recording transactions and preparing financial statements for external users.

Financial Statements

Statement of retained earnings
A statement showing the changes that have occurred in retained earnings during a particular time period.

Statement of changes in financial position (SCFP)
A statement showing the sources and uses of working capital, or resources, or cash during the fiscal year.

Income statement
A financial report summarizing the entity's progress during a time period; summarizes revenue earned and expenses incurred, and calculates net income for the period.

Net income
The excess of revenues over expenses during a period of time.

Net loss
The excess of expenses over revenue for a period of time.

Balance sheet
A financial report showing the assets, liabilities, and equities of an entity on a specific date; also referred to as a *statement of financial position* or *a statement of financial condition*.

Accrual method of accounting
Method of accounting that recognizes revenues when they are earned and expenses when they are incurred; ignores when cash is received or paid in recognizing revenues or expenses; also referred to as accrual basis of accounting.

A standard format for financial statements has been developed by accountants and the users of accounting reports. Two of the most widely used statements are the income statement and the balance sheet. These are discussed in the sections which follow. Two additional statements, **the statement of retained earnings** and **the statement of changes in financial position**, are introduced subsequently in chapters 4 and 16, respectively. These four main financial statements are prepared by accountants and are usually accompanied by supplementary information in notes.

The **income statement** communicates the inflow of assets (called *revenues*) and the outflow or consumption of assets (called *expenses*) resulting from the entity's activities. An excess of inflows over outflows is called **net income**. An excess of outflows over inflows is called a **net loss**.

The **balance sheet** communicates the balances of what the entity owns (called *assets*), what the entity owes (called *liabilities*), and the difference between the assets and the liabilities, called *equity*. The equity amount represents the balance that belongs to the owners of the entity.

The Income Statement

The income statement can be compared to a movie camera with a counter that continually records transactions of an entity; the counter accumulates these transactions while the camera records them. The income statement, however, is very selective, in that it accumulates only the revenue and expense transactions of the entity. When the camera stops, the counter shows the accumulated total of all these revenue and expense transactions.

In the adjacent income statement of Bluebeard Computer Corporation (BCC), the camera was started on November 1, and was stopped at November 30, and the counter shows a net income of $2,000. In this income statement the expenses of the November time period are deducted from the revenue of the same time period. Identifying expenses and revenues with a time period is referred to as the **accrual method of accounting**.

Bluebeard Computer Corporation
Income Statement
For the Month Ended November 30, 19X1

Revenue		
Repair Revenue		$7,000
Expenses		
Rent Expense	$ 600	
Salaries Expense	2,500	
Supplies Used	1,200	
Truck Expense	700	
Total Expenses		5,000
Net Income		$2,000

When the camera begins again in December, the counter continues to accumulate revenue and expense transactions; that is, it adds the December transactions to those of November.

One film is used for each 12-month time period. At the end of the year, the exposed film is removed and a new film is inserted for the next 12 months. When the new film is inserted, the counter in the camera is automatically reset to zero; in this way only the transactions of the new year are accumulated. The income statement is therefore referred to as a period-of-time financial statement.

What Is Revenue?

Revenue An inflow of assets to an entity in return for services performed or goods sold during that period.

Revenue consists of the inflow of assets to an entity in return for services performed or goods sold during that period. It is expressed in terms of dollars. In the case of Bluebeard Computer Corporation, the services performed are computer repairs.

What Are Expenses?

Expenses An outflow of assets or the resources of an entity used up, or obligations incurred during a time period, in the course of performing revenue-earning services.

Expenses represent either an outflow or consumption of assets, or the resources belonging to the entity that have been used up, or the obligations incurred in performing the revenue-earning services. The Bluebeard Computer Corporation uses parts, for example, to make repairs; these parts are a resource of the entity used up in performing repairs. These expenses represent the outflow or consumption of assets needed to earn the $7,000 revenue.

What Is Net Income?

The difference between revenue and expenses is called net income. It is a guide for the reader of the income statement as to how profitably the activities of the entity are being conducted; it is a measure of success of the entity. The net income calculation is also used in calculating taxes payable to government, and it is one criterion used to determine the amount of dividends to be paid. (*Dividends* are payments made by a corporation to its owners and are never included in an income statement.)

Net income is the difference between revenue and expense. The accumulated net income that has not been paid as dividends is referred to as retained earnings. The accounting for dividends is further discussed in Chapter 5; the preparation of a statement of retained earnings is illustrated at the fiscal year-end of Bluebeard Computer Corporation, discussed in Chapter 5.

The Balance Sheet

The balance sheet can be compared to a snapshot camera that produces a picture of the entity at a point in time. In the adjacent balance sheet of Bluebeard Computer Corporation, the snapshot was made on November 30. It shows the corporate assets, liabilities, and equity on that date. A balance sheet can be compiled whenever necessary but is *always* taken at the end of the corporation's business year. The balance sheet is therefore referred to as a point-in-time financial statement.

The economic resources owned by the entity are listed as assets on the balance sheet; these assets are individually described and their cost is indicated. Those having a claim against these assets are listed as liabilities and equities. Note that the total amount of assets equals the total claims against those assets. The date of the balance sheet is important because it identifies the date at which the assets owned and the existing claims against the assets are listed.

Bluebeard Computer Corporation
Balance Sheet
At November 30, 19X1

Assets		Liabilities		
Cash	$ 5,000	Bank Loan	$ 5,000	
Accounts Receivable	3,000	Accounts Payable	1,000	
Equipment	2,000	Total Liabilities		$ 6,000
Truck	8,000			
		Equity		
		Common Stock	$10,000	
		Net Income	2,000	12,000
		Total Liabilities and		
Total Assets	$18,000	Equity		$18,000

The term *balance sheet* is widely used in Canada. However, other titles that are more descriptive of the statement's purpose are also used: *statement of financial position* and *statement of financial condition*.

What Is an Asset?

An asset was broadly defined at the beginning of this chapter as being anything of value owned by the entity. Assets include tangible resources, such as equipment and a truck, as well as other resources, such as accounts receivable and patents. To be called assets, they must have some future value to the entity in generating revenue; the recorded asset cost does not necessarily indicate the asset's current value, the cost of replacing the asset, nor how much it could be sold for if offered for sale. Assets are recorded at cost because cost is an objective amount resulting from arm's-length bargaining between a buyer and seller. Accounts receivable, for example, represent an amount due to be collected for goods sold or services rendered.

What Is a Liability?

A liability was defined at the beginning of this chapter as an obligation to pay some asset in the future, or to provide a service or goods at some later date. Until the obligation is paid, creditors have a claim against the assets of the entity. For example, a bank loan is an obligation to repay cash in the future including the amount borrowed as well as interest. Accounts payable are obligations to pay a supplier for goods purchased or services rendered.

What Is Equity?

Owners' equity represents the amount of net assets owing to the owners of the entity. In the case of Bluebeard Computer Corporation, this equity belongs to shareholders; it is shareholders who own a corporation. Equity is the balance that remains after liabilities are deducted from assets. In BCC's November 30 balance sheet, equity is calculated as $12,000 ($18,000 assets minus $6,000 liabilities).

What Is Common Stock?

Common stock
The class of shares that is a basic ownership unit in a corporation. Ownership carries the right to vote and to share in dividends.

Common stock represents all the common shares that are the ownership interest of shareholders in the net assets (assets minus liabilities) of the corporation. A share certificate (sometimes referred to as a stock certificate) represents a unit of ownership in the corporation; it is nothing more than an elaborately printed piece of paper indicating a particular investor's writ of ownership. A typical share certificate is illustrated in Figure 1-1.

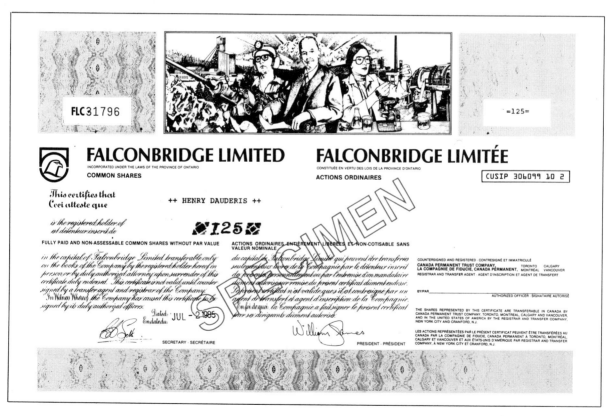

Figure 1-1   A typical share certificate

Conceptual Issue 1-1

Social Responsibility

Robert H. Anderson, University of Regina

There is more to a business operation than accounting reports show. As illustrated by Figure 1 (on p. 1), accounting deals with transactions that at present are limited to financial transactions which accountants view as economic events. Thus the accounting model introduced in Figure 1 is limited to what can be objectively measured in dollars. The net income, often referred to as profit, does not show the effect on the corporation of everything it does; it only summarizes the financial transactions. One of the unreported aspects is social responsibility.

Social responsibility is the need for all individuals and institutions, governments, not-for-profit organizations, corporations, and other businesses to assess the effect of decisions and actions taken from those decisions, on the entire social system. That most basic and important concept of accounting, the entity concept, no longer applies in its accounting meaning. Social responsibility concerns the total costs and benefits to a larger entity, society, not solely to the accounting entity. Some attempts have been made to develop social responsibility performance measurement systems or social responsibility accounting systems, that is, a systematic assessment of and reporting on those parts of an organization's activities that have a social impact. Very little is done in actual practice.

The interest in and concern about social responsibility has grown from two major forces that are related to each other. The first is an increasing awareness by the public of the power and control that corporations have which leads to a need for accountability to the public. The second is an increasing decline in the popularity (or increase in the unpopularity) of business. Because the public is generally better educated, questioning, discerning, and informed, the public holds increased social, moral, and economic expectations of corporations; widespread doubts have developed about how responsible business corporations in particular are, resulting mainly from the power and control corporations can exercise.

Research over the past 25 years shows that significantly fewer Canadians view business favourably than was the case in the early 1960s, while many more view business unfavourably over the same period. Part of this decline in business acceptability is a result of media communication of the flaws in business people and their organizations, particularly in relation to the issues of the environment and bribery. Environmental damage that can be directly attributed to a specific firm is an instant news item. A cartoon in the New Yorker expresses the bribery issue well, showing a smiling corporate executive saying, "It looks as if, this year, our kickbacks will exceed our bribes!" This common view of corporations contributes to their declining popularity. Also contributing is the largeness, inflexibility, and conservatism of business institutions especially in the area of consumer affairs. The matter of a small consumer fighting a huge corporation over a defective product induces distrust of the corporation and cheers for the individual. This lack of acceptability leads to a need for business to be able to explain its role more understandably. For corporations, this does not mean to not consider profits; profit-making remains an important social responsibility. It does mean making profits in a socially acceptable way, that is, in a positive, constructive manner — not by taking advantage of corporate power.

Similar social responsibilities exist for not-for-profit institutions as well as for individuals, and, in particular, professionals. Society expects that anyone privileged with professional status ought to use his/her talents for something more than individual advancement and benefit.

The main arguments for having organizations accept increased social responsibility can be summarized as follows:

• It will serve their interests in the long run by promoting a better public image, providing a better operational environment, and ensuring the long-run viability of business. Corporations exist at the will of society and must produce social benefits if they are to survive. In the past, if a product was salable, it was considered socially acceptable; this is no longer so.

• Corporations are more likely to have the resources—both human and financial—to solve social problems.

• Corporations should seek to balance power with responsibility. The public and government may be more tolerant of concentrated corporate economic power if increased social responsibility goes with it.

• Increased social responsibility will help business to avoid further government intervention and regulation. Social action, either through corporate acceptance or through government intervention, is inevitable. If corporations initiate the action, they'll have more effect in determining what it will be. Also prevention is easier than curing; governments seem to concentrate on curing.

• The public now expects more of business and, as part of the public, so do shareholders. They have diverse ownership and individual interests and thus benefit or suffer from corporate activities in the environment external to the corporation.

• Increased social responsibility may provide hidden profit opportunities for corporations. Sometimes problems turn into profits. For example, pollution-control requirements have already brought profit opportunities to many corporations making the necessary equipment.

There are, however, equally strong arguments against corporations accepting increased social responsibility:

• Corporations should be concerned only with profit maximization, as this is their fundamental purpose. The costs of social involvement could drive marginal firms out of business, in turn, increasing social costs not only through lost jobs but through giving the surviving firms more concentrated powers.

• Corporations already have enough power; social power should not be added, especially with the current lack of accountability. Also, since co-ordinated efforts among numerous corporations are often needed to accomplish social objectives, this co-operation would further increase concentration and power.

• Corporations do not have the required social skills. They are equipped to do only certain jobs well and should concentrate on those jobs. Such is the basis of the North American competitive economic system.

• With a basic need for profit, can corporate managers be relied on to continue to be socially responsible in difficult economic times? Often social costs outweigh social benefits, especially when considered in terms of a single firm; social responsibility programs are likely to be dropped quickly when business drops off.

• Managers are not very good at recognizing public consensus on social concerns and their priorities. If managers are to serve the interests of society as a whole, then ultimately they must be controlled by governments that can determine politically what social priorities exist.

Whether they should or not, corporations have, for the most part, accepted some sort of social responsibility. They already spend money on, or allocate employee time to, social action programs, athletic sponsorship, or community services without expecting any income as a result of these expenditures. Therefore, what is important is to formulate accounting principles for measuring, reporting, and auditing social programs.

Three basic assumptions underly an increased public demand for social responsibility and the increased corporate need for some attempt at measurement and accountability. The first assumption is that management wants socially responsible behaviour. This aim is not always obvious in actions taken, particularly with respect to protection of the environment. However, it is true that corporate management generally supports socially responsible behaviour. The second assumption is that finances limit social investments. That is, corporations do not have unlimited money to spend on socially responsible activities: a sound assumption. The third assumption is that increased social performance requires improved efficiency in order to compensate for the second assumption of scarce resources. That is, some method of measuring the effectiveness of spending on social objectives would help to allocate scarce resources.

A report on the measurement of social responsibility performance can range from a simple, totally subjective report, that describes actions taken, to a complex report completely in dollars. The following list illustrates the range of complexity that such reports may take:

• a word summary of activities performed (sometimes called an *inventory*)

• a word summary of objectives and activities and an assessment of the extent to which the activities met the objectives

• a simple statement of costs or outlays on socially responsible activities

• a program management approach (similar to the second type of report, except it includes spendings; it shows the activities and programs, the amount spent on each, and whether the objectives of the activities and programs have been met)

• a cost or outlay statement showing both improvements and detriments (what was done and what is not yet done) and cost estimates for these (this produces what is sometimes called a *socio-economic operating statement*)

• a statement of costs compared to benefits for all activities and programs undertaken (this is the most complex, most complete, and most difficult report to prepare).

The ultimate in reporting on the performance of social responsibility is to produce the last type of report; accountants should be pressing to reach that stage. A major factor in starting the process of social responsibility accounting is to concentrate on a small number of key issues when first reporting on social responsibility performance. Then specific results will be quickly and easily seen.

The reports discussed above have been difficult for accountants to accept for several reasons. First, they lack objectivity; that is, they are not made up of solid, provable figures. Different people could see the results in different ways. Accounting data have always been assessed on their objectivity. A second difficulty is that social responsibility measures are often qualitative, that is, word descriptions; reports may simply be in terms of "good", "better", "worse", "satisfactory". Accountants and people who use accounting reports prefer quantitative measures, that is, in quantities, usually, in dollars. In many cases, then, social responsibility performance measurement reports would be opinions and hard to compare. Finally, the shifting nature of social responsibility makes measurement and comparison difficult. Social targets are moving targets. What was not required five years ago becomes expected today and will be legally required five years from now. Is a corporation socially responsible if it meets legal requirements? Or does corporate social action have to be above minimum legal standards? If legal standards increase, does a corporation's social responsibility decrease? These questions are currently unanswerable.

Why should introductory financial accounting students be concerned about the issue of corporate social responsibility? Students need to be aware that published financial statements do not contain all that is necessary to know about a corporation. A naïve belief in the accuracy and usefulness of net profit as the sole measure of corporate success leads to two errors: first the assumption that financial health is adequately measured by reported net income and, second, the discarding of efforts at measuring social responsibility performance merely because they lack precision or objectivity. If the social impacts of a corporation's activities are not included in the formal measurement process, then these impacts are not likely to be considered in a corporation's planning decisions or performance evaluations.

The long-term aim should be a system of social responsibility accounting that records, regularly and routinely, in the same way economic events are reported, the corporation's social impact on products, environment, employees, and the community. This information is necessary both for management's internal use and for its external reporting.

Courtesy of Robert Anderson.

Proprietorship and Partnership Equity

The preceding discussion of owners' equity relates to a corporate form of business organization. A business entity can also be a sole-owner **proprietorship** or a multiple-owner **partnership**. The only significant difference in the balance sheet of a proprietorship or a partnership is in the treatment of owners' equity. A Capital account is used to record owner contributions to the business. Any owner withdrawals, usually called *drawings*, reduce this Capital account; net income earned by the business increases the Capital account. No distinction is made in the balance sheet between owner capital contributions and net income earned and retained in the business, as does occur with the corporate form of organization. The owners' equity of a proprietorship and a partnership appears on the balance sheet as follows:

Proprietor's Equity			Partners' Equity	
Bruce Bluebeard, Capital	$12,000		Bruce Bluebeard, Capital	$ 8,000
			Bill Dill, Capital	4,000
			Total	$12,000

A partnership has the added advantages over a proprietorship of a greater amount of capital contributed by the several partners and the different abilities that they bring to the management of the business. The primary disadvantage of a partnership is that each owner can be held personally responsible for all the debts of the business.

Neither a proprietorship nor a partnership pays income tax itself to government as does a corporation; rather, the proprietor and each partner personally pay income tax on the net income of the business in addition to his/her other income.

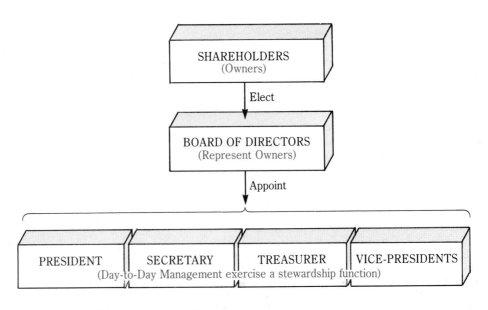

Figure 1-2   Corporate organization

Corporate Organization

Board of directors
Elected representatives of a corporation's shareholders.

Shareholders do not usually participate in the day-to-day management of a business. They participate indirectly through the election of a **board of directors**, although a shareholder may become a member of the board, or a corporate officer, or both. The board of directors also does not participate in the day-to-day management of the corporation but delegates this responsibility to the officers of the corporation, the president, secretary, treasurer, and vice-presidents. This delegation of responsibility is illustrated in Figure 1-2.

Shareholders usually meet annually to vote for a board of directors — either to re-elect the current directors or to elect new directors. The board of directors meets monthly or quarterly to review the operations of the corporation and to set policies for future operations. Based on the performance of the corporation, the board may decide to distribute some assets, usually in the form of cash, as a dividend to shareholders.

B.   The Accounting Model

Luca Pacioli
The first person to publish a description of double-entry record keeping, designed to ensure the accuracy of transactions being recorded. His book, *Arithmetic, Geometry and Proportion*, was published in 1494 in Italy.

Double-entry record keeping system
The method of accounting that recognizes the dual nature of each transaction and is used in conjunction with the accounting equation in recording transactions.

Accounting equation
The foundation on which accounting is developed and the basic formula for the balance sheet. It expresses the dollar amounts of assets, liabilities, and equities and can be stated as ASSETS = LIABILITIES + EQUITY.

Equity
Claims against assets of the entity; consists of creditor claims and owner claims.

The mechanics used in the accounting process were first published in 1494 by a Franciscan friar living in Italy. In his book *Arithmetic, Geometry and Proportion*, **Luca Pacioli** included a description of a **double-entry record keeping system** designed to ensure the accuracy of transactions being recorded. As early as 1200, a more primitive version of this recording system was in use in Venice, and by Pacioli's time the double-entry system was widely used. Although Pacioli is often given credit for its invention, it is doubtful that he originated the double-entry model, often referred to as the *accounting equation*. It is more likely that he either refined the recording practice of the day or integrated the system into the wider mathematical context of his book.

The **accounting equation** states that the total assets belonging to an entity must always equal the total claims (called **equities**) against those assets. The equality between assets and equities is shown by an equals sign. The equation is expressed as follows:

$$ASSETS = EQUITIES$$

The use of the word *equities* in this expression of the accounting equation includes claims of both **creditors** (anyone to whom the business owes money) and owners against the assets of the entity.

There is another way of expressing the relationship between assets and equities that is equally correct:

$$ASSETS = SOURCES\ OF\ ASSETS$$

Since assets have to be received from some source, this form of the equation emphasizes the contribution of assets by various individuals, including creditors and owners.

Creditors' claims to the assets of the entity (primary claims) equal the amount owed to them. The owners' claims (residual claims) consist of the amount left after the entity has taken into consideration the amounts due to everyone else. The accounting equation is therefore expanded into this form:

ASSETS	=	LIABILITIES	+	EQUITY
(economic resources owned by an entity)		(creditors' claims to assets = primary claims)		(owners' claims to assets = residual claims)

Creditors
Individuals to whom money is owed by an entity; often referred to as *primary claims*.

The word *equity*, as used in this expression of the accounting equation, refers only to owners' equity; this restricted use of the word is the more widely accepted in accounting literature.

This basic accounting model forms the foundation on which accounting is built. In addition to providing this foundation, it also expresses an equality between the assets and the total claims against those assets.

The Accounting Equation Illustrated

The following example illustrates the use of the equation. Assume that a business owns one asset, a truck, which has a purchase price of $8,000, and that $3,000 has been paid at the purchase date, with a $5,000 balance due to the bank (a creditor) remaining. The equation now appears in the following form:

$$\text{ASSETS} = \text{LIABILITIES} + \text{EQUITY}$$
$$\$8,000 = \$5,000 + \$3,000$$

In this situation the entity owns $8,000 of assets (truck), a creditor (the bank that lent the money) has a primary claim of $5,000, and the owners have residual claims (the balance remaining) of $3,000. It is clear that the *asset* total of $8,000 *equals* the total of the *equity* side of the equation, $5,000 + $3,000.

Since owners are interested in knowing the amount of their equity in an entity, financial statements are designed to show the amount left for them after all other claims have been recognized. Owners' claims are expressed as the difference between total assets and total liabilities. The accounting equation is often stated in the following manner to emphasize owners' claims:

$$\text{ASSETS} - \text{LIABILITIES} = \text{EQUITY}$$
$$\$8,000 - \$5,000 = \$3,000$$

Net assets
The excess of assets over liabilities; often referred to as *equity*.

Since total assets minus total liabilities also equals net assets, it is obvious that net assets is synonymous with the owners' equity interest in total assets. The $3,000 difference between assets and liabilities can also be referred to as **net assets**.

Financial Structure

The accounting equation therefore expresses a relationship between assets owned by the entity and the claims against those assets. Although shareholders own a corporation, shareholders alone do not finance the corporation; creditors also finance a part of its activities. Creditors and shareholders together are said to form the financial structure of a corporation. What is Bluebeard Computer Corporation's financial structure like?

Accounting Equation				
ASSETS	=	LIABILITIES	+	EQUITY
$18,000	=	$6,000	+	$12,000

BCC has a low reliance on debt in its financial structure, and therefore creditors have only a small claim against its assets. Analysts and investors are concerned with the financial structure of a corporation; that is, with the proportion of shareholders' claims against the assets of a corporation as compared with creditors' claims. What is the proportion of shareholders' and creditors' claims to the assets of BCC?

This proportion is important because the long-term financial strength of the corporation depends on its financial structure. In any given situation, a corporation is said to be *underfinanced* if it has inadequate equity capital; it is said to be *overfinanced* if shareholder capital is excessive. The proportion of shareholders' to creditors' claims is calculated by dividing shareholders' equity by total liabilities. Here is relevant financial information to calculate this proportion for BCC:

		19X1
Equity	(a)	$12,000
Total Liabilities	(b)	$ 6,000
Equity to Debt	(a ÷ b)	2 : 1

These calculations tell us that Bluebeard has $2 equity for each $1 of liabilities. Shareholders, therefore, are currently financing the bulk of BCC's operations. This fact can be a cause for concern.

> On the one hand, management's reliance on shareholder financing is good. Creditors are usually willing to extend additional financing for business operations when shareholders finance the bulk of a corporation's activities. Shareholders are thereby spared from the purchase of additional shares to finance expansion. On the other hand, management's reliance on shareholder financing is poor policy. Interest does not usually have to be paid to short-term creditors (trade accounts payable) and the corporation thereby has the free use of credit for business operations. Shareholders can invest less in a corporation when it has a greater reliance on creditor financing.

The proportion of shareholders' and creditors' claims is a management decision. In the final analysis, a reasonable balance has to be maintained. Although there is no fixed rule for an adequate proportion, there are ways of designing an optimum balance. This balance involves the weighing of **leverage** (the proportion of debt) against the risk involved and is the subject of studies in finance; it is not usually attempted in an accounting course. What is attempted, however, is an evaluation of an existing financial structure, which is discussed further in chapters 5 and 15.

Leverage
The use of borrowed capital in an attempt to earn more in the business than the rate of interest paid on the borrowed capital.

This involves an analysis of the corporation's solvency (its ability to pay debts as they become due) and the efficiency with which it conducts its operations. Solvency is analyzed using balance sheet data primarily, while net income is the starting point in evaluating the efficiency of operations. These topics are discussed in chapters 5 and 15.

Real Life Example 1-1

All in the Family

. . . let's think of the government as a family with a take-home annual income of $30,000.

The family has a lot of expenses. There's Grandmother who needs help. Raising the children takes money. So the family is spending more than it makes in a year. Quite a bit more. Total spending is $45,000, some $15,000 more than income.

That's the family deficit, the amount that's being added to its debt in a year. The family already owes quite a bit, what with the mortgage on the house, the unpaid balance on the car, and the credit card debts.

All in all, the family owes $72,000. Some family members worry about this debt and especially about the way it's rising. Ten years ago, they say, the family owed only $25,000.

Others pooh-pooh this concern.

There's general agreement around the dinner table that they're spending too much on interest and that it's going up too fast. Two years ago, the family paid out about $7,000 in interest. Last year it was $8,000. Now it's $10,000. But there isn't agreement on what to do about it.

Some . . . think expenses have to be cut, starting with the money they send to Grandmother and what they spend on the children.

They're prepared for cuts right down the line. Steak will disappear from the table and hamburger and beans will take its place. But the family deficit can't be brought down without cutting what it spends on members too young or too old to work.

Others say income has to go up. (On the federal scene, these are advocates of higher taxes.) Some say the teenagers should quit school to go to work.

This last tactic is shortsighted, according to others at the dinner table. If the young people quit and get poor-paying jobs, they'll never earn as much as they would by getting proper training.

It would make more sense, they say, to run a bigger deficit now to pay for a good education. Then the deficit will come down when the youngsters are earning high pay.

People of this opinion in the larger world of federal finance are those who advocate a "stimulative deficit" to produce better growth and higher federal revenue later.

Michael Wilson is like the father who has to produce a plan he knows won't please everyone. He just hopes it won't make the family too angry with him.

He knows it will be hard to satisfy the folks who think the children — and Grandmother — are spoiled rotten and a little hardship would be good for them. What he needs is a plan that suggests the family has turned from its spendthrift ways and is prepared to slash its deficit, even if only by about $2,000 in the coming year.

(Those well able to think in billions need only multiply all amounts of money in this column by 2,222,222 to translate it into the amounts of money actually involved in the federal budget.)

. . . Normal people can't visualize a billion of anything.

Imagine, for example, watching a mass marathon. A hundred people a minute run past — or 6,000 in an hour. They pass day and night, summer and winter. It would take 20 years for a billion people to pass.

You get some idea of the immensity. But the idea is still hazy.

If Wilson talks about Canada's gross national product — the output of the country — he'll be in the $400-billion range. That's more than $1 billion a day, or $46 million an hour or $760,000 a minute or $13,000 a second.

Source D. McGillvray, "Federal Finance in Family Terms, *The* (Montreal) *Gazette*, November 1, 1984, p. C-1.

C. Transactions Analysis

Documents
The raw data of the financial transactions of an entity; also referred to as *source documents*. They include: bank deposit slips, cancelled cheques, sales invoices, purchase invoices, insurance policies, contracts of the entity, and utility bills.

Accountants view financial transactions as economic events which change components within the accounting equation. These changes are usually measured by reference to **documents**; documents provide objective and verifiable data, so that anyone can make the same measurements using these documents. Documents can be prepared internally and externally. An internally prepared document supporting the purchase of supplies is called a *purchase order*; the supplier's invoice is the externally prepared document supporting the purchase. The financial transactions resulting in changes within the accounting equation are then recorded. Analysis of financial transactions are illustrated next; the following expanded accounting equation is used for this transaction analysis:

ASSETS	=	LIABILITIES	+	EQUITY

Cash + Accounts Receivable + Equipment + Truck = Bank Loan + Accounts Payable + Common Stock + $\begin{bmatrix} + \text{ Revenue} \\ - \text{ Expenses} \end{bmatrix}$

Assets are broken down into four groups:

1. Cash, which includes coins, currency, and cheques
2. Accounts Receivable, which consists of amounts due from customers for services rendered by Bluebeard Computer Corporation
3. Equipment, which is used for repairing computers
4. A truck, which permits the repairman to conduct his business.

Liabilities consist of a bank loan and accounts payable, amounts owed to creditors resulting from obligations incurred by the corporation in exchange for the acquisition of an asset.

Equity represents assets less liabilities, and is broken down into:

1. Common stock, which represents the investments of shareholders in the corporation
2. Revenues, which represent the performance of repair services by the corporation in exchange for assets of the customers (asset inflows)
3. Expenses, which represent an outflow or consumption of assets from the corporation incurred in earning the revenue.

Notice that the above expression of the accounting equation incorporates the different accounting categories discussed in sections A and B of this chapter: assets, liabilities, equity, revenue, and expenses. The transactions analysis illustrated here is in accordance with Pacioli's double-entry system.

Double-Entry Accounting

Pacioli's double-entry model reflects the dual nature of each transaction: each one affects at least two different items within the equation. If one item within the equation is changed, then another item must also be changed to balance it. In this way, the equality of the equation is maintained. For example, if there is an increase in an asset, then there must be a decrease in another asset or a corresponding change in a liability or equity. This is the essence of double-entry record keeping. The equation itself always remains in balance after each transaction.

The operation of double-entry accounting is illustrated in Figure 1-3, which shows seven transactions of Bluebeard Computer Corporation, an entity formed to perform computer repairs for customers and recently incorporated under the Canada Business Corporations Act (CBCA).

Note the effect of each transaction on the accounting equation; a change in one item within the equation always results in another change elsewhere within the equation. The equality of the equation is maintained in this way.

Each of these November transactions represents an exchange of something of value in return for something else of value or the incurring of an obligation to be paid in assets at a future date. Figure 1-3 summarizes these transactions and their effect on the accounting equation.

Transaction Number and Date	Description of Transaction	Effect on the Accounting Equation		
		ASSETS	= LIABILITIES +	EQUITY
1. Nov. 1	*Bluebeard Computer Corporation issued 1,000 shares of common stock for $10,000 cash.* This transaction has a dual nature: the asset Cash is increased while the equity Common Stock is also increased.	(+)		(+)
2. Nov. 2	*The corporation purchased $3,000 of equipment on account. This purchase on account represents an obligation for the corporation, to be paid at a later date.* The increase of the asset Equipment is one side of this transaction; the obligation to pay for this asset at a later date is the other side of the transaction. The obligation results in an increase in the liability Accounts Payable.	(+)	(+)	
3. Nov. 3	*The corporation purchased a delivery truck for $8,000, paying $3,000 cash and incurring a bank loan for the balance.* In this transaction, the asset cash is decreased, while the asset Equipment is increased; the liability Bank Loan is also increased.	(−)(+)	(+)	
4. Nov. 14	*The corporation paid $2,000 on account to the creditor in Transaction 2. This payment on account represents a part payment of the obligation incurred by the corporation when the equipment was purchased.* The asset Cash is decreased as one side of this transaction; the other side of the transaction decreases the obligation Accounts Payable.	(−)	(−)	
5. Nov. 20	*Equipment that had cost $1,000 was sold for $1,000 cash.* In this transaction, the asset Cash is increased, while the asset Equipment is decreased.	(+)(−)		
6. Nov. 27	*Computer repairs of $7,000 were made for customers during the month as follows: $4,000 worth of repairs were made for cash and $3,000 worth of repairs were made on account; that is, payment will be received at a later date for these repairs.* On one side of this transaction, the Cash and Accounts Receivable assets of the corporation increase; there is also an increase in equity of the other side of the transaction.	(+)(+)		(+)
7. Nov. 29	*The corporation paid operating expenses for the month as follows: $600 for rent; $2,500 for salaries; $1,200 for supplies used; and $700 for truck expenses (oil, gas, etc.).* The dual nature of this transaction consists of a decrease in the asset Cash on one side of the transaction, and on the other side, the decrease of computer repair revenue recorded in Transaction 6.	(−)		(−)

Figure 1-3   **Effects of transactions on the accounting equation of Bluebeard Computer Corporation in November**

Each of these November transactions represents an exchange of something of value in return for something else of value or the incurring of an obligation to be paid in assets at a future date. Figure 1-3 summarizes these transactions and their effect on the accounting equation.

Illustrative Problem — Double-Entry Accounting

The double-entry recording of each of BCC's November transactions (in Figure 1-3) is illustrated in the following section.

Transaction 1 (November 1)

Bluebeard Computer Corporation issued 1000 shares of common stock for a total of $10,000 cash.

Analysis: This is the corporation's first transaction. The issuance of common shares results in cash being received by the corporation. The asset Cash is therefore increased by this transaction. The equity Common Stock is also increased by $10,000 from this transaction.

Recording: When the amounts are entered into the accounting equation, the transaction has been recorded according to Pacioli's double-entry system and appears as follows:

ASSETS				=	LIABILITIES		+	EQUITY		
Cash	+	Accounts Receivable + Equipment + Truck		=	Bank Loan	+ Accounts Payable	+	Common Stock	+	+ Revenue / − Expenses
+$10,000								+$10,000		

Notice that this transaction does not affect the liabilities component of the equation.
Note: In this and following transactions, the plus and minus signs are used to show the direction of change in each item caused by the transaction.

Transaction 2 (November 2)

Equipment to be received November 30 was purchased for $3,000 on account. The equipment is said to be purchased on account because it will be paid for at a later date.

Analysis: An asset is acquired and a liability incurred in this transaction. The asset Equipment is acquired here and is therefore recorded as an increase. By the purchase of equipment, a liability is incurred, and is thus recorded as an increase on the other side of the equation.

Recording: When the amounts are entered into the accounting equation, it shows the following balances:

ASSETS				=	LIABILITIES		+	EQUITY		
Cash	+	Accounts Receivable + Equipment + Truck		=	Bank Loan	+ Accounts Payable	+	Common Stock	+	+ Revenue / − Expenses
		+$3,000				+$3,000				

Transaction 3 (November 3)

A repairman's truck to be delivered on November 3 was purchased for $8,000; BCC paid $3,000 cash and incurred a $5,000 loan for the balance.

Analysis: One asset is exchanged in this transaction; an obligation to pay an asset in the future is also incurred. The asset Truck is acquired by this purchase and is therefore recorded as an increase. The asset Cash is decreased by the purchase of the truck. A liability is incurred in connection with the truck purchase and is recorded as an increase on the other side of the equation.

Recording: When the amounts are entered into the accounting equation, it appears as follows:

ASSETS				=	LIABILITIES		+	EQUITY		
Cash	+ Receivable + Equipment + Truck	=	Bank Loan	+	Accounts Payable	+	Common Stock	+	+ Revenue / − Expenses
−$3,000	+$8,000		+$5,000						

Notice that the equation is in balance after the recording of this transaction.

Transaction 4 (November 14)
The corporation paid $2,000 on account to the creditor in Transaction 2.
Analysis: This payment decreases Accounts Payable, a liability, because the $2,000 is
due to a creditor of the corporation.
The payment of cash also decreases an asset.
Recording: When the amounts are entered into the accounting equation, it shows the
following balances:

	ASSETS			=	LIABILITIES		+	EQUITY	
Cash	Accounts Receivable	Equipment	Truck	= Bank Loan +	Accounts Payable	+	Common Stock	+	[+ Revenue − Expenses]
− $2,000					− $2,000				

Transaction 5 (November 20)
Unnecessary equipment that had cost $1,000 was sold for $1,000 cash and will be deliv-
ered to the purchaser on November 30.
Analysis: One asset is exchanged for another in this transaction. The asset Cash is
increased by $1,000 from the sale of the equipment.
The asset Equipment is decreased in this transaction.
Recording: When the amounts are entered into the accounting equation, it appears as
follows:

	ASSETS			=	LIABILITIES		+	EQUITY	
Cash	Accounts Receivable	Equipment	Truck	= Bank Loan +	Accounts Payable	+	Common Stock	+	[+ Revenue − Expenses]
+ $1,000		− $1,000							

This equipment was sold at cost. If it had been sold at a price above its cost, equity
would have been increased by the amount of the gain.

Transaction 6 (November 27)
A total of $7,000 worth of computer repairs were made for customers by the corporation
during the first month of business activities.
Analysis: An analysis of these revenue-creating activities reveals that the company
earned $4,000 from cash customers and also earned $3,000 for repairs made on account.
These activities increase two assets: the asset Cash is increased by $4,000 and the
asset Accounts Receivable is increased by $3,000. The total revenue earned during the
month is $7,000 and this increases equity.
Recording: When the amounts are entered into the accounting equation, it shows the
following balances:

	ASSETS			=	LIABILITIES		+	EQUITY	
Cash	Accounts Receivable	Equipment	Truck	= Bank Loan +	Accounts Payable	+	Common Stock	+	[+ Revenue − Expenses]
+ $4,000	+ $3,000								+ $7,000

Equity is only temporarily increased by this transaction, because the expenses incurred
to make these repairs must be deducted from revenue so that net income for the month
can be calculated. It is the net income that actually increases equity.

Transaction 7 (November 29)

Paid operating expenses that were incurred during the month to earn the repair revenue described in Transaction 6. These expenses consist of rent, $600; salaries expense, $2,500; supplies used, $1,200; and truck expense, $700 (for oil, gas, etc.).

Analysis: These expenses, summarized here as one transaction for illustrative purposes, reduce the assets and equity of the accounting equation.

Recording: When the paid amounts are recorded in the equation, the asset Cash is reduced by $5,000 ($600 + $2,500 + $1,200 + $700) and equity is reduced by the same amount, leaving the accounting equation as follows:

	ASSETS			=	LIABILITIES		+	EQUITY	
Cash	Accounts Receivable	Equipment	Truck	=	Bank Loan	Accounts Payable	+	Common Stock	+ [+ Revenue / − Expenses]
− $5,000									− $ 600
									− 2,500
									− 1,200
									− 700

The above expenses reduce repair revenue to determine net income for the month.

The increases and decreases recorded in the preceding transactions of Bluebeard Computer Corporation can now be totalled to show a final amount for each category in the expanded accounting equation. A transactions worksheet, as shown in Figure 1-4, is useful for illustrative purposes, but is not prepared in actual practice.

Accounting Time Periods

Financial statements are prepared at regular intervals — usually monthly or quarterly — and at the end of each 12-month period. The timing of these financial statements is determined by the needs of management in running the entity. Financial statements may also be required by outside parties, such as bankers, before the granting of loans to the entity can be considered. It is also customary for corporations listed on stock exchanges to prepare quarterly accounting reports for the use of shareholders, investors, and other interested parties in evaluating the progress of these corporations.

Calendar Year-End

Year-end
The last day of the fiscal year, or of the calendar year.

Interim financial statement
A financial report prepared monthly or quarterly; always for a time period of less than 12 months.

An entity operates on the basis of 12-month time periods. Accounting reports, called the annual financial statements, are prepared at the end of each 12-month period, which is known as the **year-end** of the entity. Companies having a year-end that coincides with the calendar year are said to have a December 31 year-end. While financial statements can also be prepared quarterly or monthly (these are commonly referred to as **interim financial statements**), they are always prepared at the calendar year-end, December 31.

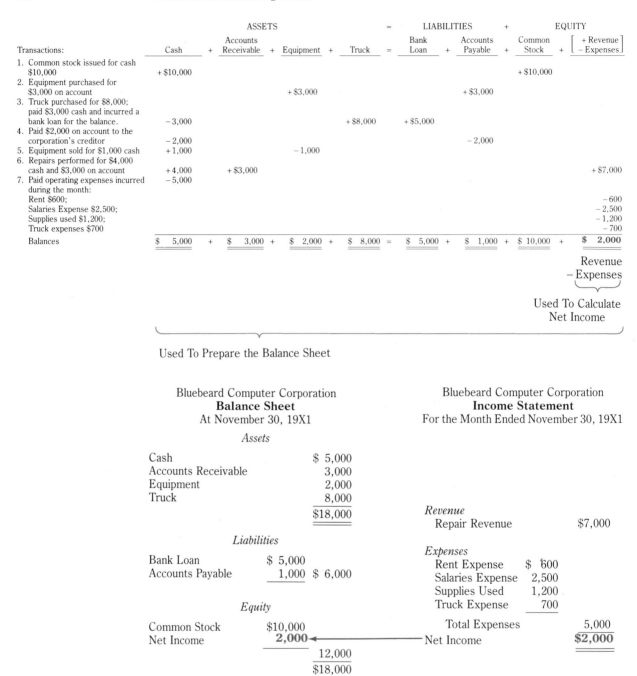

Transactions:	ASSETS				=	LIABILITIES		+	EQUITY	
	Cash	+ Accounts Receivable	+ Equipment	+ Truck	=	Bank Loan	+ Accounts Payable	+	Common Stock	+ [+ Revenue − Expenses]
1. Common stock issued for cash $10,000	+ $10,000								+ $10,000	
2. Equipment purchased for $3,000 on account			+ $3,000				+ $3,000			
3. Truck purchased for $8,000; paid $3,000 cash and incurred a bank loan for the balance.	− 3,000			+ $8,000		+ $5,000				
4. Paid $2,000 on account to the corporation's creditor	− 2,000						− 2,000			
5. Equipment sold for $1,000 cash	+ 1,000		− 1,000							
6. Repairs performed for $4,000 cash and $3,000 on account	+ 4,000	+ $3,000								+ $7,000
7. Paid operating expenses incurred during the month:	− 5,000									
Rent $600;										− 600
Salaries Expense $2,500;										− 2,500
Supplies used $1,200;										− 1,200
Truck expenses $700										− 700
Balances	$ 5,000	+ $ 3,000	+ $ 2,000	+ $ 8,000	=	$ 5,000	+ $ 1,000	+	$ 10,000	+ $ 2,000

Revenue
− Expenses

Used To Calculate
Net Income

Used To Prepare the Balance Sheet

Bluebeard Computer Corporation
Balance Sheet
At November 30, 19X1

Assets

Cash	$ 5,000
Accounts Receivable	3,000
Equipment	2,000
Truck	8,000
	$18,000

Liabilities

Bank Loan	$ 5,000	
Accounts Payable	1,000	$ 6,000

Equity

Common Stock	$10,000	
Net Income	2,000	
		12,000
		$18,000

Bluebeard Computer Corporation
Income Statement
For the Month Ended November 30, 19X1

Revenue

Repair Revenue		$7,000

Expenses

Rent Expense	$ 600	
Salaries Expense	2,500	
Supplies Used	1,200	
Truck Expense	700	
Total Expenses		5,000
Net Income		$2,000

Figure 1-4   Transactions worksheet for Bluebeard Computer Corporation for November

Fiscal Year-End

Fiscal year
A 12-month accounting period that may or may not coincide with the calendar year.

Companies whose year-end does not coincide with the calendar year are said to operate on a **fiscal year**. For example, some corporations have a June 30 fiscal year-end; others choose a year-end that coincides with their natural year. A *natural year* ends when business operations are at a low point. A ski resort will probably have a year ending in late spring or early summer, when its business operations are at their lowest point: for example, April 30. Although interim financial statements can also be prepared quarterly or monthly, annual financial statements are always prepared at the fiscal year-end, in the case of the ski resort, April 30. The inter-relationship of the interim and year-end financial statements is illustrated in Figure 1-5.

Note that Bluebeard Computer Corporation's fiscal year-end coincides with the calendar year ending December 31. Because BCC began operations on November 1, 19X1, its first year-end consists of only two months. Each subsequent fiscal year will comprise 12 months.

The headings of the financial statements shown in this chapter are designed to identify the entity for which the statements are being prepared: Bluebeard Computer Corporation; the name of the statement, either income statement or balance sheet; and the date of the statements, November 30, 19X1.

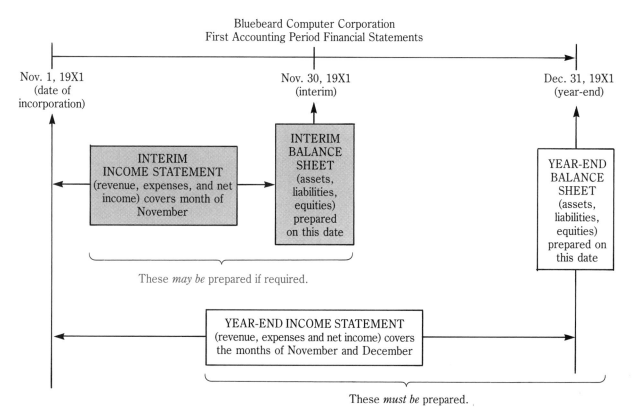

Note: This two-month year-end will occur only once; afterward, a company will have a 12-month year and choose a year-end date, such as December 31.

Figure 1-5   The relationship of interim and year-end financial statements

The *income statement* is dated *For the Month Ended November 30, 19X1* because it is intended to show the performance of the entity over the November time period. The *balance sheet* is dated *At November 30, 19X1* because it is designed to show the financial position of the entity at a particular point in time — November 30.

The Time-Period Assumption

Periodicity concept
The preparation and issuance of financial statements on a timely basis; used as a measure of performance and accomplishment for decision-making purposes. Also called the *time-period assumption.*

The time-period assumption requires the preparation of timely and useful financial statements. Underlying this assumption, however, is the concept that the entity's activities can actually be broken into meaningful time periods. Although necessary for financial reporting, this concept — also called the **periodicity concept** — results in accounting measurement problems that require compensation through the use of accrual accounting and the matching concept. As noted earlier, the accrual method of accounting aligns expenses and revenues with a particular time period; under this method, the cost of assets transferred to customers or consumed during the period are considered as expenses; the revenue generated by these expenses is included in the income statement of the same time period. In this way, expenses incurred are matched with revenue generated. The application of these concepts is explained and illustrated further in Chapter 3.

Discussion Questions

1. Explain, using an example, what is meant by the term *financial transactions*.
2. What is the entity concept of accounting? Why is it important?
3. How does an accountant select business transactions that are translated into accounting information applicable to a particular entity?
4. What are financial statements?
5. What is the purpose of an income statement? a balance sheet? How do they inter-relate?
6. Define the terms *revenue* and *expense*, as they are understood by accountants.
7. What is net income? Why is it a useful measure for readers of financial statements?
8. What are assets? Where do they appear in financial statements?
9. What do the terms *liability* and *equity* refer to? In which way can they both be referred to as equity?
10. Why are financial statements prepared at regular intervals? Who are the users of these statements?
11. What is a year-end? How does the timing of year-end financial statements differ from that of interim financial statements?
12. How does a fiscal year differ from a calendar year?
13. Define the accounting process. What are the three steps in this accounting process?
14. Distinguish between financial and managerial accounting.
15. What is the accounting model? How does it work?
16. Why is the accounting equation expanded when financial transactions are recorded? Illustrate, using the example of Bluebeard Computer Corporation.
17. The accounting model is often referred to as a double-entry accounting system. Explain how it works.
18. What is the financial structure of an entity?
19. What is the importance of the proportion of shareholders' and of creditors' claims against the assets of the entity?
20. Is management's reliance on shareholder financing good or bad for the business? Explain.
21. Refer to Real Life Example 1-1, ''All in the Family'': comment on financial structure, debt to equity, leverage and solvency as they are discussed in the chapter.
22. Refer to Conceptual Issue 1-1, ''Social Responsibility'': how might accountants quantify corporate social responsibility? How subjective would this accounting be? Do you favour rigid guidelines for accountants in the quantifying of social actions, or do you believe accountants should be left to judge each case on its own merits?

Discussion Cases

Discussion Case 1-1:   Rodolph and Marmaduke

Scene: The great hall of that fine old English castle, Dogsberry Towers. The date is 1291. As the curtain rises, that good, simple-minded old knight, Sir Rodolph the Uninspired, is discovered behind a large table littered with bits of paper, slate, and sharp stones (the recording implements of the time), among which the old fellow is shuffling about, pausing from time to time to scratch a figure laboriously, with much licking of pointed stones. Finally, he gives up in exasperation and bangs loudly on the table with a tankard.

RODOLPH: What ho, without there! Fetch me another double mead — standing up.
VOICE WITHOUT: Coming, sire.
[*A servant shuffles in with a tankard.*]
ROD.: And where is my steward Marmaduke? Is he not yet arrived?

SERVANT: I was on the point of showing him in, sire.
[*He does so. Enter Marmaduke.*]
ROD.: Dear Marmaduke! I am so glad to see you. Something terrible has happened — you see before you a ruined man.
MARMADUKE: [*Incredulously.*] A ruined man? But, my lord, you are one of the wealthiest men in Christendom.
ROD.: I was once, but I am sinking fast. I have it all here. [*He fumbles about and finally emerges with a piece of slate.*] Yes, since you made up the last statement of my affairs a few years ago, my wealth has declined. Here, let me see . . . [*reads*] from 812 to 533.
MAR.: From 812 to 533? But what figures are these?
ROD.: [*Excitedly.*] Well, they are my own invention. You see, I listed down everything I owned — just as you showed me. But when I was finished, I wanted to see whether I was

going ahead or behind. So [*with an expression of delight at his own cunning*] I added all the things up. Last time, I had 812 things; this time 533. It's as simple as that—bankruptcy in a few more years, at this rate.

MAR.:   But you can't do that. That's like adding barrels of ale and goblets of wine.

ROD.:   Well, what's wrong with that? Three barrels and two goblets make five things, right?

MAR.:   [*Effort at control*] I am a member of the guild of stewards, after serving the customary 25-year apprenticeship. May I respectfully suggest that you leave these counting matters to me.

ROD.:   [*Piteously*] But you had taught me to add . . . and I thought you would be so pleased.

MAR.:   [*Relenting.*] Look, my lord. Would you rather have three horses and one rabbit, or one horse and ten rabbits?

ROD.:   Naturally, I would rather have three horses and one rabbit.

MAR.:   Quite right. You see, you would be better off with four animals than with eleven [*his voice gradually rises as he loses his control*] because they are not the same kind of animal! [*He continues more calmly.*] You see, the reason you had so many things at the time of the first count was that you had just bought 500 exotic birds.

ROD.:   They were a passing fancy of my wife's. I can deny her nothing.

MAR.:   Whereas, they are all gone now, my lord.

ROD.:   [*Indulgently.*] She changed her mind, the little dear.

MAR.:   So you see, if you disregard the birds—which you didn't like anyway—you have actually increased your possessions from 312 to 533.

ROD.:   But then, I lost some large items, too. After all, that bastard Guido the Provocative burned down one of my best manor houses.

MAR.:   On the other hand, however, in a reprisal raid you took from him half his holdings.

ROD.:   I counted that. I added in a half for that.

MAR.:   That's just fine: you get half Guido's holdings and you lose 500 birds—so it's a net loss of 499½. As a matter of fact, the guild is very worried about this. There is some nut —from Edinburgh, of course (wouldn't you know it)—who is going about the kingdom advocating a new idea in which you value everything and add it all up to a big total. Our Conduct and Discipline Committee think they can hang a witchcraft charge on him. This whole idea of his involves the introduction of new mathematical techniques, such as long division. And of course the guild believes that long division is too erratic and too subjective a process to be relied on for accounting. Our Research Committee has got out a pronouncement saying that it has considered the use of long division and has concluded that it is inappropriate at this time.

ROD.:   [*Shyly.*] Do you think that your guild members would be interested in my idea of just counting things?

MAR.:   I'm afraid not, my lord. At best, they might endorse it as an alternate procedure, which is what they do when they want to go out of their way to be patronizing.

[*Curtain.*]

Source   Adapted from Howard Ross, *Financial Statements: A Crusade for Current Values* (Toronto: Pitman, 1969), pp. 30–33.

For Discussion

1. Rodolph, a separate entity, has been counting his assets. Has he also been accounting for them? Why or why not?
2. The process of valuing assets requires the use of some common denominator in order that different kinds of assets can be added together. Is the common denominator in use today better than that used by Rodolph? Why or why not?

Discussion Case 1-2:   The Financial Treadmill

It's a Saturday morning early in 1992. Last night, on CBC's *The National*, an excited reporter relayed the news that it's probably going to cost you a record of 25 percent to renew the mortgage on your house next week.

This morning you're reading in *The Paper* the grim news that five more Montreal companies folded this past week, done in by the soaring cost of bank credit.

Today your friendly dealer will call you to say it's going to cost a staggering 32 percent to finance that great new car you have your eye on.

And on Monday your travel agent will tell you regretfully that she's going to have to tack a big surcharge on the bill for that Caribbean getaway you've been planning for months.

Why? "It's the Canadian dollar. You do know it's only worth 45 cents U.S. now, don't you?"

Is this a likely prospect? It could happen, according to financial experts, if Canada's national government goes on borrowing money to pay its bills at its current rate—one dollar out of every three it spends.

They point to the recent decision to rule out using any money saved from social programs to reduce the government's huge annual financial deficit.

The result, in time, would be soaring interest rates and a collapsing dollar—unless the government later takes even more drastic action than the admittedly tough moves needed now.

Why would that matter to the rest of us? After all, as taxpayers and consumers of government services we just owe the money to ourselves, don't we?

The trouble is that right now, in order to pay its bills, the Canadian government has to borrow and re-borrow billions of dollars each month in the country's financial markets.

And, unlike the conscripted dollars that come in from taxes, that money is handed over only voluntarily.

The government cannot easily compel investors to lend it their savings. It has to offer a sufficiently high interest rate to make the idea attractive to them. And that interest has to be paid year in and year out.

For the moment, Ottawa's financial managers are not having much trouble — although their demand for money is keeping interest rates higher for everybody than they would be otherwise.

That's partly because there's not a great deal of competition from business firms and individual Canadians for the available credit in the economy.

But it would be a mistake to be complacent about the situation, the experts warn.

The danger is that each month's borrowing brings the government closer to starting a sort of financial doomsday machine. It would happen this way, the experts explain.

Ottawa has already run up a debt of $165 billion, equal to $6,600 for every man, woman, and child in the country and $24,000 for the average family.

Just paying the interest on that huge debt already absorbs a big chunk of the government's annual revenue — roughly 28 percent last year, and approaching 30 percent this year.

That's bad enough.

But, worse still, that annual interest bill jumps each year as Ottawa adds to the national debt at the rate of $30 billion to $35 billion a year.

Within a year or so, possibly as soon as next year, the entire amount the government borrows will be needed just to pay the interest on what it's borrowed previously.

It's as if you asked your banker to lend you the money to pay your credit-card interest bill, then kept on spending and never paid anything back.

And, once you get onto that treadmill, the amount of your income that has to go on paying interest climbs with startling speed.

The arithmetic is inexorable.

On a plausible scenario painted by a Toronto-based consulting economist, Nuala Beck, the government would have to spend half its revenue on interest as soon as 1988. And two years later, Ottawa's annual interest bill would approach 60 percent of its revenue.

That's assuming the government does nothing to reduce its deficit and continues to borrow on today's scale.

In those circumstances, the government would eventually be paralysed by its interest bills.

There would then effectively be only one way out. Ottawa would have to order the Bank of Canada to print enough money for it to pay its bills.

The result of that would be soaring inflation, sky-high interest rates, and a shrunken dollar, a fate that's befallen many countries already this century.

Source   "Is Deficit Destroying our Economy?", *The* (Montreal) *Gazette*, February 9, 1985, p. B-1.

For Discussion

1. Compare and contrast the use of leverage in a business setting with/to borrowing on the part of governments.
2. What options does the government have other than printing enough money to pay its bills?
3. What types of problems may government accountants face that their counterparts in private business will not face?

Discussion Case 1-3: Farmers' Finances

Study Shows Farmers Earn Twice as Much as Average Canadian

Farmers earn twice as much as the average Canadian, but pay one-quarter as much in income tax, says a study recently released by the federal government.

The white paper, prepared at the request of Finance Minister Michael Wilson, appears to debunk many farmers' claims that they are an impoverished group that needs more financial help.

The study found that:

• Farmers are nine times as wealthy as the average Canadian. The average farm is worth $508,000, of which $417,000 is debt-free; the average Canadian family, however, has a net worth of only $47,000. The largest one-third of farms are considerably more valuable than the average. They have an average $891,000 worth of land and buildings and nearly $700,000 of that is fully paid for.

• Farmers had an average taxable income of $16,964 in 1981, compared with $12,961 for average business people and $15,382 for all tax filers. But the figures underestimate farm incomes by as much as 100 percent because of the special tax deductions that farmers are allowed to use.

• There are so many of these deductions that the average farmer pays only 4 percent of his/her income to the federal and provincial governments. This compares with 14.9 percent for other businesses and 15.6 percent for salaried workers. In addition, the study said, "a significant proportion of high-income" farmers pay no income tax at all.

• Farm land is apparently a very good investment. The value of rural real estate jumped by 1184 percent between 1960 and 1983, while the Toronto Stock Exchange 300 composite index rose 360 percent in the same period. Land prices peaked in about 1981–82, but have softened by only 4 percent since then.

• Farmers get a high return on their investment. Between 1975 and 1983, the average return on farm equity was 19.3 percent, nearly twice the rate for Canada Savings Bonds and substantially higher than for many other industries.

• Farm bankruptcies have received a great deal of publicity in recent years, but the failure rate is only one-fifth as high as for businesses in general. The number of failures reached a record high in 1984, but the bankruptcy rate represented less than 0.2 percent of all farms. At this rate, it would take 500 years for all Canadian farms to go under.

• Some farmers are undoubtedly in severe financial distress, but they represent a small minority of the industry. According to one financial measure cited in the study, about 3.2 percent are considered in the distress category and about 7500 farmers are considered virtually beyond hope. For the latter group debt costs exceed 40 percent of their sales. By comparison, 91 percent of all farms are considered to be in a relatively strong financial position because they have an equity rate of more than 50 percent.

• The authors of the study were perplexed by two discrepancies that showed up in their survey. Apparently, 450 000 Canadians claim to be farmers for tax purposes, although there are only 318 000 farms in the country. To further confuse the issue, the number of farms declined by 112 000 between 1966 and 1981, but the number of farm tax-filers increased by more than 100 000. This would indicate that many Canadians are aware of the lucrative tax write-offs available to agriculture.

Source   Oliver Bertin, *The Globe and Mail*. February 23, 1985, p. 1.

Globe Compounded Distortion in Report

A finance department discussion paper presents an extremely misleading picture of farm incomes and a story in *The Globe and Mail* compounds the distortion, Don Knoerr, president of the Canadian Federation of Agriculture, said yesterday.

The *Globe* story said farmers earn twice as much as the average Canadian, a conclusion based "on improper calculations and misleading statements," Mr. Knoerr said in a statement.

"The fact is, the farm operator's average income in 1981 was less than the average income of the civilian labour force," Mr. Knoerr said. In 1984, the average farmer likely earned less than $10,000.

The story in Saturday's newspaper was based on a discussion paper, promised last November and released three weeks ago, on three farm tax issues the Conservatives have promised to reform.

The discussion paper makes no mention of the government's promise and basically argues against introducing "agribonds" to raise funds for struggling and starting farmers, reforming tax laws for part-time farmers and ending capital gains on farmlands.

It paints a favourable picture of farm incomes compared with those of non-farmers by blending farmers' on-farm and off-farm incomes together.

Mr. Knoerr said the Finance Department inflates farm incomes by adding in the rise in value of farmland and farm assets, money that is available only when farmers sell their farms. It does not help them pay bills or maintain their family, he said.

Mr. Knoerr told the commons agriculture committee that, in addition, the department bases its statements on figures for 1971 to 1981, ignoring the steady drop in land values since then.

Brigid Pyke, the federation's first vice-president, said the finance department paper and the *Globe* story made "a ludicrous comparison" in saying the average farmer was worth $508,000, compared with $47,000 for the average Canadian.

"That's like saying what right does a construction worker have to drive a $250,000 earth mover when the average Canadian is driving a $9,000 car?"

She said the finance department paper was full of factual errors that begged misinterpretation and the *Globe* story did that.

Source   *The* (Montreal) *Gazette*, February 28, 1985, p. 8.

For Discussion

1. Comment on the views expressed in both articles above. Which view can be supported or disputed by what you have learned in Chapter 1?
2. Would the use of a balance sheet and an income statement be useful in discussing these issues? Support your answer.
3. A farm operator owns assets, has debts, and produces an income, while another tax filer might work for an organization. What similarities and differences does this pose for the analysis of each as an accounting entity?

Comprehension Problems

Comprehension Problem 1-1

The following list covers all possible transactions that can occur in accounting. Notice that each transaction has a dual effect.

Types of Accounting Transactions

	ASSETS	=	LIABILITIES	+	EQUITY
1.	(+)				(+)
2.	(+)		(+)		
3.	(+)(−)				
4.	(−)				(−)
5.	(−)		(−)		
6.			(+)		(−)
7.			(−)		(+)
8.			(+)(−)		
9.					(+)(−)

The dual effect of each transaction illustrated above maintains the equality of the accounting equation.

Required: Study the following transactions and identify, using the accounting equation, the effect of the transaction. Use a (+) to denote an increase and a (−) to denote a decrease. Some of the transactions do not involve accounting.

A = L + E

Example:

(+)   (+)   Issued common shares for cash

_____ Purchased a truck for cash
_____ Incurred a bank loan as payment for equipment
_____ Made a deposit for electricity service
_____ Paid rent expense
_____ Signed a new union contract that provides for increased wages
_____ Hired a messenger service to deliver letters during a mail strike and wrote a letter of complaint to the prime minister about the strike
_____ Received a collect telegram from the prime minister; paid the messenger
_____ Billed customers for services performed
_____ Made a payment on account
_____ Received a payment on account
_____ Collected cash from a customer
_____ Paid for truck expenses (gas, oil, etc.)
_____ Made a monthly payment on the bank loan; this payment included a payment on part of the loan and also an amount of interest expense. (*Hint:* This transaction affects more than two parts of the accounting equation.)

Comprehension Problem 1-2

Refer to the list of accounting transactions in Comprehension Problem 1-1.

Required: Study the following transactions and identify, by number (1 to 9) the type of transaction. Some transactions do not involve accounting.

Example:
| 1 | Issued common shares for cash |

_____ Paid an account payable
_____ Borrowed money from a bank and issued a note
_____ Collected an account receivable
_____ Collected a commission on a sale made today
_____ Paid for an advertisement in a newspaper
_____ Borrowed cash from the bank
_____ Signed a contract to purchase a computer
_____ Received a bill for supplies used during the month
_____ Received a payment on account
_____ Sent a bill for repairs made today
_____ Sold equipment for cash
_____ Purchased a truck on account
_____ Requested payment of an account receivable that is overdue
_____ Settled a union dispute by increasing vacations from four to six weeks
_____ Recorded the amount due to the landlord as rent
_____ Received the monthly telephone answering service bill

Comprehension Problem 1-3

A transaction worksheet of McGill Erectors Limited shows the following recorded transactions during January 19X1.

	Cash	+	Accounts Receivable	+	Supplies	+	Equipment	+	Truck	=	Accounts Payable	+	Common Stock	+	[+ Revenue − Expense]
a.	+$5,000												+$5,000		
b.							+$1,000				+$1,000				
c.					+$300						+ 300				
d.			+$3,500												+$3,500
e.	− 350														− 350
f.	+1,000		− 1,000												
g.	− 500										− 500				
h.	− 2,000								+8,000		+ 6,000				
i.	− 2,500														− 500
															−1,200
															− 800
j.					− 200										− 200

Additional information: transaction (e) involved rent for the month of January and transaction (i) involved advertising, salaries, and truck repairs, in that order.

Required:
1. Describe each of the above transactions.
2. Calculate the total for each column at the end of January.

Comprehension Problem 1-4

The following information is taken from the records of Jackson Music Corporation at April 30, 19X1.

Accounts Payable	$7,000	Insurance Expense	$ 300
Accounts Receivable	6,000	Interest Expense	500
Cash	1,000	Rent Expense	700
Common Stock	8,500	Truck	8,000
Equipment	4,000	Truck Expense	600
Fees Earned	8,100	Wages Expense	2,500

Required: Prepare an interim income statement and an interim balance sheet for April 30, 19X1.

Comprehension Problem 1-5

The following financial statements have been prepared from the records of Clampton Strings Inc.

Clampton Strings Inc.
Income Statement
May 31, 19X1

Service Revenue		$6,500
EXPENSES		
Advertising Expense	$ 200	
Equipment	2,000	
Truck Expense	500	
Wages Expense	3,300	6,000
		$ 500

Clampton Strings Inc.
Balance Sheet
May 31, 19X1

Accounts Payable	$5,000
Accounts Receivable	4,000
Cash	3,000
Common Stock	8,000
Equipment Rental Expense	300
Truck	6,200
Net Income	500
Total	$ 0

Required: Prepare Clampton's interim financial statements in correct and proper form.

Problems

Problem 1-1

Following are the asset, liability, and equity balances of Herman's Services Corporation at January 31, 19X1, its first month of operations.

ASSETS		=	LIABILITIES	+	EQUITY	
Cash	$1,300		Bank Loan	$8,000	Common Stock	$2,000
Accounts			Accounts		Service Revenue	7,500
Receivable	2,400		Payable	1,000	Advertising Expense	500
Prepaid					Commissions Expense	720
Insurance	550				Insurance Expense	50
Supplies	750				Interest Expense	80
Truck	9,000				Rent Expense	400
					Supplies Used	100
					Telephone Expense	150
					Wages Expense	2,500

Required:
1. Prepare an interim income statement for the month ending January 31, 19X1 in proper form. Record the expenses in alphabetical order.
2. Prepare an interim balance sheet at January 31, 19X1 in proper form.

Problem 1-2

The following is an alphabetical list of data from the records of Financial Services Corporation at March 31, 19X1.

Accounts Payable	$9,000	Equipment Rental Expense	$ 500
Accounts Receivable	3,900	Fees Earned	4,500
Advertising Expense	300	Insurance Expense	400
Cash	3,100	Interest Expense	100
Common Stock	2,000	Truck Expense	700
Equipment	5,000	Wages Expense	1,500

Required: Prepare an interim income statement and an interim balance sheet for March 31 in proper form. Record the expenses on the income statement in alphabetical order.

Problem 1-3

The following financial statement was prepared from the records of Annuity Reports Inc. at August 31, 19X1.

Annuity Reports Inc.
Financial Statement
At August 31, 19X1

Cash	$ 400	Accounts Payable	$ 7,800
Accounts Receivable	3,800	Common Stock	3,200
Supplies	100	Service Revenue	6,000
Equipment	8,700		
Advertising Expense	300		
Interest Expense	500		
Maintenance Expense	475		
Supplies Used	125		
Wages Expense	2,600		
	$17,000		$17,000

Required:
1. What kind of statement is this?
2. Using the above data, prepare an interim income statement and balance sheet as discussed in this chapter.

Problem 1-4

The following balances appeared on the transactions worksheet of Wyde Tables Inc. on April 1, 19X1.

	ASSETS			=	LIABILITY	+		EQUITY	
	Accounts	Prepaid			Accounts		Common		+ Revenue
Cash +	Receivable +	Rent +	Supplies =		Payable	+	Stock	+	− Expense
$1,400	$3,600	$1,000	$350		$2,000		$4,350		

The following transactions occurred during April:
a. Collected $2,000 cash on account
b. Billed $3,000 to customers for tables rented to date
c. Paid the following expenses: advertising, $300; salaries, $2,000; telephone, $100
d. Paid half of the accounts payable
e. Received a $500 bill for April truck expenses
f. Collected $2,500 on account
g. Billed $1,500 to customers for tables rented to date
h. Transferred $500 of prepaid rent to rent expense
i. Counted $200 of supplies still on hand (recorded the amount used as an expense).

Required: Record the opening balances and the above transactions on a transactions worksheet as discussed in this chaper and calculate the total of each column at the end of April. (Use the headings above on your worksheet.)

Problem 1-5

The following transactions occurred in Brock Accounting Services Inc. during August 19X1, its first month of operations.

Aug. 1   Issued common shares for $3,000 cash
Aug. 1   Borrowed $10,000 cash from the bank
Aug. 1   Paid $8,000 for a used truck
Aug. 4   Paid $600 for a one-year truck insurance policy effective August 1 (recorded as Prepaid Insurance since it will benefit more than one month)
Aug. 5   Collected $2,000 fees from a client for work performed
Aug. 7   Billed $5,000 fees to clients for services performed to date
Aug. 9   Paid $250 for supplies used to date
Aug. 12   Purchased $500 supplies on account (recorded as an asset)
Aug. 15   Collected $1,000 of the amount billed August 7
Aug. 16   Paid $200 for advertising in *The News* during the first two weeks of August
Aug. 20   Paid half of the amount owing for the supplies purchased August 12
Aug. 25   Paid the following expenses: rent for August, $350; salaries, $2,150; telephone, $50; truck, $250
Aug. 28   Called clients for payment of the balance owing from August 7
Aug. 29   Billed $6,000 fees to clients for services performed to date
Aug. 31   Transferred the amount of August's truck insurance to Insurance Expense
Aug. 31   Counted $100 of supplies still on hand (recorded the amount used as an expense).

Required:

1. Record the above transactions on a transaction worksheet, as discussed in this chapter, and calculate the total of each column at the end of August. Use the following headings on your worksheet:

ASSETS					=	LIABILITIES	+		EQUITY		
Cash	Accounts Receivable	Prepaid Insurance	Supplies	Truck	=	Bank Loan	Accounts Payable	Common Stock	+ Revenue − Expense		

2. Prepare an interim income statement at August 31 in proper form. Identify the revenue earned as Fees Earned. Record the expenses in alphabetical order.

Problem 1-6

The following transactions took place in Maison Renovations Inc., during June 19X1, its first month of operations.

Jun. 1   Issued common stock for $8,000 cash
Jun. 1   Purchased $5,000 equipment on account
Jun. 2   Collected $600 cash for repairs completed today
Jun. 3   Paid $20 for supplies used June 2
Jun. 4   Purchased $1,000 supplies on account (recorded as an asset)
Jun. 5   Billed customers $2,500 for repairs completed to date
Jun. 8   Collected $500 of the amount billed June 5
Jun. 10   Paid half of the amount owing for equipment purchased June 1
Jun. 15   Sold excess equipment for $1,000 on account (the same amount as the original cost of this equipment)
Jun. 18   Paid for the supplies purchased June 4
Jun. 20   Received a bill for $100 for electricity used to date (recorded as Utilities Expense)
Jun. 22   Paid $600 to the landlord for June and July rent (recorded as Prepaid Rent, since it will benefit more than one month)
Jun. 23   Signed a union contract
Jun. 25   Collected $1,000 of the amount billed June 5

Jun. 27   Paid the following expenses: advertising, $150; telephone, $50; truck expense (rental, gas), $1,000; wages, $2,500

Jun. 30   Billed $2,000 for repairs completed to date

Jun. 30   Transferred the amount for June rent to Rent Expense

Jun. 30   Counted $150 of supplies still on hand (recorded the amount used as an expense).

Required:

  1. Record the above transactions on a transactions worksheet and calculate the total of each column at the end of June. Use the following headings on your worksheet.

  2. Prepare an income statement and a balance sheet for June 30 in proper form. Identify the revenue earned as Repair Revenue. Record the expenses on the income statement in alphabetical order.

Alternate Problems

Alternate Problem 1-1

The following asset, liability, and equity accounts are taken from the transactions worksheet of Appelbaum Services Corporation at December 31, 19X1, its first month of operations.

ASSETS		=	LIABILITIES		+	EQUITY	
Cash	$ 1,000		Accounts Payable	$17,000		Common Stock	$25,000
Accounts Receivable	9,000		Salaries Payable	2,000		Fees Earned	13,600
Prepaid Taxes	2,250					Advertising Expense	1,000
Land	10,000					Insurance Expense	250
Building	25,000					Property Tax Expense	200
Equipment	5,800					Salaries Expense	3,000
						Telephone Expense	100

Required:

  1. Prepare an interim income statement for the month ending December 31, 19X1 in proper form. Record the expenses in alphabetical order.

  2. Prepare an interim balance sheet for December 31, 19X1 in proper form.

Alternate Problem 1-2

The following is an alphabetical list of data from the records of Managerial Services Inc. at September 30, 19X1.

Accounts Payable	$2,200	Repair Revenue	$6,550
Accounts Receivable	6,000	Rent Expense	400
Advertising Expense	50	Salaries Expense	2,350
Cash	700	Supplies Used	100
Common Stock	5,000	Telephone Expense	75
Equipment	2,000	Truck Expense	325
Maintenance Expense	250	Wages Expense	1,500

Required: Prepare an interim income statement and an interim balance sheet for September 30 in proper form. Record the expenses on the income statement in alphabetical order.

Alternate Problem 1-3

The following financial statement was prepared from the records of Compound Connections Corporation at November 30, 19X1.

Compound Connections Corporation
Financial Statement
At November 30, 19X1

Cash	$ 750	Bank Loan	$5,000
Accounts Receivable	2,200	Accounts Payable	3,000
Prepaid Insurance	550	Common Stock	1,000
Supplies	300	Repair Revenue	5,000
Equipment	6,000		
Advertising Expense	200		
Commissions Expense	1,500		
Insurance Expense	50		
Rent Expense	450		
Wages Expense	2,000		
	$14,000		$14,000

Required:
1. What kind of financial statement is this?
2. Using the above data, prepare an interim income statement and balance sheet, as discussed in this chapter.

Alternate Problem 1-4

The following amounts appeared on the transactions worksheet of Hampstead Tool Rentals Inc. on May 1, 19X1.

ASSETS					=	LIABILITY +		EQUITY	
Cash	+ Prepaid Insurance	+ Supplies	+ Equipment	+ Truck	=	Accounts Payable	+ Common Stock	+	$\begin{bmatrix} +\text{Revenue} \\ -\text{Expense} \end{bmatrix}$
$1,600		$400	$3,000	$7,000		$4,000	$8,000		

The following transactions occurred during May:
a. Collected $5,000 cash for tool rental during the month (Hampstead does not rent tools on account)
b. Paid $500 rent expense
c. Paid $1,500 on account
d. Paid $600 for a one-year insurance policy effective May 1 (recorded as Prepaid Insurance, since it will benefit more than one month)
e. Purchased used truck for $5,000 on account
f. Paid the following expenses: advertising, $300; salaries, $2,500; telephone, $150; truck, $550
g. Transferred the amount of May's insurance to Insurance Expense
h. Estimated $200 of supplies to have been used during May.

Required: Record the above transactions on a transactions worksheet as discussed in this chapter and calculate the total of each column at the end of May. Use the headings above on your worksheet.

Alternate Problem 1-5

Electrical Contractors Corp. was incorporated on May 1, 19X1 and had the following transactions during its first month of operations.

May 1	Issued common shares for $5,000 cash
May 1	Paid $1,500 in advance for three months' rent: May, June, and July (recorded as Prepaid Rent, an asset)
May 2	Purchased $1,000-worth of supplies on account (recorded as an asset)
May 3	Billed a customer $1,500 for repairs performed
May 4	Paid $50 for an advertisement in *The News*
May 5	Received $250 cash for work completed today
May 10	Collected the amount billed on May 3
May 15	Paid $500 on account to a creditor
May 18	Borrowed $2,000 cash from the bank
May 20	Signed a major contract for work to be done in June
May 22	Purchased for cash $3,000-worth of equipment
May 25	Billed customers $3,500 for work completed to date
May 27	Paid the following expenses: electricity, $75; telephone, $25; and wages, $2,000
May 31	Transferred the amount of May's rent from Prepaid Rent to Rent Expense
May 31	Counted $200-worth of supplies still on hand; the rest had been used during May.

Required:

1. Record the above transactions on a transactions worksheet and calculate the total of each column at the end of May. Use the following headings on your worksheet.

ASSETS					=	LIABILITY	+		EQUITY		
Cash +	Accounts Receivable +	Prepaid Rent +	Supplies +	Equipment =		Bank Loan +		Accounts Payable +	Common Stock +	+ Revenue	− Expense

2. Prepare an interim income statement for the month of May. Identify the revenue earned as Repair Revenue. Record the expenses in alphabetical order.

Alternate Problem 1-6

Nick's Snow Removal Inc. was incorporated on December 1, 19X1 and had the following transactions during its first month of operations.

Dec. 1	Issued common shares for $6,000 cash
Dec. 1	Purchased a used truck for $9,000: paid $4,000 cash, balance due January 15
Dec. 2	Purchased on account a $2,000 snowplough to be attached to the truck (recorded as an increase in the cost of the truck)
Dec. 3	Billed customers $5,000 for December snow removal (customers will always be billed at the beginning of each month)
Dec. 5	Purchased on account salt, sand, and gravel for $500 (recorded as supplies)
Dec. 6	Paid truck expenses of $200
Dec. 7	Paid $360 for a one-year truck insurance policy effective December 1 (recorded as Prepaid Insurance)
Dec. 14	Paid $1,500 in wages for two weeks
Dec. 16	Paid $40 traffic ticket (recorded as Truck Expense)
Dec. 20	Received a bill for $350-worth of truck expenses
Dec. 24	Purchased tire chains for $100 on account (recorded as Truck Expense)
Dec. 24	Collected $3,500 of the amount billed December 3
Dec. 27	Paid for the purchase made on December 5
Dec. 28	Collected $400 for snow removal performed today for a new customer
Dec. 28	Paid $1,500 in wages for two weeks
Dec. 30	Called customers owing $1,500 billed December 3

Dec. 31   Transferred the amount of December's truck insurance to Insurance Expense
Dec. 31   Counted $100-worth of salt, sand, and gravel still on hand (recorded the amount used as an expense)
Dec. 31   Recorded wages for three days applicable to December in the amount of $450 (enter amount owing in Wages Payable column).

Required:
1. Record the above transactions on a transactions worksheet and calculate the total of each column at the end of December. Use the following headings on your worksheet.

		ASSETS			= LIABILITY +		EQUITY	
Cash +	Accounts Receivable +	Prepaid Insurance +	Supplies +	Truck =	Accounts Payable +	Wages Payable +	Common Stock +	[+ Revenue − Expense]

2. Prepare an income statement and a balance sheet in proper form for December 31. Identify the revenue as Service Revenue. Record the expenses in alphabetical order.

Decision Problem

Decision Problem 1-1

Herman's Services Corporation (described in Problem 1-1) and the Appelbaum Services Corporation (described in Alternate Problem 1-1) are involved in similar, competing business activities. You are considering investing some money in one of these two businesses. While the Appelbaum Services Corporation is larger, it appears to you that Herman's Services Corporation has more activity during business hours. Both Appelbaum and Herman's have provided you with the information that was contained in Problem 1-1 and Alternate Problem 1-1. While you would want more information if you were actually investing in these corporations, base your responses solely on the information provided.

Required:

1. Comment on the financial structure of both Herman's Services Corporation and the Appelbaum Services Corporation.
2. Which of the two corporations is more efficient in its business activities?
3. How much of the bank loan must Herman's Services Corporation repay each month in order to pay it back in full but remain solvent? (The payment is due on February 1, 19X1.)
4. What further information would you, as a user of financial information for investment purposes, want to be provided with?

GAAP and the Accounting Process

Accounting information is prepared and communicated in accordance with accepted practice and pronouncements by authoritative accounting bodies. The following questions introduce the scope of this chapter's subject matter.

1. What is the framework of principles that has received general acceptance within the Canadian business community and accounting profession?
2. Has the accounting profession in Canada actually agreed on a definitive list of fundamentals underlying the accounting process?
3. What are the authoritative accounting bodies in Canada? How do they interact in issuing pronouncements relating to accounting?
4. Is the Canadian dollar a stable unit of measure? Is it the most appropriate measure for transactions and for the reporting of accounting information?
5. Financial statements are prepared on the basis of historical cost. Why is historical cost used to measure financial transactions?
6. In what way does accrual accounting match revenue with expenses?
7. When do accountants assume that revenue is earned?
8. What is the function of the auditor's report in relation to generally accepted accounting principles?
9. What is the impact of conservatism and consistency in situations where a choice is made between equally defensible accounting principles?
10. What qualities is financial information expected to have?
11. How are accounts used in the accounting process?
12. What are the meanings of the terms *debit* and *credit*? Should they be associated with "good" and "bad" or "increase" and "decrease"?
13. How does use of debits and credits facilitate and control the accounting process?
14. What is the function of a trial balance? a general journal? a general ledger?
15. What are the sequential steps performed by the accountant in converting economic data into financial information?

A. Generally Accepted Accounting Principles

Generally accepted accounting principles (GAAP)
A set of accounting principles and practices that have become generally accepted and are used by accountants in the preparation of financial statements.

Financial statements are prepared according to a number of assumptions about the entity and about the environment within which the entity operates, and according to a number of accounting practices. A consensus has been arrived at over the years as to how assets, liabilities, and equities should be recorded and communicated. This consensus is necessary because of the wide range of users of financial statements, most of whom are external to the firm; these include shareholders, investors, creditors, customers, unions, governments, and the general public. Within the entity itself, management needs the financial statements for decision making and problem solving.

The framework of principles that has received general acceptance within the business community and accounting profession is referred to as **generally accepted accounting principles** (usually shortened to GAAP). These principles are reviewed in detail in the following sections, and for this text's purposes are referred to as assumptions.

Generally Accepted Assumptions

Assumption 1: The Entity

Each entity is seen as an individual unit of accountability separate from the owners of the entity. Separate records are kept for the transactions of each entity; the assets and obligations of each entity are kept separate from the assets and obligations of those who own it. This assumption was introduced in Chapter 1.

As noted earlier, a corporation is a legal entity; although there are a few exceptions concerning personal guarantees and bankruptcy laws, the assets of the corporation cannot be used to pay the obligations of the owners and vice versa. No legal distinction exists, however, between the assets and obligations of a proprietorship and its owner or a partnership and its owners. In these cases, personal assets of the owner(s) may be used to pay the entity's obligations; the assets of the entity may be used to pay personal obligations of the owner(s). Nevertheless, separate records are still maintained for the entity and for its owner(s).

Assumption 2: The Going Concern

Each entity is assumed to have an unlimited life; that is, it is assumed to continue operating indefinitely. This assumption is necessary because it provides the foundation for the periodic accounting reports that measure the entity's performance; such performance reports cannot wait until the end of the entity's life, when it is assumed to be indefinite. This assumption therefore leads to the periodicity assumption and the resulting need for accrual accounting and the matching assumption (as introduced in Chapter 1 and further discussed in Chapter 3).

Assumption 3: The Stable Unit of Measure

Transactions occur continuously within an entity. In Canada, these transactions are completed in terms of Canadian dollars. These dollar amounts are assumed to be the most appropriate measure for transactions and for reporting of accounting information. Under this concept, the dollar is assumed to be constant over time. In fact, it has been unstable as rapid inflation (and devaluation of the dollar) has occurred. An example of chronic inflation is illustrated in Real Life Example 2-1.

Some accountants have proposed that constant-dollar accounting be used, so that all historical dollars — because they have had different purchasing powers — are converted to end-of-the-current-year dollars. This process would include constructing a general price index that would be used to restate financial statement items from prior years in current-year common dollars.

One obvious advantage of constant-dollar accounting is its elimination of the impact of inflation on financial statement information, with all the benefits that result. One of the serious disadvantages, some experts claim, is that the cost of converting this information may exceed the benefits gained.

Although constant-dollar accounting would be an interesting solution to the impact of inflation, the accounting profession has not yet embraced it within its GAAP. An example of how factors external to the entity can challenge the foundations of GAAP is illustrated in Real Life Example 2-1.

Assumption 4:   Historical Cost

The cost of an acquired asset is measured either by the cost paid or the value of the asset given in exchange, or by the amount of the liability assumed when an asset is acquired in exchange for a liability. Financial statements are based on historical cost measures of financial transactions. Cost is seen as a reasonable measure of an acquired asset because it is objectively determined, usually as a result of arms-length bargaining; this procedure minimizes opportunities for its manipulation in financial statements.

Subsequent to the acquisition of an asset, its recorded cost is not changed even though the measurement unit — the dollar — has become unstable through inflation. Assume that, on a later date, Bluebeard pays $15,000 for another truck that is identical to the $8,000 truck it currently owns, and that the difference in price is solely a result of the impact of inflation. While this example is hypothetical, it illustrates that subsequent financial statements would report two identical assets, each having a different cost. The difference in this case would be attributable to a change in the dollar measurement unit resulting from inflation.

Use of historical cost is appropriate when the entity is a going concern. Its use is inappropriate in the case of a ''gone concern'', or bankrupt entity, for which the use of **liquidation values** is necessary.

Liquidation values
The valuation of assets at their net realizable value; based on the assumption that the entity will go out of business and will sell its assets.

Assumption 5:   Periodicity

It is assumed that an entity's business activities can be broken down into meaningful reporting periods so that performance reports (financial statements) can be prepared. Reports can be prepared monthly, quarterly, or for any other useful time period; they must always be reported annually. The application of this assumption is introduced in Chapter 1 with the preparation of an income statement and a balance sheet. The preparation of a statement of retained earnings is illustrated in Chapter 4 and a statement of changes in financial position in Chapter 16.

Assumption 6:   Accrual Accounting and Matching

The measurement of net income for an accounting time period requires the matching of expenses incurred and revenue generated during that particular time period. The cost of assets transferred to customers or consumed during the period are considered as expenses; the revenue generated by these expenses is included in the income statement of the same period. Matching is accomplished through use of the accrual method

Real Life Example 2-1

When Inflation Rate Is 116 000%, Prices Change by the Hour

A courier stumbles into Banco Boliviano Americano, struggling under the weight of a huge bag of money he is carrying on his back. He announces that the sack contains 32 million pesos, and a teller slaps on a notation to that effect. The courier pitches the bag into a corner.

"We don't bother counting the money any more," explains Max Leow Stahl, a loan officer standing nearby. "We take the client's word for what's in the bag." Pointing to the courier's load, he says, "That's a small deposit."

At that moment, the 32 million pesos — enough bills to stuff a mail sack — were worth only $500. Today, less than two weeks later, they are worth at least $180 less. Life's like that with quadruple-digit inflation.

A 116 000% Rate?

Bolivia's inflation rate is the highest in the world. In 1984, prices zoomed 2700%, compared with a mere 329% the year before. Experts are predicting the inflation rate could soar as high as 40 000% this year. Even those estimates could prove conservative. The central bank last week announced January inflation of 80%; if that pace continued all year, it would mean an annual rate of 116 000%.

Prices go up by the day, the hour or the customer. Julia Blanco Sirba, a vendor on this capital city's main street, sells a bar of chocolate for 35 000 pesos. Five minutes later, the next bar goes for 50 000 pesos. The [5 cm] 2 in. stack of money needed to buy it far outweighs the chocolate.

Changes in the dollar exchange rate — and thus in vendors' own prices — pass by word of mouth. One egg costs 10 000 pesos this week, up from 3000 pesos last week.

Bolivians aren't yet lugging their money about in wheelbarrows, as the Germans did during the legendary hyperinflation of the Weimar Republic in the 1920s, when prices increased 10 billionfold. But Bolivia seems headed in that direction.

Tons of paper money are printed to keep the country of 5.9 million inhabitants going. Planeloads of money arrive twice a week from printers in West Germany and Britain. Purchases of money cost Bolivia more than $20 million last year, making it the third-largest import, after wheat and mining equipment.

Weighing In

The 1000-peso bill, the most commonly used, costs more to print than it purchases. It buys one bag of tea. To purchase an average-size television set with 1000-peso bills, customers have to haul money weighing more than [30 kg] 68 lb. into the showroom. (The inflation makes use of credit cards impossible here, and merchants generally don't take cheques, either.) To ease the strain, the government in November came out with a new 100 000-peso note, worth $1. But there aren't enough in circulation to satisfy demand.

"This isn't even good as toilet paper," says pharmacist Ruth Aranda, holding up a 100-peso bill. Indeed, she points out, admission to a public toilet costs 300 pesos.

Three years ago, she says, she bought a new luxury Toyota auto for what she now sells three boxes of aspirin for.

"We're headed for the garbage can," says Jorge von Bergen, an executive of La Papelera S.A., a large paper-products company, who lugs his pocket-money around in a small suitcase. "When it comes to inflation, we're the international champs."

Mr. von Bergen says his wife has to take the maid along to the market to help carry the bales of cash needed for her shopping. But all that money buys so little that Mrs. von Bergen easily carries her purchases back home on her own.

Food shortages abound, and fights break out as people try to squeeze into line to buy sugar at several times the official price. Some companies have resorted to barter.

The situation has upset all phases of life in Bolivia. Private banks were closed a few days ago because of worries about executive safety. Strikes frequently close the factories. Many shops have closed. Because pesos are practically worthless, dollars now are being demanded for big-ticket purchases. People get their dollars from the 800 or so street-side money vendors who line Avenida Camacho, long La Paz's Wall Street. Banking, in effect, has moved outside.

Wages have risen 1500% since President Hernan Siles Zuazo took over from the military in 1982, but inflation has more than offset the gains, yielding a 25% decline in real terms. The result is that there were 540 strikes in Bolivia last year and 35 days of general strikes when virtually nothing functioned.

In one incident, state-hospital doctors struck, so state-hospital patients took to the streets on crutches, demanding medical care. The government caved in and gave the doctors a raise. In one recent week, not much different from others, workers in 34 factories took 180 business executives hostage in wage disputes. Some weren't released for three days.

President Siles Zuazo's government, meanwhile, has gone through 74 ministers and six cabinets in its two years in office, but it still hasn't presented a comprehensive economic plan or budget. It has announced several devaluations and several austerity plans, without much effect. It is expected to announce more such actions soon.

. . .

The current crisis dates to the late 1970s, when large oil reserves the country thought it had didn't materialize and when large international loans began to come due. Meanwhile, the price of tin, the second-largest legal export, collapsed, and the market for the largest legal export, natural gas, turned sour because of the problems of its main customer, Argentina.

Source Sonia L. Nazario, *The Wall Street Journal*, February 7, 1985, p. 1.

A Bolivian peso, circa 1920

A German 200-million note from the Weimar Republic

of accounting, which is further illustrated in this chapter; the use of Pacioli's debit and credit methodology to control its accuracy is discussed and illustrated in section B of this chapter. The application of matching to measure net income is developed and illustrated in more detail in Chapter 3 and subsequent chapters.

Assumption 7:   Revenue Realization

Revenue realization is concerned with establishing the point at which the revenue of the entity is earned. Although revenue has unquestionably been earned by the time the service is completed or the goods are exchanged and cash is collected, accountants generally assume that revenue is earned at an earlier point — after the service has been performed or the goods have been exchanged but before payment has been received. This point can be objectively determined, thereby avoiding the need for subjective estimates. In actual practice, it is convenient to recognize revenue at the point when an invoice is prepared and sent to the customer. The application is discussed further in Chapter 3.

There are exceptions to this assumption. Revenue can sometimes be realized before the service has been completed or the goods have been exchanged, for example, in the case of a long-term construction contract where revenue, expenses, and net income can be recognized by a method called percentage of completion.

Revenue can sometimes be realized after the service has been performed or the goods have been exchanged. A typical case involves the use of the installment method, whereby revenue is recognized in proportion to the percentage of accounts receivable collected.

Although these seven assumptions are said to be generally accepted, it is important to note that the accounting profession has yet to agree on a definitive list of the fundamentals underlying the accounting process. This lack of agreement exists because of the nature of these assumptions, which:

> are not derivable from physical science or natural law; they are, rather, conventions, related to certain necessarily pragmatic postulates, whose existence and validity derive from public exposure, debate, and acceptance. Generally accepted accounting principles, . . . in short, are not discovered, but declared. Their existence cannot forerun their utterance and acceptance by the profession itself.[1]

Because accounting principles are declared rather than discovered, accounting literature and practice include variations and differences, which result in some lack of precision in financial statements.

Figure 2-1 summarizes the way the seven accounting assumptions relate to the accounting process.

The entity's financial transactions are recorded in accordance with these assumptions; the content of financial statements is influenced by the operating cycle concept, which identifies certain activities that are repeated regularly during the accounting time period. The sequence of activities takes the following form:

1. Operations begin with some cash on hand.
2. This cash is used to make purchases and to pay expenses.
3. Revenue is earned as repair services are performed. (An account receivable may result.)
4. Cash is collected.

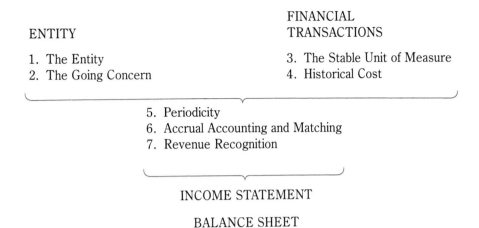

Figure 2-1   **Inter-relationships of accounting assumptions**

Operating cycle
The cash-to-cash
sequence of events for
the revenue-producing
operations of an entity.

This cash-to-cash sequence is referred to as the **operating cycle**. Chapter 3 discusses the impact of this operating cycle on financial statement disclosure and the identification of revenue with different time periods.

Qualities of Accounting Information

Accounting converts transactions of an entity into financial statement information. The framework of principles involved in the preparation of these statements was discussed in the preceding pages. The subsequent reporting of this financial information is intended to facilitate decision making by its users. Accordingly, it is necessary to understand what qualities this information is expected to have. One of the qualities is relevance. The information has to be timely and useful; it should reduce uncertainty associated with decision making. Another quality is reliability; the user should be able to depend on the information and employ it in order to evaluate alternatives. Accountants use materiality as a test when deciding to disclose certain relevant information; although relevant, the disclosure of immaterial information is more likely to hinder than help the user of financial statements. The information must also be comparable to similar information of previous accounting time periods and to the statements of other entities in the same industry.

Often, GAAP permits a choice between equally defensible alternate accounting principles in a given business situation. When making a choice, the accountant may often practice conservatism. Once the choice is made, the accounting profession requires consistency to ensure usefulness of the information.

Conservatism

Conservatism represents the accounting profession's preference for prudence when dealing with conditions involving uncertainty and risk. When making a choice between equally defensible alternatives, the accountant chooses the alternative that will produce the least favourable result for the entity. Therefore, when estimating the useful life of Bluebeard's equipment and truck, for example, BCC's accountant should use the lowest estimate if two or more equally defensible estimates are available.

With conservative estimates, the asset cost expires more quickly, producing the least favourable result because it translates into a lower net income figure and a lower unexpired asset balance reported in the balance sheet. More discussion of this issue appears in chapters 3 and 9. Other examples involving a choice between equally defensible estimates are introduced throughout this book.

In the past, an extreme application of conservatism required the selection of an alternative that ''anticipates no profit and provides for all possible losses''. The intent, then, was for financial statements to avoid favourable exaggeration; an understatement of reported net income and balance sheet amounts was intended to protect users making decisions from this information. Today, the emphasis is on the fair presentation of financial statement information; therefore, the focus is on a choice only between equally defensible alternatives. The choice of an alternative simply to produce the least favourable result is not in accordance with GAAP.

Consistency

The usefulness of financial statements is enhanced by the consistent use of accounting principles chosen from among alternatives. Consistency requires that these selected accounting principles be used for each accounting time period. In this way, there is a uniformity in financial information produced by the entity; changes between accounting time periods can then be attributed to operations and not to changes in the selection of accounting principles. Comparability of financial statement information from one time period to another of the same entity and among different entities is thereby enhanced.

Changes in accounting principles are discouraged unless such changes improve financial statement reporting or are required because of changed conditions. Such changes must be disclosed in the financial statements; this disclosure is usually made through notes to the financial statements.

Limitations on the Disclosure of Useful Accounting Information

Financial statements are prepared and distributed at regular accounting time periods so that useful information is available for decision making. Useful information is not always reported. The accountant uses materiality to decide whether particular items of information need be disclosed. The accountant, in addition, makes a cost-benefit judgement, which also limits the disclosure of useful information.

Materiality

Some information may not be sufficiently large in amount or importance to affect the judgement of a reasonably knowledgeable user. For example, the cost of a calculator is not material when compared to the cost of Bluebeard's truck. Although both are theoretically assets until their useful life expires, the calculator cost would never be shown as an asset in an accounting report; rather, it would be expensed when purchased.

In actual practice, no clear cut distinction can be drawn between material and immaterial amounts. Each case has to be considered on its own merits. As a matter of expediency, policies are usually established within the entity to facilitate consistent recording of certain transactions. Their subsequent disclosure is influenced by materiality.

Cost-Benefit Judgements

Useful information is not always reported because the costs associated with its preparation exceed the expected benefits. Therefore, the decision to prepare inflation-adjusted financial statements in addition to historical cost financial statements is influenced by cost-benefit considerations. As with materiality, individual, highly subjective judgement is required in the application of the cost-benefit decisions; accountants have developed, and use, consistent guidelines in actual practice to minimize this subjective element.

Accounting Standards Committee (AcSC)
A committee responsible for issuing pronouncements relating to accounting; exposure drafts are used to obtain views on proposed recommendations.

CICA Handbook
A codification of research pronouncements and accounting principles published by the CICA; has been given a quasi-legislative weight in Canada.

Chartered Accountant (CA)
A professional accountant who has passed the CICA national examination and satisfied all other requirements for admittance.

Canadian Institute of Chartered Accountants (CICA)
The national professional accounting association of Chartered Accountants in Canada.

Canadian Certified General Accountants' Association of Canada (CGAAC)
The national professional accounting association of Certified General Accountants in Canada.

Certified General Accountant (CGA)
A professional accountant who has passed the CGA national examination and satisfied all other requirements for admittance.

The Accounting Profession and the Development of GAAP

A number of authoritative accounting organizations are concerned with the formulation of generally accepted accounting principles.

The **Accounting Standards Committee** (AcSC) is responsible for the issuance of pronouncements relating to accounting. Membership in AcSC includes representatives from organizations such as the Canadian Institute of Chartered Accountants (CICA), the Financial Analysts Federation, the Financial Executives Institute of Canada, the Canadian Certified General Accountants' Association, and the Society of Management Accountants. In developing Canadian accounting standards and research, the AcSC uses exposure drafts to obtain the views of members and the business community on proposed recommendations.

Research pronouncements and accounting principles are published in the **CICA Handbook** and represent standards to be adhered to. (The setting of accounting standards where none existed is discussed in Real Life Example 2-2.) The fact that the *CICA Handbook* has received general acceptance in the formulation of accounting principles makes the Canadian experience somewhat different from that in other parts of the world, as has been observed:

> In all the world, we are unique, because we have been singled out as the professional body responsible for developing accounting standards for Canadian business by the Canadian Business Corporations Act, some provincial corporations acts, and securities regulations. Such recognition is noteworthy, but the quasi-legislative weight of the *CICA Handbook* must not obscure the fact that the status of our standards must be maintained as it was earned: by treating standard setting as an independent, professional responsibility. The profession developed the handbook as a guide to best practice for its own members, for the protection of its own standards. Implicit in these standards, however, is the basic goal of protecting the public. Developing standards based on a complex professional body of knowledge but directed toward the needs of a wide group of users is a test of professional judgement.[2]

The dominant group of accountants is composed of **Chartered Accountants** (CAs) who are members of the **Canadian Institute of Chartered Accountants** (CICA). An important group of public accountants is the **Certified General Accountants' Association of Canada** (CGAAC). Its members use the designation **Certified General Accountant** (CGA). Although CGAs practise accounting in certain provinces, many specialize in management, government accounting, and taxation.

Conceptual Issue 2-1

Standard Setting

Ross Denham, University of Alberta

Standard setting in Canada and elsewhere has become a positive, important, complex, and powerful force in the accounting profession. But it also comes in for its fair share of pressure and criticism by governments, their agencies, corporate executives, members of the accounting profession, and a variety of others having a stake in financial reporting. The pressures are natural and the criticisms are valuable in such an evolutionary process. They confirm the impact of the process on society and the fact that a responsible, continual evaluation of the process by the profession is essential.

I believe that the standard-setting process is an important activity operating in a dangerous environment. . . . The standard-setting process is an essential part of the profession because it provides society with established, widely recognized financial reference points. If standards are credible and respected, informed groups can use them as guidance for making judgements on financial representations. Standards also signal how accountants and others are likely to react under given conditions, as well as become triggers for action when violated. Of importance, too, is the fact that the process helps the profession protect its self-regulatory authority: operative standards are one defence against calls for technical regulation or supervision by external bodies.

The significance of the process can be judged in other ways, too. Legislative and regulatory recognition is given to the resulting policies, which implies they are of major social significance and engender confidence in the activity. The fact that the *CICA Handbook*, for example, is given legislative weight in the Canada Business Corporations Act and in the practices and requirements of various regulatory bodies indicates that the process is valued, respected, and accepted at an official level. Unfortunately, it also reduces the possibility of quick reaction to events or frequent changes.

It may be argued by some that the branching occurring in the process is further evidence of its continuing significance. Look-alike, standard-setting activities exist today in which government and international accounting environments are subject to critical overview by the private sector. A relatively new committee in Canada deals with public-sector accounting and auditing. This, it is noted, is in addition to the traditional Accounting Standards Committee (AcSC) and the Auditing Standards Committee (AuSC). Similarly, the Governmental Accounting Standards Board (GASB) has recently come into being in the United States. Furthermore, and certainly not least important, Canadians have been instrumental in the development and support of an International Accounting Standards Committee (IASC), which introduces and harmonizes standards across national boundaries and extends them into less developed nations. Finally, in addition to the CICA's financial accounting standard setting, the Certified General Accountants Association of Canada now sets standards for its members and the Society of Management Accountants does so in the management accounting area.

An example illustrates the nature of the challenges and indicates that political, technical and economic complexities can converge in the process.

In Canada, a recent clash between the Canadian government and several oil companies, on the one hand, and the keepers of professional accounting standards, on the other, centred on how to account for Petroleum Incentive Program grants (PIP) under the National Energy Program (NEP). Conventional accounting policy requires that the grants be matched with the expenditures to which they relate. If grants are received in a period prior to the one in which the related expenditures are made, the grants should be capitalized. The government and several oil companies, however, wanted the grants shown as income items when they are received, which would be prior to the period of actual expenditures. Clearly, such a practice has the effect of enhancing profits ''early'' to the detriment of profits in later periods. Some argued that such a recognition policy is necessary because it should (or arguably, it does) make corporate financing easier than it might otherwise be. That, in turn, encourages expanded exploration activity by oil firms. Such results, one might well suspect, will reflect well on one of the major economic initiatives of the government of the day and, not incidentally, enhance the success of the controversial NEP.

There are different perspectives and little agreement concerning the precise nature of the standard-setting process and the way it operates in Canada and elsewhere. At least four major ways of looking at its orientation or rationale seem to exist in everyday thought or in the literature: (1) as a mainly pragmatic process; (2) as a process in which a social/economic/political orientation predominates and the resulting standards have an impact in that context; (3) as one founded on certain absolutes pertaining to concept, logic, and neutrality; and (4) as a key process in the management of the discipline's substance. Likely, the four are not exhaustive nor discrete.

Standard setters can provide an indispensable service to the profession by imposing theory on practice and observing the impact of practice on theory. They also can seek to support practices through certain kinds of research. In this way, they become a major linking force for theory, research, and practice in accounting. This link is not new in Canada; it is just not very explicit sometimes. A rededication of standard setters to the spirit of policy setting and practice that will emerge from research and theoretical fundamentals should be welcome. Such an approach may be expected to strengthen accounting practice and enhance the ability of standard setters to confront the challenges and dangers facing the standard-setting process today.

Source   Ross A. Denham, ''Standard Setting under Pressure'', *CAMagazine*, May 1985, pp. 36–45.

SMA
The national professional accounting association of certified management accountants in Canada.

CMA
A professional accountant who has passed the FAE national examination and satisfied all other requirements for admittance.

Order des comptables agréés du Québec
The provincial association of chartered accountants in Quebec.

FASB
A United States group formed in 1973 to issue research pronouncements and accounting principles; exposure drafts are used to obtain views on proposed recommendations.

SEC
An agency of the U.S. federal government that is influential in the development of accounting principles and reporting practices. It focuses on securities traded on U.S. stock exchanges.

CPA
A professional accountant who has passed the Uniform CPA Examination and satisfied all other professional requirements for admittance.

AICPA
The national professional accounting association of Certified Public Accountants in the United States.

CAAA
An organization in Canada primarily for academic accountants; is also open to anyone interested in accounting and accounting education.

AAA
An organization in the United States primarily for academics in accounting.

The dominant group of management accountants is the **Society of Management Accountants** (SMA), whose members use the designation **Certified Management Accountant** (CMA). The SMA develops managerial accounting education materials and publishes special studies dealing with areas of management accounting.

Each Canadian organization is incorporated under federal legislation and has associations in every province. Everyone who holds membership in a provincial association is automatically a member of the national group and membership is fully portable between provinces. The first accounting body in North America was formed in Canada in 1880 and was called the Association of Accountants in Montreal (now the **Ordre des comptables agréés du Québec**). Its formation is discussed in Real Life Example 2-2.

In addition to these bodies, each province has a securities commission or other government body that exercises a considerable amount of control in the securities markets, particularly in the area of prospectuses. These provincial commissions have formally defined generally accepted accounting principles for financial disclosure as those pronouncements that are set out in the *CICA Handbook*.

The **Financial Accounting Standards Board** (FASB) is the leading independent non-government body in the United States responsible for the development and issuance of financial accounting standards. A large part of the GAAP in use today was established by the FASB. In addition, it has focused on the development of a conceptual framework of accounting to re-evaluate basic accounting theory. This FASB conceptual framework has been referred to as the constitution for accounting. CAs and other public accountants in Canada are strongly influenced by these and other American accounting pronouncements and research.

The Securities and Exchange Commission (SEC) is a government body in the United States which issues pronouncements and regulations that form part of GAAP. Large Canadian public corporations listed on American stock exchanges are affected by these pronouncements and regulations. The SEC mandate focuses on the identification of information that must be disclosed by listed corporations and on the establishment of accounting procedures to be used in making these disclosures. Fortunately, the SEC generally relies on the accounting profession to establish accounting procedures.

The dominant group of accountants in the United States is comprised of **Certified Public Accountants** (CPAs), who are members of the **American Institute of Certified Public Accountants** (AICPA). The AICPA was formerly responsible for the development of GAAP; in 1973 this role was undertaken by the then–newly created FASB.

The **Canadian Academic Accounting Association** (CAAA) is an association formed for accountants in academic work but open to anyone interested in accounting and accounting education. The CAAA encourages the improvement of accounting education, sponsors various types of accounting research, and publishes its semi-annual publication *Contemporary Accounting Research*. As well, many Canadians in academic work are also members of the **American Accounting Association** (AAA), whose objectives are similar to those of the CAAA.

The Auditor's Report

When year-end financial statements are published, they are usually accompanied by an **auditor's report**. The auditor's report indicates that the statements have been examined by an independent, professional accountant who is legally permitted to do so, and that the statements present fairly the financial position of the entity and the results of its operations for a particular time period. The independent, professional accountant, usually referred to as the *auditor*, also indicates whether the financial statements have been prepared in accordance with generally accepted accounting principles and whether these accounting principles have been used in a consistent way. If there is a violation of GAAP in the financial statements, then the auditor's report is modified so as to alert readers to the violation. For an example of an auditor's report, see Circo Craft's annual report in Real Life Example 5-2 in Chapter 5.

Real Life Example 2-2

Philip S. Ross: Setting Accounting Standards

Philip S. Ross was born in Belfast, Ireland, in 1827. His father, a Scot, was a regular army officer. Ross regarded Scotland as his home and there got his education and his early accounting experience.

In 1853, he emigrated to Canada, a common solution for an ambitious Scot of limited means in the 19th century. Ross's father had left the army and was working as a bookkeeper in Glasgow. He had little he could give Ross to help him establish himself. Even that little Ross would not accept. He was then, and remained all his life, fiercely independent and proud.

When Ross had paid for his passage to Canada, he had $25 left. Although the 1853 dollar was a lot more robust than the dollar is today, the sum still only represented wages for two to three months; it was hardly a lavish start for a 26-year-old in a new life in a new country.

Ross went first to Perth, Ont., where he stayed for about a year, and then moved to Montreal. He worked as an accountant for a drug wholesaler and later for the Canada Marine Works.

In 1858, he started practice as a public accountant, even though a major depression had enveloped Canada in 1857.

His brother, safe in Glasgow, thought this a foolish move — throwing away a salary of $300 — but Ross's father encouraged him in his gamble. "Hope high, persevere in a straight honest path and I have no fears that in the end your labours will be rewarded."

Public accounting in 1858 bore little resemblance to the profession we have today. In the first place, there was little auditing done. Most of the business enterprises were small, run by one person or a tiny group of partners. What few public companies there were usually had two shareholders deputed to act as auditors, for professional accountants were regarded as too expensive for such routine matters.

Sidelines

Most of an accountant's time would be spent on bankruptcy work. The use of credit, in a cash-poor society, was widespread, with the consequent prevalence of business failures. However, no accountant really expected to live on his practice alone. He would have some sideline providing steady income between professional accounting engagements.

To help support his family and provide for his brothers left behind in Scotland, Ross offered to act as a forwarding agent trans-shipping cargoes.

In 1860, he went into business as a ship's chandler, with first one and later both his brothers. After only three years' operation, he was forced into bankruptcy through a fraud by an associate. Ross could have escaped at 35¢ on the dollar, but his pride forced him to pay off the full $30,000 from the scanty revenues of his accounting practice. Eventually, the chandlery business recovered and continued until 1879, when Ross devoted himself full-time to accountancy.

Ross's attitude to life is well illustrated by his marriage. He wrote back to the Presbyterian minister in his hometown in Scotland, enclosing a list of three women, and asked the minister to propose marriage and to ship the one who accepted to Canada. The minister did as he was asked and Christina arrived in 1856. Within half an hour of her disembarking the ship, Ross married her, and the marriage lasted, happily, for more than 50 years.

Ross worked alone until 1884. A contemporary has left a

B. Accounts in the Accounting Process

The dual nature of accounting transactions is explained and illustrated in the preceding chapter. There, the November transactions of Bluebeard Computer Corporation are first analyzed to determine the changes in each item in the accounting equation brought about by each transaction. Increases and decreases in each item are then recorded in a series of expanded accounting equations, in which the following headings appear: Cash, Accounts Receivable, Equipment, Truck, Bank Loan, Accounts Payable, Common Stock, and Revenue less Expenses. Next, the dollar amounts of each transaction are recorded on a transaction worksheet and two financial statements are prepared from the totals calculated on the worksheet. These financial statements can communicate financial information of BCC, a legal entity, to interested parties.

The record keeping and the calculation of these totals was a convoluted process. Can

description of him sitting in skullcap and slippers performing his audit. He was sparing with words. His report for the Montreal Protestant School Board for 1872 read, in its entirety: "Audited, found correct and fully vouched."

But he was building up his practice. In 1876 he got the audit for Sun Life Assurance Co., then a struggling junior insurance company, and, in 1880, a fledgling Bell Telephone appointed him as its first auditor. His successors have continued to hold these appointments ever since.

In the 1880s, Ross acquired his first employee. Later in the decade he took three of his sons into the practice. He retired from management of the firm in 1890, although he continued active as a chartered accountant for some years after that.

When Ross started to practise accountancy, and for some 20 years thereafter, there were no standards. Anyone who wanted to could become an accountant, and the business community was unprotected against incompetent practitioners.

In the 1870s, Ross, together with another accountant and friend, James Court, set out to create an association of accountants in Montreal and, in 1879, they called a meeting to form the first formal grouping of accountants in North America. This association in the direct ancestor of *l'Ordre des comptables agréés du Québec*.

Ross, Court, and the other 11 accountants who attended the initial meeting wanted to discipline the chaos of the Montreal accounting scene, to provide the accountants themselves with tangible evidence of their competence and to protect the business public.

The group got its charter from the Quebec Legislature in July 1880. Accountants were now "chartered" with the power to establish their own entrance requirements. Further, the chartered accountants could discipline their members to ensure they maintained standards.

James Court became the first president of the association, with Ross the vice-president. Court died in 1883 and Ross succeeded him as president, holding that office for 13 years — far longer than any of his successors.

Ross had no interest in public affairs. His view was: "Thank God I was never minded to get mixed up in politics and that dirty business." He was devoted to his family, his firm, and his profession.

He took an active part in the charitable work of the Presbyterian Church and, in particular, the Montreal Sailors' Institute. That institution sought to provide visiting sailors with safe recreation and relaxation away from the usual temptations of the dockyard.

Ross died in 1907. Summing up his life the Montreal *Herald* said: "In Mr. Philip Simpson Ross there passed away a citizen whose whole life, while unpretending and uneventful, illustrated to an exceptional degree the courage, the probity, the private generosity, and high principle."

Building on the founder's work, his successors have created one of the world's leading firms of public accountants. In 1958, P.S. Ross merged with George A. Touche & Co. to become Touche Ross, now the fifth largest public accounting firm in Canada with 1550 partners and professional staff operating from 35 offices. Internationally, the firm practises in 87 countries.

Source   Philip Creighton, "Philip S. Ross: Setting Accounting Standards where None Had Existed," *The Financial Post Special Report*, April 28, 1984, p. B5.

Account
An accounting record designed to classify and accumulate the dollar effect of financial transactions.

T-account
The form of an account that is used in accounting courses and elsewhere to illustrate the accumulation of financial information.

Debit
The left side of a T-account.

Credit
The right side of a T-account.

you imagine CP Rail or any other large entity recording its millions of financial transactions during the course of a time period in this manner? In actual practice, even small entities usually use a more efficient and convenient method. The widespread use of computers has revolutionized this record-keeping and calculation process. However, a manual methodology that is more efficient than that used in the preceding chapter is introduced in this chapter.

Each accounting transaction is actually recorded in, and accumulated by, an **account**. A separate account is used for each asset, liability, equity, each type of revenue, and each type of expense. A simplified account, often used graphically, is a **T-account** (because it resembles the letter T). The term **debit** is used to describe the left side of the account, the term **credit** the right side.

Debit	*Credit*
(always the left side)	(always the right side)

While the terms *debit* and *credit* had a specific meaning in their Latin roots and were used as recently as A.D. 1200, today the accountant uses them to mean "place an amount on the left side of an account" for debit and "place an amount on the right side of an account" for credit. Other than this, these terms have no other meaning in accounting. Students tend to associate "good" and "bad" or "increase" and "decrease" with *credit* and *debit*, but this is not a valid association and it should be avoided. For convenience, debit is often abbreviated as "Dr." and credit as "Cr."

In the case of the November transactions of BCC, a separate T-account would be prepared for each of: Cash, Accounts Receivable, Equipment, Truck, Bank Loan, Accounts Payable, Common Stock, Repair Revenue, Rent Expense, Salaries Expense, Supplies Used, and Truck Expense. Each transaction of the corporation affects more than one of these accounts. In fact, if a transaction affects the left side of one account, it also affects the right side of another account, and vice versa. This matching is *always* true of all accounting transactions. For example, study these three types of transactions.

Type of Transaction	An Asset Debit (increase)	Credit (decrease)	A Liability Debit (decrease)	Credit (increase)	Equity Debit (decrease)	Credit (increase)
1. An increase in An Asset and an increase in Equity.	X					X
2. An increase in An Asset and an increase in A Liability.	X			X		
3. A decrease in An Asset and a decrease in A Liability.		X	X			

Notice that, in each type of transaction affecting the accounts shown, a change on one side of a T-account always results in a change on the other side of another account. This dual feature of the debit-credit mechanism is common to every accounting transaction that is recorded in accounts; it is part of the double-entry model.

Although the evolution of this mechanism is unknown, a set of rules has gradually developed to record transactions in a manner that results in an equality of debits with credits. These rules are not self-evident truths, but rather a methodology that has become generally accepted. They have to be learned before double-entry record keeping as it is practised today can be mastered.

The *type* of account determines whether a debit represents an increase or a decrease in a particular transaction or whether a credit represents an increase or a decrease.

> The pattern of recording increases and decreases is common to accounts representing *assets* and *expenses*.

This guideline can be explained using the graphic T-account.

Debit (always the left side)	*Credit* (always the right side)
A debit records an increase in assets and expenses.	A credit records a decrease in assets and expenses.

> The pattern of recording increases and decreases is common to accounts representing *liabilities, equity,* and *revenues*.

This guideline can be explained using the graphic T-account.

Debit (always the left side)	*Credit* (always the right side)
A debit records a decrease in liabilities, equity, and revenues.	A credit records an increase in liabilities, equity, and revenues.

Students often have difficulty at first with this debit-credit, increase-decrease methodology. The following summary shows how debits and credits are used to record increases and decreases in various types of accounts.

ASSETS EXPENSES	LIABILITIES EQUITY REVENUES
Increases are DEBITED. Decreases are CREDITED.	Increases are CREDITED. Decreases are DEBITED.

As you use this system over time, you'll find that the debit-credit system used in recording transactions becomes second nature. However, the summary given above is repeated on some of the following pages where transactions of BCC are recorded to help you become familiar with the process. Refer to it as often as you find necessary.

> Accounting converts the transactions of an entity into financial statement information. In this conversion process, transactions are analyzed and recorded, summarized, and subsequently communicated to interested individuals. The equality of debits with credits is used to control the accuracy of this process. The basic accounting model is used not only to organize the transactions but also to communicate financial statement information. Accounting is essentially an art; it is not a science.

C. Transactions Analysis Using Accounts

Every business is involved in the analysis and recording of financial transactions. Accountants use the debit and credit system as a shorthand to keep track efficiently of the thousands of different financial events that occur during a time period.

The use of this debit and credit shorthand can be illustrated in the recording of the November transactions of Bluebeard Computer Corporation that were first examined in section C of Chapter 1 (Figure 1-3). The transactions are analyzed and recorded, then are summarized by account.

The analysis and recording process involves use of accounting procedures; the focus, however, is on the accounting process and how GAAP are applied in the records of an entity so that useful information is made available for decision making.

Illustrative Problem — The Debit-Credit Mechanism and Use of Accounts

The adjacent November transactions for Bluebeard Computer Corporation are used to illustrate the debit-credit mechanism and use of accounts. Where each transaction is discussed, the data are accumulated in the conceptual T-accounts to the right of the text.

Transaction Number Date	Description of Transaction	Application of Debit-Credit Methodology	
		Debit	*Credit*
1. Nov. 1	Bluebeard Computer Corporation issued 1,000 shares of common stock for $10,000 cash.	Cash	Common Stock
2. Nov. 2	The corporation purchased $3,000-worth of equipment on account.	Equipment	Accounts Payable
3. Nov. 3	The corporation purchased a repairman's truck for $8,000; paid $3,000 cash and incurred a $5,000 bank loan for the balance.	Truck	Cash Bank Loan
4. Nov. 14	The corporation paid $2,000 on account to a creditor in transaction 2.	Accounts Payable	Cash
5. Nov. 20	Equipment costing $1,000 was sold for $1,000 cash.	Cash	Equipment
6. Nov. 27	Computer repairs amounting to $7,000 were made for customers during the month as follows:		
	$4,000 of repairs were made for cash	Cash	Repair Revenue
	$3,000 of repairs were made on account.	Accounts Receivable	
7. Nov. 29	The corporation paid operating expenses for the month as follows:		
	$600 for rent	Rent Expense	Cash
	$2,500 for salaries	Salaries Expense	
	$1,200 for supplies used	Supplies Used	
	$700 for truck expenses (oil, gas, etc.)	Truck Expense	

REFER TO THE FOLLOWING AS YOU ANALYZE EACH TRANSACTION

ASSETS	LIABILITIES
EXPENSES	EQUITY
	REVENUES
Increases are DEBITED.	Increases are CREDITED.
Decreases are CREDITED.	Decreases are DEBITED.

Transaction 1 (November 1)
Bluebeard Computer Corporation issued 1,000 shares of common stock for a total of $10,000 cash.

Analysis: This is the corporation's first transaction. The issuance of common shares results in cash being received by the corporation. An asset account, Cash, is therefore increased by this transaction.

Debit: An asset is increased by a debit.

    Debit   Cash   10,000

Cash	
Debit	*Credit*
10,000	

An equity account, Common Stock, is also increased by $10,000 from this transaction.

Credit: An equity is increased by a credit.

    Credit   Common Stock   10,000

Common Stock	
Debit	*Credit*
	10,000

Transaction 2 (November 2)
Equipment to be received November 30 was purchased for $3,000 on account.

Analysis: An asset is acquired and a liability incurred in this transaction. The asset Equipment is acquired here and is therefore recorded as an increase in the Equipment account.

Debit: An asset is increased by a debit.

    Debit   Equipment   3,000

Equipment	
Debit	*Credit*
3,000	

By the purchase of equipment, a liability is incurred and is therefore recorded as an increase.

Credit: A liability is increased by a credit.

    Credit   Accounts Payable   3,000

Accounts Payable	
Debit	*Credit*
	3,000

Transaction 3 (November 3)
A truck for the repairman to be delivered on November 3 was purchased for $8,000; paid $3,000 cash and incurred a $5,000 bank loan for the balance.

Analysis: One asset is exchanged in this transaction; an obligation to pay an asset in the future is also incurred. An asset Truck is acquired from this purchase and is therefore recorded as an increase in the Truck account.

Debit: An asset is increased by a debit.

    Debit   Truck   8,000

Truck	
Debit	*Credit*
8,000	

The asset Cash is decreased by the purchase of the truck.

Credit: An asset is decreased by a credit.

    Credit   Cash   3,000

Cash	
Debit	*Credit*
10,000	
	3,000

REFER TO THE FOLLOWING AS YOU ANALYZE EACH TRANSACTION

ASSETS	LIABILITIES
EXPENSES	EQUITY
	REVENUES
Increases are DEBITED.	Increases are CREDITED.
Decreases are CREDITED.	Decreases are DEBITED.

A liability, bank loan, is incurred in the acquisition of the asset truck.
Credit: An obligation is increased by a credit.
>   Credit   Bank Loan   5,000

Bank Loan	
Debit	*Credit*
	5,000

Transaction 4 (November 14)
The corporation paid $2,000 on account to a creditor.

Analysis: This payment decreases Accounts Payable, a liability account, because the $2,000 is due to a creditor of the corporation.
Debit: A liability is decreased by a debit.
>   Debit   Accounts Payable   2,000

Accounts Payable	
Debit	*Credit*
	3,000
2,000	

The payment also decreases the asset Cash.
Credit: An asset is decreased by a credit.
>   Credit   Cash   2,000

Cash	
Debit	*Credit*
10,000	3,000
	2,000

Transaction 5 (November 20)
Unnecessary equipment that had cost $1,000 was sold for $1,000 cash. The equipment was to be delivered on November 30.

Analysis: One asset is exchanged for another in this transaction. The asset Cash is increased by $1,000 from the sale of the equipment at its original cost.
Debit: An asset is increased by a debit.
>   Debit   Cash   1,000

Cash	
Debit	*Credit*
10,000	3,000
	2,000
1,000	

The asset Equipment is decreased in this transaction.
Credit: An asset is decreased by a credit.
>   Credit   Equipment   1,000

Equipment	
Debit	*Credit*
3,000	
	1,000

Transaction 6 (November 27)
A total of $7,000-worth of computer repairs were made for customers by the corporation during its first month of business activities.

Analysis: An analysis of these revenue-creating activities reveals that the company earned $4,000 from cash customers and also earned $3,000 for repairs made on account. These revenue activities increase two asset accounts: the asset Cash is increased by $4,000 and the asset Accounts Receivable is increased by $3,000.
Debit: Both of these assets are increased by a debit.
>   Debit   Cash   4,000
>   Debit   Accounts Receivable   3,000

Cash	
Debit	*Credit*
10,000	3,000
1,000	2,000
4,000	

Accounts Receivable	
Debit	*Credit*
3,000	

The total revenue earned during the month is $7,000 and this increases revenue of the corporation.
Credit: An increase of revenue is recorded by a credit.
>   Credit   Repair Revenue   7,000

Repair Revenue	
Debit	*Credit*
	7,000

REFER TO THE FOLLOWING AS YOU ANALYZE EACH TRANSACTION

ASSETS	LIABILITIES
EXPENSES	EQUITY
	REVENUES
Increases are DEBITED.	Increases are CREDITED.
Decreases are CREDITED.	Decreases are DEBITED.

Transaction 7 (November 29)

Operating expenses were incurred and paid during the month to earn the repair revenue described in transaction 6. These expenses consist of: rent, $600; salaries expense, $2,500; supplies used, $1,200; and truck expenses, $700 (for oil, gas, etc.).

Analysis: These expenses, summarized here as one transaction for illustrative purposes, are recorded as increases.

Debit: Expenses are increased by a debit.

Debit	Rent expense	600
Debit	Salaries Expense	2,500
Debit	Supplies Used	1,200
Debit	Truck Expense	700

Rent Expense

Debit	Credit
600	

Salaries Expense

Debit	Credit
2,500	

Supplies Used

Debit	Credit
1,200	

Truck Expense

Debit	Credit
700	

Note that each expense is recorded in a separate expense account. Each type of expense is always recorded in its own individual T-account. The total payment of these expenses amounts to $5,000 ($600 + $2,500 + $1,200 + $700) and since they have been paid in cash, the Cash account, an asset account, is decreased by $5,000.

Credit: An asset is decreased by a credit.

Credit	Cash	5,000

Cash

Debit	Credit
10,000	3,000
1,000	2,000
4,000	
	5,000

Because the expenses have been summarized here as one transaction for illustrative purposes, the total payment is also summarized. In actual practice, each paid expense would be recorded individually by a debit to the appropriate expense account and a credit to Cash. Since the transactions are summarized here, only one credit of $5,000 is made to Cash.

Trial Balance Preparation

Footing
A total of a column of figures.

After the November transactions of Bluebeard Computer Corporation have been analyzed and recorded, the T-accounts are totalled in a process called **footing**, as shown in the following diagram; that is, each account with more than one transaction on the debit or credit side is totalled and the difference between the debit balance and the credit balance is calculated. In the case of the Cash account in the diagram, the balance of $5,000 is called a *debit balance*. In the following T-accounts, the numbers in parenthesis refer to the transaction numbers used in the preceding pages; the date of the transaction generally would be inserted here.

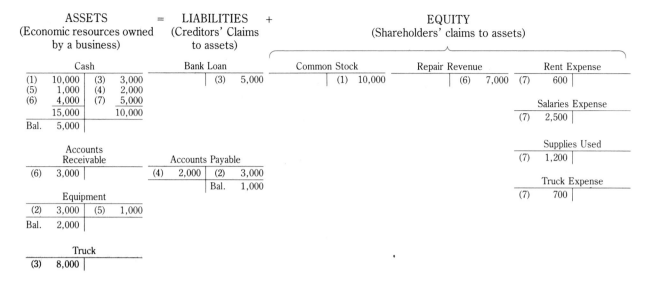

Trial balance
A list of each account together with its individual debit or credit balance; used to establish the equality of debits with credits before the preparation of financial statements.

A **trial balance** lists and totals all the debit and credit account balances in a two-column schedule. It is prepared after all transactions for the accounting period (November, in this case) have been recorded in appropriate accounts. The end of the month is the usual time for trial balance preparation, although it can be prepared any time that the mathematical accuracy of the T-account balances needs to be checked.

The form and content of a trial balance is illustrated below, using the account labels and account balances of Bluebeard Computer Corporation.

Bluebeard Computer Corporation
Trial Balance
November 30, 19X1

	Account Balances		
	Debit	*Credit*	
Cash	$ 5,000		
Accounts Receivable	3,000		
Equipment	2,000		
Truck	8,000		
Bank Loan		$ 5,000	
Accounts Payable		1,000	
Common Stock		10,000	
Repair Revenue		7,000	
Rent Expense	600		These accounts are used to prepare the Income Statement.
Salaries Expense	2,500		
Supplies Used	1,200		
Truck Expense	700		
	$23,000	$23,000	
	Total	Total	
	Debit =	Credit	

Since a double-entry system has been used in recording the transactions of Bluebeard Computer Corporation, the total of debit account balances must equal the total of credit account balances. The trial balance establishes that this equality actually exists, but it does not ensure that each item has been entered in the proper account. Neither does it ensure that all items that should have been entered, have in fact been entered. Both of these errors could have occurred and the trial balance would still balance. In addition, a transaction may have been recorded twice. Nevertheless, a trial balance is prepared before the financial statements are begun.

Preparation of Financial Statements

An interim income statement is a statement to be prepared before the entity's year-end from the revenue and expense accounts listed in the trial balance.

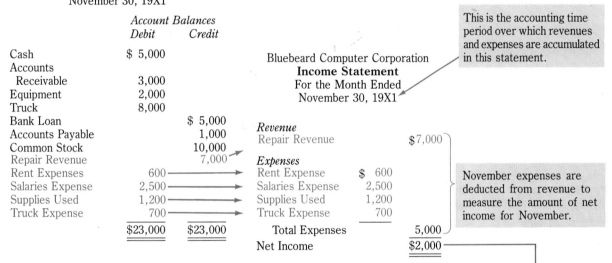

The interim balance sheet is prepared next. The assets, liabilities, and equities belong in the balance sheet.

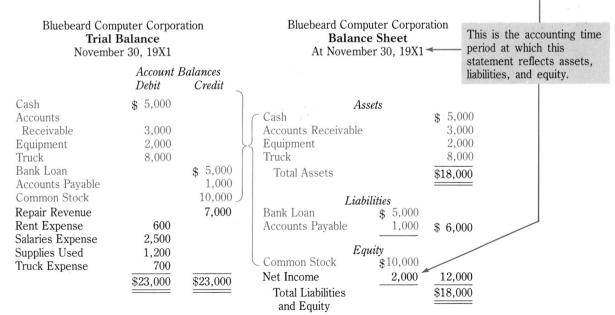

Note that the actual format of the balance sheet can vary. Two commonly used formats are the *account form* and the *report form*. They are illustrated below so that you can compare them. The same information is conveyed by both formats.

Balance Sheet Formats

Account Form				Report Form	
Assets	$xxx	*Liabilities*	$ xx	*Assets*	$xxx
		Equity	x		
	$xxx		$xxx		$xxx
				Liabilities	$ xx
				Equity	x
					$xxx

Assets appear on the left side, and liabilities and equity appear on the right side when the account form is used.

Assets are presented first, with liability and equity items following when the report form is used.

D. Using Formal Accounting Records

The preceding analysis of financial transactions included a debit and credit entry for each transaction as well as the accumulation of dollar amounts in T-accounts. Formal accounting records are kept in a general journal and general ledger.

A **general journal** is a ruled form used to record chronologically the debit and credit analysis of the entity's financial transactions (see Figure 2-2). It is often referred to as a book of original entry. **Journalizing** is the process of recording a financial transaction (called an **entry**) in the journal. In addition to a general journal, formal accounting records also include specialized journals, which are discussed in Chapter 6.

A **general ledger** is a ruled form used to maintain all the accounts of the entity in one place. **Posting** is the process of transferring amounts from the journal to a ledger account. Because amounts recorded in the journal eventually end up in a ledger account, the general ledger is sometimes referred to as a book of final entry.

Recording Transactions in the General Journal

A general journal provides a complete record of transactions in chronological order in one place. Each transaction is recorded first in the journal. The November transactions of Bluebeard Computer Corporation are recorded in its general journal in Figure 2-2. The journalizing procedure follows a number of steps.

1. The year is recorded at the top and the month is entered on the first line of page 1. This information is repeated only on each new journal page used to record transactions.
2. The date of the first transaction is entered in the second column, on the first line. The day of each transaction is always recorded in this second column.
3. The name of the account to be debited is entered in the description column on the first line. Accounts to be debited are always recorded before accounts to be credited. The amount of the debit is recorded in the debit column. A dash is often used by accountants in place of .00 cents.

General journal
A chronological record of an entity's financial transactions; often referred to as a *book of original entry*.

Journalizing
The process of recording a transaction in a journal.

Journal entry
An entry recorded in the general journal with at least one debit and one credit.

General ledger
A book that contains the asset, liability, equity, revenue, and expense accounts of an entity; often referred to as a *book of final entry*.

Posting
The process of transferring amounts from the journal to a ledger account.

4. The name of the account to be credited is on the second line of the description column and is indented about one-quarter of the column. Accounts to be credited are always indented in this way in the journal. The amount of the credit is recorded in the credit column. Again, a dash is used in place of .00 cents.
5. An explanation of the transaction, usually referred to as a journal entry narrative, is entered also in the description column, on the next line. It is not indented.
6. A line is usually skipped after each journal entry to separate individual journal entries and the date of the next entry recorded. It is unnecessary to repeat the month (November here) as long as it is unchanged from that recorded at the top of the page.

BCC's first two journal entries have one debit and credit. An entry can also have more than one debit or credit, in which case it is referred to as a **compound entry**. The entry of November 3 is an example of a compound entry.

The positioning of the debit-credit entry is similar in some respects to a programming language. This entry instructs:
Post $10,000 to the debit side of the Cash account (increasing cash by $10,000) and
Post $10,000 to the credit side of the Common Stock account (increasing this equity by $10,000).

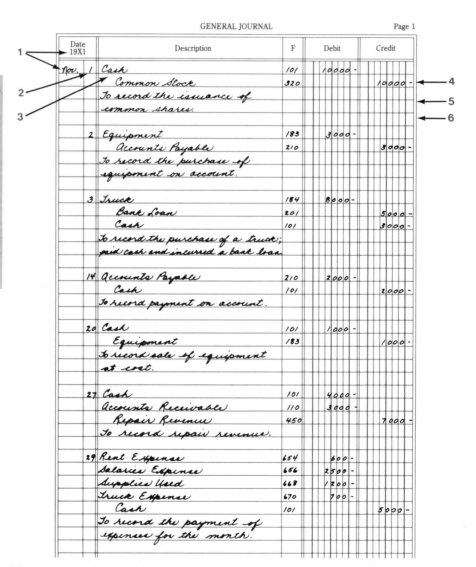

Figure 2-2   **General journal transactions for BCC in November**

Posting Transactions in the Ledger

Ledger account
An account kept in a book called a ledger.

The **ledger account** is a more formal variation of the T-account and is used by companies with a manual accounting system. Ledger accounts are kept in the general ledger, often a loose-leaf binder. Debits and credits recorded in the general ledger are posted to appropriate ledger accounts so that the balance of each account can be found easily at any time. The posting of amounts and recording of other information is illustrated in Figure 2-3, using the first transaction of Bluebeard Computer Corporation.

The journal connects the transaction with the ledger.

The ledger is a device to classify and store transactions.

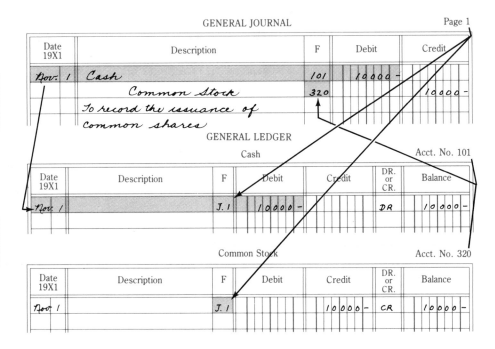

Figure 2-3   A transaction posted in general ledger

1. The date and amount are posted to the appropriate ledger account. Here the debit Cash entry is posted to the Cash ledger account and the credit Common Stock entry to the Common Stock ledger account.
2. The journal page number is recorded in the folio (F) column of each ledger account as a cross reference. In this case, the posting has been made from journal page 1; the reference is recorded as J.1.
3. The appropriate ledger account number is recorded in the folio (F) column of the general journal to indicate the posting has been made to that particular account. Here the debit Cash entry has been posted to Account No. 101 and the credit Common Stock entry to Account No. 320.

Following the posting process, a balance is calculated for each ledger account. A notation is recorded in the Dr./Cr. column indicating whether the balance in the account is a debit or credit. This manual posting is a slow process. Many accounting departments, especially in large companies, use specially designed mechanical equipment where the volume of transactions justifies their use; a posting machine is one example of such equipment. More recently, computers have replaced most of these posting machines, since the accumulation of debit and credit amounts by account is most efficiently performed by a computer.

In this and subsequent chapters either the conceptual T-account or the more formal three-column ledger account can be used in completing assignment material. Both types of accounts are used in subsequent chapters, although your instructor may prefer use of one or the other.

Chart of Accounts

Chart of accounts
A list of account names and numbers used in the general ledger; usually found in financial statement presentation order.

The ledger accounts used by an entity are organized using a chart of accounts. Typically accounts are grouped within asset, liability, equity, revenue, and expense classifications; a number is assigned to each account to be used by the entity. Flexibility exists in the chart of accounts through the inclusion of gaps in the numerical sequence, so that subsequent accounts can be added. Here is the chart of accounts for Bluebeard Computer Corporation.

Bluebeard Computer Corporation
CHART OF ACCOUNTS

Balance Sheet Accounts

101–199 *Asset Accounts*
101 Cash
106 Temporary Investments
110 Accounts Receivable
116 Interest Receivable
120 Notes Receivable
150 Merchandise Inventory
160 Prepaid Advertising
161 Prepaid Insurance
162 Prepaid Rent
173 Supplies
180 Land
181 Building
182 Furniture
183 Equipment
184 Truck

200–299 *Liability Accounts*
201 Bank Loan
210 Accounts Payable
214 Loans Payable
222 Interest Payable
226 Salaries Payable
231 Property Taxes Payable
236 Utilities Payable
237 Wages Payable

300–399 *Equity Accounts*
320 Common Stock
340 Retained Earnings
350 Dividends
360 Income Summary

Income Statement Accounts

400–499 *Revenue Accounts*
450 Repair Revenue
460 Revenue (for other types not identified within the operating revenue category)
470 Service Revenue
480 Subscriptions Revenue

600–699 *Expense Accounts*
610 Advertising Expense
615 Commissions Expense
630 Equipment Rental Expense
631 Insurance Expense
632 Interest Expense
641 Maintenance Expense
642 Miscellaneous Expense
650 Office Supplies Used
651 Property Tax Expense
654 Rent Expense
656 Salaries Expense
668 Supplies Used
669 Telephone Expense
670 Truck Expense
676 Utilities Expense
677 Wages Expense

800–899 *Other Accounts*
830 Income Tax Expense

The use of these accounts is explained in Chapter 4.

A common practice is to have the accounts arranged in a manner that is compatible with the order of their use in financial statements. Although it is not a rigid rule to number accounts in this manner, it does have considerable advantage and is recommended in this text. (List accounts in the above sequence when completing assignment material for this text that requires the preparation of financial statements. The above accounts and account numbers are applicable to all the assignment material in this and the following chapters.)

The Accounting Cycle

In the preceding pages, the November transactions of Bluebeard Computer Corporation were used to demonstrate the sequential steps performed by the accountant in converting economic data into financial information. This conversion was carried out in accordance with the basic double-entry accounting model established by Luca Pacioli in 1494. These sequential steps can be visually summarized as follows:

Step 1: Transactions Are Analyzed and Recorded.
Journalizing consists of analyzing transactions as they occur, to see how they affect the accounting equation, and then recording the transactions chronologically in the general journal.

Step 2: Transactions Are Summarized by Account.
Posting consists of transferring debits and credits from the general journal to the appropriate ledger accounts.

Step 3: The Equality of Debits with Credits Is Established To Ensure Accuracy.
Preparing a trial balance consists of listing account names and balances to prove the equality of total debit balances with total credit balances.

Step 4: The Summarized Trans-actions Are Communicated
Preparing financial statements at this point consists of using the data listed in the columns of the trial balance to prepare the income statement and the balance sheet.

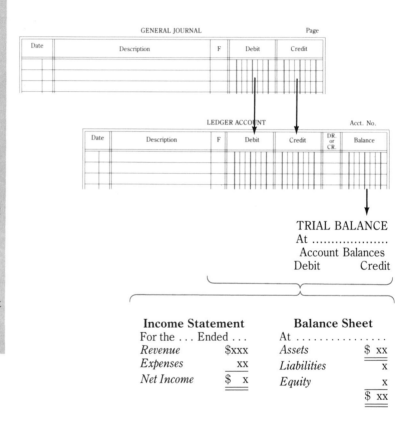

The sequence just described, beginning with the journalizing of the transactions, and ending with the communication of financial information in financial statements, is commonly referred to as the **accounting cycle**. Although the number of steps is expanded somewhat in chapters 3 and 4, the basic sequence is not changed; these additional steps are needed because of the large number of transactions facing the modern corporation and the special accounting procedures needed for the artificial time periods within which financial information is communicated.

Accounting cycle
The individual steps required to process accounting information during an accounting period.

Discussion Questions

1. What are generally accepted accounting principles (GAAP)?
2. The dollar is seen as the most appropriate measure for the analysis and recording of transactions in Canada. Is its use valid in these days of rapid inflation: why or why not?
3. What is the realization concept?
4. How does the matching concept attempt to determine most accurately the income of a business?
5. What are the qualities that accounting information is expected to have?
6. Name the North American accounting organizations concerned with the formulation of accounting principles.
7. What is the *CICA Handbook*? How does the CICA separate the Canadian experience in formulating accounting principles from that in other parts of the world?
8. What is an auditor's report? What does it indicate?
9. Why is the use of a transactions worksheet impractical in actual practice?
10. What is an account? How are debits and credits used to record transactions?
11. Students tend to associate ''good'' and ''bad'' or ''increase'' and ''decrease'' with credits and debits. Is this a valid association? Explain.
12. The pattern of recording increases and decreases is common to asset and expense accounts. Explain, using an example.
13. The pattern of recording increases and decreases is common to liabilities, equity, and revenues. Explain, using an example.
14. Summarize the rules for using debits and credits to record assets, expenses, liabilities, equity, and revenues.
15. What is a trial balance? Why is it prepared?
16. How is a trial balance used to prepare financial statements?
17. A general journal is often called a book of original entry. Why?
18. The positioning of a debit-credit entry in the general journal is similar in some respects to programming methods. Explain, using an example.
19. What is a ledger? Why is it prepared?
20. What is a chart of accounts? What is the advantage of arranging the accounts in a manner that is compatible with the order of their use in financial statements?
21. List the steps in the accounting cycle.
22. Define accounting.
23. Is accounting an art or a science?
24. Refer to Discussion Case 1-1 in Chapter 1. Accountants refer to GAAP when valuing assets shown on a balance sheet. Identify the accounting principles that relate directly to Sir Rodolph and explain the application of each principle in Sir Rodolph's cases.
25. Compare and contrast standard setting as it is discussed in Conceptual Issue 2-1 and Real Life Example 2-2. What is the role of standards? What is the effect of the *CICA Handbook* having a quasi-legislative weight in the federal and provincial business corporations and securities acts?

Discussion Cases

Discussion Case 2-1: Ivan and Igor, Wheat Growers

Many, many years ago, there lived a feudal landlord in a small province of Central Europe. The landlord, called the Red-Bearded Baron, lived in a castle high on a hill, and this benevolent fellow was responsible for the well-being of many peasants who occupied the lands surrounding his castle. Each spring, as the snow began to melt and thoughts of other, less influential men turned to matters other than business, the baron would decide how to provide for all his serf-dependents during the coming year.

One spring, the baron was thinking about the wheat crop of the coming growing season. ''I believe that 30 acres of my land, being worth 5 bushels of wheat per acre, will produce

enough wheat for next winter,'' he mused, ''but who should do the farming? I believe I'll give Ivan the Indefatigable and Igor the Immutable the task of growing the wheat.'' Whereupon Ivan and Igor, two serfs noted for their hard work and not overly active minds, were summoned for an audience with the landlord.

''Ivan, you will farm on the 20-acre plot of ground, and Igor will farm the 10-acre plot,'' the baron began. ''I will give Ivan 20 bushels of wheat for seed and 20 pounds of fertilizer. (Twenty pounds of fertilizer are worth 2 bushels of wheat.) Igor will get 10 bushels of wheat for seed and 10 pounds of fertilizer. I will give each of you an ox to pull a plough, but you will have to make arrangements with Feyador, the plough-maker, for a plough. The oxen, incidentally, are only three years old and have never been used for farming, so they should have a good 10 years of farming ahead of them. Take good care of them, because an ox is worth 40 bushels of wheat. Come back next fall and return the oxen and the ploughs along with your harvest.''

Ivan and Igor genuflected and withdrew from the Great Hall, taking with them the things provided by the baron.

The summer came and went, and after the harvest Ivan and Igor returned to the Great hall to account to their master for the things given them in the spring. Ivan, pouring 223 bushels of wheat onto the floor, said, "My lord, I present you with a slightly used ox, a plough broken beyond repair, and 223 bushels of wheat. I, unfortunately, owe Feyador the ploughmaker, 3 bushels of wheat for the plough I got from him last fall. And, as you might expect, I used all the fertilizer and seed you gave me last spring. You will also remember, my lord, that you took 20 bushels of my harvest for your own personal use."

Igor, who had been given 10 acres of land, 10 bushels of wheat, and 10 pounds of fertilizer, spoke next. "Here, my lord, is a partially used ox, the plough for which I gave Feyador the ploughmaker 3 bushels of wheat from my harvest, and 105 bushels of wheat. I, too, used all my seed and fertilizer last spring. Also, my lord, you took 30 bushels of wheat several days ago for your own table. I believe the plough is good for two more seasons."

"Fellows, you did well," said the Red-Bearded Baron. Blessed with this benediction and not wishing to press their luck further, the two serfs departed hastily.

After the servants had taken their leave, the Red-Bearded Baron, watching the two hungry oxen slowly eating the wheat piled on the floor, began to contemplate what had happened. "Yes," he thought, "they did well, but I wonder which one did better?"

Source W.T. Andrews, Jr., "Another Improbable Occurrence", *The Accounting Review*, April 1974. Reprinted with permission of the author and the editor of *The Accounting Review*.

Required: Assuming that a bushel of wheat is the standard measure in use in this province of Central Europe, prepare:

1. A separate balance sheet at the beginning of the spring season for Ivan and for Igor.
2. A separate income statement for the harvest season for Ivan and for Igor.
3. A separate balance sheet at the end of the fall season for Ivan and for Igor.
4. If the Red-Bearded Baron was willing to give the serf who achieved the greater gain a bonus of one bushel of wheat, which serf would receive the bonus?

Consider using each of the following measures of efficiency in making your decision:

a.	$\dfrac{\text{Net Income}}{\text{Number of Acres}}$	c.	$\dfrac{\text{Net Income}}{\text{Owner's Equity}}$
b.	$\dfrac{\text{Net income}}{\text{Total Assets Employed}}$	d.	$\dfrac{\text{Net Income}}{\text{Bushels of Wheat Grown}}$

Discussion Case 2-2: Flick of a Pen

For years, there has been an argument between the auditor-general and the government over the fact that a large part of federal revenue and spending are "off-budget". The items were included in the government's non-budgetary accounts and any deficits — or surpluses — did not show up in the budgetary deficit.

The debate does not affect the federal government's statement of its financial requirements. Whether a deficit item is recorded on or off the budget, it still represents money Ottawa must raise to meet its commitments.

In his last three annual reports to parliament, [Auditor-General] Dye has argued with increasing forcefulness that several off-budget items, along with their accumulated deficits, should be folded into the government's main books.

The Tories have not accepted all his advice and it shows in Mr. Dye's opinion and observatations attached to the 1983–84 accounts.

Despite the government's changes, Mr. Dye still has several reservations with Ottawa's accounting policies.

He continues to complain that there is fragmented reporting of government activities, that some assets are reported in excess of their value, and that some liabilities have not been recorded.

Had the government accepted all his recommendations, it would have added another $5.2 billion to last year's deficit and almost $20 billion to Ottawa's accumulated deficit.

As it was, the extraordinary item helped push the government's accumulated deficit — which represents all the deficits piled up since Confederation — to $157 billion.

A key complaint of Mr. Dye's is that over $8 billion in federal revenue and spending flows through what are called "specified purpose accounts", such as unemployment insurance and Canadian ownership accounts.

The government argues that these must be kept separate because the law says so.

Mr. Dye said he does not believe that consolidation of the special accounts into the main books "requires legislative amendment, and my legal counsel concurs".

With a simple change in the way it keeps its books, the federal government has tacked $5.2 billion on to the deficit for the 1983–84 fiscal year.

Mr. Wilson told the Commons that the Conservative

government had accepted some accounting advice from Mr. Dye.

The changes, he said in an accompanying document, added $300 million to the 1983–84 deficit and would continue to add between $500 million and $800 million a year in the future.

What he did not say was that the government would also pull into its budgetary accounts so-called ''off-budget'' deficits from previous years.

The accumulation of those shortfalls added up to $4.9 billion which, along with the $300 million for 1983–84, totals $5.2 billion, and has been brought into last year's deficit under the heading ''extraordinary item''.

The biggest item is $1.9 billion, which is set aside to cover vacation and termination benefits for federal employees. Previously, these were recorded as they were paid and no allowance was made for the fact that many employees allowed their holiday time to build up over the years.

Another $1.7 billion of the total converts some government loans outstanding — mainly to less developed countries — to grants, recognizing they will probably never be repaid. Mr. Dye still thinks another $1 billion should be written off in this fashion.

In addition, $1.15 billion in losses by the two government-owned aircraft companies — Canadair Ltd. and de Havilland Aircraft of Canada, Ltd. — are also brought into the budgetary deficit.

The other $450 million is a one-shot item to cover money the government expects to have to pay for statutory items like fiscal stabilization and the Crow's Nest benefit payments.

The effect of these changes, according to the public accounts released yesterday, is to raise Ottawa's total budgetary deficit last year to $37.5 billion, not the $31.8 billion cited by Mr. Wilson on November 8.

Mr. Wilson's figure of $31.8 billion included the $300 million he mentioned in his documents, but not the $4.9 billion deficit backlog.

Adding the backlog brings the deficit figure to $36.7 billion, leaving an $800 million discrepancy between Mr. Wilson's figures and those reported yesterday.

The reason for the difference, as he explained on November 8, is $800 million in revenue generated last year by the Canadian Ownership Special Charge, a levy at the gasoline pumps introduced to finance the Petro-Canada takeover of Petrofina Canada Inc., but still in effect long after the acquisition was paid for.

Mr. Wilson, like his predecessor, treats the COSC revenue as a budgetary item, but the people who keep the public accounts treat it as non-budgetary revenue.

Effectively, that reduces budgetary revenue by $800 million and tacks the same amount on to the budgetary deficit. It is that bit of arithmetic which produces the $37.5 billion deficit.

Source   ''Flick of a pen adds $5.2-billion to deficit'', *The Globe and Mail*, December 8, 1984, p. B-1.

For Discussion

1. A framework of accounting principles has received general acceptance within the business community and accounting profession. This acceptance doesn't seem to sit well with the federal government, if the auditor-general has reservations about the federal government's accounting policies. What are the implications of: (a) reporting some assets in excess of their value? and (b) not recording some liabilities?

2. Is the 1983–84 deficit $31.8 billion or $37.5 billion? Explain your answer.

3. Financial statements of business entities are prepared according to a number of assumptions and a number of accounting practices. Which of these (discussed in section A of Chapter 2) appear not to be followed by the federal government?

4. The government could argue that Unemployment Insurance and other programs are not similar to what accountants call ''contingent liabilities'', since any potential problems can be remedied simply by raising premiums. Discuss.

Discussion Case 2-3:   The Osborne Collapse

Mr. Osborne started Osborne Computer with $1 million in seed money from Mr. Melchor's firm and several private investors. Prior to that he was a successful author of microprocessor textbooks and had been head of data processing at the Shell Oil Development Company. The 44-year-old Mr. Osborne is described as charming, persuasive, egotistical, and supremely confident.

Attracting capital into Osborne Computer was never a problem — at least until near the time it declared bankruptcy. Besides the seed money, there was a $1.6-million financing in late 1981 that helped kick off the company's marketing drive. With sales booming, Osborne Computer found venture capital firms clamouring for its private offering the following spring. Virtually all of the same venture firms that participated in that deal lined up again in early April of 1983 to ink their names to another commitment of almost $9 million. The company's earnings problems had not yet come to their attention.

Yet even after hearing the bad earnings news, the venture capitalist and other investors still had hope, and they came up with an additional $11 million in June. Within a matter of weeks, however, investment bankers were not able to find new investors for a further $20 million, which the company considered necessary to speed its I.B.M. compatible product from drawing board to market.

While Mr. Osborne may have sparked enthusiasm among investors, it was the 59-year-old Mr. Melchor who inspired confidence. He had been in charge of Hewlett-Packard's Palo Alto, Calif., division, and was dabbling in venture capital before going into it full time about 15 years ago.

Usually preferring to act alone or with only one other small venture capital firm when providing seed financing for a new company, Mr. Melchor was one of the original founders of Rolm, Verbatim, and Triad Systems, all successes. In addition, he can point to a string of successful start-up investments, such as Biomation, Kaspar Instruments, Consolidated Video Systems, and Telecommunications Technology, all of which have been sold to larger companies.

Typically, only the investors in the initial seed stages of a company's financing—Mr. Melchor at Osborne, for example — sit on the board and play an active role in monitoring the company's progress. And if the company starts to flounder, they are the ones who rally board support for a change in top management. At Osborne Computer, investors expected Mr. Melchor to play that role if necessary—he was their security belt.

As David Anderson of Sutter Hill Ventures in Palo Alto said, "In this type situation, where our involvement was less than $750,000 and where there were highly qualified investors from earlier rounds of financing, we trusted them to manage our investment."

Venture capitalists are also swayed by who else is in on the deal. Thomas Unterberg of L. F. Rothschild, Unterberg, Towbin, for instance, noted that Osborne Computer "was going great guns and a lot of our friends were investors". Among those friends, he said, were Mr. Melchor, Mr. Oshman, Mr. Noyce, and Benjamin Rosen of Sevin-Rosen Partners. Mr. Unterberg said he put about $1 million of his firm's venture capital funds into Osborne, including about $100,000 of his own money.

Another factor that apparently prompted investors to jump on the bandwagon was the expectation that a public offering of the company's stock was just around the corner.

Whether too much was expected of Mr. Melchor by other venture capitalists is one of the big unanswered questions. As one of the lead investors, he served as the company's chairman in 1982 and played a hand in all of its financings, Mr. Melchor maintains that he personally did not solicit much of the money raised, but rather provided the company with lists of prospective investors. Those who were interested then discussed the deals and the company's prospects with Mr. Osborne or his fellow executives.

Altogether the venture firms in which Mr. Melchor is either the general partner or an adviser control about $17 million, $2 million of which was invested in Osborne. In addition, Mr. Melchor said he put $1.25 million of his own family's money into the company's last deal.

But did he do enough to correct the deficiencies in the company itself? Mr. Melchor is quick to point out that "the chairman of the company has no authority". But "collectively" he added, "the board could probably have done a hell of a lot more in forcing the issues earlier."

Mr. Osborne, however, insists that "if you take a look at the record of right and wrong decisions, we did damned well — as good as anyone." He added that the game plan he directed was "to put the pedal to the metal and go for it before I.B.M. killed our market."

It was not until the fall of last year, however, that the board convinced Mr. Osborne to step aside as chief executive officer. Ostensibly the change was made to bring in more professional management in preparation for a public offering of securities that, as it turned out, never came to pass. The new chief executive was Robert Jaunich 2d, who was wooed to Osborne from the presidency of the Consolidated Foods Corporation.

In retrospect, if the move to replace Mr. Osborne had been made six months earlier, admits Mr. Melchor, "the company would probably be O.K. today". Certainly a public offering might have been possible if Mr. Jaunich had been on board last year. And the money it raised, some analysts believe, might have been enough to weather this year's financial storms and speed up introduction of an I.B.M. compatible model.

One of the series of problems that unfolded this past spring — and one that helped convince investment bankers to drop the idea of taking the company public—was a requirement by auditors. According to Mr. Melchor, the auditors determined that heavy reserves needed to be set up to account for losses stemming from the premature announcement of a new model computer. As a result, Osborne lost more than $8 million for the year ending February 28, compared with a loss of only $1 million for the year ending November 1982.

Much of the investor-initiated lawsuit focuses on the lack of financial information available to the investor group when the company asked it in March 1983 to purchase about $9 million in stock warrants. Mr. Melchor maintains that the company's earnings problems did not surface until late April and that he "immediately called a meeting of investors".

In order to reconstruct what went wrong, Mr. Melchor said, "I have gone back and tried to talk to all who were involved." So far the lesson he has been reminded of is that "quite often the entrepreneur who starts a fast-growth company is not the person who should manage the growth".

To William Egan of Burr, Egan & Deleage, a Boston and San Francisco venture capital firm that put $1.8 million into Osborne, the company's meteoric rise and fall shows "dramatically the importance of a strategic decision", such as reacting to I.B.M.'s entry into personal computers. He added that without a seat on the board, "We did not play an important role in Osborne."

Other investors in Osborne say they come away from the experience with greater respect for the topsy-turvy nature of the personal computer field. "Today's winners are not necessarily those of tomorrow," said Sutter Hill's Mr. Anderson.

Miss Dyson of Rosen Research, however, contends that investors would not be licking their wounds today if they had done more homework on the company in the first place. "What happened at Osborne," she says, "is not a warning against problems in the microprocessor industry. It's really a warning for people who invest carelessly."

To venture capital firms the financing deal for the Osborne

Computer Corporation was an offer they simply couldn't refuse. Barely 12 months after introducing the world's first portable computer, Osborne's sales hit a sizzling $70-million-a-year clip. At the helm was the charismatic British computer whiz Adam Osborne, and sitting in the watchdog role as chairman was Jack L. Melchor, a respected venture capitalist whose string of successful technology investments in Silicon Valley was practically without equal.

And now Osborne Computer had decided to give up 18 percent of its ownership to raise $10 million from private investors to stoke the furnace further. There was even talk that investment bankers would be creating a public market for Osborne's stock within a matter of months.

"Everyone wanted in on the offering in the worst way. It was the hottest private deal around," recalls Sanford Robertson of Robertson, Colman & Stephens, a San Francisco brokerage firm whose venture capital operation participated.

But these days venture capitalists, including Mr. Robertson, are wishing they had refused the offer. Osborne Computer, which was born in early 1981, filed for bankruptcy in September, leaving its investors exposed to a potential loss of at least $30 million.

Most of that investment was made on behalf of wealthy individuals and corporate pension plans which are partners in funds managed by 10 technology-oriented venture capital firms — Melchor Venture Management, G.T. Technology Investors, Technology Venture Investors, the venture capital operations of L.F. Rothschild, Unterberg, Towbin and Smith Barney, Harris Upham, Sutter Hill Ventures, Montgomery Ventures, Burr, Egan & Deleage, Sevin-Rosen Partners, and Hambro America.

Also exposed on its own are the pension and profit-sharing plans of the Hewlett-Packard Corporation. That company's president, John Young, is a participant in Mr. Melchor's Portolla II, a venture fund that also invested in Osborne. Also in Portolla II are a number of other executives from leading technology companies, such as Robert Noyce, vice-chairman of Intel, and M. Kenneth Oshman, president of Rolm, who was also a director of Osborne Computer.

Venture capital, of course, is by nature a risky business and even the best firms have their share of losers. But the speed with which Osborne fell — after a spectacular, though shortlived, rise — has caught the industry by surprise, especially because the company appeared to be on a fast track to success. Usually when a venture capital-backed company fails, it loses its seed money and perhaps an initial round of financing. Osborne Computer went through five separate rounds of financing and, as it looks now, could rank as one of the largest losses in the history of the United States venture-capital industry.

There is another unusual aspect to the Osborne financing: a number of venture firms and other investors are suing the company's auditor and many of its officers and directors, including Mr. Osborne himself, for alleged false and misleading financial information. One of the defendants in that suit is Mr. Melchor, which gives it the added twist that venture capitalists are suing one of their own fraternity, something rarely done in this close-knit world.

How could a company off to such an auspicious start end up in such a mess? And why did such sophisticated technology investors miss the early warning signals that in retrospect seem to have been so obvious? More important, what investment lessons are there to be learned — not just by venture capitalists but by any investor in one of the overnight wonders of the technology industry?

In part, of course, Osborne Computer stumbled and fell because of the shakeout under way in the personal computer business. Even giant Texas Instruments had to concede a week and a half ago that it could not make a go of it on the home computer battlefront. In the portable computer field Osborne stood alone when it introduced its first product. Now more than 50 companies are chipping away at the market.

Nevertheless, what the venture capitalists missed in their assessment of Osborne was that it was poorly managed and ill-prepared for growth and the competition that inevitably would head its way. As Esther Dyson, president of Rosen Research, a publisher of a newsletter for the personal computer industry, said: "There was a typical non-business mentality at Osborne."

Not only did other companies, notably Kaypro, enter that market with a lower-priced portable computer with at least as much all-inclusive software, but also the I.B.M. personal computer, introduced in late 1981, fast became the technology standard-bearer by which other personal computers were judged. Osborne did not react fast enough to adopt I.B.M.'s state of the art technology or to come out with a portable model that customers would find compatible with their I.B.M. personal computer at home or in the office, added Alexander Stein of Data Quest, a San Jose technology-oriented consulting firm.

Even last spring when Osborne did come up with a more sophisticated version of its original product, Mr. Osborne made the mistake of announcing it too soon, according to Mr. Stein. As a result, sales of the existing models dried up immediately, inventories had to be written off and it was more than a month before the new model was able to generate sales again. That episode and the lack of an I.B.M. compatible product to sell this past summer created a cash-flow problem that eventually forced the company into bankruptcy.

Source: Fred R. Bleakley, "The Osborne Collapse," *New York Times*, Nov. 6, 1983, Section 3, Page 1.

For Discussion

1. Each entity is assumed to have an unlimited life, as referred to in the going-concern assumption. Yet Osborne Computer Corporation became a "gone concern". What is a gone concern and how does one affect the application of accounting assumptions and practices in the preparation of financial statements?

2. What role does the auditor play in relation to audited financial statements? Why would the auditor be sued in the Osborne failure?

3. Corporate organization was discussed in section A and Figure 1-2 of Chapter 1. What role would the board of directors have played in relation to shareholders of Osborne?

Discussion Case 2-4:   Regulating Accounting

Canadian companies registered with the United States Securities and Exchange Commission (SEC) are being asked to include information on the effects of changing prices in accordance with *CICA Handbook* section 4510.

A letter from Clarence Sampson, SEC chief accountant, stating the commission's view is reproduced below.

January 13, 1984
Mr. R.D. Thomas, FCA
General Director of Research
Canadian Institute of Chartered Accountants

Dear Mr. Thomas:
This letter responds to your request regarding the supplementary information on the effects of changing prices which Canadian registrants should include in filings with this Commission. A recent letter to a Canadian chartered accounting firm provided the following staff position.

Section 4510 of the Canadian Institute of Chartered Accountants Handbook closely parallels Statement of Financial Accounting Standards No. 33 (''FAS 33'') in both scope and content. Both standards specify certain supplemental information which, although not technically a part of the generally accepted accounting principles governing the recognition, measurement, and display of the elements constituting the primary financial statements, is considered beneficial to users of financial reports, especially the reports of large publicly held enterprises.

The staff believes that Canadian and other non-domestic registrants should include information on the effects of changing prices where standards are in effect in the respective countries of such registrants. Accordingly, since *CICA Handbook* section 4510 was issued in December 1982, it appears that those Canadian registrants to which section 4510 is directly applicable (ie, large publicly held enterprises which meet the threshold test of the section) should include the specified information in SEC filings which include annual financial statements for 1983 and later calendar years and for fiscal years ending after 1983.

Sincerely,
[Signed: Clarence Sampson]

Courtesy of the CICA.

For Discussion

1. The *CICA Handbook* has received general acceptance in the formulation of accounting principles in Canada. For instance, in the letter reproduced above, the United States Securities and Exchange Commission is asking the CICA to include specified information with financial statements. Discuss the implications of the *CICA Handbook* formulated GAAP requiring the approval of foreign government agencies, such as the SEC.
2. The *CICA Handbook* incorporates Canadian GAAP and has a quasi-legislative weight in Canada. How does the Canadian experience differ from that in the United States?
3. What concession does the SEC appear to be making in relation to section 4510 of the *CICA Handbook*?

Comprehension Problems

Comprehension Problem 2-1

The following is a chart of accounts for George's Multiple Repair Services Ltd.

Balance Sheet Accounts

Assets
101 Cash
110 Accounts Receivable
161 Prepaid Insurance
173 Supplies
183 Equipment
184 Truck

Liabilities and Equity
201 Bank Loan
210 Accounts Payable
320 Common Stock

Income Statement Accounts

Revenue
450 Repair Revenue

Expenses
631 Insurance Expense
654 Rent Expense
668 Supplies Used
670 Truck Expense
678 Utilities Expense

Required: Indicate the account number for each debit and credit required in the following transactions. (The first transaction is done for you.)

Account Numbers
Debit   Credit

Example:

Debit	Credit	
101	320	Issued common shares for cash
_____		Purchased repair supplies (asset) on account
_____		Paid rent expense for the current month
_____		Paid cash for equipment
_____		Purchased a truck by signing a bank loan
_____		Received an invoice from hydro for electricity used to date
_____		Made a payment for the purchase of repair supplies made earlier (in the second transaction)
_____		Billed customers for services provided to date
_____		Received a payment on account
_____		Made a monthly payment toward the bank loan
_____		Sold excess equipment at its cost for cash
_____		Collected cash for services performed today
_____		Paid the hydro bill received in the sixth transaction
_____		Borrowed additional cash from the bank
_____		Made a physical count of the repair supplies purchased in the second transaction: half of the supplies have been used to date.

Comprehension Problem 2-2

Required: Using the chart of accounts in the text of this chapter, indicate the account number for each debit and credit required in the following transactions. (The first transaction is done for you.) Refer to the following as you analyze each transaction:

ASSETS	LIABILITIES
EXPENSES	EQUITY
	REVENUES
Increases are DEBITED.	Increases are CREDITED.
Decreases are CREDITED.	Decreases are DEBITED.

Account Numbers
Debit   Credit
Example:

Debit	Credit	
101	320	Issued common shares for cash
_____		Purchased a truck for cash
_____		Incurred a bank loan as payment for equipment
_____		Made a deposit for electricity service
_____		Paid rent expense
_____		Signed a new union contract that provided for increased wages
_____		Hired a messenger service to deliver letters during a mail strike and wrote a letter of complaint to the prime minister about the strike
_____		Received a collect telegram from the prime minister; paid the messenger
_____		Billed customers for services performed
_____		Made a payment on account
_____		Received a payment on account
_____		Collected cash from a customer
_____		Paid for truck expenses (gas, oil, etc.)
_____		Made a monthly payment on the bank loan; this payment included a payment on part of the loan and also on amount of interest expense. (*Hint:* This transaction affects more than two parts of the accounting equation.)

Comprehension Problem 2-3

Required: Using the chart of accounts in the text of this chapter, indicate the account number for each debit and credit required in the following transactions. (The first transaction is done for you.) Refer to the following as you analyze each transaction.

ASSETS	LIABILITIES
EXPENSES	EQUITY
	REVENUES
Increases are DEBITED.	Increases are CREDITED.
Decreases are CREDITED.	Decreases are DEBITED.

Account Numbers
Debit   Credit
Example:

101	320	Issued common shares for cash
_____		Paid an account payable
_____		Borrowed money from a bank and issued a note
_____		Collected an account receivable
_____		Collected a commission on a sale made today
_____		Paid for an advertisement in a newspaper
_____		Borrowed cash from the bank
_____		Signed a contract to purchase a computer
_____		Received a bill for supplies used during the month
_____		Received a payment on account
_____		Made a payment on account
_____		Sent a bill for repairs made today
_____		Sold equipment for cash
_____		Purchased a truck on account
_____		Requested payment of an account receivable that is overdue
_____		Settled a union dispute by increasing vacations from four weeks to six weeks
_____		Recorded the amount due to the landlord as rent
_____		Received the monthly telephone answering service bill.

Comprehension Problem 2-4

This transactions worksheet of McGill Erectors Limited shows these recorded transactions during January 19X1.

	Cash	+	Accounts Receivable	+	Supplies	+	Equipment	+	Truck	=	Accounts Payable	+	Common Stock	+	[+ Revenue / − Expense]
a.	+$5,000												+$5,000		
b.							+$1,000				+$1,000				
c.					+$300						+ 300				
d.			+$3,500												+$3,500
e.	− 350														− 350
f.	+1,000		− $1,000												
g.	− 500										− 500				
h.	− 2,000								+8,000		+6,000				
i.	− 2,500														− 500
															− 1,200
															− 800
j.			− 200												− 200

Additional information applicable to the above transactions: transaction (e) involved rent and transaction (i) involved advertising, salaries, and truck expenses in that order.

Required:
1. Open ledger accounts for the following: Cash, Accounts Receivable, Supplies, Equipment, Truck, Accounts Payable, Common Stock, Revenue, Advertising Expense, Rent Expense, Salaries Expense, Supplies Used, Truck Expense.
2. Prepare journal entries to record the January transactions. Post these entries to the ledger accounts.
3. Prepare a trial balance at January 31.

Comprehension Problem 2-5

This transactions worksheet is for Fortunato Corporation at March 31. Each line represents a transaction during the month.

			ASSETS				=	LIABILITY		+		EQUITY		
Transaction	Cash	+	Accounts Receivable	+	Prepaid Rent	+	Equip- ment =	Bank Loan	+	Accounts Payable	+	Common Stock	+	[+ Revenue − Expense]
1.	+ $5											+ $5		
2.	− 3						+ $6			+ $3				
3.	− 2				+ $2									
4.	+ 4		+ $2											+ $6
5.	+ 1						− 1							
6.										+ 3				− 3 (supplies)
7.			+ 1											+ 1
8.					− 1									− 1 (rent)
9.										+ 2				− 2 (truck)
10.	− 1									− 1				

Required:
1. Prepare journal entries for the ten transactions.
2. Post the journal entries to T-accounts.
3. From the T-accounts, prepare a trial balance. List expenses in alphabetical order.
4. Calculate the total of each asset, liability, and equity column on the worksheet; prove that the total of assets equals the total of liabilities and equity.
5. What is the relationship of the equality of transactions entered on the worksheet and the equality of debits with credits on the trial balance?

Comprehension Problem 2-6

The following T-accounts show the relationship of increases and decreases with debits.

Trans-action	Assets		Liabilities	
	Debit (increase)	*Credit* (decrease)	*Debit* (decrease)	*Credit* (increase)
1.	x			

Trans-action	Common Stock		Revenues		Expenses	
	Debit (decrease)	*Credit* (increase)	*Debit* (decrease)	*Credit* (increase)	*Debit* (increase)	*Credit* (decrease)
1.		x				

Required: For each of the following transactions, indicate which accounts are debited and which are credited. (Transaction 1 is done for you)

1. Issued common shares for cash
2. Paid cash for a truck
3. Paid for prepaid rent, an asset
4. Borrowed cash from the bank
5. Received a bill for extermination services performed last week
6. Collected cash for services performed last week
7. Billed customers for services performed last week
8. Sold excess equipment at its cost
9. Repaid part of the bank loan
10. Made a payment for electricity service
11. Paid cash for truck expenses
12. Received a bill for repair supplies used during the month
13. Made a payment on account
14. Received a payment on account
15. Received a note from a customer in payment of his account.

Comprehension Problem 2-7

The following accounts are taken from the ledger of Trust Ned Inc. at the end of July, its first month of operation.

Cash *No. 101*		Bank Loan *No. 201*		Insurance Expense *No. 631*	
1,000	9,000		10,000	1,200	
10,000	900				
1,500	50			Interest Expense *No. 632*	
2,000	75			600	
	600				
	2,200				

Accounts Receivable *No. 110*		Accounts Payable *No. 210*		Rent Expense *No. 654*	
3,000	1,500		1,200	300	
			100		

Prepaid Rent *No. 162*		Common Stock *No. 320*		Salaries Expense *No. 656*	
900	300		1,000	2,200	

Truck No. 184	Repair Revenue No. 450	Telephone Expense No. 669
9,000	3,000 2,000	75

	Advertising Expense No. 610	Utilities Expense No. 676
	50	100

Required:
1. Prepare journal entries for the transactions recorded in the ledger accounts.
2. From the ledger accounts appearing above, prepare a trial balance.

Comprehension Problem 2-8

The following trial balance has been prepared from the ledger of MacDonald Voyages Inc.

MacDonald Voyages Inc.
Trial Balance
January 31, 19X1

	Account Balances	
	Debits	*Credits*
Cash	$ 60	
Accounts Receivable	140	
Supplies	10	
Equipment	300	
Bank Loan		$100
Accounts Payable		20
Common Stock		250
Service Revenue		990
Fees Earned		885
Advertising Expense	200	
Salaries Expense	800	
Supplies Used	20	
Telephone Expense	10	
Utilities Expense	5	
Wages Expense	700	

Required:
1. Calculate the total debits and credits.
2. From the accounts in the trial balance, prepare an interim income statement and an interim balance sheet.

Problems

Problem 2-1

The following account balances are taken from the records of Pana-Micro Inc. at October 31, 19X1.

Accounts Payable	$9,000	Insurance Expense	$ 500
Accounts Receivable	6,000	Repair Revenue	19,000
Advertising Expense	2,200	Supplies Used	800
Bank Loan	5,000	Telephone Expense	250
Cash	1,000	Truck	9,000
Common Stock	2,000	Truck Expense	1,250
Commissions Expense	4,500	Wages Expense	4,000
Equipment	7,000	Wages Payable	1,500

Required:
1. Prepare a trial balance at October 31.
2. Prepare an interim income statement for October 31 in proper form.
3. Prepare an interim balance sheet at October 31 in proper form.

Problem 2-2

The following ledger accounts were prepared for Coquitlam Tool Rentals Corporation during the first month of operations ending May 31, 19X1. No journal entries were prepared in support of the amounts recorded in the ledger accounts.

Cash		Equipment		Commissions Expense	
5,000	1,000	2,000	800	1,100	
2,000	500				
1,500	300				
1,200	600				
800	400				
	3,500				

		Accounts Payable		Rent Expense	
		600	1,000	400	
			150		
			1,100		

Accounts Receivable		Common Stock		Salaries Expense	
3,000	1,500		5,000	3,500	
2,500	1,200				

Prepaid Advertising		Revenue		Supplies Used	
500	250		3,000	100	
			2,000		
			2,500		

Supplies		Advertising Expense		Telephone Expense	
300	100	250		150	

Required:
1. Reconstruct the transactions that occurred during the month and prepare journal entries to record these transactions.
2. Calculate the balance in each account and prepare a trial balance at May 31, 19X1.

Problem 2-3

The following trial balance was prepared for Draimin Consultants Corp. at January 31, 19X1, its first month of operations, by a newly hired clerk who has insufficient training.

Draimin Consultants Corp.
Trial Balance
January 31, 19X1

	Account Balances	
	Debits	*Credits*
Accounts Payable	$ 9,000	
Accounts Receivable		$ 8,000
Advertising Expense	150	
Bank Loan		3,625
Cash	2,000	
Common Stock		7,000
Equipment		4,000
Furniture		1,000
Interest Expense	200	
Maintenance Expense		250
Prepaid Advertising	300	
Repair Revenue	9,500	
Rent Expense		400
Salaries Expense		2,600
Salaries Payable		1,500
Supplies Used	350	
Telephone Expense	125	
Truck	9,000	
Truck Expense		750
Wages Expense		1,500
	$30,625	$30,625

Required:
1. Prepare a corrected trial balance at January 31. List the accounts by the sequence in the chart of accounts in the text and record the amounts in their proper debit-credit positions.
2. How is it possible that the debit-credit totals amount to $30,625 in both trial balances? (Assume that individual amounts are correct.)

Problem 2-4

The following balances appeared in the general ledger of Wyde Tables Inc. at April 1, 19X1.

Cash	$1,400	Accounts Payable	$2,000
Accounts Receivable	3,600	Common Stock	4,350
Prepaid Rent	1,000		
Supplies	350		

The following transactions occurred during April:
a. Collected $2,000 cash on account
b. Billed $3,000 to customers for tables rented to date
c. Paid the following expenses: advertising, $300; salaries $2,000; telephone, $100
d. Paid half of the accounts payable
e. Received a $500 bill for April truck expenses
f. Collected $2,500 on account
g. Billed $1,500 to customers for tables rented to date
h. Transferred $500 of prepaid rent to rent expense
i. Counted $200-worth of supplies on hand; recorded the amount used as an expense.

Required:
1. Open ledger accounts for the following and enter the April 1 balances: Cash, Accounts Receivable, Prepaid Rent, Supplies, Accounts Payable, Common Stock, Revenue, Advertising Expense, Rent Expense, Salaries Expense, Supplies Used, Telephone Expense, Truck Expense.
2. Prepare journal entries to record the April transactions. Post these entries to the ledger accounts.
3. Prepare a trial balance at April 30.
4. Prepare an interim income statement and interim balance sheet at April 30 in proper form.

Problem 2-5

The following transactions occurred in Brock Accounting Services Inc. during August 19X1, its first month of operations.

Aug. 1	Issued common shares for $3,000 cash
Aug. 1	Borrowed $10,000 cash from the bank
Aug. 1	Paid $8,000 for a used truck
Aug. 4	Paid $600 for a one-year truck insurance policy effective August 1 (recorded as Prepaid Insurance)
Aug. 5	Collected $2,000 cash fees from a client for work performed today (recorded as Revenue)
Aug. 7	Billed $5,000-worth of fees to clients for services performed to date (recorded as Revenue)
Aug. 9	Paid $250 for supplies used to date
Aug. 12	Purchased $500-worth of supplies on account (recorded as an asset)
Aug. 15	Collected $1,000 of the amount billed on August 7
Aug. 16	Paid $200 for advertising in *The News* during the first two weeks of August
Aug. 20	Paid half of the amount owing for the supplies purchased on August 12
Aug. 25	Paid the following expenses: rent for August, $350; salaries, $2,150; telephone, $50; truck, $250
Aug. 28	Called clients for payment of the balance owing from August 7
Aug. 29	Billed $6,000-worth of fees to clients for services performed to date (recorded as Revenue)
Aug. 31	Transferred the amount of August's truck insurance to Insurance Expense
Aug. 31	Counted $100-worth of supplies still on hand (recorded the amount used as an expense).

Required:
1. Open ledger accounts for the following: Cash, Accounts Receivable, Prepaid Insurance, Supplies, Truck, Bank Loan, Accounts Payable, Common Stock, Revenue, Advertising Expense, Insurance Expense, Rent Expense, Salaries Expense, Supplies Used, Telephone Expense, Truck Expense.
2. Prepare journal entries to record the August transactions. Post these entries to the ledger accounts.
3. Prepare a trial balance at August 31.
4. Prepare an interim income statement and interim balance sheet at August 31 in proper form.

Problem 2-6

The following transactions took place in Maison Renovations Inc. during June 19X1, its first month of operations.

Jun. 1 Issued common shares for $8,000 cash
Jun. 1 Purchased $5,000-worth of equipment on account
Jun. 2 Collected $600 cash for repairs completed today
Jun. 3 Paid $20 for supplies used on June 2
Jun. 4 Purchased $1,000-worth of supplies on account (recorded as an asset)
Jun. 5 Billed customers $2,500 for repairs collected to date
Jun. 8 Collected $500 of the amount billed on June 5
Jun. 10 Paid half of the amount owing for equipment purchased on June 1
Jun. 15 Sold on account excess equipment for $1,000 (its original cost)
Jun. 18 Paid for the supplies purchased on June 4
Jun. 20 Received a $100 bill for electricity used to date (recorded as Utilities Expense)
Jun. 22 Paid $600 to the landlord for June and July rent (recorded as Prepaid Rent)
Jun. 23 Signed a union contract
Jun. 25 Collected $1,000 of the amount billed on June 5
Jun. 27 Paid the following expenses: advertising, $150; telephone, $50; truck expense (for rental and gas), $1,000; wages, $2,500
Jun. 30 Billed $2,000 for repairs completed to date
Jun. 30 Transferred the amount for June's rent to Rent Expense
Jun. 30 Counted $150-worth of supplies still on hand (recorded the amount used as an expense).

Required:
1. Open ledger accounts for the following: Cash, Accounts Receivable, Prepaid Rent, Supplies, Equipment, Accounts Payable, Common Stock, Repair Revenue, Advertising Expense, Rent Expense, Supplies Used, Telephone Expense, Truck Expense, Utilities Expense, Wages Expense.
2. Prepare journal entries to record the August transactions. Post these entries to the ledger accounts.
3. Prepare a trial balance at June 30.
4. Prepare an interim income statement and balance sheet at June 30 in proper form.

Alternate Problems

Alternate Problem 2-1

The following account balances are taken from the records of Geosign Repairs Corp. at November 30, 19X1:

Accounts Payable	$5,000	Rent Expense	$ 700
Accounts Receivable	6,000	Repair Revenue	8,350
Advertising Expense	500	Salaries Expense	3,000
Bank Loan	4,500	Salaries Payable	1,000
Cash	2,000	Supplies	500
Common Stock	8,000	Supplies Used	250
Commissions Expense	1,500	Truck	8,000
Equipment	3,500	Truck Expense	900

Required:
1. Prepare a trial balance at November 30.
2. Prepare an interim income statement for November 30 in proper form.
3. Prepare an interim balance sheet at November 30 in proper form.

Alternate Problem 2-2

The following accounts were prepared for Etobicoke Garage Inc. during the first month of operations ending July 31, 19X1. No journal entries were prepared in support of the amounts recorded in the ledger accounts.

Cash		Truck	Advertising Expense
3,000	1,000	7,000	100
1,500	400		
1,200	600		
2,000	300		
	1,100		
	3,200		

Accounts Receivable		Accounts Payable		Insurance Expense
2,500	1,200	300	6,000	50
3,500	2,000	1,100	500	
			200	
			100	

Prepaid Insurance		Common Stock	Rent Expense
600	50	3,000	400

Supplies		Revenue	Supplies Used
500	150	2,500	150
		1,500	
		3,500	Salaries Expense
			3,200

	Truck Expense
	200

Required:
1. Reconstruct the transactions that occurred during the month and prepare journal entries to record these transactions.
2. Calculate the balance in each account and prepare a trial balance at July 31, 19X1.

Alternate Problem 2-3

The following trial balance was prepared for Houde Services Corp. at March 31, 19X1, its first month of operations, by a part-time clerk who has insufficient training.

Trial Balance
March 31, 19X1

	Account Balances	
	Debits	*Credits*
Accounts Payable	$ 5,000	
Accounts Receivable		$ 3,000
Bank Loan		3,550
Cash	1,500	
Common Stock	3,000	
Equipment	2,000	
Fees Earned	6,900	
Insurance Expense	50	
Interest Expense		100
Rent Expense		600
Truck		8,000
Truck Expense		
Utilities Expense		200
Wages Expense		3,000
	$18,450	$18,450

Required:
1. Prepare a correct trial balance at March 31. List the accounts by the sequence in the chart of accounts in the text and record the amounts in their proper debit-credit positions.
2. How is it possible that the debit-credit totals amount to $18,450 in both trial balances? (Assume that individual amounts are correct).

Alternate Problem 2-4

The following balances appeared in the general ledger of Hampstead Tool Rentals Inc. on May 1, 19X1.

Cash	$1,600	Accounts Payable	$4,000
Supplies	400	Common Stock	8,000
Equipment	3,000		
Truck	7,000		

The following transactions occurred during May:
a. Collected $5,000 cash for tool rental during the month (Hampstead does not rent tools on account.)
b. Paid $500 rent expense
c. Paid $1,500 on account
d. Paid $600 for a one-year insurance policy effective May 1
e. Purchased a used truck for $5,000 on account
f. Paid the following expenses: advertising, $300; salaries, $2,500; telephone, $150; truck, $550
g. Transferred the amount of May's insurance to Insurance Expense.
h. Estimated $200 of supplies to have been used during May.

Required:
1. Open ledger accounts for the following and enter the May 1 balances: Cash, Prepaid Insurance, Supplies, Equipment, Truck, Accounts Payable, Common Stock, Revenue, Advertising Expense, Insurance Expense, Rent Expense, Salaries Expense, Supplies Used, Telephone Expense, Truck Expense.

2. Prepare journal entries to record the May transactions. Post these entries to the ledger accounts.
3. Prepare a trial balance at May 31.
4. Prepare an interim income statement and interim balance sheet at May 31.

Alternate Problem 2-5

Electrical Contractors Corp. was incorporated on May 1, 19X1 and had the following transactions during its first month of operations.

May 1 Issued common shares for $5,000 cash
May 1 Paid $1,500 for three months rent in advance: May, June, and July (recorded as Prepaid Rent)
May 2 Purchased $1,000-worth of supplies on account (recorded as an asset)
May 3 Billed a customer $1,500 for repairs performed
May 4 Paid $50 for an advertisement in *The News*
May 5 Received $250 cash for work completed today
May 10 Collected the amount billed on May 3
May 15 Paid $500 on account to a creditor
May 18 Borrowed $2,000 cash from the bank
May 20 Signed a major contract for work to be done in June
May 22 Purchased $3,000-worth of equipment; paid cash
May 25 Billed customers $3,500 for work completed to date
May 27 Paid the following expenses: electricity, $75; telephone, $25; wages, $2,000
May 31 Transferred the amount of May's rent from Prepaid Rent to Rent Expense
May 31 Counted $200-worth of supplies still on hand; the rest had been used during May.

Required:
1. Open ledger accounts for the following: Cash, Accounts Receivable, Prepaid Rent, Supplies, Equipment, Bank Loan, Accounts Payable, Common Stock, Repair Revenue, Advertising Expense, Rent Expense, Supplies Used, Telephone Expense, Utilities Expense, Wages Expense.
2. Prepare journal entries to record the May transactions. Post these transactions to the ledger accounts.
3. Prepare a trial balance at May 31.
4. Prepare an interim income statement and interim balance sheet at May 31 in proper form.

Alternate Problem 2-6

Nick's Snow Removal Inc. was incorporated on December 1, 19X1 and had the following transactions during its first month of operations.

Dec. 1 Issued common shares for $6,000 cash
Dec. 1 Purchased a used truck for $9,000: paid $4,000 cash, balance owing until January 15
Dec. 2 Purchased a $2,000 snow plough on account (recorded as an increase in the cost of the truck)
Dec. 3 Billed customers $5,000 for December snow removal (Nick's customers are billed at the beginning of each month.)
Dec. 5 Purchased salt, sand, and gravel for $500 on account (recorded as Supplies)
Dec. 6 Paid truck expenses of $200
Dec. 7 Paid $360 for a one-year insurance policy effective December 1 (recorded as Prepaid Insurance)
Dec. 14 Paid $1,500 for two weeks wages
Dec. 16 Paid $40 traffic ticket (recorded as Truck Expense)
Dec. 20 Received a bill for $350-worth of truck expenses
Dec. 24 Purchased tire chains for $100 on account (recorded as Truck Expense)

Dec. 24 Collected $3,500 from customers billed on December 3
Dec. 27 Paid for the purchase made on December 5
Dec. 28 Collected $400 for snow removal performed today for a new customer
Dec. 28 Paid $1,500 for two weeks wages
Dec. 30 Called customers owing $1,500 billed on December 3 and not yet paid
Dec. 31 Transferred the amount of December's truck insurance to Insurance Expense
Dec. 31 Counted $100-worth of salt, sand, and gravel still on hand (recorded the amount used as an expense)
Dec. 31 Recorded three days wages applicable to December 29, 30, and 31, to be paid in January.

Required:
1. Open ledger accounts for the following: Cash, Accounts Receivable, Prepaid Insurance, Supplies, Truck, Accounts Payable, Wages Payable, Common Stock, Service Revenue, Insurance Expense, Supplies Used, Truck Expense, Wages Expense.
2. Prepare journal entries to record the December transactions. Post transactions to the ledger accounts.
3. Prepare a trial balance at December 31.
4. Prepare an income statement and a balance sheet at December 31 in proper form.

Decision Problem

Decision Problem 2-1

Ron McCharles, a second-year business student at the University of Alberta, has had a hard time finding an enjoyable summer job that pays well. He has therefore decided to begin his own business for the summer. He and two high school friends meet and decide to establish a home repair company. Ron will run the business side of the operations while his two friends, Warren MacDonald and Dave Victor, who are enrolled in the technology program at the Northern Alberta Institute of Technology, will do the majority of the home repairs with Ron filling in whenever he can.

A corporation is formed and issues $1,000 of common stock to each student and receives a total of $3,000 cash for these shares on June 1st.

The three decide to call their corporation the Mic Mac & Vic Corp. (MMV). MMV agrees to rent a van from Jim Stephens for $200 per month; under this agreement, MMV will be liable for all fuel and repair bills. After this transaction, the corporation is ready to begin business.

The business proved to be successful from the start. Ron, a Marketing major, spent most of his time promoting the business, making sales calls, and writing up estimates. Ron devoted little effort toward establishing an accounting system or keeping formal accounting records. He had not particularly liked his first accounting course at the U of A and thought that MMV could do with only a chequebook. So that all transactions would pass through the chequebook, Ron arranged with the local Canadian Tire Store, McBride's Shell Service Station, and Bittners Hardware to pay all bills by cheque.

On August 31, the students had completed their summer's work and were preparing to return to school. All payments from customers had been received and all bills had been paid. The students agreed that Warren's sister, Betty MacDonald, a third-year accounting student at NAIT, would determine the financial position of MMV at August 31.

From the records, Betty discovered that receipts from customers for the summer totalled $35,542. The materials bought for use by MMV amounted to $24,500, with $2,500 of unused material, such as paint, lumber, nails, and electrical fixtures remaining; of these 80 percent could be returned for full credit, while 20 percent had to be expensed. Other expenses incurred were $75 for advertising, and $375 for fuel and oil for the van. Luckily, the van did not need any repairs. As well, the students paid themselves $1,500 each on August 1. The Bank balance for MMV on August 31 showed a total of $8,492.22. The unused supplies had not yet been returned for credit.

Required:
1. Prepare two balance sheets: one dated June 1, and one dated August 31.
2. Prepare an income statement for MMV for the three months ended August 31.
3. If each student worked 190 hours per month from June 1 through August 31, how successful have they been?
4. Betty was also asked to make recommendations to Ron, Warren, and Dave since they plan to resume the business next summer. What should Betty suggest to these entrepreneurs?

GAAP and the Operating Cycle: Part One

Each business entity has a series of financial transactions that occur continuously during the accounting time period. As noted in Chapter 2, such repeated activities comprise the operating cycle.

1. What is the basic sequence of an operating cycle?
2. How can incomplete cycles exist at the end of an accounting time period?
3. What theoretical problems are involved with revenue recognition? In actual practice, at what point is revenue recognized?
4. How should a payment received before a service is performed be recorded?
5. How should cost outlays that are made continuously during the operating cycle be recorded?
6. How do financial statements made at the end of an accounting time period accurately reflect cost outlays, even if these may have been inaccurately stated during the accounting period?
7. How is it possible to manipulate the operating results and financial position of an entity?
8. What is the relationship between accrual accounting and the matching concept?
9. What are three categories of expenses requiring alignment with revenue? How is this accomplished through the recording of adjusting entries?
10. What are mixed balance sheet accounts, incorrect statement accounts, and accruals?

A. The Operating Cycle

Financial transactions that occur continuously during an accounting time period are part of a sequence of activities. In Bluebeard Computer Corporation, this sequence of activities takes the following form:

> 1. Operations begin with some cash on hand.
> 2. This cash is used to purchase supplies and to pay expenses incurred while performing computer repairs.
> 3. Revenue is earned as repair services are performed. (An accounts receivable may result.)
> 4. Cash is collected.

This cash-to-cash sequence of events is commonly referred to as an operating cycle, as described in Chapter 2. This cycle is illustrated in Figure 3-1.

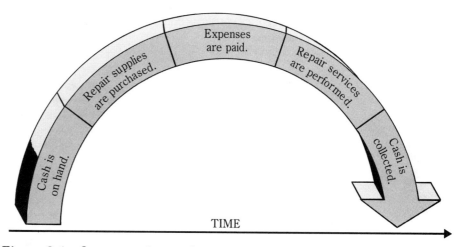

Figure 3-1   One operating cycle

Figure 3-1 refers to only one operating cycle. In actual practice, many cycles of this type are under way simultaneously, and the cycles overlap. The overlapping of these cycles during an accounting time period is illustrated in Figure 3-2.

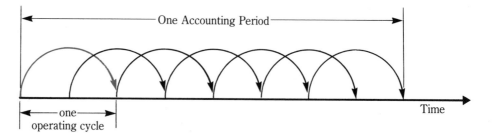

Figure 3-2   Overlapping operating cycles

As some transactions in one cycle are being completed, others are only beginning. For example, while repairs are being completed in one cycle, repair supplies are being purchased for use in another cycle; while expenses are being paid in one cycle, repairs are beginning in another cycle; and, while all this is going on, cash is being collected and being paid out continuously. A similar operating cycle exists for every entity, whether it provides a service, buys and sells merchandise, or manufactures products. Although the cycle of each type of entity may have different components, the basic sequence remains the same.

Under the going-concern assumption, any incomplete cycles, which exist at the beginning and end of each operating cycle, will be completed during the unlimited life of the entity. Accordingly, the use of historical costs to prepare financial statements is a reliable measure of financial transactions as they are completed, because it is objectively determined and can be verified by reference to documents.

Accountants are obviously concerned with the accurate recording of all these transactions. However, the recording of some transactions causes more theoretical problems than the recording of others. For example, the choice of a point at which revenue can be said to be earned causes numerous problems for accountants; the point at which an asset becomes an expense is not always clear-cut either. Later in this chapter, we examine further some transactions of Bluebeard Computer Corporation, in order to focus on two major categories of transactions that cause recording problems for accountants. These two categories are:

> 1. Transactions involving services performed or goods sold by the business and the establishment of *the point at which revenue is earned* from these services.
> 2. Transactions involving cost outlays and expenses incurred to earn those revenues.

Revenue Recognition

Revenue recognition
Revenue is recognized as having been earned when the service is completed or the goods sold.

Revenue recognition is concerned with establishing the point at which the revenue of a business is actually earned.

1. Is revenue earned when cash from the service is collected?
2. Is some revenue earned throughout the complete accounting cycle, while the service is being completed? If so, how is an estimate accurately made?
3. Is revenue earned only when the service has been completed?

Although revenue has unquestionably been earned by the time the service is completed and the cash is collected, accountants generally assume that service is earned at an earlier point — when the service is completed but payment, in the form of cash, has not yet been made. This point can be more objectively determined than subjective estimates. In actual practice, it is convenient to recognize revenue at the point when an invoice is prepared and sent to the customer. A transaction of this type creates an asset called accounts receivable, which is exchanged for the asset cash when payment is received.

In some cases, a deposit or advance payment is obtained *before* the service is performed. When an advance payment is received, accountants use the following accepted practice to record this type of receipt consistently:

> 1. The receipt is recorded as a *liability* if the service is not expected to be completed before the end of the current accounting period.
> 2. The receipt is recorded as a *revenue* if the service is expected to be completed during the current accounting period.

Recording Cost Outlays

Cost outlays are made continuously during the accounting time period and are recorded at cost, that is, at the amount paid. Each cost outlay is recorded either as an *asset*, if it can be used to produce future revenues, or as an *expense*, if it does not have the potential to produce future revenues. The following practice is often used by accountants to record cost outlays consistently:

> 1. The cost is recorded as an *asset* if it will be incurred in producing revenue in future accounting time periods.
> 2. The cost is recorded as an *expense* if it will be consumed during the current accounting period.

This inter-relationship between assets and expenses is illustrated in Figure 3-3.

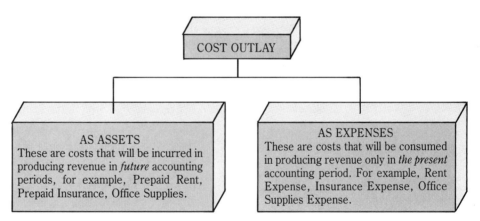

Figure 3-3   The inter-relationship of assets and expenses

Theoretically, any cost outlay that has a future value—that is, if it will be used in producing revenue in future accounting time periods — should be recorded as an asset. In actual practice, an arbitrary rule is usually adopted to facilitate the need to keep track of assets which expire in the future:

> If the future value of the asset benefits more than solely the current accounting period, then it is recorded as an *asset*. If the future value of the asset expires during the current accounting period, then it is recorded as an *expense*.

In this way the financial statements prepared at the end of the time period accurately reflect the status of the cost, although the cost outlay may be inaccurately stated during the accounting period. Thus, while the payment of rent on November 1 is an asset during November, it is properly reflected as an expense at November 30, if it was originally recorded as rent expense on November 1.

In actual practice, some large entities record all cost outlays of one kind as assets and all cost outlays of another kind as expenses. Varying practices depend on the accounting policies adopted by the particular entity. If this practice is followed during the accounting period, then the expired portion of assets and the unexpired portion of expenses must be accurately reflected in the financial statements at the end of the accounting period. Adjusting journal entries, explained in sections D and E of this chapter, are prepared to record the proper end-of-period status of such items.

The Need for Consistency

An overall concern of the accountant in recording revenues and cost outlays is that the income statement and balance sheet accurately reflect the operating results and financial position of the entity at the end of the period.

One possible manipulation of an entity's operating results and financial position results when different accounting policies and rules are used from one accounting period to another. Although many revenues and expenses can be recorded properly in more than one way, the accounting practice of consistency requires that the same policies and rules be used from one time period to another. In this way, there is uniformity in the financial information recorded and reported in financial statements. Such uniformity means that changes in the operating results and financial position of an entity are caused by its operations and not by changes in accounting policies and rules. Changes in these policies and rules are discouraged unless the change results in improved reporting in financial statements. (Any such change must be noted in the financial statements.)

B. Transactions Analysis Involving Cost Outlays and Revenue Recognition

The December transactions of Bluebeard Computer Corporation will be used to demonstrate record keeping using the cost outlay and revenue recognition assumptions made by accountants. November transactions 1 to 7 were previously recorded and discussed in chapters 1 and 2; this chapter continues with December transactions 8 to 14. The adjacent summary of these December transactions appears with a guide to which assumption — cost outlay or revenue recognition — is being discussed in each transaction.

Illustrative Problem —
Cost Outlay and Revenue Recognition Analysis

The analysis and recording of each transaction is described in detail in the following pages. The numbers in parentheses in T-accounts refer to the transaction number. The posted ledger accounts appear to the right of the text.

Transaction Number Date	Description of Transaction	Application of Accounting Assumption	
		Cost Outlay	Revenue Recognition
8. Dec. 1	Bluebeard Computer Corporation paid $1,200 for a comprehensive one-year insurance policy, effective December 1.	ASSET	
9. Dec. 3	The corporation received $600 as an advance payment for the part-time rental of the corporation truck for three months as follows: $200 for December, $200 for January, $200 for February.		LIABILITY
10. Dec. 5	The corporation purchased on account $900-worth of repair supplies expected to be used during December.	EXPENSE	
11. Dec. 16	The corporation performed $5,000-worth of repairs for a customer who signed a 60-day, 12-percent, interest-bearing note as payment.		REVENUE
12. Dec. 26	The corporation received $2,000 from a customer for repairs that are expected to be done before the end of December.		REVENUE
13. Dec. 31	Additional computer repairs were made for customers during December as follows: $9,395-worth were repairs made for cash, $500-worth were repairs made on account.		REVENUE
14. Dec. 31	Miscellaneous expenses were paid during the month: $600, rent expense; $2,500, salaries; $700, truck; and $300, utilities.	EXPENSE	

REFER TO THE FOLLOWING AS YOU ANALYZE EACH TRANSACTION

COST OUTLAY	REVENUE RECOGNITION
The cost is recorded as an ASSET if it will be used in producing revenue in future accounting time periods.	*The receipt is recorded as a LIABILITY* if the service is not expected to be completed before the end of the current accounting time period.
The cost is recorded as an EXPENSE if it will be used up during the current accounting period.	*The receipt is recorded as a REVENUE* if the service is expected to be completed during the current accounting period.

Transaction 8

Bluebeard Computer Corporation paid $1,200 for a comprehensive one-year insurance policy, effective December 1.

Analysis: Since the one-year period will not expire by the time financial statements are prepared at December 31, the insurance cost is considered to be an asset at the payment date.

Journal Entry: The asset account, Prepaid Insurance, is increased by this transaction. (A debit records an asset increase.) Payment of the insurance results in a decrease in the asset account, Cash. (A credit records an asset decrease.) The journal entry appears as follows:

Prepaid Insurance

(8) 1,200 |

Dec. 1	Prepaid Insurance	161	1,200	
	Cash	101		1,200
	To record payment for one-year policy.			

Cash

| (8) 1,200

REFER TO THE FOLLOWING AS YOU ANALYZE EACH TRANSACTION	
COST OUTLAY	REVENUE RECOGNITION
The cost is recorded as an ASSET if it will be used in producing revenue in future accounting time periods.	*The receipt is recorded as a LIABILITY* if the service is not expected to be completed before the end of the current accounting time period.
The cost is recorded as an EXPENSE if it will be used up during the current accounting period.	*The receipt is recorded as a REVENUE* if the service is expected to be completed during the current accounting period.

Transaction 9

The corporation signed a contract for the use of its truck on a part-time basis and received an advance payment of $600 for use of the truck as follows: $200 for December, $200 for January, and $200 for February.

Analysis: The revenue relating to this cash receipt will not be earned by the end of the current accounting period. Therefore, it is considered to be a payment received in advance of its being earned.

Journal Entry: An asset account, Cash, is increased at the time the contract is signed. (A debit records an asset increase.) A liability account, Unearned Rent, is increased by this transaction. (A credit records a liability increase.) The journal entry appears as follows:

			Cash	
			(9) 600	

Dec. 3	Cash	101	600	
	Unearned Rent	248		600
	To record advance payment for three months truck rental.			

Unearned Rent

	(9) 600

Transaction 10

The corporation purchased on account $900-worth of supplies expected to be used during December.

Analysis: Since the repair supplies are expected to be used during the current accounting period, the cost of the supplies is considered to be an expense.

Journal Entry: An expense account, Supplies Used, is increased by this transaction. (An expense is increased by a debit.) A liability account, Accounts Payable, is increased by the transaction. (A liability is increased by a credit.) The journal entry appears as follows:

Supplies Used

(10) 900	

Dec. 5	Supplies Used	668	900	
	Accounts Payable	210		900
	To record purchase of supplies.			

Accounts Payable

	(10) 900

Transaction 11

The corporation performed $5,000-worth of repairs for a customer who signed a 60-day, 12-percent, interest-bearing note as payment. The $5,000 principal and interest will be paid at the end of 60 days.

Analysis: These repairs were completed before the end of December; revenue has therefore been earned and must be recorded.

Journal Entry: An asset account is increased by this transaction. (An asset increase is recorded by a debit.) A revenue account, Repair Revenue, is increased by this transaction. (A revenue increase is recorded by a credit.) The journal entry appears as follows:

			Notes Receivable	
			(11) 5,000	

Dec. 16	Notes Receivable	120	5,000	
	Repair Revenue	450		5,000
	To record payment for repairs by note.			

Repair Revenue

	(11) 5,000

Transaction 12

The corporation received $2,000 from a customer for repairs that are expected to be done before the end of December.

Analysis: Since the repairs are expected to be done before the end of the current accounting period, the $2,000 is recorded as a revenue.

Journal Entry: An asset account, Cash, is increased in this transaction. (An asset is increased by a debit.) A revenue account, Repair Revenue, is also increased by the transaction. (A revenue is increased by a credit.) The journal entry appears as follows:

Cash

(12) 2,000	

Dec. 26	Cash	101	2,000	
	Repair Revenue	450		2,000
	To record payment for repairs to be made in December.			

Repair Revenue

	(12) 2,000

Transaction 13

An additional $9,895-worth of computer repairs were made for customers during December; $9,395-worth of repairs were made for cash; $500-worth of these repairs were made on account.

Analysis: These revenue activities affect two asset accounts. The asset accounts, Cash and Accounts Receivable, are increased by the revenue earned during the month. Because three accounts are involved in this transaction, a compound journal entry is necessary.

Journal Entry: The asset accounts, Cash and Accounts Receivable, are increased by this transaction. (Assets are increased by a debit.) A revenue account, Repair Revenue, is increased by this transaction. (A revenue is increased by a credit.) The journal entry appears as follows:

Cash

(13) 9,395	

Accounts Receivable

(13) 500	

Dec. 31	Cash	101	9,395	
	Accounts Receivable	110	500	
	Repair Revenue	450		9,895
	To record repairs made during December.			

Repair Revenue

	(13) 9,895

REFER TO THE FOLLOWING AS YOU ANALYZE EACH TRANSACTION

COST OUTLAY	REVENUE RECOGNITION
The cost is recorded as an ASSET if it will be used in producing revenue in future accounting time periods.	*The receipt is recorded as a LIABILITY* if the service is not expected to be completed before the end of the current accounting time period.
The cost is recorded as an EXPENSE if it will be used up during the current accounting period.	*The receipt is recorded as a REVENUE* if the service is expected to be completed during the current accounting period.

Transaction 14

Paid expenses incurred during the month to earn the repair revenue. These expenses consist of: Rent Expense for December, $600; Salaries Expense for four weeks in December, $2,500; Truck Expense for gas, oil, etc., $700; and Utility Expense, $300.

Analysis: These expenses, summarized here for demonstration, are applicable to the current accounting period, since their cost has been used up during the month.

Journal Entry: In actual practice, each paid expense would be recorded individually as the payment was made. Each expense is increased in this transaction. (An increase in an expense is recorded by a debit to each expense account.) An asset account, Cash, is decreased by these expenses. (A decrease in an asset is recorded by a credit.) Since the transactions are summarized here, only one credit of $4,100 is made to the Cash account. The journal entry appears as follows:

Dec. 31	Rent Expense	654	600	
	Salaries Expense	656	2,500	
	Truck Expense	670	700	
	Utilities Expense	676	300	
	Cash	101		4,100

To record miscellaneous expenses paid.

Rent Expense
(14) 600

Salaries Expense
(14) 2,500

Truck Expense
(14) 700

Utilities Expense
(14) 300

Cash
(14) 4,100

C. The Accounting Process — Review of Steps 1–3

In this chapter so far, three individual steps of the accounting process have been discussed. The first two steps occur continuously through the time period; the third step occurs only at the end of the period and is taken in order to prove transactions during the time period have been recorded accurately.

Step 1: **Transactions Are Analyzed and Recorded in the Journal**
The general journal provides a complete record of a corporation's transactions, listed in chronological order. Because this journal is the first place a transaction is recorded, the general journal is commonly referred to as a *book of original entry*.

GENERAL JOURNAL

19X1				
Dec. 1	Prepaid Insurance	161	1,200	
	Cash	101		1,200
	To record payment for one-year policy.			
3	Cash	101	600	
	Unearned Rent	248		600
	To record advance payment for three months truck rental.			
5	Supplies Used	668	900	
	Accounts Payable	210		900
	To record purchase of supplies.			
16	Notes Receivable	120	5,000	
	Repair Revenue	450		5,000
	To record payment for repairs by note.			
26	Cash	101	2,000	
	Repair Revenue	450		2,000
	To record payment for repairs to be made in December.			
31	Cash	101	9,395	
	Accounts Receivable	110	500	
	Repair Revenue	450		9,895
	To record repairs made during December.			
31	Rent Expense	654	600	
	Salaries Expense	656	2,500	
	Truck Expense	670	700	
	Utilities Expense	676	300	
	Cash	101		4,100
	To record miscellaneous expenses paid.			

Step 2:   The Journal Entries Are Posted to Ledger Accounts

When the posting of December transactions has been completed, the ledger accounts are footed and a net debit or credit balance calculated for each account. In the case of the Cash account, for example, a debit balance of $11,695 remains at the end of December. (The ledger accounts for Bluebeard Computer Corporation follow.) The conceptual T-account is used in place of the more formal ledger account, in order to emphasize the relationship between the accounting equation and the accounts that fall under each equation component. Because of space limitations, the November transactions are not repeated here; rather the November 30 balance of each account is carried forward from Chapter 2 (under "Trial Balance Preparation").

| ASSETS | = | LIABILITIES | + | EQUITY |

Cash   *No. 101*

Bal.	5,000	(8)	1,200
(9)	600	(14)	4,100
(12)	2,000		
(13)	9,395		
	16,995		5,300
Bal.	11,695		

Accounts Receivable   *No. 110*

Bal.	3,000	
(13)	500	
Bal.	3,500	

Notes Receivable   *No. 120*

(11)	5,000	

Prepaid Insurance   *No. 161*

(8)	1,200	

Equipment   *No. 183*

Bal.	2,000	

Truck   *No. 184*

Bal.	8,000	

Bank Loan   *No. 201*

	Bal.	5,000

Accounts Payable   *No. 210*

	Bal.	1,000
	(10)	900
	Bal.	1,900

Unearned Rent   *No. 248*

	(9)	600

Common Stock   *No. 320*

	Bal.	10,000

Repair Revenue   *No. 450*

	Bal.	7,000
	(11)	5,000
	(12)	2,000
	(13)	9,895
	Bal.	23,895

Rent Expense   *No. 654*

Bal.	600	
(14)	600	
Bal.	1,200	

Salaries Expense   *No. 656*

Bal.	2,500	
(14)	2,500	
Bal.	5,000	

Supplies Used   *No. 668*

Bal.	1,200	
(10)	900	
Bal.	2,100	

Truck Expense   *No. 670*

Bal.	700	
(14)	700	
Bal.	1,400	

Utilities Expense   *No. 676*

(14)	300	

Note: The highlighted items are the December 31 balances.

Step 3: The Equality of Debits with Credits Is Established by the Trial Balance

The account balances are listed in the trial balance to establish the equality of total debit balances with total credit balances. The following December trial balance is for the Bluebeard Computer Corporation.

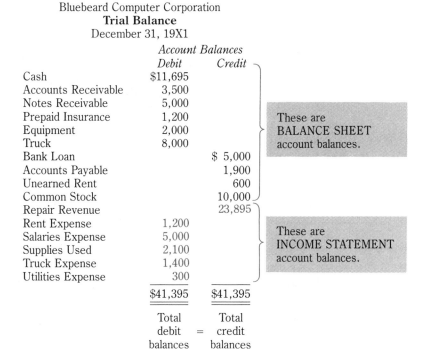

Bluebeard Computer Corporation
Trial Balance
December 31, 19X1

	Account Balances	
	Debit	*Credit*
Cash	$11,695	
Accounts Receivable	3,500	
Notes Receivable	5,000	
Prepaid Insurance	1,200	
Equipment	2,000	
Truck	8,000	
Bank Loan		$ 5,000
Accounts Payable		1,900
Unearned Rent		600
Common Stock		10,000
Repair Revenue		23,895
Rent Expense	1,200	
Salaries Expense	5,000	
Supplies Used	2,100	
Truck Expense	1,400	
Utilities Expense	300	
	$41,395	$41,395
	Total debit balances	= Total credit balances

These are BALANCE SHEET account balances.

These are INCOME STATEMENT account balances.

D.   Mixed Balance Sheet Accounts

Accrual Accounting and the Matching Concept

At the beginning of this chapter, the transactions of business entities were shown to comprise a sequence of events, identified as an operating cycle. Each entity's accounting time period consists of a series of such cycles. As the transactions in one operating cycle are completed, other cycles are beginning; still others are in progress. Financial statements are prepared on the basis of data originating with fully completed and partially completed cycles. Accrual accounting, as described in Chapter 1, matches expenses with revenues of a particular time period. The matching of revenues with expenses is the objective; the accrual method of accounting is the basis on which accounts are adjusted to reach the objective. Under this method, the cost of assets transferred to customers or consumed during the period are considered as expenses; these expenses are matched with the revenues generated by these expenses and are included in the income statement of the same period.

Reported net income, therefore, results from the application of accrual accounting and the matching concept. Their relationship within an accounting time period can be illustrated as in Figure 3-4.

Since only the cost of assets transferred to customers or consumed during the period are considered as expenses, any expenses relating to other accounting periods are excluded from the calculation of net income for the current time period — except for certain extraordinary items that do not occur regularly and are material in amount; these are discussed in Chapter 5.

For accrual accounting, three different categories of expenses require alignment with revenue. They can be distinguished as follows:

Category 1
The cost of goods (either items sold or services provided) transferred to customers can be easily aligned as expenses incurred in the same period that revenue is generated. For example, at Bluebeard Computer Corporation, the use of parts in repairing computers can be identified with revenue generated by the repairs that required those parts.

Category 2
The cost of assets only partially consumed during the time period is not always easily aligned with revenue generated. For example, Bluebeard's equipment and truck were used to generate revenue in November and December 19X1 but were not fully used up during its first months of operation; that is, they still have some future benefit. Accordingly, the amount used up of the useful ''life'' of the equipment and the truck must be estimated, and this estimate allocated as an expense incurred in generating the revenue of that time period. The estimate is often not easily calculated in actual practice.

Category 3
The cost of some expenses incurred during the period is also not always identified easily with revenue generated. For example, the president of Bluebeard maintains that part of his salary benefits future time periods; for instance, his time spent soliciting future customers in November and December resulted in no generation of revenue during that time period. His accountant agrees. However, in this and similar cases, his salary is recorded as a 19X1 expense, the time period in which his services as an employee are

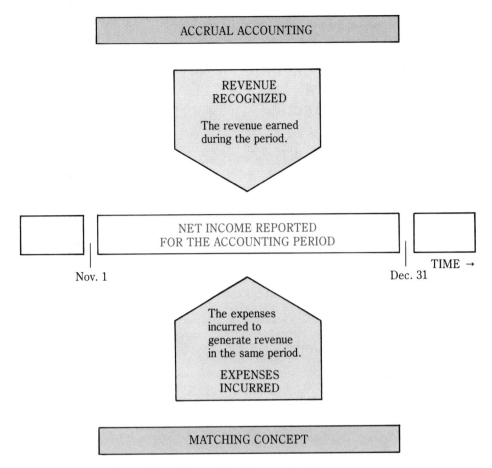

Figure 3-4   **The relationship among accrual accounting, the matching concept, and net income reported for one accounting period**

performed. This practice is in accordance with GAAP because no future benefit can be identified clearly with salary expense; therefore, the salary does not qualify as an asset, the only other way it could have been recorded.

These categories relate to the accrual method of accounting. An alternate method, used primarily by full-time farming and fishing entities, is referred to as the cash basis of accounting. Under this method, cash payments and cash receipts are aligned with a particular time period. The excess of cash receipts over cash payments indicates a positive cash flow and an excess of cash payments over cash receipts, a negative cash flow. However, cash receipts are seldom the same as revenue earned; customarily, for example, credit is extended to customers that are permitted to pay at a later date. Similarly, cash payments are seldom the same amount as expenses incurred because of the purchase of services and goods on account. As a result, the cash basis of accounting, while it measures cash flow, fails to provide an accurate measurement of net income; its use, therefore, is not recommended by GAAP. From this introduction, you can see that the matching concept is difficult to achieve in practice; for a further discussion, see the following Conceptual Issue 3-1.

Conceptual Issue 3-1

The Matching Principle: Why It's So Hard to Achieve in Practice

by Ross Skinner

In an exchange economy, the goal of productive activity is to sell a product or service for more than its cost of production. In accounting, income is the difference between costs (sacrifices) and revenues (benefits). If one visualizes a business in the form of a single venture, income over its entire lifetime will be the difference between cash receipts (excluding capital paid in) and cash disbursements (excluding capital withdrawn or return on capital, such as dividends, paid out). It is natural, therefore, to think of revenue as an inflow of assets — ultimately, cash—in exchange for the product of the enterprise.

This discussion oversimplifies matters. An enterprise may receive cash other than in exchange for product or service, or as a capital contribution. For example, if an asset is destroyed by fire, the insurance proceeds would not represent payment for the productive activity of the enterprise. It is still true that over the lifetime of an enterprise the excess of cash receipts over cash disbursements (excluding cash associated with capital transactions) will equal the net gain. But that net gain will consist of (1) the excess of revenues from productive activity over costs of earning those revenues, together with (2) miscellaneous gains or losses on events or activities that are not part of the main activity of the enterprise.

When speaking of the lifetime of an enterprise from initial cash investment to ultimate cash realization, it is possible to talk solely about movements in cash. Accounting for a period shorter than enterprise lifetime, however, presents a problem. At any given point of time, the enterprise will have delivered product or services for which it has not yet received payment. Conversely, it may have received payment for which it has not yet satisfied its obligation to deliver. It will also have incurred other costs and acquired rights or items that may reasonably be expected to be rewarded by the receipt of cash in a future exchange transaction. Moreover, it may not yet have paid for goods or services it has received. Thus, estimation of income for a period based on transactions is considerably more difficult than determination of income for a completed business lifetime. Such estimation requires that

The Need for Adjusting Entries

The trial balance of Bluebeard Computer Corporation at December 31 includes cost outlays that have been recorded as *assets* of the corporation. These cost outlays are recorded as assets during an accounting period if they can be used to produce future revenue. At the end of the period, an accounting measurement is required. The amount of the asset that has expired during the period must be calculated and that amount transferred to *expense*. In this way, revenues for the period are matched with expenses incurred to earn that revenue.

The December 31 trial balance of the corporation also includes receipts that have been recorded as *liabilities*. These receipts are recorded as liabilities during an accounting period if they have not been earned when received. At the end of the period, an accounting measurement is also required. The amount of the liability that has been earned during the period must be calculated and the amount transferred to *revenue*. In this way, revenues for the period are matched with expenses incurred to earn that revenue.

Mixed accounts
Accounts containing both a balance sheet and income statement portion at the date of adjusting entry preparation.

Adjusting entry
An adjustment made at the end of an operating cycle to update the accounts of an entity; the adjustment is required by the matching concept.

Mixed Asset and Liability Accounts

The asset and liability accounts referred to above are called **mixed accounts** by accountants. They are given this name because they include both a *balance sheet* portion and an *income statement* portion at the end of the accounting period. The income statement portion must be removed from the account by an **adjusting entry**.

non-capital cash inflows of past, present, and future periods be assigned to periods in which they are ''earned''. Similarly, non-capital cash outflows of past, present, and future periods must be assigned to the period in which any benefit from them is used up. That is, the goal of income accounting under the transaction-based model is to provide rules for assigning revenues and expenses from operating transactions, and gains and losses from peripheral activities to accounting periods.

Because income accounting associates cash flows with time periods, it automatically results in recognizing assets and liabilities. For example, a cash receipt today that is associated with revenue of a future period must be recorded as unearned revenue—a liability to deliver product or service in the future. A cash disbursement today associated with revenue of future periods must be recorded as an asset — an expectation of future benefit. In other words, asset and liability recognition (and changes in assets and liabilities previously recognized) can result from income accounting conventions as well as the conventions governing initial recognition of asset and liabilities.

It is convenient to summarize here the definitions of elements of financial statements provided by the FASB. These definitions make a useful distinction whereby revenues and expenses are described as the outcome of the primary business operations, and gains and losses are described as the result of incidental or peripheral events or activities.

• Assets are probable future economic benefits obtained or controlled by a particular entity as a result of past transactions or events.

• Liabilities are probable future sacrifices of economic benefits arising from present obligations of a particular entity to transfer assets or provide services to other entities in the future as a result of past transactions or events.

• Revenues are inflows or other enhancements of assets of an entity or settlements of its liabilities (or a combination of both) during a period from delivering or producing goods, rendering services, or other activities that constitute the entity's ongoing major or central operations.

• Expenses are outflows or other using up of assets or incurrences of liabilities (or a combination of both) during a period from delivering or producing goods, rendering services, or carrying out other activities that constitute the entity's ongoing major or central operations.

• Gains are increases in equity (net assets) from peripheral or incidental transactions of an entity and from all other transactions and other events and circumstances affecting the entity during a period, except those that result from revenues or from investments by owners.

• Losses are decreases in equity (net assets) from peripheral or incidental transactions of an entity and from all other transactions and other events and circumstances affecting the entity during a period, except those that result from expenses or from distributions to owners.[1]

Source   Courtesy of Ross Skinner.

Illustrative Problem — Unmixing Asset and Liability Accounts

The following balance sheet accounts of Bluebeard Computer Corporation require this kind of adjustment at December 31:

Partial Trial Balance
December 31, 19X1

	Account Balances	
	Debit	Credit
a. Prepaid Insurance	$1,200	
b. Unearned Rent		$600

This is a LIABILITY account balance.

These accounts are analyzed and it is determined that adjusting entries for items a and b need to be prepared.

Each of the above accounts is analyzed in the following manner:

Step 1
At the end of the accounting period, determine which portion of the mixed account belongs in the balance sheet and which belongs in the income statement.

Step 2
The portion that does not belong in the asset or liability account must be transferred out. An adjusting entry is made in the general journal and posted to the proper accounts to accomplish this transfer.

(a)

In December, the company paid for a 12-month insurance policy, effective December 1 (transaction 8).

The general ledger shows the following Prepaid Insurance account:	This balance resulted from the recording of the following journal entry:

Prepaid Insurance
(asset)   No. 161

| 1,200 | |

Prepaid Insurance   1,200
   Cash   1,200

At December 31, only one month of the policy has expired.

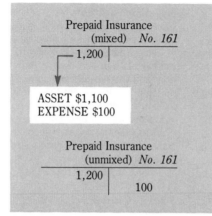

Step 1:
At the end of the accounting period, Prepaid Insurance is a mixed account; $1,100 is still an asset; $100 has expired and is, therefore, an expense.

Step 2:
The expired amount of $100 does not belong in this account. Therefore an adjusting journal entry is required to transfer out of Prepaid Insurance.

This is the adjusting journal entry:

Dec. 31   Insurance Expense   631   100
            Prepaid Insurance   161   100
        To record insurance expense for December.

This adjusting entry transfers the expired $100 of prepaid insurance to the Insurance Expense account. The balance remaining in the Prepaid Insurance account after the entry is posted ($1,200 − $100) represents the unexpired asset that will benefit future periods.

When the adjusting entry is posted, the expense portion is transferred as follows:

An expense account, Insurance Expense, is increased by the expired $100. An expense is increased by a debit.	An asset account, Prepaid Insurance, is decreased by the $100 that has expired during December. An asset is decreased by a credit.

(b)

On December 3, the corporation signed a contract for the use of its truck on a part-time basis and received an advance payment of $600 for use of the truck as follows: $200 for December, $200 for January, and $200 for February (transaction 9).

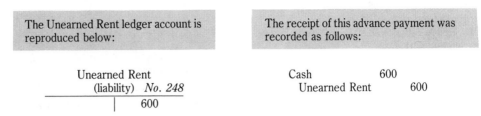

The Unearned Rent ledger account is reproduced below:

The receipt of this advance payment was recorded as follows:

Unearned Rent (liability) *No. 248*		Cash	600	
	600	Unearned Rent		600

This advance payment was recorded as unearned, since it was received before it was earned. At December 31, however, one month of the rent has been earned.

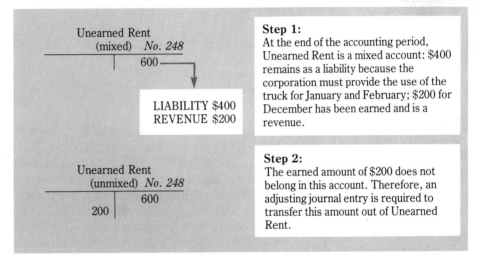

Step 1:
At the end of the accounting period, Unearned Rent is a mixed account: $400 remains as a liability because the corporation must provide the use of the truck for January and February; $200 for December has been earned and is a revenue.

Unearned Rent (mixed) *No. 248* — 600

LIABILITY $400
REVENUE $200

Step 2:
The earned amount of $200 does not belong in this account. Therefore, an adjusting journal entry is required to transfer this amount out of Unearned Rent.

Unearned Rent (unmixed) *No. 248*
200 | 600

This is the adjusting journal entry:

Dec. 31	Unearned Rent	248	200	
	Rent Earned	440		200
	To record rental earned during December.			

This adjusting entry transfers the $200 of rent earned to revenue. The balance remaining in Unearned Rent after the entry is posted ($600 − $200) represents the unearned amount that will be earned in future periods.

When the adjusting entry is posted, the revenue element is removed from the mixed account as follows:

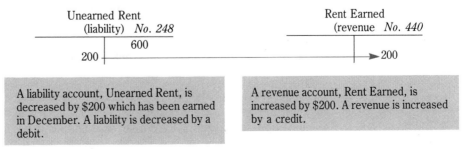

Unearned Rent (liability) *No. 248*			Rent Earned (revenue *No. 440*	
	600			
200				200

A liability account, Unearned Rent, is decreased by $200 which has been earned in December. A liability is decreased by a debit.

A revenue account, Rent Earned, is increased by $200. A revenue is increased by a credit.

Mixed Fixed Assets

Depreciation
The decline in the useful life of a fixed asset.

Depreciation expense
That part of the original cost of a fixed asset allocated to a particular accounting period.

Accumulated depreciation
The total amount of an asset's original cost that has been allocated to expense since the asset was acquired. The account where these expenses are entered is called an asset *valuation account* or *contra-asset account*.

Valuation account
An account that is deducted from another account to modify the recorded amount of that latter account; sometimes called a *contra account*.

Contra account
An account used to accumulate amounts that are related; sometimes called a *valuation account*.

Useful life
An estimate of the time during which an asset will be used by the entity; the term is used in connection with a fixed asset.

Scrap value
The estimated amount for which the asset can be sold at the end of its useful life; also called *salvage value*.

The mixed portion that had expired was transferred from the asset account in the case of insurance or rent. The expired portion of a fixed asset, however, is handled in a different manner. *Accountants do not unmix fixed asset accounts.*

> 1. The expired portion of the cost of a fixed asset is called **depreciation**. The periodic expired cost, called **depreciation expense**, requires no periodic cash outlay but, nevertheless, is a continuous expense of operating the business.
>
> 2. The amount of depreciation is not transferred from the asset account, since both the original cost and recorded depreciation are relevant pieces of information to readers of financial statements. Therefore, two new accounts are used to record the estimated depreciation.

Journal entries used to record depreciation take the following form:

Depreciation Expense	XX	
Accumulated Depreciation		XX

The Depreciation Expense account records the amount of estimated expense that belongs to the accounting period under consideration. This account is shown on the income statement as an expense. The amount of **accumulated depreciation** is deducted from the asset on the balance sheet to disclose the net book value of the asset; accordingly, it is referred to as a **valuation account** or **contra account**. The balance in the Accumulated Depreciation account represents the amount that the asset has expired.

The amount of depreciation is calculated using an estimate of the **useful life** of the asset and its subsequent **scrap value**. The calculation is illustrated in the examples that follow.

Illustrative Problem — Mixed Fixed Asset Accounts

The following fixed assets of Bluebeard Computer Corporation consist of mixed balances at the end of the accounting period:

Partial Trial Balance
December 31, 19X1

		Account Balances	
		Debit	Credit
c.	Equipment	$2,000	
d.	Truck	8,000	

Each account is analyzed in the following manner:

Step 1
At the end of the accounting period, determine the amount of depreciation expense.

Step 2
The estimated depreciation is *not* transferred from the asset account; rather, an adjusting journal entry is prepared using two new accounts, one of which is a contra-asset account. Note that a contra–fixed asset account *always has a credit balance*.

(c)

BCC owns $2,000-worth of equipment (transactions 2 and 5).

> The Equipment ledger account appears as follows:

Equipment (asset) *No. 183*
| 2,000 |

> This account balance resulted from two journal entries, which are summarized below for illustrative purposes only:

| Equipment | 2,000 | |
| Cash | | 2,000 |

Calculation of Depreciation

$$\frac{\text{Cost} - \text{Salvage Value}}{\text{Useful life}}$$

$$\frac{\$2,000 - \$200}{60} = \$30$$

The equipment was recorded as a fixed asset because it has a useful life of 60 months and will have a scrap value of $200. Although this equipment had been purchased in November, it was used in December. At December 31, one month of the net asset cost has expired. The depreciation expense for the equipment in December is calculated as $30 [($2,000 − 200) ÷ 60 = $30]. This estimate is calculated using the **straight-line method of depreciation**.

Straight-line method of depreciation
A method in which equal amounts of depreciation expense are recorded for each time period over the useful life of the asset.

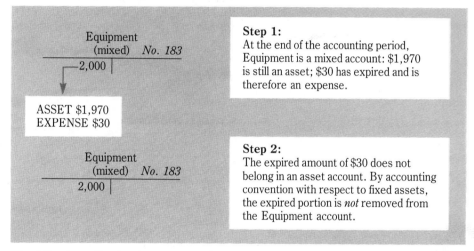

Equipment (mixed) *No. 183*
| —2,000 |

ASSET $1,970
EXPENSE $30

Step 1:
At the end of the accounting period, Equipment is a mixed account: $1,970 is still an asset; $30 has expired and is therefore an expense.

Equipment (mixed) *No. 183*
| 2,000 |

Step 2:
The expired amount of $30 does not belong in an asset account. By accounting convention with respect to fixed assets, the expired portion is *not* removed from the Equipment account.

The following adjusting journal entry is made:

Dec. 31	Depreciation Expense — Equipment	623	30	
	Accumulated Depreciation — Equipment	193		30
	To record depreciation for December.			

This adjusting entry records the $30 of depreciation on equipment. The mixed balance remains in the Equipment account.

When the adjusting entry is posted, the accounts appear as follows:

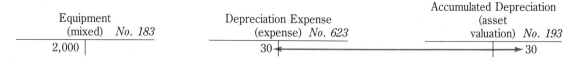

Equipment (mixed) *No. 183*
| 2,000 |

Depreciation Expense (expense) *No. 623*
| 30 ← |

Accumulated Depreciation (asset valuation) *No. 193*
| → 30 |

> This account remains unchanged.

> An expense account, Depreciation Expense, is increased by $30 that has expired. An expense is increased by a debit.

> The valuation account, Accumulated Depreciation, is also increased by the $30 that has expired. This valuation account is increased by a credit.

(d)

BCC owns a truck for which it paid $8,000 (transaction 3).

The truck ledger account appears as follows:	The truck purchase journal entry appears as follows:

Truck
(asset)   *No. 184*
————————
8,000 |

Truck   8,000
  Bank Loan   5,000
  Cash   3,000

The truck was recorded as a fixed asset because it has a useful life of 60 months; it will have a scrap value of $800. At December 31, two months of the truck cost have expired. The depreciation expense for the truck by December 31 is calculated as: ($8,000 − $800) ÷ 60 months × 2 months = $240; this estimate is calculated using the straight-line method of depreciation.

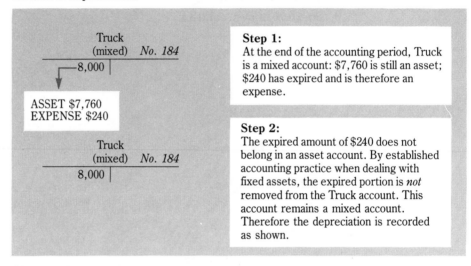

Step 1:
At the end of the accounting period, Truck is a mixed account: $7,760 is still an asset; $240 has expired and is therefore an expense.

Step 2:
The expired amount of $240 does not belong in an asset account. By established accounting practice when dealing with fixed assets, the expired portion is *not* removed from the Truck account. This account remains a mixed account. Therefore the depreciation is recorded as shown.

The following adjusting journal entry is made:

Dec. 31   Depreciation Expense — Truck   624   240
         Accumulated Depreciation — Truck   194   240
         To record depreciation for December.

This adjusting entry records the $240 of depreciation on trucks. The mixed balance remains in the Truck account. Depreciation expense is shown on the income statement as an expense.

When the adjusting entry is posted, the accounts appear as follows:

Truck (mixed) *No. 184*	Depreciation Expense (expense) *No. 624*	Accumulated Depreciation (asset valuation) *No. 194*
8,000 |	240 ◄———	———► 240
This account remains unchanged.	An expense account, Depreciation Expense, is increased by $240, which has expired. An expense is increased by a debit.	The valuation account, Accumulated Depreciation, is also increased by $240 that has expired. This valuation account is increased by a credit.

E. Mixed Income Statement Accounts

The trial balance of Bluebeard Computer Corporation at December 31 includes a receipt that has been recorded as a revenue of the corporation.

> Receipts are recorded as *revenues* during an accounting period if they are expected to be earned during the period. If, in fact, they have not been earned by the end of the period, an accounting measurement is required. The amount of revenue unearned must be calculated and the unearned revenue recognized as a *liability* at the end of the period. In this way, only revenues earned during the period are matched with expenses incurred to earn those revenues.

The trial balance of the corporation also includes a cost outlay that has been recorded as an expense of the corporation.

> Cost outlays are recorded as *expenses* during an accounting period if they are expected to be used up (that is, if they are expected to expire) during the period. If, in fact, they have not been completely consumed by the end of the accounting period, an accounting measurement is required. The amount of the expense that has not expired must be calculated and the unexpired amount recognized as an *asset* at the end of the period. In this way, revenues for the period are matched with expenses incurred to earn those revenues.

The revenue and expense accounts referred to above are also mixed accounts, since they include both an income statement portion and a balance sheet portion at the end of the period.

Illustrative Problem — Unmixing Income Statement Accounts

The following income statement accounts of Bluebeard Computer Corporation require adjustment at December 31:

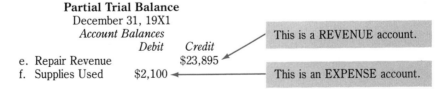

Partial Trial Balance
December 31, 19X1
Account Balances

	Debit	Credit	
e. Repair Revenue		$23,895	This is a REVENUE account.
f. Supplies Used	$2,100		This is an EXPENSE account.

These accounts are analyzed and adjusted as follows:

Step 1
At the end of the accounting period, determine which portion of the mixed account belongs in the balance sheet and which belongs in the income statement.

Step 2
The portion that does not belong in the revenue or expense account must be transferred out. An adjusting entry is made in the general journal and posted to the proper accounts to make the transfer.

(e)

BCC received $2,000 on December 26 for repairs to be made in December (transaction 12). According to its best estimates, the company would begin the repairs in January and hopefully have the work completed by mid-February.

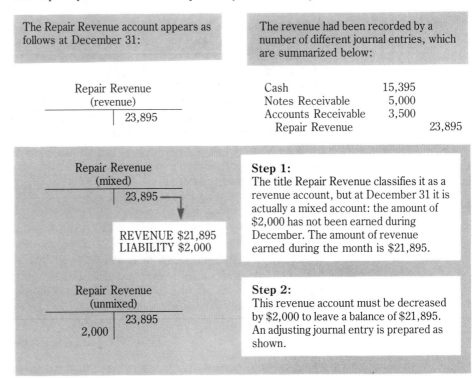

| The Repair Revenue account appears as follows at December 31: | The revenue had been recorded by a number of different journal entries, which are summarized below: |

Repair Revenue
(revenue)
| 23,895

Cash   15,395
Notes Receivable   5,000
Accounts Receivable   3,500
    Repair Revenue   23,895

Repair Revenue
(mixed)
| 23,895

REVENUE $21,895
LIABILITY $2,000

Step 1:
The title Repair Revenue classifies it as a revenue account, but at December 31 it is actually a mixed account: the amount of $2,000 has not been earned during December. The amount of revenue earned during the month is $21,895.

Repair Revenue
(unmixed)
| 23,895
2,000 |

Step 2:
This revenue account must be decreased by $2,000 to leave a balance of $21,895. An adjusting journal entry is prepared as shown.

This is the adjusting journal entry:

Dec. 31 Repair Revenue   450   2,000
             Unearned Repair Revenue   247   2,000
         To record unearned repair revenue
         at December 31.

The revenue, Repair Revenue, is decreased by the $2,000 that has not yet been earned. In this way, the mixed revenue account is split into two portions: the unearned amount is transferred to the balance sheet liability account; what remains in the account is the income statement portion.

When this adjusting entry is posted, the unearned portion is transferred from the mixed account as follows:

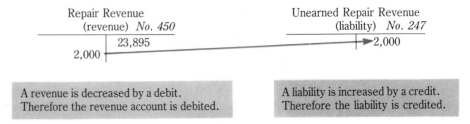

Repair Revenue
(revenue) *No. 450*
| 23,895
2,000 |

Unearned Repair Revenue
(liability) *No. 247*
| ►2,000

| A revenue is decreased by a debit. Therefore the revenue account is debited. | A liability is increased by a credit. Therefore the liability is credited. |

(f)

BCC purhased $2,100-worth of supplies to be used during November and December (transactions 7 and 10). Since these supplies were expected to be used during that accounting period, their cost was recorded as an expense.

The Supplies Used account appears as follows at December 31:	This expense had been recorded by a number of different journal entries, which are summarized below:

Supplies Used (expense) No. 668		Supplies Used	2,100	
2,100		Cash		1,200
		Accounts Payable		900

At December 31, a physical count of inventory of supplies showed that $495-worth of supplies were still on hand, indicating that not all the supplies were used during the two months.

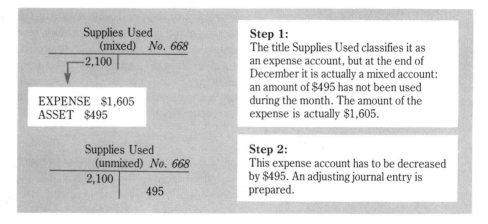

Step 1:
The title Supplies Used classifies it as an expense account, but at the end of December it is actually a mixed account: an amount of $495 has not been used during the month. The amount of the expense is actually $1,605.

Step 2:
This expense account has to be decreased by $495. An adjusting journal entry is prepared.

This is the adjusting journal entry:

Dec. 31	Supplies	173	495	
	Supplies Used	668		495
	To record unused supplies at December 31.			

When the adjusting entry is posted, the unexpired portion is transferred from the mixed account as follows:

An asset is increased by a debit. Therefore the asset account, Supplies, is debited.	An expense is decreased by a credit. Therefore the expense account, Supplies Used, is credited.

F. Accruals

Accruals
Items that accumulate or increase and are recognized to increase usually during the adjustment phase of the accounting cycle.

Accrued expenses
An increase in expenses during the current accounting period, which is due to be paid in a future accounting period.

Accrued revenues
An increase in revenues during the current accounting period, which is due to be received in a future accounting period.

Some revenues and expenses increase as time passes and are therefore said to accrue. An **accrual** is an item that increases with the passage of time and is often used by accountants in reference to adjusting entries. Several examples of items that accrue on a day-to-day basis are the following:

Revenues that Accrue	*Expenses that Accrue*
Interest Earned	Interest Expense
Rent Earned	Rent Expense
	Salaries Expense

These revenues are usually recorded when cash is received.	These expenses are usually recorded when cash is paid.

Interest, as an example, accrues (increases) daily but is received or paid only at certain specified times: perhaps monthly, in the case of banks, or at the due date of a note when the principal and interest are paid. No accounting problem is caused by the fact that these items have not been recorded during the accounting period, but accounting principles require that revenues earned and expenses incurred during the period must be matched in the accounts. Accordingly, at the end of the period, an adjusting journal entry is made so that revenues are properly matched with expenses of the same period.

> During the accounting period, regular business transactions are recorded as they occur. At the end of the period, the accountant may find that ledger account balances are incomplete. In the case of revenue and expense items that accrue, some new amounts must be brought into the accounts. The adjusting entries to accomplish this balance are referred to as *accruals*.

Illustrative Problem — Recording Accruals

The following accounts of Bluebeard Computer Corporation require an accrual at December 31:

Income Statement Account	*Balance Sheet Account*
Interest Earned	Interest Receivable
Salaries Expense	Salaries Payable
Interest Expense	Interest Payable
Income Tax Expense	Income Tax Payable

The accounts are discussed and adjusting entries are prepared in the following pages, under headings g, h, i, and j.

Unrecorded Revenues

Unrecorded revenues consist of revenues that have been earned during the accounting period but that are not due to be collected until sometime in the next period.

(g)

Bluebeard Computer Corporation performed $5,000-worth of repairs for one of its customers, who signed a 60-day, 12-percent, interest-bearing note dated December 16.

   Although interest accrues daily on the $5,000 loan, the interest is actually received only at the maturity date of the note, February 14, when the amount due (principal plus interest) is paid by the customer. At December 31, the end of the accounting period for BCC, interest has been earned for 15 days in December (December 16–31), as shown in Figure 3-5, but this interest earned has not yet been recorded by the company.

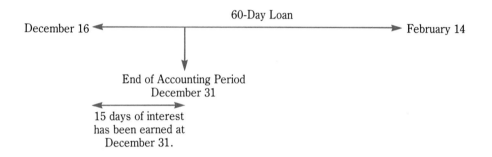

Figure 3-5   Interest earned during an accounting period

The formula for computing interest is show below:

$$\text{Interest} = \text{Principal} \times \text{Interest rate} \times \frac{\text{Elapsed time in days}}{365}.$$

The interest revenue accrued at December 31 is computed as follows:

$$\text{Interest} = \$5,000 \times 0.12 \times \frac{15}{365} = \$24.66 \text{ (or \$25 rounded for illustrative purposes).}$$

   The principal multiplied by the interest rate equals the total interest for one year ($5,000 × 0.12 = $600); the interest for a year ($600) multiplied by the elapsed fraction of a year (15/365) is the interest revenue for 15 days ($600 × 15/365), or $25. The use of 365 days in the formula, ignoring leap years, is consistent with commercial practice, the primary reason being simplicity of calculation.

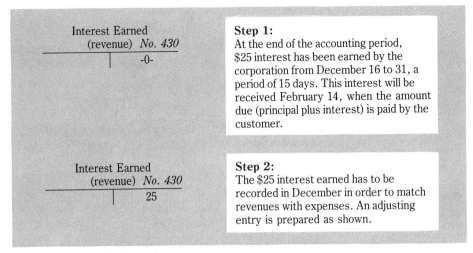

This is the adjusting journal entry:

Dec. 31	Interest Receivable	116	25	
	Interest Earned	430		25
	To record interest accrued at December 31.			

This adjusting entry enables BCC to include in income of the period the interest earned, even though the payment has not yet been received. The entry created an accrued receivable — that is, a receivable for an income earned during an accounting period but collectible in another accounting period.

When the adjusting entry is posted, the accounts appear as follows:

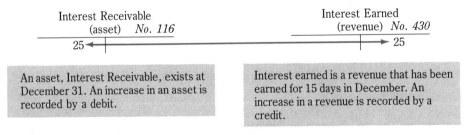

Other adjusting entries for various revenues, which have been earned by the company during the accounting period but have not been received or are not due to be collected until some time in the next period, are recorded in a manner similar to the adjustment for interest earned. The amount earned must be calculated and is recorded in the accounts by the following type of journal entry:

Receivable	XX	
Earned		XX
To accrue revenue.		

Unrecorded Expenses

Unrecorded expenses are expenses that have been incurred during the accounting period but have not been paid during the accounting period or that are not due to be paid until some time in the next period.

(h)

At December 31, the end of the accounting period for Bluebeard, salary expense had been incurred for three days in December, as shown in Figure 3-6, but this expense had not been recorded.

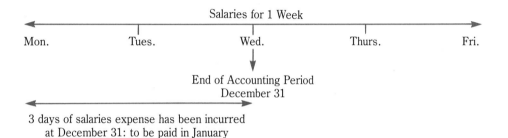

3 days of salaries expense has been incurred
at December 31: to be paid in January

Figure 3-6 Salary expense incurred but not paid during one accounting period

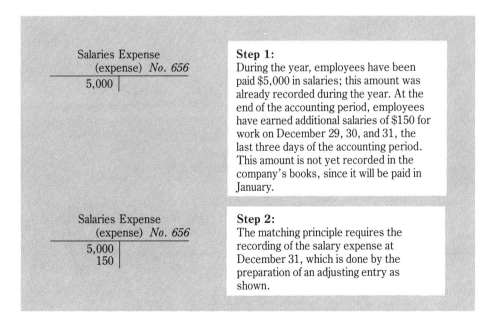

Salaries Expense
(expense) *No. 656*

| 5,000 | |

Step 1:
During the year, employees have been paid $5,000 in salaries; this amount was already recorded during the year. At the end of the accounting period, employees have earned additional salaries of $150 for work on December 29, 30, and 31, the last three days of the accounting period. This amount is not yet recorded in the company's books, since it will be paid in January.

Salaries Expense
(expense) *No. 656*

| 5,000 | |
| 150 | |

Step 2:
The matching principle requires the recording of the salary expense at December 31, which is done by the preparation of an adjusting entry as shown.

This is the adjusting entry:

Dec. 31	Salaries Expense	656	150	
	Salaries Payable	226		150
	To record salaries accrued at December 31.			

This entry enables the company to include in expense all salaries earned by employees, even though not all salaries have yet been paid. The entry creates an accrued liability — that is, a liability for an expense incurred during one accounting period (December) but payable in another accounting period (January).

When the adjusting entry is posted, the accounts appear as follows:

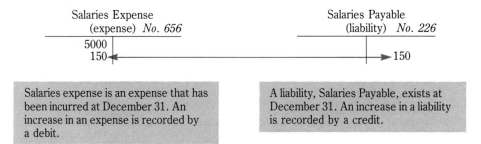

Salaries expense is an expense that has been incurred at December 31. An increase in an expense is recorded by a debit.

A liability, Salaries Payable, exists at December 31. An increase in a liability is recorded by a credit.

(i)

Bluebeard Computer Corporation had incurred a $5,000 bank loan in the purchase of a truck in November. The interest rate was 12-percent per annum. Although interest accrues daily on this bank loan, no interest has yet been paid at the end of the accounting time period.

At December 31, the end of the accounting period for BCC, interest has accrued for 58 days to December 31 (November 3 to December 31), but this interest expense has not yet been recorded by the company.

The interest expense accrued at December 31 is computed as follows:

$$\text{Interest} = \$5,000 \times 0.12 \times \frac{58}{365} = \$95.34 \text{ (or \$95 rounded for illustrative purposes)}$$

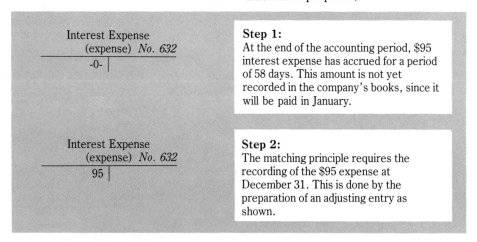

Step 1:
At the end of the accounting period, $95 interest expense has accrued for a period of 58 days. This amount is not yet recorded in the company's books, since it will be paid in January.

Step 2:
The matching principle requires the recording of the $95 expense at December 31. This is done by the preparation of an adjusting entry as shown.

This is the adjusting entry:

Dec. 31	Interest Expense	632	95	
	Interest Payable	222		95
	To record interest accrued at December 31.			

The entry creates an accrued liability — that is, a liability for an expense incurred during the current accounting period but payable in another accounting period (January).

When the adjusting entry is posted, the accounts appear as follows:

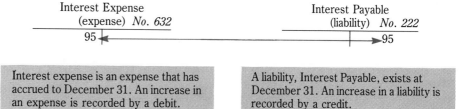

Interest Expense (expense) *No. 632*	Interest Payable (liability) *No. 222*
95	95

Interest expense is an expense that has accrued to December 31. An increase in an expense is recorded by a debit.	A liability, Interest Payable, exists at December 31. An increase in a liability is recorded by a credit.

Other adjusting entries for expense (such as utilities, telephone, and so on) that have been incurred by the company during the accounting period but that are not due to be paid until the next period are recorded in a manner similar to the adjustment for salary and interest expenses. The amount of the expense must be calculated and then recorded in the following type of entry:

Date	Expense	XX	
	Expense Payable		XX
	To accrue an expense.		

Recording Taxes

Another adjustment that is required for Bluebeard Computer Corporation involves the recording of $6,000 estimated income taxes due to the government. This payment is necessary because a corporation is taxed as an entity separate from its shareholders.

(j)

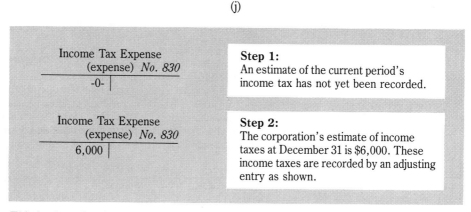

Income Tax Expense (expense) *No. 830*	**Step 1:** An estimate of the current period's income tax has not yet been recorded.
-0-	

Income Tax Expense (expense) *No. 830*	**Step 2:** The corporation's estimate of income taxes at December 31 is $6,000. These income taxes are recorded by an adjusting entry as shown.
6,000	

This is the adjusting entry:

Dec. 31	Income Tax Expense	830	6,000	
	Income Tax Payable	260		6,000
	To record estimated income taxes at December 31.			

When the adjusting entry is posted, the accounts appear as follows:

Income Tax Expense (expense) *No. 830*	Income Tax Payable (liability) *No. 260*
6,000 ◄─────────────────────────────►	6,000

| Income Tax Expense is an expense that has been incurred. An expense is increased by a debit. | Income Tax Payable is a liability that has accrued at December 31. A liability is increased by a credit. |

The above adjusting entry enables the company to show the income taxes applicable to the income earned during the period. However, not all organizations are required to pay income tax; a case in point is not-for-profit organizations. Some accounting differences in not-for-profit organizations are elaborated on in Real Life Example 3-1.

Real Life Example 3-1
Significant Accounting Differences

Unlike the profit sector, the bottom line of which is a profit and loss picture, non-profit organizations are, in the main, concerned with showing full use of income from grants, donations, and fund-raising events. But in Revenue Canada's books, the line between profit and non-profit has become increasingly smudged. Paragraph 149 (1)(1) of the Income Tax Act exempts non-profit organizations from income tax, provided they operate exclusively for any purpose except profit, with no income payable or otherwise made available to members. And yet, one of the criteria determining a profit-oriented association is whether "the main activity carries on a trade or business". Thus, an association of handicapped people making a business of recycling paper could be subject to tax. So could such groups as the YWCA, operating fitness sessions and sports facilities.

The government issued Interpretation Bulletin 496, "Non-profit Organizations", in February 1983, but subsequent discussions with accountants show that no single objective test is applied to investigations. Rather, each case is individually reviewed, and evaluation is subjective.

Equally confusing is the area of non-monetary donations. Items can be receipted for tax deduction, but services cannot. Thus, a restaurant donating prepared food can be receipted at the menu (or retail) value, unless a supplier donates the ingredients; then, the supplier can be receipted, but the restaurant cannot claim its cooking and preparation time. In other areas, it's difficult to establish fair market value for tax receipts.

Standards and guidelines for non-profit accounting procedures are noticeably absent. For instance, assets are capitalized in some cases, not in others. The same lack of consensus applies to property depreciation.

Endowments and other bequests often carry conditions governing their specific use, requiring equally specific accounting procedures. The non-profit sector also faces more accountability than the profit sector in the area of trust funds and their relative specific uses.

Investment by non-profit groups for long-range revenue is increasing but in some cases engenders ethical problems. Accountants for CUSO and Oxfam, for example, must screen all investments for South African connections, in accordance with the groups' stand against apartheid.

Source   C. Potter, "Charitable and Non-profit Organizations", *CGA Magazine*, August 1985, p. 31.

G. The Accounting Process — Steps 4–6

In this chapter, six individual steps of the accounting process have been reviewed. The first two steps occur continuously through the time period; the third to sixth steps occur at the end of the accounting period.

Step 4: *The Account Balances Are Analyzed and Adjusted Entries Prepared*

As is the case with the December transactions (recorded in section B of this chapter), the adjusting entries are also recorded in the journal of the Bluebeard Computer Corporation at the end of December.

The caption *Adjusting Entries* is written in the journal on the line following the last regular journal entry of the corporation.

After the adjusting entries have been posted, the mixed elements in the accounts have been eliminated. Account numbers are recorded in the folio column to indicate that the amounts have been posted to the particular account involved.

Step 5: *The Adjusting Entries Are Posted to Ledger Accounts*

When the December adjusting entries have been posted to the ledger accounts, the ledger accounts are footed and any debit or credit balances are calculated. For example, the Prepaid Insurance account has a debit balance of $1,100 after it has been footed.

Step 6: *An Adjusted Trial Balance Is Prepared To Prove the Equality of Debits and Credits*

Adjusted trial balance
A listing of accounts and their balances after the posting of adjusting entries to the accounts of the entity.

A trial balance prepared after the posting of adjusting entries to the ledger would contain the accounts and account balances shown below. Note that new accounts have been included as required by the adjusting entries, and that this trial balance is labelled as an **adjusted trial balance** to distinguish it from the *unadjusted* trial balance prepared earlier.

The purpose of any trial balance is to establish the equality of debits and credits, to ensure the accuracy of the mechanical process of recording transactions and the posting of journal entries to the ledger.

The trial balance, or in this case, the adjusted trial balance, is useful to the accountant in the preparation of financial statements. The accountant could prepare these statements directly from the ledger accounts, but the trial balance or adjusted trial balance is a convenient summary of this information for the preparation of financial statements.

Bluebeard Computer Corporation
Adjusted Trial Balance
December 31, 19X1

	Account Balances	
	Debit	*Credit*
Cash	$11,695	
Accounts Receivable	3,500	
Interest Receivable	25	
Notes Receivable	5,000	
Prepaid Insurance	1,100	
Supplies	495	
Equipment	2,000	
Truck	8,000	
Accumulated Depreciation — Equipment		$ 30
Accumulated Depreciation — Truck		240
Bank Loan		5,000
Accounts Payable		1,900
Interest Payable		95
Salaries Payable		150
Unearned Repair Revenue		2,000
Unearned Rent		400
Income Tax Payable		6,000
Common Stock		10,000
Interest Earned		25
Repair Revenue		21,895
Rent Earned		200
Depreciation Expense — Equipment	30	
Depreciation Expense — Truck	240	
Insurance Expense	100	
Interest Expense	95	
Rent Expense	1,200	
Salaries Expense	5,150	
Supplies Used	1,605	
Truck Expense	1,400	
Utilities Expense	300	
Income Tax Expense	6,000	
	$47,935	$47,935

Chart of Accounts

The following accounts are used in the assignment material in this chapter and throughout the text.

100–199 *Current Assets*
100 Petty Cash
101 Cash
106 Temporary Investments
110 Accounts Receivable
111 Allowance for Doubtful Accounts
116 Interest Receivable
120 Notes Receivable
150 Merchandise Inventory
160 Prepaid Advertising
161 Prepaid Insurance
162 Prepaid Rent
170 Office Supplies
171 Repair Supplies
172 Service Supplies
173 Supplies

Fixed Assets
180 Land
181 Building
182 Furniture
183 Equipment
184 Trucks
191 Accumulated Depreciation — Building
192 Accumulated Depreciation — Furniture
193 Accumulated Depreciation — Equipment
194 Accumulated Depreciation — Truck

200–299 *Current Liabilities*
201 Bank Loan — Current
210 Accounts Payable
214 Loans Payable
215 Mortgage Payable — Current
220 Notes Payable — Current
221 Dividends Payable
222 Interest Payable
226 Salaries Payable
231 Property Tax Payable
236 Utilities Payable
237 Wages Payable
240 Unearned Advertising

242 Unearned Commissions
244 Unearned Fees
246 Unearned Interest
247 Unearned Repair Revenue
248 Unearned Rent
249 Unearned Revenue
250 Unearned Subscriptions
260 Income Tax Payable

Long-Term Liabilities
271 Bank Loan — Long-Term
272 Bonds Payable — Long-Term
275 Mortgage Payable — Long-Term
280 Notes Payable — Long-Term

300–399 *Shareholder's Equity*
320 Common Stock
340 Retained Earnings
350 Dividends
360 Income Summary

400–499 *Revenue*
410 Commissions Earned
420 Fees Earned
430 Interest Earned
440 Rent Earned
450 Repair Revenue
460 Revenue (for other types not identified within the revenue category)
470 Service Revenue
480 Subscription Revenue

500–549 *Sales Accounts*
500 Sales
508 Sales Returns and Allowances
509 Sales Discounts

550–599 *Purchases Accounts*
550 Purchases
558 Purchases Returns and Allowances
559 Purchases Discounts
560 Transportation In

600–699 *Expenses*
       610 Advertising Expense
       613 Bad Debt Expense
       615 Commissions Expense
       620 Delivery Expense
       621 Depreciation Expense — Building
       622 Depreciation Expense — Furniture
       623 Depreciation Expense — Equipment
       624 Depreciation Expense — Truck
       630 Equipment Rental Expense
       631 Insurance Expense
       632 Interest Expense
       641 Maintenance Expense
       650 Office Supplies Used
       651 Property Tax Expense
       652 Miscellaneous General Expense
       653 Miscellaneous Selling Expense
       654 Rent Expense
       655 Repair Supplies Used
       656 Salaries Expense
       657 Salespersons' Salaries Expense
       668 Supplies Used
       669 Telephone Expense
       670 Truck Expense
       676 Utilities Expense
       677 Wages Expense

700–749 *Other Gains and Revenues*
       732 Interest Income

750–799 *Other Losses and Expenses*
       760 Loss on Sale of Equipment

800–899 *Other Accounts*
       830 Income Tax Expense

Discussion Questions

1. What is an operating cycle? How does it function?
2. In what manner do operating cycles overlap in actual practice? Use an example to explain.
3. The recording of some transactions causes more problems than the recording of others. Identify and explain two categories of such transactions.
4. Why is it important to identify the point at which the revenue of a business is actually earned?
5. When a deposit or advance payment is received, what is the accepted practice used by accountants to record its receipt? Identify and explain the practice.
6. Define cost outlay.
7. Identify and explain the accepted practice used by accountants to record cost outlays.
8. Is consistency an accounting principle or practice? What is its importance?
9. What are adjusting entries and why are they required? Why are some accounts described as being "mixed"?
10. What is the general method used in unmixing asset accounts? Identify and describe the steps involved.
11. What is the general method used in unmixing liability accounts? Identify and describe the steps involved.
12. Accountants do not unmix fixed asset accounts. Why?
13. Depreciation Expense and Accumulated Depreciation are two accounts used in relation to fixed accounts. Why are they used?
14. Under what circumstances are cash receipts recorded as revenues?
15. Under what circumstances are cost outlays recorded as expenses?
16. What is the general method used in unmixing income statement accounts?
17. What is meant by the term *to accrue*? Give examples of items that accrue.
18. List the steps in the accounting cycle.
19. Which steps in the accounting cycle occur continuously throughout the accounting period?
20. Which steps in the accounting cycle occur at the end of the accounting period? Explain how they differ from the other steps.
21. Refer to Conceptual Issue 3-1. Accountants sometimes use the term *unearned revenue*; is this term a contradiction? Where would it fit in to the FASB definitions?

Discussion Cases

Discussion Case 3-1:   The Bottom Line

"Everybody is talking GAAP, GAAP, GAAP," said Martin Ives, vice-chairman and director of research for the Governmental Accounting Standards Board, a private non-profit group that sets the GAAP guidelines. "I remember when."

"When" was before 1982. That was the last year New York state reported its financial operations on a cash basis accounting system. Revenues were recorded at the time they came in and expenditures at the time they went out.

That system allowed politicians to distort the financial condition of the state government honestly by moving receipts and disbursements from one fiscal year to another, by delaying payments or by speeding up collections.

For example, the state's fiscal year ends March 31. If the state ordered and received $100 million-worth of widgets in February, it could wait to pay for them until April 1, thereby pushing the $100 million disbursement into the next fiscal year.

When the books for the year ended March 31 were reviewed, the $100 million would not show up, even though the widgets had been ordered and put into use that year. In other words, the cash system made it possible to run today's operation by pushing some costs into tomorrow's budget.

Looking for a Better Way

Nowhere was this technique more artfully employed than in aid to local school districts. By the late 1970s, it had become impossible to assess accurately the state's fiscal health. More and more officials began to look for an accurate way to determine it.

Under GAAP, expenditures are recorded when they are incurred rather than when the cheque is written. Revenues are recorded when they are due, rather than when the money is actually received.

So, if the state receives $100 million in widgets in February, they are charged agaist that fiscal year, even if the state doesn't get around to paying the bill until the next year.

When in the late 1970s state auditors began to analyze the accounts under GAAP, they realized how big New York's deficits had become. GAAP accounting did not help to eradicate the accumulated deficit (which now amounts to $4 billion), but it did define the size of it.

Source Jeffrey Schmalz, ''Sometimes There's Just No Settling on the Bottom Line'', *The New York Times*, March 17, 1985, p. 6-E.

For Discussion

1. Identify the previous method of accounting used by New York and explain how it worked. What is the method used since 1982 called?
2. Refer to Discussion Case 2-2 (in Chapter 2) and discuss the method of accounting used by the Canadian federal government. Is it in accordance with GAAP?

Discussion Case 3-2:   Montreal Artist Rues Day Taxman Brought his Slippers

At 8:30 on a Monday morning, 53-year-old Montreal sculptor Yves Trudeau looked out his window and saw The Taxman pacing back and forth in front of his house.

Nervous (''I thought I could be arrested''), yet confident that he had nothing to hide, Trudeau opened the door.

The taxman came in, hung up his coat, put on his bedroom slippers, and stayed.

He came again each day, for three weeks.

He said he had the power of the RCMP (though in truth he doesn't) Trudeau recalls, demanded to see the house from roof to cellar, and sat down at the dining room table. He scoured through receipts, cancelled cheques, everything, all the while sitting in the middle of the house in his bedroom slippers.

''I couldn't stand it,'' says Trudeau. ''Every half hour he would ask my wife a question. She panicked.'' Finally, Trudeau called his accountant with an ultimatum: ''Take him out of my house or I'll kill him.''

In the end, the sculptor of 30 years had to cough up $6,000 in back taxes.

Trudeau is one of the hundreds of artists across Canada who say that Revenue Canada is persecuting them.

When Toni Onley in Vancouver threatened to torch $1 million-worth of his works in October, that's exactly what he was trying to tell the country.

These artists claim that, although the Income Tax Act has never had a section dealing specifically with them, things had gone along merrily for years, with them paying taxes according to the way that law was applied in *practice*.

Suddenly, the artists say, Revenue Canada changed its interpretation of the same laws, reprogrammed its trusty computers, and began demanding thousands of dollars in back taxes which the artists almost always don't have. Now, the computer tells the taxman, if an artist isn't making a profit on his art, he/she is merely a ''hobbyist'', not an artist at all. So he can't deduct the cost of his materials.

On the other hand, says the computer, if they *are* making a profit, they are to be treated exactly the same way as a businessperson manufacturing widgets. That means, for one thing that, until a piece of work is sold, an artist cannot write off the cost of producing it.

Under these rules, artist Emily Carr, who didn't make a profit with her work, would have been considered a hobbyist by Revenue Canada. . . .

What makes it complex is, that, until recently, artists were informally allowed a dual status which, they say, worked. They used to be able to hold another job to support their art and at the same time be considered self-employed so they could deduct the costs of supplies, travel, instruments, whatever.

Now artists feel they are the victims of a streamlined computer program that turns a blind eye to the precarious life of Canada's artists. The facts show that an artist almost always needs a second job to survive. In 1982, the average income of a self-employed professional writer was approximately $6,100; a visual artist $2,100; a professional actor $9,100. The poverty line for a single person living in cities of more than 500 000 in Canada was $8,970 that year. The average annual income of self-employed artists fell from $4,835 in 1974 to $4,352 in 1980.

Miserable facts

With these miserable facts to live with, artists feel that Revenue Canada threatens to cut off the country's creative juices which, ironically, many other departments in Ottawa have done much to encourage.

No one, with the possible exception of Revenue Canada, can say exactly how many artists consider themselves to be victims of the tax department. But Jane Condon, national director of an Ottawa group called Canadian Artists' Representation which claims to speak for 800 visual artists, says: ''Based on our experience, the number who have contacted this office directly would indicate that hundreds of visual artists have been affected.''

Condon says it is particularly hard to know how many artists have been harassed by the tax department because: ''Nobody really wants to talk about money — how much they make and how much they pay in taxes except in a very general sense. So getting people to talk about it is not easy.''

In fact, most of the artists who eventually went public thought they were isolated cases until Onley captured media attention last October. Onley decided to burn his paintings because a tax officer suggested that by destroying "inventory" (like any other manufacturer), the artist could write off the expenses he incurred in producing them.

Communications Minister Francis Fox telegraphed Onley and asked him to wait while Fox presented "the concern of Canada's artists to the minister of national revenue".

The tax department is giving some writers a hard time, too. Dale Thomson, McGill University political science professor, former vice-principal, and author of political biographies was nabbed by Revenue Canada who, he says, treated him in a "crude, callous and indifferent" way.

Source Brenda Zosky Proulx, "The Day the Taxman Brought his Slippers", *The* (Montreal) *Gazette*, January 7, 1984, pp. A-1, A-4.

For Discussion

1. Should an artist who is making a profit be treated differently from one who is not? Why or why not?
2. Accrual accounting aligns expenses with revenues of a time period. Under this method, the cost of assets transferred to customers or used up during the period are considered as expenses; these expenses are matched with the revenue generated by these expenses and are included in the income statement of the same time period. How does accrual accounting apply in the position of the tax collector that, "until a piece of work is sold, artists cannot write off the cost of production"?
3. How does the destruction of "inventory" justify the writing off of the expenses incurred in producing paintings? Is the cash method or the accrual method more appropriate for artists? Why or why not?

Discussion Case 3-3: Airline in a Tailspin

For a man who heads an airline, Frank Borman is the ultimate pilot. His celestial exploits are legendary: America remembers how he read from the Bible on Christmas Eve as he commanded the first manned orbit of the moon. Since then, Mr. Borman's sights have become more terrestrial. For nearly a decade, he has headed chronically troubled Eastern Air Lines, the nation's third-largest carrier. But, in that time, Mr. Borman has failed to break the cycle of crisis that continues to haunt Eastern and has steered the airline dangerously close to financial disaster.

Trouble struck again this month—the most serious Eastern has ever faced. The airline fell into technical default to its bankers over its inability to draft a new employee wage contract. Eleventh-hour negotiations eventually produced the needed agreement, but deeper problems remain. Eastern has been unprofitable since 1979 and it is unclear when—and if—it will begin making money. The airline has racked up $380 million in losses over the last five years, and its debt has swelled to a staggering $2.5 billion. Labour relations are touchy, at best, and the goodwill that Mr. Borman once enjoyed is now long gone.

"When Borman came in, he had a wealth of good will from employees, and that's been totally dissipated," said D. Quinn Mills, a labour expert and professor at the Harvard Business School. "That's happened in little pieces over the last two to three years. He's not very effective in that job any longer and that's unfortunate." . . .

For his part, Mr. Borman predicts a rosy future for his company and himself. "I'm confident we will emerge from 1985 and this decade as a tough, competitive and successful company," said Mr. Borman, 55, in his spacious office decorated with models of new planes and paintings of old ones. "The average Eastern employee knows I care about him and his future. If I didn't think the employees felt that way, I'd leave and I don't intend to leave."

Such optimism notwithstanding, many lay the blame for

Eastern's current problems squarely on Mr. Borman. . . . Critics contend Mr. Borman spent money for the latest aircraft when the airline could not afford to do so—amassing the huge debt that now hangs like a noose. His blunt manner has only antagonized labour — "like oil and water," said one analyst—just when the airline dearly needs labour concession. Given such deep-rooted labour and financial problems, it is virtually impossible to foretell how the drama at Eastern will play out.

Eastern's continued inability to make money leaves it vulnerable on many fronts: to a recession, low-cost competitors and any unforeseen events that may come its way. Its financial weakness has forced Mr. Borman to yield an extraordinary amount of control to Eastern's lenders and its employees — who now hold the trump cards and are playing them with skill. Employees own 25 percent of the company and hold four seats on the board. Yet even this level of employee involvement still wasn't enough to stave off the frantic negotiations earlier this month, as labour battled the company and the bankers turned up the heat.

When Mr. Borman took over as chief executive officer in 1975, the company was, even then, teetering on bankruptcy. He upgraded its aging fleet, streamlined its routes, improved its service and turned in four straight years of record profits. But that success began to sour in the early 1980s, as the impact of deregulation unfolded and hit Eastern harder than most other airlines. . . .

With fuel prices hitting new highs in the mid-1970s, Mr. Borman directed Eastern on a highly controversial aircraft-buying spree, incurring enormous debt to buy new Airbuses and Boeing 757s. This has given Eastern the newest and most fuel-efficient fleet in the American skies — just as fuel prices have fallen to lows not seen in many years. The debt for those purchases consumes about $235 million in interest expense annually, pushing Eastern's debt-to-equity ratio to a precipitous 8 : 1. As a result, the first 6½ cents of every dollar earned at Eastern goes to repay that debt. "Their financial situation is very serious," said Hans Plickert, an analyst with E.F. Hutton. "They're highly leveraged and their expenses virtually eat up all their revenues."

Mr. Borman strongly defends his aircraft purchases, particularly the Boeing 757, which he claimed has been "profitable from the day it hit the property." Debt aside, Mr. Borman maintained: "If you don't have the latest equipment in a free market, it doesn't matter how friendly your people are. They're not working at People Express wages." Analysts say it is difficult to fault Eastern for miscalculating the direction of oil prices and that a modern fleet is an admirable goal. Despite this, they still question whether Eastern mortgaged its future with these planes.

"Whether the airplane acquisitions were a good or a bad move is not the question. Eastern simply couldn't afford it," said one banker close to the company. . . .

The well-publicized labour negotiations that spanned the last several weeks were among Eastern's darkest hours — a crisis that some say Mr. Borman precipitated, one that Mr. Borman blames on the unions. What is particularly distressing is that it came after a year of tenuous labour *rapprochement*, resulting from the revolutionary 1984 wage agreement in which the employees gave up a scheduled 18 percent increase and accepted a one-year wage freeze in return for 25 percent of Eastern's stock and four seats on its board. This trade-off reflected a belief by the workers that concessions on their part would be required to keep Eastern viable and their jobs secure. Still, the unions were awaiting the lifting of the wage freeze scheduled for December 31, 1984.

At the same time, Eastern had to submit to its lenders, by December 31, 1984, a new business plan — which included a final determination of Eastern's 1985 wage costs. Eastern is chronically in violation of covenants to its loan agreements that require it to maintain a certain degree of financial health. But each year Eastern's bankers grant the airline a waiver that, in effect, makes these violations meaningless. Whether this waiver would be extended for yet another year depended on Eastern's ability to produce a 1985 wage contract.

Negotiations between Eastern and its unions were going nowhere as the due date approached and on December 31, Mr. Borman threw down the gauntlet. He announced that the wage freeze would be continued and that the 18 percent increase would not be instituted. It was an action that infuriated the unions, put the two sides in court, and stopped the negotiations cold.

Eastern claims it had no choice — it couldn't afford the $22 million-a-month to cover the higher wages and the unions were being obstinate besides. The unions say that Mr. Borman was not only obligated to provide the 18 percent, but it would also have been a good-faith gesture to rebuild trust between the two sides and smooth negotiations.

Eastern Air Lines
(All dollar amounts in thousands, except per-share data)

Three months ended Dec. 31	**1984**	**1983**
Revenues	$1,117,558	$984,707
Net income	10,700	(54,800)
Earnings per share	$0.09	—

Year ended Dec. 31	**1984**	**1983**
Revenues	$4,363,898	$3,942,134
Net income	(37,900)	183,700)
Earnings per share	–	–

Total assets (Sept. 30, 1984)	$3,653,620
Current assets	868,410
Current liabilities	984,436
Long-term debt	1,487,488
Stock price, Feb. 15, 1985, N.Y.S.E. consolidated close	5¾
Stock price (52-week range)	6¾–3½
Employees (Dec. 31, 1984)	40.806
Headquarters	Miami
(loss)	

Eastern's Tailspin

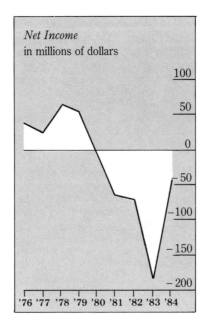

Net Income
in millions of dollars

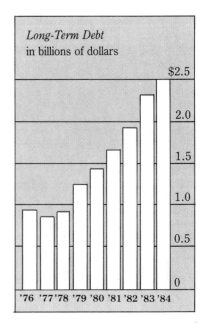

Long-Term Debt
in billions of dollars

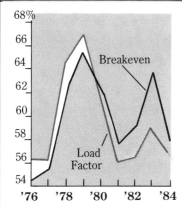

It Is Flying Closer To the Breakeven Point . . .
Eastern's passenger load factor vs. its breakeven load factor; both in percent

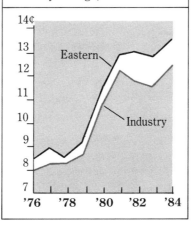

Its Yield Is Better Than the Industry's . . .
Eastern's revenue yield per revenue passenger mile vs. the industry average; in cents

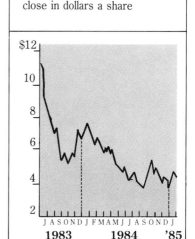

But Its Stock Price Is Very Depressed
Eastern's weekly N.Y.S.E. close in dollars a share

But the real danger was more than a simple labour tiff. The lenders had agreed to extend their December 31 deadline for an agreement — the day when the waiver would expire — by one month. But, January 31 came and went and there was still no wage contract. This put Eastern into technical default on its bank loans — meaning that it was still making its interest payments, but, with its waiver dead, it now was obligated to prove a level of financial health that it clearly could not show. As a result, the lenders could force acceleration of payment on Eastern's debt, a move that would bankrupt the company.

While it was doubtful the banks would do that, the specter of bankruptcy was beginning to send ripples of fear through ticket agents and passengers. Bookings began to dip — and a dip in revenues could have sunk the company as surely as the bankers. Some $300 million in outstanding tickets were held by Eastern passengers. Had they cashed them in — a form of a run on Eastern's bank — the $360 million in cash and short-term securities that Eastern carries on its balance sheet could have quickly been wiped out. And, while most lenders were refraining from calling their loans due, had one bolted, it is likely others would have followed and the rush would have been on.

Mr. Borman is repeatedly described as being autocratic, of running his operation like a military bureaucracy and of being irritatingly direct. Many say he has lost credibility with his workers through a series of well-publicized flip-flops. In the midst of tough labour talks in 1983, Mr. Borman threatened bankruptcy and said he would take a strike, only to back down on both counts. . . .

As part of the 1984 wage freeze, the employees began to participate in — and help direct — a massive productivity program. The savings from the wage freeze, plus an estimated $50 million in productivity savings helped account for a remarkable turnaround in Eastern's 1984 financial performance. Operating earnings, which had been about $100 mil-

lion in the red, swung by some $300 million in one year's time to reach a $189.6 million operating profit for the year.

Eastern closed the year with two consecutive quarters of net profit, although for the whole year it lost $37.9 million on revenues of $4.3 billion. This compares with a $183 million loss in 1983 on revenues of $3.9 billion. For 1985, the company is boldly predicting it will produce a profit — some $90 million. Yet past predictions of profitability have failed to come true.

But even more than the numbers, 1984 marked a tentative beginning of better labour relations. Machinists began to do more work in-house that Eastern formerly sent out — and paid a higher bill. Employees were cited for the smooth workings and quick turnaround time at Eastern's new facility in Kansas City. Flight attendants and pilots were flying additional hours and employees in some cities would drop off lost luggage on their way home for a small fee, less than the cost of taxis that Eastern have formerly used.

Source Leslie Wayne, ''Frank Borman's Most Difficult Days'', *The New York Times*, February 17, 1985, Section 3, p. 1. (Includes graphs.)

For Discussion

1. As a user of financial information how do you assess the health of Eastern Airlines? Do you share Frank Borman's enthusiasm for the future of the company he heads?
2. In the graphs comparing Eastern Airlines to the rest of the industry, Eastern appears to be doing as well as many of its competitors. As an investor, what conclusions would you make about the data that were presented?
3. As an potential investor in Eastern Airlines, where would you look to obtain financial information to add to what has been presented?

Comprehension Problems

Comprehension Problem 3-1

The following are account balances of Sirois Limited.

Account Title	Amount in Trial Balance	Balance After Adjustment
Interest Receivable	$ -0-	$110
Prepaid Insurance	1,800	600
Interest Payable	-0-	90
Salaries Payable	-0-	450
Unearned Rent	700	200

Required:
1. Enter the unadjusted balance for each account in the following T-accounts: Interest Receivable, Prepaid Insurance, Insurance Expense, Interest Payable, Interest Expense, Salaries Payable, Salaries Expense, Unearned Rent, and Rent Earned.
2. Enter the adusted balance in the appropriate T-account.
3. Reconstruct the adjusting entry that must have been recorded for each account and prepare these adjusting entries.

Note: For general journal entries throughout solutions for this chapter, do not include explanation lines.

Comprehension Problem 3-2

The following ledger accounts are taken from the books of the Lupton Corporation at the end of its fiscal year, December 31, 19X6:

Cash			Depreciation Expense			Common Stock	
750	50		2				400
950	150						
90	50		**Insurance Expense**			**Retained Earnings**	
	24		2				350
	20						
	70		**Repair Supplies**			**Office Supplies Used**	
			145	80		25	

Accounts Receivable			Furniture			Rent Expense	
228	90		150			50	

Prepaid Insurance			Accumulated Depreciation			Repair Supplies Used	
24	2			2		80	

Office Supplies			Accounts Payable			Telephone Expense	
50	25		70	145		20	

Repair Revenue	
	950
	228

Required:
1. Indicate the amounts that represent adjustments made at December 31.
2. Prepare the adjusting entries made at December 31.

Comprehension Problem 3-3

The trial balance of Whyte Corporation, before and after the posting of adjusting entries, follows.

	Trial Balance		Adjustments		Adjusted Trial Balance	
	Dr.	*Cr.*	*Dr.*	*Cr.*	*Dr.*	*Cr.*
Cash	$ 4,000				$ 4,000	
Accounts Receivable	5,000				5,000	
Prepaid Insurance	3,600				3,300	
Prepaid Rent	1,000				500	
Truck	6,000				6,000	
Accumulated Depreciation						$ 1,500
Accounts Payable		$ 7,000				7,400
Salaries Payable						1,000
Unearned Rent		1,200				600
Common Stock		2,700				2,700
Revenue		25,000				25,000
Rent Earned						600
Advertising Expense	700				700	
Commissions Expense	2,000				2,000	
Depreciation Expense					1,500	
Interest Expense	100				500	
Insurance Expense					300	
Rent Expense	5,500				6,000	
Salaries Expense	8,000				9,000	
Totals	$35,900	$35,900			$38,800	$38,800

Required:
1. Indicate the debit or credit difference between the trial balance and the adjusted trial balance.
2. Prepare the adjusting entries that had been recorded in a general journal.

Problems

Problem 3-1

Lalonde Contractors Corp. was incorporated on December 1, 19X1 and had the following transactions during December.

Part A

Dec. 1   Issued common shares for $5,000 cash
Dec. 1   Paid $1,200 for three months rent: December, January, and February
Dec. 1   Purchased a used truck for $10,000 on account
Dec. 1   Purchased on account $1,000-worth of supplies, which are expected to be used during the month (recorded as expense)
Dec. 3   Paid $1,800 for a one-year truck insurance policy, effective December 1
Dec. 5   Billed customers $4,500 for work completed to date
Dec. 6   Collected $800 for work completed today
Dec. 14   Paid the following expenses: advertising, $350; interest, $100; telephone, $75; truck, $425; wages, $2,500
Dec. 14   Collected $2,000 of the amount billed December 5
Dec. 20   Billed customers $6,500 for work completed to date
Dec. 23   Signed a $9,000 contract for work to be performed in January
Dec. 28   Paid the following expenses: advertising, $200; interest, $150; truck, $375; wages, $2,500
Dec. 29   Collected a $2,000 advance on work to be done in January (The policy of the corporation is to record such advances as revenue at the time they are received.)
Dec. 31   Received a $100 bill for electricity used during the month (recorded as utilities expense).

Required:
1. Open ledger accounts for the following: Cash, Accounts Receivable, Prepaid Insurance, Prepaid Rent, Truck, Accounts Payable, Common Stock, Revenue, Advertising Expense, Interest Expense, Supplies Used, Telephone Expense, Truck Expense, Utilities Expense, Wages Expense.
2. Prepare journal entries to record the December transactions. Post the entries to the ledger accounts.

Part B

At December 31, the following information is made available for the preparation of any required adjusting entries.
a. One month of the Prepaid Insurance has expired.
b. The December portion of the December 1 rent payment has expired.
c. A physical count indicates that $350-worth of supplies are still on hand.
d. The amount collected on December 29 is unearned at December 31.
e. Three days of wages for December 29, 30, and 31 are unpaid; the unpaid amount of $1,500 will be included in the first Friday wages payment in January.
f. The truck has an estimated useful life of 4 years with an estimated salvage value of $880.

Required:
3. Open additional ledger accounts for the following: Supplies, Accumulated Depreciation, Wages Payable, Unearned Revenue, Depreciation Expense, Insurance Expense, Rent Expense.
4. Prepare all necessary adjusting entries. Post the entries to the ledger accounts.
5. Prepare a trial balance at December 31.

Problem 3-2

Part A

The following transactions are from the records of Gilbert Services Corp. during the month of January 19X1. The company started operations with $15,000 cash and $15,000-worth of common shares.

a. Purchased a truck for $15,000 cash
b. Collected three months advertising revenue amounting to $12,000 (recorded as revenue)
c. Paid $600 for a one-year insurance policy, effective January 1
d. Received two months of interest amounting to $150 (recorded as a revenue)
e. Purchased $500-worth of supplies on account (recorded as an expense)
f. Received three months of commissions amounting to $900 (recorded as revenue)
g. Invested $5,000 temporarily idle cash in a term deposit (debited Temporary Investments)
h. Paid $5,000 for equipment
i. Received $900 for a three-month sublet of some office space
j. Paid $3,000-worth of wages during the month.

Required:
1. Open ledger accounts for the following: Cash, Temporary Investments, Prepaid Insurance, Equipment, Truck, Accounts Payable, Unearned Advertising, Commissions Earned, Rent Earned, Supplies Used, Wages Expense, Common Stock, Revenue and Interest Earned.
2. Prepare journal entries to record the January transactions. Post the entries to the ledger accounts.

Part B

At the end of the month, the following information is made available for the preparation of any required adjusting entries.

k. The truck purchased in transaction a on January 1 has a useful life of five years and an estimated salvage value of $1,500.
l. One-third of the advertising has been earned.
m. The January portion of the insurance policy has expired.
n. Half of the two months of interest has been earned.
o. A physical count indicates $200-worth of supplies are still on hand.
p. The January component of the commissions has been earned.
q. An amount of $50 interest is accrued on the term deposit; this amount will be included with the interest payment to be received at the end of February.
r. The equipment, purchased in transaction h on January 1, is expected to have a useful life of four years and an estimated salvage value of $200.
s. One-third of the three-month sublet has been earned.
t. Three days of wages amounting to $150 remain unpaid; the amount will be included in the first Friday payment in February.

Required:
3. Open additional ledger accounts for the following: Supplies, Accumulated Depreciation — Equipment, Accumulated Depreciation — Truck, Wages Payable, Depreciation Expense — Equipment, Depreciation Expense—Truck, Insurance Expense, Interest Receivable, Unearned Interest, Unearned Rent, Unearned Commissions, Unearned Revenue, Supplies and Unearned Commissions.
4. Prepare all necessary adjusting entries. Post the entries to the ledger accounts.
5. Prepare a trial balance at January 31.

Problem 3-3

The following unrelated accounts are extracted from the records of Cowansville Corp. at December 31, its fiscal year-end.

	Balance	
	Unadjusted	Adjusted
a. Prepaid Rent	$ 300	$ 600
b. Wages Payable	500	700
c. Income Tax Payable	-0-	1,000
d. Unearned Commissions	2,000	3,000
e. Unearned Revenue	25,000	20,000
f. Advertising Expense	5,000	3,500
g. Depreciation Expense — Equipment	-0-	500
h. Supplies Used	850	625
i. Truck Expense	4,000	4,500

Required: For each of the above unrelated accounts, prepare the adjusting entry that was probably made.

Problem 3-4

The trial balance of Hitchcock Films Corp. includes the following account balances at December 31, 19X1, its fiscal year-end. No adjustments have yet been recorded.

	Debit	Credit
Prepaid Rent	$ 1,500	
Equipment	2,500	
Unearned Advertising		1,000
Insurance Expense	900	
Supplies Used	600	
Telephone Expense	825	
Wages Expense	15,000	

The following information is available:
a. A physical count of supplies indicates that $300-worth of supplies have not yet been used at December 31.
b. A $75 telephone bill has not yet been received or recorded.
c. One day of wages amounting to $125 remains unpaid and unrecorded at December 31; the amount will be included with the first Friday payment in January.
d. The equipment was purchased December 1; it is expected to last 2 years and its estimated salvage value is $100. No depreciation has yet been recorded.
e. The prepaid rent is for December 19X1 and for January and February 19X2.
f. Half of the advertising has been earned at December 31.
g. The $900 amount in Insurance Expense is for a one-year policy, effective July 1, 19X1.

Required: Prepare all necessary adjusting entries.

Problem 3-5

The trial balance of Stratus Services Inc. includes the following account balances at December 31, its fiscal year-end. No adjustments have yet been recorded.

Temporary Investments	$10,000
Prepaid Insurance	600
Supplies	500
Bank Loan	5,000
Subscription Revenue	9,000
Salaries Payable	500
Rent Expense	3,900
Truck Expense	4,000

The following information is available:

a. The Temporary Investment balance represents an investment of temporarily idle cash in interest-bearing investments; an amount of accrued interest amounting to $250 has not yet been recorded.
b. The $600 prepaid insurance is for a one-year policy, effective September 1.
c. A physical count indicates that $300-worth of supplies are still on hand.
d. Interest on the bank loan is paid on the fifteenth day of each month; the unrecorded interest for the last 15 days of December amounts to $25.
e. The Subscription Revenue is for six-month subscriptions to the corporation's *Investment Trends* report; the subscriptions began December 1.
f. Three days of salary amounting to $300 remain unrecorded at December 31.
g. The monthly rent amounts to $300.
h. A bill for December truck expenses has not yet been received; an amount of $400 is estimated as owing.

Required: Prepare all necessary adjusting entries.

Problem 3-6

The following accounts are taken from the record of Harrison Forbes Inc. at the end of its first twelve months of operations, December 31, 19X1.

In addition to the balances in each set of accounts, additional data are provided for adjustment purposes if applicable. Treat each set of accounts independently of the others.

a.

Truck		Depreciation Expense — Truck		Accumulated Depreciation — Truck	
7,000		600			600

Additional information: The truck was purchased July 1 and has a useful life of 4 years and an estimated salvage value of $1,000.

b.

Unearned Rent		Rent Earned	
	-0-		6,000

Additional information: The monthly rental revenue is $500. A part of Harrison's office was sublet during the entire 12 months at $500 per month.

c.

Supplies		Supplies Used	
		1,250	

Additional information: A physical inventory indicated $300-worth of supplies to be still on hand.

d.

Prepaid Rent	Rent Expense
1,200	4,400

Additional information: The monthly rent is $400.

e.

Wages Expense	Wages Payable
6,000	500

Additional information: In addition to these balances, unrecorded wages at December 31 amount to $250.

f.

Bank Loan	Interest Expense	Interest Payable
8,000	600	100

Additional information: The bank loan bears interest at 10 percent. The money was borrowed on January 1, 19X1.

g.

Utilities Expense	Utilities Payable
1,200	200

Additional information: The December bill has not yet been received or any accrual made; the amount owing at December 31 is estimated at $150.

h.

Prepaid Insurance	Insurance Expense
600	600

Additional information: A $1,200 one-year insurance policy had been purchased effective April 1, 19X1; there is no other insurance policy in effect.

i.

Unearned Rent	Rent Earned
900	300

Additional information: The Unearned Rent balance is applicable to the months of November and December 19X1 and for January 19X2.

j.

Unearned Revenue	Revenue
-0-	25,200

Additional information: An amount of $2,000 has not been earned at December 31.

Required: Prepare all necessary adjusting entries.

Alternate Problems

Alternate Problem 3-1

Multi-Publishers Corp. was incorporated at June 1, 19X1 and had the following transactions during its first month of operation.

Part A

Jun. 1   Issued common shares for $10,000 cash
Jun. 1   Purchased equipment for $6,500 on account
Jun. 2   Purchased on account $750-worth of supplies, which are expected to last three months (recorded as an asset)
Jun. 3   Paid two months of newspaper advertising for $500
Jun. 5   Collected $12,000 of three-month subscriptions to its *PC REVIEW* magazine, effective June 1
Jun. 14 Paid the following expenses: telephone, $350; rent for June, $500; salaries, $3,000
Jun. 16 Collected $5,000 from advertisers for the June edition of *PC REVIEW* magazine
Jun. 18 Paid half of the equipment purchased June 1
Jun. 20 Paid $2,000 for supplies used
Jun. 28 Paid the following expenses: telephone, $250; salaries, $3,000
Jun. 30 Received a $200 bill for electricity used during the month (recorded as a utilities expense).

Required:
1. Open ledger accounts for the following: Cash, Prepaid Advertising, Supplies, Equipment, Accounts Payable, Unearned Subscriptions, Common Stock, Advertising Revenue, Advertising Expense, Rent Expense, Revenue, Salaries Expense, Telephone Expense, Utilities Expense, Supplies Used.
2. Prepare journal entries to record the June transactions. Post the entries to the ledger accounts.

Part B

At June 30, the following information is made available for the preparation of any required adjusting entries.
a. The June portion of advertising paid on June 3 has expired.
b. One month of the subscriptions collected June 5 has been earned.
c. A physical count indicates that $100-worth of supplies are still on hand.
d. A 5 percent commission is owed on the June portion of the subscriptions collected June 5.
e. Two days of salary for June 29 and 30 are unpaid; the unpaid amount will be included in the first Friday salary payment in July. The salary for each day during the week amounts to $300.
f. The equipment purchased on June 1 has an estimated useful life of 5 years and is estimated to have a salvage value of $500.

Required:
3. Open additional ledger accounts for the following: Accumulated Depreciation, Salaries Payable, Unearned Subscriptions, Advertising Expense, Commissions Expense, Depreciation Expense, Subscription Revenue, Supplies Used.
4. Prepare all necessary adjusting entries. Post the entries to the ledger accounts.
5. Prepare a trial balance at June 30.

Alternate Problem 3-2

Breen Productions Inc. began operations January 1, 19X1 with $50,000 cash and $50,000-worth of common shares.

Part A

The following are from the transactions of Breen Productions Inc. during January 19X1.
a. Paid salaries of $15,000 during the month
b. Purchased on account $750-worth of supplies (recorded as an asset)
c. Paid $8,000 for equipment
d. Invested $10,000 temporarily idle cash in a term deposit (debited Temporary Investments)
e. Paid $1,200 for a one-year insurance policy, effective January 1 (recorded as an asset)
f. Collected $6,000-worth of one-year subscriptions, beginning January 1 (recorded as unearned revenue)
g. Paid $1,500 for three months of rent (recorded as an asset)
h. Collected $600 for a two-month sublet of part of the company's warehouse, effective January 1 (recorded as unearned revenue)
i. Paid $7,000 for a used truck.

Required:
  1. Open ledger accounts for the following: Cash, Temporary Investments, Prepaid Insurance, Prepaid Rent, Supplies, Equipment, Truck, Accounts Payable, Unearned Rent, Unearned Subscriptions, Salaries Expense, Common Stock.
  2. Prepare journal entries to record the January transactions. Post the entries to the ledger accounts.

Part B

At the end of the month, the following information is made available for the preparation of any required adjusting entries.
j. Two days of salary amounting to $1,000 remain unpaid; the amount will be included in the first Friday salary payment in February.
k. A physical count of supplies indicates that $250-worth are still on hand.
l. The equipment, purchased in transaction c on January 1, has useful life of 3 years and an estimated salvage value of $800.
m. An amount of $100 interest is accrued on the term deposit; this amount will be included with the interest payment of February 28.
n. One month of the insurance policy has expired.
o. The January portion of the subscriptions has been earned.
p. The January portion of the rent payment has expired.
q. Half of the sublet has been earned.
r. The truck, purchased in transaction i on January 1, has a useful life of 4 years and an estimated salvage value of $1,000.

Required:
  3. Open additional ledger accounts for the following: Interest Receivable, Salaries Payable, Accumulated Depreciation — Equipment, Accumulated Depreciation — Truck, Interest Earned, Rent Earned, Subscription Revenue, Depreciation Expense — Equipment, Depreciation Expense — Truck, Insurance Expense, Rent Expense, Supplies Used.
  4. Prepare all necessary adjusting entries. Post the entries to the ledger accounts.
  5. Prepare a trial balance at January 31.

Alternate Problem 3-3

The following unrelated accounts are from the records of Bedford Inc. at December 31, its fiscal year-end.

	Balance	
	Unadjusted	Adjusted
a. Prepaid Insurance	$ 500	$ 300
b. Supplies	850	400
c. Accumulated Depreciation — Truck	-0-	1,200
d. Salaries Payable	2,500	2,600
e. Unearned Fees	5,000	1,000
f. Income Tax Payable	-0-	3,500
g. Revenue	50,000	45,000
h. Commissions Expense	4,000	5,500
i. Interest Expense	800	850

Required: For each of these unrelated accounts, prepare the adjusting entry that was probably recorded.

Alternate Problem 3-4

The trial balance of Eastwood Productions Corp. includes the following account balances at December 31, 19X1, its fiscal year-end. No adjustments have been recorded.

	Debit	*Credit*
Prepaid Insurance	$ 1,800	
Truck	19,000	
Unearned Commissions		$ 9,000
Rent Earned		-0-
Advertising Expense	5,000	
Salaries Expense	25,000	
Supplies Used	900	

The following information is available:
a. A physical count indicates that $200-worth of supplies have not yet been used at December 31.
b. The prepaid insurance consists of a one-year policy, effective October 1.
c. The truck was purchased on July 1; it is expected to have a useful life of 6 years and its estimated salvage value is $1,000. No depreciation has been recorded during the year.
d. The unearned commissions at December 31 actually amount to $7,500.
e. Two days of salary amounting to $200 remain unpaid at December 31; the amounts will be included with the first Friday's payment in January.
f. A rent payment has not yet been received for a sublet of part of a warehouse for two weeks during December. Payment of the $300 has been promised for the first week in January.
g. A $300 bill for December advertising has not yet been received or recorded.

Required: Prepare all necessary adjusting entries.

Alternate Problem 3-5

The trial balance of Bishop Court Corp. includes the following account balances at December 31, 19X1, its fiscal year-end. No adjustments have yet been recorded.

Temporary Investments	$15,000
Prepaid Rent	1,200
Bank Loan	7,500
Unearned Subscriptions	9,000
Insurance Expense	2,400
Salaries Expense	75,000
Supplies Used	600
Utilities Expense	-0-
Supplies	-0-

The following information is available:
a. Accrued interest on the temporary investment amounts to $40 at December 31.
b. The prepaid rent is for the months of November and December 19X1, and January 19X2.
c. Accrued interest on the bank loan amounts to $40 at December 31.
d. One-third of the subscriptions remain unearned at December 31.
e. Insurance expense includes the cost of a one-year insurance policy, effective January 1, 19X1 and the cost of a one-year renewal, effective January 1, 19X2. The premium cost for each year is $1,200.
f. Two days of salary have not yet been accrued at December 31; the usual salary for a five-day week is $2,500.
g. A physical count indicates that $100-worth of supplies are still on hand at December 31.
h. A $200 bill for electricity has not yet been received or recorded for December.

Required: Prepare all necessary adjusting entries.

Alternate Problem 3-6

The following accounts are taken from the records of Erma Brooks Ltd. at the end of its first twelve months of operations, December 31, 19X1. In addition to the balances in each set of accounts, additional data are provided for adjustment purposes, if applicable. Treat each set of accounts independently.

a.

Prepaid Rent		Rent Expense	
-0-		5,200	

Additional information: The monthly rent is $400.

b.

Bank Loan		Interest Expense		Interest Payable	
	10,000	850			-0-

Additional information: Unpaid interest on the bank loan amounts to $150.

c.

Supplies		Supplies Used	
-0-		800	

Additional information: Supplies still on hand amount to $300.

d.

Salaries Expense		Salaries Payable	
5,000			-0-

Additional information: Salaries owing at December 31 amount to $1,000.

e.

Prepaid Advertising		Advertising Expense	
800		3,000	

Additional information: Prepaid Advertising at December 31 amounts to $1,200.

f.

Equipment		Depreciation Expense — Equipment		Accumulated Depreciation — Equipment	
7,000		500			500

Additional information: The equipment was purchased on July 1 and has a useful life of 5 years with an estimated salvage value of $1,000.

g.

Unearned Rent		Rent Earned	
	-0-		10,000

Additional information: Unearned Revenue at December 31 amounts to $2,500.

h.

Prepaid Insurance		Insurance Expense	
100		500	

Additional information: The monthly insurance amounts to $50; $600 was paid for a one-year policy effective January 1, 19X1.

i.

Utilities Expense		Utilities Payable	
875			-0-

Additional information: The December bill has not yet been received; the amount owing has been estimated at $225.

Required: Prepare all necessary adjusting entries.

Decision Problem

Decision Problem 3-1

Joe Campbell, a friend of your father's is considering investing in one of two construction corporations. Both began operations on January 1, 1985 and have been in operation for two years. Campbell shows you the following information on each corporation and asks you for your opinion on the financial health of each.

Glionna Construction Corporation

Sales payment received 1985	$1,622,500
Expenses 1985	2,427,400
Accounts Receivable (Dec. 31, 1985)	1,947,600
Sales Payment Received 1986	947,400
Expenses 1986	1,747,400
Accounts Receivable (Dec. 31 1986)	3,427,400

Montreal Builders Ltd.

Sales payment Received 1985	$1,240,000
Expenses 1985	977,200
Accounts Receivable (Dec. 31, 1985)	142,500
Sales Payment Received 1986	1,625,500
Expenses 1986	1,222,000
Accounts Receivable (Dec. 31, 1986)	247,000

Campbell also tells you that all of Glionna Construction's accounts receivable are for the construction of a new post office building in Pictou on June 1. If Glionna does not complete the building on time, there will be a 5-percent penalty levied on the amount that remains to be paid. All construction is ahead of schedule, though, and no problems are anticipated.

Montreal Builders Ltd., Campbell tells you, builds for the residential market and does renovations to existing houses. Currently, it has six projects in progress. As he is leaving, Campbell gives you two final pieces of information; Glionna expects expenses for the first six months of 1987 to be $750,000 and is bidding on another post office construction project it is likely to get. Campbell says that the manager of Montreal Builders is complaining about some of its customers being late in paying their bills.

Required:
1. From the information provided, what can you tell Joe Campbell?
2. What can you deduce about the credit practices of each company?
3. Should Campbell be worried about the large amount of accounts receivable for Glionna Construction Ltd.?
4. Discuss the matching principle as it relates to these two entities.
5. What other information should Campbell consider before investing?

GAAP and the Operating Cycle: Part Two

The accountant follows a sequence of steps in transforming transaction dollar amounts into financial statement information.

1. What are the steps that occur continuously during the accounting time period?
2. What steps occur whenever interim or year-end financial statements are prepared?
3. Which steps occur only at the fiscal year-end?
4. How does a worksheet assist in the preparation of financial statements?
5. Why are closing entries prepared, and what exactly is the closing procedure?
6. What is the purpose of a post-closing trial balance?
7. What are reversing entries, and why are they prepared?
8. How does preparation of reversing entries minimize the possibility of errors?
9. What is a simple rule useful in the preparation of reversing entries for accruals?
10. How does the preparation of reversing entries transfer amounts to their proper location?

A. The Worksheet

Worksheet
A multi-column schedule used to organize the many details that are brought together when financial statements are being prepared; facilitates the preparation of financial statements.

Accountants usually use a columnar schedule to aid in preparing financial statements. This columnar schedule is called a **worksheet**. In Chapter 3, a trial balance for Bluebeard Computer Corporation was prepared as a separate schedule, following the recording and posting of the corporation's December transactions. As an alternate practice, the trial balance could be recorded directly on the worksheet. The arrangement of a typical worksheet consists of a series of debit and credit columns, as shown in Figure 4-1.

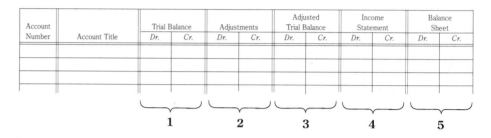

Figure 4-1   The worksheet

The columns on the worksheet are explained below.

> 1. The debit and credit account balances are entered in these columns directly from the general ledger.
> 2. The adjusting entries for the period are recorded on the worksheet in the second pair of debit and credit columns.
> 3. The amounts in the preliminary trial balance and adjustment columns are combined, and the new balances are recorded in this third pair of debit and credit columns; these totals are referred to as an adjusted trial balance.
> 4. The revenue and expense account balances listed in the adjusted trial balance columns are transferred to the income statement debit and credit columns. The income statement will later be prepared from the amounts listed in these columns.
> 5. The asset, liability, and equity account balances listed in the adjusted trial balance columns are transferred to the balance sheet debit and credit columns. The statement of retained earnings and the balance sheet will later be prepared from the amounts listed in these columns.

The worksheet is not a formal accounting record, as are the journal and ledger. Rather, it is an intermediate step that bridges the gap between the accounting records and the financial statements. (See Figure 4-2.)

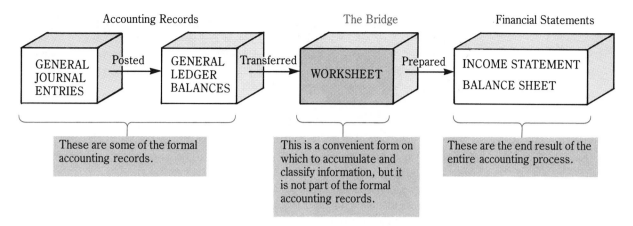

Figure 4-2 The function of the worksheet

The worksheet organizes the many details that are brought together when statements are being prepared. It also provides an opportunity to check financial data, since its debit and credit column totals prove the equality of the account balances. An error is indicated whenever total debits do not equal total credits in any pair of columns. The worksheet is also a convenient place to calculate the net income or net loss for the period. The worksheet gives the accountant a preview of the final financial statements before these statements are prepared.

A worksheet is unnecessary in actual practice if there are only a few accounts in the trial balance and if only a few adjusting entries are required. The worksheet is very useful, however, when numerous accounts and adjustments must be organized before financial statements are prepared. In the case of the Bluebeard Computer Corporation, the December 31 worksheet might not be used by an experienced accountant, although its use may be convenient.

In the next few pages, a worksheet for BCC at December 31 is prepared to demonstrate the methodology. The use of the worksheet in the preparation of the corporation's year-end financial statements is also examined.

Recording a Trial Balance in the Worksheet

When all December transactions are journalized and posted, a trial balance is prepared on the worksheet to prove the equality of debit and credit balances in the ledger. The trial balance is recorded directly on the worksheet, to reduce the duplication that would otherwise result from preparing the trial balance elsewhere and then transferring the identical information to the worksheet. Figure 4-3 illustrates the four steps required in worksheet preparation, which are discussed next.

Step 1: The Trial Balance Is Recorded Directly in the Worksheet

Accountants often refer to this trial balance as the *unadjusted trial balance*, because the adjusting entries required to match revenues with expenses are not yet included in the account balances. The preparation of financial statements from an unadjusted trial balance would cause misleading information to be communicated.

Following the recording of the unadjusted trial balance in the worksheet, the adjusting entries are entered in the second pair of columns (as in Figure 4-3).

Step 2: The Adjustments Are Recorded in the Appropriate Columns of the Worksheet

The adjustments recorded on the worksheet are identified by the following key letters:

(a) The December expense portion of prepaid insurance
(b) The December revenue portion of unearned rent
(c) Depreciation of the equipment during December
(d) Depreciation of the truck during December
(e) The amount of unearned revenue in December
(f)   Repair supplies not used in December
(g) Interest earned on note during December
(h) Salaries accrued at December 31
(i)   Interest expense on bank loans
(j)   Estimated income taxes at December 31.

These are the adjustments that were prepared in Chapter 3.

Step 3: The Trial Balance Columns Amounts Are Combined with the Adjustments Columns Amounts

The accountant uses the worksheet to organize the many details that have to be brought together from the ledger and the schedule of adjustments before the financial statements can be prepared. Following the recording of adjusting entries on the worksheet, an adjusted trial balance is calculated in the third pair of columns.

Step 4: The Amounts in the Adjustments Columns Are Transferred to the Income Statement and Balance Sheet Columns

The adjusted trial balance columns amounts are transferred either to the income statement columns or to the balance sheet columns in this way:

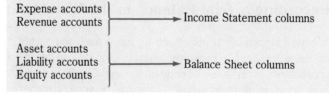

Expense accounts
Revenue accounts ────────► Income Statement columns

Asset accounts
Liability accounts ────────► Balance Sheet columns
Equity accounts

WORKSHEET
For the Period Ended December 31, 19X1

Account Number	Account Title	Trial Balance Dr.	Trial Balance Cr.	Adjustments Dr.	Adjustments Cr.	Adjusted Trial Balance Dr.	Adjusted Trial Balance Cr.	Income Statement Dr.	Income Statement Cr.	Balance Sheet Dr.	Balance Sheet Cr.
101	Cash	11,695				11,695				11,695	
110	Accounts Receivable	3,500				3,500				3,500	
120	Notes Receivable	5,000				5,000				5,000	
161	Prepaid Insurance	1,200			(a) 100	1,100				1,100	
183	Equipment	2,000				2,000				2,000	
184	Truck	8,000				8,000				8,000	
201	Bank Loan		5,000				5,000				5,000
210	Accounts Payable		1,900				1,900				1,900
248	Unearned Rent		600	(b) 200			400				400
320	Common Stock		10,000				10,000				10,000
340	Retained Earnings		0								
450	Repair Revenue		23,895	(e) 2,000			21,895		21,895		
654	Rent Expense	1,200				1,200		1,200			
656	Salaries Expense	5,000		(h) 150		5,150		5,150			
668	Supplies Used	2,100			(f) 495	1,605		1,605			
670	Truck Expense	1,400				1,400		1,400			
676	Utilities Expense	300				300		300			
	Totals	41,395	41,395								
631	Insurance Expense			(a) 100		100		100			
440	Rent Earned				(b) 200		200		200		
623	Deprec. Exp.–Eqpmt.			(c) 30		30		30			
193	Accum. Deprec.–Eqpmt.				(c) 30		30				30
624	Deprec. Exp.–Truck			(d) 240		240		240			
194	Accum. Deprec.–Truck				(d) 240		240				240
247	Unearned Repair Rev.				(e) 2,000		2,000				2,000
173	Supplies			(f) 495		495				495	
116	Interest Receivable			(g) 25		25				25	
430	Interest Earned				(g) 25		25		25		
226	Salaries Payable				(h) 150		150				150
632	Interest Expense			(i) 95		95		95			
222	Interest Payable				(i) 95		95				95
830	Income Tax Expense			(j) 6,000		6,000		6,000			
260	Income Tax Payable				(j) 6,000		6,000				6,000
	Totals			9,335	9,335	47,935	47,935	16,120	22,120	31,815	25,815
	Net Income							6,000			6,000
	Totals							22,120	22,120	31,815	31,815

Total Debit Balances = Total Credit Balances

Figure 4-3   The Worksheet Illustrated

The equality of these columns is proved to help insure that no errors have been made.

Balancing the Worksheet

The income statement and balance sheet debit and credit columns are now totalled. The difference between the totals of the income statement columns is the net income of $6,000 at December 31; a net income exists because the total of the credit column exceeds the total of the debit expenses column. The $6,000 difference is entered in the income statement debit column and in the balance sheet credit column, as shown below.

Entering Net Income on this line brings the columns into balance. This is the self balancing feature of the accounting equation.

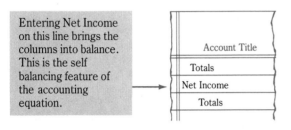

Account Title	Adjusted Trial Balance		Income Statement		Balance Sheet	
	Dr.	Cr.	Dr.	Cr.	Dr.	Cr.
Totals	47,935	47,935	16,120	22,120	31,815	25,815
Net Income			6,000			6,000
Totals						

The next step in the completion of the worksheet is the addition of the income statement and balance sheet columns.

Each column is totalled.

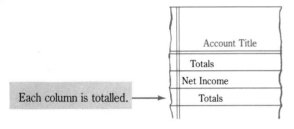

Account Title	Adjusted Trial Balance		Income Statement		Balance Sheet	
	Dr.	Cr.	Dr.	Cr.	Dr.	Cr.
Totals	47,935	47,935	16,120	22,120	31,815	25,815
Net Income			6,000			6,000
Totals			22,120	22,120	31,815	31,815

Note that the totals in the two income statement columns are equal, and that the totals in the two balance sheet columns are also equal. These balances indicate the equality of debits and credits that has been maintained in recording the trial balance and adjustments in the worksheet. The fact that debits equal credits indicates that all calculations in the worksheet are mathematically correct.

If the worksheet reveals that expenses exceed revenues during a period (that is, when there is a net loss), the procedure to be followed is as follows:

Account Title	Adjusted Trial Balance		Income Statement		Balance Sheet	
	Dr.	Cr.	Dr.	Cr.	Dr.	Cr.
Totals	50,000	50,000	8,000	5,000	42,000	45,000
Net Loss				3,000 ◄──► 3,000		
Totals			8,000	8,000	45,000	45,000

In this case, a $3,000 net loss exists, since the total of the income statement debit column exceeds that of the income statement credit column. The $3,000 difference is recorded in the income statement credit column and in the balance sheet debit column.

B. Preparation of Financial Statements from the Worksheet

The data listed in the income statement and balance sheet columns of the worksheet are used to prepare the financial statements of Bluebeard Computer Corporation at the end of December. In the following pages, extracts from the worksheet are used to demonstrate the tie-in between the worksheet and end-of-period financial statement preparation.

Income Statement Preparation

The income statement is prepared from the amounts in the income statement columns of the worksheet. Notice in the illustration (Figure 4-4) that all the amounts contained in the income statement columns are rearranged and repeated in the formal statement.

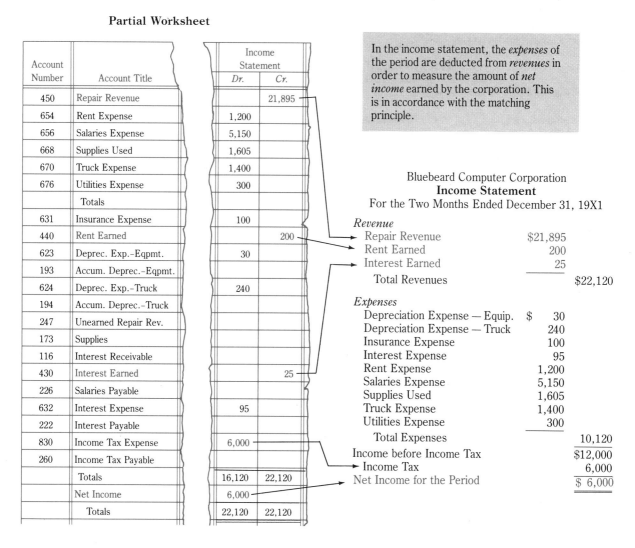

Partial Worksheet

Account Number	Account Title	Income Statement Dr.	Income Statement Cr.
450	Repair Revenue		21,895
654	Rent Expense	1,200	
656	Salaries Expense	5,150	
668	Supplies Used	1,605	
670	Truck Expense	1,400	
676	Utilities Expense	300	
	Totals		
631	Insurance Expense	100	
440	Rent Earned		200
623	Deprec. Exp.-Eqpmt.	30	
193	Accum. Deprec.-Eqpmt.		
624	Deprec. Exp.-Truck	240	
194	Accum. Deprec.-Truck		
247	Unearned Repair Rev.		
173	Supplies		
116	Interest Receivable		
430	Interest Earned		25
226	Salaries Payable		
632	Interest Expense	95	
222	Interest Payable		
830	Income Tax Expense	6,000	
260	Income Tax Payable		
	Totals	16,120	22,120
	Net Income	6,000	
	Totals	22,120	22,120

In the income statement, the *expenses* of the period are deducted from *revenues* in order to measure the amount of *net income* earned by the corporation. This is in accordance with the matching principle.

Bluebeard Computer Corporation
Income Statement
For the Two Months Ended December 31, 19X1

Revenue

Repair Revenue	$21,895	
Rent Earned	200	
Interest Earned	25	
Total Revenues		$22,120

Expenses

Depreciation Expense — Equip.	$ 30	
Depreciation Expense — Truck	240	
Insurance Expense	100	
Interest Expense	95	
Rent Expense	1,200	
Salaries Expense	5,150	
Supplies Used	1,605	
Truck Expense	1,400	
Utilities Expense	300	
Total Expenses		10,120
Income before Income Tax		$12,000
Income Tax		6,000
Net Income for the Period		$ 6,000

Figure 4-4 Income statement preparation

Real Life Example 4-1

How Your Tax Dollars Are Spent

How many Canadians does it take to pay the interest on the national debt?

About 515 400.

The average Canadian worker produces about $32,400-worth of wealth in a year. But the federal government will need about $16.7 billion in the coming year just to pay the interest on its debt. So it takes the full-time work of more than half a million Canadians to pay the interest.

How many Canadians does it take to defend the country? About 334 000.

Of these, 81 000 are in the armed forces. Another 37 000 are civilian workers for the defence department.

And 216 000 are the ordinary Canadians whose full-time work would be needed to produce the $7 billion the government plans to spend for defence.

These are only some of the fascinating figures that can be derived from the spending estimates tabled Tuesday in the Commons by Donald Johnston, president of the Treasury Board.

Johnston outlined plans to spend $76.3 billion in the fiscal year starting April 1. That's $145,000 a minute or $8.7 million an hour, day and night for the 365 days. And the total is growing larger, minute by minute. . . . When Allan MacEachen produced his first fiscal forcast in 1980, federal spending in the coming year was expected to be $142,000 a minute.

Another way of looking at the growth of government spending is to figure out how many Canadians, working full time, it would have taken to pay the interest on the national debt in past years.

In 1979, it would have taken 335 000. In 1980, it would have taken 384 000. And last year, it would have taken 490 000.

If it now takes more than half a million Canadians just to pay the interest on the debt, how many does it take to keep the whole federal government running?

About 2 794 400.

Of that total, 439 000 are working directly for the government, including the 60 000 in the Canada Post Corporation and 81 000 in the armed forces.

The other 2 355 400 are ordinary working Canadians whose combined output would be needed to pay the cost of the government in the coming year.

But even these numbers can produce some sobering statistics. For example, the Canadian economy — even in its weakened state — now produces about $1 billion of output a day. This means that when the fiscal year opens April 1, it would take the entire output of the country — of all Canadians — until June 17 to pay the cost of the federal government, even according to Johnston's underestimates.

And, if we were then able to go on working to pay off the $130-billion national debt, spending nothing on our own living, it would take us until October 25 to do it. The last time Canadians had that kind of government burden was just after the Second World War, which was financed mainly with borrowed money.

Source D. McGillvray, ''Working for the Nation's Interest'', *The* (Montreal) *Gazette*, February 28, 1982, p. D-2.

A sole proprietor pays personal income tax on business income; a partner pays personal income tax on his/her share of a partnership's income. Accordingly, the income statement of a proprietorship or partnership does not include an income tax calculation. A corporation, however, pays income tax as a percentage of income from operations; for illustrative purposes, this rate is assumed to be 50 percent. (In a sense, it can be said that government is a silent partner in every business. How government uses its share of business income, which it collects as income tax, is reviewed in Real Life Example 4-1.) Shareholders do not pay income tax on the corporation's income; rather, they are subject to tax only on the amount of cash dividends received by them.

Statement of Retained Earnings and Balance Sheet Preparation

Retained earnings
Net income that is not paid out as dividends; net income that is reinvested in the entity for expansion and growth of the entity.

Retained earnings represent the net income of a corporation which has been retained in the business; this amounts to $6,000 for Bluebeard Computer Corporation at December 31, 19X1. The statement of retained earnings is the financial statement which, in effect, links the income statement with the balance sheet. Net income (or net loss) reported in the income statement is added (or deducted, if a loss) to any opening Retained Earnings account balance (less any dividends paid, as illustrated in Chapter 5) in calculating the ending Retained Earnings amount reported on the balance sheet. In this way, the statement of retained earnings reconciles the opening Retained Earnings amount with the ending Retained Earnings amount appearing in the balance sheet. There is no opening retained earnings in the case of Bluebeard Computer Corporation, since it only began operations during the year. The $6,000 Retained Earnings balance at December 31, 19X1 becomes the opening Retained Earnings amount on January 1, 19X2.

The statement of retained earnings and the balance sheet are prepared from amounts in the balance sheet columns of the worksheet. Preparation of these financial statements is facilitated by using these worksheet columns, since all necessary financial information is already listed there. (See Figure 4-5.)

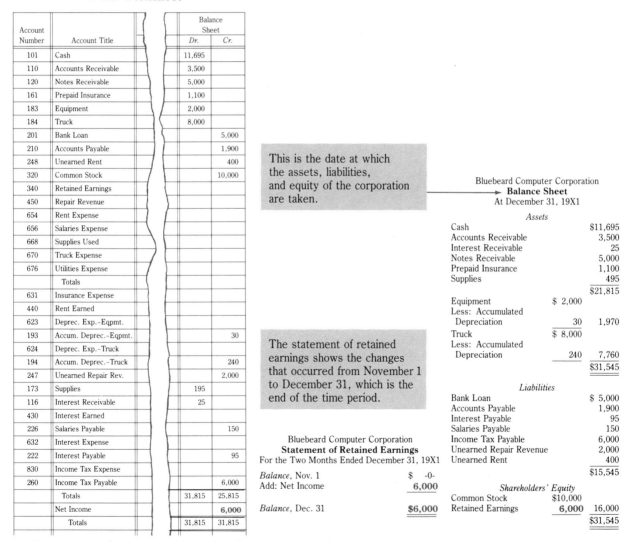

Figure 4-5   Statement of retained earnings and balance sheet preparation

Care must be taken in the preparation of financial statements from a worksheet. The debit/credit relationship shown on the worksheet is not emphasized by these statements, although it is obviously present. In the balance sheet for example, Accumulated Depreciation—Truck, with a credit balance of $240, is deducted from Truck, which has a debit balance. Care must also be taken to use each amount just once and in its proper debit/credit relation.

C. Closing the Books

Closing entries
The entries that reduce revenue and expense balances to zero in preparation for the next fiscal year.

Temporary accounts
Accounts that accumulate data for a fiscal year and are closed at the end of the fiscal year; also called *nominal accounts*. All revenue and expense accounts are temporary accounts.

Permanent accounts
Accounts that have a continuing balance from one fiscal year to another; also called *real accounts*. All balance sheet accounts are permanent accounts.

At the end of a fiscal year, following the recording of all entries that belong to that operating period, the revenue and expense accounts have accumulated all the amounts affecting the business; these *revenue* and *expense accounts* must now be reduced to zero balances, so that they can begin to accumulate the amounts that belong to a new fiscal year. It is customary in business record-keeping that these accounts accumulate amounts for a time period not exceeding one year. Therefore, **closing entries** are made to transfer the balances from these **temporary accounts**. **Permanent accounts** are those that have a continuing balance from one fiscal year to the next. The different types of temporary and permanent accounts are listed below.

At the end of the fiscal year, these accounts must be closed; that is, they must have a zero balance when the new fiscal year begins.

Temporary Accounts	*Permanent Accounts*
Revenue Accounts	Asset Accounts
Expense Accounts	Liability Accounts
	Common Stock Account
	Retained Earnings Account

The Closing Procedure

Income summary
A temporary account used to accumulate all revenue and expense balances at the end of the fiscal year. This account summarizes the net income (or loss) for the period and is closed to the Retained Earnings account.

An intermediate summary account called **Income Summary** is used to close the revenue and expense accounts. The balances in these accounts are transferred to the Income Summary account. Since December 31 is the year-end of Bluebeard Computer Corporation, closing journal entries are prepared at this date. The closing procedure for these accounts is illustrated in Figure 4-6 and explained below.

Entry 1: **Closing the Revenue Accounts**
The revenue accounts are closed in one compound closing journal entry to the Income Summary account. (All revenue accounts with credit balances are debited to bring them to zero. Their balances are transferred to the Income Summary account.)

Entry 2: **Closing the Expense Accounts**
The expense accounts are closed in one compound closing journal entry to the Income Summary account. (All expense accounts with debit balance are credited to bring them to zero. Their balances are transferred to the Income Summary account.)

Entry 3:   Closing the Income Summary Account

The Income Summary account is next closed to the Retained Earnings account.

The caption *Closing Entries* is written in the general journal on the line following the last adjusting entry. Unlike regular transaction entries, which require analysis and judgement, the closing process is purely mechanical and involves only the shifting and summarizing of amounts already recorded in the worksheet.

The balance in the Income Summary account is transferred to Retained Earnings because the net income (or net loss) belongs to the shareholders.

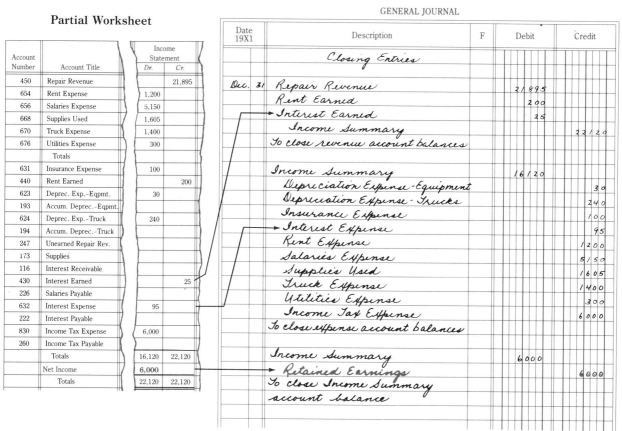

Partial Worksheet

Account Number	Account Title	Income Statement Dr.	Income Statement Cr.
450	Repair Revenue		21,895
654	Rent Expense	1,200	
656	Salaries Expense	5,150	
668	Supplies Used	1,605	
670	Truck Expense	1,400	
676	Utilities Expense	300	
	Totals		
631	Insurance Expense	100	
440	Rent Earned		200
623	Deprec. Exp.–Eqpmt.	30	
193	Accum. Deprec.–Eqpmt.		
624	Deprec. Exp.–Truck	240	
194	Accum. Deprec.–Truck		
247	Unearned Repair Rev.		
173	Supplies		
116	Interest Receivable		
430	Interest Earned		25
226	Salaries Payable		
632	Interest Expense	95	
222	Interest Payable		
830	Income Tax Expense	6,000	
260	Income Tax Payable		
	Totals	16,120	22,120
	Net Income	6,000	
	Totals	22,120	22,120

GENERAL JOURNAL

Date 19X1	Description	F	Debit	Credit
	Closing Entries			
Dec. 31	Repair Revenue		21,895	
	Rent Earned		200	
	Interest Earned		25	
	Income Summary			22,120
	To close revenue account balances			
	Income Summary		16,120	
	Depreciation Expense–Equipment			30
	Depreciation Expense–Trucks			240
	Insurance Expense			100
	Interest Expense			95
	Rent Expense			1,200
	Salaries Expense			5,150
	Supplies Used			1,605
	Truck Expense			1,400
	Utilities Expense			300
	Income Tax Expense			6,000
	To close expense account balances			
	Income Summary		6,000	
	Retained Earnings			6,000
	To close Income Summary account balance			

Figure 4-6   Closing Entries

Posting the Closing Entries to the Ledger

As Entries 1 and 2 are posted to the ledger, the balances in all revenue and expense accounts are transferred to the income summary account. The transfer of these balances is shown in Figure 4-7. Notice that a zero balance remains in each revenue and expense account after the closing entries are posted.

Closing Revenue and Expense Accounts

Following the closing of the revenue and expense accounts to the Income Summary account, the balance in the Income Summary account is equal to the net income of $6,000.

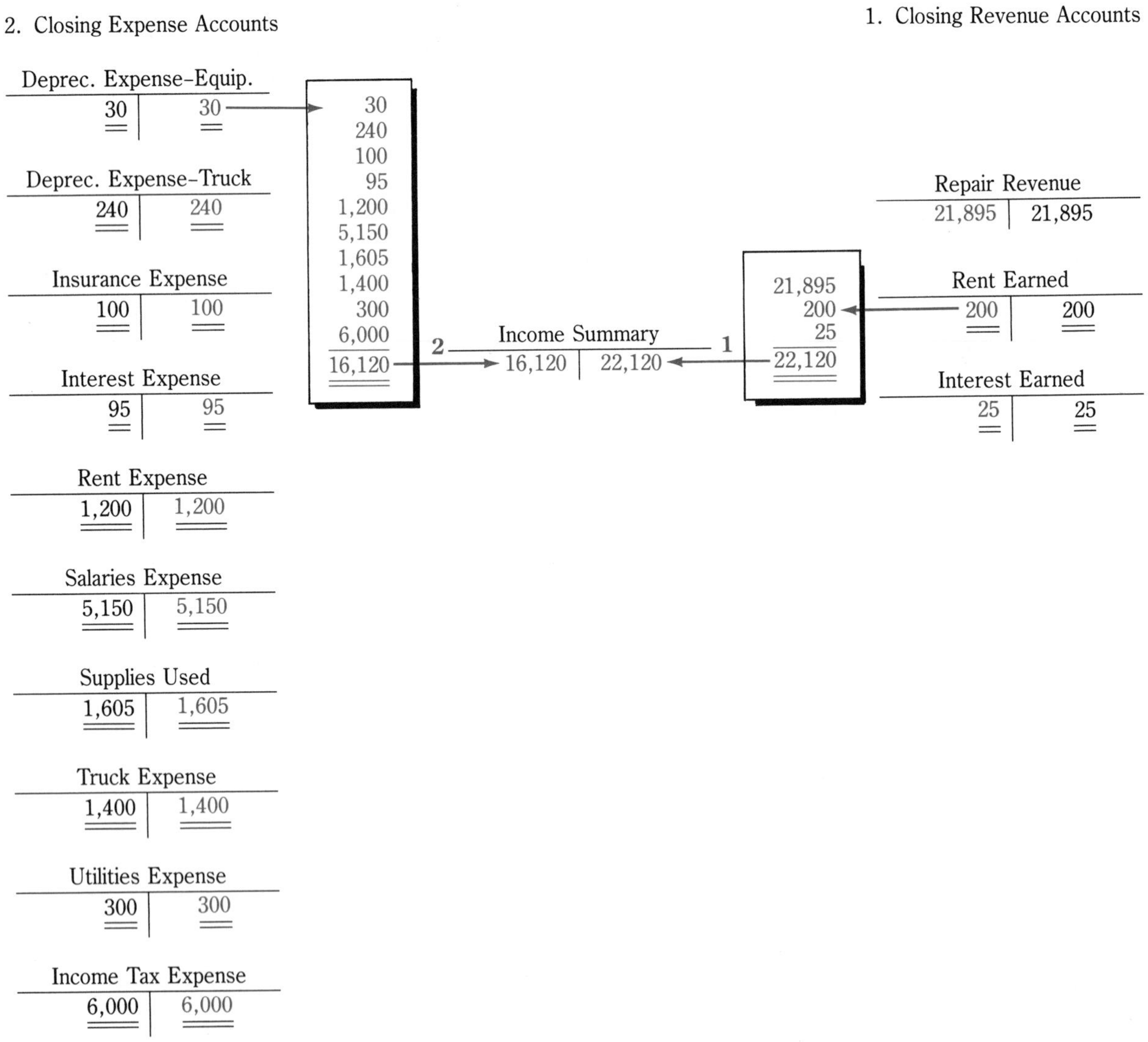

2. Closing Expense Accounts   1. Closing Revenue Accounts

Figure 4-7   Closing revenue and expense accounts

Closing the Income Summary Account

The Income Summary account is now closed to Retained Earnings.

3. Closing Income Summary Account

Income Summary			Retained Earnings

Income Summary		3	Retained Earnings
16,120	22,120		6,000
6,000			Bal. 6,000
22,120	22,120		

Figure 4-8   Closing Income Summary Account

The Post-closing Trial Balance

Post-closing trial balance
A listing of accounts and their balances after all temporary accounts have been closed; all temporary accounts should have a zero balance.

A **post-closing trial balance** is prepared immediately following the posting of closing entries and before the posting of transactions for the next accounting time period. The purpose of its preparation is to ensure that the debits and credits in the general ledger are equal and that all revenue and expense accounts have in fact been closed. Here is the post-closing trial balance of Bluebeard Computer Corporation.

Bluebeard Computer Corporation
Post-Closing Trial Balance
At December 31, 19X1

	Account Balances	
	Debit	*Credit*
Cash	$11,695	
Accounts Receivable	3,500	
Interest Receivable	25	
Notes Receivable	5,000	
Prepaid Insurance	1,100	
Supplies	495	
Equipment	2,000	
Truck	8,000	
Accumulated Depreciation — Equipment		$ 30
Accumulated Depreciation — Truck		240
Bank Loan		5,000
Accounts Payable		1,900
Interest Payable		95
Salaries Payable		150
Income Tax Payable		6,000
Unearned Repair Revenue		2,000
Unearned Rent		400
Common Stock		10,000
Retained Earnings		6,000
	$31,815	$31,815

Note that only balance sheet accounts still have a balance that is carried forward to the next accounting time period. All revenue and expense accounts begin the new time period with a zero balance, so that they can be used to accumulate amounts belonging to that new time period. Accordingly, the accounting model, A = L + E, is not only the model for the balance sheet but is also the model for the post-closing trial balance.

D.   The Sequence of Steps in the Accounting Process

The periodicity, or time period, concept was introduced and its application explained in the preceding chapters; it assumes that an entity's business activities can be broken into meaningful accounting time periods, for which financial statements are prepared. Certain accounting measurement problems result from the periodicity concept; accrual accounting and application of the matching of revenues with expenses is illustrated in Chapter 3.

The accounting process is the way in which the dollar amount of transactions during the accounting time period is transformed into financial statement information. A sequence of steps is followed by the accountant during the time period; as noted in Chapter 2, these steps are collectively referred to as the accounting cycle. This sequence of steps is shown in its relation to the accounting time period of Bluebeard Computer Corporation in Figure 4-9.

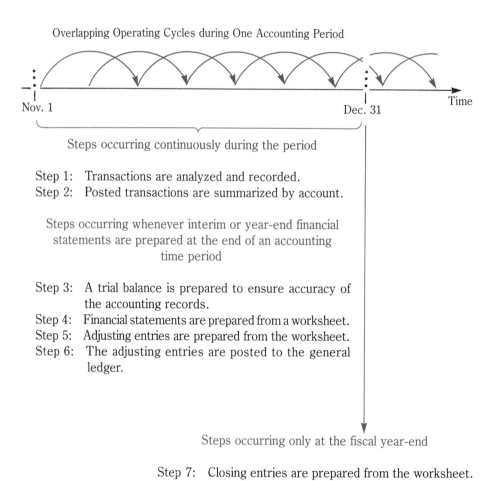

Overlapping Operating Cycles during One Accounting Period

Nov. 1   Dec. 31   Time

Steps occurring continuously during the period

Step 1:   Transactions are analyzed and recorded.
Step 2:   Posted transactions are summarized by account.

Steps occurring whenever interim or year-end financial
statements are prepared at the end of an accounting
time period

Step 3:   A trial balance is prepared to ensure accuracy of the accounting records.
Step 4:   Financial statements are prepared from a worksheet.
Step 5:   Adjusting entries are prepared from the worksheet.
Step 6:   The adjusting entries are posted to the general ledger.

Steps occurring only at the fiscal year-end

Step 7:   Closing entries are prepared from the worksheet.
Step 8:   Closing entries are posted to the general ledger.
Step 9:   A post-closing trial balance is prepared.

Figure 4-9   Sequence of steps through an accounting period

APPENDIX: Reversing Entries

Reversing entries
Entries made at the beginning of a new accounting time period to reverse an adjusting entry made in the immediately preceding accounting time period. The use of reversing entries facilitates the subsequent recording of transactions in the new accounting time period.

During the 19X1 accounting period, regular business transactions of Bluebeard Computer Corporation were recorded as they occurred. At the end of the period, BCC's accountant found it necessary to prepare adjusting journal entries so that expenses incurred would be matched with the revenue generated during the same accounting period. Adjusting entries were prepared for mixed balance sheet accounts, mixed income statement accounts, and accruals. The preparation of these entries was discussed in Chapter 3.

Reversing entries are prepared at the beginning of the next accounting time period —January 1, 19X2, in this case— to reverse certain adjusting entries made at the previous year-end, December 31, 19X1 for Bluebeard Computer Corporation. The following guidelines can be formulated about the need for reversing entries; each general rule is dicussed next.

1. The preparation of reversing entries for accrual adjustments is recommended for problem solving in this text.
2. Reversing entries are **always** prepared for mixed income statement account adjustments.
3. Reversing entries are **never** prepared for mixed asset account adjustments.

The use of reversing entries promotes the efficient operation of the accounting function, particularly in large corporations where numerous routine transactions are recorded.

Accrual Adjustments

One category of adjusting entries illustrated in Chapter 3 is accruals. At the end of the accounting period, the accountant of Bluebeard Computer Corporation had found that some ledger accounts were incomplete because some revenues and expenses accrue. No accounting problem is caused by the absence of these items during the accounting period; the matching concept requires, however, that they be recorded when financial statements are prepared. The following BCC accounts required an accrual adjustment at December 31:

Income Statement Accounts	*Balance Sheet Accounts*
Interest Earned	Interest Receivable
Salaries Expense	Salaries Payable
Interest Expense	Interest Payable
Income Tax Expense	Income Tax Payable

These are the accounts that are reversed. (In practice, however, reversing entries for accruals are optional.)

When no reversing entry is prepared, the following procedure, using BCC's adjusting entry (h) as an example, can be followed. Three days of salary amounting to $150 was incurred in December 19X1 but was payable at the end of the week — which was in January 19X2. The accountant recorded an accrual at December 31, so that revenues would match expenses incurred during the same period.

19X1 Accrual Entry			19X2 Payment of Salary		
Salaries Expense	150		Salaries Expense	100	
Salaries Payable		150	Salaries Payable	150	
			Cash		250

Here, the recording of the 19X2 salary payment was not recorded in the normal way; the accountant had to recall the previously recorded 19X1 accrual entry. Since additional analysis of this transaction is needed, this is an inefficient recording practice.

Note that the amount of expense applicable to January is only $100, the salary for the two days of the first week of January. In effect, the original 19X1 credit to Salaries Payable is reduced to a zero debit in recording the 19X2 payment.

Preparation of Reversing Entries for Accruals

Reversing entries are prepared at the beginning of a new fiscal year; they reverse an accrual recorded in the immediately preceding year. To demonstrate, take the salary accrual prepared as adjusting entry (h) once more as an example.

19X1 Accrual Entry			19X2 Reversing Entry			19X2 Payment of Salary		
Salaries Expense	150		Salaries Payable	150		Salaries Expense	250	
Salaries Payable		150	Salaries Expense		150	Cash		250

The recording of the 19X2 salary payment was made in the normal way; it was not necessary for the accountant to recall the previously recorded 19X1 accrual entry. Therefore, the reversing entry is a more efficient accounting practice.

Note that, when the reversing and salary payment entries are posted to ledger accounts, the amount of expense applicable to January is only $100, the salary for two days of January. This is the same amount that resulted in the preceding example, where a reversing entry was not prepared, although the January entry was different.

	Salaries Expense			Salaries Payable	
	Dr	Cr		Dr	Cr
Bal. (Jan. 1, 19X2)	-0-				150
Reversing entry		150		150	
				150	150
Payment of salary	250				
Salary expense	100				

The use of a reversing entry therefore results in the same salary expense figure in the next accounting period under both methods.

The non-use of reversing entries depends on accountants having to recall previously recorded adjusting entries. Using reversing entries permits accountants to record subsequent payments in the normal way, thereby minimizing errors.

Other reversing entries applicable to accruals of Bluebeard Computer Corporation recorded in December are next prepared for adjusting entries (g), (i), and (j).

	19X1 Adjusting Entry			19X2 Reversing Entry			19X2 Cash Payment or Cash Receipt		
(g)	Interest Receivable	25		Interest Earned	25		Cash	100	
	Interest Earned		25	Interest Receivable		25	Interest Earned		100
(i)	Interest Expense	94		Interest Payable	94		Interest Expense	99	
	Interest Payable		94	Interest Expense		94	Cash		99
(j)	Income Tax Expense	6,000		Income Tax Payable	6,000		Income Tax Expense	6,000	
	Income Tax Payable		6,000	Income Tax Expense		6,000	Cash		6,000

The use of this simple rule may be useful in the preparation of reversing entries for accruals: *reverse any previous year's adjusting entry* (19X1 for Bluebeard) *that follows with a cash payment or cash receipt the next year* (19X2 for Bluebeard). Notice that all the reversing entries in the examples here resulted in a debit or a credit to Cash in the subsequent accounting period.

Mixed Income Statement Account Adjustments

A mixed revenue account, as discussed in Chapter 3, includes an unearned amount, such as unearned rent, for example. The unearned amount is therefore recognized as a liability and is transferred to a liability account at the end of the period. Similarly, a mixed expense account includes an unexpired amount; the unexpired amount is recognized as an asset and is transferred to an asset account at the end of the period. Adjusting entries are prepared for mixed accounts so that revenues generated during the period are matched with expenses incurred to earn that revenue. Reversing entries are always prepared at the beginning of the next accounting period in order to return balances in mixed asset and liability accounts to their proper, before adjustment, location. The unexpired portion of one year's expense will usually expire in the subsequent year. The unearned portion of one year's revenue will usually be earned in the next year. Therefore, reversing entries transfer these amounts to their proper—original, before adjustment—location; any confusion that might otherwise result in further record-keeping is removed.

Illustrative Problem—Reversing Entries for Mixed Income Statement Accounts

Reversing entries are always used to reverse adjustments previously made to mixed income statement accounts. BCC's adjusting entry (e) can provide an example: $2,000 was received in December for repairs that were not done by December 31, 19X1; the repairs are currently scheduled to be made in January or February 19X2. An adjusting entry was prepared at December 31, so that revenues earned would match expenses incurred during the same period.

The following reversing entry is made on January 1, 19X2 to return the repair revenue amount to its original location.

19X1 Adjusting Entry			19X2 Reversing Entry		
Repair Revenue	2,000		Unearned Repair Revenue	2,000	
Unearned Repair Revenue		2,000	Repair Revenue		2,000

This reversing entry returns to its proper location the amount expected to be earned as revenue in 19X2. In this way, all revenue earned in 19X2 will be recorded in the same account, Repair Revenue.

The other BCC mixed income statement amount recorded in December that required an adjustment resulted in adjusting entry (f). A physical inventory of repair parts showed that supplies costing $600 were still on hand, thereby indicating that all supplies had not been used during the month. The original purchase of these parts had been recorded as an expense. The following reversing entry is made:

19X1 Adjusting Entry			19X2 Reversing Entry		
Supplies	600		Supplies Used	600	
Supplies Used		600	Supplies		600

This reversing entry returns to its proper location the amount expected to be used up in 19X2. In this way, all supplies used in 19X2 will be recorded in the same account, Supplies Used.

Mixed Balance Sheet Account Adjustments

A mixed asset account includes an amount that has expired during the period. Accordingly, its expired portion is transferred to expenses through an adjusting entry. A mixed liability account includes an amount that has been earned during the period. Therefore, the expired portion is transferred to revenue by an adjusting entry. No reversing entry is required at the beginning of the next accounting period because the balances remaining in the balance sheet accounts are already in their proper location. Regular business transactions can continue to be recorded in these accounts, and, as required, subsequent adjusting entries will remove the expired portion of asset accounts and the earned portion of liability accounts before preparation of the next year's financial statements.

Review of the Accounting Cycle

The accounting cycle consists of steps occurring continuously during its time period, steps occurring whenever financial statements are prepared, and steps occurring only at the fiscal year-end. These steps are reviewed below.

Steps occurring continuously during the accounting time period.

Step 1: Transactions Are Analyzed and Recorded
Journalizing consists of analyzing transactions as they occur to see how they affect the accounting equation and then recording the transactions chronologically in the general journal.

Step 2: Transactions Are Summarized by Account
Posting consists of transferring debits and credits from the general journal to the appropriate ledger accounts. A balance is calculated after the recording of each debit and credit entry.

Steps occurring whenever financial statements are prepared

Step 3: The Equality of Debits with Credits Is Established To Ensure Accuracy
Preparing a trial balance consists of listing account names and balances to prove the equality of total debit balances with total credit balances. These balances are listed directly onto the worksheet. The worksheet is then completed.

Step 4: The Summarized Financial Information Is Communicated to Interested Parties
Preparing financial statements consists of using the data listed in the adjusted trial balance columns of the worksheet to prepare the income statement, the statement of retained earnings, and the balance sheet.

Step 5: Adjusting Journal Entries Are Prepared from the Adjustment Columns of the Worksheet
Preparing adjusting journal entries consists of recording in the books the necessary adjustments to match revenues with expenses.

Step 6: The Adjusting Entries Are Posted to the Ledger
Posting adjusting entries involves transferring debits and credits from the general journal to the appropriate ledger accounts. A balance is calculated after the posting of each debit and credit entry.

Step 7: **Closing Journal Entries Are Prepared from the Worksheet**
Closing journal entries involves closing all revenue and expense accounts and transferring net income (loss) to retained earnings.

Step 8: **The Closing Entries Are Posted to the Ledger**
Posting of closing entries consists of transferring debits and credits from the general journal to the appropriate ledger accounts. A balance is calculated after the posting of each debit and credit entry.

Step 9: **The Equality of Debits with Credits Is Established To Ensure Accuracy**
Preparing a post-closing trial balance consists of listing account names and balances to prove the equality of total debit and credit balances.

Step 10: **Reversing Entries Are Prepared and Posted to the Ledger**
Reversing entries are prepared after the closing process but before the beginning of the next accounting time period.

Steps occurring only
at the fiscal year-end

Discussion Questions

1. Accountants usually use a columnar schedule to aid in preparing financial statements. What is this columnar schedule called and how is it used?
2. Is the worksheet a formal accounting record, as are the journal and the ledger?
3. Under what circumstances is the use of a worksheet unnecessary?
4. Why is a trial balance recorded directly on a worksheet in actual practice? How do accountants refer to this trial balance?
5. Describe how the income statement and balance sheet columns of a worksheet are balanced.
6. The debit/credit relationship shown on the worksheet is not shown in the financial statements. Explain.
7. Customarily, in business record-keeping, income state-ment accounts accumulate amounts for a time period not exceeding one year. Why is this custom necessary?
8. Identify which accounts are temporary and which are permanent.
9. What are the entries used to close the books at the fiscal year-end?
10. What is the Income Summary account, and why is one used?
11. Why is a post-closing trial balance prepared?
12. List the accounting steps when a worksheet is used.
13. Refer to Real Life Example 4-1: how would the form of business organization affect the amount of tax that the government can collect? If both the corporation and its shareholders pay tax in a corporate form of ownership, is this practice not, in effect, double taxation?

Discussion Cases

Discussion Case 4-1: Enormous Successful Corporation

Consolidated Year-End Balance Sheet

Assets

CURRENT ASSETS	19X6	19X5
Cash	$ 3,253,747,801	$1,157,353,991
Certificates of Deposit (*note A*)	3,000	41,664,812
Accounts Receivable (*note B*)	41,664,812	3,000
Other (*note C*)	24	24
Securities	806,459,528	317,655,290
	$ 4,101,875,165	$1,516,677,117
Less: Allowance for Doubtful Accounts (*note D*)	(41,664,812)	(39,969)
Inventories (*note E*)	821,000,001	721,000,002
Prepaid Expenses	89,997,765	1,630,599,553
Total Current Assets (*note F*)	$ 4,971,208,120	$3,868,236,704
Property, Plant, and Equipment (*note G*)	189,292,654	136,834,769
Intangibles	5	
Other Assets	4,896,977,562	4,996,997,562
Total Assets	$10,057,478,341	$9,002,069,035

Liabilities and Shareholders' Equity

CURRENT LIABILITIES	19X6	19X5
Current Maturities of Long-Term Debt (*note H*)	$ 4,285,314	$ 4,385,414
Short-Term Notes Payable	624,833,824	624,833,826
Accounts Payable	432,198,765	198,765,432
Income Taxes Payable (*note I*)	321,987,654	87,654,321
Salaries, Wages, Commissions, etc.	160,998,827	160,998,837
Other	100,000,000	90,000,000
Total Current Liabilities	$ 1,644,304,384	$1,166,637,830
Deferred Income Taxes	$ 877,766,655	$ 988,877,766
Commitments and Contingent Liabilities (*note J*)	523,412	412,632,412
SHAREHOLDERS' EQUITY		
Preferred Stock	305,816,903	245,355,077
Common Stock	436,258	436,278
Additional Paid-In Capital (*note K*)	7,242,630,729	6,288,129,672
Accumulated Deficit	(14,000,000)	(100,000,000)
	$ 7,534,883,890	$6,433,921,027
Total Liabilities and Shareholders' Equity	$10,057,478,341	$9,002,069,035

To Our Shareholders:

We are pleased to announce that 19X6 was a very good year for your company, ENORMOUS SUCCESSFUL CORPORATION. In spite of uncertainties in Guatemala and a clouded outlook in Paterson, New Jersey, your company's assets increased by $1,055,409,306, easily keeping pace with liabilities. Our product groups improved their mix; our subsidiaries were written down; and our divisions were written *up*. Much of this success is a result of your company's decision in 19X1 to continue the operations of Bushey Dynamics, which had been operating at a sizable loss for as long as anyone could remember. Bushey is still presenting a debit profile, and its negative input produced this year a $480,000,000 tax-loss carry-over which justified the inclusion in "Other Assets" of a $748 extraordinary credit from the reserve taken the previous year for estimated write-down assets in 19X2. But why pat ourselves on the back? This balance sheet speaks for itself!

Covington Hornchurch
Chairman and President

NOTES

A: Certificates of Deposit

Cycil Hornchurch, a Director of your company, recommended that these certificates be withdrawn from the Second National Bank of Flat Bluff, Kentucky, because last May 24th a teller at the Second National Bank treated Mrs. Hornchurch with extreme disrespect.

B: Accounts Receivable

This is the amount outstanding on a loan made by your company to Tory Hornchurch, Jr., a promising young pork-belly trader. (To explain the amusing coincidence in surnames, Tory Hornchurch, Sr., is your Chairman's second-youngest brother.) The first repayment installment of $11,000,000, plus .002 percent interest, is expected any day now.

C: Other

This amount is a refund owed your company by the New York Telephone Company. Your company has written them eight letters about this item, since February, 19X5, and it is starting to get a little "hot under the collar".

D: Doubtful Accounts

A precautionary listing, based on the fact that no one has heard from Tory Hornchurch, Jr., since he left for Peru's Urubamba Valley last August "to photograph a rare species of butterfly" (his exact words).

E: Inventories

Inventories are computed under the first-in, first-out method for the hard, fast-spinning, and breakable products group; under the last-in, last-out method for the slimy products group; and under the half-in, half-out method for the tall, skinny, pulverized products group. It should also be noted that, in 19X6, Porcumpansen-Bushey, one of our subsidiaries, changed its night for closing up shop and taking inventory from the first Monday of each month to the *second Tuesday*.

F: Discontinued Operations

Every once in a while your company decides to discontinue an operation. Last March, for example, Bushey Dynamics stopped making wire rakes; in May, the Hornchurch Oilstone

Factory floated away. In such cases, assets are usually diminished.

G: Property, Plant, and Equipment

Property, plant, and equipment consists of land, buildings, machinery, furniture, and fixtures. Last March, Biff Klassfelder, the Treasurer of ENORMOUS SUCCESSFUL CORPORATION, prepared a detailed list of your property, plant, and equipment, but it now appears that this list has somehow been obtained by Sheikh Abdul Hamanhi, of Qatar, who has promised to return it soon. Forehandedly, Biff had also written the totals on the inside of a matchbook. Property, plant, and equipment are carried at cost, naturally. Depreciation is on the straight-line method for financial statement purposes and on the bent-line method for tax purposes. Expenditures for repairs and minor betterments (such as the bells in our standby maintenance-inventory-exchange sub-office, which now go "ding" instead of "grr") are charged against operations.

H: Long-Term Debt

The composition of long-term debt as of December 31, 19X6 is as follows:

IOUs held by Sheikh Hamanhi	$314,285,414,275
Mortgages on land and buildings (due 19X8)	$975,314,453
Time payments on the Assistant Treasurer's Cadillac	$4,010
Total	$315,260,732,738

I: Income Taxes

Your company and its subsidiaries file consolidated state and federal income tax returns, which are very, very complicated.

J: Commitments and Contingent Liabilities

As of December 31, 19X6, your company and its subsidiaries are obligated to pay $654,523,412 in fees to Claus F. Bushey and his brother, Bernie. Bernie Bushey, to be sure, owes $654,523,412 to Cyril Hornchurch, who has a tax-loss carryforward from a 19X4 sale of wire rakes to the Greek & Italian Canned Salad & Spinach Corporation, of Harrisburg, Pennsylvania, which is owned by Claus F. Bushey's daughter-in-law. In addition, the Porcumpansen Corporation, which is a partly owned subsidiary of the Greek & Italian Canned Salad & Spinach Corporation and of K.C. Bushey and Sons, Inc. — a division of Bushey Dynamics — has contracted to have a two-car garage and sauna constructed at your company's executive Rest and Rehabilitation Center, at Gerber's Lake, at an estimated cost of $312,500. This facility will be leased to Dr. Cyril Hornchurch, Jr., Inc., a wholly owned subsidiary, at a rent yet to be determined. Meantime, Biff Klassfelder

is listing our commitments and contingent liabilities in the $523,412 range.

As for the anti-trust suit that has been filed by the Justice Department against our Porcumpansen Low-Flying Avionics division, your company's lawyers cannot, of course, predict on which side the Supreme Court will come down, but your company does not believe in any case that the $2,500,000 judgment would have a lasting adverse effect on your company's operations, because Porcumpansen Low-Flying Avionics is carried on the books of its parent company, the Porcumpansen Corporation, at no value, and because Moleff-Dynamics (the parent company of the Porcumpansen Corporation) has not guaranteed the operations of Porcumpansen's subsidiaries, on the ground of "incomprehensibility".

K: Additional Paid-In Capital

If Biff Klassfelder didn't put exactly the right amount on this line, liabilities would not equal assets.

Source: Adapted from James Munves, "Annual Report", *The New Yorker*, March 7, 1977, pp. 32–33.

For Discussion

1. The transactions for an entity are first analyzed and then recorded; they are next summarized by account. From a review of the balance sheet and notes of the Enormous Successful Corporation, what observations can you make about the accounting process underlying the preparation of its balance sheet?

2. a. One concern of shareholders centres on the quality of management and the compensation it receives. From your reading of the preceding balance sheet and notes, what judgements can you make about these features at ESC? Provide specific details to support your answer.

   b. One concern of investors (which includes shareholders) is the way decisions about investments are made in a particular entity. How would you, as an investor in ESC, react to this balance sheet? Provide specific examples to support your answer.

3. For the reader of financial statements who is unfamiliar with accounting, how useful is any balance sheet and notes? Would an income statement be more useful?

4. Howard Ross has been quoted as saying about users of financial statements that: "Users get used to using what they are given. Investors who cannot get by with the information available are, I suppose, eliminated by a sort of Darwinian process — through losing the stuff to invest with." Comment on this observation.

Discussion Case 4-2: Ford Motor Company

On May 28, 1972, Richard Grimshaw, then 13, was offered a lift in a new Ford Pinto by a friend of his family, Mrs. Lily Gray. They were heading for the southern California desert resort of Barstow on Interstate Route 15 when Gray's Pinto stalled because of a faulty carburetor and was hit from behind by another car.

The Pinto's gas tank, located only 7 in. (18 cm) behind the rear bumper was ruptured by the impact. Fumes from the gas that escaped mixed with air in the passenger compartment, a spark ignited the mixture and the Pinto was enveloped in flames.

Lily Gray was so badly burned that she died in hospital two days later. Richard suffered 90 percent burns; he lost four fingers. Miraculously, he survived. After 52 operations he has now a new nose and ear, but his face will always be a mass of twisted scar tissue and there are more operations to come.

"In each case the gas tank was buckled and gas spewed out. In each case, the interior of the vehicle was totally gutted by the ensuing fire. It is our opinion that three such conflagrations (all experienced by one rental agency in a six-month period) demonstrates a clear and present safety hazard to all Pinto owners."

Shortly before Richard's case began, Dr. Leslie Ball — former safety chief for the NASA manned space program and founder of the International Society of Reliability Engineers — had publicly asserted that "the release to production of the Pinto was the most reprehensible decision in the history of American engineering".

Ball was particularly scathing about the design and location of the Pinto's gas tank. There were, he said, a large number of European and Japanese cars in the same price and weight range as the Pinto which were more safely designed. Most used a "saddle style" gas tank placed above the car's back

---

BENEFITS:
Savings — 180 burn deaths, 180 serious injuries, 2100 burned vehicles
Unit Cost — $200,000 per death, $67,000 per injury, $700 per vehicle
Total — 180 × $200,000 + 180 × $67,000 + 2100 × $700 = *$49.5 million*

COSTS:
Sales — 11 million cars, 1.5 million light trucks
Unit Cost — $11 per car, $11 per truck
Total Cost — 11,000,000 × $11 + 1,500,000 × $11 = *$137 million*

These are the confidential calculations that convinced a southern California jury that Ford Motor Company had knowingly sold cars with a potentially lethal design fault. The formula illustrated is taken from a 1972 Ford memo.

He has also been awarded $128 million in damages, the highest-ever personal injury award. The award was made after a jury heard how Ford had calculated the cost of building greater safety into its cars against the probable amount the company would save in protecting car owners from death or injury by burning.

Based on the probability of 180 burn deaths in a year, and 180 severe burn injuries, Ford came up with a "unit cost" of $200,000 per death, $67,000 per injury and $700 per vehicle, for a total of $49.5 million.

The cost of altering cars and light trucks to conform with safety standards then being proposed by the United States Congress to prevent gas tanks exploding after an accident was put at $137 million. Ford's engineers concluded that such changes would not be "cost effective".

Richard's legal team had access to valuable background material before the case began. The hazards presented by the design and positioning of the Pinto's gas tank had been investigated by several independent organizations since the model went into production in August 1970.

A study in 1973 by the University of Miami's accident analysis unit, examining four years of car crashes, had singled out the Pinto for comment. Under the heading "Gas Tank Integrity/Protection (Ford Pinto)", the Miami unit observed:

axle, out of the line of direct impact. The basic patent on the saddle-tank, Ball noted, was owned by Ford.

And the greatest damage to Ford's case was done by its own analysis of the price of building greater safety into Ford cars against the expected benefit derived from saving Ford owners from death or injury by burning.

Some common measure was required to make the comparison.

The memo noted: "the measure typically chosen is dollars". Ford's calculations of the value of a human life were based on a 1972 study by the National Highway Traffic Safety Administration (NHTSA) which sought to establish the cash cost of death in a car crash by breaking down and valuing ten separate components.

"Future productivity losses" were so much, medical costs so much, insurance administration and legal expenses so much. There was even a figure — $10,000 — for "Victim's pain and suffering" though the NHTSA steadfastly refused to say how it had been arrived at.

The overall "societal cost" came to $200,000. Ford also allowed a figure of $67,000 for non-fatal burn injuries.

From official statistics, Ford extracted the figure of 180 deaths per year from burns in rollover accidents.

Where some experts disagree with Ford is in its further estimate that numbers emerging alive from such accidents, but suffering severe burns, would also be 180 a year. Some authoritative studies have put this figure 10 times higher at 1,800 a year.

Based on the benefits of saving 180 lives and preventing another 180 people from being burned, with an allowance for the cost of damaged cars, Ford put the total benefits of a design change at slightly less than $50 million. That was set against the costs — $11-worth of modifications per Ford vehicle sold — of $137 million.

That, Ford's engineers observed, was almost three times greater than the benefits, "even using a number of highly favourable benefit assumptions". They could not envisage any developments which "could make compliance with the rollover requirement cost effective".

On the heels of that chilling memo, the Santa Anna jury heard something of the background to Ford's decision to place the Pinto's gas tank in such an exposed position.

First, Richard Grimshaw's lawyers produced their star: "defector" Harley F. Copp, a senior design engineer with Ford for 20 years, retired at the time of the trial.

Against a stream of objections from Ford's team of lawyers, Copp demonstrated with blackboard, wall chart, and models to the evident discomfort of his former employers (helped by occasional indulgence from the bench: "I will allow hearsay" the judge declared at one point, "provided it is reliable hearsay").

Copp had worked on Ford's successful Capri range in which the gas tank rode, saddle-style, above the back axle; he was certain that this was the safest design (Ford had, in fact, considered using the Capri design on the Pinto).

What could a designer like him do, Richard's lawyers asked, if "corporate management" specified the location of the gas tank? "Follow corporate policy," Copp replied.

Had Ford's top management, in fact, issued a design directive for the Pinto's tank? "Behind the rear axle, beneath the floor." Could Copp estimate how much extra it would have cost to place the Pinto's tank above the axle? "About $9 more per car."

Copp's testimony was reinforced by more memos from Ford's confidential files, demonstrating, Richard's lawyers argued, how Ford had disregarded danger signals in its rush to get the Pinto onto the lucrative United States small car market. (The company's share of this market had been declining at an alarming rate in the face of competition from European and Japanese models.)

Shortly after Pinto's production began, several Capris with saddle-style tanks came through crash tests with flying colours; next day, Capris with modified tanks placed, like the Pinto's, behind the rear axle were crash-tested and leaked gas in every case.

Like every company in the ferociously competitive small-car market, Ford was exceedingly price conscious.

A Ford U.S. engineer told the American magazine *Mother Jones* that the Pinto was rigidly governed by "the limits of 2000" — it was not to weigh more than 2000 lb. (907 kg) and not to cost more than $2,000. (The magazine, named after the formidable Mary Harris Jones, self-styled "hell-raiser", was the first to publish some of the Ford documents used in Richard Grimshaw's case.)

A $25 increase in production costs could price a compact out of its market; so could a marginal reduction in sales features, such as the size of the trunk. "Do you realize that, if we put a Capri-type tank in the Pinto, you could only get one set of golf clubs in there?" another Ford engineer told the magazine.

It took the jury in Richard Grimshaw's case one minute to reject Ford's argument that the speed at which Gray's Pinto had been hit — from 50 to 65 mph — was the chief cause of the tragedy rather than any deficiency in the design of its gas tank. (The jury concluded that the speed at impact was 35 mph at the most.)

Punitive damages verdicts in California have, in the past, invariably come unstuck in subsequent courts of appeal, and Ford said two weeks ago that it would continue to fight against "this unreasonable and unwarranted award".

Ford's position is that every Pinto it manufactured had met or surpassed the government safety standards applicable at the time, and Pintos produced since September 1976 meet the revised rear-impact standards introduced since Richard was involved in his accident.

Source: Philip Jacobson and John Barnes, *The* (Montreal) *Gazette*, February 17, 1978, pp. 1 and 4.

For Discussion

Management is concerned with planning and controlling to accomplish the goals and objectives of the entity. On the basis of the information given in this case:

1. What appear to be the goals and objectives of this business entity?
2. Identify the planning activities that took place, as revealed at the trial.
3. Recalculate the savings that would result if the number of serious burns were 1800 rather than 180. How does this compare with the $137 million total cost amount?
4. Identify the controlling activities of the entity that took place, as revealed in the article.
5. Did management achieve the goals and objectives of this entity?

Discussion Case 4-3: Pension Time Bomb

Over the past few years the consequences of the massive demographic changes that have occurred since the end of the Second World War have been coming home to roost in such forms as changes in housing demand — shifting from four-bedroom homes to townhouses and condominiums — and sweeping changes in dining-out habits.

Shrinking population

But the changes are just beginning, reflecting the fact that, except for immigration, Canadians are not having children fast enough to avoid population shrinkage. As of 1982 the average number of children for each Canadian woman of child-bearing years was 1.7, a statistic that has been dropping steadily since 1956, when a woman of child-bearing age had 3.9 children on average.

This decline alone would increase the average age of the population. But the population is aging even faster than the decline in births would indicate.

Since 1930, male life expectancy has increased by 10 years, to about 70 years. For women the increase has been even greater: by 15 years, to an expectancy of 78.

By the year 2000, it is expected that male infants will have a life expectancy of 72 years, and female infants 81 years.

The greying of Canada will present a number of challenges to existing institutions, not the least of which will be pensions.

The Canada Pension Plan, and its Quebec counterpart, are essentially pay-as-you-go systems. When you and I retire, most, if not all, of our public pension payments will come from contributions made by those who are still working.

In principle, it is an equitable arrangement: We now support the elderly on Canada-Quebec pensions. Our children will support us. And their children will support them.

Fewer children

The trouble is that while you and I have a lot of children to support us, our children have chosen to have fewer children. By the time today's 18-year-old retires, there will be four Canadian workers to make up his/her pension. Today there are about 16 workers for each retired person.

Already, the future is overtaking us. In the early days, contributions to the plans exceeded benefits paid out, with the surplus mostly lent to the provinces at favourable interest rates.

Last year, contributions fell short of payments by about $1.2 billion, which was funded by drawing on the surpluses of earlier years. But those past surpluses will evaporate in a few years.

To keep the pension scheme on a pay-as-you-go basis will require substantial increases in CPP/QPP contributions. With a labour force that is about to start shrinking, those increases will have to be large indeed.

It has been called the "greying of America" and federal figures released this week illustrate dramatically how costly that phenomenon has become in Canada.

Payments under the Canada and Quebec Pension plans were being pumped out to elderly people almost as quickly as contributions were coming in from working Canadians in 1982–82, figures released by Statistics Canada show.

Almost two million people were paid a total of $4.1 billion under the plans in the year ending March 31, 1983, almost a seven-fold increase over the 331 000 people who received $189.6 million-worth of benefits under the plans in 1971–72.

The most disturbing sign perhaps is that contributions to the plans in 1982–83 totalled only $4.4 billion, a mere $300 million more than what was needed to pay retirement, disability, and survivor benefits under the plans.

By contrast, contributions were about six times greater than payments in 1971, the agency said.

While the figures point to trouble down the road unless the schemes are revamped, the evidence shows they are self-financing for the time being.

"We've got a bit of a breathing space," Eden Cloutier, an economist with the Economic Council of Canada, said in an interview. "The real crunch is a few years down the road when the retiring labour force exceeds new entries."

In other words, when the baby boomers start retiring in 2011, there probably will not be enough offspring from the declining birthrate of the last decade entering the labour force to pay for the benefits needed to support the over-65 crowd.

Cloutier described the Statistics Canada figures as unsurprising, but a welcome body of evidence for people looking into the whole pension issue.

Source Seymour Friedland, "Pensions bear a time bomb", *The* (Montreal) *Gazette*, April 19, 1984, p. B-1.

Source "Pension payment statistics point to trouble down road", *The* (Montreal) *Gazette*, April 12, 1984, p. D-7.

For Discussion

1. Comment on the policy of having present contributions pay for those who have retired. Should each individual be responsible for his/her own pension? Why or why not?
2. How could the payment of future pensions be better provided for?

Discussion Case 4-4: The 1980 Winter Olympic Games

The first independent financial analysis of the 1980 Winter Olympics in Lake Placid showed an operating loss of $4,366,029.

The financial review, made at the insistence of government officials, also showed claims against the Lake Placid Olympic Organizing Committee of $21.5 million, arising mainly from construction disputes.

The unaudited financial statement was made by the accounting firm of Peat, Marwick and Mitchell. The indications are that the audited report of the Olympic Committee's books would not be more than $500,000 off the statement issued.

The statement said that it cost $60.8 million to administer and operate the games, with the major expenses in operations, $19.4 million, and marketing, $17 million.

The revenues — including television rights, $13 million; marketing and licensing contracts, $17.7 million; ticket sales, $12.2 million, and contributions, $7.4 million — totalled $56.4 million.

The report also showed construction costs of $72 million, most of which was paid by government. In addition, although the report did not mention it, an additional $40 million was contributed for improvement and renovation of government-owned facilities at Mount Van Hoevenberg, where the bobsled run was held, and at White Face Mountain, where the downhill speed skiing races and the slalom competitions were held.

The most expensive construction items were the $17.9 million housing complex for athletes at Ray Brook, which has just been converted into a prison; a new field-house in Lake Placid Village, $14.9 million, and the ski jumps, $5.9 million.

A footnote in the report also showed that the organizers had obligated themselves to pay $1.5 million as a fee and $2.3 million in costs to the Gilbane Construction Company, which supervised the construction.

Most of the claims against the committee are in $21.5 million in suits, filed or pending, by construction contractors. But, general counsel for the committee feels that these are exaggerated and it has included a reserve fund for potential damages within the $8.5 million it has requested from government.

Source   Harold Faber, *The New York Times*, October 5, 1980, p. 51.

A Profit-Cost Statement
For the Winter Olympics

Revenues

Television Rights	$13,092,221
Marketing and Licensing	17,750,993
International Olympic Comm.	1,000,000
Contributions	7,368,835
Miscellaneous	590,177
Ticket Sales (net)	12,224,145
Accommodations	2,421,260
Proceeds on Disposal of Assets	751,605
Investment Income	625,710
Restricted Gifts	656,339
Total Revenues	$56,481,285

Administrative Costs

Executive	$ 8,897,343
Protocol	4,104,769
Marketing	17,014,290
Engineering and Construction	5,412,260
Operations	19,439,569
Press and Public Affairs	2,836,914
Sports	3,089,034
Other	53,135
Total Costs	$60,847,314
Deficit	$4,336,029

For Discussion

1. Accountants usually assume that an entity is a going concern. Is the entity, the 1980 Winter Olympic Games, a going concern? Explain.

2. A cost outlay is usually recorded as an expense if it does not have the potential to produce future revenues. Why is the illustrated financial statement called a *profit-cost statement*? Explain.

3. The construction costs of $72 million have been excluded from the profit-cost statement. Is this acceptable from the point of view of matching of expenses with revenues? Why or why not?

4. An amount of $40 million-worth of improvements and renovations of government-owned facilities is excluded from the financial statements of the games. On the basis of what accounting principle could this be justified? Explain.

Comprehension Problems

Comprehension Problem 4-1

The following is an incomplete worksheet of Bernotas Corporation at its fiscal year-end, June 30, 19X2.

Worksheet
For the Year Ended June 30, 19X2

Account Number	Account Title	Trial Balance Dr.	Trial Balance Cr.	Adjustments Dr.	Adjustments Cr.	Adjusted Trial Balance Dr.	Adjusted Trial Balance Cr.	Income Statement Dr.	Income Statement Cr.	Balance Sheet Dr.	Balance Sheet Cr.
	Cash	600								?	
	Accounts Receivable	?								1,500	
	Prepaid Insurance	600			?					200	
	Prepaid Rent	400			?					200	
	Supplies	750			?					500	
	Truck	5,000								?	
	Accounts Payable		?								?
	Common Stock		1,000								?
	Revenue		9,000							?	
	Advertising Expense	450						450			
	Rent Expense	2,400		?				?			
	Telephone Expense	300						300			
		12,000	12,000								
	Insurance Expense			?				400			
	Supplies Used			?				250			
	Depreciation Expense			?				?			
	Accumulated Deprec.				?						450
	Totals			1,300	1,300			4,450	?	8,000	?
	Net Income for Year							?			?
	Totals							9,000	9,000	?	8,000

Required: Complete this worksheet.

Note: For solutions in this chapter, consult the master chart of accounts in Chapter 3 when necessary. Complete solutions requiring reversing entries only if The Appendix was studied in your course.

Comprehension Problem 4-2

The following ledger accounts are taken from the books of Tetu Inc. at its year-end, December 31, 19X1.

Revenue		Advertising Expense		Rent Expense	
	10,000	200		2,400	

	Interest Expense		Salaries Expense	
	100		5,000	

Required:
1. Prepare the closing entries, including all T-accounts.
2. Post these closing entries to the ledger accounts.
3. Balance and rule the accounts.

Comprehension Problem 4-3

The following ledger accounts and additional information are taken from the records of Cristhop Corp. at the end of its fiscal year, December 31, 19X1.

Cash		Supplies		Advertising Expense	
Bal. 900		Bal. 700		Bal. 200	

Accounts Receivable		Common Stock		Salaries Expense	
Bal. 2,000			Bal. 3,800	Bal. 4,500	

Prepaid Insurance		Revenue		Telephone Expense	
Bal. 1,200			Bal. 7,750	Bal. 250	

Additional information:
a. The prepaid insurance is for a one-year policy, effective July 1, 19X1.
b. A physical count indicated that $500-worth of supplies are still on hand.
c. A $50 December telephone bill has not yet been received or recorded.

Required:
1. Record all necessary adjusting entries for the general journal.
2. Post the adjusting entries to the necessary ledger accounts.
3. Prepare all closing entries.
4. Post the closing entries to the applicable ledger accounts. Balance and rule each account closed.
5. Prepare the necessary reversing entries.
6. Post the reversing entries to the applicable ledger accounts.

Problems

Problem 4-1

The adjusted trial balance of Umma Services Inc. follows.

Partial Worksheet
For the Year Ended December 31, 19X1

Account Title	Adjusted Trial Balance	
	Dr.	Cr.
Cash	500	
Accounts Receivable	10,000	
Truck	11,000	
Accumulated Deprec.		2,500
Bank Loan		10,000
Accounts Payable		6,000
Common Stock		1,000
Revenue		27,000
Advertising Expense	1,500	
Commissions Expense	5,000	
Depreciation Expense	2,500	
Insurance Expense	1,200	
Interest Expense	750	
Rent Expense	3,600	
Salaries Expense	10,000	
Supplies Used	250	
Telephone Expense	200	
Totals		
Net Income for Year		
Totals		

Required:
1. Calculate the totals of the adjusted trial balance debit and credit columns.
2. Complete the income statement and balance sheet columns of the worksheet.
3. Prepare the formal year-end income statement of the corporation.
4. Prepare all closing entries.

Problem 4-2

The following partial worksheet and additional information are taken from the records of Davey Pencils Inc. at the end of its first year of operations.

Partial Worksheet
For the Year Ended December 31, 19X1

Account Title	Trial Balance Dr.	Trial Balance Cr.
Cash	3,300	
Accounts Receivable	4,000	
Prepaid Insurance	1,200	
Supplies	500	
Truck	8,500	
Accounts Payable		5,000
Unearned Rent		2,400
Common Stock		6,000
Revenue		16,600
Advertising Expense	200	
Commissions Expense	1,000	
Interest Expense	400	
Rent Expense	3,600	
Salaries Expense	7,000	
Telephone Expense	300	
Totals		
Insurance Expense		
Supplies Used		
Depreciation Expense		
Accumulated Deprec.		
Salaries Payable		
Rent Earned		
Totals		
Net Income for Year		
Totals		

The following additional data are available:
a. Prepaid insurance at December 31 amounts to $600.
b. A physical count indicates that $300-worth of supplies are still on hand at December 31.
c. The truck was purchased on July 1 and has a useful life of 4 years with an estimated salvage value of $500.
d. One day of salaries for December 31 is unpaid; the unpaid amount of $200 will be included in the first Friday payment in January.
e. The unearned rent represents six months rental of some warehouse space, effective October 1.
f. A $100 bill for December telephone charges has not yet been received or recorded (record in Accounts Payable).

Required:
1. Prepare all necessary adjusting entries.
2. Complete the worksheet.
3. Prepare all necessary reversing entries.

Problem 4-3

The following columns are taken from the workseet of Staedtler Service Corporation:

Partial Worksheet
For the Year Ended December 31, 19X1

Account Title	Income Statement		Balance Sheet	
	Dr.	Cr.	Dr.	Cr.
Cash			650	
Prepaid Insurance			1,100	
Supplies			700	
Equipment			3,000	
Accumulated Deprec.				250
Accounts Payable				2,000
Unearned Revenue				750
Income Tax Payable				725
Common Stock				1,000
Revenue		11,750		
Advertising Expense	400			
Commissions Expense	1,500			
Depreciation Expense	250			
Insurance Expense	100			
Rent Expense	2,400			
Salaries Expense	5,000			
Supplies Used	300			
Telephone Expense	350			
Income Tax Expense	725			
Totals				
Net Income for Year				
Totals				

Required:
1. Complete the worksheet income statement and balance sheet columns.
2. Prepare all closing entries.
3. Prepare a post-closing trial balance.

Problem 4-4

The following entries are extracted from the records of Village Cleaners Inc.

GENERAL JOURNAL   Page 1

Date 19X1	Description	F	Debit	Credit
	Closing Journal Entries			
Dec. 31	Revenue		30 000 -	
	Income Summary			30 000 -
	To close revenue account.			
31	Income Summary		25 000 -	
	Advertising Expense			500 -
	Commissions Expense			5 000 -
	Insurance Expense			1 200 -
	Rent Expense			3 600 -
	Truck Expense			4 700 -
	Wages Expense			10 000 -
	To close expense accounts.			
31	Income Summary		5 000 -	
	Retained Earnings			5 000 -
	To close the Income Summary account.			

Required: Using the data in the journal closing entries, complete the income statement and the statement of retained earnings for the year-end, December 31, 19X1. (The Retained Earnings January 1 balance is $10,000.)

Problem 4-5

The following post closing trial balance and closing entries are taken from the records of Côte St Luc Services Corporation.

Post-closing Trial Balance
December 31, 19X1

	Account Balances	
	Debit	Credit
Cash	$ 3,500	
Accounts Receivable	7,500	
Supplies	1,000	
Truck	13,000	
Accumulated Depreciation		$ 3,000
Bank Loan		2,000
Accounts Payable		10,000
Common Stock		3,000
Retained Earnings		7,000
	$25,000 =	$25,000

GENERAL JOURNAL   Page 1

Date 19X1	Description	F	Debit	Credit
	Closing Journal Entries			
Dec 31	Revenue		28000 -	
	Income Summary			28000 -
	To close revenue account.			
31	Income Summary		21000 -	
	Advertising Expense			1500 -
	Depreciation Expense			3000 -
	Salaries Expense			10000 -
	Supplies Used			500 -
	Telephone Expense			2000 -
	Truck Expense			4000 -
	To close expense accounts.			
31	Income Summary		7000 -	
	Retained Earnings			7000 -
	To close the Income Summary accounts.			

Required: Using the data given, complete the income statement, the statement of retained earnings (with a zero January 1 balance), and the balance sheet for the year-end at December 31, 19X1.

Alternate Problems

Alternate Problem 4-1

The adjusted trial balance of Elam Services Ltd. follows.

Partial Worksheet
For the Year Ended Decemer 31, 19X1

Account Title	Adjusted Trial Balance Dr.	Adjusted Trial Balance Cr.	Income Statement Dr.	Income Statement Cr.	Balance Sheet Dr.	Balance Sheet Cr.
Cash	2,500					
Accounts Receivable	9,000					
Equipment	5,500					
Accumulated Deprec.		600				
Bank Loan		5,000				
Accounts Payable		6,000				
Common Stock		3,000				
Revenue		17,300				
Advertising Expense	200					
Commissions Expense	3,000					
Depreciation Expense	600					
Interest Expense	500					
Rent Expense	2,400					
Salaries Expense	7,500					
Supplies Used	400					
Telephone Expense	300					
Totals						
Net Income for the Year						
Totals						

Required:
1. Calculate the totals of the adjusted trial balance debit and credit columns.
2. Complete the income statement and balance sheet columns of the worksheet.
3. Prepare the formal year-end income statement of the corporation.
4. Prepare all closing entries.

Alternate Problem 4-2

The following partial worksheet is taken from Dutoit Movers Corp. at the end of its first year of operations.

Partial Worksheet
For the Year Ended December 31, 19X1

Account Title	Trial Balance Dr.	Trial Balance Cr.
Cash	1,500	
Accounts Receivable	7,000	
Prepaid Rent	1,200	
Supplies	100	
Equipment	3,500	
Accounts Payable		6,000
Unearned Commissions		3,000
Common Stock		1,000
Revenue		20,000
Advertising Expense	850	
Commissions Expense	3,600	
Interest Expense	550	
Rent Expense	4,400	
Supplies Used	700	
Wages Expense	6,600	
Totals		
Depreciation Expense		
Accumulated Deprec.		
Wages Payable		
Unearned Revenue		
Interest Payable		
Totals		
Net Income for the Year		
Totals		

The following additional data are available:
a. Prepaid rent represents rent for the months of December 19X1 and January and February 19X2.
b. A physical count indicates that $200-worth of supplies are on hand at December 31.
c. The equipment was purchased on July 1 and has a useful life of 3 years with an estimated salvage value of $500.
d. Wages for December 30 and 31 are unpaid; the unpaid amount of $300 will be included in the first Friday payment in January.
e. Revenue includes $2,500 received for work to be started in January 19X2.
f. Unrecorded interest expense amounts to $150.

Required:
1. Prepare all necessary adjusting entries.
2. Complete the entire worksheet.
3. Prepare all reversing entries.

Alternate Problem 4-3

The following columns are taken from the worksheet of Drapeau Polish Inc.

Partial Worksheet
For the Year Ended December 31, 19X1

Account Title	Income Statement Dr.	Income Statement Cr.	Balance Sheet Dr.	Balance Sheet Cr.
Cash			2,700	
Prepaid Rent			900	
Supplies			600	
Equipment			5,000	
Accum. Depreciation				500
Accounts Payable				4,500
Unearned Revenue				1,500
Income Tax Payable				850
Common Stock				1,000
Revenue		14,500		
Advertising Expense	300			
Depreciation Expense	500			
Interest Expense	100			
Rent Expense	2,400			
Supplies Used	400			
Truck Expense	2,500			
Utilities Expense	600			
Wages Expense	6,000			
Income Tax Expense	850			
Totals				
Net Income for Year				
Totals				

Required:
1. Complete the worksheet income statement and balance sheet columns.
2. Prepare all closing entries.
3. Prepare a post-closing trial balance.

Alternate Problem 4-4

The following entries are extracted from the records of Aztec Repairs Corp.

GENERAL JOURNAL

Page 1

Date 19X1	Description	F	Debit	Credit
	Closing Journal Entries			
Dec 31	Revenue		14400 -	
	Income Summary			14400 -
	To close revenue account			
31	Income Summary		12400 -	
	Advertising Expense			300 -
	Interest Expense			1000 -
	Maintenance Expense			700 -
	Salaries Expense			8000 -
	Supplies Used			2000 -
	Telephone Expense			400 -
	To close expense accounts			
31	Income Summary		2000 -	
	Retained Earnings			2000 -
	To close the Income Summary account			

Required: Using the data in the journal closing entries, complete the income statement and the statement of retained earnings (with January 1 balance of $5,000) for the firm's year-end, December 31, 19X1.

Alternate Problem 4-5

The following post-closing trial balance and closing entries are taken from the records of Globe Services Corporation.

	Account Balances	
	Debit	Credit
Cash	$ 2,500	
Accounts Receivable	10,000	
Prepaid Insurance	600	
Equipment	9,000	
Accumulated Depreciation		$ 1,000
Bank Loan		8,000
Accounts Payable		7,000
Common Stock		2,500
Retained Earnings		2,600
	$22,100 =	$22,100

GENERAL JOURNAL   Page 1

Date 19X1	Description	F	Debit	Credit
	Closing Journal Entries			
Dec. 31	Revenue		12750 –	
	Income Summary			12750 –
	To close revenue account			
31	Income Summary		10150 –	
	Advertising Expense			450 –
	Depreciation Expense			1000 –
	Insurance Expense			600 –
	Rent Expense			2400 –
	Supplies Used			700 –
	Wages Expense			5000 –
	To close expense accounts			
31	Income Summary		2600 –	
	Retained Earnings			2600 –
	To close the Income Summary account			

Required: Using the data given, complete the income statement, the statement of retained earnings (with a zero January 1 balance), and the balance sheet for the year-end, December 31, 19X1.

Review Problems

Review Problem 4-1

The following account balances are taken from the ledger of Andersen Services Corporation at the end of its fiscal year, June 30, 19X5. The corporation began operation on May 1, 19X5.

Account Balances

	Debit	Credit
Cash	$ 6,600	
Accounts Receivable	3,400	
Notes Receivable	2,000	
Service Supplies	1,000	
Prepaid Rent	2,400	
Office Supplies	750	
Equipment	12,000	
Accounts Payable		$ 3,600
Notes Payable		2,200
Common Stock		16,000
Revenue		8,335
Maintenance Expense	260	
Telephone Expense	45	
Utilities Expense	80	
Wages Expense	1,600	
Totals	$30,135	$30,135

At the end of June, the following additional information is made available:
a. The Notes Receivable account represents a 60-day, 20-percent, interest-bearing note signed by a customer on June 30.
b. The monthly rent is $600.
c. A physical count shows that office supplies on hand are worth a total of $375 and service supplies on hand are worth a total of $600.
d. Equipment acquired on May 1 has an estimated useful life 5 years and a salvage value of $1,200.
e. The bank loan bears interest at 20 percent; interest amounting to $75 and applicable to May and June has not yet been accrued.
f. Wages of employees earned but not paid are $300.

Required:
1. Record the trial balance on the worksheet. Enter the following account titles on the worksheet: Service Supplies Used, Rent Expense, Office Supplies Used, Depreciation Expense — Equipment, Accumulated Depreciation — Equipment, Interest Expense, Interest Payable.
2. Complete the worksheet, using the additional information.
3. From the worksheet, prepare an income statement, a statement of retained earnings, and a balance sheet.
4. From the worksheet, prepare and post the adjusting and closing journal entries.
5. From the ledger, prepare a post-closing trial balance.
6. Prepare all necessary reversing entries.

Review Problem 4-2

The general ledger of Robinson Limited showed the following balances at the end of its first 12-month time period:

Robinson Limited
Trial Balance
At August 31, 19X3

	Debits	Credits
Cash	$ 12,000	
Accounts Receivable — Advertisers	2,500	
Accounts Receivable — Subscribers	1,100	
Prepaid Insurance	-0-	
Supplies	2,500	
Land	15,000	
Building	60,000	
Equipment	20,000	
Furniture	3,000	
Accumulated Depreciation — Building		-0-
Accumulated Depreciation — Equipment		-0-
Accumulated Depreciation — Furniture		-0-
Accounts Payable		$ 2,600
Notes Payable		1,800
Unearned Advertising		1,200
Unearned Subscriptions		800
Salaries Payable		-0-
Interest Payable		-0-
Mortgage Payable		47,600
Common Stock		52,100
Retained Earnings		-0-
Income Summary	-0-	-0-
Advertising Revenue		37,900
Subscriptions Revenue		32,700
Advertising Expense	4,300	
Depreciation Expense — Building	-0-	
Depreciation Expense — Equipment	-0-	
Depreciation Expense — Furniture	-0-	
Interest Expense	2,365	
Insurance Expense	1,800	
Salaries Expense	33,475	
Supplies Used	15,800	
Utilities Expense	2,860	
Totals	$176,700	$176,700

At the end of August, the following additional information is available:
a. The company's insurance coverage is provided by a single comprehensive 12-month policy that began on March 1, 19X3.
b. Supplies on hand total $2,850.
c. The building has an estimated useful life of 50 years.
d. The equipment has an estimated useful life of 11 years and an estimated salvage value of $2,400.
e. The furniture has an estimated useful life of 11 years and an estimated salvage value of $300. (*Round your answer to the nearest dollar.*)
f. Interest of $9 on the note payable for the month of August will be paid on September 1, when the regular $50 payment is made.
g. Unearned advertising as of August 31 is determined to be $450.

h. Unearned subscriptions as of August 31 are determined to be $2,800.

i. Salaries that have been earned by employees but are not due to be paid to them until the next payday (in September) amount to $325.

j. Interest of $199 on the mortgage payable for the month of August will be paid on September 1, when the regular $300 payment is made.

Required:

1. Record the trial balance in proper order on a worksheet.
2. Complete the worksheet, using the additional information.
3. From the worksheet, prepare an income statement, a statement of retained earnings, and a balance sheet.
4. From the worksheet, prepare and post the adjusting and closing journal entries.
5. From the ledger, prepare a post-closing trial balance.
6. Prepare all necessary reversing entries.

The Revenue-Expenditure Cycle

Part II focuses on the revenue-expenditure cycle of a merchandising entity. Revenue consists of sales of merchandise on account with the subsequent collection of cash. Expenditure involves both the purchase of merchandise on account and the subsequent payment of cash, not only for purchases but also for selling, general, administrative, and other expenses. Recording the distinct transactions of sales and collections, and of purchases and payments is the subject matter of Chapter 5. The calculation and relationship of gross profit to sales is explained. The chapter includes a discussion of inventory and the need to recognize it in the financial statements in order to facilitate the evaluation of the entity's operations during a particular time.

The volume of transactions facing most entities requires the establishment of accounting systems to process mass transactions. Special journals, usually referred to as books of original entry, can be grouped within the sales and collections, and the purchases and payment cycles identified in Chapter 5. A payroll cycle is also introduced in Chapter 6. The objectives of accounting systems include accurate recording of information in the appropriate special journal and accurate accumulation of amounts in the general ledger and subsidiary ledgers.

Internal control systems are designed to ensure this accuracy; they are also designed to maximize efficiency and to control the entity's assets. The sales and collections cycle is completed with the collection of cash; the purchase and payments cycle, as well as the payroll cycle, are completed with the payment of cash. The control of cash is an area of concern for obvious reasons; internal control and controls designed to protect cash are described in Chapter 7.

GAAP have an impact on each of the cycles; an accountant should be concerned with whether the information produced by each cycle is in accordance with generally accepted accounting principles. Sales on account involve the extension of credit; unfortunately, not every account receivable is collectible. A good internal control system is designed to minimize bad debt losses. Accountants apply the matching concept to align bad debt expenses with revenues of the same accounting period. The use of the accrual method of accounting to make this alignment and the methods of calculating estimated bad debt expenses round out the discussion of the revenue-expenditure cycle.

Accounting for Merchandising Operations

The accounting for a merchandiser differs from that required for a service business for decision-making purposes. Classified financial statements of merchandising operations facilitate short-term solvency analyses and analyses of operational efficiency.

1. In what way is the matching principle emphasized in the income statement prepared for a merchandising firm?
2. What is the usefulness of the gross profit calculation?
3. What is the sequence of events in the sales and collection cycle?
4. What accounts are used to modify sales revenue?
5. What is the sequence of events in the purchase and payment cycle?
6. How is the cost of goods sold calculated?
7. What is the periodic inventory system, and how does it differ from the perpetual inventory system?
8. How is ending inventory recorded in the accounts under the periodic inventory system?
9. What internal control features are incorporated in the perpetual inventory system?
10. How do closing entries for a merchandiser differ from those prepared for a service business?
11. What are the advantages of classified financial statements?
12. What is the distinction between selling expenses and general and administrative expenses?
13. How do extraordinary items differ from prior-period adjustments?
14. What is the distinction between current items and non-current items disclosed in the balance sheet?
15. What is short-term solvency analysis, and why is it important?
16. How can the efficiency with which an entity uses its assets be established?

A. The Calculation of Gross Profit

Merchandising
The activity of buying and selling goods that are already made.

Gross profit
The excess of the sales price over the net cost of the goods sold, also referred to as *gross margin*.

The income statement for a merchandising firm differs from that prepared for entities providing a service. The differences result from the fact that **merchandising** involves the purchase and subsequent resale of goods; matching the cost of the goods sold with the sales revenue generated from this sale is emphasized in the income statement. An income statement for a merchandising entity discloses this matching of cost with revenue in a different manner from that used by a service business; it shows the calculation of a **gross profit**, the excess of sales revenue over the cost of goods sold. A simple gross profit analysis was made for management of Bluebeard Computer Corporation when they were evaluating the start of their merchandising operations. The data involved the purchase for resale (rather than for internal use by BCC) of a portable computer for $2,000. They decided to sell the computer for $3,000. A gross profit calculation was prepared as follows:

Partial Income Statement

Sales	(a)	$3,000
Cost of Goods Sold		2,000
Gross Profit	(b)	$1,000
Gross Profit (%)	(b) ÷ (a)	33⅓%

Cost of goods sold
Accounting term used to describe the cost of merchandise sold during an accounting period.

The $1,000 gross profit is essentially a subtotal calculation, which is usually shown separately in the income statement. This calculation is particularly useful in establishing the spread between the **cost of goods sold** (a computer, which cost BCC $2,000 in this case) and revenue from its sale (the selling price of $3,000).

In the BCC example, the spread, which amounts to $1,000, is the gross profit. The word "gross" is used by accountants to indicate that other expenses incurred in running the business must still be deducted from this amount before net income for the accounting period is established. In other words, the gross profit of $1,000 represents the amount of sales revenue that remains to pay operating expenses, interest expense, and income tax.

A gross profit percentage can be calculated to express the relationship of gross profit to sales. The sale of the portable computer that cost $2,000 results in a 33⅓ percent gross profit. Users of financial statements are interested in establishing this percentage in order to evaluate the performance of this entity with other entities in the same industry; they also want to know whether the percentage is increasing or decreasing from one accounting time period to another. For decision-making purposes, it is important to identify the reasons causing a change. Of necessity, the change in a gross profit percentage must be attributable to a change in either the sales price or the cost, or possibly a combination of both. An illustration of the many facets that make up the cost of goods sold is given in Real Life Example 5-1.

Real Life Example 5-1

The Price is Right

We can estimate what it would cost to produce a typical small PC [personal computer] software package in the customary vinyl folder: about $5 a copy, exclusive of overhead and the mental effort expended to create the software itself.

Now let's look at what you can sell your product for. If you don't know the practices of distribution and mark-ups — and most of us really don't — then you may be in for some shocks.

For the moment, we'll ignore the official list price of your product, or what it ought to be. We'll come back to that subject later. Instead, let's consider everything in terms of a percentage of the list price as is the custom in discussions of distribution and pricing.

Slicing Up the Pie

If we're lucky enough to sell our software to the end-user at 100 percent of the list price, that's all gravy for us. Unfortunately, we can't get it very much of the time. If we want to sell as many copies of our programs as possible and make as much money as possible, we have to get retailers, distributors, discounters, and others involved and give each a slice of the pie. As it turns out, they expect a bigger slice than most people imagine.

It's customary for a retail store to buy its goods at roughly 60 percent of the list price. It sounds as though they're getting 40 percent of your customer's dollar, but retailers have rent, salespeople to pay, and lots of overhead costs. Retailers don't bank much of their 40 percent cut.

The same holds true, by the way, of the mail-order discounters. Discounters save overhead and pass it on to the end-user. They typically sell at about 70 to 75 percent of the list price and cover their costs and profit on a margin of 10 to 15 percent, instead of the retailer's 40 percent.

If you're lucky enough to be selling directly to retailers and not being buried alive in the process, then you're doing very nicely to be getting up to 60 percent of the list price of your programs. There is a good reason, though, why software distributors exist. Distributors act as buffers between software producers and computer retail stores. A retail store can turn to a distributor for one-stop shopping instead of ordering from dozens of suppliers and trying to keep track of who ships quickly and reliably and who takes frightfully long to send the goods. From the point of view of a retailer, the distributor smooths out the uneven response time from software producers. Budding software producers like us get a lot from distributors as well: one source of orders instead of a

B.   The Sales and Collection Cycle

Sales
An account used to accumulate revenue transactions wherein merchandise is sold to others.

A retail or wholesale merchandising entity accumulates revenue in a **Sales** account. Sales of merchandise on account result in an accounts receivable; the subsequent collection of cash completes the sales and collection cycle, which is sometimes identified as the revenue cycle. The distinct transactions making up this cycle are influenced by marketing techniques that are designed to increase sales. For example, a customer may be permitted to return merchandise if it is not satisfactory; an allowance may be given if the merchandise is damaged or differs cosmetically from that ordered. Collection techniques also affect the transactions in this cycle; discounts may be permitted for prompt payment. These techniques are monitored by management through the creation of special general accounts designed for a merchandising or a manufacturing business for sales returns and allowances or for sales discounts.

The sequence of events in the sales and collection cycle is illustrated in Figure 5-1.

Sales

Revenue resulting from the sale of merchandise is recorded in a Sales (revenue) account. An accounts receivable results when the sale is made on account. The sale of Bluebeard's portable computer for $3,000 on account is recorded as follows:

Accounts Receivable	3,000	
Sales		3,000

flood of phone calls from many stores, a sales force that knows all those computer stores, and an accounting department that knows how to pay its bills.

Distributors get their own slice of pie. Retailers buy from the distributors at about 60 percent of list, and the distributors expect to buy from us at no more than 40 percent of list. Often they will require a price as low as 35 or even 30 percent.

The Publisher's Piece

If you end up selling your product for about 35 percent of the list price, you make a lot less profit than you might have expected. Let's suppose that you've created a game or some other piece of software that can't sell for a high ticket price. Typical game prices are $30, $35, $40 tops. Let's slice up the pie on a $30 product.

The customer pays 100 percent, $30. The retailer pockets 40 percent, $12, to cover costs and profit, passing on $18 to the distributor, who pockets 25 percent or $7.50. You get your 35 percent, some $10.50. But unlike everyone else, you've got the actual production cost, which we ball-park at $5, so your gross profit is a mere $5.50. For you, though, that's just a gross — out of it you have to cover your overhead, including any advertising you might be doing. Whatever is left is your profit as software author and software publisher — not sudden riches in anyone's book.

We've been assuming all along that you're both author and publisher of your own software. What if you don't plan on wearing both hats? Perhaps you've written something and you'd just as soon let someone else have the hassles of publishing it.

Although any kind of deal can be struck, the software publishing business has settled down to some stable standards that closely match the customs of the book publishing business. An often-quoted figure is a royalty to the author of 15 percent of the publisher's gross. That's not, as many people assume, 15 percent of the list price. In the case of software publishing, it's typically 15 percent of 35 percent of the list — or a net royalty of about 5 percent of list. For our hypothetical $30 software package, the royalty would be about $1.50 on each copy. That's far from a fat slice of the pie, but the author is relieved of all the business of making and selling and is responsible just for creating (which the business world never considered an important activity anyway).

It should be clear now why so much software is priced in the hundreds of dollars. It takes lots of investment in teams of programmers and in advertising to get big, serious software onto the streets. While a kitchen table software house might be able to thrive on a gross profit of $5 or $10, Ashton-Tate, MicroPro, and Peachtree can't. If a software publisher needs $100 gross profit to pay those hungry programmers, then his/her product is going to have a list price in the $300 to $400 range.

Source Peter Norton, ''Make Sure the Price Is Right'', *P.C. Magazine*, June 26, 1984.

The Sales account is a revenue account, similar to the Repair Revenue account used when BCC had not begun merchandising operations; the normal balance of the Sales account is a credit balance. It is commonly referred to as gross sales because it excludes amounts resulting from sales returns and allowances or from sales discounts. Only sales of merchandise purchased for resale are recorded in this account. The disposal of other corporate assets, such as equipment or a truck, are not credited to the Sales account; rather, the cost of these assets is removed from the appropriate asset account with a gain or loss being recognized.

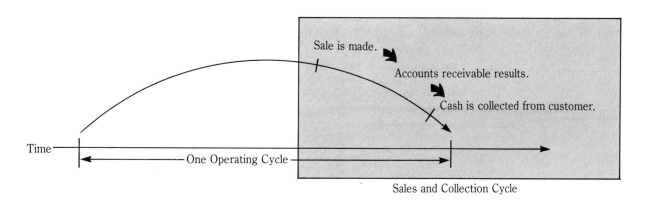

Figure 5-1 The sales and collection cycle

Other accounts involved in keeping track of the revenue-generating activities of a merchandising firm are contra accounts. They are contra accounts because they are deducted from Sales; in this way a net sales amount is calculated for a particular accounting time period. As noted in the introduction, these additional accounts are identified as Sales Returns and Allowances, and Sales Discounts.

Sales Returns and Allowances

Sales Returns and Allowances
A contra account to sales; goods returned by customers or price adjustments allowed to customers are recorded in this account.

It is not unusual for merchandise to be returned to the retailer by the customer. It may be the wrong model, it may be defective, or the merchandise may have been damaged in shipment; a reduction in the sales price may result. The amount of merchandise returns and allowances given on merchandise is accumulated in a **Sales Returns and Allowances** contra account. A $100 allowance for damage to a BCC computer during shipment to a customer is recorded by the following entry:

Sales Returns and Allowances	100	
Accounts Receivable		100

A separate account is used to accumulate the amount of sales returns and allowances for purposes of control. A large balance in this account is a signal to management of a potential problem that requires study and resolution.

The Sales Returns and Allowances account is a Sales contra account and is deducted from the Sales balance when preparing an income statement. In this way, the reported sales revenue is reduced by the amount of returns and allowances. Accounts Receivable is credited (assuming the original sale was made on account), since the amount owing from the customer is reduced.

Sales Discounts

Sales Discounts
A contra account to Sales; cash discounts taken by customers if payment is made within a certain discount period are recorded in this account.

Another Sales contra account, **Sales Discounts**, accumulates sales discounts. These may apply to a sale made on account, if the customer pays within a time period that is specified on the sales invoice. For example, the sales terms may require payment within 30 days. However, a discount is often permitted if payment is made earlier. The exact terms are stated on the sales invoice of Bluebeard Computer Corporation as "2/10, n30". This short form means that the amount owed must be paid within 30 days; however, if the customer chooses to pay within 10 days, a 2 percent discount can be deducted by the customer from the amount owed.

Consider the sale on account of BCC's $3,000 personal computer (less the $100 return for damage), with the above terms. Payment within 10 days entitles the customer to a $58 discount, calculated as follows: ($3,000 − $100 allowance) = $2,900 × 0.02 = $58. Note that the discount percentage is applied directly to the selling price involved. BCC receives $2,842 cash ($2,900 − $58) and prepares the following entry, if payment is made within the discount period.

Cash	2,842	
Sales Discounts	58	
Accounts Receivable		2,900

The Sales Discounts account is also a Sales contra account and is deducted from the Sales balance when preparing an income statement. In this way, the reported sales revenue is reduced by the amount of the discount; in effect, sales discounts are considered as a reduction of the selling price.

If Bluebeard had sold a computer and subsequently allowed a $100 allowance and $58 discount, these amounts would be deducted from sales in the calculation of net sales as follows:

Sales			$3,000
Less:	Sales Returns and Allowances	$100	
	Sales Discounts	58	158
Net Sales			$2,842

Because they are usually immaterial in amount, the amounts of the Sales Returns and Allowances and Sales Discounts contra accounts are often omitted on income statements of merchandisers; their disclosure consists simply of the net Sales amount.

C. The Purchase and Payment Cycle

A merchandising entity usually makes its purchases of items for resale on account; the subsequent payment of cash completes the purchase and payment cycle, which forms part of a broader revenue expenditure cycle that encompasses selling, general and administrative, and other expenses. The distinct transactions of the purchase and payment cycle are the focus of this section. For example, purchasing activities include the occasional return to a supplier of merchandise; often an allowance is given by a supplier for damaged merchandise. These transactions result in the reduction of the amount due to the supplier. If the amount has already been paid, then an asset, an Accounts Receivable, results. Purchase activities involve the payment of transportation associated with the purchase. Payment activities also include the availability of discounts for prompt payment. These activities are monitored by management through the special general ledger accounts for purchases returns and allowances, purchases discounts, and transportation in. The sequences of events in the purchase and payment cycle is illustrated in Figure 5-2.

It is important to note that, in actual practice, the cash payment may follow the collection of cash resulting from sale of the item; the actual sequence of cash payments and cash collections is influenced by the length of time between delivery from a supplier and sale to a customer. Purchases, the calculation of the cost of goods sold, and the accounting for inventory are discussed in the following sections.

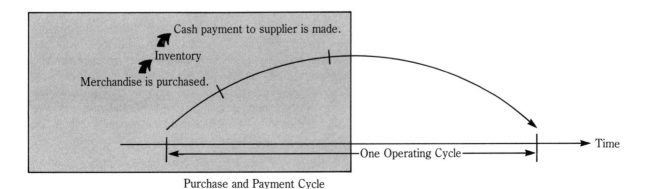

Purchase and Payment Cycle

Figure 5-2   The purchase and payment cycle

Purchases

Purchases
Expense accounts used to accumulate the purchase cost of merchandise held for resale.

The cost of merchandise from suppliers is recorded in the *Purchases* account. An account payable results when the purchase is made on account. When BCC purchases a portable computer from its supplier on account, the transaction is recorded as follows:

Purchases	2,000	
Accounts Payable		2,000

Only the purchase of merchandise for resale is recorded in the Purchases account; the Purchases account has a debit balance. Purchases of supplies to be used in the business or purchases of other assets are recorded in other more appropriate accounts, as was discussed in preceding chapters.

Establishing Cost of Goods Sold

Merchandise inventory
Goods held for resale by a retailer or a wholesaler.

In order to establish the cost of goods sold in an accounting period, the number of items for sale must be controlled. An important difference between a merchandising firm and a service business relates to the existence of **inventory**, in this case, any merchandise for sale held by the entity between delivery from the supplier and sale to a customer. It is not unusual to have merchandise on hand at the end of an accounting time period; such merchandise is called ending inventory. For example, assume that Bluebeard Computer Corporation made the following purchases and sales during a particular time period:

Purchases	5	portable computers at $2,000 each
Less: Sales	−3	portable computers at $3,000 each
Ending Inventory	2	portable computers at $2,000 each

The gross profit calculation for that time period would be as follows:

Gross Profit Calculation

	Units		*Dollars*
Sales (net)	3		$9,000
Cost of Goods Sold:			
Cost of Purchases	5	$10,000	
Less: Ending Inventory	−2	4,000	
Total Cost of Goods Sold	3		6,000
Gross Profit			$3,000

The format used for this calculation is patterned after the income statement. The units included in this calculation are not actually indicated on an income statement; they are shown here to demonstrate that sales of 3 units are matched with the purchase cost of 3 units in the calculation of gross profit. The remaining 2 units comprise ending inventory.

In this example, the cost of ending inventory is deducted from the cost of the 5 units purchased; in this way, the cost of the 3 units sold is matched with the sales revenue generated from their sale. An understanding of the deduction methodology used in the calculation of cost of goods sold can be facilitated by the following comparison:

Conventional Method		*Income Statement Method*	
Units Purchased	5	Units Purchased	5
Less: Units Sold	3	*Less:* Ending Inventory	2
Equals: Ending Inventory	2	*Equals:* Units Sold	3

The gross profit amount is a subtotal calculation on the income statement; its disclosure is designed to facilitate evaluation of an entity's operations during a particular time period. Its disclosure is not required, but is often made. The gross profit may not be disclosed for any number of reasons; one often cited is marketing strategy: management often doesn't want competitors to have this information.

Opening Inventory

The ending inventory of one accounting time period becomes the opening inventory of the next accounting time period. Assume that Bluebeard Computer Corporation had the following transactions in the next accounting time period:

Opening Inventory	2 portable computers at $2,000 each
Purchases	6 portable computers at $2,000 each
Sales	5 portable computers at $3,000 each

The gross profit calculation disclosed on the interim income statement of both accounting periods appears below. Note that the ending inventory in Period 1 becomes the opening inventory of Period 2.

	Period 1		Period 2	
	Units	*Dollars*	*Units*	*Dollars*
Sales (net)	3	$9,000	5	$15,000
Cost of Goods Sold:				
Opening Inventory	0		2	$ 4,000
Cost of Purchases	5	$10,000	6	12,000
Goods Available	5		8	$16,000
Less: Ending Inventory	−2	4,000	−3	6,000
Total Cost of Goods Sold	3	6,000	5	10,000
Gross Profit		$3,000		$ 5,000

Again, although units are not actually included in an income statement, they are shown here to emphasize the matching of costs with revenues. In Period 2, 8 portable computers are available for sale; 3 are not sold and are indicated as ending inventory. The cost of the 5 portable computers sold is matched with the revenue generated from the sale of these 5 portable computers.

Students usually find it difficult to follow the income statement calculation of cost of goods sold. This calculation can be further illustrated as follows:

	Opening Inventory
+	Cost of Purchases
=	Cost of Goods Available for Sale
−	Ending Inventory
=	Cost of Goods Sold.

This discussion has focused on purchases and inventory in the calculation of cost of goods sold. There are, however, several other accounts also used in merchandising operations.

> There are two contra accounts deducted from purchases in the calculation of net purchases. These accounts are:
> 1. Purchases Returns and Allowance, and
> 2. Purchases Discounts.
> There is also an account which is included in the cost of purchases for the accounting time period. This account is:
> 3. Transportation In.

These additional accounts are necessary in merchandising operations to accumulate amounts for activities related to the purchase of merchandise for resale. These accounts provide additional information for decision-making purposes.

Purchases Returns and Allowances

Purchases Returns and Allowances
A contra account to Purchases; goods returned to suppliers or price adjustments allowed by suppliers are recorded in this account.

Assume that one computer sent to Bluebeard by a supplier is slightly damaged. When purchased merchandise is not satisfactory, it may be returned to the supplier, or an allowance that reduces the purchase amount may be received from the supplier. The amount of purchases return or allowance is accumulated in a separate **Purchases Returns and Allowances** account. If the account has not yet been paid, a $100 allowance for BCC would be recorded by the following entry:

Accounts Payable	100	
Purchases Returns and Allowances		100

Accounts Payable is debited, as the item was supplied on account and has not yet been paid for.

A separate account is used to accumulate purchases returns and allowances for purposes of control. A large balance signals management that a particular supplier or group of suppliers may require attention. For instance, investors in the stock of Verbatim — a Sunnyvale, California manufacturer of floppy disks — were recently startled to learn that one of the company's largest customers had returned some $2 to $3 million-worth of disks. Industry sources report that the Verbatim customer in question was IBM and that the disks were rejected because Verbatim had changed the design of the disk jacket so that its corners were more pointed than on the disks previously supplied by the manufacturer.[1]

The Purchases Returns and Allowances account is a Purchases contra account and is deducted from the amount of Purchases when preparing an income statement. In this way, the reported purchase cost is reduced by the amount of returns and allowances.

Purchases Discounts

Purchases Discounts
A contra account to Purchases; cash discounts taken if payment is made within a certain discount period.

Another Purchases contra account, **Purchases Discounts**, accumulates purchases discounts. These may apply to purchases made on account, if payment is made within a time period specified in the supplier's invoice. For example, the terms on the $2,000 invoice for one portable computer received by Bluebeard indicates "1/15, n45". This shorthand means that the $2,000 must be paid within 45 days; however, if payment is made within 15 days, a 1 percent discount can be taken.

Consider the slightly damaged computer received by BCC. If the 1/15, n45 terms apply to its purchase, and the accounting policy of the company is to take advantage of such discounts, Bluebeard will make the payment within 15 days. The supplier's terms entitle Bluebeard to deduct $19 calculated as follows: $(\$2,000 - \$100) = \$1,900 \times 0.01 = \$19$. Therefore, an $1,881 cash payment is made to the supplier and is recorded as follows:

Accounts Payable	1,900	
Purchases Discounts		19
Cash		1,881

The Purchases Discounts account, a Purchases contra account, is deducted from the amount of Purchases in the income statement. In this way, the cost of purchases is reduced by the discounts taken.

Transportation In

fob shipping point
A term indicating that title to shipped goods passes when the goods leave the shipping point.

fob destination
A term indicating that title to shipped goods passes when the goods reach their destination.

Transportation In
Expense account used to accumulate freight charges on merchandise purchased for resale; these charges are added to the purchase cost of this merchandise.

The purchase invoice for merchandise usually indicates who will pay for the cost of transporting it. The term "fob" (meaning "free on board") is commonly used: **fob shipping point** means the purchaser pays, and **fob destination** means the supplier pays.

Assuming that Bluebeard's supplier sells on the basis of fob shipping point, the transportation cost is the responsibility of Bluebeard and its cash payment would be recorded as follows:

Transportation In	125	
Cash		125

The **Transportation In** account is added to the cost of Purchases in the income statement. In this way the reported cost of purchases is increased by the amount for transportation.

An alternate way of accounting for transportation could have been used in this case. Although Bluebeard is responsible for the costs involved, the shipment could have been "freight prepaid" by the supplier. In this case, the supplier would have paid the transportation and BCC would have to reimburse the supplier. Of course, no discount for prompt payment would apply in this situation.

Alternatively, if Bluebeard purchased from a supplier whose terms were fob destination, and the shipment had been sent "freight collect", then BCC would deduct the transportation charges owed to that supplier.

Cost of purchases
Purchases less purchases returns and allowances and purchases discounts, plus transportation in; also referred to as cost of goods purchased.

The composition of the **cost of purchases** made during the accounting period is therefore calculated as: purchases less purchases returns or allowances and purchases discounts plus transportation in. The cost of BCC's purchased computer is as follows:

Purchases		$2,000
Less: Purchases Returns and Allowances	$100	
Purchases Discounts	19	119
Net purchases		$1,881
Add: Transportation In		125
Total Cost of Goods Purchased		$2,006

The cost of goods purchased can also be indicated as Cost of Purchases on the income statement.

Inventory

The Periodic Inventory Method

Periodic inventory method
A method whereby a record of the opening inventory and purchases during the period is kept. Ending inventory is calculated by physically counting the goods on hand and assigning a cost to these goods; all goods not on hand at the end of the period are assumed to have been sold.

Accounting for purchases, as described here, is in accordance with an inventory control system called the **periodic inventory method**. Merchandise purchased for resale is recorded into a Purchases account; whenever financial statements are prepared, a physical count is made to determine the amount of inventory on hand. The amount of goods sold during the accounting period is calculated at the time these financial statements are prepared, as discussed earlier. Therefore, the change in inventory between the beginning and end of an accounting time period is recorded only periodically, usually at year-end. The inter-relationship of inventory disclosed in the income statement and balance sheet can be illustrated as follows:

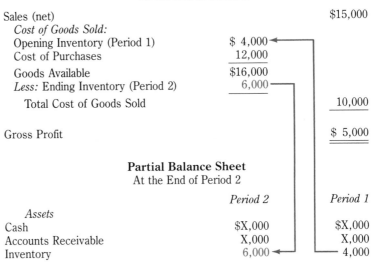

Partial Income Statement
At the End of Period 2

Sales (net)		$15,000
Cost of Goods Sold:		
Opening Inventory (Period 1)	$ 4,000	
Cost of Purchases	12,000	
Goods Available	$16,000	
Less: Ending Inventory (Period 2)	6,000	
Total Cost of Goods Sold		10,000
Gross Profit		$ 5,000

Partial Balance Sheet
At the End of Period 2

	Period 2	Period 1
Assets		
Cash	$X,000	$X,000
Accounts Receivable	X,000	X,000
Inventory	6,000	4,000

A physical count of inventory requires careful planning and accurate inventory-taking procedures. For instance, pre-numbered inventory tags can be attached to all inventory items; quantities are recorded on these tags; the numerical sequence of the completed tags is subsequently checked to ensure that all counted quantities are accounted for.

The periodic inventory system is most useful where many different or low value items are kept in stock and where maintaining detailed records would be expensive.

The Perpetual Inventory System

Perpetual inventory system
A method of inventory valuation in which purchases and sales are recorded as they occur and a continuous balance of inventory on hand is calculated in terms of units and often in terms of cost. The cost of goods sold is determined for

Under the **perpetual inventory system** a continuous balance of inventory on hand is calculated in terms of units and, often, in terms of cost. As a purchase is received, the quantity received is added to the quantity recorded as being on hand. When inventory is sold, the sold units are deducted and a new balance of inventory on hand is calculated. Inventory on hand at the end of the accounting period is counted to verify the quantities actually on hand. One cause of fluctuations in the gross profit percentage can be inventory losses through theft and errors; management control over inventory, if this is the case, needs to be strengthened.

The perpetual inventory system, therefore, incorporates an important internal control feature. Losses resulting from theft and error can easily be determined when the actual

each sale and is recorded. A physical count at the end of the period is used to verify the quantities that should be on hand.

quantity counted is compared with the quantities that ought to be on hand. This advantage is reduced, however, by the time and expense required for continuously updating the inventory records. Computerization makes this record-keeping easier and less expensive, particularly when the inventory system is tied into the sales system, so that inventory is updated whenever a sale is recorded. The actual procedures involved in a perpetual inventory system and the impact of inventory errors on the income statement are further discussed in Chapter 8.

Purchase and Payment: Related Recording

Debit and Credit Memos

Debit or credit memo
A document issued to alter an amount between seller and purchaser.

The return of merchandise, the granting of an allowance, or the discovery of an invoicing error are among the reasons for the preparation of a document referred to as a **debit** or **credit memo**. The accounting for such memos involves a different account when dealing with sales, as opposed to purchases. The Accounts Receivable account is debited or credited when a sales-related memo is issued; a purchase-related memo involves Accounts Payable. A debit or credit memo can be issued by either the seller or the purchaser.

Seller-Issued Memos
• A debit memo issued by a seller results in a debit to the customer's Accounts Receivable account. The increase in the amount due from the customer could be, for instance, the result of a calculation error in an original invoice which undercharged the customer.
• A credit memo issued by a seller results in a credit to the customer's Accounts Receivable account. This decrease in the receivable may be, for instance, the result of an allowance for damaged goods granted to the customer.

Purchaser-Issued Memos
• A debit memo issued by a purchaser results in a debit to the supplier's Accounts Payable account. This decrease in the amount owed to the supplier may be, for instance, a result of a pricing error in an original invoice which overcharged the purchaser.
• A credit memo issued by a purchaser credits the supplier's Accounts Payable account. This credit memo increases the amount owed the supplier.

Trade Discounts

Trade discount
A percentage or dollar amount used to calculate the actual sales or purchase price of merchandise.

The preceding discussion of sales and purchases involved use of an established dollar amount for price. In actual practice, these amounts are often determined through use of a suggested list price in conjunction with a catalogue indicating the merchandise offered. **Trade discounts** from the suggested list price are used to calculate prices for different categories of buyers and for different quantities. For example, a 30 percent discount may be offered to colleges and universities, and a different discount percentage to retailers. Trade discounts can be in terms of a percentage or dollar amount deducted from the suggested list price.

A Bluebeard software package with a suggested list price of $250 less a 20 percent discount would be priced at $200 = ($250 × 20% trade discount).

The sale to a BCC customer of this software would be recorded as follows:			The purchase by BCC from a supplier of this software would be recorded as follows:		
Accounts Receivable	200		Purchases	200	
Sales		200	Accounts Payable		200

The amount of the trade discount, $50 in this case, is not recorded in the books and should not be confused with cash discounts offered for prompt payment; the recording of cash discounts for both sales and purchases was discussed previously.

D.   Completion of the Worksheet

As in the case of a service business, the completion of a worksheet for a merchandising firm organizes the many details that must be brought together when financial statements are being prepared. As well, the worksheet gives the accountant a preview of the final statements before they are actually prepared.

The adjacent completed worksheet is for Bluebeard Computer Corporation for 19X3. Note that the opening inventory is extended to the income statement debit column. Ending inventory is recorded directly on the worksheet as a credit in the income statement columns and as a debit in the balance sheet columns.

Note that the worksheet for a merchandising firm differs in one respect from that of the service business: the treatment of inventory.

1. Opening inventory appears in the trial balance as $80,000. This amount has not changed during the year because Bluebeard follows the periodic inventory system in recording the purchase of merchandise for resale in the Purchases Account. The Merchandise Inventory account remains unchanged until the closing entries are recorded.
2. The opening inventory amount is transferred to the income statement debit column because it is later used in the calculation of the cost of goods sold sub-total, which appears in the income statement.
3. The amount of ending inventory is recorded directly on the worksheet:
    a. as a credit in the income statement columns because it is later used in the calculation of cost of goods sold; in this calculation, it is deducted from the cost of goods available for sale, and
    b. as a debit in the balance sheet columns because it represents the amount of inventory at year-end; an asset appearing in the balance sheet requires a debit balance.

The recording of the ending inventory amount into the records is discussed later in this chapter.

After the recording of ending inventory in the worksheet, the columns are added and balanced, as explained in Chapter 4. Note that there are no adjusted trial balance columns; this set of columns is simply an intermediate step between the recording of adjustments and the transfer of adjusted balances to the income statement and balance sheet columns. Omission of the adjusted trial balance columns reduces the time required to complete the worksheet without any corresponding loss of accuracy.

Bluebeard Computer Corporation
Worksheet
For the Year Ended December 31, 19X3

Account Number	Account Title	Trial Balance Dr.	Trial Balance Cr.	Adjustments Dr.	Adjustments Cr.	Adjusted Trial Balance Dr.	Adjusted Trial Balance Cr.	Income Statement Dr.	Income Statement Cr.	Balance Sheet Dr.	Balance Sheet Cr.
101	Cash	10,800								10,800	
110	Accounts Receivable	26,000								26,000	
150	Merchandise Inventory	80,000						80,000	120,000	120,000	
161	Prepaid Insurance	2,400			(a) 1,200					1,200	
183	Equipment	13,600								13,600	
193	Accum. Deprec.–Eqpmt.		–		(b) 1,600						1,600
201	Bank Loan — Current		39,000								39,000
210	Accounts Payable		25,000								25,000
260	Income Tax Payable		–		(c) 15,000						15,000
271	Bank Loan—Long-Term		48,500								48,500
320	Common Stock		10,000								10,000
340	Retained Earnings		21,750								21,750
350	Dividends	4,250								4,250	
500	Sales		308,500						308,500		
508	Sales Returns and										
	Allowances	6,000						6,000			
509	Sales Discounts	2,500						2,500			
550	Purchases	240,000						240,000			
558	Purchases Returns and										
	Allowances		12,600						12,600		
559	Purchases Discounts		2,400						2,400		
560	Transportation In	15,000						15,000			
610	Advertising Expense	10,000						10,000			
615	Commissions Expense	15,000						15,000			
620	Delivery Expense	6,000						6,000			
632	Interest Expense	10,000						10,000			
654	Rent Expense	3,600						3,600			
656	Salaries Expense	20,000						20,000			
669	Telephone Expense	1,080						1,080			
676	Utilities Expense	1,520						1,520			
	Totals	467,750	467,750								
623	Deprec. Expense–Eqpmt.			(a) 1,200				1,200			
631	Insurance Expense			(b) 1,600				1,600			
830	Income Tax Expense			(c) 15,000				15,000			
	Totals			17,800	17,800			428,500	443,500	175,850	160,850
	Net Income for the Year							15,000			15,000
	Totals							443,500	443,500	175,850	175,850

Closing Entries

The recording of adjusting entries from the worksheet and subsequent preparation of closing entries, as illustrated in Chapter 4, also applies to merchandisers. At the end of a fiscal year, the revenue and expense accounts are reduced to a zero balance, so that they can begin to accumulate amounts of the new fiscal year. Closing entries are prepared to close these income statement accounts; dividend accounts are also closed at the end of the corporate year.

The closing process for merchandisers includes new Sales and Purchases accounts, as well as their contra accounts. The closing procedure remains the same as for service entities; all accounts listed in the income statement columns are transferred to the Income Summary account. This includes the debit balance relating to opening inventory and the credit balance relating to the ending inventory.

Under the periodic inventory system, the opening inventory is removed, and ending inventory recorded, as part of the closing process. The following T-account illustrates how this occurs.

	Merchandise Inventory *No. 150*	
Jan. 1 Opening bal.	80,000	
Less: Opening inventory (closing entry posted)		80,000
Bal.	-0-	
Add: Ending inventory	120,000	
Dec. 31 Ending bal.	120,000	

The closing entries prepared for Bluebeard Computer Corporation at December 31, 19X3 are shown in Figure 5-3. Note the inclusion of the Merchandise Inventory opening and ending balances.

Entry 1
The revenue accounts are closed in one compound closing journal entry to the Income Summary account. (All revenue accounts with credit balances are debited to bring them to zero. Their balances are transferred to the Income Summary account.)

Entry 2
The expense accounts are closed in one compound closing journal entry to the Income Summary account. (All expense accounts with debit balances are credited to bring them to zero. Their balances are transferred to the Income Summary account.)

Entry 3
The Income Summary account is next closed to the Retained Earnings account.

Entry 4
The dividend account is closed directly to the Retained Earnings account. Since Dividends is not an expense account, it is not closed to Income Summary; rather, it is closed

directly to Retained Earnings, because dividends are a distribution of earnings made by the corporation to its owners, the shareholders.

GENERAL JOURNAL

Date 19X1		Description	F	Debit	Credit
		Closing Entries			
Dec	31	Merchandise Inventory (ending)	150	120 000 -	
		Sales	500	308 500 -	
		Purchases Returns	558	12 600 -	
		Purchases Discounts	559	2400 -	
		Income Summary	360		443 500 -
		To record ending inventory and			
		to close income statement			
		accounts with a credit balance.			
	31	Income Summary	360	428 500 -	
		Merchandise Inventory (opening)	150		80 000 -
		Sales Returns and Allowances	508		6000 -
		Sales Discounts	509		2500 -
		Purchases	550		240 000 -
		Transportation In	560		15 000 -
		Advertising Expense	610		10 000 -
		Commissions Expense	615		15 000 -
		Delivery Expense	620		6000 -
		Depreciation Expense - Equipment	623		1600 -
		Insurance Expense	631		1200 -
		Interest Expense	632		10 000 -
		Rent Expense	654		3600 -
		Salaries Expense	656		20 000 -
		Telephone Expense	669		1080 -
		Utilities Expense	676		1520 -
		Income Tax Expense	830		15 000 -
		To record opening inventory and			
		to close income statement			
		accounts with a debit balance.			
	31	Income Summary	360	15 000 -	
		Retained Earnings	340		15 000 -
		To close Income Summary account.			
	31	Retained Earnings	340	4250 -	
		Dividends	350		4250 -
		To close Dividend account.			

Figure 5-3   Closing entries

E.   Classified Financial Statements

Classification
The grouping of accounts on financial statements by category.

Accountants are concerned with the application of GAAP to the recording of financial transactions; the impact of GAAP on the accounting process has been the focus of preceding chapters. This section focuses on the preparation of financial statements, that is, the disclosure in financial statements of financial information recorded in the company's books. The issues involved include financial statement preparation and **classification** (the way accounts are grouped). Real Life Example 5-2 includes the financial statements for 1985 for Circo Craft Co. Inc.

The Classified Income Statement

In actual practice, the income statement of a merchandising firm is usually classified, that is, revenues and expenses are broken into categories with subtotals provided for each classification. This classification highlights inter-relationships of important amounts by making the information readily available.

The importance of the gross profit subtotal was previously discussed; it represents the amount of sales revenue that remains to pay expenses necessary to operate the business (operating expenses) and financing expenses, such as interest expense and the amount paid to the entity's silent partner, the government, as income tax expense. The balance is the bottom line — the net income amount. Net income represents the return on shareholders' investment and the amount available for dividends to shareholders. For bankers, the net income represents the ability of the entity to expand its operations through debt financing and its ability to support increased interest charges that result from increased debt. For labour unions, the entity's net income is an indication of what they perceive as a basis for increased salary demands in labour negotiations.

Operating expenses
Expenses incurred in the operation of the business, except items classified as *other expenses* or as *income tax expense*.

The adjacent classified income statement of Bluebeard Computer Corporation for the year ended December 31, 19X3 also includes the classification of **operating expenses** into two categories: selling expenses and general and administrative expenses.

Selling expenses — those incurred to sell the merchandise — are classified as part of operating expenses. General and administrative expenses are those incurred to administer the merchandising operations. While most operating expenses are easily distinguished as one or the other category, some require allocation; for example, rent expense may include both the sales area and the office. Sometimes, classification is made on the basis of expediency, particularly if the amounts involved are not material; insurance expense, which covers both the sales area and office space, has not been allocated by Bluebeard.

Interest expense is classified separately because of the impact that financing the entity's activities through debt has on the bottom line calculation of net income.

The 19X3 year-end income statement illustrates all the major classifications required for Bluebeard. Other entities may require further classifications indicating other subtotals to highlight important inter-relationships relevant to specific aspects of their operations.

In actual practice, the financial statements would indicate not only the 19X3 data, but the comparative data for the preceding year, 19X2 in this case. These are then referred to as comparative financial statements; comparative amounts would be provided in each of the financial statements prepared. (See the financial statements for Circo Craft in Real Life Example 5-2 for an example.)

Often a condensed income statement is reproduced in published annual reports. One such condensed statement could be designed as shown on page 200.

Bluebeard Computer Corporation
Income Statement
For the Year Ended December 31, 19X3

Sales			$308,500
Less: Sales Returns and Allowances		$ 6,000	
Sales Discounts		2,500	8,500
Net Sales			$300,000
Cost of Goods Sold:			
Opening Inventory (Jan. 1)		$ 80,000	
Purchases	$240,000		
Less: Purchases Returns and Allowances $12,600			
Purchases Discounts 2,400	15,000		
Net Purchases	$225,000		
Add: Transportation In	15,000		
Cost of Goods Purchased		240,000	
Cost of Goods Available		$320,000	
Ending Inventory (Dec. 31)		120,000	
Total Cost of Goods Sold			200,000
Gross Profit			$100,000
Operating Expenses:			
Selling Expenses:			
Advertising Expense	$ 10,000		
Commissions Expense	15,000		
Delivery Expense	6,000		
Total Selling Expenses		$ 31,000	
General and Administrative Expenses:			
Depreciation — Equipment	$ 1,600		
Insurance Expense	1,200		
Rent Expense	3,600		
Salaries Expense	20,000		
Telephone Expense	1,080		
Utilities Expense	1,520		
Total General and Administrative Expenses		29,000	
Total Operating Expenses			60,000
Income from Operations			$ 40,000
Financing Costs:			
Interest Expense			10,000
Income (before income tax)			$ 30,000
Income Tax			15,000
Net Income for the Year			$ 15,000

Bluebeard Computer Corporation
Income Statement
For the Year Ended December 31, 19X3

Net Sales		$300,000
Costs and Expenses:		
Cost of Goods Sold	$200,000	
Selling, General and Administrative	58,400	
Depreciation	1,600	260,000
Income from Operations		$ 40,000
Financing Costs:		
Interest Expense		10,000
Income (before income tax)		$ 30,000
Income Tax		15,000
Net Income for the Year		$ 15,000

Note that, for disclosure purposes, in accordance with GAAP, the depreciation has been shown separately from the amount of general and administrative expenses. The total amount still agrees with the selling and general and administrative expenses reported on the preceding classified income statement.

Extraordinary Items

A further category of items requires special income statement classification. This category comprises unusual items that do not occur regularly and that are material in amount; they are referred to as extraordinary items, examples of which are provided in the *CICA Handbook*, section 3480. They include: (a) the sale or abandonment of a plant or significant segment of the entity, (b) sale of investments not acquired for resale, (c) expropriation of property by government or other regulatory bodies, and (d) the effects of earthquakes, floods, or other similar events.

Because extraordinary items by definition do not occur regularly, separate income statement classification of resulting gains and losses facilitates the evaluation of an entity's normal business activities. Therefore, extraordinary gains and losses are classified on the income statement below the net income for the period. Income tax on income from operations has already been deducted in the calculation of net income for the period; income tax applicable to extraordinary items is classified with the extraordinary item, so that it is separate from income tax applicable to income from operations.

The accountant is also concerned with calculation of the earnings per share of common stock (EPS). One calculation of EPS is made using net income from operations. (The EPS calculation is discussed in detail later in this chapter.)

The Statement of Retained Earnings

The net income (or loss) for the period, as well as dividends for the accounting time period, are reported in the statement of retained earnings. This statement is a link between the income statement and balance sheet. The balance of the Retained Earnings account represents the earnings of the entity that have not been distributed to share-holders as dividends.

Since its inception in 19X1 until the beginning of 19X3, Bluebeard Computer Corporation has retained $21,750. It earned $15,000 in 19X3 and paid $4,250 cash dividends to shareholders during the year. A **dividend** results in the reduction of retained earnings, which consists of net income earned in the current or prior periods. The asset Cash is decreased by the payment, and the shareholders' equity item, Retained Earnings, is also decreased. During 19X3, BCC declared and paid a $4,250 dividend authorized by its board of directors. This payment was recorded by the following entry:

Dividend
A distribution to corporate shareholders; can consist of cash, property of the corporation, or shares of stock.

Dividends	4,250	
Cash		4,250

The pattern of recordng dividend payments is similar to that used for assets and expenses. Debits record an increase in assets, expenses, and dividends.

The 19X3 ending amount of earnings retained in the business amounts to $32,500 ($21,750 + $15,000 − $4,250). This amount of retained earnings is represented by assets held by the corporation; these assets are available not only for use in the future expansion of the business but also to absorb any losses that may occur. If a net loss had occurred in 19X3, the amount of loss would have been deducted from the opening Retained Earnings balance of $21,750.

The adjacent statement of retained earnings is for Bluebeard Computer Corporation for the year ended December 31, 19X3. Note that the Dividends balance is deducted on the statement.

Bluebeard Computer Corporation
Statement of Retained Earnings
For the Year Ended December 31, 19X3

Balance (Jan. 1)	$21,750
Add: Net Income for the Year	15,000
Total	$36,750
Less: Dividends	4,250
Balance (Dec. 31)	$32,500

The net income for the year is taken from the income statement illustrated in an earlier section. This statement discloses the changes during the year to the Retained Earnings account reported in the balance sheet at December 31, 19X3.

Prior-Period Adjustments

Prior-period adjustments
Gains and losses that are applicable to the net income reported in prior years; disclosed in the statement of retained earnings.

An additional category of amounts, referred to as **prior-period adjustments**, are also reported in the statement of retained earnings. This category relates to gains or losses that constitute changes in the net income reported in the prior year. They are excluded from the current year's income statement; they are disclosed in the statement of retained earnings because the net income (or loss) of the prior year is included in the opening Retained Earnings balance.

The recording of adjustments to net income reported in prior periods is restricted by the *CICA Handbook*, section 3600, and is meant to appear infrequently in actual practice. Prior-period adjustments are recorded in the case of non-recurring items, consisting of

adjustments or settlements of income taxes and settlements of claims resulting from litigation, for example. Items are prior-period adjustments only if they have all of the following four characteristics:
• if they are specifically identified with and directly related to the business activities of particular prior periods
• if they are not attributable to economic events, including obsolescence, occuring subsequent to the date of the financial statements for such prior periods
• if they depend primarily on decisions or determinations by persons other than management or owners
• if they could not be reasonably estimated prior to such decisions or determinations.
The more complex aspects of the treatment of prior-period adjustments are the subject matter of intermediate accounting courses.

The Classified Balance Sheet

The merchandiser's balance sheet, like that of a service entity, is prepared from amounts in the balance sheet columns of the worksheet. The classification of accounts into meaningful categories is designed to facilitate the analysis of balance sheet information. Assets and liabilities are customarily classified as either current or long-term.

Current Assets

Current assets is a category which groups certain asset accounts in order of their liquidity, with Cash listed first:

1. Cash, the most liquid asset
2. Temporary Investments, the investment of temporarily idle cash
3. Accounts Receivable that are due to be collected within one year — not as easily converted into cash as temporary investments
4. Notes Receivable that are due to be collected within one year — not as easily converted into cash as accounts receivable.
5. Merchandise Inventory that is expected to be sold within one year — not as easily converted into cash as accounts or notes receivable.

The current asset category also includes accounts whose future benefit is expected to expire in a short period of time. These are not expected to be converted into cash:

6. Prepaid Expenses that will expire in the next year
7. Supplies that will be used during the next year.

For convenience, all prepaid expense and supplies accounts are grouped together into one amount on the balance sheet as Prepaid Expenses. This grouping is convenient, because the amounts are usually small and their individual disclosure would provide no meaningful information to the reader of financial statements.

Long-Term Assets

Long-term assets are commonly referred to as fixed assets in Canada. Fixed assets are customarily listed in the inverse order of their liquidity, with Land shown first.

8. Land on which buildings have been constructed, the least liquid asset
9. Buildings used in the business
10. Equipment installed in the buildings
11. Trucks used in the business.

Since the cost of depreciable assets is allocated to operations over their useful life, the accumulated depreciation contra accounts can be individually deducted from the appropriate fixed asset account in the calculation of a net fixed asset amount. For disclosure purposes however, all accumulated depreciation accounts are usually added together and a lump sum total is deducted from the total fixed asset amount on the balance sheet.

Land that is vacant or other fixed assets that are idle are excluded from the fixed assets category and are disclosed separately as Other Assets.

Current Liabilities

Current liabilities is a category which groups certain liability accounts in order of their due dates, with any bank loans shown first:

1. Bank Loans that are payable on demand or due within the next fiscal year, the most current obligation
2. Accounts Payable, obligations that must be paid within a relatively short period of time
3. Accruals (often small in amount compared with accounts payable) usually grouped with accounts payable and disclosed as ''Accounts Payable and Accruals''
4. The current portion of long-term debt, listed in order of due date in relation to other current liabilities
5. Income tax liabilities usually follow the Accounts Payable and Accruals amount.

The current liability category also includes accounts that represent the unearned portion of amounts received from customers, or that represent obligations to provide goods or services within the next year.

Long-Term Liabilities

The category of long-term liabilities includes all debt not due to be paid within the next year, such as non-current loans, mortgages, and bonds. Reference has been made to the next year in the distinction of assets and liabilities as either current or long-term. Where the operating cycle of the entity is longer than one fiscal year — the manufacture and aging of scotch, for example — exceptions to the one-year rule are permitted.

Equity

The equity category of the classified balance sheet consists of two major accounts: Common Stock and Retained Earnings. Additional subdivisions within the equity category are discussed in Chapter 10.

The following balance sheet illustrates the classification of Bluebeard Corporation's accounts.

Bluebeard Computer Corporation
Balance Sheet
At December 31, 19X3

Assets			*Liabilities*		
CURRENT ASSETS			CURRENT LIABILITIES		
Cash	$ 10,800		Bank Loan — Current	$39,000	
Accounts Receivable	26,000		Accounts Payable	25,000	
Inventory	120,000		Income Tax Payable	15,000	
Prepaid Insurance	1,200				
Total Current Assets		$158,000	Total Current Liabilities		$ 79,000
FIXED ASSETS			LONG-TERM LIABILITIES		
Equipment	$ 13,600		Bank Loan — Long Term		
Accum. Depreciation	1,600		(note 1)		48,500
Total Fixed Assets		12,000			
			Total Liabilities		$127,500
			Shareholders' Equity		
			Common Stock (note 2)	$10,000	
			Retained Earnings	32,500	
			Total Shareholders' Equity		42,500
			Total Liabilities and		
Total Assets		$170,000	Shareholders' Equity		$170,000

Following its financial statements, a corporation discloses what accounting policies it has followed in their preparation. These policies are summarized to facilitate the review and analysis of the financial statements. The matters covered could include revenue recognition, valuation of inventories, the accounting treatment of fixed asset expenditures, the accounting for income taxes, and other issues significant to the business. Any changes in accounting policy from previous years must be noted.

In addition to a discussion of accounting policies, information that helps users of financial statements to understand individual items are indicated through disclosures in notes. These notes may explain extraordinary items or prior-period adjustments, if any, details about income tax matters, transactions with related companies, commitments entered into by the company, and events subsequent to the data of the financial statements which are important and may affect the reader's interpretation.

The 19X3 financial statements of Bluebeard Computer Corporation include the following notes relating to the terms of its bank loan and a description of its common stock.

Note 1 — Bank Loan
The bank loan consists of a 12-percent demand bank loan. Under the terms of this bank loan, Bluebeard has pledged its accounts receivable and inventory as collateral. In addition, certain personal guarantees have been made by one of the shareholders of Bluebeard, and certain insurance policies have been assigned to the bank.

Account form balance sheet
A balance sheet where the liabilities and equities are listed to the right of the assets.

Report form balance sheet
A balance sheet in which the sections for liabilities and equities are listed below those for the assets.

Note 2 — Common Stock

The authorized capital of the company is comprised of an unlimited number of common shares without nominal or par value, of which 10 000 shares are issued and outstanding. The rights of the shareholders include the right to vote at any meeting of shareholders, to receive any dividends as and when declared by the directors of the company, and to receive the remaining property of the company on dissolution.

Balance Sheet Form

The balance sheet can be presented in either the **account form**, that is, with the liabilities and equities presented to the right of the assets, or in the **report form**, with the liabilities and equities presented below the assets. Both formats are acceptable; the account form seems slightly more popular in published financial statements.[2]

F. Evaluation of the Entity

Solvency
The ability to pay current liabilities as they become due.

Accountants, analysts, and investors often talk about the solvency of a company. What does this mean? The term **solvency**, when applied to a company, refers to its ability to pay current liabilities as they become due. Why is it important to know whether a company is solvent? If a company is insolvent, then it is unable to pay its creditors who have provided goods and services on account. The implications of being insolvent are:

> 1. Current Liabilities
> — Creditors can refuse to provide any further goods or services on account.
> — Creditors can sue for payment.
> — Creditors can put the company into bankruptcy.
> 2. Long-Term Liabilities
> — Creditors can refuse to lend additional cash.
> — Creditors can demand repayment of their long-term debts under some circumstances.
> 3. Shareholders' Equity
> — Shareholders risk the loss of their investment if the corporation is placed into bankruptcy.

At the present time, Bluebeard Computer Corporation is a solvent corporation. What is the structure of BCC's creditor financing? An analysis of the company's balance sheet reveals the following liabilities:

	19X3
Current Liabilities	$79,000
Long-Term Liabilities	48,500

This information indicates that the company's management relies on both short-term and long-term creditor financing. If the bank decides not to continue lending money to BCC, its ability to pay its other liabilities as they become due may be compromised. Management needs to be able to analyze its short-term solvency.

Short-Term Solvency Analysis

Ratio
The quotient resulting when one number is divided by another.

Ratios are one way of evaluating any company's solvency. Two commonly used ratios are introduced and explained below:

Ratio analysis
Analysis of inter-relationships of different financial statement items as a method of financial statement evaluation.

Short-Term Solvency Analysis	*Indicates*
1. The Current Ratio	How many current asset dollars exist to pay current liabilities. This ratio is only a crude measure of solvency.
2. The Acid-Test Ratio	Whether the company is able to meet the immediate demands of creditors. This ratio is a more severe measure of solvency. Inventory and prepaid items are excluded from the calculation.

The Current Ratio

Current ratio
Current assets divided by current liabilities; also called the *working capital ratio*.

An overall analysis of solvency is made by a ratio labelled the **current ratio**. Is the firm able to repay short-term creditors? The current ratio answers this question by expressing a relationship between current assets and current liabilities — current assets are divided by current liabilities. These are the relevant BCC financial data required to calculate this ratio:

		19X3
Current Assets	(a)	$158,000
Current Liabilities	(b)	$ 79,000
Current Ratio	(a ÷ b)	2 : 1

The results of this calculation are an indication of how many current asset dollars exist to pay current liabilities. $2 of current assets exists in 19X3 to pay each $1 of current liabilities. Is $2 adequate? Unfortunately, there is no one current ratio which indicates whether an amount is adequate. There are three possibilities in any given situation; these are given in Figure 5-4.

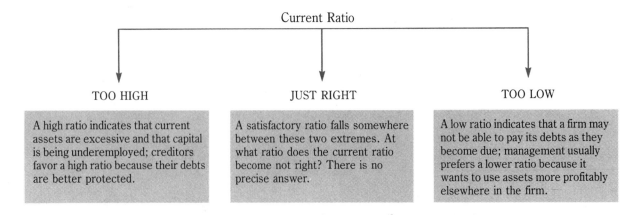

Current Ratio

TOO HIGH

A high ratio indicates that current assets are excessive and that capital is being underemployed; creditors favor a high ratio because their debts are better protected.

JUST RIGHT

A satisfactory ratio falls somewhere between these two extremes. At what ratio does the current ratio become not right? There is no precise answer.

TOO LOW

A low ratio indicates that a firm may not be able to pay its debts as they become due; management usually prefers a lower ratio because it wants to use assets more profitably elsewhere in the firm.

Figure 5-4   Current ratio analysis

In the past, a current ratio of two-to-one (2 : 1) was considered necessary. For example, if there were $2 of current assets to pay each $1 of current liabilities, an entity's management would have thought these current assets could shrink considerably and the firm would still be able to pay its debts. By this guide, the current ratio of Bluebeard Computer Corporation would be acceptable.

Today, however, analysts generally agree that no one ratio is sufficient for all businesses, and that other factors — such as the composition of current assets, the credit terms extended to customers, or the credit terms extended by suppliers—must also be considered to arrive at an acceptable ratio.

Dun and Bradstreet, as well as various trade publications, provides a range of current ratios that may be applicable to companies in a particular industry at one point in time. It is noteworthy that the adequacy of a current ratio depends on other developments within a company and, while a particular ratio may be satisfactory one year, it may not be adequate the next year.

Composition of Specific Items in Current Assets

In the following example, each company has a 2 : 1 current ratio. Is each company as able to repay its short-term creditors?

	A Corp.	B Corp.
CURRENT ASSETS		
Cash	$ 1	$10
Accounts Receivable	2	20
Inventory	37	10
Total Current Assets	$40	$40
Current Liabilities	$20	$20
Current Ratio	2 : 1	2 : 1

Each company has equal dollar amounts of current assets and current liabilities, but their debt-paying abilities are not equal. Company A must first sell some inventory and collect the resulting accounts receivable, or it can immediately sell its inventory as a single lot for cash, probably for less than its cost. This type of shrinkage is provided for in the 2 : 1 current ratio. The current ratio is, therefore, only a rough indicator of how able a firm is to pay its debts as they become due. The criticism of this ratio is that it doesn't consider the components of current assets in analyzing the solvency of a firm.

The Acid-Test Ratio

Acid-test ratio
Quick current assets divided by current liabilities; also called the *quick* ratio.

Quick current assets
Assets that can be quickly converted into cash; usually includes cash, temporary investments, and accounts receivable.

A more severe test of solvency is provided by the so-called **acid-test ratio**, which is often called the *quick ratio*. It provides an indication of instant solvency — the ability to meet the immediate demands of creditors. To calculate this ratio, current assets have to be broken down into quick and non-quick current assets.

Quick Current Assets:

Cash
Temporary Investments
Accounts Receivable — Trade

These current assets are considered to be readily convertible into cash.

Non-quick Current Assets:

Inventory
Prepaid Items

Cash could not be obtained immediately from these current assets.

Inventory and prepaid items are not usually convertible into cash in a short period of time. They are therefore excluded from **quick current assets** in the calculation of this ratio. The acid-test ratio is calculated by dividing the total of quick current assets by current liabilities. These are the relevant BCC financial data used to calculate the acid-test ratio:

		19X3
Quick Current Assets	(a)	$36,800
Current Liabilities	(b)	79,000
Acid-Test Ratio	(a ÷ b)	0.47 (rounded)

This ratio indicates how many quick asset dollars (cash, temporary investments, and trade accounts receivable) exist to pay each $1 of current liabilities. As can be seen, there are $0.47 of quick assets in the Bluebeard Computer Corporation to pay each $1 of current liabilities.

What Is an Adequate Acid-Test Ratio?

Analysts generally consider that a one-to-one (1 : 1) acid-test ratio is adequate to ensure that a firm is able to pay its current obligations. However, this is a fairly arbitrary guideline and is not necessarily reliable in all situations. A lower ratio than 1 : 1 can often be found in successful companies.

A company tries to keep a reasonable balance in its current assets among cash, receivables, and inventory. Unfortunately, there is no one indicator of what this balance really is. The balance is acceptable when debts are being paid. The "end of the rope" comes when current liabilities are not being paid; in such a case a reasonable balance does not exist.

What Is the Relationship between the Current Ratio and the Acid-Test Ratio?

When taken together, these ratios give the financial statement reader a better understanding of the inventory implications for a company. While the current ratio may be favourable, the acid-test ratio may be such that it alerts the reader to the non-quick current assets of the company.

G.   Analysis of Operations Efficiency

Each entity uses its assets as resources to earn net income. However, some entities do so more successfully than others. How can the efficiency with which a company is using its assets be established?

An evaluation of an entity's operations efficiency can be established through the calculation and study of relevant ratios. Of particular interest is the current status of the entity, the record of the entity over a number of years, and a comparison of the entity's financial performance with that of others in the same industry and in other industries.

The net income earned is the starting point for this ratio analysis. The efficient use of assets can be measured by expressing net income as a return on assets, on shareholders' equity, on sales, and on each share. An additional measurement used in the stock market to evaluate the selling price of shares relates the selling price to the share's earnings.

Analysis of Operations Efficiency:	Indicates:
1. Return on Total Assets	How efficiently a company uses its assets as resources to earn net income.
2. Return on Shareholders' Equity	The adequacy of net income as a return on shareholders' equity.
3. Return on Sales	The percentage of sales revenue earned by the business after payment of creditor interest and government income tax.
4. Return on Each Share	The amount of net income that has been carried for each share of common stock.
5. Price-Earnings Ratio	The reasonableness of market price in relation to per share earnings.

The relationship of the first three of these ratios to the balance sheet and income statement of an entity is shown in Figure 5-5.

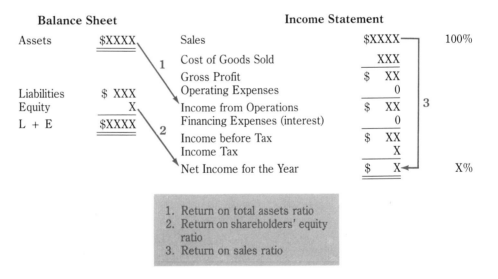

Figure 5-5   Relationship of three ratios to financial statements

Return on Total Assets Ratio

An efficient use of assets should result in a higher return on these assets; a less efficient use should result in a lower return. The return on total assets ratio is designed to measure the efficiency with which assets are used. The ratio is calculated as follows:

$$\frac{\text{Income from Operations}}{\text{Average Total Assets}}$$

Attention is focused on net income from operations, which is the amount earned by the entity from the use of its assets. Expenses not applicable to operations of the entity, such as interest (expenses to finance the entity) and income taxes (expenses on income due to the government) are excluded. Average total assets are used in the calculation because the amount of assets used varies during the year.

Return on Shareholders' Equity Ratio

The assets of an entity are financed by both creditors and shareholders. In return for their share of financing, creditors are paid interest. Shareholders have claim to whatever remains after interest is paid to creditors and income taxes are paid to government. This return on shareholders' equity is measured through the following ratio:

$$\frac{\text{Net Income for the Year}}{\text{Average Shareholders' Equity}}$$

Net income after interest and income taxes is used in this calculation because only the balance remains to shareholders. Average equity is used because the amount of equity can vary during the year.

Return on Sales Ratio

The efficiency, or *productivity*, of each sales dollar is established through the calculation of the return on sales. This percentage of sales revenue retained by the entity — after payment of creditor interest expenses and government income taxes — is an index of performance that can be used to compare this entity with others in the same industry, or in other industries. The percentage return on sales is calculated as follows:

$$\frac{\text{Net Income for the Year}}{\text{Sales}}$$

Return on Each Share: Earnings per Share

The return to shareholders discussed earlier indicates the return on assets financed by shareholders. This return to shareholders can also be expressed on a per-share basis. That is, the amount of net income can be divided by the number of common shares outstanding in order to establish how much net income has been earned for each share of stock. This return per share is calculated as follows:

$$\frac{\text{Net Income for the Year}}{\text{Number of Common Shares Outstanding}}$$

This expression of net income as a per-share amount is widely quoted in financial circles and, as noted, is called earnings per share (EPS). If preferred shareholders exist, their claims on net income are deducted before net income is divided by the number of shares of common stock outstanding:

$$\frac{\text{Net Income for the Year } - \text{ Preferred Dividends}}{\text{Number of Common Shares Outstanding}}$$

Earnings per share is of particular interest to investors because of its importance in influencing share market values. For this reason, in actual practice, EPS must be disclosed on the income statement or in a note to the statements.

Price–Earnings Ratio

The price–earnings ratio is calculated by dividing the market value of a share by earnings per share:

$$\frac{\text{Market Price per Share}}{\text{Earnings per Share}}$$

This ratio indicates the reasonableness of market price in relation to per-share earnings.

Real Life Example 5-2

Circo Craft Co. Inc.

Hans Muhlegg says it was with "a lot of guts and ignorance" that he founded a company in 1973 to manufacture sophisticated printed circuit boards for electronic equipment manufacturers.

Those two factors have combined to make Circo Craft Co. Inc. a multi-million dollar success story with profits expected to reach $6.6 million on projected sales of as much as $36 million for 1984.

Muhlegg, a German-born mining engineer, and Renato Cervini, who completed his studies at a polytechnical institute in Rome, formed Circo Craft after both men decided to leave their employer, a local circuit board manufacturer, 11 years ago.

A few thousand dollars — what Circo Craft president Muhlegg calls "really zilch" — rented them a manufacturing facility in Montreal and some essential equipment.

"We had a lot of customer contacts and it seemed like a good idea with a lot of potential," Muhlegg, 42, said in an interview at his luxuriously appointed executive office, complete with fireplace. Cervini, 37, works as vice-president of the company.

Circo Craft is considered one of Canada's largest independent manufacturers of printed circuits, which are widely used in telecommunication, computer, and other electronic equipment.

Printed circuits are metallic patterns, bonded to a special board, which conduct electric current between electronic components. Circuits patterns can be printed on both sides of a board, and boards can be laminated together to form multiple layers.

Both those products are manufactured at the firm's plant in Granby, which has undergone its fifth expansion this year into a [3800 m²] 41 000-square-foot facility, and at a [6000 m²] 65 000-square-foot plant opened in Kirkland in May 1982. In June, the firm purchased a [13 000 m²] 140 000-square-foot plant in Pointe Claire. It plans to begin production this spring of hybrid circuits, a cross between printed circuits and more complex integrated circuits.

Earlier this year the federal government gave Circo Craft a $999,000 grant to expand the Kirkland plant and another $1.1 million for the start-up of the Point Claire facility.

Almost all of the firm's business is in the Canadian market, although there are plans to expand into the United States. There are an estimated 50 independent manufacturers in Canada and about 1 500 in the United States.

In 1983, according to Muhlegg, Circo Craft held an estimated 18 per cent of printed circuit production by independent producers in Canada.

"We stayed low key for a long time, but then after a while, our competitors woke up and by then it was too late," said Muhlegg.

"Business is tough enough, without looking over your shoulder at your competitors all the time. We don't ignore them, but we don't worry about them either," he said.

The firm's financial growth has been steady. In 1973, the first year of operation, sales were $380,000. Within five years, they had jumped to $2.4 million. Last year, sales reached $19 million.

Circo Craft went public in October, pre-selling almost all of the 2.8 million shares at $8.25 each. The additional capital allowed the firm to pay off some of its long-term debt and expand the manufacturing plants.

Selling off roughly one-quarter of their interests in the company left Muhlegg with control at about 55 percent and Cervini with about 23 percent.

In an unusual move, the firm gave each of its then-400 employees the means to purchase shares: $500 cash plus $300 for each year of service. The move cost the company's treasury about $500,000 — but Muhlegg said it has paid handsome dividends in terms of employee productivity.

Circo Craft's incentive-oriented treatment of staff, now about 500, ranges from bi-annual salary increases and merit bonuses to the construction of a sports playing field behind the Kirkland plant.

Muhlegg's worth as a team player was put to the test last year during a company soccer game. He broke his foot trying, without success, to win the game.

[The 1985 annual report for Circo Craft Co. Inc. follows.]

Source Fran Halter, "Founder of Circuit Board Manufacturer Says Firm Started on Guts, Ignorance", *The* (Montreal) *Gazette*, November 14, 1984, p. C-1.

APPENDIX: Circo Craft Inc. 1985 Annual Report

Circo Craft

ANNUAL REPORT

1985

FINANCIAL HIGHLIGHTS

	1985	1984	1983
Operations (millions of dollars)			
Sales	**$ 45.3**	$ 37.3	$ 19.6
Operating margin	**16.8**	15.3	7.2
Pre-tax earnings	**8.5**	9.3	3.1
Net earnings	**5.3**	6.6	2.6
Financial Position (millions of dollars)			
Working capital	**$ 9.5**	$ 12.2	$ 4.9
Shareholders' equity	**34.7**	29.4	7.0
Total assets	**49.8**	40.8	19.9
Per share (in dollars)			
Net earnings	**$ .44**	$ .64	$ .26
Closing shareholders' equity	**2.88**	2.44	.70
Key Ratios			
Return on sales	**11.8%**	17.8%	13.1%
Return on average equity	**16.6%**	36.4%	44.6%
Current ratio	**2.5**	2.6	2.1
Other Statistics (millions of dollars)			
Capital expenditures	**$ 15.5**	$ 12.0	$ 3.6
Cash flow from operations	**8.8**	8.8	3.9

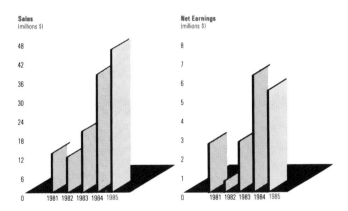

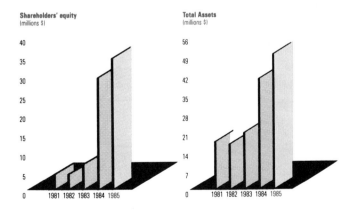

FINANCIAL REVIEW

Total and fixed assets
(millions $)

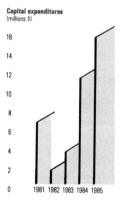

Total assets
Fixed assets

Capital expenditures
(millions $)

Operating Results

Sales in 1985 increased by 21.4 percent compared to the previous year to reach a record level of $45.3 million. Total operating margin increased by $1.5 million or 9.5 percent as a result of increased sales volume. However, as a percentage of sales, operating margins declined from 41.1 percent in 1984 to 37.1 percent in 1985 as a result of increased manufacturing costs related to the expanded facilities and the lower rate of utilization of such facilities in the initial year of production.

Selling, general and administrative expenses also increased during 1985 due to the expansion of the sales force required in order to establish a strong position in foreign markets and insure continued close client relations. As well, Circo Craft emphasized building a strong managerial base to support further growth.

Depreciation expenses also increased sharply during the year, again because of the major expansion of the Company's production facilities and the purchase of new equipment to allow the fabrication of more complex double-sided and multilayer printed circuits. Depreciation expense of $2.4 million in 1985 was 57.4 percent higher than for the previous year.

Research and development costs increased by 76.9 percent in 1985, largely in support of the increase in the complexity of Circo Craft's products. A total of $506,000 net of Government tax credits was spent on research and development in 1985, up from $286,000 in 1984. These funds were used for various projects including the development of new material applications, such as the use of copper for hybrid circuitry.

Interest income, net of interest paid on long-term debt contributed $563,000 to Circo Craft's earnings during 1985, compared to an expense of $532,000 in 1984. This was due to the initial public offering made by the Company in the fourth quarter of 1984 that enabled Circo Craft to reduce debts and retain a strong cash position throughout 1985.

Although anticipated, start-up costs of $1,445,000, associated with the new hybrid production facility also had a very significant impact on earnings in 1985.

As a result of these factors and particularly the hybrid start-up costs, earnings before income taxes were $8.5 million in 1985, compared with $9.3 million in 1984.

Despite the slightly lower pre-tax earnings level in 1985, the provision for income taxes increased by 18.5 percent from $2.7 million in 1984 up to $3.2 million in 1985. This represents an effective income tax rate of 37.4 percent, compared to 28.9 percent in the previous year. The increase results primarily from a change in accounting policy for investment tax credits, based on recommendations of the Canadian Institute of Chartered Accountants effective January 1, 1985.

Under the new method of reporting investment tax credits, income tax reductions related to purchases of fixed assets are deducted from the cost of such assets. The investment tax credits were previously applied as a reduction of income taxes. This change resulted in a decrease in net earnings of $988,000, or $0.08 per share.

Net earnings per share for 1985, as a result, were 44 cents compared to 64 cents per share in 1984. It should be noted that per share calculations for 1985 are based on a weighted monthly average of 12,072,700 common shares outstanding compared to 10,425,897 shares in 1984.

For 1985, Circo Craft had a return on sales of 11.8 percent and a return on average shareholders' equity of 16.6 percent. While lower than last year, it is important to note that these results were achieved despite a major industry downturn and a substantial increase in overhead related to the increase in production capacity. Circo Craft however was one of the most profitable companies in the industry in North America in 1985.

Capital Expenditures

Circo Craft's capital expenditures during 1985 were $15.5 million and totalled $27.5 million over the last two years. These expenditures were part of a significant expansion program aimed at increasing total plant capacity, acquiring additional sophisticated equipment to allow the fabrication of more complex products and the diversification of the company's client and geographic sales base. Capital expenditures necessary to complete the current investment program, due to be completed by mid 1986, are estimated at $5 million.

Capital expenditures-net during 1985 were financed as follows:

- Use of the residual proceeds from the initial public offering by Circo Craft in 1984, which had been held in term deposits .... $ 4.8 million
- Increase in long-term debt .... 4.0 million
- Partial use of funds generated by operations .... 6.7 million

$15.5 million

Government assistance to be received by the Company in connection with this capital expenditure program amounts to $3.1 million. Of this total, $1.2 million was received on February 14, 1986 by way of an issue of second preference shares by the Company and $1.9 million will be received in the form of grants.

Capitalization

The Company remains in a very strong financial position, with long-term debt accounting for only 12 percent of total capitalization. This enables the Company to complete the current capital expenditure program as well as limits exposure to interest rate fluctuations.

Shareholders' equity increased during the year by 18.1 percent to $34.7 million and was equal to 69.8 percent of total assets as at December 31, 1985.

Working Capital and Cash Flow from Operations

Working capital declined from $12.2 million at the end of 1984 to $9.5 million on December 31, 1985. This reduction is largely attributed to the utilization of $4.8 million of short-term deposits used to fund the 1985 capital expenditures program.

Significant cash flow of $8.8 million generated by the operations in 1985, equaled the record high achieved in 1984 and enabled us to maintain an excellent current ratio of 2.46, which provides a strong liquidity position to support increased sales in 1986.

Capitalization (at December 31)	**1985**		1984		1983	
	million	%	million	%	million	%
Long-term debt, including current portion	$ 5.2	(12.0)	$ 1.2	(3.6)	$ 7.2	(45.0)
Deferred income taxes	$ 3.4	(7.9)	2.4	(7.3)	1.8	(11.2)
Common shareholders' equity	34.7	(80.1)	29.4	(89.1)	7.0	(43.8)
	$43.3	(100.0)	$33.0	(100.0)	$16.0	(100.0)

Quarterly Financial Data (unaudited)	1st Quarter	2nd Quarter	3rd Quarter	4th Quarter	Total
	(in thousands of dollars, except per share data)				
1985					
Sales	$11,363	$11,250	$10,623	$12,081	$45,317
Operating Margin	3,743	4,301	4,014	4,729	16,787
Net Earnings	1,566	1,298	1,190	1,278	5,332
Net Earnings per common share (dollars)	0.13	0.11	0.10	0.10	0.44
1984					
Sales	$ 8,190	$ 9,502	$ 8,266	$11,377	$37,335
Operating Margin	3,702	3,879	3,413	4,338	15,332
Net Earnings	1,755	1,604	1,452	1,824	6,635
Net Earnings per common share (dollars)	0.18	0.16	0.15	0.15	0.64
1983					
Sales	$ 4,121	$ 4,473	$ 4,441	$ 6,558	$19,593
Operating Margin	1,427	1,560	1,696	2,495	7,178
Net Earnings	539	406	563	1,062	2,570
Net Earnings per common share (dollars)	0.05	0.04	0.06	0.11	0.26

STATEMENT OF EARNINGS

for the year ended December 31, 1985

	1985		1984
	(thousands of dollars except per share amounts)		
Sales	$ 45,317	$	37,335
Cost of Sales	28,530		22,003
Operating Margin	16,787		15,332
Selling, General and Administrative Expenses	4,481		2,890
Other Expenses (Income)			
Depreciation	2,407		1,529
Research and development costs	506		286
Start-up costs – Hybrid Division (note 9)	1,445		—
Interest on long-term debt	78		1,056
Interest income – net (note 3)	(641)		(524)
Share purchase assistance	—		468
Exchange loss on repayment of long-term debt	—		292
	3,795		3,107
Earnings before Income Taxes	8,511		9,335
Provision for Income Taxes (note 10)	3,179		2,700
Net Earnings for the Year	$ 5,332	$	6,635
Earnings per Share (note 11)	$ 0.44	$	0.64

B A L A N C E   S H E E T

as at December 31, 1985

		1985		1984
		(thousands of dollars)		
Assets				
Current Assets				
Short-term deposits	$	**1,975**	$	6,816
Accounts receivable (note 4)		**6,839**		5,271
Income taxes recoverable		**619**		—
Inventories (note 5)		**6,256**		7,687
Prepaid expenses		**288**		190
		15,977		19,964
Fixed Assets (note 6)		**33,806**		20,868
	$	**49,783**	$	40,832
Liabilities				
Current Liabilities				
Bank indebtedness (note 4)	$	**661**	$	610
Accounts payable and accrued liabilities		**5,787**		5,692
Income taxes		**—**		1,448
Current portion of long-term debt (note 7)		**16**		13
		6,464		7,763
Long-Term Debt (note 7)		**5,212**		1,229
Deferred Income Taxes		**3,361**		2,426
		15,037		11,418
Shareholders' Equity				
Share Capital (note 8)	$	**17,100**	$	17,100
Retained Earnings		**17,646**		12,314
		34,746		29,414
	$	**49,783**	$	40,832

Signed on behalf of the board

Hans-Karl Muhlegg
Director

Peter David Kyle
Director

Auditors' Report to the Shareholders

We have examined the balance sheet of Circo Craft Co. Inc. as at December 31, 1985 and the statements of earnings, retained earnings and changes in financial position for the year then ended. Our examination was made in accordance with generally accepted auditing standards, and accordingly included such tests and other procedures as we considered necessary in the circumstances.

In our opinion, these financial statements present fairly the financial position of the company as at December 31, 1985 and the results of its operations and the changes in its financial position for the year then ended in accordance with generally accepted accounting principles applied, except for the change in the method of accounting for investment tax credits referred to in note 2, on a basis consistent with that of the preceding year.

Chartered Accountants

Coopers & Lybrand

Montreal, Quebec
February 7, 1986

Chartered Accountants

Dellaire, Alain, Brodeur, Destrelleur

Granby, Quebec
February 7, 1986

STATEMENT OF RETAINED EARNINGS
for the year ended December 31, 1985

	1985	1984
	(thousands of dollars)	
Balance – Beginning of year	$ 12,314	$ 7,045
Net earnings for the year	5,332	6,635
	17,646	13,680
Dividends	—	594
Share issue expenses – net	—	772
	—	1,366
Balance – End of year	$ 17,646	$ 12,314

STATEMENT OF CHANGES IN FINANCIAL POSITION
for the year ended December 31, 1985

	1985	1984
	(thousands of dollars)	
Source of Funds		
Net earnings for the year	$ 5,332	$ 6,635
Items not affecting working capital –		
Depreciation	2,407	1,529
Deferred income taxes	935	600
Loss on disposal of fixed assets	88	33
Provided from operations	8,762	8,797
Proceeds on disposal of fixed assets	124	137
Increase in long-term debt	4,000	—
Proceeds on issue of common shares	—	17,099
	12,886	26,033
Application of Funds		
Acquisition of fixed assets – net	15,557	11,951
Decrease of long-term debt	17	5,378
Dividends	—	594
Share issue expenses – net	—	772
	15,574	18,695
Increase (Decrease) in Working Capital	(2,688)	7,338
Working Capital – Beginning of Year	12,201	4,863
Working Capital – End of Year	$ 9,513	$ 12,201

NOTES TO FINANCIAL STATEMENTS

for the year ended December 31, 1985

1. Accounting Policies

Inventories

Inventories are valued at the lower of cost and market. Cost is determined on the first-in, first-out basis for raw materials and maintenance supplies. The cost of work in process inventories includes the cost of raw materials, direct labour and applicable manufacturing overhead, excluding depreciation. Market is defined as replacement cost for raw materials and net realizable value less cost to complete for work in process.

Fixed assets and depreciation

Fixed assets are reported at cost less accumulated depreciation. Cost is reduced by applicable investment tax credits. Assets acquired prior to 1982 are depreciated using the diminishing balance method at rates varying between $2^1/2$% and 15%. Assets acquired after 1981 are depreciated using the straight-line method at rates varying between $2^1/2$% and 20%.

Government grants relating to the acquisition of fixed assets are credited to the cost of acquisition.

Foreign exchange

Monetary assets and liabilities are translated into Canadian dollars at December 31 exchange rates and non-monetary assets and liabilities at the exchange rates prevailing when the assets were acquired and liabilities incurred. Sales and expenses, with the excep-

tion of depreciation, are translated at average monthly rates. Depreciation is translated at the rates used in the translation of the relevant asset accounts. Translation gains and losses are included in determining net earnings in the year in which the exchange rate changes.

Income taxes

The company follows the tax allocation method of providing for income taxes.

Deferred income taxes result primarily from the difference between capital cost allowance claimed for income tax purposes and depreciation recorded for accounting purposes.

Investment tax credits

Investment tax credits earned subsequent to January 1, 1985 are accounted for using the cost reduction method. Under this method, credits arising from the acquisition of fixed assets are deducted from the cost of the related assets and credits relating to current expenditures are included in the determination of net earnings for the current year.

Investment tax credits earned prior to December 31, 1984 are recognized as a reduction in the provision for income taxes in the year in which such items are claimed for tax purposes.

2. Change in Accounting Policy

The company has adopted the recommendations of the Canadian Institute of Chartered Accountants for investment tax credits effective January 1, 1985 as set out in note 1. These recommendations are being applied

prospectively with respect to investment tax credits earned subsequent to the effective date.

Net earnings decreased by $988,000 or $0.08 per share as a result of this change.

3. Government Assistance

The company obtained the following government grants:
- Department of Regional Economic Expansion

    An amount of $537,000 (1984 – $740,000) relating to the acquisition of certain fixed assets has been credited to the cost of acquisition.
- Société de développement industriel du Québec

An amount of $427,000 (1984 – $237,000) representing a rebate of interest paid on long-term debt and bank indebtedness in prior years has been included with interest income in the statement of earnings. As at December 31, 1985 the unrealized interest rebate relating to future years amounted to $979,000.

NOTES TO FINANCIAL STATEMENTS
for the year ended December 31, 1985

4. Security for Bank Indebtedness

The accounts receivable have been pledged as security for bank indebtedness.

5. Inventories

	1985		1984
	(thousands of dollars)		
Raw materials	$ 3,434	$	4,383
Work in process	1,802		2,734
Maintenance supplies	1,020		570
	$ 6,256	$	7,687

6. Fixed Assets

	1985			1984
	Cost	Accumulated depreciation	Net	Net
	(thousands of dollars)			
Land and non-depreciable assets	$ 857	$ —	$ 857	$ 1,037
Buildings	17,342	586	16,756	8,861
Machinery and equipment	24,144	6,239	17,905	12,218
Vehicles	437	170	267	274
Deposits on machinery and equipment	88	—	88	334
	$ 42,868	$ 6,995	35,873	22,724
Less: Government grants – net of accumulated amortization of $897,000			2,067	1,856
			$ 33,806	$ 20,868

7. Long-term debt

	1985		1984
	(thousands of dollars)		

a) Long-term debt is comprised of the following:

	1985		1984
Term loan bearing interest at an annual rate of prime plus ½% repayable in monthly instalments of $142,000 commencing in January 1987	$ 4,000	$	—
Balance of purchase price bearing interest at an annual rate of 9%, secured by a first mortgage on a certain property, repayable in monthly instalments of $10,350 including principal and interest commencing in July 1984 and due in June 1989	1,228		1,242
	5,228		1,242
Less: Current portion	16		13
	$ 5,212	$	1,229

7. Long-Term Debt (continued)

The aggregate amount of payments required in each of the next five years to meet retirement provisions is as follows:

Year ending December 31, 1986	$ 16,000	
1987	1,721,000	
1988	1,723,000	
1989	613,000	
1990	23,000	

b) The term loan is guaranteed by a demand debenture in the amount of $6,800,000. Under the terms of a Trust Deed, this debenture is secured by a specific charge of a second rank on a certain property.

8. Share Capital

a) As at December 31, 1985 the authorized share capital consists of the following:

An unlimited number of First Preferred shares, without nominal or par value, issuable in series

An unlimited number of Second Preferred shares, without nominal or par value, issuable in series

An unlimited number of Common shares, without nominal or par value

The directors are responsible for defining the rights, privileges, restrictions and the conditions attached to each series of the First and Second Preferred shares upon their issuance.

b) The issued and paid capital stock as at December 31, 1985 consists of the following:

	1985	1984
	(thousands of dollars)	
12,072,700 Common shares	**$17,100**	$17,100

c) The company intends to issue Second Preferred shares, Series A in connection with the financial assistance amounting to $1,200,000 to be received from the Government of Quebec by the Company for costs incurred for the installation of the thick-film hybrid circuits facility. Such shares, to be issued in 1986 given the start-up of commercial production of thick-film hybrid circuits in late 1985, will be non-voting and entitled to receive, as and when declared, an aggregate non-cumulative preferential dividend of $1 and, upon liquidation, to receive an aggregate amount of $1. The company will covenant to issue such shares only for the purposes of such financial assistance and to repurchase such shares at their issue price upon request of the holder thereof if the majority of the common shares or more than half of the assets of the company are transferred, within five years following the granting of such financial assistance, to an enterprise whose head office is not located in the Province of Quebec or to an individual who does not reside therein.

9. Start-up Costs – Hybrid Division

Start-up costs, net of revenues of $98,000 relating to the pre-production of thick-film hybrid circuits, have been expensed in these financial statements. Commercial production of thick-film hybrid circuits began late in 1985 and accordingly depreciation of the related equipment and facility will begin in 1986.

NOTES TO FINANCIAL STATEMENTS
for the year ended December 31, 1985

10. Income Taxes

The company's provision for income taxes includes the following:

	1985	1984
	(thousands of dollars)	
Current	$2,244	$2,100
Deferred	935	600
	$3,179	$2,700

The company's effective income tax rate is calculated as follows:

	1985	1984
	%	%
Combined basic federal and provincial income tax rate	42.25	41.50
Increase (decrease) in income tax rate resulting from:		
Manufacturing and processing reduction	(6.00)	(6.00)
Investment tax credit	—	(7.99)
Inventory allowance	(0.98)	(0.44)
Other	2.08	1.85
	37.35	28.92

11. Earnings per Share

Earnings per share is calculated using the weighted average number of Common shares outstanding during the respective fiscal years: 12,072,700 and 10,425,897 common shares in 1985 and 1984 respectively.

12. Legal Proceedings

The company has been named defendant in 1982 in a legal action claiming $531,878 for unpaid amounts relating to the construction of its Kirkland plant. An amount of $385,176 has been recorded as accounts payable as at December 31, 1985. Furthermore, the company has initiated a legal action of its own claiming $533,000 for damages due to unrespected specifications in the contract. The amount recorded as accounts payable is deemed by management to be sufficient to cover the eventuality of an unfavorable judgement.

13. Major Clients

Approximately 57% (1984 – 69%) of the company's sales were to an unrelated multinational corporation which has several divisions responsible for their own purchasing decisions.

14. Related Party Transactions

Shop supplies and machinery and equipment purchased from an affiliated company at fair market value are as follows:

	1985	1984
	(thousands of dollars)	
Machinery and equipment	$ 1,049	$ 1,575
Shop supplies	$ 390	$ 452

15. Commitments

Capital expenditures committed at December 31, 1985 amount to approximately $3,275,000.

SELECTED DATA – 10 YEARS

For the year	1985	1984	1983
Operations (thousands of dollars)			
Sales	45,317	37,335	19,593
Cost of Sales	28,530	22,003	12,415
Operating Margin	16,787	15,332	7,178
Depreciation	2,407	1,529	1,151
Interest (Income) Expense – net	(563)	532	776
Pre-tax Earnings	8,511	9,335	3,113
Income Taxes	3,179	2,700	543
Net Earnings	5,332	6,635	2,570
Balance Sheet (thousands of dollars)			
Total Assets	49,783	40,832	19,888
Current Assets	15,977	19,964	9,272
Current Liabilities	6,464	7,763	4,409
Working Capital	9,513	12,201	4,863
Shareholder's Equity	34,746	29,414	7,046
Long-Term Debt	5,212	1,229	6,607
Cash Flow (thousands of dollars)			
Cash Flow from Operations	8,762	8,797	3,857
Capital Expenditures – net	15,557	11,951	3,647
Cash Dividends	—	594	—
Key Financial Ratios			
Current Ratio	2.5	2.6	2.1
Net Earnings as a Percentage of Sales	11.8	17.8	13.1
Return on Average Shareholders' Equity	16.6	36.4	44.6
Sales/Fixed Assets	1.34	1.82	1.85
Sales/Total Assets	0.91	0.92	0.98
Per Share Data* (dollars)			
Net Earnings	$0.44	$0.64	$0.26
Dividends Paid	—	0.06	—
Shareholder's Equity	2.88	2.44	0.70
Other Information			
Number of Employees at Year-End			
– Printed Circuit Division	455	465	317
– Hybrid Division	70	15	—
– Total	525	480	317
Total Square Footage of Plant Facility			
– Printed Circuit Division	175,000	110,000	100,000
– Microelectronics Division	40,000	—	—
– Available Future Expansion	115,000	142,000	—
– Total	330,000	252,000	100,000

*By a certificate of amendment dated
August 24, 1984, the outstanding
common shares of the company were
subdivided into 10,000,000 common
shares. Per share data for the years
1973 to 1983 have therefore been
calculated based on the assumption that
10,000,000 shares were issued and
outstanding.

1982	1981	1980	1979	1978	1977	1976
11,893	12,195	7,196	6,010	2,617	1,693	1,169
8,334	7,282	4,688	3,848	1,859	1,271	816
3,559	4,913	2,508	2,162	758	422	353
610	176	149	114	57	32	23
586	40	63	18	38	22	18
897	3,689	1,646	1,512	270	141	137
389	1,206	645	475	59	30	30
508	2,483	1,001	1,037	211	111	107
16,079	17,540	4,982	3,448	1,491	1,004	735
7,441	9,618	3,260	2,152	886	626	474
3,561	5,222	1,394	1,079	573	323	298
3,880	4,396	1,866	1,073	313	303	176
4,476	4,594	2,363	1,462	588	377	266
6,265	6,395	794	560	234	263	135
1,580	3,559	1,238	1,402	322	148	143
1,362	6,387	609	852	314	179	24
627	252	100	163	—	—	—
2.1	1.8	2.2	1.9	1.6	1.9	1.6
4.3	20.4	13.9	17.3	8.1	6.6	9.2
11.2	71.4	52.3	101.2	43.7	34.5	50.4
1.38	1.54	4.18	4.64	4.33	4.48	4.48
0.74	0.70	1.44	1.74	1.76	1.69	1.59
$0.05	$0.25	$0.10	$0.10	$0.02	$0.01	$0.01
0.06	0.02	0.01	0.02	—	—	—
0.45	0.46	0.23	0.15	0.06	0.04	0.03
156	167	112	135	120	119	119
—	—	—	—	—	—	—
156	167	112	135	120	119	119
100,000	35,000	35,000	30,000	20,000	20,000	13,000
—	—	—	—	—	—	—
—	65,000	—	—	—	—	—
100,000	100,000	35,000	30,000	20,000	20,000	13,000

A S S I G N M E N T   M A T E R I A L S

Discussion Questions

1. How does the income statement prepared for a merchandising firm differ from that prepared for a service business?
2. What relationship does a gross profit calculation express? Explain, using an example.
3. How does the gross profit appear on an income statement? Could its calculation be omitted from the income statement?
4. Is the gross profit always disclosed on the income statement? Why or why not?
5. Contrast and explain the sales and collections cycle and the purchase and payment cycle.
6. What contra accounts are used for Sales and Purchases? What are their functions?
7. How is cost of purchases calculated?
8. List the components of the cost of goods sold calculation.
9. Contrast the differences between the periodic inventory method and the perpetual inventory system.
10. How is ending inventory recorded on the worksheet of a merchandiser under the periodic inventory method? Illustrate your answer, using a $10,000 ending inventory as an example.
11. Explain how ending inventory is recorded in the accounts of a merchandiser.
12. Why is interest expense classified separately on the income statement?
13. What items are referred to as extraordinary? How are they disclosed?
14. What are prior-period adjustments? How do they differ from extraordinary items?
15. What categories of assets and liabilities are indicated on a classified balance sheet?
16. What are the implications for a firm to be insolvent?
17. What are financial ratios, and why are they calculated?
18. Distinguish between the current ratio and the acid-test ratio.
19. Is any one current ratio or acid-test ratio adequate for all businesses? Why or why not?
20. What ratios are relevant for an evaluation of an entity's operations efficiency?
21. Refer to Real Life Example 5-1: what factors are disclosed regarding pricing by small and large organizations? How are these factors represented in the financial statements?

Discussion Cases

Discussion Case 5-1:   Majestic Contractors Limited

The following information is extracted from the 1984 annual report of Majestic Contractors Limited, a company listed on the Toronto Stock Exchange (formerly, Majestic Wiley).

Majestic is one of North America's leading dryland cross-country pipeline contractors. Originally formed in 1954, the company, through amalgamation, was listed on the Toronto Stock Exchange in May 1974. The company has been involved in all major pipeline systems in Canada and several in the United States, and has developed valuable expertise in arctic construction in both Canada and Alaska. The corporation has also completed projects in India, Malaysia, and the Middle East.

The company owns a large fleet of well-maintained pipeline construction equipment. Our resources are particularly suited to big-inch pipe from 508-mm to 1067-mm diameter and larger.

In 1982, the company acquired 51 percent of a new high-tech company called Majestic Laser Systems Ltd. This company has a mandate to undertake research and development projects within the general field of laser materials processing, using high-powered lasers.

Report to Shareholders

This year marks the company's thirtieth year in business. During this period Majestic has developed into one of North America's premier big-inch pipeline contractors. Currently our emphasis has shifted to the international market, where we expect to become a major participant in 1985.

Revenues were $59,403,000 for the year ended December 31, 1984, compared with $28,928,000 the previous year. The net loss was $(1,093,000) or $(0.13) per share, compared with a net loss of $(2,741,000) or $(0.33) per share in 1983. Cash flow from operations was $2,041,000, compared with $677,000 in the previous year. The loss sustained in 1984 was primarily attributable to high start-up costs incurred by our 49-percent–owned Saudi company and a significant loss sustained on a project in Quebec.

On August 19, 1984, the company announced its intention to purchase up to 421 277 shares (5 percent) of its common stock through the facilities of the Toronto Stock Exchange. Majestic believes that at the current market price range, the common shares represent a worthwhile investment and an appropriate use of company funds. At December 31, 1984, the company has purchased for cancellation 169 500 common shares at prices ranging from $3.20 to $3.35.

On December 19, 1984, the Board of Directors declared a cash dividend of $0.25 per share, payable on the thirty-first day of January, 1985 to shareholders at the close of business on the eighteenth day of January, 1985.

Canadian Operations

The Canadian division has successfully completed the first season's work on the Norman Wells project in the first quarter for Interprovincial Pipeline (NW) Ltd. and has started the second phase of this project, which will be completed in March 1985.

During the second quarter, we were awarded, in joint venture with Charles Duranceau Limitée and Legault & Touchette Inc., two projects by Gaz Inter Cité Québec Inc. for the installation of 70 km of 406.4-mm gas pipeline and 36 km of 101.6-mm to 254-mm gas pipeline. These projects were completed in October 1984 and substantial losses were incurred. A claim has been submitted to the owner and settlement is anticipated during the first half of 1985.

We also received an award from Union Gas Limited for the construction of 17 520 m of 1067-mm gas pipeline in Ontario which was successfully completed in the third quarter.

Westcoast Transmission Company Limited awarded the company a contract for the replacement and relocation of various sections of 762-mm and 914-mm gas pipeline near Hope, British Columbia in the third quarter. This project was completed in December 1984.

United States Operations

Our United States division received an award from Minnesota Pipeline Company for the construction of 79 km of 406.4-mm gas pipeline, consisting of eight loops. Profitable completion of this project occurred in September 1984.

International Operations

Majestic International Contractors Limited received approval from the Saudi authorities in March 1984 to incorporate a new Saudi company called Abahsain Majestic Pipeline Company Limited, with Majestic International Contractors Limited owning 49 percent of the issued shares. This company completed two small projects during 1984 and is at present working on a 338-km pipeline project scheduled for completion in September 1985. Margins are very tight at present and higher than expected start-up costs have resulted in a loss being incurred in 1984. The company submitted a tender on February 9, 1985 for construction of 1201 km of 1422.4-mm crude oil pipeline, which is divided into four contracts. Construction award, to the successful bidders, is scheduled for March 1985.

The company, in joint venture with a large Indian contractor, submitted a tender on July 16, 1984 for construction of 1700 km of 457-mm to 914.4-mm gas pipeline. Award of this project to the successful bidders is scheduled for the second quarter of 1985.

The company also profitably completed its management contract in Malaysia in the fourth quarter. The project was managed by our United States division.

Laser Operations

Our 51-percent–owned subsidiary, Majestic Laser Systems Ltd. successfully tested its laser at an output of 23 kW during 1984. Another 18–24 months of development time will be required before the unit is marketed. In order to reduce Majestic's 100 percent funding requirement, the company is looking at various funding alternatives to continue the project. The power output level reached to date is significant and will allow metals up to 1 inch [25.4 mm] thickness to be welded in a single pass at very high speeds. Majestic Contractors Limited has provided $2.2 million-worth of funding for this project to date, excluding government grants.

Other Operations

The company's 50/50 joint venture with Goodbrand Construction Limited completed two projects for Metro Canada Limited for the elevated guideway for the Edmonds and Kingsway sections of the Advanced Light Rail Transit System in the Greater Vancouver area.

The company, in joint venture with Perini International Corporation, will serve as facilities subcontractor to Sperry Corporation, under that company's recently awarded $79.7 million U.S. contract with the United States Airforce to upgrade the nation's North Warning System against bomber or cruise missile attack. Phase I of this design/construct work along the Arctic Circle in Eastern Canada calls for a 42-month program to develop two radar sites.

Outlook

We are optimistic that our concentrated efforts directed toward the international market will provide profitable new work for the company during 1985. Experience gained in the Middle East and Malaysia during 1984 will help to make us more competitive on future bids. If we are successful on the India or Saudi bid, much of our surplus equipment will be profitably utilized.

In North America, we are cautiously optimistic that a more normal level of activity will resume by the fourth quarter and continue during 1986. Margins will continue to be depressed during 1985.

Management Changes

During the year, the board of directors approved several management changes to adjust our corporate structure to our current needs. The most significant promotions were: Mr. G.M. Oswald (formerly Vice-President, Canadian Operations) became Senior Vice-President, Pipeline Operations;

Norman A. Harrison (formerly Vice-President, Finance and Treasurer) became Senior Vice-President, Finance and Administration; Kenneth R. Austin (formerly Vice-President, Engineering, U.S.) became Vice-President, U.S. Operations; Leo G. Ziehr (formerly General Superintendent) became Vice-President, Canada; and Michael J. Finlayson (formerly Manager of Construction) became Vice-President, Special Projects.

The directors wish to thank our dedicated staff for their extra efforts during a difficult year.

February 21, 1985

[signed]

A. J. Cressey   J.M. Bankes
President and   Chairman of the Board
Chief Executive Officer

Summary of Accounting Policies
December 31, 1984 and 1983

Accounting Principles

The consolidated financial statements are prepared in accordance with accounting principles generally accepted in Canada and, therefore, conform in all material respects with the standards of the International Accounting Standards Committee.

Principles of Consolidation

The financial statements are expressed in Canadian dollars and include the accounts of the company, its 100-percent-owned subsidiary, Majestic International Contractors Limited, its 51-percent-owned subsidiary, Majestic Laser Systems Ltd. and its pro-rata share, utilizing the proportionate consolidation method, of the assets, liabilities, revenues, and expenses of joint ventures. Details for joint ventures have not been provided as the amounts are not material. All significant intercompany transactions and balances have been eliminated in consolidation.

Majestic International Contractors Limited owns 49 percent of Abahsain Majestic Pipeline Company Limited, a Saudi Arabian company. In the consolidated financial statements, this investment is accounted for on the equity method, with the company's share of revenues ($2,024,000) and costs ($3,916,000) included in "Revenues" and "Cost of operations", respectively, in the consolidated statements of loss.

Translation of Foreign Currencies

The United States division is an integrated foreign operation. The United States division accounts stated in foreign currencies have been translated into Canadian dollars as follows:
a) as to current assets (except for prepaid expenses) and current liabilities (except for deferred contract revenue) at the exchange rate at the balance sheet date;
b) as to all other assets, liabilities, and non-current deferred income taxes, at the approximate rate of exchange at the time the transaction occurred; and
c) as to revenues and expenses, at the average rate of exchange for the year, except for items relating to balance sheet accounts that are translated at historical exchange rates.

All translation gains and losses related to the United States division are included in the statement of loss in accordance with generally accepted accounting principles applicable in Canada.

Majestic International Contractors Limited is a self-sustaining foreign operation. The accounts of this subsidiary stated in foreign currencies have been translated into Canadian dollars as follows:
a) Assets and liabilities at the rate of exchange in effect at the balance sheet date.
b) Revenue and expense items at the rate of exchange in effect on the dates on which such items are recognized in income during the period.

The resulting translation adjustments are deferred and shown as a separate component of shareholders' equity.

Accounting for Construction Contracts

Profits from construction contracts are recognized for accounting purposes on the percentage of completion method. The percentage of completion is determined by relating the actual cost of work performed to date, to the current estimated total cost of the respective contracts. When the current estimated costs to complete indicate a loss, such a loss is recognized immediately for accounting purposes. Revisions in costs and earnings or loss estimates during the course of the work are reflected during the accounting period in which the facts that cause the revision become known. Income from claims is recorded in the year such claims are resolved.

Unbilled work represents the excess of contract costs and profits or losses recognized to date, on the percentage of completion accounting method, over billings to date. Deferred contract revenue represents the excess of billings to date over the amount of contract costs and profits or losses recognized to date, on the percentage of completion accounting method.

Property and Equipment

All property and equipment is recorded at cost. The cost and the accumulated depreciation of property and equipment which is retired or sold are removed from the accounts and the gain or loss is recorded in the Consolidated Statement of Loss.

Depreciation is provided primarily on the declining balance method over the useful lives of the assets, which are estimated to be 10 to 25 years for buildings, 3 to 10 years for construction equipment, and 10 years for other assets.

Income Taxes

The recovery of income taxes recognizes the tax effects of all income and expense transactions included in each year's financial statements regardless of the year the transactions are reported for tax purposes.

Investment tax credits relating to the scientific research investment contract were applied to reduce income taxes payable in the year in which it was purchased.

Deferred income taxes arising from items in current assets or current liabilities are classified as a current liability.

The non-current deferred income taxes arise primarily from the difference between the depreciation claimed for tax purposes and the depreciation recorded in the accounts, as well as from the scientific research investment contract.

SUMMARY OF CONSOLIDATED INCOME STATEMENTS
(in thousands, except for per share amounts)

	1984	1983	1982	1981	1980	1979	1978	1977	1976	1975	1974
Revenues	$59,403	$28,928	$136,420	$158,798	$51,646	$29,563	$48,514	$48,612	$125,093	$108,106	$32,049
Cost of operations	61,554	33,547	117,286	124,050	52,999	30,866	44,588	45,010	117,699	98,582	30,871
Gross profit (loss) from operations	(2,151)	(4,619)	19,134	34,748	(1,353)	(1,303)	3,926	3,602	7,394	9,524	1,178
General & administrative expenses	3,183	4,346	5,104	6,003	3,921	2,650	2,540	2,157	1,700	1,861	2,078
Income (loss) before other income	(5,334)	(8,965)	14,030	28,745	(5,274)	(3,953)	1,386	1,445	5,694	7,663	(900)
Other income, net	3,184	2,569	1,791	1,105	3,782	2,646	2,931	964	304	(453)	(88)
Income (loss) before income taxes	(2,150)	(6,396)	15,821	29,850	(1,492)	(1,307)	4,317	2,409	5,998	7,210	(988)
Income taxes (recovery)	(1,057)	(3,655)	7,624	15,025	(1,161)	(867)	1,627	1,147	3,179	3,676	99
Net income (loss)	$(1,093)	($2,741)	$ 8,197	$ 14,825	$ (331)	$ (440)	$ 2,690	$ 1,262	$ 2,819	$ 3,534	$(1,087)
Earnings (loss) per common share	$ (0.13)	$ (0.33)	0.98	$ 1.77	$ (0.40)	$ (0.53)	$ 0.33	$ 0.15	$ 0.34	$ 0.43	$ (0.13)
Weighted average common shares outstanding used in per-share calculations	8,397	8,393	8,378	8,360	8,307	8,281	8,273	8,272	8,270	8,262	8,255

Note: Majestic Wiley Contractors Limited was formed by amalgamation effective May 1, 1974. The above income statement for the year ended December 31, 1974 is unaudited and has been restated to reflect operations both prior to and subsequent to amalgamation during 1974.

Notes to Consolidated Financial Statements
December 31, 1984 and 1983

3. Other income, net

	1984	1983
Income from short-term investments	$1,780,000	$2,298,000
Royalties from scientific research investment contract	1,407,000	1,326,000
Amortization of cost of scientific research investment contract	(1,250,000)	(1,250,000)
Foreign exchange gains	896,000	32,000
Interest expense	(91,000)	(74,000)
Other	442,000	237,000
	$3,184,000	$2,569,000

6. Business Segment Information

The Company operates in one industry segment, that being construction. Its operations are conducted principally in Canada and the United States. The operations and identifiable assets by geographic region for the years ended December 31, 1984 and 1983 are as follows:

	CANADA	FOREIGN	TOTAL
1984			
Revenues	**$47,911,000**	**$11,492,000**	**$59,403,000**
Operating Loss	**$(2,665,000)**	**$(2,669,000)**	**$(5,334,000)**
Other income, net			**3,184,000**
Recovery of income taxes			**1,057,000**
Net loss			**$(1,093,000)**
Identifiable assets	**$28,333,000**	**$10,797,000**	**$39,130,000**
1983			
Revenues	$14,395,000	$14,533,000	$28,928,000
Operating Loss	$(3,126,000)	$(5,839,000)	$8,965,000)
Other income, net			2,569,000
Recovery of income taxes			3,655,000
Net loss			$(2,741,000)
Identifiable assets	$34,887,000	$ 8,657,000	$43,544,000

Loss per Share

Computations of loss per share are based on the weighted average number of shares outstanding during the respective years (1984 — 8 397 391 shares; 1983 — 8 392 657 shares). The additional number of shares issuable upon the potential exercise of employees' stock options has not been included, since the effect would not be material.

Pension and Incentive Compensation Plans

The company has two non-contributory pension plans which cover its executive, professional, administrative, and clerical employees, subject to certain specified service requirements. An actuarial valuation is prepared every three years. The actuarial valuations as at December 31, 1982 for the Canadian plan and December 31, 1983 for the United States plan indicate that there is no unfunded liability in either plan.

The company has an incentive compensation plan which provides for payment to be made to certain key employees based on performance goals. Amounts accrued under this plan are charged to income in the current year and are payable over a period of years, subject to approval of the board of directors. The amount not currently payable is immaterial.

Scientific Research Investment Contract

In 1982, the company purchased a scientific research investment contract. This investment qualifies as a research and development expense for income tax purposes. Under the Income Tax Act, there is a permanent tax saving that has been applied to reduce the cost of the investment in the financial statements.

The contract entitles the company to guaranteed semi-annual royalty payments from 1983 to 1986. The cost of the investment and the related income taxes are being amortized over the life of the guaranteed royalty payments.

Research and Development Costs

Research and development costs, net of any related grants from government incentive programs, are charged against income during the year.

For Discussion

1. The comparative income statements of this entity show the gross profit (loss) from operations over a period of eleven years. What does a comparison of gross profit (loss) indicate for Majestic? Explain in your own words what a "gross loss" means.
2. The income statement does not indicate the reasons for the change during the period but these reasons may be more important than the amounts involved. Is there any information provided elsewhere that is useful for interpreting the performance of Majestic?
3. Make an analysis of the information contained in the balance sheet to establish the solvency of the entity. Calculate appropriate short-term solvency ratios.
4. Compare the segment information provided in note 6 to the financial statements. How do you view the profitability of operations in Canada compared with those in the United States?

SUMMARY OF CONSOLIDATED BALANCE SHEETS

	1984	1983	1982	1981*	1980	1979	1978	1977	1976	1975	1974
Current assets	$22,724	28,405	36,242	50,115	$24,106	$20,555	$21,557	$15,990	$17,687	$10,824	$ 9,002
Current liabilities	(7,360)	(5,949)	(14,628)	(29,337)	(11,667)	(6,363)	(6,351)	(2,863)	(9,720)	(5,468)	(6,251)
Working capital	15,364	22,456	21,614	20,778	12,439	14,192	15,206	13,127	7,967	5,356	2,751
Mortgage receivables	–	–	–	–	38	44	49	50	–	–	–
Property and equipment — net	10,233	12,294	15,187	17,757	9,764	8,707	10,079	12,322	15,997	18,968	21,964
Operating authorities and other assets	–	–	–	–	190	192	193	193	193	193	194
Long-term debt					–	–	(1,500)	(3,073)	(3,116)	(5,209)	(9,200)
Deferred income taxes	(5,593)	(5,611)	(5,986)	(4,364)	(2,510)	(3,029)	(3,571)	(3,198)	(2,885)	(3,975)	(3,920)
Shareholders' equity	26,177	31,984	34,644	34,817	$19,921	$20,106	$20,456	$19,421	$18,156	$15,333	$11,789

*Note   After 1980, Mortgage Receivables are included in Current Assets.

Discussion Case 5-2:   Joe, the Restaurateur

Joe, the restaurateur, adds a rack of peanuts to the counter, hoping to pick up a little extra profit in the usual course of business. He is interviewed by his Accountant/Efficiency Expert.

EFF. EX.   Joe, you said you put in these peanuts because some people ask for them, but do you realise what this rack of peanuts is costing you?

JOE   It ain't gonna cost. 'Sgonna be a profit. Sure, I hadda pay $25 for a fancy rack to holda bags, but the peanuts cost 6¢ a bag and I sell 'em for 10¢. Figger I sell 50 bags a week to start. It'll take 12½ weeks to cover the cost of the rack. After that I gotta clear profit of 4¢ a bag. The more I sell, the more I make.

EFF. EX.   That is an antiquated and completely unrealistic approach, Joe. Fortunately, modern accounting procedures permit a more accurate picture which reveals the complexities involved.

JOE   Huh?

EFF. EX.   To be precise, those peanuts must be integrated into your entire operation and be allocated their appropriate share of business overhead. They must share a proportionate part of your expenditures for rent, heat, light, equipment depreciation, decorating, salaries for your waitresses, cook,——

JOE   The cook? What'sa he gotta do wit'a peanuts? He don' even know I got 'em!

EFF. EX.   Look, Joe, the cook is in the kitchen, the kitchen prepares the food, the food is what brings people in here, and the people ask to buy peanuts. That's why you must charge a portion of the cook's wages, as well as part of your own salary to peanut sales. This sheet contains a carefully calculated costs analysis which indicates the peanut operation should pay exactly $1,278 per year toward these general overhead costs.

JOE   The peanuts? $1,278 a year for overhead? the nuts?

EFF. EX.   It's really a little more than that. You also spend money each week to have the windows washed, to have the place swept out in the mornings and keep soap in the washroom. That raises the total to $1,313 per year.

JOE (thoughtfully)   But the peanut salesman said I'd make money—put 'em on the end of the counter, he said—and get 4¢ a bag profit——

EFF. EX. (with a sniff)He's got an accountant. Do you actually know what the portion of the counter occupied by the peanut rack is worth to you?

JOE   Ain't worth nothing. No stool there—just a dead spot at the end.

EFF. EX.   The modern cost picture permits no dead spots. Your counter contains 60 square feet [5.6 m²] and your counter business grosses $15,000 a year. Consequently, the square foot [0.1 m²] of space occupied by the peanut rack is worth $250 per year. Since you have taken that area away from general counter use, you must charge the value of the space to the accountant.

JOE   You mean I gotta add $250 a year more to the peanuts?

EFF. EX.   Right. That raises their shares of the general operating costs to a grand total of $1,563 per year. Now, then, if you sell 50 bags of peanuts per week, these allocated costs will amount to 60¢ per bag.

JOE   WHAT?

EFF. EX.   Obviously, to that must be added your purchase price of 6¢ per bag, which brings the total to 66¢. So you see, by selling peanuts at 10¢ per bag you are losing 56¢ on every sale.

JOE   Somethin's crazy!

EFF. EX.   Not at all! Here are the figures. They prove your peanut operation cannot stand on its own feet.

JOE (brightening)   Suppose I sell lotsa peanuts — thousand bags a week 'stead a fifty?

EFF. EX. (tolerantly)   Joe, you don't understand the problem. If the volume of peanut sales increases, your operating costs will go up — you'll have to handle more bags, with more time, more depreciation, more everything. The basic principle of accounting is firm on that subject! "The Bigger the Operation the More General Overhead Costs that Must Be Allocated." No, increasing the volume of sales won't help.

JOE   Okay. You so smart, you tell me what I gotta do.

EFF. EX. (condescendingly)   Well — you could first reduce operating expenses.

JOE   How?

EFF. EX.   Move to a building with cheaper rent. Cut salaries. Wash the windows biweekly. Have the floor swept only on Thursday. Remove the soap from the washrooms. Decrease the area value of your counter. For example, if you can cut your expenses 50 percent that will reduce the amount allocated to peanuts from $1,563 down to $781.50 per year, reducing the cost to 36¢ per bag.

JOE (slowly)   That's better?

EFF.EX.   Much, much better. However, even then you would lose 26¢ per bag if you charge only 10¢. Therefore, you must also raise your selling price. If you want a net profit of 4¢ per bag you would have to charge 40¢.

JOE (flabbergasted)   You mean even after I cut operating costs 50 percent, I still gotta charge 40¢ for a 10¢ bag of peanuts? Nobody's that nuts about nuts! Who'd buy 'em?

EFF. EX.   That's a secondary consideration. The point is, at 40¢ you'd be selling at a price based upon a true and proper evaluation of your then-reduced costs.

JOE (eagerly)   Look! I gotta better idea. Why don't I just throw the nuts out — put 'em in a ash can?

EFF. EX.   Can you afford it?

JOE   Sure. All I got is about 50 bags of peanuts — cost about three bucks — so I lose $25 on the rack, but I'm outa this nasty business and no more grief.

EFF. EX. (shaking head)   Joe, it isn't quite that simple. You are in the peanut business! The minute you throw those peanuts out you are adding $1,563 of annual overhead to the rest of your operation. Joe — be realistic — can you afford to do that?

JOE (completely crushed)   It'sa unbelievable! Last week I was a make money. Now I'm in a trouble — justa because I think peanuts on a counter is a gonna bring me some extra profit — justa because I believe 50 bags of peanuts a week is a easy.

EFF. EX. (with raised eyebrow)   That is the object of modern cost studies, Joe — to dispel those false illusions.

Source   "Peanuts — or The Higher Control of Business", *Cost and Management*, IV, 4 (July–August, 1970), p. 63. (Reprinted from the *New York Certified Public Accountant*, June, 1960.)

For Discussion

1. For financial statement purposes, some expenses have been shown in Chapter 5 to be common to both the selling and administrative functions; these expenses have to be apportioned between these functions on some equitable basis. In this case, the accountant/efficiency expert also believes that costs must further be apportioned among the types of items sold in the restaurant to enable Joe to make accurate business decisions. Is the accountant/efficiency expert correct? Why or why not?

2. If you prepared an income statement for Joe without any peanut sales and a second income statement showing the sale of 50 bags of peanuts a week, which income statement would show a larger net income? Why?

3. How accurate a picture has the accountant/efficiency expert given Joe? Does Joe make $0.04 a bag or doesn't he?

Discussion Case 5-3:   Cheque, Please.

At most restaurants, you get what you pay for, but at Juliano's Family Restaurant, it's the other way around. With no prices on the menu, customers are asked to pay what their palates — and conscience — tell them.

Whatever the inspiration, the results have been stupendous. Never mind the marketing textbooks and their pricing strategies; for Juliano's, having no prices has led to an increase of 25 percent to an average of $6,000 per month. Patronage has also soared at the 48-seat eatery. Thus far, most customers are "coming pretty close to the prices I had," Juliano says. Only two diners have left without leaving anything.

When looking for a place to open a restaurant in 1983, Juliano found three places he could afford, but the two best spots could not be secured. By default, Juliano decided to take a former waterbed shop, which he leases for $800 a month. He spent $20,000 for used kitchen equipment, furniture and minor repairs. "When we opened in December, we had $400," he said.

When Juliano decided to remove his prices, "We didn't have anything to lose." He alerted two local newspapers, which promptly dispatched two reporters to the scene. Subsequent stories attracted the Associated Press and a National TV network with the story of the restaurant with no prices racing across the country.

Lest you think that this might go too far, Juliano drew the line when he recently hired two employees. He is leaving the salaries to his discretion.

Source   Adapted from: " 'Price-less' menu brings Juliano's customers" *Restaurant News*, by Marilyn Alva, April 22, 1985 and "We can Name Lots of Restaurants That Wouldn't Dare Attempt This" by Terrence Roth, *Wall Street Journal*, Feb. 21, 1985, p. 35e.

For Discussion

1. Discuss the matching principle as it relates to Juliano's Family Restaurant.

2. Could the increase in patronage at the restaurant be a result of the novelty of Juliano's pricing structure? Do you think this trend is likely to continue? why or why not? If you were a bank loan officer and Juliano approached you for a business loan, how would you react to his proforma financial statements?

Comprehension Problems

Comprehension Problem 5-1

The following income statement was prepared by the new accountant of the Careless Company Limited.

<table>
<tr><td>(1)</td><td colspan="3" align="center">Careless Company Limited</td></tr>
<tr><td>(2)</td><td colspan="3" align="center">**Income Statement**</td></tr>
<tr><td>(3)</td><td colspan="3" align="center">December 31, 19X5</td></tr>
<tr><td></td><td></td><td colspan="2" align="center">($000)</td></tr>
<tr><td>(4)</td><td>Sales less: Returns and Allowances</td><td>$9,440</td><td></td></tr>
<tr><td>(5)</td><td>Purchases: Discounts Earned</td><td>10</td><td>$9,450</td></tr>
<tr><td>(6)</td><td>*Deduct:* Cost of Goods Sold:</td><td></td><td></td></tr>
<tr><td>(7)</td><td>Inventory (Dec. 31, 19X5)</td><td>$ 880</td><td></td></tr>
<tr><td>(8)</td><td>*Add:* Purchases</td><td>5,860</td><td></td></tr>
<tr><td>(9)</td><td>Delivery Expense</td><td>360</td><td></td></tr>
<tr><td>(10)</td><td>Goods Available for Sale</td><td>$7,100</td><td></td></tr>
<tr><td>(11)</td><td>Inventory (Jan. 1, 19X5)</td><td>750</td><td>6,350</td></tr>
<tr><td>(12)</td><td>Operating Profit</td><td></td><td>$3,100</td></tr>
<tr><td>(13)</td><td>*Deduct:* Expenses:</td><td></td><td></td></tr>
<tr><td>(14)</td><td>Salaries</td><td>$1,220</td><td></td></tr>
<tr><td>(15)</td><td>Utilities</td><td>210</td><td></td></tr>
<tr><td>(16)</td><td>Insurance</td><td>190</td><td></td></tr>
<tr><td>(17)</td><td>Transportation In</td><td>205</td><td></td></tr>
<tr><td>(18)</td><td>Property Tax</td><td>43</td><td></td></tr>
<tr><td>(19)</td><td>Miscellaneous Expenses</td><td>260</td><td>2,428</td></tr>
<tr><td>(20)</td><td>Net Income (before income tax)</td><td></td><td>672</td></tr>
<tr><td>(21)</td><td>Income Tax</td><td></td><td>312</td></tr>
<tr><td>(22)</td><td>Net Income for the Year</td><td></td><td>$ 360</td></tr>
</table>

Required:
1. Identify the errors in the income statement by referring to the assigned line numbers and briefly explain why they are errors.
2. Prepare a new income statement correcting the errors you discovered.

Note: Throughout assignment material for this chapter, refer to the master Chart of Accounts provided in Chapter 3.

Comprehension Problem 5-2

The following is the incomplete worksheet of Liebman Inc., at the end of its fiscal year March 31, 19X6:

LIEBMAN INC.
Worksheet
For the Year Ended March 31, 19X6

Account Title	Trial Balance Dr.	Trial Balance Cr.	Adjustments Dr.	Adjustments Cr.	Adjusted Trial Balance Dr.	Adjusted Trial Balance Cr.	Income Statement Dr.	Income Statement Cr.	Balance Sheet Dr.	Balance Sheet Cr.
Cash	?				7,500				7,500	
Accounts Receivable	14,300				14,300				?	
Notes Receivable	1,525				?				?	
Merchandise Inventory	?				?		21,200	20,500	?	
Prepaid Insurance	850			?	610				610	
Prepaid Rent	4,200			?	2,100				2,100	
Office Supplies	190			?	55				55	
Equipment	2,500			?	2,500				2,500	
Accum. Deprec.–Eqpmt.		1,600		?		1,660				1,660
Furniture	4,500				4,500				4,500	
Accum. Dep.–Furniture		1,560		?		?				?
Accounts Payable		8,950				?				?
Notes Payable		4,200				?				?
Common Stock		25,000				?				?
Retained Earnings		10,610				?				?
Dividends	2,600				2,600				2,600	
Sales		?				?		?		
Sales Returns and Allow.	3,175				3,175		3,175			
Sales Discounts	1,295				1,295		1,295			
Purchases	77,050				77,050		77,050			
Purchases Returns and Allowances		2,290				2,290		2,290		
Transportation In	1,635				1,635		1,635			
Advertising Expense	5,540				5,540		5,540			
Miscellaneous General Expense	635				635		635			
Salesperson's Salaries	7,950				7,950		7,950			
General Selling Expense	4,660				4,660		4,660			
	161,305	161,305								
Insurance Expense			?		240		240			
Rent Expense			?		2,100		2,100			
Office Supplies Used			?		135		135			
Deprec. Expense–Eqpmt.			?		60		60			
Deprec. Expense–Furniture			?		250		250			
Income Tax Expense			800		?		?			
Income Tax Payable				800		?				?
Totals			3,585	3,585	162,415	162,415	?	129,885	?	?
Net Income							?			?
							?	129,885	?	56,190

Required: Complete the worksheet for the missing amounts.

Comprehension Problem 5-3

The following closing entry is taken from the journal of J.J. Jones Inc. at December 31, 19X4:

GENERAL JOURNAL

Date 19X4		Description	F	Debit	Credit
Dec.	31	Sales		161 000 -	
		Purchases, Returns and Allowances		1 500 -	
		Inventory (Dec. 31)		13 500 -	
		Purchases			84 000 -
		Rent Expense			18 000 -
		Advertising Expense			13 600 -
		Delivery Expense			4 800 -
		Office Supplies Used			6 400 -
		Miscellaneous General Expense			11 650 -
		Inventory (Jan. 1)			11 250 -
		Income Summary			26 300 -
		To close revenue and expense			
		accounts and to set up ending			
		inventory.			

Required: Prepare an income statement in proper form.

Comprehension Problem 5-4

The following transactions relating to Dominion Ltd. took place in November of the current year.

Nov. 1 Dominion purchased merchandise on account from Miller Ltd., terms 1/10, n/30, $600.
Nov. 2 Dominion sold merchandise on account to Jones, terms 2/10, 1/15, n/60, $800.
Nov. 4 Purchased office supplies on account, 1/15, n/30, $230.
Nov. 5 Purchased $1,500 of office equipment, paying $300 in cash and signing a promissory note payable for the balance.
Nov. 7 Dominion received a memorandum for unsatisfactory merchandise purchased from Miller Ltd. on November 1 and returned for credit, $100.
Nov. 8 Purchased merchandise on account from SDR Company Ltd., terms 1/10, n/60, $500.
Nov. 9 Paid for the merchandise purchased on November 1.
Nov. 10 Sold merchandise to Brown on account, terms 1/10, n/30, $1,000.
Nov. 12 Issued a $200 memorandum to customer Brown, who purchased merchandise on November 10 and returned a portion for credit.
Nov. 14 Jones, the customer who made the purchase on November 2, paid cash today for that purchase.
Nov. 18 Brown sent in a cheque this date to pay in full the balance owed Dominion.

Required: Prepare journal entries to record the November transactions.

Comprehension Problem 5-5

The following account balances are extracted from the records of Gibbons Distributors Inc. at December 31, 19X4, its fiscal year-end.

Merchandise Inventory (Jan. 1, 19X4)	6,000
Merchandise Inventory (Dec. 31, 19X4)	5,000
Transportation In	1,000
Delivery Expense	2,500
Sales	47,000
Purchases	29,500
Sales Returns	1,550
Purchases Returns	1,205
Sales Discounts	450
Purchases Discounts	295
Interest Expense	1,200

Required: Calculate the gross profit for Gibbons; use the classified income statement form.

Problems

Problem 5-1

The following data pertain to Kitchener Hardware Inc. for the year ended December 31, 19X9.

Sales Salaries	$ 16,400
Office Salaries Expense	6,200
Sales	157,500
Transportation In	2,200
Rent Expense (selling space)	9,600
Rent Expense (office space)	1,200
Rent Payable	800
Sales Discounts	1,500
Depreciation Expense — Equipment (office)	320
Delivery Expense	2,700
Purchases	97,300
Sales Returns and Allowances	1,300
Merchandise Inventory (Jan. 1)	15,500
Advertising Expense	1,800
Insurance Expense	130
Merchandise Inventory (Dec. 31)	17,900
Purchases Discounts	1,100
Store Supplies Used	850
Purchases Returns and Allowances	550
Office Supplies Used	250
Depreciation Expense — Equipment (store)	1,550
Dividends	2,500

Required: Prepare a classified income statement.

Problem 5-2

The following information is extracted from the income statement columns of the worksheet of Ontario Limited at December 31, 19X4.

Merchandise Inventory	184,000	200,000
Sales		781,600
Sales Returns and Allowances	16,400	
Sales Discounts	16,480	
Purchases	364,000	
Purchases Returns and Allowances		15,200
Purchases Discounts		4,800
Transportation In	6,560	
Salaries — Salespersons	88,000	
Advertising Expense	15,600	
Delivery Expense	69,200	
Miscellaneous Selling Expense	15,000	
Salaries — Office	80,000	
Property Taxes	13,500	
Sundry Expense	32,440	
Supplies Used	9,060	
Interest Income		840
Insurance Expense	11,160	
Depreciation Expense	22,080	
Interest Expense	2,112	
Income Tax Expense	18,530	
Totals	964,122	1,002,440
Net Income for the Year	38,318	
	1,002,440	1,002,440

Required:
1. Prepare an income statement in proper form (record Sundry Expense and Depreciation Expense as General and Administrative Expense).
2. Prepare all necessary closing journal entries.

Problem 5-3

The income statement of Tonto and Silver Limited is presented below.

Income Statement
For the Year Ended December 31, 19X8

($000)

Sales			$2,500
Cost of Goods Sold			
Opening Inventory (Jan. 1)		$ 500	
Purchases		1,415	
Transportation In		25	
Cost of Goods Available		$1,940	
Ending Inventory (Dec. 31)		340	
Total Cost of Goods Sold			1,600
Gross Profit			$ 900
OPERATING EXPENSES			
Selling			
Advertising Expense	$ 40		
Miscellaneous Selling Expense	75		
Total Selling Expenses		$ 115	
General and Administrative Expenses:			
Depreciation Expense	$ 28		
Insurance Expense	6		
Miscellaneous General Expense	86		
Rent Expense	48		
Utilities Expense	50		
Wages Expense	385		
Total General and Administrative Expenses		603	
Total Operating Expenses			718
Income from Operations			$ 182
Financing Costs			
Interest Expense		$ 161	
Other Revenue			
Interest Earned	$ 80		
Rent Earned	70	150	11
Income (before income tax)			$ 171
Income Tax			35
Net Income for the Year			$ 136

Required: Prepare closing journal entries at December 31, 19X8.

Problem 5-4

Beacon Hill Corp. was incorporated on July 2, 19X2 to operate a merchandising business. All its sales on account are made according to the following terms: 2/10, n/30. Its transactions during July 19X2 are as follows:

Jul. 2   Issued common shares for $5,000 cash to George Hill, the incorporator and sole shareholder of the corporation

Jul. 2   Purchased $3,500 merchandise on account from Westmount Pencils Ltd. for terms 2/10, n/30

Jul. 2   Sold $2,000-worth of merchandise on account to Hampstead Tool Rentals Inc.

Jul. 3   Paid Concordia Rentals Corp. $500 for July rent

Jul. 5   Paid Westwood Furniture Ltd. $1,000 for equipment

Jul. 8   Collected $200 for a cash sale made today to Byron Peel

Jul. 8   Purchased $2,000 merchandise on account from MacDonald Distributors Inc. for terms 2/15, n/30

Jul. 9   Received the amount due from Hamstead Tool Rentals Inc. for the July 2 sale (less discount)

Jul. 10 Paid Westmount Pencils Ltd. for the July 2 purchase (less discount)

Jul. 10 Purchased $200-worth of merchandise on account from Peel Products Inc. for terms n/30

Jul. 15 Sold $2,000-worth of merchandise on account to Condor Products Corp.

Jul. 15 Purchased $1,500-worth of merchandise on account from Draper Door Inc. for terms 2/10, n/30

Jul. 15 Received a credit note memo from MacDonald Distributors Inc. for $100-worth of defective merchandise included in the July 8 purchase

Jul. 16 Condor Products Corp. returned $200-worth of merchandise: issued a credit memo

Jul. 20 Sold $3,500-worth of merchandise on account to Pine Promotions Ltd.

Jul. 20 Paid MacDonald Distributors Inc. for half the purchase made July 8 (less credit note, less discount on payment)

Jul. 24 Received half the amount due from Condor Products Corp. in partial payment for the July 15 sale (less discount on payment)

Jul. 24 Paid Draper Doors Ltd. for the purchase made July 15 (less discount)

Jul. 26 Sold $600 merchandise on account to Daytona Sales Ltd.

Jul. 26 Purchased $800-worth of merchandise on account from Gold & Silver Co. for terms 2/10, n/30

Jul. 31 Paid Real-Quick Transport Co. $350 for transportation to our warehouse during the month. (All purchases are fob shipping point.)

Required: Prepare journal entries to record the July transactions.

Problem 5-5

Lucerne Sales Corp. was incorporated on May 1, 19X1 to operate a merchandising business. All its sales on account are made according to the following terms; 2/10, net 30. Its transactions during May 19X1 are as follows:

May 1   Issued common shares for $2,000 cash to Harry Jones, the incorporator and sole share-holder of the corporation

May 1   Received $10,000 from the Second Canadian Bank as a demand bank loan

May 1   Paid Cadillac Corp. $1,500 for three months rent in advance — May, June, and July (recorded as an asset)

May 1   Paid Avanti Equipment Ltd. $5,000 for equipment

May 1   Purchased $2,000-worth of merchandise on account from St Luc Wholesalers Ltd. for terms 2/10, n/30

May 1   Sold $2,500-worth of merchandise on account to Montreal West Distributors

May 2   Purchased $1,800-worth of merchandise on account from Rosedale Products Ltd. for terms n/30.

May 2   Sold $2,000-worth of merchandise on account to Terrebonne Sales Inc.

May 3   Collected $500 for a cash sale made today to Irwin Peabody

May 5   Paid All Province Insurance Inc. $1,200 for a one-year insurance policy, effective May 1 (recorded as an asset)

May 5   Sold $1,000-worth of merchandise on account to Brock Stores Corporation

May 6   Terrebonne Sales Inc. returned $500-worth of merchandise: issued a credit memo

May 8   Received a credit memo from St Luc Wholesalers Corp. for $300-worth of defective merchandise included in the May 1 purchase and returned subsequently to St Luc

May 8	Purchased $2,800-worth of merchandise on account from Elmhurst Novelties Ltd. for terms 2/15, n/30
May 9	Received the amount due from Montreal West Distributors from the May 1 sale (less discount)
May 9	Paid St Luc Wholesalers Corp. for the May 1 purchase (less discount)
May 10	Sold $400-worth of merchandise on account to Western Warehouse
May 11	Received the amount due from Terrebonne Sales Inc. (less the May 6 credit memo and discount)
May 13	Paid Express Corporation $100 for transportation in
May 15	Purchased $1,500-worth of merchandise on account from Hudson Distributors Inc. for terms 2/10, n/30
May 15	Sold $1,500-worth of merchandise on account to Roxboro Outlets Inc.
May 15	Paid $500 in commissions to Harry Jones, *re*: sales invoices nos. 1, 2, and 3
May 19	Paid Rosedale Products Inc. for the May 2 purchase
May 19	Purchased $1,200-worth of merchandise on account from Mid-Island Stores Corp. for terms 1/10, n/30
May 22	Purchased $600-worth of merchandise on account from Quick Sales Co. for terms n/30
May 22	Paid to Elmhurst Novelties Inc. for the May 8 purchase (less discount)
May 24	Paid to Express Corporation $150 for transportation in
May 25	Sold $900-worth of merchandise on account to Kirkland Centres Ltd.
May 26	Received the amount due from Brock Stores Corporation
May 27	Paid $200 to Yale Deliveries Ltd. for deliveries made to customers
May 28	Collected $300 for a cash sale made today to Joe Montclair
May 28	Made a $200 cash purchase from Ballantyne Sales Inc. today; issued cheque #11 (debited purchases)
May 28	Sold $900-worth of merchandise on account to Lachine Wharf Corp.
May 29	Purchased $100-worth of merchandise on account from Sidekicks Inc.
May 29	Paid Speedy Ltd. $300 for deliveries (debited account 620)
May 29	Paid Impetus Advertising Agency $400 for advertising materials used during May
May 29	Paid Hydro-Bec $100 for electricity
May 29	Paid Harry Jones $350 commission, *re*: sales invoices nos. 4, 5, 6, and 7.
May 30	Collected $1,000 on account from Roxboro Outlets Inc.
May 31	Paid Mid-Island Stores Corp. $700 on account
May 31	Paid Harry Jones $100 for dividends declared today.

Required: Prepare journal entries to record the May transactions.

Problem 5-6

The following accounts and account balances are taken from the worksheet of Kapoor Enterprises Ltd. at December 31, 19X6, its fiscal year-end.

	Balance Sheet	
Account Title	*Dr.*	*Cr.*
Cash	2,000	
Accounts Receivable	8,000	
Merchandise Inventory	19,000	
Prepaid Insurance	1,000	
Land	5,000	
Buildings	25,000	
Equipment	20,000	
Accum. Deprec. — Buildings		1,000
Accum. Deprec. — Equipment		4,000
Bank Loan (due 19X7)		5,000
Accounts Payable		7,000
Income Tax Payable		3,000
Mortgage Payable (due 19X9)		50,000
Common Stock		3,000
Retained Earnings		2,000
Dividends	1,000	
Totals	81,000	75,000
Net Income		6,000
Totals	81,000	81,000

Required:
1. Using the above information, prepare a classified balance sheet.
2. Make the following calculations:
   a. The proportion of shareholders to creditors claims on the assets of Kapoor.
   b. The current ratio.
   c. The acid-test ratio.
3. Assume that you are the loan officer of the bank where Kapoor has applied for a 120-day loan of $10,000. Would you grant the loan? Why or why not?
4. If the loan were granted, calculate to current ratio and acid-test ratio immediately following the receipt of the loan on January 2, 19X7.

Problem 5-7

The following closing entries were prepared for Ferries Products Inc. at December 31, 19X3, the end of its fiscal year. (The journal entry narratives have been omitted.)

Dec. 31	Merchandise Inventory	6,000	
	Sales	31,000	
	Purchases Returns	575	
	Purchases Discounts	225	
	Income Summary		37,800
31	Income Summary	32,800	
	Merchandise Inventory		4,000
	Sales Returns		690
	Sales Discounts		310
	Purchases		22,500
	Transportation In		300
	Operating Expenses		5,000

31	Income Summary	5,000	
	Retained Earnings		5,000
31	Retained Earnings	1,000	
	Dividends		1,000

Required:
1. Post and rule the above Merchandise Inventory (with a January 1 balance of $4,000) and Income Summary accounts to T-accounts.
2. Using the data in the preceding closing entries, complete the income statement column of a worksheet. Calculate the debit and credit and the net income.
3. Calculate the gross profit, using the classified income statement form.

Problem 5-8

The following trial balance has been extracted from the records of Diane Jewellery Inc. at December 31, 19X5, its fiscal year-end. The balances for Merchandise Inventory and Retained Earnings have not changed during the year.

	Account Balances	
	Dr.	*Cr.*
Cash	$ 750	
Accounts Receivable	12,000	
Merchandise Inventory	6,000	
Prepaid Rent	-0-	
Office Supplies	-0-	
Equipment — Office	4,400	
Accum. Depreciation		-0-
Bank Loan		$ 5,000
Accounts Payable		12,540
Income Tax Payable		2,400
Common Stock		2,000
Retained Earnings		1,500
Dividends	900	
Sales		50,000
Sales Returns	1,500	
Sales Discounts	500	
Purchases	35,000	
Purchases Returns		1,700
Purchases Discounts		300
Transportation In	1,000	
Advertising Expense	1,700	
Commissions Expense	4,800	
Delivery Expense	650	
Depreciation Expense	-0-	
Insurance Expense	350	
Interest Expense	600	
Office Supplies Used	350	
Rent Expenses	1,950	
Telephone Expense	300	
Utilities Expense	290	
Income Tax Expense	2,400	
Totals	$75,440	$75,440

Required:
1. Record the trial balance on a worksheet.
2. Prepare adjusting entries for the following and record them on the worksheet.
   a. $1000 of the accounts receivables not yet recorded have just been received.
   b. A physical count of supplies indicates that $100-worth are still on hand.

    c. No depreciation has yet been recorded on the office equipment. An amount of $400 is estimated applicable to 19X5.

    d. The December telephone bill has not yet been received. An amount of $60 is estimated as owing. Record as Accounts Payable.

3. Complete the worksheet. A physical count of inventory indicates that $8,000-worth of merchandise is still on hand at December 31, 19X5.

4. From the worksheet, prepare the following financial statements in good form:

    a. Classified income statement (The advertising, commissions, and delivery expenses are considered as selling expenses.)

    b. Statement of retained earnings.

    c. Classified balance sheet.

5. From the worksheet, prepare all necessary closing entries.

6. Make calculations to answer the following questions:

    a. What is the proportion of shareholder to creditor claims on the assets of the corporation?

    b. What is the current ratio?

    c. What is the acid-test ratio?

7. Assume that you are the loan officer of a bank to which the corporation has applied for an additional 3-month $10,000 bank loan. Would you grant the loan? Why or why not?

8. If the loan were granted on January 2, 19X6, calculate the working capital, current ratio, and acid-test ratio immediately following receipt of the loan.

Alternate Problems

Alternate Problem 5-1

The following information relates to the Interprovincial Colossus Corporation for the current year.

a. Merchandise inventory on hand January 1 is $100,000.

b. During the year, purchased merchandise on account for $200,000 for terms 2/10, n/30. Half of the purchases were paid within the discount period.

c. Paid freight on merchandise purchased, $8,000.

d. Damaged merchandise with an invoice price of $4,000 was returned to the supplier. A cash refund for the returned amount less discount was received. This merchandise was part of the purchase in transaction b which had been paid within the discount period.

e. An allowance of $2,750 was granted customers because merchandise was not satisfactory. Cheques were issued to the several customers.

f. The ending inventory was $80,000 at cost.

Required:

1. Prepare journal entries where necessary for each of the transactions. (Omit explanation lines and assume the company uses periodic inventory method.)

2. Prepare the necessary closing entries based on the above information.

3. What was the cost of goods sold? (December 31 is year-end.)

Alternate Problem 5-2

Southern Corporation supplies you with the following information applicable to the current year. The year-end is December 31.

Transportation In	$ 3,000
Delivery	2,000
Sales	100,000
Merchandise Inventory (Jan. 1)	12,000
Merchandise Inventory (Dec. 31)	15,000
Purchases	70,000
Office Supplies Used	7,000
Purchases Discounts	4,000
Purchases Returns and Allowances	6,000
Sales Returns and Allowances	10,000
Supplies	5,000

Required:
1. Prepare in proper form a partial income statement including sales, cost of goods sold, and gross profit.
2. Prepare closing entries required for the above data.

Alternate Problem 5-3

Sim Co. Products Inc. was incorporated on April 1, 19X1 to operate a merchandising business. All its sales on account are made according to the following terms: 2/10, n30. Its transactions during April 19X1 are as follows.

Apr. 1   Issued common shares for $3,000 cash to Rosco Simcoe, the incorporator and sole shareholder of the corporation

Apr. 1   Purchased $4,000-worth of merchandise on account from Beaconsfield Wholesalers Inc. for terms 2/10, n/30

Apr. 1   Sold $3,000-worth of merchandise on account to Ahuntic Products Corp.

Apr. 2   Collected $500 for a cash sale made today to George Kirkland

Apr. 2   Purchased $750 merchandise on account from Dorval Wholesalers Ltd. for terms n/30

Apr. 2   Sold $1,200-worth of merchandise on account to Chambly Stores Inc.

Apr. 5   Received half the amount due from Ahuntic Products Corp. for the April 1 purchase (less discount on payment)

Apr. 8   Received the amount due from Chambly Stores Inc. for the April 2 purchase (less discount)

Apr. 9   Paid Beaconsfield Sales Inc. for the April 1 purchase (less discount on payment)

Apr. 10   Purchased $2,000-worth of merchandise on account from Carlton Distributors Inc. for terms 2/15, n/30

Apr. 11   Sold $500-worth of merchandise on account to Presidential Sales Inc.

Apr. 12   Presidential Sales Inc. returned $100-worth of merchandise: issued a credit memo

Apr. 15   Received a credit memo from Dorval Wholesalers Ltd. for $150-worth of defective merchandise included in the April 2 purchase and subsequently returned

Apr. 15   Purchased $1,500-worth of merchandise on account from Atwater Distributors Inc. for terms 2/10, n/30

Apr. 19   Purchased $1,250-worth of merchandise on account from Kildare Sales Ltd. for terms n/30

Apr. 20   Sold $2,000-worth of merchandise on account to Salaberry Corp.

Apr. 20   Received the amount due from Presidential Sales Inc. for the April 11 purchase (less return and less discount)

Apr. 22   Paid Carlton Distributors Inc. for the April 10 purchase (less discount on payment)

Apr. 24   Paid Atwater Distributors Inc. for the April 15 purchase (less discount on payment)

Apr. 27   Sold $800-worth of merchandise on account to Bishop Emporium Corp.

Apr. 30   Paid Rapid Delivery Inc. $200 for deliveries made to customers during the month (debited account 620)

Apr. 30   Paid Truck Forwarders Ltd. $500 for transportation to our warehouse during the month. (All purchases are fob shipping point.)

Required: Prepare journal entries to record the April transactions.

Alternate Problem 5-4

Rockland Wholesalers Inc. was incorporated on March 1 to operate a merchandising business. All its sales on account are made according to the following terms: 2/10, n/30.

Mar. 1   Issued common shares for $410,000 cash to Michael Strong, the incorporator and sole shareholder of the corporation
Mar. 1   Paid Brunswick Fixtures Inc. $4,000 for equipment
Mar. 1   Purchased $2,100-worth of merchandise on account from Mid-Island Stores Corp. for terms 2/10, n/30
Mar. 2   Sold $2,000-worth of merchandise on account to Kirkland Centers Ltd.
Mar. 2   Collected $300 for a cash sale made today to Irving Clayton
Mar. 3   Purchased $500-worth of merchandise on account from Quick Sales Co. for terms 1/10, n/30
Mar. 4   Sold $2,500-worth of merchandise on account to Western Warehouse
Mar. 4   Kirkland Centres Ltd. returned $200-worth of merchandise: issued a credit memo
Mar. 5   Purchased $1,400-worth of merchandise on account from St Luc Wholesalers Corp. on account for terms n/30
Mar. 6   Received a credit memo from Mid-Island Stores Corp. for $100-worth of defective merchandise included in the March 1 purchase and subsequently returned to Mid-Island
Mar. 6   Sold $1,500-worth of merchandise on account to Lachine Wharf Corp.
Mar. 7   Purchased $600-worth of merchandise on account from Brock Stores Corporation for terms 2/15, n/30
Mar. 8   Received the amount due from Kirkland Centres Ltd. (less credit memo, less discount)
Mar. 10   Paid Quick Sales Co. for the March 3 purchase (less discount)
Mar. 11   Received $7,500 from the Third Canadian Bank as a demand bank loan
Mar. 12   Paid Fairview Realty Corp. $1,000 for two months rent, March and April (recorded as an asset)
Mar. 12   Sold $700-worth of merchandise on account to Hudson Distributors Inc.
Mar. 13   Received the amount due from Western Warehouse (less discount)
Mar. 15   Paid Michael Strong $350 for commissions earned to date
Mar. 15   Paid Mid-Island Stores Corporation $1,000 on account
Mar. 15   Purchased $1,000-worth of merchandise on account from Rosedale Products Ltd. for terms 2/15, n/30
Mar. 18   Paid Brock Stores Corporation for half of the March 7 purchase (less discount on payment)
Mar. 19   Collected $100 for a cash sale made today to Al Trudeau
Mar. 20   Purchased $1,200-worth of merchandise on account from Sheraton Centers Inc. for terms n/30
Mar. 20   Paid $400 for a cash purchase from Roslyn Distributors Inc. (debited purchases)
Mar. 20   Sold $600-worth of merchandise on account to Sidekicks Inc.
Mar. 21   Paid St Luc Wholesalers Corp. $700 on account
Mar. 22   Received $500 on account from Lachine Wharf Inc.
Mar. 23   Paid All City Insurance Ltd. $2,400 for a one-year insurance policy, effective March 1 (recorded as an asset)
Mar. 24   Paid $300 for a cash purchase from C.K.U. Emporium (debited purchases)
Mar. 25   Sold $1,400-worth of merchandise on account to Elmhurst Novelties Inc.
Mar. 26   Purchased $700-worth of merchandise on account from Grand Markets Ltd. for terms 2/10, n/30
Mar. 30   Paid D-Liver Corp. $500 for deliveries (debited account 620)
Mar. 30   Paid Michael Strong $400 for commissions earned to date
Mar. 30   Paid Bell-Bec $75 for the monthly telephone bill
Mar. 30   Paid Johnson Visuals Ltd. $250 for advertising materials used during the month
Mar. 31   Paid Michael Strong $200 for dividends declared today.

Required: Prepare journal entries to record the March transactions.

Alternate Problem 5-5

The following journal closing entries were prepared for Skinner Services Ltd. at December 31, 19X7, its fiscal year-end. (The journal entry narratives have been omitted.)

Dec. 31	Merchandise Inventory	7,000	
	Sales	34,000	
	Purchases Returns	1,760	
	Purchases Discounts	240	
	Income Summary		43,000
31	Income Summary	40,000	
	Merchandise Inventory		6,000
	Sales Returns		660
	Sales Discounts		340
	Purchases		24,000
	Transportation In		1,000
	Operating Expenses		8,000
31	Income Summary	3,000	
	Retained Earnings		3,000
31	Retained Earnings	750	
	Dividends		750

Required: Calculate the gross profit, using the form of a classified income statement.

Alternate Problem 5-6

The following accounts and account balances are taken from the worksheet of Eckel Promotions Corp. at December 31, 19X6, its fiscal year-end.

	Income Statement	
	Dr.	Cr.
Merchandising Inventory	3,000	4,000
Sales		52,000
Sales Returns	1,480	
Sales Discounts	520	
Purchases	37,000	
Purchases Returns		1,130
Purchases Discounts		370
Transportation In	500	
Advertising Expense	1,250	
Insurance Expense	600	
Rent Expense	1,800	
Salary Expense	6,350	
Income Tax	2,500	
Totals	55,000	57,500
Net Income	2,500	
Totals	57,500	57,500

Required: Prepare the classified income statement.

Alternate Problem 5-7

The following trial balance has been extracted from the records of Van der Aa Merchants Inc. at December 31, 19X2, its fiscal year-end. The balances for Merchandise Inventory and Retained Earnings have not changed during the year.

	Account Balances	
	Dr.	*Cr.*
Cash	$ 1,500	
Accounts Receivable	5,000	
Merchandise Inventory	5,000	
Prepaid Insurance	1,300	
Prepaid Rent	600	
Equipment — Office	12,500	
Accumulated Depreciation		-0-
Bank Loan		$ 10,000
Accounts Payable		8,350
Income Tax Payable		3,600
Common Stock		3,000
Retained Earnings		2,000
Dividends	600	
Sales		75,000
Sales Returns	2,250	
Sales Discounts	750	
Purchases	60,000	
Purchases Returns		9,400
Purchases Discounts		600
Transportation In	2,000	
Advertising Expense	1,800	
Commissions Expense	7,200	
Delivery Expense	1,600	
Depreciation Expense	-0-	
Insurance Expense	1,100	
Interest Expense	1,200	
Rent Expense	3,300	
Telephone Expense	550	
Utilities Expenses	100	
Income Tax Expense	3,600	
Totals	$111,950	$111,950

Required:

1. Record the above trial balance on a worksheet.
2. Prepare adjusting entries for the following and record them on the worksheet.

   a. The balance in Prepaid Rent consists of rent for the months of December 19X2 and January 19X3.

   b. Interest on the bank loan applicable to the month of December amounts to $100. This amount has not yet been recorded. Record as Interest Payable.

   c. No depreciation has yet been recorded on the office equipment. An amount of $500 is estimated applicable to 19X2.

   d. The December telephone bill has not yet been received. An amount of $50 is estimated as owing. Record as Accounts Payable.

   e. The balance in Prepaid Insurance includes an amount applicable to December 19X2 and the twelve months of 19X3.

3. Complete the worksheet. A physical count of inventory indicates that $10,000-worth of merchandise is on hand at December 31, 19X2.
4. From the worksheet, prepare the following financial statements in proper form:

   a. Classified income statement (The advertising, commission and delivery expenses are considered as selling expenses.)

   b. Statement of retained earnings

   c. Classified balance sheet.

5. From the worksheet, prepare all necessary journal closing entries.
6. Make calculations to answer the following questions:
   a. What is the proportion of shareholder to creditor claims on the assets of the corporation?
   b. What is the current ratio?
   c. What is the acid-test ratio?
7. Assume that you are the loan officer of a bank to which the corporation has applied for an additional 6-month $5,000 bank loan. Would you grant the loan? Why or why not?
8. If the loan were granted on January 2, 19X3, calculate the working capital, current ratio, and acid-test ratio immediately following receipt of the loan.

Review Problems

Review Problem 5-1

The following information is made available to you for John Stone Inc. The year-end of the company is April 30.

John Stone Inc.
Balance Sheet
At April 30, 19X1

Assets			Liabilities	
CURRENT ASSETS			Accounts Payable	$ 10
Cash		$ 20	Unearned Revenue	15
Accounts Receivable		30	Total Liabilities	$ 25
Inventory of Merchandise		25		
Prepaid Insurance		16	Shareholders' Equity	
Total Current Assets		$ 91	Common Stock	10
FIXED ASSETS			Retained Earnings	146
Equipment	$96			
Accum. Deprec. — Equipment	6	90		
Total Assets		$181	Total Equities	$181

May Transactions:

May 2	Sales on Account	$100
May 6	Purchases on Account	55
May 8	Collection of Accounts Receivable	95
May 12	Payment of Accounts Payable	40
May 15	Dividends	20
May 16	Sales Returns and Allowances	2
May 23	Purchases Returns and Allowances	1
May 27	Payment of Wages During May	10
May 27	Payment of Other Expenses	8

Data for adjustment:
a. Accrued unpaid wages on May 31 amounted to $1.
b. A one-year insurance policy was purchased on January 1, 19X1.
c. Equipment has an estimated service life of 4 years.
d. The necessary deliveries were made to all customers who had paid in advance. All unearned revenue was earned in May.
e. A physical count of inventory was made on May 31, 19X1, and its cost was determined to be $20.

Required:
1. Journalize the May transactions.
2. Post to appropriate general ledger accounts.
3. Prepare a trial balance on a worksheet.
4. Complete the worksheet.
5. Prepare in proper form the balance sheet and the income statement at May 31.
6. Journalize the adjusting entries.
7. Post the adjusting entries.
8. Prepare a trial balance from the adjusted ledger accounts.

Review Problem 5-2

Nu-Vogue Hat Shop maintained incomplete records. After investigation, you uncovered the following assets and liabilities:

Assets

	19X6	
	January 1	*December 31*
Cash	$ 2,680	$ 2,060
Accounts Receivable	13,400	13,660
Inventory	6,200	7,600
Equipment (net of depreciation)	10,400	11,200
Prepaid Insurance	240	120
	$32,920	$34,640

Liabilities

Accounts Payable	$ 2,000	$ 4,400
Bank Loan		6,000
Accrued Liabilities	180	100
	$ 2,180	$10,500
Common Stock	1,600	4,000
Retained Earnings	29,140	20,140
	$32,920	$34,640

An analysis of cash inflow and outflow showed:

Collections from Customers	$17,940
Proceeds of Bank Loan	6,000
Additional Common Stock Issued	2,400
Payment to Creditors	12,200
Payment of Expenses (selling)	9,000
Refunds on Sales	700
Dividends	3,000
Interest on Bank Loan	60
Purchase of Equipment	2,000

Required:
1. Compute the net income (or loss) by analyzing the changes in retained earnings.
2. Prepare an income statement in proper form.

Accounting Systems

An accounting system is designed to produce timely and accurate records. The use of special journals and control and subsidiary accounts facilitates the recording of accounting information and its communication to management for decision making.

1. How does the volume of business transactions influence the design of special journals?
2. What common features are used in the design of all special journals?
3. Into what operating cycles can special journals be grouped?
4. What business documents are used by accountants in the sales and collection cycle?
5. What documents are involved in the purchase and payment cycle?
6. How are records designed to record the acquisition and subsequent payment of employee services?
7. What is the inter-relationship between the general ledger and subsidiary ledgers?
8. How does accounting information flow through subsidiary and control accounts?
9. How does a one-write system function?
10. What is the impact of computers on accounting procedures that lead to management decision making?

A. Special Journals

Special journals
Multi-column journals specially designed not only to record similar transactions chronologically but also to reduce the writing of repetitious information. They are collectively referred to as *books of original entry*; the general journal is used to record transactions that cannot be recorded in any special journal.

In the preceding chapter, the general journal was introduced and used to record each financial transaction of Bluebeard Computer Corporation. This procedure was useful for explaining the fundamentals of the accounting process, but it is practical only when a business has a small number of transactions.

The volume of transactions facing most entities makes it impractical to record each transaction in a general journal. It is not inconceivable for even a small business to have 200 to 300 customers and perhaps 50 to 100 suppliers of goods and services. Consider the number of journal entries that would be required to record sales and purchases on account, cash sales and cash purchases, cash receipts and cash disbursements, and payroll transactions. Recording these transactions in a general journal would be time consuming; the additional labour of posting entries to the general ledger would become overwhelming, increasing the possibility of posting errors so that the ledger does not balance.

In actual practice, transactions are grouped into a number of classifications common to most business entities and recorded in various **special journals** as indicated below:

Transaction:	*Recorded in:*
Sales or services on account	Sales Journal
Collection of cash	Cash Receipts Journal
Purchases on account	Purchases Journal
Payment of cash	Cash Disbursements Journal
Payroll	Payroll Journal

Most entities maintain a separate journal in each of these categories, often collectively referred to as *books of original entry*. The frequency with which certain types of transactions occur determines how many and what types of journals the entity will use.

The common feature in the actual design of all special journals is the use of multiple columns for debit and credit entries and for the recording of related information. In addition to reducing the time required for posting transactions, the use of multiple columns reduces the need to repeat information. Although the actual layout of the columns differs among entities and is also influenced by the availability of mechanical devices or electronic data processing, the following types of columns are always present:

Columns for Information:	*Columns for Recording Debits and Credits:*
Date of transaction	Accounts to be debited or credited
Name of other party involved	
Other details relevant to the transaction	Amount actually debited or credited for each transaction
Other details relevant to the posting information	

Although the arrangement of columns may differ from one entity to another, the column sequence used in this chapter is designed to emphasize the information to be recorded for each transaction and the equality of debits and credits. Once the methodology of special journals is understood, any variation in format can be easily accommodated by any accountant.

The use of special journals permits an efficient division of duties among employees. For example, while one employee is recording transactions in one journal, another can be recording other transactions in another journal. In this way, the recording process is expedited.

The accounting system of each entity is organized to achieve certain objectives, which include the accurate recording of accounting information in the appropriate special journal. An additional objective is the accumulation of amounts in the appropriate general ledger and any **subsidiary ledgers** used by the entity. Internal control systems are designed to ensure this accuracy; they are also designed to maximize efficiency and to control the entity's assets. The control of cash is one area of particular concern for obvious reasons; internal controls are designed to protect it and also to ensure its accurate recording. These are more fully described in Chapter 7. Control of inventory was discussed briefly in Chapter 5. To help maintain bookkeeping accuracy, a **control account** that accumulates balances of particular accounts in a subsidiary ledger is maintained. In these ways, management can keep an eye on operating efficiency through its accounting system.

Special journals can be grouped within a number of operating cyles continuously occurring within the entity. These cycles comprise major areas of the entity's activities; the preceding discussion has identified major categories of financial transactions and the applicable special journals.

The cycles focused on in this chapter, as in Chapter 5, are the sales and collection cycle and the purchase and payment cycle. The discussion in section A of this chapter begins with the inception of transactions in each of these cycles. Section B focuses on the flow of data through the entity's accounts. Both are a part of the accounting process and lead to the reporting of information useful to users of financial statements; the preparation of these statements was the emphasis of the preceding chapters.

GAAP has an impact on each of these cycles because acountants are concerned with whether the information produced by each cycle is in accordance with generally accepted accounting principles.

Subsidiary ledger
A group of homogenous accounts kept in a separate ledger, which correspond to related ledger control accounts in the general ledger; examples include an accounts receivable subsidiary ledger and an accounts payable subsidiary ledger.

Control account
A general ledger account, a balance in which equals the total of many account balances in a related subsidiary ledger.

The Sales and Collection Cycle

This cycle focuses on sales, accounts receivable, and the subsequent collection of cash. Transactions in this cycle begin with the preparation of a sales invoice, which is a source document. The collection of cash occurs to end this cycle; the source document here is the deposit slip stamped by the bank as evidence of the deposit of cash and cheques received. This information is recorded in the appropriate special journals, which are posted to the general ledger and a subsidiary customer ledger. (The inter-relationship of the general and subsidary ledgers is discussed in section B.) The accounting process applicable to this cycle is illustrated in Figure 6-1.

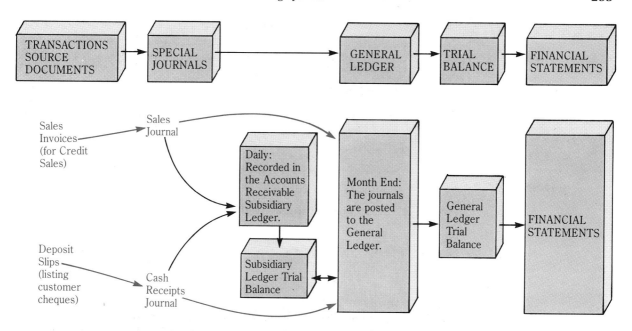

Figure 6-1   The accounting process of the sales and collection cycle

The Sales Journal

Sales journal
A special journal used to record all sales on account.

All sales on account are recorded in the **sales journal**. (Cash sales are recorded in the cash receipts journal.) Figure 6-2 is an extract from the sales journal of Bluebeard Computer Corporation, in which January sales have been recorded and the columns totalled. The single column in this sales journal is designed for recording the debit to the Accounts Receivable account for each sale and the credit to the Sales account.

Every entry in the sales journal includes a debit to Accounts Receivable and a credit to Sales. Recall that a sale would have been recorded in BCC's general journal as follows:

Jan. 5	Accounts Receivable	1,000	
	Sales		1,000
	To record a sale on account		

Note that, in the sales journal, this transaction would be recorded on a single line, with a single entry recording debit and credit. Since such a sale can be recorded in a special journal, it need not be recorded in the general journal.

SALES JOURNAL   Page 1

Date		Sold To	Invoice Number	Terms	F	Accts Rec — Dr. Sales — Cr.
19X3 Jan.	5	Devco Marketing Ltd.	301	net 30		1,000
	9	Perry Co. Ltd.	302	2/10, net 30		200
	10	Horngren Corp.	303	2/10, net 30		650
	19	Bendix Inc.	304	1/10, net 45		100
		Totals				1,950
A		B	C	D	E	F

Figure 6-2   Sales journal illustrated

The columns in the sales journal shown in Figure 6-2 are explained below:

Columns for Information:
A   The date of the sales invoice is recorded in the Date column.
B   The name of the customer is recorded in the Sold To column. (This column is also often called the Account Debited column.)
C   The sales invoice number is recorded in the Invoice Number column. Sales invoices are recorded in numerical sequence and all sales invoice numbers, including cancelled sales invoices, must be recorded.
D   The terms of the sale are listed in the Terms column. If the same terms are extended to all customers this column can be left out.
E   The use of this column is explained in section B of this chapter.

Column for Recording of Sales on Account:
F   The amount in this column is debited to Accounts Receivable and credited to Sales.

Other columns, if needed, could be added to the sales journal that appears here. For example, there could be a credit column for Sales Tax or columns for crediting sales by department or by product. In such cases, there would be a debit column for Accounts Receivable.

The Cash Receipts Journal

Cash receipts journal
A special journal used to record all receipts of cash.

All *receipts of cash* are recorded in the **cash receipts journal**. Figure 6-3 is a page from the cash receipts journal of Bluebeard Computer Corporation, after January cash receipts have been recorded and the columns totalled. The columns used in this journal are designed to record the debits to the Cash and Sales Discounts accounts and the credits to Accounts Receivable, as well as to other accounts that might be affected.

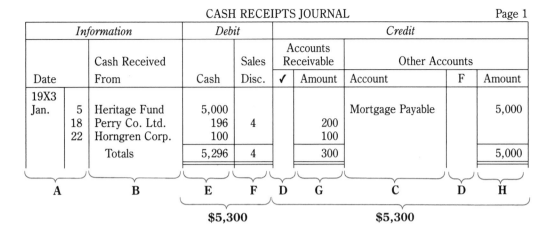

Figure 6-3   **Cash receipts journal illustrated**

The columns in the cash receipts journal shown in Figure 6-3 are explained below:

Columns for Information:
A   The date of the receipt is recorded in the date column.
B   The source of the cash receipt is written in the Cash Received From column. Cash receipts in payment of customers' accounts are shown individually, while cash sales are recorded as a daily total or weekly total amount, depending on the frequency and the dollar value of the transactions.
C   The Other Accounts Credit column is used to record the name of general ledger acccounts for which no special column has been provided. When applicable, cash sales are recorded here.
D   The use of this column is explained in section B of this chapter.

Columns for Recording Receipts of Cash:

Columns for Debits
E   The amount of cash actually received is recorded in the Cash columns.
F   Any cash discount granted a customer is recorded in the Sales Discount column.

Columns for Credits
G   The amount of accounts receivable paid by the customer is recorded in this column; the amount recorded is the total of cash received plus any sales discounts granted to the customer.
H   This column is for credits to general ledger accounts for which no special column has been provided in the cash receipts journal.

Every entry in the cash receipts journal includes a debit to Cash; any other debit or credit entry depends on the transaction involved. For example, the receipt of a $5,000 mortgage would have been recorded in BCC's general journal as follows:

```
Jan. 5     Cash                              5,000
               Mortgage Payable                        5,000
               To record payment of mortgage.
```

Note that this transaction is recorded on a single line in the cash receipts journal, and that the equality of the debit and credit is still maintained through the use of the journal columns. The receipt of cash is recorded in the Debit Cash column; since there is no special column for mortgage payable, the account name and amount are entered in Other Accounts. Since the cash receipt is now recorded in a special journal, it is not recorded in the general journal.

The receipt of cash within the discount period would have been recorded in BCC's general journal as follows:

```
Jan. 18    Cash                              196
           Sales Discounts                     4
               Accounts Receivable                      200
```

In this case, Perry Co. Ltd. paid its account within 10 days and, accordingly, BCC deducted 2 percent from the $200 amount of the sale ($200 × 0.02 = $4). Since this cash receipt is now recorded on a single line in a special journal, it is not recorded in the general journal.

Other columns could be added to the cash receipts journal to meet the specific needs of another entity. For example, a Cash Sales column could be added for an entity that has frequent cash sales.

Since special journals are designed to facilitate not only the recording but also the posting process, the sequence of the Debit and Credit columns is often reversed in actual practice; that is, the Credit columns are placed before the Debit columns, as illustrated in Figure 6-4.

CASH RECEIPTS JOURNAL   Page 1

Date			Credit					Debit	
			Accounts Receivable		Other Accounts				Sales
			F	Amount	Account	F	Amount	Cash	Disc.

Figure 6-4   Alternate cash receipts journal

The posting process and the subsidiary accounts receivable ledger are explained in section B of this chapter.

The Purchase and Payment Cycle

This cycle focuses on purchases, accounts payable, and cash payments; these are discussed in this section. (The acquisition of, and payment for, employee services is discussed in section C.) Transactions in this cycle begin with the preparation of a purchase requisition and purchase order within the entity. The recording begins with an invoice from the supplier involved, which is the source document. The payment of cash completes this cycle; the source document here is the cheque prepared by the entity. These source documents are recorded in the appropriate special journals, the transaction then being posted to the general ledger and a subsidiary suppliers ledger. (The inter-relationship of the general and subsidiary ledgers is discussed in section B.) The accounting process applicable to this cycle is illustrated in Figure 6-5.

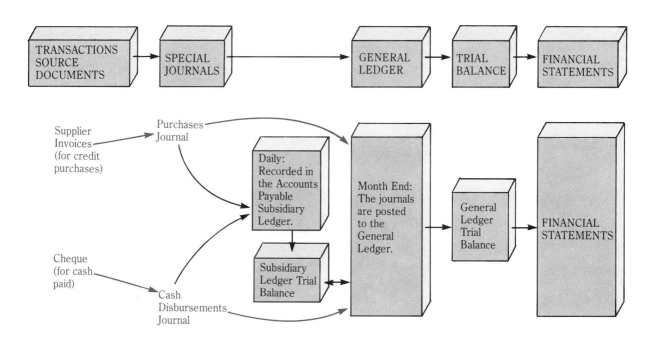

Figure 6-5   The accounting process of the purchase and payments cycle

During the month, purchases on account and payments on account are posted from the purchases journal and the cash disbursement journal to an accounts payable subsidiary ledger. The total debit and credit column balances in both the purchases and the cash disbursement journals are posted to the general ledger at the end of each month.

The Purchases Journal

All *purchases on account of merchandise for resale by the entity* are recorded in the **purchases journal**. (Cash purchases are recorded in the cash disbursements journal.) Figure 6-6 is a page from the purchases journal of Bluebeard Computer Corporation in which January purchases have been recorded and the column totalled.

PURCHASES JOURNAL   Page 1

Date		Purchased From	Terms	F	Purchases — Debit Accts Pay. — Credit
19X3 Jan.	3	Pemberton Ltd.	2/10, net 30		600
	4	Kensington Ltd.	net 30		350
	11	Canark Co. Ltd.	net 30		500
	26	Jaycor Ltd.	2/10, net 30		250
					1,700
A		B	C	D	E

Figure 6-6   Purchases journal illustrated

The columns in the purchases journal shown in figure 6-6 are explained below:

Columns for Information:
A The date of the supplier's invoice is recorded in the Date column.
B The name of the supplier is recorded in the Purchased From column. (This column is also often called the Account Credit column.)
C The terms of purchase are listed in the Terms column.
D The use of this column is explained in section B of this chapter.

Columns for Recording Purchases on Account:
E The amount of the purchase is recorded in the column as a debit to Purchases and a credit to Accounts Payable.

Every entry in the purchases journal includes a debit to the Purchases account and a credit to Accounts Payable. The purchase from Pemberton Ltd. would have been recorded in BCC's general journal as follows:

Jan. 3	Purchases	600	
	Accounts Payable		600
	To record purchase on account from Pemberton Ltd.		

Note that this transaction is recorded on a single line in the purchases journal, with debit and credit recorded by a single entry.

Other columns could be added to meet specific needs. For example, a debit column for each department might be added, or for classes of products.

Separate columns are frequently used for debits and credits. Since special journals are designed to facilitate not only the recording but also the posting process, the sequence of the debit and credit columns is often reversed in actual practice; that is, the Credit columns are placed before Debit columns, as illustrated in Figure 6-7.

PURCHASES JOURNAL   Page 1

Date		F	*Credit*	*Debit*		
			Accounts Payable	Purchases		
				A	B	C

Figure 6-7   Alternate purchases journal

The posting procedure and the subsidiary accounts payable ledger are explained in section B of this chapter.

The Cash Disbursements Journal

Cash disbursements journal
A special journal used to record all payments made by cheque. Payments of cash are usually handled as part of a petty cash fund.

All *payments of cash made by cheque* are recorded in the **cash disbursements journal**. Payments made in bills and coins are usually handled as part of a petty cash fund (which is discussed in Chapter 7). Figure 6-8 is a page from the cash disbursements journal of Bluebeard Computer Corporation, in which January cash disbursements have been recorded and the columns totalled. The columns in this cash disbursements journal are designed for recording debits to accounts applicable in a particular transaction and the credit to Cash.

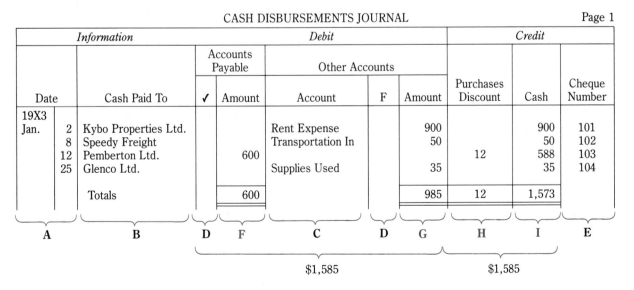

Figure 6-8   Cash disbursements journal illustrated

The columns in the cash disbursements journal shown in Figure 6-8 are explained below:

Columns for Information:
A The date recorded on the cheque is recorded in the Date column.
B The name of the payee is recorded in the Cash Paid To column.
C The Other Accounts Debit column is used to record the name of the general ledger accounts for which no special column has been provided.
D The use of this column is explained in section B of this chapter
E The cheque number is recorded in the Cheque Number column.

Columns for Recording Payments of Cash:
Columns for Debits
F The amount of the accounts payable paid to the supplier is recorded in this column; the amount recorded is the total of the actual cheque amount plus any purchase discount taken.
G This column is for debits to general ledger accounts for which no special column has been provided in the cash disbursements journal.

Columns for Credits
H Any cash discount taken is recorded in the Purchases Discount column.
I The actual amount of the cheque is recorded in the Cash column.

Every entry in the disbursements journal consists of a debit to some account and a credit to Cash. The payment to Pemberton Ltd. on January 12 would have been recorded in BCC's general journal as follows:

Jan. 12	Accounts Payable	600	
	Purchases Discounts		12
	Cash		588
	To record payment, less discount		
	of amount due Pemberton Ltd.		

In this case, Bluebeard paid Pemberton within 10 days and accordingly deducted $12 from the $600 amount of the purchase made on January 3 ($600 $\times$ 0.02 = $12). Since this cash receipt is now recorded on a single line in a special journal, it is not recorded in the general journal.

Other columns could be added to the cash disbursements journal to meet the specific needs of another entity, based on the frequency with which certain cash disbursements occur.

The General Journal

When special journals are used, the general journal is still used to record all other transactions that cannot be recorded in any of the special journals. For example, sales returns, purchases returns, and adjusting and closing entries continue to be recorded in the general journal.

The three January entries in the general journal of Bluebeard Computer Corporation (in Figure 6-9) illustrate its use for transactions that cannot be recorded in a special journal.

Date		Description	F	Debit	Credit
19X3					
Jan.	12	Sales Returns and Allowances	508	100	
		Accounts Receivable	110✓		100
		To record return from Horngren Corp.			
	27	Accounts Payable	210✓	50	
		Purchases Returns and Allowances	558		50
		To record goods returned to Jaycor Ltd.			
	31	Depreciation Expense — Trucks	624	200	
		Accumulated Depreciation — Truck	194		200
		To record depreciation for January.			

GENERAL JOURNAL — Page 10

Note that a (✓) is entered into the Folio column (F) to indicate that the posting has also been made to the account of the customer and the supplier. This procedure is necessary whenever a control account is used.

Figure 6-9   General journal illustrated

Other Special Journals

Additional special journals can also be designed as required by an entity. In the sales and collections cycle, for example, a sales returns and allowances journal may be a labour-saving journal; in the purchases and payments cycle, a purchases returns and allowances journal may improve efficiency. The frequency with which these transactions occur determines the need for such additional special journals; the volume of other types of transactions would determine the need for other special journals.

B.   The General Ledger and Subsidiary Ledgers

An entity often has a large number of customers; a department store, for example, may have in excess of 50 000 credit customers for whom detailed financial information has to be maintained. If each customer had an account in the general ledger, the general ledger would become unwieldy. For this reason, a subsidiary accounts receivable ledger is designed to include each customer's account; only one Accounts Receivable account — in this case, the control account — is kept in the general ledger. After all transactions for the month have been recorded, the total of the accounts receivable subsidiary ledger should be equal to the balance in the control account:

GENERAL LEDGER	ACCOUNTS RECEIVABLE SUBSIDIARY LEDGER		
Accounts Receivable	Bendix Inc.	Devco Marketing Inc.	Horngren Corp.
1,650	100	1,000	550

CONTROL TOTAL = SUBSIDIARY TOTAL
$1,650 $1,650

Other subsidiary ledgers, such as a subsidiary fixed assets ledger, can also be created to control volume.

A trial balance of the accounts receivable subsidiary ledger (also called a schedule of accounts receivable) is prepared at the end of the month to check that the subsidiary ledger total agrees with the Accounts Receivable control account in the general ledger.

Bluebeard Computer Corporation
Schedule of Accounts Receivable
January 31, 19X3

Bendix Inc.	$ 100
Devco Marketing Inc.	1,000
Horngren Corp.	550
Total	$1,650

The Flow of Accounting Information through the Accounts

Accounting information is initially recorded in special journals, as illustrated in section A. This information is next accumulated in both subsidiary and control accounts; this procedure is referred to as a flow of accounting information through the accounts of an entity. This flow for each cycle can be illustrated by looking at the posting process, that is, how the information flows through both control and subsidiary accounts.

Flow through the Sales and Collection Cycle Accounts

Flow through the Accounts Receivable Control Account

Each amount in the Accounts Receivable columns of the sales journal and the cash receipts journal is posted to the accounts receivable subsidiary ledger—usually daily. This posting updates the balance of each customer's account and makes the information readily available. (The "S1" refers to page 1 of the Sales journal.)

Accounts Receivable			*No. 110*		Sales			*No. 500*
19X3					19X3			
Jan. 31	S1	1,950			Jan. 31	S1	1,950	

At the end of each month, each debit and credit total appearing in the cash receipts journal is also posted to the appropriate general ledger account. The general ledger account number is placed in parentheses below each total in the cash receipts journal to indicate that the posting has been done. (See Figure 6-10.)

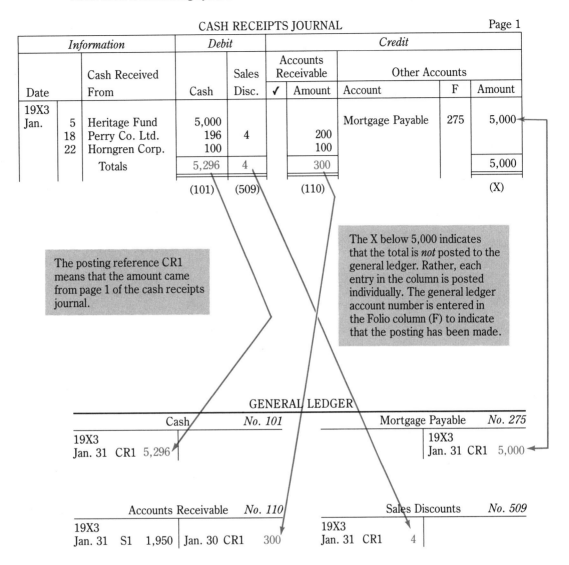

Figure 6-10   Cash receipts journal transactions posted to the general ledger

Flow through the Subsidiary Accounts

Each amount in the Accounts Receivable columns of the sales journal and the cash receipts journal is posted to the accounts receivable subsidiary ledger — usually daily. This posting updates the balance of each customer's account and makes the information readily available for trial balance preparation.

Note that the Folio column (F) is used to indicate postings to the accounts receivable subsidiary ledger. A check (✓) is entered to indicate that the posting has been done.

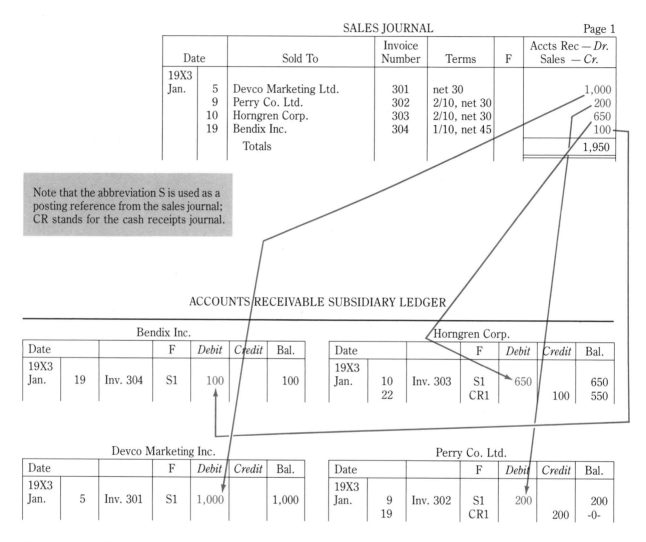

SALES JOURNAL Page 1

Date		Sold To	Invoice Number	Terms	F	Accts Rec — Dr. Sales — Cr.
19X3 Jan.	5	Devco Marketing Ltd.	301	net 30		1,000
	9	Perry Co. Ltd.	302	2/10, net 30		200
	10	Horngren Corp.	303	2/10, net 30		650
	19	Bendix Inc.	304	1/10, net 45		100
		Totals				1,950

Note that the abbreviation S is used as a posting reference from the sales journal; CR stands for the cash receipts journal.

ACCOUNTS RECEIVABLE SUBSIDIARY LEDGER

Bendix Inc.

Date			F	Debit	Credit	Bal.
19X3 Jan.	19	Inv. 304	S1	100		100

Horngren Corp.

Date			F	Debit	Credit	Bal.
19X3 Jan.	10	Inv. 303	S1	650		650
	22		CR1		100	550

Devco Marketing Inc.

Date			F	Debit	Credit	Bal.
19X3 Jan.	5	Inv. 301	S1	1,000		1,000

Perry Co. Ltd.

Date			F	Debit	Credit	Bal.
19X3 Jan.	9	Inv. 302	S1	200		200
	19		CR1		200	-0-

Figure 6-11 Posting of sales journal entries to accounts receivable subsidiary ledger

Flow through the Purchase and Payments Cycle Accounts

Flow through the Accounts Payable Control Account

At the end of each month, each debit and credit total appearing in the purchases journal is posted to the appropriate general ledger account. The general ledger account number is placed in parentheses below each total in the purchases journal to indicate that the posting has been done. (The "P1" refers to page 1 of the Purchases journal.)

	Purchases		*No. 550*		Accounts Payable		*No. 210*
19X3					19X3		
Jan. 31	P1	1,700			Jan. 31	P1	1,700

At the end of each month, each debit and credit total appearing in the cash disbursements journal is also posted to the appropriate general ledger account. The general ledger account number is placed in parentheses below each total in the cash disbursements journal to indicate that the posting has been done.

CASH DISBURSEMENTS JOURNAL

Page 1

	Information			*Debit*				*Credit*		
			Accounts Payable		Other Accounts					
Date	Cash Paid To	✓	Amount	Account	F	Amount	Purchases Discount	Cash	Cheque Number
19X3									
Jan. 2	Kybo Properties Ltd.			Rent Expense	654	900		900	101
8	Speedy Freight			Transportation In	560	50		50	102
12	Pemberton Ltd.	✓	600				12	588	103
25	Glenco Ltd.			Supplies Used	668	35		35	104
	Totals		600			985	12	1,573	
			(210)			(X)	(559)	(101)	

> The posting reference CD1 means that the amount came from page 1 of the cash disbursements journal.

> The X below the 985 total indicates that this total is *not* posted to the general ledger. Rather, each entry is posted individually. The general ledger account number is entered in the Folio column (F) to indicate that the posting has been made.

GENERAL LEDGER

		Cash		*No. 101*			Transportation In		*No. 560*			Accounts Payable		*No. 210*
19X3				19X3		19X3					19X3		19X3	
Jan. 31	CR1	5,296		Jan. 31 CD1	1,573	Jan. 31	CD1	50			Jan. 31 CD1	600	Jan. 31 P1	1,700

		Supplies Used		*No. 668*			Rent Expense		*No. 654*			Purchases Discounts		*No. 559*
19X3						19X3							19X3	
Jan. 31	CD1	35				Jan. 31	CD1	900					Jan. 31 CD1	12

Figure 6-12   Posting of cash disbursement journal entries to general ledger

Flow through the Subsidiary Accounts

Each amount in the Accounts Payable columns of the purchase journal and the cash disbursements journal is posted to the accounts payable subsidiary ledger — usually daily. This posting updates the balance of each creditor's account and makes the information readily available. The date of the entry in the subsidiary ledger account is the invoice date, which is needed if a discount is to be taken.

PURCHASES JOURNAL   Page 1

Date		Purchased From	Terms	F	Purchases — Dr. Accts Pay. — Cr.
19X3					
Jan.	3	Pemberton Ltd.	2/10, net 30	✓	600
	4	Kensington Ltd.	net 30	✓	350
	11	Canark Co. Ltd.	net 30	✓	500
	26	Jaycor Ltd.	2/10, net 30	✓	250
		Totals			1,700

> Note that the abbreviation P is used as a posting reference from the purchases journal; CD stands for the cash disbursement journal.

> Note that the Folio column (F) is used to indicate postings to the accounts payable subsidiary ledger. A check (✓) is entered to indicate that the posting has been made.

ACCOUNTS PAYABLE SUBSIDIARY LEDGER

Canark Co. Ltd.

			F	Debit	Credit	Bal.
19X3						
Jan.	11		P1		500	500

Kensington Ltd.

			F	Debit	Credit	Bal.
19X3						
Jan.	4		P1		350	350

Jaycor Ltd.

			F	Debit	Credit	Bal.
19X3						
Jan.	26		P1		250	250

Pemberton Ltd.

			F	Debit	Credit	Bal.
19X3						
Jan.	3		P1		600	600
	12		CD1	600		-0-

Figure 6-13 Posting of purchases journal entries to accounts payable subsidiary ledger

A trial balance of the accounts payable subsidiary ledger (also called a schedule of accounts payable) is prepared at the end of the month to check that the subsidiary ledger total agrees with the Accounts Payable control account in the general ledger.

Bluebeard Computer Corporation
Schedule of Accounts Payable
January 31, 19X3

Canark Co. Ltd.	$ 500
Jaycor Ltd.	250
Kensington Ltd.	350
Total	$1,100

The One-Write System

Recording in the cash disbursements journal and posting to the subsidiary accounts payable journal can be simplified in actual practice through the use of a one-write system. In addition to postings to a cash disbursements journal and subsidiary accounts payable journal, a one-write system can also be used to prepare the actual cheque used for payments. Similar one-write systems are also available for the sales and collections cycle and for the payroll cycle. A one-write system is represented in Figure 6-14.

The one write system organizes input and eliminates transposition errors, and establishes a clear audit trail. Some systems also allow the user to attach cheques to eliminate rewriting.

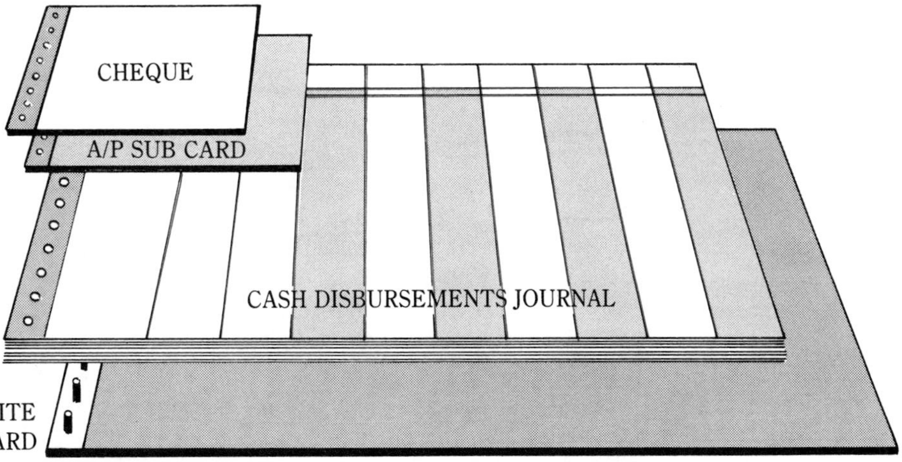

Figure 6-14   The one-write system for the payment cycle

C. The Payroll Cycle

The payroll cycle focuses on the acquisition of employee services and their subsequent payment. Transactions in this cycle begin with the preparation for each employee of a daily time card, which is translated into an amount of earnings for each pay period; the document used to make this calculation is the source document in this cycle. The calculation of a net pay amount leads to the payment of cash to each employee. When the payment is made by cheque, the cheque becomes the source document that ends this cycle.

The Payroll Journal

Payroll journal
A special journal used to record the payment of salaries or wages.

The payment of *salaries* or wages is recorded in the **payroll journal** each pay period; these payments can be by cheque or in cash. Figure 6-15 is a page from the payroll journal of Bluebeard Computer Corporation, in which the January payroll has been recorded and the columns totalled. The columns in the payroll journal are designed to meet the needs of BCC and are arranged to emphasize the recording of debits and credits applicable to each pay.

PAYROLL JOURNAL　　　　　　　　　　　　　　　　　　　　　　　Page 1

Information							Debit			Credit											
Week Ending				Hours		Rate		Gross Pay			Income Tax		Deductions								
Mo.	Day	Yr.	Employee Name	Reg.	OT	Reg.	OT	Sales	Delivery	Office	Fed.	Prov.	UIC	Pension	Health	1	2	3	Total	Net Pay	Chq. No.
1	5	X3	J. Abbott					400			42	54	6	7					109	291	101
1	5	X3	N. Ait							300	26	33	5	5					69	231	102
1	5	X3	R. River	40					250		18	24	4	4					50	200	103
						6.25		400	250	300	86	111	15	16					228	722	

　A　　　B　　C　　D　　　F　F　F　G　G　H　H　　H　I　I　I　J　K　E

Figure 6-15　Payroll journal illustrated

The columns used in the payroll journal shown in Figure 6-15 are explained below:

Columns for Information:

A　The date recorded on the payroll cheque is recorded in the Date column.

B　The name of the employee is recorded in the Employee Name column.

C　The hours worked during the week are recorded in the Regular Hours column and in the Overtime Hours column if applicable.

D　The earnings of each employee are calculated and recorded in the Regular Earnings column and the Overtime Earnings column, if applicable.

E　The payroll cheque number is recorded in the Cheque Number column.

Columns for Recording Payroll:

F　The amount of the gross pay (before deductions) is recorded in the column that represents the appropriate pay category — sales, delivery, or office.

G　The amount of income tax applicable to the gross pay of each employee is recorded in these columns. In some provinces it is not necessary to show the federal and provincial portions of the income tax deduction.

H　The amount of deductions for unemployment insurance, government pension plan, and health insurance are recorded in these columns. These deductions are usually paid to governments monthly.

I　Other deductions that may be made are recorded in these columns: for example, group insurance, union dues, Canada Savings Bonds. These deductions are later paid to the appropriate jurisdictions.

J　The total deductions are calculated here.

K　The difference between gross pay and the total deductions is calculated and recorded here. This is the actual amount — net pay — received by the employee.

Each entry in the payroll journal includes a debit to the Gross Pay account and credits to the appropriate deductions accounts and to Net Pay. Note that the pay for R. River is recorded on a single line in BCC's payroll journal and that the equality of debits and credits is maintained through the use of journal columns. Gross pay is recorded in the delivery column in the case of R. River, who delivers computer parts to customers. In this way, a breakdown of payroll is prepared for management information. Since each pay is recorded in the payroll journal it is not recorded in the general journal.

Other columns are often found in payroll journals designed to meet the varying needs of entities.

Flow through the Control Account

At the end of the pay period, the totals for gross pay, deductions, and the net pay are posted from the payroll journal to the general ledger. The totals from the payroll journal are reproduced in Figure 6-16 to illustrate the posting. Note that the account numbers are recorded below the column totals posted to the general ledger.

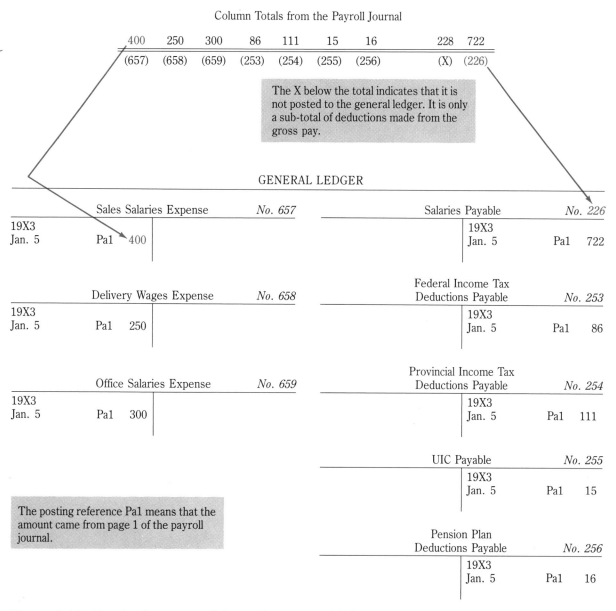

Figure 6-16   Posting from payroll journal to general ledger

Often the payroll journal is not posted directly to the general ledger but rather serves as the basis for an entry in the general journal, which is subsequently posted to the general ledger. The BCC journal entry to record the January 5, 19X3 payroll in this manner is shown below:

Jan. 5	Sales Salaries Expense	657	400	
	Delivery Wages Expense	658	250	
	Office Salaries Expense	659	300	
	Federal Income Tax Deductions Payable	253		86
	Provincial Income Tax Deductions Payable	254		111
	UIC Payable	255		15
	Pension Plan Deductions Payable	256		16
	Salaries Payable	226		722
	To record payroll for the week ending January 5, 19X3.			

Recording Payroll-Related Taxes

Employers are required by law to make contributions on behalf of their employees for unemployment insurance, government pension, and health insurance, in addition to the amounts deducted from employees' salaries or wages. For example, the Unemployment Insurance Act provides for a payroll-related tax on employers at the rate of 1.4 of the amount deducted from employees. For Bluebeard Computer Corporation, this amounts to $21 ($15 × 1.4) for each employee. The Canada Pension Plan also requires employers to pay an amount equal to that deducted from employees; BCC, in this instance, is required to pay $16. In addition to these, government health insurance plans require employers to make contributions at a specified rate.

The employer contribution for payroll-related taxes is always subject to modification because of the changing needs of these government-administered plans. Accordingly, it is assumed for illustrative purposes that the employer is required to pay an amount equal to that deducted from employees except in the case of health insurance, where the employer is assumed to pay the entire amount. The BCC contribution for the January 5, 19X3 payroll period is therefore calculated as follows:

	Employee Deductions	Employer Contribution	Total Paid to Government
Unemployment Insurance	15	21	36
Government Pension	16	16	32
Government Health Insurance	–	28	28
Total	31	65	96

The BCC contributions for the pay period ending January 5, 19X3 are recorded in the general journal as follows:

Jan. 5	Payroll Taxes Expense	653	65	
	UIC Payable	255		21
	Pension Plan Deductions Payable	256		16
	Health Insurance Deductions Payable	257		28
	To record payroll-related taxes for the payroll period ending January 5, 19X3.			

Employee payroll deductions and employer contributions are usually paid to government in the following month. If a balance remains unpaid when financial statements are being prepared, it is classified as a current liability on the balance sheet.

Flow through the Subsidiary Accounts: Individual Employee Records

Although the payroll journal records payroll transactions, it does not accumulate payroll data for each employee. Such cumulative individual employee data must be furnished to both the government and each employee at the end of every calendar year; in addition, Bluebeard Computer Corporation is required to keep track of individual employee deductions for unemployment insurance, government pension, and health plan contributions, since these deductions are no longer made once the maximum amount has been paid.

Individual employee earnings record
The payroll document used to record and accumulate individual employee payroll data.

In order to aid the accumulation of the individual employee's earnings data, the **individual employee earnings record** is used. Each is a copy of the columns appearing in the payroll journal; the data recorded in the individual record are usually identical to those recorded in the payroll journal, as shown in Figure 6-17.

INDIVIDUAL EMPLOYEE EARNINGS RECORD

Date Started: Social Insurance No.:   Employee No.:
Date Left: Marital Status: Income Tax Exemption:
Reason: Dependents: Rate:

			Information			Hours	Earnings	*Debit*				*Credit*													*Deductions*		
Week Ending			Employee Name					Gross Pay			Income Tax			Deductions											*Accumulation*		
Mo.	Day	Yr.		Reg./OT	Reg./OT	Sales	Delivery	Office	Fed.	Prov.	UIC	Pension	Health	1	2	3	Total	Net Pay	Chq. No.	UIC	Pension	Health
1	5	X3	J. Abbott			400			42	54	6	7					109	291	101	6	7	

INDIVIDUAL EMPLOYEE EARNINGS RECORD

Date Started: Social Insurance No.:   Employee No.:
Date Left: Marital Status: Income Tax Exemption:
Reason: Dependents: Rate:

			Information			Hours	Earnings	*Debit*				*Credit*													*Deductions*		
Week Ending			Employee Name					Gross Pay			Income Tax			Deductions											*Accumulation*		
Mo.	Day	Yr.		Reg./OT	Reg./OT	Sales	Delivery	Office	Fed.	Prov.	UIC	Pension	Health	1	2	3	Total	Net Pay	Chq. No.	UIC	Pension	Health
1	5	X3	N. Ait					300	26	33	5	5					69	231	102	5	5	

INDIVIDUAL EMPLOYEE EARNINGS RECORD

Date Started: Social Insurance No.:   Employee No.:
Date Left: Marital Status: Income Tax Exemption:
Reason: Dependents: Rate:

			Information			Hours	Earnings	*Debit*				*Credit*													*Deductions*		
Week Ending			Employee Name					Gross Pay			Income Tax			Deductions											*Accumulation*		
Mo.	Day	Yr.		Reg./OT	Reg./OT	Sales	Delivery	Office	Fed.	Prov.	UIC	Pension	Health	1	2	3	Total	Net Pay	Chq. No.	UIC	Pension	Health
1	5	X3	R. River	40		250		250	18	24	4	4					50	200	103	4	4	

Figure 6-17   **Payroll journal — individual employee records**

D. Computerized Accounting Systems

A typical Canadian entity processes numerous routine accounting jobs, most of which involve some sort of record-keeping. In small companies, all records may be kept manually, while a large corporation, such as General Motors or Seagram's, may have a totally computerized system. Bookkeepers may take care of the payroll, sales orders, inventory control, accounts receivable and payable, and the general ledger either manually or through automated processing. Computerized accounting may involve numerous systems with specific programs tailored to the entity's particular needs.

Payroll System

Payroll system
A computer system that assists in the preparation of salary cheques, maintains payment records, and provides reports related to payroll activities.

A **payroll system** would accumulate data for individual employees in order to compute deductions for provincial and federal taxes, unemployment insurance, pension, and health insurance. The system would, on the pay day, produce a paycheque for each employee, like the computer-printed statement of earnings and deductions illustrated in Figure 6-18. Notice that this statement notifies the employee that his/her paycheque has been automatically deposited in his/her bank account. Each employee's deductions are accumulated by the payroll system, so that reports for managerial purposes and for reporting taxes withheld for Revenue Canada and other govenment agencies can be prepared through the system. In addition, the payroll system can communicate with the general ledger system so that it can incorporate the payroll data and summarize the financial status of the organization.

```
              Bluebeard Computer Corporation
           STATEMENT OF EARNINGS AND DEDUCTIONS

NAME: R. River          S.I.N.: 244-897-153        EMPLOYEE NO.: 05225

| EARNINGS    | HRS/UNITS | AMOUNT  | DEDUCTIONS        | YEAR TO DATE  |
| Regular     | 40        | $250    | * Fed. Tax $18 *  | Gross $250    |
| Txb Benefit | -0-       | .00     | * Prov. Tax $24 * | UIC  $4       |
| Overtime    | 0         | .00     | *UIC Contr. $4 *  | F. Tax $18    |
|             |           |         | * Pension $4 *    | P. Tax $24    |

TOTAL EARNINGS: $250.00       TOTAL DEDUCTIONS: $50.00
WEEK ENDING: X3/01/05         NET PAY: $200.00

NOTE: Deposited at Queen and University Royal Bank Branch.
```

Figure 6-18   A computerized statement of earnings for individual paycheque.

Sales Order Entry System

Sales order entry system
A computer system that initiates shipping orders, keeps track of back orders, and produces various reports.

All merchandisers have some sort of organized procedure for processing customers' orders as they are received either in person, by telephone, or by mail. This procedure is called the **sales order entry system**. Large merchandisers have computerized their sales order entry system. Each order contains the customer's name, as well as a description of and the quantity of items to be sold. A good system can be designed to permit fast processing of orders, to update the inventory on hand, and to flag bad credit risks. Retail stores face special problems when dealing with sales order entry and inventory levels. A grocery store, for example, may sell one tin of soup to a customer who may never shop at the same store again. Computerized systems have helped these retailers control these problems (see Real Life Example 6-1).

Conceptual Issue 6-1

Boolean Mathematics

The inner workings of the modern computer run on a much more basic logic than the debit and credit system you have learned thus far in this course. The foundation of the logic system that operates the modern computer is based on the work of mathematician George Boole. In his lifetime, George Boole was considered to be somewhat of a disappointment as a mathematician after showing much promise as a youth. At 16, he became an assistant master in a private school. A brilliant teacher, he later became Professor of Mathematics at Queen's College, Cork, Ireland.

He began his investigations of experimental mathematics while at Queen's when a fantastic new scheme came to him — a system of mathematics and algebra using only ones and zeros that was a perfect plan of logic. Boole envisioned sets and subsets, unions, intersections, universals, and complements. The system fit together nicely.

In 1847 he wrote a statement describing his new system and in 1854 he published his monumental work on Boolean Algebra. This brought Boole only frustration and disappointment; no one cared or even pretended to be interested. Who, it seemed, would be interested in a primitive system using only ones and zeros?

For almost a century, Boole's work lay unused; then in the late 1940s scientists and engineers created a device capable of processing decimal numbers. It had one problem though: it kept adding two and two and getting five. What was required was a system of mathematics based on ones and zeros — a system suitable to the on/off states inherent in computer hardware. With this advance, Boole's system and the modern computer became a perfect match.

Today almost every digital computer performs its mathematical computations in circuitry based on Boole's scheme. From kindergarten to college, students are studying new math. And for the modern accountant in a computer environment, the most important mathematical scheme that exists is the Boolean system of algebra.

Real Life Example 6-1
Computers in the Supermarket

One comprehensive use of computers by merchandisers is in the supermarket. Most items of merchandise are printed with the Universal Product Code (UPC), a series of bars and numbers that can be decoded by an optical scanner. A cashier passes each UPC over the optical scanner; the decoded information is displayed on the cash register. The computer records the sale, gives the customer an itemized receipt, and updates the inventory to preserve the perpetual inventory system. A further benefit is more efficiently produced information required for ordering and selecting products.

This decoding-inventory system is expensive: between $100,000 and $150,000 per store. It has met with opposition from retail clerks who fear job losses and from consumer groups that want to prevent shopper exploitation by supermarkets that stop marking prices on individual items. Conversely, supermarket executives argue that this new system will cut retailer costs by millions and, thus, eventually benefit consumers through lower food costs. UPC symbols now appear on an estimated 92 percent of all packaged grocery goods and the use of optical scanners is increasing.

Inventory Control System

Inventory system
A computer system used to monitor inventories and minimize inventory costs.

As mentioned, a routine job that can be handled through computer procedures is inventory control. A computerized inventory control system can accumulate the number of units of each product purchased for inventory, deduct each item sold or used, and ensure that proper quantities of products are kept in stock. Automatic updates reduce the number of time-consuming manual counts needed to control inventory.

When a customer requests a product, the order is entered by a clerk into the sales order entry system; if there is a sufficient number to fill the order, the goods are made available for shipment. The appropriate data are relayed to the accounts receivable system, which produces an invoice for the customer. If the goods are not in stock, the customer's order may be placed on back-order and the inventory control system will produce a notice to this effect indicating when the customer can expect the goods to be delivered.

A good inventory control system should be designed to maintain an economical inventory level; it should have a warning procedure to notify managers when stock levels are too low. Most inventory control systems contain a variety of mathematical routines to help managers calculate an economical inventory level for each product.

Accounts Receivable System

Accounts receivable system
A computer system which bills customers, maintains records of amounts due from customers, and generates reports on overdue amounts.

The accounts receivable for a large merchandiser must be tracked efficiently. The high volume of transactions can be handled by an accounts receivable system to control customers' purchases, payments, unpaid accounts, and account balances. The system can be designed to calculate and print customers' purchases, payments, unpaid accounts, and account balances. The system can be designed to calculate and print customers' bills and management reports. Other output can include sales analyses that describe changing sales pattern and reports of current and past due accounts. A more detailed presentation of accounts receivable is discussed in section C of Chapter 7.

Accounts Payable System

Accounts payable system
A computer system which provides control over payments to suppliers, issues cheques to suppliers, and provides information necessary for effective cash management.

The accounts payable a merchandiser owes to its suppliers can also be handled by a computerized system designed for the individual entity. An accounts payable system can control bills and invoices received and generate cheques to pay the bills in much the same way that the payroll system operates.

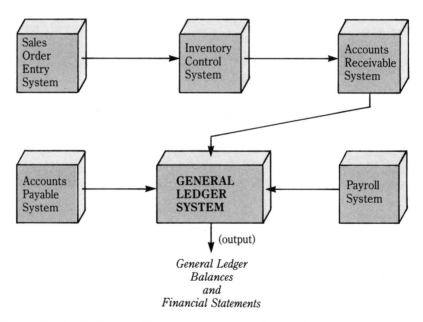

Figure 6-19   Relationships among accounting systems

General Ledger System

General ledger system
A computer sysem which keeps track of all financial summaries, produces ledger balances, and financial statements.

The **general ledger system** in a computerized merchandising operation can determine whether the books balance, and produce general ledger balances and financial statements.

Once a company has decided to computerize one or more of its routine activities, it must decide whether to develop its own software or by a software package from a vendor. A computerized system developed by the company can have the advantage of being designed precisely for the company's particular needs. Vendor-supplied software, on the other hand, is quite inexpensive; for example, a general ledger package that operates on the IBM-PC is currently retailing for as little as $200. Regardless of which way a company decides to go, it must be sure that the general ledger system will be compatible with other systems that the entity's computer already runs. Figure 6-19 illustrates the inter-relationships of the various systems discussed in this section; the importance of the general ledger system is clear.

Management Uses of Computerized Accounting Systems

Management information system (MIS) An information system designed to aid in the performance of management functions.

Decision support system (DSS) An information system that managers can use easily that provides highly refined information to help make non routine decisions.

Spreadsheet A program that allows the user to create a large two-dimensional table and manipulate data in many different ways.

While the automation of routine data-processing tasks undoubtedly reduces accounting and other clerical expenses, the computer can do much more than perform these programs. The computer's efficient organization of information can assist many levels of management in their decision-making roles. Again, programs can be designed to suit a particular entity's needs. For instance, based on trends in the historical sales results accumulated by the sales order entry system, forecasts for future sales can be calculated. A system that both reports routine data processing and generates information is called a **management information system** (MIS). Lately, **decision support systems** have also been introduced; unlike MIS, these systems permit the user to pose questions while the user is online. One of the most popular microcomputer applications of decision support systems is spreadsheet analysis. For an example of a spreadsheet, see Figure 6-20.

Spreadsheet

A **spreadsheet** is a table of columns and rows, as shown in Figure 6-20. Various commercial spreadsheets, such as Visicalc, Supercalc, and Lotus 1-2-3-, perform many of the same functions, and operate using similar logic; however, some spreadsheet software packages may have additional features that others are lacking. A spreadsheet program prepares the computer to accept tables, values, or mathematical formulas into the pre-established spreadsheet cells.

In this case, the payroll information (in Figure 6-15) from BCC's January 5 payroll journal has been entered into the spreadsheet program. The real advantage of a spreadsheet program is that, if a single datum changes, the entire spreadsheet is recalculated by the program. For instance, if the hourly wage of R. River is increased to $9.00 per hour, the user enters the new rate and the program automatically recalculates any amounts in the spreadsheet that are affected by the change. This is a simple example. A spreadhseet, such as Lotus 1-2-3 with 2043 rows and 254 columns, can perform calculations that would take hours with a calculator.

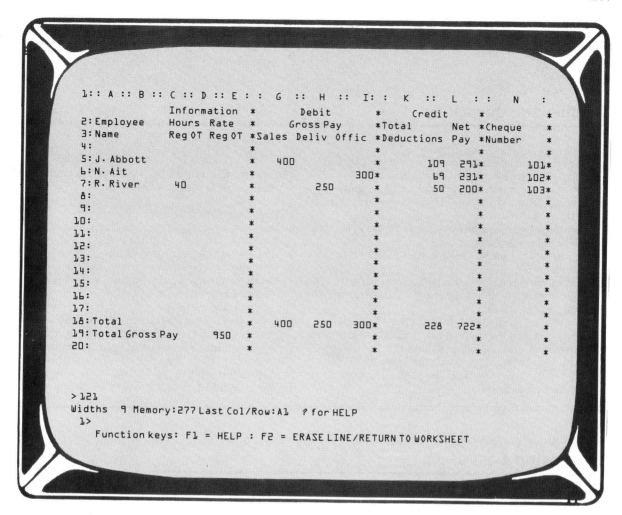

```
 1: : A : : B : : C : : D : : E : :  G  : :  H  : :  I : :  K  : :  L  : :  N   :
                Information   *        Debit     *     Credit   *            *
 2: Employee    Hours Rate   *     Gross Pay    *Total       Net *Cheque     *
 3: Name        Reg OT Reg OT *Sales Deliv Offic *Deductions Pay *Number     *
 4:                          *                  *            *            *
 5: J. Abbott              *  400             *      109  291*      101*
 6: N. Ait                 *             300*       69  231*      102*
 7: R. River   40          *       250       *       50  200*      103*
 8:                        *                *            *            *
 9:                        *                *            *            *
10:                        *                *            *            *
11:                        *                *            *            *
12:                        *                *            *            *
13:                        *                *            *            *
14:                        *                *            *            *
15:                        *                *            *            *
16:                        *                *            *            *
17:                        *                *            *            *
18: Total                 *  400  250  300*      228  722*            *
19: Total Gross Pay   950 *                *            *            *
20:                       *                *            *            *


> 121
Widths  9 Memory:277 Last Col/Row:A1   ? for HELP
  1>
     Function keys: F1 = HELP : F2 = ERASE LINE/RETURN TO WORKSHEET
```

Figure 6-20   A spreadsheet

Discussion Questions

1. Special journals are often referred to as books of original entry. What are the advantages in using them?
2. What is the common feature in the actual design of all special journals? What types of columns are always present?
3. How does the use of special journals permit a better division of duties among employees?
4. In what special journal are cash sales recorded? cash purchases?
5. Special journals are designed to facilitate not only the recording but also the posting process. Explain how this improvement is achieved.
6. In order for special journals to facilitate the posting process, the sequence of the debit and credit columns is often reversed in actual practice. Explain how this column rearrangement facilitates the posting process.
7. What entries are recorded in the general journal when special journals are in use?
8. What is a control account? a subsidiary ledger?
9. Posting to subsidiary ledgers is often done on a daily basis, while posting to control accounts is done only at month-end. Why?
10. What is a source document?
11. How does a payroll journal differ from a cash disbursements journal?
12. How are employer-related payroll taxes recorded?
13. What is an employee earnings record, and why is it used?
14. For each of the computerized systems detailed in the text identity the inputs, what occurs to the data ''in'' the computer, and the output.
15. Some people argue that computers are intelligent and capable of decision making. Others argue that computers are simply dumb machines that execute what they are programmed to do. Take one side of this argument and support your position.
16. What are the limitations, if any, of spreadsheet programs?

Discussion Cases

Discussion Case 6-1:   The Missing Millions

The [Quebec] provincial auditor-general has discovered chaos in the record-keeping process of five Quebec school boards, according to a preliminary report made public yesterday by Finance Minister Jacques Parizeau.

Gerard Larose studied the operations of 5 of the province's 250 boards after he was asked by Parizeau to find out how the education system could have mislaid hundreds of millions of dollars in the past three years.

Larose, who will require several months to make a more thorough study, says he found immediately that many school-board records and administration were a shambles.

He says he also found that the education ministry was unable to verify or keep track of the number of students and teachers in Quebec schools, or of the correct salary levels for some teachers.

As Parizeau revealed in his budget speech a week ago last night, the result was a $500 million ''hole'' in the education budget.

It was accounted for partly by excess salary payments and by allowances to one board for students who, for example, had moved away and were registered with some other school board as well.

Commenting on Larose's preliminary report at a news conference yesterday, Parizeau observed that the system of funding school boards in Quebec has been ''rotting merrily on the vine for 15 years'' and requires a complete overhaul.

In Montreal meanwhile, Jacques Mongeau, chairman of the Quebec Federation of Catholic School Boards, called his own news conference and blamed Education Minister Jacques-Yvan Morin for the mislaying of the money.

Mongeau said he'd welcome a public inquiry into the education budget because such an inquiry would exonerate the school boards.

He said that Morin and other ministry officials ''simply miscalculated the cost of what they told us to do.''

For example, he said, the ministry told the boards to integrate handicapped pupils into the general student population. ''A good idea,'' Mongeau said yesterday, ''but it cost money and the education ministry didn't realize how much.''

Some boards might have submitted confusing financial statements, but that was because they received inadequate guidance from the ministry, he said.

In Quebec, Parizeau said he had ordered the study by the auditor-general of primary and secondary teaching when it became clear last November that the discrepancy between figures for 1977–78 and 1978–79 were too great to be explainable.

Larose's preliminary report said that: there is virtually no control over the information on the number of teachers in the school system. As Parizeau said in the budget speech, the government does not know how many teachers it has, how much experience they have, or how many students they teach.

In one regional school board, 75 percent of the personnel files do not confirm teachers' experience.

In a local school board, only 10 percent of the personnel files confirm the years of experience.

The ministry of education has little way of knowing how many students are enrolled on September 30, and the auditor-general could give no opinion about how many students there had been enrolled on September 30 for the last three years.

More than 10 000 students were enrolled in more than one school board during 1978–79 which, according to Parizeau, resulted in an overpayment to school boards of between $25 and $30 million.

Delays in closing the books were such that two of the five school boards had not completed the bookkeeping for the school year of 1977–78.

The school board filing system is so inadequate that there were more than one copy of some documents while others could not be located.

The school boards on the island of Montreal have been so late in filing the financial documents that the government requires that the Ministry of Finance estimates that they owe $1 million in penalties.

Parizeau told a news conference that the government had inherited $500 million in school board arrears from the outgoing Liberal government when it took office in 1976.

"Perhaps we didn't sufficiently ask ourselves the question 'Was this an accident?' " Parizeau said.

He said that, by last November, the government had managed to pay off the amount in arrears.

"I was feeling pretty pleased with myself," he said. "I admit that I fell over when I realized that — 'Yoohoo!' — there was another $500 million that had to be dealt with."

Parizeau broke down the $500 million as consisting of $300 million in outstanding bank loans to school boards over the last three years that had to be paid, and an additional, unforeseen $200 million that had to be added to the budget for the next year. The budgetary hole developed in part because the school boards had been receiving funding on the basis of how many students were enrolled, and on a salary chart which calculated the number of teachers, their years of education, and their years of experience.

As the bookkeeping was months and even years behind, school boards would send estimates — and borrow money to make up the difference.

When Parizeau became aware of the problem, he commissioned the study by the auditor-general, and used the preliminary study in the preparation of his budget speech.

The result was a dense, complex document of 13 pages. Quipped Parizeau: "If it were easy to understand, it would have been discovered quickly."

Source Graham Fraser, "Why Hundreds of Millions Went Missing", *The* (Montreal) *Gazette*, April 2, 1980.

For Discussion

1. What do you think caused the record-keeping process to fail?
2. Discuss in detail the need for and use of some sort of specialized journals in accounting for the school boards:
   a. at the school board level
   b. at the education ministry.
3. Explain the advantages of control and subsidiary ledgers in this situation.
4. The press had reported that the cost per pupil in Quebec stands at roughly $500 per child per year higher than in Ontario. What additional information would you require to evaluate this difference?

Discussion Case 6-2: Tax Probe Uncovers 347 Evaders and $56 million in Single Fraud

Officials in the department of national revenue have wrapped up their inquiry into the biggest income-tax evasion scheme ever uncovered in Canada, after two years of digging by investigators who, at the peak, numbered 150 persons.

The racket involved 347 companies and unreported incomes of $56.8 million. Both figures are records, according to a source in the department. So are the number of investigators and the money which will be recovered.

The fraud involved the selling of false invoices and became known as the Shildan affair after a small Montreal knitter, Shildan Knitting Mills Ltd., one of the linchpins.

Under the scheme no merchandise changed hands. When the vendor was paid he/she retained a commission, usually from 6 percent to 10 percent of the invoice value, and remitted the balance to the owner or owners of the buying company.

According to the scheme, a vendor operating a limited company would make out a normal invoice for $10,000 to a buyer, which issues a cheque for the full amount but never receives any merchandise. The vendor would then cash the cheque, keep $1,000 commission, and give the $9,000 balance to the buyer.

Principals of both companies in this fictitious example would thus be able to divert cash from their companies into their own pockets. For the buyer there is a further advantage: $10,000 marked on the false invoice is an expense that reduces the company's taxable income.

Severance Quarrel

The fraud came to light when a Shildan employee quarreled with Shildan's president over his severance pay. Early in 1976 the employee tipped off the Toronto Dominion Bank, from which the president had a loan of $1.33 million, as well as several federal agencies.

The tale sounded so unlikely that it was originally scorned. However, in the face of growing rumors the Toronto Dominion sent its agents to investigate Shildan in May 1976 and on July 8 the knitter was declared bankrupt. The deficiency was $1.5 million.

At a bankruptcy hearing, the president admitted Shidan had sold phony invoices worth $18 million from August 1974, when it was incorporated, through May 1976. The company netted from $300,000 to $400,000 in commissions on the transactions. Shildan's president also admitted he had begun selling false invoices in 1969.

He testified that three dummy companies had been set up to handle the accommodation invoices, as they are called by the revenue department.

Source Alan D. Gray, "Income tax probe uncovered 347 evaders and $56 million", *The* (Montreal) *Gazette*, July 7, 1978, p. 31.

For Discussion

1. What sort of tax or other controls can the federal government impose to prevent frauds of this kind?
2. Comment on the role of accountants within and external to Shildan Knitting Mills Ltd. Could the Shildan accountants have discovered this fraud?
3. If you were auditing Shildan and discovered the company's part in this fraud, what would you do?

Discussion Case 6-3:   Making Dough with a PC

The Deerfield Bakery is managed by Karl Schmitt, whose family has been in the baking business since his great-grandfather began the tradition in Germany. From there the family moved to Chicago where it operated the bakery until moving to the present location 11 years ago.

Schmitt became part owner of the store in 1979 when he gave up his career as an actuary and brought with him the programming skills he gained in the business world.

Like many small business owners, Schmitt hoped that computers would bring greater efficiency to his operation, while preserving a craft that had been handed down through the family. But computerization didn't happen overnight; Schmitt experimented with both hardware and software to build the right system.

"We started with a Texas Instruments computer, but by 1980 we had outgrown it," he recalled. As more and more of the bakery's operations were automated, the business needed a machine with greater capabilities, so he turned to the Apple III. However, he had problems with the hardware so he bought a Commodore PET, but found it didn't meet his needs, either. When IBM announced its PC, Schmitt decided to wait for it. He bought one of the first PCs available in his area. Since the initial purchase, he has bought three more. Two of the PCs are used in the store in place of cash registers. The sales personnel punch in a code, which corresponds to the type of item and the price. The computer calculates the applicable tax, the total bill, and the change due. The printer produces a receipt. The computers also keep track of the various products and remind employees of their duties in other parts of the shop. The two other PCs are located in the company office upstairs from the shop. Both machines have combination clock calendars, printer interface and memory expansion cards, 320K disk drives, light pens, and colour/graphics boards.

Schmitt has added a VOX board to upgrade one of the PCs to 14 megabytes. "I've written the programs so they can be run on floppies," he said. "I don't use the hard disk for original copy — it is more of a backup. If one machine goes down, I can run the program on the other machine on a floppy disk. This way, all of the programs can run on any of the PCs."

Programming for Baking

Finding the right software wasn't easy, either. When Schmitt began to computerize his business, he used off-the-shelf programs to handle accounts receivable and payable and other accounting procedures. However, he discovered that many of them did not adequately meet the needs of a small business.

"It's natural for commercial programmers to take the applications from large businesses — that's what they've done," he said. Unfortunately, a small business can't really use them, or, it isn't economical to do so.

As an experienced computer programmer, Schmitt was not deterred by the lack of available commercial programs geared to his industry. He decided to write his own software, which could be tailored to the bakery's specific needs. He has written more than 60 programs in BASIC, which do anything from printing out recipes for each day's baking to making lists of how to decorate specialty cakes. According to Schmitt, he chose BASIC over COBOL or FORTRAN because it can be written quickly, and it can be compiled. Compiled programs execute quickly. While it is true that some of these functions would be performed by commercial programs, Schmitt believes that writing his own saved time and money.

There are also other advantages to customized programming. "Some commercial programs are designed to be so flexible that they are neither easy nor fast to operate" said Schmitt. "Part of what I expect from computers is speed. If a program doesn't run quickly, you've saved labor but thrown away the savings on the time spent operating it. Some programs are so user-friendly that they are cumbersome to use."

One problem that Schmitt remedied with his own software was slow printing speed. A commercial program he had used took 45 minutes to print cheques because of pauses built into the software; his program, however, can produce cheques as quickly as his Anadex dot-matrix printer can generate them. His accounting software consists of three programs chained together, and it handles tasks that once required 12 commercial programs.

The advantages of writing your own software are many, but most small-business owners probably don't have programming experience as extensive as Schmitt's. However, he believes that even a short, simple customized program can be helpful and he recommends at least giving it a try.

Schmitt has considered marketing his software but decided against it because each operation's needs are so specific. "Someone else using our programs would run into the same problems I had with the commercial programs," he explained.

With the right hardware and software in place, the store can get down to the business of baking. Schmitt's programs include those for accounts receivable, bread recipes, cake recipes, and billing for wholesale accounts. He also uses programs for listing each type of decorative cake, determining price codes and one for tallying cake orders to determine quantities of ingredients.

Getting Down to Baking

Not every program is used every day, but most of them are central to the bakery's operations. When a customer calls in an order, the information is jotted down and later entered on the computer, where it is sorted by field (name, address, telephone number, type of order, price, and so forth). For example, this system allows you to examine all chocolate sheet cake orders at one time. At the end of the day, the telephone orders are combined with those from the wholesale customers (the bakery also sells some of its goods to supermarkets), and with the order of goods to stock the store. The computer will develop a recipe from this information, using another program.

Using this information the computer or an operator can decide to make, for example, [50 kg] 110 lb. of white bread loaves. The computer then creates a recipe and determines quantities for the necessary ingredients. In this case the recipe calls for [0.78 kg] 1.72 lb. of yeast, [2.46 kg] 5.43 lb. sweetened and condensed milk, [15.43 kg] 34.02 lb. of water, [29.14 kg] 64.25 lb. of flour, [0.4 kg] 0.9 lb. of diamalt, [0.57 kg] lb. of salt, and [0.33 kg] 0.72 lb. of shortening. If prepared sweetened and condensed milk is unavailable, the computer automatically includes a recipe for it. It also provides other help-ful hints for preparation. For instance, the program knows that flour in the United States comes in 100-pound sacks, so, in addition to calling for the required 64.25 pounds, it will note that you can simply remove 35.75 pounds of flour from the 100-pound sack. The recipe includes more than one set of mixing directions, each geared to a different machine in the bakery. The program specifies how long the mixing procedure will take, according to the machine used. A printout of the recipe is given to each baker when he begins work. For cakes or specialty items, the program will provide a decorations list along with a cake recipe.

"One of the biggest problems we had in the past," said Schmitt, "was misfiling of orders. A customer who had ordered a cake would come into the store, and we wouldn't have the cake ready—a sure way to damage your reputation. With the computer we print a list for the decorators each day, and all of the cakes are decorated to order.

"This is a prime example of the computer's value," he continued. "Management becomes easy when you have an alphabetical list of the cakes that have been ordered for a particular day. Without a computer, preparing a list like this one is such a time-consuming, tedious activity that many small businesses don't take the time to do it."

The Deerfield Bakery uses its PCs to keep track of more than 700 different confections and about 1000 designs for cakes, which can cost up to $300 or $400. It also offers 18 different types of bread ranging from plain white to zucchini. In addition, each type of bread is available in a number of forms, such as muffins, loaves, and rolls. Each form requires a different proportion of ingredients. On a typical day the bakery will make from 30 to 40 different doughs. "When you include cake fillings, icings, and garnishes, you use more than 50 ingredients," said Schmitt. "It used to take up to 2 hours to total manually the next day's needs and then calculate the quantities. With the computer the process moves as quickly as punching the keyboard."

Source Michael Muskal, "Making Dough with the P.C.", *P.C. Magazine*, February 7, 1984.

For Discussion

1. What are some advantages and disadvantages of Karl Schmitt writing his own accounting computer programs?
2. Would you incorporate controls into Schmitt's system? If so, what sort of controls?
3. Can you pinpoint potential limitations in Schmitt's system?

Comprehension Problems

Comprehension Problem 6-1

Apex Auto Supplies Ltd. sells to 300 customers on a regular basis. On July 31, 19X2, the Accounts Receivable balance is $40,000. The following transactions occur during the month of August:

Sales on Account	$53,000
Cash payments received for Sales on Account	39,000
Sales Discounts — Sales on Account	300
Cash Sales	16,700
Salespersons' Salaries	1,700

Required: Prepare the Accounts Receivable control account for the month of August. (*Hint:*   You may find it useful to rearrange the above data into a cash receipts journal format before preparing your Accounts Receivable control account.)

Note: For assignment material in this chapter, refer when necessary to the master chart of accounts in Chapter 3.

Comprehension Problem 6-2

Collreem Sales Inc. was incorporated on May 1, 19X1 to operate a merchandising business. Its sales journal, cash receipts journal, and general journal follow.

SALES JOURNAL   Page 1

Date		Sold To	Invoice Number	Terms	F	Accts Rec. — Dr. Sales — Cr.
19X1						
May	1	Bloomfield Products Corp.	1	2/10, n/30		6,000
	2	Garland Stores Inc.	2	2/10, n/30		2,400
	11	Summit Sales Inc.	3	2/10, n/30		1,000
	20	Willowdale Corp.	4	2/10, n/30		4,000
	27	Cardinal Emporium Corp.	5	2/10, n/30		1,600
		Totals				15,000
						(110) (500)

CASH RECEIPTS JOURNAL   Page 1

Information		Debit			Credit			
				Accounts Receivable		Other Accounts		
Date	Cash Received From	Cash	Sales Disc.	✓	Amount	Account	F	Amount
19X1								
May 1	Common Stock	6,000				Common Stock	320	6,000
2	Harvey Pann	1,000				Sales (cash)	500	1,000
5	Bloomfield Products Corp.	2,940	60		3,000			
8	Garland Stores Inc.	2,352	48		2,400			
20	Summit Sales Inc.	784	16		800			
	Totals	13,076	124		6,200			7,000
		(101)	(509)		(110)			(X)

GENERAL JOURNAL   Page 1

Date 19X1	Description	F	Debit	Credit
May 12	Sales Returns and Allowances	508	200 -	
	Accounts Receivable	110		200 -
	To record return from Summit			
	Sales Inc.			

Required:
1. Open accounts receivable subsidiary accounts for each customer.
2. Post the appropriate information and amounts from each journal.
3. Calculate the balance in each accounts receivable subsidiary account.

Comprehension Problem 6-3

Lakeside Trading Corp. keeps a subsidiary ledger for accounts payable with a control account in the general ledger. On March 31, 19X2, its balance sheet contained the following data:

Inventory	$60,000
Accounts Payable	35,000
Notes Payable	5,000

Transactions during the month of April:

Purchases on Account	$27,000
Cash Purchases	400
Purchases Returns and Allowances — Purchases on Account	300
Purchase Discounts — Purchases on Account	900
Cash Paid on Account	44,100
Transportation In — Paid in Cash	200
Note Payable — Paid in Cash	5,000

Required:
1. Calculate the Accounts Payable column total in the following cash disbursements journal. (Individual amounts have already been entered.)

CASH DISBURSEMENTS JOURNAL   Page 7

| Information | | Debit | | | | | Credit | | |
| | | Accounts Payable | | Other Accounts | | | | | |
Date	Cash Paid To	✓	Amount	Account	F	Amount	Purchases Discount	Cash	Cheque number
19X2 Apr. 28	EZ Express			Transportation In	560	200		200	51
29	Peel Products Inc.			Purchases	550	400		400	52
30	Maxum Corporation			Note Payable	220	5,000		5,000	53
	Totals		?			5,600	900	49,700	
			(210)			(X)	(559)	(101)	

2. Prepare the Accounts Payable control account for April using the data from the journal and the other transactions during April, where applicable.

Comprehension Problem 6-4

Rapid Sales Inc. was incorporated on June 2, 19X1 to operate a merchandising business. Its sales and purchases during June are recorded below.

PURCHASES JOURNAL   Page 1

Date		Purchased From	Terms	F	Purchases — Dr. Accts Pay. — Cr.
19X1 Jun.	2	Atwater Pencils Ltd.	2/10, n/30		7,000
	8	Hymus Distributors Inc.	2/15, n/30		4,000
	10	Park Products Inc.	n/30		400
	15	MacKay Door Inc.	2/10, n/30		3,000
	26	Coolbrooke Co.	2/10, n/30		1,600
					16,000
					(550) (210)

CASH DISBURSEMENTS JOURNAL

Page 1

| Information | | | Debit | | | | Credit | | |
Date	Cash Paid To	✓	Accounts Payable — Amount	Other Accounts — Account	F	Amount	Purchases Discount	Cash	Cheque number
19X1									
Jun. 3	Concordia Rentals Corp.			Rent Expense	654	1,000		1,000	1
5	Westwood Furniture Ltd.			Equipment	183	2,000		2,000	2
10	Atwater Pencils Ltd.		7,000				150	6,850	3
20	Hymus Distributors Inc.		1,900				38	1,862	4
24	MacKay Doors Ltd.		3,000				60	2,940	5
31	Real Quick Transport Co.			Transportation In	560	700		700	6
	Totals		11,900			3,700	248	15,352	
			(210)		(X)		(559)	(101)	

GENERAL JOURNAL

Page 1

Date		F	Debit	Credit	Bal.
19X1					
Jun. 15	Accounts Payable	210	200		
	Purchases Returns and Allowances	558		200	
	To record goods returned to Hymus Distributors Inc.				

Required:
1. Open accounts payable subsidiary accounts for each supplier.
2. Post the appropriate information and amounts from each journal.
3. Calculate the balance in each accounts payable subsidiary account.

Problems

Problem 6-1

The following accounts payable subsidiary ledger accounts have been posted during March 19X2 from two books of original entry.

ACCOUNTS PAYABLE SUBSIDIARY LEDGER

Avon Stores Inc.

Date			F	Debit	Credit	Bal.
19X2 Bal.		(purchase made Feb. 2, 19X2, terms n/30)				1,000
Mar.	15		P.3		500	
	17		P.3		750	
	20		CD.7	1,000		

Clanranald Novelties Ltd.

Date			F	Debit	Credit	Bal.
19X2						
Mar.	3		P.3		1,500	
	12		CD.7	1,500		
	26		P.3		1,250	

Fulton Place Products Inc.

Date			F	Debit	Credit	Bal.
19X2						
Mar.	25		P.3		3,000	
Mar.	31		CD.7	1,500		

Otterburn College Inc.

Date			F	Debit	Credit	Bal.
19X2 Bal.		(purchase made Feb. 10, 19X2, terms n/30)				2,000
Mar.	20		P.3		400	
	31		CD.7	1,600		

Richmond Renovators Corp.

Date			F	Debit	Credit	Bal.
19X2						
Mar.	10		P.3		900	
	24		CD.7	900		

Required:
1. Calculate and record the balance in each of the above accounts.
2. Using the information in these accounts, complete the purchases journal and calculate the column total.

PURCHASES JOURNAL   Page 3

Date		Purchased From	Terms	F	Purchases — Dr. Accts Pay. — Cr.
19X2 Mar.	3		2/10, n/30		
	10		2/15, n/30		
	15		n/30		
	17		n/30		
	20		n/30		
	25		2/10, n/30		
	26		2/10, n/30		
					(550) (210)

3. Using the information in the subsidiary ledger accounts, complete the cash disbursements journal and calculate all column totals. Assume that all cash disbursements in March were for the payment of accounts payable.

CASH DISBURSEMENTS JOURNAL   Page 7

Information		Debit						Credit		
		Accounts Payable		Other Accounts						
Date	Cash Paid To	✓	Amount	Account	F	Amount	Purchases Discount	Cash	Cheque number
19X2									
	Totals								
			(210)			(X)	(559)	(101)	

4. Open general ledger accounts for Cash, Accounts Payable, Purchases, and Purchases Discounts. Post the column totals of the purchases journal and cash disbursements journal.
5. Prepare a schedule of accounts payable at March 31, 19X2. The total should agree with the balance in the general ledger Accounts Payable account. The February 28, 19X2 balance in this control account amounted to $3,000.

Problem 6-2

The following accounts receivable subsidiary ledger accounts have been posted during January, 19X3 from two books of original entry.

ACCOUNTS RECEIVABLE SUBSIDIARY LEDGER

Atwater Marketers Corp.

Date			F	Debit	Credit	Bal.
19X3 Bal.						5,250
Jan.	15		S.6	1,000		

Coolbrooke Distributors Ltd.

Date			F	Debit	Credit	Bal.
19X3 Jan.	6		S.6	500		
	9		S.6	250		
	15		CR.9		500	

Hymus Sales Corp.

Date			F	Debit	Credit	Bal.
19X3 Bal.						1,500
Jan.	2		S.6	1,200		
	11		CR.6		2,700	

Mackay Products Inc.

Date			F	Debit	Credit	Bal.
19X3 Bal.						200
Jan.	7		S.6	800		
	10		CR.9		200	

Park Extension Ltd.

Date			F	Debit	Credit	Bal.
19X3 Bal.						900
Jan.	18		CR.9		900	
	25		S.6	600		

TransCanada Sales Inc.

Date			F	Debit	Credit	Bal.
19X3 Jan.	10		S.6	400		
	14		S.6	300		
	19		CR.9		400	

Required:
1. Calculate and record the balance in each of the accounts.
2. Using the information in the accounts, complete the sales journal and calculate the column total.

SALES JOURNAL　　　　　　　　　　　　　　　　Page 6

Date		Sold To	Invoice Number	Terms	F	Accts Rec. — Dr. Sales — Cr.
19X3 Jan.	2		31	2/10, n/30		
				2/10, n/30		
				2/10, n/30		
				2/10, n/30		
				2/10, n/30		
				2/10, n/30		
				2/10, n/30		
				2/10, n/30		
				2/10, n/30		
						(110)　(500)

3. Using the information in the subsidiary ledger accounts, complete the cash receipts journal and calculate all column totals. Assume that all cash receipts in January were from the collection of accounts receivable. Note that all eligible customers took discounts.

CASH RECEIPTS JOURNAL　　　　　　　　　　　　　　　　Page 9

Information			Debit		Credit				
					Accounts Receivable		Other Accounts		
Date		Cash Received From	Cash	Sales Disc.	✓	Amount	Account	F	Amount
19X3 Jan.	10								
		Totals							
			(101)	(509)		(110)			(X)

4. Open general ledger accounts for Cash, Accounts Receivable, Sales, and Sales Discounts. Post the column totals of the sales journal and cash receipts journal.

5. Prepare a schedule of accounts receivable at January 31, 19X3; the total should agree with the balance in the general ledger Accounts Receivable account. The January 1, 19X3 balance in this control account amounted to $7,850.

Problem 6-3

Beacon Hill Corp. was incorporated on July 2, 19X1 to operate a merchandising business. Its sales and purchases during July are recorded below.

SALES JOURNAL   Page 1

Date		Sold To	Invoice Number	Terms	F	Accts Rec. — Dr. Sales — Cr.
19X1 Jul.	2	Hampstead Tool Rentals. Inc.	1	2/10, n/30		2,000
	15	Condor Products Corp.	2	2/10, n/30		2,000
	20	Pine Promotions Corp.	3	2/10, n/30		3,500
	26	Daytona Sales Ltd.	4	2/10, n/30		600
	31	Argyle Inc.	5	2/10, n/30		1,900
						10,000
						(110) (500)

PURCHASES JOURNAL   Page 1

Date		Purchased From	Terms	F	Purchases — Dr. Accts Pay — Cr.
19X1 Jul.	2	Westmount Pencils Ltd.	2/10, n/30		3,500
	8	MacDonald Distributors Inc.	2/15, n/30		2,000
	10	Peel Products Inc.	n/30		200
	15	Draper Door Inc.	2/10, n/30		1,500
	26	Gold & Silver Co.	2/10, n/30		800
					8,000
					(550) (210)

Other transactions during the month were as follows:

Jul. 2   Issued common shares for $5,000 cash to George Hill, the incorporator and sole shareholder of the corporation

Jul. 3   Issued cheque no. 1 to Concordia Rentals Corp. for $500 in payment of July rent

Jul. 5   Issued cheque no. 2 to Westwood Furniture Ltd. for $1,000 in payment for equipment

Jul. 8   Collected $200 for a cash sale made today to Byron Peel

Jul. 9   Received the amount due from Hampstead Tool Rentals Inc. for the July 2 sale (less discount)

Jul. 10   Issued cheque no. 3 to Westmount Pencils Ltd. in payment for the July 2 purchase (less discount)

Jul. 15   Received a credit note memo from MacDonald Distributors Inc. for $100-worth of defective merchandise included in the July 9 purchase.

Jul. 16   Condor Products Corp. returned $200-worth of merchandise (issued a credit memo)

Jul. 20   Issued cheque no. 4 to MacDonald Distributors Inc. in payment of half the purchase made July 8 (less credit note, less discount on payment)

Jul. 24   Received half the amount due from Condor Products Corp. in partial payment for the July 15 sale (less discount on payment)

Jul. 24   Issued cheque no. 5 to Draper Door Inc. in payment of the purchase made July 15 (less discount)

Jul. 31   Issued cheque no. 6 to Real Quick Transport Co. for $350 in payment for transportation to our warehouse during the month (All purchases are fob shipping point.)

Required:

1. Record the July transactions in the following journals:
   a. cash receipts journal
   b. cash disbursements journal
   c. general journal.
2. Calculate the total of each column in the cash receipts and cash disbursements journals. For each journal, ascertain whether total debits equal total credits.
3. Open subsidiary ledger accounts for each of the customers listed in the sales journal and post the sales transactions and appropriate cash receipts transactions to these accounts.
4. Open subsidiary ledger accounts for each of the suppliers recorded in the purchases journal and post the purchase transactions to these accounts.
5. Post the appropriate entries from the general journal to the subsidiary accounts receivable and subsidiary accounts payable accounts.
6. Open the following general ledger control accounts:
   a. accounts receivable
   b. accounts payable.

   Post all appropriate balances from the cash receipts and cash disbursements journals and the appropriate amounts from the general journal.
7. Prepare a schedule of accounts receivable; the total should agree with the Accounts Receivable control account.
8. Prepare a schedule of accounts payable; the total should agree with the Accounts Payable control account.

Problem 6-4

Lucerne Sales Corp. was incorporated on May 1, 19X1 to operate a merchandising business. Its sales and purchases journals for May are reproduced below.

SALES JOURNAL   Page 1

Date		Sold To	Invoice Number	Terms	F	Accts Rec. — Dr. Sales — Cr.
19X1						
May	1	Montreal West Distributors	1	2/10, n/30		2,500
	2	Terrebonne Sales Inc.	2	2/10, n/30		2,000
	5	Brock Stores Corporation	3	2/10, n/30		1,000
	10	Western Warehouse	4	2/10, n/30		2,400
	15	Roxboro Outlets Inc.	5	2/10, n/30		1,500
	25	Kirkland Centres Ltd.	6	2/10, n/30		700
	28	Lachine Wharf Corp.	7	2/10, n/30		900
						11,000
						(110) (500)

PURCHASES JOURNAL   Page 1

Date		Sold To	Terms	F	Purchases — Dr. Accts Pay. — Cr.
19X1					
May	1	St Luc Wholesales Corp.	2/10, n/30		2,000
	2	Rosedale Products Ltd.	n/30		1,800
	8	Elmhurst Novelties Inc.	2/15, n/30		2,800
	15	Hudson Distributors Inc.	2/10, n/30		1,500
	19	Mid-Island Stores Corp.	1/10, n/30		1,200
	22	Quick Sales Co.	n/30		600
	29	Sidekicks Inc.	2/15, n/30		100
					10,000
					(550) (210)

Other transactions during the month were as follows:

May   1   Issued common shares for $2,000 cash to Harry Jones, the incorporator and sole shareholder of the corporation

May   1   Received $10,000 from the Second Canadian Bank as a demand bank loan

May   1   Issued cheque no. 1 to Cadillac Corp. for $1,500 in payment for 3 months rent in advance — May, June, and July (recorded as a asset)

May   1   Issued cheque no. 2 to Avanti Equipment Ltd. for $5,000 in payment for equipment

May   3   Collected $500 for a cash sale made today to Irwin Peabody

May   5   Issued cheque no. 3 to All Province Insurance Inc. for $1,200 in payment for a one-year insurance policy, effective May 1 (recorded as an asset)

May   6   Terrebonne Sales Inc. returned $500 of merchandise (issued a credit memo)

May   8   Received a credit memo from St Luc Wholesalers Corp. for $300-worth of defective merchandise included in the May 1 purchase and returned subsequently to St Luc

May   9   Received the amount due from Montreal West Distributors from the May 1 sale (less discount)

May   9   Issued cheque no. 4 to St Luc Wholesalers Corp. in payment of the May 1 purchase (less discount)

May 11   Received the amount due from Terrebonne Sales Inc. (less the May 6 credit memo and discount)

May 13   Issued cheque no. 5 to Express Corporation for $100 in payment for transportation in

May 15   Issued cheque no. 6 for $500 commissions to Harry Jones, *re* sales invoices nos. 1, 2, and 3

May 19   Issued cheque no. 7 to Rosedale Products Ltd. in payment for the May 2 purchase

May 22   Issued cheque no. 8 to Elmhurst Novelties Inc. in payment for the May 8 purchase (less discount)

May 24   Issued cheque no. 9 to Express Corporation for $150 in payment for transportation in

May 26   Received the amount due from Brock Stores Corporation

May 27   Issued cheque no. 10 for $200 to Yale Deliveries Ltd. for deliveries made to customers

May 28   Collected $300 for a cash sale made today to Joe Montclair

May 28   Made a $200 cash purchase from Ballantyne Sales Inc. today (issued cheque no. 11; debited purchases)

May 29   Issued the following cheques:
no. 12 to Speedy Ltd. for $300 in payment for deliveries (debited account 620)
no. 13 to Impetus Advertising Agency for $400 in payment for advertising materials used during May
no. 14 to Hydro-Bec for $100 in payment for electricity
no. 15 to Harry Jones for $350 commissions, *re*: sales invoices nos. 4, 5, 6, and 7

May 30   Collected $1,000 on account from Roxboro Outlets Inc.

May 31   Issued cheque no. 16 to Mid-Island Stores Corp. for $700 on account

May 31   Issued cheque no. 17 to Harry Jones for $100 in payment of dividends declared today.

Required:
1. Record the May transactions in the following journals:
   a. cash receipts journal
   b. cash disbursements journal
   c. general journal.
2. Calculate the total of each column in the cash receipts and cash disbursements journals. For each journal, ascertain whether total debits equal total credits.
3. Open subsidiary accounts receivable accounts for each of the seven customers recorded in the sales journal, and post the sales transactions and appropriate cash receipts transactions to these accounts.
4. Open subsidiary accounts payable accounts for each supplier listed in the purchases journal, and post the purchases transactions and appropriate cash disbursements transactions to these accounts.
5. Post all appropriate entries from the general journal to the subsidiary accounts receivable and subsidiary accounts payable accounts.
6. Open the following general ledger control accounts:
   a. accounts receivable,   b. accounts payable.
   Post all appropriate balances from the cash receipts and disbursements journals, and appropriate amounts from the general journal.
7. Prepare a schedule of accounts receivable accounts; the total should agree with the Accounts Receivable control account.
8. Prepare a schedule of accounts payable accounts; the total should agree with the Accounts Payable control account.

Problem 6-5

The following payroll information for the week ending June 7, 19X2 is taken from the records of Sim and Son Personnel Services Inc.

Gross Pay	$3,000
Deductions from Employees:	
Unemployment Insurance	60
Income Tax	600
Pension Plan	40
Health Insurance	50

Required:
1. Calculate the amount of net pay
2. Prepare the journal entry to record the payroll deductions.
3. Prepare the journal entry to accrue the empoyer-related payroll taxes. Assume that the employer pays on a 1 : 1 ratio for pension plan and health insurance and on a 2 : 1 ratio for unemployment insurance.

Problem 6-6

The partially completed payroll journal of Jackson Thrills Inc. for the week ending March 20, 19X1 is reproduced below.

PAYROLL JOURNAL   Page 1

Information								Debits			Credits										
				Hours		Rate		Gross Pay			Deductions										
Week Ending											Income Tax										
Mo.	Day	Yr.	Employee Name	Reg.	OT	Reg.	OT	Sales	Delivery	Office	Fed.	Prov.	UIC	Pension	Health	1	2	3	Total	Net Pay	Chq. No.
03	20	X2	Carl Edge							450	51	65	6	8							
03	20	X2	Ry. R. Son	40		12.50			500		61	77	6	8							
03	20	X2	Al Nate					350			33	43	6	6							

Required:
1. Complete the payroll journal by calculating the total and net pay columns; add each column to check that total debits equal total credits.
2. Post the amounts in the payroll journal to the appropriate general ledger accounts. (Use account numbers assigned in this chapter.)
3. Prepare a journal entry to record the employer's share of contributions. Assume that the employer is required to pay an amount equal to that deducted from employees for UIC and pension. In the case of health insurance, where the employer is assumed to pay the entire amount, calculate as 3 percent of gross pay.

Alternate Problems

Alternate Problem 6-1

The following accounts payable subsidiary ledger accounts have been posted for July 19X5 from two books of original entry.

ACCOUNTS PAYABLE SUBSIDIARY LEDGER
Bessborough Warehouse Inc.

Date			F	Debit	Credit	Bal.
19X5 Jul.	15		P.10		2,000	
	24		CD.15	1,000		
	29		CD.15	1,000		
	31		P.10		500	

Crescent Shops Ltd.

Date			F	Debit	Credit	Bal.
19X5 Bal.		(purchase made June 3, 19X5, terms n/30)				3,000
Jul.	10		P.10		250	
	30		CD.15	1,500		

Peel Stadium Corp.

Date			F	Debit	Credit	Bal.
19X5 Bal.		(purchase made June 15, 19X5, terms n/30)				850
Jul.	20		P.10		250	
	25		CD.15	550		

St. Lawrence Downtown Inc.

Date			F	Debit	Credit	Bal.
19X5 Jul.	9		P.10		1,500	
	23		CD.15	750		
	25		P.10		500	
	30		CD.15	750		

Walkley Cabinets Ltd.

Date			F	Debit	Credit	Bal.
19X5 Jul.	2		P.10		600	
	11		CD.15	600		

Required:
1. Calculate and record the balance in each of the accounts.
2. Using the information in the accounts, complete the purchases journal and calculate the column total.

PURCHASES JOURNAL   Page 10

Date		Purchased From	Terms	F	Purchases — Dr. Accts Pay. — Cr.
19X5					
July	2		2/10, n/30		
	9		2/15, n/30		
	10		n/30		
	15		2/10, n/30		
	20		n/30		
	25		2/15, n/30		
	31		2/10, n/30		
					(550) (210)

3. Using the information in the subsidiary ledger accounts, complete the cash disbursements journal and calculate all column totals. Assume that all cash disbursements in July were for the payment of accounts payable. A sample Cash Disbursements Journal can be found on page 297 or in the *Working Papers* which accompanies the text.
4. Open general ledger accounts for Cash, Accounts Payable, Purchases, and Purchases Discounts. Post the column totals of the purchases journal and cash disbursements journal.
5. Prepare a schedule of accounts payable at July 31, 19X5; the total should agree with the balance in the general ledger Accounts Payable account. (The July 1, 19X5 balance of the control account amounted to $3,850.)

Alternate Problem 6-2

The following accounts receivable subsidiary ledger accounts have been posted during June 19X4 from two books of original entry.

ACCOUNTS RECEIVABLE SUBSIDIARY LEDGER
Bloomfield Centres Corp.

Date			F	Debit	Credit	Bal.
19X4						
Bal.						500
Jun.	1		S.8	400		
	6		S.8	600		
	14		CR.5		500	

Cardinal Cards Corp.

Date			F	Debit	Credit	Bal.
19X4						
Jun.	5		S.8	100		
	10		S.8	300		
	22		CR.5		400	

Earnscliffe Distributors Corp.

Date			F	Debit	Credit	Bal.
19X4						
Bal.						2,000
Jun.	1		CR.5		1,000	
	10		S.8	200		

Garland Products Inc.

Date			F	Debit	Credit	Bal.
19X4						
Jun.	7		S.8	800		
	21		CR.5		800	

Summit Sales Inc.

Date			F	Debit	Credit	Bal.
19X4						
Jun.	14		S.8	200		
	20		S.8	750		
	30		CR.5		200	

Willowdale Sales Ltd.

Date			F	Debit	Credit	Bal.
19X4						
Bal.						2,500
Jun.	15		S.8	1,500		
	30	Payment on account	CR.5		1,000	

1. Calculate and record the balance in each of the accounts.
2. Using the information in the accounts, complete the sales journal and calculate the column total. Note that all June sales journal entries are posted to the accounts and that terms for all sales are 2/15, net 30.
3. Using the information in the subsidiary ledger accounts, complete the cash receipts journal and calculate all column totals. Assume that all cash receipts in June were from the collection of accounts receivable. Note that all eligible customers took discounts.
4. Open general ledger accounts for Cash, Accounts Receivable, Sales, and Sales Discounts. Post the column totals of the sales journal and cash receipts journal.
5. Prepare a schedule of accounts receivable at June 30, 19X4; the total should agree with the balance in the general ledger accounts receivable account. The June 1, 19X4 balance in this control account amounted to $5,000.

PURCHASES JOURNAL   Page

Date	Purchased From	Terms	F	Purchases — Dr. Accts Pay. — Cr.
				(550) (210)

CASH DISBURSEMENTS JOURNAL   Page

Information			Debit				Credit		
		Accounts Payable		Other Accounts					
Date	Cash Paid To	✔	Amount	Account	F		Purchases Discount	Cash	Cheque number
	Totals								
			(210)			(X)	(559)	(101)	

Alternate Problem 6-3

Sim Co. Products Inc. was incorporated on April 1, 19X1 to operate a merchandising business. Its sales and purchases during April are now recorded below.

SALES JOURNAL   Page 1

Date		Sold To	Invoice Number	Terms	F	Accts Rec. — Dr. Sales — Cr.
19X1 Apr.	1	Ahuntic Products Corp.	1	2/10, n/30		3,000
	2	Chambly Stores Inc.	2	2/10, n/30		1,200
	11	Presidential Sales Inc.	3	2/10, n/30		500
	20	Salaberry Corp.	4	2/10, n/30		2,000
	27	Bishop Emporium Corp.	5	2/10, n/30		800
						7,500
						(110) (500)

PURCHASES JOURNAL   Page 1

Date		Purchased From	Terms	F	Purchases — Dr. Accts Pay. — Cr.
19X1 Apr.	1	Beaconsfield Sales Inc.	2/10, n/30		4,000
	2	Dorval Wholesalers Ltd.	2/15, n/30		750
	10	Carlton Markers Corp.	n/30		2,000
	15	Atwater Distributors Inc.	2/10, n/30		1,500
	19	Kildare Sales Ltd.	n/30		1,250
					9,500
					(550) (210)

Other transactions during April were as follows:

Apr. 1   Issued common shares for $3,000 cash to Rosco Simcoe, the incorporator and sole shareholder of the corporation

Apr. 2   Collected $500 for a cash sale made today to George Kirkland

Apr. 5   Received half the amount due from Ahuntic Products Corp. for the April 1 purchase (less discount on payment)

Apr. 8   Received the amount due from Chambly Stores Inc. for the April 2 purchase (less discount)

Apr. 9   Issued cheque no 1 to Beaconsfield Sales Inc. in payment for the April 1 purchase (less discount on payment)

Apr. 12   Presidential Sales Inc. returned $100-worth of merchandise (issued a credit memo)

Apr. 15   Received a credit memo from Dorval Wholesalers Ltd. for $50-worth of defective merchandise included in the April 2 purchase and subsequently returned

Apr. 20   Received the amount due from Presidential Sales Inc. for the April 11 purchase (less return, less discount)

Apr. 22   Issued cheque no. 2 to Carlton Markers Corp. in payment for the April 10 purchase (less discount on payment)

Apr. 24   Issued cheque no. 3 to Atwater Distributors Inc. on account in partial payment of the April 15 purchase (less discount on payment)

Apr. 30   Issued cheque no. 4 to Rapid Delivery Inc. for $200 in payment for deliveries made to customers during the month (debited account 620)

Apr. 30   Issued cheque no. 5 to Truck Forwarders Ltd. for $500 in payment for transportation to our warehouse during the month (All purchases are fob shipping point.)

Required:
1. Record the April transactions in the following journals:
   a. cash receipts journal
   b. cash disbursement journal
   c. general journal.
2. Calculate the total of each column in the cash receipts and cash disbursements journals. For each journal, ascertain whether total debits equal total credits.
3. Open subsidiary ledger accounts for each of the customers recorded in the sales journal, and post the sales transactions and appropriate cash receipts transactions to these accounts.
4. Open subsidiary ledger accounts for each of the suppliers recorded in the purchases journal, and post the purchase transactions and appropriate cash disbursements transactions to these accounts.
5. Post all appropriate entries from the general journal to the subsidiary accounts receivable and subsidiary accounts payable accounts.
6. Open the following general ledger control accounts:
   a. accounts receivable,   b. accounts payable.
   Post all appropriate balances from the cash receipts and disbursements journals, and appropriate amounts from the general journal.
7. Prepare a schedule of accounts receivable; the total should agree with the Accounts Receivable control account.
8. Prepare a schedule of accounts payable; the total should agree with the Accounts Payable control account.

Alternate Problem 6-4

Rockland Wholesalers Inc. was incorporated on March 1 to operate a merchandising business. Its sales and purchases journals for March are reproduced below.

SALES JOURNAL   Page 1

Date		Sold To	Invoice Number	Terms	F	Accts Rec. — Dr. Sales — Cr.
19X1						
Mar.	2	Kirkland Centres Ltd.	1	2/10, n/30		2,000
	4	Western Warehouse	2	2/10, n/30		2,500
	6	Lachine Wharf Corp.	3	2/10, n/30		1,500
	12	Hudson Distributors Inc.	4	2/10, n/30		1,700
	20	Sidekicks Inc.	5	2/10, n/30		600
	25	Elmhurst Novelties Inc.	6	2/10, n/30		1,400
	29	Terrebonne Sales Inc.	7	2/10, n/30		300
						10,000
						(110) (500)

PURCHASES JOURNAL   Page 1

Date		Purchased From	Terms	F	Purchases — Dr. Accts Pay. — Cr.
19X1					
Mar.	1	Mid-Island Stores Corp.	2/10, n/30		2,100
	3	Quick Sales Co.	1/10, n/30		500
	5	St Luc Wholesalers Corp.	n/30		1,400
	7	Brock Stores Corporation	2/15, n/30		600
	15	Rosedale Products Ltd.	2/15, n/30		1,000
	20	Sheraton Centres Inc.	n/30		1,200
	26	Grand Markets Ltd.	2/10, n/30		700
					7,500
					(550) (210)

Other transactions during March were as follows:

Mar. 1   Issued common shares for $10,000 cash to Michael Strong, the incorporator and sole shareholder of the corporation

Mar. 1   Issued cheque no. 1 to Brunswick Fixtures Inc. for $4,000 in payment for equipment

Mar. 2   Collected $300 for a cash sale made today to Irving Clayton

Mar. 4   Kirkland Centres Ltd. returned $200-worth of merchandise (issued a credit memo)

Mar. 6   Received a credit memo from Mid-Island Stores Corp. for $100-worth of defective merchandise included in the March 1 purchase and subsequently returned to Mid-Island

Mar. 8   Received the amount due from Kirkland Centres Ltd. (less credit memo, less discount)

Mar. 10   Issued cheque no. 2 to Quick Sales Co. in payment for the March 3 purchase (less discount)

Mar. 11   Received $7,500 from the Third Canadian Bank as a demand bank loan

Mar. 12   Issued cheque no. 3 to Fairview Realty Corp. for $1,000 in payment for 2 months rent: March and April (recorded as an asset)

Mar. 13   Received the amount due from Western Warehouse (less discount)

Mar. 15 Issued cheque no. 4 to Michael Strong for $350 — commissions earned to date

Mar. 15 Issued cheque no. 5 to Mid-Island Stores Corporation for $1,000 on account

Mar. 18 Issued cheque no. 6 to Brock Stores Corporation in payment for half of the March 7 purchase (less discount on payment)

Mar. 19 Collected $100 for a cash sale made today to Al Trudeau

Mar. 20 Made a $400 cash purchase from Roslyn Distributors Inc.; issued cheque no. 7 in payment (debited Purchases)

Mar. 21 Issued cheque no. 8 to St Luc Wholesalers Corp. for $700 on account

Mar. 22 Received $500 on account from Lachine Wharf Corp.

Mar. 23 Issued cheque no. 9 to All City Insurance Ltd. for $2,400 in payment for a one-year insurance policy, effective March 1 (recorded as an asset)

Mar. 24 Made a $300 cash purchase from CKU Emporium; issued cheque no. 10 (debited Purchases)

Mar. 30 Issued the following cheques:

no. 11 to D-Liver Corp. for $500 for deliveries (debited account 620)

no. 12 to Michael Strong for $400 — commissions earned to date

no. 13 to Bell-Bec for $75 in payment for the monthly telephone bill

no. 14 to Johnson Visuals Ltd. for $250 in payment for advertising materials used during the month

Mar. 31 Issued cheque no. 15 to Michael Strong for $200 in payment of dividends declared today

Required:

1. Record the March transactions in the following journals:
   a. cash receipts journal
   b. cash disbursements journal
   c. general journal.
2. Calculate the total of each column in the cash receipts and cash disbursements journals. For each journal, ascertain whether total debits equal total credits.
3. Open subsidiary accounts receivable accounts for each of the customers recorded in the sales journal, and post the sales transactions and appropriate cash receipts transactions to these accounts.
4. Open subsidiary accounts payable accounts for each of the customers recorded in the purchases journal, and post the purchase transactions and appropriate cash disbursements transactions to these accounts.
5. Post the appropriate entries from the general journal to the subsidiary accounts receivable and subsidiary accounts payable accounts.
6. Open the following general ledger control accounts:
   a. accounts receivable,   b. accounts payable.
   Post all appropriate balances from the cash receipts and disbursements journals, and appropriate amounts from the general journal.
7. Prepare a schedule of accounts receivable accounts; the total should agree with the Accounts Receivable control account.
8. Prepare a schedule of accounts payable accounts; the total should agree with the Accounts Payable control account.

Alternate Problem 6-5

The following payroll information for the week ending January 1, 19X1 is taken from the records of Sandblom Authoring Corporation.

Gross Pay	$4,500
Deductions from Employees:	
Unemployment Insurance	80
Income Taxes	900
Pension Plan	60
Health Insurance	80

Required:

1. Calculate the amount of net pay.
2. Prepare the journal entry to record the payroll deductions.
3. Prepare the journal entry to accrue the employer-related payroll taxes. Assume that the employer contributes on a 1 : 1 ratio for the pension plan and health insurance and on a 2 : 1 ratio for unemployment insurance.

Alternate Problem 6-6

The partially completed payroll journal of George and Father Corp. for the week ending April 15, 19X3 is reproduced below.

PAYROLL JOURNAL   Page 1

Information							Debits			Credits											
Week Ending				Hours		Earnings		Gross Pay			Deductions										
			Employee Name								Income Tax									Net Pay	Chq. No.
Mo.	Day	Yr.		Reg.	OT	Reg.	OT	Sales	Delivery	Office	Fed.	Prov.	UIC	Pension	Health	1	2	3	Total		
04	15	X3	G. Williams							300	30	40	6	8							
04	15	X3	G. Vanier	40		10			400		50	70	6	8							
04	15	X3	Mac Gill					500			60	80	6	8							

Required:

1. Complete the payroll journal by calculating the total and net pay columns; add each column to check that total debits equal total credits.
2. Post the amounts in the payroll journal to the appropriate general ledger accounts. (Use the account numbers assigned in this chapter.)
3. Prepare a journal entry to record the employer's share of contributions. Assume that the employer is required to pay an amount equal to that deducted from employees for UIC and pension; in the case of health insurance, where the employer is assumed to pay the entire amount, calculate as 3 percent of gross pay.

Review Problems

Review Problem 6-1

This problem completes the accounting cycle for Lucerne Sales Corp. previously introduced in Problem 6-4. Complete Problem 6-4 before attempting this review. At the end of May, 19X1, the following additional information is available for the preparation of adjusting entries.

a. The May portion of the payment made by cheque no. 1 has expired.
b. There is accrued interest of $150 on the bank loan at May 31, which has not yet been recorded.
c. Depreciation on the equipment for May amounts to $50.
d. A $50 bill for May telephone expenses has not yet been received or recorded.
e. The May portion of the payment made by cheque no. 3 has expired.

A physical count of inventory on May 31 indicates that $2,000-worth of inventory is still on hand. The periodic inventory method is used by the corporation. The fiscal year-end of Lucerne is May 31.

Required:
1. Open general ledger accounts for the following: Cash, Accounts Receivable, Merchandise Inventory, Prepaid Insurance, Prepaid Rent, Equipment, Accumulated Depreciation, Bank Loan, Accounts Payable, Interest Payable, Utilities Payable, Common Stock, Retained Earnings, Dividends, Income Summary, Sales, Sales Returns, Sales Discounts, Purchases, Purchases Returns, Purchases Discounts, Transportation In, Advertising Expense, Commissions Expense, Delivery Expense, Depreciation Expense, Insurance Expense, Interest Expense, Rent Expense, Telephone Expense, Utilities Expense.
2. Post the following journals to the general ledger accounts:
   a. sales journal   d. cash disbursements journal
   b. purchases journal   e. general journal.
   c. cash receipts journal
3. Prepare and record a trial balance on a worksheet.
4. Prepare and record all necessary adjusting journal entries on the worksheet.
5. Complete the worksheet.
6. Prepare the following financial statements from the worksheet:
   a. income statement   c. balance sheet
   b. statement of retained earnings
7. Post the adjusting entries to the general ledger.
8. Prepare closing entries and post to the general ledger. Rule all closed accounts.
9. Prepare a post-closing trial balance.
10. Prepare any required reversing entries and post to the general ledger.

Review Problem 6-2

This problem completes the accounting cycle for Rockland Wholesalers Inc. previously introduced in Alternate Problem 6-4. Complete Alternate Problem 6-4 before proceeding. At the end of March, 19X1, the following additional information is made available for the preparation of adjusting entries.

a. Depreciation on the equipment for March amounts to $25.
b. There is $100 accrued interest on the bank loan at March 31, which has not yet been recorded.
c. The March portion of the payment made by cheque no. 3 has expired.
d. The March portion of the payment made by cheque no. 9 has expired.
e. A $100 bill for March electricity service has not yet been received or recorded.

A physical count of inventory on March 31 indicates that $1,000-worth of inventory is still on hand. The periodic inventory method is used by the corporation. The fiscal year-end of Rockland is March 31.

Required:
 1. Open general ledger accounts for the following: Cash, Accounts Receivable, Merchandise Inventory, Prepaid Insurance, Prepaid Rent, Equipment, Accumulated Depreciation, Bank Loan, Accounts Payable, Common Stock, Retained Earnings, Dividends, Income Summary, Sales, Sales Returns, Sales Discounts, Purchases, Purchases Returns, Purchases Discounts, Transportation In, Advertising Expense, Commissions Expense, Delivery Expense, Depreciation Expense, Insurance Expense, Interest Expense, Rent Expense, Telephone Expense, Utilities Expense.
 2. Post the following journals to the general ledger accounts:
    a. sales journal   d. cash disbursements journal
    b. purchases journal   e. general journal
    c. cash receipts journal
 3. Prepare and record a trial balance on a worksheet.
 4. Prepare and record all necessary adjusting journal entries on the worksheet.
 5. Complete the worksheet.
 6. Prepare the following financial statements from the worksheet:
    a. income statement   c. balance sheet.
    b. statement of retained earnings
 7. Post the adjusting entries to the general ledger.
 8. Prepare closing entries and post to the general ledger. Rule all closed accounts.
 9. Prepare a post-closing trial balance.
10. Prepare any required reversing entries and post to the general ledger.

Decision Problem

Decision Problem 6-1

The North Star Corporation is a long-established family business, selling a limited line of highly priced, profitable merchandise to a few customers. The books of account consist of a general journal and a general ledger. The bookkeeper, who was somewhat set in his ways, has been with the company since it started and has provided accurate and timely statements every month.

In February of this year, the granddaughter of the original owner, having obtained her Bachelor of Commerce (Marketing major) degree, entered the business. She was aggressive and wanted to see the business expanded. Within six months, she had taken on several new lines that added numerous new customers. The volume of transactions increased from 200 to 2000 per month. By the end of August, with the accounting statements for May 31 still not available, the bookkeeper had a nervous breakdown.

Required:
 1. What do you think might be the impact on the company of not having interim financial statements prepared?
 2. Discuss in detail the recommendations you would have made with respect to the accounting system, if you had been the accountant and had observed the change over this period in the company's expansion policy.

Cash and Receivables

The collection of cash completes the sales and collection cycle. Management is responsible for the design of an effective system of internal control to safeguard the cash asset. Sales on account involve the extension of credit; the amount of uncollectible accounts must be estimated in order to match expenses with revenues.

1. What constitutes a good system of internal cash control?
2. How does the preparation of a bank reconciliation facilitate control over cash?
3. What is the imprest petty cash system and how is it used to control this fund?
4. How is the estimation of uncollectible accounts receivable part of the matching concept?
5. How are uncollectible accounts disclosed on financial statements?
6. Is bad debts expense classified in the income statement as a selling or a general and administrative expense?
7. What are the different methods used for calculating estimates for uncollectible accounts receivable?
8. How is an ageing of accounts receivable used in estimating uncollectible accounts?
9. How are credit balances in accounts receivable classified on the balance sheet?

A.   The Concept of Internal Control

The accounting process transforms the dollar amounts of transactions into financial statement information for communication purposes. The steps involved in and the generally accepted accounting principles applied to this accounting process have been discussed. The way transactions are processed in an accounting system was illustrated in the preceding chapter. Internal controls must be applied to the accounting system to ensure that transactions processing results in reliable records and that assets of the entity are protected. **Internal control** is defined as:

Internal control
The system used to ensure accurate record keeping and the timely preparation of financial statements, in order to safeguard the assets of the entity and to promote efficiency.

> the plan of organization and all the co-ordinate systems established by management of an enterprise to assist in achieving management's objective of ensuring, as far as practical, the orderly and efficient conduct of its business, including the safeguarding of assets, the reliability of accounting records, and the timely preparation of financial information (*CICA Handbook*).

Although not formally a part of financial accounting, internal control is useful in understanding the accounting process. Real Life Example 7-1 describes the disastrous consequences resulting from a breakdown in internal control.

One part of a good system of internal controls is the accounting system, which must be designed to produce timely, accurate records. The chart of accounts is an important control; it describes what type of transaction should be recorded in each account. For

---

Real Life Example 7-1

Jaggard the Blackguard

The newspapers are calling him "Jaggard the blackguard" and "the greedy old man of Grays".

However, a certain man-in-the street admiration is evident for the old codger who bamboozled the bookkeepers for 40 years, made off with $6 million, and spent the whole works on slow horses, fast cars, and women. Counting the unpaid interest on his haul, financial experts say he hurt the Grays Building Society — a type of mortgage-and-loan institution — to the tune of about $16.8 million.

Harold Jaggard, 79 when he quietly ended his life a year ago, pulled off what is being called the biggest one-man swindle ever perpetrated in Britain. The end for Jagggard, boss of the building society, came when a comptometer operator checking the books muttered, "There's something gone wrong here."

Jaggard quietly put on his hat and went home. He drew a warm bath, wrote a note, and downed a handful of pills.

An official report by two inspectors later state: "His forgery was astounding in its scale, audacious in its execution, and consistently successful. By it, he hoodwinked the auditors for more than 40 years."

Harold Jaggard was born in the east end of London, the son of a dock worker. He joined Grays as an assistant secretary in 1923. Later in life, he began gambling and tapping company funds to cover his losses. He also spent lavishly on a string of mistresses and went through three wives. When he became boss of Grays, he instructed the staff to make entries in pencil in the ledgers. Where ink was necessary, he specified a type that erased easily.

Over the years, he replaced staff members with youngsters right out of school and trained them in his own unique bookkeeping habits. Each year, the auditors came around at precisely the same date and Jaggard took the books home, where he kept one ledger ahead of them, making corrections as he went along.

Last year, however, the auditors came early and the comptometer operator, working on ledger No. 6, was told "jump to No. 12". Forty years of deception was over. At the end, Jaggard had exactly $3,600 in the bank.

[The Grays Building Society did not have accurate records; its assets were obviously not protected against theft or loss.]

Source   Canadian Press, *The* (Montreal) *Gazette*, May 19, 1979.

example, assets are classified and recorded in asset accounts, and expenses are classified and recorded in expense accounts. In addition, financial statements, prepared according to generally accepted accounting principles, are useful not only to external users in evaluating the progress of the entity, but also to management making decisions. The design of accounting records and documents is an important aspect of control. Financial information is entered and summarized in records and transmitted by documents. A good system of internal control requires that these records and documents be prepared at the time a transaction takes place or as soon as possible afterward, since they become less credible and the possibility of error increases with the passage of time. The documents should also be consecutively pre-numbered, to provide a control for missing documents.

Another aspect of internal control is the use of a procedures manual that sets out the procedures necessary for proper record-keeping. Employees must be trained in the application of control procedures; they must also be competent to carry out their responsibilities. Incompetent or dishonest employees can make even the best control procedures ineffective.

Management is responsible for the installation and operation of internal controls. This responsibility is often acknowledged in published annual reports, as in the example shown in Figure 7-1. Failure to provide an adequate division of duties can have serious consequences to the entity's wealth, as illustrated in Real Life Example 7-2.

LOBLAW COMPANIES LTD.

[with Auditor's Report]

Responsibility for Financial Reporting

The management of Loblaw Companies Limited is responsible for the preparation and integrity of the financial statements and related financial information of the Company. The financial statements and other financial information in this report have been prepared by the management of the Company in accordance with generally accepted accounting principles and, where necessary, utilizing management's judgements and best estimates.

To help fulfil its responsibility and to assure integrity of financial reporting, management maintains a system of internal controls encompassing all financial records. These controls, which include a comprehensive budgeting system and timely periodic reporting of financial information, provide reasonable assurance that assets are safeguarded and transactions and events are properly recorded. To augment the internal control systems, the Company maintains a program of internal audits co-ordinated with the external auditors.

Ultimate responsibility for financial statements to shareholders rests with the board of directors. An audit committee of non-management directors is appointed by the board to oversee the fulfilment by management of its responsibilities in the preparation of financial statements and financial control of operations. The audit committee reviews financial statements with management and reports to the directors prior to the approval of the audited financial statements for publication.

Thorne Riddell, independent auditors appointed by the shareholders, review the financial statements in detail and meet separately with both the audit committee and management to discuss their findings, including the fairness of financial reporting and the results of their review of internal controls. The shareholders' auditors report directly to shareholders and their report also appears on this page.

Richard J. Currie   Sheldon Douglass
President   Vice President, Financial Services

Figure 7-1   Statement of responsibility of Loblaw management, from its annual report

Real Life Example 7-2

Secretary Takes Home $39,000 a Week

A petite blonde secretary, who rode to work in a limousine while her employer took the subway, was arrested yesterday and charged with stealing $384,451 from the boss's chequing account.

During last summer, the indictment said, Jeanne Jantzen, 26, was cashing cheques at the rate of $39,000 a week.

District Attorney Frank Hogan said the boss, real estate man Paul Yanowicz, did not notice for two years and four months because Miss Jantzen, who had the authority to sign cheques, kept the accounts balanced. Then, Hogan said, an accountant mentioned to Yanowicz that, while his chequing accounts balanced, he seemed to be taking a lot of money out of the business account and putting it in his personal one.

Yanowicz replied, Hogan said, that he took only $250 at a time to which the accountant pointed out that the accounts showed he took $7,250 at a time.

Assistant District Attorney Leonard Newman, chief of the frauds bureau, said Miss Jantzen and another employee had joint authority to sign cheques. When Yanowicz asked for $250, he said, Miss Jantzen would get the other employee to sign for the requested amount then take the business account cheque, raise the amount by $7,000, sign it herself and deposit this in Yanowicz's personal account. Then, Newman said, Miss Jantzen would draft a $250 cheque on the personal account, go through the signing process again, raise this cheque to $7,250, cash it, give Yanowicz $250 and keep $7,000 for herself.

Source   Associated Press, *The Montreal Star*, November 24, 1971, p. 19.

B.   Cash Collections and Payments

Cash
Anything that will be accepted by a bank for a deposit; serves as a unit of account, a medium of exchange, and a store of purchasing power. Includes cash in the bank, cash on hand, and petty cash.

The widespread use of banks for the deposit of **cash**, collection of negotiable instruments such as notes receivable and the payment of cheques not only facilitates cash transactions between entities, but also provides a safeguard for each entity's cash assets. Currency can take any of a number of different forms; for a somewhat unusual form, see Real Life Example 7-3.

This involvement of banks as intermediaries between entities has accounting implications. Usually, the cash balance in the accounting records of a particular entity differs from the bank cash balance of that entity at any time period. The differences are usually attributable to the fact that, at the given time period, cash transactions recorded in the accounting records have not yet been recorded by the bank and, conversely, cash transactions recorded by the bank have not yet been recorded in the entity's accounting records.

Bank reconciliation
A comparison of the items shown on the bank statement with entries made in the records of the entity. A schedule called a bank reconciliation is prepared to explain the differences and to reconcile the amounts of cash shown by the bank and the entity's books.

Control over cash requires an accounting for the different book and bank cash balances; this accounting is accomplished through the preparation of a schedule frequently referred to as a **bank reconciliation**. The cash balance reported in the accounting records and bank are established at a particular time, usually month-end. The balance of cash according to the entity's books appears in the general ledger Cash account; the cash according to the bank is reported in a bank statement. The bank reconciliation process calculates an adjusted book cash balance and adjusted bank cash balance. These adjusted amounts must agree.

The following are reconciling items usually appearing in the bank reconciliation; they are discussed in detail in later sections of this chapter.

Book Reconciling Items:	Bank Reconciling Items:
1. Collection of Negotiable Instruments	1. Outstanding Deposits
2. NSF Cheques	2. Outstanding Cheques
3. Bank Charges	3. Bank Errors.
4. Book Errors.	

Book Reconciling Items

Collections are often made by a bank on behalf of its customers; these collections are frequently recorded in the entity's books only after receipt of the bank statement.

Bank service charges for cheques paid and other services provided are deducted from the customer's bank account; these reductions of cash are also customarily recorded in the entity's books following receipt of the bank statement.

Cheques returned to the bank because there were not sufficient funds to cover them cannot be credited to the customer. These NSF cheques frequently appear on the bank statement as a reduction of cash. (Such amounts must be re-demanded by the entity.) In addition, cheques received by the entity and deposited in its account may be returned by the cheque-maker's bank, because they are stale-dated, unsigned, illegible, or show the wrong account number. These relevant NSF cheques must be deducted from the balance of Cash appearing in the entity's books.

Book recording errors can occur. They usually surface when the bank statement arrives and the bank reconciliation is prepared; the result may be either an increase or a decrease of the Cash balance.

Bank Reconciling Items

Cheques are recorded by the entity as a reduction of Cash at the date of their preparation; in actual fact, the cost is not paid until the cheque is cleared by the bank. Cheques that are recorded in the entity's books as cash disbursements but are not yet paid by the bank are referred to as *outstanding cheques*. When a depositor requests that a cheque be certified, the bank deducts the amount of the cheque from the depositor's balance and deposits it in a special account of the bank. When the certified cheque comes to the bank it is deducted from this special account and not from the depositor's balance. Cash receipts are recorded as an increase of cash when they are received; however, the bank records an increase in cash only when it actually receives the deposit. There is usually a time interval between the recording of cash in the books and the receipt of a deposit by the bank. Outstanding deposits consist of amounts that are not yet recorded by the bank.

Bank errors sometimes occur. These errors may increase or decrease the bank cash balance; the bank is responsible for the correction of these errors.

Bluebeard Computer Corporation banks at the Second Chartered Bank. The entity's bank account is carried as a liability in the records of the bank, since the amount is owed to BCC. Accordingly, credit memos included with the bank statement are for items that have also increased the bank balance. Debit memos included with the bank statement are for items that have also decreased the bank balance. These credit and debit memos must be taken into consideration when BCC prepares its bank reconciliations.

Real Life Example 7-3

Yap Currency

On this tiny South Pacific island, life is easy and the currency is hard.

Elsewhere, the world's troubled monetary system creaks along; floating exchange rates wreak havoc in currency markets, and devaluations are commonplace. But on Yap the currency is as old as a rock. In fact, it *is* rock. Limestone to be precise.

For nearly 2000 years the Yapese have used large stone wheels to pay for major purchases, such as land, canoes and permission to marry. Yap is a United States trust territory, and the dollar is used in grocery stores and gas stations. But reliance on stone money, like the island's ancient caste system and the traditional dress of loincloths and grass skirts, continues.

Buying property with stones is "much easier than buying it with U.S. dollars," says John Chodad, who recently purchased a building lot with a [76 cm] 30-inch stone wheel. "We don't know the value of the U.S. dollar." Others on this [60 k²] 37-square-mile island [850 km] 530 miles southwest of Guam use both dollars and stones. Venito Gurtmag, a builder, recently accepted a [1.2 m] 4-foot-wide stone disk and $8,700 for a house he built in an outlying village.

Stone wheels don't make good pocket money, so for small transactions, Yapese use other forms of currency, such as beer. Beer is proffered as payment for all sorts of odd jobs, including construction. The 10 000 people on Yap consume 40 000 to 50 000 cases a year, mostly of Budweiser. In fact, Yapese drink so much that sales taxes on alcoholic beverages account for 25 percent of local tax revenue.

Basket of Currencies

Besides stone wheels and beer, the Yapese sometimes spend *gaw*, consisting of necklaces of stone beads strung together around a whale's tooth. They also can buy things with *yaw*, a currency made from large sea shells. But these are small change.

The people of Yap have been using stone money ever since a Yapese warrior named Anagumang first brought the huge stones over from limestone caverns on neighbouring Palau, some 1500 to 2000 years ago. Inspired by the moon, he fashioned the stone into large circles. The rest is history.

Yapese lean the stone wheels against their houses or prop up rows of them in village "banks". Most of the stones are [0.76 to 1.5 m] 2½ to 5 feet in diameter, but *some* are as much as [3.6 m] 12 feet across. Each has a hole in the centre so it can be slipped onto the trunk of a fallen betel-nut tree and carried. It takes 20 men to lift some wheels.

By custom, the stones are worthless when broken. You never hear people on Yap musing about wanting a piece of the rock. Rather than risk a broken stone — or back — Yapese tend to leave the larger stones where they are and make a mental accounting that the ownership has been transferred — much as gold bars used in international transactions change hands without leaving the vault of the New York Federal Reserve Bank.

The worth of stone money doesn't depend on size. Instead, the pieces are valued by how hard it was to get them here. The earlier stones, brought by war canoe by Anagumang and

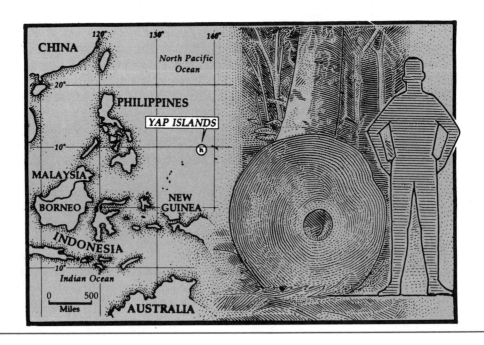

his descendants, are the most precious because they cost many lives to bring in during the heady days of what historians now call the Yap empire. Although the heavily laden Yapese canoes were fitted with outriggers, they often capsized during the [450 km] 280-mile ocean voyage from Palau.

Next in value are some stones cut on Palau in the 1870s by David Dean O'Keffe, a shipwrecked American sailor who escaped from the island and returned later with a Chinese junk. Mr. O'Keffe, who helped transport the boulders in return for Yapese help in processing dried coconut, ultimately ran the island as a self-styled emperor. His exploits were portrayed in a book — and later a movie — titled "His Majesty O'Keffe". (To the dismay of Yapese chiefs, the movie was made on Fiji.) According to Andrew Roboman, Yap's paramount chief, the O'Keffe disks are worth about half as much as pre-O'Keffe stones.

Finally, there are a few mechanically chiseled stone wheels brought in without problems by German traders in the late 1800s and early 1900s. But Chief Roboman says the value of these has hit rock bottom.

There are some decided advantages to using massive stones for money. They are immune to black-market trading, for one thing, and they pose formidable obstacles to pickpockets. In addition, there aren't any sterile debates about how to stabilize the Yapese monetary system. With only about 6600 stone wheels remaining on the island, the money-supply level stays put. "If you have it, you have it," shrugs Andrew Ken, a Yapese monetary thinker.

But stone money has its limits. Linus Ruuamau, the manager of one of the island's few retail stores, won't accept it for general merchandise. And Al Azuma, who manages the local Bank of Hawaii branch, the only conventional financial institution here, isn't interested in limestone deposits or any sort of shell game. So the money, left uninvested, just gathers moss.

But stone money accords well with Yapese traditions. "There are a lot of instances here where you cannot use U.S. money," Mr. Burtmaga says. One is the settling of disputes. Unlike most money, stones sometimes *can* buy happiness, of sort; if a Yapese wants to settle an argument, he brings his adversary stone money as a token. "The apology is accepted without question," Mr. Chodad says. "If you used dollars, there'd be an argument over whether it was enough."

Mr. Ken presented shell money to his future father-in-law last year to win his daughter's hand. Dollars would never have done. "I couldn't pay cash," Mr. Ken says. "They would have been insulted."

But it may not be that way much longer. Despite Yap's firm resistance, progress is threatening the island's traditions.

Just three decades ago, Yap was little changed from the way it had been for centuries, in spite of colonization by Spain, Germany and Japan. The years after the Second World War brought roads, cars, motorboats and store-bought clothes, not to mention beer. Although the Yapese did turn down offers by American and Japanese companies to build western-style tourist hotels, and some customs remain (women still walk several paces behind men, for instance), the island's traditions face a potent new threat: United States television programs are providing a "Sunset Strip" model for youth.

Yapese teenagers, torn between old and new cultures, have taken to heavy drinking and to driving around aimlessly. Delinquency has risen sharply, a serious matter in a population where the median age is 15. Suicide also is up. "It reminds me of what happened to the U.S. a couple of decades ago," says John Mooteb, a Yapese psychologist who serves as the island's probation officer. "Except here, the kids don't run away."

The youth problem is spurring plans to bolster Yap's anemic economy through a 15-year development program designed to attract investment and increase jobs. Sen. Joe Tamag, Yap's biggest entrepreneur and the chairman of the legislature's economic-development committee, is hoping to attract light industry and possibly even some tourism. But "we will be very selective on tourists," he cautions.

Right now, the Yapese are optimistic. The island is part of the Federated States of Micronesia, a trust territory the United States administers for the United Nations, but it is to gain a wide measure of autonomy under a planned "free association compact" with Washington. Yap will continue to receive American money, and Governor John Mangefel is counting on budgeting about $4 million a year for economic development. (At present, most of the Yap government's money comes from an annual U.S. $11.4 million appropriation; local tax revenues run about $1.6 million a year.)

How all this will affect the stone money isn't clear. Most Yapese think the island will continue to rely on big wheels for another decade or more — at least until the older generation dies or changes its ways.

But the stalwarts are more positive about tradition. Mr. Ken, who owns several of the large stone wheels, is trying to persuade the Yap government to start a stone money exchange so Yapese can trade in their boulders for dollars, or buy them back, whenever they wish. "We're losing because we can't liquidate," Mr. Ken complains.

Meanwhile, Yap's stone money may be about to take on international significance. Just yesterday, Washington received notice that Tosiho Nakayama, the president of Micronesia, plans to bring a stone disk when he visits the United States next month. It will be flown by Air Force jet.

Officials say Mr. Nakayama intends the stone as Micronesia's symbolic contribution toward reducing the United States budget deficit. Plans are to have the rock accepted formally by Vice-President George Bush, who is said to be the administration's formost expert on voodoo economics.

Source Art Pine, "Fixed Assets, or: Why a Loan in Yap Is Hard To Roll over", *The Wall Street Journal*, Ed. Edition, V, no. 1 (March 29, 1984).

Illustrative Problem — Bank Reconciliation

Assume that a bank reconciliation is prepared by Bluebeard Computer Corporation at April 30. At this date, the general ledger Cash account shows a balance of $21,929 and includes the cash receipts and disbursements shown in Figure 7-2.

Cash   Acct. No.

Date 19X1	Description	F	Debit	Credit	DR. or CR.	Balance
Mar. 31	Balance				DR	20 673 —
Apr. 30	April cash receipts	CR	9482 —		DR	30 155 —
30	April cash payments	CP		8226 —	DR	21 929 —

Figure 7-2   Bluebeard's Cash Account at April 30

Extracts from BCC's accounting records are reproduced with the bank statement for April in Figure 7-3. Note the existence of outstanding cheques from the preceding month's bank reconciliation (March).

PER COMPANY BOOKS

Outstanding Cheques at March 31:

Cheque No.	Amount
580	$4,051✓
599	196✓
600	7✓

Cash Disbursements for the Month of April:

Cheque No.	Amount
601	$ 24✓
602	1,720✓
603	230✓
604	200✓
605	2,220✓
606	287
607	1,364
608	100
609	40
610	1,520
611	124✓
612	397✓

Cash Receipts for the Month of April:

Date	Amount
April 5	$1,570✓
10	390✓
23	5,000✓
28	1,522✓
30	1,000✓

March 31 outstanding cheques compared with cheques cashed to see if still outstanding at April 30.

Cash disbursements compared with cheques cashed to locate outstanding cheques.

Cash receipts compared with deposits to locate outstanding deposits.

PER BANK RECORDS

The Bank Statement
It is customary for banks to send depositors a monthly statement together with the cancelled cheques and notices of bank charges and credits. The statement shows the activities for the month; it should list:
1. Beginning balance;
2. Deposits received and credits to the account;
3. Cheques paid and other charges to the account;
4. Ending balance.

The bank statement for the month of April was as follows:

Second Chartered Bank
Statement of Account
with Bluebeard Computer Corporation

Cheques			Deposits	Date	Balance
				April 1	24,927
4,051✓				2	20,876
196✓	24✓	230✓	1,570✓	6	21,996
200✓			390✓	11	22,186
124✓	397✓	7✓		16	21,658
2,220✓	180	NSF		21	19,258
1,720✓	31		5,000✓	26	22,507
6 SC			1,522✓	29	24,023

CC — Certified Cheque   DM — Debit Memo
NSF — Not Sufficient Funds   CM — Credit Memo
SC — Service Charge   OD — Overdraft

Figure 7-3   The Relationship of Company and Bank Records

The bank reconciliation underscores the reciprocal relationship between the bank's records and the depositor's. For each entry in the depositor's books, there should be a counterpart in the bank's books.

In the Books:	*In the Bank*:
1. All cash receipts are recorded by a debit to Cash.	1. When the bank receives the cash, it credits the depositor's account.
2. All cash disbursements are recorded by a credit to Cash.	2. When the bank pays the cheque, it debits the depositor's account.

The five steps in reconciling the cash per books (Figures 7-2 and 7-3) with cash per bank (Figure 7-3) are as follows.

Step 1

The cheques paid by the bank in April are matched. Any cancelled cheques retained with the bank statement are compared with cheques recorded as cash disbursements.

The bank reconciliation from the preceding month is inspected for the existence of any outstanding cheques at March 30.

In the Books:	*In the Bank*:
These cheques were recorded in March; therefore, the Cash balance per books is correctly stated.	These outstanding March cheques may or may not have been paid by the bank in April. If some of the cheques have not yet been paid by the bank in April, the bank balance is overstated at April 30 by the amount of these cheques.

In fact, the March outstanding cheques were paid by the bank in April; no adjustment is therefore required in the April 30 bank reconciliation—the cash balance per books and per bank are correctly stated in relation to these March outstanding cheques.

The returned cancelled cheques are compared with the cheques recorded in the April cash disbursements journal. This comparison indicates that the following cheques are outstanding because they have not yet been paid by the bank.

Cheque No.	Amount
606	$ 287
607	1,364
608	100
609	40
610	1,520

In the Books:	*In the Bank*:
These cheques were recorded in April; therefore, the Cash balance per books is correctly stated.	These outstanding cheques were not paid by the bank in April; therefore, the bank balance is overstated at April 30.

In reconciling the cash balance per books and per bank, the outstanding cheques must be deducted from the bank account's cash balance.

Step 2

Debit memos made by the bank must be examined.

In the Books:	*In the Bank:*
If these debit memos have not yet been recorded in April, then the Cash balance per books is overstated at April 30.	The bank has already made deductions from the cash balance per bank when these debit memos were recorded.

In reconciling the cash balance per books and per bank, these debit memos must be deducted from the Cash balance per books, if they were not recorded.

An examination of the April 30 bank statement shows that the bank had deducted the NSF cheque of John Donne for $180.

In the Books:	*In the Bank:*
The cheque of John Donne had originally been recorded as a cash receipt (a payment on account). During April, no entry was made regarding this returned cheque; therefore, the Cash balance per book is overstated at April 30.	The cheque of John Donne was originally deposited in the bank. However, John Donne's bank did not pay this cheque because of insufficent funds in Donne's account. The cheque was returned to BCC's bank and was then deducted from the company's cash balance.

In reconciling the cash balance per books and bank, this returned cheque must be deducted from the Cash balance per books. (A notice must be sent to Donne to request payment again, preferably by certified cheque.)

An examination of the April 30 bank statement also shows that the bank had deducted a service charge of $6 during April.

In the Books:	*In the Bank:*
This service charge was not deducted from the Cash balance per books during April; therefore, the Cash balance per books is overstated at April 30.	This service charge has already been deducted from the cash balance per bank.

In reconciling the cash balance per books and bank, this service charge must be deducted from the Cash balance per books.

Step 3

Deposit in transit
Deposit made too late to appear on the current bank statement.

The deposits shown on the bank statement are compared with the amounts recorded in the cash receipts journal. This comparison indicates that the April 30 cash receipt amounting to $1,000 is not included as a deposit in the bank statement. This amount is an outstanding deposit, or a **deposit in transit**.

Cash Receipts for the Month of April:

Date	Amount
Apr. 5	$1,570✓
10	390✓
23	5,000✓
28	1,522✓
30	1,000

The bank statement for the month of April was as follows:

Second Chartered Bank
Statement of Account
with Bluebeard Computer Corporation

Cheques			Deposits	Date	Balance
				Apr. 1	24,927
4,051✓				2	20,876
196✓	24✓	230✓	1,570✓	6	21,996
200✓			390✓	11	22,186
124✓	397✓	7✓		16	21,658
2,220✓	180 NSF			21	19,258
1,720✓	31		5,000✓	26	22,507
6 SC			1,522✓	29	24,023

In the Books:	*In the Bank*:
The April cash receipts have been recorded in the books during April.	The April cash receipts have been deposited in the bank during April; however, the April 30 deposit was not recorded by the bank in April. Therefore, the cash balance per bank is understated at April 30.

In reconciling the cash balance per books and per bank, the outstanding deposit must be added to the cash balance per bank.

Step 4

The March bank reconciliation is inspected for outstanding deposits at March 31.

In the Books:	*In the Bank*:
The cash receipts of March had been recorded in the books during March.	Any outstanding deposits at March 31 should have been recorded by the bank in April. If any March deposit is outstanding at April 30, an investigation should be made.

In reconciling the cash balance per books and per bank, any March outstanding deposit should be investigated. In fact, there were no deposits in transit at March 31.

Step 5

Any errors in the books or in the bank account that become apparent during the reconciliation process must be taken into consideration.

In the Books:	*In the Bank*:
Any error recorded in the books requires a correction in the Cash balance per books.	Any error recorded in the bank statement requires a correction in the cash balance per bank.

In reconciling the cash balance per books and per bank, any book error must be added or subtracted from the Cash balance per books; any bank error must be added or subtracted from the cash balance per bank.

An examination of the April 30 bank statement shows that the bank had deducted, in error, a cheque from Lou Board for $31. The bank indicated it would make a correction in May's bank statement.

In the Books:	*In the Bank*:
This cheque of Lou Board does not belong to Bluebeard and does not require any change on the books.	This cheque of Lou Board should not have been deducted from the account of Bluebeard; therefore, the cash balance per bank is understated at April 30.

In reconciling the cash balance per books and per bank, this bank error must be added to the cash balance per bank.

Bank Reconciliation
At April 30, 19XX

Cash per Books, Apr. 30		$21,929	Cash per Bank Statement, Apr. 30		$24,023
			Add: Outstanding Deposit		1,000
			Cheque Deducted in Error		31
					$25,054
Less: Bank Charges	$ 6		Less: Outstanding Cheques		
NSF Cheques	180	186	*Cheque No.*	*Amount*	
			606	$ 287	
			607	1,364	
			608	100	
			609	40	
			610	1,520	3,311
Adjusted Cash Balance, Apr. 30		$21,743	Adjusted Cash Balance, Apr. 30		$21,743

———— These Balances Must Agree.————

Errors and adjustments in the "per books" section require journal entries in the general journal to correct the books, so that the cash is shown at $21,743.	Outstanding deposits and cheques should pass through the bank in May, thereby adjusting the cash balance in the bank. Other errors and adjustments must be reported to the bank so that they can make the necessary corrections to Bluebeard's account.

A bank reconciliation is prepared after the above five steps have been completed; as shown below, it accounts for the difference between the cash per books ($21,929) and the cash per bank ($24,023), and calculates adjusted cash balances at April 30. The adjusted Cash balance in the books of BCC is the reported amount of cash in its interim balance sheet. The adjusted balance represents the actual cash that belongs to BCC the amount that can still be withdrawn from the bank. The adjusted cash balance which appears in the books of Bluebeard is illustrated in the general ledger account in Figure 7-4.

Updating the Accounting Records

The preparation of the bank reconciliation must be followed by an updating of the accounting records. As a general rule, every reconciling item used in the calculation of an adjusted cash balance per books requires the preparation of an adjusting journal entry to update the accounting records. A reconciling item added to the book Cash balance requires a debit to Cash and a deduction from the bank cash balance requires a credit to Cash. The following journal adjusting entries are prepared at April 30.

Apr. 30	Bank Charges Expense	6	
	Cash		6
	To record bank service charge for April.		
30	Accounts Receivable — NSF cheque	180	
	Cash		180
	To record amount due from John Donne.		

Note that these adjusting entries include all book reconciling items. The general ledger Cash account is then brought up to date, as illustrated in Figure 7-4.

Cash   Acct. No. 101

Date 19X1		Description	F	Debit	Credit	DR. or CR.	Balance
Mar.	31	Balance				DR	20673 -
Apr.	30	April cash receipts	CR	9482 -		DR	30155 -
	30	April cash payments	CP		8226 -	DR	21929 -
	30	Bank charge expense	J1		6 -	DR	21923 -
	30	NSF cheque	J1		180 -	DR	21743 -

> This is the adjusted cash balance shown in the bank reconciliation.

Figure 7-4 Updated cash account in the general ledger

Note that the balance in the general ledger Cash account is the same as the adjusted cash balance calculated on the bank reconciliation. Bluebeard doesn't make any adjusting entries for bank reconciling items. The outstanding deposit and outstanding cheques will probably be paid by the bank in May. Adjustments for bank errors are made by the bank.

Petty Cash Transactions

The payment of small bills by cheque is not only inconvenient but also costly. The payment of postage due on some incoming mail, for example, might be less than the bank
charge to process payment of a cheque. It is therefore useful to have a relatively small
amount of cash on hand to pay small disbursements; this cash is usually referred to as a
petty cash fund. There are different ways of handling such petty cash transactions;
the imprest system is discussed in the following sections. Under this **imprest petty
cash system**, a fixed petty cash fund is maintained, being increased or decreased in
amount according to needs.

Establishing the Petty Cash Fund

Under the imprest system, a regular cheque is prepared in the amount of the petty cash
fund; this cheque can be payable either to the Petty Cash account or to the custodian of
the fund. If the fund is found subsequently to be too small, it can be increased; it can be
decreased if changed circumstances result in its being too large. It is only in these cases
that the Petty Cash general ledger account is affected.

Establishing the Fund		Increasing the Fund		Decreasing the Fund	
Petty Cash	200	Petty Cash	100	Cash	50
Cash	200	Cash	100	Petty Cash	50
The amount of the fund is established by this entry.		The additional debit increases the fund to $300.		The credit of $50 decreases the fund to $250.	

The above transactions affect the size of the petty cash fund; they do not involve the
record of disbursements paid out of the fund.

Reimbursing the Petty Cash Fund

Payments are made out of the fund as required; payments should be supported by a
petty cash voucher signed by the recipient of the payments, in addition to any supporting documents, such as a taxi receipt. When the amount of cash has been reduced to a
pre-determined level, say $10 or $20, then the petty cash fund is reimbursed for the
total amount of payments made. A regular cheque is prepared in the total amount of all
these payments and is made payable to Petty Cash or to the custodian, as the practice
may be.

  The cheque is recorded in the cash disbursements journal with the appropriate expense
accounts debited. For example, the following compound journal entry would record the
following payments: delivery charges totalling $35, light bulbs and other building mainte-
nance items totalling $14, miscellaneous general expenses totalling $31 (including a $30
amount for postage and a $1 shortage in the petty cash fund), and miscellaneous office
supplies amounting to $45. Because there is no specific postage account in BCC's ledger
(as noted on its chart of accounts), the $30 postage payment is recorded as Miscella-
neous General Expense.

Delivery Expense	35	
Maintenance Expense	14	
Miscellaneous General Expense	31	
Office Supplies Used	45	
Cash		125
To replenish the petty cash fund.		

The shortage in a fund is usually recorded in a miscellaneous account. The petty cash vouchers and supporting documents should be cancelled at the time of reimbursement in order to prevent their reuse for duplicate reimbursements. The vouchers and shortage (or excess, as sometimes occurs) should be approved by a responsible employee.

Responsibility for the fund should be delegated to only one person, who should be held accountable for its contents. At any given time, the petty cash amount should consist of cash and supporting vouchers, all totalling the Petty Cash Fund amount.

C. Completion of the Sales and Collections Cycle — Accounts Receivable

Accounts receivable
An asset arising from the sale of goods or services to customers on account; an account receivable originating from a loan made to an officer or employee of the entity as excluded from accounts receivable as explained above and must be disclosed separately in the financial statements.

Transactions in the sales and collections cycle were introduced in Chapter 5. In this cycle, sales mare made, sales on account result in the creation of an **accounts receivable**, and the collection of cash completes the cycle. This section discusses the accounting treatment required when cash is not collected to complete the cycle; uncollected accounts receivable result in a cycle being completed with bad debts.

The extension of credit to an entity's customers produces this uncollectibility. The expectation of increased profits resulting from increased sales is a strong motivation to extend credit to customers. Also, competition may make the extension of credit a necessary business practice. Unfortunately, not every accounts receivable is collected; uncollected accounts receivable are often referred to as bad debts.

A risk inherent in the sales and collections cycle, therefore, includes the possibility that some accounts receivable will not be collected. The existence of a good internal control system is designed to minimize bad debt losses. One such control is to permit sales on account only to credit-worthy customers; however, at some point, the decision of who is credit-worthy involves a trade-off between increasing this entity's sales, and its profit, or risking an increase in competitors' sales and potential profit. Even so, each entity realizes that a certain percentage of all credit sales will never be collected and some may be collected long after the sale was made.

Accountants applying the matching concept to this cycle must align expenses of a particular time period with revenues of the same time period. The accrual method of accounting is used as the vehicle in making this alignment for bad debts expense. For this alignment, use is made of an **Allowance for Doubtful Accounts** account to estimate potential uncollectibles; this account is a contra account to Accounts Receivable and is disclosed on the balance sheet as follows.

Allowance for doubtful accounts
A contra asset (valuation) account, showing the estimated amount of accounts receivable that may not be collected.

Partial Balance Sheet
At December 31, 19X4

Current Assets:		
Cash		$ 5,000
Temporary Investments		10,000
Accounts Receivable	$25,000	
Less: Allowance for Doubtful Accounts	1,400	23,600
Inventory		50,000
Prepaid Expenses		3,450
Total Current Assets		$92,050

Conceptual Issue 7-1

The Cost of Control

by James Gaston, Price Waterhouse

If there is one activity modern business considers exempt from cost controls, it's controls themselves.

Most managers wouldn't dream of expanding production or embarking on an advertising campaign without demanding cost estimates to justify such expenditures. Yet, they never stop to question the cost or necessity of the staggering number of controls designed to ensure the accuracy of financial and operational data; the reasonableness of assumptions used as a basis for budgets and cash flow projections; the safety of assets; and employee compliance with company policies.

Doubts about the need for all these controls are usually dispelled by controllers or auditors, who raise the spectre of disastrous losses the company might suffer if an error were to occur or remain undetected.

While such a danger may indeed exist, its size, the likelihood it will happen, and its potential impact should all be weighed against the amount of money being spent to prevent it.

An expenditure of $3,000 is justified if it prevents a loss of $10,000 or more. But if the loss isn't likely to exceed $1,000, then controls of that magnitude make no more sense than an expensive insurance policy on a car that can be sold only for scrap.

To minimize the cost of controls without exposing their business to unjustifiable risks, managers should answer the following questions:

What potential errors need to be controlled? Many businesses have elaborate controls without being quite sure what it is they're trying to prevent. As a first step, compile an inventory of risks and their possible consequences.

Which controls deserve the highest priority? Once you've identified the risks, categorize them as (1) totally unacceptable, (2) controllable, providing the cost does not outweigh the losses you're trying to prevent, and (3) acceptable, therefore requiring no further action.

If you start by developing controls for unacceptable risks, you may achieve other controls as a bonus.

Let's say that supplying customers with parts quickly and efficiently is the cornerstone of your business. If you can control your perpetual inventory records well enough, you will probably get as a by-product the financial information needed to make the right production and purchasing decisions.

Risks

What are the odds that expensive errors will occur? The less likely the risk, the less money you'll need to spend to prevent it.

If you've dealt with most of your suppliers for years—and they're reliable — the arithmetic on their purchase invoices isn't likely to be wrong. While you may want to keep checking prices, there's probably no need to have your staff check every addition and multiplication—unless unusual circumstances come to your attention.

How important are the errors being found? Ask your employees who perform control activities to keep track of the dollar savings they achieve. How much money did you save last year by having them check prices on all purchase invoices, or by cross-checking all the freight bills with shipping records? How much did you spend to achieve these savings? The answers may surprise you.

Can you recoup the cost of an error after it has occurred? Most control systems combine preventive features with detective ones, so errors slipping through the preventive screen will later be caught.

If you're satisfied an error can be corrected once it's found, consider reducing the amount of money you spend preventing it from occurring in the first place.

Spend less time checking and reviewing sales tax exemption certificates, for example, if you are reasonably sure your customers will reimburse you should Revenue Canada challenge the exemptions.

Are you a victim of the "all or nothing" syndrome? Applying the sme controls to all your transactions, regardless of their nature or size, wastes time and money. In the case of purchase invoices, for instance, check all invoices over a certain dollar value, as well as those from new suppliers.

Sampling

With the rest, statistical sampling will provide all the information you need to project the dollar value of undetected errors. Using that calculation, then decide whether it is worthwhile to check individually all invoices for small purchases.

Can you mechanize your control procedures? Because computers can perform control activities faster and more accurately than humans, all businesses, regardless of size, should consider computerizing. For example, computer systems can check a series of documents for missing numbers, or match receiving report quantities with purchase invoices.

Should you contract out your controls? Outside agencies will verify your costs either on a fee basis, or for a percentage of the money saved. In addition to routine applications, such as purchase invoices and inventory, some agencies check advertising, freight or sales tax costs.

Of course, periodically review the fees you pay to ensure your staff couldn't perform the same duties at a lower cost.

Source James Gaston, "How to check if your control systems are worth the cost", *The Financial Post*, March 24, 1984, p. 18.

As can be seen, the contra Allowance for Doubtful Accounts account reduces Accounts Receivable to the amount that is expected to be collected. Because the estimated uncollectible amount is usually immaterial, it is not disclosed on the balance sheet; instead only the net amount collectible is shown. Where the estimated uncollectible amount is significant, this information can be disclosed in the statement or in a note.

The estimated uncollectible amount is subsequently used in writing off actual bad debts as they occur. At the balance sheet date, only an estimated uncollectible amount appears in the Allowance for Doubtful Accounts account; no Accounts Receivable amount has been written off at this date. However, the estimated bad debts expense for the accounting period is matched with revenues of that same period through an entry used to record the bad debts expense for the year.

Bad debts expense is usually classified in the income statement as a general and administrative expense since—for internal control purposes—the sales department should not authorize credit. This arrangement avoids a possible conflict between the approval of credit and the primary objective of a sales department, increasing the sales, particularly when sales bonuses are calculated on sales volume or remuneration includes a commission component. At year-end, the Bad Debts Expense account is closed to the Income Summary.

Estimating Uncollectible Accounts Receivable

The use of an allowance account matches expenses and revenues and helps management to estimate sales and uncollectibles realistically. Once the estimate of uncollectible accounts is made, a journal entry is prepared with a debit to Bad Debts Expense and a credit to Allowance for Doubtful Accounts. Two different methods can be used to calculate the estimated amount; both follow the matching concept. One method focuses on the income statement, while the other focuses on the balance sheet.

Income Statement Method:	*Balance Sheet Method:*
This method assumes that a certain percentage of sales on account made during the accounting time period will result in bad debts. In order to match all expenses with sales revenue, an estimate of bad debts is made at the end of the accounting period on the basis of bad debts experienced in prior years (or expected this year) in relation to credit sales.	This method assumes that a certain amount of accounts receivable will not be collected in the next accounting period. In order to establish the amount that is expected to be collected (often called the realizable value of the receivables), an estimated uncollectible amount is calculated using an ageing schedule. In this way, the net collectible amount can be reported on the balance sheet.
This estimated bad debts expense is calculated independent of any current balance in the Allowance for Doubtful Accounts account.	The estimated bad debts expense is the difference between the current allowance balance and the amount required at the end of the accounting period.

The Income Statement Method

Under this method, estimated bad debts expense is calculated by applying an estimated loss percentage to net sales for the accounting time period involved. The percentage used can be calculated using actual losses experienced in prior years.

Year	Net Sales	Accounts Written Off	Loss Percentage
19X1	$150,000		
19X2	200,000		
19X3	250,000		
	$600,000	$3,000	0.005 = 0.5%

The average loss over these years is ½ of 1%. If management anticipates that similar losses may be applicable to 19X4, the estimated bad debts expense is calculated as follows: 19X4 sales $300,000 × .005 = $1,500 estimated uncollectible accounts receivable. Under the income statement method, this $1,500 is recorded as the estimated uncollectible accounts receivable by the following entry:

Dec. 31	Bad Debts Expense	1,500	
	Allowance for Doubtful Accounts		1,500

When posted to the allowance account, the new account balance becomes $1,750.

The balance remaining in the account is $250.	The estimated balance of $1,500 is added to the existing balance.

Allowance for Doubtful Accounts			Allowance for Doubtful Accounts	
	Bal. 250			Bal. 250
				1,500
				1,750

Note that this method calculates the estimated uncollectible amount for the current year; it matches revenues for the year. In this way, the emphasis of the income statement method is on matching expenses with revenues; the remaining balance in the allowance account does not influence the amount of bad debts expense for the accounting period.

The Balance Sheet Method

Ageing of accounts receivable
The detailed analysis of trade accounts receivable, by time elapsed since the creation of the receivable.

The estimated bad debt expense can be calculated by first accumulating the uncollectible amount with an ageing schedule. An **accounts receivable ageing** is illustrated in the following schedule when each account is classified as either not yet due or past due by the number of days indicated at the top of each column.

ANALYSIS OF ACCOUNTS RECEIVABLE BY AGE
December 31, 19X4

Customer	Total	Not Yet Due	1–30	31–60	61–90	Over 90
Bendix Inc.	$ 1,000					$1,000
Devco Marketing Inc.	6,000	$ 1,000	$3,000	$2,000		
Horngren Corp.	4,000	2,000	1,000	–	$1,000	
Perry Co. Ltd.	5,000	3,000	1,000	–	1,000	
Others	9,000	4,000	–	–	5,000	
Totals	$25,000	$10,000	$5,000	$2,000	$7,000	$1,000

Each account balance is listed and extended to the appropriate not-yet-due or past-due columns. An estimated loss percentage is then applied to each total, thereby calculating the estimated uncollectible amount as follows.

Calculation of Uncollectible Amount
December 31, 19X4

	Accounts Receivable	Estimated Loss Percentage	Uncollectible Amount
Not yet due	$10,000	1%	100
Past due:			
1–30 days	5,000	3%	150
31–60 days	2,000	5%	100
61–90 days	7,000	10%	700
Over 90 days	1,000	40%	400
Totals	$25,000		$1,450

The estimated loss percentage can be calculated on the basis of prior experience with past due accounts — they usually become less collectible the longer they remain uncollected. The above calculation indicates that $1,450 is estimated as uncollectible at December 31, 19X4.

Under the balance sheet method, as noted, the estimated bad debts expense consists of the difference between the current balance remaining in the Allowance for Doubtful Accounts account and the estimated uncollectible amount required at year-end.

The balance remaining in the account is $250.	The estimated uncollectible amount is $1,450.	An amount of $1,200 must be recorded to bring the account to $1,450.

Allowance for Doubtful Accounts	Allowance for Doubtful Accounts	Allowance for Doubtful Accounts
Bal. 250	Bal. 250 ___ 1,450	Bal. 250 1,200 ___ 1,450

Under the balance sheet method, therefore, the calculation of the bad debts expense amount of $1,200 in this case is dependent on whatever balance remains at the end of the accounting time period.

The amount is recorded by the following journal entry.

Dec. 31	Bad Debts Expense	1,200	
	Allowance for Doubtful Accounts		1,200

This entry records the amount required to bring the balance in the allowance account to the $1,450 estimated uncollectible amount; it thereby applies the matching concept to the sales and collections cycle in a different manner from that used in the income statement method. Although both methods match expenses with revenues, one result may differ from the other.

Writing Off Bad Debts

Once the estimated uncollectibles are in place, accounts receivable that are not collected in the subsequent year are written off to the allowance account. The example provided here is based on the uncollectible amount calculated by the balance sheet method. Assume that the account of Bendix Inc. becomes uncollectible by Bluebeard as a result of the bankruptcy of Bendix. The uncollectible account receivable is removed by this entry:

Apr. 1	Allowance for Doubtful Accounts		1,000	
	Accounts Receivable			1,000
	To write off uncollectible account			
	from Bendix Inc.			

Note that the write-off is made to the contra allowance account, which is debited. In this way, both the Allowance for Doubtful Accounts account and Accounts Receivable are reduced.

Accounts Receivable		Allowance for Doubtful Accounts	
Bal. 25,000			Bal. 1,450
	1,000	1,000	

The $1,000 write-off reduces both Accounts Receivable and the allowance account. The balance remaining in the allowance account represents the estimated amount of other accounts receivable that may also become uncollectible. Note that the use of an allowance account for the write-off of an uncollectible account does not affect the net Accounts Receivable amount.

	Before Write-Off	*Following Write-Off*
Accounts Receivable	$25,000	$24,000
Less: Allowance for Doubtful Accounts	1,450	450
Net Accounts Receivable	$23,550	$23,550

Note also that the Bad Debts Expense balance is not affected by the Bendix account receivable write-off. The Bad Debts Expense account was debited to record the estimated bad debt expense and was closed to Income Summary at year-end.

The amount estimated as an allowance for doubtful accounts seldom agrees with that actual amount that actually proves uncollectible. A credit balance remains in the allowance account if fewer bad debts occur during the year than are estimated. There is a debt balance in the allowance account if more bad debts occur during the year than are estimated. Subsequently an adjusting entry is prepared to set up the uncollectible balance that remains.

Collection of Amounts Previously Written Off

When Bendix Inc. went bankrupt, its debt to Bluebeard Computer Corporation was written off in anticipation that there would be no recovery of the amount owed. Later, an announcement is made that 25 percent of amounts owed by Bendix would in fact be paid by the trustee handling the bankruptcy. This new information requires the reinstatement of the amount *expected* to be collected by BCC — $250 in this case. This transaction is recorded by this journal entry.

Accounts Receivable	250	
Allowance for Doubtful Accounts		250

This entry reverses part of the amount previously written off and sets up the amount collected as a receivable. As a result, both accounts are increased.

Accounts Receivable		Allowance for Doubtful Accounts	
Bal. 25,000			Bal. 1,450
	1,000	1,000	
250			250

Since Bendix Inc. is a bankrupt entity (a gone concern) its credit-worthiness is no longer an issue. It may occur, however, that the previously written off amount of an entity is reinstated and further sales contemplated. The reinstatement of the accounts receivable when full payment is anticipated has an effect on that customer's future credit worth. Therefore, Bluebeard records recoveries on each customer's subsidiary ledger account as a credit reference.

The actual collection of the reinstated amount is recorded by a second journal entry.

Cash	250	
Accounts Receivable		250

The collection is thereby recorded in the normal manner.

Credit Balances in Accounts Receivable

Accounts receivable subsidiary account balances usually have a debit balance because amounts are receivable from customers. Occasionally a credit balance occurs in some accounts as a result of double payment, merchandise being returned, or an allowance granted. Theoretically, the total amount of credit balances should be classified on the balance sheet as a liability, since the individual amounts are actually owing to the customers involved, in accordance with the concept of materiality. In actual practice, the net amount is usually shown as part of the Accounts Receivable total on the balance sheet, unless the credits would materially misrepresent the amount reported.

Instalment Accounts Receivable

The sale of merchandise on account was discussed under the assumption that a single payment will be made. In actual practice, payments often consist of periodic payments usually on a monthly basis; these are referred to as *instalment accounts receivable*. Department stores, such as Eatons and The Bay, often have instalment accounts receivable. Because payment is made over a period of time under the instalment method, it requires special rules in order to be recognized as revenue from sales. Often a portion of revenue is recorded as earned only as the payments are received; however, there are many possible variations. The accounting for instalment sales is usually dealt with in more advanced accounting courses.

Discussion Questions

1. What is an entity's internal control?
2. What is cash?
3. What different forms can currency take?
4. How does the preparation of a bank reconciliation strengthen the internal control of cash?
5. What different reconciling items appear in a bank reconciliation?
6. What are the steps in preparing a bank reconciliation?
7. What is an NSF cheque?
8. What is a deposit in transit?
9. What is an imprest petty cash system?
10. What is the difference between establishing and replenishing the petty cash fund?
11. How does use of an Allowance for Doubtful Accounts account match expense with revenue?

12. How is bad debt expense classified in the income statement?
13. How does the income statement method calculate the estimated amount of uncollectible accounts?
14. What is an ageing schedule for bad debts, and how is it used in calculating the estimated amount of uncollectible accounts?
15. How are credit balances in accounts receivable reported on the financial statements?
16. What is the role of the accountant in establishing and maintaining controls in organizations? Refer to Real Life Examples 7-1 and 7-2 when discussing your answer.

Discussion Cases

Discussion Case 7-1:   Cash on the Balance Sheet

The following is a letter to a professional accounting journal. It discusses the question of whether the cash balance in the books or the cash balance in the bank is the right cash balance to be shown on the balance sheet.

SIR — Traditionally, accountants show in balance sheets against the above heading the balance as shown in the firm's cashbook. This figure is often at variance with the balance shown in the books of the firm's bankers owing usually to unpresented cheques and lodgements not credited.

It is submitted that, in the context of showing "a true and fair view", cash at bank (and bank overdraft) should be the unadjusted but, nevertheless, reconciled bank balance according to the firm's bankers.

While cheques are unpresented, there is always the possibility that they may be stopped or held over. It would seem, therefore, that the only accurate balance is that as shown in the bank statement.

I should be interested in your readers' views on this subject.
Yours faithfully,
DATESEC

Source   Letter to the editor, *The Accountant*, August 28, 1965, p. 280.

For Discussion

Use the bank reconciliation in section B of this chapter to discuss this case.
1. Usually there is a difference between the balance of cash shown in the books of an entity and the balance of cash shown by the bank statement. Accountants reconcile these different amounts when they prepare a bank reconciliation. Which is the correct balance of cash at the end of a time period — the balance per books or the balance per bank? Why?
2. If the cash balance per bank were used as the amount reported in the balance sheet, how would the following items be handled
   a. Outstanding cheques?   b. Outstanding deposits?
3. Using the bank reconciliation in this chapter, prepare a bank reconciliation in accordance with the view that the cash balance shown in the bank statement is the proper cash balance to be reported in the balance sheet. (Note that the cash balance per books and the cash balance per bank would still be reconciled. Only the reconciling items used would change.)

Discussion Case 7-2: When American Money Wasn't Worth a Thing

The founder of *The Gazette*, Fleury Mesplet, might have left Montreal, and never have set up his newspaper, if his money had been worth anything. In that early spring of 1776, he needed someone to transport himself, his wife, his printing press and all his belongings out of the country. He was willing to pay. But no one in Montreal would have taken his money.

For about half a year (from the late autumn of 1775 till the early spring of 1776), Montreal was an American city. It had been seized by an American army of invasion sent northward by the government established in Philadelphia by the 13 colonies.

These were the colonies that had declared their independence and thrown off the rule of the British government. They were the nucleus of the United States that was to be.

This revolutionary government in Philadelphia called itself the Continental Congress. It issued its own paper money, backed by the combined credit of the 13 colonies. These paper bills were known as "continentals".

Money Not Trusted

Fleury Mesplet had been sent to Montreal by the Continental Congress to print revolutionary propaganda. He had with him such paper money. But he was to find, as did the American army of invasion, that in Canada such money was not trusted.

If the American Revolution were to fail and be suppressed, the paper money its Congress had issued would be worthless. When the American army of invasion tried to buy supplies in Canada, it soon found that its paper money would not be accepted. The expression "not worth a continental" showed the contempt in which it was held.

Often the American troops could buy what they needed only if they had "hard cash"—not paper, but metal coins, especially gold or silver. But the American supply of hard cash was insufficient.

Desperate measures were taken to compel the acceptance of the Congress's paper money. On March 4, 1776, Benedict Arnold, commanding the American army besieging Quebec, issued a proclamation to the inhabitants of the countryside.

"On account of the present scarcity of gold and silver coin," the proclamation declared, "and the very great outlay of our army before Quebec, we deem it expedient to make current a sufficient quantity of the paper money issued by order of the Hon. Congress. . . .

"We declare . . . that . . . every person who shall refuse to receive it at par, and without any discount, shall be considered an enemy . . . and be treated as such."

The Americans were not relying on such threats alone. They were doing what they could do borrow "hard cash" from some merchants in Montreal who were supporting the revolution.

Their chief source of "hard cash" was the merchant, James Price. Being a revolutionary enthusiast, he lent "hard money" to the Americans in Montreal, up to a total of £20,000 — a huge sum in those times.

The Americans were trying to borrow cash from another Montreal merchant of revolutionary sympathies. He was William Heywood.

. . .

The soldiers would not re-enlist unless they were paid in hard cash, not in the paper money of Congress. Being paid in such paper money was as bad for them as not being paid at all, for in Canada it would buy them nothing, not even a drink in a tavern.

Benedict Arnold wrote to the merchant Heywood:

"Col. Bedel acquaints me he has an opportunity of re-enlisting 70 or 80 men provided he can procure £thirty in hard money. . . . If you can possibly procure me the money, I shall esteem it a great favour and will replace it out of the first cash which arrives."

Many in Montreal who had lent money to the Americans, or had supplied goods on the promise of payment, felt a surge of hope that they might be paid at last. The Continental Congress was sending special commissions to Montreal, headed by Benjamin Franklin, one of the most eminent and revered leaders of the revolution.

This commission, clothed with prestige and authority, was expected to take charge of American affairs in Canada. The hope was that it would also bring with it a war chest of gold and silver.

Actually, the commissioners were coming with high prestige but with little else. They soon realized what meagre confidence was felt in Canada in the paper money of Congress. "Not the most trifling service can be procured," the commissioners wrote to the Congress, "without an assurance of instant pay in silver or gold."

When Franklin and his fellow-commissioners had sailed up Lake Champlain, they sent a courier on to Benedict Arnold in Montreal to inform him of their arrival at St. John's. This courier, however, could not take the ferry across the St. Lawrence River to Montreal because he had nothing but paper money. In the same way, carriages could not be sent to bring the commissioners from St. John's; paper money was not accepted as payment.

In the end, the courier crossed the river and the carriages were sent to St. John's only because a sympathizer with the revolutionary cause in Montreal was ready to put up the hard cash.

As soon as the commissioners were established at the Château de Ramezay, creditors crowded in upon them, demanding to be paid in silver or gold. Franklin appealed to Congress to send £20,000 to Montreal with the "utmost dispatch." But the treasury of the Congress in Philadelphia could not meet the demand.

Benjamin Franklin quickly saw the hopelessness of trying to maintain the American invasion of Canada. Despair was spreading among the American troops. They had given up the siege of Quebec and were in disorderly retreat up the St. Lawrence.

Franklin and the other commissioners left Montreal and headed south. Fleury Mesplet, brought to Montreal to do printing for them, might have joined the hurried exodus. But his paper money could not even buy for him the means of escape.

Great Faith

Mesplet had always placed a great faith in this paper money. While in business in Philadelphia, before coming to Montreal, it was "well known to the whole town" that he had "sold goods in the way of his trade, for Continental Currency, and that he even gave gold and silver in exchange for paper money."

He was to realize, however, that this paper money of Congress did not have the same status in Montreal as it had in Philadelphia. Since he could not use it to buy the means of escape, he was immobilized and had to stay. Because he stayed, he was to become Montreal's first printer and the founder of Montreal's first paper.

Source Edgar Andrew Collard, "When money wasn't worth a thing", *The* (Montreal) *Gazette*, November 24, 1984, p. B-2.

For Discussion

1. If you were an accountant contemporary to these circumstances, how would you account for "continentals", "hard cash", gold, and silver?
2. Comment on why gold and silver are recognized as legitimate forms of currency to this day.

Discussion Case 7-3: Signing a Company Cheque

Here's a rude shock for business people who routinely pen their signatures on hundreds of company cheques a year: If they sign a company cheque and it bounces at the bank, they could be held personally liable by the individual or firm for whom the money was intended.

No matter that the name of the firm is clearly printed over the space reserved for the signature.

The law is clear: whether it's a cheque or a promissory note, there must be some written evidence on the document to indicate the person signing it is doing so in a representative capacity.

In other words, a signature alone is all that's necessary to make the individual personally liable for the payment.

The best way to avoid trouble is for the signatory to write the word 'per' after the company name and before his/her own signature to show the individual is signing on the company's behalf. As an extra precaution, the signer should also add his/her company title — president, manager, secretary, for example.

The reason for these rules of "strict liability" lies in the negotiable nature of cheques and promissory notes. Because the documents can be "sold" or "negotiated," their commercial integrity must be maintained; the holder of the instrument must be confident that the person(s) behind the signature can be held responsible for payment.

This might seem pretty ridiculous to a business person who feels he/she is hauled into court, along with his/her company, as a defendant in a case concerning a bounced cheque, the business person will simply tell the judge that he/she intended to sign the cheque on behalf of the firm. The judge, he/she thinks, will throw the case out of court.

The trouble is, however, that unless it's demonstrated to the court there's doubt as to whether, in fact, he was signing in a personal capacity, he won't be allowed to do any explaining.

The cheque or note will have to speak for itself. And if there's nothing on it to limit his personal liability, the case could go against him/her.

There has been considerable confusion in this area of the law—not as far as the basic principle is concerned, but because of its application in various cases.

In one Ontario Appeal Court case, it was ruled that the signatures appearing on a promissory note under the printed company name had nothing to show there was any connection between them and the company.

There was nothing ambiguous as to the intentions of the persons signing, so no proof of intention was allowed and the signatories were held personally liable.

However, a British Columbia Supreme Court judge looked at two signatures beneath a stamped company name and decided there was certainly some doubt as to whether the parties had signed the note in a representative capacity.

He then allowed proof to be made as to the intention of the defendants. Once it was established that they had, indeed, signed as representatives of the company, it was ruled they were not to be held personally liable.

Then there was an Ontario case where the signatories got off the hook because the company name stamp also imprinted two lines for signatures, followed by titles. The judge ruled there was clearly a connection between the company name and the lines — enough, anyway, to show the representative character of the signatures.

And, to confuse the issue further, an Ontario Supreme Court judge once held that a cheque on which the company name was printed in two places — at the top of the document and above the space reserved for the signature—was obviously a company cheque.

Because the company's name was so much in evidence, the court decided there was a considerable doubt as to whether the defendant had signed in his personal capacity, as the plaintiff claimed.

Evidence was therefore allowed for the defendant to prove his intent to sign as a representative of the firm.

But why expose yourself to personal liability and a rough day in court when the law provides you with ironclad protection? The next time you uncap your pen to deal with a company cheque, make sure you add a couple of strategic scribbles before and after your signature.

Source Claire D. Bernstein, "Signing a company cheque", *The* (Montreal) *Gazette*, December 4, 1982.

For Discussion

1. How would the issues raised in the case affect your decisions if you were the signing officer of a proprietorship? a partnership? a corporation?
2. If a cheque from The Government of Canada bounces, can the individual who signed it be held accountable?

Comprehension Problems

Comprehension Problem 7-1

The bookkeeper for Hooper Corporation prepared the following bank reconciliation.

Hooper Corporation
Bank Reconciliation at May 31

Cash per Books (May 31)	$4,343	Cash per Bank Statement (May 31)	$5,590
Less: Bank Service Charges	6	*Add:* Deposit in Transit	1,314
Adjusted Cash Balance (May 31)	$4,337	Total	$6,904

Less: Outstanding Cheques:		
Cheque No.	*Amount*	
680	$ 476	
690	891	
695 (certified cheque for $500)		
701	1,200	2,567
Adjusted Cash Balance (May 31)		$4,337

Required:
1. How did the bookkeeper determine the amounts to be added or deducted?
2. Why is cheque no. 695 excluded from the total of outstanding cheques?
3. What adjusting entry will be necessary at May 31?

Note: Consult, when necessary, the master chart of accounts in Chapter 3.

Comprehension Problem 7-2

The cash balance shown in the general ledger Cash account of Delta Ltd. at December 31 is reconciled with the cash balance reported in the bank statement using the following types of adjustments:
a. Additions to the reported general ledger cash balance.
b. Deductions from the reported general ledger cash balance.
c. Additions to the reported cash balance per the bank's statement.
d. Deductions from the reported cash balance per the bank's statement.
e. Information that has no effect on the current bank reconciliation.

Required:
1. Using the letters a to e from the list, indicate the appropriate adjustment for each of the following pieces of information derived from Delta's December bank statement.
2. Add a check mark if the item requires an adjusted journal entry on the books of Delta at December 31.

_____ A customer's cheque has been returned marked NSF. Delta Ltd. had no prior knowledge of this.
_____ A cheque for $930 deposited by Delta was recorded in error by the Delta bookkeeper as $390.
_____ A company deposit dated December 31 does not appear on the bank statement.
_____ Bank charges of $35 are shown on the bank statement.
_____ Cheque no. 821 for $663.90, issued on December 14 for the purchase of equipment, has been entered incorrectly by the bank as $636.90.
_____ Delta obtained a loan from the bank, which was not entered in the books of the company.
_____ The account of I. Payslo was written off to the allowance account as uncollectible.
_____ Cheques outstanding on the November reconciliation remain unreturned by the bank.
_____ A note collected by the bank was not reported previously to Delta.
_____ The bank has charged Delta, in error, with a $500 cheque that should have been charged to Deltoid Ltd.

Comprehension Problem 7-3

The following information is taken from the records of NATE Corporation for 19X4:

	Jan. 1	Dec. 31
Accounts Receivable — Trade	$630	?
Allowance for Doubtful Accounts	16	?
Sales for the Year		$4,270
Accounts Receivable Collected during the Year		4,131

The following additional information is available:

a. Among the Accounts Receivable collections was the recovery in full of a $7 receivable from James Knight, a customer whose account had been written off as worthless late in 19X3. During 19X4 it was necessary to write off $16 as doubtful accounts.

b. At December 31, 19X4 the accounts receivable included $100 of past-due accounts. After careful study of all past-due accounts, the management estimated that the probable loss was 10 percent of all past-due accounts and that, in addition, 2 percent of the other 19X4 accounts receivable might prove uncollectible.

c. The accounts receivable collected during the year includes $7 received from James Knight.

Required:

1. Prepare journal entries for all 19X4 transactions relating to accounts receivable.
2. Prepare the general ledger postings for the Accounts Receivable — Trade at December 31.
3. Calculate the balance in Allowance for Doubtful Accounts at December 31, *before* the adjusting entry for doubtful accounts at December 31.
4. Prepare the necessary adjusting entry at December 31 for the Allowance for Doubtful Accounts.
5. What amount should appear in the income statement at December 31 as bad debts expense for the year?

Problems

Problem 7-1

The reconciliation of the cash balance per bank statement with the cash balance per general ledger usually results in one of five types of adjustments. These are:

a. Additions to the reported general ledger cash balance
b. Deductions from the reported general ledger cash balance
c. Additions to the reported cash balance per the bank statement
d. Deductions from the reported cash balance per the bank statement
e. Information that has no effect on the current reconciliation.

Required:

1. Using the above letters a to e from the list, indicate the appropriate adjustment for each of the following items that apply to XYZ Ltd. for December.

_____ The company has received a $3,000 loan from the bank, which was not recorded in the books of the company.

_____ A $250 cheque, certified on December 27, was not returned with the bank statement.

_____ Cheques amounting to $4,290, shown as outstanding on the November reconciliation, still have not been returned by the bank.

_____ A $1,000 collection made by the bank has not been previously reported to XYZ.

_____ The bank has erroneously charged XYZ with an $1,100 cheque, which should have been charged to XXZ Ltd.

_____ A $350 cheque made out by ABC Company and deposited by XYZ has been returned by the bank marked NSF; this is the first knowledge XYZ has of this action.

_____ A cheque for $840 by KLM Ltd., a customer, which has been deposited in the bank, was erroneously recorded by the bookkeeper as $730.

_____ A $600 bank deposit of December 31 does not appear on the statement.

_____ Bank service charges amounting to $75 are reported to XYZ.

_____ The company declared a $1,500 cash dividend to shareholders on December 15.

2. Prepare a bank reconciliation using the data given above. On December 31, the Cash account of XYZ Ltd. showed a balance of $84,293. The bank statement showed a balance of $90,568.

3. Prepare journal entries required to adjust the Cash account of XYZ Ltd. to the reconciled balance.

Problem 7-2

The following is information for the Vancouver Company Ltd.

a. Balance per the bank statement dated December 31 is $25,430.

b. Balance of the cash account on the company books at December 31 is $11,040.

c. A cheque for $840 that had been deposited in the bank was erroneously recorded by the bookkeeper as $930.

d. A cheque for $2,100 deposited on December 21, is returned by the bank marked NSF; no entry has been made on the company records to reflect the returned cheque.

e. Among the cancelled cheques is one for $345 given in payment of an account payable; the bookkeeper had recorded the cheque at $480 in the company records.

f. Bank service charges for December amount to $50.

g. The bank erroneously charged the Vancouver Company account for a $10,000 cheque of the Victoria Company; the cheque was found among the cancelled cheques returned with the bank statement.

h. The bank had collected a $15,000 note plus accrued interest amounting to $75; $15,075 was credited to Vancouver's account; a collection fee of $10 was debited to Vancouver Company's account.

i. Bank deposit of December 3 for $1,570 does not appear on the bank statement.

j. Outstanding cheques at December 31; no. 197, $4,000; no. 199, $9,000.

Required:

1. Prepare a bank reconciliation statement at December 31.

2. Prepare the necessary adjusting journal entries to make the Cash account agree with the bank reconciliation adjusted cash balance at December 31.

Problem 7-3

The Ross Corporation prepares a bank reconciliation every month. The general ledger Cash account contained the following details at the end of December.

Cash   No. 101

Date		Description	F	Debit	Credit	DR. or CR.	Balance
Nov.	30	Balance					11300
Dec.	31		CR. 16	7300			18600
	31		CD. 12		8450		10150

The December 31 bank statement showed:
a. Total cheques paid in December — $9,280
  (i) A cheque for $70 issued in December was the only one outstanding.
  (ii) Included in the cheques paid total was a cheque actually drawn on Ross Sales
      Inc. bank account, but which had been charged to Ross Corporation in error. — 400
b. Total deposits recorded by the bank during December — 7,000
c. Bank charges not recorded by company
  (i) Collection fee — 4
  (ii) NSF cheque returned (received from a customer for a credit sale) — 76
d. Additional credits on bank statement not recorded by the company
  (i) Note receivable collected — 500
  (ii) Interest on investments — 100

Required:
1. Determine the unreconciled bank balance at December 31.
2. Prepare the necessary adjusting journal entries to make the Cash account agree with the bank reconciliation adjusted cash balance at December 31.

Problem 7-4

The following figures appeared in the Allowance for Doubtful Accounts account during the current year.

Allowance for Doubtful Accounts

(a)	900	Bal. Beginning Year 1	2,400
(b)	800	(c)	600
(d)	1,100		

An analysis of the accounts receivable indicates that, at the end of the year, $3,100 of the accounts are uncollectible.

Required: Reconstruct the entries for the year and prepare the adjusting entry at the end of the year.

Problem 7-5

Tilbury Carpet Centre Ltd. reports to its shareholders the following balances on its December 31, 19X2 year-end report:

Notes Receivable from Customers	$ 20,000	
Accrued Interest on Notes Receivable	400	
Accounts Receivable	84,000	
	$104,400	
Less: Allowance for Doubtful Accounts	(2,000)	$102,400

The following occurred in January 19X3:
a. Accounts of $1,200 were written off as uncollectible.
b. An account for $300 previously written off was collected.
c. A customer's note for $250 was written off against the allowance account.
d. An analysis of the aged accounts receivable indicated a need for an allowance of $3,500 to cover the possiblity of uncollectible accounts.

Required: Prepare journal entries to record the above items.

Problem 7-6

At December 31, 19X3, the Wawa Lumber Company Ltd. balance sheet had a balance of $1,268,800 in trade accounts receivable. In addition, a contra account showed an Allowance for Doubtful Accounts balance of $32,400. Credit sales for 19X4 were $8,540,000, with collections of the receivables amounting to $8,262,560, including $15,600 that Wawa had written off as uncollectible in December 19X3, from Superior Lumber Ltd. During 19X4, Wawa wrote off $33,660 as uncollectible.

On November 1, 19X4, a customer with a $720,000 balance in accounts receivable sent $200,000 in cash (included in the cash collections) and a 12-percent 6 months note for the balance. The account was considered to be collectible.

At December 31, 19X4, Wawa's year-end, the balance in trade accounts receivable included $200,580 of past due accounts, which management estimated would result in a 10 percent loss, based on past experience. In addition, it was management's policy to set up an allowance on current accounts receivable equal to 2 percent of the balance outstanding.

Required:
1. Prepare general journal entries for all 19X4 transactions relating to notes and accounts receivable.
2. Prepare all adjusting entries at December 31, 19X4. (Include explanations, showing calculations.)
3. Show the amount which should appear in the 19X4 income statement as Bad Debts Expense.
4. What is the total for the Allowance for Doubtful Accounts account?

Alternate Problems

Alternate Problem 7-1

The preparation of the bank reconciliation is an important function of the accountant at Long Life Ltd. Normally, five types of adjustments are used.
a. Additions to the reported general ledger cash balance
b. Deductions from the reported general ledger cash balance
c. Additions to the reported cash balance per the bank statement
d. Deductions from the reported cash balance per the bank statement
e. Information that has no effect on the current bank reconciliation.

Required:
1. Using the letters a to e from the list, indicate the appropriate adjustments for each of the following pieces of information derived from Long Life Ltd.'s January bank statement.

_____ A bank collection of $2,000 was not previously reported to Long Life.
_____ A certified cheque amounting to $500 and dated January 15 was not returned with the January bank statement.
_____ The January 31 $1,000 deposit arrived too late at the bank to be included in the January statement.
_____ The $225 cheque of Phantom Truckers has been returned with the voucher, marked NSF; the Long Life people are surprised.
_____ A cheque received for $540 was deposited by the accounts receivable clerk as $450.
_____ A debit memo for $13 for service charges is received with the bank statement.
_____ A $10,000 loan received from the bank is included in the bank statement only.
_____ A $150 December cheque has still not been paid by the bank.
_____ The bank has credited Long Life with a $2,000 deposit that should have been credited to Long Life Insurance.

2. Prepare a bank reconciliation using the data given above. On January 31, the Cash account of Long Life Ltd. showed a balance of $24,848. The bank statement showed a balance of $37,850.

Alternate Problem 7-2

The following items relate to the activities of Eastern Company Ltd.
a. At June 30, the Cash account shows a balance of $1,200.
b. The June bank statement shows a balance of $64.
c. Of four cheques not returned by the bank in May, one still has not been returned in June: cheque no. 208 in the amount of $80.
d. Eastern deposited cash received on June 29 (in the amount of $1,000) and June 30 (in the amount of $200) in the night depository as June 29 and 30, a Saturday and Sunday, respectively; these deposits do not appear on the bank statement.
e. On checking the cheques returned with the bank statement, Eastern found the following: cheque no. 214 properly made out for $45 was coded as a debit to office expense and a credit to cash for $54; cheque of Western Company in the amount of $200 was incorrectly processed through Eastern's bank account by the bank.
f. Bank service charge for the month totalled $5.
g. A cheque no. 261 for $180 written in June was not returned with the cancelled cheques.

Required:
1. Prepare a bank reconciliation at June 30.
2. Prepare the necessary adjusting journal entries to make the Cash account agree with the bank reconciliation adjusted cash balance at June 30.

Alternate Problem 7-3

Paper Book Shop Ltd. effectively controls their cash by depositing receipts on a daily basis and making all disbursements by cheque. After all the posting for the month of November was completed, the cash balance in the general ledger was $4,209. The statement received from the Guaranteed Bank showed the balance to be $4,440. The following data are available for the purpose of reconciling these balances.

a. Cash receipts for November 30 amounting to $611 have been placed in the night depository and do not appear on the bank statement.

b. Credit and debit notes previously not available to Paper Book are included with the other vouchers. A debit memo for an NSF cheque, originally received as payment for an account receivable of $130, is included. A debit memo for bank charges of $6 is also included. A credit memo advises Paper Book Shop Ltd. that $494 has been deposited to the account, the net proceeds of a collection the bank had made on behalf of Paper Book Shop Ltd. on a $500 note.

c. Cheques written during November but not included with the vouchers: no. 1154, $32; no. 1192, $54; no. 1193, $83; no. 1194, $109.

d. Cheque no. 1042 for $494 was returned with the vouchers but a check of the cheque register indicates the amount recorded was $548; the cheque had been charged to office expense.

e. Cheques outstanding at the end of October included cheque no. 1014 for $152 and no. 1016 for $179. Cheque no. 1016 was paid in the bank statement; cheque no. 1014 was not.

Required:
1. Prepare a bank reconciliation at November 30.
2. Prepare the necessary adjusting journal entries required to make the Cash account agree with the bank reconciliation adjusted cash balance at November 30.

Alternate Problem 7-4

The General Co. Ltd. has, since inception, estimated its bad debts at 1 percent of net credit sales. During 19X5, General decided to calculate the required balance for the allowance account at year-end, December 31, by ageing its accounts receivable. The review suggested a required balance of $7,200. The following data, which already have been recorded in the company's books, are also available:

	19X4	19X5
Accounts Written Off		
On March 14, 19X4 (Brown)	$600	
On March 30, 19X5 (Smith)		$300
Recoveries of Accounts Written Off		
On June 5, 19X5 (Brown)		400

The Allowance for Doubtful Accounts account reported the following balances: January 1, 19X4 — $1,500, and January 1, 19X5 — 3,900.

Required: Prepare journal entries to record
1. The amount of bad debts expense for the year 19X4.
2. The bad debts expense on December 31, 19X5.
3. The collection from Brown on June 5, 19X5.

Alternate Problem 7-5

On January 1, the accounts receivable account balance of Carlton Iron Works Inc. was $265 and an allowance for doubtful accounts was $7. The firm's credit sales during the year were $2,105 and cash collections from customers amounted to $2,025. Among these collections was the recovery in full of a $3 receivable from James Walburn, a customer whose account had been written off as worthless in the previous year. During the current year it was necessary to write off as uncollectible customers' accounts totalling $8.

At December 31, the accounts receivable included $40 of past-due accounts. After careful study of all past-due accounts, the management estimated that the probable loss contained therein was 20 percent and that, in addition, 2 percent of the current accounts receivable might prove uncollectible.

Required:
1. Calculate the balance of the Accounts Receivable account at December 31.
2. Prepare the necessary adjusting entry for the bad debts at December 31.
3. What amount should appear in this year's income statement as Bad Debts Expense?
4. Show the balance sheet presentation of accounts receivable at December 31.

Alternate Problem 7-6

The Baker Company Ltd. has followed the income statement method in providing for possible bad debt losses. Currently, they use ½ of 1 percent of net sales for the setting up of their allowance for doubtful accounts. At January 1, the allowance account had a balance of $55 CR. During the year, the following occurred:

Jan. 22   One customer, the Red Shirt Company, had declared bankruptcy and no payment could be expected. Balance of the Red Shirt Co. account was $9.

Mar. 17   The Green Hills Company sent a cheque for $2. This account had been written off last year.

Dec. 31   A year-end examination showed that $19 of accounts were written off as uncollectible.

The following is a portion of the income statement of the Baker Company Ltd., for the current year ended December 31.

Partial Income Statement

Sales		$4,500
Less: Returns and Allowances	$400	
Discounts Allowed	100	500
		$4,000

Required:
1. Prepare journal entries for the above transactions (*include* explanation).
2. Prepare the adjusting entry at December 31.
3. What is the balance in the Allowance for Doubtful Accounts account for December 31? Show details.
4. Would the sales manager be the appropriate person to approve the general write-off of uncollectible accounts at year-end? Why?
5. Why does the accountant of the Baker Company Ltd. provide for bad debt losses in preparing his annual statements?

Decision Problems

Decision Problem 7-1

You have been given the following bank reconciliation of AB Ltd. at November 30 and asked to review the value of outstanding cheques at November 30 and of cheques written from December 1 to 15.

You obtained a bank statement and cancelled cheques from the bank on December 15. Cheques issued from December 1–15 per the books were worth $11,241. Cheques returned by the bank on December 15 amounted to $29,219. Of the cheques outstanding at November 30, $4,800-worth were not returned by the bank with the December 15 statement, and,

of those issued per the books in December, $3,600 were not returned.

Required:
1. Using the information relating to cheques, compare the cheques returned by the bank on December 15, with the cheques outstanding on November 30 and issued in December.
2. Suggest at least three possible explanations for any discrepancy that exists.

Bank Reconciliation
at November 30

Cash per Books	$12,817	Cash per Bank	$15,267
		Add: Outstanding Deposits	18,928
			$34,195
		Less: Outstanding Cheques	(21,378)
		Adjusted Cash Balance	$12,817

Decision Problem 7-2

The internal control procedures for cash transactions in the Algonquin Corporation were not adequate. James Shifty, the cashier-bookkeeper, handled cash receipts, made small disbursements from the cash receipts, maintained accounting records, and prepared the monthly reconciliations of the bank account. At November 30, the bank statement showed a balance of $17,500. The outstanding cheques were as follows:

Cheque No.	Amount
7062	$268.55
7183	170.00
7284	261.45
8621	175.19
8623	341.00
8632	172.80

There was also an outstanding deposit of $3,347.20 at November 30.

The Cash balance as shown on the company records was $20,258.31, which included some cash on hand. The bank statement for November included $200 arising from the collection of a note left with the bank; the company's books did not include an entry to record this collection.

Recognizing the weakness existing in internal control over cash transactions, Shifty removed the cash on hand and then prepared the following reconciliation in an attempt to conceal his theft.

Balance per Books	$20,258.31	Balance per Bank	$17,500.00
		Add: Outstanding Deposit	3,347.30
			$20,847.30
		Less: Outstanding Cheques	

Cheque No.	Amount	
8621	$175.19	
8623	341.00	
8632	172.80	(588.99)
Adjusted Cash Balance		$20,258.31

Required:
1. Calculate the amount of cash taken by Shifty.
2. Explain how Shifty attempted to conceal his theft of cash.

The Conversion Cycle

Part III focuses on the conversion of an entity's resources acquired through expenditures. Conversion refers not only to the resale of assets but also to their use and consumption. Inventory and fixed assets are included in this category; their use or consumption in manufacturing operations usually represents a substantial amount of the entity's resources.

Inclusion of inventory in the calculation of cost of goods sold was introduced in Chapter 5 where focus was on its use for resale. Chapter 8 discusses the different accounting methods for calculating inventory cost and the impact of inflation on financial statement disclosure of inventory cost. Accountants have a choice of inventory systems and estimation methods for inventory calculation.

Fixed assets are often used in the operations of an entity. A truck, for example, can be used for deliveries, a building for storage of unsold inventory. Chapter 9 deals with establishing the cost of long-term assets and their depreciation over their estimated useful lives; it also includes a comparison of depreciation allocation assumptions.

In a manufacturing entity, inventory — often called raw materials — is transformed through production into finished goods ready for sale. An intermediate inventory production stage is referred to as work in process. Finished goods and work-in-process cost normally include material, labour, and overhead components. Fixed assets, as used in manufacturing operations, form part of the overhead cost. Chapter 18 discusses the accounting required for manufacturing operations.

Inventory

Inventory is usually a major financial statement amount. Matching cost of goods sold with revenue and inventory valuation in the balance sheet are particularly important.

1. In what way can the actual flow of goods differ from the flow of costs?
2. What compromises are made by accountants when calculating the cost of inventory?
3. What impact does the practice of consistency have on changing from one cost flow assumption to another?
4. How is the laid-down cost of goods calculated?
5. What meaning is attributed by accountants to the word *market* when calculating inventory at the lower of cost and market?
6. What impact does the use of different cost flow assumptions have on financial statements?
7. What is the relationship between the cost of ending inventory and the resulting net income?
8. How is current cost information recommended to be disclosed on financial statements?
9. What is the distinction between a trading gain and a holding gain?
10. What different methods can be used to calculate inventory?

A. Calculation of Inventory Costs

There are two problems in determining inventory. The first involves calculating the quantity of inventory at the end of an accounting period: usually not difficult. The other problem involves assigning the most appropriate cost to this quantity. Choosing the most appropriate cost *can* be difficult.

The cost of inventory can be determined in several different ways. Consider the following: five gadgets are purchased for resale on different dates during a period of rising prices.

> 1st purchase: 1 gadget at $1
> 2nd purchase: 1 gadget at $2
> 3rd purchase: 1 gadget at $3
> 4th purchase: 1 gadget at $4
> 5th purchase: 1 gadget at $5.

At the end of the accounting period, four of these gadgets have already been sold and only one gadget remains in ending inventory. What is the cost of the one remaining gadget in ending inventory? Is it $1, $2, $3, $4, or $5?

According to generally accepted accounting principles, as recommended in the *CICA Handbook* (section 3030.09), the inventory cost should be the one that "results in the fairest matching of costs against revenues", with due regard to its usefulness as a measure of balance sheet inventory cost. What gadget cost in inventory results in the fairest matching? Why aren't costs fairly matched against revenues when any one of the gadget costs is used for inventory? or are they? Which cost is the most useful measure of the balance sheet cost? How are inventories normally costed? How would cost be assigned to the gadget in inventory in actual practice? If a method is chosen to measure net income best, what effect is there on the amount then shown on the balance sheet as inventory cost?

These are some of the questions that must be dealt with when considering ending inventory costs; they are discussed in this chapter. Sections A and B look at the methods used to calculate inventory costs. Section C discusses the calculation of inventory cost under each of the periodic and perpetual systems. Section D covers the estimation of inventory costs when a physical inventory count is impossible or impractical.

Specific Identification

Specific identification
A method of inventory costing in which goods are identified with their purchase cost; an assumption on the flow of costs is not necessary when this method is used.

Flow of goods
The sequence in which purchased goods are sold; includes FIFO, LIFO, and average sequences.

Each inventory item is identified with its purchase cost under this method. **Specific identification** costing is most practical when inventory consists of relatively few, expensive items, particularly when individual units can be checked with serial numbers, as in the case of motor vehicles. Its usefulness is limited when inventory consists of a large number of inexpensive items purchased at various times during the period at different prices; in this case, the expense involved in calculating specific identification costs is not cost effective. Consequently, a method of assigning costs to inventory items based on an assumed **flow of goods** is usually adopted. Once chosen, the method must be followed consistently so as to match costs with revenues and for inventory balance sheet valuation purposes.

There is another feature of specific identification that is objectionable to accountants. There is the possibility of *profit enhancement opportunities* being available to management: when inventory purchase costs are increasing for identical units, management can show a larger net income by "selecting" for sale units that cost less; similarly, net income can be reduced if management "selects" for sale units that cost more.

The Actual Flow of Goods

Assigning the cost to inventory is easy under the specific identification method because the cost of each item sold is known. Inventory costing would be even easier if the price of goods did not change; in this case, the same cost would always apply and it would not be necessary to key the cost of each item separately — it would be the same for each one.

Prices of goods *do* change. Therefore, costs have to be assigned to closing inventory according to a flow of goods. What are the different flows of goods that accountants have identified? There are three possible ways to analyze the flow of goods: they are known as **first in, first out** (FIFO); **last in, first out** (LIFO); and the **average** method. The actual flow of goods depends on the conditions that exist in various companies.

The FIFO Assumption

Assume that a company purchases and sells eggs. Their perishable nature requires a flow of goods which ensures that the first eggs on hand are sold first; the eggs acquired next are next to be sold; and so on. This is a FIFO flow of goods. This flow can be thought of as a "conveyor belt" flow of goods. As each lot of eggs is purchased, it is placed on the "conveyor belt", as shown in Figure 8-1, for sale.

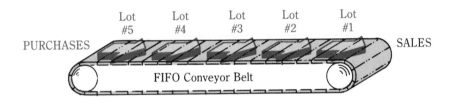

Figure 8-1   The FIFO flow of goods

Lot No. 1 is sold first. It is the first in; therefore it is the first out. Lot No. 2 is the next lot to be sold, and so on. A flow of costs which assumes that the first goods on hand (Lot No. 1) are the first to be sold is obviously the best method of calculating inventory cost in this situation. In addition to the egg example, a FIFO flow of goods is desirable where drugs, photo films, and other time-dated items make up inventory; a FIFO flow of costs is the most suitable accounting assumption in these situations.

The LIFO Assumption

Assume that a company purchases and sells coal. As coal is purchased, it is dumped on each preceding purchase, with the result that a pyramid of coal is formed, as illustrated in Figure 8-2.

FIFO (first in, first out)
Either an actual flow or an assumed flow can be used in relation to the flow of goods or costs or both; the first goods purchased are assumed to be the first goods sold.

LIFO (last in, first out)
Either an actual flow or an assumed flow can be used in relation to the flow of goods or costs or both; the last goods purchased are assumed to be the first goods sold.

Average
Either *weighted* or *moving* average; an average is calculated by dividing an amount by a quantity.

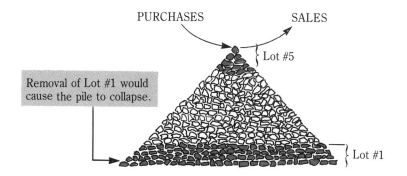

Figure 8-2   The LIFO flow of goods

As can be seen, coal at the top of the pile is the first to be sold. If an attempt were made to remove coal at the bottom, a dangerous landslide of coal could result. Therefore, the last purchased (at the top) is sold first, and the physical flow of goods is called a LIFO flow. A flow of costs which assumes that the last goods purchased (coal at the top of the pile) are the first to be sold is obviously the best method of calculating inventory cost in this type of situation.

The Average Assumption

In actual practice, an average may be used in both the egg and coal business, since goods purchased on different dates are mixed in common storage facilities and specific identification of each inventory item is impractical. Further, such costs as shipping and handling may not be readily assignable to specific items. The average method does not assume any particular flow of goods but is a reasonable compromise.

One of the problems in dealing with inventory was earlier identified as the need to calculate the quantities of goods in closing inventory. The calculating itself is not particularly difficult. But once the quantity of goods has been determined, an assumption must be made:

1. These goods have resulted from a FIFO flow of goods during the accounting period, or
2. These goods have resulted from a LIFO flow of goods during the accounting period, or
3. These goods are mixed at the end of the period and an average assumption is the most reasonable compromise.

The Actual Flow of Costs

Flow of costs
The sequence in which costs are assigned to merchandise sold and remaining in inventory; includes FIFO, LIFO, and average cost sequences.

Once the flow of goods has been recognized, the **flow of costs** can be determined and costs can easily be assigned to closing inventory. The calculation of inventory cost under each of the three methods follows. The purchase of five gadgets is used to illustrate the calculation of the ending inventory under the three flow-of-goods assumptions.

FIFO Cost Assumption

Since the FIFO flow of goods assumes that the first units on hand are the first to be sold, the units acquired next are the next to be sold, and so on, the calculation of inventory cost should correspond to this flow of goods. For example, the FIFO cost of one gadget remaining in ending inventory (four gadgets have been sold) would be $5, calculated as follows.

1st purchase: 1 gadget at $1   (1st to be sold)
2nd purchase: 1 gadget at $2   (2nd to be sold)
3rd purchase: 1 gadget at $3   (3rd to be sold)
4th purchase: 1 gadget at $4   (4th to be sold)
5th purchase: 1 gadget at $5   (ending inventory is the cost of this purchase).

Thus, the first four gadgets purchased are the first four gadgets sold; the cost of the one remaining gadget in closing inventory is the cost of the fifth gadget purchased.

FIFO is a popular method in actual practice because, in most merchandising entities, it coincides with the actual flow of goods and is not susceptible to the type of manipulation by management possible under the specific identification method.

LIFO Cost Assumption

Since the LIFO flow of goods assumes that the last unit purchased is the first to be sold, the calculation of inventory cost has to correspond to this flow of goods. The LIFO cost of one gadget remaining in ending inventory (four gadgets have been sold) would be $1, calculated as follows.

1st purchase: 1 gadget at $1   (ending inventory is the cost of this purchase)
2nd purchase: 1 gadget at $2   (4th to be sold)
3rd purchase: 1 gadget at $3   (3rd to be sold)
4th purchase: 1 gadget at $4   (2nd to be sold)
5th purchase: 1 gadget at $5   (1st to be sold).

Thus the last four gadgets to be purchased are the first four gadgets to be sold; the cost of the one remaining gadget in closing inventory is the cost of the first gadget purchased.

As long as the ending inventory quantity is maintained or increased, the first costs are not related to the cost of gadgets sold and, therefore, do not appear on the income statement. However, if the ending inventory quantity is sold, then first costs *are* included in the income statement.

Average Cost Assumption

Since the average cost method does not assume any particular flow of goods, the cost of each gadget sold is simply a computed average cost of all gadgets purchased. The calculation of this average depends on whether a *periodic* (weighted average) or *perpetual* (moving average) inventory system is in use. (The moving average costing procedure is discussed further in section D.)

Assuming a periodic inventory system, the average cost (called weighted average) of a gadget would be $3 ($1 + $2 + $3 + $4 + $5 = $15 ÷ 5 units = $3 per unit). Note that the ending inventory cost is computed by dividing the total cost of units available for sale ($15) by the quantity of units available for sale (5 units).

The average cost assumption is popular in actual practice because it is easy to calculate. It is also particularly well suited to situations in which inventory is mixed in common storage facilities, for example, oil. In such cases, average cost is representative of all costs incurred in filling the oil storage tanks. The average cost amount calculated usually falls between the costs calculated by FIFO and LIFO and is a compromise between these two methods.

The calculation of inventory cost under each of the three methods is summarized below:

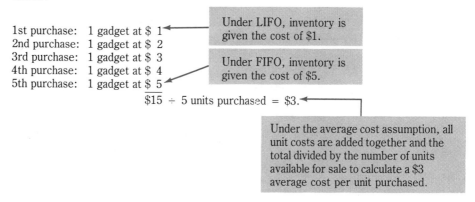

1st purchase: 1 gadget at $ 1
2nd purchase: 1 gadget at $ 2
3rd purchase: 1 gadget at $ 3
4th purchase: 1 gadget at $ 4
5th purchase: 1 gadget at $ 5

$15 ÷ 5 units purchased = $3.

Under LIFO, inventory is given the cost of $1.

Under FIFO, inventory is given the cost of $5.

Under the average cost assumption, all unit costs are added together and the total divided by the number of units available for sale to calculate a $3 average cost per unit purchased.

Inventory Costing Practice in Canada

Studies of financial statements prepared by the CICA indicate that FIFO costing is the most frequently used method to calculate cost. While the LIFO costing method is not permitted for Canadian income tax purposes, Canadian companies may use this method for inventory costing provided they use a method acceptable to Canadian tax authorities for income tax purposes.

Accounting Compromises

Accountants make a number of compromises between what is conceptually correct and what is done in practice when calculating the cost of inventory. One of these involves use of an assumed flow of costs that differs from the actual flow of goods. Another involves what is referred to as laid-down cost, discussed later.

Mismatched Flow of Costs with Flow of Goods

The previous paragraphs focused on the different ways that goods can flow through an entity. Inventory costs should be calculated on the FIFO basis where there is a FIFO flow of goods and on the LIFO basis where there is a LIFO flow of goods; an average method should be used when an average is the most reasonable assumption that can be made about the flow of goods.

In actual practice, however, the flow of costs assumed by management in calculating the cost of ending inventory may not be the same as the actual movement of goods.

- A FIFO cost flow can be assumed where a LIFO flow of goods actually exists, or
- A LIFO cost flow can be assumed where a FIFO flow of goods actually exists, or
- Any other combination of one cost flow with a different flow of goods may be used.

This mismatching of the actual flow of costs with the movement of goods can result in a substantial miscalculation of net income or represent, in some cases, *profit enhancement opportunities*.

> The use of an assumed flow of costs that differs from the actual flow of goods is permitted by generally accepted accounting principles.

The recommendation in the *CICA Handbook* is that the cost flow method that results in the fairest matching of costs with revenues be used in calculating cost, regardless of whether the method corresponds to the physical flow of goods.

Although use of the most suitable cost flow assumption is encouraged by GAAP, emphasis is also placed on the consistent use of the assumption selected. The accountant's practice of consistency does not prevent a change from a cost flow assumption that is no longer suitable. Rather, it is designed to facilitate meaningful year-to-year comparisons of operating results and balance sheet valuation. Accordingly, where the cost flow assumption has changed, the *CICA Handbook* (section 3030.13) recommends that the effect of the change on net income should be disclosed in notes to the financial statements.

Laid-Down Cost

Laid-down cost
(of inventory) Includes every cost incurred by the purchaser to get the merchandise to his or her place of business.

The discussion in this chapter so far emphasizes the calculation of inventory cost. For a wholesale or retail business, inventory is generally understood to mean *goods owned and available for sale to customers*; it is recommended in the *CICA Handbook* (section 3030.05) that this cost be the **laid-down cost**. This laid-down cost includes the invoice price of the goods (less purchase discounts) plus transportation in, insurance while in transit, and any other expenditure made by the purchaser to get the merchandise to his place of business.

The cost of merchandise available for sale is usually considered as the laid-down cost. In the following partial income statement (based on the one in section E of Chapter 5), which amount is the laid-down cost?

All merchandise a company has for sale during the accounting period is sometimes called a *pool of costs*.

This is the laid-down cost.

Cost of Goods Sold:			
Opening Inventory			$ 80,000
Purchases		$240,000	
Less: Purchases Returns and			
Allowances	$12,600		
Purchases Discounts	2,400	15,000	
Net Purchases		$225,000	
Transportation In		15,000	
Cost of Goods Purchased			240,000
Cost of Goods Available			$320,000
Ending Inventory (Dec. 31)			120,000
Total Cost of Goods Sold			$200,000

The pool of goods available for sale is divided into two categories at the end of an accounting period.

If transportation in and other such costs are insignificant in relation to the invoice price of the merchandise, a proportionate amount should theoretically be added to the cost of ending inventory. In actual practice, these costs are often significant and are hence considered as expenses of the accounting period in which they were incurred and are not allocated to ending inventory. Similarly, purchase discounts are not usually deducted from inventory.

The exclusion of these items from ending inventory is also in accordance with the practice of conservatism subscribed to by accountants. Although these laid-down costs are usually omitted for convenience from the calculation of ending inventory, their exclusion is justified by the practice of conservatism, which permits the mis-statement of an item if the end result is less favourable in its impact on net income and/or asset valuation. It is interesting to note that the accountant's view of conservatism was considered peculiar by Professor Henry Rand Hatfield, an eminent accountant, whose own view was:

> The accountant transcends the conservatism of the proverb "Don't count your chickens before they are hatched", saying "Here are a lot of chickens already safely hatched but, for the love of Mike use discretion and don't count them all, for perhaps some will die".[1]

It is noteworthy that this attitude represents extreme conservatism and the observation was made 60 years ago; not all accounting policies today emphasize this extreme conservatism.

Lower of Cost and Market

As discussed, historical cost is the generally accepted method used for inventory costing. The use of replacement cost is in accordance with GAAP when the replacement cost of an inventory item in the market place decreases, for whatever reason, in relation to the cost of that item recorded in the books of the company.

Market
The cost of replacing an asset on the open market.

The term **market** in this context means the cost of replacing the goods and the CICA has observed that:

> in view of the lack of precision in meaning, it is desirable that the term "market" not be used in describing the basis of valuation. A term more descriptive of the method of determining market, such as replacement cost, net realizable value, or net realizable value less normal profit margin, would be preferable (section 3030.11).

LOCAM (lower of cost and market)
A method of inventory valuation that calculates inventory cost at *cost* or *market*, whichever is lower; the term is also used in relation to temporary investments.

LOCAM, as applied on a unit-by-unit basis and on a group inventory basis, is illustrated below.

	Total Cost	Total Market	Unit Basis	Group Basis
Item X	$1,250	$1,200 ——→$1,200		
Item Y	1,400	1,500	1,400	
Total	$2,650	$2,700		$2,650
Ending Inventory (LOCAM)			$2,600	$2,650

On the basis of these calculations (any of the inventory cost assumptions — FIFO, LIFO, average — discussed previously can be used as "cost"), the valuation of ending inventory can be either $2,600 or $2,650. Under the unit basis, the lower of cost and market is selected for each item, while, under the group basis LOCAM, which is total cost of $2,650 in this example, an increase in Item Y is offset by a decrease in Item X. However, both methods, as well as sub-totals of different categories, are acceptable in the calculation of LOCAM.

The use of LOCAM is usually supported with an assumption that retail selling prices are expected to decline as inventory purchase cost declines. This assumption, however, is not always correct; and if declines in sales price do occur, they are not always proportional to the decline in inventory purchase cost, that is, "market". The accountant's practice of conservatism is therefore invoked to justify use of LOCAM, although balance sheet valuation of inventory and measurement of net income is initially adversely affected. The business community seems to demand conservatism on the part of accountants.

This approach was adopted in the days when conservatism was a dominant consideration for asset valuation. What it means is that, when the goods in inventory can be replaced for an amount that is less than their assumed cost, the inventory should be costed at this lower amount. A more accurate matching of costs and revenues in the next accounting period also results from this recognition of the lower cost of ending inventory, if sales prices are falling.

LOCAM is most useful when inventory costs are decreased because of obsolesence or damage.

B. Impact of Different Inventory Cost Flows

The application of different cost flow assumptions was illustrated in section A. If the cost of purchases did not increase during the period, then each method would allocate similar amounts to cost of goods sold and ending inventory. A problem arises, however, when purchase cost fluctuates during the accounting period. Typically, in a period of rapid inflation, cost increases can be significant. The resulting impact on the income statement and balance sheet are described next.

Impact on the Income Statement

When purchase costs are increasing, each cost flow method results in a different amount of ending inventory, cost of goods sold amount, and net income.

An example can be drawn from an analysis made for management of Bluebeard Computer Corporation. Three different cost flows were considered: FIFO, LIFO, and weighted average (average cost). Use was made of the data from section A concerning the purchase costs increase from $1 to $5 during the period; the result was a total purchase cost of $15 ($1 + $2 + $3 + $4 + $5). These increases reflected the period of rapidly rising purchase costs, which had occurred recently. It was further assumed in the analysis that sales prices were also rising, and that four gadgets had been sold for a total of $20 ($2 + $4 + $6 + $8). Expenses were assumed to remain constant at $6.

Note that the differences in net income are not caused by differences in the physical flow of goods; rather, they result from assumptions made about the flow of costs.

	FIFO Cost Flow		LIFO Cost Flow		Weighted Average Cost Flow	
Sales		$20		$20		$20
Cost of Goods Sold:						
Purchases	$15		$15		$15	
Less: Ending Inventory	5		1		3	
Total Cost of Goods Sold		10		14		12
Gross Profit		$10		$ 6		$ 8
Operating Expenses		6		6		6
Net Income		$ 4		$ -0-		$ 2

As can be seen, the impact of different cost flow assumptions is dramatic. FIFO maximizes income when purchase costs are rising and may result in a distorted net income amount. LIFO minimizes net income when purchase costs are rising and results in a more accurate matching of current revenue with current costs; it also tends to approximate inflation-adjusted accounting. Unfortunately, it also results in an unrealistic amount of inventory reported on the balance sheet. Weighted Average results in a net income figure between those for FIFO and LIFO.

> The choice of a particular inventory costing assumption can result in substantially different amounts of net income when purchase costs are fluctuating (and inventory turns over quickly).

In view of the impact that different cost flow assumptions can have on the financial statements, GAAP requires that the cost flow assumption used by an entity be disclosed in its financial statements.

A relationship between the cost of an ending inventory and the resulting net income is also apparent from the analysis. The FIFO method, with a larger ending inventory value ($5), also has the largest net income ($4). The LIFO method, with a smaller ending inventory value ($1), also has the lowest net income ($0). Therefore, we can conclude that, if ending inventory is higher or increases, net income also is higher or increases; if ending inventory is lower or decreases, net income also is lower or decreases.

If ending inventory

   cost increases ⬆   net income will increase. ⬆   income taxes will increase. ⬆

If ending inventory

   cost decreases ⬇   net income will decrease. ⬇   income taxes will decrease. ⬇

The ability to predict this relationship between net income and changes in the cost of ending inventory is important for business decisions.

> 1. If the objective of management is to increase reported net income, then that inventory method should be adopted which gives the highest ending inventory.
> 2. If the objective of management is to minimize income taxes, then that inventory cost method should be adopted which results in the lowest ending inventory.

The Canadian federal and provincial governments, aware of the implications of this choice and the popularity it would have with businesses wishing to reduce income taxes, must have considered the advisability of permitting the use of LIFO inventory costing for income tax purposes. This consideration probably did not take long.

LIFO costing is not permitted for income tax reporting in Canada. This policy does not mean that LIFO costing cannot be used in business. It simply means that this method cannot be used in the calculation of income taxes. Therefore, a business using LIFO costing in its records has to recalculate LIFO inventory cost to FIFO, average, or another acceptable method for income tax purposes.

During a period of falling prices, FIFO results in the lowest ending inventory cost; LIFO would produce the opposite results.

Phantom Profits

The comparison of the effects of FIFO and LIFO costing methods on net income (discussed above) show that a larger net income results when FIFO costing is used during a period of increasing prices. In the example, the net income on sales was $4 using FIFO and actually nil using LIFO. That is, FIFO showed profits of $4 more than LIFO.

	FIFO	*LIFO*
Net Income	$4	$-0-

Phantom profits
(from inventory)
A term used to describe the extra profits reported under the FIFO method of assigning costs to inventory, as compared with the LIFO method, during a period of rising prices (costs).

Such profits are sometimes referred to as **phantom profits**. The word "phantom" implies that these profits are an illusion.

Why are the extra profits under FIFO an illusion? Under FIFO, earlier costs are included in cost of goods sold. In the income statement these *earlier* costs are matched with *current* sales prices, with the result that there is no real profit under LIFO and a phantom profit of $4 under FIFO.

Under LIFO, the most recent costs are included in cost of goods sold. In the income statement these *more recent* costs are matched with *current* sales prices, and a closer matching of costs with revenue is achieved. Therefore LIFO costing, it is claimed, is more realistic with respect to the measurement of income.

In actual practice, a good matching occurs under LIFO only when purchases and sales occur frequently and in approximately the same quantity.

Impact on the Balance Sheet

Despite its advantages in matching inventory costs with revenue in the income statement, a major disadvantage of LIFO costing is its understatement of the inventory figure that appears on the balance sheet. This disadvantage in turn limits the significance and usefulness of this financial statement.

The gadget data used in the preceding discussions are repeated here to compare the inventory values that appear on the balance sheet as an asset, under each of the three cost assumptions.

	FIFO	*LIFO*	*Weighted Average*
Ending Inventory	$5	$1	$3

As is obvious, LIFO provides an unrealistic ending inventory value. If this comparison of ending inventory under the three cost assumptions is representative of what occurs in actual practice — which it tends to be when prices are rising — care has to be exercised by the reader of financial statements in interpreting the amounts reported in the financial statements.

> Full disclosure of the inventory costing assumption used in the financial statements is essential, because inventory is often the largest single item in the current assets section of the balance sheet.

The differences between the cost flow assumptions and their impact on the income statement and balance sheet are compared in the adjacent table.

Comparison of Cost Flow Assumptions

	FIFO	*LIFO*	*WEIGHTED AVERAGE*	*SPECIFIC IDENTIFICATION*
Physical Flow vs Cost Flow	The flow of goods approximates the flow of costs in most cases.	The flow of goods does not approximate the flow of costs in most cases.		The flow of goods is the same as the flow of costs since costs are identified with specific goods.

INCOME STATEMENT:

— Matching of costs with revenues.	The earlier costs in opening inventory and earlier purchases are matched with current revenues	Emphasizes the matching of the most current costs with current revenues.	An average cost for the period is matched with revenues.	The actual cost of each item sold is matched with the revenue resulting from the sale.
— Net Income Determination	Maximizes income when prices are rising because the earlier (and lower) costs are included in cost of goods sold.	Minimizes net income when prices are rising because more current, and therefore higher, costs are included in cost of goods sold.	When prices are rising, results in a net income figure which is less than the FIFO calculation but more than the LIFO calculation.	When prices are rising (or falling), the user can arrange to sell identical higher-cost or lower-cost items.
	Therefore FIFO can result in a distorted net income figure.	Therefore LIFO results in a more accurate net income figure.	Therefore weighted average results in a net income figure which is between FIFO and LIFO.	Therefore specific identification can be more susceptible to net income manipulation.

BALANCE SHEET:

— Inventory Valuation	Approximates replacement cost (particularly when inventory turnover is rapid) since ending inventory consists of most current costs.	Consists of the earliest costs which may not approximate current replacement cost.	Consists of average cost which is more current than that calculated under LIFO but which does not approximate replacement cost as well as that occurring under FIFO.	The actual cost of each item in inventory is included in inventory.
	Therefore FIFO results in a more current balance sheet inventory figure.	Therefore LIFO can result in a distorted balance sheet inventory figure.		

C.   Inventory Systems

There are four different methods that can be used to calculate inventory. Two of these methods are based on calculations made by the company: the periodic inventory method and the perpetual inventory method. Two are based on estimates made by the company: the gross profit method and the retail inventory method. They are shown in Figure 8-3.

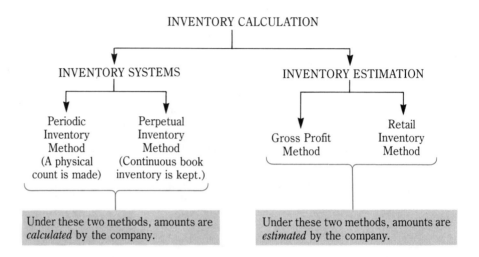

Figure 8-3   Methods for Calculating Inventory

These four different quantity calculation methods are discussed in the remaining part of this chapter.

Periodic Inventory System

Under the periodic inventory system, as discussed in Chapter 5, the inventory is determined by a physical count. Therefore, the change in inventory is recorded only periodically, usually at the end of each year. A physical count requires careful planning and inventory-taking procedures: numbered inventory tags are attached to all inventory items; quantities counted are recorded on these tags; and the numerical sequence of the completed tags is subsequently checked to ensure that quantities are accounted for. The inventory descriptions and quantities are next transferred to inventory summary sheets, which also have blank columns for the entry of costs and the calculation of total costs.

Chartered accountants and other independent auditors make test counts during a physical count to satisfy themselves that inventory quantities to be used to calculate total inventory cost are correct. Following the physical count, costs are assigned to the units in inventory. As discussed, specific identification, FIFO, LIFO, or average (weighted) costing can be used.

Perpetual Inventory System

The perpetual inventory system, as discussed in Chapter 5, requires a continuous balance of inventory on hand to be calculated in terms of units and often also in terms of cost. The use of this system requires maintaining a subsidiary inventory record; an example of a subsidiary accounts receivable record was illustrated in Chapter 6. An example of a subsidiary inventory record with recorded purchases and sales in terms of units is illustrated in Figure 8-4.

	Purchased		Sold		Balance		
	Quantity	Unit Cost	Quantity	Unit Cost	Quantity	Unit Cost	Total Cost
Purchase #1	1				1		
Sale #1			1		0		
Purchase #2	1				1		
Purchase #3	1				2		
Sale #2			1		1		
Purchase #4	1				2		
Sale #3			1		1		
Purchase #5	1				2		
Sale #4			1		1		

Figure 8-4   Inventory record card

As each purchase is received, the quantity received and the balance on hand are recorded in the appropriate columns. When inventory is sold, units sold are recorded in the units sold column; a new balance on hand is also calculated and recorded. Thus, a change in inventory quantity is recorded each time a purchase or sale is made. The inventory at the end of an accounting period is one unit in Figure 8-4.

A physical count is made periodically to verify the quantities are actually on hand.

Note the availability of columns for cost calculations. As purchases and sales are made, costs are assigned to the goods using whatever cost flow assumption is in use.

Illustrative Problem — FIFO Costing under the Perpetual System

The purchases and sales from Figure 8-4 are repeated, incorporating unit costs.

	Purchased		Sold		Balance		
	Quantity	*Unit Cost*	*Quantity*	*Unit Cost*	*Quantity*	*Unit Cost*	*Total Cost*
Purchase #1	1	1			1	× 1	= 1
Sale #1			1	1	0	× 0	0
Purchase #2	1	2			1	× 2	2
Purchase #3	1	3			2 ⟶ 1 × 2 ⟶ 1 × 3 }		5
Sale #2			1	2	1	× 3	3
Purchase #4	1	4			2 ⟶ 1 × 3 ⟶ 1 × 4 }		7
Sale #3			1	3	1	× 4	4
Purchase #5	1	5			2 ⟶ 1 × 4 ⟶ 1 × 5 }		9
Sale #4			1	4	1	× 5	= 5

Figure 8-5   Inventory record card using FIFO costing

Under FIFO, the earliest purchase costs are assigned to sales. Note that the cost of ending inventory under the perpetual system is the same as the calculation for FIFO under the periodic inventory system. When FIFO is used as the cost flow assumption, the calculation of ending inventory under the perpetual and periodic system will always be the same. (This correlation is not the case for LIFO or weighted average costing.)

Illustrative Problem — LIFO Costing under the Perpetual System

The example in Figure 8-4 is repeated in Figure 8-6, using the LIFO cost flow assumption.

Under LIFO, the cost of ending inventory is assumed to consist of the first unit purchased and not sold. In the case of Purchase #1, only one unit was on hand at the time of the sale. Therefore, the cost of $1 left the system when Sale #1 was made. The first unit purchased and still on hand is Purchase #2 for $2.

	Purchased		Sold		Balance		
	Quantity	*Unit Cost*	*Quantity*	*Unit Cost*	*Quantity*	*Unit Cost*	*Total Cost*
Purchase #1	1	1			1	× 1	= 1
Sale #1			1	1	0	0	0
Purchase #2	1	2			1	2	2
Purchase #3	1	3			2 ⟶ 1 × 2 ⟶ 1 × 3 }		5
Sale #2			1	3	1	× 2	2
Purchase #4	1	4			2 ⟶ 1 × 2 ⟶ 1 × 4 }		6
Sale #3			1	4	1	× 2	2
Purchase #5	1	5			2 ⟶ 1 × 2 ⟶ 1 × 5 }		7
Sale #4			1	5	1	× 2	= 2

Figure 8-6   Inventory record card using LIFO costing

The ending inventory cost under LIFO with the perpetual inventory system differs from that calculated under LIFO with the periodic system as follows:

	LIFO Periodic	LIFO Perpetual
Ending Inventory	$1	$2

The difference in amounts calculated is attributable to the fact that, under LIFO/perpetual, the most recent cost immediately prior to a sale leaves the system when the sale is actually made. Under LIFO/periodic, the calculation is made at year-end; therefore, the most recent cost at that date leaves the system. In periods of rising prices, LIFO/perpetual usually produces a higher ending inventory amount than LIFO/periodic.

Illustrative Problem — Moving Average Costing under the Perpetual System

The calculation of ending inventory under moving average costing is illustrated in Figure 8-7, using the same data as before.

	Purchased		Sold		Balance		
	Quantity	Unit Cost	Quantity	Unit Cost	Quantity	Unit Cost	Total Cost
Purchase #1	1	1			1	× 1	= 1
Sale #1			1	1	0	0	0
Purchase #2	1	2			1	2	2
Purchase #3	1	3			2	× 2.50	5
Sale #2			1	2.50	1	× 2.50	2.50
Purchase #4	1	4			2	× 3.25	6.50
Sale #3			1	3.25	1	× 3.25	3.25
Purchase #5	1	5			2	× 4.125	8.25
Sale #4			1	4.125	1	× 4.125	= 4.125

Figure 8-7   Inventory record card using moving average costing

The moving average is calculated as follows:

1 × $2.00	=	$2.00
1 × $3.00	=	$3.00
2		$5.00
Average	=	$2.50

1 × $2.50	=	$2.50
1 × $4.00	=	$4.00
2		$6.50
Average	=	$3.25

1 × $3.25	=	$3.25
1 × $5.00	=	$5.00
2		$8.25
Average	=	$4.125

Under moving average, a weighted average is calculated each time a purchase is made. Accordingly, a weighted average is calculated after purchases #3, #4, and #5. The ending inventory cost is $4.125 under moving average costing; under weighted average costing, ending inventory amounts to $3. In periods of rising prices, moving average usually produces a higher ending inventory than weighted average.

Inventory Systems Compared

The results produced by each of the cost flow assumptions under both periodic and perpetual systems are compared; these results also assume that prices are rising.

	FIFO		LIFO		Average	
	Periodic	*Perpetual*	*Periodic*	*Perpetual*	*Periodic*	*Perpetual*
Ending Inventory	$5	$5	$1	$2	$3	$4.125

Ending inventory is always the same under both systems. FIFO always produces the highest ending inventory amount (and therefore income) when prices are rising because ending inventory consists of the most recent costs.

Ending inventory usually differs under both systems; LIFO/ periodic usually produces a lower amount because ending inventory is calculated at the end of the period under periodic; under perpetual, the inventory balance is calculated after each sale. LIFO always produces the lowest ending inventory amount (and therefore income) when prices are rising.

Ending inventory usually differs under both systems; periodic/weighted average usually produces a lower amount than perpetual/moving average. Under periodic, one average cost is calculated for the whole period; under perpetual, an average is calculated following each purchase. An average method produces an ending inventory amount that is between the amounts for FIFO and LIFO.

The amount of difference between LIFO costs calculated on either the periodic or the perpetual system and between FIFO costs calculated on either system will correspond to the magnitude of the change in prices during the period and to the rapidity of inventory turnover.

When prices are falling, the results produced under the different cost flow assumptions are reversed. LIFO produces the highest ending inventory, and FIFO the lowest. The average method produces an amount between those under LIFO and FIFO.

Under the periodic inventory method, the quantity of the ending inventory is determined by a complete physical count; the quantity in inventory is not readily available during the accounting period. When a perpetual inventory method is used, a continuous book inventory is kept for each type of item in inventory. The quantity in inventory is readily available at any time under this method.

The perpetual inventory incorporates an internal control feature that is lost under the periodic inventory method. Losses resulting from theft and error can easily be determined when the actual quantity of goods on hand is compared with the quantities shown in the inventory records as being on hand. This advantage is offset, however, by the time and expense required to update the inventory records continuously, particularly where there are thousands of different items of various sizes in stock. Computerization makes this record-keeping easier and less expensive, particularly when the inventory accounting system is tied in to the sales system in such a way that inventory is updated whenever a sale is recorded.

The perpetual inventory system also requires that the cost of inventory sold — which is an expense — be recorded periodically, so that a dollar amount of inventory is accurately shown in the general ledger.

The journal entries required under the FIFO/perpetual and FIFO/periodic systems differ for Purchase #1 and Sale #2, as illustrated below. Under the perpetual system, purchases are debited to the asset account Merchandise Inventory. Under the perpetual system, when a sale is made, the cost of inventory is recorded as an expense.

Periodic Inventory			*Perpetual Inventory*		
Purchases	1		Merchandise Inventory	1	
Accounts Payable		1	Accounts Payable		1
To record Purchase #1.			To record Purchase #1.		
Accounts Receivable	2		Accounts Receivable	2	
Sales		2	Sales		2
To record Sale #1.			To record Sale #1.		
			Cost of Goods Sold	1	
			Merchandise Inventory		1
(No Entry Required)			To record the cost of Sale #1.		

Inventory Errors

A physical inventory count usually results in the discovery of shortages and excesses (overages). The use of a perpetual inventory system results in better inventory control, since these differences are isolated when the counted quantity is compared with the quantity that should be on hand according to the perpetual inventory record.

The following comparative income statements illustrate the impact of an error in ending inventory one year and its impact the following year. A constant amount of sales, purchases, and inventory is assumed to highlight the impact of a $1,000 ending inventory understatement in 19X6 and the resulting $1,000 opening inventory understatement in 19X7.

	19X6		19X7	
		Ending Inventory Under-	Opening Inventory Under-	
	Correct	*Stated*	*Stated*	*Correct*
Sales	$30,000	$30,000	$30,000	$30,000
Cost of Goods Sold:				
Opening Inventory	$ 2,000	$ 2,000	$ 1,000	$ 2,000
Purchases	20,000	20,000	20,000	20,000
Goods Available for Sale	$22,000	$22,000	$21,000	$22,000
Ending Inventory	2,000	1,000	2,000	2,000
Total Cost of Goods Sold	$20,000	$21,000	$19,000	$20,000
Gross Profit	$10,000	$ 9,000	$11,000	$10,000

As can be seen, income is misstated in both 19X6 and 19X7 when ending inventory is erroneously recorded, because the ending inventory of 19X6 is the opening inventory of 19X7. The opposite occurs when inventory is overstated. The effect of inventory errors on both ending and opening inventory can be shown as follows:

Effect of Error on:

	INCOME STATEMENT		BALANCE SHEET
Type of Error	*Cost of Goods Sold*	*Income*	*Ending Inventory*
1. Ending Inventory Understated (↓)			
1st year — ending inventory (↓)	↑	↓	↓
2nd year — opening inventory (↓)	↓	↑	not applicable
2. Ending Inventory Overstated (↑)			
1st year — ending inventory (↑)	↓	↑	↑
2nd year — opening inventory (↑)	↑	↓	not applicable

If found in 19X6, the error could be corrected by the following journal entry prepared according to the perpetual inventory system:

Merchandise Inventory	1,000	
Cost of Goods Sold		1,000

The debit and credit entries would be reversed, if the error had been an overstatement rather than an understatement.

D. Estimating Inventory Costs

The periodic and perpetual inventory systems have the following procedure in common: both begin with quantities of items that are either listed on cards (perpetual) or counted during a physical count (periodic), and costs are assigned to the counted units; a total dollar amount of inventory is subsequently calculated. By this means, individual inventory items are summed to get an inventory total amount.

The next two inventory systems to be discussed differ from these two in that they do not begin with inventory quantities that are then used to arrive at an inventory dollar amount. Rather, these methods calculate only the total dollar amount of inventory and do not consider quantities. How is this possible? By *estimating* the inventory dollar amount, using financial data of the firm. There are two reasons why estimating inventory is useful.

Reason 1:   Useful for Inventory Control

Under the periodic inventory system, a physical inventory count determines the quantity of items on hand. When costs are assigned to these items and these individual costs are added, a total inventory amount is calculated. Is this dollar amount correct? Should it be larger? How can one tell if an inventory shortage exists for comparison with the physical amount calculated? An estimate of what the amount should be is one answer.

Reason 2:   Useful for the Preparation of Interim Financial Statements

Where a perpetual inventory system is not used, estimating the inventory amount offers a means of determining a company's inventory at frequent intervals, thereby avoiding the cost and inconvenience of taking a physical count each time monthly statements are being prepared.

Calculating Gross Profit

Two methods used to estimate the inventory dollar amount are the *gross profit method* and the *retail inventory method*.

Both the gross profit method and retail inventory method are based on a calculation of the gross profit rate in the income statement. The following partial income statement shows how to calculate the gross profit rate (percentage).

Sales		$1,000	100%	
Cost of Goods Sold:				
Opening Inventory	$100			
Net Purchases	700			
Cost of Goods Available for Sale	$800			
Estimated Ending Inventory	200			The gross profit in this case is
Total Cost of Goods Sold		600	60%	
Gross Profit		$400	40%	40% ($400 ÷ $1,000)

Here, the gross profit is $400. This is the profit left over after the cost of the goods sold ($600) is deducted from net sales ($1,000). As calculated, the gross profit is 40 percent of net sales.

The word *gross* is used by accountants in this case to indicate that the operating expenses necessary to run the business must still be deducted before (net) profit can be calculated. As is shown, the gross profit is 40 percent of the net sales ($1,000 $\times$ 40% = $400).

> The calculation of the gross profit rate is the first step in making an estimate of the ending inventory amount.

Ending inventory estimation also requires an understanding of the relationship of ending inventory with cost of goods sold. As can be seen in the following comparative examples, data from the preceding partial income statement has been removed.

Cost of Goods Sold:	
Opening Inventory	$100
Net Purchases	700
Goods Available for Sale	$800
Estimated Ending Inventory	?
Total Cost of Goods Sold	$600

Cost of Goods Sold:	
Opening Inventory	$100
Net Purchases	700
Goods Available for Sale	$800
Estimated Ending Inventory	200
Total Cost of Goods Sold	?

How much of the $800-worth of goods that the company had available to sell, is still not sold at December 31 (that is, how much is in ending inventory)? How do you calculate the dollar amount of this inventory?

It had	$800
It sold	600
∴ It still has	$200

How much of the $800-worth of goods that were available to be sold, have been sold? And how do you calculate the dollar amount of this inventory at December 31?

It had	$800
It still has	200
∴ It must have sold	$600

In these two examples, two questions are posed: What is the amount of cost of goods sold at December 31? and What is the amount of ending inventory at December 31? What should now be obvious is that once one of these two questions is answered, the answer to the other question can be easily calculated. The cost of goods sold and ending inventory are two sides of the same coin. Knowing this relationship will make it easier to understand how estimating inventory works in the gross profit and retail inventory method.

Gross Profit Method

Gross profit method
A method of estimating the amount of inventory without taking a physical count. This method can be used to verify the reasonableness of the actual inventory calculated, but it is not usually acceptable for calculating the amount of inventory to be reported in financial statements.

The **gross profit method** assumes that the *rate* (percentage) of gross profit on sales remains approximately the same from year to year. Therefore, if this rate (percentage) can be calculated, the dollar amount of inventory can be estimated easily. Assume that, during the previous two years, Bluebeard Computer Corporation has averaged a gross profit rate of 40 percent, as shown below.

| | Prior Years | | | This Year |
	1	*2*	*Totals*	
Sales	$400	$600	$1,000	$2,000
Cost of Goods Sold	200	400	600	?
Gross Profit	$200	$200	$ 400	? ← Calculated as $800.
Gross Profit Rate (%)	50%	33⅓%	40%	40% assumed

In this case, with the assumption made by the gross profit method, the gross profit rate for Year 3 is 40 percent, and the gross profit is calculated at $800 ($2,000 sales × 40% gross profit). Therefore, cost of goods sold must be the difference between $2,000 and $800; that is, $1,200. The income statement for Year 3 now can be completed.

| | Prior Years | | | This Year |
	1	*2*	*Totals*	
Sales	$400	$600	$1,000	$2,000
Cost of Goods Sold	200	400	600	1,200
Gross Profit	$200	$200	$ 400	$ 800
Gross Profit Rate (%)	50%	33⅓%	40%	40% assumed ← These amounts are calculated based on the assumed GP rate.

Using these figures, the partial income statement for Year 3 appears as follows, after the inclusion of the opening inventory and purchases amounts:

Sales		$2,000
Cost of Goods Sold:		
Opening Inventory	$ 200	
Net Purchases	1,100	
Cost of Goods Available for Sale	$1,300	
Estimated Ending Inventory	?	
Total Cost of Goods Sold		1,200
Gross Profit		$ 800

This information is always given to students for problem solving. In actual practice, if necessary, these amounts can also be reconstructed from company and other records.

How much is the ending inventory at December 31? It must be $100, the difference between the goods the company had available to sell ($1,300) and the amount it actually sold ($1,200).

The gross profit method of estimating inventory is particularly useful in situations where goods have been stolen or destroyed by fire; in these cases it is obviously impossible to make a physical inventory count.

Retail Inventory Method

Retail inventory method
A method of estimating the amount of inventory without taking a physical count; converts retail value of inventory to cost.

Under the **retail inventory method** both the cost and selling prices of goods purchased (called *retail* prices) are recorded and are available at the time of inventory estimation.

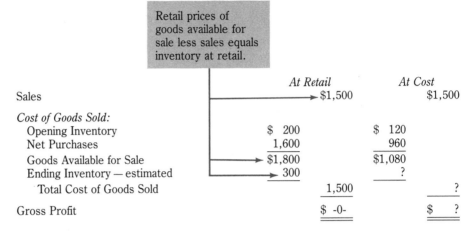

Retail prices of goods available for sale less sales equals inventory at retail.

		At Retail	At Cost
Sales		$1,500	$1,500
Cost of Goods Sold:			
Opening Inventory	$ 200		$ 120
Net Purchases	1,600		960
Goods Available for Sale	$1,800		$1,080
Ending Inventory — estimated	300		?
Total Cost of Goods Sold		1,500	?
Gross Profit		$ -0-	$?

As can be seen, the ending inventory at retail is easily calculated by deducting sales during the period ($1,500) from the goods available for sale priced at retail ($1,800). How much is the ending inventory at retail for this company?

It sold	$1,500	(using retail sales prices)
It had available	1,800	(using retail cost of goods available prices)
∴ It must still have	$ 300	(this is the ending inventory at retail prices)

How much is the ending inventory at cost? Ending inventory at retail is converted to cost by applying the cost percentage to the $300 ending inventory at retail prices. First, the cost percentage is calculated.

	Cost	Retail
Opening Inventory	$ 120	$ 200
Net Purchases	960	1,600
Goods Available for Sale	$1,080	$1,800

The cost percentage is the ratio of cost of goods available to the retail price of those goods.

Cost Percentage (Ratio of Cost to Retail)
= $\frac{\$1,080}{\$1,800}$ = 60%.

Then the cost percentage is used to convert the $300 ending inventory at retail prices.

The retail inventory of $300 is converted to cost inventory of $180 using the cost percentage.

Ending Inventory at Retail = $300
Estimated Ending Inventory at Cost (60% of $300) = $180

The retail inventory method of estimating ending inventory is commonly used by department stores where inventory is taken at the selling price. It is easy to calculate and produces a relatively accurate cost of ending inventory, provided that no change in the cost percentage has occurred during the current period. This method results in an average cost of ending inventory, because the cost percentage is an average and therefore makes no assumption that goods are sold in any particular order.

Certain terms such as *mark-ups* and *mark-downs* have become associated with the retail inventory method but are more appropriately dealt with in a more advanced accounting course. For purposes of this text, mark-ups and mark-downs are ignored in the calculation of the cost percentage.

Inventory Estimation Systems Compared

Both the gross profit method and the retail inventory method are based on calculation of the gross profit rate. The gross profit method uses past experience as a basis; the retail inventory method uses current experience, which is more reliable and therefore preferable.

APPENDIX: The Current Cost Model

The *CICA Handbook* recommends that certain current cost information relating to both the income statement and the balance sheet be disclosed as supplementary information to financial statements based on historical cost. In the case of inventories, cost of goods sold should be measured on a current cost basis, using current costs at the date of sale (section 4510.38). The balance sheet inventory valuation should also be measured on a current cost basis, using current costs at the balance sheet date (section 4510.42).

The use of current costs in record-keeping, or the incorporation of current costs into the body of financial statements, is not included among the *CICA Handbook* recommendations. Availability of current cost supplementary information is seen as adequate for the financial statement reader to assess the impact of changing prices on the entity's need to set aside funds for inventory replacement and thereby maintain its level of **operating capability**. The objective of the current cost model is the maintenance of operating capability; this capability at the end of the accounting period must be the same as at the beginning of the period before income was earned.

Operating capability
The ability to operate at the same level at year-end as existed at the beginning of the year.

Impact on the Income Statement

The cost flow analysis made for management at Bluebeard Computer Corporation is further developed to consider the impact of current costs. Following the recommendation in the *CICA Handbook*, the current cost to replace each of the four units at the time of each sale was used; the total current cost of these four units amounted to $18. With this additional datum, income measurement using the FIFO and LIFO cost flow assumptions was compared with that resulting when current costs were used. BCC's executives are astounded with the results.

| | Measurement of Income | | |
	FIFO Cost Flow	LIFO Cost Flow	Current Cost Model
Sales	$20	$20	$20
Cost of Goods Sold:			
Purchases	$15	$15	
Ending Inventory	5	1	
Total Cost of Goods Sold	10	14	18
Gross Profit	$10	$ 6	$ 2
Operating expenses	6	6	6
Net Income (Loss)	$ 4	$-0-	$(4)

This further analysis indicates that using FIFO not only produces a phantom profit of $4 but also that the current cost calculation indicates BCC would be losing its ability to operate at the same level in the future; that is, its operating capability would be reduced. Eventually, it might even be unable to replace inventory without increased borrowing. Even worse, the $4 Net Income under FIFO might be considered by shareholders to be available for the payment of dividends. Employees might also feel justified in asking for increased remuneration and bonuses, while government would, regardless, continue to collect income taxes on these phantom profits.

It is true that the LIFO cost flow assumption produces a more realistic measurement of income than FIFO. However, only the current cost model indicates that BCC is losing its operating capacity and might be unable to replace inventory without increased borrowing.

Impact on the Balance Sheet

The impact of balance sheet inventory valuation for Bluebeard was also calculated. Following the recommendation in the *CICA Handbook*, the current cost to replace ending inventory at the balance sheet date was calculated; the current cost of the 1 unit in ending inventory at the balance sheet date was $7. With this additional datum, a comparison of balance sheet inventory valuation yielded the following:

	FIFO Cost Flow	LIFO Cost Flow	Current Cost Model
Ending Inventory	$5	$1	$7

The management at BCC are aware that the LIFO cost flow assumption generally produces an unrealistic ending inventory amount when prices are rising. They are surprised that FIFO, which is generally supposed to approximate replacement cost, could still be so short of the mark in their case. The current cost model calculation of ending inventory reinforces further the fact that BCC will lose its operating capability if it continues to operate at the same level in the future.

Income Measurement and Asset Valuation

The choice between a cost flow assumption and the use of current cost involves the continuing controversy between the importance of income measurement and of asset valuation. If prices were stable, this controversy would not exist: each cost flow assumption and the current cost model would produce approximately the same result. A problem arises, however, because prices fluctuate.

Real Life Example 8-1

Barbecon

Barbecon is a medium-sized public company. We have a divisionalized organization and operate three basic businesses: the distribution of printing paper to the graphic arts industry, the manufacture of envelopes for printers and consumers, the manufacture and distribution of social stationery.

Our suppliers hit us with a series of significant paper price increases that created a perplexing situation. The most satisfying result was an unprecedented burst of profit; we were suddenly making money at almost twice the rate as any time in the company's 100-year history. This, unfortunately, was the only good news. Although profits were extraordinary, we were pressing bank lines to the limit. The investment required to maintain physical inventory levels jumped with each price increase. Stockpiling in anticipation of further increases compounded the problem.

Cash was not the only concern. Each successive increase generated illusory, but fully taxable, inventory profits. Our directors asked whether we should distribute part of these profits as dividends. Our managers expected these windfall gains to be included in bonus calculations, even though they were not a reflection of operating performance. Earnings had never been better. But, instead of prosperity, capital erosion, cash flow problems, and misleading financial rsults were the order of the day.

We needed a method of accounting that would both explain the effects of rapid paper price increases on our organization and be easily understood and practical in application. Current cost accounting satisfied these requirements.

The basic principle of current cost accounting is that we do not recognize profits until provision is made to replace physical operating capacity. In the case of inventory, for example, physical capital maintenance means splitting historical cost gross margins in two and distinguishing between **trading** and **holding gains** (see below).

In the concept of holding gains, we found the explanation for both our exceptional profit performance and our cash flow problems. Our historical cost accounting system recognized inventory holding gains as earnings. As a result, we enjoyed enriched margins when we sold old inventory at current prices. This sounds logical, but it misrepresented the economic reality of the situation. Inventory gains are not profits. They do not represent distributable earnings. When prices rise, a company must spend additional money to maintain physical operating capacity. Our historical cost earnings were overstated by the amount of the inventory profits. These holding gains represent the cost of maintaining our business capital at existing levels.

Once we recognized that inventory gains are not distributable, we understood why we had *cash flow* problems. Inventory gains are not cash gains; the extra cash generated by selling old stock at current prices disappears when the cash is used to replenish inventory at higher replacement costs. If the need to maintain physical capital is not explicitly recognized in pricing policies, real earnings fall. Businesses are forced to finance the same level of inventory through increased borrowing.

The effects of inflation on our company were significant, and we decided it was essential for us to integrate current cost accounting into our management information system. Because the merchant side of our business was the most susceptible to the distortions of inflation, it became our starting point.

Source   Richard S. Clark, "Current Cost Accounting . . . One Company's Case", *CAMagazine*, July 1980, p. 25.

THE COMPONENTS OF GROSS PROFIT

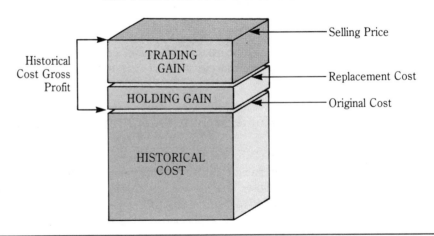

Income Measurement

When prices are rising, FIFO can result in a distorted net income figure because earliest — usually lower — costs are matched with current — usually higher — sales prices. LIFO, on the other hand, results in a more accurate net income calculation because more current — and usually higher — costs are matched with these same current — and usually higher — sales prices.

Trading gain
During a period of inflation, the difference between the sale price of an asset and its current replacement cost.

The use of current costs at the date of sale, as is recommended in the *CICA Handbook*, would appear to satisfy best the *CICA Handbook* recommendation that "the method selected for determining cost should be one which results in the fairest matching of costs against revenues regardless of whether or not the method corresponds to the physical flow of goods" (section 3030.09). On the surface, it would appear that no fairer matching than current cost with current revenue would be possible.

Asset Valuation

When prices are rising, FIFO results in a more current — and usually higher — balance sheet inventory figure, while LIFO can result in a less current — usually lower — balance sheet amount, because the earliest cost may not even approximate current replacement value.

Holding gain
During a period of inflation the difference between the original and replacement cost of an asset.

Again, use of current cost at the balance sheet date in this case — to value ending inventory, as is recommended in the *CICA Handbook* — results in the most current balance sheet inventory cost amount. In this way, problems associated with cost flow assumptions are avoided.

The Matching Concept in Perspective

As explained earlier, the emphasis of the current cost model is its concern with the maintenance of the entity's operating capability, which should be the same at the end of an accounting period as it was at the beginning.

A dilemma for the accounting profession centres on the historical cost concept. It is retained for financial statement purposes because historical costs are objectively determined — even though the measure used, the stable dollar concept, is invalid in periods of rapid inflation. Although current cost data are more relevant, the objection to their incorporation into the body of financial statements is that their determination of current costs is generally a subjective process, based in some cases, on management's estimates and assumptions. One wonders if the choice is in reality between being approximately right or precisely wrong.

Although current cost data are more relevant, their use in record-keeping, as well as their incorporation into financial statements, is not included among the *CICA Handbook* recommendations. As noted, the availability of current cost supplementary information is assumed to be adequate for the financial statements reader. A review of published supplementary information leads one to question the validity of this assumption.

A Word of Caution

In addition to the recommendations for the measurement of cost of goods sold and ending inventory using current costs, there are also certain other effects associated with changing prices. These relate to the impact of financing or other adjustments that may alleviate, at least in part, the loss of operating capability during the year.

A more complete treatment of these topics is usually the subject matter of advanced accounting courses and is not attempted here. Caution must also be exercised in generalizing to other situations the impact of price changes on Bluebeard Computer Corporation. Different circumstances can be expected to yield different results.

The current cost model is in an experimental state at the present time and is under constant evaluation. No general concensus has yet emerged concerning the usefulness of the information generated; it is expected, however, to provide useful insights into the operations of each entity using the model.

Discussion Questions

1. Explain the importance of maintaining inventory levels for: (a) management, (b) accountants, (c) investors and creditors.
2. What is meant by the laid-down cost of inventory?
3. How does a flow of goods differ from a flow of costs? Do generally accepted accounting principles require that the flow of costs be similar to the movement of goods? Explain.
4. What factors are considered in costing inventory? Which of these factors is most difficult to determine? Why?
5. Under the LIFO cost flow assumption, do ending inventories consist of the earliest or most recent costs? Do cost of goods sold include the earliest or most recent costs?
6. In recent years, the cost of goods acquired has been increasing because of inflation. What problems for financial reporting have resulted?
7. In a period of rising prices, which method of inventory valuation will result in the highest net income figure? the highest ending inventory amount?
8. Assume that you are paid a year-end bonus according to the amount of net income earned during the year. When prices are rising, would you prefer to value inventories on a FIFO or a LIFO basis? Explain, using an example to support your answer. Would your choice be the same if prices were falling?
9. Why is consistency in inventory valuation necessary? Does the application of the consistency principle preclude a change from LIFO to FIFO? Explain.
10. The ending inventory of CBCA Inc. is overstated by $5,000 at December 31, 19X4. What is the effect on 19X4 net income? What is the effect on 19X5 net income assuming that no other inventory errors have occurred during 19X5?
11. For Questions 11 and 12, refer to Real Life Example 8-1. What are phantom profits? Where do they come from?
12. What is a holding gain? a trading gain? How do they differ? Use an example to explain the difference.
13. How does the use of current costs eliminate the need for any cost-flow assumption?
14. What is the primary reason for the use of the LOCAM method of inventory valuation? What does the term *market* mean? What is recommended in the *CICA Handbook* regarding use of this term?
15. When inventory is valued at LOCAM, what does *cost* refer to?
16. What is the generally accepted method used for inventory valuation?
17. When can inventory be valued at less than cost?
18. When should ending inventory be shown at cost, even though cost is higher than replacement cost?
19. What are the objections against LOCAM? Evaluate these objections.
20. LOCAM assumes that retail prices will decline when inventory cost declines. Is this realistic? Why or why not?
21. A book inventory is required under the perpetual inventory system. What is the difference between a book inventory and a physical inventory?
22. What internal control feature of the perpetual inventory method is lost under the periodic inventory method? Would you recommend that a hardware store use the perpetual inventory method? Why or why not?
23. What procedure do the periodic and perpetual inventory systems both have in common?
24. Discuss the methods available to cost inventory under each of the periodic and perpetual inventory systems.
25. Why is estimating inventory useful?
26. Contrast the journal entries required under the periodic and perpetual inventory systems.
27. Do the gross profit and retail inventory methods use inventory quantities to calculate the dollar amount of inventory?
28. How does the calculation of ending inventory differ from the gross profit method to the retail inventory method? Use an example to illustrate.
29. When is the use of the gross profit method particularly useful?
30. Does the retail inventory method assume any particular movement of inventory? What cost flow is calculated under this method?

Discussion Cases

Discussion Case 8-1:   Control Data's Fall from Grace

It appeared to be quite a scoop. About three weeks ago, WTCN-TV, the NBC affiliate in Minneapolis, broadcast an interview with a man identified as "a former high-level Control Data Corporation executive". He said the big data-processing company was suffering from low morale and technical problems and would soon lay off 5000 employees.

The broadcast was laced with intrigue. The man's voice was disguised and his face hidden from view — undermining the credibility, Control Data says, of the whole report. Nonetheless, the broadcast caused an uproar in Minneapolis, where Control Data employs nearly 18 000 people.

The company's switchboard was inundated with anxious calls. Control Data issued a memo to its employees, assuring them no lay-off was in the offing. And Richard C. Reid, Control Data's spokesman, still insists that there are "no plans for that at all".

But not even Reid could deny the broadcast's main point: Control Data, one of the giants of the computer industry, is in trouble.

Once a leading maker of mainframe computers, disk drives, and other data-processing gear, it has failed to keep up with sweeping changes in just about every market in which it competes. Analysts say its products have been late to market, costly, or out of touch with customer demand. The result has been a drop in profits and market share that is so steep that, some say, Control Data may never catch up.

. . .

Control Data's problems with [13 cm] 5¼-inch disk drives have been unnerving. The company's competitors rushed to market with the little units in 1977, when they became the storage device of choice for personal computer makers. Control Data did not produce its first 5¼-inch drive until 1980.

Early in 1981, many domestic manufacturers began producing 5¼-inch drives overseas in anticipation of an onslaught of lower-cost drives from Japan. That onslaught has now occurred. In the last six months alone, wholesale prices have fallen to about $75 a drive from $150. Control Data, however, did not move its production offshore until last year. Moreover, the rest of the industry began producing smaller units known as half-height drives in early 1983. Control Data's half-height versions did not appear until late that year.

The result, experts say, is that Control Data is stuck with a huge inventory of overpriced 5¼-inch drives that it must sell at a loss.

Source Eric N. Berg, "Control Data's Fall from Grace", *The New York Times*, February 17, 1985, p. 4-F.

For Discussion

1. In light of this article, how would you, as potential investor, view the stated inventory on Control Data's published financial statements?
2. Should Control Data sell its inventory at a loss or hold it to wait for prices to rise? Explain.

Discussion Case 8-2:   Steel Service Centres

The warehouse area of Denman & Davis in the industrial city is piled neatly to its high ceilings with tonnes of steel — bars, angles, lattices, beams, flat sheets and rolls. If the company were a steel producer, the huge inventory would probably augur sluggish sales. But for Denman & Davis, the huge stock means business is thriving.

Denman & Davis is a steel service centre, a steel industry middleman that buys steel from both domestic and foreign mills and cuts and shapes it to customers' specifications. It is a veritable "supermarket for metal", as its president, David N. Deinzer, put it. And it, along with hundreds of other steel service centres, represents one of the few oases of profits in the disaster area that is the steel industry. The steel industry's troubles have actually provided the boost that the service centres needed to catapult themselves out of being simply warehouses for metal — a function that some have performed

since the late 1890s — into the more profitable business of customer service.

For example, the domestic mills are in a cost squeeze and are concentrating on fewer products and high-volume runs.

The centres are benefiting not only from the steel producers's retrenchment, but also from the nationwide push among all manufacturing companies to pare raw materials inventories to the bone. There is a "just-in-time revolution" going on in inventory control, much of it patterned on the Japanese system of "kanban", which stresses a supplier/customer relationship in which vendors and distributors deliver raw materials so frequently that the supply on hand need never exceed more than one shift's requirements.

The service centres, thus, have become the inventory management specialists of the steel industry. They will hold the inventories for any number of steel users and deliver them on a pre-arranged schedule. And they will take a hefty mark-up for their troubles.

Most of the service centres spend a lot of time working directly with the customers' line managers, working out detailed schedules to reassure them that their needed raw materials will indeed be in the pipeline when they are needed. Through the trade association, the centres are trying to standardize part numbers and nomenclature to make it easier for customers to place orders. And most are wrestling with customers to get even more co-ordination of their production schedules with the service centre's own inventory.

Source Daniel F. Cuff, "Steel Service Centres: Oases in a Profit Desert", *The New York Times*, March 17, 1985, p. 8-F.

For Discussion

1. Comment on the merits of the "just-in-time" inventory system.
2. Because many manufacturing companies are trying to hold their raw material inventories to the lowest possible levels, the opportunity exists for competitors to take advantage. Such competing firms could stress customer service and high inventory levels. How would an investor evaluate the difference between two competing companies by their published financial statements?

Comprehension Problems

Comprehension Problem 8-1

The following transactions took place in BM Limited in 19X4:

Opening Inventory	2000 units @ $0.50
Purchases	1000 units @ $2.00
	500 units @ $1.00
	1000 units @ $2.50
Sales	2000 units

1. Ending inventory under LIFO/periodic would be:
   a. $3,000   c. $2,660
   b. $5,000   d. $2,000.
2. Ending inventory under FIFO/periodic would be:
   a. $3,333   c. $5,000
   b. $2,660   d. none of these.
3. Ending inventory under weighted average would be:
   a. $5,000   c. $3,000
   b. $3,333   d. none of these.
4. Cost of goods sold under LIFO/periodic would be:
   a. $2,660   c. $3,000
   b. $4,000   d. none of these.
5. Cost of goods sold under FIFO/periodic would be:
   a. $4,000   c. $2,660
   b. $1,000   d. none of these.
6. Cost of goods sold under weighted average would be:
   a. $2,667   c. $3,100
   b. $1,000   d. none of these.

Note: Answer problems regarding the current cost model only if the Appendix was studied in your course.

Comprehension Problem 8-2

The following transactions took place during January 19X7 in Kingsly Inc.; the company sold 200 units during this month.

	Units	Unit Cost
Opening Inventory	100	$1
Purchase #1	10	1
Purchase #2	20	2
Purchase #3	30	3
Purchase #4	40	4
Purchase #5	50	5

Required: Calculate the cost of goods on hand, cost of goods sold, and ending inventory by completing the schedule for each of:
1. FIFO/periodic   2. LIFO/periodic

	Goods on Hand			−	Goods Sold			=	Ending Inventory		
	Units	Unit Cost	Total Cost		Units	Unit Cost	Total Cost		Units	Unit Cost	Total Cost
Inventory (Jan. 1)	100	× $1	= $100								
Purchase #1											
Purchase #2											
Purchase #3											
Purchase #4											
Purchase #5											

Comprehension Problem 8-3

Choose the method of inventory valuation that corresponds to each of the statements that follow.

1. FIFO   2. LIFO   3. Weighted Average.

	Statement
3	Matches actual flows of goods with actual flow of costs in most cases
1	Matches new costs with new prices
2	Matches old costs with new prices
2	Results in phantom profits in a period of rising prices
2	Results in the lowest net income in periods of falling prices
3	Best matches current costs with current revenues
3	Does not assume any particular flow of goods
3	Results in the same inventory valuation, regardless of whether a periodic or perpetual inventory system is used
3	Best suited for situations in which inventory consists of perishable goods
2	Not accepted for income tax purposes in Canada
1	Emphasizes income determination
2	Emphasizes balance sheet valuation
3	Values inventory at approximate replacement cost
1	Results in lower income in a period of deflation
2	Results in higher income in a period of deflation

Comprehension Problem 8-4   (CGA adapted)

Listed below are four common accounting errors. Using the format shown, indicate the effect, if any, of each of the errors on the company's statements for the items shown. The company uses a periodic inventory method.

| | | 19X2 Statements | | | | | 19X3 Statements | | |
Errors:	Open. Invent.	End. Invent.	*19X2 Total Assets*	*19X2 Net Income*	Open Invent.	End. Invent.	*19X3 Total Assets*	*19X3 Net Income*
1. Goods bought in 19X2 were included in December 31 inventory, but purchases and liability were not recorded until early 19X3.	-0-							
2. Goods bought in 19X3 were included in December 31, 19X2 inventory, and purchases were recorded in 19X2.	-0-							
3. Goods were bought in 19X2 and purchases were recorded in that year; however, the goods were not included in the December 31 inventory as they should have been.	-0-							
4. Goods bought in 19X2 were excluded from December 31 inventory, and purchases were recorded early in 19X3.	-0-							

Required: Use a + (plus sign) to denote that an item is too high as a result of the error, a − (minus sign) to denote that it is too low, and a 0 (zero) to indicate no effect. The answer for the 19X2 opening inventory is indicated.

Comprehension Problem 8-5

Dunn Inc. sells golf balls. The following data are available regarding transactions relating to Brand X during the month of January:

	(a)	(b)	(c)	(d)	(e)	(f)	(g)	(h)	(i)
Jan. 1 bal.							100	(j)	100
Jan. 7 (k)	20	1.10	(l)				100	1.00	
							20	1.10	(n)
Jan. 14 Purchase	200	(m)	300				100		
							20		
							200	(o)	422
Jan. 19 Sale				100					
Jan. 22 Purchase	(p)	1.00	120						
Jan. 23 (q)				220					
Jan. 29 Sale				10					

Required:
1. Complete the schedule.
2. If Dunn were to use a LIFO/perpetual inventory system, what would the ending inventory amount to?
   a. $113.10   c. $135.50
   b. $111.00   d. $110.00
3. If a FIFO/perpetual inventory system were used, what would be the value of the ending inventory?
   a. $110.00   c. $133.10
   b. $111.10   d. $135.50
4. If a weighted average system of inventory were used, what would be the cost of Brand X golf balls available for sale at the end of January?
   a. $110.00   c. $133.10
   b. $111.00   d. $135.50
5. Which method would yield an inventory of $133.10?
   a. LIFO/perpetual   c. Weighted average
   b. FIFO/perpetual   d. Moving average
6. Under which of the following methods is the ending inventory lowest?
   a. LIFO/perpetual   c. Moving average
   b. FIFO/perpetual   d. Weighted average
7. If Dunn wishes to show the highest net income, which method of inventory evaluation should it choose?
   a. LIFO/perpetual   c. Weighted average
   b. FIFO/perpetual   d. Moving average
8. Under which method would the cost of goods sold be lowest?
   a. Weighted average   c. LIFO/perpetual
   b. FIFO/perpetual

Comprehension Problem 8-6

The records of Qonqa Corporation show the following information for 19X4. Sales during the period were $276,000. Opening inventory amounted to $26,000 at cost and $80,000 at retail. Purchases were $200,000 at retail and $90,000 at cost. The company paid $4,000 for transportation in.

Required: Choose the best answer for each of

1. Gross profit at retail was:
   - a. $157,720
   - b. $153,720
   - c. -0-
   - d. none of the above

2. The ending inventory at retail was:
   - a. -0-
   - b. $4,000
   - c. $1,720
   - d. $9,333

3. The cost percentage would be calculated as follows:
   - a. $\dfrac{280,000}{120,000}$
   - b. $\dfrac{120,000}{280,000}$
   - c. $\dfrac{116,000}{280,000}$
   - d. $\dfrac{280,000}{116,000}$

4. The ending inventory at cost was:
   - a. $1,720
   - b. $9,333
   - c. $4,000
   - d. -0-

5. The gross profit at cost was:
   - a. $157,720
   - b. -0-
   - c. $153,770
   - d. none of the above

6. The following are all characteristics of the retail method except:
   - a. Results in an average cost of ending inventory
   - b. Assumes goods are sold in a particular order
   - c. Is commonly used by department stores.

Problems

Problem 8-1

The following purchases were made during 19X8 at Hooper Corporation. The opening inventory consisted of 50 units at $1 each.

		Units	Unit Cost
Apr.	15	200	$2
May	25	200	$3
Jun.	7	200	$4
Oct.	15	200	$5

Required:
1. Calculate the number of units for opening inventory, purchases, and goods available for sale. Also calculate cost of goods available for sale at December 31, 19X8, under each of: FIFO/periodic, LIFO/periodic, and weighted average flows of goods.
2. If there are 200 units on hand at December 31, 19X8, calculate the cost of this inventory under each of: FIFO/periodic, LIFO/periodic, and weighted average flows of goods.
3. Calculate the number of units for goods available for sale, ending inventory, and goods sold. Calculate also the cost of goods sold under each of: FIFO/periodic, LIFO/periodic, and weighted average flows of goods.
4. The president of Hooper Corporation has asked you to consider the implications of using a weighted average cost flow method when in fact a LIFO flow of goods exists in the company. He is concerned that reported income does not reflect the real income of the firm. Prepare some calculations comparing the effect on income of:
   a. Using a weighted average cost flow method when there is LIFO flow of goods.
   b. Using a FIFO cost flow method when there is a LIFO flow of goods.
   c. Using a LIFO cost flow method when there is a LIFO flow of goods.
   What method of cost flow would you recommend in this case? Why?

Problem 8-2

The following data are taken from the records of Bethune Inc. for the month of January 19X8.

	Purchases			Sales	
	Units	Unit Cost		Units	Unit Price
Opening Inventory	25	$5			
Purchase #1	15	4	Sale #1	30	$6
Purchase #2	10	3	Sale #2	20	4
Purchase #3	35	2	Sale #3	50	2
Purchase #4	40	1			

Required:
1. Calculate the amount of inventory at the end of January assuming that inventory is costed using FIFO/periodic.
2. How would the ending inventory differ if it was costed using LIFO/periodic?
3. Calculate the amount of gross profit under each of the above costing methods. Which method matches inventory costs more closely with revenues? Why?
4. Assume that the LIFO costing method was permitted in Canada for income tax purposes and that the income tax was calculated at 50 percent of net income. Would more income tax be payable under the FIFO or LIFO method? Explain why.

Problem 8-3

Roxan Corporation sells three products. The inventory valuation of these products is shown below for years 19X3 and 19X4.

	19X3			19X4		
	Cost	*Market*	*Unit Basis (LOCAM)*	*Cost*	*Market*	*Unit Basis (LOCAM)*
Product X	$14,000	$15,000	?	$15,000	$16,000	?
Product Y	12,500	12,000	?	12,000	11,500	?
Product Z	11,000	11,500	?	10,500	10,000	?
Total	?	?	?	?	?	?

The partial comparative income statements for the two years follow:

	19X3		19X4	
Sales		$240,000		$280,000
Cost of Goods Sold:				
Opening Inventory	$ 20,000		$?	
Purchases	240,000		260,000	
Goods Available for Sale	$?		$?	
Ending Inventory	?		?	
Total Cost of Goods Sold		?		?
Gross Profit		$?		$?

Required:

1. If Roxan values its inventory using LOCAM, unit basis, complete the 19X3 and 19X4 cost, market, and LOCAM calculations, and the partial income statements for 19X3 and 19X4.
2. Complete the partial income statements, if Roxan uses LOCAM, group basis to value its inventory.
3. Complete the partial income statements, as if the inventory were valued at cost.
4. Which two methods of inventory valuation would yield the same gross profit for 19X3 and 19X4?
   a. Cost and LOCAM, unit basis
   b. Cost and LOCAM, group basis
   c. Cost basis.
5. Which two methods yield the maximum reported profit?

Problem 8-4

The Southern Company Limited made the following purchases during the year.

Jan. 7	8000 units @ $12.00 = $ 96,000	Jul. 04 16000 units @ $12.60 = $201,600
Mar. 30	9000 units @ $12.40 = $111,600	Sep. 02 6000 units @ $12.80 = $ 76,800
May 10	12000 units @ $12.00 = $144,000	Dec. 14 7000 units @ $12.70 = $ 88,900.

Closing inventory at December 31 amounted to 15 000 units. Selling price during the year was stable at $16 per unit. Opening inventory at January 1 amounted to 4000 units at $11.90 per unit.

Required:
1. Prepare a schedule of inventory as at December 31, under both a FIFO/periodic and LIFO/periodic.
2. Prepare an income statement showing sales, cost of goods sold and gross profit on both a FIFO and LIFO basis, using the above data.
3. Which method of inventory valuation matches revenues more closely with costs in this company under current conditions? Why?
4. The company is concerned about the continually increasing cost of its purchases. In January of the next year the cost price of each unit was $13. You are asked to explain the concept of phantom profits to the president. What will you say?

Problem 8-5

The controller of Westminster Products Ltd. has asked your help in forecasting the effect of rising and falling prices on income when FIFO and LIFO costing are used. The following inventory data are made available.

Opening Inventory	100 units at $10 = $1,000
Purchases	500 units at $12 = $6,000
Ending Inventory	250 units.

Partially completed income statements are presented.

	Rising Prices FIFO	LIFO	Falling Prices FIFO	LIFO
Sales	$5,000	$5,000	$5,000	$5,000
Cost of Goods Sold:				
Opening Inventory	$1,000	$?	$?	$?
Purchases	6,000		?	?
Total Goods Available	$7,000	$?	$?	$?
Ending Inventory	3,000	?	?	?
Total Cost of Goods Sold	4,000	?	?	?
Gross Profit	$1,000	$?	$?	$?

The statement for FIFO rising prices has been completed. The ending inventory is calculated as follows for FIFO — 250 units at $12 = $3,000.

Required:
1. Complete the statement for LIFO rising prices using the data provided. (Note that you have to recalculate the ending inventory cost.)
2. Complete the statement for FIFO falling prices by assuming that purchases were made at $8 per unit. (Note that this changes cost of purchases and ending inventory cost.)
3. Complete the statement for LIFO falling prices by assuming that purchases were made at $8 per unit. (Note that this changes cost of purchases and ending inventory cost.)
4. Assume that LIFO costing was permitted in Canada for income tax purposes and that income tax was 50 percent of income. Which costing method would be most advantageous from the company's point of view when prices are rising? when prices are falling?

Problem 8-6

MacDonald Products Corp. sells gadgets. During the month of January 19X3, the number of gadgets purchased and sold is shown below:

			Purchases			Sales			Balance		
			Units	Unit Cost	Total Cost	Units	Unit Cost	Total Cost	Units	Unit Cost	Total Cost
Jan.	1	Balance	100	$1							
	3	Purchase	100	1							
	8	Purchase	200	2							
	10	Sale				200	$3				
	15	Purchase	300	3							
	20	Sale				500	5				
	27	Purchase	400	1							

Required:
1. Calculate the cost of the month-end inventory under each of the following costing assumptions:
   a. FIFO/perpetual;   b. LIFO/perpetual;   c. Moving average.
2. Prepare the journal entries required under the perpetual inventory method for the LIFO costing method.
3. Prepare the journal entries required under the periodic inventory method for the LIFO costing method.
4. Why are different journal entries prepared under each method?

Problem 8-7

The Kamloops Retail Company Ltd. has consistently averaged 39 percent gross profit. The company's inventories, which are on a periodic basis, were recently destroyed by fire. The following data are available:

Sales	$305
Purchases	175
Opening Inventory	25
Sales Returns	5
Purchases Returns	5
Delivery Expense	8
Transportation In	3
Repairs to Delivery Truck	3
Selling Commissions	6
Administrative Expenses	3

Required:
1. Calculate the estimated ending inventory.
2. Prepare journal entries (with explanation lines) to record
   a. The destruction of the inventory by fire
   b. The recovery of $30 from the insurance company
3. Why did the insurance recovery exceed the inventory cost?

Problem 8-8

The president of Segovia Corporation is concerned that the year-end inventory amounting to $5,000 at cost is less than expected. Although a physical count was made and the costing was accurately calculated using FIFO, the president asks you to estimate the year-end inventory using the following data:

	At Retail	At Cost
Sales for the Year	$160,000	
Sales Returns	10,000	
Purchases for the Year	164,000	$80,000
Purchases Returns	4,000	2,000
Transportation In		1,000
Opening Inventory	20,000	11,000

Required:
1. Calculate the estimated ending inventory at retail.
2. Calculate the cost percentage (ratio of cost to retail).
3. Calculate the estimated ending inventory at cost.
4. Calculate the amount of inventory lost during the year.
5. Assuming that the current replacement cost of the inventory is covered by insurance, calculate the amount paid by the insurer if
   a. the current replacement cost is 25 percent greater than the inventory FIFO cost, and
   b. the insurer pays 80 percent of the current replacement cost.
6. Prepare the journal entry to record the amount recovered from the insurer.

Alternate Problems

Alternate Problem 8-1

The following transactions took place during January 19X6 at Kelly Corp. The opening inventory consisted of 100 units at a total cost of $100.

			Units	Total Cost
Jan.	5	Purchase #1	100	$ 100
Jan.	9	Purchase #2	200	400
Jan.	16	Purchase #3	300	900
Jan.	26	Purchase #4	400	1,600

Units sold during the month were as follows:

			Units	Total Cost
Jan.	10	Sale #1	200	$ 600
	17	Sale #2	500	1,500

Required:
1. Calculate the cost of ending inventory and the cost of goods sold under each of
   a. FIFO/periodic
   b. LIFO/periodic
   c. Weighted average
   d. Specific identification (assume that the 700 units sold were identified as being made from the 100 units in opening inventory, the 200 units purchased on January 9, and the 400 units purchased January 26).
2. The accountant of Kelly Corp. is concerned that the LIFO cost flow method used by the company does not represent the FIFO flow of goods that exists in this company. What are the implications of mismatching cost flow and the flow of goods? Make some calculations to support your answer.

Alternate Problem 8-2

The Howell Company Ltd. is considering the use of different methods of calculating their ending inventory. The following data are applicable to its December operations:

	Purchases			*Sales*	
Dec.	4	1000 units @ $2.50	Dec.	5	600 units
	11	800 units @ $2.60		12	500 units
	23	1600 units @ $2.30		17	500 units
	29	900 units @ $2.40		27	400 units
				31	600 units

Required:
1. Calculate the amount of ending inventory under each of
   a. FIFO/periodic;   b. LIFO/periodic;   c. Weighted average/periodic.
2. Which method presents the most appropriate balance sheet valuation of inventory? Explain, using appropriate amounts to support your answer.
3. Which method results in the most realistic income statement? Why?

Alternate Problem 8-3

Shanghai Corporation began operating on January 2, 19X1. The following table shows the valuation of its inventory, using four different inventory valuation methods:

	LIFO	*FIFO*	*Market*	*LOCAM*
Dec. 31, 19X1	$ 9,200	$10,000	$ 9,600	$8,900
Dec. 31, 19X2	9,100	9,000	8,800	8,500
Dec. 31, 19X3	10,300	11,000	12,000	10,900

Required:
1. Which inventory method shows the highest net income for 19X1?
   a. LIFO   c. Market
   b. FIFO   d. LOCAM
2. Which inventory method shows the highest net income for 19X2?
   a. LIFO   c. Market
   b. FIFO   d. LOCAM
3. For 19X3, how much higher or lower would net income be if FIFO valuation were used instead of LOCAM?
   a. $100 lower   e. $1,000 higher
   b. $100 higher   f. $1,000 lower
   c. $400 higher   g. $1,400 higher
   d. $400 lower   h $1,400 lower
4. Which inventory method shows the lowest net income for the three years combined?
   a. LIFO   c. Market
   b. FIFO   d. LOCAM
5. On the basis of the data in this problem, the movement of inventory prices was:
   a. Up in 19X1 and down in 19X3
   b. Up in both 19X1 and 19X3
   c. Down in 19X1 and up in 19X3
   d. Down in both 19X1 and 19X3

Alternate Problem 8-4

The Single Product Company Ltd. had the following inventory transactions for the month of December:

Nov. 30	Inventory of	20 units @ $4.60
Dec. 8	Purchased	80 units @ $5.00
Dec. 15	Purchased	40 units @ $5.30
Dec. 22	Purchased	60 units @ $5.60
Dec. 31	Purchased	40 units @ $5.50

By December 31, 190 of the units had been sold by Single.

Required:
1. Calculate the cost of the ending inventory using each of
   a. FIFO/periodic;   b. LIFO/periodic;   c. Weighted average.
2. The prices of the company's purchases have been increasing during the month and the controller is concerned about the possible existence of phantom profits under the FIFO method of costing inventory. If the sales price of each unit was $7 during December, prepare calculations necessary to isolate the existence of phantom profits.

Alternate Problem 8-5

The following transactions took place in the month of May at Crown Corporation. The opening inventory consisted of 50 units at $10. On May 2, the company purchased 60 units at $12. On May 10, it sold 10 units. On May 22, it purchased an additional 100 units at $15. On May 24, 150 units were sold.

Required:
1. Calculate the cost of goods sold for each of LIFO/perpetual, FIFO/perpetual, and moving average inventory methods.
2. Calculate the cost of goods sold under each of LIFO/periodic, FIFO/periodic, and weighted average inventory methods.

Alternate Problem 8-6

Janus Products Inc. sells television sets. The following information relates to January 19X7 purchases and sales of Brand X 20-inch [50 cm] colour television sets.

			Purchases			Sales			Balance		
			Units	Unit Cost	Total Cost	Units	Unit Cost	Total Cost	Units	Unit Cost	Total Cost
Jan.	1	Balance	6	$400							
	2	Sale				1	$600				
	3	Purchase	2	450							
	7	Sale				2	700				
	10	Sale				1	650				
	15	Purchase	3	500							
	20	Sale				4	750				
	25	Purchase	1	500							
	29	Sale				1	800				

Required:
1. Calculate the cost of the month-end inventory under each of
   a. FIFO/perpetual;   b. LIFO/perpetual;   c. Moving average
2. Prepare the journal entries required under the perpetual inventory method for each of
   a. FIFO/perpetual;   b. LIFO/perpetual;   c. Moving average

Alternate Problem 8-7

The Kenilworth Mall housed the premises of the Handy Hardware Company Ltd. On the morning of November 1, fire gutted the hardware store and some of the other tenant shops. Handy Hardware had been a popular location for homeowners and had, as a result, consistently earned a gross profit on net sales of 40 percent over the year. Appropriate data to date were as follows:

Sales	$1,220
Purchases	700
Purchases Returns	20
Sales Returns	16
Delivery Expense	30
Transportation In	12
Administrative Expense	8
Opening Inventory (Jan. 1)	100
Advertising Expense	20
Salaries	85
Sales Discounts	4

Required:
1. Calculate the estimated closing inventory.
2. Prepare the entries required to show the claim set up by Handy Hardware and the collection of a settlement in full of $60.
3. Did the insurance settlement exceed the inventory cost? Why?

Alternate Problem 8-8

University Men's Shop Corp. takes a year-end physical inventory at marked selling prices and reduces the total to a cost basis for year-end statement purposes. University also uses the retail method to estimate the amount of inventory that should be on hand at year-end. By comparison of the two totals, it is able to determine inventory shortages resulting from theft. The following information at the end of December is available.

	At Retail	At Cost
Sales	$234,680	
Sales Returns	3,740	
Opening Inventory	36,200	$24,420
Purchases	239,800	166,770
Purchases Returns	3,900	2,830
Inventory Count (Dec. 31)	40,900	

Required:
1. Use the retail method to estimate the year-end inventory at cost.
2. Use the retail method to reduce the shop's year-end physical inventory to a cost basis.
3. Prepare a schedule showing the inventory shortage at cost and at retail.

Supplementary Problems

Supplementary Problem 8-1

The following partial income statements have been prepared for Jackson Video Inc.

	19X2		19X3		19X4
Sales		$3,000		$7,000		$10,000
Cost of Goods Sold:						
Opening Inventory	$1,000		$ 4,000		$ 8,000	
Purchases	5,000		9,000		11,000	
Total Goods Available	$6,000		$13,000		$19,000	
Ending Inventory	4,000		8,000		12,000	
Total Cost of Goods Sold		2,000		5,000		7,000
Gross Profit		$1,000		$2,000		$ 3,000

Subsequent to the preparation of these income statements, two inventory errors were found: (a) the 19X2 ending inventory was overstated by $1,000, and (b) the 19X3 ending inventory was understated by $1,000.

Required:
1. Prepare corrected income statements for the three years, using the comparative format above.
2. What is your explanation for the difference in the 19X3 gross profit?
3. Is the balance of retained earnings at the end of 19X4 affected by the errors?

Supplementary Problem 8-2

The following transactions took place during January 19X9 at Kendriff Inc. The opening inventory consisted of 100 units of Brand X at $10 per unit. The following purchases were made during the month:

		Units	Unit Cost
Jan.	3	200	$10
	11	400	9
	19	500	8
	24	600	7
	30	200	6

During the month, 1700 units were sold for $12 each.

Required:
1. Calculate the cost of ending inventory and cost of goods sold under each of FIFO/periodic, LIFO/periodic, and weighted average.
2. Calculate the gross profit under each of the above methods.
3. Under what circumstances will the cost of inventory under the LIFO assumption result in a lower net income than the FIFO assumption? in a higher net income than the FIFO assumption?

Supplementary Problem 8-3

The following transactions took place during January 19X7 at Dana Corp.

Jan.	1	Opening Inventory	200	$1
	10	Purchase #1	200	$2
	15	Sale #1	200	
	20	Purchase #2	300	$3
	25	Sale #2	400	
	30	Purchase #3	300	$3

Required:
1. Calculate ending inventory and cost of goods sold under each of
   a. FIFO/perpetual;   b. LIFO/perpetual.
2. Calculate the cost of the January 15 and 25 sales using the moving average assumption.
3. How much would the cost of the January 15 and 25 sales amount to under the weighted average assumption? Why does this cost differ from that calculated in 2, above?
4. Which inventory cost assumption would you choose:
   a. to relect the probable flow of goods?
   b. to report the lowest net income for the month?

Supplementary Problem 8-4

Peel S.T. Corporation prepares monthly financial statements; it made a physical inventory count in January and February but intends to use the gross profit method of estimating inventory in March and April. Partial income statements appear below.

	January		February		March		April	
Sales		$40,000		$60,000		$50,000		$75,000
Cost of Goods Sold:								
Opening Inventory	$?		$?		$?		$?	
Purchases	50,000		30,000		20,000		40,000	
Total Goods Available	$ 60,000		$ 70,000		$ 50,000		$ 60,000	
Ending Inventory	?		?		?		?	
Total Cost of Goods Sold		20,000		40,000		?		?
Gross Profit		$?		$?		$?		$?

Required:
1. Calculate the gross profit percentage to be used in estimating March and April ending inventories.
2. Using the percentage calculated in 1, complete the partial income statements for March and April.
3. A physical count was made at April 30 and the inventory was accurately costed at $10,000. The controller, sceptical of estimates, attributes the differences to the gross profit percentage used to estimate ending inventory. Under what circumstances would you agree? disagree?

Supplementary Problem 8-5

The following data are taken from the records of the Turner Promotions Ltd.

Opening Inventory		Transportation in	500
At retail	7,000	Purchases Returns	
At cost	5,000	At retail	2,000
Purchases		At cost	1,500
At retail	25,000	Sales	22,000
At cost	16,000	Sales Returns	1,000

1. Calculate the estimated ending inventory at cost, using the retail inventory method.
   a. Calculate the ending inventory at retail.
   b. Calculate the cost percentage (ratio of cost to retail).
   c. Calculate the ending inventory at cost.
2. Calculate the ending inventory at cost, using the gross profit method. A gross profit rate of 35 percent is considered reasonable in the circumstances.
3. Explain why the ending inventory would be different under the two methods.

Supplementary Problem 8-6

Part A

The accountant of Loyola Inc. is concerned about the inventory in its bookstore. A physical count at May 31, 19X8 showed that $10,000 inventory (at cost) was on hand. The following information for the year then ended is available.

	At Retail	At Cost
Sales for the Year	$62,500	
Sales Returns	2,500	
Opening Inventory	14,000	$10,000
Purchases for the Year	55,000	39,000
Purchases Returns	3,000	2,000
Transportation In		1,000

Required:
1. Calculate the estimated ending inventory at retail.
2. Calculate the cost percentage (ratio of cost to retail).
3. Calculate the May 31, 19X8 estimated ending inventory at cost.
4. Why is the inventory calculated in 3, above, different from the physical count at May 31?

Part B

The controller of Sir George Corp. is calculating the amount of inventory lost during the year ended May 31, 19X8. A physical count was not made at May 31 due to circumstances beyond his control. The following information for the year then ended is available from its general ledger.

Sales for the Year	$50,000
Sales Returns	5,000
Opening Inventory	6,000
Purchases for the Year	35,000
Purchases Returns	3,000
Purchases Discounts	2,000
Transportation In	1,500
Delivery Expense	1,000
Depreciation Expense — Truck	400
Insurance Expense	100

The following are partial income statements of Sir George Corp. for years 19X5 to 19X7 (amounts are in thousands of dollars).

	19X5	19X6	19X7	Totals
Sales	$20	$30	$40	$
Cost of Goods Sold	10	20	30	
Gross Profit	$10	$10	$10	$

Required: Using the gross profit method, calculate the May 31, 19X8 estimated ending inventory at cost.

Decision Problems

Decision Problem 8-1

Consider the controversy that exists as to whether LIFO, FIFO, average, or some other cost is most appropriate in measuring income for a period and asset position at the end of a period.

Required:
1. Discuss the extent to which this controversy is (or is not) solved by switching to some form of current value ac-

counting. For simplicity, assume the replacement cost version of current value.
2. Illustrate your analysis, using the following data. Use a perpetual inventory system to demonstrate that there is no arbitrary choice in measuring cost of goods sold and inventory position.

Inventory of Laser Class Sailboats

		In	Out	Balance
19X1				
Jan. 31	Bought	5 @ $1,000		5 @ $ ____
May 30	Bought	10 @ $1,200		15 @ $ ____
July	Sold		12 @ $ ____	3 @ $ ____
Nov. 30	Bought	2 @ $1,300		5 @ $ ____
19X2				
Jan. 31	Bought	4 @ $1,300		9 @ $ ____
May 30	Bought	10 @ $1,400		19 @ $ ____
July	Sold		15 @ $ ____	4 @ $ ____

Decision Problem 8-2

The president's assistant of TSOE Limited asks you to come to a board of directors meeting to explain some accounting problems to the members of the board. He indicates that the questions will be concerned with the problems of inventories. As the controller of the firm, you are fully aware that the corporation has used the lower of FIFO cost and market value in accounting for the inventory. At the board meeting the following questions are raised. How would you answer them?

1. What is the objective of determining the cost of the inventory and cost of goods sold in accordance with the principles of the LIFO method?
2. Are there some accounting assumptions or conventions that are responsible for the development of this method?
3. What effect would the adoption of this method have on the financial statements?

Decision Problem 8-3

The records of the Redgrave Trading Corporation show the following data about item A. The balance on January 1 was 200 units at $10 per unit. The selling price was $15 per unit throughout the year.

| | | Purchases | |
	Units	Purchase Price per Unit	Sales Units
Jan. 12	100	$11	
Feb. 1			200
Apr. 16	200	$12	
May 1			100
Jul. 15	100	$14	
Nov. 10			100
Dec. 5	200	$17	
	600		400

Required:
1. Calculate the cost of the ending inventory under the FIFO method when a perpetual inventory system is followed.
2. Calculate the cost of the ending inventory under the LIFO method when perpetual inventory records are maintained. Prepare a perpetual inventory card.
3. The company has experienced a period of rapidly rising prices for its purchases during the year. If selling price has remained fairly constant during this period because of heavy competition in the marketplace, what effect will result from the use of FIFO, as compared to LIFO, on:
   a. the income statement,   b. the balance sheet.
4. Assume that the sale of February 1 was on credit to customer B, that perpetual inventory records were maintained, and the LIFO method was used. Prepare the required journal entry or entries to record the sale and the cost of the goods sold February 1.

Fixed Assets

Fixed assets are used in the normal operating activities of the business and are expected to provide benefits for a period in excess of one year. Depreciation is calculated to allocate a part of fixed asset cost over its useful life.

1. What is the distinction between capital expenditures and revenue expenditures?
2. How do generally accepted accounting principles prescribe what amount should be capitalized?
3. How should a corporation record the cost of an asset it has constructed?
4. What is the distinction between a betterment and an extraordinary repair?
5. What is the primary objective of recording periodic depreciation?
6. What different methods can be used in the calculation of depreciation?
7. What is the maximum amount of depreciation on fixed assets that is permissible for income tax purposes?
8. Is the value of services rendered by a fixed asset in the first year of its life the same as in its last year?
9. What is the impact on fixed assets of the changing purchasing power of the dollar through inflation?
10. How does current cost accounting provide for the maintenance of operating capacity?

A. Establishing Cost of Fixed Assets

At the time of its acquisition, a long-term asset can be thought of as a bundle of services that will be used up over a period of years. Each year, as a part of this bundle of services is used up, a part of its cost is written off. Eventually the asset is all used up and is no longer useful. At this point, the asset is disposed of. This life cycle of a fixed asset is illustrated in Figure 9-1.

USEFUL LIFE OF THE ASSET

ASSET ACQUISITION ⎯⎯⎯⎯⎯⎯⎯→ ASSET DISPOSAL

The cost of the asset is arbitrarily allocated to depreciation over the useful life of the asset.

Figure 9-1   Life cycle of a fixed asset

Capital Expenditures

Capital expenditures consist of the asset cost less any applicable cash discounts, plus any additional costs involved in preparing the asset for use. Assume that equipment is purchased for a net price of $20,000, transportation costs $500, installation requiring special wiring costs $1,000, construction of a cement foundation costs $2,500, and test runs to debug the equipment cost $2,000. The total cost of the asset, then, is $26,000. In addition to the purchase price or invoice cost of the asset acquired, the costs to prepare the asset for use are also **capitalized**. The various costs that may be incurred in the course of acquiring and preparing the asset for use are listed below.

(to) Capitalize
To record an expenditure as an asset, rather than as an expense; often referred to as a *capital expenditure*.

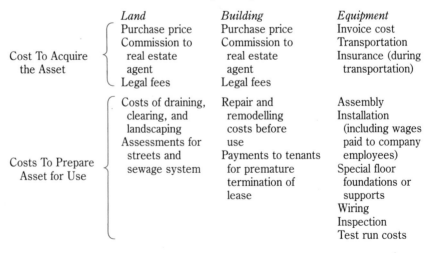

Capital Expenditures

	Land	*Building*	*Equipment*
Cost To Acquire the Asset	Purchase price Commission to real estate agent Legal fees	Purchase price Commission to real estate agent Legal fees	Invoice cost Transportation Insurance (during transportation)
Costs To Prepare Asset for Use	Costs of draining, clearing, and landscaping Assessments for streets and sewage system	Repair and remodelling costs before use Payments to tenants for premature termination of lease	Assembly Installation (including wages paid to company employees) Special floor foundations or supports Wiring Inspection Test run costs

There are well-established principles for determining what amounts should be included in the cost of the asset in most situations.

> Generally accepted accounting principles require that all costs benefitting future accounting periods in which the asset will be used, be included in the cost of the asset.

The preceding types of cost are clear examples of expenditures made in the course of acquiring the asset and preparing it for use. However, other expenditures are often more difficult to allocate. These are discussed next.

Land

In addition to the costs listed in the preceding schedule, the cost of land will be increased by the cost of removing any useless structures found on the land. This cost is reduced by the proceeds, if any, obtained from the sale of the scrap. Assume that the total cost of land is $100,000 before an additional $15,000 cost to raze an old building: $1,000 is expected to be received for salvaged materials. The cost of the land is $114,000.

Total Cost of Land		$100,000
Razing Costs for Building	$15,000	
Less: Salvage Proceeds	1,000	14,000
		$114,000

Frequently, land and useful buildings are purchased for a lump sum. If the buildings will be used for business purposes, the purchase price must be apportioned between the land and buildings, because buildings are subject to depreciation. Land does not usually depreciate, since its utility for building or for other purposes does not diminish. The purchase price is usually allocated to the acquired assets on the basis of their market values. Assume that a lump sum of $150,000 is paid for land and buildings. This cost can be allocated as follows:

	Market Value	*Percent of Total Market Value*	*Cost Allocation*
Land	$ 50,000	25%	$ 37,500 ($150,000 × 25%)
Building	150,000	75%	112,500 ($150,000 × 75%)
Total	$200,000	100%	$150,000

The allocation can also be made on some other basis; it may be based on municipal assessed values or on estimates made by a professional appraiser.

As stated earlier, land does not normally depreciate. An exception to this rule occurs where non-renewable mineral deposits or oil are to be removed from the land during future accounting periods. In such cases, the mineral deposit component of the land is subject to depletion, which is deducted from the asset account as the non-renewable resource is removed from the land. Further discussion of this topic is in Section F of this chapter.

Building and Equipment

When an asset is purchased, its cost includes the net purchase price plus all costs to prepare the asset for use. In some cases, a business may construct its own building or equipment. In the case of a building, for example, cost includes all pertinent expenditures, including costs for excavation, building permits, insurance and property taxes during construction, engineering fees, the cost of labour incurred by having company employees supervise and work on the construction of the building, and the cost of any interest incurred to finance the construction during the construction period.

The cost of an asset constructed by the company is never recorded at the amount that it would have cost to have someone else construct the same building or piece of equipment. Accounting principles do not permit the recording of an unrealized profit — from construction of an asset at less than purchase cost, in this case.

In some cases, one asset is exchanged for another asset. Assume that a piece of land acquired several years ago at a cost of $25,000 is exchanged for a piece of equipment owned by another company. At the time of the exchange, the **fair market value (FMV)** of the land is $50,000 and the FMV of the equipment is $60,000. What is the cost of the equipment?

The rule followed by most accountants in this type of situation requires that the cost of the asset acquired (equipment) be the FMV of the asset given up (land, FMV $50,000); if the FMV of the land cannot be established or is not clear, then the FMV of the asset acquired (equipment, FMV $60,000) is used.

Fair market value (FMV)
The price or cost of an asset negotiated between two parties dealing at arm's length.

Real Life Example 9-1

Buy or Lease?

Should You Buy or Lease Space?

There is no best, least expensive, route to acquiring business space. Each company must decide from among a broad spectrum of financial and non-financial options and considerations.

Without denying the importance of non-financial and even emotional factors, however, you should explore your financial options on their own merits. One of the biggest decisions any company can make is whether to lease or buy.

Both owning and leasing have benefits and drawbacks. A company's existing circumstances, projected position, and goals can turn some of the intrinsic benefits of one into drawbacks, and vice versa.

Buying Takes Capital

To buy space usually takes a lot of initial capital as well as borrowing ability. The purchase uses funds that you could invest in other areas, within or outside the company.

The major advantage of buying include tax benefits, depreciation's contribution to cash flow, the possibility of appreciation in value, and of course the warm feeling that comes from owning something of value.

But the property investment is only as liquid as the real estate marketplace, on which also depends the owner's future freedom to move or to rent out excess space. While ownership gives a company control over the management and use of the space, it also imposes responsibilities and requires attention that the company might more productively give to its primary business.

Leasing: Pay As You Go

Leasing does not require a major capital outlay. Leasing preserves the company's existing capital and borrowing power

for other investments, but lease payments aren't likely to appreciate in value.

You can often negotiate favourable settlements or terms if you must move out of or change leased space early. You may even be able to negotiate some tax benefits. But these benefits will rarely match those of ownership.

Though a tenant usually exercises less control over leased space than owned space, degrees of control are negotiable in leases. The tenant also does not have to be concerned with building management. That's the property owner's responsibility.

The decision to lease or buy may rest on your choice of location. It is harder to buy a prime location than to rent one.

Assessing Future Costs Today

To evaluate and compare the financial elements of the buying or leasing option, you must assign a value to each element of a lease and to each element of the cost of buying. To make the comparison's outcome comprehensible, if inexact, you must measure the value in today's dollars. Be aware, though, that no amount of forecasting can produce a precise dollar comparison that will remain valid for 15 or 20 years. Inflation and interest rates are only two of the many variables that one cannot accurately foresee. The future is risk by another name.

Net present value (NPV), however, is a useful tool for analyzing future costs in today's dollars. NPV should be viewed as an index, rather than a dollar figure. It represents the present value of future payments discounted at the opportunity rate, i.e., the projected loss from not investing the same money elsewhere.

Source Marita Thomas, "Facilities Planning, Evaluation and Acquisition for Smaller Corporations", *Inc. Magazine*, September 1984, p. 111.

One exception to this rule occurs when one asset is traded in for a similar asset—an old piece of equipment for a new piece of equipment, for example. This topic is treated in Section C of this chapter.

Capital and Revenue Expenditures

Expenditure
A cash disbursement to obtain an asset, goods, or services.

Any cash disbursements is referred to as an **expenditure**. All expenditures made to purchase an asset and for its preparation for use are capitalized. When these expenditures are debited to an asset account, they are said to be capitalized and are referred to as capital expenditures. An expenditure of this kind produces an asset.

> Generally accepted accounting principles require expenditures to be capitalized when they will benefit more than one accounting period, and when they are significant in amount, and when they can be measured with reasonably objective evidence.

For capital expenditures, a distinction is often made between a betterment and an extraordinary repair. A *betterment* results in a change to the asset that increases its efficiency; the estimated useful life of the asset does not change. For example, if a tape drive in a personal computer is replaced by a disk drive, the cost of the betterment is added to the existing asset cost and is depreciated over the existing asset's useful life. The cost of the replaced part and accumulated depreciation attributable to it are removed from the accounts.

An *extraordinary repair* results in a change of the estimated useful life of the asset. The cost is debited to accumulated depreciation rather than to asset cost, since it is viewed as reducing the previously recorded depreciation. The resulting net asset cost is then depreciated over the asset's remaining useful life. The accounting procedures in establishing the revised depreciation charges are discussed later in this chapter.

Revenue expenditure
An expenditure recorded as an expense to be matched with the current period's revenue; often thought of as routine maintenance expenses, as opposed to a capital expenditure that is recorded as an asset.

Not all asset-related expenditures incurred after the purchase of an asset are capitalized. Other expenditures, called **revenue expenditures**, result in an addition to an expense account. Examples of these expenditures include the cost of replacing parts of an asset (eg, in the case of a truck, new tires, new muffler, new battery), continuing expenditures for maintaining the asset in good working order (eg, oil changes, antifreeze, transmission fluid changes), and costs of renewing structural parts of an asset (eg, repairs of collision damage, repair or replacement of rusted parts).

> An expenditure made to maintain an asset in satisfactory working order is a *revenue expenditure* of the accounting period in which the expenditure was made.

Although some revenue expenditures will benefit more than one accounting period, they do not increase the serviceability of the asset beyond its original useful life, and therefore are treated as normal maintenance costs.

Three criteria should be considered when establishing a policy to distinguish between capital and revenue expenditures incurred after the purchase and installation of an asset.

Asset-Related Expenditures Following Purchase of the Asset

Criterion	Capital Expenditure	Revenue Expenditure
1. Life of the Part	Will benefit two or more accounting periods.	Will benefit the current accounting period.
2. Expenditure for Repairs	Will prolong the useful life of the asset beyond the original estimate; make it more valuable or more adaptable.	Will not prolong the useful life of the asset beyond the original estimate; doesn't make it more valuable or more adaptable.
3. Materiality of the Expenditure	Dollar amount of expenditure is large, is not made often, and will benefit two or more accounting periods.	Dollar amount of expenditure is small, is made relatively often, and does not materially affect net income.

The concept of *materiality* enters into the distinction between capital and revenue expenditures. As a matter of expediency, an expenditure of $200 that has all the characteristics of a capital expenditure would probably be expensed rather than capitalized in an entity such as General Motors, because the effort to capitalize and depreciate the item is so much greater than the benefits to be derived. Policies are established by many companies to resolve the problem of distinguishing between capital and revenue expenditures. For example, all capital expenditures in excess of $1,000 are capitalized; all capital expenditures under $1,000 are expensed.

B.   The Nature of Depreciation

It is unfortunate but true that the new sportscar you would like to purchase or are thinking of purchasing will wear out — probably in five to seven years. The engine will begin to break down; the five on the floor will become two-and-a-half; the imitation leather seats will tear; within five years, depending on where you live, the car will rust through. Meantime (probably within two years), the price of gas will have increased to such an extent that you will not be able to afford the car's 3 km/L (9 mi./gal.), and you will be forced to purchase a mini-bike — a case of technological obsolescence in action.

Unfortunately, **tangible assets** come to the end of their usefulness, whether from physical deterioration (cars, lawn mowers) or obsolescence caused by such factors as technology (monaural record players), or the enactment of prohibitory laws (pinball machines). A classic description of the nature of depreciation — introduced in Chapter 3 — was given by Professor Henry Rand Hatfield, an eminent accountant, when he wrote:

> All machinery is on an irresistible march to the junk heap, and its progress, while it may be delayed, cannot be prevented by repairs.[1]

The role of depreciation is to recognize this limited useful life and to allocate the cost of the asset over its useful life; that is, over the accounting periods expected to receive benefits from its use.

Assume that a machine acquired for $20,000 will have an estimated useful life of 5 years, after which time it will be scrapped for $2,000. The company has purchased for $20,000 a 5-year bundle of services, part of which will be used up each year, as shown in Figure 9-2.

Tangible assets
Assets of a physical and relatively permanent nature, acquired for use in the regular operations of an entity: for example, land, building, equipment, and trucks.

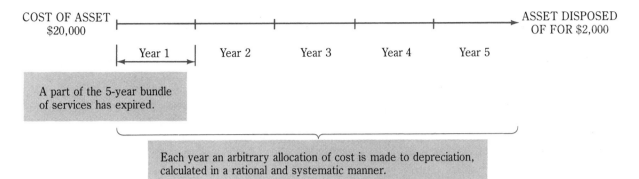

Figure 9-2   Allocation of cost over the useful life of an asset

Each year, part of the bundle of services of the asset is allocated to expense. The problem is: how do you measure the benefits that flow from an asset? Without this information (and it is difficult to obtain in practice) how do accountants rationally allocate the cost of an asset to a particular accounting period? The answer is that they can't! In actual practice, an estimate is made.

Assets included within the non-current asset category for fixed assets are:

1. Depreciable tangible assets, such as buildings and equipment. **Depreciation** is the term used to describe the allocation of a tangible asset's cost to expense over its useful life.
2. Depreciable natural resource assets, such as oil and coal. **Depletion** is the term used to describe the allocation of a natural resource's cost to expense over its useful life.
3. Depreciable intangible assets, such as patents and goodwill. **Amortization** is the term used to describe the allocation of an asset's cost to expense over its useful life.
4. Other assets, such as investment assets and non-production assets.

Fixed Asset Cost Allocation Methods

Income determination is a primary objective of the depreciation process.

> According to generally accepted accounting principles, a firm should adopt the method of allocating the cost of an asset to depreciation expense that produces the most appropriate matching of depreciation costs with revenues earned.

The most frequently used methods to allocate asset cost over its estimated useful life are:

- Usage methods
- Time-based methods : Straight-line method
                       : Declining balance method
                       : Capital cost allowance.

Depreciation
The expiration of a fixed asset's usefulness; the process of allocating the cost of a fixed asset to each accounting period that will benefit from its use. The amount recorded during an accounting period depends on an estimate of (1) the asset's useful life; (2) the asset's scrap value; and (3) the method of depreciation used.

Depletion
Physical exhaustion of a natural resource; the process of allocating the cost of a natural resource to each accounting period receiving benefits. The exhaustion of part of the natural resource results in an allocation of cost to expense.

Amortization
The process of allocating the cost of an asset to each accounting period receiving benefits; usually used in the case of intangible assets.

Usage Methods

Usage methods
(of depreciation) Depreciation is calculated on the
basis of the use made of
the asset during the
period.

Salvage value
The amount of asset cost
expected to be recovered
when the asset is
eventually sold, traded in,
or scrapped.

Usage methods of calculating depreciation are useful when wear and tear is the major cause of depreciation, and when the amount of asset use may vary from period to period. Depreciation is calculated on the basis of an equal amount charged for each unit produced, each hour worked, each kilometre driven, each tonne hauled. Assume that a machine costing $20,000 has a **salvage value** of $2,000 and is expected to have an estimated productive life of 10 000 units. If 1500 units were processed during the current period, the depreciation expense for the period would be $2,700.

$$\frac{\text{Cost} - \text{Salvage value}}{\substack{\text{Number of units of}\\\text{estimated productive life}}} = \substack{\text{Depreciation}\\\text{per unit}} \times \substack{\text{Number of units}\\\text{produced}} = \substack{\text{Depreciation expense}\\\text{for the period}}$$

or, using the figures given:

$$\frac{\$20,000 - \$2,000}{10\ 000\ \text{units}} = \$1.80 \times 1500\ \text{units} = \$2,700\ \text{depreciation expense.}$$

Usage methods assume that the asset will contribute to the earning of revenues in relation to the amount of use during the accounting period. Therefore, the depreciation expense under this method records the decline in the capacity of the asset during the period.

Time-Based Method: Straight-Line

The straight-line method — introduced briefly in Chapter 3 — ignores asset usage and assumes that the asset will contribute to the earning of revenues equally during each period; that is, each period will receive services of equal value. Therefore, equal amounts of depreciation are recorded during each year of its useful life.

The straight-line method is, therefore, appropriate for assets that make an equal contribution to operations during each year of their productive life. It is not appropriate when the asset does not contribute uniformly to operations during each year of its life.

> Under the straight-line method, depreciation expense for each accounting period remains the same dollar amount during the useful life of the asset.

The straight-line method can be calculated as follows:

$$\frac{\text{Cost} - \text{Salvage value}}{\text{Estimated useful life}} = \text{Depreciation expense.}$$

Assume that the same $20,000 machine used earlier, with an estimated service life of 5 years and an estimated net salvage value of $2,000, is depreciated on the straight-line method. The annual depreciation charge is:

$$\frac{\$20,000 - \$2,000}{5} = \$3,600.$$

Figure 9-3 illustrates the arbitrary method of allocating costs in the straight-line method.

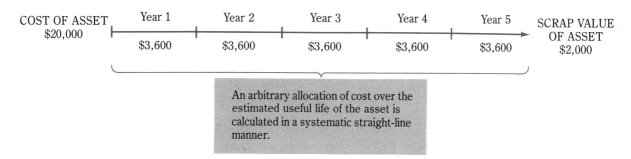

Figure 9-3   Allocation of cost using the straight-line method

The straight-line method considers depreciation as a function of time and its main advantage is its simplicity of calculation. Since it is usually difficult to judge what the pattern of an asset's use will be, this method is the one that is least likely to be subject to bias.

Time-Based Method: Declining Balance

Declining balance method
(of depreciation) Depreciation is calculated on the assumption that during the useful life of an asset, each period receives unequal benefits from the use of the asset; a constant rate is applied to the remaining carrying value of each period.

The **declining balance method** of allocating fixed asset costs assumes that the asset will contribute more to the earning of revenues in the earlier stages of its useful life than in the later stages. Accordingly, more depreciation is recorded in earlier years with the depreciation expense gradually decreasing each year. Because more depreciation is calculated initially, it is often referred to as an accelerated depreciation method.

The declining balance method is most appropriate where assets experience high technological obsolescence in the early part of their useful life (for example, computers) or where the value of the service rendered is not the same in the first year when the asset (for example, a machine) is new and efficient, as in the last year when it is nearly broken down.

Under the declining balance method, depreciation expense becomes smaller each year during the useful life of the asset.

Note, however, that some accountants consider that the amount of maintenance required in later years of the assets life may equal the difference between the lower depreciation amount calculated under the declining balance method and the amount which would result under the straight-line method. Accordingly, the total of depreciation and maintenance expense may result in virtually equal amounts of expense during future years.

Under the declining balance method, a constant rate is applied to the balance of the *net book value*, also called the *net carrying value* (cost less accumulated depreciation). This rate is calculated in actual practice by a somewhat involved mathematical formula, designed to measure best the amount of depreciation to be recorded for each accounting period. The method of calculating such a rate is complex and accordingly is left for coverage in a quantitative methods course. For our purposes, a rate can be calculated at double the straight-line rate (double declining balance), at one-and-one-half times the straight-line rate (150 percent declining balance), or in any other manner appropriate in the circumstances.

For example, the $20,000 machine has an estimated useful life of 5 years. The straight-line rate is 20 percent calculated by dividing 100 percent by 5 years (100% ÷ 5 = 20%). In order to calculate the declining balance rate, this straight-line rate of 20% is doubled to obtain the double-declining balance rate (20% × 2 = 40%); it is multiplied by one-and-one-half times to obtain a 150%-declining balance rate (20% × 1½ = 30%).

For income tax purposes, the rate cannot exceed the maximum allowed by official government regulations. It is important to note that declining balance rate is applied to the net book value, that is the carrying value, of the asset before any deduction for salvage value. However, the asset is not depreciated below its salvage value. In other words, in the example used, depreciation expense would not be recorded once the net book value is $2,000, since the asset has an estimated salvage value of $2,000 and, therefore, will not depreciate below this amount. A 40 percent depreciation rate—double the straight-line rate of 20 percent—applied to the carrying value remaining at the end of each year gives the following results for the 5 years. (Note that salvage value is ignored in the amount being depreciated.)

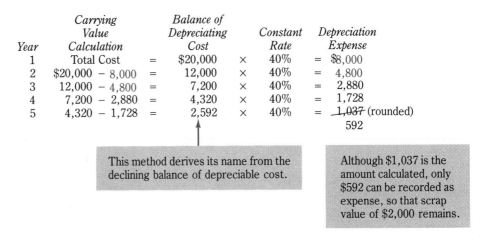

Year	Carrying Value Calculation		Balance of Depreciating Cost		Constant Rate		Depreciation Expense
1	Total Cost	=	$20,000	×	40%	=	$8,000
2	$20,000 − 8,000	=	12,000	×	40%	=	4,800
3	12,000 − 4,800	=	7,200	×	40%	=	2,880
4	7,200 − 2,880	=	4,320	×	40%	=	1,728
5	4,320 − 1,728	=	2,592	×	40%	=	~~1,037~~ (rounded)
							592

This method derives its name from the declining balance of depreciable cost.

Although $1,037 is the amount calculated, only $592 can be recorded as expense, so that scrap value of $2,000 remains.

Figure 9-4 illustrates the arbitrary method of allocating costs in the declining balance method.

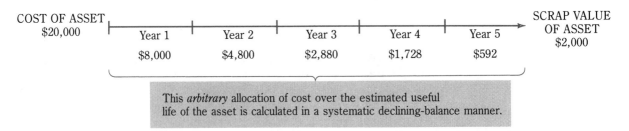

Figure 9-4   Allocation of costs using the declining-balance method

For income tax purposes, depreciation is referred to as **capital cost allowance**. Depreciable assets are grouped into classes and can be depreciated at any rate up to a maximum allowed by official regulations. For example, automobiles and trucks may be depreciated at a maximum rate of 30 percent, calculated on the balance at year-end. Equipment may be depreciated at a maximum rate of 20 percent. Each class of assets is treated separately and is subject to a specific maximum depreciation rate. This system minimizes disputes between the taxpayer and the income tax authorities.

Actual Practice versus GAAP

The most important part of the cost allocation process is the recognition of the portion of the asset services that have expired. In actual practice, there is considerable evidence that the value of services rendered by an asset in the first year of its life is not the same as in its last year. An apartment building, for example, commands greater rent and occupancy when it is new than when it is older. Similarly, a lathe produces fewer rejects in its initial year than in its later years. This phenomenon has resulted in a belief among many accountants that depreciation of assets should be recorded so that a larger amount of depreciation is allotted to earlier years and a smaller amount to the later years. The depreciation pattern can therefore be illustrated as a curve, as shown in Figure 9-5.

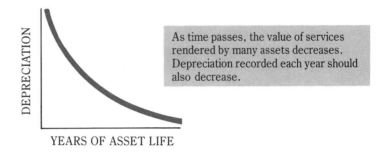

As time passes, the value of services rendered by many assets decreases. Depreciation recorded each year should also decrease.

Figure 9-5   The depreciation curve

This diagram reflects the belief that the efficiency of an asset is greater during its initial years and less during its later years. The accounting problem becomes one of allocating the expired part of the asset cost to a particular accounting period. This allocation is essentially arbitrary.

The declining-balance method using income tax depreciation rates is popular because it is acceptable for income tax purposes. Many firms have adopted this method for book purposes in order to reduce the inconvenience of maintaining two different calculations of depreciation — one for book purposes and another for income tax purposes.

Use of a declining balance method with depreciation rates permitted by the income tax authorities is in accordance with generally accepted accounting principles if the cost allocation pattern conforms with the pattern of depreciation. In this case, net income will properly show the earning power of the company.

Unfortunately, some firms use the income tax declining balance method for accounting purposes even when its use does not produce the most appropriate matching of fixed asset costs with revenues. This practice is in fact, a stretching of principles, but it is accepted by accountants. The fact that the estimate of the useful life of fixed assets and the allocation of depreciation are arbitrary tends to justify this departure from generally accepted accounting principles.

One adverse result of using the income tax method of depreciation is the possibility that a distorted net income figure will be produced. This figure might mislead investors who are attempting to evaluate the entity's performance and to compare its performance with that of another entity, which uses a different depreciation method.

C.   Depreciation Allocation Assumptions Compared

Cost Allocation Methods Compared

Useful life
(of an asset) An estimate
of the time over which an
asset will benefit the
operations of an entity.

As discussed, the role of depreciation is to allocate to expense the cost of limited-life fixed assets over their estimated useful lives. A problem arises, however, with predicting the **useful life** of an asset. The approaches to this problem taken by the different cost allocation methods are various.

Approach 1:   Usage Method of Cost Allocation
This method attempts to relate the amount of cost allocated as an expense to the actual physical use of the asset. A unit cost is computed by dividing depreciable cost (cost less salvage value) by the expected output: for example, total units to be produced, total tonnes to be hauled, total hours to be worked. The amount of depreciation expense for any accounting period is found by multiplying the calculated unit cost by the number of units produced or used during that period. Depreciation, therefore, depends on the amount that the asset is used. The validity of this method depends on the accuracy of the estimate made of total units to be produced, total tonnes to be hauled, or total hours to be worked. Unfortunately, estimates are subject to considerable error.

Time-Based Methods of Cost Allocation

Two other methods are widely used in actual practice to allocate the cost of limited life assets. Both ignore the actual amount an asset was used during the accounting period, and each makes an assumption about how cost should be allocated over the useful life of the asset.

Approach 2:   Straight-Line Method
This method assumes that each period receives services of equal value from the asset. Therefore, equal amounts of cost are allocated as depreciation expense to each period.

Approach 3:   Declining Balance Method and Capital Cost Allowance
This method assumes that the asset will contribute more to the earning of revenues in the earlier years of useful life than in later stages. Therefore, larger amounts are allocated as depreciation expense to earlier periods and smaller amounts to later periods.

A comparison of the straight-line method and declining balance method is made in Figure 9-6 over 5 years, using each method.

As illustrated in Figure 9-6, the declining-balance method records a larger amount of depreciation in Years 1 and 2, and a progressively smaller amount in Years 3, 4, and 5. However, both methods allocate the total $18,000 depreciable cost of the asset expense over the 5-year period. This periodic allocation of cost is often graphed to show the dollars of depreciation each year.

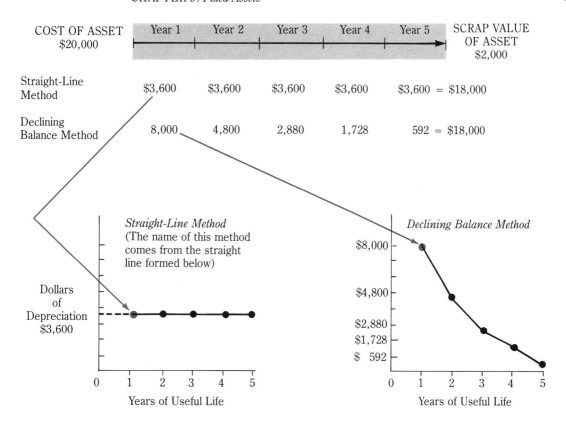

Figure 9-6   Comparison of Straight-Line and Declining Balance Methods

Matching Fixed Asset Costs with Revenues

Generally accepted accounting principles require the entity to choose the method of allocating cost that best matches expired fixed asset costs with revenues. Therefore, the matching concept, as applied to fixed asset cost allocation, stresses the calculation of net income and not the balance sheet valuation of the asset.

The effect of the straight-line and declining balance methods on net income is illustrated below. Which is the most appropriate method of allocating costs?

COST OF ASSET IS $20,000	Year 1	Year 2	Year 3	Year 4	Year 5	SCRAP VALUE OF ASSET IS $2,000
Straight-line method		$3,600	$3,600	$3,600	$3,600	$3,600
Declining balance method		8,000	4,800	2,880	1,728	592
Reduction in net income, using declining balance method		$4,400	$1,200			
Increase in net income, using declining balance method				$ 720	$1,872	$3,008

In actual practice, it is very difficult to predict accurately such issues as estimated useful life and scrap value. These and other issues, such as the value of service rendered by an asset during different years, complicates the identification of the most appropriate method of allocating fixed asset costs.

Use of the declining balance method for income tax purposes decreases net income and, therefore, results in less income taxes during Years 1 and 2; it increases net income and, therefore, results in more income taxes during Years 3, 4, and 5. Thus, there is delayed payment of income taxes when this method is used. If income taxes are assumed to be 50 percent, then this firm will delay payment of income taxes amounting to $2,800.

$$
\begin{array}{lll}
\text{Year 1} & \$4,400 \times 50\% & = \$2,200 \\
\text{Year 2} & \$1,200 \times 50\% & = \$\ \ 600 \\
& \text{Total Taxes Delayed} & \ \ \$2,800 \\
\end{array}
$$

These delayed income taxes in Years 1 and 2 are usually seen as an interest-free loan to the taxpayer. In actual practice, as business operations expand, more fixed assets are acquired and, in some cases, continue the delay of income taxes almost indefinitely. A problem arises, however, when capital expenditures are reduced; at that point the income taxes must be paid.

Phantom Profits

One problem affecting depreciation that accountants have been unable to solve is the changing purchasing power of the dollar through inflation and the resulting effect on net income.

> In matching depreciation costs with revenues in the income statement, revenues are stated in dollars that have this year's purchasing power, while depreciation costs are stated in terms of old dollars, that is, dollars that had a different purchasing power.

Assume that a machine was acquired 10 years ago at a cost of $100,000; the identical machine would cost $200,000 today. During this 10-year period, the selling prices of the firm have also increased proportionately. In recording current sales revenue and matching these with 10-year-old costs, the firm shows a larger net income than it would if there were no inflation. The reported net income includes two different components: the normal income from operations and an income from comparing old costs with current revenues — a holding gain. As noted in Chapter 8, this holding gain is referred to as phantom profits. Recall that income taxes are calculated on the total net income, which includes these phantom profits; therefore, income tax, in real dollars, is paid on phantom profits.

D. Depreciation and Financial Statements

Fixed Assets on the Balance Sheet

The objective of the depreciation process is that the appropriate allocation of cost be matched with revenues for net income determination. The resulting balance sheet valuation of fixed assets is a secondary consideration. What are the implications of this emphasis?

- Depreciation allocation methods are all based on estimates, and estimates are subject to error. Accordingly, the undepreciated cost, net book value, shown on the balance sheet will in all probability be incorrect anyway. Therefore, why should we be particularly concerned about the balance sheet value of fixed assets?
- Depreciation for a time period varies considerably, depending on the allocation method used. Accordingly, the undepreciated cost shown on the balance sheet of a firm can also vary considerably. Using amounts calculated earlier in this chapter, equipment would appear on the balance sheet at the end of Year 1 as follows:

	Under Straight-Line Method	*Under Declining Balance Method*
Fixed Assets:		
Equipment	$20,000	$20,000
Less: Accumulated Depreciation	3,600	8,000
Net Book Value	$16,400	$12,000

- Historical cost is the commonly used basis for recording and depreciating fixed assets; its popularity is based on the fact that it is an objectively determined amount.
- Some readers misunderstand the significance of the undepreciated cost shown on the balance sheet. They assume that it represents the cost to replace the asset at the end of its useful life. However, because of inflation, the expenditure needed to replace the asset will probably exceed the original cost paid ($20,000) by a substantial amount, with the result that a financing problem occurs when the asset must be replaced.

Trends in Reporting Fixed Asset Depreciation

Disclosure requirements for fixed assets are stated in the *CICA Handbook*. The CICA suggests that fixed asset cost and accumulated depreciation be disclosed on the balance sheet, or in a note, and that the accumulated depreciation should be deducted from fixed assets, which preferably should be disclosed by major category (sections 3060.02 and 3060.03).

Studies of balance sheets prepared by leading corporations show that there is increasing support for the segregation of fixed assets but not for the segregation of accumulated depreciation.

The income statement should also disclose the amount of depreciation and the methods and rates used in its calculation, according to the CICA. Where the amount of depreciation is significant, separate amounts for each type of fixed asset should be disclosed.

Partial Year Depreciation

Assets may be both purchased and sold during the accounting year. Should depreciation be calculated for a whole year in such a case? The answer depends on individual circumstances and corporate accounting policy. A number of practices can be chosen. One is to record half a year's depreciation regardless of when an asset purchase or sale occurs during the year. Another alternative is to calculate partial depreciation from the month of asset purchase or sale. In the case of an asset purchased June 7, for example, depreciation for seven months would be recorded if the corporate fiscal year coincided with the calendar year. If the asset purchase had been made June 17, then only six months depreciation would be recorded. The general rule to be followed in this case is the recording of depreciation from the month of acquisition (June) if the asset was purchased during the first half of the month (June 7); depreciation would be calculated from the next month (July) if the asset purchase was made during the second half of the month (June 17). For problem-solving purposes in this text, it is recommended that this practice be used.)

The annual calculation of straight-line depreciation for the $20,000 machine with an estimated useful life of 5 years and an estimated salvage value of $2,000 can be contrasted with partial year depreciation.

Purchase Jan. 1	*Purchase Jun. 7*	*Purchase Jun. 17*
The depreciation is allocated among five years as follows: ($20,000 − $2,000) ÷ 5 years = $3,600 per year.	The depreciation is allocated as follows: $3,600 per year × 7/12 months = $2,100	The depreciation is allocated as follows: $3,600 per year × 6/12 months = $1,800.

Deprec. Expense 3,600
    Accum. Deprec.   3,600
	Deprec. Expense 2,100
	    Accum. Deprec. 2,100
		Deprec. Expense 1,800
		    Accum. Deprec. 1,800

This example shows the recording of partial depreciation when an asset is purchased. Partial depreciation must also be recorded when asset disposal occurs.

Group Depreciation

Group rate
Depreciation calculated on a group of homogeneous fixed assets taken as a whole, as opposed to calculating depreciation on invididual assets.

Composite rate
Depreciation calculated on a group of nonhomogeneous (heterogeneous) assets taken as a whole, as opposed to calculating depreciation on individual assets.

The preceding examples discussed the calculation of depreciation for individual assets. In actual practice, depreciation is usually calculated on a group basis, particularly when the assets are similar. In this situation, a **group rate** is used; an average useful life is calculated and applied to the total asset cost. A group rate can also be calculated when there is a mixture of dissimilar assets. In this case, the rate is referred to as a **composite rate**.

The calculation of group rates can be complex and is beyond the subject matter of this chapter. Advanced accountancy courses examine not only the methodology used to establish group rates but also the ramification of having assets replaced before the expiration of their estimated useful lives.

Revision of Depreciation Charges

The useful life of an asset is estimated at the time an asset is acquired and, as is the case with any estimate, it is subject to considerable error.

Equipment	Accumulated Depreciation	
20,000	Year 1 3,600	Total accumulated depreciation is $7,200.
	Year 2 3,600	

This machine that cost $20,000 had been estimated to have a useful life of 5 years and a scrap value of $2,000. At the end of the first 2 years, it was discovered that the asset would have a useful life of 10 years, but that scrap value would amount to only $1,000. At the end of 2 years, the remaining undepreciated cost of the asset was $12,800 (cost of $20,000 − $7,200 accumulated depreciation to date). In fact, the proper accumulated depreciation should be $3,800.

	Revised Estimates	Original Estimates
Equipment Cost	$20,000	$20,000
Less: Revised Scrap Value	1,000	2,000
Amount To Be Depreciated	$19,000	$18,000
Estimated Useful Life	10 years	5 years
Annual Depreciation	$ 1,900	$ 3,600
Accumulated Depreciation for Two Years	$ 3,800	$ 7,200

> An excessive amount of depreciation has been recorded in Years 1 & 2.

What is the proper accounting procedure for this situation? The accepted procedure in Canada is to leave unchanged the depreciation recorded to date and to revise the annual depreciation to be recorded over the remaining estimated life of 8 years. This method is easy to apply. The amount of depreciation to be recorded in each of the remaining years is calculated as follows:

Actual Book Value ($20,000 − 7,200)	$12,800
Actual Scrap Value	1,000
Undepreciated Amount over Remaining 8 Years	$11,800
Depreciation for Each of the Next 8 Years Is $11,800 ÷ 8 Years =	$ 1,475

Accordingly, $1,475 would be recorded as the depreciation expense in the current year and in each of the next 7 years. Obviously there is a substantial difference between $1,475 and $3,600 recorded in each of the 2 preceding years; however, the overcharge of depreciation in Years 1 and 2 is offset by an undercharge of depreciation in the remaining 8 years. (If accurate information had been available at the outset, each year would have had a depreciation expense of $1,900.)

Another more complicated method, which differs in its approach to depreciation revisions, is also acceptable in the United States. It involves a correction of prior years earnings and is properly dealt with in a more advanced accounting course.

E.   Disposal of Fixed Assets

The disposal of a fixed asset requires the elimination from the balance sheet of both its cost and accumulated depreciation. As discussed, partial depreciation must be recorded when an asset disposal occurs. The sale, or abandonment, and trade-in of assets are discussed next.

Sale or Abandonment of Fixed Assets

When an asset has reached the end of its useful life it can be either sold or abandoned. In either case, the asset cost and accumulated depreciation are removed from the records, following the recording of any partial depreciation that may be appropriate.

Recall the calculation of straight-line depreciation for the $20,000 machine with an estimated useful life of 5 years and an estimated salvage value of $2,000. Assume that the general ledger accounts of the equipment and its related accumulated depreciation amount contain the following entries:

. Equipment	Accumulated Depreciation
Year 1 20,000	Year 1 3,600
	Year 2 3,600
	Year 3 3,600
	Year 4 3,600
	Year 5 3,600

When a fully depreciated asset is abandoned, or simply thrown away, the asset is written off. If there are any proceeds from a sale of the asset, a gain or loss may be recognized.

Assume that the same machine is sold at the end of Year 5, when accumulated depreciation amounted to $18,000. Book value at this date was $2,000 ($20,000 cost − $18,000 accumulated depreciation). Three different situations are possible.

Sale at Book Value
The asset is sold for $2,000. The journal entry to record the sale is:

Cash	2,000	
Accum. Deprec.	18,000	
Equipment		20,000

Sale above Book Value
The asset is sold for $3,000. The journal entry to record the sale is:

Cash	3,000	
Accum. Deprec.	18,000	
Gain on Disposal		1,000
Equipment		20,000

Sale below Book Value
The asset is sold for $1,000. The journal entry to record the sale is:

Cash	1,000	
Accum. Deprec.	18,000	
Loss on Disposal	1,000	
Equipment		20,000

In each of these cases, the cash proceeds must be recorded (by a debit) and the cost and accumulated depreciation must be removed from the accounts. At this point the debits of the journal entry must equal the credits. A credit difference represents a gain on disposal; a debit difference represents a loss on disposal.

Disposal Involving Trade-In

Trade-in
The exchange of one
asset for another.

Trade-in allowance
The amount allocated to
an asset being exchanged
for another asset; often
the trade-in allowance is
not realistic.

It is a common practice to exchange a used asset as a **trade-in** when a new asset is acquired. Usually a **trade-in allowance** is applied to the sales price of the new asset, and the purchaser pays the difference. If the trade-in allowance approximates the fair market value of the used asset on the open market, the new asset is recorded at its list price. If the trade-in allowance is not realistic—as is usually the case, particularly in the case of motor vehicles — the new asset is recorded at its cash market price.

$$\text{Cost of New Asset} = \text{Cash Paid} + \text{Fair Market of Asset Traded in.}$$

If there is a difference between this calculated fair market value of the asset traded in and the book value of the asset traded-in, then a gain or loss results.

Assume that the same machine that cost $20,000 and has an accumulated depreciation of $18,000 at the end of Year 5 is traded in for a new machine with a list price of $25,000. A trade-in allowance of $2,000 is given on the old machine, which has a fair market value of $1,000. In this case, the cost of the asset is calculated as follows:

$$\text{Cash paid} + \text{Fair Market Value of Asset Traded in} = \text{Cost of New Asset}$$
$$= \$24,000$$

$$\$23,000 \quad + \quad \$\ 1,000$$

List Price:	$25,000
Trade-in:	2,000
Cash Paid:	$23,000

The journal entry to record the purchase of the new machine and trade-in of the old follows:

Equipment (new)	24,000		
Accumulated Depreciation	18,000	Debits = $42,000	A debit difference
Loss on Disposal of Equipment	1,000		means a loss
Equipment (old)		20,000	of $1,000.
Cash		23,000	Credits = $43,000

In this entry, the cost of the new machine ($24,000) is entered into the accounts, the accumulated depreciation and cost of the old machine is removed from the accounts, and the amount of cash paid is recorded. At this point the total debits equal $42,000 ($24,000 + $18,000) and total credits equal $43,000 ($20,000 + $23,000), with debit shortage of $1,000 ($42,000 debits versus $43,000 credits). The debit difference of $1,000 represents a loss on disposal.

F.   Depletion of Natural Resources

Natural resources include timberlands, mines, oil wells, and natural gas deposits. They are recorded in asset accounts at cost. These natural resources are sometimes referred to as wasting assets because the resource in most cases is not renewable and, once extracted, the asset value is reduced. This expiration of the asset is recorded in the books as depletion. (Natural resources deplete, while non-natural assets depreciate.) The journal entry usually takes the following form:

Depletion Expense	xxx	
Accumulated Depletion — Mine		xxx

Theoretically, the depletion becomes a part of the inventory cost, which includes labour and other costs of extracting the ore (overhead). Therefore, depletion is a part of the cost of goods sold on the income statement. In the balance sheet, Accumulated Depletion — Mine is deducted from the cost of the mine resource:

Property:

Gold Mine	$xx,xxx	
Less: Accumulated Depletion	xxx	$xx,xxx

The periodic depletion charge is usually calculated on a usage basis called *units of production*. A depletion cost per unit is multiplied by the number of units extracted in order to calculate the periodic depletion expense. For example a mine having an estimated 100 000 tonnes of nickel would have a cost of $3 per tonne if its cost less salvage value amounted to $300,000 ($350,000 cost − $50,000 salvage value). If 20 000 tonnes are extracted during the year, the depletion would amount to $60,000.

$$\frac{\$350,000 \text{ cost} - \$50,000 \text{ salvage value}}{100\ 000 \text{ tonnes}} = \$3 \text{ per tonne} \times 20\ 000 \text{ tonnes}$$

$$= \$60,000$$

The depletion for the year would be recorded in the general journal this way:

Depletion Expense	60,000	
Accumulated Depletion — Mine		60,000

In the example, the output of the mine was measured in tonnes. Usually the marketing unit is used as the unit of production in calculating depletion expense — *board metres* or *(feet)* of lumber, *tonnes* of ore, *barrels* of oil, and *cubic metres* (or *feet*) of natural gas.

APPENDIX: The Current Cost Model

The *CICA Handbook* (section 4510.42) recommends that current cost fixed asset data be disclosed as supplementary information to historical cost based financial statements. The balance sheet fixed asset valuation should use current costs at the balance sheet date.

Impact on the Balance Sheet

This calculation of fixed asset current cost can be illustrated from an analysis made for management of Bluebeard Computer Corporation. Two different years were considered. Fixed assets were assumed to cost $20,000, had an estimated useful life of 5 years, and a salvage value of $2,000; a straight-line method of depreciation was used. It was further calculated that year-end fixed asset current cost was $28,000 in Year 1.

	Asset Valuation	
	Under Historical Cost December 31, Year 1	*Under Current Cost* December 31, Year 1
Balance Sheet		
Fixed Assets	$20,000	$28,000
Less: Accumulated Depreciation	3,600 (18%)	5,040 (18)%
Carrying Value	$16,400	$22,960

> In Year 1, accumulated depreciation amounts to 18% of fixed asset cost. Under the historical cost assumption, depreciation expense amounts to $3,600 per year. Note that the calculation of depreciation expense is different under the current cost model.

> In Year 1, the 18% is used to calculate accumulated depreciation ($28,000 × 18% = $5,040). Under the current cost model, depreciation expense can amount to $5,040.

As can be seen, fixed asset current costs result in entirely different cost, accumulated depreciation, and carrying value amounts. A more complete discussion of current cost accounting is beyond the scope of this chapter; it is usually the subject matter of more advanced accounting courses.

A number of different measurement techniques have been suggested to calculate the current cost of fixed assets. These include the use of price indices and appraisals; engineering estimates of the impact of technological change and other factors can also be considered. Because the calculation of these current costs is in an experimental stage, further refinements to current techniques are expected as experience in their calculation and use develops. The same estimated useful life and straight-line depreciation method is used as in the historical cost calculation presented here.

Calculation of current costs is essentially a subjective process; here it is based on management's estimates and assumptions regarding matters such as replacement costs, and impacts of technology.

Impact on the Income Statement

The analysis prepared in Chapter 8 for management of Bluebeard Computer Corporation showed the impact of current cost calculations on net income when inventory purchase costs are increasing. This analysis is developed in this chapter to consider the impact of current cost on depreciation expense. The same sales, cost of goods sold and gross profit data were used for this new analysis.

With the additional straight-line depreciation data, a comparison of net income was prepared under the historical cost assumption the current cost model. The BCC executives were stunned by the results.

	Historical Cost	Current Cost
Sales	$20,000	$20,000
Cost of Goods Sold	10,000	18,000
Gross Profit	$10,000	$ 2,000
Operating Expenses:		
Depreciation	$ 3,600	$ 5,040
Other Expenses	2,400	2,400
	$ 6,000	$ 7,440
Operating Income (loss)	$ 4,000	($ 5,440)
Income Tax (50%)	2,000	2,000
Net Income (loss)	$ 2,000	($ 7,440)

The *CICA Handbook* (section 4510.38) recommends that current costs information relating to depreciation expense and its impact on the reported net income figure be disclosed as supplementary information to historical cost based financial statements.

This further analysis clearly shows a wider spread between the phantom profit produced under the historical cost assumption and the increased loss under the current cost model. Bluebeard's executives had been told that, under current cost accounting, depreciation expense is viewed as the part of the asset that has been used during the year. On the basis of the above net income (loss) calculations, it is apparent that the company would be unable to replace its fixed assets without additional borrowing; it is losing its ability to operate at the same level in the future.

Even worse, income tax estimated at 50 percent and calculated at $2,000, would be paid on the historical cost calculation of operating income while, in fact, there was an operating loss under the current cost model. The payment of income tax on these phantom profits is not at all satisfactory.

The current cost model indicates that Bluebeard is losing its operating capacity and will eventually be unable to replace its fixed assets without increased borrowing.

The Historical Cost Dilemma

As explained, the emphasis of the current cost model is its concern with the maintenance of the entity's operating capability, which should be as great at the end of the accounting period as it was at the beginning.

A dilemma for the accounting profession centres on the historical cost concept. As noted earlier, it is retained for financial statement purposes because historical costs are objectively determined — even though the measure used, the stable dollar concept, is invalid during periods of rapid inflation. Although current cost figures are more relevant, their incorporation into the body of financial statements is questioned because the determination of current costs is generally a subjective process, based, in some cases, on management's estimates and assumptions.

Although current costs seem more relevant, their use in record-keeping or incorporation into the body of financial statements is not included among the *CICA Handbook* recommendations. As explained before, the availability of current cost supplementary information is assumed to be adequate for financial statement readers to assess the impact of changing prices or the entity's ability to maintain its level of operating capability. A review of published supplementary information leads some experts to question the validity of this assumption.

A Word of Caution

In addition to the recommendations for the measurement of depreciation expense and fixed assets using current costs, there are also certain other effects associated with changing prices. These relate to the impact of financing and other adjustments that may alleviate, at least in part, the loss of operating capability. There is also the use of recoverable amounts in certain cases which, in effect, is an exception to the use of current costs.

A more complete treatment of these topics is usually the subject matter of advanced accounting courses. Caution must also be exercised in generalizing to other situations the impact of price changes on Bluebeard Computer Corporation. Different circumstances can be expected to yield different results.

The current cost model is in an experimental state at the present time and is being evaluated. No general concensus has emerged concerning the usefulness of the information generated; however, it is expected to provide useful insights into the operations of each entity using the model.

APPENDIX: Intangible Assets

Intangible assets
Non-physical rights and expected benefits that come from the ownership of intangible assets: for example, patents, copyrights, trademarks, and goodwill.

Fixed assets are referred to as tangible assets because they have physical substance. Another major category of assets do not have physical substance; these are referred to as intangible assets. The *CICA Handbook* (section 3080.01) recommends that the major categories of **intangible assets**, such as goodwill, franchises, patent rights, copyrights, and trademarks, should be shown separately. Other assets — for example, accounts receivable, pre-paid expenses, and investments — although they do not have a physical substance as such, are reported under other asset classifications in the balance sheet. They are never called intangible assets.

Intangible assets, as discussed in this section, are sometimes referred to as "soft assets" because of the uncertainty associated with their estimated useful lives. This uncertainty makes allocating their cost over the accounting periods that will be benefitted difficult. Where an intangible asset is acquired other than through payment of cash or its equivalent, the *CICA Handbook* recommends that the basis of valuation should be fully disclosed (section 3080.02). The *Handbook* further recommends that the amount of amortization for the current period and the basis of amortization should also be disclosed (section 3080.04).

Intangible assets share two additional characteristics: they are all long-term assets and, as detailed later, they all bestow certain legal rights.

Patents

Patent
A seventeen-year exclusive right granted by the federal government to an inventor to produce and sell his/her invention.

Patents are intangible assets that affect how the entity produces its products. A **patent** is granted by the federal government and gives the holder an exclusive legal privilege to produce and sell a product for a period of 17 years. The useful life of the patent may be less than 17 years because of changes in technology or in the marketplace. On the other hand, modifications to the original product can result in a new patent being granted, in effect, extending the original 17-year life of the original patent. Patents can be purchased or sold.

Real Life Example 9-2

Computer Clones

IBM Canada Ltd. has obtained an injunction against a Montreal company, Spirales Computers, to prevent it from selling an "IBM clone" computer called the Copan PC 301. According to evidence filed by IBM in obtaining the junction, a chip in the PC 301 is a copy of one in the IBM Personal Computer.

This is a good time to explain the difference between a compatible computer and a clone. Not every microcomputer that runs the same software as the IBM PC is really an IBM clone. Most of them simply run the MS-DOS operating system (which is essentially the same as the PC-DOS operating system on the IBM) and therefore most of the software that works on the PC. The hardware is not the same.

A real clone is an illegal copy of the PC or any other computer. It doesn't have to be identical; it's a clone if some part of it was copied directly from another computer (usually the IBM

PC or the Apple II). This is what IBM is claiming the Copan PC 301 is. Such computers may be illegal because they infringe patents and/or copyrights.

The law is not terribly clear on this point, though, because — particularly in the area of computer software — Canadian legislation is somewhat behind the times. Our Copyright Act is about 60 years old and says nothing about software. . . .

The Spirales case will be an interesting one because it will determine what IBM and companies like IBM can do about the clones in Canada. Users of established PC–compatible machines like the Hyperion, Compaq, Columbia and so forth need not worry, however.

Source   Grant Buckley, "Personal Computers", *The* (Montreal) *Gazette*, May 26, 1984, p. I-6.

Patents are recorded at cost. If purchased from an inventor, the patent's cost is easily identified; if developed internally, the patent's cost includes all expenditures incurred in the development of the patent, with the exception of those expenditures classified as research and non-deferable development costs. The detailed coverage of the distinction between expenditures to be classified as either patent or research and development costs is the subject matter of advanced accounting courses. In addition to the capitalization of the legal and registration costs associated with the patent, the costs of any successful patent infringement lawsuits would be included in the Patent account.

Because of changes in technology and in the marketplace, a conservative estimate is usually made for a patent's useful life. A straight-line method of amortization is usually used and is recorded directly to the asset account.

Patent Amortization Expense	XXX	
Patent		XXX

Copyrights

Copyright
The exclusive right granted by the federal government to publish a literary or artistic work; exists for the lifetime of the author and an additional fifty years after his/her death.

A **copyright** is another intangible asset that confers on the holder an exclusive legal privilege: in this case, the federal government grants control over a published or artistic work for the life of the artist and 50 years afterward. This control extends to the reproduction, sale, or other use of the copyrighted material.

While the cost to obtain a copyright is minimal, the purchase of a copyrighted work can be substantial. Purchased copyrights are recorded at cost; this cost is amortized over the estimated useful life of the copyright, which is often less than its legal life. As is the case with patents, the costs of any successful copyright infringement lawsuits or out-of-court settlements are added to the cost of the assets and amortized over its remaining useful life. An interesting example of copyright infringement involving personal computers is found in Real Life Example 9-2.

Trademarks

Trademark
A legal right granted by the federal government to use a symbol or a word to identify a company or one of its products or services.

A **trademark** is a symbol or a word used by a company to identify itself or one of its products in the marketplace. Symbols are often logos printed on company stationery or displayed at company offices, on vehicles, or in advertising. Well-known word examples are Coke and CN. The right to use a trademark can be protected by registering it with the registrar of trademarks. Normally a trademark does not diminish in value through the passage of time or usage but is affected by its success or lack of success. Trademarks are usually carried at cost and not amortized. Two unusual issues involving trademarks are discussed in Real Life Example 9-3.

Franchises

Franchise
A legal right to render a service or to produce a good.

A **franchise** is a legal right granted by an entity or a government to sell particular products or to provide certain services in a given territory using a specific trademark or trade name. In return for the franchise, the franchisor often pays a fee that constitutes his/her franchise cost. McDonalds is one example of a franchised fast-food chain. The right to manufacture and sell Coke is another example.

Another example of a franchise is one granted by government for the provision of certain services within a given geographical location: for example, television stations authorized by the Canadian Radio-television and Telecommunications Commission, telephone services authorized in a particular province, or garbage collection authorized within a given community.

Real Life Example 9-3

Trademarks

An example of a trademark that was once widely used by RCA, discontinued in 1968, and is once again being used, follows.

Remember Nipper? He first appeared in 1901 on the first RCA gramophone ad—"His Master's Voice". Now RCA has gone to the dog again—he has been collared as the logo for all new RCA audio and video products.

But wait, that's not the tail-end of the story. Nipper was a real fox terrier pooch born near Bristol, England, in 1884, and he really did look into a gramophone that way. He was captured on canvas by Francis Barraud, the brother of Nipper's real master, who died. Times were ruff, so Barraud sold the painting and rights to RCA for £100. Nipper died in 1895, but his bonefied replicas live on. However, reproducing him will not come as cheap. It's estimated that the logo, along with the ad campaigns, will put the bite on RCA for some $8 million a year — and that's nothing to shake a stick at.

In some cases, a trademark is not issued, as in the following case.

No doubt much to entertainer Johnny Carson's relief, the phrase "Here's Johnny" is not an acceptable trademark for portable toilets.

A "john" might be a portable toilet or "a client of a lady of negotiable virtue", a Federal Court of Canada ruling said yesterday. But "Here's Johnny" is just too readily associated with Johnny Carson and The Tonight Show to be allowed as a trademark for portable toilets, Mr. Justice Patrick Mahoney said.

Carson had appealed a decision by the registrar of trademarks to allow William Reynolds of St. Catharines to use the trademark for his business of renting portable outhouses.

The judge hinged his decision on a section of the Trade Marks Act that says no one shall adopt a trademark that may falsely suggest a connection with any living individual. He accepted as evidence a random survey in which people surveyed where handed a card bearing the words "Here's Johnny" and were asked, "What does this mean to you?". Of those surveyed, 63 percent mentioned Carson or the Johnny Carson Show. While it was clear a significant number of people connected the phrase with Carson, there was no connection between Reynolds or the talk-show host, Judge Mahoney said.

As in the case of patents and copyrights, the cost of a franchise should be amortized over its useful life. In addition to the payment of a franchise fee that is capitalized, a franchise agreement usually requires annual payments. These payments, when incurred, are considered as an operating expense.

Secret Processes

Secret processes are not normally subject to amortization because they are assumed to have an unlimited life. Real Life Example 9-4 illustrates how important a secret process can be to a corporation. If the process will benefit the business as long as it is a going concern, then the cost of the process should not be amortized.

Research and Development Costs

Research and development activities are distinguished as follows in the *CICA Handbook*, section 3450.02:

> Research is planned investigation undertaken with the hope of gaining new scientific or technical knowledge and understanding. Such investigation may or may not be directed towards a specific practical aim or application. In this case, it is recommended that the research costs be expensed during the period in which they are incurred.

Real Life Example 9-4

The Coca-Cola Secret

The Coca-Cola Company says the secret formula for its cola flavouring ingredients is kept in a bank vault, which can be opened only by a vote of the board of directors. The formula for the soft drink long known by its trademark "Coke", the company adds, is known by only two senior chemists who are currently active at Coca-Cola (and apparently by one who has retired).

Early in 1985, in a brave marketing move, the company announced that it was discontinuing production of Coca-Cola and would replace it with a new Coke. This move followed several months of heatedly aggressive advertising campaigns by Coca-Cola and its competitors. One month after launching this new cola, the company changed once more in response to a massive consumer-testing effort; this time, it announced plans to bring back the former soft drink and market it under the name "Coca-Cola Classic", while retaining the new Coke as its flagship brand.

What's in that cola bottle? To start with, it apparently contains 99.8 percent water and sugar. After that, the mystery begins. The name "Coca-Cola" itself gives the best clue to the drink's principal flavouring ingredients, the coca leaf and the cola nut. In addition, the formula contains a complex blend of flavours and additives, with none standing out as a distinctive taste.

A modest amount of research turned up the following putative recipe for Coca-Cola Classic, which the company declines to confirm or dispute but which outside experts find reasonable:

Water, sugar, caramel (for colouring), caffeine, phosphoric acid, cinnamon, nutmeg, vanilla, glycerin, lavender, lime juice, other citrus oils and fluid extract of guarana (which comes from the roasted, chestnut-like seed of a Brazilian tree, and contains caffeine and tannin).

Finally, there is the so-called secret ingredient, "merchandise No. 5": Three parts coca leaves (with the cocaine removed) to one part cola nut.

In the late 1800s, Coke apparently contained a trace of cocaine, left over in the coca leaf after the "decocainizing" process. Shortly after 1900, however, the removal of cocaine from the leaf came under government supervision and, ever since, the drink has had to stand on its own as a pick-me-up.

Today, the coca flavouring for both colas is said to be extracted from coca leaves imported by the Stepan Chemical Company's Maywood, N.J. division. The cocaine, some [900–1350 kg] 2000 to 3000 lb. a year, is reportedly sold for medicinal uses.

Whatever the ingredients, they remain Coca-Cola's secret — and the life blood of the corporation.

Development is the translation of research findings or other knowledge into a plan or design for new or substantially improved materials, products, processes, systems or services prior to the commencement of commercial production or use. These expenses should also be written off as incurred unless they meet certain circumstances set out in Section 3450.21 in which case they should be capitalized and amortized over future periods.

Because of the difficulty in meeting all the criteria set out in the *CICA Handbook*, most research and development expenses tend to be written off as incurred. The detailed coverage of research and development expenditures is the subject matter of more advanced accounting courses.

Goodwill

Goodwill is an example of an intangible asset that may or may not appear in an entity's books. This apparent inconsistency results because there may have been no purchased cost of goodwill and, under GAAP, it cannot be recorded as an asset, even though the entity may have superior earning power, better business locations, particularly effective management, or a secret process that set it apart from its competitors. **Goodwill** is seen as a composite of all these and other factors that individually, cannot be valued.

Goodwill is recorded only when it is purchased; it usually arises in a business consolidation and is calculated as the difference between the purchase cost of an interest in another entity and the acquiring company's interest in its net assets. The detailed coverage of goodwill is further discussed in Chapter 17. The *CICA Handbook* (section 1580.58) recommends that the amount of goodwill should be amortized over its useful life using a straight-line amortization method; the period should not exceed 40 years.

Organization Costs

Expenditures made to incorporate or to establish the entity are referred to as *organization costs*. These costs are usually seen as having a benefit over the life of the entity and, therefore, are considered as an asset. (This issue is discussed further in Chapter 10.) In actual practice, the amount involved is small in relation to total assets; it is usually written off. The *CICA Handbook* recommends that when organization costs are amortized, the amortization be disclosed.

Goodwill
The value attached to the ability of an entity to make superior earnings as compared with other entities in the same industry; this value is usually not recognized in the financial statements of the entity, unless the entity is purchased; when purchased, it is recorded at acquisition cost and amortized over its remaining useful and legal life.

Discussion Questions

1. The cost of an asset is said to be capitalized. What does this mean?
2. How does a capital expenditure differ from a revenue expenditure? Assume that you have purchased a minicomputer for business use; illustrate, using examples, capital and revenue expenditures associated with the computer.
3. CBCA Inc. has purchased land and buildings for a lump sum. What does this mean? What is the acceptable manner of accounting for a lump sum purchase?
4. When one fixed asset is exchanged for another, how is the cost of the newly acquired asset determined?
5. Contrast the accounting for a betterment and an extraordinary repair. Given an example of each.
6. How does the concept of materiality affect the distinction between a capital and a revenue expenditure?
7. Fixed assets are often thought of as a bundle of services to be used over a period of years. The value of these services in the first year of the useful life of such assets it is claimed, is not the same as in later years. Using a car as an example, indicate whether you agree or disagree.
8. Define tangible assets. How do they differ from intangible assets?
9. Distinguish among depreciation, depletion, and amortization. Give an example of each.
10. Assume that you have recently purchased a new sports car. Is a usage or a time-based method preferable in recording depreciation? Why?
11. Why is salvage value ignored when depreciation is calculated according to the declining balance method but not the straight-line method? Is this inconsistent? Why or why not?
12. What is the derivation for the declining balance method of depreciation? the straight-line method?
13. How is the double-declining balance rate of depreciation calculated for an asset that is expected to have a 5-year useful life?
14. What is capital cost allowance? Why is it a useful method of depreciation calculation?
15. The use of the capital cost allowance method, it is claimed, sometimes involves a stretching of accounting principles. Explain how this might occur. What are the disadvantages of this method?
16. When referring to fixed asset cost allocation, do generally accepted accounting principles stress balance sheet valuation or net income calculation? Explain.

17. a. The payment of income tax is often delayed through the use of capital cost allowance. Does this delay constitute an interest-free loan? If so, when will this loan be repaid?
    b. What are phantom profits in relation to fixed assets, and where do they come from?
18. a. Why don't accountants use the replacement cost of an asset when calculating periodic depreciation?
    b. Your friend is concerned that the calculation of depreciation relies too much on the use of estimates that are usually erroneous. Your friend believes that accountants should be precise. Do you agree that accountants are imprecise in the use of estimates for depreciation? Why or why not?
19. What is the commonly used basis for the recording and depreciating of fixed assets? What other methods could be used?
20. What is the proper accounting procedure to be followed in Canada when previously estimated useful life of an asset is found to be erroneous? Why is more accurate information unavailable when fixed assets are initially acquired?
21. What is a trade-in? Explain whether one is or is not the same as the sale of an asset.
22. Why is the trade-in allowance, particularly in the case of a car, usually unrealistic? Why would a dealer give more trade-in allowance on a used car than it is worth?
23. What are wasting assets? Give some examples. Explain whether all assets aren't wasting.
24. Why is a declining balance method unrealistic for natural resources? What method is permitted for income tax purposes in Canada?
25. What is a patent? Does a patent's useful life usually correspond to its useful life? Why or why not? Support your answer with an example.
26. How does a copyright differ from a trademark? Give an example of each.
27. Why are secret processes not usually subject to amortization? Explain whether or not this practice is inconsistent with generally accepted accounting principles.
28. What is recommended in the *CICA Handbook* for intangible asset valuation and disclosure?
29. What is goodwill? Why is an entity's goodwill usually not recorded in its books?

Discussion Cases

Discussion Case 9-1: J. R.'s Ranch

In the 1950s, Quaker Oats promoted its cereals with an unusual offer: the purchaser of a box of Quaker Oats was entitled to an inch-square [6.5 cm²] piece of land in the Yukon. Now the same gimmick is being used to popularize not cereal but a serial. According to an advertisement in the *National Enquirer*, $25 will purchase a square foot [0.1 m²] of land in J. R.'s South Fork Ranch, the place where the television show *Dallas* was filmed.

"South Fork Ranch is mine," said J. R. Duncan, owner of 8,712,000 square feet [246 700 m²] of Texas soil, who was christened Joseph Rand Duncan, giving him the same initials as the popular *Dallas* character, J. R. Ewing. "By coincidence," said Duncan, "I have not been shot."

"We have actual deeds we send out with the documents to transfer the land to the new buyer," Duncan said, contrasting his land sale with the Quaker Oats giveaway, in which the individual deeds weren't formally registered.

Duncan said he was selling grazing land in the southeastern section of the ranch. Those who buy the land will have only limited rights to it. Although Duncan has built a separate entrance for the new ranch partners, there will be no picnic tables or kiddie rides. In fact, Duncan said he still intended to have his cattle graze the land. Duncan has also arranged to pay property taxes so the city clerk will not have to send thousands of assessment bills around the world.

As part of the deal for shooting on the ranch, Lorimar Productions, the makers of *Dallas*, have granted Duncan exclusive world-wide marketing rights for products carrying the South Fork name. Besides the obligatory T-shirts, belt buckles, and hatbands, Duncan has licensed the company to sell South Fork dirt and another gentleman to sell pieces of the fence.

"He's going to pay me to tear down my fence and cut it up in little pieces for wall plaques and desk weights," Duncan said. "And then he is going to build me a new fence. I'll tell you, I'm open to new ideas."

Source *The New York Times*, December 21, 1980, s. 3, p. 19.

For Discussion

1. Would you pay $25 for a square foot of J. R.'s South Fork Ranch? Consider the following in your answer.
   a. Your use of this land
   b. Novelty value among your friends
   c. Possible increase in value in the future as a collector's item.
   d. Other similar implications, including future land taxes applied to you if there were a default on tax payment.
2. How much would Duncan receive for the land if all 8,712,000 square feet were sold? How would this compare to the probable current market value of this land?
3. If South Fork dirt is sold, would a part of the proceeds constitute a sale of land, depletion expense recovered, or something else? How would Duncan account for this? Prepare a few journal entries to illustrate your solution to this question.
4. (a) Is the original fence generally considered by accountants as part of the cost of the land, a land improvement, equipment or something else? (b) If this land is sold as indicated in this article, what is the proper journal entry to record the sale? (c) If a new fence is going to be built on J. R.'s ranch by the purchaser of the old fence at no charge to Duncan, what is the proper journal entry, if any, to record the new fence? Discuss and illustrate with appropriate journal entries, if applicable. (d) Explain, using your knowledge of accounting theory, why the new fence would not be recorded, if you support this view.
5. What is your estimate of Duncan's probable success in
   a. Selling a square foot of J. R.'s ranch
   b. Selling South Fork dirt
   c. Selling wall plaques and desk weights made from the fence on South Fork.

Discussion Case 9-2:   Canada's Secret Computer Centre

The building looks like one of those nondescript factories that dot the west end of Mississauga, near Toronto, where that industrial playground fades off into its drowsy suburbs. Nothing is manufactured there and, despite the building's size (60,000 square feet or 5575 m²), hardly anyone ever enters or leaves through its imposing shock-sensored doors.

This is the headquarters of Combac Management Corp., one of the more esoteric offshoots of our computer age. Except for its president, a bearded former Winnipegger of Icelandic origin named Gunnar Helgason, and his secretaries, the building is deliberately kept empty — empty, that is, but for the banks of silent sentinels in its lower level. This is a "computer back-up centre", quietly financed by three dozen of Canada's big-ticket corporations. Except for a similar arrangement in Philadelphia, it is the largest facility of its kind in the free world.

It has yet to be used, but its very existence — which has been kept secret because of potential security risks — indicates how dependent Canadian companies have become on their electronic software and hardware. "It's not a published statistic," Helgason told me in an exclusive interview, "but all it would take for the chartered banks to lose financial control of their operations would be 36 hours with their computers down. The Bank of Montreal, for example, is one of the largest private users of computer power in the world today. As the capacities of these computers get larger and faster, the dependency of business people on these machines is growing exponentially. If a computer goes down, it can bring a company to its knees."

It's to provide for such emergencies, whatever their cause, that Helgason created his enterprise. "It's a place where company executives temporarily deprived of their own computer can almost immediately get back to business. We even have a war room for them with audio-visual facilities from which the president and his senior people can operate."

The Mississauga location was chosen because it is near Toronto International Airport, so that the facility is readily available to firms across Canada. Helgason refuses to list his clients, all of whom have insisted on a confidentiality clause in their contracts. The building bristles with closed-circuit television sets, and every window has its own shatter-guard system which will go off at the sound of a scratch. Fire detection and prevention includes not only the standard sprinkler system but heat, smoke and ionization detectors which can report a blaze in its incipient stages. Any fire will trigger clouds of Halon gas — an inert substance (kept in tanks in the building's basement) that deprives fire of oxygen. A 900-circuit telephone switchboard has been installed, and there is a large (eerily vacant) cafeteria, as well as an infirmary for medical emergencies. As many as half a dozen companies can be accommodated at any one time. "In an atomic war, of course," Helgason admits, "all bets are off. Countries and economies can be crippled by attacking just their computer systems. Any intelligent insurrection would pick data centres as prime targets.

"Computers can also be hit during thunderstorms; if an installation's lightning arresters and surge protectors should fail, a bolt out of the sky can zap high voltage into a computer's front end, rendering it useless. Every Canadian company of any size now depends on at least one data centre, and without a back-up facility like this their hands would be tied in the event of any emergency. But it's just too expensive for each company to operate its own back-up system."

Space is allocated for future application of laser, fibre optics and satellite communication facilities. Helgason refuses to discuss the operational details of any of his clients but he has been briefed on the critical time path of each of their decision-making processes and knows how long any company could survive without computer access. "One of our users," he says, "has recently finished a cost analysis of not being able to use their data centre. They have a total of 200 applications running on their computers, and *one* of those applications alone would cost the company $12 million a month if they weren't able to process."

The facility is owned by a limited company named Combac, with 61 partners, many of them major Canadian investors who estimate that it would cost about $10 million to duplicate the Mississauga computer centre. Its heart is a specially acclimatized area with a mammoth IBM-compatible installation (a V-8 Amdahl) and a tape library capable of holding 25 000 reels of tape. (The computer is now being upgraded to a larger model.)

Helgason loosely classifies himself as a financial consultant. He was invited to leave the University of Manitoba after two years of science courses for playing cards once too often in the students' union. He then became a chartered accountant, worked for Manitoba Hydro, Ducks Unlimited, Coopers & Lybrand and Thorne Riddell. He has packaged tax shelters, sold MURBS and now has interests in half a dozen Journey's End Motels, as well as doing the syndication packaging for Golden Griddle restaurants, and dealing in Florida real estate. His most interesting venture (with a partner, Frank Dwyer) is Manu-Comp Systems, which sells computer software to doctors and dentists. He is also a partner in New Age Softwear Ltd., which has developed a new computer language that will allow machines to communicate with one another. (That's referred to in the trade as "a fourth-generation system interface".)

At 38, Helgason claims he really doesn't "work" any more. "I've retired," he says. "That's the way I look at it."

He spends most of his time in that big empty building in Mississauga, planning for a day that may never come — when he could be running the decision-making centre of industrial Canada.

Source   Peter C. Newman, "Canada's Secret Computer Centre", *Maclean's*, September 19, 1983.

For Discussion

Tangible assets come to the end of their useful lives; depreciation is recorded in recognition of the assets' useful life. How should depreciation be recorded for Combac's computers? What issues would you consider in your decision?

Discussion Case 9-3: Carpar

Carpar, a Windsor company producing auto parts, acquired a robot for its assembly line because it found its human workers could not perform at peak efficiency throughout the 8-hour day and produce uniform quality. At the same time that prices for its products were falling, costs were rising. The average worker cost Carpar $55,000 per year in salary and benefits. The company employs 12 people, 10 of whom are directly involved in production. Annual sales are worth about $1 million.

In February 1986, it bought the playback articulated robot to perform the coating operation, at a cost of $110,000. The robot is used on two 12-hour shifts and is operated by a worker with one year of experience. His job is to take the work from the conveyor to the jig, attach it, and remove it when the coating is finished, a process which takes 25 seconds in total. There are two other employees who are in charge of robot teaching and maintenance. The maintenance cost of the robot is estimated to be $6,000 per year for the 10-year life of the robot. The robot can coat 3200 pieces in 8 hours, as opposed to the 800 turned out by experienced workers. This result represents a 400 percent increase in productivity.

For Discussion

1. What would be the most appropriate method of depreciation to allocate the robot's cost over its full useful life?
2. Robots, which can be classified as fixed assets, can be depreciated over their useful life. Employees, who perform the same tasks, improve their work skills over time and receive remuneration according to their skill development, cost of living, and seniority. Compare and contrast the income statement bottom line implications of using robots contrasted to using human employees.
3. Currently, major league baseball teams are allowed to depreciate their players' contracts over their expected playing careers for income tax purposes. Comment on this practice as it relates to GAAP.

Discussion Case 9-4: Bionics

Artificial knees. Artificial hips. Artificial blood. Artificial ears. Artificial arteries. Artificial hearts. Such are the wondrous products of the ultimate business: the replication of the human body. Substitutive medicine — replacing real parts with fake ones — has blossomed into one of the most important trends in health care and has, in turn, spawned a fast-growing community of manufacturers that try to replace the irreplaceable.

More than a million people have artificial parts implanted inside them every year. Individuals in excruciating pain from arthritis now walk more peacefully with artificial hips. Victims of atherosclerosis, a form of hardening of the arteries, have had their circulation bettered by vascular grafts. Cataract patients see because of intraocular lenses. Years in the future, anything may be possible, since the consuming belief of medical researchers is that everything in the body will ultimately be duplicated by parts flowing out of a factory.

Ear — *$8,000–12,000*
Lens Implant — *$300*
Wrist — *$280–295*
Heart — *$50,000–80,000*
Heart Valve — *$2,000*
Knee — *$1,500–2,000*
Finger Joint — *$99*
Leg or Arm — *$1,000–3,000*
Ankle — *$700*
Blood Vessel — *$300*
Toe Joint — *$92–99*
Shoulder and Knee Ligament — *$200–500*
Shoulder — *$900*
Elbow — *$1,200*
Hip — *$1,000–2,000*

Design proliferation characterizes the industry. Need a knee? Choose from hundreds. A lens? Hundreds to pick from. Differences are usually too subtle for the eye to detect. Ask about how perfectly the fake parts work, and the answers from executives are like this: "There is no ideai heart valve" or "There are over 300 designs for the knee and we haven't found the perfect solution yet."

An artificial part in place, patients may be liberated from pain, but they are often foolhardy, expecting it to be as good as new.

Talking about artificial joints, Frank Lewis, director of engineering at Richards, says: "How long one lasts depends on the surgeon's skill, the type of implant, and the patient. The most important are the patients. What do they do after they get the prosthesis? Do they go jogging? Do they go mountain climbing? These people are out of pain for the first time, so they tend to abuse the new joints. I think the *Six Million Dollar Man* on television didn't help any. You would think the artificial joint would be stronger because it's metal rather than bone. But the bone reheals itself. The metal just wears down. And you can't do maintenance. You can't get in there and give it a shot of grease."

For all its promise, the artificial body parts business is laden with risks. There is a rising tide of transplants of living organs. What's more researchers might strike it big with a miracle drug that will tame one of the horrid diseases that cause patients to seek new parts. A Pfizer official commented: "If our pharmaceutical division comes up with a drug that cures arthritis, then I guess we send our prosthesis division down the tubes."

The list of products runs on and on, until the bionic human is nearly complete.

Need some bones? Calcitek, a division of Intermedics, makes a fake bone mineral fashioned out of hydroxylapatite. "When you implant any form of this synthetic bone mineral, it fools the bone into believing it is real bone," explains Dr. Michael Jarcho, the company's president. "So the actual living bone grows and attaches itself to the substance." Though currently restricted to dental applications, the substance is expected to spread to orthopaedic applications and be used as a bone graft substitute.

Need blood? Green Cross, a Japanese drug company, has Fluosol, an artificial blood. Still years away from distribution, Fluosol is not without drawbacks, for instance carrying no white cells to combat infections. But in emergency situations it could be a life-saver.

Musing about the hunt for new and better products as the clatter from the Howmedia parts factory reverberated in the background, Dave Fitzgerald said, "You gotta wonder sometimes if maybe we live too long. But, as long as people get older this market gets bigger. As you get older, your parts wear down. That's what it really comes down to. This whole business is the wearing down of parts. As long as they wear out, we'll put in new ones."

Source   *The New York Times*, November 20, 1983, p. 1-F.

For Discussion

1. In accounting terms, would you view the purchase of an artificial joint as a capital expenditure or as a revenue expenditure? Why?
2. Comment on the accounting issues involved in the sale of transplant organs.
3. In Canada, people donate blood voluntarily to Red Cross reserves; in the United States, people are paid for giving blood. Comment on accounting issues for the Red Cross that differ between the two countries, regarding blood collection.

Discussion Case 9-5:   Air Canada's "Newest" Aircraft

Air Canada's newest aircraft, unveiled yesterday, is also one of its oldest — a sign of tough economic times.

They used to be called DC-8s in the 1960s, but with a facelift and four new CFM-56 engines, they are now known as DC-8 Super 73s.

Six are being refurbished for cargo service in a $147-million program, mainly because it would cost more than twice as much to replace them with new aircraft.

Without the new engines, they, like hundreds of DC-8s and Boeing 707s, would be grounded by tough aircraft noise-abatement rules that take effect in 1986.

Air Canada is one of only four companies in the world doing the re-engining itself and hopes to get outside contracts for similar jobs. It would like the Canadian Forces to re-engine its four 707s, or even better, buy some of Air Canada's surplus DC-8s — it has 19 to sell — and have the airline do the work.

"This is an expertise we paid to acquire and we hope to use it to our advantage," said Pierre Jeanniot, the airline's executive vice-president.

The work was to be performed by Cammacorp of California, but was reclaimed by Air Canada during the recession, allowing the recall of 65 laid-off mechanics.

Source   Canadian Press, "A DC-8 by any other name . . .", *The* (Montreal) *Gazette*, November 8, 1983, p. D-1.

For Discussion

1. Recall the claim that tangible assets are on an "irresistible march to the junk heap". How does the re-emergence of the DC-8 square with this claim?
2. What would be the appropriate cost allocation method?

Comprehension Problems

Comprehension Problem 9-1

Accountants distinguish between capital and revenue expenditures when referring to cash disbursements made for asset-related reasons. The debit entry for such expenditures can be made to any one of the following accounts:

Balance Sheet Accounts

a. Land	d. Trucks
b. Buildings	e. Automobiles
c. Equipment	f. Accumulated Depreciation

Income Statement Accounts

g. A revenue account   h. An expense account.

Required: For each transaction, indicate the account to be debited.

Example:

b	Architect fees to design building
h	Battery purchased for truck
c	Cash discount received on payment for equipment
A	Commission paid to real estate agent to purchase land
c	Cost of equipment test runs
B	Cost to remodel building
B	Cost to replace manual elevator with automatic elevator
A	Cost of sewage system
c	Equipment assembly expenditure
C	Expenditures for debugging of equipment
h	Installation of air-conditioner in automobile
h	Insurance paid during construction of building
A	Legal fees associated with court case to defend title to land purchased
h	Oil change for truck
A	Payment for landscaping
A	Proceeds received on demolition of useless building on land purchased
A	Removal of useless structure expenditures
h	Repair made to building after moving in
h	Repair of collision damage to truck
h	Repair of torn imitation leather seats in automobile
h	Replacement of rusted fender on automobile
h	Replacement of transmission on automobile
C	Special floor foundations for installation of equipment
h	Tires purchased for truck
C	Transportation expenditures to bring equipment to plant.

Note: Answer problems regarding intangible assets or current costs only if the Appendixes were studied in your course.

Comprehension Problem 9-2

Atlantic Limited purchased a $30,000 depreciable asset with a 5-year life expectancy and no salvage value. Two alternative methods of depreciating this asset are presented below.

	Depreciation	
Year	Method A	Method B
1	$6,000	$12,000
2	6,000	7,200
3	?	?

Required:
1. Identify the method of depreciation and compute the depreciation expense for the third year under each depreciation method.
2. The controller of Atlantic considers the difference in annual depreciation to be nothing more than a change in the estimate of depreciation required; he proposes to use Method B for Years 1 and 2 and Method A for Years 3, 4, and 5. In this way, he can deduct the maximum depreciation each year over the life of the asset. Is his proposal acceptable? Why or why not?
3. What factors should be considered in choosing a method of depreciation?

Comprehension Problem 9-3

Brinks Limited purchased a truck on January 1, 19X4. The following details are made available:

Cost	Useful Life	Salvage Value	Depreciation Method
$10,500	5 years	$500	Capital Cost Allowance (30%)

In 19X5, the company paid $3,500 for gas and oil, a tune-up, new tires, and a battery. On January 1, 19X5 the company also paid $4,000 to install a lift on the back of the truck (consider this addition as a betterment). The year-end of the company is December 31.

Required: Prepare journal entries to record
1. The purchase of the truck.
2. Depreciation for 19X4.
3. The 19X5 expenditures relating to the truck.
4. Depreciation for 19X5.
5. Do you think that using the income tax capital cost allowance method of calculating depreciation involves a "stretching" of accounting principles in this case? Why or why not?

Comprehension Problem 9-4

The Alberta Corporation purchased three milling machines on January 1, 19X3 and immediately placed them in service. The following information relates to this purchase:

	Machine 1	Machine 2	Machine 3
Cost	$7,500	$7,500	$7,500
Salvage Value	-0-	1,200	300
Useful Life	5 Years	6 Years	8 Years

The company uses the straight-line method of depreciation. Five years after the purchase, Machine 1 was sold for $500. Management elected to re-evaluate the estimated useful life and the salvage value estimates of the remaining machines. They came to the conclusion that Machine 2 had a remaining useful life of 2 years as of January 1, 19X8; salvage value remained unchanged. Machine 3 had a remaining useful life of 5 years but, likely, no salvage value.

Required: Prepare journal entries required during 19X8
1. To record the sale on January 1, 19X8
2. To record the revised depreciation expense for Machine 2 at December 31, 19X8.
3. To record the revised depreciation expense for Machine 3 at December 31, 19X8.

Comprehension Problem 9-5

The following equipment and accumulated depreciation accounts appear in the general ledger of the Big Corporation at December 31, 19X6.

Equipment   No. 183

Date 19X6	Description	F	Debit	Credit	DR. or CR.	Balance
Jan. 1	Machine #1		5000 -		dr	5000 -
Jan. 1	Machine #2		10000 -		dr	15000 -

Accumulated Depreciation-Equipment   No. 193

Date 19X6	Description	F	Debit	Credit	DR. or CR.	Balance
Dec. 31	Depreciation 19X6			1500 -	Cr	1500 -

At the time of purchase, the equipment was expected to have a useful life of 10 years with no salvage value at the end of that time. A straight-line method of depreciation has been used by the company in 19X6. On January 1, 19X7, it was discovered that the equipment would in fact last only 4 more years.

Required:

1. Calculate the depreciation required in 19X7, using the new facts concerning the revised useful life of the equipment.
2. Prepare the entry to record depreciation in 19X7 in the general ledger.
3. Post the accumulated depreciation part of the entry in 2, above, to the ledger and calculate the new balance in the account.
4. When you consider the substantial difference between the depreciation amounts in 19X6 and 19X7, what is your impression of the validity of the information conveyed to the reader of Big Corporation's balance sheet in 19X6 as compared with 19X7? How much should the depreciation amount have been in each year if the actual 5-year useful life of the equipment had been known in 19X6?

Comprehension Problem 9-6

A truck was purchased by Eric's Transport Inc. on June 30, 19X3.

Cost	Useful Life	Salvage Value	Depreciation Method
$13,500	6 Years	$1,500	Capital Cost Allowance (30% declining balance)

Required:
1. Calculate the depreciation for 19X3 and 19X4.
2. Using the information calculated in 1, prepare journal entries if the truck is sold January 2, 19X5 for cash for:
   a. $6615   b. $7615   c. $5615.
3. Do you think that using the income tax capital cost allowance method of calculating depreciation involves a "stretching" of accounting principles in this case? Why or why not?
4. Assume that the old truck was traded in for a new truck instead of being sold; prepare the journal entry to record the trade-in on January 2, 19X5. The list price of the new truck is $15,000. The old truck had a fair market value of $5,000. Eric's Transport Inc. traded in the old truck and paid an additional $7,500 cash in acquiring the new truck.

Comprehension Problem 9-7

Assets included within the fixed asset category usually include the following:
a. Depreciable Tangible Assets
   Depreciation is the term used to describe the allocation of a tangible asset's cost to expense over its useful life.
b. Depreciable Natural Resource Assets
   Depletion is the term used to describe the allocation of a natural resource's cost to expense over its useful life.
c. Depreciable Intangible Assets
   Amortization is the term used to describe the allocation of an intangible asset's cost to expense over its useful life.

Required: For each asset listed, indicate the proper term used to describe the allocation of the asset's cost to expense — depreciation, depletion, or amortization. Indicate with an "x" any asset that does not depreciate, deplete, or amortize.

Example:

__a__ Apartment building

X Cash	X Land improvements
b Coal mine	B Mineral deposit
A Capital expenditures related to apartment building	B Natural gases
C Copyright	B Oil well
X Cost of useless structure removed from land owned	C Patent
A Cost to debug equipment	A Pin ball machine
C Edsel car	X Revenue expenditure related to truck
A Equipment	C Secret processes
A Floor supports for equipment	A Sports car
C Franchise	A Tools
B Gold mine	C Timberlands
C Goodwill	C Trademark
X Land	A Truck.

Problems

Problem 9-1 (SMA adapted)

The following items relate to the acquisition of a new machine by the Hamilton Group Inc. On the right-hand side is a number of possible accounting treatments; on the left-hand side is a number of independent accounting situations.

Situation

_____ Invoice price of new machine, net of the cash discount offered

_____ Cash discount on the above, which has not yet been taken

_____ Anticipated first year's savings in operating costs from use of new machine

_____ Two-year service contract on operations of new machine paid in full

_____ Cost of materials used while testing new machine

_____ Cost of installing sound insulation in wall near machine so that nearby office employees will not be disturbed by it

_____ Cost of removing machine that new machine replaces.

Accounting Treatment

(1) Debit Machinery account

(2) Debit an expense account for the current period

(3) Debit an asset other than the machine and amortize the asset separately from the machine

(4) Credit Machinery account

(5) An accounting treatment other than the above. Explain what account would be appropriate.

Required: Indicate the appropriate accounting treatment for each situation. Record any assumptions that you think might be necessary for any given situation.

Problem 9-2

Fun City Amusement Park Ltd. acquired a new amusement ride, on which it took a July 1 delivery. The following details apply to the purchase.

Cost per supplier's invoice	$20,000
(The invoice provided a 1% cash discount if paid within 30 days. Paid for above item on July 15.)	
Payment on July 4 to Howe Construction Ltd. for cement base for new ride	4,000
Transportation paid on purchase, July 5	520
Insurance paid on ride July 5 — 3-year term	90
Installation costs, July 6	188
Alterations to new ride	900
(This was covered up to 25% by the vendor under terms of its guarantee. Bill received and paid, July 5.)	

Required:

1. Prepare journal entries to record the activities of Fun City in acquiring its new ride.
2. Calculate the carrying value of the asset after accounting for the above.

Problem 9-3

Kappa Corporation purchased a piece of machinery at the beginning of 19X5. The following information is made available.

Cost	Useful Life	Salvage Value	Depreciation Method
$90,000 installed	9000 units	-0-	usage

Output during 19X5 and 19X6 was 2000 and 3000 units, respectively.

Required:
1. Calculate the depreciation expense for 19X5 and 19X6.
2. What is the balance of accumulated depreciation at the end of 19X6?
3. What is the net amount of the machinery shown on the balance sheet at the end of 19X6?
4. Prepare a partial comparative balance sheet for Kappa Corporation at the end of 19X6.

Problem 9-4

Mulroney Corp. purchased a business microcomputer on January 1, 19X3. The company year-end is December 31. The following information is made available.

Cost	Useful Life	Salvage Value	Depreciation Method
$5,000	4 years	$1,000	(to be discussed)

Required:
1. Calculate the depreciation expense for a 4-year period under each of these depreciation methods; straight-line, double-declining balance (calculate the rate), and capital cost allowance (30%).

YEAR	Depreciation Expense		
	STRAIGHT LINE	DOUBLE DECLINING BALANCE	CAPITAL COST ALLOWANCE
1			
2			
3			
4			
TOTAL			

2. Since computers are subject to rapid changes in technology, the president asks you to explain what impact potential changes may have on the microcomputer's useful life. What factors should you cover in your explanation?
3. Which method of depreciation would you recommend in this case? Why?

Problem 9-5

Liebman Trucks Inc. purchased a delivery van on January 1, 19X3. The following information is available.

Cost	Useful Life	Salvage Value	Depreciation Method
$11,000	4 Years	$2,000	(to be discussed)
	(consisting of 75 000 km)		

The truck covered 20 000 km in 19X3.

Required:

1. Calculate the depreciation for 19X3 under each of the following methods:
   a. Usage
   b. Straight-line
   c. Single-declining balance
   d. Double-declining balance
   e. Capital cost allowance (30%).
2. Compare the depreciation expense, accumulated depreciation, and net book value for 19X3 for each of these methods:
   a. Usage
   b. Straight-line
   c. Single-declining balance
   d. Double-declining balance
   e. Capital cost allowance.
3. Which of these methods can be used for income tax purposes? Why?
4. Which method would result in the lowest income taxes paid in 19X3? Calculate the income tax saving in 19X3 if the income tax rate is 50 percent. (*Hint*: The maximum allowable depreciation for income tax purposes cannot exceed the amount calculated using the CCA method.)
5. Which method results in the lowest income taxes paid in 19X6? Show details to support your answer. (Assume that the income tax rate is 50 percent.)
6. Is it fair to try to save on income taxes in 19X3?

Problem 9-6

The Ontario Co. Ltd. purchased a machine on January 1, 19X6 for $23,000. Transportation charges paid by Ontario amounted to $600 and another $1,400 cost was incurred for installation. The estimated salvage value of the machine is $1,000.

Required:

1. Calculate the depreciable cost of the machine.
2. In journal entry form, record the depreciation each year of the expected life of the machine under:
   a. Straight-line method (estimated life 3 years)
   b. Declining balance method (at 40% rate).
3. On January 1, 19X7, Ontario changed the life estimate on the machine from a total of 3 to a total of 5 years. Salvage value remains at an estimated $1,000. You are required to calculate the depreciation that should be recorded in 19X7 and each year thereafter. The company used a straight-line method.

Problem 9-7

On January 1, 19X1, Niedvaras Inc. purchased a machine for $30,000. The engineers had established a life duration for that machine of 20 years. The scrap value is estimated to be 10 percent of the original cost. On January 1, 19X8, experts were hired to review the expected life and scrap value of the machine. Here are the findings:

New Estimated Life   15 years
New Estimated Scrap Value $6,000

Depreciation has not yet been recorded in 19X8. Assume that the straight-line method of depreciation is used.

Required:
1. Calculate the book value of the machine at December 31, 19X7.
2. Calculate the undepreciated cost of the machine at January 1, 19X8, assuming that the straight-line method of depreciation is used.
3. Calculate the amount of depreciation expense to be recorded at December 31, 19X8, and prepare the necessary journal entry.
4. If the current replacement value of the machine is $51,000, comment on the existence of phantom profits in this company. Make some calculations to support your answer.

Problem 9-8 (SMA adapted)

Part A

Littleman Manufacturing Inc. started business on May 1, 19X4. It commenced operations by signing a 20-year lease for a factory building. The year-end of the company is December 31. On May 5, 19X4, the company purchased equipment for $130,000. The equipment had an estimated useful life of 4 years, or a production of 100 000 units, with a salvage value of $10,000. The equipment over three years produced the following numbers of units: 19X4 — 12 000; 19X5 — 30 000; and 19X6 — 20 000.

   On January 4, 19X7, the company traded in all the original equipment on new equipment. The company traded in its old equipment and paid cash ($140,000) to receive delivery of the new equipment. The company had used the units-of-output (usage) method of calculating the depreciation on the manufacturing equipment. The fair market value of the original equipment was $60,000 at the date of the trade.

Part B

On January 5, 19X5, Littleman Manufacturing Inc. was able to buy a nearby warehouse for the storage of its finished product. The cost included: land, $50,000; building, $300,000. The company signed a 10-year mortgage for $320,000 and paid the balance in cash. The building had a useful life of 50 years with no salvage value. On June 28, 19X9, the warehouse was totally destroyed by fire. Owing to a strike by the company employees at the time, the warehouse was empty and the company received $270,000 from the insurance company as settlement in full for the building. The building was depreciated on a straight-line basis.

Required: Prepare journal entries to record the transactions on the following dates
   1. May 5, 19X4 (part A)   3. January 5, 19X5 (part B)
   2. January 4, 19X7 (part A) 4. June 28, 19X9 (part B).

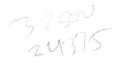

Problem 9-9

A bank manager, a friend of yours, discusses with you the matter of goodwill, which appears so often in financial statements. She mentions that she does not think that such an account should appear in the financial statements, particularly since the rules for evaluation and presentation vary from one company to another.

Required:
1. What is goodwill? Name some factors or situations that justify recording it.
2. Give the essential condition(s) that would justify showing goodwill in the financial statements.

Alternate Problems

Alternate Problem 9-1

Nickelbelt Corp. operates a plant building adjacent to its office building. The plant building is old and requires continuous maintenance and repairs. On the first day of the current fiscal period, the Plant Building account shows a $250,000 balance and the Accumulated Depreciation account shows a $150,000 balance. During the year, the following expenditures relating to the plant building were incurred:

a. Continuing, frequent, and low-cost repairs	$26,000
b. Overhaul of the plumbing system (old costs not known)	17,000
c. New storage shed attached to the plant building (estimated life, 10 years)	48,000
d. Replaced an old shingle roof with a new tile roof (cost of the old shingle roof was $30,000)	60,000
e. Unusual infrequent repairs	10,000

Required:
1. Prepare journal entries to record each of items (a) to (e).
2. Explain your treatment of each item.

Alternate Problem 9-2

The City Ballet Inc. is a public company incorporated 6 years ago. The company gives ballet courses to more than 1000 students annually and presents several shows each year. The directors decided in 19X2 to construct their own building to be used for the school and the shows. In June 19X4, the company purchased and paid for land worth $60,000. An old building was standing on the site. The processes of tearing down the old building and constructing City Ballet's building took one year.

On December 1, 19X4, the metropolitan municipality made a donation of $55,000 toward the land purchased by the company. At that date, the municipal valuation of the land was $50,000 and its fair market value was $70,000. The company paid $8,800 to raze the old building; it sold some of the lumber and bricks for $1,000. Legal fees of $600 were paid for title search. During construction, the following amounts were paid:

Land survey	$ 200
Building plans	2,000
Liability insurance during construction	350
Landscaping	1,500
Property taxes (Jun. 1, 19X4 to Jun. 30, 19X5)	1,500
Architect fees paid	1,200

The contractor's charge was $675,000. The City Ballet paid the contractor in two instalments: $300,000 at the end of 6 months and the balance at the completion of the construction. The first payment was financed by borrowing from the bank at 7 percent for 6 months.

Required:
1. How should the grant of $55,000 be accounted for?
2. Calculate the cost of the land to be shown on the 19X5 balance sheet.
3. Calculate the cost of the building to be shown on the 19X5 balance sheet.

Alternate Problem 9-3

Little Hectare Limited purchased the following equipment on January 1, 19X2:

Cost	Useful Life	Salvage Value	Depreciation Method
$6,000	5 Years	$300	(to be discussed)

Required:
1. Calculate the total depreciation for the 5-year period 19X2–19X6, under each of these depreciation methods: straight-line and double-declining balance.
2. Both methods of calculating depreciation are used in actual practice. List the advantages of
   a. The straight-line method
   b. The double-declining balance method.

Alternate Problem 9-4

Turner Inc., a speculative mining organization, purchased a machine on April 1, 19X4. The following information is made available:

Cost	Useful Life	Salvage Value	Depreciation Method
$40,000	3 years (consisting of 100 000 tonnes)	$4,000	(to be discussed)

The machine has an estimated life in production output of 100 000 tonnes. Actual output was: Year 1 — 40 000 tonnes; Year 2 — 20 000 tonnes; Year 3 — 10 000 tonnes. The year-end of the company is March 31.

Required:
1. Calculate the depreciation expense and the net book value at year-end for the 3-year period under each of these depreciation methods: straight-line, double-declining balance, capital cost allowance (20%), and usage.
2. Assume that the machine is no longer useful at the end of 3 years and must be sold. Although depreciation has been recorded based on machine usage as calculated in 1, above, the president believes that it could have been used to process an additional 30 000 tonnes. He fears that an excessive amount of depreciation has been charged against income during the 3 years and that the company has issued incorrect financial statements. Do you agree? Why or why not?

Alternate Problem 9-5

Simon Inc. purchased its first piece of equipment on January 1, 19X6. The following information pertains to this machine:

Cost	Useful Life	Salvage Value	Depreciation Method
$11,000	5 Years	$1,000	(to be discussed)

As the chief accountant for the company, you are faced with making a choice of a depreciation method to be used.

Required:
1. Calculate the straight-line and double-declining balance method depreciation for 19X6, 19X7, and 19X8.
2. Using the format provided, complete comparative partial income statements and balance sheets at December 31 for both the straight-line and declining balance methods of depreciation.

Partial Income Statement	19X6	19X7	19X8
Net Income before Depreciation and Income Taxes	$30,000	$25,000	$35,000
Depreciation Expense	?	?	?
Income from Operations	$?	$?	$?
Income Taxes (50%)	$?	$?	$?
Net Income for the Year	$?	$?	$?
Partial Balance Sheet			
Equipment	$?	$?	$?
Less:			
Accumulated Depreciation	?	?	?
Net Book Value	$?	$?	$?

3. Which depreciation method should be used for deferral of income taxes? Explain.

Alternate Problem 9-6

The Lambton Carpet Centre purchased a cutting machine at the beginning of 19X4 for $46,000. Lambton paid additional charges of $1,200 and $2,800 for freight and installation, respectively. Salvage value was estimated at $2,000.

Required:
1. Calculate the depreciable cost of the machine.
2. In journal form, record the depreciation for each year, using
   a. Straight-line method (with a life estimate of 3 years)
   b. Declining balance method (at 40% rate — depreciate for only 3 years).
3. On January 19X5, Lambton revised the life estimate on the machine from a total of 3 years to a total of 5 years. Estimated salvage remained at $2,000. Calculate the depreciation that should be recorded in 19X5 and each year thereafter. Use the straight-line method of depreciation.

Alternate Problem 9-7

On the first business day of the new year 19X1, Woodslee Truckers Ltd. purchased for cash a new truck from its local dealer. The truck was a heavy-duty type, and records indicated it should have a 10-year life span but no salvage value. The vehicle cost $12,000. During the first week of January, 19X5, the truck was repaired and rebuilt. The total cost was $3,200, of which $2,400 was for additions (considered as a betterment) and $800 for ordinary repair. The former increased the efficiency of the truck, but no change was contemplated in life expectancy or salvage value. On April 1, 19X6, the truck was completely wrecked. Beta Insurance Co. settled the claim for $4,000.

Required: Prepare journal entries for
1. Purchase of the truck
2. Depreciation of the truck (straight-line method)
3. 19X5 transaction involving rebuilding
4. 19X5 depreciation
5. 19X6.

Alternate Problem 9-8

The following account appears in the general ledger of the S. Hudas Corp. at December 31, 19X4.

Equipment   No. 183

Date 19X4	Description	F	Debit	Credit	DR. or CR.	Balance
Jan. 1	Machine #1		6400 -		dr	6400 -

Accumulated Depreciation — Equipment   No. 193

Date 19X4	Description	F	Debit	Credit	DR. or CR.	Balance
Dec. 31	Depreciation for 19X4			1000 -	Cr	1000 -
19X5						
Dec. 31	Depreciation for 19X5			1000 -	Cr	2000 -

Machine No. 1 was estimated to have a useful life of 6 years, with an estimated salvage value of $400. On January 1, 19X6, Machine No. 1 was traded in for Machine No. 2. The list price of Machine No. 2 was $8,000 and the S. Hudas Corp. received a trade-in allowance of $4,500.

Machine No. 2 is estimated to have a useful life of 8 years, with an estimated salvage value of $1,000. The fair market value of machine No. 1 was $4,000 at the date of the trade-in.

Required:
1. Prepare a journal entry to record the trade-in of Machine No. 1 for Machine No. 2.
2. Post the appropriate parts of the entry prepared in 1, above, to the general ledger accounts, and calculate the new balance in each account.
3. The installation cost of Machine No. 2 amounted to $500 and was recorded in the Maintenance Expense account when paid. Prepare a correcting entry at December 31, 19X6.
4. Prepare the entry to record the depreciation for 19X6. (The correcting entry required in 3, above, has already been made.) Post the appropriate part of this entry to the Accumulated Depreciation account, and calculate the new balance in that account.

Alternate Problem 9-9

In accounting, certain intangible assets are subject to the process of amortization, whereas others are not. Listed below are three intangibles that an accountant might encounter:
1. Trademarks
2. Patents
3. Goodwill.

Required: Explain the accounting treatment you would suggest for each, incorporating in your answer reasons for the suggested treatment.

Supplementary Problems

Supplementary Problem 9-1

Four machines were purchased by Alpha Co. Ltd. during 19X4 and 19X5. Machine A was finally placed in use at the end of August 19X4. The cost was $26,400, the estimated life 8 years, and the estimated salvage value $2,400. Depreciation was to be on a straight-line basis. The company year-end is December 31.

Machine B was ready for use October 1, 19X4. Depreciation was to be on a units of production basis. The cost was $23,600, with a 5-year life expectancy and an estimated salvage value of $3,600. Estimated production over the 5 years would be 50 000 units. In 19X4, 3000 units were produced, 11 500 in 19X5 and 12 000 during 19X6. Machines C and D were purchased for $34,200 in April 19X5 and were in production on July 1 of that year. The following additional information about Machines C and D is available:

Machine	Appraised Value	Salvage Value	Estimated Life	Installation Cost	Depreciation Method
C	$16,000	$1,000	6 Years	$ 500	Straight-line
D	20,000	1,600	10 Years	1,000	Declining balance

1. For each of the four machines, calculate the total amount to be charged to depreciation and the depreciation for 19X4, 19X5, and 19X6. Assume that double the straight-line rate was used for the declining balance depreciation.)
2. Prepare journal entries to record payment and to record installation for Machines C and D. Installation costs were paid on the date they were placed in service.
3. Prepare a compound journal entry to record the 19X6 depreciation on the four machines.

Supplementary Problem 9-2 (SMA adapted)

The comparative statements for Reliable Enterprises Corporation are as follows

Income Statements

	19X4	19X3
Sales	$600,000	$540,000
Cost of Goods Sold	360,000	324,000
Gross Profit	$240,000	$216,000
Operating Expenses	150,000	140,000
Net Income	$ 90,000	$ 76,000

Statement of Retained Earnings

	19X4	19X3
Balance (Jan. 1)	$256,000	$200,000
Add: Net income	90,000	76,000
	$346,000	$276,000
Less: Dividends	30,000	20,000
Balance (Dec. 31)	$316,000	$256,000

In 19X4, Reliable decided to switch its depreciation method from the declining balance to the straight-line method. The differences in the two methods are:

	19X4	19X3
Declining balance	$58,000	$65,000
Straight-line	40,000	40,000
Difference	$18,000	$25,000

The income statement for 19X4 includes $58,000 in depreciation expense. Also, it was discovered that there was an overstatement of $20,000 in the 19X3 ending inventory balance. Reliable uses a periodic inventory system. 19X4 ending inventory is correct.

Required: Correct the financial statements.

Supplementary Problem 9-3

Corporations X and Y are identical in almost every respect. Both began business during the first days of January, 19X6, with equipment costing $40,000, and having a 10-year life with no salvage value. Neither X nor Y added to equipment during 19X6. At year-end, Corporation X decided to depreciate its equipment using the declining balance method at double the straight-line rate, while company Y chose straight-line depreciation. On December 31, before depreciation was recorded, the ledgers included the following items:

	Company X	Company Y
Sales	$75,000	$75,000
Salaries Expense	7,000	7,000
Rental Expense	2,500	2,500
Other Expenses	300	300

During 19X6, both purchased merchandise as follows:

Jan. 6	400 units @ $12.50/unit
Mar. 13	1200 units @ $12.00/unit
Jun. 28	800 units @ $13.50/unit
Oct. 10	800 units @ $14.00/unit
Dec. 20	400 units @ $15.00/unit

Corporation X priced its 440 units of ending inventory on a LIFO basis, while Corporation Y used FIFO for its 440-unit ending inventory.

Required: Prepare an income statement for X and for Y, showing the results for 19X6. Show your calculations of the inventory as a note to the statement.

Supplementary Problem 9-4

On January 1, 19X2, Sanilac Construction Corporation purchased for $120,000 cash a new excavating machine for use in its business. The new machine was expected to have a useful life of 10 years with no salvage value. On January 2, 19X5, a device was added to the machine, increasing its output by 10 percent. The cost was $5,600 cash. This addition brought no change to either life expectancy or salvage value. The machine was overhauled (considered as an extraordinary repair) during the first week of January 19X9 for $36,000. The salvage value still remained the same, but the life expectancy was increased by 3 years.

Required: Prepare journal entries to record
  1. The original purchase
  2. Depreciation for 19X2 (straight-line; the year-end is December 31.)
  3. The addition to the equipment
  4. The depreciation for 19X5
  5. The overhauling of the equipment
  6. The depreciation for 19X9.

Supplementary Problem 9-5

On January 1, 19X1, Northern Construction Limited purchased new heavy-duty equipment and placed it in service. The cost to the company was $60,000 cash. The equipment was expected to have no salvage value after a life expectancy of 10 years. On January 1, 19X4, a device was added to the equipment that increased its output by approximately 20 percent. The cost was $2,800. This addition brought no change to either life expectancy or salvage value.

The equipment was overhauled (considered as an extraordinary repair) during the first week of January 19X8, for $18,000 cash. The salvage value still remained the same, but the life expectancy increased by 3 years. On July 1, 19X9, the equipment was a total loss following a fire. The insurance company arranged for settlement and paid the company $20,000.

Required: Prepare journal entries to record
  a. Depreciation for 19X1 (straight-line; year-end is December 31.)
  b. The addition to the equipment account after the January 2 addition
  c. The depreciation for 19X3, 19X4, 19X5, 19X6, and 19X7
  d. The overhauling of the equipment in January 19X8
  e. The depreciation for 19X8
  f. The fire loss and settlement on July 1, 19X9.
  2. Post the appropriate part of these entries to the ledger accounts, Equipment and Accumulated Depreciation — Equipment, and calculate the balance in each account.

Supplementary Problem 9-6

The Essex Manufacturing Co. Ltd., which uses the straight-line method of depreciation, purchased three pieces of equipment (Machine A, Machine B, and Machine C) on the first day of business in January 19X3. Details of the acquisition are as follows:

	Machine A	Machine B	Machine C
Original Cost	$30,000	$30,000	$30,000
Estimated Salvage	-0-	4,800	1,200
Life Expectancy	5 Years	6 Years	8 Years

During the first week of business in 19X8, Machine A was sold for $2,000. This encouraged management to re-examine the useful life expectancy and the expected salvage value of Machines B and C. Management decided that Machine B had a remaining life of 2 years as of January 2, 19X8, and that the salvage expectation was about right. Machine C, on the other hand, had a remaining life of 5 years and, likely, there would be no scrap value.

Required: Prepare journal entries required in 19X8 to record
  1. Sale of Machine A
  2. Depreciation on Machines B and C as at December 31, 19X8.

Supplementary Problem 9-7

The Ingenio Corp. applied for and received in 19X6 a patent on a new manufacturing process for aluminium tubing. Research costs amounting to $40,000 were incurred in 19X6, and $30,000 of research costs were incurred in 19X5. The following expenses were also incurred:

	19X6	19X5
Cost of drawings	$1,000	$2,000
Legal fees	500	3,000
Patent application	200	—
Cost of testing	2,500	500
Fees paid to an engineer	2,000	3,000
Estimated salary for time spent on project:		
President	5,000	2,000
Treasurer	2,000	7,000

Required:
1. On the basis of the above information, calculate the cost of the patent at the end of 19X5 and 19X6.
2. Give the balance sheet presentation of the patent at the end of 19X5 and 19X6. (assume that the patent was not used in 19X5 nor in 19X6.)
3. What is the legal life of this patent?

Decision Problems

Decision Problem 9-1

Riverside Construction Company Ltd. purchased a farm from J. B. Smith. Riverside and Smith completed the transaction under the following terms: a cheque from Riverside to Smith for $140,000; mortgage on property assumed by Riverside, $100,000. Legal, accounting, and brokerage fees amounted to $20,000.

It was Riverside's intention to build homes on the property after sub-dividing. Crops on the farm were sold for $6,000; a house, to be moved by the buyer, was sold for $1,600; barns were razed at a cost of $6,000, while salvaged lumber was sold for $4,400. The property was cleared and levelled at a cost of $10,000.

The necessary property was turned over to the township for roads, schools, churches, and playgrounds. Riverside still expected to secure a total of 500 lots from the remaining land.

Required: Prepare a schedule showing the cost to Riverside of the 500 lots.

Decision Problem 9-2

Newold Ltd. commenced construction of a new plant on July 1, 19X1. All construction activities were completed by March 31, 19X2, after which time the plant went into operation. Total cost incurred during the construction period included:

	(000s)
Cost of Land (includes the cost of an old building on it)	$ 55
Engineering Fees:	
Analysis of the sub-soil	$ 8
Construction supervision	50
Analysis of the electrical system	30
Planning of a new production process (required in order to use new equipment that will be installed in the new building)	45
	$ 133
Subcontractor's Charges:	
Demolition of the old building	$ 3
Wages and material (excluding landscaping)	531
Landscaping	4
	$ 538
Charges Included in the Company's Operating Accounts:	
Wages of employees on construction site	$ 460
Construction materials	1,267
Taxes and interest (payable in advance, for the entire year commencing July 1, 19X1)	18
	$1,745

The company is to receive a government grant of $200,000 for having selected a recommended site as the actual location of the new plant.

Required: As controller of Newold Ltd., determine which of the above costs should properly be included in the cost of the new plant accounts. Briefly explain why you would include or exclude each cost item.

Decision Problem 9-3

The Beta Corp. manufactures light fixtures for the wholesale trade. A major piece of machinery is a drill press that cost $220,000 on January 1, Year 1. This press is being depreciated, using the declining balance method of depreciation; it has an estimated $20,000 scrap value and an estimated useful life of 4 years. As of January 1, Year 3, the company will change its depreciation method to straight-line. Management thinks that this method will provide a better matching of revenues and expenses. The company has a December 31 year-end.

Required:
1. Prepare a schedule of depreciation for Years 1, 2, 3, and 4, using the declining balance method and the straight-line method. Calculate the difference for each year between the methods. (The declining balance rate is calculated at 50 percent.)
2. The controller of Beta notes that the estimate of yearly depreciation using the declining balance method will differ from the estimate of depreciation using the straight-line method. She considers the change to be nothing more than a change in the estimate of depreciation required. Do you agree that this change from declining balance to straight-line method is really a change in the estimate of depreciation required? Why or why not?

Decision Problem 9-4

Jackson Mines Ltd., incorporated March 31, 19X1, had an asset, land, bearing recoverable ore deposits, estimated by geologists to contain 800 000 tonnes. The cost of this land was $450,000, and it was estimated to be worth $50,000 after extraction of the ore. During this year, mine improvements totalled $17,500. Various buildings and sheds were constructed at a cost of $22,500. During the year, 35 000 tonnes were mined. Of this tonnage, 6500 tonnes were on hand unsold on March 31, 19X2, the balance having been sold for cash at $4.50 per tonne. Expenses incurred and paid during the year, exclusive of depletion and depreciation, were as follows:

Mining	$84,000
Delivery	9,250
Administration	8,800

It is believed that buildings and sheds will be useful over the life of the mine only; therefore, depreciation should be recognized in terms of mine output.

Required: Prepare an income statement for the year ended March 31, 19X2.

Decision Problem 9-5

Z Ltd. was incorporated on January 1, 19X3 and on that date purchased these assets:

Land	$100,000
Buildings	150,000
Equipment	75,000
Trucks and Automobiles	30,000

On December 14, 19X3, the president of Z Ltd. asks you for advice in selecting a realistic depreciation policy for the company. The president informs you that the subject has been discussed with the manager and the bookkeeper and that the following views have been expressed:

President — No depreciation should be provided for land and buildings, because the inherent increase in land values will more than compensate for any physical deterioration of the buildings. Equipment, trucks, and automobiles should be written off in the year of purchase in order to ensure that they will be purchased only in years when there are sufficient profits to absorb the costs of such fixed assets.

Manager — No depreciation should be provided for land, because land is not used to earn profits. Buildings and equipment should be written off over the estimated useful lifes of the assets — 40 years for buildings and 10 years for equipment. Trucks and automobiles should be written off over a period of 3 years, since the company intends to trade them in for new ones every 3 years.

Bookkeeper — No depreciation should be provided for land, because few companies ever depreciate land and, therefore, any write-offs would not conform to generally accepted accounting principles. All other fixed asset costs should be written off by the declining balance method, calculated on the following annual rates:

Buildings	8%
Equipment	25%
Trucks and Automobiles	35%

Required: What is your advice to the president of Z Ltd. as to the most acceptable depreciation policy for the company? Explain your comments on the validity of each of the views expressed by the president, the manager, and the bookkeeper.

The Financing Cycle

Equity and debt comprise the financing cycle of the entity. Equity financing, the subject of chapters 10, 11, and 12, includes capital contributions by owners and earnings made and retained in the entity.

Chapter 10 discusses how corporations use different types of share capital to obtain capital, and the recording of these transactions. Retained earnings of the entity can be either restricted or unrestricted for dividend payments; other components comprising shareholders' equity must also be disclosed in the balance sheet.

Chapter 11 discusses matters related to dividend declaration and payment. Both creditors and shareholders are interested in the amount of assets that can be distributed as dividends. Stated capital and restricted retained earnings represent assets that are not available for distribution as dividends. These exceptions are intended to protect creditors; they prevent shareholders from withdrawing assets as dividends to the point where assets become insufficient to pay creditors. They are also intended to ensure the continued operation of the business.

Equity transactions for a partnership are recorded differently from those of corporations. Chapter 12 reviews these different equity transactions.

Chapter 13 deals with accounting for an entity's efforts to obtain long-term debt in order to finance operations. Bond issues are an important source of debt financing. The proportion of debt to equity varies from one entity to another. There are many factors influencing management's choice between the issue of equity and debt. The advantages and disadvantages must be weighed according to the risk involved.

Shareholders' Equity

Corporations finance their operations through issues of share capital. The financial statement reader is interested in shareholders' equity information to answer such questions as:

1. What types of different classes of shares does the corporation have available to interest investors?
2. How much is the corporation's stated capital?
3. What are the different rights of shareholders in this corporation?
4. What dividends are preferred shareholders entitled to if dividends are declared by the corporation?
5. How much are the claims of preferred shareholders in the event of liquidation?
6. What is the status of corporate shares at year-end?
7. What is the maximum amount of dividends that could be declared by the corporation?
8. What is the amount of retained earnings actually available for dividends?
9. Have any assets of the corporation been revalued?
10. Are there any unusual components of shareholders' equity?
11. What is the book value of common shares?

A. The Corporate Structure

The accounting equation expresses a relationship between assets owned by a corporation and the claims against those assets by creditors and shareholders. The accounting for assets and their financial statement disclosure was discussed in preceding chapters. The accounting for shareholders' equity is covered in this chapter. Corporate accounting for equity focuses on the distinction between the two main sources of shareholders' equity, illustrated in Figure 10.1.

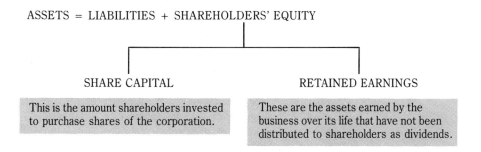

Figure 10-1   Share capital and retained earnings

These two basic components are discussed in detail in order to explain the main features of corporate accounting and the guidelines used by accountants for shareholders' equity disclosure.

Corporate Characteristics

The distinguishing characteristics of the corporation are that it is created by law, it has an unlimited life, it has limited liability, it can acquire capital easily, and it pays income tax on earnings.

Creation by Law

Canada Business Corporations Act (CBCA)
Statute regulating federally incorporated companies.

In Canada, an entity can become a corporation under either federal or provincial law. Each province has a corporations act that regulates the formation of corporations. Federal incorporation is made under the **Canada Business Corporations Act**, (CBCA). One difficulty in gathering information about a corporation is that these laws differ. This makes it hard to determine the rights and obligations of any one corporation or shareholder. The corporation is also subject to these government regulations:

1. It must file reports with government.
2. It cannot distribute profits arbitrarily but must treat all shares of the same class alike.
3. It is subject to special taxes and fees.

Nevertheless, a corporation's advantages far outweigh its disadvantages.

Unlimited Life

A corporation has an existence separate from that of its owners. Individual shareholders may die, but the corporate entity continues. The life of a corporation comes to an end only when it is dissolved, becomes bankrupt, or has its charter revoked. In general, it has many of the rights and responsibilities that an individual citizen has. It can own property, for instance; it can sue and be sued.

Limited Liability

The corporation's owners are liable only for the amount that they have invested in the corporation. If the corporation fails, its assets are used to pay creditors. If insufficient assets exist to pay all debts, there is no further liability on the part of shareholders. For the protection of creditors, the limited liability of a corporation must be disclosed in its name. The words *Limited*, *Incorporated*, or *Corporation* (or the abbreviations Ltd., Inc., or Corp.) must be used as the last word of the name of a company incorporated federally or provincially, except in Quebec, where only the French terms *Limitée* or *Incorporée* (or the abbreviations Ltée or Inc.) must be used, regardless of where the company was incorporated. Federally and provincially incorporated companies were formerly required to use the word "Limited" to indicate the limited liability of corporate shareholders in Canada. However, the Canada Business Corporations Act and the British Columbia Companies Act also permit the use of the words "Incorporated" or "Corporation" to indicate this limited liability. Companies incorporated in Ontario are permitted to use the word "Incorporated" in place of "Limited". Because satisfaction of creditor claims is limited to corporate assets, the extent of credit tends to be limited to the level of corporate assets or some relationship to them.

Ease of Acquiring Capital

A corporation is a multiple-ownership organization and *shares* are the ownership units. The issue of shares allows many individuals to participate in the financing of a corporation. Both small and large investors are able to participate because of the ease with which ownership can be transferred — shares are simply purchased or sold.

There are many different types of shares. Differences exist with regard to voting rights, dividend rights, liquidation rights, and other preferential features. The rights of each shareholder depend on the class or type of shares held, and the amount of ownership by each shareholder depends on the number of shares he/she holds in relation to total shares outstanding. Through the issue of shares on stock markets like the Toronto Stock Exchange, large amounts of capital can be raised.

Income Taxes on Earnings

That corporations should pay income tax is understandable. However, individual shareholders are also taxed on dividends. This is double taxation. The federal government recognizes this fact and allows taxpayers a dividend tax credit and investment income exemption to minimize the effect of the taxation. Large corporations are taxed at one of two rates, depending on the amount of taxable income. This form of taxation is more advantageous than the escalating rates applied to individual taxpayers, which increase as earnings increase.

Rights of Shareholders

Share certificate
A unit of corporate ownership; usually either common or preferred.

Ownership of a **share certificate** carries with it certain rights. These rights are printed on the certificate itself if they differ between classes of shares. (Figure 1-1 in Chapter 1 is a typical share certificate.) Each share in a class must be treated like every other share in that class with respect to whatever rights and privileges attach to it. The rights and privileges usually attached to common stock are:

1. The right to participate in the management of the corporation by voting at shareholders meetings. (This participation includes voting to elect a board of directors.) Each share corresponds to one vote.
2. The right to participate in dividends when they are declared by the corporation's board of directors.
3. The right to participate in a distribution of assets on liquidation of the corporation.
4. The right to appoint auditors.

These rights attach to each common shares unless otherwise restricted in the articles of incorporation or letters patent. In some cases these rights are restricted in other classes of shares.

Any shareholder of a corporation formed under the Canada Business Corporations Act also has additional rights if he/she is entitled to vote at an annual meeting. Such shareholders — except in very small corporations — can submit a proposal to raise any matter at an annual meeting and have this proposal circulated to other shareholders at the corporation's expense. If the corporation intends to make fundamental changes in its business, a shareholder may require the corporation to buy his/her shares at their fair value. In addition, shareholders can apply to the courts for an appropriate remedy if they find themselves oppressed or find their interests unfairly disregarded by the corporation.

Board of Directors

Shareholders usually meet annually to vote for a board of directors — either to re-elect the current directors or to vote in new directors. Individual directors do not participate in daily management. The board of directors meets monthly or quarterly to review the operations of the corporation and to set policies for future operations. Based on the performance of the corporation, the board may decide to distribute some assets as a dividend to shareholders. It may also decide that some percentage of the net assets of the corporation legally available for dividends should be made unavailable for dividends; in this case a restriction on the distribution of assets is created. Such restrictions are discussed in section C of this chapter. The relationship between a board of directors and its corporation's management is discussed in Real Life Example 10-1.

Real Life Example 10-1

Independence of the Board of Directors

The board of directors must assure itself that the long-run interests of the corporation are being served and that management is acting in a responsible manner. To assess management's performance objectively, board members must be independent of those responsible for operating the corporation. Further, as key factors in an internal "credibility-added" function, board members must also appear to outsiders to be independent. When he was chairman of the United States Securities and Exchange Commission, Harold M. Williams suggested on several occasions that the following groups should not be allowed board membership: management, major customers and suppliers of goods and services, commercial bankers, outside counsel, investment brokers, and any other individuals whose positions might raise conflict of interest questions in the minds of reasonable third parties. Williams would, however, allow the corporation's chief executive officer (CEO) board membership as long as he/she did not chair the board. Although that suggested criterion for membership would

improve the perception of the board's independence, the CEO's membership could have the effect of neutralizing the board's real independence.

Admission to the boardroom is a recognition of success. Good sense, effective judgment, initiative, and the right connections are universally regarded as desirable traits in new board members. Chief executive officers consider one other ingredient essential—loyalty. Loyalty develops rather naturally in novice board members; the initial board appointment understandably generates a sense of gratitude, a desire to be accepted quickly, and a recognition of an obligation to those who supported the selection. Any misplaced sense of self-importance quickly evaporates along with the mystique usually associated with the boardroom setting. A lesson soon learned after admission into the inner corporate circle is that the probability of success as a board member is significantly improved if operating management — particularly the CEO — is enthusiastically supported. Admission into the corridors of

Corporate Terminology

Students sometimes have difficulty with the specialized meaning of terms required for corporate accounting, especially such terms as *value*; it has different meanings for non-accountants and accountants.

The Meaning of "Value"

Value
An accounting term that refers to the amount at which an item appears in the general ledger. Value can be cost value, LOCAM, net realized value, no par–value, book value.

The word **value**, in accounting terminology, usually refers to an amount that appears in the general ledger accounts of a business or in its financial statements. The word *value* does not express what an item is actually "worth" if offered for sale on the market. Study the following examples.

> 1. *Assets are nomally recorded at cost.*
> Value here refers to the cost of assets, not to their worth; cost is the way the value of assets is determined.
>
> 2. *Inventories are sometimes recorded at the lower of cost and market (LOCAM).*
> The value of inventories is the amount calculated under the LOCAM rules. LOCAM does not intend to convey what this inventory is worth if resold; rather, it is a method by which a dollar amount of inventory is determined.

The word *value* is used by accountants to quantify assets and liabilities in money terms; it is also used in relation to share capital. *Value* has a precise meaning when used to describe the shares issued by a corporation.

corporate power is, after all, a prestigious position worth holding on to.

To neutralize the support-of-management syndrome and replace it with effectiveness, the independence of the board vis-à-vis management must be established uncompromisingly. No member of management, particularly the CEO, should be allowed voting status on the board. Allowing the CEO membership would only perpetuate the status quo. Not permitting the CEO membership will neutralize his/her influence over board members and support the development of their real independence and ultimate effectiveness.

Membership restrictions, however, should not be allowed to erode the board's accessibility to management and vice versa. The CEO and other senior corporate operating managers should be present, by invitation, at most board meetings, and their opinions, comments, and views given significant consideration. The CEO should be able to request board meetings to consider topics of timely importance. Most senior operating executives will have little difficulty with the concept of reporting to a board over which they exert no formal control; convincing the board to approve major undertakings is no more than they would expect to have to accomplish, given their role within the corporation. Board scrutiny of their activity represents accountability commensurate with authority and position.

To some, however, the transition may not be palatable. What of the CEO who owns 51 percent of the voting stock in a public company? Is it reasonable to ask such a corporate head to remove himself as a voting member from the board? One response is that removal is the cost attached to using the securities markets to raise capital. Borrowing from or selling stock to the public necessitates increased accountability and, to discharge that accountability effectively, the CEO must report to, as opposed to direct the activity of, a board that has the requisite level of autonomy necessary to function in a responsible manner. When a company seeks or uses outside funds, shareholders should insist on the independence of the board of directors. The responsibility for establishing an effective internal monitoring system over operating management can then begin from a base of real as well as perceived objectivity.

Source "The Inside Story on Financial Statement Credibility", Donald S. Johnston and Morley Lemon, *CAMagazine*, June 1984, pp. 53–54.

Market Value

Market value of a share is the price at which a share is trading on the stock market. In one manner of speaking, this amount *can* be considered to represent what shares are worth.

Book Value

Book value of a share is the amount determined by dividing shareholders' equity by the number of shares outstanding. If 1000 common shares are outstanding and shareholders' equity totals $50,000, each of the 1000 shares has a book value of $50. Book value *does not* connote the worth of shares.

Three different classes of terms can be identified. These are shown in Figure 10-2 and are discussed later in this section.

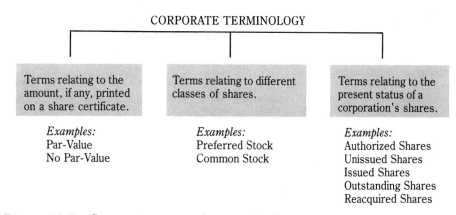

Figure 10-2 Corporate accounting terminology

Share Values

The word *value*, for corporate accountants, takes on a precise meaning indicated by its preceding adjective. For example, *market* indicates the precise meaning of *value* in market value. In each of the above examples, *value* only refers to an amount: a market amount in one case and a book amount in the other. Printed on a corporation's shares, the word *value* is explained by the adjectives *par* and *no par*.

Par-Value

Par-value
An amount specified in a corporate charter, which becomes the minimum at which a share can be sold by the corporation.

Par-value is an amount specified in a corporation's charter. It is a monetary amount printed on each share of the corporation, and it bears no relationship to the market value or book value of the share. Only in some provincial jurisdictions is the issue of par-value shares still permitted; the issue of these shares is authorized at the time these companies are incorporated. Par-value shares must be sold at or above par-value. For all practical purposes, par-value shares cannot be sold for less than par in Canada—except in some mining situations. The accounting for these shares is influenced by the par-value amount, as illustrated in section B of this chapter.

No Par-Value

No par-value
The term used in reference to shares that do not have a par-value.

No par-value is the term used in situations where no amount is specified for shares in a corporation's charter. The amount received from the issuance of a share is considered as the minimum amount that has to be paid to the issuing corporation by the original purchaser of a share.

Under the CBCA and some provincial jurisdictions, the issue of only no par-value shares is permitted in companies incorporated under their legislation. This restriction is imposed in the belief that par-values are arbitrary and can be misleading to the unsophisticated investor; also, their use can result in unnecessary accounting complications. Some provinces permit the issue of both par-value and no par-value shares; the issue of such shares is authorized at the time these companies are incorporated in these provincial jurisdictions.

Classes of Shares

Preferred stock
A class of shares that has a preference over common stock. Holders of preferred shares are entitled to payment of dividends before common shareholders and usually have a prior claim on a corporation's assets on liquidation.

All corporations issue common stock. Some corporations, in order to appeal to as large a group of investors as possible, also issue **preferred stock**. Different classes of shares permit different risks to be assumed by different classes of shareholders in the same company.

Of the two groups of investors, common shareholders normally accept a larger element of risk that the corporation will be successful. In return for this risk-taking, they expect that they will receive dividends and/or an increase in the market value of their shares. To accomplish these goals, common shareholders usually exercise voting control of the corporation.

Preferred shareholders typically assume less risk than common shareholders. They are also entitled to a limited amount of dividends and are given little or no real influence in the control of the corporation. Sometimes a corporation may issue only common stock but will divide it into classes to represent different voting rights or dividend privileges. Such shares are usually identified as *class A* and *class B* stock, as opposed to common and preferred. In this case, only one of these classes represents the basic ownership interest in the corporation. The particular features of both common and preferred shares and the rights they confer on their owners are indicated in the corporation's articles of incorporation. Although these may vary somewhat, certain typical features of this ownership can be stated.

Rights of Common Shareholders:

1. They have the right to vote on matters requiring owner approval. This right includes the election of the board of directors, who appoint the officers of the corporation, declare dividends, etc.

2. They are entitled to dividends only after preferred shareholder claims have been satisfied. Common shareholders, however, have the potential for receiving substantial dividends if the corporation is successful.

3. They receive the balance of assets, if any, after all other claims have been satisfied. No such balance usually exists to be distributed to common shareholders if the corporation becomes bankrupt.

Rights of Preferred Shareholders:

1. They do not normally have the right to vote for the board of directors and, therefore, do not have a voice in the control of the corporation. (One exception sometimes occurs when there is a default on dividends by the corporation, in which case they may have the right to vote for directors.)

2. They are entitled to the receipt of dividends before any payments are made to common shareholders. Preferred shareholders, therefore, have more assurance of receiving dividends, although there is usually a limit on the amount of these dividends.

3. In the event of the corporation's dissolution, preferred shareholders usually have a preferred claim on the assets of the corporation. This claim on assets cannot, however, exceed the stated value of the shares issued.

Status of Shares

At the time of incorporation under the Canada Business Corporations Act and in some provincial jurisdictions, a company indicates in its articles of incorporation the permitted issue of either an unlimited number of shares or a designated number of shares. If a designated number of shares, usually referred to as **authorized stock**, is indicated in the articles of incorporation, then the amount of authorized shares can be shown in the accounts and in the Shareholders' Equity section of the balance sheet as follows:

Authorized stock
The designated number of shares of share capital that a corporation may issue.

Recording in the Accounts:

GENERAL JOURNAL

19X1
Apr. 1   Memorandum
         Authorized under the CBCA to issue 10 000 common
         shares of no-par-value.

GENERAL LEDGER
Common Stock   *No. 320*

19X1
Apr. 1 Authorized to issue 10 000 common shares, no par-value.

Balance Sheet Presentation:

Shareholders' Equity
    Common Stock, No Par-Value
       Authorized — 10 000 Common Shares

Some provinces limit the number of authorized shares a corporation can issue. In the examples used in this text, and in the problem assignments, it is assumed that the charters of all the corporations limit the number of shares that can be issued, unless otherwise indicated. This provision eliminates the need to distinguish continually between jurisdictions that limit the number of issued shares and those that do not.

The shares of a corporation can have a different status at different points in time — **unissued** or **issued**, issued and **outstanding**, or issued and in the treasury. The meaning of these terms is summarized in Figure 10-3.

Unissued stock
The shares of share capital that a corporation is authorized to issue but has not yet issued.

Issued stock
The cumulative total number of authorized shares that has been issued in the name of shareholders; issued stock may or may not actually be in the hands of shareholders.

Outstanding stock
Authorized shares that have been issued and are actually in the hands of shareholders.

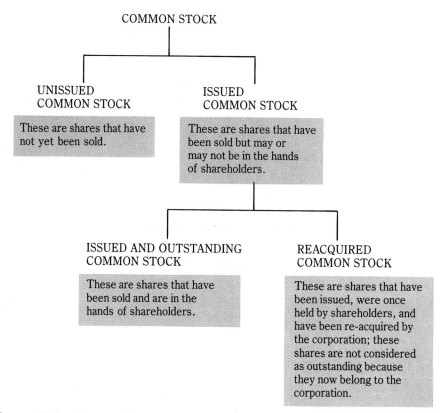

Figure 10-3   Status of common stock

Students are sometimes confused by these different classifications. Take sufficient time to understand the distinctions before continuing with this chapter.

B.   Share Capital Transactions

Share capital
A generic classification for all shares, common and preferred.

Share capital refers to all of a corporation's preferred and common stock. (Share capital is also called *capital stock*.) The recording of share capital transactions is influenced by the legislation of the jurisdiction under which the company is incorporated. The provisions of the Canada Business Corporations Act are used to illustrate the recording of stock transactions and to explain the various applications of the provisions. Note, however, that the Ontario Act has been designed so that there is some uniformity between Ontario legislation and the CBCA. The following discussion is also applicable to other provinces where similar legislation has been proclaimed. Following this, accounting for share capital in companies provincially incorporated of CBCA-incompatible jurisdiction are discussed.

Incorporation under the CBCA and CBCA-Compatible Provincial Legislation

Stated value
The amount received from the sale of shares; a term used in the CBCA to refer to the amount of capital that cannot be paid to shareholders as a dividend.

The term **stated value** is used in the CBCA to indicate a restriction on the return of share capital to shareholders; it consists of the amount recorded as share capital in the books of the corporation, as shown in Figure 10-4. Shareholders' investment in a corporation is often seen as a margin of safety for creditors, because the limited liability feature of corporations restricts claims against the corporation to corporate assets.

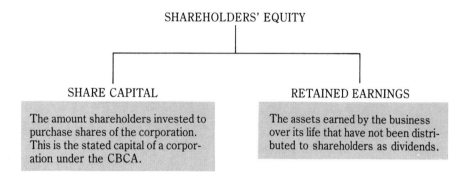

Figure 10-4   Sub-classes of shareholders' equity

A legal limit on shareholder withdrawals of share capital assures creditors that corporate losses, should they occur, will be absorbed from the capital contributed by shareholders up to the amount of the corporation's stated capital; any remaining loss will be absorbed by creditors.

Recording Share Transactions

As explained, some jurisdictions only permit the issue of no par-value shares. The accounting for no par-value stock is discussed next.

Assume that the following three transactions took place at the New Canada Corporation, which has an authorized capital consisting of an unlimited number of no par-value common shares.

Transaction 1
New Canada sells 1000 shares for $10,000 cash. The journal entry to record this transaction reads:

Cash	10,000	
Common Stock		10,000

Transaction 2

A further 2500 shares are issued for land and buildings that have a fair market value of $35,000 and $50,000, respectively. The journal entry to record this transaction reads:

Land	35,000	
Buildings	50,000	
Common Stock		85,000

Transaction 3

Organization costs
Organization costs consist of fees for incorporation, for lawyers, and other costs incurred to establish the business. Such costs are an intangible asset, not an equity item.

Next, 500 shares are issued to the organizers of the corporation in payment of their services valued at $5,000. (These are **organization costs**, discussed in an earlier chapter.) The journal entry to record this transaction reads:

Organization Costs	5,000	
Common Stock		5,000

The shareholders' equity section of the New Canada Corporation balance sheet shows the following items after these three transactions:

Shareholders' Equity

Common Stock, No Par-Value	
Authorized — An Unlimited Number of Shares	
Issued and Outstanding — 4000 Common Shares	$100,000

The amount of stated capital in this example is $100,000; this amount is not available for the payment of dividends.

Transaction 4

Reacquired shares
Issued and outstanding shares that have been repurchased by the corporation; also referred to as *treasury shares*.

The CBCA permits a corporation to reacquire some of its shares, provided that the purchase does not cause insolvency. The Act requires the **reacquired shares** to be restored to the status of authorized but unissued stock, and also requires the appropriate stated capital account to be reduced by the payment.

Assume that 1000 shares are repurchased. The use of an average per-share amount is recommended in the *CICA Handbook* (section 3240.18) in accounting for reacquired shares. The calculation for the reacquisition of New Canada's shares is made from the balances immediately preceding the reacquisition.

$$\frac{\text{Stated Capital Balance}}{\text{Number of Shares Issued}} = \frac{\$100,000}{4000} = \$25 \text{ average per share.}$$

The weighted average cost of 1000 shares, therefore is $25,000 (1000 shares $\times$ $25 average per share).

As can be seen, this weighted average amount is identical to the amount paid by the corporation. In actual practice, the payment is either in excess of or below the weighted average. The accounting required in these cases are discussed in section D in Chapter 11.

The journal entry for the 1000 shares, that are repurchased for $25,000, reads:

Common Stock	25,000	
Cash		25,000

The reacquired shares are restored to the status of authorized but unissued stock. The shareholders' equity section of the balance sheet now appears as follows:

Shareholders' Equity

Common Stock, No Par-Value
    Authorized — An Unlimited Number of Shares
    Issued and Outstanding — 3000 Common Shares $75,000

As permitted by the Act, the reacquired 1000 shares are removed from the issued shares, and the stated capital amount, common stock, is reduced by $25,000.

Transaction 5

At a later date, 10 000 shares are issued for $150,000. The journal entry reads:

Cash	150,000	
Common Stock		150,000

The shareholders' equity section of the balance sheet for the New Canada Corporation now shows the following entries:

Shareholders' Equity

Common Stock, No Par-Value
    Authorized — An Unlimited Number of Shares
    Issued and Outstanding — 13 000 Common Shares $225,000

The amount of stated capital amounts to $225,000 following transaction 5; this amount is not available for the payment of dividends.

Incorporation under CBCA-Incompatible Provincial Legislation

In some provinces, the issue of both par-value and no par-value common shares is permitted in companies incorporated under their legislation. Preferred shares, however, must have a par-value.

Issue of No Par-Value Shares

The accounting for the issue of no par-value shares is identical to that for companies incorporated under the CBCA. The five transactions of the New Canada Corporation illustrated earlier would be recorded in the same manner, if New Canada had been incorporated in a non-CBCA province.

Issue of Par-Value Shares

The accounting for par-value shares requires the creation of new general ledger accounts for amounts received in excess of par-value for each share.

Issue at a Premium

Assume that a corporation is organized with an authorized capital of $100,000, consisting of 10 000 common shares of $10 par-value each; assume further that 3000 shares are sold for $15 each. In this case, $5 has been received for each share in excess of its $10 par-value.

Transaction 6

Assume that a corporation issued 3000 $10 par-value shares at $15 (that is, at a premium of $5). This is the entry to record the sale of these shares:

Cash	45,000	
Common Stock		30,000 (3000 shares @ $10 par value)
Premium on Common Stock		15,000 (3000 shares @ $5 premium)

The issue of shares above par-value requires the amount over par to be credited to the Premium on Common Stock account. The shareholders' equity section of the balance sheet shows the following items, following the recording of transaction 6.

Shareholders' Equity

Common Stock, $10 Par-Value	
Authorized — 10 000 Shares	
Issued and Outstanding — 3000 Shares	$30,000
Premium on Common Stock	15,000

The use of a Premium on Common Stock account for the excess paid over par-value results in the common stock being shown at par-value on the balance sheet, as well as the amount actually contributed for the shares.

A separate premium account is used for each class of shares. In Canada, this premium on par-value shares is one element of contributed surplus; it is always classified separately within the shareholders' equity section of the balance sheet.

The accounting required when shares have par-value is contrasted with the accounting required when shares have no par-value in the journal entries below.

Transaction	Par-Value Share (If the share had a $10 par-value)			No Par-Value Share (if the share had no par-value)		
Issued 3000 Common shares for $45,000.	Cash	45,000		Cash	45,000	
	Common Stock		30,000	Common Stock		45,000
	Premium on Common Stock		15,000			

Issue at a Discount

The issue of par-value shares at a discount can result in the assumption of a liability by the holder of these shares for the amount of the discount. This contingent liability rests with the person who owns the shares at the time a corporation needs money and not with the investor who originally purchased the shares. This liability creates a messy situation when and if the discount becomes due. For all practical purposes, par-value shares cannot be sold at a discount in Canada (except in some specific mining situations).

Transaction 7

Assume that a corporation issued 1000 shares with a par-value of $10 at $8 each. The entry to record the sale of these shares reads:

Cash	8,000	
Discount on Common Stock	2,000	
Common Stock		10,000

The issue of these shares below par-value requires the $2 discount to be debited to Discount on Common Stock. This account records the difference between the issue price per share and the par-value per share. The amount of the discount is shown as a deduction in the shareholders' equity section of the balance sheet, and indicates the existence and the amount of the contingency applicable to holders of these shares.

Shareholders' Equity
Common Stock, $10 Par-Value
Authorized — 10 000 Shares
Issued and Outstanding — 4000 Shares $40,000
Premium on Common Stock   15,000
Discount on Common Stock   (2,000)

Notice that the premium and discount accounts are not offset against each other. Separate accounts are always maintained, since an off-set would conceal the existence of the discount contingent liability.

The accounting required when par-value shares are issued at a discount is contrasted with the accounting required when they are issued at a premium in the journal entries below.

Transaction	*Share Issued at Discount* *(The shares are issued for $8 each)*		*Share Issued at Premium* *(The shares are issued for $15 each)*	
Issued 1000 shares with a par value of $10.	Cash	8,000	Cash	15,000
	Discount on		Premium on	
	Common Stock	2,000	Common Stock		5,000
	Common Stock		10,000	Common Stock		10,000

Reacquired Shares

Companies incorporated in some provinces and under the CBCA are permitted to reacquire some of their own shares. However, unlike the requirements of the CBCA, provincial requirements legislate that these reacquired shares can be either cancelled or reissued. If all the reacquired shares are not cancelled and have not be reissued, they are called **treasury stock**. The cost of treasury stock is deducted from the total Shareholders' Equity on the balance sheet. They are *never* shown as an asset on the balance sheet. Reacquired shares are discussed further in Chapter 11.

Treasury stock
Reacquired shares that have not been cancelled and have not been reissued.

Components of Shareholder Contributions

The accounting for share capital transactions requires new terminology and also new accounts. One of the new accounts required when par-value shares are issued in excess of par has been labelled the *Premium on Common Stock* account; it is also referred to as a **Contributed Surplus** account. The latter is recommended in the *CICA Handbook*. The distinction between stated capital and contributed surplus is illustrated in Figure 10.5.

Contributed surplus
A category of surplus that usually refers to the amount of premium received on the issue of par value shares; also includes donated capital and distributable surplus.

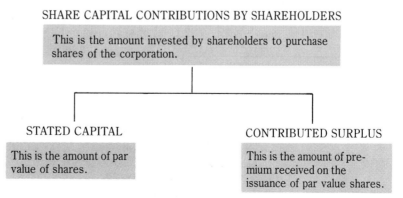

Figure 10-4   Stated Capital and Contributed Surplus

Legally, the amount of assets represented by stated capital must be kept in the corporation for the protection of creditors. When no par-value shares are issued, the entire amount received by the corporation is considered to be stated capital. The amount of assets represented by contributed surplus, in most cases, can technically be considered eligible for dividend distributions.

Stock Splits

Stock split
An action taken by a corporation to increase the number of shares outstanding; involves the exchange of originally issued shares for a larger number of new shares; a stock split reduces the per-share market value of the stock.

The corporation may find its shares selling at a high price on the stock market, thereby putting them beyond the reach of many investors. To solve this problem, management may opt for a **stock split** to increase the marketability of a corporation's shares; the corporation issues, for example, three new shares to replace each old share. The old outstanding share certificates are *called in* and three new certificates are issued as replacements for each old share. The number of outstanding shares has now been tripled and the market price of each share tends to decrease to one-third of its former market price. This increase in shares and the change in market price is illustrated, using the data of the New Canada Corporation:

	Number of Shares Outstanding	Total Common Stock on Balance Sheet	Market Price per Share (Assumed)
Before Stock Split	13,000	$225,000	$75
After Stock Split (3 for 1)	39,000	225,000	25

This information appears in the financial statements of the corporation.

This information is available from the Toronto Stock Exchange.

As can be seen, the number of outstanding shares triples and the market price of each share decreases proportionately. The shareholders' equity section of the New Canada Corporation would be shown on the balance sheet as follows:

Before Split:
Shareholders' Equity
Common Stock, No Par-Value
  Authorized — An Unlimited Number
    of Shares
  Issued and Outstanding —
  13 000 Shares $225,000

After Split:
Shareholders' Equity
Common Stock, No Par-Value
  Authorized — An Unlimited Number
    of Shares
  Issued and Outstanding —
  39 000 Shares $225,000

Notice that the amount of shareholders' equity has not changed. The only change is the increase in issued and outstanding shares from 13 000 to 39 000. Since there is no change in the $225,000 of shareholders' equity, no debit-credit entry is required to record the stock split. A memorandum should be recorded, however, indicating the new number of shares outstanding.

Common Stock   Acct. No. 201

Date 19X1	Description	F	Debit	Credit	DR. or CR.	Balance
	Memorandum *The outstanding shares were increased from 13 000 to 39 000 by a 3-for-1 stock split.*					

Real Life Example 10-2

This Stock Split Is 4799 for 1

Tribune Co. yesterday announced a 4799-for-1 stock split as part of its move to become a publicly held company.

The company, owner of the *Chicago Tribune* and *New York Daily News* newspapers and the Chicago Cubs baseball team, will distribute 4799 shares of stock for each of the existing 7393 shares, said Stanton Cook, president and chief executive. The shares will be distributed October 3 to shareholders of record as of the close of business yesterday, he said. The company's current shares of stock are privately held and not publicly traded.

After the distribution, the stock will be listed on the New York Stock Exchange. A spokesman for the company said about 33.5 million shares would be outstanding and each is expected to be worth between $20 and $25.

The spokesman said Tribune Co. also is waiting for final government approval of its public statement of registration. The statement was filed about a month ago when the company announced that it would become a publicly held company.

Tribune also is planning to offer 5.5 million shares of additional common stock, which is expected to sell for between $22 and $26 a share, the spokesman said. That sale is contingent upon distribution of the common stock to current shareholders, he added.

In addition to the *Tribune*, the *Daily News*, and the Cubs, the company owns newspapers in Florida; WGN-TV in Chicago and several other broadcast properties; and operations in cable television, entertainment and newsprint, and forest products.

Source Associated Press, *The* (Montreal) *Gazette*, February 27, 1983.

In the preceding example, the common stock had no par-value. When the shares being split have a par-value, it is necessary to change the par-value amount in proportion to the amount of the stock split. For example, if the stock split involves 2 new shares for each old share, the par-value of the share would be halved. This change is necessary because the total amount of the share capital does not change. Only the number of shares changes. The par-value of the shares must be adjusted so that the new number of shares outstanding multiplied by the decreased par-value still equals the previous amount of share capital.

Remember that the purpose of a stock split is to increase the marketability of a share and, thereby, to permit more investors to own shares of the corporation. The advantage to the corporation is the wider ownership base.

Sometimes, management decides to effect a **reverse stock split**; in this case, the old shares are called in and fewer new shares are issued. This action may be taken when management considers that the market price of the stock is too low. A contraction of the number of shares outstanding increases the market price.

Reverse stock split
An action taken by a corporation to decrease the number of shares outstanding; involves the exchange of originally issued shares for a smaller number of new shares; a reverse stock split increases the per-share market value of the stock.

C. Retained Earnings Restrictions

Retained earnings, as introduced in Chapter 4, represent the assets earned by a business over its life that have not been distributed as dividends to shareholders. Rather, these assets have been reinvested; that is, they have been ploughed back into the business.

The Retained Earnings account normally has a credit balance. If the Retained Earnings account has a debit balance, the corporation has incurred a **deficit**; that is, its expenses have exceeded revenues, or excessive dividends have been paid. The result of a deficit is that no assets of the corporation can be used for the payment of dividends.

Deficit
A debit balance in the Retained Earnings account of a corporation.

Restricted and Unrestricted Retained Earnings

Restricted retained earnings
The assets of a corporation represented by an amount of retained earning that is not available for dividends.

Unrestricted retained earnings
An amount of retained earnings representing assets of the corporation that are available for dividends, also known as *free retained earnings*.

The assets represented by retained earnings can be either **restricted** or **unrestricted** for dividend distributions. Study Figure 10-6 to better understand the concept of restricted and unrestricted retained earnings.

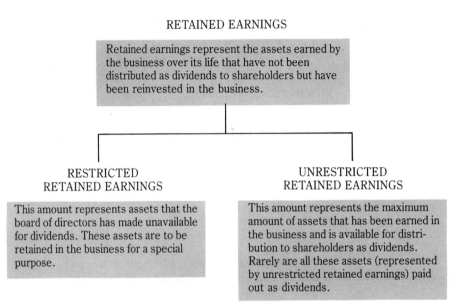

RETAINED EARNINGS

Retained earnings represent the assets earned by the business over its life that have not been distributed as dividends to shareholders but have been reinvested in the business.

RESTRICTED RETAINED EARNINGS

This amount represents assets that the board of directors has made unavailable for dividends. These assets are to be retained in the business for a special purpose.

UNRESTRICTED RETAINED EARNINGS

This amount represents the maximum amount of assets that has been earned in the business and is available for distribution to shareholders as dividends. Rarely are all these assets (represented by unrestricted retained earnings) paid out as dividends.

Figure 10-6   Restricted and unrestricted retained earnings

Assume that a corporation has $120,000 of retained earnings at the balance sheet date. The board of directors passes a resolution to restrict $70,000 for a plant expansion. The balance remains unrestricted for dividend purposes, although the directors have not yet decided whether to pay dividends this year. The $70,000 restricted amount remains a part of retained earnings; the full cycle of the restriction for plant expansion is shown in Figure 10-7.

As can be seen, the creation of a restriction on retained earnings divides the $120,000 amount into a restricted component of $70,000 and an unrestricted component of $50,000. The latter amount is sometimes called *free retained earnings*.

Students sometimes do not understand why the unrestricted retained earnings of $50,000 cannot be paid out as dividends. Unrestricted retained earnings are an equity and not an asset; only assets can be paid out as dividends. The $50,000 equity amount is represented by assets in the company, but these assets consist of receivables, inventory, and fixed assets. Retained earnings amounts need not necessarily be matched with cash asset amounts. It is possible—but rare—that a fixed asset dividend could be issued. To understand this relationship of assets and dividends better, study the following examples.

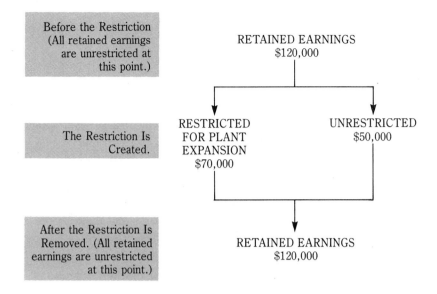

Figure 10-7   Restriction for plant expansion: creation and removal

Cash dividends are possible.		Cash dividends are not possible. (Only a fixed asset dividend is possible but this is highly improbable.)	
Assets		*Assets*	
Cash	$150,000	Fixed Assets	$150,000
Equity		*Equity*	
Common Stock	$ 30,000	Common Stock	$ 30,000
Retained Earnings	120,000	Retained Earnings	120,000
	$150,000		$150,000

When cash is not available to pay dividends, then, dividends cannot be paid. Even when cash is available, dividends may still not be paid. The growth of a corporation is dependent to some extent on the retention of earnings within the corporation and their investment in corporate assets, and their use for working capital and other purposes.

Restrictions on Retained Earnings

The creation of special restrictions on retained earnings is made by the board of directors to indicate management's intention to use assets for a particular purpose; such assets are unavailable for dividends. These restrictions do not in any way alter the total amount of retained earnings or the total amount of shareholders' equity.

The journal entry to record the creation of the above $70,000 restriction for plant expansion reads:

Retained Earnings	70,000	
Retained Earnings — Restricted		
for Plant Expansion		70,000

This restriction does not reduce the total retained earnings but rather records a portion of these earnings in an account specifically designated to indicate its purpose — plant expansion. The restricted amount is still part of retained earnings; it is classified as retained earnings in the shareholders' equity section of the balance sheet.

It is important to understand that recording a restriction for plant expansion does not set up some kind of cash fund for the expansion. The restriction is an equity account; it is represented by corporate assets, but these assets may be fixed assets, accounts receivable, or some other assets.

Removing a Restriction on Retained Earnings

When the special restriction account has served its purpose and the requirement for which it was set up no longer exists, the amount in the restricted account is returned to the Retained Earnings account from which it was created. The entry setting up the restriction is reversed. The entry to return the restricted amount for plant expansion to Retained Earnings is:

Retained Earnings — Restriction for		
Plant Expansion	70,000	
Retained Earnings		70,000

Note that any restriction is created *within* the Retained Earnings account. The construction of the plant is recorded in the normal manner. Assume that the plant expansion is paid for in cash. The construction and payment is recorded in the journal as follows.

Plant	70,000	
Cash		70,000

This journal entry records the actual plant expenditure. It also shows that restricted retained earnings are *not* used to pay for the plant. The expenditure is paid with the asset cash. The restriction account is reversed when the plant has been built, because dividends are no longer restricted by the need for a plant expansion. *Dividends are now restricted by the lower amount of corporate cash.*

Are restrictions of retained earnings the best means for indicating and explaining management's intentions? Probably not! Most financial statement readers are not sufficiently familiar with accounting terminology to appreciate the nature of retained earnings restrictions. In addition, the use of the word *restriction* (or *appropriation*, as is used in some cases), is misleading. Nothing tangible has been restricted or appropriated as such. Rather, the restriction only indicates management's intention to use $70,000 of corporate assets for plant expansion at some time in the future. A note to the financial statements and an explanation of management's intentions in the president's letter to shareholders are probably more meaningful to the average investor. The reference to a note and the note itself can take the following form:

Retained Earnings (*Note 1*) $120,000

Notes to Financial Statements
Note 1:   The board of directors has established a $70,000 restriction on retained earnings for a plant expansion. The assets represented by this amount are therefore not available for dividend purposes. The plant expansion is discussed further in the president's letter to shareholders.

The use of notes has become more popular in recent years. Note disclosure and balance sheet disclosure of the actual restriction in the shareholders' equity section are equally acceptable alternates.

Use of the Word "Reserve" to Indicate a Restriction

Reserve
A term referring to a restriction of retained earnings.

The word **reserve** is often used in actual practice to indicate management's desire to retain within the company a portion of corporate assets for some purpose rather than distribute these assets to shareholders in the form of a dividend. Like the word *value*, *reserve* holds a specific meaning for accountants. Unfortunately, misuse of this term in the past has created a lot of confusion. Formerly *reserve* was applied to valuation and liability accounts, as shown in the following examples:

Former Usage:	*Current Terminology:*
Reserve for Bad Debts	Allowance for Doubtful Accounts
Reserve for Depreciation	Accumulated Depreciation
Reserve for Income Taxes.	Provision for Income Taxes.

The term *reserve* was also used for restrictions of retained earnings and continues to be used in this sense today. However, the former usage of the term *reserve* for valuation and liability accounts suggests an inaccurate meaning to most people whenever this term is used. Therefore, in this text, "restriction for plant expansion" is used instead of "reserve for plant expansion". Other examples of preferred usage are shown below.

Current Usage of the Term "Reserve":	*Preferred Terminology:*
Reserve for Plant Expansion	Restriction for Plant Expansion
Reserve for Contingencies	Restriction for Contingencies
Reserve for Replacement of Machinery.	Restriction for Replacement of Machinery.

D. Other Components of Shareholders' Equity

The emphasis in corporate accounting is on the distinctions among various sources of shareholders' equity. The accounting for share capital and for premium on the issue of shares (also referred to as contributed surplus) was illustrated in the earlier sections of this chapter. The availability of retained earnings for the payment of dividends to shareholders and the use of retained earnings restrictions to indicate the unavailability of corporate assets for dividend payments was also discussed. These are all sources of shareholders' equity. There remain to be discussed two other components of shareholders' equity: *donated capital* and *appraisal increase*.

Donated Capital

The earlier discussion of share capital described the contribution of capital to a corporation by shareholders through the purchase of shares. Capital can also be contributed to a corporation by parties other than shareholders. For example, land or cash is sometimes given by a municipality or province to a corporation as an inducement to locate a plant within its boundaries. This is, in effect, a donation to the corporation, and the asset received belongs to the corporation once contractual agreements have been fulfilled. Assume that a corporation receives from a municipality free of charge a plant site on which to locate its plant. An independent appraiser values this donated land at $50,000, and the board of directors accepts this amount as its fair market value. The following journal entry is made by the corporation:

Land	50,000	
Donated Capital — Land		50,000

Donated capital
A contribution of capital to a corporation by parties other than shareholders.

This **donated capital** is classified as a part of contributed surplus in shareholders' equity on the balance sheet. Other assets given to a corporation by donation are recorded in the accounts and classified in a similar manner.

Appraisal Increase

Appraisal increase
The increase that results when corporate assets are revalued upward.

An **appraisal increase** occurs when corporate assets — usually land and buildings — are revalued upward to reflect current market values. The usefulness of historical cost is limited when there is a continuing increase in price levels. A wide disparity develops between original cost and market (or replacement) values.

The recording of an appraisal increase, however, violates generally accepted accounting principles, which require that assets be recorded at cost; they also require that only revenues realized by a market transaction be shown in the financial statements. Although recording an appraisal is permitted when a corporate reorganization occurs, these appraisal increases are rarely recorded in other circumstances. The journal entry to record the appraised difference between cost and market increases assets by a debit and credits the Appraisal Increase account.

Assume that a corporation's land, which had been recorded at $100,000 cost in the accounts, was appraised at $250,000. The increase in value to $250,000 would be recorded as follows:

Land — Appreciation in Value	150,000	
Appraisal Increase		150,000

Following this entry, the Land account continues to show its original cost of $100,000, and the new account, Land — Appreciation in Value, shows the $150,000 increase.

The official CICA position is that long-term asset values should not be revalued upward in normal circumstances. However, where an appraisal has been recorded:

1. Future depreciation charges should be based on the appraised amount and
2. The appraisal increase credit must be left indefinitely in the financial statements and must be transferred to Retained Earnings in amounts not exceeding the increase in depreciation charges or the realization of the increase through a sale of the asset.

The appraisal increase results in a larger shareholders' equity amount, and this increase comes neither from capital contributions of shareholders nor from corporate earnings. Therefore, the appraisal amount of $100,000 should be classified in the financial statements separately from contributed surplus or retained earnings. Usually it is shown as the last item in the shareholders' equity section.

Components of Shareholders' Equity

The total composition of shareholders' equity can now be diagrammed as shown in Figure 10-8.

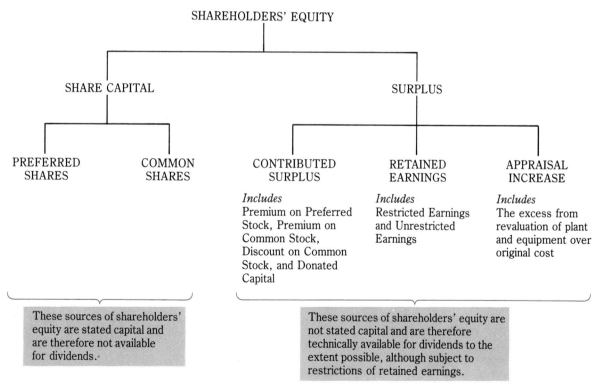

Figure 10-8   The components of shareholders' equity

Notice the breakdown of equity into two major classifications — share capital and surplus. *Surplus* is another of those accounting terms often found in financial statements but not

Surplus
A generic term referring to the part of equity that is not share capital.

recommended by the accountancy profession. As shown in Figure 10-8, **surplus** is a generic term and includes contributed surplus, retained earnings, and appraisal increase. Because of its widespread use in Canada, the word *surplus* is used in this text, but only as a generic term.

Former Usage:	Current Terminology:
Donated Surplus	Donated Capital
Earned Surplus	Retained Earnings
Appraisal Surplus.	Appraisal Increase.

The term *contributed surplus* is currently accepted for usage in Canada to denote capital contributions of shareholders in excess of par, donations of capital, and other shareholder-related items not detailed here.

E.   Book Value

Book value
The amount of net assets represented by one share of stock. When referring to common stock, book value represents the amount not claimed by creditors and preferred shareholders; when referring to preferred stock, book value represents the amount that preferred shareholders would receive if the corporation were liquidated.

The **book value** of a share is the amount determined by dividing shareholders' equity by the number of shares outstanding:

$$\frac{\text{Shareholders' Equity}}{\text{Number of Shares Outstanding}} = \text{Book Value}.$$

This calculation is easy when only one class of shares exists in the corporation. Some complications occur, however, when two or more classes of shares are outstanding. If both preferred and common shares are outstanding, the shareholders' equity must be divided between both classes of shares. Preferred shares are allocated the amount that they would receive if the corporation were liquidated. The common shares receive the balance, if any remains.

Liquidating Value of Preferred Shares

Cumulative dividend
An undeclared dividend that accumulates and has to be paid in the future before any dividends can be paid on common shares.

The liquidating value of a preferred share is always printed on the share certificate. It can be the par-value of the share. It can also be an amount higher than this par-value. Some preferred shares are entitled to dividends that are in arrears. This involves a *cumulative dividend* feature that is attached to some preferred shares.

For the problems that follow this chapter, no cumulative dividend feature is assumed to exist. Therefore, the liquidating value of the preferred shares is the par-value of the shares unless a liquidating value is indicated in the problem narrative.

Calculation of Share Book Value

The calculation of the book value of preferred and common shares can be illustrated by using the following shareholders' equity data:

Shareholders' Equity

Preferred Stock, 5%, $10 Par-Value		
Authorized — 5000 Shares		
Issued and Outstanding — 1000 Shares		$ 10,000
Common Stock, No Par-Value		
Authorized — 200 000 Shares		
Issued and Outstanding — 60 000 Shares		20,000
Retained Earnings		105,000
Total Shareholders' Equity		$135,000

Note: There are $5,000-worth of dividends in arrears on the preferred shares.

Book value is calculated as follows:

Preferred Shares		*Common Shares*	
Dividends in Arrears	$ 5,000	Total Shareholders' Equity	$135,000
Liquidating Value	10,000	*Less:* Preferred Claims	15,000
Total	$15,000	Balance	$120,000
Shares Outstanding	1000	Shares Outstanding	60 000
Book Value per Share	$15	Book Value per Share	$ 2

A change in book value from one period of time to another may be significant in some circumstances, since it indicates a change in dollar equity per share. Comparison of book value with market value gives an insight into investors' evaluations of the corporation.

Some shares regularly sell for less than their book value on the Toronto Stock Exchange. This does not necessarily mean they are a bargain investment. The market price of a share is related to such factors as the company's earnings, dividend record, future potential to generate earnings, and so on. A higher book value than market price of a share may be interpreted as investor judgement that a corporation's shares are a poor investment.

Illustrative Problem: Shareholders' Equity Classification and Interpretation

The trial balance of the New Carlisle Corporation at December 31, 19X1 included the following accounts:

Mortgage Payable	$5,000
Retained Earnings	1,570
Premium on Preferred Stock	10
Allowance for Doubtful Accounts	30
Common Stock, No Par-Value, 15 000 Shares Authorized:	
Issued and Outstanding, 10 000 Shares	5,000
Preferred Stock, 6% Par-Value $1	
500 Shares Authorized and Issued	500
Restriction for Income Tax Litigation	700
Accumulated Depreciation	600
Donated Surplus — Land	375
Restriction for Contingencies	2,500
Appraisal Surplus — Land	400

A partial balance sheet can now be prepared from the trial balance items:

New Carlisle Corporation
Partial Balance Sheet
At December 31, 19X1
Shareholders' Equity

SHARE CAPITAL:
  Preferred Stock, 6%, $1 Par-Value
    Authorized, Issued and Outstanding —
    500 Shares. $ 500
  Common Stock, No Par-Value
    Authorized — 15 000 Shares
    Issued and Outstanding — 11 000 Shares   5,000
      Total Share Capital $ 5,500

SURPLUS:
  Contributed Surplus
    Premium on Preferred Stock $ 10
    Donated Capital — Land   375
      Total Contributed Surplus $ 385
  Retained Earnings
    Restricted
      For Income Tax Litigation $ 700
      For Contingencies   2,500
             $3,200
    Unrestricted   1,570
      Total Retained Earnings   4,770
  Appraisal Increase — Land   400
      Total Surplus   5,555
      Total Shareholders' Equity $11,055

Note the form used in the classification of the sources of shareholders' equity. The proper display of each item makes it easier for readers to understand the corporation's financial situation.

The reader of financial statements is interested in information contained in shareholders' equity, to answer the questions that introduced the chapter:

1. What types of different classes of shares does the corporation have available to interest investors?
2. How much is the corporation's stated capital?
3. What are the different rights of shareholders in this corporation?
4. What dividends are preferred shareholders entitled to if dividends are declared by the corporation?
5. How much are the claims of preferred shareholders in the event of liquidation?
6. What is the status of corporate shares at year-end?
7. What is the maximum amount of dividends that could be declared by the corporation?
8. What is the amount of retained earnings actually available for dividends?
9. Have any assets of the corporation been revalued?
10. Are there any unusual components of shareholders' equity?
11. What is the book value of common shares?

The discussion of the answers to these questions will be related to Figure 10-9 showing the composition of New Carlisle Corporation's shareholders' equity.

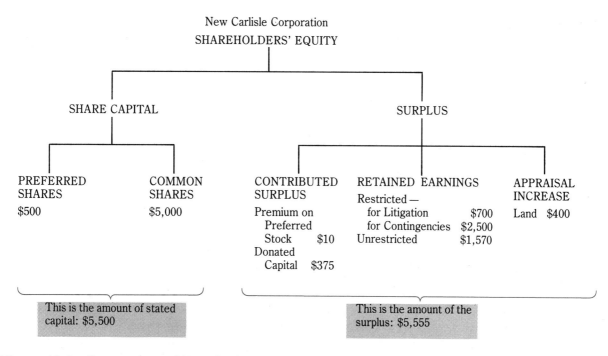

Figure 10-9 Components of New Carlisle shareholders' equity

Question 1: What Different Classes of Shares Does the Corporation Have Available?

There are both preferred and common shares. The preferred shares have a par-value of $1 each and are entitled to 6% dividends if dividends are declared. The common shares are no par-value.

Question 2: How Much Is the Corporation's Stated Capital?

An amount of $5,500 of the shareholders' equity of $11,055 exists as a margin of safety for creditors and for the operation of the corporation. This $5,500 cannot be withdrawn by shareholders as dividends. Any corporate losses in excess of the surplus total will first be absorbed by common shareholders to the extent of $5,000 and next by preferred shareholders to the extent of $500.

Questions 3, 4 and 5: What Are the Rights of Preferred Shareholders?

The corporate charter indicates all particular features applicable to preferred shares. Based on the information contained in shareholders' equity, preferred shareholders are entitled to dividends of $30 ($500 × 6%) before any dividend payments are made to common shareholders. They also have a claim of $500 to the assets of the corporation in the event of liquidation *before* distribution of assets, if any remain, to common shareholders. Reference should be made to the preferred share certificate itself to ascertain whether preferred shares have any voting rights in this corporation.

Question 6: **What Is the Status of Corporate Shares at Year-End?**

Since the status of shares can change from one year to the next, readers of financial statements, particularly shareholders, are interested in the status of corporate shares. A reading of shareholders' equity indicates that all 500 authorized preferred shares and 10 000 of the 15 000 authorized common shares have been issued by the corporation and are outstanding (that is, in the hands of shareholders). The corporation may wish to increase the authorized preferred shares at some time in the future and must apply to government for authorization to increase the number of authorized shares.

It is important for shareholders in Canada to review the issue of shares by a corporation, since the so-called *pre-emptive right of shareholders* in the United States does not exist in Canada unless specifically included in the company's charter. That is, existing shareholders do not have to be given first opportunity to purchase newly issued shares. The effect is that the relative shareholding percentage of an investor can be changed from, for example, 10 percent of the corporation to 5 percent, as illustrated in the following example:

Before Issue of New Shares:	*After Issue of New Shares:*
Investor A owns 1000 common shares of New Carlisle Corporation. This is a 10% ownership (1000 / 10 000 shares).	The company issues 10 000 new shares to other investors. Investor A now owns 1000 of 20 000 shares, which now gives A only a 5% ownership.

Question 7: **What Is the Maximum Amount of Dividends that Can Be Declared?**

The maximum amount of dividends depends on the amount of cash or assets that are available to be distributed to shareholders at any one point in time. For example, it would be hard to distribute receivables as dividends to shareholders. It would be less difficult to distribute inventory.

Assuming that cash was available, $5,555 less retained earnings restrictions of $3,200 ($700 + $2,500) could theoretically be issued as dividends. This is an amount of $2,355 ($5,555 − $3,200).

Question 8: **What Is the Amount of Retained Earnings Actually Available for Dividends?**

The total amount of earnings that has been retained in New Carlisle is $4,770. However, a total of $3,200 has been restricted by the board of directors. The corporation therefore anticipates the possible need of $3,200 of assets for income tax litigation settlement purposes and for other contingencies. This amount of assets is therefore not available as dividends.

The amount available for dividends is $1,570. Although $1,570 in dividends could theoretically be paid from retained earnings, there may not be sufficient cash in the corporation to pay this amount. Further, the financial strength of New Carlisle could be jeopardized by the payment of such a large amount.

Question 9: **Have Any Assets of the Corporation Been Revalued?**

The corporation has recorded an unrealized increase in land amounting to $400. Except in the case of reorganization, this type of revaluation is not in accordance with generally accepted accounting principles. GAAP require that assets be recorded at cost and that only revenues realized by a market transaction be recorded. The reader of New Carlisle's financial statement should review the accounting treatment of the appraisal increase.

Question 10:   Are There Any Unusual Components of Shareholders' Equity?

A review of contributed surplus indicates that $375 of capital has been donated to the company in the form of land. This may indicate that a plant construction has occurred recently. There is also a premium on preferred shares, which has been paid by the original purchasers of these shares from the corporation. This premium is a normal component of contributed surplus.

Question 11:   What Is the Book Value of Common Shares?

A review of the preferred share description does not indicate any amount at which these shares are redeemable. There is also no liquidating value specified. Therefore, it can be assumed that these shares are only entitled to their $1 par-value if the corporation is liquidated. Book value can be calculated as follows:

Total Shareholders' Equity	$11,055
Less: Preferred Claims	500
Available for Common Shares	$10,555
Common Shares Outstanding	10 000
Book Value per Common Share	$1.06 (rounded)

APPENDIX: Stock Subscriptions

Stock subscription
An agreement to purchase share capital from a corporation with payment to be made at a later date; subscribed stock becomes issued but is not outstanding until fully paid for and given to shareholders.

These discussions of share capital transactions assumed that full payment was received and that shares were issued at once. However, these exchanges happen only in the case of small or closely held corporations. In actual practice, shares can be sold through a **stock subscription**, with payment being made later. The subscriber signs an agreement whereby he/she agrees to buy a certain number of shares and to make certain specified payments.

Subscriptions under the CBCA and CBCA-Compatible Provincial Legislation

In these jurisdictions, share certificates are issued only when full payment for the subscribed share is made. In fact, legally, the subscriber is not considered to be a shareholder.

No entry is made in the books of the corporation at the time an agreement is made with the subscriber; the first entry occurs when cash is received from the subscriber. A debit is made to Cash and a credit is made to a liability account; the use of a liability account indicates that no shares are issued to the subscriber as payments for shares are received by the corporation. Assume that New Carlisle Corporation, as a corporation incorporated under the CBCA, accepts subscriptions for 1000 common shares at a total subscription price of $1,500 to be paid in two instalments of $750 each. At this point, a memorandum entry similar to the following can be prepared.

Common Stock   Acct. No. **320**

Date 19X1	Description	F	Debit	Credit	DR. or CR.	Balance
	Memorandum					
	Accepted subscriptions					
	for 1 000 common shares					
	at a total subscription					
	price of $1,500.					

The acceptance of the subscription is not recorded in the accounts and no amount should appear in the shareholders' equity section of the balance sheet, since the subscriber is not considered to be a shareholder.

When the first instalment of $750 is received, it is recorded as follows:

Cash	750	
Payments for Stock Subscriptions		750
Received first instalment on		
common shares subscribed.		

A liability account is credited, because the $750 is not considered to be payment for shares.

The journal entry to record collection of the second instalment is:

Cash	750	
Payments for Stock Subscriptions		750
Received second instalment on common		
shares subscribed.		

The shares have now been paid for in full, and the common shares can be issued to the subscriber. The following journal entry records the issue of the shares:

Payments for Stock Subscriptions	1,500	
Common Stock		1,500

The subscriber has now acquired the full status of a shareholder, and once he/she actually receives the shares, the shares are referred to as issued and outstanding.

A balance sheet prepared at this time shows the increase in issued and outstanding shares from 10 000 shares to 11 000 shares.

New Carlisle Corporation
Partial Balance Sheet
At December 31, 19X1
Shareholders' Equity

SHARE CAPITAL:
Preferred Stock, 6%, No Par-Value
  Authorized, Issued and Outstanding—500 Shares $ 500
Common Stock, No Par-Value
  Authorized—15 000 Shares
  Issued and Outstanding—11 000 Shares   6,500
         $7,000

Subscriptions under CBCA-Incompatible Provincial Corporations Acts

When subscriptions are received, the corporation debits a receivable account, Subscriptions Receivable, for the subscriptions price of the shares. A temporary share capital account, Common Stock Subscribed, is credited for the par-value of the shares, if they have a par-value. The use of a temporary account indicates that the sale of the shares has not been completed. A premium, if any occurs, is treated in the same manner as under CBCA incorporation. Assume that New Carlisle Corporation is a CBCA-incompatible provincially incorporated company and that subscriptions are received for the same 1000 common shares. A total subscription price of $1,500 is to be paid in two equal instalments of $750 each. The entry to record the subscription is:

Subscriptions Receivable	1,500	
Common Stock Subscribed		1,500
Received subscriptions for 1000		
common shares at a total		
price of $1,500.		

Note that the total subscription price is debited to a special receivable account and a special temporary equity account is credited. Note also that the Common Stock Subscription account represents shares that are classified as unissued shares. The subscriber to the stock does not acquire full status of a shareholder until full payment is received. If no par-value shares are involved, the temporary Stock Subscribed account is credited for the full amount. If a balance sheet is prepared at this point, the subscribed shares are shown as follows:

Shareholder's Equity

SHARE CAPITAL:	
Preferred Stock, 6%, $1 Par-Value	
Authorized, Issued and Outstanding—500 Shares	$ 500
Common Stock, No Par-Value	
Authorized — 15 000 Shares	
Issued and Outstanding — 10 000 Shares	5,000
Subscribed but Not Issued — 1000 Shares	1,500
	$7,000

The collection of the first instalment is recorded as follows:

Cash	750	
Subscriptions Receivable		750
Received first instalment		
on common shares.		

At this point, the shares are still unissued and the subscriber does not acquire full status of a shareholder. The journal entry to record collection of the second instalment is:

Cash	750	
Subscriptions Receivable		750
Received second instalment		
on common shares.		

The shares have now been fully paid for and the company is permitted to issue the subscribed shares to the subscriber. A journal entry is required to transfer these common shares from the temporary Common Stock Subscribed equity account to the permanent Common Stock account. The transfer is made by the following entry:

Common Stock Subscribed	1,500	
Common Stock		1,500

The subscriber has now acquired the full status of a shareholder. The temporary equity account now has a zero balance and does not appear in the shareholders' equity section of the balance sheet.

Shareholders' Equity

Common Stock, No Par-Value
  Authorized — 15 000 Shares
  Issued and Outstanding — 11,000 Shares $6,500

If preferred stock is also subscribed for, the same accounts would be used, except that the temporary equity account would be Preferred Stock Subscribed; any premium would also be recognized at the time of the subscription. The entry to record a subscription of preferred stock would take the following form:

Subscriptions Receivable	XXX	
Preferred Stock Subscribed		XX
Premium on Preferred Stock		X
Received subscriptions for *?* shares		
of preferred stock at *?* per share.		

The accounting procedures required when a corporation falls under the jurisdiction of a CBCA-incompatible province are contrasted with federal jurisdiction (the CBCA) below.

CBCA-Incompatible

Transaction	*Provincial Jurisdiction*			*The CBCA*		
1. Subscription received for 1000 common shares; total subscription $1,500.	Subscriptions Receivable Common Stock Subscribed	1,500	1,500	No entry is made.		

2. The first instalment of $750 received.	Cash
	  Subscriptions Receivable
		750	750	Cash
				  Payment for Stock
				  Subscriptions
					750	750

3. The second instalment of $750 is received.	Cash
	  Subscriptions Receivable
		750	750	Cash
				  Payments for Stock
				  Subscriptions
					750	750

4. The common shares are issued.	Common Stock Subscribed
	  Common Stock
		1,500	1,500	Payments for Stock
				Subscriptions
				  Common Stock
					1,500	1,500

Discussion Questions

1. What are some advantages and disadvantages of the corporate form of organization?
2. What is meant by the limited liability feature of corporations? How does it influence creditors?
3. In what way is there double taxation for a corporation? Are there tax advantages with a corporate form of organization?
4. What rights are attached to common shares? Where are these rights indicated?
5. What are the typical features of incorporation?
6. What is a board of directors and whom does it represent? Are the directors involved in the daily management of the entity?
7. Corporate accounting involves the use of specialized terminology. Explain:
   a. The different terms relating to the amount, if any, printed on a share certificate
   b. The different classes of shares
   c. The different terms relating to the current status of a corporation's shares.
8. The word *value* has a specific meaning for accountants. What exactly does it mean? Give examples of different uses.
9. Distinguish between par-value stock and no par-value stock. What does the CBCA require?
10. In what way is stock "preferred"? In which way is it similar to common stock? Different from common stock?
11. Distinguish among authorized, unissued, issued, and outstanding shares.
12. What is stated value? Why is it used in the CBCA jurisdictions?
13. Distinguish between premiums on common stock and discounts on common stock. Is it legal in Canada to issue shares at a discount? Is a premium income?
14. Describe the accounting treatment of reacquired shares as required in the CBCA. Can these shares be resold? Explain.
15. Differentiate between treasury shares and shares reacquired under the CBCA. Why would a corporation purchase its own shares?
16. *Contributed surplus* is a generic term. What does it include? Must the assets represented by contributed surplus be legally kept in the corporation for the protection of creditors?
17. Why do corporations sometimes opt for a stock split? What is a reverse stock split?
18. Assume a 2-for-1 stock split occurs. Explain
    a. The effect on the par-value of each share split
    b. The effect on the total amount of issued and outstanding shares.
19. In what way have retained earnings been ploughed back into an entity?
20. What is the difference between restricted and unrestricted retained earnings? Why would some retained earnings be restricted? Prepare the journal entry used to make a restriction.
21. Are restrictions of retained earnings the best method for indicating and explaining management's intentions? Explain.
22. What does the term *reserve* mean? What is a reserve for bad debts? A reserve for depreciation?
23. Define *donated capital*. How does it differ from share capital? Where is donated capital classified in the balance sheet?
24. What is the justification for the creation of an appraisal increase? Is it in accordance with generally accepted accounting principles? Why or why not?
25. Identify the major components of the shareholders' equity section of a balance sheet. Why are these components distinguished?
26. What does book value of shares represent? How is it calculated?
27. A corporate entity has both preferred and common classes of shares. How is the book value of common shares calculated in this case? What is meant by the liquidating value of preferred shares?
28. Does the book value change from year to year? Of what value is its calculation to the reader of financial statements?
29. The market price of a share is less than its book value; is it a bargain? Why or why not?
30. Refer to Real Life Example 10-1. What is the function of the Board of Directors? What are the similarities between the Board of Directors and the firm's auditors in their relationship with the firm's shareholders?

Discussion Cases

Discussion Case 10-1: Why Own Stock if you Can't Vote?

Non-voting ownership has grown into a peculiarly Canadian monster. It's not new and, in particular cases in the past, it seemed like a good idea at the time. Even necessary.

What is new for Canada's more than 2 million shareholders, and the health of the investment climate, is this: There now are so many companies with limited or non-voting stock that almost everyone has begun to worry about it.

And some thought is being given in corporate boardrooms and the financial community to what should be done about the problem of the emasculated shareholder. It's accompanied by the fear that the government might do it if others won't.

It's no small problem. Isn't it wrong to invite investors to put their money into a company's common shares — taking the risks — yet deprive them of the advantages of the voting power that normally would go with such ownership?

Certainly, the ideal of shareholder democracy goes out the window. In any crunch over corporate control or management policy, the owners of a non-voting stock might find themselves without an effective voice.

That could be true of their power to influence management and the important (voting) owners, and in receiving a take-over bid, if any. In some cases, a takeover bidder is free to offer a fat price only for the voting shares. That leaves the non-voters out in the cold though their stock might otherwise be identical.

Even Voters Are Restricted

In other cases, companies put a ceiling on the number of voting shares that can be voted by one person or group. That often is designed to keep management in control, though the managers might have little of their own money in the company.

These and other developments are increasingly pressing. Billions of dollars worth of non-voting stock — or shares of limited voting power — have been issued by scores of Canadian companies. Meanwhile, the real clout in these corporations rests with sometimes relatively small amounts of voting shares.

Broadly, there's concern that the practice could make Canadians less enthusiastic about investing. And these new doubts almost certainly will slow the trend. Some companies will either give up any idea of voting curbs or decide to sweeten their non-voting shares.

Ways To Help Non-voters

The latter can be done in various ways. Non-voting stock can be given more advantages in receiving dividends. There can be an explicit guarantee that non-voters will share the benefits of any takeover bid. Or they can be given selected voting rights — in the event of a takeover or in naming directors to represent themselves.

Some foreign stock exchanges won't list common shares that don't have full voting rights. They don't fit their ideas of what capitalism is all about. The Toronto Stock Exchange has about 125 such issues. About 80 are non-voting with the remainder having some kind of limitation. In the stock lists, they appear with a small "f" after them, referring to an explanatory footnote usually accompanying the table.

Some critics think that's not enough. Aside from those who'd ban voting curbs, or narrow their scope, others would like to see these issues listed in a separate table to make the distinction more obvious to the average investor.

Source Jack McArthur, "Why own stock if you can't vote?", *The* (Montreal) *Gazette*, November 17, 1983, p. 8-9.

For Discussion

1. What are the advantages, if any, of non-voting shares?
2. For an investor with a small amount of money would the effect of voting shares be negligible?
3. What issues should small and large investors be concerned with concerning the type of shares that a company is offering?

Discussion Case 10-2: CP Stock Split

Canadian Pacific Ltd. of Montreal, one of Canada's most widely held companies, is planning a three-for-one split of ordinary shares and preferred shares, its first split since 1971 and only its third since 1930.

The news is a "pleasant surprise" for the company's thousands of shareholders, one Toronto analyst said. At the end of 1984, CP LTD. had about 47 000 shareholders.

Shareholders will be asked at the annual meeting May 1 to approve the split on the 3-for-1 basis. Previous splits were 5 for 1 in 1971 and 4 for 1 in 1930.

The company also reported profit for the year ended December 31, 1984, rose to $5.21 a share from $1.98 a year earlier. The analyst said the 1984 figure was generally higher than expected and about 30 cents a share above his estimate. Total 1984 profit rose to $375 million from $143 million in 1983.

The shares, which have swung widely in the 14 years since the last split, have risen sharply this year from $50 at the end of 1984. The price was as low as $24.87 in 1982.

The shares have often been promoted by analysts as offering investors "a piece of Canada" because of the company's widespread interests. It is involved, directly and through subsidiaries, in rail, truck, telecommunications, airline, hotel and shipping enteprises. A subsidiary, Canadian Pacific Enterprises Ltd. of Calgary, has natural resource and manufacturing interests.

CP LTD. said it plans to redeem, "as soon as practicable," all 7.25 per cent cumulative redeemable series A preferred shares outstanding at $10 a share, plus acrrued and unpaid dividends to the date of redemption.

The number of shareholders in CP LTD. is among the half-dozen highest in Canada, analysts said. Others include Bell Canada Enterprises Inc. of Montreal, with the largest number, Imperial Oil Ltd. of Toronto and British Columbia Resources Investment Corp. of Vancouver.

Source George Linton, "Rare CP Ltd. stock split surprises shareholders", *The Gazette*, February 13, 1985, p. B-12.

For Discussion

1. Equity is unchanged by a stock split. Why would CP investors view this split as a "pleasant surprise"?
2. "The CP LTD. stock split is like taking a twenty-dollar bill to the bank and getting two tens in return." Comment on this statement.

Discussion Case 10-3: A Reverse Stock Split

Askin Service Corp. and Motor Oil Refinery Holding Co. of Chicago have reached an agreement in principle for the combination of the two companies.

Askin, which has been reducing its retail operations and has announced a plan to enter the energy field, would issue 10 520 298 common shares and warrants to purchase another 450 000 in the transaction, which would result in a transfer of control to the Chicago firm.

Askin currently has 818 922 shares outstanding and warrants to buy 400 000 additional shares.

Askin said the companies are considering a possible reverse split to reduce the shares outstanding of the combined company. The transaction is subject to the approval of a definite contract by the boards of Askin and Motor Oil Refinery and the shareholders of Askin.

For Discussion

1. The company is reported to be considering a reverse stock split. What are the implications of this decision for the market price of shares, the number of shareholders and the shareholder base, and the number of shares outstanding?
2. A student friend, a major in hotel administration, is having difficulty understanding the idea of a stock split. Someone has suggested using, instead of shares, a banana to be split. How is it comparable and how is it not comparable?
3. Prepare a short example of a reverse stock split, using a banana split to get the idea across.

Discussion Case 10-4: Conversion of Debt to Equity in Massey-Ferguson Ltd.

Massey is currently in the process of trying to raise $700 million to pay off some of its $2.6 billion in debts. Besides the government-guaranteed issue of $200 million in shares, Massey is getting $150 million from the Canadian Imperial Bank of Commerce, partly in fresh equity and partly through the conversion of debt to equity.

The company is also asking its 250 lenders to forgive $350 million in interest on loans in exchange for equity in the company.

For Discussion

1. If creditors agree to accept shares in the corporation in place of the interest owing, what would be the journal entry on the books of:
   a. Massey-Ferguson Ltd.?   b. The creditors?
2. Is the interest and debt forgiven by the issue of shares, or do the shares pay the interest? Explain.

Comprehension Problems

Comprehension Problem 10-1

The shareholders' equity section of Fatemech Corporation's balance sheet at December 31, 19X3 is given below.

Shareholders' Equity

SHARE CAPITAL:
  Preferred Stock, $50 par-value
    Authorized — 100 shares
    Issued and Outstanding — ? Shares $3,200
  Common Stock, no par-value
    Authorized — 2000 Shares
    Issued and Outstanding — 800 Shares   1,680
      Total Share Capital $4,880

SURPLUS:
  Contributed Surplus
    Premium on Preferred stock $256
  Retained Earnings   600
    Total Surplus   856
    Total Shareholders' Equity $5,736

Required:
1. How many preferred shares are outstanding?
2. What is the average price received for each issued preferred share?
3. What is the average price received for each issued common share?
4. What is the total stated capital of the company?
5. Is it likely that the corporation is incorporated under the CBCA? How can you tell?

Note: Answer problems involving stock subscriptions only if the Appendix was studied in your course.

Comprehension Problem 10-2

The ledger accounts of Waldo Corp. have the following amounts recorded during December:

Cash		Land		Building	
30,000	5,000	10,000	4,000	12,000	
15,000	8,000			8,000	
7,000	6,000				
4,000					
14,000					

Preferred Stock, No Par-Value		Common Stock, No Par-Value	
6,000	15,000	5,000	30,000
	14,000		22,000
			7,000

Required: Reconstruct the transactions that occurred during December and prepare the journal entries to record these transactions.

Comprehension Problem 10-3

The ledger accounts of Tetu Service Corporation have the following amounts recorded during March:

Cash		Preferred Stock, $10 Par-Value	Premium on Preferred Stock
40,000	5,000	20,000	5,000
3,400		3,000	400
2,000			

Land		Common Stock, $1 Par-Value	Premium on Common Stock
12,000	2,000	13,000	2,000
		10,000	

	Discount on Common Stock
	3,000

Required:
1. Reconstruct the transactions that occurred during March and prepare the journal entries to record these transactions.
2. How many preferred and common shares have been issued?

Comprehension Problem 10-4

The following is a classification of assets, liabilities, and equities that appear on the balance sheet of Nagys Inc.

Balance Sheet Accounts

Assets	*Liabilities and Equities*
a. Current Assets	f. Current Liabilities
b. Fixed Assets	g. Long-Term Liabilities
c. Intangibles	h. Preferred Stock
	i. Common Stock
	j. Contributed Surplus
	k. Retained Earnings
	l. Appraisal Increase

Required: Using this classification, indicate where each of the following would be presented or disclosed on the balance sheet.

a	Allowance for Doubtful Accounts
h	Authorized Preferred Shares
j	Donated Capital
k	Restriction for Plant Expansion
j	Premium on Preferred Stock
l	Appraisal Increase
h	Restriction for Contingencies
i	Common Shares Authorized
h	Par-Value of Preferred Shares
j	Discount on Common Stock
b	Accumulated Depreciation
a	Prepaid Insurance
k	Unrestricted Retained Earnings
f	Salaries Payable
l n B	Land — Appraisal Increase

Comprehension Problem 10-5

The following are captions for sub-totals appearing in the shareholders' equity section of the balance sheet for Vasil Corporation.

a. Total Share Capital
b. Total Contributed Surplus
c. Total Retained Earnings
d. Total Surplus

Required: For each event listed below, indicate, in the format provided, whether each sub-total is increased (↑) or decreased (↓). Indicate with an X if there is no change to a particular sub-total. Consider each event to be unrelated to the others, unless otherwise indicated.

	a	b	c	d
Example:				
Issued common stock at par	↑	x	x	x
Issued common stock at a premium				
Created a restriction on retained earnings for contingencies				
Split 2 for 1 the common stock of the corporation				
Created an allowance for doubtful accounts				
Received a donation of land from the province				
Issued common stock at a discount				
Recorded an appraisal increase in an asset of the corporation				
Issued par-value preferred stock at a premium				
Recorded a net income for the year from operations				
Issued no par-value common stock				
Removed the restriction on retained earnings for contingencies				
Recorded a net loss for the year from operations				

Comprehension Problem 10-6

The shareholders' equity section of Dresden Manufacturing Limited's balance sheet at December 31, 19X6 is shown below:

Shareholders' Equity

SHARE CAPITAL:
Preferred Stock, 8%, $1 Par-Value
Authorized — 500 Shares
Issued and Outstanding — 300 shares $300
Common Stock, No Par-Value
Authorized — 100 Shares
Issued and Outstanding — 20 Shares   500

Total Share Capital $800

Retained Earnings   192

Total Shareholders' Equity $992

Required:

1. Calculate the book value per share of
   a. The preferred shares,   b. The common shares. (No dividends are in arrears at December 31.)
2. Assume that the common stock was split 2 for 1 on January 2, 19X7 and that there was no change in any other account at that time. Calculate the new book value of common shares immediately following the stock split.

Comprehension Problem 10-7

Wade Inc. received a charter that authorized it to issue 100 shares of common stock. The following transactions were completed during 19X6:

Jan. 5 Sold and issued 30 shares of common stock for a total of $150

Jan. 12 Exchanged 50 shares of common stock for assets listed at their fair market values: Machinery — $100; Building — $100; Land — $50

Jan. 30 Subscriptions were received on 10 shares of common stock at $6 each. Downpayments amounting to 20 percent accompanied the subscription contracts

Feb. 28 Received payment of the balance due on the subscriptions of Jan. 30; the stock was then issued

Dec. 31 Closed the net income of $41 to retained earnings

Dec. 31 Paid a total dividend on common stock of $20.

Required:
1. Prepare journal entries for the 19X6 transactions, assuming that
   a. Wade was incorporated under the CBCA
   b. Wade was incorporated in a CBCA-incompatible province and the common stock had a par-value of $5.
2. Assuming that Wade had been incorporated under the CBCA, prepare the shareholders' equity section of the balance sheet at
   a. January 31,　　b. February 28,　　c. December 31.
3. Assuming that Wade had been incorporated in a CBCA-incompatible province, prepare the shareholders' equity section of the balance sheet at
   a. January 31,　　b. Feburary 28,　　c. December 31.

Problems

Problem 10-1

Price Inc. was incorporated on June 1 and was authorized under its provincial charter to issue the following shares — 20 000, 5% preferred shares of $5 par-value, and 10 000, common shares of no par-value.

Required:
1. Prepare journal entries to record the following June transactions:
   a. Issued 3000 preferred shares for $6 cash each
   b. Issued 5000 preferred shares for $5 cash each
   c. Issued 2000 common shares for $2 cash each
   d. Issued 1000 common shares for $1 cash each
   e. Issued 500 common shares for land valued at $1,500.
2. Prepare the shareholders' equity section of the balance sheet at June 30.
3. On July 15, the common stock was split 2 for 1. Assuming no other transactions occurred since June 30, prepare the shareholders' equity on July 15 following the stock split.

Problem 10-2

Following is the shareholders' equity section of Carlos's Book Mart Inc. shown before and after a stock split on April 15.

Before Split		**After Split**	
Shareholders' Equity		*Shareholders' Equity*	
Common Stock, No Par-Value		Common Stock, No Par-Value	
Authorized — 5000 Shares		Authorized — ? Shares	
Issued and Outstanding —		Issued and Outstanding —	
1000 Shares	$100,000	? Shares	$?

On April 15, the company decided to increase the marketability of its shares by opting for a 5 for 1 stock split.

Required:
1. Complete the shareholders' equity section of the balance sheet after the split.
2. Joe Carlos, the president, asks you to record a memorandum indicating the new number of shares. Record the appropriate journal memorandum.
3. How would a reverse stock split of 1 for 2 on April 15 affect the common stock? Record your answer using this schedule form.

	Number of Shares Outstanding	*Total Common Stock on Balance Sheet*	*Market Price per Share*
Before Stock Split	1000	$100,000	$200
After Stock Split			

4. On the basis of the information given in the shareholders' equity section (before split), would a stock split or reverse stock split be most appropriate? Explain.

Problem 10-3

The trial balance of Montclair Limited at December 31, 19X2 included the items listed below:

Mortgage Payable	$10,000
Premium on Preferred Stock	20
Common Stock, No Par-Value, 500 Shares	
Authorized and Issued	10,000
Allowance for Doubtful Accounts	40
Restriction for Contingencies	1,400
Accumulated Depreciation	1,200
Retained Earnings	3,140
Preferred Stock, 7%, $1 Par-Value	
1000 Shares Authorized and Issued	1,000
Capital Arising from Donation of Plant Site	750
Restriction for Plant Extension	200
Income Tax Payable	400

Required: Prepare the shareholder's equity section of the balance sheet in proper form.

Problem 10-4

The shareholder's equity section of the balance sheet of Alexandria Limited, as at December 31, 19X1, shows the following amounts:

Shareholders' Equity

SHARE CAPITAL:
Preferred Stock, 8%, No Par-Value
    Authorized — 1,000 shares
    Issued and Outstanding — 150 Shares $15,000
Common Stock, No Par-Value
    Authorized — 10,000 Shares
    Issued and Outstanding — 4,800 Shares   24,000

    Total Share Capital $39,000

SURPLUS:
Retained Earnings
    Restricted for Plant Expansion $12,000
    Unrestricted   28,000

    Total Retained Earnings   40,000

    Total Shareholders' Equity $79,000

Alexandria Limited is incorporated under the CBCA. The following transactions occurred during 19X2:

a. Reacquired 400 shares of common stock at $10 each
b. Split the common stock 2 for 1
c. Issued for $3 cash each, an additional 200 shares of common stock
d. The board authorized a further addition of $5,000 to the retained earnings restricted for plant expansion
e. Net income of $19,500 was transferred from Income Summary to Retained Earnings.

Required:
1. Prepare journal entries for the 19X2 transactions.
2. Prepare the shareholders' equity section of the balance sheet at December 31, 19X2.

Problem 10-5

The following is the shareholders' equity section of the balance sheet of Red River Foods Limited at December 31, 19X5.

Shareholders' Equity

SHARE CAPITAL:		
Common Stock, Par-Value $10		
Authorized — 500 Shares		
Issued and Outstanding — 300 Shares		$3,000
SURPLUS:		
Contributed Surplus		
Premium on Common Stock	$ 70	
Retained Earnings	500	
Total Surplus		570
Total Shareholders' Equity		$3,570

Required:
1. What is the book value per common share?
2. On December 31, the Red River common shares traded at a high of $24. What is the explanation of this price, related to your answer in 1, above?
3. The premium on common shares resulted from a July 1 transaction. If the shares had a no par-value, how would the $70 premium have been recorded?
4. Is this corporation incorporated under the CBCA? How can you tell?

Problem 10-6

Big City Carpet Corporation was not incorporated January 2, 19X5 under the Canada Business Corporations Act; it was authorized to issue an unlimited number of no par-value common shares. Big City's year-end is December 31. The following transactions occurred during 19X5:

Jan. 2 Issued 2 shares for $4 cash each

Jan. 2 Issued 5 shares of common stock to Black for carpet-cutting equipment — Black paid $10 for the equipment last year; the book value for Black was $9, but current market value is $15

Jan. 25 Subscriptions for 10 shares of the common stock were accepted at $4 per share; a 25% cash payment accompanied the subscription

Jul. 2 The balance due on the common stock subscription was collected, and the shares were issued.

Required:
1. Prepare journal entries to record the 19X5 transactions.
2. Prepare the shareholders' equity section of the balance sheet at
   a. January 31,   b. July 31.

Problem 10-7

Academy Limited received a charter authorizing it to issue 30 shares of $100 par-value, 10% preferred stock and 50 shares of $10 par-value common stock. During the month of January, 19X4, following receipt of the charter, the following transactions took place:

Jan. 5 Sold 20 shares of common stock at par for cash; the shares were issued immediately
Jan. 10 Accepted subscriptions for 20 shares of common stock at par; a 50% downpayment accompanied the subscription
Jan. 15 The promoters of Academy accepted 1 share of common stock for their services to the company; the board of directors valued their services at $100
Jan. 20 In exchange for 2 shares of preferred stock, the company received land and building with fair market values of $50 and $150, respectively
Jan. 25 The balance due on the January 10 subscription was collected and the shares were issued
Jan. 30 Subscriptions were accepted on the balance of the common stock at par; a 50% down-payment accompanied the subscriptions.

Required:
1. Prepare journal entries to record the January transactions.
2. Prepare the shareholders' equity section of the balance sheet at January 31, 19X4.

Alternate Problems

Alternate Problem 10-1

Waterhouse Corporation was incorporated on May 1, 19X3. The following transactions occurred during the month.

May 1 Issued 1000 preferred shares for $3 cash each
May 2 Issued 2000 common shares for $5 cash each
May 5 Issued 1500 common shares for $2 cash each
May 10 Issued 1000 preferred shares for $1 cash each
May 15 Issued 3000 preferred shares for $2 cash each
May 21 Issued 5000 common shares for $3 cash each.

Part A

Assume that Waterhouse was incorporated under the CBCA and was authorized to issue an unlimited number of preferred shares of no par-value and common shares of no par-value.

Required:
1. Prepare journal entries to record the May transactions.
2. Prepare the shareholders' equity section of the balance sheet at May 31, 19X3.

Part B

Assume that Waterhouse was incorporated under CBCA-incompatible provincial jurisdiction authorizing the issue of the following shares — 10 000: 8% preferred shares of $2 par-value, and 20 000: common shares of $3 par-value.

Required:
3. Prepare journal entries to record the May transactions.
4. Prepare the shareholders' equity section of the balance sheet at May 31, 19X3.

Alternate Problem 10-2

Micro-Small Software Inc. was incorporated under the CBCA on April 15, 19X4 to design instruction software for colleges and universities. The following transactions occurred during April.

Apr. 15   Received a corporate charter authorizing the issue of an unlimited number of no par-value common shares
Apr. 16   Issued 5000 common shares for $10,000 cash
Apr. 20   Issued 10 000 common shares for land to be used for the construction of a building; the shares were selling for $3 each on this date
Apr. 25   Issued 1000 common shares for $4 cash each
Apr. 30   Reacquired 1000 common shares for $2,750.

Required:
1. Prepare journal entries to record the April transactions.
2. Prepare the shareholders' equity section of the balance sheet at April 30.
3. Assume that on May 25 the stock was split 2 for 1. How would the stock split affect the common stock? Record your answer using the following schedule form.

	Number of Shares Outstanding	*Total Common Stock on Balance Sheet*	*Market Price per share*
Before Stock Split			$6
After Stock Split			

Alternate Problem 10-3

The trial balance of Fredericton Limited at December 31, 19X6 includes the following items:

Retained Earnings	$ 5,700
Allowance for Doubtful Accounts	7,500
Common Stock, No Par-Value,	
10 000 Shares Authorized and Issued	50,000
Dividends Payable	1,000
Premium on Preferred Stock	2,500
Mortgage Payable	35,000
Restriction for Contingencies	5,000
Preferred Stock, 7%, $100 Par-Value,	
100 Shares Authorized and Issued	10,000
Capital from Land Donation	1,200
Appraisal Increase — Land	2,000
Income Tax Payable	500

Required: Prepare in proper form the shareholders' equity section of the balance sheet as at December 31.

Alternate Problem 10-4

Quality Pools Limited was incorporated in a CBCA-incompatible province on July 20, 19X4. The company has selected the calendar year as its accounting year. It has received a corporate charter authorizing the issue of the following share capital— (a) 5000 shares of $10 par-value, 6% preferred, and (b) 50 000 shares of no par-value common. The following transactions occurred during 19X4.

Jul.   20   Issued 6000 shares of common stock for $39,000 cash
Aug. 11   Issued 3000 shares of preferred stock for $33,000 cash
Sept. 7   Received a $50,000 plant site from the city of Pointe Claire in return for an obligation to establish a plant in that municipality's industrial park

Oct. 30 Issued 3000 shares of common stock to a contractor and also paid him $50,000 cash for construction of a building valued at $75,000.

Nov. 5 Recorded an appraisal of the corporation's land and building; cost $125,000, appraisal value of $175,000 (Land increase $30,000, building increase $20,000)

Nov. 18 Split the common stock 4 for 1

Dec. 31 Net income for the year after income tax was $25,000 (make the closing entry)

Dec. 31 Established a retained earnings restriction of $10,000 for expansion of the corporation's building.

Required:
1. Prepare journal entries to record the 19X4 transactions.
2. Show the Preferred Stock ledger account, as it would appear in the general ledger at December 31.
3. Prepare the shareholders' equity section of the balance sheet at December 31.

Alternate Problem 10-5

The shareholders' equity section of the Prairie Machine Company Limited balance sheet at December 31, 19X3 appears below:

SHARE CAPITAL:
Preferred Stock, 6%, $100 Par-Value, Liquidation Value $101
  Authorized — 10 Shares
  Issued and Outstanding — 8 Shares $ 800
Common Stock, No Par-Value
  Authorized — 200 shares
  Issued and Outstanding — 80 Shares   860
    Total Share Capital $1,660

SURPLUS:
Contributed Surplus
  Premium on Preferred Stock $ 48
Retained Earnings
  Restricted for Plant Expansion $200
  Unrestricted   900
    Total Retained Earnings   1,100
    Total Surplus   1,148
    Total Shareholders' Equity $2,808

Required:
1. Calculate the average price received for each outstanding preferred share.
2. What is the book value of a common share? (No dividends are in arrears as at December 31, 19X3.)
3. a. Why do you think the directors established a restriction for plant expansion by restricting part of the retained earnings.
   b. Assume that the plant expansion was completed by June 30, 19X4 and that the new facilities were all paid for. What entry would be made to the restriction?

Alternate Problem 10-6

The following are selected accounts (with normal balances) taken from the general ledger of the Southeast Manufacturing Co. Ltd., at December 31 of the current year.

Loan Payable to Shareholders	$150
Common Stock Subscribed	25
Premium on Preferred Stock	8
Common Stock	100
Subscriptions Receivable — Common Stock	6
Preferred Stock	50
Discount on Common Stock	5
Retained Earnings	300
Capital from Land Site Donation	100

The following additional information is available: (a) Preferred stock is 6%, $1 par-value; authorized 200 shares, and (b) Common stock is $1 par-value; authorized 200 shares.

Required: Prepare the shareholders' equity section of the balance sheet at December 31.

Alternate Problem 10-7

Ojibway Corporation was not incorporated under the CBCA, which authorized it to issue an unlimited amount of common stock. The following transactions occurred during 19X1 and 19X2:

19X1

Mar. 20   Issued 200 shares of common stock for $2,000

Apr. 1   Accepted the following assets at their indicated fair market value for an additional 200 shares: Inventory — $250, Furniture — $150, Machinery — $400, Building — $700. Land — $500.

Sept. 30   Accepted subscriptions for 100 common shares at $12 each; the subscriptions were accompanied with a 25% cash payment

Dec. 31   The Income Summary account was closed; Ojibway had suffered a loss of $65 during the period.

19X2

Jan. 31   Collected the remaining 75% of the balance due on the September 30 subscriptions, and the shares were issued.

Required:
1. Prepare journal entries to record the 19X1 and 19X2 transactions.
2. Prepare the shareholders' equity section of the balance sheet at
    a. December 31, 19X1,
    b. January 31, 19X2.

Supplementary Problems

Supplementary Problem 10-1

Part A

Rosedale Corp. is incorporated under the CBCA and is authorized to issue an unlimited number of shares of 5% preferred stock and 30 000 common shares. Rosedale earned $40,000 during 19X7. The following shareholders' equity sections are for 19X6 and 19X7.

At December 31, 19X6		At December 31, 19X7	
Shareholders' Equity		*Shareholders' Equity*	
SHARE CAPITAL:		SHARE CAPITAL:	
Common Stock, No Par-Value		Common Stock, No Par-Value	
Authorized — 30 000 Shares		Authorized — 30 000 Shares	
Issued and Outstanding—1000 Shares	$10,000	Issued and Outstanding—5000 Shares	$10,000
Retained Earnings	25,000	Retained Earnings	50,000
	$35,000		$60,000

Required: Explain what changes occurred in shareholders' equity during 19X7.

Part B

During 19X8, Rosedale had the following equity account transactions:
a. Issued 6000 preferred shares to a contractor and also paid him $30,000 for the construction of a building valued at $66,000
b. Issued 5000 common shares for $5,000 cash; used the proceeds to pay for new equipment
c. Established the following restrictions and allowances during the year:

Restriction for Plant Expansion	$15,000
Accumulated Depreciation—building	5,000
Allowance for Doubtful Accounts	3,000
Restriction for lawsuit	8,000

d. Net income for the year after income tax (and after all other transactions) was $30,000. (Make the closing entry.)

Required:
1. Prepare journal entries to record the 19X8 transactions.
2. Prepare the shareholders' equity section of Rosedale's balance sheet at December 31, 19X8.

Part C

During 19X9, Rosedale had the following equity account transactions:
a. Acquired for $11,000 cash, and cancelled, 1000 preferred shares
b. Settled the lawsuit for $5,000; the $8,000 restriction was returned to retained earnings
c. Paid a $3,000 cash dividend
d. Net income for the year after income tax and after all other transactions was $40,000. (Make the closing entry.)
e. The common stock was split 2 for 1.

Required:
1. Prepare journal entries to record the 19X9 transactions.
2. Prepare the shareholders' equity section of Rosedale's balance sheet at December 31, 19X9.

Supplementary Problem 10-2

Corning Limited was incorporated in 19X1 with authorized common stock of 100 shares, par-value $5 each. All the shares were subsequently issued at $5 per share. By the end of December, 19X2, the book value of the outstanding shares had increased to $7.50 per share as a result of an increase in retained earnings; at this time, the market value of the shares were $8.25 per share. On action by the board of directors, approved by the shareholders, the capital structure was changed to 400 common shares with a par-value of $1.25 each; the new certificates were issued on a 4 for 1 basis.

At the end of 19X6, the capital structure was again changed to 500 shares with a par-value of $1 each, and new certificates were issued in exchange for those outstanding. Immediately before this latest change, shareholders' equity consisted of the following:

Share Capital (par-value $1.25)	$500
Retained Earnings	60

Required:
1. Prepare journal entries to record each revision of the share capital.
2. Show the shareholders' equity section of the balance sheet following the second change.
3. Indicate the book value per share following the second change.

Supplementary Problem 10-3

Green Hectares Limited was incorporated in a CBCA-incompatible province on July 2, 19X1. The company's year-end is December 31. The company's net income was $20,000 and $35,000 for the years 19X1 and 19X2, respectively. The following transactions occurred:

a. Received a corporate charter authorizing the issue of 30 000 common shares with a par-value of $20 per share and 5000 shares of 5% preferred stock with a par-value of $100 per share
b. The preferred shares were issued on the following dates:
   July 2, 19X1 — 800 shares at $100 per share
   October 3, 19X1 — the preferred stock was split 4 for 1
   June 1, 19X2 — 100 shares at $26.25 per share
   January 30, 19X3 — 400 shares at $28.50 per share
c. The common shares were issued as follows:
   July 2, 19X1 — 5000 shares for $100,000
   June 1, 19X2 — 1000 shares for $22,000
   October 15, 19X2 — 1000 shares for $23,000
   January 15, 19X3 — 1000 shares for $25,000
   January 20, 19X3 — the common shares were split 2 for 1

Required:
1. Prepare the shareholders' equity section of the balance sheet at December 31, 19X2.
2. The restricted retained earnings and allowance accounts at December 31, 19X3 include the following:

Restricted for Plant Expansion	$10,000
Accumulated Depreciation — Building	7,000
Allowance for Doubtful Accounts	2,500
Restricted for Contingencies	3,000

The company's income since incorporation totalled $70,000. No dividends have been declared. Prepare the shareholders' equity section of the balance sheet at December 31, 19X3.

Dividend Distributions

The amount of a corporation's retained earnings is an important input for management decisions regarding dividend declaration. Dividends reduce retained earnings.

1. What components of shareholders' equity represent assets that are available for dividend payments?
2. Why would a corporation choose not to declare dividends?
3. At what point does a dividend become a legal liability of the corporation?
4. How are declared dividends disclosed?
5. Which shares of the corporation have a preference to dividends?
6. Do undeclared dividends in any of the corporation's shares accumulate?
7. Which features are included with certain classes of shares to make them more attractive to investors?
8. Does a stock dividend have any effect on the investor's portfolio?
9. Does a stock dividend change the investor's percentage of corporate ownership?
10. How does the corporation record a stock dividend?

A. Dividends

Components of Shareholders' Equity

Dividend
A distribution to corporate shareholders; can consist of cash, property of the corporation, or shares.

Shareholders' equity comprises assets contributed by shareholders and also assets earned and retained in the corporation. The distinction between the sources of these assets is important. The difference relates to the availability of assets for **dividend** payments to corporate shareholders. Figure 11-1 distinguishes between the components of shareholders' equity representing assets that are available for dividend payments and those representing assets that are not available.

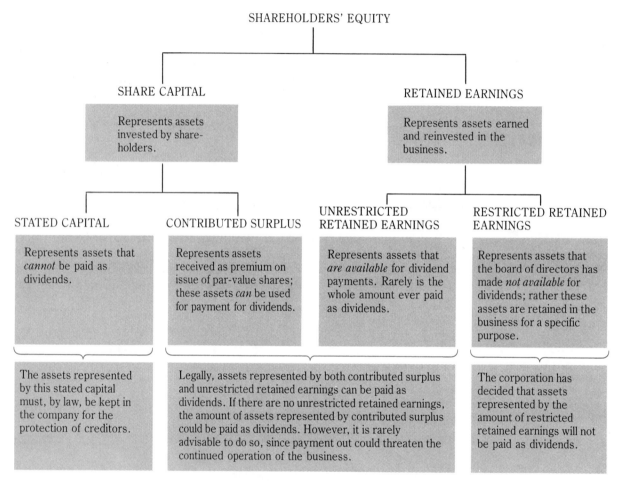

Figure 11-1   Components of shareholders' equity

Both creditors and shareholders are interested in the amount of assets that can be distributed as dividends. Stated capital and restricted retained earnings represent assets that are not available for distribution as dividends. These categories are intended to protect creditors because they prevent shareholders from withdrawing assets as dividends to the point where assets become insufficient to pay creditors; they are also intended to ensure the continued operation of the business.

Shareholders' equity is classified in Figure 11-1 to emphasize the distinction between assets that are available for dividends and assets that are not available for dividends. However, such a diagram is not published by corporations in their financial statements. Rather, the reader of financial statements must understand the information on the balance sheet and in its notes and must be able to interpret it.

There are different provisions concerning the legality of dividend payments in each of the provincial companies acts and in the federal CBCA. The classification of sources of shareholders' equity in Figure 11-1 assumes that the assets represented by the stated capital of a corporation are the only ones that cannot be paid out as dividends. However, in any specific situation, reference must always be made to the appropriate legislation.

Dividend Policy

Sometimes a board of directors may choose not to declare any dividend. There may be financial conditions in the corporation that make the payment impractical or impossible, even though the corporation has unrestricted retained earnings.

Consideration 1:   There May Not Be Adequate Cash
Corporations regularly reinvest their earnings in assets in order to make more profits. Growth occurs in this way and reliance on creditor financing can be minimized.

Consideration 2:   Policy of the Corporation May Preclude Dividend Payments
Some corporations pay no dividends. They reinvest their earnings in the business. Shareholders benefit through increased earnings, which are translated into increased market prices for the corporation's shares. The pressure from shareholders for the corporation to provide dividends is reduced in this way. This type of dividend policy is often found in growth-oriented corporations.

Consideration 3:   No Legal Requirement that Dividends Have To Be Paid
The board of directors may decide that no dividends should be paid. If shareholders are dissatisfied, they can elect a new board or, failing that, sell their shares.

Consideration 4:   Dividends May Be Issued in Shares of the Corporation Rather than in Cash
Stock dividends may be issued to conserve cash or to increase the number of shares to be traded on the stock market. Stock dividends are discussed in section C of this chapter.

The difficulty faced in deciding on the declaration of a dividend is discussed in Real Life Example 11-1.

Real Life Example 11-1

A Tough Call: The Dividend

Du Pont's board of directors will gather tomorrow in one of the ornate rooms at the chemical company's headquarters in Wilmington, Del., for what has become an annual fall ritual: the vote on whether to award an extra dividend on top of the $0.60 quarterly dividend.

Some analysts believe the vote will indicate just how difficult the board expects the next couple of quarters to be. With the economy in such straits, and Du Pont's chemical business having a difficult time, there are some questions as to whether the board will part with the traditional bonus, which has been as high as $0.75 and has been paid in eight out of the last 11 years. Last year shareholders received an extra $0.35.

"No one knows what will happen," said a spokesman for Du Pont. "The finance committee will consider it first because they have all the information on earnings and the economy,

and then they will send the recommendation onto the full board, which meets right after the finance committee."

The decision might produce a lively debate between the board members who are large shareholders and need the dividends, like the three Seagram representatives, and the more frugal-minded executives of Du Pont, according to William Young, a vice-president at Dean Witter Reynolds.

Most analysts think the odds are high that the extra dividend will be awarded simply because it does not really cost Du Pont all that much — around $80 million if $0.35 is awarded, according to Young — and not awarding the special payment could alienate shareholders who have stuck by the company during a difficult year.

Source *The New York Times*, November 14, 1984, p. 27-f.

Dividend Declaration

Dividends can be paid only if they have been officially declared by the board of directors. The board must pass a formal resolution authorizing the dividend payment. Notices of the dividend are then published. It is noteworthy that once a dividend declaration has been made public, the dividend cannot be rescinded. At this point, the dividend becomes a liability and must be paid. An example of a dividend notice is shown in Figure 11-2.

Bluebeard Computer Corporation
Dividend Notice
On May 25, 19X1 the Board of Directors of Bluebeard Computer Corporation declared a semi-annual dividend of $0.50 per share on common shares. The dividend will be paid on June 26, 19X1 to shareholders of record on June 7, 19X1.

By Order of the Board
[signed]
Lee Bluebeard
Secretary

May 25, 19X1

Figure 11-2   A typical dividend notice

Date of dividend declaration
The date on which the dividend is declared.

Date of record
Dividends are paid to the shareholder who owns the shares at this date.

Date of payment
The date on which dividends are actually paid.

Three different and important dates are associated with the dividend. Usually dividends are declared on one date, the **date of dividend declaration**; they are payable to shareholders on a second date, the **date of record**; and the dividend itself is actually paid on a third date, the **date of payment**.

Date of Dividend Declaration

The dividend declaration provides an official notice of the dividend. It specifies the amount of the dividend and which shareholders will receive the dividend. The liability for the dividend is recorded in the books of the corporation at its declaration date. Shareholders become creditors of the corporation until the dividend is paid.

Date of Record

Shareholders who own the shares on the date of record will receive the dividend even if they have sold the share before the dividend is actually paid. This date is usually a week or two after the date of declaration. This is important for corporations whose shares are actively traded on the stock market. Investors whose names appear in the shareholders' ledger on the date of record will receive the dividend. Shares sold on the stock market after the date of record are sold *ex-dividend*, that is, without any right to the dividend.

Date of Payment

The dividend is actually paid on this date to investors whose names appear in the shareholders' ledger on the date of record. This date is several weeks after the date of record, in order to allow share transfers to be recorded to the date of record and dividend cheques to be prepared.

Accounting for Dividends

Cash dividend
A dividend paid in cash.

Property dividend
A dividend paid in property of the corporation.

Dividends are usually paid as **cash dividends**. They can also be paid in other assets of the corporation, or in shares of the corporation itself. (The latter case is discussed in section C.) When dividends are declared in assets other than cash, they are usually referred to as **property dividends**. Property dividends usually create problems in dividing the property pro-rata (in proportion) so that it can be distributed to shareholders in proportion to the number of shares they own. Usually, inventory of the corporation and temporary investments are the first assets to be considered for property dividends. The journal entries for cash dividends and property dividends take the following form:

Cash Dividends			**Property Dividends**		
At the declaration date			*At the declaration date*		
Dividends	xx		Dividends	xx	
Dividends Payable		xx	Dividends Payable		xx
At the payment date			*At the payment date*		
Dividends Payable	xx		Dividends Payable	xx	
Cash		xx	Inventory		xx
			Investments		xx

B. Shareholder Preference to Dividends

Preferred shareholders are usually entitled to dividends before any dividends are distributed to common shareholders. They may also have other dividend preferences, depending on what rights have been attached to preferred shares at the date of incorporation. Two additional preferences can be:
- The accumulation of undeclared dividends from one year to the next — referred to as *cumulative dividends*, as compared with *non-cumulative dividends*, which do not accumulate.
- The participation of preferred stock with common stock in dividend distributions beyond the usual preferred dividends — referred to as a *participating* feature of preferred stock as compared with a *non-participating* feature.

The relationships among these dividend preferences are shown in Figure 11-3.

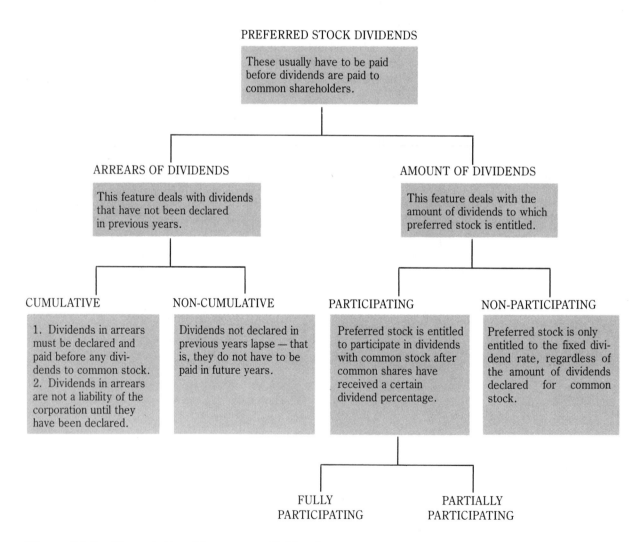

Figure 11-3   The relationships among dividend types

Cumulative Dividend Preferences

Cumulative preferred stock
Stock on which undeclared dividends accumulate and have to be paid in the future before any dividends can be paid on common shares.

The **cumulative** preference means that an unpaid dividend accumulates from year to year and is payable from future earnings if a dividend declaration is made by the entity. These accumulated dividends must be paid before any dividends are paid on common stock. The unpaid dividends are usually referred to as *dividends in arrears*. Dividends in arrears are not recorded as a liability on the balance sheet of the company unless and until they have been declared by the board of directors. Note disclosure of dividends in arrears must, however, be made in the financial statements.

Case 1:   Preferred Shares with a Cumulative Preference
Assume that George Williams Inc. declared dividends totalling $92,000 when the shareholders' equity section of its balance sheet contained the following classes of shares:

Preferred stock, $100 Par-Value,
        8% Cumulative
   Authorized — 3000 Shares
   Issued and Outstanding — 2000 Shares $200,000
Common Stock, $10 Par-Value
   Authorized — 35 000 Shares
   Issued and Outstanding — 30 000 Shares $300,000 $500,000

A note to the balance sheet indicates that there were two years of preferred dividends in arrears. How much of the $92,000 cash dividend is paid to each class of shares? The preferred shares are entitled to $16,000 dividends per year ($200,000 × 8%) whenever dividends are declared. Because these shares have a cumulative preference, they are also entitled to dividends in arrears.

Non-cumulative preferred stock
Stock on which a dividend, if not declared in a given year, will not accumulate to be received at a later date.

Shareholder Preference to Dividends		**Dividend Distribution**		
		To Preferred	*To Common*	*Balance*
	Total Dividend Declared			$92,000
1st Preference:	Arrears ($16,000 × 2 Years)	$32,000	–	60,000
2nd Preference:	Current Year — Preferred	16,000	–	44,000
	Balance to Common	–	$44,000	-0-
	Total	$48,000	$44,000	

The cumulative preference has resulted in the payment to preferred shareholders of dividends unpaid in the previous two years; this amounts to $32,000. For the current year, preferred shareholders receive only $16,000, compared with $44,000 paid to common shareholders. The normally cautious preferred shareholder is usually content with a smaller share of the profits as long as there is a reasonably certain return. The cumulative feature ensures that, if any dividends are declared by the corporation, the preferred shareholder will be paid.

Participating preferred stock
Stock entitled to participate in dividends with common stock after common have received a certain dividend percentage.

If a preferred stock is **non-cumulative**, a dividend not declared by the board of directors in any one year is lost forever.

Participating Dividend Preferences

Non-participating preferred stock
Stock not entitled to participate in additional dividends after receiving the specified dividend percentage to which they are entitled.

A **participating** feature is sometimes added to preferred stock to make it more attractive to shareholders. This feature permits, under certain circumstances, the shareholders' participation in the earnings of the entity in excess of the stipulated rate. The extent of this participation can be limited or unlimited. **Non-participating** preferred stocks do not receive a share of additional dividends.

Case 2: Preferred Shares That Are Partially Participating

Assume that the preferred shares of George Williams Inc. were participating up to 10 percent. This means that after common shareholders have received a payment equivalent to the normal preferred claim — 8 percent in this case — the participating preferred stock is entitled to receive an additional amount of excess dividends up to an additional 2 percent (ie, 10 percent in all) of the par-value of the preferred stock. In other words, once common shareholders receive 8 percent of the par-value of their shares in dividends, preferred shareholders are entitled to a pro-rata share of excess dividends up to 10 percent.

Shareholder Preference to Dividends		Dividend Distribution		
		To Preferred	*To Common*	*Balance*
	Total Dividend Declared			$92,000
1st Preference:	Arrears ($16,000 × 2)	$32,000	–	60,000
2nd Preference:	Current Year — Preferred 8%	16,000	–	44,000
3rd Preference:	Current Year — Common 8% to Match Preferred 8% ($300,000 × 8%)	–	$24,000	20,000
4th Preference:	Current Year — 1% to Each Class			
	($200,000 × 1%)	2,000	–	15,000
	($300,000 × 1%)	–	3,000	
5th Preference:	Current Year — Additional 1% to Each Class = 10% to Each Class	2,000	3,000	10,000
	Balance to Common	–	10,000	-0-
	Total	$52,000	$40,000	

In this case, preferred shareholders received $52,000, compared with $40,000 for common shareholders. If there had been insufficient dividends declared to pay $24,000 ($300,000 × 8%) for the current year in the third preference above, however, the participating feature would not have come into effect for preferred shareholders. Notice also that there were sufficient dividends to pay more than 10 percent of par-value to common shareholders, who received the balance of $10,000 after the fifth preference.

Case 3: Preferred Shares that Are Fully Participating

Case 2 presented the calculation of dividends when preferred shareholders were partially participating in dividends. Preferred stock may also be fully participating. What would the dividend distribution be if preferred shareholders were fully participating with common shareholders in George Williams Inc., rather than being limited to 10 percent participation?

Shareholder Preference to Dividends		Dividend Distribution		
		To Preferred	*To Common*	*Balance*
	Total Dividend Declared			$92,000
1st Preference:	Arrears ($16,000 × 2)	$32,000	–	60,000
2nd Preference:	Current Year — Preferred 8%	16,000	–	44,000
3rd Preference:	Current Year — Common 8% to Match Preferred 8%	–	$24,000	20,000
4th Preference:	Current Year — the Balance Is Distributed in Proportion of Each Class of Shares to Total Stated Capital			
	Preferred — $\frac{\$200,000}{\$500,000} \times \$20,000 =$	8,000		
	Common — $\frac{\$300,000}{\$500,000} \times \$20,000 =$		12,000	-0-
	Total	$56,000	$36,000	

In this case, preferred shareholders receive $56,000 compared with $36,000 for common shareholders. Obviously, the fully participating preference allows preferred shareholders to receive more dividends than common shareholders.

Investments in shares of a corporation carry with them an element of risk that the investment may be lost if the corporation is unsuccessful. Different classes of shares are therefore used to appeal to investors with differing willingness to take risks. In the case of George Williams Inc., the preferred shareholders have less risk than the common shareholders. The preference features attached to the stock have made it perform quite well in the cases above. Common shareholders have received less with the participating feature than was given to preferred shareholders. These examples have been used to illustrate the different preferences that can be given to preferred stock. In actual practice, fully participating features are seldom provided for preferred shares. While cumulative features occur, participating features are rarely found.

C. Stock Dividend Distributions

Stock dividend
A dividend paid in shares of the corporation instead of cash.

A **stock dividend** is a dividend payable to shareholders in shares of the declaring corporation; these shares are given in place of a cash dividend. In this way, the declaring corporation is able to reinvest its earnings in the business and reduce the need to finance its activities through borrowing.

Assume that the Sherbrooke Corporation declares a 10 percent, common stock dividend to common shareholders. At the time of this declaration, the shareholders' equity of the corporation consists of the following:

Shareholders' Equity

Common Stock, No Par-Value		
Authorized — 20 000 Shares		
Issued and Outstanding — 5000 Shares	$ 25,000	
Retained Earnings	100,000	$125,000

At the date of dividend declaration, the common shares of the corporation were trading on the Toronto Stock Exchange at $4.

In this case, the stock dividend is expressed as a percentage of the outstanding common stock. The stock dividend amounts to 500 shares (5000 outstanding shares $\times$ 10%). This means that an investor owning 1000 shares receives 100 new shares when the dividend is issued.

Is There Any Dollar Effect on the Investor's Portfolio?

Theoretically, the market value of the common shares should fall somewhat to compensate for the increased number of shares. For example, the market price of the share would, theoretically, decrease as follows:

	Before *Stock Dividend*	*After* *Stock Dividend* *(Theoretically)*
Market Price of Common Share	$4	A New, Lower Market Value
Total Market Value of Shares		
1000 Shares × $4	$4,000	
1100 Shares × New Market Price		$4,000

Theoretically, the total market value of the common shareholding would remain the same, at $4,000. In reality, the market price rarely decreases proportionately to the percent of the stock dividend. Usually, if the stock dividend is not large in relation to the total of outstanding shares, no change in the market value of the shares occurs.

A distinction is usually made between a small stock dividend, (of approximately 20 percent of outstanding shares) which does not tend to affect the market price of that stock, and large stock dividends, which result in a proportionate decrease in the stock's market value. An extreme example of a 100 percent stock dividend would tend to reduce by half the market value of that stock. In this case, the total market value of the investor's portfolio remains the same. However, since the market price of the stock is materially reduced, a large stock dividend—one in excess of 20 to 25 percent—is usually regarded as a stock split. There is no agreement in the accounting profession regarding the recording of a large dividend; further discussions are usually dealt with in advanced accounting courses. What is important at this level is to be aware that there is a difference between the accounting for what is regarded as a stock dividend and for a stock split. A stock dividend results in the transfer (capitalization) of retained earnings to share capital. No such transfer occurs when there is a stock split.

The CICA has not recommended any particular handling of stock dividends. In accordance with generally accepted accounting principles, the fair market value of stock dividends is transferred to share capital from retained earnings, since the CBCA requires that shares be issued at their fair market value.

For example, since the market value of shares rarely changes when a stock dividend is small, an investor in shares of the Sherbrooke Corporation would see the market value of his/her shares as follows:

	Market Value of Investor Shares	
	Before Stock Dividend	*After Stock Dividend*
Common Shares — 1000 × $4	$4,000	
Common Shares — 1100 × $4		$4,400

That is, the investor sees his/her total market value of common shares increase by $400. No journal entry is made by the investor on receipt of a stock dividend, since there is no dividend income. The investor simply increases the number of shares owned in the corporation and, of course, has 100 additional share certificates. The investor's total cost of shares in Sherbrooke Corporation remains the same as was originally paid for the 1000 shares.

Investment in Sherbrooke Corporation

	Before Stock Dividend		After Stock Dividend	
	Cost	Shares Owned	Cost	Shares Owned
	$5,000	1000 shares	$5,000	1100 shares

Cost per Share
$5,000 ÷ 1000 Shares $5
$5,000 ÷ 1100 Shares $4.55 (approx.)

As can be seen in these calculations, the $5,000 cost of this investor's shares is allocated over 1000 shares before the stock dividend and over 1100 shares after the stock dividend. The cost of the shares continues to be $5,000 in total.

Is There Any Change in the Investor's Percentage of Corporate Ownership?

Since a stock dividend is issued to all shareholders, each shareholder has a larger number of shares after the stock dividend, but his/her ownership percentage of the company and his/her dollar equity in the company remains the same, as illustrated in the following example.

Assume that there are 5 shareholders in Sherbrooke Corporation, each of whom owns 1000 shares before the stock dividend. Each of these shareholders receives a 10 percent stock dividend, that is, 100 new shares.

Corporate Ownership

	Before Stock Dividend		After Stock Dividend	
Shareholders	Shares	Percent	Shares	Percent
A	1000	20%	1100	20%
B	1000	20%	1100	20%
C	1000	20%	1100	20%
D	1000	20%	1100	20%
E	1000	20%	1100	20%
	5000	100%	5500	100%

Each shareholder has received 100 new shares but his/her ownership percentage of the company remains 20 percent. Each shareholder holds more shares but the *percentage of ownership remains the same, as do the net assets of the company.*

Assuming that each of the 5 investors had originally paid the same amount to the corporation for his/her shares, their corporate ownership in dollars before and after the stock dividend appears as follows:

Corporate Ownership

	Before Stock Dividend		After Stock Dividend	
Shareholders	Shares	Dollar Equity	Shares	Dollar Equity
A	1000	$ 25,000	1100	$ 25,000
B	1000	25,000	1100	25,000
C	1000	25,000	1100	25,000
D	1000	25,000	1100	25,000
E	1000	25,000	1100	25,000
	5000	$125,000	5500	$125,000

Since each shareholder owns 20 percent of the company, the share of shareholders' equity owned by each is $25,000 ($125,000 total equity × 20%). No assets are received by the corporation when the additional shares are issued as a stock dividend, and therefore *the total equity remains unchanged* at $125,000.

Conceptual Issue 11-1

The Fine Line between Dividends and Stock Splits

by Alfred L. Kahl and William F. Rentz, University of Ottawa

If a firm wants to reduce the price of its stock, should a stock split or a stock dividend be used? Stock splits are generally used after a sharp price run-up, when a large price reduction is sought. Stock dividends are frequently used on a regular annual basis to keep the stock price more or less constrained. For example, if a firm's earnings and dividends are growing at about 10 percent per year, the price would tend to go up at about that same rate, and it would soon be outside the desired trading range. A 10 percent annual stock dividend would maintain the stock price within the optimal trading range.

Although the economic effects of stock splits and dividends are virtually identical, accountants treat them somewhat differently. On a 2-for-1 split, the shares outstanding are doubled, and the stock's par value (if any) is halved. This treatment is shown in the adjacent table, section 2, for Carson Computer Corporation, using a pro forma 19X7 balance sheet. With a stock dividend, the par value is not reduced, but an accounting entry is made transferring capital from retained earnings to common stock and to paid-in capital. The transfer from retained earnings is calculated as follows:

$$\begin{pmatrix} \text{Dollars} \\ \text{transferred} \\ \text{from} \\ \text{retained} \\ \text{earnings} \end{pmatrix} = \begin{pmatrix} \text{Number} \\ \text{of shares} \\ \text{outstanding} \end{pmatrix} \begin{pmatrix} \text{Percentage} \\ \text{of the stock} \\ \text{dividend} \end{pmatrix} \begin{pmatrix} \text{Market} \\ \text{price of} \\ \text{the stock} \end{pmatrix}$$

For example, if Carson, selling at $60, declared a 20-percent stock dividend, the transfer would be:

Dollars transferred = (50 million)(0.2)($60) = $600,000,000.

As shown in section 3, of this $600 million transfer, $10 million is recorded in common stock and $590 million in additional paid-in capital. Retained earnings are reduced to $1.25 billion.

Price Effects

Several empirical studies have examined the effects of stock splits and stock dividends on stock prices. The findings of the Barker study[1] are presented next. When stock dividends were associated with a cash dividend increase, the value of the company's stock six months after the ex-dividend date had risen by 8 percent. On the other hand, where stock dividends were not accompanied by cash dividend increases, stock values fell by 12 percent, which approximated the percentage of the average stock dividend.

Price Effects of Stock Dividends
Price at Selected Dates

	Six Months prior to Ex-Dividend Date	At Ex-Dividend Date	Six Months after Ex-Dividend Date
Cash dividend increase	100%	109%	108%
No cash dividend increase	100%	99%	88%

Accounting for Stock Dividends

The market price of the shares is used to record a stock dividend. This market price is usually the closing market price per share on the day preceding the declaration of the stock dividend. If the shares are not traded on the stock exchange, then a fair market value can be sought from expert appraisers. The recording of a stock dividend requires a transfer from Retained Earnings to Common Stock. This transfer is illustrated in Figure 11-4.

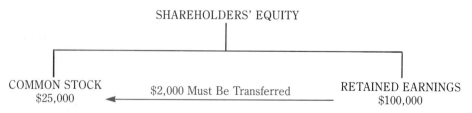

Figure 11-4 Transfer from Retained Earnings to Common Stock

Carson Computer Corporation Shareholders' Equity Accounts, Pro Forma, 19X7/12/31

1. **Before a stock split or a stock dividend:**

Common stock (60 million shares authorized, 50 million outstanding, $1 par)	$ 50,000,000
Additional paid-in capital	100,000,000
Retained earnings	1,850,000,000
Total common shareholders' equity	$2,000,000,000

2. **After a 2-for-1 stock split:**

Common stock (120 million shares authorized, 100 million outstanding, $0.50 par)	$ 50,000,000
Additional paid-in capital	100,000,000
Retained earnings	1,850,000,000
Total common shareholders' equity	$2,000,000,000

3. **After a 20 percent stock dividend:**

Common stock (60 million shares authorized, 60 million outstanding, $1 par)[a]	$ 60,000,000
Additional paid-in capital[b]	690,000,000
Retained earnings[b]	1,250,000,000
Total common shareholders' equity	$2,000,000,000

[a]Shares outstanding are increased by 20 percent, from 50 million to 60 million.
[b]A transfer equal to the market value of the new shares is made from retained earnings to additional paid-in capital and common stock: Transfer = (50 million shares)(0.2)($60) = $600 million.

These data seem to suggest that stock dividends are seen for what they are — simply additional pieces of paper — and that they do not represent true income. When stock dividends are accompanied by higher earnings and cash dividends, investors bid up the value of the stock. However, when stock dividends are not accompanied by increases in earnings and cash dividends, the dilution of earnings and dividends per share causes the price of the stock to drop by about the same percentage as the stock dividend. The fundamental determinants of price are the underlying earnings and dividends per share.

Since the stock is recorded at market value, the amount of transfer from Retained Earnings to Common Stock is $2,000 (500 stock dividend shares × $4 market value). The $2,000 transfer to Common Stock means that this amount becomes a part of stated capital and the assets represented by the $2,000 are no longer available for the payment of future cash dividends.

After the transfer has been recorded, shareholders' equity appears as shown in Figure 11-5.

This transfer reduces Retained Earnings and increases Common Stock by the same $2,000 amount. Total shareholders' equity, however, remains unchanged. This result of the stock dividend differs from the distribution of a cash dividend, which reduces both Retained Earnings and Cash and results in a *lower* total shareholders' equity after the cash dividend distribution.

Capitalization of retained earnings
The transfer of an amount from Retained Earnings to a share capital account as in the case of a stock dividend.

The transfer of retained earnings to a share capital account, Common Stock, is often referred to by accountants as a **capitalization of retained earnings**. The share capital of the corporation has been increased, even though no new assets have been acquired by the corporation.

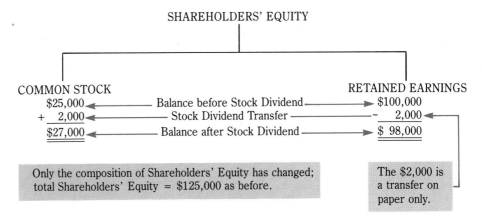

Figure 11-5   Shareholders' equity after dividend transfer

Two journal entries at different dates are required to record the stock dividend. The original dividend declaration would be recorded as follows:

Retained Earnings	2,000	
Stock Dividend To Be Issued		2,000
To record the declaration of a		
10% common stock dividend.		

When a stock dividend is declared, the debit could be made to Stock Dividends rather than Retained Earnings. At the year-end of the corporation, this Stock Dividend account would be closed to Retained Earnings in the same way a Cash Dividend account is closed. The closing entry for a stock dividend would be:

Retained Earnings	2,000	
Stock Dividends		2,000
To close the Stock Dividends account.		

No assets are required for a stock dividend and therefore an equity account is credited. The entry is comparable to the entry required for a cash dividend that reduces Retained Earnings and credits a cash-payable account. If a balance sheet is prepared at this point, a declared cash dividend is shown as a current liability. In the case of a stock dividend, the Stock Dividends To Be Issued account is not a liability of Sherbrooke Corporation, because there is no liability incurred by a corporation declaring and issuing shares as a dividend. If financial statements are prepared between the declaration and payment of stock dividends, the Stock Dividends To Be Issued account is shown as an addition to share capital.

Shareholders' Equity

Share Capital:		
Common Stock, No Par-Value		
Authorized — 20 000 Shares		
Issued and Outstanding — 5000 Shares	$25,000	
To Be Issued as a Stock Dividend — 500 Shares	2,000	$ 27,000
Retained Earnings		98,000
		$125,000

Dividends, as noted, are usually declared on one date, payable to shareholders of record on a second date, and actually paid on a third date. In the case of the stock dividend made by Sherbrooke Corporation, the dividend was declared on December 15, payable to common shareholders of record on December 20, 19X1. The stock dividends were issued January 10, 19X2. The journal entry to record the stock dividend issue is shown below:

```
19X2
Jan. 10   Stock Dividends To Be Issued                    2,000
              Common Stock                                          2,000
          To record the issue of
          the stock dividend declared
          December 15, 19X1.
```

Illustrative Problem: Dividend Distribution Considerations

The sources of shareholders' equity are disclosed in the following partial balance sheet of Brand X Inc.:

Shareholders' Equity

		(000s)	
Share Capital:			
Preferred Stock, $1 Par Value, 6% Cumulative			
and Participating to 7%			
Authorized — 500 Shares			
Issued and Outstanding — 200 Shares		$200	
Common Stock, No Par-Value			
Authorized — 2500 shares			
Issued and Outstanding — 250 Shares		300	
Total Share Capital			$500
Surplus:			
Contributed Surplus			
Premium on Preferred Stock	$ 5		
Donated Capital — Land	25		
Total Contributed Surplus		$ 30	
Retained Earnings			
Restricted for Contingencies	$ 20		
Unrestricted	250		
Total Retained Earnings		270	
Total Surplus			300
Total Shareholders' Equity			$800

Notes:
1. The dividends on preferred stock are one year in arrears.

Case 1:   A Dividend Is Declared

The board of directors declared a dividend of $50 on December 1, 19X3 to shareholders of record on December 20, which was to be paid on January 15, 19X4. How much of the dividend is payable to each class of shareholders?

There is one year of dividends in arrears owing to preferred shareholders. The annual dividend of 6 percent amounts to $12 ($200 × 6%); this amount must be paid before any other dividends are paid. Since the $50 dividend declared exceeds the $12 dividend in arrears, the dividends for 19X3 can also be calculated at the same time. Care must be taken to apply the participating feature accurately.

Shareholder Preference to Dividends		Dividend Distribution		
		To Preferred	*To Common*	*Balance*
	Total Dividend Declared			$50
1st Preference:	19X2 Arrears ($200 × 6%)	$12	–	38
2nd Preference:	19X3 Preferred Dividend	12	–	26
3rd Preference:	19X3 Common Dividend ($300 × 6%) to Match Preferred	–	$18	8
4th Preference:	19X3, 1% to Each Class			
	($200 × 1%)	2	– ⎫	
	($300 × 1%)	–	3 ⎬	3
	Balance to Common	–	3 ⎭	-0-
	Total	$26	$24	

How Are Declared Dividends Disclosed on the Balance Sheet?

Once dividends have been declared, they become a legal liability of the declaring corporation. If declared dividends have not been paid at year-end, the liability for dividends is included in the current liability section of the balance sheet.

Case 2:   Cash Dividends and Stock Dividends

On June 30, 19X4 the board of directors declared a $35 cash dividend to shareholders of record on July 15, payable July 31. The amount of dividend payable to each class of shares is illustrated below.

Shareholder Preference to Dividends		Dividend Distribution		
		To Preferred	*To Common*	*Balance*
	Total Dividend Declared			$35
1st Preference:	19X4 Preferred Dividend ($200 × 6%)	$12	–	23
2nd Preference:	19X4 Common Dividend ($300 × 6%) to Match Preferred	–	$18	5
3rd Preference:	19X4 – 1% to Each Class			
	($200 × 1%)	2	– ⎫	
	($300 × 1%)	–	3 ⎬	-0-
	Total	$14	$21	

In this case, both classes of shares have received 7 percent dividends. Although a larger dollar amount is shown as paid to common shareholders, this does not mean that a greater return was earned by them. There is simply a larger common share capital on which to calculate dividends.

On December 15, 19X4, the board of directors declared a 10 percent common stock dividend to common shareholders of record December 31 to be distributed January 20, 19X5. The market price of common shares was $5 on the Toronto Stock Exchange at the close of December 14. This price was accepted by the board of directors as a fair market value for recording the stock dividend. Why was this stock dividend only applicable to common shareholders?

Preferred shareholders are entitled to an annual 6 percent dividend and are entitled to participate with common shareholders to 7 percent. These preferences have already been met with the dividend declared June 30, 19X4. Therefore any other dividends are applicable to common shareholders only, who are to receive all the 10 percent common stock dividend.

Stock Dividend or Stock Split?

Stock dividends under 20 percent are considered to be stock dividends rather than stock splits under guidelines issued by the AICPA. Since no contradictory CICA guidelines exist, accountants are usually influenced by the 20 percent recommendation. Therefore, this 10 percent common stock dividend is to be recorded as a stock dividend. The stock dividend is calculated as follows:

$$\text{Common Shares Outstanding} \times \text{10\% Common Stock Dividend} = \text{Stock Dividend}$$

$$250 \text{ Shares} \times 10\% = 25 \text{ Shares.}$$

The fair market value of the stock dividend is calculated as follows:

$$\text{Common Stock Dividend} \times \text{Fair Market Price per Share} = \text{Value of Dividend}$$

$$25 \text{ Shares} \times \$5 = \$125.$$

The amount of the stock dividend is therefore calculated at $125.

How Does the Corporation Record This Stock Dividend?

The recording of this stock dividend requires a transfer of $125 from Retained Earnings to Common Stock (capitalization of retained earnings). The following journal entry is made at the date the stock dividend is declared:

19X4			
Dec. 15	Retained Earnings	125	
	Stock Dividend To Be Issued		125
	To record the declaration of a		
	100% common stock dividend.		

This entry records the declaration of the stock dividend. The actual common shares are not yet issued to shareholders.

If a balance sheet is prepared at December 31, 19X4, the stock dividend to be issued is shown as a part of the common stock, as follows:

Shareholders' Equity

SHARE CAPITAL:
Common Stock, No Par-Value
  Authorized — 2500 Shares
  Issued and Outstanding — 250 Shares $300
  To Be Issued as a Stock Dividend — 25 Shares   125 $425

The issue of the stock dividend in 19X5 is recorded by the following journal entry:

```
19X5
Jan. 20   Stock Dividend To Be Issued                    125
              Common Stock                                       125
          To record the issue of the stock
          dividend declared December 15, 19X4.
```

The common share certificates are issued to shareholders on this date.

Is the Stock Dividend Income to the Shareholders Receiving it?

No, a stock dividend is simply a distribution of shares to shareholders. The shareholders' percentage ownership of the corporation remains the same; the amount of shareholders' equity is unchanged.

Each shareholder has more shares after a stock dividend. However, no assets of the corporation have been issued to shareholders. Therefore, there is no income involved.

Some shareholders may perceive a stock dividend as income, but technically it is not. Theoretically, the market value of common shares should fall somewhat to compensate for the increased number of shares outstanding. In reality it rarely decreases proportionately to the percent of the stock dividend, if at all. Therefore, an increase in the market value of a shareholder's investment occurs. Study the following example, in which an investor owns 100 shares, to understand how this increase occurs.

Shareholder Investment

	Before Stock Dividend			After Stock Dividend		
	Shares Owned	Cost	Market	Shares Owned	Cost	Market
Investment in Shares	100	$120		110	$120	
Cost per Share						
$120 ÷ 100 Shares		$1.20				
$120 ÷ 110 Shares					$1.09 approx.	
Market Price per Share			$5			$5
Market Value of Shares						
$5 × 100 Shares			$500			
$5 × 110 Shares						$550

In this example, with the assumption of no fall in market price of the common shares, this investor is $50 ahead ($550 − $500) after the stock dividend. This is a gain as far as investors are concerned, although no gain has been realized by them. However, a gain may be realized when these additional shares are sold; any such gain (or loss) would be reflected in the entry recording the sale.

APPENDIX: Reacquisition of Shares

The reacquisition of shares by a corporation from its existing shareholders — either through purchase or through other circumstances, such as in settlement of a debt or the purchase of a dissident shareholder's shares — results in the creation of what is commonly referred to as treasury stock.

The method of accounting for reacquired shares is influenced by the legislation of the jurisdiction under which the business entity is incorporated. The CBCA permits a corporation to reacquire some of its shares subject to a number of conditions. Generally, the Act requires reacquired shares to be cancelled and the appropriate share account to be reduced in amount. Corporations falling under CBCA-incompatible provincial jurisdiction are subject to different regulations; therefore, the treatment of these reacquired shares differs from the method required under the CBCA.

Figure 11-6 illustrates some of the differences relating to the reacquisition of shares and their subsequent handling required by different jurisdictions.

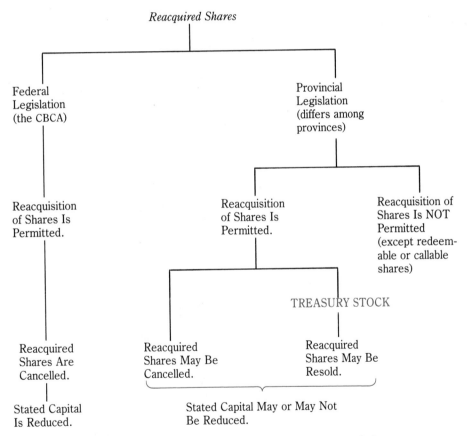

Figure 11-6   Differences relating to the reacquisition of shares

Generally, reacquired shares do not receive dividends and do not confer on the holder the right to vote. The provisions of the CBCA are used first to illustrate the accounting for reacquired shares and to explain applications of these provisions. Following, the handling of treasury stock for CBCA-incompatible provincially incorporated corporations are discussed.

Incorporation under the CBCA

As mentioned, corporations falling within the jurisdiction of the CBCA are permitted to reacquire their own shares — that is, purchase or otherwise receive their own shares from existing shareholders of the corporation. This reacquisition is subject to conditions, such as a solvency test, and to certain other exceptions, which permit the corporation to hold its own shares without the need to cancel them. Generally, these exceptions are applicable when such shares are held as collateral for loans, as in the case of financial institutions, and when the corporation is a legal representative.

The handling of reacquired shares is influenced by the recommendations of the AcSC, as published in the *CICA Handbook*. The use of an ''average per share amount'' is recommended in accounting for reacquired shares (section 3240.18). This weighted average dollar amount per share is calculated for the class of shares (for example, common stock) at the date of acquisition. The calculation is made from the balances preceding the reacquisition and is calculated as follows:

$$\frac{\text{Stated Capital Balance for the Class of Shares}}{\text{Number of Shares Currently Issued}}.$$

Assume that only two common share transactions have occurred.

Transaction	*1 Share Issued for $10*		*1 Share Issued for $12*	
Issued 2 No Par-Value Common Shares	Cash	10	Cash	12
	Common Stock	10	Common Stock	12

The weighted average can be calculated as follows:

$$\frac{\text{Stated Capital}}{\text{Number of Shares}} = \frac{\$10 + \$12}{1 + 1} = \frac{\$22}{2} = \$11 \text{ per share.}$$

> This $11 weighted average of common shares is used in preparing journal entries for the reacquired shares.

There are only three alternatives when shares are reacquired — that is, purchased from existing shareholders. The amount paid by the corporation to the shareholders can be identical to the weighted average amount; usually, it is either in excess or below the weighted average.

The accounting required when shares are reacquired and cancelled in each of these circumstances is shown next, using the $11 weighted average.

Share Reacquired for $11 (weighted average is $11)		*Share Reacquired for $13* (weighted average is $11)		*Share Reacquired for $9* (weighted average is $11)	
Common Stock 11		Common Stock 11		Common Stock 11	
Cash	11	Retained Earnings 2		Contributed Surplus	2
		Cash	13	Cash	9

> In actual practice, ''Contributed Surplus'' would be more fully described; one example is ''Contributed Surplus — Gain on Reacquisition of Common Stock''.

The difference between weighted average and the reacquisition payment illustrated above follows the recommendations of the AcSC.

1. For a reacquisition payment in excess of weighted average (*CICA Handbook*, section 3240.15), the payment is to be split as follows:

    (a) The weighted average amount is to be debited to the class of shares involved ($11 in this case).

    (b) The excess ($2 in this case) is to be debited to Retained Earnings, unless there is an existing gain in contributed surplus from a previous reacquisition of shares of that same class. (In this latter case, the debit of $2 would be applied to that contributed surplus amount with any remaining balance being debited to Retained Earnings.)

2. For a reacquisition payment below weighted average (*CICA Handbook*, section 3240.17), the payment is to be split as follows:

    (a) The weighted average amount is to be debited to the class of shares involved ($11 in this case).

    (b) The excess (also $2 in this case) is to be credited to Contributed Surplus.

The CBCA also requires that reacquired stock be cancelled and that, if the articles of incorporation limit the number of authorized shares, the reacquired shares be restored to the status of authorized but unissued stock.

In the rare case where reacquired shares have not been cancelled by the balance sheet date, the reacquired shares would be labelled as treasury stock on the balance sheet and their cost would be deducted from shareholders' equity.

Partial Balance Sheet
At December 31, 19X2

Shareholders' Equity

	Case 1	Case 2	Case 3
Common Stock, No Par-Value			
Issued 2 Shares	$ 22	$ 22	$ 22
Retained Earnings (assumed)	100	100	100
	$122	$122	$122
Less: Treasury Stock — At Cost	11	13	9
Total Shareholders' Equity	$111	$109	$113

Note that 2 shares are still shown as being issued. The cost of the treasury stock is deducted from shareholders' equity. This disclosure is in accordance with the recommendation of the AcSC that no adjustment be made to the equity accounts until the treasury stock has been sold (or cancelled).

Restrictions on the Reacquisition of Shares

Although the CBCA permits a corporation to reacquire shares, it also restricts any such reacquisition if the corporation is insolvent or if the reacquisition will cause insolvency — that is, if it will affect the corporation's ability to pay its debts as they become due. The various solvency tests applicable in different situations are complex and are the subject of more advanced accounting courses.

Incorporation under CBCA-Incompatible Provincial Legislation

Provincially incorporated corporations are subject to a variety of regulations — different not only from the requirements of the CBCA but also varying from province to province. While the CBCA permits the issue of only no par-value shares, corporations falling within provincial jurisdiction are usually permitted to issue both par-value and no par-value shares. Thus, the possible existence of contributed surplus from the issue of par-value shares in excess of par, or the establishment of distributable surplus in the case of no par-value shares (where permitted), introduces an additional wrinkle. More significant, however, is the opportunity to hold reacquired shares without an obligatory cancellation requirement. The permitted variations further complicate the accounting for treasury stock.

When shares are cancelled in the case of provincially incorporated corporations, the accounting treatment recommended by the AcSC is similar to that illustrated for cancellation of shares under the CBCA. In both cases an amount is allocated to the stated capital component with any resulting excess being allocated to contributed surplus and/or retained earnings.

A difference exists however, when reacquired shares are permitted to be held and subsequently resold. This subsequent sale of treasury shares can be made at the same amount as the reacquisition; often, however, the sale is made in excess of or below the reacquisition cost.

The following illustration uses the same data as the CBCA example — no par-value shares and the same reacquisition cost — to compare the journal entries required.

Share Reacquired for $11		*Share Reacquired for $13*		*Share Reacquired for $9*	
Treasury stock	11	Treasury stock 13		Treasury stock 9	
Cash	11	Cash	13	Cash	9

Note that the purchase cost of the share is debited to treasury stock in each case. This Treasury Stock account is not an asset, since a corporation cannot own part of itself. The Treasury Stock account is a contra equity account and the cost of treasury stock is deducted from shareholders' equity, as shown below:

Partial Balance Sheet
At December 31, 1982

Shareholders' Equity

	Case 1	Case 2	Case 3
Common Stock, No Par-Value			
Issued 2 Shares	$ 22	$ 22	$ 22
Retained Earnings (assumed)	100	100	100
	$122	$122	$122
Less: Treasury Stock — At Cost	11	13	9
Total Shareholders' Equity	$111	$109	$113

Note that 2 shares are still shown as being issued. The cost of the reacquired shares is deducted from shareholders' equity. This disclosure is in accordance with the recommendation of the AcSC that no adjustment be made to the equity accounts until the reacquired shares are cancelled.

This disclosure is in accordance with the AcSC recommendation that "the shares should be carried at cost and shown as a deduction from shareholders' equity until cancelled or sold".

It is also necessary to restrict an amount of retained earnings equal to the amount of treasury stock, so that some assets are not available for dividend distributions. The creation and removal of restrictions on retained earnings is more fully explained in section C of Chapter 10.

When the reacquired share is subsequently sold, the sale can be at any price, including the original reacquisition cost; more often than not, it is either in excess of or below the acquisition cost. The accounting required when shares are resold in each of these circumstances is shown below.

Share Resold for $11 (previously reacquired for $11)			*Share Resold for $16* (previously reacquired for $13)			*Share Resold for $6* (previously reacquired for $11)		
Cash	11		Cash	16		Cash	6	
Treasury Stock		11	Contributed Surplus		3	Retained Earnings	3	
			Treasury Stock		13	Treasury Stock		9

The difference between the cost of reacquiring the share and the proceeds from its subsequent sale, as above, follows the recommendations of the AcSC (*CICA Handbook*, section 3240.11) as follows:

1. For a sale of reacquired stock in excess of cost, the excess amount ($3 in this case) is credited to Contributed Surplus, as shown here. The Contributed Surplus credit would be more fully described as "Contributed Surplus — Gain on Sale of Treasury Stock".

2. For a sale of reacquired stock below cost, the difference (also $3 in this case) is debited to Retained Earnings, if there is no existing contributed surplus from any previous sale or cancellation of shares. (If there were such a previous balance, the debit of $3 would be applied to that existing Contributed Surplus account; any remaining balance would be debited to Retained Earnings, if there was insufficient contributed surplus. This example illustrates the case where there is no existing contributed surplus from any previous sale or cancellation of shares.

Gains or losses on treasury stock are never reported in the income statement.

Discussion Questions

1. Shareholders' equity represents the net assets of a corporation. Distinguish between assets that are available for dividend purposes and those that are not. Stated capital represents which assets?
2. When making a decision involving the declaration of dividends, what are some of the main considerations used by a board of directors?
3. If a corporation is making a substantial net income each year, why might it not pay any dividends?
4. Distinguish among the date of dividend declaration, the date of record, and the date of payment.
5. Is a corporation legally required to declare a dividend? At what point do dividends become a liability of the corporation?
6. What is the difference in accounting between cash dividends and property dividends? Give a sample journal entry for each.
7. Explain the different dividend preferences that may be attached to preferred shares. Why would preferred shares have these preferences over common shares? Does it mean that purchasing preferred shares is better than purchasing common shares?
8. What are arrears of dividends? Are they a liability of the corporation?
9. Distinguish between a stock dividend and a cash dividend. Which is preferable, from a shareholder's point of view? Why?
10. How does a stock dividend differ from a stock split?
11. Is there any dollar effect on an investor's portfolio when a stock dividend is declared and paid? Why or why not?
12. Does a stock dividend result in a change in an investor's percentage of corporate ownership? Explain, using an example.
13. What does a capitalization of retained earnings refer to, when made in relation to the declaration and payment of a stock dividend?
14. How is a stock dividend recorded at the date of declaration? at the date of payment?
15. Can a corporation own shares in itself? under what circumstances? What are the conditions set out in the CBCA?
16. Are all reacquired shares actually treasury shares? Explain.
17. How is the accounting for reacquired shares handled under the CBCA?
18. What is the recommendation of the AcSC in the calculation of a cost applicable to reacquired shares?
19. Under the CBCA, how are reacquired shares recorded when they are reacquired at an amount in excess of their weighted average cost? when they are reacquired at an amount below their weighted average cost?
20. When treasury stock is resold, how are the proceeds from the sale recorded when they exceed the purchase cost of the shares? What are the recommendations of the AcSC applicable to these solutions?
21. Refer to Real Life Example 11-1 and Conceptual Issue 11-1. What should the investor in an entity look for: dividends or stock price? Discuss.

Discussion Cases

Discussion Case 11-1: Bank of Montreal

The Bank of Montreal plans to provide shareholders with various options for enlarging their holdings.

Under the plan, shareholders could receive dividends in three ways: as a cash dividend as at present; as a cash dividend that would be reinvested automatically in the bank's common shares at a discount of 5 percent from the average market price over a determined period; and as a stock dividend.

In addition, common shareholders would be entitled to purchase shares directly from the bank at the average market price, subject to a limitation of $5,000 a shareholder a quarter.

The plan is subject to regulatory approval and the waiver of pre-emptive rights by shareholders, which will be voted upon at the annual meeting January 19.

For Discussion

1. What are the advantages and disadvantages of each of the following three different forms of dividends proposed by the Bank of Montreal:
   a. Cash dividends?
   b. Reinvested cash dividends?
   c. Stock dividends?
2. Which form of dividend would you prefer? Why?
3. Bank of Montreal shareholders apparently have a pre-emptive right. What does this mean?
4. (a) What effect on shareholder percentage ownership would result under each of the three dividend forms?
   (b) What would be the amount of shareholders' equity?
   (c) What amount of assets would remain in the bank after the dividend?

Discussion Case 11-2: Canada Development Corporation

Canada Development Corp. says holders of the company's class B preferred shares registered at the close of business on February 27 will receive one bonus common share for each class B preferred share held.

As a result, an additional 1 380 000 common shares will be in the hands of 13 400 shareholders, increasing by 60 per cent the number of CDC common shares on the stock market.

A CDC spokesperson said the move would decrease the federal government's share in the company's voting stock to 48.7 percent from 49.9 percent.

When issued in 1975, each class B preferred share carried the right to receive 2 bonus common shares. The first of these was distributed in the fall of 1979, one year ahead of schedule. This second distribution comes more than four years earlier than the originally scheduled date of October 1, 1985.

H. Anthony Hampson, president, said the decision to issue the second bonus common share was based on the board's desire to increase the number of shares available for trading.

Hampson said early distribution of the bonus shares should not be taken as an indication of any change with respect to dividend policy on common shares, and the company plans to continue to invest earnings in profitable, high-growth industries.

"The board continues to believe that the best return on shareholders' equity can be attained by this policy of expanding the corporation's investments in strong companies oriented to the future," Hampson said.

The company said other conditions of the class B preferred shares have not changed as a result of the decision. This includes the dividend rate and the right to convert each class B preferred share into 10 common shares at any time at the holder's option.

For Discussion

1. Is this second bonus share a stock split or a stock dividend? Refer to the guideline issued by the AICPA in this chapter.
2. What journal entry, if any, would be made on the books of the CDC?
3. Would the market price of the preferred or common shares be affected by this bonus share distribution? Explain.

Discussion Case 11-3:   International Harvester Co.

Massey-Ferguson Ltd., you're not alone.

Chicago-based International Harvester Co. is also plagued by a staggering debt load, climbing interest rates, weak markets and high-cost plants. But officials of International Harvester expect to muddle through the beginning of 1981. The chairman and chief executive of the beleaguered farm-equipment maker, Archie McCardell, even says he expects the company's setback to be brief.

The market penetration of the 150-year-old company reached new highs in trucks and farm equipment in recent months, he said in a recent interview, and the company rebounded vigorously between April, when a six-month strike ended, and the current lull. McCardell expects the company to benefit also from a record number of new and updated products that would hit the market next year.

But most important, according to company executives, is that cost-cutting measures and operating efficiencies are finally beginning to show their effects. These changes, they said, will reduce annual operating costs by U.S. $400 million from the level of three years ago.

The strike settlement, McCardell said, gave the company work rules and labour costs that are now comparable to those of Harvester's competition. Several operations have been sold, phased out or cut back, ending losses of more than $25 million annually. Strict new inventory-control guidelines were adopted after the company learned during the strike that it could get by on less inventory. As a result, Harvester says, working capital requirements were $800 million less in 1980 than they would have been under previous practices.

The distance Harvester still has to go, however, was highlighted early this month, when Harvester directors decided to reduce the quarterly dividend to shareholders by more than 50 percent to $0.30 a share. The move upset many investors, who had held the stock for its traditionally generous dividends.

Three days before the board meeting, McCardell ignored his own prediction that the company, which lost $397.3 million in the year ended October 31, would suffer a loss in the first quarter. He said that the dividend cash requirements were inconsequential. "It's only $80 million a year," McCardell said.

McCardell, who was wooed from the presidency of the Xerox Corp. to Harvester three years ago, was awarded a controversial $1.7-million bonus a few months ago on the strength of 1979 earnings of $369.6 million on record revenues of $8.4 billion. This fiscal year, sales plunged to $6.3 billion under the impact of a six-month-long strike and a faltering economy.

With the mounting possibility of a severe cash crunch facing the company early next year, an event that could require putting more of the company's assets on the auction block, Harvester directors agreed to cut the dividend.

That was the latest of a series of austerity measures and strategy changes for the company. This fall Harvester cancelled a $100-million preferred stock issue and chopped $150 million from next year's capital and research budgets, the cornerstones of McCardell's revival strategy.

McCardell conceded that "over the years we had lost a lot of our operating flexibility", a condition for which he blamed union work rules. "We were undercapitalized and couldn't borrow, so we had a lot of old plants and equipment," he continued, a condition for which he blamed the dividend policy and high wages rates. "And we were not as wise as we could have been in our use of working capital."

The company's staggering debt load of $2.2 billion, about a quarter of which is tied to movements in the prime rate, is expected to help push the company into the red in the first quarter. High interest rates will also depress Harvester's sales volume. McCardell said, however, that he expected interest rates to peak sometime in January, which would relieve the credit pressures later in the year.

In addition to weak markets and climbing interest expenses, International Harvester is saddled with high-cost plants. In addition, the company makes nearly all its products for mature markets with slow growth rates. Its common stock is selling at less than 50 percent of book value.

For Discussion

1. If the strike settlement gave the company labour costs that are comparable to those of Harvester's competition, it appears that its labour costs had been lower than those of competitors in the past. Therefore, labour costs would necessarily be a larger expense to the company in the future. In view of "weak markets and climbing interest rates, high cost plants, mature markets with slow growth rates", would you tend to agree with McCardell's belief that the company's set-back will be brief? Why, or why not? (In your decision, consider market penetration of trucks and farm equipment and the introduction of new products to be introduced during the following year. Also do not ignore the $150 million chopped from the capital and research budget.)

2. Why do you think Harvester cancelled a $100-million preferred stock issue? Consider its undercapitalization and difficulty in borrowing at the time of the article in evaluating the implications of this cancellation.

3. The common stock was reported to be selling at less than 50 percent of book value. Why was this so? Consider in your answer the fact that the company had old plant and equipment that should be considerably depreciated in the books of the company, leaving a low net book value of these assets. Is the stock of a company with such a lower market price a "real bargain"?

4. Evaluate the stewardship of this company. Consider in your evaluation:
   a. The company learned during the strike that it could get by on less inventory.
   b. The company has a number of old buildings and much old equipment.
   c. The company has traditionally declared generous dividends.

   Include the role of both the board of directors and management in your evaluation.

5. Dividends were only $80 million a year in this company. Yet many investors had held the stock for its "traditionally generous dividends." There seems to be a contradiction here. What is it? Couldn't the company issue stock dividends? Why or why not?
6. Is the payment of the "traditionally generous dividends" part of the company's misfortune? Why or why not?
7. The name of Harvester does not contain any word indicating limited liability of shareholders. Does this mean that shareholders may be responsible for claims of creditors?

Harvester Losses Mount

International Harvester Co., struggling to emerge from a financial crisis, yesterday reported a net loss of $534 million for its first quarter ended January 31.

The loss was attributed primarily to a $479-million write-off of assets in its money-losing farm equipment division, which it sold to Tenneco Inc. during the period. (All figures are in U.S. funds.)

Chicago-based Harvester said that its continuing operations, consisting of its medium-and heavy-duty truck and diesel engine businesses, earned $42 million during the quarter. Those same operations reported a loss of $5 million during the first quarter of fiscal 1984.

Harvester, which announced in November that it would sell its farm-equipment operations to Houston-based Tenneco for $430 million in cash and stock, said yesterday the actual price at the close of the sale on January 31 came to $488 million, including $301 million in cash and $187 million in Tenneco preferred stock.

But that price was still far below the value at which the division had been carried on Harvester's books. As a result, Harvester was forced to write off the difference, including the value of its big Farmall tractor plant in Rock Island, Ill., which was not purchased by Tenneco and is being closed.

Harvester also said that its farm-equipment division suffered a $97-million operating loss for the quarter before it was turned over to Tenneco.

Source "Harvester losses mount", *The* (Montreal) *Gazette*, February 23, 1985, p. C-8.

For Discussion

8. As a shareholder, how would you evaluate the performance of Harvester and its future potential?

Discussion Case 11-4: Shareholders Win on Ford's Profit

While Chrysler Canada Ltd. of Windsor offered a $500 bonus to employees for their help in setting record profits last year, Ford Motor Co. of Canada Ltd., Oakville, Ont., will be thanking its shareholders.

Ford of Canada yesterday announced a profit of $433.5 million on sales of $12.1 billion, almost triple the 1983 performance of $152.6 million in profit from sales of $8.6 billion.

With that large jump in profits, Ford of Canada's board of directors approved an extra dividend of $10 a share in addition to raising the company's annual dividend to $4 from $3 a share for shareholders of record March 1, 1985. Ford Motor Co. of Detroit owns approximately 89 percent of the 8.3 million outstanding common shares of Ford of Canada.

Source Christopher Waddell, "Shareholders win on Ford's profit", *The Globe and Mail*, February 20, 1985, p. B-5.

For Discussion

1. As a potential investor, on the basis of this article, would you be more likely to invest in Chrysler or Ford? Why?
2. How does Ford of Canada's relationship to its American parent affect its dividend policy?
3. Comment—from an accounting perspective—about the effects of foreign ownership on Canadian businesses.

Comprehension Problems

Comprehension Problem 11-1

The following is a dividend announcement published in a financial newspaper on October 27, 19X2:

Cavendish Limited
At a meeting held on October 25, 19X2, the board of directors
declared a cash dividend of $1.00 per share on the outstanding
Common Shares, payable on January 2, 19X3 to shareholders
of record at the close of business on November 30, 19X2.
W. S. Golden
Secretary

Required:
1. What is the dividend declaration date?
2. What is the significance of the words "shareholders of record at the close of business on November 30, 19X2"?
3. If there are 5000 common shares outstanding, prepare the journal entries necessary for declaration and payment of dividends.

Note: Do not attempt problems regarding reacquired shares unless your accounting course included The Appendix.

Comprehension Problem 11-2

The shareholders' equity section of the Jaleh Company Ltd.'s balance sheet as at December 31, 19X1 is given below.

Shareholders' Equity

SHARE CAPITAL:		
Preferred Stock, $50 Par-Value, 6% Cumulative		
Authorized — 10 000 Shares		
Issued and Outstanding — (*Note 1*) Shares	$32,000	
Common Stock, No Par-Value		
Authorized — 200 000 Shares		
Issued and Outstanding — 80 000 Shares	16,800	
Total Share Capital		$48,800
SURPLUS:		
Contributed Surplus		
Premium on Preferred Stock	$25,600	
Deficit	(60,000)	(34,400)
Total Shareholders' Equity		$14,400

Note 1: The number of shares issued and outstanding has been omitted on purpose.
Note 2: In the past, the directors have followed the practice of paying dividends semi-annually.

Required:
1. How many preferred shares are outstanding?
2. The last semi-annual dividend on preferred shares was paid last year. No dividends have been declared in 19X1. Show how this would be disclosed on the balance sheet as at December 31, 19X1.
3. The directors of the Jaleh Company Ltd. are anxious to commence dividend payments to all shareholders as soon as possible. What is the minimum net income after taxes that must be earned in the six months ending June 30, 19X2, before any dividends could possibly be paid to the common shareholders?

Comprehension Problem 11-3

The following note appeared on the balance sheet of Fidelity Data Limited:

As of December 31, 19X2, dividends on the 5% cumulative
preferred shares, par-value $100, were in arrears to the extent
of $15 per share and amounted in total to $15,000.

Required:
1. Does the amount of the arrears appear as a liability on the December 31, 19X2 balance sheet? Explain your answer.
2. Is Fidelity Data Limited necessarily in a deficit position? (A deficit position occurs when there is a debit balance in the Retained Earnings account.) Explain your answer.
3. The comptroller of Fidelity Data projects net income after taxes for the 19X3 fiscal year of $35,000. When the company last paid dividends, the directors allocated 50 percent of current year's net income after taxes for dividends. If dividends on preferred shares are resumed at the end of 19X3 and the established policy of 50 percent is continued, how much will be available for dividends to the common shareholders if the profit projection is realized?

Comprehension Problem 11-4

The shareholders' equity section of the Prairie Machine Company Limited balance sheet as at December 31, 19X3 appears below.

Shareholders' Equity

SHARE CAPITAL:			
Preferred Stock, $100 Par-Value, 6%			
Authorized — 10 Shares			
Issued and Outstanding — (*Note 1*) Shares		$ 800	
Common Stock, No Par-Value			
Authorized — 200 Shares			
Issued and Outstanding — 80 Shares		860	
Total Share Capital			$1,660
SURPLUS:			
Contributed Surplus			
Premium on Preferred Stock		$ 48	
Retained Earnings			
Restricted for Contingencies	$200		
Unrestricted	900		
Total Retained Earnings		1,100	
Total Surplus			1,148
Total Shareholders' Equity			$2,808

Note 1: Number of shares omitted deliberately.

Required:
1. Prepare the journal entry to record the declaration of the semi-annual preferred share dividend on December 28, 19X3.
2. Assume the directors declared a common stock dividend of 10 percent on January 2, 19X4, distributable January 30 to shareholders of record on January 23; the fair market value of Prairie Machine common stock was $15 per share. No shares had been issued after the December 31, 19X3 figures were prepared. Prepare journal entries to record the declaration and issue of the stock dividend.

Comprehension Problem 11-5

The Brock Company Limited has outstanding shares as follows: (a) 2000 shares of 6%, $100 par-value preferred stock; and (b) 5000 shares of $100 par-value common stock. At December 31, 19X1 there were no dividends in arrears. During the five following years, the company's dividend declarations were as follows:

19X2	$70,000	19X5	$12,000
19X3	42,000	19X6	54,000
19X4	6,000		

Required:

1. Calculate the dividend distribution for 19X2, using the form that follows, assuming the preferred stock is cumulative and fully participating.

Shareholder Preference to Dividends	Dividend Distribution		
	To Preferred	*To Common*	*Balance*
Total Dividend Declared			$70,000
1st Preference: Arrears			
2nd Preference: Current Year — Preferred 6% × $200,000			
3rd Preference: Current Year — Common 6% × $500,000			
4th Preference: Current Year — The Balance Is Distributed in Proportion of Each Class of Shares to Total Stated Capital			
Preferred			
Common			
Total			

2. Calculate (a) for 19X3 to 19X6 the amount of dividends for each class-stock, assuming that the preferred stock is cumulative and fully participating; and (b) for 19X2 to 19X6 the amount of dividends for each class of stock, assuming:
   - The preferred is non-cumulative and fully participating
   - The preferred is cumulative and non-participating
   - The preferred is non-cumulative and non-participating.

   Record your answers using the form that follows.

Year		Cumulative and Fully Participating	Non-cumulative and Fully Participating	Cumulative and Non-participating	Non-cumulative and Non-participating
19X2	Preferred				
	Common				
19X3	Preferred				
	Common				
19X4	Preferred				
	Common				
19X5	Preferred				
	Common				
19X6	Preferred				
	Common				

Problems

Problem 11-1

Using the format shown, indicate the effect in terms of assets, liabilities, and shareholders' equity of the items given. For no change indicate 0; for increase, +; and for a decrease, −.

	Assets	Liabilities	Shareholders' Equity
a. Declaration of a stock dividend			
b. Declaration of a cash dividend			
c. Issue of new shares in place of old shares associated with a stock split			
d. Distribution of stock dividend in (a)			
e. Payment of cash dividend in (b)			

Problem 11-2

The ABM Company Ltd. had outstanding share capital as follows: (a) 1000 shares 6% preferred, par-value $100, and (b) 5000 shares common stock, par-value $100. For the years 19X3 to 19X7, net income was $48,000, $32,000, $3,000, $10,000, and $40,000, respectively. The company policy is to pay out all net income as dividends. There were no dividends in arrears on December 31, 19X2.

Required: Calculate for 19X3 to 19X7, using the form that follows, the amount of dividends for each class of stock, assuming:
a. The preferred is cumulative and non-participating
b. The preferred is cumulative and fully participating
c. The preferred is non-cumulative and fully participating
d. The preferred is non-cumulative and non-participating.

	Cumulative and Non-participating	Cumulative and Fully Participating	Non-cumulative and Fully Participating	Non-cumulative and Non-participating
19X3 Preferred				
Common				
19X4 Preferred				
Common				
19X5 Preferred				
Common				
19X6 Preferred				
Common				
19X7 Preferred				
Common				

Problem 11-3 (SMA adapted)

Mulroney Enterprises Ltd. was incorporated February 20, 19X4 with the following authorized share capital: (a) 9% preferred shares, cumulative, redeemable, non-participating, $100 par-value, 2000 shares authorized; (b) 50,000 common shares, no par-value. The following transactions occurred during the first two years of operation:

19X5
Jan. 3 Issued the following shares for cash: 1000 preferred shares for $103 per share and 10 000 common shares for $11 per share
Dec. 20 Declared a regular cash dividend of $9 on the outstanding preferred shares payable January 6, 19X6 and a 5 percent stock dividend on the outstanding common shares to be distributed January 12, 19X6 (current market value of the common shares is $15 per share)

19X6
Mar. 1 The company announced a stock split of all common shares on the basis of four new common shares for each outstanding share; the new shares are to be issued March 31, 19X6 (current market value of the common stock is $18)
Dec. 20 Declared a cash dividend of $0.10 payable on January 6, 19X7 to the common shareholders of record January 2, 19X7; also declared the regular dividend on the preferred shares.

Other Information:
• Net income for the year ended December 31, 19X5 $32,000
• Net income for the year ended December 31, 19X6 $45,000.
(Record the closing entry for each year.)

Required:
1. Prepare journal entries to record the 19X5 and 19X6 transactions.
2. Prepare the shareholders' equity section of the balance sheet at December 31, 19X6 in proper form.
3. Calculate the book value of a preferred share and a common share at December 31, 19X6.

Problem 11-4 (CGA adapted)

The shareholders' equity section of the balance sheet of Boyle Services Inc. at December 31, 19X7 appears below.

Shareholders' Equity

SHARE CAPITAL:
  Preferred Stock, 6%
    Authorized — 1000 Shares, $10 Par Value, Cumulative Non-participating
    Issued and Outstanding — 40 Shares $ 400
  Common Stock
    Authorized — 4000 Shares, $1 Par Value
    Issued and Outstanding — 2000 Shares   2,000
      Total Share Capital $2,400

SURPLUS:
  Contributed Surplus
    Premium on Common Stock $ 300
  Retained Earnings   900
      Total Surplus   1,200

      Total Shareholders' Equity $3,600

The following transactions occurred during 19X8.

Feb. 15   Declared the regular semi-annual dividend on its preferred stock and a $0.05 per-share dividend in the common stock to holders of record March 5, payable April 1

Apr. 1   Paid the dividends declared February 15

May 1   Declared a 10 percent stock dividend to common shareholders of record May 15 to be issued June 15, 19X6 (The common stock closed at a price of $2 on this date on the Toronto Stock Exchange; this price was designated by the board as the fair market value.)

Jun. 15   Paid the dividends declared May 1

Aug. 15   Declared the regular semi-annual dividend on preferred stock and a dividend of $0.05 on the common stock to holders of record August 31, payable October 1

Oct. 1   Paid the dividends declared August 15

Dec. 15   Declared a 10 percent stock dividend to common shareholders of record December 20 to be issued on January 15, 19X9 (The common stock closed at a price of $3 on this date on the Toronto Stock Exchange; this price was designated by the Board as the fair market value.)

Dec. 31   Net income for the year ended December 31, 19X8 was $1,400. (Record the closing entry.)

Required:
1. Prepare journal entries to record the 19X8 transactions.
2. Prepare the shareholders' equity section of the balance sheet at December 31, 19X8 in proper form.

Problem 11-5

At December 31, 19X3, the shareholders' equity section of the balance sheet for the Walkerville Automotive Corporation totalled $2,207,000. Following are the balances of various accounts at that date.

			('000s)
4% Preferred Stock, Par $10	Authorized	100 shares	
	Issued	50 shares	$500
Premium on Preferred Stock			7
Common Stock, $15	Authorized	100 shares	
Par-Value	Issued	50 shares	750
Restriction for Plant Extension			150
Restriction for Retirement of Bonds			200
Retained Earnings			600

Following are the transactions that occurred during the year 19X4.

Mar. 20   The regular semi-annual preferred dividend was declared payable April 1

Apr. 1   Payment of previously declared dividend

Jun. 15   The regular semi-annual common dividend of $0.40 per share was declared payable July 10

Jul. 10   Payment of the previously declared dividend

Sep. 20   Regular semi-annual preferred dividend was declared payable October 1

Oct. 1   Payment of previously declared dividend

Nov. 15   The board of directors met today and appropriated an additional $50 for the restriction for plant extension, another $50 for the restriction for the retirement of bonds, and $25 restriction for contingencies relating to an impending court case

Dec. 15   The regular semi-annual common dividend of $0.40 per share was declared payable January 10. In addition, a 10 percent stock dividend was declared on the common shares outstanding to shareholders of record December 20, the stock to be issued January 20. The market price of the stock was $20, which the directors consider to be the fair value.

Required:
1. Prepare journal entries for the 19X4 transactions.
2. Prepare the shareholders' equity section of the balance sheet at December 31, 19X4, assuming profit for the year amounted to $165.

Problem 11-6

The following selected transactions pertain to activities of Victoria Ltd., a company incorporated in British Columbia, whose authorized share capital is 400 000 common shares, each having a par-value of $10; 300 000 common shares have been issued at $12 each.

19X4

Feb. 7   Purchased 2000 shares of the company's own stock on the open market at $8.50 per share

Apr. 14   Sold half the purchase of February 7 to an investment company at a price of $5 per share.

19X5

Sep. 12   Purchased for retirement 19 000 shares of the company's own stock on the open market at $11 per share

Sep. 22   The board of directors of Victoria declared a stock dividend of 1 percent to shareholders of record October 15 to be distributed November 1, 19X5.
          The market value is still unchanged at $11 per share.

Required: Prepare journal entries to record these transactions.

Problem 11-7

The comparative shareholders' equity sections for Walker Corporation balance sheets at December 31, 19X2 and 19X3 follow.

Shareholders' Equity

	19X3	19X2
SHARE CAPITAL:		
Preferred Stock, 9%, No Par-Value		
Issued — 96 Shares	$96	$ 96
Common Stock, No Par-Value		
Issued — (19X3) 24 Shares; (1982) ? Shares	48	70
Total Share Capital	$144	$166
SURPLUS:		
Contributed Surplus		
Premium on Preferred Stock	$ 6	$ 6
Gain on Sale of Treasury Stock — Common	6	–
Donated Capital — Land	8	8
Total Contributed Surplus	$ 20	$ 14
Retained Earnings		
Restricted For Contingencies	$ 2	–
For Plant Additions	19	–
For Treasury Stock	33	–
Unrestricted	6	$ 20
Total Retained Earnings	$ 60	$ 20
Appraisal Increase — Building	7	7
Total Surplus	87	41
Total Share Capital and Surplus	$231	$207
Less: Treasury Stock — Common At Cost	33	–
Total Shareholders' Equity	$198	$207

Required:

1. Is the above corporation incorporated under the CBCA? Explain.
2. Assuming that only 6 Treasury Stock common shares were sold in 19X3, how many common shares were issued and outstanding at December 31, 19X2?

3. Is there any difference between the weighted average price of common shares at December 31, 19X3 and at December 31, 19X2?
4. Calculate the purchase cost of the Treasury Stock common shares reacquired in 19X3, assuming they were reacquired altogether.
5. Assuming that 6 Treasury Stock common shares were sold in 19X3, calculate the price per share sold.
6. Assuming that no dividends were declared in 19X3, calculate the net income for the year earned by Walker Corporation.

Alternate Problems

Alternate Problem 11-1

Required: Using the format shown, indicate the effects in terms of assets and shareholders' equity of the items below. For no change indicate 0; for increase, +; for decrease, −.

	Assets	Shareholders' Equity
a. Declaration of a cash dividend		
b. Declaration of a stock dividend		
c. Payment of the cash dividend in (a)		
d. Distribution of stock dividend in (b)		
e. Issue of new shares in place of old shares in connection with a stock split.		

Alternate Problem 11-2

The Retained Earnings account of the ABC Co. Ltd. was $400,000 on January 1, 19X5. During the following years, the company's dividend declarations were as follows:

19X5	$48,000	19X7	$ 2,000	19X9	$42,000
19X6	30,000	19X8	14,000		

ABC Co. Ltd. had outstanding shares as follows: (a) 1000 shares 8% preferred stock, par-value $100; and (b) 2000 shares common stock, par-value $100.

Required: Calculate for 19X5 to 19X9, using the form given, the amount of dividends for each class, assuming:

a. The preferred is cumulative and non-participating
b. The preferred is cumulative and fully participating
c. The preferred is non-cumulative and fully participating
d. The preferred is non-cumulative and non-participating.

Year	Cumulative and Non-participating	Cumulative and Fully Participating	Non-cumulative and Fully Participating	Non-cumulative and Non-participating
19X5 Preferred				
Common				
19X6 Preferred				
Common				
19X7 Preferred				
Common				
19X8 Preferred				
Common				
19X9 Preferred				
Common				

Alternate Problem 11-3 (SMA adapted)

Neanderthal Company Ltd., a progressive company in the glue business, has the following capital:
100 000 class A, 10% cumulative, non-participating, preferred shares, par-value $100. These shares have a preference as to dividends over all other shares.
50 000 class B 5% non-cumulative, fully participating preferred shares, par-value $100. These shares participate equally with common shares after common dividend of $3.
450 000 common shares no par-value, $45,000,000.

The company distributes 75 percent of net income earned each year. However, the company pays dividends on both classes of preferred shares up to the point at which further payment would place the company in a deficit position. (A deficit position occurs when there is a debit balance in Retained Earnings.) All dividends are declared at the end of the fiscal year and are payable on January 15 of the following year. The balance of the Retained Earnings January 1, 19X4 and net income each year is shown in the schedule.

Required: Calculate the amount of dividends declared each year to complete the schedule.

Neanderthal Company Ltd.
Schedule of Distribution of Dividends
For the Years Ended December 31, 19X4 to 19X7

	19X4	19X5	19X6	19X7
Balance (Jan. 1)	$1,200,000	$?	$?	$?
Add: Income (Loss)	4,000,000	(1,000,000)	(2,000,000)	7,000,000
Balance Available				
for Distribution	$5,200,000	$?	$?	$?
Dividends:				
Class A Pref.				
Class B Pref.				
Participation				
Common				
Participation				
Total Dividends				
Balance (Dec. 31)				

Alternate Problem 11-4 (SMA adapted)

On January 1, 19X3, the Kildonan Corporation Ltd. began operations. It had authorization to issue 20 000 no par-value common shares and 10 000 no par-value, cumulative, redeemable preferred shares. The dividend on preferred shares is $1 per year. 4000 no par-value common shares were issued for $120,000 on January 1, 19X3. The Retained Earnings balance on December 31, 19X3 was $145,000. During 19X4 the following transactions occurred.

Feb. 15   Issued 1000 preferred shares at $8 each
Mar. 1   Acquired a parcel of land adjacent to the present building, having an appraised market value of $40,000 in exchange for 1500 common shares
Jun. 1   Declared a $5 cash dividend on outstanding common shares and the annual cash dividend on outstanding preferred shares payable July 1, 19X4
Dec. 1   Declared a 10 percent common stock dividend to common shareholders (The market value of common stock on this day was $35 per share; the dividend was payable on December 20, 19X4.)
Dec. 31   Net income for the year was $98,000. (Record the closing entry.)

Required:
1. Prepare journal entries to record the 19X4 transactions.
2. Prepare the statement of retained earnings at December 31, 19X4 in proper form.
3. Prepare the shareholders' equity section of the balance sheet at December 31, 19X4 in proper form.

Alternate Problem 11-5

On December 31, 19X4, the shareholders' equity section of the Fingal Company Limited balance sheet was as follows:

Shareholders' Equity

SHARE CAPITAL:

Preferred Stock, $100 Par-Value, 6% Cumulative and Non-participating — Authorized 5000 Shares Issued and Outstanding — 200 Shares	$20,000	
Common Stock, $10 Par-Value Authorized — 2000 Shares Issued and Outstanding — 100 Shares	1,000	
Total Share Capital		$21,000

SURPLUS:

Contributed Surplus		
Premium on Common Stock	$ 150	
Retained Earnings	5,450	
Total Surplus		5,600
Total Shareholders' Equity		$26,600

During 19X5, Fingal engaged in the following transactions.

Mar. 15   Declared the regular semi-annual $3 per-share dividend on the preferred stock and $0.50 per-share dividend on the common stock

Apr. 30   Paid the dividends previously declared

Sep. 15   Declared the regular semi-annual $3 per-share dividend on the preferred stock and a $0.50 per-share dividend on the common shares

Oct. 30   Paid the dividends previously declared

Dec. 15   Declared a 10 percent common stock dividend distributable on January 15 to shareholders of record January 10, 19X6 (The common shares were trading and closed on the Toronto Stock Exchange December 15 at $18 per share; this amount was approved by the board for the dividend.)

Required: Prepare journal entries to record the 19X5 transactions.

Alternate Problem 11-6

Data pertaining to the Accumatic Company Ltd. are given below. Accumatic has an authorized capital of 1 million common shares of $20 par-value and functions in a jurisdiction where it is possible to repurchase its own shares.

19X6
Jan. 2   Issued 600 000 common shares for $24 cash per share.

19X7
Feb. 15   Purchased 4000 shares of the company's stock in the open market at $17 per share

Jun. 30   Sold 2000 shares purchased February 15 at a price of $10 per share.

19X8
Sep. 2   Purchased for retirement 38 000 shares of the company's stock at $22 per share

Sep. 30   Declared a stock dividend of 2 percent to shareholders of record October 30 to be distributed November 15; the market value was unchanged from September 2.

Required: Prepare journal entries to record these transactions.

Alternate Problem 11-7

The following transactions were recorded in the journal of Clayton Computer Products Inc. during 19X3.

1. Cash   1,500
      Common Stock   1,500
    To record the issue of 1000 no par-value common shares.

2. Cash   22,000
      Preferred Stock   20,000
      Premium on Preferred Stock   2,000
    To record the issue of 200, $? par value,
    6% cumulative, non-participating, preferred shares
    (authorized 800 shares).

3. Cash   500
      Common Stock   500
    To record the issue of 1000 no par-value common shares.

4. Treasury Stock — Common   200
      Cash   200
    To record reacquisition of 100 common shares.

5. Cash   75
      Gain on Sale of Treasury Stock   25
      Treasury Stock — Common   50
    To record sale of ? common shares held as treasury stock.

6. Cash   90
    Gain on Sale of Treasury Stock   25
    Retained Earnings   5
      Treasury Stock — Common   120
    To record sale of ? common shares held as treasury stock.

7. Common Stock   10
    Retained Earnings   10
      Treasury Stock — Common   20
    To record cancellation of ? common shares held as treasury stock.

Other Data: Retained Earnings at December 31, 19X3 amounted to $1,115 before any adjustment from the preceding transactions

Required:
1. Is Clayton incorporated under the CBCA? Why or why not?
2. What is the weighted average price of the common shares?
3. What is the par-value of the preferred shares? How much was each preferred share issued for?
4. What is the reacquisition cost of each common share?
5. How many treasury common shares were sold in transaction 5? Is the Gain on Sale of Treasury Stock reported in the income statement?
6. How many treasury common shares were sold in transaction 6? Why is Retained Earnings debited?
7. How many treasury common shares were cancelled in transaction 7? Why is Retained Earnings debited rather than Gain on Sale of Treasury Stock?
8. Prepare the shareholders' equity section of the balance sheet at December 31, 19X3 after transaction 7 is recorded.

Supplementary Problems

Supplementary Problem 11-1

Sharp Furniture Limited pays dividends on the issued and outstanding preferred and common shares twice a year. In December, 19X2, the directors declared the semi-annual dividend on preferred shares and $0.60 per share on the common. The dividends are to be paid January 31. 19X3. The shareholders' equity at December 31, 19X2 consisted of the following:

Preferred Shares, $50 Par Value, 5% Cumulative
　Issued and Outstanding 5000 Shares
Common Shares — No Par Value,
　Issued and Outstanding 30 000 Shares
Retained Earnings $560,000.

In 19X3 the following transactions affecting the company's shares took place.

Jan. 31　Paid the dividends declared in December, 19X2
Mar. 31　Sold 10 000 common shares at $30 per share
Jun. 28　Declared the regular semi-annual dividend on preferred shares and a dividend of $0.60 per share on common shares
Jul. 31　Paid the dividends declared in June
Sep. 21　Declared a 10 percent stock dividend on outstanding common shares to be issued October 31 to the shareholders of record October 12; market price of $31 to be used
Oct. 31　Issued the stock dividend declared in September
Dec. 28　Declared the regular semi-annual preferred share dividend and a cash dividend of $0.50 per share on common shares outstanding.

Required:
　1. Prepare journal entries to record the 19X3 transactions.
　2. If Sharp Furniture had a net profit of $100,000 in 19X3, what is the balance of Retained Earnings after closing the books on December 31, 19X3?

Supplementary Problem 11-2

Axworthy Productions Ltd. had the following shareholders' equity at January 1, 19X7:

Common stock, $10 par-value,	
1000 shares outstanding	$10,000
Premium on common stock	1,000
Retained earnings	9,000
Total shareholders' equity	$20,000

Part A

The following transactions occurred during the year.

Jun. 1　Declared a cash dividend of $1 per share to common shareholders of record June 15, payable June 30
Jun. 30　Paid the dividend declared June 1
Dec. 1　Declared a 10 percent stock dividend to common shareholders of record December 15 to be issued January 1, 19X8; the fair market value was designated by the board at $20 per share
Dec. 31　Net income for the year amounted to $5,000. (Record the closing entry.)

Required:

1. Prepare journal entries to record the 19X7 transactions.
2. Compute the book value per share at January 1, 19X7.
3. Prepare the shareholders' equity section of the balance sheet at December 31, 19X7 in proper form.
4. Compute the book value per share at December 31, 19X7.
5. Prepare the shareholders' equity section of the balance sheet at January 1, 19X8 immediately following the issue of the stock dividend.
6. Compute the book value per share at January 1, 19X8 immediately following the issue of the stock dividend.

Part B

The following transactions occurred during 19X8.

Feb. 15   Declared a cash dividend of $1 per share to common shareholders of record March 1, payable March 15
Mar. 15   Paid the dividend declared February 15
Jun. 30   The common stock was split on the basis of 2 new common shares for each outstanding share; the market value of each share was designated by the board at $40 per share at the date of the split. (The new shares are to be issued July 23.)
Jul. 23   Issued the new common shares
Dec. 31   Net income for the year amounted to $8,000. (Record the closing entry.)

Required:

7. Prepare journal entries to record the 19X8 transactions.
8. Prepare the shareholders' equity section of the balance sheet at December 31, 19X8 in proper form.
9. Compute the book value per share at December 31, 19X8.
10. What are the advantages of a stock split to shareholders?

Supplementary Problem 11-3 (SMA adapted)

The shareholders' equity section of Waterloo Computers Inc. balance sheet at January 1, 19X6, is as follows:

	Shareholders' Equity
Common Stock, $5 par-value	$2,000,000
Premium on Common Stock	1,600,000
Retained Earnings	4,800,000
Total Shareholders' Equity	$8,400,000

On April 15, a 5 percent stock dividend was declared, payable June 1 to shareholders of record on May 15. On July 1, a 2 for 1 stock split was announced. Net income for the year was $2,400,000. The fair market price of Waterloo's shares were as follows:

Apr. 15 $12   Jun. 1 $15
May 15   14   Jul. 1   8

Required:

1. What was the issue price per share of the shares outstanding January 1, 19X6, assuming they were all issued at one time?
2. How much was the dollar change in retained earnings as a result of the stock dividend? Explain.
3. How much was the dollar change in shareholders' equity as a result of the stock dividend? Explain.
4. How much was the dollar change in shareholders' equity as a result of the stock split? Explain.
5. Prepare the shareholders' equity section of the balance sheet at December 31, 19X6 in proper form.

6. If Mary Munroe, a shareholder, owned 20 common shares at January 1, 19X6, what was the dollar amount of her equity in Waterloo at April 14, immediately before the declaration of the stock dividend at June 1?; immediately after the stock dividend had been paid?
7. How did the declaration of a stock split on July 1 affect Mary Munroe?
8. What are the advantages and disadvantages of a stock dividend
   a. to Waterloo Computers Inc.?   b. to Mary Munroe?
9. What are the advantages and disadvantages of a stock split
   a. to Waterloo Computers Inc.?   b. to Mary Munroe?

Decision Problems

Decision Problem 11-1

The Wayne-Kett Plastics Company Limited was incorporated in June 19X2. Preferred shares were issued in January, 19X4 for $100 per share and carried a $6 per share cumulative dividend up to January 1, 19X7. The last audited balance sheet showed the following accounts (summarized):

Balance Sheet
At June 30, 19X7

Cash	$ 22,000
Other Current Assets*	152,000
Temporary Investments	60,000
Fixed Assets	620,000
Intangible Assets	30,000
Other Assets	16,000
	$900,000
Current Liabilities	$ 76,000
Long-Term Loans	120,000
Preferred Shares — $100 par value	100,000
Common Shares (30 000 Shares)	300,000
Retained Earnings	304,000
	$900,000

*Accounts Receivable $72,000
 Merchandise Inventory $80,000

The board of directors had not declared a dividend since incorporation; instead, the profits were used to expand the company. The board is planning to declare a year-end dividend (December, 19X7).

Required:
1. If the required dividend on the preferred and $0.50 per share on the common shares was to be paid in December, what amount would be required? Prepare the necessary journal entry (entries) for the declaration of such dividends.
2. If the dividends are paid in 19X7 as proposed in 1, above, the company expects to implement the following policy: retain 50 percent of net income for expansion and pay 50 percent in dividends. Determine the necessary 19X8 net income to implement the policy if a $1 per share dividend is to be paid on the common shares.

Decision Problem 11-2

Toward the end of the current year, the board of directors of the London Corporation Ltd. is presented with the following shareholders' equity section of the balance sheet.

Shareholders' Equity

SHARE CAPITAL:
Common Stock, No Par-Value
Authorized — 5000 Shares
Issued and Outstanding —

1500 Shares		$30,000
SURPLUS:		
Contributed Surplus		
Premium on Common Stock	$18,000	
Retained Earnings	24,000	
Total Surplus		42,000
Total Shareholders' Equity		$72,000

London Corporation Ltd. has paid dividends of $3.60 per share in each of the last five years. After careful consideration of the company's cash needs, the board of directors declared a stock dividend of 300 shares of common stock. Shortly after the stock dividend had been distributed and before the end of the year, the company declared a cash dividend of $3 per share.

James Brown owned 360 shares of London Corporation common stock, which he acquired several years ago. The market price of this stock when the stock dividend was declared was $60 per share.

Required: Answer the following questions, showing calculations.

1. What is Brown's share (in dollars) of the net assets of London Corporation Ltd. before the stock dividend action? What is his share after the stock dividend action? Explain why there is (or is not) any change as a result of the stock dividend.
2. What are the probable reasons why the market value of Brown's stock differs from the amount of net assets per share shown on the books?
3. Compare (with comment) the amount of cash dividends that Brown receives this year with dividends received in previous years.
4. On the day the common stock went ex-dividend (with respect to the stock dividend), its quoted market value fell from $60 to $50 per share. Did this represent a loss to Brown? Explain.
5. If the London Corporation Ltd. had announced that it would continue its regular cash dividend of $3.60 per share on the increased number of shares outstanding after the stock dividend, would you expect the market value of the common stock to react in any way different from the change described in 4, above? Why?

Partnerships

Although partnerships record asset and liability transactions in the same manner as corporations, equity transactions are recorded in a manner unique to partnerships.

1. How do the characteristics of a partnership differ from those of a corporation?
2. What unique accounting characteristics are required for a partnership?
3. What kind of entity is a partnership?
4. How are partnership assets owned by partners?
5. What are the different methods used to divide partnership profits and losses?
6. How do partnership financial statements differ from those of a corporation?
7. What are alternate methods used for admission of new partners?
8. How is the withdrawal of a partner accounted for?
9. How is a partnership liquidated?
10. What is the *Garner* v. *Murray* rule regarding partnerships, and when is it used?

A. Partnership Characteristics

Partnership
An unincorporated form of business organization in which the entity is owned by two or more persons.

A **partnership** combines the abilities and capital of any number of individuals who together own and operate a business. Although a partnership is a business entity, it is not a legal entity as is a corporation; that is, a partnership has a limited life. Partnerships also have a number of unique characteristics; therefore, accounting for partners' equity differs from accounting for shareholders' equity. Whereas previous chapters in this part focus on accounting for equity in the corporate form of business organization, this chapter discusses the accounting treatment of partnership equity.

Characteristics that influence equity accounting for a partnership include limited life, unlimited liability, mutual agency, co-ownership of assets, and sharing of profits and losses.

Limited Life

Partnership agreement
A written contract indicating how profits and losses are to be divided, how the partnership can be dissolved, and other matters relating to the partners.

The life of a partnership may be limited by a clause in the **partnership agreement** stipulating that the partnership will terminate after a particular period of time or completion of the partnership objective. More often, however, an existing partnership is dissolved when a new partner is admitted, or an existing partner withdraws or dies. Partner dissolution does not necessarily mean that the business is also dissolved; usually the business continues under a new partnership agreement. Accounting for partnership capital therefore involves issues related to the formation and dissolution of partnerships and to the allocation of the profits and losses to the individual partners.

Unlimited Liability

While a partnership business is an entity that exists separately from its owners, it does not have a separate legal life, as a corporation does. Each partner is personally liable for debts that the partnership cannot pay. In the event that a partner is unable to pay his/her share of partnership debts, the other partners can be called on to pay personally for such debts. Accounting for partnerships includes issues related to the payment of partnership debts from personal assets of individual partners. Liability can be limited: partners can be designated as ''limited'' or ''general''.

Mutual Agency

Unless otherwise stated in the partnership agreement, each partner is able to make decisions that are legally binding, not only on the partnership, but also on the other partners. The only exception involves activities that fall outside the normal activities of the partnership. For example, a partnership formed to sell used cars would not normally include the buying and selling of footwear; in this case, used-car partners would not be legally bound to footware contracts signed by only one of the partners. A clear understanding of mutual agency implications is important, since it focuses on one of the pitfalls of the partnership form of business organization. Real Life Example 12-1 discusses this and other problem areas for unwary partners.

Real Life Example 12-1

Why Partnerships Break up

Two and a half years ago, four of us started out on a great adventure together — our own consulting partnership. For six months, we struggled along with no clients. Then we hit the big time: a $1.3-million contract. But somehow our success at attracting clients was greater than our ability to work together harmoniously. This April, our original partnership broke up. The experience was one of the toughest I've ever gone through—but it taught me some valuable lessons about what makes a partnership succeed.

When it became apparent, after several attempted salvage operations, that there were irreconcilable differences in our partnership, we called in our attorney. "Splitting up a partnership," he said, "is just like a divorce without the kids." He meant to reassure us with the comment about kids, but I found that the dissolution of a partnership can be just as emotional as a divorce. Like ours, many partnerships consist of friends and former colleagues, and many other partnerships include relatives. Couple these personal relationships with the intense involvement required to run a small business, and you can see why a failing partnership creates misunderstandings, bruised egos, bitterness, hurt feelings, and anger.

Of course, no one puts together a partnership thinking about the unpleasantness of breaking it up. The key is to recognize that a partnership arrangement is subject to some stresses that are not found in other corporate structures. After our partnership broke up, I began to analyze our experiences and, I found that there were three basic rules that were responsible for our successes when we heeded them, and for our problems when we didn't.

Rule 1: Share and Share Alike

Very simple, right? Most partners have every intention of doing just that. The problem is to make reality conform with the intent. Unfortunately, as George Orwell pointed out, some of us are more equal than others. Human nature being what it is, some people are more exploitative or manipulative, and some are more easily exploited and manipulated.

Because of various backgrounds and experiences, partners may have different opinions on what risk is justifiable, how money should be managed, and what the work ethic really means. Before you sign your name to a partnership agreement, assess just how everyone views such questions. This will provide a good indication of how equal everyone is likely to be three months or three years later.

Also ask if each partner can contribute enough money. Our experience confirmed that there are those months when the cash flow slows to a trickle or does not flow at all. When that happens, the partners may have to do without. Most partners may agree to such a sacrifice in the excitement of beginning a new venture, but when it comes time to actually go without pay, some partners simply may not be able to do so. The ledger sheet may eventually be brought back into balance, but the psychological effects of unequal sacrifice will probably remain.

Set aside at least one meeting to discuss nothing but the personal ability of each partner to persevere through periods of reduced income. This is not a time to be timid or to worry about being "impolite". Spell out what will be expected of each partner (and it had better be much the same for each) if the worst case occurs. If you have the time, continue to talk about personal financial positions on a regular basis.

The need for the partners to contribute *themselves* equally to the company is even more important than how much money they can contribute. In many cases, partnerships are formed because one partner can contribute something that the other partners cannot, and that's what a good partnership is all about. But a merger of disparate specialists, no matter how good they are in their particular areas, has a distinct disadvantage. In young, small businesses, everyone has to do a little bit of everything. In our case, the four partners were the entire company for the first six months. That meant that each of us had to raise money, keep the books, research and produce our services, type, make coffee, get the mail, and sweep the steps. If your partners will not share in such tasks — especially when everyone's personal hard work is the only thing that will earn money—friction and failure are inevitable. The only safeguard is to spell out from the start who is going to do what, making sure that the tasks and levels of effort are reasonably equitable.

There is no secret of success: It's hard work. If your partners don't see it that way, beware. If everyone is committed to lots of hard work, determine exactly how hard it is going to be. Is everyone going to do his share of overtime? If one of your partners loves golf, sailing, skiing, or even church or service organizations more than anything else, does that mean more than the company? Remember, your partners are not likely to change their characters or habits just because you are now a partnership.

But if recreation and outside interests are recognized by the partnership as desirable aspects of the partners' lives, spell it out so that time legitimately taken away from the company is available to everyone in equal portions. One week for a partner to serve as a counselor at scout camp should be matched with one week for the other partners, whether it be for running marathons, lying on a sunny beach, or working for the United Way.

Rule 2: Get it in Writing

In each of the cases mentioned above, your best bet is to get it in writing. Write down who is going to do what tasks. Write down how much everyone is going to work. Write down how much money each partner will invest and where that money will come from. Write down how much money in wages will be given up when there is limited income. Write down your

Why Partnerships Break up (Cont.)

goals and expectations for marketing, production, and routine management. Write down a plan to monitor progress. Write down who will go to training sessions, seminars, and conferences. Write down who will get what perquisites.

All of this writing serves three related purposes: planning, record keeping, and protection. Writing everything out will allow you to encounter and solve many of your problems before they jeopardize your company or destroy your friendships. Once you get going, you should continue to plan on paper. A record of your agreements on goals, policies, and procedures protects the company in general and the partners in particular. If you have agreed to limit spending on a particular marketing target, and the marketing partner exceeds the limit with no results, a reprimand is in order. It's especially important to keep written records because, if worst comes to worst — if the partnership falters and the separation is contested — the record will protect the partners who are not at fault by showing exactly who did what.

Let's say you have three basic goals. You want to hold administrative costs to 20 percent, you want to produce three handmade bamboo fly rods and 150 flies per week, and you want to double the demand for your products within three months. Develop and write the plan in outline fashion, in as much detail as you can imagine. Start with the goal: three rods and 150 flies. Decide who will be responsible: Partner A. Decide who will do the work: Partner A (75%) and Partner B (25%). Allocate the time to accomplish the task: one week. Plan what will be done if the target of doubling your demand in three months is not met; record at least five options. When each goal is developed and addressed in this fashion, write

the whole thing up formally, and have each partner sign it. If this is done for each main goal, no one aspect of the business should get so far off the track that it endangers the other aspects of the company itself.

These written plans are the basis for the overall operation of the company. They provide the focus for the management meeting you should hold at least once a week. To make these meetings worth anything, a recording secretary must keep complete and objective minutes. These minutes must then be reviewed at each subsequent meeting so that everyone is satisfied that interim operating procedures are mutually acceptable.

Like a report outline, company plans provide frameworks for action. Don't deviate from them capriciously. As circumstances dictate change, review your plans with all of the partners. Some seemingly simple change that you're sure is appropriate may be seen quite differently by another partner.

While this may all sound ominously formal, structured, and time-consuming, it is much more costly in both time and dollars to proceed on an ill-defined course or, worse, to operate at cross-purposes with your partners. If you fail to write everything down (and there are always plenty of good excuses for not doing it), and things start to go wrong, be assured that no one will agree on what was said six months ago.

Rule 3: Don't Lie

Generally, none of us tells big lies that lead to fraud or other criminal acts. But there are those little white lies — more pleasant ways of putting the truth, or simply lack of candor — that can occur, and they can be devastating to a partnership.

There is a great deal of pressure to dismiss, ignore, or avoid

Co-Ownership of Assets

Unless the partnership agreement specifies otherwise, all assets contributed to the partnership by individual partners are jointly owned by all partners. Each partner, therefore, has a claim against all partnership assets up to the amount of his/her capital balance. Therefore, partnership assets are often sold on liquidation to facilitate their distribution to partners in the form of cash.

Sharing of Profits and Losses

The partnership agreement usually stipulates the manner in which profits and losses will be shared. If no such provision is specified, then partners share all profits and losses equally. Accounting issues related to the division of profits and losses are discussed in section B of this chapter.

Advantages of a Partnership

A partnership has several advantages over other forms of business organizations. It can be easily formed through provincial registration, without the legal process and costs involved in incorporation. A partnership is less subject to government supervision; there

bad news. Bad news, however, is not necessarily a sign of personal failure, nor is it usually the result of some totally external factor inflicted on the company by unknown agents. Instead, it is information that must be addressed in the context of your company plans. Only if you get sound and adequate information can you overcome problems.

If one partner is responsible for raising money, and all of the partners have agreed that a certain action is dependent on raising $30,000 from normally acceptable sources, it is not really a favour to the company if the money-raiser gets $10,000 from selling his car, $10,000 from his kindly old aunt, and $10,000 from a loan shark, and neglects to tell you that it didn't come from the bank. The consequences of such efforts, even if they happen to have some short-term advantages, are detrimental to company planning because they are based on false premises. It is always possible that the banks are refusing your loan request for a good reason, a reason that the company should be aware of. If the company is going beyond conventional sources for loans, it had better be a partnership decision. In this example, there is the additional danger that personal concerns will adversely affect company performance. Your company should not be forced into making decisions based on a partner's having to walk to work, getting into disputes with relatives, or being threatened with bodily harm.

It's particularly easy to lie to yourself about employee relations. If the employees are not producing, you must find out why and face the consequences. Most people find it difficult to fire employees, and many managers have trouble urging, cajoling, or demanding the required work from employees. Use the style that best suits you when it comes to supervision, but don't lie to yourself. In most cases, you simply can't afford to "wait three more months" for an employee to get the hang of it. And, in fact, it does the employee little good to assume that his work is acceptable when it is not. Employees must understand clearly what is expected of them and then be given adequate opportunity and support to meet those goals. If the person is not suited for the position, send him on his way with suggestions for more appropriate employment. Delay only compounds the problem and your level of stress.

You may also notice a tendency to oversell yourself or the company. This is lying. Some people can work 112 hours a week, but most of us can't. You can't plan effectively if you don't assess your capabilities realistically. The same is true at the company level. You really don't gain anything by selling what you can't deliver, and there's no better method for shutting off the flow of contracts.

Lying or not confiding in your other partners is harmful mainly because it denies your business the chance to benefit from all your partners' experience. You are partners because each one of you is bright, talented, and full of useful contributions to the company. Don't fail to use your own resources by hiding unpleasant situations from your partners. They may not think the situation is as grave as you do.

Partnerships are a great way to combine resources, and much of their effectiveness comes from a merger of human and intangible qualities. Your accountant, attorney, or banker can be invaluable with corporate and financial concerns, but it is your partners who are your greatest assets. Choose them wisely, ask hard questions, and don't take them — or yourself — for granted. You have to work at your partnership as much as you do at your business.

Source Stephen G. Thomas, "Why Partnerships Break Up", *Inc. Magazine*, 1984.

---

are fewer government regulations and less paper work regarding partnerships than corporations. Because a partnership is not a legal entity, it is not subject to corporate income tax; individual partners file personal income tax returns, which include their allocation of partnership profits. Since a partnership includes at least two, and often more, individuals, it has access to more capital and expertise than does a proprietorship.

Disadvantages of a Partnership

A partner has to answer to other partners for his/her actions and has mutual agency and unlimited liability. Therefore, individual partners are legally liable for the financial debt arising from actions of other partners. (Recall that corporations are legally liable for their own actions and have limited liability.) A partnership is dissolved on the death or withdrawal of a partner, although the business may continue with new partners. This arrangement is more cumbersome than the selling of shares in a corporation. Also, a corporation usually has access to a larger amount of capital, since it appeals to more investors, particularly those who want to make a good investment but do not want to get involved with running the business. In addition, corporate tax rates can be more favourable than personal tax rates; moreover, dividends received by a corporate shareholder are taxed more favourably than the earnings of business income.

Partnership Accounting

Business transactions for a partnership are recorded in the same manner as those for a corporation. The only significant difference between a partnership or a proprietorship and corporation is in the treatment of owners' equity. A **Capital** account is used to record owner contributions to a partnership or a proprietorship. Partner or owner withdrawals, called **drawings** reduce the Capital account(s). Individual Capital accounts and Drawings accounts are maintained for each partner. The Drawings account balance is closed to each partner's Capital account at the end of the accounting time period.

Capital account
A permanent account used to record the capital investment and withdrawals of each partner and his/her allocation of the profits and losses of the partnership; the Drawings account of each partner is closed to his/her Capital account at the end of each fiscal year.

Partnership Capital Accounts

Partner investments in a partnership are recorded into a Capital account. Each partner has an individual account that is credited with capital contributions to the partnership. The following entry records a $5,000 cash investment by partner **A**.

Cash	5,000	
A, Capital		5,000
To record investment by **A**.		

If non-cash assets are contributed, then the appropriate asset account is debited.

    Partner withdrawals of assets from the partnership are recorded in each partner's Drawings account. If partner **A** withdraws $1,000 cash, for example, the following entry is recorded:

A, Drawings	1,000	
Cash		1,000
To record drawings by **A**.		

Drawings account
A temporary account used to record the withdrawal of cash or assets by a partner during the fiscal year; this account is closed to the partner's Capital account at the end of the fiscal year.

At year-end, each partner's Drawings account is closed to his/her Capital account. The following closing entry would close partner **A**'s Drawings account, assuming no further drawings have been made.

A, Capital	1,000	
A, Drawings		1,000
To close **A**'s Drawings account.		

> The Drawings account is closed directly to the Capital account of each partner.

Proprietorship Accounting

Proprietorship
An unincorporated form of business organization, in which the entity is owned by one person.

A **Proprietorship** business is owned by one individual who usually also manages the operation. The proprietorship is a business entity that is handled as a separate entity from its owner, although it is not a legal entity, as is a corporation. Proprietor investments in the business are recorded in a Capital account in the same way as in a partnership. Proprietor withdrawals from the business are also recorded as drawings; the Drawings account balance is closed to the Capital account at year-end.

B. Division of Partnership Profits and Losses

Partnership profits and losses are divided equally among partners, if no profit and loss sharing ratio is indicated in the partnership agreement. Otherwise, the ratio specified in the agreement is used; this ratio can be fixed, such as 3 : 2 or ⅔ to ⅓, for example. Profits and losses may also be shared according to a formula specified in the agreement. This formula usually considers three factors: a return to each partner for the amount of his/her capital invested in the partnership, a payment to each partner for services rendered, and a further division of any remaining profit (or resulting loss) in the profit and loss sharing ratio. Although a partnership agreement may not include separate calculations for each of these factors, the ratio should be calculated after considering their impact on each partner's remuneration.

Division Using a Fixed Ratio

The division of profits and losses according to a fixed ratio is appropriate when each partner makes an equal contribution to the business. Ideally, each partner would have an equal amount of capital invested in the partnership and would devote an equal amount of time and effort in the business. However, usually the amount of capital differs, and time and effort devoted to the business is unequal. The initial calculation of a fixed ratio inclusion in the partnership agreement would consider the weight of these factors.

Assuming that **A** and **B** share profits in the ratio of 3 : 2, a $15,000 profit would be divided and recorded by the following entry.

Income Summary	15,000	
A, Capital (3/5 × 15,000)		9,000
B, Capital (2/5 × 15,000)		6,000
To record division of partnership profits.		

Division Using Capital Balances

An alternate method of allocating partnership profits and losses uses partners' Capital balances. This method is most suitable where large amounts are invested by partners and where profits are mainly attributable to these invested amounts. Use of this method must be specified in the partnership agreement; otherwise, profits and losses are divided equally among partners.

Assuming that use of Capital balances are indicated in the **A** and **B** partnership agreement and that these balances amount to $10,000 for each partner, the $15,000 profit would be divided equally in this case (by coincidence). It is recorded as follows:

Income Summary	15,000	
A, Capital		7,500
B, Capital		7,500
To record division of partnership profits.		

Note that the partnership agreement should indicate whether the opening, ending, or average Capital balances are to be used in dividing profits and losses. Each balance would result in a different amount calculated unless the capital invested in the partnership by each partner did not change during the year. The use of opening or ending Capital balances, however, may not be an equitable method in many circumstances.

Division Using Salary and Interest Allocations

Salaries to partners
A mechanism used for
dividing a portion of the
income of the partnership
among partners. Such a
division recognizes the
value of services rendered
by each partner; this is
not the same as a salary
expense.

**Interest on partners'
Capital balance**
A mechanism used for
dividing a portion of the
income of the partnership
among partners having
different capital
investments.

Since the time and effort devoted by individual partners to the business is often unequal and the amount of Capital balance varies among partners, another allocation method can be chosen. Profits and losses can be divided using an allocation through **partner salary** and **interest on capital balances** to each partner, in accordance with individual contributions. Any remaining profits and losses can be divided through the profit and loss sharing ratio. The salary and interest allocations are not deducted as expenses on the income statement; *salary* and *interest* used here refer only to individual factors used in dividing profits and losses among partners.

Before beginning their partnership, **A** and **B** recognize that **A** deserved more salary compensation because of his technical skills and the fact that he had been earning more than **B**. Accordingly, the following salary allocations were specified in their partnership agreement: $7,000 to **A** and $5,000 to **B**. The agreement also indicated that 12 percent interest should be allocated to their Capital balances and that any remaining profit and loss should be shared in the ratio of 3 : 2.

The following calculation shows how a $15,000 profit is divided according to these provisions of the **A** and **B** partnership agreement. Remember that these salary and interest amounts have not been paid to partners; rather they are a calculation for allocating partnership net income to partners.

	A	B	Total
Amount of Profit To Be Allocated to Partners			$15,000
Interest Allocation:			
A: $10,000 × 12%	$1,200		
B: $10,000 × 12%		$1,200	2,400
Balance			$12,600
Salary Allocation	7,000	5,000	12,000
Balance			$ 600
Balance Allocated in Profit and Loss Sharing Ratio:			
A: $600 × 3/5	360		
B: $600 × 2/5		240	600
Balance			-0-
Allocated to Partners	$8,560	$6,440	

The following entry records this profit allocation between **A** and **B**:

Income Summary	15,000	
A, Capital		8,560
B, Capital		6,440

If the $15,000 partnership income had been inadequate to cover the salary and interest allocated to **A** and **B**, the difference would have been allocated in the profit and loss sharing ratio. Assuming that partnership net income had amounted to $9,000, the following calculation of amounts allocated to the partners would be made:

	A	B	Total
Amount of Profit To Be Allocated to Partners			$ 9,000
Interest Allocation:			
A: $10,000 × 12%	$ 1,200		
B: $10,000 × 12%		$ 1,200	2,400
Balance			$ 6,600
Salary Allocation	7,000	5,000	12,000
Balance			($ 5,400)
Balance Allocated in Profit and Loss Sharing Ratio:			
A: $5,400 × 3/5	(3,240)		
B: $5,400 × 2/5		(2,160)	5,400
Balance			-0-
Allocated to Partners	$4,960	$4,040	

These calculations illustrate the allocation of partnership net income using a combination of interest and salary elements, with any remaining balance being allocated to partners according to their profit and loss sharing ratio. Alternately, the partnership agreement may only provide for allocation of a salary, with the remaining balance being allocated according to the profit and loss sharing ratio. In actual practice, the agreement may also provide periodic drawings to individual partners, equal to their salary allocation; the Drawings account is closed to each partner's capital account at year-end.

Partnership Financial Statements

Partnership and proprietorship financial statements are similar. The income statement of a partnership might include this allocation of income to individual partners:

A and B
Income Statement
For the Year Ended December 31, 19X4

Sales		$150,000
Cost of Sales		
Net Income for the Year		$ 15,000
Net Income Allocation:		
A	$8,560	
B	6,440	$ 15,000

Statement of partners' capital
A statement required in partnership accounting, summarizing the changes that occurred in partners' capital during the period.

A **statement of partners' capital** replaces the statement of retained earnings. It shows partner contributions to the business, changes in capital resulting from net income (or loss) allocations, and drawings representing withdrawals during the period. The partners' capital statement for **A** and **B** would appear as follows:

A and B
Statement of Partners' Capital
For the Year Ended December 31, 19X3

	A	B	Total
Capital Balance (Jan. 1)	$ 5,000	$ 5,000	$10,000
Add: Investments during 19X3	5,000	5,000	10,000
Net Income for the Year	8,560	6,440	15,000
	$18,560	$16,440	$35,000
Less: Drawings	7,000	5,000	12,000
Capital Balance (Dec. 31)	$11,560	$11,440	$23,000

It is assumed in this statement of partners' capital that each partner made additional $5,000 investments during the year and that net income is divided using salary and interest allocations.

The balance sheet of a partnership shows the Capital balance of each partner if there are only a few partners. Otherwise, only a total Capital amount is indicated, with details appearing in the statement of partners' capital. Note that no distinction is made between owner capital contributions and net income earned and retained in the business, as occurs in corporate financial statements. The owners' equity of **A** and **B** may appear as follows on the balance sheet:

Partners' Equity

A, Capital	$11,560
B, Capital	11,440
Total Equity	$23,000

C.   Admission of a New Partner

The admission of a new partner results in the creation of a new partnership. Although the business of the former partnership need not discontinue, the former partnership ceases to exist with the admission of a new partner. Since the liability, agency, and profit sharing arrangements will be altered, a new partnership agreement is required.

For illustrative purposes, the following balance sheet data are used for the **A** and **B** partnership.

Assets		*Liabilities and Equity*		
Cash	$ 5,000	Liabilities		$ 7,000
Other Assets	22,000	**A**, Capital	$10,000	
		B, Capital	10,000	20,000
	$27,000			$27,000

A new partner, **C**, wants to enter the **A** and **B** partnership. He can be admitted either by purchasing an existing partner's interest or by contributing assets to the partnership. In either case, the admission of a new partner must be approved by the existing partners.

Purchase of an Existing Partner's Interest

Assume **C** is going to purchase **B**'s interest in the **A** and **B** partnership. The purchase of an existing partner's interest in a partnership is a private transaction between the new partner and the existing partner who is selling his/her interest in the partnership. The new partner **C** makes a payment to the existing partner **B**, who in turn transfers his/her partnership interest. This type of purchase does not affect the assets of the partnership. Only an entry recording the change in ownership is made in the partnership books. The following entry illustrates the recording of **C**'s purchase of **B**'s interest.

B, Capital	10,000	
C, Capital		10,000
To record transfer of **B**'s partnership interest to **C**.		

C could have paid $15,000 or $5,000 to **B** for his/her ownership interest; because the purchase is a private transaction between **B** and **C**, the amount paid is not reflected in the entry made in the partnership records. **C** could also have purchased half of **B**'s interest. In this case, only half of **B**'s interest would be transferred to **C** by the following entry:

B, Capital	5,000	
C, Capital		5,000
To record transfer of half **B**'s partnership interest to **C**.		

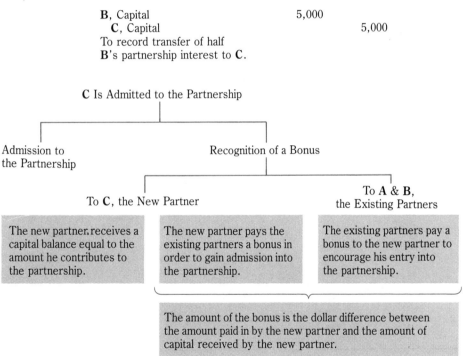

Figure 12-1 **Admission of a new partner**

Investment in the Partnership

Rather than purchase an existing partner's interest, the new partner could contribute cash and/or other assets in return for a partnership interest. This method differs from the purchase of an existing partner's interest; in this case, both the assets and equity of the partnership are increased. Assume the same data exist in the **A** and **B** balance sheet. Assume in this case that **C** contributes assets at their fair market value of $10,000 (referred to as *Other Assets* for illustrative purposes) to the partnership for a one-third interest in the partnership capital after his investment. This investment is recorded as follows:

Other Assets	10,000	
C, Capital		10,000
To record C's investment in the partnership.		

The **A**, **B** and **C** partnership balance sheet, following the investment, appears as follows:

Assets		Liabilities and Equity		
Cash	$ 5,000	Liabilities		$ 7,000
Other Assets				
($22,000 + $10,000)	32,000	A, Capital	$10,000	
		B, Capital	10,000	
		C, Capital	10,000	30,000
	$37,000			$37,000

Note that **C**'s $10,000 investment results in a $10,000 Capital balance; the total partnership capital amounts to $30,000, of which **C** has a one-third ownership interest.

C may receive more or less than a $10,000 Capital balance. Under some circumstances, a bonus may be given either to the new partner or to the existing partners. The admission of a new partner and the recognition of a bonus is shown in Figure 12-1.

Bonus to the New Partner

The partnership may want to add a new partner who can bring with him/her certain technical skills, management abilities, or some other desirable business strengths. To entice a desirable individual, a bonus may be offered in excess of the amount invested by the new partner. In this case, the existing partners allocate a portion of their capital to **C**.

Assume that **C** invests assets at their fair market value of $4,000 into the partnership for a one-third ownership interest. The new total capital amounts to $24,000; of this amount, $8,000 (one-third) belongs to **C**. The calculation of these amounts is illustrated below:

A, Capital	$10,000
B, Capital	10,000
Existing Capital	$20,000
Investment by C	4,000
Capital of New Partnership (a)	$24,000
C's Capital (a × ⅓)	$ 8,000

The new partner's bonus is recorded as follows:

Other Assets	4,000	
A, Capital	2,000	
B, Capital	2,000	
C, Capital		8,000

The $4,000-worth of assets invested by **C** results in an $8,000 Capital balance by reducing the capital of both **A** and **B**. In this journal entry, it is assumed that **A** and **B** share profits and losses equally; accordingly, they both have an equal $2,000 capital reduction.

The partnership balance sheet following the recording of **C**'s investment would appear as follows:

Assets		Liabilities and Equity		
Cash	$ 5,000	Liabilities		$ 7,000
Other Assets				
($22,000 + $4,000)	26,000	A, Capital	$8,000	
		B, Capital	8,000	
		C, Capital	8,000	24,000
	$31,000			$31,000

Note that the profit and loss sharing ratio is the same as the Capital balance ratio only if the partnership agreement fails to indicate a particular profit and loss sharing ratio, or if the partners have, in fact, agreed to share profits and losses according to their Capital balance ratio.

Bonus to Existing Partners

If the partnership business is particularly successful and profitable, the existing partners may require the new partner to pay them a bonus as an admission requirement. In this case, the new partner has less capital than his/her contribution of assets to the partnership; a portion of this contribution is allocated to existing partners. The calculation of this allocated amount follows.

Assume that **C** invests assets at their fair market value of $13,000 in the partnership for a one-third ownership interest. The new total capital amounts to $33,000; of this amount, $11,000 (one-third) belongs to **C**.

A, Capital	$10,000
B, Capital	10,000
Existing Capital	$20,000
Investment by C	13,000
Capital of New Partnership (a)	$33,000
C's Capital (a × ⅓)	$11,000

The bonus to existing partners is recorded as follows:

Other Assets	13,000	
A, Capital		1,000
B, Capital		1,000
C, Capital		11,000

The $13,000 invested by **C** results in an $11,000 Capital balance; the balance is allocated to **A** and **B** in their profit sharing ratio, which they are assumed to share equally. Accordingly, both **A** and **B** receive a $1,000 increase in each of their Capital balances as a result of **C**'s $13,000 investment in the partnership.

The partnership balance sheet, following the recording of **C**'s investment, would appear as follows:

Assets		Liabilities and Equity		
Cash	$ 5,000	Liabilities		$ 7,000
Other Assets				
($22,000 + $13,000)	35,000	A, Capital	$11,000	
		B, Capital	11,000	
		C, Capital	11,000	33,000
	$40,000			$40,000

Note that the profit and loss sharing ratio is the same as the Capital balance ratio only if the partnership agreement is silent on a particular profit and loss sharing ratio or the partners have in fact agreed to share profits and losses in the same ratio as their Capital balances.

D.   Withdrawal of an Existing Partner

The withdrawal of a partner can be accounted for as a sale to a new partner, as a sale to one or more of the existing partners, or through a payment of partnership assets to the withdrawing partner. The balance sheet below shows the **A**, **B**, and **C** partnership:

Assets		Liabilities and Equities		
Cash	$ 5,000	Liabilities		$ 7,000
Other Assets	32,000	**A**, Capital	$10,000	
		B, Capital	10,000	
		C, Capital	10,000	30,000
	$37,000			$37,000

Sale to a New Partner

This method is similar to the one discussed earlier of the purchase of an existing partner's interest to admit a new partner. One partner sells his/her interest to another person. There is no change in either the assets or the capital of the partnership as a result of this transaction. Payment for the ownership interest is a private transaction; of course, the existing partners must approve the new arrangement.

Sale to the Remaining Partners

An alternate method is for the withdrawing partner to sell his/her ownership interest to the remaining partner(s). This transaction is also private. The assets and the total equity of the partnership are not altered. An entry is made to record the change in the partnership books. If **C** wants to withdraw and **A** and **B** both purchase **C**'s interest, the following entry would be recorded:

C, Capital	10,000	
A, Capital		5,000
B, Capital		5,000
To record transfer of **C**'s partnership interest to **A** and **B**.		

Although more or less than $10,000 may have been paid personally by **A** and **B** to **C**, the record to transfer **C**'s ownership is based on the recorded balance.

Payment from Partnership Assets

A third method involves the withdrawing partner being paid the amount of his/her Capital balance. This causes no recording difficulties. If the payment is made in cash, the following entry would be prepared:

C, Capital	10,000	
Cash		10,000
To record **C**'s withdrawal from partnership.		

Usually, however, the withdrawing partner may receive either more or less than his/her recorded Capital balance. The difference can result from undervalued or overvalued partnership assets, anticipated future profitable operations in excess of normal return, or inter-personal difficulties. As a result, the partners calculate an agreed amount that is due to **C**; the difference is treated as a bonus to either the withdrawing partner or the remaining partners. That is, the Capital balances of the remaining partners absorb the difference in the remaining partners' profit and loss sharing ratio. In this case, the two remaining partners are assumed to share the difference equally.

If **C** is paid $2,000 more than his Capital balance, the Capital balances of both **A** and **B** would each be reduced by $1,000.

C, Capital	10,000	
A, Capital	1,000	
B, Capital	1,000	
Cash		12,000

To record **C**'s withdrawal from the partnership.

C, therefore, receives a total of $12,000, represented by the $10,000 Capital balance and a bonus of $2,000, which is paid equally by **A** and **B**.

If **C** is paid $3,000 less than his Capital balance, the Capital balances of both **A** and **B** would be increased by $1,500.

C, Capital	10,000	
A, Capital		1,500
B, Capital		1,500
Cash		7,000

To record **C**'s withdrawal from the partnership.

C receives $7,000 in cash; the $3,000 difference, shared equally by **A** and **B**, increases their Capital balances.

An alternate method of calculating the payment from partnership assets involves an appraisal of partnership assets and the recording of adjustments to Capital balances in the partners' profit and loss sharing ratio. The withdrawing partner is paid the amount of his/her adjusted Capital balance. The recording of appraisal values is not in accordance with generally accepted accounting principles; GAAP's historical cost concept requires that assets be recorded at their historical cost. Therefore, although the withdrawing partner can have a revalued Capital balance resulting from changed asset values, total partnership assets cannot be revalued.

On the death of a partner, the partnership business may be continued under a new partnership agreement; settlement of the deceased partner's ownership interest is made in accordance with provisions in the partnership agreement.

E. Liquidation of a Partnership

Liquidation
Closure of an entity through sale of the assets, payment of creditors, and distribution of remaining cash to owners.

The **liquidation** of a partnership results in a termination of the partnership business; its assets are sold, debts are paid, and any remaining cash (or unsold assets) is distributed to the partners in settlement of their Capital balances. The amount of cash available to partners is influenced by the sale of partnership assets at a gain or loss. The following partnership post-closing balance sheet at January 1, 19X4 illustrates the accounting for the liquidation of the **A**, **B**, and **C** partnership.

Assets		Liabilities and Equity		
Cash	$ 5,000	Accounts Payable		$ 7,000
Other Assets	32,000	**A**, Capital	$10,000	
		B, Capital	10,000	
		C, Capital	10,000	30,000
	$37,000			$37,000

For purposes of this section, profits and losses are assumed to be shared in a ratio of 5 : 3 : 2.

Gains on Sale of Assets

Each partner's share of gains realized on the sale of assets is recorded as an increase in his/her Capital account. If other assets are sold for $42,000, the following entry is prepared to record the gain.

Cash	42,000	
Gain on Realization of Assets		10,000
Other Assets		32,000
To record the gain on sale of other assets.		

The $10,000 gain is then divided among the partners in their 5 : 3 :2 profit and loss sharing ratio.

Gain on Realization of Assets	10,000	
A, Capital		5,000
B, Capital		3,000
C, Capital		2,000
To record the division of the gain from sale of other assets.		

The liabilities are then paid; the journal entry to record the payment follows.

Accounts Payable	7,000	
Cash		7,000
To record payment of liabilities.		

At this point, the partnership balances would appear as shown next.

Assets		*Equities*	
Cash	$40,000	**A**, Capital	$15,000
		B, Capital	13,000
		C, Capital	12,000
	$40,000		$40,000

The following entry is prepared to record payment of the three Capital account balances:

A, Capital	15,000	
B, Capital	13,000	
C, Capital	12,000	
Cash		40,000
To record payment of Capital accounts.		

Note that all Capital account balances are zero, following the distribution of cash.

Loss on Sale of Assets

Realization
Conversion of assets to cash.

In this case, losses resulting from the **realization** of assets — their conversion to cash — are also allocated to partners in their profit and loss sharing ratio. The discussion that follows deals with the situation in which each partner's Capital balance is sufficient to absorb his/her share of the loss. The subsequent discussion covers the situation in which one of the partner's Capital balance is insufficient to absorb his/her share of the loss.

Adequate Amount of Capital Balances

Assume that the sale of the $32,000-worth of other assets in the example given earlier realizes only $22,000. The following entry records the sale:

Cash	22,000	
Loss on Realization of Assets	10,000	
Other Assets		32,000
To record loss on sale of assets.		

The $10,000 loss is then allocated to each partner in accordance with the 5 : 3 :2 profit and loss sharing ratio.

A, Capital	5,000	
B, Capital	3,000	
C, Capital	2,000	
Loss on Realization of Assets		10,000
To record the division of loss from sale of assets.		

The payment of liabilities is then recorded.

Accounts Payable	7,000	
Cash		7,000
To record payment of accounts payable.		

The partnership balances are next calculated.

Assets		*Equities*	
Cash	$20,000	**A**, Capital	$ 5,000
		B, Capital	7,000
		C, Capital	8,000
	$20,000		$20,000

The following entry records the distribution of cash to the partners:

A, Capital	5,000	
B, Capital	7,000	
C, Capital	8,000	
Cash		20,000
To record payment of		
Capital accounts.		

Note that the balance in each Capital account is zero following the distribution of cash.

Inadequate Amount of Capital Balances

Partnership assets may have to be sold at a considerable loss, resulting in a debit balance in one partner's account following allocation of the loss. Assume that sale of the previous $32,000-worth of other assets realizes only $8,000. The following entry records the sale:

Cash	8,000	
Loss on Realization of Assets	24,000	
Other Assets		32,000
To record loss on sale of assets.		

This $24,000 loss is next allocated to each partner in accordance with the 5 : 3 : 2 profit and loss sharing ratio.

A, Capital	12,000	
B, Capital	7,200	
C, Capital	4,800	
Loss on Realization of Assets		24,000
To record the division of loss		
from sale of assets.		

The payment of liabilities is then recorded.

Accounts Payable	7,000	
Cash		7,000
To record payment of accounts payable.		

The partnership balances now appear as follows:

Assets		*Equities*	
Cash	$6,000	A, Capital	$(2,000)
		B, Capital	2,800
		C, Capital	5,200
	$6,000		$6,000

As can be seen, **A** has a debit balance in his Capital account. **A** would be expected to contribute $2,000 cash to the partnership to make up this debit balance. If **A** does not contribute this amount, then this $2,000 debit balance is allocated to the remaining partners in their agreed profit and loss sharing ratio, in this case 3 : 2. The following entry illustrates the allocation of **A**'s debit balance to **B** and **C**.

B, Capital	1,200	
C, Capital	800	
A, Capital		2,000
To record allocation of A's debit balance.		

At this point, the partnership balances are:

Assets		*Equities*	
Cash	$6,000	B, Capital	$1,600
		C, Capital	4,400
	$6,000		$6,000

The distribution of cash to **B** and **C** would be recorded by the following entry.

B, Capital	1,600	
C, Capital	4,400	
Cash		6,000
To record payment of Capital accounts.		

Liquidation Statement

A liquidation statement can be prepared to show the progress of the liquidation over a period of time. The data involving the sale of $32,000-worth of other assets for $8,000, allocation of loss to the partners, payment of liabilities, allocation of **A**'s debit balance to **B** and **C**, and final distribution of cash, are summarized in the following statement.

A, B, and C
Statement of Partnership Liquidation
For the Month of January, 19X3

	Cash	Other Assets	Liabilities	A	B	C
Balance (Jan. 1)	$5,000	$32,000	$7,000	$10,000	$10,000	$10,000
Sale of Other Assets	8,000	(32,000)				
Allocation of Loss ($24,000)				(12,000)	(7,200)	(4,800)
	$13,000	-0-	$7,000	($ 2,000)	$ 2,800	$ 5,200
Payment of Liabilities	(7,000)		(7,000)			
	$ 6,000		-0-			
Allocation of **A**'s Debit Balance				2,000		
B: 3/5 × $2,000					(1,200)	
C: 2/5 × $2,000						(800)
				-0-	$ 1,600	$ 4,400
Distribution of Cash	(6,000)				(1,600)	(4,400)
	-0-				-0-	-0-

Garner v. *Murray* **Rule**

Garner v. Murray rule
Derived from an English legal case which ruled that a deficiency in a partners' Capital account must be allocated to the other partners in the ratio of their Capital accounts immediately before the date of liquidation.

A profit and loss sharing ratio was specified in the partnership agreement of **A**, **B**, and **C**. Therefore, the debit Capital balance of **A** could be allocated to **B** and **C** in an agreed manner. If the partnership agreement did not specify such a ratio, then the ***Garner* v. *Murray* rule**, from a 1904 United Kingdom law case, might be applied. According to this case (which may not be applicable in Canada today), the debit balance in one partner's Capital account would be allocated to the remaining partners in the ratio of their Capital accounts immediately before the date of liquidation. It may be assumed for problem solving in this text that the debit balance would be allocated in the profit and loss sharing ratio.

Discussion Questions

1. Identify and briefly explain five unique characteristics of a partnership.
2. What are the advantages and disadvantages of a partnership?
3. How does accounting for a partnership differ from that for a corporation?
4. How are partnership profits and losses divided among partners?
5. Why are salary and interest allocations included in the division of profits and losses?
6. How are partners' Capital balances disclosed in the balance sheet?

7. What is a partnership bonus? How is it calculated when a new partner is admitted?
8. Distinguish between the sale of a withdrawing partner's interest to a new partner and its sale to his/her existing partner(s).
9. Explain how a debit balance in one partner's Capital account is handled if that partner is unable to contribute additional assets to cover the debit balance.
10. How does the *Garner* v. *Murray* rule require a debit balance to be handled when that partner is unable to make up the amount?

Discussion Case

Discussion Case 12-1:   To Incorporate or Not?

Adam, Porter, and Ida Clark own and operate as partners a family business known as Clarks' Raiders. Along with ten employees and equipment valued at about $200,000, they travel the carnival and rural fair circuit each summer with a crowd-thrilling automobile stunt show. Business is seasonal, and each of the three owns a home in the Maritimes, where the families are located permanently. The partners feel that they could double the amount of annual revenue with the addition of more equipment and the hiring and training of two or three more drivers. Ida and Porter are in favour of such action, but Adam is hesitant. He points out that twice during the past season, a car ran into a section of bleachers, causing damages amounting to thousands of dollars; it was fortunate that the costs did not run into the hundreds of thousands. He has heard something about limited liability of the corporate form of business but really doesn't understand what it would mean to Clarks' Raiders. All three partners agree to seek your advice.

For Discussion: Using this partnership, what are some advantages and disadvantages of changing to the corporate form of business?

Comprehension Problems

Comprehension Problem 12-1

You are given the following data for the partnership of B. B. Smith and C. Clearwater.

B. B. Smith and C. Clearwater
Trial Balance
December 31, 19X4

Cash	$ 41,000	
Accounts Receivable	68,400	
Inventory (Jan. 1, 19X4)	22,500	
Accounts Payable		$ 45,800
B. B. Smith, Capital		30,000
B. B. Smith, Drawings	7,000	
C. Clearwater, Capital		20,000
C. Clearwater, Drawings	5,000	
Sales		322,000
Purchases	168,000	
Purchases Returns & Allowances		3,000
Rent Expense	36,000	
Advertising Expense	27,200	
Delivery Expense	9,600	
Office Expense	12,800	
Other Store Expense	23,300	
	$420,800	$420,800

Inventory at December 31, 19X4, amounted to $27,000. Each partner had added $10,000 capital during the year; the opening credit balance in each capital account had been Smith $20,000 and Clearwater $10,000. The partners share profits and losses equally.

Required:
1. Prepare closing entries at year-end, omitting explanation lines.
2. Prepare an income statement for the year.
3. Prepare a statement of partners' capital for the year.

Statement of Partners' Capital
For the Year Ended December 31, 19X4

	Smith	Clear-water	Total
Capital Balance, January 1	$	$	$
Add: Investments during 19X4			
Net Income for the Year			
	$	$	$
Deduct: Drawings			
Capital Balance, December 31	$	$	$

Comprehension Problem 12-2

A partnership of **R**, **S**, and **T** has sold all of its assets and paid out all of its cash to its creditors. There are no cash or other assets remaining in the partnership. The following liability and capital balances remain. (Figures shown in parentheses reflect the partners' profit and loss sharing percentage.)

Liabilities and Partners' Equity

Liabilities	$21,000 Cr.
R, Capital (40%)	66,000 Dr.
S, Capital (20%)	20,000 Cr.
T, Capital (40%)	25,000 Cr.

Required: (Treat 1 and 2 independently of each other.)
1. Assuming all partners are personally bankrupt, briefly explain what the creditors of the partnership may do.
2. Assume the following information regarding the personal solvency of the partners:

	Assets	Liabilities
R	$ 6,000	$28,000
S	38,000	14,000
T	7,000	8,000

Indicate the course of action that you expect the creditors to take, given the above circumstances.

Comprehension Problem 12-3

The following balance sheet is for the partnership of Allan, Billie, and Carrie.

Allan, Billie and Carrie
Balance Sheet
At November 1, 19X2

Assets		*Liabilities and Partners' Equity*	
Cash	$ 20,000	Liabilities	$ 50,000
Other Assets	180,000	Allan, Capital (40%)	37,000
		Billie, Capital (40%)	65,000
		Carrie, Capital (20%)	48,000
	$200,000		$200,000

Figures shown parenthetically reflect agreed profit and loss sharing percentages. The partnership is dissolved and liquidated by selling the other assets for $100,000 and paying off the creditors.

Required: The partners are unclear as to how to divide the proceeds of liquidation. You have been handling the accounting for the partnership, so they ask you to prepare the schedule of partnership liquidation (use the format shown in section E of the chapter).

Statement of Partnership Liquidation
For the Month of November, 19X2

	Cash	Other Assets	Liabilities	Allan	Billie	Carrie
Balance, Nov. 1, 19X2	$	$	$	$	$	$
Sale of Other Assets Allocation of Loss ($)						
	$	-0-	$	$	$	$
Payment of Liabilities	( )		( )			
	$		-0-			
Distribution of Cash	( )			( )	( )	( )
	-0-			-0-	-0-	-0-

Problems

Problem 12-1

On January 1, 19X3, XYZ partnership had Capital balances of $60,000, $100,000 and $20,000 for **X**, **Y**, and **Z** respectively. In 19X3 the partnership reported net income of $40,000. None of the partners withdrew any assets in 19X3. The partnership agreed to share profits and losses as follows:

a. A monthly salary allowance of $2,000, $2,500, and $4,000 to **X**, **Y**, and **Z** respectively.
b. An annual interest allowance of 10 percent to each partner based on his/her capital balance at the beginning of the year.
c. Any remaining balance to be shared in a 5 : 3 : 2 ratio (X : Y : Z).

Required:
1. Using the form from section B of the chapter, prepare a schedule to allocate the 19X3 net income to partners.
2. Assume all the income statement accounts for 19X3 have been closed to the Income Summary account. Prepare the entry to record the division of the 19X3 net income.

	X	Y	Z	Total
Amount of Profit to be Allocated to Partners				$
Interest Allocation				
X:$ x %	$			
Y:$ x %		$		
Z:$ x %			$	
Balance				$
Salary Allocation				
Balance				$
Balance Allocated in Profit and Loss Sharing Ratio				
X:$ x				
Y:$ x				
Z:$ x			$	
Balance				-0-
Allocated to Partners	$	$	$	

Problem 12-2

X and **Y** have decided to establish a partnership in a local mall. They are evaluating two plans for a profit and loss sharing agreement:

Plan A **X** to receive a salary of $15,000 per year, the balance to be divided in their Capital balance ratios of $50,000 for **X** and $100,000 for **Y**.

Plan B **X** to receive a salary of $1,000 per month, 8 percent per year interest each on their investments and the balance equally.

Required: Calculate the division under each plan in the following schedule, assuming: (a) a profit of $60,000 per year, and (b) a loss of $30,000 per year.

Profit and Loss Sharing Plan	Division with Profit of $60,000		Division with Loss of $30,000	
	X	Y	X	Y
Plan A:				
Salary				
Balance				
Plan B				
Salary				
Interest				
Balance				

Problem 12-3

G, **H**, and **F** are partners, sharing profits equally. They decide to admit **Q** for an equal partnership with one-quarter of the total capital. The balances of the partners' Capital accounts are:

G, Capital	$30,000
H, Capital	26,000
F, Capital	19,000
	$75,000

Required: Prepare journal entries to record admission of **Q**, using the bonus method:
1. Assuming the bonus is paid to the new partner; **Q** invests $15,000.
2. Assuming the bonus is paid to existing partners; **Q** invests $45,000.

Problem 12-4

The **A**, **B**, and **C** partnership, the balance sheet for which is shown below, has decided to liquidate. The general ledger shows the following balances on March 1, 19X3:

Cash	$ 10,000
Other Assets	125,000
Accounts Payable	10,000
A, Capital	25,000
B, Capital	37,500
C, Capital	62,500

Proceeds from the sale of non-cash assets during March were $42,500.

Required: Prepare a statement of partnership liquidation. Net income and losses are shared equally; the partners have no other assets.

Alternate Problems

Alternate Problem 12-1

Partners **A** and **B** are subject to the following agreement for the sharing of profits/losses:
a. Annual salaries are allowed — $12,000 to **A**, $14,000 to **B**.
b. Interest at 10 percent is allowed on original capital contributions of $100,000 from **A**, and $70,000 from **B**.
c. Any remainder is to be split in the ratio of 3 : 2.

Required: How much net income must be earned by the partnership for **A** to be allocated a total of $47,000? (Use the form from section B of the chapter.)

Alternate Problem 12-2

Meyer and Roberts have decided to open a business partnership. Meyer is familiar with the business and is expected to spend a good deal of time running it. Roberts, on the other hand, will be the "financial" person of the partnership. They have the ramifications of changes in the net income under discussion. The following plans for sharing profits and losses are being considered:

Plan A   Salary with balance equally: Meyer's salary $10,000 per year, Roberts's nil.
Plan B   Salary, interest on investment and balance equally: Meyer $10,000 salary, Roberts nil, both to receive 10 percent per year on beginning investment. Beginning investments: Meyer $50,000, Roberts $200,000.

Required: Calculate the division under each plan (using form in Problem 12-2), assuming: (a) a profit of $150,000, and (b) a loss of $25,000.

Alternate Problem 12-3

Crane and Davis are partners sharing profits and losses 60 percent and 40 percent respectively. On July 1, their interests in the firm are as follows: Crane $23,000, Davis $18,600. Hughes is admitted as a partner on the investment of $16,000.

Required: Record the investment by Hughes in journal form, assuming:
a. The new partner is given credit for the actual investment made.
b. The new partner is given a ⅓ interest, a bonus being given to Hughes.
c. The new partner is given a ¼ interest, a bonus being given to the existing partners.

Alternate Problem 12-4

A, B, C, and D have a partnership sharing profits 40 percent, 30 percent, 20 percent, and 10 percent respectively. Assume all partners are unable to contribute any amount to the partnership. The audited balance sheet is:

A, B, C, and D Partnership

Balance Sheet

At January 1, 19X3

Assets		*Liabilities and Partners' Equity*	
Cash	$ 4,000	Liabilities	$20,000
Non-current assets	54,000	A, Capital	4,000
		B, Capital	9,600
		C, Capital	18,400
		D, Capital	6,000
	$58,000		$58,000

The partnership is liquidated during the month of January 19X3, and the non-cash assets realize $26,000.

Required: Prepare a statement of partnership liquidation.

Decision Problems

Decision Problem 12-1

Kemp, Staub, and Thompson were partners in Tiger Sports. The partnership agreement provides that each partner shall receive an interest allowance of 9 percent of his/her Capital balances and a salary allowance as follows: Kemp $20,000; Staub $18,000; and Thompson $10,000. Thompson, who manages the stores in the off season, receives a bonus of 20 percent of the income in excess of $18,000 after partners' interest and salary allowances. The balance remaining is to be divided equally. The Capital balances at the beginning of the year were: Kemp—$120,000, Staub—$110,000, and Thompson—$170,000.

Required: Prepare
1. The journal entry to divide net income of $144,000.
2. The journal entry to divide net loss of $6,000.

Decision Problem 12-2

The post-closing trial balance for the Jones, Smith, and Scott Partnership at June 30, 19X3 contains the following items:

Cash	$10,800
Accounts Receivable	16,200
Notes Receivable	3,200
Merchandise Inventory	21,600
Prepaid Insurance	2,200
Equipment	35,200
Accumulated Depreciation—Equipment	8,200
Accounts Payable	10,260
Notes Payable	8,640
Wages Payable	2,700
Jones, Capital	23,760
Smith, Capital	23,760
Scott, Capital	11,880

On July 1, 19X3, the province issued a charter establishing the Jones, Smith and Scott Corporation authorized to issue 100 000 shares of share capital with a par-value of $20 a share.

Required:
1. Record on the books of the new corporation the following 19X3 transactions:

Jul. 2   The corporation took over all assets and liabilities of the Jones, Smith, and Scott Partnership. Prepare a journal entry to record the above asset and liability accounts and the issue of an appropriate number of shares at par to Jones, Smith, and Scott for the amount of their capital.

Jul. 3   Jones, Smith, and Scott invested $500,000 additional cash in the corporation and were issued (at par) 10 000, 10 000, and 5000 shares respectively.

Jul. 5   An additional 25 000 shares were issued at par to numerous individuals for cash.

Dec. 20   Jones, Smith, and Scott Corporation paid a $0.60 per share cash dividend.

2. Assume that in addition to the transactions in 1 above, Jones, Smith, and Scott Corporation had after-tax earnings of $262,180 in the fiscal year ended June 30, 19X4. Prepare the shareholders' equity section of the balance sheet at June 30, 19X4.

The Debt Financing Cycle

A corporation often incurs debt in order to finance its operations. Bond issue is an important source of long-term capital.

1. What are bonds, and what rights are attached to bond certificates?
2. What are the impacts of different financing methods on the earnings per share of common shareholders?
3. What are the advantages of debt financing for common shareholders? the disadvantages?
4. What types of bonds are available to satisfy various borrowing situations and investor preferences?
5. Why would investors pay a premium for a corporate bond? a discount?
6. How are bonds and related premiums or discounts disclosed on the balance sheet?
7. What accounting procedures are used by accountants to handle bonds?
8. How is the amortization of bond premiums recorded in the books? of bond discounts?
9. What is the effective interest method of amortization, and how does it differ from the straight-line method?
10. What is the purpose of a bond sinking fund?

A. The Decision to Issue Bonds

Bond
A debt security requiring the payment of a sum of money at some date in the future, together with periodic interest payments during the life of the bond.

Bond indenture
A legal document specifying the terms with which the issuing corporation will comply.

Trustee
An intermediary between a corporation issuing bonds and the bondholders.

Corporations acquire long-term capital through issue of shares and bonds. In Chapter 11, the acquisition of capital from share capital issues is discussed. This chapter discusses the acquisition of capital — that is, the financing of the corporation — through issues of bonds.

A **bond** is a debt security that requires a future payment of money, as well as periodic interest payments during its life. A contract called a **bond indenture** is prepared between the corporation and the future bondholders. It specifies the terms with which the corporation will comply. One of these terms may be a restriction on further borrowing by the corporation. A **trustee** is appointed to be an intermediary between the corporation and the bondholder.

Rights of Bondholders

Ownership of a bond certificate carries with it certain rights. These rights are printed on the actual certificate and vary among bond issues. The various characteristics applicable to bond issues are the subject of more advanced courses in finance and are not treated here. It is appropriate to point out, however, that individual bondholders always acquire two rights.

1. It is the right of the bondholder to receive the face value of the bond at a specified date in the future, referred to as the *maturity date*; and
2. It is the right of the bondholder to receive periodic interest payments, usually semi-annually, at a specified percent of the bond's face value.

Bond Authorization

Every corporation is legally required to follow a well-defined sequence in authorizing a bond issue. The bond issue is presented to the board of directors by management and must be approved by shareholders. Legal requirements must be complied with and disclosure is required in the financial statements of the corporation.

Shareholder approval is an important step because bondholders are creditors with a prior claim on the assets of the corporation if liquidation occurs. Further, dividend distributions may be restricted during the life of the bonds, for which shareholder acceptance is necessary. These restrictions are usually reported to the reader of financial statements through note disclosure.

Recording the Bond Authorization

Assuming that Bluebeard Computer Corporation decides to issue bonds amounting to $30 million to finance its expansion, the amount of authorized bonds, their interest rate, and their maturity date can be shown in the accounts as follows:

General Journal
Memorandum

19X1
Jan. 1   Authorized to issue $30,000,000 of 12%
3-year bonds due January 1, 19X4.

General Ledger
Bonds Payable
(Due January 1, 19X4)

19X1
Jan. 1   Authorized to issue $30,000,000 of 12%
3-year bonds, dated January 1. 19X1

> Different general ledger accounts are opened for each type of bond approved. The caption used for the bonds payable should generally indicate the type of bonds involved in the issue.

Bond Issues in the Financial Statements

Each bond issue is disclosed separately in the financial statements because each issue may have different characteristics. The descriptive information disclosed to readers of financial statements includes the interest rate and maturity date of the bond issue. Also disclosed in a note are any restrictions imposed on the corporation's activities in the bond indenture and the assets pledged, if any.

The Bond Financing Decision

Cash Required in the Immediate and the Foreseeable Future

Most bond issues are sold in their entirety when market conditions are favourable. However, more bonds can be authorized in a particular bond issue than will be immediately issued (sold). Authorized bonds, like authorized share capital, can be issued whenever cash is required. They do not have to be issued immediately.

Important Terms of the Bonds

The interest rate of the bonds, their maturity date, and other important provisions — such as converitibility into share capital and restrictions on future dividend distributions of the corporation — are also considered. The success of a bond issue often depends on the proper combination of these and other similar features.

Assets of the Corporation to Be Pledged

The pledging of mortgageable assets is an important consideration for bondholders because it safeguards their investment. It is important to the corporation because the pledging of all these assets may restrict future borrowings. The total amount of authorized bonds is usually a fraction of the mortgageable assets, for example, 50 percent. The difference is the margin of safety to bondholders, since it permits the proceeds from the sale of these assets to shrink substantially but still permit reimbursement of bondholders should the need arise.

Other Methods of Raising Cash

Various alternate methods of raising cash, such as issues of common or preferred stock, are also reviewed by management in order to distinguish them from issuing bonds.

There are many factors influencing management in its choice between the issue of bonds and the issue of share capital. One of the most important considerations is the potential effect of each of these financing methods on the present owners of the corporation, that is, the common shareholders. How would their earnings per share be affected?

Consider the example of Bluebeard Computer Corporation, which has 100 000 common shares outstanding, is a growth company, and is profitable. BCC requires $30 million in cash to finance its seventh new plant, complete with new equipment. Management is currently reviewing three financing options:

1. Issue 12-percent bonds, due in three years
2. Issue 8-percent preferred stock.
3. Issue an additional 200 000 shares of common stock.

Erecting a new plant and placing it in operation should result in a net income of $6 million before interest financing expenses, if any, and income taxes (assumed to be 50 percent of net income and calculated after the deduction of interest expenses from net income).

Management has prepared the following analysis to compare and evaluate each financing option. Study the details of this schedule and consider which plan is most attractive to the common shareholders.

	Plan 1: Issue Bonds	Plan 2: Issue Preferred Shares	Plan 3: Issue Common Shares
Net Income before Interest and Income Taxes	$6,000,000	$6,000,000	$6,000,000
Less:			
Bond Interest Expense	3,600,000	-0-	-0-
Earnings before Taxes	$2,400,000	$6,000,000	$6,000,000
Less:			
Income Tax at 50 percent	1,200,000	3,000,000	3,000,000
	$1,200,000	$3,000,000	$3,000,000
Less:			
Preferred Dividends at 8 percent	-0-	2,400,000	-0-
Net Available to Common Shareholders	$1,200,000	$ 600,000	$3,000,000
Number of Common Shares Outstanding	100,000	100,000	300,000
Earnings per Share on Each Common Stock	$12	$6	$10

On Study, it becomes clear that Plan 1, the issue of bonds, has several advantages for existing common shareholders.

Advantage 1: Earnings per Share

Earnings per share
A dollar amount calculated by dividing income available to common shareholders by the number of common shares outstanding.

If the additional long-term financing were acquired through the issue of bonds (Plan 1), the corporate **earnings per share** (EPS) on each common share would be $12. This EPS is greater than the EPS earned through financing with either preferred or additional common shares. On this basis alone, the issue of bonds is more financially attractive to existing common shareholders. However, there are other notable advantages to long-term financing with bonds.

Real Life Example 13-1

Assessing Corporate Capital Needs

The first step in determining how much capital a company needs and how it should be raised begins with the business plan. . . . A business plan forces managers to examine questions of growth and capital requirements. Drawing up pro formas makes obvious how much money the company will need to meet its goals.

Management then needs to ask whether the company can generate the capital needed from internal sources. It is usually preferable to reinvest excess cash than give up owners' equity or saddle the firm with more debt.

If the company cannot internally generate enough funds, management should ask if it should reduce its goals and thus eliminate the need for external financing. Does management want the company to grow so quickly that it will need outside funding — and its burdens?

If the answer is yes, management must address these questions:
1) How much capital is needed?
2) When is it needed?
3) What will the company do if it cannot raise the funds? It is foolhardy to make the commitments required for growth and then find out the capital to fulfil them can't be raised. Plan ahead for contingencies.
4) Who in the company will manage the program? It is important to assign responsibilities early on and to establish a timetable.
5) Will the company require outside help to raise the funds? Typically, any major effort will involve auditors and counsel.
6) How much management time and corporate cash will a successful capital raising program require? Will the drain on either

Advantage 2:   Control of the Corporation

Bondholders have no vote in the corporation. If common shares were issued there might be a loss of management control by existing shareholders because corporate ownership would be distributed over a larger number of shareholders. In the BCC case, outstanding common shares would increase from 100 000 to 300 000 shares.

Advantage 3:   Income Tax Expenses

Interest financing expenses are deductible for income tax purposes. Dividend payments are distributions of retained earnings and are not deducted from net income and are not deductible for tax purposes. With a 50 percent income tax rate, the after-tax interest expense to the corporation is only 6 percent (12% $\times$ 50%). By contrast, dividends to preferred shareholders would be 8 percent and would not be tax deductible.

Advantage 4:   The Impact of Inflation

The corporation would receive $30 million with today's purchasing power. If the purchasing power of the dollar declines in three years, the $30 million borrowed would be repaid in dollars with a considerably lower purchasing power; an unrecognized gain thereby would accrue to the common shareholders.

Bond Financing Disadvantages

There are also some disadvantages in long-term financing with bonds that must be carefully reviewed by management and the board of directors. The most serious disadvantage is the possibility that the corporation might earn less than $6 million before interest expense and income taxes. The bond interest expense is a fixed amount. If net income were to fall below the $3,600,000 annual interest expense, one of the other plans might become more advantageous.

Another disadvantage is the fact that bonds have to be repaid at maturity, whether or not the corporation is financially able to do so, while shares do not have to be repaid.

Since the securities market and corporate net earnings remain uncertain, there is no mathematical formula to solve this financial problem. The financing decision requires sound judgement, based on past experiences and projected future needs.

resource be excessive? Management tasks may have to be restructured to compensate for the new demands of the financing program.

7) Will the company's business plan be good enough to convince capital sources of the company's need and its ability to fulfil whatever commitments will be required?

Debt, Equity, or Other?

Every type of financing has its advantages and disadvantages. Debt means a drain on cash flow to meet interest payments. What's more, depending on the type of debt, assets may have to be pledged as security, the lender may impose other restrictive covenants on the firm, sinking funds may have to be established and paid into, and more.

Equity, on the other hand, generally will not drain cash flow. But equity can represent a permanent forfeiture of ownership of at least part of the company. Avoiding equity give-up is often an over-riding concern of owner/managers. Some sales of equity, however, can contain buy-back provisions. Used primarily in venture capital financings, this structure gives man-

agers the opportunity to buy back some of the equity sold to venture capitalists if the company meets or exceeds some pre-determined performance criteria.

What about the other financing forms? These are the so-called off-balance-sheet techniques. Off-balance-sheet capital is often preferable to any other form because its position — off the balance sheet — does not affect either the debt or equity ratios of the company. But off-balance-sheet financing typically applies to a limited number of special situations. Moreover, it requires extensive legal and accounting expertise that may make it expensive to structure.

After carefully analyzing the pluses and minuses of each financing alternative, management should be able to decide which type it prefers. Then, the question is: Is it feasible?

Here, the advice of the firm's auditors, lawyers, and/or consultants is beneficial. Management, however, can do some of its own homework. To determine whether additional debt or equity is even a possibility, management can examine the financials of other, comparable firms.

Source *Inc. Magazine*, December 1984, pp. 193–194.

B.   Bond Characteristics and Terminology

Students sometimes encounter difficulty with the new terminology involved in accounting for bonds. Three main types of bond terminology can be identified. These are shown in Figure 13-1 and are discussed next.

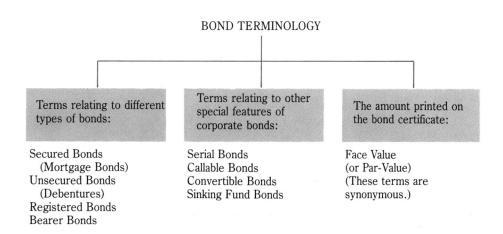

Figure 13-1   Different categories of bond terminology

Classification of Bonds

Each corporation issuing bonds has unique financing needs and attempts to satisfy various borrowing situations and investor preferences. Many types of bonds have been created to meet these varying needs. Some of the common types are described here.

Bonds Can Be Secured or Unsecured

Secured bonds are backed by mortgageable assets of the corporation. These mortgageable assets are pledged as security for the bonds, and these secured bonds are consequently referred to as *mortgage bonds*.

Unsecured bondholders are ordinary creditors of the corporation and **unsecured bonds** are secured only by the future financial success of the corporation. Such bonds are commonly referred to as *debentures*. These debenture bonds usually command a higher interest rate because of the added risk for investors.

Bonds Can Be Registered or Bearer Bonds

Registered bonds require the name and address of the owner to be recorded by the corporation or its trustee.

The title to bearer bonds passes on delivery of the bonds. Payment of interest is made when the bearer clips coupons attached to the bond and presents them to the bank.

Special Features of Bonds

Special features can be attached to bonds in order to make them more attractive to investors, as discussed next.

Varying Maturity Dates

When **serial bonds** are issued, the bonds **mature** on different dates, as indicated on the bond contract. Investors are able to choose bonds with a term that agrees with their investment plans. For example, in a $30 million serial bond issue, $10 million-worth of the bonds may mature each year for three years.

The issue of bonds with a **call provision** permits the issuing corporation to redeem, or call, the bonds before their maturity date. The bond indenture usually indicates the price at which bonds are callable. Borrowers are thereby protected in the event that market interest rates decline below the bond contract interest rate. In such an event, the higher interest rate bonds can be called to be replaced by bonds bearing a lower interest rate.

Conversion Privilege

Bonds with a conversion privilege are called **converitble bonds**; they allow the bondholder to exchange his/her bonds for a specified amount of the corporation's share capital. This feature permits the bondholder to enjoy the security of being a creditor, while having the option of becoming a shareholder if the corporation is successful.

Sinking Fund Requirement

The corporation is required to deposit funds at regular intervals, usually with a trustee, when **sinking fund** bonds are issued. This feature ensures the availability of adequate cash for the redemption of the bonds at maturity.

Secured bonds
A bond issue backed by mortgageable assets of the corporation; also referred to as *mortgage bonds*.

Unsecured bonds
A bond issue backed by the future financial success of the corporation; also referred to as *debentures*.

Serial bond
A bond issue with a special feature whereby parts of the bond issue mature on one date and other parts mature on other dates.

Maturity date
The date specified for repayment.

Call provision
A bond feature that permits the early redemption of the bond at a specified price, usually above face value.

Convertible bond
A bond that may be exchanged for common stock under certain specified conditions.

Sinking fund
A special fund into which assets are transferred in order to pay bonds at their maturity date; the fund is called 'sinking' because the transferred assets are tied up or "sunk," and cannot be used for any purpose other than the redemption of the bonds.

Restriction of Dividends

The corporation issuing bonds is required to restrict its retained earnings, thereby limiting the amount of dividends that can be paid from assets represented by retained earnings. The creation of such a restriction is discussed in Chapter 10.

In the final analysis, a bond is only as good as the quality of the assets pledged, if any, as its security and the bond interest rate. The other provisions in a bond contract are of limited or no value if the issuing corporation is in financial difficulties. A corporation in such difficulties may not be able to sell its bonds, regardless of the attractive provisions attached to them.

Face Value

Face value (of bonds) The amount to be paid at the maturity date of a bond, which is printed on a bond certificate; also referred to as *par-value* of the bond.

Bond premium The excess of the amount received by the issuer over the face value of the bond; usually results when the bond interest rate is higher than the market interest rate.

Bond discount The excess of the face value of a bond over the amount received by the issuer; usually results when the bond interest rate is lower than the market interest rate.

Market interest rate The percentage per time period paid on the open market for the use of money.

Each bond has an amount printed on the face of the bond certificate. This is called the **face value** of the bond; it is also commonly referred to as the *par-value* of the bond. When the cash received is the same as a bond's face value, the bond is said to be issued *at par*. A common face value of bonds is $1,000, although bonds of other denominations exist. A sale of a $1,000 bond for $1,000 bond for $1,000 is referred to as a sale at its par-value. A $1,000 bond is sold at a **premium** when it is sold for more than its face value. If the bond is sold for less than $1,000, then the bond has been sold at a **discount**.

With a face value of $1,000, a $30 million bond issue can be divided into 30 000 bonds. This number permits a large number of individuals and institutions to participate in corporate financing. As pointed out earlier, the opportunity to raise large amounts of capital is one of the important advantages of the corporate form of organization.

Interest paid to bondholders is *always* calculated on the face value of the bond — the contract amount — regardless of whether the bonds are issued at par, at a premium, or at a discount. For example, a $1,000 bond with a contract interest rate of 12 percent pays the following total annual interest:

$$\$1,000 \times 12\% = \$120 \text{ annual interest.}$$

This interest is usually paid semi-annually, that is, $60 every six months.

Why would investors pay a premium for a corporate bond? Why would a corporation sell its bonds at a discount? The answer to these questions lies in the relationship between the bond contract interest rate and the prevailing **market interest rate**. Figure 13-2 illustrates the relationship between the bond contract interest rate and the prevailing market interest rate.

> If the bond contract interest rate is the same as the prevailing market interest rate, *the bond will sell at par*, other things being equal.
>
> If the bond interest rate is higher than the prevailing market interest rate, *the bond will sell at a premium*, other things being equal.
>
> If the bond interest rate is lower than the prevailing market interest rate, *the bond will sell at a discount*, other things being equal.

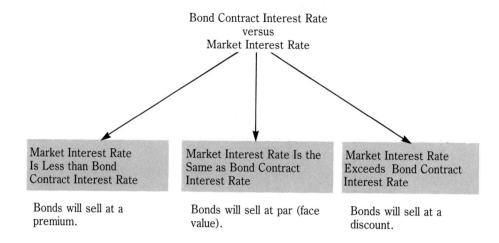

Figure 13-2   Relationship between bond contract interest rate and market interest rate

The amortization of bond premium or discount can be made by the straight-line method or by the effective interest method. These are discussed in sections C and D of this chapter, respectively.

Balance Sheet Presentation

Bonds payable are classified as long-term liabilities for disclosure on the balance sheet.

LONG-TERM LIABILITIES:

Bonds Payable
Authorized — $30,000,000, 12%, Due 19X4
Issued — $100,000

When the bonds become payable within one year from the balance sheet date, then they are classified on the balance sheet as a current liability (*CICA Handbook*, section 3210.03).

The balance of unamortized discount can be classified as a deferred charge on the assets' side of the balance sheet (*CICA Handbook*, section 3070.02). The balance of unamortized premium can be shown as a deferred credit on the liabilities side of the balance sheet. The amount amortized during the year should also be disclosed on the financial statements.

Assets		*Liabilities*	
Deferred Charge		Deferred Credit	
Discount on Bonds	$12,000	Premium on Bonds	$6,000

An acceptable alternate method advocated in the United States results in the balance of unamortized premium being added to the bonds payable balance; unamortized discount is deducted from the balance of bonds payable. This method of balance sheet disclosure is illustrated below.

LONG-TERM LIABILITIES:			LONG-TERM LIABILITIES:	
Bonds Payable			Bonds Payable	
Authorized — $30,000,000,			Authorized — $30,000,000,	
12%, Due 19X4			12%, Due 19X4	
Issued —	$100,000		Issued —	$100,000
Less: Discount on Bonds	(12,000)		Add: Premium on Bonds	6,000
	$ 88,000			$106,000

The Price of a Bond

The actual price of a bond is determined by the present value of the future cash flows associated with the bond:

1. A single amount, the face value, to be paid at maturity
2. Semi-annual interest payments during the bond life.

These future cash flows are a future value; that is, they include an interest component. This interest component can be removed through a present value (as distinguished from a future value) calculation. The price of a bond is this present value of all future cash flows resulting from that bond.

A further discussion of the time value of money, usually referred to as interest, and the method of present value calculations are further discussed in the Appendix of this chapter. Sections C and D focus on the accounting for bonds.

C. The Bond Accounting Process

Bond accounting often appears complex to students. They may be daunted by the interplay of several different variables, such as the issue of bonds between interest dates, interest dates that do not coincide with the year-end of the corporation, and the calculation of bond premiums or discounts.

Authorized bonds are issued by a corporation as cash is required. Their issue price is usually stated as a percentage of face value. An issue at 100 means 100 percent of face value; an issue at 106 means 106 percent of face value; and an issue at 88 means 88 percent of face value. Regardless of the issue price, interest is always paid as a percent as of face value. Assume that Bluebeard Computer Corporation issues 100 3-year, $1,000 bonds on January 1, 19X1; maturity date is January 1, 19X4; interest is paid each June 30 and December 31; year-end is December 31.

The Selling Price of Bonds

The bond issue proceeds include the selling price of the bonds and accrued interest, if applicable. The selling price is determined by a number of factors, including how investors view the bond contract interest rate in relation to the prevailing market interest rate.

If the bond contract interest rate is the same as that required in the market, then the bonds are usually issued at par.

If the bond contract interest rate is greater than that required in the market, then the bonds are usually sold at a premium (more than face value) to yield the investor the lower market rate.

If the bond contract interest rate is less than that required in the market, then the bonds are usually sold at a discount (less than face value) to yield the investor the higher market rate.

Recording the Bond Issue:

Cash	100,000	
Bonds Payable		100,000

Recording the Bond Issue:

Cash	106,000	
Premium on Bonds		6,000
Bonds Payable		100,000

Recording the Bond Issue:

Cash	88,000	
Discount on Bonds	12,000	
Bonds Payable		100,000

Amortizing Premiums and Discounts Using the Straight-Line Method

Where a bond premium or discount results from a bond issue, the amount of the premium or discount can be amortized in equal amounts over the life of the bond remaining from its date of sale, as shown in Figure 13-3. This method is in accordance with the straight-line method of recording of amortization. An alternate, more accurate method of amortization is discussed in section D of this chapter.

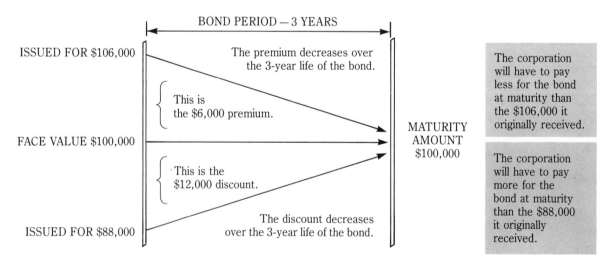

Figure 13-3 Straight-line amortization of bond premium or discount over the life of the bond issue

Interest on a Bond

Interest begins to accumulate from the previous interest payment date of the bond and is usually paid semi-annually, regardless of when the bond is actually sold. As noted earlier, interest paid to bondholders is *always* calculated on the face value of the bond, regardless of whether the bonds are issued at par, at a premium, or at a discount. For example, a $100,000 bond issue with an interest rate of 12 percent pays the following total annual interest:

$$\$100,000 \times 12\% = \$12,000 \text{ annual interest.}$$

This interest is usually paid semi-annually, that is, $6,000 every six months. Individual bondholders would receive $6,000 each semi-annually.

In this text, is recommended that bond premium and discount be amortized each time bond interest expense is recorded. The recording of amortization emphasizes that it is an adjustment of bond interest expense. The interest payments for the first year of BCC's $100,000 bond issue, together with the appropriate amortization entry are recorded below.

Payment of Interest:			*Amortization of Premium:*			*Amortization of Discount:*		
Jun. 30 Bond Interest Expense	6,000		Bond Premium	1,000		Bond Interest Expense	2,000	
Cash		6,000	Bond Interest Expense		1,000	Bond Discount		2,000
To record semi-annual bond interest.			To record amortization of bond premium.			To record amortization of bond discount.		
Dec. 31 Bond Interest Expense	6,000		Bond Premium	1,000		Bond Interest Expense	2,000	
Cash		6,000	Bond Interest Expense		1,000	Bond Discount		2,000
To record semi-annual bond interest.			To record amortization of bond premium.			To record amortization of bond discount.		

Similar entries are made each June 30 and December 31 until the bonds are retired in three years. The bond interest is entered in a separate Bond Interest Expense account, because it is usually a large amount. In this example, the interest payment date, December 31, is also the corporation's year-end. Therefore, no adjustment for interest expense is required at year-end. When the interest payment date does not coincide with the year-end, an adjusting journal entry is required at December 31 for the interest owing and any amortization required at that date. The credit part of the entry is made to Bond Interest Payable. At maturity, the bonds are retired by the payment of cash to bondholders.

19X4				
Jan. 1	Bonds Payable		100,000	
	Cash			100,000
	To record retirement of bonds.			

Remember that, before the bonds are retired, the final interest payment and applicable amortization has to be recorded.

Amortization

The amortization is made over the remaining life of the bonds from the date of sale. If the bonds are sold on January 1, the amortization at June 30 is calculated as follows:

Amortization of a Premium:			*Amortization of a Discount:*	
Premium is	$6,000(a)		Discount is	$12,000(a)
Months left are	36(b)		Months left are	36(b)
Months amortized	6(c)		Months amortized	6(c)

Calculation:			*Calculation:*	
(a ÷ b) × c			(a ÷ b) × c	
($6,000 ÷ 36) × 6 =	$1,000		($12,000 ÷ 36) × 6 =	$ 2,000

Premium Amortization Adjusting Entry:

Bond Premium	X	
Bond Interest Expense		X

Discount Amortization Adjusting Entry:

Bond Interest Expense	X	
Bond Discount		X

Amortization of premium reduces bond interest expense.

Amortization of discount increases bond interest expense.

Note that the amortization of the premium requires a debit to Bond Premium in order to decrease the $6,000 premium balance. The credit is made to Bond Interest Expense and thereby reduces the $6,000 interest expense recorded.

The credit required to amortize Bond Discount results in a debit to Bond Interest Expense. The amortization represents, therefore, an additional interest expense over the 12 percent interest rate.

These ledger accounts illustrate this reduction.

These ledger accounts illustrate this increase.

Premium on Bonds		Bond Interest Expense	
	6,000	6,000	
1,000			1,000
1,000		6,000	
2,000	6,000		1,000
	4,000	12,000	2,000
		10,000	

Discount on Bonds		Bond Interest Expense	
12,000		6,000	
	2,000	2,000	
	2,000	6,000	
12,000	4,000	2,000	
8,000		16,000	

The premium is reduced each interest period by amortization.

Amortization of a bond premium results in a decrease of bond interest expense.

The discount is reduced each interest period by amortization.

Amortization of a bond discount results in an increase of bond interest expense.

How Is the Amortization of the Premium Recorded in the Books?

It is sound accounting practice to allocate part of the premium to each semi-annual interest payment period. The effect of amortizing the premium at each interest payment date during the three years is shown in Figure 13-4. Study the effect of premium amortization on interest expense.

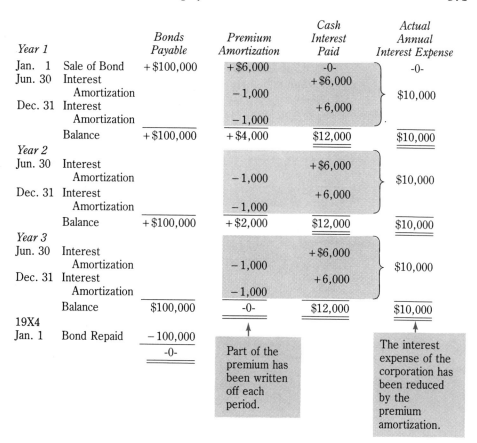

Year 1		Bonds Payable	Premium Amortization	Cash Interest Paid	Actual Annual Interest Expense
Jan. 1	Sale of Bond	+ $100,000	+ $6,000	-0-	-0-
Jun. 30	Interest			+ $6,000	
	Amortization		– 1,000		$10,000
Dec. 31	Interest			+ 6,000	
	Amortization		– 1,000		
	Balance	+ $100,000	+ $4,000	$12,000	$10,000
Year 2					
Jun. 30	Interest			+ $6,000	
	Amortization		– 1,000		$10,000
Dec. 31	Interest			+ 6,000	
	Amortization		– 1,000		
	Balance	+ $100,000	+ $2,000	$12,000	$10,000
Year 3					
Jun. 30	Interest			+ $6,000	
	Amortization		– 1,000		$10,000
Dec. 31	Interest			+ 6,000	
	Amortization		– 1,000		
	Balance	$100,000	-0-	$12,000	$10,000
19X4					
Jan. 1	Bond Repaid	– 100,000			
		-0-			

Part of the premium has been written off each period.

The interest expense of the corporation has been reduced by the premium amortization.

Figure 13-4   Effect of straight-line amortization of bond premium at each interest payment date

The total interest expense over the life of the bonds consists of $36,000 of interest less the $6,000 amortization of premium. The $6,000 premium received when the bond was sold represents a reduction of the corporation's bond interest expense during each year of the bond's life. Interest actually paid to bondholders is $36,000. The interest expense to BCC is $30,000. This decrease of $6,000 results from the favourable bond interest rate in relation to the prevailing market interest rate. In other words, receiving $106,000 on January 1, 19X1 is to the corporation's benefit as it only has to repay $100,000 on January 1, 19X4. This benefit is reflected in a reduced net annual interest expense during the life of the bonds.

Therefore, accountants record the decrease in bond interest expense as an amortization of the premium. The interest expense of $10,000 is therefore lower than the 12 percent bond interest expense of $12,000. Accordingly, whenever a corporation sells a bond for more than its face value, the corporation's total cost of borrowing is decreased.

How Is the Bond Discount Amortized in the Books?

The discount is amortized through the straight-line method by equal periodic debits to Bond Interest Expense over the three year life of the bonds. This amortization is recorded every time Bond Interest Expense is entered in the books. The effect of amortizing the discount at each interest payment date during the three years is shown in Figure 13-5. Study the effect of discount amortization on interest expense.

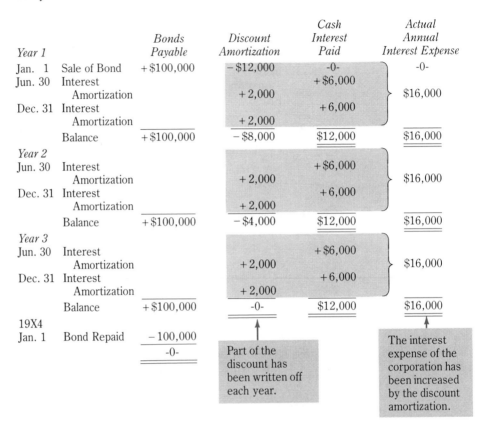

Year 1		Bonds Payable	Discount Amortization	Cash Interest Paid	Actual Annual Interest Expense
Jan. 1	Sale of Bond	+ $100,000	– $12,000	-0-	-0-
Jun. 30	Interest			+ $6,000	
	Amortization		+ 2,000		$16,000
Dec. 31	Interest			+ 6,000	
	Amortization		+ 2,000		
	Balance	+ $100,000	– $8,000	$12,000	$16,000
Year 2					
Jun. 30	Interest			+ $6,000	
	Amortization		+ 2,000		$16,000
Dec. 31	Interest			+ 6,000	
	Amortization		+ 2,000		
	Balance	+ $100,000	– $4,000	$12,000	$16,000
Year 3					
Jun. 30	Interest			+ $6,000	
	Amortization		+ 2,000		$16,000
Dec. 31	Interest			+ 6,000	
	Amortization		+ 2,000		
	Balance	+ $100,000	-0-	$12,000	$16,000
19X4					
Jan. 1	Bond Repaid	– 100,000			
		-0-			

Part of the discount has been written off each year.

The interest expense of the corporation has been increased by the discount amortization.

Figure 13-5   Effect of straight-line amortization of bond discount at each interest payment date

The total interest expense over the life of BCC's bonds consists of $36,000 interest plus $12,000 amortization of discount. The discount on the bond issue represents an increase of the corporation's bond interest expense during each year of the bond's life. Interest actually paid to bondholders is $36,000. However, the interest expense to the corporation is actually $48,000. The additional $12,000 compensates investors for the unfavourable bond interest rate in relation to the prevailing market interest rate. In other words, receiving only $88,000 on January 1, 19X1 is an additional cost to the corporation since it must repay $100,000 on January 1, 19X4. This additional cost is reflected in the increased net annual interest expense during the life of the bonds.

Therefore, in the case of bonds issued at a discount, the interest rate consists of the 12 percent bond rate plus the amortized bond discount. It is therefore higher than the bond interest rate. Accordingly, whenever a corporation sells a bond for less than its face value, the corporation's total cost of borrowing is increased because of discount amortization.

Operation of a Bond Sinking Fund

The fund set up to retire bonds is called a sinking fund because the assets in the fund are tied up or "sunk". The assets in the sinking fund cannot be used for any purpose other than the redemption of the bonds at maturity, or before maturity, if permitted in the bond indenture.

> There are three phases in the operation of a bond sinking fund:
> 1. The contributions to the fund
> 2. The earnings of the assets in the fund
> 3. The use of assets in the funds to retire bonds payable.

Each of these phases is discussed next, using the data of Bluebeard Computer Corporation. Assume that its bonds contain a sinking fund feature. Bonds amounting to $100,000 are issued on the authorization date, January 1, 19X1, and are due in three years. The bond indenture requires an annual contribution at the end of each of the three years to provide for the retirement of the bonds at maturity. Assets in the sinking fund are guaranteed by the trustee to earn 10 percent annually.

Annuity
A series of equal periodic deposits made at equal time intervals; in the case of a bond sinking fund, these deposits are made to a trustee.

The required annual contributions to the sinking fund, together with anticipated compound interest on the amount deposited, are assumed to equal the $30 million needed to retire the bonds at the end of three years. If equal amounts, each called an **annuity**, are to be deposited with the trustee and the fund is to earn 10 percent compounded annually, the annual deposit required can be calculated using an annuity table.

The following schedule accumulates the equal annual contributions and the 10 percent annual revenue earned by the assets in the sinking fund.

	Annual Contributions	10% Annual Revenue		Annual Total	Fund Balance
Dec. 31					
19X1	$30,211	-0-		$30,211	$ 30,211
19X2	30,211	(10% × $30,211 =)	$3,021	33,232	63,443
19X3	30,211	(10% × $63,433 =)	$6,346*	36,557	100,000

*Increased to adjust the fund balance to $100,000.

The annual contributions to the fund and earnings of the assets in the fund are recorded, using 19X2 amounts from this schedule.

Recording Annual Contribution:			*Recording Earnings of the Fund:*	
Bond Sinking Fund	30,211		Bond Sinking Fund	3,021
Cash		30,211	Sinking Fund Revenue	3,021

> The annual contribution is invested by the trustee.

> The earnings remain in the fund but are recorded in the books of the corporation.

The bond sinking fund is reported on the balance sheet as a long-term investment. The bond sinking fund revenue is reported on the income statement as "Other Income".

When Bluebeard management receives notice from its trustee that the bonds have been retired on January 1, 19X4, the following entry is made to remove the bond liability from BCC's books.

```
          19X4
          Jan. 1    Bonds Payable                         100,000
                        Bond Sinking Fund                             100,000
                        To record the retirement of bonds by the trustee.
```

This entry eliminates both the Bonds Payable and Bond Sinking Fund accounts.

In this example, the trustee guaranteed a 10 percent return on investments in the sinking fund and an assumption has been made that only 10 percent was earned by the fund. In actual practice, it is possible that a balance of cash may still remain in the fund. The trustee returns any such balance to the corporation, which records the receipt of cash as follows:

```
          19X4
          Jan. 1    Cash                                  XX
                        Bond Sinking Fund                             XX
                        To record receipt of balance in sinking fund.
```

Bond Redemption

The redemption, or retirement, of bonds at their maturity date requires a cash payment to bondholders; the cash payment is the face value of the bonds. The accounting entry for the retirement of Bluebeard Computer Corporation's bonds on January 2, 19X4 follows.

```
          19X4
          Jan. 1    Bonds Payable                         100,000
                        Cash                                         100,000
```

A bond issue can also be retired in whole, or in part, before its maturity date. There are several different possibilities:

1. The bonds can be repurchased on the open market if the sale is financially advantageous to the issuer.
2. A call provision is sometimes included in a bond indenture permitting early redemption at a specified price, usually higher than face value. The issuer may decide to exercise this call provision if it is financially advantageous.
3. The bondholder may be able to exercise a conversion feature if one was provided for in the bond indenture; in this case, the bonds can be converted into no par-value shares at the option of the bondholder. The conversion date can be an interest payment date if specified as such in the bond indenture, in order to simplify the accounting required in a conversion.

Whenever bonds are retired before the maturity date, the amount payable to bondholders is the face amount of the bonds or the amount required by a call provision. Any unamortized premium or discount must also be removed from the accounts. The accounting required for BCC's January 1, 19X1 issue of $100,000 face value 12% bonds has been illustrated. Suppose that $50,000 face value bonds are redeemed at 102 on December 31, 19X1, when the account balances are as follows:

19X1	Bonds Payable		Premium on Bonds	
Jan. 1		100,000		6,000
Jun. 30			1,000	
Dec. 31			1,000	
			2,000	
				4,000

Since $50,000 of the bonds are redeemed, only half of the $4,000 premium balance ($2,000) is applicable to the redeemed bonds.

The retirement by repurchase or by conversion would be recorded as follows:

Retirement by Repurchase:			*Retirement by Conversion:*		
Bonds Payable	50,000		Bonds Payable	50,000	
Premium on Bonds	2,000		Premium on Bonds	2,000	
Gain on Bond Retirement		1,000	Common Stock		52,000
Cash		51,000			

In this case, the retirement results in a gain; under different circumstances, a loss may result.	In this case, the amount of common stock is usually calculated as the carrying value of the bonds redeemed. No gain or loss is recorded.

The BCC retirement occurred on an interest payment date, December 31, 19X1; interest and premium amortization was already recorded. If the retirement had occurred between interest payment dates, then accrued interest also would be paid to the bondholders and amortization would be recorded in the issuer's books.

In addition to retirement by repurchase or conversion of bonds, it is also possible for an existing bond issue to be replaced by a new issue, usually at a lower interest rate; this is referred to as **refunding**. Outstanding bonds can also be repurchased by assets accumulated in a bond sinking fund.

Refunding
The replacing of one bond issue by a new bond issue.

Sale of Bonds between Interest Dates

Not all bonds are issued on the date when interest begins to accumulate on the bond. For example, consider the sale of an additional $50,000-worth of BCC bonds on April 1, 19X1. Interest began to accumulate on January 1 and, regardless of the date on which the bond was issued, a six-month interest payment is made to the bondholder on June 30. This payment is owing to the bondholder even though the bond has been held for only three months, from April 1 to June 30. This $50,000-worth of bonds is said to be sold at *par plus accrued interest*. The bonds could also have been sold at a premium or a discount and accrued interest. See Figure 13-6.

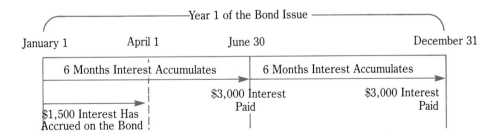

Figure 13-6   Accrued interest on bond issue

Accrued Interest on a Bond

Interest begins to accumulate from the previous interest payment date of the bond and is usually paid semi-annually, regardless of when the bond is actually sold. If the bond is sold between interest dates, the purchaser pays the accrued interest at the date of purchase.

In this case, $1,500 of interest has accrued on the bond from January 1 to April 1. When the bond is sold between interest dates specified in the bond indenture, it is accepted practice for the purchaser to pay accrued interest at the date of purchase, that is, April 1. This amount, $1,500, is returned to the investor by the corporation at the next interest date, which in this case is June 30.

Assuming reversing entries are not used, the corporation records the receipt of the accrued interest as a liability, because this amount is owing to the bondholders:

A liability account is created for the accrued interest, because this amount is owing to the bondholder.

Recording the Bond Issue:			*Payment of Interest:*		
Cash	51,500		Bond Interest Expense	1,500	
Bond Interest Payable		1,500	Bond Interest Payable	1,500	
Bond Payable		50,000	Cash		3,000

The investor pays the issue price of the bonds plus accrued interest.	The interest payment returns the accrued interest to the bondholder (previously recorded as a liability) plus the interest earned since he/she purchased the bond.

The regular semi-annual interest payment is made on June 30. For this example, the above interest calculation applies only to the $50,000 bonds issued on April 1 and excludes interest on the bonds sold January 1.

In bond transactions, the investor pays the issue price of the bonds plus an amount for accrued interest. In turn, the first interest payment is for one full interest period — six months — thereby returning to the purchaser the accrued interest paid plus the interest earned from the date of purchase to the next interest payment date.

Amortizing Premiums and Discounts

If the sale made on April 1 had been made at a premium or a discount, the amortization at June 30 would be calculated as follows:

Amortization of a Premium:		*Amortization of a Discount:*	
Premium is	$6,000(a)	Discount is	$12,000(a)
Months left are	33(b)	Months left are	33(b)
Months amortized	3(c)	Months amortized	3(c)

Calculation:	*Calculation:*
(a ÷ b) × c	(a ÷ b) × c
($6,000 ÷ 33) × 3 = $545.45 (approx.)	($12,000 ÷ 33) × 3 = $1,090.91 (approx.)

It is necessary to calculate the number of months remaining in the life of the bonds at the date bonds are sold.

If the bond has interest payment dates that do not coincide with the year-end of the issuing corporation, an adjusting journal entry is required at year-end to record interest owing at that date:

Adjusting Entry:			*Payment of Interest after Year-End:*		
Bond Interest Expense	X		Bond Interest Expense	X	
Bond Interest Payable		X	Bond Interest Payable	X	
			Cash		XX

> The bondholder receives six months of interest on the payment date. Part of the interest was recorded as an expense in the prior period; part is recorded in the current period. This entry assumes that the corporation does not use reversing entries for accruals.

D.   The Effective Interest Method of Amortization

A bond premium or discount is amortized over the bond life remaining from the date of the bond's issue. The straight-line method, as discussed in the last section, allocates an equal amount of amortization to each semi-annual interest period. The simplicity of this method makes it appropriate as an introduction to the bond accounting process.

A more theoretically acceptable method has been advocated by some accountants; it uses the market rate of interest and is commonly referred to as the effective interest method. Under this method, the amount of amortization calculated differs from one period to another. The calculation is facilitated through the preparation of an amortization table.

Essentially, an amortization table calculates the interest expense on the carrying value of the bond; in this calculation, use is made of the market rate of interest at the date of the bond issue. The difference between the market rate of interest and actual bond contract interest paid is the amortization applicable to the current period.

Note that, for this method, interest rates are usually expressed in annual rates. When semi-annual interest payments are made, the interest is compounded semi-annually; therefore, the period rate is half the annual rate, since six months is half a year.

For this discussion of the effective interest method, assume that Bluebeard Computer Corporation uses this method of amortization for the issue of its bonds on January 1, 19X1.

Calculating Interest Expense and Premium Amortization

The following amortization table is prepared for the BCC issue of $100,000 face value bonds at a premium for $110,485. The calculation begins with the $110,485 issue amount in period 1 (January 1 to June 30, 19X1); this amount is referred to as the bond carrying value. The objective of this amortization method is to reduce this carrying value to the face value of $100,000 over the life of the bonds; the decrease is shown in column E of the table.

Issue of $100,000 Bonds Payable for $110,485
Amortization Table
Using Market Interest Rate of 8%

Year	Period	A Jan. 1 Bond Carrying Value	B ([½ of 8% = 4%] × A) Using 8% Market Rate To Calculate Six-Month Interest Expense	C Actual Cash Interest Paid	D (B − C) Periodic Premium Amortization	E (A − D) Dec. 31 Bond Carrying Value
19X1	1	$110,485	(4% × $110,485 =) $4,419	$6,000	$1,581	$108,904
	2	108,904	(4% × 108,904 =) 4,356	6,000	1,644	107,260
19X2	3	$107,260	(4% × $107,260 =) $4,290	$6,000	$1,710	$105,550
	4	105,550	(4% × 105,550 =) 4,222	6,000	1,778	103,772
19X3	5	$103,772	(4% × $103,772 =) $4,151	$6,000	$1,849	$101,923
	6	101,923	(4% × 101,923) =) 4,077	6,000	1,923	100,000

Note the use of a constant interest rate under this method.	This amount is the interest expense for each 6-month period.	This amount is the amortization for each 6-month period.

In this case, the market interest rate of 8 percent, commonly referred to as the effective rate, is expressed as an annual rate. Because BCC makes semi-annual interest payments, the six-month rate is 4 percent (half of the 8 percent annual rate), which is the rate used in column B each semi-annual period. For convenience, all column B calculations are rounded to the nearest dollar.

The calculation in column D provides the premium amortization amount for each period. In period 1, for example, the difference between the $4,419 market rate interest expense (column B) and the $6,000 actual bond contract interest paid (column C) calculates the premium amortization at $1,581 (column B − column C).

Columns E and A show the decreasing carrying value of the bonds during their three-year life; these are the amounts actually used, it is claimed, in financing the entity. Accordingly, the market interest method calculates interest expense at a constant 4 percent of the bond financing in effect each period. In this way, interest expense (column B) decreases each period as less bond financing is used. From a theoretical point of view, it is preferable to show a financing interest expense that decreases (column B), as the amount of financing decreases (column A).

Recording Interest Payments and Premium Amortization

Journal entries to record interest payments and amortization of premium are made every June 30 and December 31 in the same manner as for straight-line amortization (shown in section C). The actual interest paid to bondholders amounts to $6,000 each semi-annual period; the amount of premium amortization for each period is taken from column D of the amortization table. These are the entries for period 1.

	Payment of Interest:				*Amortization of Premium:*		
Jun. 30	Bond Interest Expense	6,000			Bond Premium	1,581	
	Cash		6,000		Bond Interest Expense		1,581
	To record semi-annual				To record amortization of		
	bond interest.				bond premium.		

The entries for each remaining period are similar; only the amounts used for premium amortization differ, as shown in column D of the amortization table. After the posting of the June 30 entries, the following balances result:

Balance Sheet Accounts

Bonds Payable	Premium on Bonds
100,000	10,485
	1,581
	8,904

> The bond carrying value is $108,904 ($100,000 + $8,904) at June 30; this is the amount that appears in column E of the amortization table.

Income Statement Account

Bond Interest Expense	
6,000	
	1,581
4,419	

> This amount is the balance that was calculated in column B of the amortization table.

Calculating Interest Expense and Discount Amortization

The following amortization table is prepared for the BCC issue of $100,000 face value bonds at a discount for $90,754. The calculation begins with the $90,754 carrying value in column A. The amortization objective is to increase this carrying value to the face value of $100,000 over the 3-year life of the bond; this increase appears in column E.

The annual market interest rate in this case is 16 percent. Half this rate—8 percent—is used in the column B calculations, since interest payments are made semi-annually. For convenience, all column B calculations are rounded to the nearest dollar.

Issue of $100,000 Bonds Payable for $90,754
Amortization Table
Using Market Interest Rate of 16%

Year	Period	A *Jan. 1 Bond Carrying Value*	B ([½ of 16% = 8%] × A) *Using 8% Market Rate To Calculate Six-Month Interest Expense*	C *Actual Cash Interest Paid*	D (B − C) *Periodic Discount Amortization*	E (A − D) *Dec. 31 Bond Carrying Value*
19X1	1	$90,754	(8% × $90,754 =) $7,260	$6,000	$1,260	$ 92,014
	2	92,014	(8% × 92,014 =) 7,361	6,000	1,361	93,375
19X2	3	$93,375	(8% × $93,375 =) $7,470	$6,000	$1,470	$ 94,845
	4	94,845	(8% × 94,845 =) 7,588	6,000	1,588	96,433
19X3	5	$96,433	(8% × $96,433 =) $7,715	$6,000	$1,715	$ 98,148
	6	98,148	(8% × 98,148) =) 7,852	6,000	1,852	100,000

Note the use of a constant interest rate under this method.	This amount is the interest expense for each 6-month period.	This amount is the amortiza-tion for each 6-month period.

The calculation in column D provides the amortization amount. In period 1, for example, the difference between the $7,260 market rate interest expense (column B) and the $6,000 actual bond contract interest paid (column C) calculates the discount amortization at $1,260 (column B − column C).

Columns E and A show the increasing carrying value of the bonds during their three-year life; these are the actual amounts used, it is claimed, in financing the entity. Accordingly, the market interest method calculates interest expense at a constant 8 percent of each period's balance of bond financing. In this way, interest expense (column B) increases each period as financing increases. From a theoretical point of view, it is preferable to show a financing interest expense that increases (column B), as the amount of financing increases (column A).

Recording Interest Payments and Discount Amortization

Journal entries to record interest payments and amortization are made each June 30 and December 31 in the same manner as for the straight-line method (shown in section C). The actual interest paid to bondholders amounts to $6,000 each semi-annual period; the amount of discount amortization is taken directly from column D of the amortization table. These are the entries for period 1.

Payment of Interest				*Amortization of Discount*		
Jun. 30	Bond Interest Expense	6,000		Bond Interest Expense	1,260	
	Cash		6,000	Bond Discount		1,260
To record semi-annual bond interest.				To record amortization of bond discount.		

The entries for each remaining period are similar; only the amounts used for discount amortization differ, as shown in column D of the amortization table. After the posting of the June 30 entries, the following balances result:

Balance Sheet Accounts			Income Statement Account
Bonds Payable	Discount on Bonds		Bond Interest Expense
100,000	9,246	1,260	6,000
			1,260
	7,986		7,260

The bond carrying value is $92,014 ($100,000 − $7,986) at June 30; this is the amount in column E of the amortization table.

This amount is the balance that was calculated in column B of the amortization table.

Comparison of the Effective Interest Method with the Straight-Line Method

A comparison of the two amortization methods can be made using the data applicable to the isse of BCC's bonds at a discount; $100,000 face value bonds are issued for $90,754, resulting in a discount of $9,246 ($100,000 − $90,754). Under the straight-line method, this $9,246 discount is amortized in equal amounts over the 3-year life of the bonds. The discount is calculated for 6-month periods, because amortization is recorded at the time that semi-annual interest payments are made. The straight-line method amortization is calculated as follows:

Discount is	$9,246	(a)
Months left are	36	(b)
Months amortized	6	(c)

Calculation:
(a ÷ b) × c
($9,246 ÷ 36) × 6 = $1,541

As explained in section C of this chapter, amortization of a discount increases interest expense. Therefore, the $1,541 is added to the $6,000 interest payment to calculate the $7,541 interest expense applicable to each 6-month period.

Under the effective interest method, the $9,246 discount amortization is calculated in column D of amortization table. The relevant details are shown next to compare with the appropriate calculations under the straight-line method. For convenience, all percentage calculations are rounded.

		Effective Interest Method			Straight-Line Method		
			Interest			Interest	
		Carrying	(Expense)	(B ÷ A)	Carrying	(Expense)	
Year	Period	Value (A)	Amount (B)	%	Value	Amount	%
19X1	1	$90,754	$ 7,260	8	$90,754	$ 7,541	8.3
	2	92,014	7,361	8	92,295	7,541	8.2
19X2	3	93,375	7,470	8	93,836	7,541	8
	4	94,845	7,588	8	95,377	7,541	7.9
19X3	5	96,433	7,715	8	96,918	7,541	7.8
	6	98,148	7,852	8	98,459	7,541	7.7
			$45,246			$45,246	

Under this method the financing percentage is constant.

Under this method the financing percentage varies.

As can be seen, there is a constant financing expense of 8 percent each 6-month period (16 percent per annum) under the effective interest method. The financing rate varies from period to period under the straight-line method. Theoretically, accounting purists insist that a correct financing charge is calculated only under the effective interest method. However, others argue that, from a practical point of view, there is no material difference in the amounts calculated and the additional accuracy obtained using the market interest is not worth the effort involved. Note that the total interest expense of $45,246 for the 3-year period is the same under both methods. The straight-line method is widely used because of its simplicity. Using either of these methods is in accordance with Canadian GAAP.

This comparison involved the issue of bonds at a discount. A similar comparison for bonds issued at a premium would indicate a similar difference in the calculation of a periodic financing charge. Under the straight-line method, however, the percentage of financing charge would increase in the case of a premium, rather than decrease as here.

Accrual of Bond Interest at Year-End

In these examples, interest is paid at June 30 and December 31; here, the year-end coincided with the December 31 payment. When these two dates do not coincide, it is necessary to accrue interest at year-end and to record an appropriate amount of amortization. These adjustments are made to comply with the principle of the matching concept, which requires that all expenses be matched with revenues for that same year. The adjusting entry accruing interest requires a credit to Bond Interest Payable.

Assume that the fiscal year-end is September 30, but that interest on bonds is still paid June 30 and December 31. In this case, three months of interest has to be accrued (July, August, and September); amortization must also be recorded for three months. The amount of interest would be $3,000 ($100,000 × 12% × ¼); the amount of amortization, assuming the effective interest method is used, would be half of the appropriate semi-annual periodic amortization recorded in column D of the amortization table.

APPENDIX: Present Value Calculations

A distinction between future value and present value is useful to illustrate that interest is the time value of money. If you borrow $1 today for one year at 10 percent interest, its future value in one year is $1.10. The increase of 10 cents results from the interest on $1 for the year. Conversely, if you are to pay $1.10 one year from today, the present value is $1, since the present value calculation excludes interest to be earned in the future. The exclusion of applicable interest in calculating present value is referred to as *discounting*.

The future value of $1.10 is applicable to the first year. If the $1.10 amount at the end of the first year is borrowed for an additional year at 10 percent interest, its future value would be $1.21 ($1.10 + $0.11 interest). In this case, interest is earned on both the original $1 and on the 10 cents interest earned during the first year. This increase provides an example of compound interest: interest can be earned on interest.

If the future value of today's $1 at 10 percent interest compounded annually amounts to $1.21 at the end of 2 years, the present value of $1.21 to be paid in 2 years, discounted at 10 percent is $1. That is, the present value of $1.21 excludes interest of 21 cents.

This illustration demonstrates the two different components that exist in every future cash flow: (a) the dollar amount involved, and (b) the time value implications.

Future Cash Flows

Any cash amount to be received in the future can be discounted in a similar manner to calculate its present value, that is, the amount that excludes the interest on money. Consider Bluebeard's issue of 12-percent, $100,000–face value, 3-year bonds discussed in section D of this chapter. In this example, interest is payable semi-annually each June 30 and December 31 for three years. With this information, this future cash flow's present value can be calculated.

Since interest on the bonds is paid semi-annually, the six-month contract interest rate is 6 percent (12% × ½), as six months is half a year. Remember that interest rates are usually expressed in annual rates; these annual rates must be recalculated into period rates (half the yearly rate, in this example) whenever interest is paid for periods that are not one year.
1. The $100,000 single amount is to be paid at the end of three years; this is the face value of the bonds
2. The $6,000 semi-annual interest payments are to be paid to bondholders for 6 periods during the 3-year bond life ($100,000 face value bonds × 12% annual interest = $12,000 interest per year; the amount paid every semi-annual period is calculated at $6,000). The individual payments are referred to as an annuity.

What Is the Present Value of These Cash Flows?

The $100,000 that must be paid to bondholders in three years constitutes its future value. Therefore, it can be discounted to exclude the time value of Bluebeard's money. The $6,000 also constitutes a future value; so, the six semi-annual future payments must also be discounted.

The use of mathematical tables facilitates the discounting of future cash flows into present value dollars. The prevailing market rate of interest recalculated into period rates (half the yearly rate, in this example) is used in the calculations.

Two tables, applicable to this calculation, are:

(a) Table A: the present value of a single future amount, and (b) Table B: the present value of an annuity.

Present Value of a Single Future Amount

The present value of a single future amount — $100,000 in this case — can be calculated using Table A. Since there are six semi-annual interest payments during the three years, six periods are used in calculating the present value of the $100,000.

Table A   Present Value of 1

$$P = \frac{1}{(1 + i)^n}$$

	4%	6%	8%	10%	12%	14%	16%
1	.961538	.943396	.925926	.909091	.892857	.877193	.862069
2	.924556	.889996	.857339	.826446	.797194	.769468	.743163
3	.888996	.839619	.793832	.751315	.711780	.674972	.640658
4	.854804	.792094	.735030	.683013	.635518	.592030	.552291
5	.821927	.747258	.680583	.620921	.567427	.519369	.476113
6	.790315	.704961	.630170	.564474	.506631	.455587	.410442
7	.759918	.665057	.583490	.513158	.452349	.399637	.353830
8	.730690	.627412	.540269	.466507	.403883	.350559	.305025
9	.702587	.591898	.500249	.424098	.360610	.307508	.262953
10	.675564	.558395	.463193	.385543	.321973	.269744	.226684
11	.649581	.526788	.428883	.350494	.287476	.236617	.195417
12	.624597	.496969	.397114	.318631	.256675	.207559	.168463
13	.600574	.468839	.367698	.289664	.229174	.182069	.145227
14	.577475	.442301	.340461	.263331	.204620	.159710	.125195
15	.555265	.417265	.315242	.239392	.182696	.140096	.107927
16	.533908	.393646	.291890	.217629	.163122	.122892	.093041
17	.513373	.371364	.270269	.197845	.145644	.107800	.080207
18	.493628	.350344	.250249	.179859	.130040	.094561	.069144
19	.474642	.330513	.231712	.163508	.116107	.082948	.059607
20	.456387	.311805	.214548	.148644	.103667	.072762	.051385

Calculation 1: The Market Interest Rate Is 12 Percent (per Annum)

Since semi-annual interest payments are made, the six-month rate is half the annual rate. Therefore, the compounding rate is 6 percent (12% × ½) in this case; there are 6 periods in this 3-year bond.

According to Table A, the present value of $1 compounded at 6 percent for 6 periods, is 0.704961. The present value of the bonds is therefore calculated as follows: $100,000 × 0.704961 = $70,496 (rounded).

Calculation 2: The Market Interest Rate Is 8 Percent (per Annum)

Again since semi-annual interest payments are made, the six-month rate is half the annual rate. Therefore, the compounding rate this time is 4 percent (8% × ½); there are 6 periods in this 3-year bond.

According to Table A, the present value of $1 compounded at 4 percent for 6 periods is 0.790315. The present value of the bonds is therefore calculated as follows: $100,000 × 0.790315 = $79,032 (rounded).

Calculation 3: The Market Interest Rate Is 16 Percent (per Annum)

For these semi-annual interest payments, the six-month rate is 8 percent (16% × ½); there are 6 periods in this 3-year bond.

According to Table A, the present value of $1 compounded at 8 percent for 6 periods is 0.630170. The present value of the bonds is therefore calculated as follows: $100,000 × 0.630170 = $63,017.

Present Value of Multiple Future Amounts

The present value of multiple future amounts — in this instance, $6,000 semi-annually for 6 periods — each referred to as an annuity, can be calculated using Table B. Since BCC's payments are made semi-annually, the rate used is half the prevailing market rate of interest.

Table B   Present Value of an Annuity of 1

$$P = \left[\frac{1 - \frac{1}{(1 + i)^n}}{i} \right]$$

	4%	6%	8%	10%	12%	14%	16%
1	.961538	.943396	.925926	.909091	.892857	.877193	.862069
2	1.886095	1.833393	1.783265	1.735537	1.690051	1.646661	1.605232
3	2.775091	2.673012	2.577097	2.486852	2.401831	2.321632	2.245890
4	3.629895	3.465106	3.312127	3.169865	3.037349	2.913712	2.798181
5	4.451822	4.212364	3.992710	3.790787	3.604776	3.433081	3.274294
6	5.242137	4.917324	4.622880	4.355261	4.111407	3.888668	3.684736
7	6.002055	5.582381	5.206370	4.868419	4.563757	4.288305	4.038565
8	6.732745	6.209794	5.746639	5.334926	4.967640	4.638864	4.343591
9	7.435332	6.801692	6.246888	5.759024	5.328250	4.946372	4.606544
10	8.110896	7.360087	6.710081	6.144567	5.650223	5.216116	4.833227
11	8.760477	7.886875	7.138964	6.495061	5.937699	5.452733	5.028644
12	9.385074	8.383844	7.536078	6.813692	6.194374	5.660292	5.197107
13	9.985648	8.852683	7.903776	7.103356	6.423548	5.842362	5.342334
14	10.563123	9.294984	8.244237	7.366687	6.628168	6.002072	5.467529
15	11.118387	9.712249	8.559479	7.606080	6.810864	6.142168	5.575456
16	11.652296	10.105895	8.851369	7.823709	6.963986	6.265060	5.668497
17	12.165669	10.477260	9.121638	8.021553	6.119630	6.372859	5.748704
18	12.659297	10.827603	9.371887	8.201412	7.249670	6.467420	5.817848
19	13.133939	11.158116	9.603599	8.364920	7.365777	6.550369	5.877455
20	13.590326	11.469921	9.818147	8.513564	7.469444	6.623131	5.928841

Calculation 1: The Market Interest Rate Is 12 Percent (per Annum)
According to Table B, the present value of an annuity of $1 compounded at 6 percent (12% × ½) for 6 periods is 4.917324. The present value of an annuity of $6,000 is therefore calculated as follows: $6,000 × 4.917324 = $29,504 (rounded).

Calculation 2: The Market Interest Rate Is 8 Percent (per Annum)
Again using Table B, the present value of an annuity of $1 compounded at 4 percent (8% × ½) for 6 periods is 5.242137. The present value of an annuity of $6,000 is therefore calculated as follows: $6,000 × 5.242137 = $31,453 (rounded).

Calculation 3: The Market Interest Rate Is 16 Percent (per annum)
The present value of an annuity of $1 compounded at 8 percent (16% × ½) for 6 periods is 4.622880 according to Table B. The present value of an annuity of $6,000 is therefore calculated as follows: $6,000 × 4.622880 = $27,737 (rounded).

Calculating the Present Value of a Bond

A bond issue permits three different scenarios.

Scenario 1: *The Bond Contract Interest Rate (12%) Is the Same as the Market interest rate (12%)*

In this case, the bonds are sold at face value. An investor is willing to pay face value because the present value of the future cash flow is $100,000.

1. The $100,000 bond face value is due at the end of six periods.
   The present value of this cash flow is calculated as:
   $100,000 × 0.704961 (Table A) $ 70,496 (rounded)
2. The semi-annual $6,000 interest is to be received for six periods in total. The present value of this cash flow is calculated as:
   $6,000 × 4.917324 (Table B)   29,504 (rounded)

Total present value of these bonds is: $100,000

When the bond contract interest rate is the same as the market interest rate, the present value of all cash flows is the same as the bond's face value, other things — such as risk or inflation — being equal.

In actual practice, however, the market interest rate is not the same as the bond contract interest rate; or, some other factor (risk or inflation) creates an impact. Scenarios 2 and 3 deal with this situation.

Scenario 2: *The Bond Contract Interest Rate (12%) Is Greater Than the Market Interest Rate (8%)*

Here the bonds are sold at a premium. An investor is willing to pay more than face value because the present value of the future cash flow amounts to $110,485.

1. The $100,000 bond face value is due at the end of six periods.
   The present value of this cash flow is calculated as:
   $100,000 × 0.790315 (Table A) $79,032 (rounded)
2. The semi-annual $6,000 interest is to be received for six periods in total. The present value of this cash flow is calculated as:
   $6,000 × 5.242137 (Table B)   31,453 (rounded)

Total present value of these bonds is: $110,485

Therefore, when the bond contract interest rate is greater than the market interest rate, the present value of all cash flows is greater than the face value of the bonds, other things being equal. This excess amount, calculated as $10,485 in this example, is considered to be a premium.

Scenario 3: *The Bond Contract Interest Rate (12%) Is Less Than the Market Interest Rate (16%)*

In this case, the bonds are sold at a discount. An investor will pay less than face value because the present value of future cash flow amounts to only $90,754.

1. The $100,000 bond face value is due at the end of six periods.
   The present value of this cash flow is calculated as:
   $100,000 × 0.630170 (Table A) $63,017
2. The semi-annual $6,000 interest is to be received for six periods in total. The present value of this cash flow is calculated as:
   $6,000 × 4.622880 (Table B)   27,737 (rounded)

Total present value of these bonds is: $90,754

Therefore, when the bond contract interest rate is less than the market interest rate, the present value of all cash flows is less than the face value of the bonds, other things being equal. This difference, calculated as $9,246 ($100,000 − $90,754) in this example, is considered to be a discount.

Discussion Questions

1. A corporation can be financed in a number of ways. Explain the different ways and give examples. What factors influence management in the choice of a financing method?
2. What is a bond? a bond indenture? Why is a trustee usually necessary?
3. A bondholder has certain rights. List and explain these rights.
4. What is the significance of shareholder approval before an issue of bonds?
5. How are different bond issues reported in the financial statements of a corporation?
6. Management is considering three different financing options, the issue of preferred shares, the issue of common shares, and the issue of bonds. The directors of the corporation have concluded that attention should be devoted to observing the expected effect on earnings per common share in the selection of a financing method. What are the advantages of issuing bonds? preferred shares? common shares?
7. Three different categories of bond terminology are identified in this chapter. Identify these categories and list the major types falling within each category.
8. Why would investors pay a premium for a corporate bond? Why would a corporation issue its bonds at a discount? Explain, using the relationship between the bond contract interest rate and the prevailing market interest rate.
9. What method of balance sheet classification of bond premium or bond discount is in accordance with Canadian GAAP? How does it differ from the method used in the United States?
10. How is the actual price of a bond determined? Give an example.
11. If the bond contract interest rate is greater than that required in the market, what is the effect on the selling price of the bond? Why?
12. What are the different methods used in amortizing premiums and discounts? Explain.
13. How is the interest paid to bondholders calculated? How does this practice affect the sale of bonds between interest dates?
14. How is the amortization of bond premium recorded in the books? bond discount?
15. Explain what a bond sinking fund is. What are the three phases in its operation?
16. What are the different possibilities in the redemption of bonds before their maturity?
17. If a bond is sold between interest dates, what is the accepted practice for handling accrued interest? Why has the practice evolved in this form?
18. From a theoretical point of view, why is the effective interest method of amortization more acceptable than the straight-line method? Evaluate the usefulness of the effective interest method from a practical point of view.
19. Explain how the amortization under the effective interest method is calculated. Use an example.
20. How does the calculation of a periodic financing charge dffer from the market interest method to the straight-line method?
21. Distinguish between future value and present value. What is the time value of money? Why is it important?
22. Explain compound interest. What is its relationship to both future value and present value?
23. Why is it necessary to discount future cash flows when calculating the present value of a bond? Explain, using the different cash flows that are associated with bonds.
24. How does the use of mathematical tables facilitate the calculation of present values?
25. Contrast the calculation of present value when (a) the market interest rate is greater than the bond contract interest rate, and (b) when the market interest rate is less than the bond contract interest rate.
26. Refer to Real Life Example 13-1. Off Balance Sheet financing often involves mutual performance guarantees. What dangers does this potentially pose to a firm? Discuss how Off Balance Sheet financing conforms, or does not conform to GAAP.

Discussion Cases

Discussion Case 13-1: Ivaco Inc.

Critics say he plays too high, wide and handsome when it comes to debt, but Ivaco Inc. president Paul Ivanier has used his considerable financial skills to turn an apparent defeat into what could be a major coup.

He announced yesterday a complex $191-million issue of preferred shares and convertible debentures that he says will "lock in" a $74-million profit for his company on the 5.9 million shares of fellow steelmaker Dofasco Inc. that it owns, add about $6.5 million a year to its profit and reduce its 50 : 50 debt-to-equity ratio to 35 : 65.

Analysts believe it is a smart deal for Montreal-based Ivaco, and investors rewarded the company's class A shares with a 25 cent rise to $21.62 on the Toronto Stock Exchange and a 37 cent increase to $21.75 on the Montreal Exchange.

The issue, which Ivanier said was put together "in the past few days" and is to close in early April, pending regulatory approval, followed Tuesday's announcement by Hamilton-based Dofasco of a $325-million issue of convertible voting preferred shares.

Observers have speculated that Dofasco floated its share issue partly to dilute the 11.7 percent holding Ivaco had amassed in Dofasco and to prevent any further advance, and that the Ivaco issue is a direct response designed to enable the company either to bail out of Dofasco gracefully and profitably or to finance a further incursion into the highly regarded and profitable integrated steelmaker.

Asked about the perceived Dofasco connection, however, Ivanier said: "I don't want to tie [the Ivaco issue] to anybody."

He is keeping his options open when it comes to how Ivaco will use the proceeds from the issue, which has been bought for public distribution by McLeod Young Weir Ltd. and Gordon Capital Corp. of Toronto and Nesbitt Thomson Bongard Inc. of Montreal.

According to an Ivaco press release, the proceeds will be used for general corporate purposes, including acquisitions, investments and expansion. Ivanier said general corporate purposes might include paying down the company's long-term debt — $303.8 million at the end of 1983.

As for the notion that he might turn the tables on Dofasco and buy more of its shares, he would say only: "I'm not going to preclude myself from anything." Instead, he preferred to concentrate on the complex structure of the new issue and on the benefits he said it will bring to Ivaco.

The two components are second preferred shares and debentures, both exchangeable at any time on a one-for-one basis for the Dofasco common shares held by Ivaco at an exchange price of $32 a Dofasco share.

The exchangeable preferreds will be issued at $32 a share and carry an 8.5 percent fixed cumulative annual dividend for the first 5 years. Thereafter, the yield will be equal to the annual dividend on Dofasco common shares — based on a price of $32 a Dofasco share — plus 4 percent, calculated quarterly.

The exchangeable debentures will mature in April 2010, and bear interest at a fixed rate of 9.5 percent for the first 5 years. After that, the yield will match that of the Dofasco common share dividends, plus 5 percent, also calculated quarterly.

Ivanier said the current plan calls for a 50-50 mix of preferred shares and debentures, but that the underwriters have the right to go to a maximum of 70 percent preferreds and 30 percent debentures. The "locked-in" profit Ivaco expects to get from its Dofasco shares represents the difference between the $117 million — or average $19.50 a share — he said Ivaco paid for its Dofasco holding and the $191 million it will raise from the issue before underwriting costs.

Although Ivaco will pledge its Dofasco shares as security on the new share-debenture issue, it will continue to receive the dividends on the Dofasco shares. Ivanier said that, combined with the effects of taxation and investing the proceeds from the issue at prime, those dividends will translate into a net gain on the issue of about 3.42 percent or $6.5 million a year "as long as people do not convert".

Source John Partridge, "Ivaco's issue turns defeat to profit coup", *The Globe and Mail*, March 16, 1985, p. B-1.

For Discussion

1. Discuss the impact of this financing package on the earnings per share of common shareholders.
2. What are the advantages and disadvantages to shareholders of this share issue?

Discussion Case 13-2: Buying House Not Worth It

[1984] has not been a good year for investments.

Stock prices, despite the summer rally, are still below the September 1983 close of almost 2500 on the Toronto Stock Exchange 300 composite index. Gold is way below its level of last September.

Bonds have done better than gold, but just barely. The bellwether Government of Canada 9.5-percent issue maturing in 2003 is selling at about $780 and was over $830 a year ago.

The grimmest news for most Canadians is that home real estate is not doing well either. As far as I can tell from looking at the various surveys on housing prices, Canadian homes are worth about as much now as they were a year ago. This varies, of course, by region, but seems to be true across the nation.

Since most home ownership only makes economic sense at today's interest rates if housing is expected to appreciate, this condition not only discourages new buyers, it also encourages existing home owners to unload their "castles" if only a buyer would appear.

As a result, there is a good chance that housing prices may not simply stay flat. They could well fall as demand for homes stays flat while the supply of resale houses increases.

More Expensive than Renting

Thanks to high interest rates, most recent home buyers are paying substantially more for owned housing than they would have to pay for a rental equivalent. Further, their downpayments are not earning the interest that could have been earned if the money had been put into term deposits rather than housing.

Take today's 5-year mortgage rate of 14 percent, and the term deposit rate of about 13 percent. If housing costs $150,000, with one-third as downpayment, while equivalent housing can be rented for $900 a month, and taking into account normal real estate taxes and maintenance and assuming a personal income tax rate of 40 percent, buying a house is only justified if housing prices rise by 6.25 percent annually over the next 5 years.

Put another way, the house bought today at $150,000 would have to be worth more than $203,000 in 5 years for the buyer just to break even.

Even if the mortgage rate dropped to 12 percent, while the savings rate became 11 percent, annual appreciation would have to be 4.5 percent. Today's $150,000 house would have to be worth $187,000 in 5 years.

A 5-year mortgage rate of 8 percent has not been seen in well over a decade. But even if it miraculously reappeared, one would have to expect a $150,000 house to be worth about $165,000 in 5 years just to come out even. In order to justify buying a home if no appreciation is expected, the mortgage rate would have to be about 6 percent. Most Canadians have never seen such a low rate in their adult lives.

Look at the Prices

Greybeards like me remember those days. Back then, it used to be said, somewhat inaccurately, that selling your house at the same price you paid meant that you had lived rent-free. Fancy notions like present value were not very important when interest rates were 6 percent or less.

Instead of looking at interest rates, look at prices. At today's interest rates, how much should you be willing to pay for a house that is expected to be worth $150,000 in 5 years? The grim answer in this world of double-digit interest rates and stagnant real estate prices is less than $111,000.

The moral: when expected inflation is low and interest rates are high, today's prices can only fall.

Anyone looking at a home today had better have the courage to demand a 35-percent discount or more from asking price, or have very optimistic expectations about where interest rates are going.

Source Seymour Friedland, "Buying house not worth it", *The* (Montreal) *Gazette*, September 10, 1984, p. C-12.

For Discussion

1. Describe the changes to economic conditions since September 1984. How different would the argument for or against buying a house be now?
2. "Rent is a waste of money; you have to buy to incease your equity": comment on this statement.

Discussion Case 13-3: Stripped Bonds

Bad puns aside, the subject of stripped bonds has been attracting considerable attention in the investment community lately. Deep discount or zero coupon bonds are not new, but the latest wrinkle involves the use of bonds issued at normal commercial rates, with the bonds and their related coupons resold separately at a later date, each at significant discounts.

That raises some interesting questions, not only with regard to the tax consequences of these transactions but also as to whether Revenue Canada's views on these matters could be extended to other, more conventional bond holdings.

New Offerings

In a typical situation, an investment dealer or financial institution will acquire on the open market a substantial block of a particular issue of bonds, with all unmatured coupons attached. In the instances so far, these have been high-quality government (or government-guaranteed) bonds, issued several years earlier and having maturity dates 15 or 20 years in the future.

The dealer or financial institution will then remove the coupons from the bonds and offer each component to the public separately. In other words, the bonds will be sold without any interest coupons, but at a substantial discount that should produce a return to the investor over the remaining term of the bond roughly equivalent to a compound interest at or above current commercial interest rates.

As for the coupons, which will be sold in bearer form separately from the bonds, these would normally be in sequence of semi-annual interest payment dates. It is understood, however, that when they are sold separately, the practice is to sell the investor a block of coupons of a particular maturity date, rather than a series of coupons of consecutive payment dates.

To use an example from a recent offering of 13-percent bonds, the regular semi-annual coupons from $100,000 of bonds amounted to $6,500. If purchased approximately 4 years before their due date, these coupons were worth approximately $3,800, the difference representing a profit (interest) accruing to the investor over the intervening period. The present value (purchase price) and the resulting amount of accruing interest will, of course, vary depending on the maturity value of the particular coupon, the period of time between the purchase date and the due date and the current rate of interest at the time of purchase.

Source   Geoffrey M. Colley, ''Stripped Bonds: An Interesting Proposition'', *CA Magazine*, April 1984, p. 73.

For Discussion

1. As an investor, you are considering stripped bonds. What effect does inflation have on your decision?
2. Considering the recent conditions of inflation and financial markets, and the performance of other investments, how do you view bonds as an investment?

Discussion Case 13-4: Zero Coupons

Scene: King John's court

Chicken Little — (*Rushing in panting and excited*) The Zeros are coming! The Zeros are coming!
King John — Whoa, Little! What is all this? A one man replay of *Tora, Tora*?
C. Little — No, your illustrious eminence. I refer to the new zero coupon bonds that are selling like proverbial hot cakes on Bay and Wall Streets. It seems that, in return for a distant promise of great wealth, the well-heeled local burghers are prepared to forgo the intervening interest payments.
King John — You mean the issuer has no interest service costs during the life of the bond?
C. Little — None, your lordship.
(*Certain attending cabinet/courtiers overhearing the discussion begin to smile and move closer.*)
King John — How far into the future have the borrowers been able to push the maturity date?
C. Little — In the U.S., Fannie Mae did a $5-billion face issue of Zeros with a 40-year maturity!
King John — Far out!
C. Little — Virtually into the hereafter. (*Several cabinet/courtiers now closely listening to the dialogue begin to laugh openly and clap their hands with glee.*)

King John — How say you, Little, could our overextended Crown coffers benefit from this phenomenon?
C. Little — Of course, your grace. U.S. Secretary of the Treasury Donald Regan has already stated publicly that the U.S. intends to ''take advantage of'' this new market. If they can, we can.
King John — Donald is a smart one. He has found more wrinkles to expand the market for U.S. federal debt than Merlin has spells. But he has outdone himself on this one.
C. Little — I have more, your worship.
King John — Spill it quick, Little — I smell a master stroke here.
(*Cabinet/courtiers lean even closer in breathless anticipation*)
C. Little — Your hard-working (if not well-loved) tax collectors have cleverly ruled that the difference between the purchase price and value of maturity of these securities is considered accrued income and tax must be paid on this by the holder at least every three years.
King John — (*Incredulously*) You mean to say we can borrow money from the public — pay them no interest for its use and during the life of the bond *they have to pay us* tax on income they have not yet received?
C. Little — Absolutely, your benevolence!

King John—Zounds! The more you borrow the higher your revenue!

(*Several cabinet/courtiers now are dancing in a circle holding hands and laughing uproariously.*)

King John—This is the answer to our prayers, Little—we may raise your consultant's fee and we will consider you for the Order of the Garter Belt.

C. Little—Always pleased to be of service m'lord, but there is one minor hitch.

King John—What! A Catch 29? (Inflation-adjusted)

C. Little—Yes, your protuberance. It seems one of the provincial regulators has some misgivings about these new securities and is suggesting an explanatory document should be provided to the purchaser. According to some, such a document might dissuade a potential buyer from participating in these delightful new instruments.

King John—(*Sternly*) Which province, Little?

C. Little—Ontario, your holiness.

King John—Get [David Peterson] on the phone.

Source William Allen, "Zero coupons: A Midsummer Pipe Dream?", *The Globe and Mail*, September 1, 1984, p. B-3. (This vignette originally appeared in a newsletter from Allenvest Group Ltd. of Toronto.)

For Discussion

1. What are the advantages and disadvantages of zero coupon bonds?
2. Comment on King John's statement: "The more you borrow, the higher your revenue!"

Comprehension Problems

Comprehension Problem 13-1

Bolovision Corporation, a profitable growth company with 200 000 shares of common stock outstanding, is in need of approximately $40 million in new funds to finance required expansion. Currently, there are no other securities outstanding. Management has three options open:
a. Sell $40 million-worth of 12-percent bonds at face value
b. Sell 10 percent preferred stock: 400 000 shares at $100 per share
c. Sell another 200 000 shares of common stock at $200 per share.

Operating income (before interest and income tax) on completion of the expansion is expected to average $12 million per annum; the income tax rate is 50 percent.

Required:
1. Prepare a schedule (using the form from section A) to calculate the earnings per common share. Beginning with the amount for earnings before interest and income tax, calculate the earnings per share of common for $12 million-worth of each of bonds, preferred shares, and common shares.

	Bonds	Preferred Shares	Common Shares
Income before Interest and Tax	$12,000,000	$12,000,000	$12,000,000
Deduct Bond Interest	_____	_____	_____
Income before Tax			
Tax at 50%	_____	_____	_____
Balance			
Preferred Dividends	_____	_____	_____
Net Available to Common (a)	_____	_____	_____
Common Shares Outstanding	_____	_____	_____
Earnings per Common Share (a) ÷ (b)	_____	_____	_____

2. Which financing option is most advantageous to the common shareholders?
3. What are the advantages of issuing shares rather than bonds? of issuing bonds rather than shares?

Note: Solve problems involving present value calculation only if The Appendix was studied in your course.

Comprehension Problem 13-2

Watfor Corporation was authorized to issue $500,000 face value bonds. The corporation issued $100,000-worth of face value bonds on January 1, 19X1.

Date of Authorization January 1, 19X1	Term 3 years	Bond Contract Interest Rate 12%	Interest Payment Dates Semi-annually on June 30 and December 31

Required: Answer the questions for each of the following cases.
Case A: The bonds were issued at face value and purchased at par.
Case B: The bonds were issued for $112,000 and purchased at a premium.
Case C: The bonds were issued for $88,000 and purchased at a discount.

1. How much cash does Watfor receive for the bonds?
2. How much annual interest must the corporation pay? On what face value amount?
3. Prepare the journal entry to record the sale of the bonds.
4. Record the entries applicable to interest and straight-line amortization for June 30, 19X1 and for December 31, 19X1.

Comprehension Problem 13-3

Maple Leaf Distributors Ltd. was authorized to issue $500,000-worth of face value bonds. On January 1, 19X1, the corporation issued $200,000-worth of face value bonds for $210,152. On this date the market rate of interest was 10 percent.

Date of Authorization January 1, 19X1	Term 3 years	Bond Contract Interest Rate 12%	Interest Payment Dates Semi-annually on June 30 and December 31

Required:
1. Calculate the amount of interest paid every interest payment date.
2. Prepare an Amortization Table like the one in section D. (The carrying value at January 1, 19X1 is $210,152 and periodic interest is $10,507.) For convenience round all column B calculations to the nearest dollar. Use the effective interest method of amortization.

Issuance of $200,000 Bonds Payable for $210,152
Amortization Table
Using Market Interest Rate of 10%

Year	Period	A Jan. 1 Bond Carrying Value	B ([½ of 10% = 5%] × A) Using 10% Market Rate to calculate Six-Month Interest Expense	C Actual Cash Interest Paid	D (B–C) Periodic Premium Amortization	E (A–D) Dec. 31 Bond Carrying Value
1	1	$210,152	(5% × $210,152 =)$10,507			
	2		(5% × =)			
2	3		(5% × =)			
	4		(5% × =)			
3	5		(5% × =)			
	6		(5% × =)			

3. Calculate the financing percentage under the effective interest method of amortization for each six-month period. (Use the format in section D.) For convenience round all percentage calculations to the nearest percent.)

Year	Period	A *Jan. 1 Bond Carrying Value*	B ([½ of 10% = 5%] × A) *Using 10% Market Rate to calculate Six-Month Interest Expense*	(B ÷ A) *Financing %*
1	1	$210,152	(5% × $210,152 =)$10,507	
	2		(5% × =)	
				_____ %
2	3		(5% × =)	
	4		(5% × =)	
				_____ %
3	5		(5% × =)	
	6		(5% × =)	
				_____ %

4. Comment on the financing percentage that results in each period. Do you think that this financing percentage should remain constant from period to period? Why or why not?

Problems

Problem 13-1

The board of directors of Oligopoly Inc. has approved management's recommendation to expand the production facilities. The firm currently manufactures only heavy machinery, but plans are being developed for diversifying the corporation's activities through the production of smaller and more versatile equipment. The directors have concluded that attention should be devoted to observing the expected effect on earnings per common share in selection of a financing method. They are considering the following financing methods:
a. Sell $2 million-worth of 12-percent bonds at face value
b. Sell 8 percent preferred stock: 20 000 shares at $100 a share (no other preferred shares are outstanding)
c. Sell another 50 000 shares of common stock at $400 a share (currently 40 000 common shares are outstanding)
   Operating income (before interest and income tax) is expected to average $1,000,000 per annum following the expansion; the income tax rate is expected to be 50 percent.

Required:
1. Calculate the earnings per common share for each alternative: 12% bonds, preferred shares, and common shares.
2. Which financing method best meets the board of directors' criteria?
3. What factors should the board of directors consider, in addition to earnings per share?

Problem 13-2

Part A

Computer Stores Corporation was authorized to issue $300,000-worth of face value bonds. On January 1, 19X1, the corporation issued $150,000-worth of face value bonds for $147,000.

Date of Authorization	Term	Bond Contract Interest Rate	Interest Payment Dates
January 1, 19X1	3 years	12%	Semi-annually on June 30 and December 31

Required:
1. Calculate
   a. The amount of interest paid every interest payment date
   b. The amount of amortization to be recorded at each interest payment date (Use the straight-line method of amortization.)
2. Prepare a schedule, like the one in Figure 13-5, to show the effect of discount amortization at each interest payment date. Note that amortization is recorded each time interest expense is recorded.
3. Prepare the journal entries to record the interest and amortization at June 30, 19X1.
4. Prepare a partial balance sheet showing the bond liability and the bond discount as a deferred charge on the following dates.
   a. December 31, 19X1 (Note that the bonds are a long-term liability on this date, since they will not be redeemed in 19X2.)
   b. December 31, 19X2 (Note that the bonds are a current liability on this date, since they will be redeemed on Jan. 1, 19X4.)

Part B

The bond indenture contained a sinking fund provision requiring equal annual contributions that are transferred to a trustee who guarantees a 10 percent annual return. Annual contributions were to be made on December 31, 19X1, 19X2, and 19X3. The amount of the contributions and the 10 percent revenue in the sinking fund are calculated below.

December 31	Annual Contribution	10% Annual Revenue	Annual Total	Fund Balance
19X1	$45,317	-0-	$45,317	$ 45,317
19X2	45,317	(10% × $45,317 =)$4,532	49,849	95,166
19X3	45,317	(10% × $95,166 =)$9,517	54,834	150,000

Required: Prepare journal entries to record
5. The annual contribution in each of the three years
6. The 10 percent annual revenue in each of the three years
7. The redemption of the bonds at maturity.

Problem 13-3

On the date of bond authorization, Axel Corporation issued $100,000-worth of face value bonds.

Date of Authorization	Term	Bond Contract Interest Rate	Interest Payment Dates
January 1, 19X1	3 Years	12%	Semi-annually on June 30 and December 31

Required: Consider these three cases. Case A: the bonds are issued at face value. Case B: the bonds are issued for $103,000. Case C: the bonds are issued for $94,000. For each of them
1. Calculate
   a. The amount of interest paid every interest payment date
   b. The amount of amortization to be recorded at each interest payment date, if applicable (Use the straight-line method of amortization.)
2. Prepare journal entries to record
   a. The issue of bonds on January 1, 19X1
   b. The payment of interest on June 30, 19X1
   c. The amortization on June 30, 19X1
   d. The payment of interest on December 31, 19X1
   e. The amortization on December 31, 19X1
   f. The payment of interest on December, 19X3
   g. The amortization on December 31, 19X3
   h. The redemption of the bonds at maturity, January 1, 19X4.
3. Calculate the amount of interest expense shown in the income statement at December 31, 19X1. Is this amount the same as cash interest paid by Axel? Why or why not?

Problem 13-4

Beaver Products Inc., which uses straight-line amortization calculation, was authorized to issue $1,000,000 face value bonds. On January 1, 19X1, Beaver issued $300,000-worth of face value bonds for $272,263.

Date of Authorization	Term	Bond Contract Interest Rate	Interest Payment Dates
January 1, 19X1	3 Years	12%	Semi-annually on June 30 and December 31

Required:
1. Calculate
   a. The amount of interest paid every interest payment date
   b. The amount of amortization to be recorded at each interest payment date (Use the straight-line method.)
2. Prepare an amortization table, like the one in section D. (Note that amortization is recorded each time interest expense is recorded.)
3. Calculate the financing percentage under the straight-line method of amortization for each six month period. (For convenience round all percentage calculations to one decimal place.)
4. Comment on the financing percentage that results in each period. Do you think that this financing percentage should vary from period to period? Why or why not?

Problem 13-5

Beaver Products Inc., which uses effective interest amortization calculation, was authorized to issue $1,000,000-worth of face value bonds. On January 1, 19X1, Beaver issued $300,000-worth of face value bonds for $272,263. On this date, the market rate of interest was 16 percent.

Date of Authorization	Term	Bond Contract Interest Rate	Interest Payment Dates
January 1, 19X1	3 Years	12%	Semi-annually on June 30 and December 31

Required:
1. Calculate the amount of interest paid every interest payment date.
2. Prepare an amortization table. (The carrying value at January 1, 19X1, is $272,263 and periodic interest is $2,181.) For convenience round all column B calculations to the nearest dollar. Use the effective interest method of amortization.
3. Calculate the financing percentage under the effective interest method of amortization for each six-month period. For convenience round all percentage calculations to the nearest percent.
4. Comment on the financing percentage that results in each period. Do you think that this financing percentage should remain constant from period to period? Why or why not?

Problem 13-6

De Maisonneuve Peripherals Corp. was authorized to issue $1,000,000-worth of face value bonds. The corporation has issued $100,000-worth of face value bonds on the date of bond authorization for $107,721. The market rate of interest on the issue date was 10 percent.

Date of Authorization	Term	Bond Contract Interest Rate	Interest Payment Dates
January 1, 19X4	5 Years	12%	Semi-annually on June 30 and December 31

Required: Consider these cases. Case A: De Maisonneuve uses the straight-line method of amortization. Case B: De Maisonneuve uses the effective interest method of amortization. Prepare an amortization table to calculate the amount of amortization applicable to the first three six-month periods.

For each of the cases
1. Calculate
   a. The amount of interest paid on $100,000-worth of face value bonds every interest payment date.
   b. The amount of amortization to be recorded at each interest payment date. For convenience, round all calculations to the nearest dollar.
2. a. Prepare a schedule comparing the financing charge for the first year under both effective interest and straight-line methods. For convenience, round all percent calculations to one decimal place.
   b. Comment on the financing percentage that results under each amortization method. Which method is most appropriate? Why?
3. Prepare journal entries to record
   a. The issue of the bonds
   b. The payment of interest and amortization applicable at June 30, 19X4
   c. The payment of interest and amortization applicable at December 31, 19X4
   d. The redemption of the bonds at maturity, January 1, 19X6.

Problem 13-7

Dana's Toy Patch Inc. was authorized to issue $500,000-worth of face value bonds.

Date of Authorization	Term	Bond Contract Interest Rate	Interest Payment Dates
January 1, 19X3	5 Years	12%	Semi-annually on June 30 and December 31

The following transactions occurred during 19X3.

Jan. 31   Issued $500,000-worth of face value bonds
Jun. 30   Paid the semi-annual interest on the issued bonds and made a straight-line entry to record amortization
Dec. 31   Paid the semi-annual interest on the issued bonds and made an entry to record amortization.

Required: Consider these cases. Case A: the bonds were issued at a price to yield 12 percent. Case B: the bonds were issued at a price to yield the market rate of interest (18%). Case C: the bonds were issued at a price to yield the market rate of interest (8%). For each of the cases
  1. Calculate
      a. The amount of each semi-annual interest payment on the issued bonds
      b. The issue price of the bonds, consisting of the present value of the bond face value and the present value of the 10 semi-annual interest payments to be made during the 5-year period (For convenience, round all calculations to the nearest dollar.)
      c. The amount of amortization applicable to each interest payment date (Use the straight-line method of amortization; for convenience, round all calculations to the nearest dollar).
  2. Prepare journal entries to record the 19X3 transactions.

Alternate Problems

Alternate Problem 13-1

The financing structure of Dome Sands Corp. is currently as follows:

Current Liabilities	$200,000
Bond Payable	-0-
Preferred Stock — 8%	100,000
Common Stock — 50 000 shares	500,000
Retained Earnings	300,000

Management is considering a plant expansion costing $1,000,000. Several different factors have been considered in a selection of a financing method; the effect of alternative financing methods on earnings per common share remains to be analyzed. The following financing methods are being considered:

a.   Sell $1 million-worth of 12-percent bonds at face value
b.   Sell another 10,000 common shares at $100 per share.

Dome is a profitable growth company and operating income (before interest and tax) is expected to average $200,000 per annum; the income tax rate is 50 percent.

Required:
1. Prepare a schedule to compare the effect on earnings per common share of each of the financing options.
2. Based on earnings per common share, which method is financially advantageous to common shareholders?
3. What other factors should be considered before a final decision is made?

Alternate Problem 13-2

Part A

Mercury Software Inc. was authorized to issue $500,000-worth of face value bonds. On January 1, 19X1, the corporation issued $200,000-worth of face value bonds for $212,000.

Date of Authorization	Term	Bond Contract Interest Rate	Interest Payment Dates
January 1, 19X1	3 Years	12%	Semi-annually on June 30 and December 31

Required:
1. Calculate
   a. The amount of interest paid every interest payment date
   b. The amount of amortization to be recorded at each interest payment date (Use the straight-line method of amortization.)
2. Prepare a schedule like the one in Figure 13-4, to show the effect of premium amortization at each interest payment date. (Note that amortization is recorded each time interest expense is recorded.)
3. Prepare the journal entries to record the interest and amortization at June 30, 19X1.
4. Prepare a partial balance sheet, showing the bond liability, and the bond premium as a deferred credit, on the following dates.
   a. December 31, 19X1 (Note that the bonds are a long-term liability on this date, since they will not be redeemed in 19X2).
   b. December 31, 19X2 (Note that the bonds are a current liability on this date, since they will be redeemed on January 1, 19X4).

Part B

The bond indenture contained a sinking fund provision requiring equal annual contributions that are transferred to a trustee who guarantees a 10 percent annual return. Annual contributions are made on December 31, 19X1, 19X2, and 19X3. The amount of the contributions and the 10 percent revenue in the sinking fund are calculated in the following schedule.

December 31	Annual Contribution	10% Annual Revenue	Annual Total	Fund Balance
19X1	$60,423	-0-	$60,423	$ 60,423
19X2	60,423	(10% × $ 60,423 =) $ 6,042	66,465	126,888
19X3	60,423	(10% × 126,888 =) $12,689	73,112	200,000

Required: Prepare journal entries to record
  5. The annual contribution in each of the three years.
  6. The 10 percent annual revenue in each of the three years.
  7. The redemption of the bonds at maturity.

Alternate Problem 13-3

Andrew's Computer Corner Corp. was authorized to issue $500,000-worth of face value bonds. The corporation issued $250,000-worth of face value bonds on January 1, 19X4.

Date of Authorization	Term	Bond Contract Interest Rate	Interest Payment Dates
January 1, 19X4	3 Years	12%	Semi-annually on June 30 and December 31

Required: Consider these cases. Case A: the bonds are issued at face value. Case B: the bonds are issued for $256,000. Case C: the bonds are issued for $242,800. For each of the cases
  1. Calculate
     a. The amount of interest paid on the issued bonds every interest payment date
     b. The amount of amortization, if any, applicable to each interest payment date (Use the straight-line method of amortization.)
  2. Prepare journal entries to record
     a. The issue of the bonds
     b. The payment of interest and recording of amortization, if any, on June 30, 19X4
     c. The payment of interest and recording of amortization, if any, on December 31, 19X4.
  3. Calculate the amount of interest expense shown in the income statement at December 31, 19X4. Is this amount the same as cash paid by Andrew's in 19X4? Why or why not?
  4. On December 31, 19X4, the corporation exercised a call feature included in the bond indenture and retired the $250,000-worth of face value bonds issued January 1, 19X4. The bonds were called at 103. Prepare the December 31 journal entry to record the exercise of the call option.

Alternate Problem 13-4

Maple Leaf Distributors Ltd. was authorized to issue $500,000-worth of face value bonds. On January 1, 19X1, the corporation issued $200,000-worth of face value bonds for $210,152.

Date of Authorization	Term	Bond Contract Interest Rate	Interest Payment Dates
January 1, 19X1	3 Years	12%	Semi-annually on June 30 and December 31

Required:
1. Calculate
   a. The amount of interest paid every interest payment date.
   b. The amount of amortization to be recorded at each interest payment date. Use the straight-line method of amortization.
2. Prepare an amortization table. (Note that amortization is recorded each time interest expense is recorded.)
3. Calculate the financing percentage under the straight-line method of amortization for each six-month period. For convenience round all percentage calculations to one decimal place.
4. Comment on the financing percentage that results in each period. Do you think that this financing percentage should vary from period to period? Why or why not?

Alternate Problem 13-5

Joliette Inc. was authorized to issue $250,000-worth of face value bonds. These bonds were issued on the authorization date for $216,449. The market rate of interest on the issue date was 16 percent.

Date of Authorization	Term	Bond Contract Interest Rate	Interest Payment Dates
January 1, 19X1	5 Years	12%	Semi-annually on June 30 and December 31

Required: Consider these cases. Case A: Joliette Inc. uses the straight-line method of amortization. Case B: Joliette Inc. uses the effective interest method of amortization. Prepare an amortization table to calculate the amount of amortization applicable to the first two six-month periods.

For each of the cases
1. Calculate
   a. The amount of interest paid on the $250,000-worth of face value bonds every interest payment date
   b. The amount of amortization to be recorded at each interest payment date (For convenience round all calculations to the nearest dollar.)
2. a. Prepare a schedule to compare the financing charge for the first year under both effective interest and straight-line methods. (For convenience round all percent calculations to one decimal place.)
   b. Comment on the financing percentage that results under each amortization method. Which method is most appropriate? Why?
3. Prepare journal entries to record
   a. The issue of the bonds
   b. The payment of interest and amortization applicable at June 30, 19X1
   c. The payment of interest and amortization applicable at December 31, 19X4
   d. The redemption of the bonds at maturity, January 1, 19X6

Alternate Problem 13-6

James's Aluminum Products Inc. was authorized to issue $1,000,000-worth of face value bonds.

Date of Authorization	Term	Bond Contract Interest Rate	Interest Payment Dates
January 1, 19X7	3 Years	12%	Semi-annually on June 30 and December 31

The following transactions occurred during 19X7.

Jan. 1   Issued $100,000-worth of face value bonds

Jun. 30   Paid the semi-annual interest on the issued bonds and made an entry to record straight-line amortization

Dec. 31   Paid the semi-annual interest on the issued bonds and made an entry to record amortization.

Required: Consider these cases. Case A: the bonds were issued at a price to yield 12%. Case B: the bonds were issued at a price to yield the market rate of interest (16%). Case C: the bonds were issued to yield the market rate of interest (10%). For each of the cases

1. Calculate
   a. The amount of each semi-annual interest payment on the issued bonds
   b. The issue price of the bonds, consisting of the present value of the bond face value and the present value of the 6 semi-annual interest payments to be made during the 3-year period (For convenience, round all calculations to the nearest dollar.)
   c. The amount of amortization applicable to each interest payment date (Use the straight-line method of amortization; for convenience, round all calculations to the nearest dollar.)
2. Prepare journal entries to record the 19X7 transactions.

Supplementary Problems

Supplementary Problem 13-1

Johnson Computer Corporation was authorized to issue $150,000-worth of face value bonds. On January 1, 19X1, the corporation issued $100,000-worth of face value bonds to finance the construction of a new plant. The bonds were issued for $100,000.

Date of Authorization	Term	Bond Contract Interest Rate	Interest Payment Dates
January 1, 19X1	3 Years	12%	Semi-annually on June 30 and December 31

Required:
1. Calculate the amount of interest paid every six months.
2. Prepare journal entries to record
   a. The issue of the bonds on January 1, 19X1
   b. The payment of interest on June 30, 19X1
   c. The payment of interest on December 31, 19X1.

An additional $50,000-worth of face value bonds were issued January 1, 19X2. These bonds were issued for $48,000. Calculate the following:
3. a. The amount of interest paid on the $150,000-worth of face value of bonds every interest payment date
   b. The amount of amortization to be recorded at each interest payment date (Use the straight-line method of amortization.)
4. Prepare journal entries to record
   a. The issue of the bonds on January, 1, 19X2
   b. The payment of interest on June 30, 19X2 on the $150,000-worth of face value of issued bonds
   c. The amortization of bond discount on June 30, 19X2
   d. The payment of interest on December 31, 19X2
   e. The amortization of bond discount on December 31, 19X2.
5. Prepare a partial balance sheet at December 31, 19X2 to show the bond liability and the bond discount as a deferred charge. (Note that the bonds are to be redeemed on January 1, 19X4.)
6. Prepare a journal entry to record the redemption of the bonds at maturity, January 1, 19X4.

Supplementary Problem 13-2

Grandma's Kitchen Inc. was authorized to issue $800,000-worth of face value bonds. The corporation issued bonds of $200,000 face value for $207,200.

Date of Authorization	Term	Bond Contract Interest Rate	Interest Payment Dates
January 1, 19X7	3 Years	12%	Semi-annually on June 30 and December 31

Required: Consider these cases. Case A: the bonds are issued on January 1, 19X7. Case B: the bonds are issued on April 1, 19X7. (Note that the issue price includes accrued interest.) Case C: the bonds are issued on July 1, 19X7. For each of the cases
1. Calculate
   a. The amount of interest paid on the issued bonds every interest payment date
   b. The amount of amortization, if any, applicable to each month remaining in the life of the bonds subsequent to the issue date (Calculate separately the amortization to be recorded at each interest payment date; use the straight-line method of amortization.)

2. Prepare journal entries to record
   a. The issue of the bonds
   b. The payment of interest and recording of amortization, if any, on June 30, 19X7
   c. The payment of interest and recording of amortization, if any, on December 31, 19X7.
3. Calculate the amount of interest expense shown in the income statement at December 31, 19X7. Is this amount the same as cash paid as interest in 19X7? Why or why not?

Supplementary Problem 13-3

The following information appears in the published balance sheet of Lotus P.C. Corporation at December 31, 19X3, its fiscal year-end.

Deferred Charges:	
Discount on Bonds Payable	$ 4,000
Long-Term Liabilities:	
Bond Payable	500,000

The corporation was authorized to issued $500,000-worth of face value bonds to finance the construction of a new solar cell assembly plant. The bonds were issued on their authorization date. The corporation uses the straight-line method of amortization.

Date of Authorization	Term	Bond Contract Interest Rate	Interest Payment Dates
January 1, 19X3	3 Years	12%	Semi-annually on June 30 and December 31

Required:
1. Calculate
   a. The proceeds from the bond issue on January 1, 19X3
   b. The amount of cash interest paid in 19X3
   c. The amount of amortization recorded during 19X3
   d. The total amount of amortization to be recorded during the life of the bonds
   e. The amount of interest expense appearing in the 19X3 income statement.
2. Prepare journal entries to record
   a. The issue of the bonds on January 1, 19X3
   b. The payment of interest and recording of bond discount amortization on June 30, 19X3
   c. The payment of interest and recording of bond discount amortization on December 31, 19X3.

On January 1, 19X4, some bondholders exercised a conversion feature contained in the bond indenture; $100,000-worth of face value bonds were converted into the corporation's common shares.

3. Prepare a journal entry to record the conversion.

Supplementary Problem 13-4

Lloyd's Software House Inc. was authorized to issue $400,000-worth of face value bonds. On April 1, 19X5, the corporation issued bonds of $100,000 face value in order to purchase the rights to a word processing software package.

Date of Authorization	Term	Bond Contract Interest Rate	Interest Payment Dates
January 1, 19X5	3 Years	12%	Semi-annually on June 30 and December 31

Required: Consider these cases. Case A: the bonds are issued for $100,000, an amount which includes the accrued interest. Case B: the bonds are issued for $106,600, an amount which includes the accrued interest. Case C: the bonds are issued for $96,700, an amount which includes the accrued interest. For each of the cases
1. Calculate
   a. The amount of interest paid on $100,000 face value bonds every interest payment date
   b. The amount of accrued interest on the bonds issued April 1, 19X5
   c. The amount of amortization applicable to each month remaining in the life of the bonds, subsequent to the issue date. Calculate separately the actual amount of amortization to be recorded at each interest payment date, using the straight-line method of amortization.
2. Prepare journal entries to record
   a. The issue of bonds on April 1, 19X5 (including accrued interest)
   b. The payment of interest on June 30, 19X5
   c. The amortization on June 30, 19X5
   d. The payment of interest on December 31, 19X5
   e. The amortization on December 31, 19X5
   f. The redemption of the bonds at maturity, January 1, 19X8.
3. Calculate the amount of interest expense shown in the income statement at December 31, 19X5.
4. Prepare a partial balance sheet at December 31, 19X5, to show the bond liability and bond premium or discount, if applicable.

Supplementary Problem 13-5

Labrador Tall Grass Ltd. was authorized to issue $800,000-worth of face value bonds. On the date of authorization, the corporation issued bonds of $200,000 (face value) at a price to yield the market 18 percent rate of interest.

Date of Authorization	Term	Bond Contract Interest Rate	Interest Payment Dates
January 1, 19X2	3 Years	12%	Semi-annually on June 30 and December 31

Required:
1. Calculate
   a. The amount of each semi-annual interest payment on the issued bonds.
   b. The issue price of the bonds, consisting of the present value of the bond face value and the present value of the 6 semi-annual interest payments to be made during the 3-year period. (For convenience, round all calculations to the nearest dollar.)
   c. The amount of amortization applicable to each 19X2 interest payment date. Prepare, using the effective interest method of amortization, an amortization table for the 3 year period. (For convenience, round all calculations to the nearest dollar.)
2. Prepare journal entries to record the 19X3 transactions.
3. a. Compare the financing percentage for 19X2 under both effective interest and straight-line methods. (For convenience round all percent calculations to one decimal place.)
   b. Comment on the financing percentage that results under each amortization method. Which method is most appropriate? Why?

The Investment Cycle

Part V deals with the investment activities of an entity. These activities may be either an investment of temporarily idle cash or may involve the acquisition of a long-term position in another entity to exercise a degree of control over the other entities.

The investment cycle views equity and debt from the viewpoint of the purchaser — the investor who transfers capital to a corporation. The relative risk of investing in bonds and shares is reviewed and, differences in their accounting treatment are illustrated.

Chapter 14 deals with issues relating to both short-term and long-term bond and share investments. Chapter 17 focus on business combinations and extends the discussion begun in Chapter 14 regarding ways in which an investor acquires a controlling interest in another entity. Such an investor is actually able to control the entity, which is then referred to as a subsidiary. Although there are some exceptions, the individual financial statements of the parent and subsidiary are combined for reporting purposes, as if they were one economic entity and not two separate corporations.

The Investment Cycle

One corporation often invests in the bonds or shares of another corporation. These investments can be either temporary or long-term. Temporarily idle cash is often invested in securities that can be readily reconverted into cash as financing needs require. Shares are often purchased as long-term investments; they may be purchased to exercise a degree of control over another corporation. Relevant questions of interest to investors include:

1. Are bonds or shares a more secure form of investment?
2. What are the advantages of investing in shares of a corporation?
3. Is it true that investors have little chance of making a substantial profit on the stock market as is claimed by the efficient market hypothesis?
4. What are the alternative methods of disclosure of investments in the balance sheet?
5. What are the differences in accounting for investments in shares and bonds?
6. How are marketable securities valued for balance sheet purposes?
7. What are the different levels of investments that result in voting influence of one corporation over the operations of another corporation?
8. How does the accounting treatment of long-term investment in common shares differ, depending on the level of ownership by the investor?
9. How are bond premiums and bond discounts amortized?

A. The Investment Decision

Every corporate entity is financed by capital transferred to it by both shareholders and creditors. The preceding chapters have viewed shares and bonds from the point of view of the issuing corporations. This chapter views shares and bonds from the viewpoint of the *purchasing entity*—the investor who transfers capital into a corporation. Investments in a corporation can take various forms, as shown in Figure 14-1.

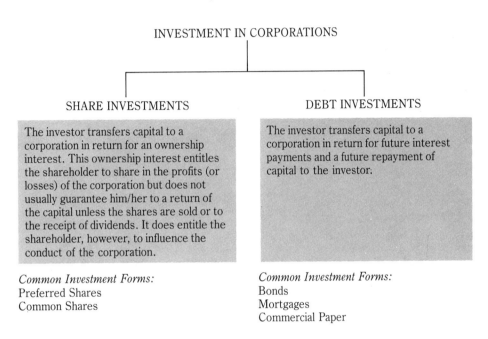

Figure 14-1   **Forms of investment in corporations**

No investor is guaranteed against a loss of invested capital if the business entity is unsuccessful. In fact, both share and debt investments can be lost if a corporation becomes bankrupt and there remain insufficient assets to be distributed to investors. Alternatively, there may be insufficient cash to pay interest to debt investors even when a corporation is not bankrupt. This, in fact, has occurred — for instance in the cases of Massey-Ferguson Ltd. and the Chrysler Corporation.

In normal circumstances, bondholders are more secure than shareholders and are able to institute legal action to obtain at least partial repayment of their capital and the interest owed them, even if this would result in the liquidation of the corporation.

Shareholders are unable to force the repayment of their investment, unless the privileges and rights attaching to the shares include a redeemable or conversion feature; usually shareholders are also unable to force a corporation to pay dividends. Why, then, would someone wish to invest in shares of a corporation? There are many reasons:

1. While it is true that an investor does risk capital, he/she also expects rewards in return. If the corporation is successful, the investor in common shares will increase the value of the investment substantially. This is *capital appreciation*.
2. The investor in common shares has a vote in the running of the corporation. The investor has an opportunity to participate in setting the goals of the corporation.

Conceptual Issue 14-1
The Efficient Markets Hypothesis

There is a passage in Lewis Carroll's *Through the Looking Glass* that sums up the stock market view of most finance professors at the University of Chicago Business School. "Here, you see," the Red Queen tells Alice, "it takes all the running you can do, to keep in the same place."

Translated into financial theory at Chicago, this means that no matter how carefully you pick your stocks, you cannot, on average, beat the market. In theory, therefore, the best plan is simply to buy all stocks in the market. This idea is known as the random walk theory, or efficient markets hypothesis, and it rests on the assumption that all important information about the real value of a stock is already incorporated in the stock's price. It is also the theory for which the Chicago Business School's finance department is famous — if the stock market presents an overly advantageous investment opportunity, the market is efficient enough to spot it quickly and bid up prices almost immediately. In other words, the market sees everything.

The efficient markets theory has inspired an almost religious frenzy among generations of doctoral candidates. For years, computer tapes have spun day and night in Chicago, as scores of researchers have tried to discover the extent to which the efficient markets hypothesis fits the real world. And almost always, the theory works.

---

3. Dividends may be declared by the corporation and may become substantial in relation to the amount of the investor's original investment. If dividends are not declared but are re-invested within the corporation, the value of the investment in common shares should increase.

Stock Market Prices

Efficient Markets Hypothesis
The theory that securities are typically in equilibrium and that they are fairly priced in the sense that the price reflects all publicly available information on the security.

It is claimed that investors have little chance of making a substantial profit on the stock market because of the **efficient market hypothesis**. This theory claims that few stocks are so undervalued that investors can yield large profits. The applicability of this theory in real life is discussed in Conceptual Issue 14-1.

Valuation of Investments

There are three different alternate methods for the disclosure of investments on the balance sheet.

Alternative 1: Original Cost
Investments are reported at their acquisition cost, which includes the original amount paid, brokerage fees, and any other acquisition costs. Under this method, the market value is disclosed on the balance sheet in parenthesis, even if market value declines below cost, provided that the decline is not expected to be permanent. This is the accepted Canadian method. In this method the temporary decline does not appear on the income statement.

Alternative 2: Lower of Cost and Market
Under this method, cost is compared with market value of the securities at each balance sheet date, and the lower of the two is used as their balance sheet value. This is the method in the United States. The actual asset account is not reduced if market is less than cost. A contra asset account (called a valuation account) is used to recognize a reduction from cost to market. In this method, the decline may be reported on the

But from time to time a researcher discovers something that the Chicago theory of efficient markets does not explain and even contradicts. Rolf Banz was such a researcher. As a Chicago graduate student in the mid-1970s, he discovered that if publicly traded companies were ranked in order of total market value, the smallest 20 percent earned abnormally high investor returns, even after adjusting for risk.

The Banz anomaly, now known as the "small-firm effect," continues to puzzle scholars of finance, especially those who adhere strongly to the efficient markets theory. But this puzzlement has not stopped some from making money on the anomaly. Thus, in 1981, a group of Chicago graduates, with the help of their professors, founded Dimensional Fund Advisors, an investment company designed to take advantage of the contradictory small-firm effect. DFA began offering a mutual fund that invested in the common stocks of some 650 companies with market values below $69 million, weighted in proportion to each company's size.

An obvious question about the fund's success is how is it affecting the Ivory Tower thinking at the famed Chicago school? According to Professor Miller, some day either the small-firm effect or the Banz theory itself will disappear. The enduring threat is that the theory is like a "barnacle" clinging to the efficient markets hypothesis. Over time, more barnacles will accumulate, until the efficient market hypothesis finally collapses and a new one takes its place. Though that may shake up the Chicago school, DFA officers will be scratching their heads all the way to the bank.

Source Claudia Rosett, Chicago School Bets on Inefficiency'', *The New York Times*, December 11, 1983.

income statement as a separate item, or following the shareholders' equity section of the balance sheet. The distinction between a short-term and a long-term investment determines where the unrealized loss should be reported. This disclosure method is discussed later in this chapter.

Alternative 3: Current Market Value

The market value at balance sheet date is taken as the value of investments, regardless of what cost is. This is not a generally accepted method of valuing these securities and is seldom used in actual practice, except by some financial institutions.

Accounting for Corporate Investments

Temporary investments
Investments of temporarily idle cash, usually in marketable securities, made for a period not exceeding one year from the balance sheet date.

Long-term investments
Investments in stocks and bonds that are not of a short-term nature.

Marketable securities
Investments in stock and bonds that are readily marketable; also includes investments in treasury bills, investment securities, and call loans.

Investments may be either **temporary** or **long-term**. The investor makes the decision. This decision affects the subsequent accounting treatment of the investment account. Although investments are always recorded at cost when the investment is made, special problems arise in the accounting for these investments after their acquisition date. Temporary and long-term investments are also classified differently on the balance sheet of the investor.

Temporarily idle cash usually earns no income unless it is invested. If the investor's objective is to invest in securities on a temporary basis and if these securities are readily marketable, then these investments are referred to as **marketable securities**, and are classified on the balance sheet as current assets immediately under cash and before accounts receivable.

Investors may decide to invest in the bonds of a corporation, or in voting or nonvoting shares of a corporation, as long-term *investments*. These investments are classified on the balance sheet as long-term assets.

The *CICA Handbook* (section 3050.03) defines Portfolio Investments as "long-term investments that are not investments in subsidiaries, joint ventures, or partnerships of the reporting enterprise, nor investments in companies that are subject to significant influence by the reporting enterprise". Both shares and bonds are included in this definition of portfolio investments.

Differences in Share and Bond Investment Accounting

The accounting for investments is influenced by a number of other considerations. The purchase of shares is always recorded at cost. However, because share purchases result in an ownership interest in the corporation, the subsequent accounting for the investment is affected by the influence that the investor is able to exert over the corporation. This matter is discussed further in Section C of this chapter.

When the investment in bonds is of a temporary nature, note that no amortization of bond premium or discount is recorded in the books of the investor. This is because the bonds are not expected to be held until maturity. The practice is further justified by the fact that the amounts involved would not be material. However, the premium or discount on bonds purchased as long-term investments is amortized. The amortization of an investor's bond premium or discount, if any, is discussed in section D of this chapter.

B.   Investments in Marketable Securities

Excess cash can be kept in a non-interest-bearing bank account or it can be invested in dividend-producing or interest-earning securites. A corporation's investment in such securities is considered temporary when its intention is to hold them for the short term and then reconvert them to cash. These securities are referred to as marketable when they are readily convertible to cash. Marketable securities usually consist of securities from government and publicly traded corporations; they may also include treasury bills, investment certificates, and call loans.

The purchase of securities is always recorded at the purchase cost, including brokerage charges and any other acquisition costs. Assume the following are initial temporary investments in Bluebeard Computer Corporation in 19X1:

Share Purchase

100 shares of BCC stock are purchased on the stock exchange for $45. Brokerage charges of $100 are paid. The purchase is recorded at cost as follows:

Marketable Securities	4,600	
Cash		4,600

To record the purchase of 100 shares at $45 per share, plus $100 brokerage charges (cost per share is $46).

Bond Purchase:

A $1,000 bond of BCC is purchased on the stock exchange at 106. Brokerage charges of $15 are paid. The purchase is recorded at cost as follows:

Marketable Securities	1,075	
Cash		1,075

To record the purchase of a $1,000 bond at 106, plus brokerage charges.

Often the purchase price of shares includes dividends that have been declared but not yet paid at the time of the purchase of shares; bonds often include interest accrued but not yet paid at the purchase date. In such cases, the entry to record the purchase separates the dividend or interest component of the purchase price.

Assume the following additional purchase of temporary investments in the Bluebeard Computer Corporation is made during 19X1. (Note: this example assumes that reversing entries are not used by the corporation.)

Share Purchase:

50 shares of BCC stock are purchased at $46 per share. Included in the purchase price is a $2 per-share dividend that has been declared but not yet paid. Brokerage charges of $50 are paid. The purchase is recorded as follows:

Marketable Securities	2,250	
Dividends Receivable	100	
Cash		2,350

To record the purchase of 50 shares at $46, including a $2 per share dividend (cost per share is $45).

When the dividend is received, it is recorded as follows:

Cash	100	
Dividends Receivable		100

To record dividend received on shares.

Bond Purchase:

$5000-worth of BCC bonds are purchased at 105 plus $200 of accrued interest. The purchase is recorded as follows:

Marketable Securities	5,250	
Bond Interest Receivable	200	
Cash		5,450

To record the purchase of $5,000-worth of bonds at 105, plus $200 accrued interest.

Note, the cost of the bonds does not include the accrued interest; the accrued interest is recorded as a separate asset.

When the semi-annual interest of $300 is received, it is recorded as follows:

Cash	300	
Bond Interest Receivable		200
Bond Interest Earned		100

To record receipt of semi-annual interest on bond.

All purchases are recorded at cost. Interest is earned on the bonds with the passage of time and is recorded as income when received or when an adjustment entry is prepared. Although dividends do not accrue with the passing of time, corporations often declare a quarterly dividend per share and it is at the date of declaration that the dividend is legally payable. The following journal entries illustrate the recording for dividend declaration and interest accrual.

Dividend Declaration:

When dividends are declared, the following entry is made:

Dividends Receivable	375	
Dividends Earned		375

To record the declaration of a $2.50 per-share dividend on 150 shares (150 shares × $2.50 = $375).

The subsequent receipt of the dividend is recorded as follows:

Cash	375	
Dividends Receivable		375

To record receipt of dividends on 150 shares.

Interest Accrual:

The accrual of interest is recorded as follows:

Bond Interest Receivable	360	
Bond Interest Earned		360

To record the accrual of interest earned on bonds

$$(\$6,000 \times 12\% \times \frac{6}{12} = \$360).$$

The subsequent receipt of interest is recorded as follows:

Cash	360	
Bond Interest Receivable		360

To record receipt of interest on $6,000-worth of bonds.

Temporary investments in bonds are not expected to be held until maturity; therefore, no amortization of any bond premium or discount is recorded. Rather, a gain or loss is recognized when the bonds are sold.

As illustrated in Chapter 11, a stock dividend consists of shares instead of cash. The stock dividend is expressed as a percentage of shares owned; for example, an investor owning 1000 shares receives 100 new shares, when a 10 percent stock dividend is issued.

No journal entry is made by the investor on receipt of a stock dividend, since there is no dividend income. The investor simply increases the number of shares owned in the declaring corporation and, of course, has 100 additional share certificates. The investor's total cost of shares remains the amount that was originally paid for the 1000 shares.

	Investment in Shares			
	Before Stock Dividend		After Stock Dividend	
	Cost	*Shares Owned*	*Cost*	*Shares Owned*
	$5,000	1000 shares	$5,000	1100 shares
Cost per Share:				
$5,000 ÷ 1000 Shares	$5			
$5,000 ÷ 1100 Shares			$4.55 (rounded)	

As seen in these calculations, the $5,000 cost of this investor's shares is allocated over 1000 shares before the stock dividend, and over 1100 shares after the stock dividend. The cost of the shares continues to be $5,000 in total; only the cost per share changes.

Theoretically, the per-share market value of the common shares should fall somewhat to compensate for the increased number of shares. For example, the market price of the share should decrease as follows:

	Before Stock Dividend	*After* Stock Dividend (theoretically)
Market Price of Common Share	$4	A New, Lower Market Value
Total Market Value of Shares:		
1000 Shares × $4	$4,000	$4,000
1100 Shares × New Market Price		$3.64 (rounded)

In reality, the market price rarely decreases proportionately to the percentage of the stock dividend. Usually, if the stock dividend is not large in relation to the total of outstanding shares, no change occurs in the per-share market value of the shares. Therefore, the investor would see the market value of these shares increase as follows:

	Market Value of Investment	
	Before Stock Dividend	*After Stock Dividend*
Common Shares:		
1000 × $4	$4,000	
1100 × $4		$4,400

That is, the investor sees the total market value of common shares increase by $400. No journal entry is made by the investor to reflect this *unrealized* increase. If a gain (or loss) on the investment is realized, it is recorded when the shares have actually been sold.

Sale of Marketable Securities

The *CICA Handbook* recommends that the cost of investments sold should be calculated on the basis of average carrying value. In this way, the difficulties of identifying the specific cost of the investments, or the calculation of a FIFO or LIFO cost, are avoided. A gain or loss results from the difference between cost and the proceeds of sale. When bonds are sold any accrued interest is included in the entry to record the sale with a credit to the Bond Interest Earned account.

Assume that the temporary investment in shares is subsequently reconverted to cash; the 150 shares are sold for $48 per share. The following entry records this transaction.

Cash	7,200	
Marketable Securities (4,600 + 2,250)		6,850
Gain on Sale of Marketable Securities		350
To record the sale of 150 shares.		

The gain on disposal of marketable securities is classified on the income statement as "other income". The gain calculated above must be considered along with the dividends received in evaluating the investment in shares.

Valuation of Marketable Securities

Canadian practice favours the valuation of marketable securities at cost and the disclosure of market values of these securities in parentheses on the balance sheet. Where a substantial decline in market value has occurred, accepted practice is to value both debt and equity securities at the lower of cost and market. In this situation, an unrealized loss from market fluctuations is recognized; an unrealized gain, however, is never recognized before the sale of the investment.

American practice favours the valuation of marketable debt securities in a manner consistent with Canadian practice. However, the recommended valuation of marketable equity securities differs: FASB Statement No. 12 advocates the LOCAM valuation of marketable securities at each balance sheet date. The total aggregate cost of marketable equity securities is compared at the balance sheet date with their aggregate market value; any decline below cost is recorded in a contra (or, valuation) account. No entry is made to the Marketable Equity Securities account.

Creation of a Valuation Account

The creation of a valuation account is discussed here, using as an example the purchase of Bluebeard Computer Corporation bonds, which cost $6,325. Assume that their market value has declined to $5,100 at the balance sheet date. An unrealized loss of $1,225 ($6,325 − $5,100) exists at this date and is recorded by the following journal entry.

Dec. 31 Unrealized Loss in Market Value of Marketable		
Equity Securities	1,225	
Allowance for Market Value Decline of		
Marketable Equity Securities		1,225

The unrealized loss account is classified in the income statement as "other expenses", below the calculation of operating income.

The allowance account is deducted from marketable securities on the balance sheet.

Assets		
Current Assets:		
Marketable Securities, at Cost	$6,325	
Less: Allowance for Market Value		
Decline of Marketable Equity Securities	1,225	$5,100

The cost of marketable securities is reduced by the unrecognized loss of $1,225 at the balance sheet date. The allowance account is referred to as a valuation account.

Adjusting the Valuation Account

A comparison of total aggregate cost with total aggregate market value is also made at the next balance sheet date. At that date, the valuation account is increased (to reflect further declines in market value) or decreased (to reflect a recovery of a recorded decline) to reflect changes in the market value of the marketable securities.

If the market value decreases $500 the following year, then this decline is recorded by the following entry:

Unrealized Loss in Market
  Value of M.E.S.   500
    Allowance for Market Value
      Decline of M.E.S.   500

In this case, the allowance account is increased by the $500 decline; the loss is classified in the income statement as "other expenses". Note that this loss is an unrealized loss.

If the market value increases $500 the following year, the increase is recorded by the following entry:

Allowance for Market
  Value Decline of M.E.S.   500
    Unrealized gain in Market
      Value of M.E.S.   500

In this case, the allowance is decreased by the $500 increase; the gain is classified in the income statement as "other income". Note that this gain is an unrealized gain.

Under the LOCAM method, market value decreases are recorded as they occur. The recovery of such decreases resulting from subsequent market value increases can be recorded up to the amount of decreases previously recorded; that is, recoveries cannot be recorded in excess of decreases originally recorded.

When marketable securities are sold, a gain or loss on the sale is recognized based on the original cost of the marketable securities and the proceeds from their sale. The balance in the unrealized loss account is ignored at the time of this recording, if there are other investments in the account. Assume that marketable equity securities with a purchase cost of $6,325 are sold for $7,000; the following entry would be made:

Cash   7,000
  Gain on Sale of Marketable Equity Securities   675
  Marketable Securities   6,325
To record sale of Bluebeard Computer
Corporation bonds.

The above gain of $675 is referred to as a realized gain, since it is the result of an objectively determined transaction; it is classified in the income statement as "other income".

Following the sale of these marketable equity securities (no marketable equity securities remain), a comparison of total aggregate cost with total aggregate market value would be made at the next balance sheet date and the accounting entries already discussed would be repeated.

C. Long-Term Intercorporate Share Investments

Intercorporate investments
Investments made by one corporation in voting common shares of another corporation, usually done to gain a voting influence over the other corporation; can also include investments in non-voting shares and bonds of the other corporation.

It is not uncommon for one corporation to invest in another corporation; such investments are commonly called **intercorporate investments**. Figure 14-2 compares the different types of intercorporate investments and the influence carried by each.

The accounting for intercorporate share investments is influenced by whether such investments provide a voting influence over another corporation or whether they are simply portfolio equity investments.

Investor Control of a Corporation

Intercorporate investments in common shares of a corporation may result in voting influence of one corporation over the operations of the other corporation (called the *investee*). Three levels of possible influence have been identified; these three levels of

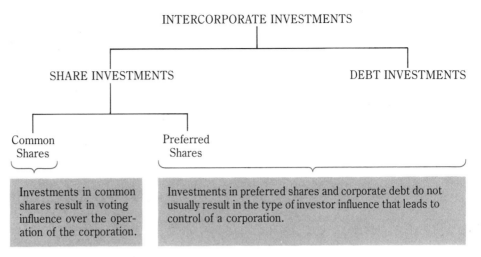

Figure 14-2   Forms of intercorporate investment

control, how they differ, and how they are accounted for are explained briefly here. (Chapter 17 continues the discussion.)

Level 1:   The under 20 Percent Level

The investor is usually seen as having little influence or control over the corporation when it has less than 20 percent ownership. The investment is reported on the financial statements of the investor at cost.

Level 2: The 20 to 50 Percent Level

In this range of ownership, it is assumed that the investor has a significant influence and control over the corporation, unless circumstances make its assumption unrealistic. The investment is reported on the financial statements of the investor under the equity method.

Level 3:   The over 50 Percent Level

In excess of 50 percent ownership, the investor is actually able to control the corporation— which is then referred to as a **subsidiary** of the investing **parent**. The financial statements of the parent and subsidiary are combined as if they were for one legal entity, not two separate corporations. The combined financial statements are then referred to as *consolidated financial statements*.

Subsidiary
An investee, controlled by another corporation, referred to as a parent, that owns 50 percent or more of the subsidiary's voting shares.

Parent
An investor corporation that owns 50 percent or more of the voting shares of a subsidiary corporation.

Note that the accounting treatment of a long-term investment in common stock (usually the voting shares) differs, depending on the level of ownership by the investor. It should be remembered that these levels are merely intended to be guidelines. In some cases, it may be possible for a corporation with less than 20 percent ownership to exert a significant influence and, in other cases, an investor with a 20–50 percent ownership may not have a significant influence. The specific circumstances must be reviewed when selecting the most appropriate accounting treatment of a corporation's long-term investment in common, or voting, shares of another corporation. An example of some of the complexities that could become involved in the choice of appropriate accounting treatment of long-term investment in shares is presented in Real Life Example 14-1.

Real Life Example 14-1

Nine Families Control 46 Percent of Stock on TSE 300

A report by the Canadian Bankers' Association showing 9 families control stock worth 46 percent of the value of the most important companies on the Toronto Stock Exchange was done to debunk the myth that the banks are increasing their control of the financial system, an association official says.

"We were getting concerned by the arguments raised by some members of the financial community that changes happening in the financial sector would cause the banks to dominate the financial system," Helen Sinclair, the association's director of public relations, said yesterday. "Underlying the whole thesis was the innuendo that the levels of concentration were increasing, which was contrary to fact. They are decreasing.

"And the arguments being levied were being levied in large part by some of these very large conglomerates which in fact really rival the banks in size."

The Canadian Bankers' Association report, completed last week, says that, if the chartered banks are removed from the calculation, the 9 families control 53 percent of the stock exchange's widely watched list of 300 companies, known as the TSE 300. This index includes about 30 companies that provide financial services.

The report says the financial empire of Peter and Edward Bronfman is already bigger than the Canadian assets of the Royal Bank of Canada, the country's largest bank. And the financial empire of Hal Jackman, through E.L. Financial Corp., is bigger than the Bank of Nova Scotia or the Toronto Dominion Bank.

A financial institution's assets are the total of its outstanding loans and mortgages as well as the value of its own portfolio investments.

While the association did not name names, a published report on the association's study said conglomerates referred to include those owned by Kenneth Thomson, the Bronfmans, Paul Desmarais, Galen Weston, Conrad and Montegu Black,

Recording Long-Term Investments in Shares

Cost is the generally accepted method of recording an investment in shares. Regardless of the ownership level that results from the share purchase, the investment is recorded at cost by the investor. After acquisition, either the cost method or the equity method can be used to record these investments. The following paragraphs explain and contrast these two methods in the case of level 1 and level 2 investor control.

Recording Method 1:   Cost
After acquisition, the investment is kept in the records of the investor at cost. The investment is reported on the balance sheet at cost. The income or losses of the issuer are ignored by the investor. Dividends are recorded as income by the investor and included in the investor's income statement.

Recording Method 2:   Equity
After acquisition, the investment is kept in the records of the investor by the cost method or, alternately, may be kept in the records by the equity method (as explained below). However, the investment is reported on the balance sheet only by the equity method. The cost of the investment is increased by the investor's share of the annual income of the issuer (or decreased by losses). This share of income is included in the income statement of the investor. The cost of the investment is reduced by the amount of dividends received by the investor. No dividend income appears on the income statement of the investor.

The important similarity to be noted between these two methods is that the investment is initially recorded at cost and may continue to be recorded on a cost basis in the day-to-day records of the investor.

the Reichmann family, as well as Ron Southern and the Seaman brothers of Calgary.

Sinclair, in Ottawa as part of an association delegation to present a brief to the House of Commons committee Loans Act, said in an interview she did not have the names on hand, but the list in the published report looked accurate.

There's no suggestion that the families we are taling about are unethical,'' she added. ''To the contrary, they are leaders in the business world.''

What the association is concerned about is the risk of self-dealing and conflict of interest that increases as conglomerates grow to take in aspects of the financial and industrial sector, Sinclair said. ''We take the view that the financial sector should be separate from the industrial sector for that reason.''

The report recommends that rules limiting the ownership of banks or their investment strategies should apply to other financial institutions. Federal law stipulates no one may own more than 10 percent of a Canadian chartered bank. Banks in turn may not own more than 10 percent of companies outside banking.

Sinclair said the report will be given to the federal government which is currently reviewing all legislation governing financial institutions. Barbara McDougall, minister of state for finance, has promised a discussion paper within a few weeks, followed by consultation and new legislation late this year.

The financial institutions have been asking for new legislation to clarify their roles. While the banks, insurance and trust companies, and investment dealers have traditionally provided separate services, they have been lobbying for the power to merge these services and provide ''one-stop-shopping'' for consumers.

The association wants its findings considered when the new legislation is drafted.

''All we're trying to do is debunk a myth which we feel is being mounted to protect the interests of certain industries to the detriment of the consumer,'' said Sinclair. ''Our whole point in the restructuring of financial services is that the consumer is the only party who really counts. And we shouldn't be re-regulating industries to protect insurance companies or to protect trust companies.''

Source Canadian Press, ''9 Families Control 46% of Stock on TSE 300'', *The* (Montreal) *Gazette*, March 20, 1985, p. C-3.

Under the equity method, regardless of how the investment account is kept in the books of the investor, the investment is reported in the financial statements on an equity basis.

Following are the journal entries that would be required under the cost and equity methods. Assume that the investment for a 100-percent ownership was $100,000, the income of the investee for the relevant year is $25,000, and dividends paid by the investee during the same period were $4,000. Note the differences.

The Cost Method			The Equity Method			Transaction
Investment in Shares	100,000		Investment in Shares	100,000		Investment in Shares
Cash		100,000	Cash		100,000	of Investee
			Investment in Shares	25,000		
(*No entry is required.*)			Income from Investee		25,000	Income of Investee
						for the Year
Cash	4,000		Cash	4,000		Receipt of Dividend
Dividend Income		4,000	Investment in Shares		4,000	from Investee

The effect of the cost and equity methods on the amounts reported in the financial statements of the investor is illustrated below:

	The Cost Method		The Equity Method	
	Balance Sheet	*Income Statement*	*Balance Sheet*	*Income Statement*
Original Investment	$100,000		$100,000	
Investment Income during the Year Reported by Investee			+25,000	+$25,000
Dividend Received from Investee during the Year		+$4,000	−4,000	
Amounts Reported by Investor	$100,000	$4,000	$121,000	$25,000

Valuation of Long-Term Investments

Canadian practice favours the balance sheet valuation of long-term investments at cost. The market value is disclosed on the balance sheet in parentheses, even if the market value of these investments declines below cost, provided that the decline is not expected to be permanent. When a permanent loss in the value of the investment has occurred, the *CICA Handbook* recommends that the investment be written down to recognize the loss. In the case of shares, a write-down of the investment would be recorded by the following entry.

Loss in Value of Long-Term Investment	X	
Investment in Shares		X

The loss account would appear in the income statement as "other losses". The written down cost of the investment is subsequently used in accounting for the investment. If there is a subsequent increase in the market value of the investment, the *CICA Handbook* recommends that the write-down of the investment should *not* be reversed.

A loss in the value of a long-term investment can arise not only in the case of a bankruptcy or an agreement to sell, but also in such situations as:
• a prolonged period during which the quoted market value of the investment is less than its carrying value
• severe losses by the investee in the current year or current and earlier years
• continued losses by the investee for a period of years
• suspension of trading in the securities
• liquidity or going concern problems of the investee
• the current fair value of the investment (an appraisal) is less than its carrying value

It should be noted that the Canadian practice differs from the American method recommended in FASB Statement No. 12. In accordance with FASB Statement No. 12, long-term portfolio equity investments are valued in a way similar to that for marketable equity securities. As with marketable equity securities, a comparison of total aggregate cost with total aggregate market value is made at each balance sheet date. Where a significant difference exists, a valuation account is created recording this difference. The following journal entry shows the recording of an unrealized loss.

Unrealized Loss in Market Value of Long-Term Investments	XX	
Allowance for Market Value Decline of Long-Term Investments		XX

The allowance account is deducted from the cost of the related long-term share investments on the balance sheet, as is the case for marketable equity securities. However, the loss account is not classified in the income statement but is classified as a contra account in the shareholders' equity section of the balance sheet.

Shareholders' Equity

Share Capital	$XXX
Retained Earnings	XXX
	XXX
Less: Unrealized Loss in Market Values	XX
of Long-term Investments	$XXX

Future market value decreases are recorded and classified in a similar manner; any future recovery of these decreases because of increases in market value are recorded as follows:

Allowance for Market Value Decline of Long-Term Investments	X	
Unrealized Loss in Market Value of Long-Term Investments		X

This future recovery reduces the amount deducted from shareholders' equity; the amount of such recoveries cannot be recorded in excess of previously recorded decreases.

When long-term share investments are sold, a gain or loss on the sale is recognized; the differences between cost and the proceeds from their sale is recorded as a gain or loss.

The sale of investments at a gain is recorded as follows:

Cash	XX	
Gain on Sale		X
Long-Term Investments		XX

The sale of investments at a loss is recorded as follows:

Cash	XX	
Loss on Sale	X	
Long-Term Investments		XX

The gain (or loss) in this case is realized and is classified in the income statement as "other income".

The CICA research study, "Accounting for Portfolio Investments", reviewed Canadian practice with the aim of identifying a common method of accounting suitable for most circumstances. One of the study's conclusions was that long-term portfolio investments in both shares and bonds should be carried at market value. This recommendation resulted from the fact that current market value represents the actual resources of the investor committed to the investment and, therefore, it provides the most realistic basis against which a return on investment can be calculated.

Although the use of current market prices would result in unrealized gains and losses being reported, there would be other advantages in valuing long-term portfolio investments and temporary investments at market value:

1. Current market values are readily available from stock exchanges and are objectively determined in the marketplace.
2. The amount of corporate resources available at the balance sheet date to pay debts would be indicated to the financial statement reader.
3. An evaluation of the effectiveness of management's investment decisions would be communicated to readers of financial statements, and the success of strategies by different corporations could be compared.

Although current market value is used in some industries, its general use is not at present in accordance with Canadian GAAP.

D. Long-Term Intercorporate Bond Investments

The accounting for long-term investments in bonds is essentially the reverse of the accounting required by the bond issues described in Chapter 13. The accounting for the long-term investments in bonds is similar to the accounting for short-term investments in bonds and the receipt of interest; the only exception is the accounting for the amortization of premiums and discounts.

Purchase Cost of Bonds

Investments in bonds are always recorded at cost; cost includes brokerage charges and any other applicable acquisition costs. The purchase price is affected by such factors as risk and the rate of inflation, but is largely determined by how investors view the bond contract interest rate in relation to the prevailing market interest rate.

1. If the bond contract interest rate is the same as that required in the market, then the bonds are usually purchased at par.
2. If the bond contract interest rate is greater than that required in the market, then the bonds are usually purchased at a premium (more than face value) to yield the investor the lower market rate.
3. If the bond contract interest rate is less than that required in the market, then the bonds are usually purchased at discount (less than face value) to yield the investor the higher market rate.

The sale of bonds by Bluebeard Computer Corporation is illustrated in section C of Chapter 13. The same data are used here as an example of an investor's purchase of these 12-percent, 3-year, $100,000 bonds paying interest semi-annually on June 30 and December 31 of each year. Their purchase at a premium and discount is shown below:

Purchased at a Premium			*Purchased at a Discount*		
Investment in Bonds	106,000		Investment in Bonds	88,000	
Cash		106,000	Cash		88,000

Note that the cost of the purchase is recorded at cost; no separate discount or premium account is required.

Amortizing Premiums and Discounts

In actual practice, the amount of premium or discount is amortized in equal amounts over the life of the bond remaining from the purchase date. It is also accepted practice to record amortization each time a journal entry is made to record interest earned. Therefore, where bond interest earned is recorded, an appropriate amount of amortization is also recorded. The periodically recorded amortization will change the carrying value of the investment (see Figure 14-3).

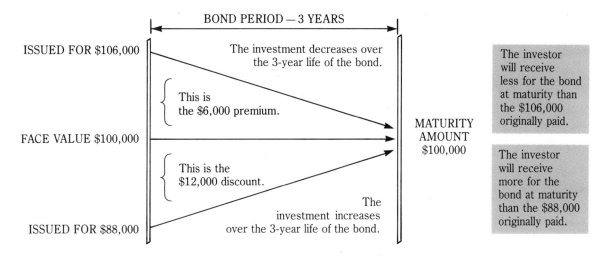

Figure 14-3 Change in carrying value over the life of the bond investment

The straight-line method of amortization is commonly used; an equal amount of amortization is allocated to each semi-annual period. The simplicity of calculation is this method's main advantage. The amortization is calculated as follows:

Amortization of a Premium		*Amortization of a Discount*	
Premium is	$6,000 (a)	Discount is	$12,000 (a)
Months left are	36 (b)	Months left are	36 (b)
Months amortized	6 (c)	Months amortized	6 (c)
Calculation:		*Calculation:*	
(a ÷ b) × c		(a ÷ b) × c	
($6,000 ÷ 36) × 6 =	$1,000	($12,000 ÷ 36) × 6 =	$2,000

The straight-line method of amortization is used in the examples here. This method is easier to use, even though the effective interest method of amortization is preferable from a theoretical point of view. Canadian GAAP permits use of either method.

When the bond is redeemed at maturity, the following journal entry is recorded:

```
19X4
Jan. 4   Cash                                  100,000
             Investment in Bonds                          100,000
         To record retirement of
         Bluebeard Computer Corporation bond.
```

The balance in the Investment in Bonds account has been reduced to face value at maturity; this entry reduces the balance in that account to zero.

How Is the Amortization of Premium Recorded in the Investor's Books?

In actual practice, the bond premium is commonly amortized using the straight-line method over the life of the bonds, until no premium remains at maturity. It is accepted practice to record amortization each time a journal entry is made to record interest. Therefore, when bond interest earned is recorded, an appropriate amount of premium amortization is also recorded. The amount of amortization applicable to each interest receipt period is calculated as follows:

$6,000 Premium ÷ 3 Years ÷ 2 Interest Payments per year =
$1,000 Amortization per Interest Period.

The journal entries to record the receipt of interest and the appropriate amortization are as follows:

Receipt of Interest			*Amortization of Premium*		
Cash	6,000		Bond Interest Earned	1,000	
Bond Interest Earned		6,000	Investment in Bonds		1,000

> This entry decreases the investment account and also the bond interest earned. The interest rate is therefore lower than the 12-percent bond interest rate.

Similar entries are made each June 30 and December 31 until the BCC bonds mature in three years. Bond interest earned is usually recorded in a separate general ledger account. Note that premium amortization reduces the bond interest earned; the yield to the investor is less than the bond contract interest rate, in this case. Consequently, the discount amortization increases the bond interest earned, thereby increasing, in excess of the bond contract interest rate, the yield to the investor.

In these examles, the December 31 interest date coincides with the investor corporation's year-end. Therefore, no adjustment for bond interest earned is required at year-end. When the interest payment date does not coincide with the fiscal year-end, an adjusting journal entry is required at December 31 for the interest earned until that date and for the appropriate amount of amortization. The adjusting entry accruing interest to December 31 requires a debit to Bond Interest Receivable.

The amortization recorded during the three-year life of the bond will reduce the Investment in Bonds account to face value, $100,000. At maturity the Investment in Bonds account appears as is shown in Figure 14-4.

Investment in Bonds

Date		Explanation	Debit	Credit	Balance
19X1					
Jan.	1	Purchase $100,000 Bond	106,000		106,000
Jun.	30	Amortization of Premium		1,000	105,000
Dec.	31	Amortization of Premium		1,000	104,000
19X2					
Jun.	30	Amortization of Premium		1,000	103,000
Dec.	31	Amortization of Premium		1,000	102,000
19X3					
Jun.	30	Amortization of Premium		1,000	101,000
Dec.	31	Amortization of Premium		1,000	100,000

Figure 14-4

The amount of premium has been amortized from the date of purchase to the date of maturity. If no amortization had been recorded, the amount of premium would be recognized as a loss in the accounting period during which the bonds mature. Such a loss would reflect only the failure to adjust the Bond Interest Earned account in earlier accounting periods.

How Is the Bond Discount Amortized in the Investor's Books?

The discount is amortized by periodic debits to the Investment in Bonds account and credits to Bond Interest Earned. Since interest is paid every six months, the periodic amortization is recorded as follows:

$12,000 ÷ 3 Years ÷ 2 Interest Payments per Year = $2,000 Amortization per Period.

Amortization is recorded every time bond interest expense is entered in the books:

Receipt of Interest:			*Amortization of Discount:*		
Cash	6,000		Investment in Bonds	2,000	
Bond Interest Earned		6,000	Bond Interest Earned		2,000

> The debit to the investment account increases the amount of the investment recorded in the books; the credit to Bond Interest Earned represents additional interest earned over the 12 percent bond interest rate.

The recording of amortization during the three-year life of the bond is shown below. Study the effect of the discount amortization on both the Investment in Bonds and the Bond Interest Earned account.

		Investment in Bonds	Cash Interest Received	Actual Annual Bond Interest Earned
19X1				
Jan. 1	Purchase of Bonds	+ $88,000		
Jun. 30	Interest Received		+ $6,000	
	Discount Amortization	+ 2,000		$16,000
Dec. 31	Interest Received		+ 6,000	
	Discount Amortization	+ 2,000		
	Balance	$92,000	$12,000	$16,000
19X2				
Jun. 30	Interest Received		+ $6,000	
	Discount Amortization	+ 2,000		$16,000
Dec. 31	Interest Received		+ 6,000	
	Discount Amortization	+ 2,000		
	Balance	$96,000	$12,000	$16,000
19X3				
Jun. 30	Interest Received		+ $6,000	
	Discount Amortization	+ 2,000		$16,000
Dec. 31	Interest Received		+ 6,000	
	Discount Amortization	+ 2,000		
	Balance	$100,000	$12,000	$16,000
19X1				
Jan. 1		− 100,000		
		-0-		

Interest received by the terms of the bond contract amounted to $12,000 per year; however, the interest earned was actually $16,000 per year. This additional interest usually compensates for the unfavourable bond interest rate in relation to the rate required in the securities market for this type of bond.

Study the following ledger accounts, which illustrate this increase over the first year of the bonds' term:

	Investment in Bonds		Bond Interest Earned	
The investment account is increased each interest period by amortization.	88,000			6,000
	2,000			2,000
				6,000
	2,000			2,000
	92,000			16,000

In the case of bonds purchased at a discount, bond interest earned consists of the 12-percent bond rate plus the amortized discount. Whenever an investor purchases bonds for less than face value, the investor's total interest earned is increased because of the discount amortization.

Comparison of Recording by the Bond Investor and the Investee

The following comparison of entries on the books of the investor and the investee illustrates the accounting for bonds. The comparison stresses the fact that the accounting for the investor is virtually the mirror image of the accounting for the investee.

	Transaction:	*Recorded by the Investor*			*Recorded by (BCC) the Investee*		
19X1							
Jan. 1	Investor purchases BCC's $100,000-worth of bonds at 106.	Investment in Bonds Cash	106,000	106,000	Cash Bonds Payable Premium on Bonds	106,000	100,000 6,000
Jun. 30	BCC pays semi-annual interest on bond. The bond premium is amortized for 6 months.	Cash Bond Interest Earned Bond Interest Earned Investment in Bonds	6,000 1,000	6,000 1,000	Bond Interest Expense Cash Premium on Bonds Bond Interest Expense	6,000 1,000	6,000 1,000
Dec. 31	BCC pays semi-annual interest on bond. The bond premium is amortized for 6 months.	Cash Bond Interest Earned Bond Interest Earned Investment in Bonds	6,000 1,000	6,000 1,000	Bond Interest Expense Cash Premium on Bonds Bond Interest Expense	6,000 1,000	6,000 1,000

ASSIGNMENT MATERIALS

Discussion Questions

1. Is an investor guaranteed against the loss of an investment? Explain.
2. How can bondholders obtain repayment of their investment? Are shareholders more secure than bondholders? Explain.
3. Why would someone prefer to invest in the shares of a corporation rather than in bonds?
4. What are three different alternative methods for investment disclosure on the balance sheet? Which is the accepted Canadian practice?
5. What are marketable securities? How are they classified on the balance sheet?
6. What are long-term investments? How are they classified on the balance sheet?
7. Is amortization of any bond premium or discount recorded for temporary investments in bonds? Why or why not?
8. If the purchase price of shares includes dividends that have been declared but not yet paid at the time of share purchase, how is the subsequent receipt of the dividend recorded? Do dividends accrue?
9. Does the price of bonds include accrued interest? How is accrued interest recorded by the investor?
10. How is the gain or loss on disposal of marketable securities classified on the income statement?
11. What is the Canadian practice in the valuation of marketable securities when there has been a substantial decrease in their market value? when there has been a substantial increase?
12. How does the accounting for marketable equity securi-

ties required under FASB Statement No. 12 differ from Canadian practice?
13. How does Canadian practice favour the long-term valuation of long-term investments when a permanent market value decline has occurred?
14. What factors can result in a permanent market value decline in a long-term investment?
15. How do incorporate investments in common shares differ from investments in preferred shares as far as investor control of a corporation is concerned?
16. Identify and discuss three levels of voting influence by an investor corporation over the investee corporation.
17. What is a subsidiary? a parent corporation?
18. Distinguish between the cost method and the equity method of accounting for long-term equity investments. What is one important similarity between these two methods?
19. Contrast the accounting period required for income earned by an investee under the cost method and under the equity method. Is there any effect on the balance sheet or the income statement under either method?
20. Explain how the price of an investment is influenced by the bond contract interest rate and the prevailing market interest rate.
21. Refer to Conceptual Issue 14-1. How would dividends and stock splits affect the Efficient Markets Hypothesis? Discuss.

Discussion Cases

Discussion Case 14-1:   New Dofasco Preferred Issue

Dofasco Inc. plans to raise $325 million through an issue of 10 million preferred shares — a move that has surprised steel industry watchers and may also have put a dent in the ambitions of the company's largest single shareholder.

Dofasco, which is based in Hamilton, Ont., announced yesterday that it plans to use the proceeds from the issue partly to help finance a previously announced $1-billion capital spending program and possibly to expand its activities both inside and outside the steel business.

The shares are cumulative, redeemable, voting preferreds and are convertible to common shares on a one-for-one basis for 10 years. The yield will be 8-percent or $2.60 a share.

Dofasco said in a press release that a preliminary prospectus relating to the issue will be filed with regulatory authorities across Canada. It also said that Dominion Securities Pitfield Ltd., Wood Gundy Inc., Burns Fry Ltd., all of Toronto, and Richardson Greenshields of Canada Ltd., Winnipeg, have agreed to buy the issue.

The issue, the steel maker's first since 1980, brought mixed reactions from several analysts, not least because when it announced its capital spending program last fall, it said it planned to finance it mostly from internally generated funds.

"I'm a little surprised they are coming in for so much money, because at the moment they don't need anything like that amount," said Gerry Reid of Toronto investment dealer Gardiner Watson Ltd.

"It's a big, big issue that will mean a lot of dilution," said Don Crook of Walwyn Stodgell Cochran Murray Ltd., also of Toronto, noting that on conversion the preferreds will add about 10 million shares to the company's 50.7 million common shares outstanding.

That 20 percent dilution may be of particular concern to Paul Ivanier, president of steel maker Ivaco Inc. of Montreal. Ivaco last year raised its holding in Dofasco to almost 12 percent from 4.6 percent.

The move made Ivaco the largest single shareholder in Dofasco and fueled speculation that Ivanier had set his sights on acquiring the minimum 20 percent his company would need to account for the holding on an equity basis.

It also prompted the normally reticent Dofasco to issue a terse statement that made it clear it did not welcome the company's advances.

A Dofasco spokesperson conceded yesterday that in order to maintain its position, Ivaco would in effect have to buy about 20 percent of the new preferred issue. He denied, however, that diluting the Ivaco presence was one of the reasons for the issue.

He said the issue was made strictly to finance the company's expansion, and that coming off a good year, the company saw this as an "opportune time" to go to the market.

Reid was not so sure. "I think sceptics will say there's a little bit of Ivanier in [Dofasco's] mind."

Ivanier has never publicly revealed his intentions toward Dofasco. And when asked yesterday whether Ivaco could afford to take a share of the new issue, or indeed whether it wants to, he would not say.

Source   John Partridge, "New Dofasco preferred issue surprises industry watchers", *The Globe and Mail*, March 13, 1985, p. B-1.

For Discussion

1. Refer to Discussion Case 13-1. How do the financial changes described affect both Dofasco and Ivaco?
2. What journal entries would Dofasco prepare for its issue of 10 million shares?
3. What are some long-term and short-term considerations for Dofasco's decision?

Discussion Case 14-2: Compound Interest

Why is growth essential?

Unless your investments beat inflation, there is no "real" growth. High growth enables the magic of compounding to work best — to generate large sums of money over time. Every additional per cent makes a big difference.

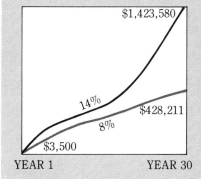

ANNUAL INVEST-MENT	% RETURN	GROWS TO AMOUNT INDICATED WITHIN:				
		10 YEARS	15 YEARS	20 YEARS	25 YEARS	30 YEARS
$1,000	8	$ 15,645	$ 29,324	$ 49,423	$ 78,954	$ 122,346
	10	17,531	34,950	63,002	108,182	180,943
	12	19,655	41,753	80,699	149,334	270,293
	14	22,045	49,980	103,768	207,333	406,737
	16	24,733	59,925	133,841	289,088	615,162
	18	27,755	71,939	173,021	404,272	933,319
	20	31,150	86,442	224,026	566,377	1,418,258
TOTAL INVESTED		$ 10,000	$ 15,000	$ 20,000	$ 25,000	$ 30,000
$3,500	8	$ 54,759	$102,635	$ 172,980	$ 276,340	$ 428,211
	10	61,359	122,324	220,509	378,636	633,302
	12	68,791	146,136	282,446	522,669	946,024
	14	77,156	174,931	363,189	725,665	1,423,580
	16	86,565	209,738	468,442	1,011,809	2,153,066
	18	97,143	251,787	605,574	1,414,952	3,266,615
	20	109,026	302,547	784,090	1,982,321	4,963,903
TOTAL INVESTED		$ 35,000	$ 52,500	$ 70,000	$ 87,500	$ 105,000
$5,500	8	$ 86,050	$161,284	$ 271,826	$ 434,249	$ 672,902
	10	96,421	192,224	346,514	595,000	995,189
	12	108,100	229,643	443,843	821,337	1,486,609
	14	121,245	274,892	570,726	1,140,330	2,237,054
	16	136,031	329,558	736,123	1,589,985	3,383,389
	18	152,653	395,665	951,616	2,223,497	5,133,252
	20	171,327	475,432	1,232,141	3,115,075	7,800,418
TOTAL INVESTED		$ 55,000	$ 82,500	$ 110,000	$ 137,500	$ 165,000

Extra growth does pay off. In a big way, through the effects of compounding. For example, $3,500 invested at 14% grows to $1,423.580 over 30 years versus just $428,211 for an investment yielding 8% over the same period. The trick, clearly, is to achieve high rates of growth without sacrificing security.

For Discussion

1. Comment on the usefulness of this type of analysis.
2. Refer to Figure 6-20. How might a spreadsheet analysis be used in this instance?

Discussion Case 14-3:   The Seagram Company Ltd.

During the months from August 1980 through August 1981, The Seagram Company Ltd. completed one of the largest corporate asset redeployments in North American business history. Boiled down to the bare essentials, the company sold, for $2.3 billion, the United States properties of its Texas Pacific Oil Company subsidiary. After a period of economic analysis and interim investment of the proceeds, Seagram obtained ownership, at a cost of $2.6 billion, of a 20 percent equity interest in E.I. du Pont de Nemours and Company, one of the most distinguished of all North American corporate entities, which itself had been enhanced by its acquisition of Conoco Inc., ninth largest oil company in the United States and the parent of giant Consolidation Coal Company.

The combined Du Pont and Conoco now ranks as North America's seventh largest industrial corporation, a company with combined revenues of $32 billion and assets of $22 billion.

Shortly after completion of the Du Pont-Conoco merger, Seagram and Du Pont signed an agreement drawn to define the future relationship between the two companies. As a general matter Seagram has the right to increase its ownership of Du Pont voting securities up to a limit of 25 percent, and Du Pont has a right of first refusal should Seagram decide to sell its Du Pont holding during the term of the agreement. Seagram has representation on Du Pont's Board of Directors and, in evidence of the growing spirit of co-operation between the two companies, Du Pont now has representation on Seagram's. The agreement's term is for 10 years, but unless Seagram gives notice of its desire to terminate, it will be automatically extended for another five.

The first six months operating results following the acquisition of Dupont shares, extracted from the second quarter report of the Seagram Company Ltd. are reproduced below:

An evaluation of these six month figures is provided below.

When liquor billionaires Charles and Edgar Bronfman signed a non-aggression pact with Du Pont's blue-blooded corporate chieftains last fall, and were admitted to the chemical company's exclusive boardroom in Wilmington, Del., it was seen as a glittering consolation prize for their failure to win one of 1981's toughest takeover struggles.

The prize is not quite so helpful, though, to the corporate performance of the Bronfman-controlled Seagram Co. and to its non-Bronfman shareholders. The wheeling and dealing that finally put the brothers among the Du Pont directors is still costing the Montreal-based company plenty.

This fact is not immediately obvious from Seagram's latest profit report, published this week and covering the six months that ended January 31. But a closer look at the situation, and a check with financial industry sources, show that so far the American venture is not earning its keep.

The Bronfmans did not set out last year to acquire a 20-percent holding in Du Pont, although that's what they got. What they really wanted was control of the ninth-biggest oil company in the United States: Conoco. Oil and liquor could mix, they figured, and they were prepared to put more than $4 billion of their own and their bankers' money on the line to prove it. (Because this is an American story, all the money is counted in U.S. dollars, which are worth 20 percent more than Canadian bucks, in case you hadn't noticed.)

A gigantic corporate rumble followed. In the end Du Pont carried the day, through a $7.4-billion merger deal with Conoco. As part of that deal, Seagram turned over to Du Pont the Conoco shares it had acquired.

Those Conoco shares cost Seagram $2.6 billion, a lot of it borrowed money. In exchange for them, the company wound

	Six Months Ended January 31 (US $000s)	
	1982	*1981*
Sales and Other Income	$1,609,225	$1,555,756
Operating Income	174,000	161,010
Interest Expense	57,935	54,596
Income from Operations before Income Taxes	116,065	106,414
Provisions for Taxes	44,569	52,186
	71,496	54,228
Interest Expense, after Taxes, Relating to Share Repurchase	(4,661)	–
Income from Dividends and Interim Investments, after Taxes	56,947	72,400
	123,782	126,628
Equity in Unremitted Earnings of E.I. du Pont de Nemours and Company	42,131	–
Discontinued Operations (after taxes)	165,913	126,628
	–	6,802
Income before Extraordinary Gain	165,913	133,430
Extraordinary Gain on Sale of Oil and Gas Properties, after Taxes	–	1,222,481
Net Income	$ 165,913	$1,355,911

up with 20 percent of Du Pont. That's the largest single block, and it should be enough to lay down the law in Wilmington. The Du Pont family owns more shares in total, but they're scattered around in smaller parcels and it would be difficult to concentrate their power effectively.

But it didn't turn out that way. The Bronfmans took just their two seats on the 31-member board of directors, a mere 6 percent, and Edgar Bronfman became one of the 10 members of the influential finance committee (10 percent). They also promised not to increase the Seagram holding to more than 25 percent, and Du Pont has the first refusal on the shares if Seagram wants to sell them.

These are not exactly the kind of terms dictated by a conqueror to the conquered.

Meanwhile, the bills are coming in. On the face of it, the six-month report looks pretty good. Profit was up a gratifying 24 percent from the comparable six-month period a year earlier.

But all of that increase came from the inclusion in the tally for the most recent period of something called "equity in unremitted earnings" of Du Pont, amounting to $42 million. This is not your ordinary person's idea of a profit. It's a peculiar device dreamed up by the accountants to show, on the books, what Seagram's share of Du Pont's profit would amount to *if it could get at it.* Showing it on the financial statements is quite legitimiate, but it's strictly a paper amount. You can't spend it, or pay off your bank loans with it.

What Seagram actually gets from Du Pont in cash is a much smaller amount in the form of dividends paid on the shares it owns. It's not easy to tell from the published numbers how much this was in the latest six-month accounting period. But it's possible to make a good guess about the probable dividend income for the full year that will end next January.

Seagram owns roughly 47 million Du Pont shares. Most American analysts figure the chemical company's profit will be equivalent to about $6 a share this year, and the dividend paid to shareholders will be about $2.60. So that means about $122 million in cash for Seagram.

But the Bronfman company has to pay interest on the money it borrowed to buy the shares, or give up interest it could earn on any of its own cash that it used for the deal. There are taxes to take into account, but a conservative estimate of the effective cost puts it not far short of $200 million — a net cash drain of close to $80 million.

There's another thing for Seagram shareholders to think about. Their company is the proud possessor of 47 million shares that cost $54 apiece less than a year ago, and are selling at about $32 now.

That's a billion-dollar drop in the value of their investment. True, everybody's suffered from the collapse of the stock market. But the fact that Seagram bought into an oil company at the height of the industry's popularity among investors didn't help.

Just possibly, the investment may turn out well in the end. But on present form it would have been more profitable, if less glamorous, for Seagram to have stayed away from U.S. adventures — and put its money in the bank instead of borrowing more.

Sources   The Seagram Company Ltd., *Annual Report 1981*, pp. 6 and 9; The Seagram Company Ltd., *Second Quarter Report, Six Months Ended January 31, 1982*, n.p.; Hugh Anderson, "Bronfman Prize Has Big Pricetag", *The* (Montreal) *Gazette*, March 13, 1982.

The Seagram Building is one of the jewels of Park Avenue—a sleek Mies Van de Rohe skyscraper of bronze and glass. At its epicenter is Edgar M. Bronfman, chief executive of the Seagram Company and son of its founder. But Seagram, the world's largest distiller, is finding liquor demand plummeting in the face of health concerns. And Bronfman, corporate scion of one of the world's wealthiest families, must now scramble to keep the business growing for the next generation and beyond.

Ironically, Seagram, a name synonymous with liquor in 175 countries, earns more from its investments than from distilled spirits. Thanks to Bronfman's abortive 1981 raid on Conoco, Seagram has gained a 22.5 percent stake—the biggest minority position — in Du Pont, the ultimate victor in the battle for Conoco. This stake provides nearly 75 percent of Seagram's earnings and, more importantly, is seen as the key to its future. Indeed, when asked what Seagram was doing to offset the drop in liquor consumption, Bronfman answered with one word: "Du Pont."

"The Bronfmans feel that distilled spirits is not going to make them terribly wealthy from here on and they are trying to locate the thing that will," said Arthur Kirsch, an analyst with Drexel Burnham Lambert. First Boston analyst Martin Romm is more blunt: "The liquor business has dried up."

The fortunes of Seagram rise and fall on the fate of E.I. du Pont de Nemours & Company, a cyclical company whose own business is weak right now. For the record, both sides proclaim fidelity. But, in private, there is intrigue between a liquor company that wants a bigger say in its investment and a chemical giant that resists any meddling. And, the big unanswered question is whether Seagram, at some point in the future, will vastly increase its Du Pont holding—and to what end. Not surprisingly, each company eyes the other, like two feudal tribes girding for a battle that may — or may not — erupt.

"It's been a four-year state of seige," said one observer familiar with both sides. Added Drexel's Kirsch: "I can't see the Bronfmans having $3 billion parked in one investment where all they get is three seats on the board. At some point, something is going to change."

Heading the Seagram side is Edgar Bronfman, 56, the tanned and lean guardian of the Bronfman dynasty, who surrounds himself with expensive art and well-paid management talent. The Bronfman family, immigrants from Czarist Russia, began their $2.8 billion business by making Canadian whiskey that found its way to America during Prohibition. Mr. Bronfman's view of Du Pont is simple: "Our intent is clearly to have an important voice."

Where Seagram's Earnings Come From

Seagram's earnings excluding extraordinary items, in millions of dollars

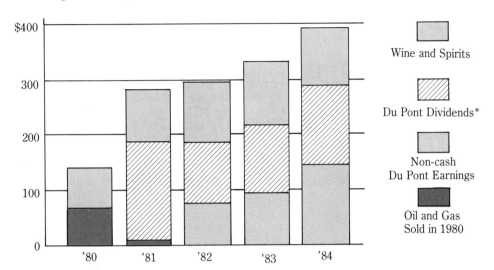

*1980 data are for gain on investments

Slower Growth for U.S. Wine and Spirits Market

Total U.S. consumption of wine and spirits, in billions of gallons

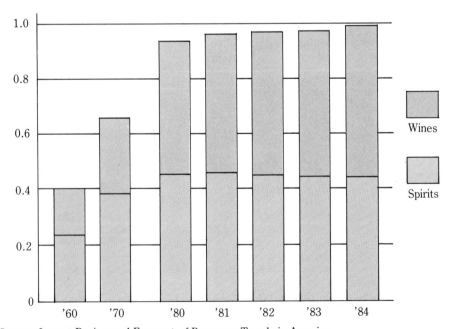

Source: Impact Review and Forecast of Beverage Trends in America

Du Pont, a $35 billion company that traces its origins to the original du Ponts who made gunpowder for the War of 1812, has long been viewed as the model of the modern corporation. Family control passed many decades ago to outside managers who oversee the making of everything from nylon to film to explosives. Du Pont, the nation's largest chemical company, is far more silent than Seagram. "There is little to be gained by getting into it," explained John R. Malloy, Du Pont's vice president for public affairs. "Our relations with Seagram are outstanding and constructive and there is not much more we can say than that."

Ties between the two companies are both formal and informal. Three Seagram representatives sit on the Du Pont board and two from Du Pont are members of the Seagram board. Edgar's brother, Charles, who is Seagram's deputy chairman, has become a close social friend of Edward G. Jefferson, Du Pont's chief executive — although some wonder whether the relationship is fueled by genuine friendship or an attempt to keep an eye on one another. Seagram receives Du Pont dividends — some $141.3 million last year — and has dedicated this cash stream to solely buying even more Du Pont shares. This money has enabled Seagram to increase its Du Pont shares from 20 percent of the company in 1981 to 22.5 percent today, and more purchases are on the way.

More than money, however, is influence. The Bronfmans say they are already involved in major decisions at Du Pont, and even though they are happy with the way Du Pont is managed, they want a bigger voice. "We see ourselves in the role of an active limited partner," said Bronfman. "We're allies of management at Du Pont to help them do a better job. We're involved in long-term decisions at Du Pont. We see eye-to-eye on the future of the company. It is superbly managed."

Others at Seagram are even more blunt. "We'd like to have a larger say in the policy direction of Du Pont," said David G. Sacks, executive vice president for administration and finance. "We are reasonable people and not a Boone Pickens or a Carl Icahn. We're Seagram Company and we operate with a certain style. We're not corporate takeovers artists. We've increased our stake to have meaningful impact on Du Pont policy."

Some within Du Pont say that the Bronfmans — despite what they say and the size of their position — play no greater a role than any other outside director. Seagram's three members — Edgar, his brother Charles and Seagram president Philip E. Beekman — have no more impact on long-term Du Pont policy than anyone else on Du Pont's 29-member board. They are not involved in the management of Du Pont and, in fact, there is little that the Bronfmans could do, since the two

AT A GLANCE

Seagram Company

All dollar amounts in thousands, except per share data

Three months ended April 30

	1985	1984
Revenues	$604,761	$625,620
Net Income	24,400	89,285
Earnings per share	$0.26	$0.99
Year ended Jan. 31	**1985**	**1984**
Revenues	$2,821,245	$2,647,552
Net Income	383,618	317,546
Earnings per share	$4.22	$3.53

Total assets, Jan. 31, 1985	$5,595,872
Current assets	1,535,084
Current liabilities	740,556
Long-term debt	780,760
Book value per share, Jan. 31, 1985	$33.50
Stock price, Aug. 9, 1985	
N.Y.S.E. consolidated close	40¾
Stock Price, 52-week range	44⅝–35⅜
Employees, Jan. 31, 1985	15,000
Headquarters	Montreal

AT A GLANCE

Du Pont

All dollar amounts in thousands, except per share data

Three months ended June 30

	1985	1984
Revenues	$8,614,000	$9,198,000
Net Income	268,000	437,000
Earnings per share	$1.10	$1.81
Year ended Dec. 31	**1984**	**1983**
Revenues	$36,218,000	$35,769,000
Net Income	1,431,000	1,127,000
Earnings per share	$5.93	$4.70

Main Lines of Business
Contribution to 1984 revenues

Oil, gas, coal	56%
Polymers, fibers	23%
Agricultural, industrial chemicals	10%
Industrial, consumer products	8%
Biomedical products	3%

Total assets, Dec. 31, 1984	$24,098,000
Current assets	8,651,000
Current liabilities	5,177,000
Long-term debt	3,421,000
Book value per share, Dec. 31, 1984	$50.06
Stock price, Aug. 9, 1985	
N.Y.S.E. consolidated close	58
Stock price, Aug. 9, 1985	61⅞–46⅛
Employees, Dec. 31, 1984	157,783
Headquarters	Wilmington, Del.

companies are in such dissimilar businesses and differ so much in size.

"The Bronfmans play no more or no less a role than any other outside director," said Andrew F. Brimmer, a board member and economic consultant. "I'm not conscious of the Bronfmans being any more active in questioning or probing than any other director. Neither they, nor any other outside director, have any management or initiating role."

Seagram stumbled into Du Pont more by accident than design. After stubbing its toes on acquisition passes at St. Joe Minerals and Conoco, Seagram ended up as the biggest shareholder of Du Pont—some 53.8 million shares valued at more than $3 billion. It got this in exchange for its Conoco stake. The Du Pont shares represent more than half of Seagram's corporate assets. Yet it is an investment that has performed well, but not spectacularly.

"It's an acquisition the Bronfmans chanced into," said Rex McCafferty, an analyst with Dominion Securities Pitfield in Toronto. "They are fighting what amounts to an environment of being in a sunset business and Du Pont gives them a stable cash flow. It hasn't been a bad investment, but it's not where I'd put my money. Liquor is in secular decline and Du Pont is large and cyclical. It's like buying a part of the U.S. economy."

On the positive side, the Du Pont contribution helps fatten a bottom line threatened by weakening liquor sales. Yet it comes at a price. Until 1984, Du Pont shares, which are now trading at about $60 a share, were selling below Seagram's average acquisition cost of $52 a share—creating hundreds of millions of dollars in paper losses. And, Seagram is in the unenviable position of having the bulk of its assets tied up in an investment that it does not actively manage.

Nor have the Du Pont returns been remarkable — except for their cyclicality. For instance, Du Pont's fiscal year 1985 earnings are expected to be weak due to a strong dollar and a sluggish economy. And Seagram's its earnings in its first quarter, ended April 30, fell to 26 cents a share from 99 cents a share in the 1984 first quarter, due largely to big write-offs taken by Du Pont. Even by Seagram's own admission, the 8 to 12 percent annual after-tax return on its Du Pont holding is "satisfactory, not spectacular", said Seagram's Sacks.

Seagram, however, dismisses each naysaying. "There's no question we could put $3 billion in something and make more money than Du Pont," said Sacks. "Maybe gold. Maybe casinos in Atlantic City. But that ignores the appreciation in the stock and right now the market price is higher than our carrying cost. We're delighted with our relationship."

All eyes, however, are where Seagram goes from here — especially now that key deadlines approach in a precisely worded standstill agreement between the two companies. The agreement was drafted after Bronfman elected to take a minority position in Du Pont rather than cash in his Conoco shares and, under its terms, Bronfman has promised not to buy more than 25 percent of Du Pont for a certain time period in exchange for three seats on the Du Pont board.

The agreement provided something for everyone. Du Pont got assurances that its biggest shareholder's appetite would be curbed for at least 10 years, until 1991. Seagram got Du Pont board representation and, under accounting rules, the vast size of its stock holdings and its board seats mean that Seagram is clearly able to claim up to 25 percent of Du Pont's earnings as its own.

For instance, in the fiscal year 1984, in addition to the cash Du Pont dividends, Seagram claimed about $141.4 million of Du Pont's earnings as its own — a percentage equal to Seagram's percentage ownership of Du Pont. This is a non-cash accounting entry that is added to Seagram's bottom line and makes the distiller look even more attractive to investors. Last year, Seagram earned $383.6 million, which included $282 million in cash and non-cash contributions from Du Pont.

The key date in the immediate future is October 1987, when Seagram must notify Du Pont whether it wants to extend the agreement for five years beyond the 1991 expiration date. If the agreement is not extended, Seagram immediately loses its Du Pont board seats and, perhaps, even its ability to claim Du Pont earnings as its own. But Seagram would be free to accumulate shares beyond the 25 percent limit starting in 1991 — perhaps as a prelude to a raid or an attempt to get an even larger bloc of Du Pont to gain an even higher premium price if sold as a single unit.

Conversely, extension of the agreement would be a signal of a continuation of the present situation. Seagram's hands as a raider would be tied, but its ability to draw upon Du Pont's earnings would be guaranteed. And, since Seagram would be barred from buying more than 25 percent of Du Pont, the enormous dividend stream that Seagram currently dedicates to buying more Du Pont could be used for other goals, perhaps other acquisitions or investments.

Right now, Bronfman is giving no hints of his intention. "What our plans are now and in 1987 are not fixed," he said. "Whether we renew the agreement or not has not been decided."

Ironically, one of the few other standstill agreements in effect at a major American company is between the Scott Paper Company, which is just down the road in Philadelphia from Wilmington-based Du Pont, and Brascan Ltd., a Toronto-based investment concern owned largely by Edgar Bronfman's cousins, Peter and Edward, generally known as the Canadian Bronfmans to distinguish them from the American branch that runs Seagram. That agreement halted Brascan's advances and limited its ownership of Scott to 25 percent in return for four board seats. Following adoption of this 1981 agreement, the Pennsylvania legislature enacted a measure to make takeovers in that state more difficult and greenmail impossible by banning the payment of premiums for large blocks of shares.

Bronfman, son of the legendary "Mr. Sam" who built Seagram, presides over a company that moved to the top of the liquor business during Prohibition and stayed there. But liquor, particularly the "brown goods" that Seagram is known for—its most famous brands are 7 Crown, V.O. Canadian and Chivas Regal — are being shunned by consumers concerned about diet and health.

Industry-wide shipments of distilled spirits fell in 1984 to a pre-1975 level of 440 million gallons a year, according to the trade publication Impact. Seagram brands have not been immune. Sales of 7 Crown and V.O. Canadian, two of its top brands, fell 4 percent last year, following even bigger declines in previous years. And no one, not even those at Seagram, believes that a turn-around is in sight.

"There's still a lot of liquor consumed, but it is declining in the long run," said First Boston's Romm. "The question is what do they do to restructure the company to lessen its dependence on liquor." Added Roy D. Burry, an analyst with Kidder, Peabody: "Seagram has a tremendous amount of product in the aging process and demand is contracting. Over time, this will generate large amounts of money. If demand goes down forever, production disappears and the company turns into a pile of cash. But I don't think that is what the Bronfmans want."

Mr. Bronfman sees his task to expand the company for his sons and for generations of Bronfmans yet to come. The Bronfman family owns about 38 percent of Seagram and Bronfman makes it clear that he wants Seagram to be the family treasure well into the next century. "And it is exactly how the next generation feels too," said Bronfman, while seated in an office decorated with a Miro tapestry and Rodin sculptures. And when Bronfman steps down as chief executive in the next four to six years, he will hand over the office to one of his sons, most likely Edgar Jr., age 30, or Sam, age 31, who already work for the company.

Yet as Bronfman looks to the future, he does not envision the day when Seagram or the Bronfmans will be out of the distilled spirits business. "The core business has its problems, but it's not all on the black side," said Bronfman.

Seagram has already begun moves to spur growth. Its overseas operations, which represent slightly under half of sales, are being expanded by products, acquisitions and forays into new markets. Under the aegis of Edgar Bronfman Jr., the domestic distilled spirits operation has been streamlined, resulting in the laying off of as many as 200 of 750 marketing and sales employees. Margins in distilled operations remain comfortable as the company sells off old products and spends less in production costs. Still, no one knows the impact of a $2-a-gallon Federal excise tax increase scheduled to go into effect on Sept. 30.

Seagram spent $237 million to buy the Wine Spectrum, makers of Sterling and Taylor California Wines, from Coca-Cola in 1984. This, combined with Seagram's existing Paul Masson wines, makes it the nation's second-largest wine producer and gives it a bigger stake in the domestic wine business, which has been reeling of late from the twin effects of a strong dollar and an oversupply of grapes. Analysts, however, say that in the long run, this investment should pay off, and, even in the short run, Seagram appears to be doing well with new products like Seagram Coolers, a wine and citrus mix.

And Bronfman talks about making a $1 billion to $2 billion acquisition of a consumer products or leisure time company, although he has no specific plans in mind. "We're not actively looking for acquisitions, but an acquisition is not beyond the scope of our imagination if the right acquisition came along and the timing was right."

With nearly 40 percent of the company in family hands and another 10 percent or so in the hands of corporate officers, Seagram is in the enviable position of being fairly impervious to an unfriendly takeover. Nonetheless, the company attempted last May to restructure Seagram's by proposing to increase its control to nearly 87 percent. The proposal sought to give the Bronfmans increased votes in exchange for a high dividend to non-Bronfman shareholders. That proposal, however, was withdrawn after opposition from non-Bronfman shareholders.

Indeed, the only threat could come from within — if members of the Bronfman family decided, over time, to sell their Seagram shares. Already, a trust representing Edgar's sister, Minda, sold more than 900 000 shares on the open market last March and some 4.9 million of her shares are now in the hands of her heirs following her death last July. As the generations continue, there will be more Bronfmans splitting the family holdings and more people with individual needs for cash that might result in a diminution of the family stake. For now, Bronfman said that he or his brother Edgar will buy the shares of any Bronfman heir who wants to sell his or her Seagram holdings.

And family ownership, he feels, is in the best interest of Seagram. "There's been a lot of criticism of American corporations where people are in their jobs a short time and don't have a long view," said Bronfman. "It's a great advantage to have a family tradition now and into the 21st century. That doesn't always justify family control, but I view it that way and it's een a good benefit to the Seagram shareholders."

Source Lesley Wayne, "The House of Seagram Puts its Faith in Chemicals," *The New York Times*, August 11, 1985, pp. F-1 and F-6.

For Discussion

1. It is assumed that the investor corporation has a significant influence and control over an investee corporation when the investor has between 20 and 50 percent ownership of the investee. From your reading of the preceding information, do you believe that Seagram has a significant influence and control over Du Pont? Why or why not?

2. Seagram reports its investment in Du Pont on the equity method. What are the journal entries that Seagram prepares to report under the equity method? Prepare sample journal entries.

3. Evaluate from a shareholder's view the fact that the Du Pont dividends received by Seagram appear to be considerably less than the cost to borrow money to purchase Du Pont shares or interest that Seagram could otherwise earn on its money. Consider both the short-term and long-term prospects.

4. Would the fact that 25 percent of Du Pont's earnings are recorded as revenue for Seagram prompt you to invest (or prevent you from investing) in the Seagram Company?

5. Suggest reasons why — from the perspective of Canadian GAAP — 20 percent stock ownership is used as the benchmark for significant influence.

6. Would you suggest that the Bronfmans divert their investment in liquor — owing to the apparently bleak future for such products? Why or why not?

Comprehension Problems

Comprehension Problem 14-1

Mountain Wagons Inc., had the following short-term investment transactions in marketable securities during 19X8.

Jan. 1   Purchased $50,000 face value, 12-percent bonds, of Crescent Restaurants Ltd., at 102, plus $1,000 brokerage fees. (Semi-annual interest is payable on June 30 and December 31.)

Apr. 15   Purchased 1000 shares of Bishop Court Inc., for $14.75 per share, plus $250 brokerage fees

May 25   Received a 10-percent stock dividend from Bishop Court Inc. (Recorded a memo entry in the Investment account noting the new number of shares held.)

Jun. 7   Received a $0.10 per-share cash dividend for the shares in Bishop

Jun. 30   Received the semi-annual interest on the Crescent bonds

Oct. 4   Sold the bonds of Crescent Restaurants Inc., at 99, less brokerage fees of $1,000 (Recorded accrued interest at this date amounting to $1,578.)

Dec. 31   The market value of a Bishop share was $10 on this date.

Required:
  1. Prepare journal entries to record the 19X8 transactions.
  2. How should the market value of Bishop shares be disclosed in the December 31, 19X8 balance sheet of Mountain Wagons Inc.
     a. According to the CICA?
     b. According to the LOCAM method? Prepare the December 31, 19X8 entry required under this method.

Comprehension Problem 14-2

Brandon Corporation purchased 20 000 shares, representing a 20-percent interest in Curtis Corporation for $10 per share on January 1, 19X8. The following transactions occurred during the year.

Apr. 15   Curtis paid a $0.25 per-share dividend

Jun. 7   Curtis distributed a 10 percent stock dividend

Oct. 4   Curtis paid a $0.15 per-share dividend

Dec. 31   Curtis reported net income of $50,000; Brandon exercises a significant control over Curtis.

Required:
  1. Prepare journal entries to record
     a. The purchase of the 20 000 shares as a long-term investment
     b. Receipt of its share of dividends paid by Curtis
     c. Brandon's share of net income reported by Curtis.
  2. Prepare an investment schedule (like the one in section C), to show the amounts reported on the balance sheet and on the income statement under the equity method.

Comprehension Problem 14-3

Cord City Inc. paid $147,000 for $150,000 face value bonds of Computer Stores Corporation. The bonds, which were acquired on January 1, 19X1 as a long-term investment, had the following features.

Date of Authorization	Term	Bond Contract Interest Rate	Interest Payment Dates
January 1, 19X1	3 years	12%	Semi-annually on June 30 and December 31

Required:
1. Calculate
   a. The amount of interest received every interest payment date
   b. The amount of amortization to be recorded at each interest payment date (Use the straight-line method of amortization.)
2. Prepare the ledger entries for the Investment in Bonds account of Cord City Inc. to show the purchase of the bonds and the semi-annual amortization amounts until redemption. (Note that amortization is recorded each time bond interest income is recorded.)

Date	Description	Debit	Credit	Balance
19X1				
Jan. 1	Purchase of Computer Stores Corporation bonds			
June 30	Amortization of Discount			
Dec. 31	Amortization of Discount			
19X2				
June 30	Amortization of Discount			
Dec. 31	Amortization of Discount			
19X3				
June 30	Amortization of Discount			
Dec. 31	Amortization of Discount			
19X4				
Jan. 1	Bonds Redeemed			

3. Prepare the journal entries to record the interest and amortization at June 30, 19X1.

Comprehension Problem 14-4

Liebman Inc. the year-end for which is January 31, acquired $50,000 face value bonds of Zilch Corporation at 103. The bonds that were acquired on January 1, 19X3 as a long-term investment had the following features.

Date of Amortization	Term	Bond Contract Interest Rate	Interest Semi-annually
January 1, 19X3	2 years	12%	on July 1 and January 2

Required:

1. Prepare a schedule (like the one in section D) for the two-year life of the bonds to show a running balance for the Investment in Bonds account. Calculate the cash interest received and the annual interest earned by Liebman.

		Investment in Bonds	Cash Interest Received	Annual Interest Income
19X3				
Jan. 1	Purchase of Bonds			
April 30	Interest Accrued and Amortization	_____	_____	_____
	Balance			
July 1	Interest Received and Amortization			
19X4				
Jan. 1	Interest Received and Amortization			
April 30	Interest Accrued and Amortization	_____	_____	_____
	Balance			
July 1	Interest Received and Amortization			
19X5				
Jan. 1	Interest Received and Amortization	_____	_____	_____
	Balance			
Jan. 1	Bond Repaid			
		-0-		

The interest income of the corporation is reduced by the premium amortization

2. Prepare journal entries to record the 19X3–19X5 transactions.
3. If the market rate of interest was 16 percent at December 31, 19X3, for how much could Liebman Inc. sell its investment in bonds?

Problems

Problem 14-1

Morton Services Inc. had the following short-term investment transactions in marketable securities during 19X7.

Jan. 1   Purchased $25,000-worth of face value 12-percent bonds of Côte St-Luc Farms Inc. at 95, plus $250 brokerage fee

Feb. 28   Purchased 200 shares of Côte Vertu Centres Ltée, for $20 each plus, $600 brokerage fee

Jun. 30   Received the semi-annual interest on Côte St-Luc bonds

Oct. 4   Received a $0.50 per-share cash dividend from Côte Vertu

Dec. 31   Received the semi-annual interest on Côte St-Luc bonds

Dec. 31   The market value of Côte St-Luc bonds was 90 at this date; shares of Côte Vertu were trading at $15 per share.

Required:

1. Prepare journal entries to record the 19X7 transactions.
2. Prepare the journal entry required at December 31, 19X7 under the LOCAM method to record an unrealized loss on marketable equity securities.
3. Prepare a partial balance sheet at December 31, 19X7 to show the short-term investments and the allowance account for marketable equity securities.
4. How should the market value decline at December 31, 19X7 be disclosed, according to CICA recommendations?
5. The shares of Côte Vertu were sold for $25 each on April 11, 19X8. Prepare journal entries to
   a. Record the sale
   b. Eliminate the allowance account.
6. Prepare a partial income statement at December 31, 19X8 to show the gain or loss on disposal of Côte Vertu shares and the unrealized gain that results from the elimination of the allowance account.

Problem 14-2

Peter Corporation (PC) purchased 20 000 shares, representing a 20-percent interest in Sol O. Sun Inc., for $100,000 on January 1, 19X7. The following transactions occurred subsequently.

19X7
Jun. 30   Sol paid $5,000 in dividends to its shareholders
Dec. 31   Sol reported net income of $5,000 for 19X7.

19X8
Jun. 30   Sol paid $50,000 in dividends to its shareholders
Dec. 31   Sol reported net loss of $75,000 for 19X8.

Required: Consider these cases. Case A: PC has a significant influence over Sol. Case B: PC does not have a significant influence over Sol. For each of these cases
  1. Prepare journal entries to record
      a. The purchase of the 20 000 shares by PC
      b. Receipt of its share of dividends paid by Sol
      c. PC's share of Sol's net income or loss, if applicable.
  2. If the market value of the 20 000 shares declined by $1 per share at December 31, 19X7, prepare the journal entry required under the LOCAM method to record an unrealized loss. Explain how this decline would be reported in the financial statements, according to the CICA recommendations. The loss is not expected to be permanent.
  3. Prepare a schedule (like the one in section C) to compare the amounts reported on the balance sheet and on the income statement of PC for 19X7 under both the cost method and the equity method.

Problem 14-3

First Canadian Corporation purchased 60 000 shares, representing a 60-percent interest in Second Municipal Limited for $360,000 on January 1, 19X7. First is assumed to have a significant influence over Second. The following data are applicable to 19X7.

	First		Second	
	Dividends Paid	*Net Income*	*Dividends Paid*	*Net Income*
	$40,000	$170,000	$20,000	$80,000

Required:
  1. Indicate the method of accounting which can be used in the records of First to account for its investment in Second. Under which method would the investment be reported in the financial statements of First?
  2. Assuming that the investment in shares of Second is maintained on the equity basis in the records of First, prepare journal entries to record
      a. The purchase of the 60 000 shares as a long-term investment
      b. The receipt of First's share of dividends paid by Second in 19X7
      c. First's share of Second's 19X7 income.
  3. a. Assume that First's investment in shares of Second is maintained on the cost basis in its records. Prepare the entries required in 19X7 under the LOCAM method, if the market value of Second's shares are $50,000 less than the amount that appears in First's investment account.
      b. Prepare a partial balance sheet at December 31, 19X7 to show the investment and allowance accounts.
  4. How would First's investment in Second be accounted for if 10 000 shares had been purchased instead of 60 000? Why?

Problem 14-4

Muller Marketing Marauders Inc., the year-end for which is December 31, acquired $75,000-worth of face value bonds of Guelph Collegiate Inc. at 98. The bonds, which were acquired on January 1, 19X3 as a long-term investment, had the following features:

Date of Authorization	Term	Bond Contract Interest Rate	Interest Payment Dates
January 1, 19X3	3 year	12%	Semi-annually on June 30 and December 31

Required:
1. Calculate
   a. The amount of interest applicable to each six-month period
   b. The amount of amortization to be recorded at each interest date (Use the straight-line method of amortization).
2. Prepare the ledger for the Investment in Bonds account of Muller, recording the purchase and the amortization of discount amounts until redemption of the bonds.
3. Using a comparative format similar to that at the end of section D, prepare all journal entries required on the books of both Muller and Guelph in 19X3. The year end for Guelph is December 31.

Problem 14-5

Mags Inc. paid $110,000 for $100,000-worth of face value bonds of Ski Limited. Both corporations have December 31 as their year-end. The bonds, which were acquired as a long-term investment on January 1, 19X1, had the following features.

Date of Authorization	Term	Bond Contract Interest Rate	Interest Payment Dates
January 1, 19X1	2 years	12%	Semi-annually on July 1 and January 1

Required:
1. Calculate
   a. The amount of interest applicable to each six-month period
   b. The amount of amortization to be recorded at each interest date (Use the straight-line method of amortization.)
2. Using a comparative format similar to that at the end of section D, prepare journal entries on the following dates for both Mags (investor) and Ski (issuer).
   a. January 1, 19X1
   b. July 1, 19X1, for interest and amortization
   c. December 31, 19X1 accrual for interest and to record amortization
   d. January 1, 19X2 for interest
   e. July 1, 19X2 for interest and amortization
   f. December 31, 19X2 accrual for interest and to record amortization
   g. January 1, 19X3 for interest
   h. January 1, 19X3 for bond redemption.

Problem 14-6

Boulevard Investment Inc., purchased $100,000-worth of face value bonds on January 1, 19X1. On the date of bond authorization, Axel Corporation issued $100,000-worth of face value bonds.

Date of Authorization	Term	Bond Contract Interest Rate	Interest Payment Dates
January 1, 19X1	3 year	12%	Semi-annually on June 30 and December 31

Required: Consider these cases. Case A: the bonds were acquired at face value. Case B: the bonds were acquired for $103,000. Case C: the bonds were acquired for $94,000. For each of these cases

1. Calculate
    a. The amount of interest received every interest payment date
    b. The amount of amortization to be recorded at each interest payment date, if applicable (Use the straight-line method of amortization.)
2. Prepare journal entries to record
    a. The acquisition of bonds on January 1, 19X1
    b. The receipt of interest on June 30, 19X1
    c. The amortization on June 30, 19X1
    d. The receipt of interest on December 31, 19X1
    e. The amortization on December 31, 19X1
    f. The receipt of interest on December 31, 19X3
    g. The amortization on December 31, 19X3
    h. The redemption of the bonds at maturity, January 1, 19X4.
3. Calculate the amount of bond interest income shown in the income statement at December 31, 19X1. Is this amount the same as cash interest received by Boulevard? Why or why not?

Alternate Problems

Alternate Problem 14-1

King Edward Estates Inc. had the following short-term investment transactions in marketable securities during 19X6 and 19X7.

19X6
Jan. 1   Purchased $100,000-worth of face value, 12-percent bonds, of Montclair Corp. at 97, plus $1,000 brokerage fees; semi-annual interest is payable on June 30 and December 31
Apr. 1   Purchased 5000 shares of Marker Stores Inc., for $5 per share, plus $250 brokerage fees
May 1   Received a $0.25 per-share cash dividend from Marker
Jun. 30   Received the semi-annual interest from Montclair; sold the Montclair bonds at 102, less brokerage fees of $1,000
Dec. 31   The market value of Marker shares was $4 per share.

19X7
Apr. 15   Sold the Marker shares for $1.50 per share, less brokerage fees of $100.

Required:
1. Prepare journal entries to record the 19X6 transactions.
2. Prepare the journal entry required at December 31, 19X6 under the LOCAM method to record an unrealized loss on marketable equity securities.

3. Prepare a partial balance sheet at December 31, 19X6 to show the short-term investment and the allowance account.
4. How would the market value decline at December 31, 19X6 be disclosed, according to CICA recommendations? (Consider it to be a substantial decline.)
5. Prepare a journal entry to record the 19X7 sale of Marker shares.
6. Prepare the journal entry to eliminate the allowance account set up at December 31, 19X6.
7. Prepare a partial income statement at December 31, 19X7 to show the gain or loss on the sale of Marker shares and the unrealized gain that results from the elimination of the allowance account.

Alternate Problem 14-2

P Corporation purchased 20 000 shares, representing a 20-percent interest, in S Limited for $500,000 on January 1, 19X4. The following financial data are applicable to S Limited.

	Dividends Paid	Net Income (Loss)
19X4	$200,000	$ 400,000
19X5	100,000	(300,000)

Part A

P Corporation does not have a significant influence over S Limited.

Required: Prepare journal entries to record
a. The purchase of the 20 000 shares as a long-term investment
b. The receipt of P Corporation's share of dividends paid in 19X4 and 19X5.

Part B

P Corporation is assumed to have a significant influence over S Limited.
Required: Prepare journal entries to record
a. The purchase of 20 000 shares as a long-term investment
b. The receipt of P Corporation's share of dividends paid in 19X4 and 19X5
c. P Corporation's share of S Limited's income.

Part C

Required: Prepare a schedule (like the one in section C) to compare the amount reported on the balance sheet and on the income statement of P Corporation in 19X4 and 19X5, under both the cost method and the equity method.

Part D

At December 31, 19X5, the market value of P Corporation's shares in S had declined permanently by $100,000.

Required: Assuming that the investment was recorded at cost in the books of P, prepare journal entries to record this permanent loss
a. In accordance with CICA recommendations
b. Using the LOCAM method.

Alternate Problem 14-3

Honest Ned's Corporation has 100 000 shares outstanding. The following data are applicable to 19X6 and 19X7.

	Dividends Paid	Net Income (Loss)
19X6	$100,000	$(300,000)
19X7	200,000	400,000

Part A

E. Tonne Inc. purchased 55 000 shares of Honest Ned's for $220,000 on January 1, 19X6.

Required:
1. Identify the relationship between these two corporations.
2. Indicate what method of accounting can be used in the records of E. Tonne Inc. for this long-term investment.
3. Assuming the cost method is used, prepare journal entries for 19X6 to record
   a. The purchase of the 55 000 shares
   b. The receipt of its share of 19X6 dividends paid by Honest Ned's
   c. E. Tonne's share of Honest Ned's 19X6 income
   d. A decline of $40,000 in the market value of Honest Ned's shares held by E. Tonne; use the LOCAM method to record the decline. Explain how this decline would be reported, according to CICA recommendations.
4. Assuming the cost method is used, prepare journal entries for 19X7 to record
   a. The receipt of E. Tonne's share of 19X7 dividends paid by Honest Ned's
   b. E. Tonne's share of Honest Ned's 19X7 income
   c. An unrealized recovery of $10,000 of the decline in market value of Honest Ned's shares held by E. Tonne. The market value of the shares had improved during the year.

Part B

Sim and Sons Ltd. purchased 35 000 shares, representing a 35-percent interest in Honest Ned's Corporation, for $160,000 on January 1, 19X7. Sim and Sons Ltd. is a fierce competitor of E. Tonne Inc. The purchase of these shares was viewed with concern by E. Tonne Inc.

Required:
5. Identify the relationship between Honest Ned's Corporation and Sim and Sons Ltd.
6. Indicate what method of accounting would be used in the records of Sim and Sons Ltd. for this long-term investment.
7. Assuming Sim and Sons Ltd. uses the equity method, prepare journal entries to record
   a. The purchase of $35,000 shares
   b. The receipt of its share of 19X7 dividends paid by Honest Ned's
   c. Sim and Sons Ltd.'s share of Honest Ned's income
   d. The sale of the 35 000 shares on January 1, 19X8 to E. Tonne Inc. at $6 per share, a price considerably above the stock market price of these shares. Why would E. Tonne Inc. pay more than market value for these shares?

Alternate Problem 14-4

Redi-Chip Corporation paid $212,000 for $200,000-worth of face value bonds of Mercury Software Inc. The bonds, which were acquired on January 1, 19X1 as a long term investment, had the following features.

Date of Authorization	*Term*	*Bond Contract Interest Rate*	*Interest Payment Dates*
January 1, 19X1	3 years	12%	Semi-annually on June 30 and December 31

1. Calculate
   a. The amount of interest received every interest payment date
   b. The amount of amortization to be recorded at each interest date (Use the straight-line method of amortization.)
2. Prepare the ledger for the Investment in Bonds account to record the purchase of, amortization regarding and redemption of the bonds. Note that amortization is recorded each time bond interest income is recorded.
3. Prepare journal entries to record the interest and amortization at June 30, 19X1.

Alternate Problem 14-5

Hampstead Fertilizer Corporation paid $207,200 for $200,000-worth of face value bonds of Grandma's Kitchen Inc. The bonds, which were acquired as a long-term investment, had the following features.

Date of Authorization	*Term*	*Bond Contract Interest Rate*	*Interest Payment Dates*
January 1, 19X7	3 years	12%	Semi-annually on June 30 and December 31

Required:

Consider these cases. Case A: the bonds were acquired on January 1, 19X7. Case B: the bonds were acquired on April 1, 19X7 and the acquisition price included accrued interest. Case C: the bonds were acquired on July 1, 19X7. For each of these cases
1. Calculate
   a. The amount of interest received every interest payment date
   b. The amount of amortization, if any, applicable to each month remaining in the life of the bonds subsequent to the issue date. Calculate separately the amortization to be recorded at each interest payment date. (Use the straight-line method of amortization.)
2. Prepare journal entries to record
   a. The acquisition of the bonds
   b. The receipt of interest and recording of amortization, if any, on June 30, 19X7
   c. The receipt of interest and recording of amortization, if any, on December 31, 19X7
3. Calculate the amount of bond interest income shown in the income statement at December 31, 19X7. Is this amount the same as cash received as interest in 19X7? Why or why not?

Supplementary Problems

Supplementary Problem 14-1

Campus Products Corporation (CPC) engaged in the following temporary investment transactions during 19X6 and 19X7:

19X6

Jan. 1   Purchased $100,000-worth of CPB's 12-percent, 3-year bonds on the interest date for 95, plus $500 brokerage fees

Feb. 1   Purchased 500 shares of Blue Sea Lake Corporation paying $25 per share, plus $200 brokerage fees

May 1   Received a $1 per-share cash dividend on the investment in Blue Sea Lake Corporation shares

Jun. 30   Received the semi-annual interest on CPB bonds

Oct. 4   Received a 10-percent stock dividend from Blue Sea Lake Corporation (Recorded a memo entry in the investment account to note the new number of shares held.)

Dec. 31   Received the semi-annual interest on CPB bonds

Dec. 31   The market value of CPB bonds on this date was 90; Blue Sea Lake Corporation shares were being traded at $20 per share.

19X7

Mar. 15   Sold $100,000-worth of CPB bonds at 92, less brokerage fees of $500 plus the accrued interest on these bonds at the time of sale

May 25   Blue Sea Lake Corporation shares were split 2 for 1; received the additional shares on this date (Recorded a memo entry in the investment account to note the new number of shares.)

Oct. 4   Received a $0.50 per-share cash dividend on the investment in Blue Sea Lake Corporation shares

Dec. 31   Blue Sea Lake Corporation shares were being traded for $27 at this date.

Required:

1. Prepare journal entries to record the 19X6 transactions.
2. Prepare a journal entry required at December 31, 19X6 under the LOCAM method to record an unrealized loss on marketable equity securities.
3. Prepare a partial balance sheet at December 31, 19X6 to show the short-term investments and the allowance account.
4. How would the market value decline at December 31, 19X6 be disclosed, according to the CICA recommendations?
5. Prepare journal entries required for 19X7 transactions.
6. Prepare the journal entry required at December 31, 19X7 under the LOCAM method to record the recovery of part of the unrealized loss on marketable equity securities recorded the previous year.
7. Does the receipt of a stock dividend represent income to Campus Products Corporation? Why or why not?
8. Prepare a partial balance sheet at December 31, 19X7 to show the short-term investment and the allowance account.

Supplementary Problem 14-2

User Hostile Limited (UHL) has 100 000 common shares outstanding. The following data are applicable to its operations for 19X3, 19X4, and 19X5.

	Dividends Paid	Net Income (Loss)
19X3	$200,000	$ 300,000
19X4	100,000	(400,000)
19X5	100,000	600,000

User Friendly Inc. (UFI) purchased 51 000 shares, representing a 51-percent interest in User Hostile Limited, for $300,000 on January 1, 19X3.

Part A

Required:

1. Identify the relationship of UHL and UFI during 19X3, 19X4, and 19X5.
2. Indicate what method of accounting can be used in the records of UFI for its investment in UHL. Under what method would the investment be reported in financial statements of UFI?
3. Assuming UFI uses the cost method, prepare journal entries to record
   a. The purchase of the 51 000 shares as a long-term investment
   b. In 19X3, the receipt of UFI's share of dividends paid by UHL
   c. In 19X3, UFI's share of UHL's income.
4. Assuming that the market value of UFI's shares in UHL has increased by $50,000 over book value at December 31, 19X3, indicate
   a. How the CICA recommendations would require the increased market value to be disclosed in UFI's financial statements
   b. How the LOCAM method would be applied.

Part B

Assume use of the cost method.

Required:

5. Prepare journal entries to record
   a. In 19X4, the receipt of UFI's share of dividends paid by UHL
   b. In 19X4, UFI's share of UHL's loss.
6. Assume that the market value of UFI's shares in UHL has decreased by $100,000 compared to book value (ignore the increase in market value in 19X3) at December 31, 19X4, and that this decline in market value is not expected to be permanent.
   a. Indicate the CICA recommended way of handing this loss in the financial statements.
   b. Prepare the entry required under the LOCAM method.

Part C

Assume use of the cost method.

Required:

7. Prepare journal entries to record
   a. In 19X5, the receipt of UFI's share of dividends paid by UHL
   b. In 19X5, UFI's share of UHL's income.
8. Assume that the market value of UHL's shares had improved over that of 19X4, and that $25,000 of the 19X4 decline had been recovered at December 31, 19X5.
   a. Indicate the CICA recommended method of handling this recovery in the financial statements.
   b. Prepare the journal entry required under the LOCAM method.

Supplementary Problem 14-3

Primeau Corporation purchased 10 000 shares, representing a 20-percent interest in Short Limited, for $400,000 on January 1, 19X3. The following transactions occurred during the year.

Mar. 31   Received the semi-annual cash dividend of $1 per share
Jun. 30   Received a 10-percent stock dividend
Sep. 30   Received the semi-annual cash dividend of $1 per share
Dec. 31   S Limited reported a net income of $100,000.

Part A

Primeau Corporation does not have a significant influence over Short Limited.

Required:
 1. Prepare entries to record
    a. The purchase of 10 000 Short Limited shares as a long-term investment
    b. The receipt of the March 31 cash dividend
    c. The receipt of the June 30 stock dividend
    d. The receipt of the September 30 cash dividend
 2. Calculate the average per-share cost in Short Limited.

Part B

Primeau Corporation is assumed to have a significant influence over Short Limited.

Required:
 3. Prepare entries to record
    a. The purchase of 10 000 Short Limited shares as a long-term investment
    b. The receipt of the March 31 cash dividend
    c. The receipt of the June 30 stock dividend
    d. The receipt of the September 30 cash dividend
    e. Primeau Corporation's share of Short Limited's income.
 4. Calculate the average per-share book value in Short Limited.

Part C

Required: Prepare a schedule (like the one in section C), to compare the amounts reported on the balance sheet and on the income statement of Primeau Corporation, under both the cost and equity methods.

Part D

At December 31, 19X3, the market value of Primeau Corporation's shares in Short was $50,000 less than their cost.

Required:
 5. Assuming that the investment was carried at cost in the books of Short and that the decline was not permanent, prepare journal entries to record the decline using the LOCAM method.
 6. How would the decline be handled, according to CICA recommendations? (The decline is not expected to be permanent.)

Supplementary Problem 14-4

Part A

Carrier Micro-Chips Inc. paid $100,000 for $100,000-worth of face value bonds of Johnson Computer Corporation on January 1, 19X1. The bonds, which were acquired as a long-term investment, had the following features.

Date of Authorization	*Term*	*Bond Contract Interest Rate*	*Interest Payment Dates*
January 1, 19X1	3 years	12%	Semi-annually on June 30 and December 31

Required:
1. Calculate the amount of interest received every six months.
2. Prepare journal entries to record
   a. The acquisition of the bonds on January 1, 19X1
   b. The receipt of interest on June 30, 19X1
   c. The receipt of interest on December 31, 19X1.

Part B

An additional $50,000-worth of face value bonds were acquired on January 1, 19X2 for $48,000.

Required:
3. Calculate
   a. The amount of interest income received on the $150,000-worth of face value bonds every interest payment date
   b. The amount of amortization to be recorded at each interest payment date (Use the straight-line method of amortization.)
4. Prepare journal entries to record
   a. Acquisition of the bonds on January 1, 19X2
   b. Receipt of interest on June 30, 19X2 on the $150,000-worth of face value issued bonds
   c. Amortization of bond discount on June 30, 19X2
   d. Receipt of interest on December 31, 19X2
   e. Amortization of bond discount on December 31, 19X2.
5. Prepare the ledger entries for the Investment in Bonds account of Carrier Micro-Chips Inc. from purchase to redemption.
6. Prepare a journal entry to record the redemption of the bonds at maturity, January 1, 19X4.

Supplementary Problem 14-5

On January 1, 19X3, Multi-Vard Inc. purchased $500,000 face value bonds of Lotus P.C. Corporation as a long-term investment. The bonds had these features.

Date of Authorization	Term	Bond Contract Interest Rate	Interest Payment Dates
January 1, 19X3	3 years	12%	Semi-annually on June 30 and December 31

The following information appears in the published balance sheet of Multi-Vard Inc. at December 31, 19X3, its fiscal year-end: "Long-Term Investments — $496,000". Multi-Vard uses the straight-line method of amortization.

Required:
1. a. The acquisition price of the bonds on January 1, 19X3
   b. The amount of cash interest paid in 19X3
   c. The amount of amortization recorded during 19X3
   d. The total amount of amortization to be recorded during the life of the bonds
   e. The amount of bond interest income appearing in the 19X3 income statement.
2. Prepare journal entries to record
   a. The acquisition of the bonds on January 1, 19X3.
   b. The receipt of interest and recording of bond discount amortization on June 30, 19X3.
   c. The receipt of interest and recording of bond discount amortization on December 31, 19X3.
3. On January 1, 19X4, Multi-Vard exercised a conversion feature contained in the bond indenture; $100,000-worth of face value bonds were converted into common stock of Lotus P.C. Corporation. Prepare a journal entry to record the conversion.

Disclosure and Financial Reporting

Financial statements report information for analysis to shareholders and other interested parties at regular intervals. Although shareholders actually own the entity, they alone do not finance it; creditors finance some of its activities and, together with shareholders, form the entity's financial structure. This financial structure is carefully evaluated by readers of financial statements to ascertain whether shareholders' equity is inadequate or excessive.

In previous discussions of an entity's financing cycle, equity and debt were viewed as alternate forms of financing operations. Management must decide the proportion of equity to debt financing. Analysis of financial statements evaluates such decisions.

Financial reporting and disclosure of information is intended to help users of financial statements to make investment decisions. Accordingly, this information is expected to be timely and useful; statement users should be able to depend on the information and employ it in evaluating investment alternatives. The information must also be comparable to information of previous accounting time periods of the entity, and to the statements of other entities in the same industry.

As discussed earlier, financial ratios constitute one way to evaluate an entity's short-term solvency. Ratio calculation is illustrated in Chapter 15. An evaluation of an entity's efficiency to earn net income can also be made through the calculation and study of relevant ratios.

The income statement, statement of retained earnings, and balance sheet are the focus of preceding chapters. The fourth financial statement, the statement of changes in financial position, is designed to show changes that have occurred during a particular accounting period. Chapter 16 discusses different definitions attached to this statement and illustrates its preparation under each definition.

Analysis of Financial Statements

Financial statements can be analyzed to evaluate a corporation's financial structure, solvency, and operations efficiency, as well as the impact of changing price levels on it.

1. What is the amount of shareholder claims against its assets compared to the amount of creditor claims?
2. Is the corporation underfinanced or overfinanced?
3. Under what circumstances is creditor financing more financially attractive than shareholder financing?
4. What are the relative advantages of short-term and long-term debt?
5. What is meant by *solvency*?
6. What are some ratios commonly used to evaluate solvency? What are some of their merits and weaknesses?
7. How long does it take a corporation to complete its revenue operating cycle?
8. How can the efficiency with which the corporation uses its assets to earn income be evaluated?
9. What is *trading on the equity?*
10. What is required for an accurate comparative analysis of corporations in different industries?
11. How can corporations that have a considerable amount of their assets tied up in fixed assets be evaluated?
12. What is a *horizontal analysis*? How does it differ from a *vertical analysis*?
13. What is the Consumer Price Index, and how does it measure a decrease in the dollar's purchasing power?
14. Why do some accountants propose that historical cost dollar amounts in financial statements be converted into constant dollars?
15. How does current cost accounting differ from constant dollar accounting?
16. What financial statement disclosure of changing prices is required by the AcSC?

A. Financial Structure: The Example of Bluebeard Computer Corporation

Financial structure
The components of an entity's equity, including creditor and shareholder capital; often referred to as the capital structure.

The accounting equation expresses a relationship between assets owned by an entity and the claims against those assets. Although shareholders own a corporation, they alone do not finance the corporation; creditors also finance some of its activities. Together, creditor and shareholder capital are said to form the **financial structure** of a corporation.

Bluebeard Computer Corporation's Financial Structure
ASSETS = LIABILITIES + SHAREHOLDERS' EQUITY
$2,486 = $1,255 + $1,231

Financial analysts and would-be investors look very carefully at the financial structure of a corporation, that is, at the amount of shareholder claims against the assets of a corporation compared to the creditor claims. BCC has a high reliance on debt in its financial structure; creditors have a substantial claim against the assets of Bluebeard.

The long-term financial strength of a corporation depends on its financial structure. In any given situation, a company is said to be *underfinanced* if there is inadequate shareholders' equity; it is considered to be *overfinanced* if shareholders' equity is excessive. The proportion of shareholder-to-creditor claims is calculated by dividing shareholders' equity by total liabilities. BCC's situation is outlined below:

		(000s)		
		19X5	19X4	19X3
Shareholders' Equity	(a)	$1,231	$1,195	$1,148
Total Liabilities	(b)	1,255	917	269
Equity to Debt	(a ÷ b)	0.98	1.30	4.27

Equity-to-debt ratio
A ratio indicating the shareholder and creditor claims to the assets of an entity.

These calculations tell us that BCC has 98 cents of shareholders' equity for each dollar of liabilities in its current year, 19X5, and that the proportion of equity financing has been decreasing since 19X3, when there was $4.27 of equity for each $1 of liabilities. In 19X5, creditors are financing a greater proportion of BCC than are shareholders. This **equity-to-debt ratio** and the trend of the financing over the three years is a cause for concern.

On the one hand, management's reliance on creditor financing is good. Additional issues of shares would require existing shareholders to share their control of BCC with new shareholders, thereby making less available to existing shareholders. Creditor financing may also be more financially attractive to existing shareholders, if it enables BCC to earn more than the interest paid on the debt.

On the other hand, management's reliance on creditor financing is troublesome. If there is too much debt, creditors may not be willing to extend additional financing, should it be necessary. This potential is one risk of excessive creditor financing. Another risk derives from the fact that interest has to be paid on this debt and repayment of the debt is required. The terms and timing of these payments are agreed to when the debt is incurred. Total earnings of BCC could be reduced if heavy interest payments have to be paid. Each of these risks could threaten the survival of the company.

The proportion of shareholder-to-creditor financing is decided by management. A reasonable balance has to be maintained. Although no specific figures can be stated as the most appropriate equity-to-debt ratio, there are techniques for discovering the optimum balance. They involve the weighing of leverage (the proportion of debt) against the risk involved; such material forms the subject matter of finance studies and cannot be covered in an accounting course. What can be attempted, however, is an evaluation of an existing financial structure.

Short-Term versus Long-Term Debt

Both short-term and long-term financing strategies have their advantages. The advantage of some short-term debt is that it does not require interest payments to creditors; for example, accounts payable do not usually require payment of interest if they are paid within credit terms. A further advantage of short-term debt is that income is not reduced by the debt. Short-term debt also has its disadvantages: payment is required in a short period of time, and an increase in the proportion of short-term debt is more risky because it has to be renewed more frequently.

Long-term debt's advantages are that payment may be made over an extended period of time, and that risk is reduced by this longer repayment period governed by a contractual agreement. The disadvantages of long-term debt are that interest payments are required to be made at specified times, and that these interest payments reduce income. As a general rule, long-term financing should be used to finance long-term assets.

The Structure of Bluebeard's Creditor Financing

An analysis of the company's balance sheet reveals the following liabilities:

	(000s)		
	19X5	19X4	19X3
Current Liabilities	$1,255	$917	$269
Long-Term Liabilities	–	–	–

This information indicates that BCC management relies solely on short-term creditor financing, part of which is $300,000-worth of accounts payable that bears no interest. The risk they have assumed is the need to replace existing liabilities, as they come due and are paid, with new liabilities. If creditors become unwilling to extend this short-term debt, the ability of Bluebeard to pay its other liabilities may be compromised. In fact, this is happening to BCC. Existing creditors have become less willing to extend new credit, and the bank is asking for the repayment of its loan. At this point, the company may have reached the end of its short-term financing rope.

Is Bluebeard Insolvent?

Solvency
The ability of an entity to pay debts as they become due.

Current liabilities
Obligations that will be paid within one year or within the normal operating cycle, whichever is longer.

Accountants, analysts, and investors often talk about the **solvency** of a company. The term, when applied to a company, refers to its ability to pay its **current liabilities** as they become due. If a company is insolvent, then it is unable to pay the creditors who have provided it with goods and services on account. These are the implications of being insolvent:

Current Liabilities:
Creditors can refuse to provide any further goods or services on account.
Creditors can sue for payment.
Creditors can put the company into receivership or bankruptcy.

Long-Term Liabilities:
Creditors can refuse to lend additional cash.
Creditors can demand repayment of their long-term debts, under some circumstances.

Shareholders' Equity:
Shareholders may be unwilling to invest in additional share capital of the company.
Shareholders risk the loss of their investment, if the company is placed in bankruptcy.

At the present time, BCC is unable to pay its creditors. Although sales are rapidly increasing and an acceptable gross profit is being earned, the company is, technically, insolvent.

A company normally keeps a reasonable balance in its current assets among cash, receivables, and inventory. Unfortunately, there is no one indicator of what a "reasonable" balance really is. The balance is acceptable when debts are being paid. And, when current liabilities are not being paid, as is the case for Bluebeard Computer Corporation, a reasonable balance does not exist.

Study the following components of Bluebeard's 19X5 current assets:

	(000s)	
Current Assets in 19X5		*% Composition*
Cash	$ 19	1.33
Marketable Securities	37	2.58
Accounts Receivable — Trade	544	37.96
Inventory	833	58.13
Total Current Assets	$1,433	100.00

Given this financial balance, BCC appears to have an overinvestment both in receivables and in inventory — together they amount to approximately 96 percent of its current assets — although a final evaluation must relate investment to sales and cost of goods sold. Consider the current debts of the company in 19X5.

Current Liabilities in 19X5	(000s)
Bank Loan	$ 825
Accounts Payable — Trade	300
Accrued Liabilities	82
Income Tax Payable	48
Total Current Liabilities	$1,255

These are the short-term creditors of BCC. Short-term solvency analysis emphasizes factors that are important to these creditors.

The short-term creditors would be particularly concerned about these factors:

1. Trade accounts payable are due within the next 60 days. Will BCC be able to pay them?

2. Bluebeard has asked its bankers for additional loans. The bankers are unwilling to provide new loans and are asking for repayment of existing bank loans.

3. How will BCC cope with accrued liabilities and income taxes payable?

Obviously, Bluebeard is in trouble!

BCC has $19,000 cash on hand and $37,000 in marketable securities (which can be converted immediately into cash) to pay current liabilities. One alternative at this time appears to be to collect receivables as quickly as it can and sell inventory at whatever price it can get. This desperate action would undoubtedly result in losses that would jeopardize the company's existence. Another alternative might be to renegotiate its short-term bank loan into a long-term bank loan.

B. Short-Term Solvency Analysis

Ratios are one way of evaluating any company's solvency. Commonly used ratios are introduced next, with a summary of the ratios and what they can be expected to indicate. Information from the following comparative Bluebeard financial statements for 19X5, 19X4, and 19X3 are used for detailed analysis of Bluebeard's financial position.

Bluebeard Computer Corporation
Balance Sheets
At December 31

(000s)

Assets

CURRENT ASSETS:	19X5	19X4	19X3
Cash	$ 19	$ 24	$ 50
Marketable Securities	37	37	37
Accounts Receivable — Trade	544	420	257
Inventory	833	503	361
Total Current Assets	$1,433	$ 984	$ 705

FIXED ASSETS:			
Land	$ 200	$ 200	$ 100
Buildings	350	350	200
Equipment	950	950	700
	$1,500	$1,500	$1,000
Less: Accumulated Depreciation —			
Buildings and Equipment	(447)	(372)	(288)
Net Fixed Assets	$1,053	$1,128	$ 712
Total Assets	$2,486	$2,112	$1,417

Liabilities and Shareholders' Equity

CURRENT LIABILITIES:	19X5	19X4	19X3
Bank Loan	$ 825	$ 570	–
Accounts Payable — Trade	300	215	$ 144
Other Liabilities	82	80	75
Income Tax Payable	48	52	50
Total Current Liabilities	$1,255	$ 917	$ 269

SHAREHOLDERS' EQUITY:			
Common Stock	$1,000	$1,000	$1,000
Retained Earnings	231	195	148
Total Shareholders' Equity	$1,231	$1,195	$1,148
Total Liabilities and Shareholders' Equity	$2,486	$2,112	$1,417

Bluebeard Computer Corporation
Combined Statements of Income and Retained Earnings
For the Years Ended December 31

	(000s)		
	19X5	19X4	19X3
Sales	$3,200	$2,800	$2,340
Cost of Goods Sold	2,500	2,150	1,800
Gross Profit	$ 700	$ 650	$ 540
Expenses	584	533	428
Net Income	$ 116	$ 117	$ 112
Opening Retained Earnings	195	148	96
	$ 311	$ 265	$ 208
Less: Dividends	80	70	60
Closing Retained Earnings	$ 231	$ 195	$ 148

Other related information included in total expenses:

Interest Expense	$ 89	$ 61	–
Income Tax Expense	95	102	$ 97

Short-Term Solvency Analysis:	*Indicates:*
1. The Current Ratio	How many current asset dollars exist to pay current liabilities. (This ratio is only a crude measure of solvency.)
2. The Acid-Test Ratio	Whether the company is able to meet the immediate demands of creditors. (This ratio is a more severe measure of solvency. Inventory and pre-paid items are excluded from the calculation.)
3. Management Decisions Relating to Receivables:	
a. Accounts Receivable Collection Period	The average time needed to collect receivables.
b. Accounts Receivable Turnover	How often during the year accounts receivable have been converted into cash.
4. Management Decisions Relating to Inventory:	
a. Number of Days of Sales in Inventory	How many days of sales can be made with existing inventory.
b. Inventory Turnover	How many times during the year inventory has been sold and replaced.
5. The Revenue Operating Cycle	How long it is between the purchase of inventory and the subsequent collection of cash.

The following financial information of BCC is used in the analysis of its short-term solvency.

		(000s)		
		19X5	19X4	19X3
CURRENT ASSETS:				
Cash		$ 19	$ 24	$ 50
Marketable Securities		37	37	37
Accounts Receivable — Trade		544	420	257
Inventory		833	503	361
Total Current Assets		$1,433	$984	$705
CURRENT LIABILITIES:				
Bank Loan		$ 825	$570	–
Accounts Payable — Trade		300	215	$144
Other Liabilities		82	80	75
Income Tax Payable		48	52	50
Total Current Liabilities		$1,255	$917	$269
Net Working Capital		$ 178	$ 67	$436

Working Capital

Working capital
The excess of current assets over current liabilities; also referred to as net working capital.

The calculation of working capital is a starting point in short-term solvency analysis. For accountants, **working capital** refers to the mathematical difference between current assets and current liabilities at a particular point in time. The calculation is most useful to the reader when it is compared with the working capital of previous years. For example, an increase in working capital informs the reader about the entity's increased ability to pay its debts.

In the above schedule, working capital is calculated at $178,000 in 19X5 and represents the amount of current assets in excess of current liabilities. This working capital indicates short-term solvency in a dollar amount; notice the dollar difference in working capital between 19X5 and 19X3.

The current ratio discussed under the next heading calculates this same short-term solvency in terms of a ratio; a ratio is usually easier to interpret than the calculation of an absolute dollar amount.

The Current Ratio

Current ratio
Current assets divided by current liabilities; indicates how many asset dollars are available to pay current liabilities. This is a *crude* measure of solvency.

Is the firm able to repay short-term creditors? The **current ratio** answers this question by expressing the working capital as a ratio of current assets to current liabilities — current assets are divided by current liabilities. The relevant BCC financial data required to calculate this ratio follows:

		(000s)		
		19X5	19X4	19X3
Current Assets	(a)	$1,433	$984	$705
Current Liabilities	(b)	1,255	917	269
Current Ratio	(a ÷ b)	1.14	1.07	2.62

The results of this calculation are an indication of how many current asset dollars exist to pay current liabilities. In 19X5, $1.14 of current assets exists to pay each $1 of current liabilities. Is $1.14 adequate? Unfortunately, no one current ratio can be identified as adequate in all situations. Figure 15-1 diagrams the possibilities.

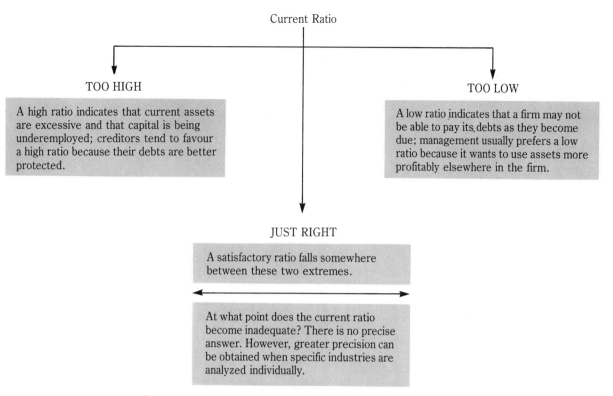

Figure 15-1   Current ratios

Bluebeard is suffering from cash shortages and is unable to pay its debts as they become due. Therefore, its current ratio of 1.14 is clearly inadequate and should be regarded unfavourably; the 19X4 ratio of 1.07 is also inadequate. Without other information, one cannot conclude whether 2.62, the 19X3 ratio, is just right or too high. Some analysts, as noted in an earlier chapter, consider that a corporation should maintain a 2 : 1 current ratio, depending on the industry in which the firm operates. For example, if there were $2 of current assets to pay each $1 of current liabilities, these current assets could shrink considerably in worth and the firm likely would still be able to pay its debts. However, it is recognized that no one current ratio is applicable to all entities; other factors — such as the composition of current assets, the credit terms extended by suppliers — must also be considered to arrive at an acceptable ratio.

Dun and Bradstreet, as well as trade publications, provide a range of current ratios that may be applicable to companies in a particular industry at a given time. Note that the adequacy of a current ratio depends on other developments within a company and that, while a given ratio may be satisfactory one year, it may not be the next year.

Composition of Specific Items in Current Assets

In the following example, each company has a 2 : 1 current ratio. Are the companies equally able to repay their short-term creditors?

	A Corp.	B. Corp.
CURRENT ASSETS:		
Cash	$ 1,000	$10,000
Accounts Receivable	2,000	20,000
Inventory	37,000	10,000
Total Current Assets	$40,000	$40,000
Current Liabilities:	$20,000	$20,000
Current Ratio	2 : 1	2 : 1

The companies have equal dollar amounts of current assets and current liabilities, but they have different debt paying abilities. A Corp. could first sell some inventory and collect the resulting receivables; or, it can immediately sell its inventory as a single lot for cash, probably for less than it cost. (This type of shrinkage is provided for in the 2 : 1 current ratio discussed previously.) Clearly, B Corp. is in a better position to repay short-term creditors.

Since the current ratio doesn't consider the components of current assets, it is only a rough indicator of how able a firm is to pay its debts as they become due. This weakness is partly remedied by another ratio, called the acid-test ratio.

The Acid-Test Ratio

Acid-test ratio
Quick current assets divided by current liabilities; indicates the ability of the entity to meet the immediate demands of creditors. This is a more severe measure of solvency than the current ratio.

Quick current assets
Assets that can be converted into cash in a short period of time, including cash, marketable securities, accounts receivable — trade, and excluding inventory and prepaid items.

A more severe test of solvency is provided by the so called **acid-test ratio**; often called the *quick ratio*, it provides an indication of instant solvency — the ability to meet the immediate demands of creditors. To calculate this ratio, current assets have to be broken down into **quick current assets** and non-quick current assets.

Quick Current Assets	Non-Quick Current Assets
Cash	Inventory
Marketable Securities	Prepaid Items
Accounts Receivable — Trade	
These current assets are considered to be readily convertible into cash.	Cash could not be obtained immediately from these current assets.

Inventory and prepaid items cannot usually be converted into cash in a short period of time. They are, therefore, excluded from quick assets in the calculation of this ratio. The acid-test ratio is derived by dividing the total of quick current assets by current liabilities. The relevant BCC financial data required to calculate this ratio follows:

		(000s)		
		19X5	19X4	19X3
Quick Current Assets	(a)	$ 600	$ 481	$ 344
Current Liabilities	(b)	1,255	917	269
Acid-Test Ratio	(a ÷ b)	0.478	0.525	1.28

This ratio indicates how many quick asset dollars (cash, marketable securities, and trade accounts receivable) exist to pay each dollar of current liabilities. As can be seen, only 47.8 cents of quick assets are available to pay each $1 of current liabilities in 19X5. This amount is clearly inadequate; 52.5 cents in 19X4 is also inadequate. The 19X3 ratio may be a reasonable guide for the adequacy of quick current assets. Of particular concern to financial analysts would be the trend of the acid-test ratio over the three years.

What is an adequate acid-test ratio? It is generally considered that a 1 : 1 acid-test ratio is adequate to ensure that a firm will be able to pay its current obligations. However, this is a fairly arbitrary guideline and is not reliable in all situations. A lower ratio than 1 : 1 can often be found in successful companies.

When taken together, the current and acid-test ratios give the financial statement reader a better understanding of a company's financial health. While the current ratio may be favourable, the acid-test ratio may alert the reader to a preponderance of non-quick assets in the company.

Management Decisions Relating to Receivables

Short-term solvency is affected by management decisions related to trade accounts receivable. Lax collection of receivables can result in a shortage of cash to pay current obligations. The effectiveness of management decisions relating to receivables is analyzed by calculating the accounts receivable collection period and the accounts receivable turnover.

Accounts Receivable Collection Period

Accounts receivable collection period ratio
Average accounts receivable is divided by net credit sales and the result is multiplied by 365 days. This ratio indicates the average time needed to collect receivables.

The acid-test ratio is a more severe test of solvency than the current ratio, since it calculates how many quick current asset dollars exist to pay current liabilities. But the acid-test ratio can also be misleading, if accounts receivable are high because of slow receivables collection. The calculation of the **accounts receivable collection period** establishes the average time needed to collect an amount. This figure indicates the efficiency of collection procedures when the collection period is compared with the firm's sales terms (in BCC's case, net 30). To calculate this ratio, average annual accounts receivable are divided by the net credit sales and the result is multiplied by 365 days. The relevant BCC financial data required to make the calculation appear next.

		(000s)	
		19X5	19X4
Net Credit Sales	(a)	$3,200	$2,800
Average Accounts Receivable [(Opening Balance + Closing Balance) ÷ 2]	(b)	482	338
Total Days in the Year	(c)	365	365
Average Collection Period [b ÷ a) × (c)]		55 days	44 days

When Bluebeard's 30-day sales terms are compared to the 55-day collection period, it is obvious that an average 25 days sales (55 days − 30 days) have gone uncollected beyond the regular credit period in 19X5. Moreover, the trend is toward an increase in this collection period over that of the previous year. Therefore, some overextension of credit and possibly ineffective collection procedures are indicated by this ratio. Quicker collection would improve BCC's cash position.

Whether the increase in collection period is good, bad, or just right depends on other factors, such as increasing sales or increasing profits. Therefore, the average collection period is subject to further interpretation before a conclusion can be made. The ratio does provide, however, an indication of the effectiveness of credit and collection procedures in 19X5.

Accounts Receivable Turnover

A further insight into the quality of trade accounts receivable is provided through the calculation of the **accounts receivable turnover**. This ratio indicates how often accounts receivable have been converted into cash during the year. The higher the turnover, the less investment exists in accounts receivable.

Higher Turnover Indicates:
1. Accounts receivable are more liquid.
2. Accounts receivable have decreased in relation to sales.
3. Investment in accounts receivable has decreased in relation to sales.

Lower Turnover Indicates:
1. Accounts receivable are less liquid.
2. Accounts receivable have increased in relation to sales.
3. Investment in accounts receivable has increased in relation to sales.

The accounts receivable turnover is calculated by dividing net credit sales during the year by average accounts receivable. The relevant BCC financial data required to calculate this ratio follow.

		(000s)	
		19X5	19X4
Net Credit Sales	(a)	$3,200	$2,800
Average Accounts Receivable [(Opening Balance + Closing Balance) ÷ 2]	(b)	482	338
Accounts Receivable Turnover	(a ÷ b)	6.64 times	8.28 times

As can be seen, the accounts receivable turnover has decreased during 19X5; that is, accounts receivable were converted into cash fewer times during the year than in the previous year. This simply means that trade receivables are less liquid in 19X5. The danger exists that they were less collectible in 19X5, because older receivables may be buried in the total amount of receivables.

Management Decisions Relating to Inventory

The acid-test ratio showed how short-term solvency is affected by management decisions involving inventory, since an overinvestment in inventory can reduce the amount of cash available to pay current liabilities. The effectiveness of management decisions relating to inventory can be analyzed by the number of days of sales in inventory and the inventory turnover.

Number of Days of Sales in Inventory

If current assets are tied up in inventory, then accounts payable cannot be paid within the discount period, a situation that would not be beneficial for the company. One method of analyzing whether there is an over-investment in inventory is to calculate how many days of sales can be made with the existing inventory. The **number of days of sales in inventory** is calculated by dividing average inventory by the cost of goods sold and

---

Accounts receivable turnover ratio
Net credit sales is divided by average accounts receivable. This ratio indicates how often during the year accounts receivable have been converted into cash.

Number of days of sales in inventory ratio
The average inventory is divided by cost of goods sold and the result is multiplied by 365 days. This ratio indicates how many days of sales can be made with existing inventory.

multiplying the result by 365 days. The relevant BCC financial data required to calculate this ratio are reproduced below:

		(000s)	
		19X5	19X4
Cost of Goods Sold	(a)	$2,500	$2,150
Average Inventory [(Opening Balance + Closing Balance) ÷ 2]	(b)	668	432
Days in the Year	(c)	365	365
Number of Days of Sales in Inventory	[(b ÷ a) × (c)]	97.5 days	73.3 days

There are more days of sales in 19X5 inventory, which means that Bluebeard is increasing its investment in inventory. In 19X5, 97.5 days of sales in inventory indicates that BCC can handle approximately 3 months of sales with its existing inventory.

Inventory Turnover

Inventory turnover
Cost of goods sold is divided by average inventory. This ratio indicates how many times during the year inventory has been sold and replaced.

An **inventory turnover ratio** can also be calculated for Bluebeard to measure how many times inventory has been sold and replaced during the year. This analysis is important because a gross profit is earned each time inventory is turned over. The ratio is calculated by dividing cost of goods sold by average inventory. The relevant BCC financial data required to calculate this ratio are reproduced below:

		(000s)	
		19X5	19X4
Cost of Goods Sold	(a)	$2,500	$2,150
Average Inventory [(Opening Balance + Closing Balance) ÷ 2]	(b)	668	432
Inventory Turnover	(a ÷ b)	3.74 times	4.98 times

Inventory has turned over fewer times in 19X5 than in 19X4. In other words, inventory was sold and replaced less often in 19X5. Usually a high turnover is considered favourable, and a low turnover is considered troublesome. However, the situation is more complex.

A high turnover is usually a sign of good inventory management, because the amount of assets tied up in inventory is lower, and an optimum amount of inventory is being purchased. A high turnover is also important for controlling inventory losses owing to obsolescence or deterioration. A fast turnover tends to indicate that these problems will be avoided. With a high turnover, inventory-related expenses such as insurance and taxes are lower because less storage space is being used for inventory. It should be noted, however, that high turnover can have negative consequences if turnover becomes so rapid that, at any one point in time, items are out of stock that customers want to purchase.

A low turnover is usually a sign of poor inventory management, because an excessive investment in inventory ties up assets that could be used for other purposes, and an excessive amount of inventory is being purchased. Further, a low turnover tends to indicate that problems will be encountered in obsolescence (consider styling in women's shoes) or deterioration (consider groceries). Such inventories may become unsaleable. However, the positive aspect of low turnover is that there can be shorter delivery time to customers, and customers can always count on items being in stock. Customers remain satisfied and loyal.

Whether Bluebeard's reduced turnover is positive or negative depends on management's objectives. Is management increasing inventory to provide for increased sales in 19X6, or is inventory being poorly managed?

Inadequate information precludes a precise answer. Consider, however, the following factors:

Analyst's Questions:	*Facts:*
1. Is inventory turnover decreasing because of inadequate sales volume?	Sales volume is rapidly increasing.
2. Is an excessive inventory being purchased?	Sales are expected to increase in 19X6. Therefore, the 19X5 inventory should be considered in relation to anticipated 19X6 sales.
3. Are slow-moving items responsible for the decreasing turnover?	Bluebeard sells computer hardware and software, which are much in demand.

Based on this analysis, it would appear that the increased days of sales in inventory and the decreased inventory turnover can be explained in relation to Bluebeard's anticipated 19X6 sales. The problem appears to be not so much an overinvestment in inventory in relation to sales, but an overinvestment in inventory in relation to the financial strength of the corporation. In the final analysis, a reasonable balance between inventory, sales, and the company's financial strength has to be maintained. Management must decide how to strike this balance. The calculation of inventory ratios can only give an insight into the quality of these management decisions.

What Is an Adequate Inventory Turnover?

Since no management aims to tie up assets in inventory, it is important for managers to uncover the underlying circumstances when turnover is low. Is the company ''stuck'' with its inventory (as automobile manufacturers were at one time with their big cars)? Or has the company stockpiled inventory (such as oil) because of anticipated shortages or price increases?

Turnovers vary from industry to industry and a firm's performance should be compared with industry averages. However, a problem with industry averages occurs when information in published financial statements is incomplete—for example, cost of goods sold is not often shown separately. Accordingly, sales, rather than cost of goods sold, is often used in actual practice to make calculations and comparisons. The resulting ratio, however, does not give the actual inventory; it gives the sales dollars from average inventory. Such a figure may not be entirely useful for judging performance.

The Revenue Operating Cycle

Revenue operating cycle
The average number of days to turn over

Every business repeats a **revenue operating cycle** over and over again. Inventory is purchased, an accounts receivable occurs when a sale is made, and cash is generated when the receivable is collected. This cycle is illustrated in Figure 15-2.

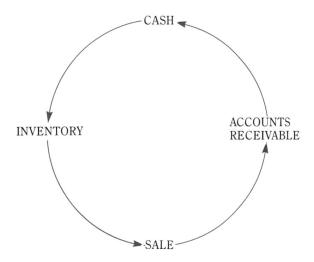

Figure 15-2   The revenue operating cycle

inventory is added to the average number of days to collect receivables. This figure indicates the number of days that elapse between the purchase of inventory and the subsequent collection of cash.

How much time elapses at Bluebeard between the purchase of inventory and the subsequent collection of cash? That is, how long does it take BCC to complete one revenue operating cycle? The amount of time required to complete a single cycle can be calculated using the number of days it takes to turn over inventory and the number of days it takes to collect receivables that result from sales. The relevant BCC financial data required to calculate this ratio follows.

	19X5	19X4
Average Number of Days To Turn Over Inventory	97 days	73 days
Average Number of Days To Collect Receivables	55 days	44 days
Number of Days to Complete Cycle	152 days	117 days

In 19X5, 152 days were required to complete this cycle, compared to 117 days in 19X4. If accounts payable are due within 60 days, it is obvious that BCC will not be able to pay these liabilities with cash from the revenue operating cycle. Moreover, the situation in 19X5 is worse than it was in 19X4.

What Is Causing Bluebeard's Financial Problems?

The company is faced with financing its sales to customers and maintaining an adequate inventory in relation to sales, without having the financial strength to do so. Although inventory turnover could be improved, it is doubtful that accounts receivable could be collected much more rapidly. BCC is experiencing rapid growth and is not able to cope with its solvency requirements.

The company has relied too much on short-term financing for its expansion and increased receivable and inventory requirements. BCC is no longer able to rely on this short-term financing and must reconsider its short-term and long-term financing objectives and requirements.

The preceding analysis used the financial data of Bluebeard Computer Corporation to introduce the calculation of solvency ratios and to discuss the merits and weaknesses of these ratios. The ratios that can be used to analyze the operations efficiency of a company are discussed next.

C. Analysis of Operations Efficiency

Every company uses its assets as resources to earn net income. However, some companies do so more successfully than others. An evaluation of a company's efficiency can be made through the calculation and study of relevant ratios. Ratios can reveal the current financial status of a company, show the trend in its performance over a number of years, and compare its performance with others in the same industry. However, the calculation of ratios does not indicate the state of such factors as labour relations, product quality, and the impact of the company's operations in the environment.

The net income earned is the starting point for this analysis. The efficient use of assets can be judged by calculating net income as: a return on assets, a return on shareholders' equity, a return per share and a return on sales. The reasonableness of a company's investment in fixed assets is also important. The following is a summary of the ratios used to analyze operations efficiency.

Analysis of Operating Efficiency:	*Indicates:*
1. Return on Total Assets	How efficiently a company uses its assets as resources to earn net income.
2. Return on Shareholders' Equity	The adequacy of net income as a return on shareholders' equity.
a. Trading on the Equity	The use of borrowed money to generate a higher return in the business than the rate being paid on the borrowed money.
b. Bondholder Protection: Times Interest Earned Ratio	The ability of a company to pay interest to long-term creditors.
3. Return on Each Share: Earnings per Share	The amount of net income that has been earned on each share of common stock.
a. Price-Earnings Ratio	The reasonableness of market price in relation to per-share earnings.
b. Dividend Yield	The return that can be expected from an investment in a company's shares.
4. Return on Sales	The percentage of sales revenue left in the business after payment of expenses, creditor interest, and government income taxes.
5. Management Decisions Relating to Fixed Assets	
a. Sales to Fixed Assets Ratio	The adequacy of sales in relation to the investment in fixed assets.
b. Fixed Asset to Shareholders' Equity Ratio	The amount of shareholders' equity tied up in fixed assets.

Return on Total Assets

Return on total assets ratio
Income from operations is divided by average total assets. This ratio indicates how efficiently a company uses its assets as resources to earn net income.

An efficient use of assets should result in a higher return on these assets; a less efficient use results in a lower return. The **return on total assets ratio** is designed to measure the efficiency with which assets are used. The ratio is calculated by the following formula:

$$\frac{\text{Income from Operations}}{\text{Average Total Assets}}$$

This ratio focuses attention on income from operations, which is the amount earned by the company from the use of company assets. Expenses not applicable to operations of the company are excluded, such as expenses to finance the company (interest) and expenses on income due to government (income taxes). Average total assets are used in the calculation because the amount of assets used varies during the year.

Return on Shareholders' Equity

Return on shareholders' equity ratio
Net income for the year is divided by average shareholders' equity. This ratio indicates the adequacy of net income as a return on shareholders' equity.

The assets of a company are financed by both creditors and shareholders. In return for their share of financing, creditors are paid interest. Shareholders receive whatever remains after interest is paid to creditors and income taxes are paid to government. This **return on shareholders' equity** is calculated as a ratio by using the following formula:

$$\frac{\text{Net Income for the Year}}{\text{Average Shareholders' Equity}}$$

Net income after interest and income taxes is used in this calculation because only the balance remains to shareholders. Average equity is used because the amount of equity can vary during the year.

Trading on the Equity

Trading on the equity
A calculation made to indicate the ability of borrowed money to generate a higher return in the business than the rate being paid on the borrowed money.

Trading on the equity is not, strictly speaking, a ratio, but it is closely related to the return on shareholders' equity, which in turn is influenced by the use of long-term credit or financing. This use of borrowed funds can generate a higher return than the rate used to borrow the funds. Consider the following example, involving Companies H and D:

	Company H	Company D
Total Assets	$400,000	$400,000
Long-Term Liabilities (12%)	–	200,000
Equity	400,000	200,000

Although both H and D have the same amount of assets. Company H has no long-term liabilities, while Company D has $200,000-worth of 12-percent long-term liabilities. If both companies have $100,000 net income from operations, do they have a similar return on shareholders' equity?

	Company H	Company D
Income from Operations	$100,000	$100,000
Interest Expense ($200,000 × 12%)	–	24,000
	$100,000	$ 76,000
Income Tax (50% assumed)	50,000	38,000
Net Income for the Year	$ 50,000	$ 38,000

Notice that the use of long-term creditor financing resulted in a lower income figure for Company D, because of the interest expense. Now consider the implications of this lower income as a return on shareholders' equity:

		Company H	Company D
Income from Operations	(a)	$100,000	$100,000
Net Income for the Year	(b)	50,000	38,000
Total Assets	(c)	400,000	400,000
Shareholders' Equity	(d)	400,000	200,000
Return on Total Assets	(a ÷ c)	25%	25%
Return on Shareholders' Equity	(b ÷ d)	12.5%	19%

The return on total assets is 25 percent for both companies; however the return on shareholders' equity is considerably greater (19 percent) for Company D. This means that Company D borrowed funds at 12 percent to earn 25 percent in its business and this resulted in a 6.5 percent gain to shareholders. That is, trading on the equity magnified the return on shareholders' equity by 6.5 percent.

There is, however, risk involved in trading on the equity. While it magnifies the return on equity when the return on borrowed funds exceeds the cost of borrowing those funds, the opposite occurs when the cost of the borrowed funds exceeds the return on those borrowed funds. In general, companies with stable earnings can carry more debt in their financial structure than companies with fluctuating earnings.

Bondholder Protection: Times Interest Earned Ratio

Times interest earned ratio
Income from operations is divided by interest expense. This ratio indicates the ability of an entity to pay interest to long-term creditors.

Bondholders and other long-term creditors are aware that their funds are used for leverage and that there is a risk that the cost of borrowed funds may exceed the return made by the borrowing company on those borrowed funds. Therefore, they are interested in the **times interest earned ratio**, which is designed to measure the ability of a company to pay interest. It indicates the amount by which income from operations could decline before a default on interest would result. The ratio is calculated by the following formula:

$$\frac{\text{Income from Operations}}{\text{Interest Expense}}$$

Income tax is excluded in the calculation of this ratio because taxes are paid after interest. Income from operations is presumed to be income *before* the deduction of interest on debts. For 19X5, then, Bluebeard's income from operations is $300,000, composed of net income of $116,000, interest expense of $89,000, and income tax expense of $95,000.

Return on Each Share: Earnings Per Share

The return to shareholders calculated above indicates the overall return on assets financed by shareholders. This return to shareholders can also be expressed on a per-share basis. That is, the amount of net income can be divided by the number of common shares outstanding to establish how much net income has been earned for each share of stock. This ratio is calculated by the following formula:

$$\frac{\text{Net Income for the Year}}{\text{Number of Common Shares Outstanding}}$$

This expression of net income as a per-share amount is widely quoted in financial circles and, as noted in Chapter 13, is commonly referred to as earnings per share (EPS). Because of widespread interest in EPS, the AcSC of the CICA has recommended its inclusion in financial statements and has also issued guidelines for its preparation in certain complex situations. These guidelines cover the treatment of extraordinary items in the income statement and the convertibility of bonds and preferred shares into common stock. *A full explanation of the CICA guidelines in such cases is the subject matter of more advanced studies in accounting and is not attempted in this text*. You should be aware, however, that, if there are preferred shareholders, their claims on net income are deducted to calculate the amount available for common shareholders. The ratio formula would then be used in the following modified form:

$$\frac{\text{Net Income for the Year} \ - \ \text{Preferred Dividends}}{\text{Number of Common Shares Outstanding}}$$

Price-to-Earnings Ratio

Price-to-earnings ratio The market price per share is divided by earnings per share. This ratio indicates the reasonableness of market price in relation to per share earnings.

Earnings per share is of particular interest to investors because of its importance in influencing share market values. Additional measurements used in the stock market to evaluate the selling price of shares are the price-to-earnings ratio and the dividend yield. The **price-to-earnings ratio** is calculated by dividing the market value of a share by earnings per share:

$$\frac{\text{Market Price per Share}}{\text{Earnings per Share}}$$

This ratio indicates the market price in relation to per-share earnings. In fact, it only indicates investors' beliefs as to whether a particular share is over- or under-valued.

Dividend Yield

Dividend yield Dividends per share is divided by market price per share. This ratio indicates the return that can be expected from an investment in a company's shares.

The **dividend yield ratio** is calculated by dividing annual dividends per share by a share's current market price.

$$\frac{\text{Dividends per Share}}{\text{Market Price per Share}}$$

This ratio indicates how large a return can be expected from an investment in the company's shares.

Return on Sales

Return on sales Net income for the year is divided by net sales. This ratio indicates the percentage of sales revenue left in the business after payment of expenses, creditor interest, and government income taxes.

The efficiency, or productivity, of each sales dollar is established through the calculation of the **return on sales ratio**. This percentage of sales revenue retained by the company — after payment of operating expenses, creditor interest expenses, and government income taxes — is an index of performance that can be used to compare the company to others in the same industry. This ratio is calculated by the following formula:

$$\frac{\text{Net Income for the Year}}{\text{Net Sales}}$$

Note that each industry has different acceptable returns on sales. Consider these returns on sales.

Food		Steel	
Company	*Return on Sales*	*Company*	*Return on Sales*
Oshawa Group Limited	1.02	Stelco Inc.	7.5
Steinberg Inc.	1.24	Algoma Steel Corp. Ltd.	10.3
Loblaw Companies Limited	0.48	Dofasco Inc.	9.54

The comparison of return on sales between different industries is meaningless if other characteristics of each industry are not considered. Sales volume, accounts receivable turnover and inventory turnover vary from industry to industry.

Industry		Ratios	
	Sales Volume	*Receivables Turnover*	*Inventory Turnover*
Food	high	not applicable	high
Steel	high	low	low

Any comparison of companies in different industries has to take distinctive industry characteristics into consideration for an accurate analysis. It is particularly difficult to evaluate the financial performance of so-called conglomerates, such as Canadian Pacific Enterprises Limited, and Genstar Limited. In the financial statements of such conglomerates, products in different industries are combined and one return on sales is calculated. This ratio is virtually meaningless and an informative comparison with other companies cannot easily be made.

Publicly owned corporations falling within the jurisdiction of the Securities and Exchange Commission (SEC) in the United States are required to report separately the financial status of each different type of business. The CICA also has requirements for the reporting of segmented information. From this information, a more useful analysis can be made through the calculation of an individual return on sales for each component of the conglomerate. Canadian corporations falling within SEC jurisdiction include Brascan Limited, Nu-West Inc., Alcan Aluminum Limited, Cadillac-Fairview Corp. and Massey-Ferguson, Ltd.

Management Decisions Relating to Fixed Assets

Corporations usually have a considerable amount of their assets tied up in fixed assets that are used to produce products to be sold. The financial strength and success of these corporations depends on the reasonableness of their investment in these assets.

An analysis of these investment decisions can be made by calculating the ratio of sales to fixed assets and the ratio of fixed assets to shareholders' equity.

Sales to Fixed Assets Ratio

Ratio of sales to fixed assets
Net sales is divided by average fixed assets. This ratio indicates the adequacy of sales in relation to the investment in fixed assets.

Are sales adequate in relation to the investment in fixed assets? The calculation of the **ratio of sales to fixed assets** provides one answer to this question by establishing the number of sales dollars earned for each dollar invested in fixed assets. The ratio is calculated by the following formula:

$$\frac{\text{Net Sales}}{\text{Average Net Fixed Assets}}$$

From the comparative balance sheet of Bluebeard Computer Corporation, the average net fixed assets for 19X4 would be calculated as $712,000 + $1,128,000 ÷ 2 = $920,000. The sales to fixed assets ratio would be the 19X4 sales, $2,800,000, divided by $920,000, or 3.04.

A low ratio in relation to other companies in the same industry may indicate their overinvestment in these assets or inefficiency in their use. The financial position of the company can be jeopardized by such errors in judgement; they are difficult to correct in the short run. It is important to recognize that results obtained by this ratio may be affected by one or both of the following factors:

1. Fixed assets are recorded at historic cost, while sales are made at current (inflation increased) prices.
2. The age of the fixed assets can distort a comparison of companies. Two companies with the same investment can show entirely different results because the different age of their assets results in differing net amounts for fixed assets in their financial statements.

Fixed Assets to Shareholders' Equity Ratio

Ratio of fixed assets to shareholders' equity
Average net fixed assets is divided by average shareholders' equity. This ratio indicates the amount of shareholders' equity tied up in fixed assets.

How much of shareholders' equity is tied up in fixed assets? The **ratio of fixed assets to shareholders' equity** calculates the amount of equity tied up in these assets and thus indicates what amount of equity is left over for working capital purposes. The ratio is calculated by the following formula:

$$\frac{\text{Average Net Fixed Assets}}{\text{Average Shareholders' Equity}}$$

There is no magic formula to indicate the proper amount of working capital to be provided by shareholders' equity. It is expected, however, that some part of working capital should be provided by shareholders' equity.

D. Bluebeard Computer Corporation's Performance

The following financial information from Bluebeard Computer Corporation is used in the calculation of ratios in this section. The ratios help to establish how efficiently the company uses its assets as resources to earn net income.

		19X5	19X4	19X3
Income from Operations	(a)	$300	$280	$209
Financing Charges — Interest		(89)	(61)	(–)
Income Tax		(95)	(102)	(97)
	(b)	$116	$117	$112
Average Fixed Assets — Net				
[(Opening and Closing Balances) ÷ 2]	(c)	$1,091	$ 920	–*
Total Assets				
[(Opening and Closing Balances) ÷ 2]	(d)	$2,299	$1,765	–*
Shareholders' Equity				
[(Opening and Closing Balances) ÷ 2]	(e)	1,213	1,172	–*
Sales	(f)	3,200	2,800	2,340
Common Shares Outstanding	(g)	100	100	100

Calculation of Selected Ratios:

		19X5	19X4	19X3
1. Return on Total Assets	(a ÷ d)	13%	15.9%	–*
2. Return on Shareholders' Equity	(b ÷ e)	9.6%	9.98%	–*
3. Return on Each Share	(b ÷ g)	$1.16	$1.17	$1.12
4. Return on Sales	(b ÷ f)	3.6%	4.2%	4.8%
5. a. Sales to Fixed Assets Ratio	(f ÷ c)	2.93	3.04	–*
b. Fixed Assets to Shareholders' Equity Ratio	(c ÷ e)	0.90	0.78	–*

*The figure for 19X2 is not available for calculation of an average for 19X3.

Return on Total Assets

Bluebeard's net income was 13 percent of average total assets in 19X5, a decrease from 15.9 percent in 19X4. This decrease is disappointing not only because it seems to indicate a less efficient use of company assets, but also because the decrease has occurred during a period of rapidly expanding sales. Although total average assets have increased almost 30 percent (from $1,765,000 to $2,299,000 in 19X5) its net income has remained virtually unchanged. It may be that the investment in fixed assets during this period has not yet begun to pay off. In all probability, however, there are other efficiency factors affecting this disappointingly decreased return on total assets.

Return on Shareholders' Equity

In 19X5, Bluebeard earned a 9.6 percent return on shareholders' equity (represented by common stock and retained earnings) compared to 9.98 percent in 19X4. Is a 9 to 10 percent return adequate? It is consistent with previous years. A comparison with other companies in the same industries and the industry average would give an indication of Bluebeard's relative performance. Such averages are published by Dun and Bradstreet and in other trade publications.

Return on Each Share

Bluebeard's EPS has remained relatively constant over the three-year period because their expansion was financed by debt.

Return on Sales

Bluebeard has a lower return on sales in 19X5 than 19X4; this decline should be viewed with some concern. Comparison has to be made with other firms in the same industry to evaluate BCC's performance. The return on total assets and on equity should also be examined when appraising the efficiency of asset use.

A low return on sales is not necessarily unfavourable, if it is accompanied by a high return on shareholders' equity. What is unsettling in BCC's case is that both return on sales and return on shareholders' equity are declining. It is important to isolate the reasons for this decline in Bluebeard's performance. A **gross profit percentage** is widely used to establish whether additional sales are being made as a result of lower sales prices. A study of BCC's gross profit shows the following:

Gross profit percentage
Gross profit is divided by sales. This ratio indicates the percentage of sales revenue that is left to pay operating expenses, creditor interest, and government income taxes.

		(000s)		
		19X5	19X4	19X3
Sales	(a)	$3,200	$2,800	$2,340
Cost of Goods Sold		2,500	2,150	1,800
Gross Profit	(b)	$ 700	$ 650	$ 540
Gross Profit (%)	(b ÷ a)	21.9%	23.2%	23.1%

Bluebeard's gross profit percentage has remained fairly constant over the three-year period. Therefore, the decrease in the return on sales must be occurring within the operating expense category.

Management Decisions Relating to Fixed Assets

It is important to analyze the reasonableness of Bluebeard's increased investment in fixed assets in the current circumstances.

Sales to Fixed Assets Ratio

In 19X5, BCC made $2.93 of sales for each dollar invested in fixed assets, a little less than the $3.04 it earned in 19X4. Much will depend on the results of 19X6. Sales have been rapidly expanding and market acceptance of any computer related innovation is assured; this growth is more important than the ratios. The fixed asset expansion does not appear unwise in the circumstances.

Fixed Assets to Shareholders' Equity Ratio

What does appear unwise is Bluebeard's method of financing its expansion. Consider the amount of shareholders' equity tied up in this expansion, calculated as follows:

		(000s)	
		19X5	19X4
Average Net Fixed Assets	(a)	$1,091	$ 920
Average Shareholders' Equity	(b)	1,213	1,172
Fixed Assets to Shareholder's Equity	(a ÷ b)	0.90	0.78

A significant change has occurred between 19X4 and 19X5. The amount of shareholders' equity tied up in fixed assets has increased from $0.78 for each dollar invested in plant and equipment to $0.90; therefore less working capital is being provided by shareholders' equity. The proportion of $0.90 to each dollar in fixed assets is not necessarily troublesome in itself. What is dangerous is the shortage of working capital.

E.   Trends

Trend analysis
The comparison of the data for several years when analyzing financial statements.

In evaluating the various ratios used in this chapter, attention is frequently focused on **trends** that have become apparent. Most public companies provide comparative ratios with their financial statements. The period of comparison usually is not less than 5 years and often covers 10 years or more. Such comparisons permit a better evaluation of a company's financial strength and profitability. They also aid comparisons with other companies in the same industry, with the industry average, and with companies in other industries. Each July, Dun and Bradstreet publishes *Key Business Ratios* for various Canadian corporations. Moody's and Standard and Poor's reporting services also provide for financial information covering extended periods of time.

Percentages can be used to analyze amounts appearing in financial statements. They can be calculated horizontally and vertically.

Horizontal Analysis:	*Vertical Analysis:*
The balance for 19X5 can be compared with the balance for 19X4. The difference, or change, is shown as a dollar amount and also as a percentage. The percentage is calculated by dividing the dollar amount of change by the older of the two amounts being compared.	Each amount on a financial statement can be expressed as a percentage of a base. Net sales is the base in the income statement, total assets is the base for assets, and total equities is the base for equities in the balance sheet. Financial statements prepared in this manner are referred to as *common size statements.*

Horizontal analysis
The analysis of financial statements through the calculation of percentage changes in statement components over two or more years.

Vertical analysis
The analysis of the composition of a financial statement through the restating of all items in the statement as percentages; comparison of the percentage between two or more years shows the change in composition of the statement components; such restated statements are often called common size statements.

Horizontal and **vertical analyses** of the balance sheets and statements of income of Bluebeard Computer Corporation follow:

Horizontal Analysis: Balance Sheets

	19X5	19X4	Change Amount	Change Percent
Current Assets	$1,433	$ 984	+ $449	+ 45.63
Fixed Assets	1,053	1,128	− 75	− 6.65
Total	$2,486	$2,112	+ $374	+ 17.71
Current Liabilities	$1,255	$ 917	+ $338	+ 36.86
Shareholders' Equity	1,231	1,195	+ 36	+ 3.01
Total	$2,486	$2,112	+ $374	+ 17.71

Notice the special columns introduced here. Analysis of the changes indicates a large increase in current assets together with a large increase in current liabilities. There was a small decline in fixed assets and a small increase in shareholders' equity. The percentage change must always be interpreted together with the dollar amount of change to avoid incorrect conclusions; percentages can sometimes be misleading.

Vertical Analysis: Balance Sheets
Common Size Percentages

	19X5	19X4
Current Assets	57.64	46.59
Fixed Assets	42.36	53.41
Total	100.00	100.00
Current Liabilities	50.48	43.42
Shareholders' Equity	49.52	56.58
Total	100.00	100.00

In the common size balance sheets, it is clear that the composition of the assets has changed with an overall shift to current assets in 19X5. It is also shown that an increase in current liabilities has occurred. Vertical analysis places the balance sheet components in comparable terms through the conversion of all dollar amounts into percentages.

Horizontal Analysis: Income Statements

	19X5	19X4	Change Amount	Percent
Sales	$3,200	$2,800	+400	+14.29
Cost of Goods Sold	2,500	2,150	+350	+16.28
Gross Profit	$ 700	$ 650	+50	+7.69
Expenses	584	533	+51	+9.57
Net Income	$ 116	$ 117	−1	−0.85

Vertical Analysis: Income Statements
Common Size Percentages

	19X5	19X4
Sales	100.00	100.00
Cost of Goods Sold	78.12	76.79
Gross Profit	21.88	23.21
Expenses	18.25	19.04
Net Income	3.63	4.17

Consider the income statement and note that, although sales and gross profit increased, net income decreased. This decrease in net income resulted from an increase in cost of goods sold and expenses. The increased sales were insufficient to offset the increased cost of merchandise and increased expenses.

Looking at the income statement, note the relative change in the components of the statement. For example, cost of goods sold increased in 19X5 relative to sales, while expenses in 19X5 relative to sales decreased. The decrease in expenses, however, was insufficient to offset a decrease in net income.

The percentages calculated become more informative when compared to earlier years. Further analysis is usually undertaken in order to establish answers to the following questions:

Horizontal Analysis:
1. What caused this change?

2. Is the change favourable or negative?

These and other similar questions call attention to weak areas and help to spot trends in financial strength and profitability.

Vertical Analysis:
1. How do the percentages of this company compare with other companies in the same industry? in other industries?

2. Why is there such a large portion of assets tied up in current assets?

These and other similar questions call attention to areas that may require further study.

In fact, the published financial statements of actual companies tend to reduce the amount of information that can be used for analysis so that competitors will be left in the dark as much as possible. Accordingly, gross profits are often not shown separately and cost of goods sold is combined with operating expenses to prevent its calculation by the reader. The lack of individual breakdowns of salaries, audit fees, promotion expenses, and so on also prevent the statement reader from obtaining a detailed picture of a corporation's activities. Therefore, shareholders, analysts and others are left in the dark. The calculation of all of the percentages and ratios that are possible from the figures provided will shed at least some light on the situation.

F. Review of Ratios

The ratios covered in this chapter are summarized next.

Reliance on Debt:	**Calculation of Ratio:**	**Indicates:**
Equity-to-Debt Ratio	$\dfrac{\text{Shareholders' Equity}}{\text{Total Liabilities}}$	What the proportion of shareholder to creditor financing is.
Short Term Solvency Analysis:		
1. The Current Ratio	$\dfrac{\text{Current Assets}}{\text{Current Liabilities}}$	How many current asset dollars exist to pay current liabilities. (This is only a crude measure of solvency.)
2. The Acid-Test Ratio	$\dfrac{\text{Quick Current Assets}}{\text{Current Liabilities}}$	Whether the company is able to meet the immediate demands of creditors. (This is a more severe measure of solvency. Inventory and prepaid items are excluded from the calculation.)
3. Management Decisions Relating to Receivables:		
a. Accounts Receivable Collection Period	$\dfrac{\text{Average Accounts Receivable}}{\text{Net Credit Sales}} \times 365$	What the average time needed to collect receivables is.
b. Accounts Receivable Turnover	$\dfrac{\text{Net Credit Sales}}{\text{Average Accounts Receivable}}$	How often during the year accounts receivable have been converted into cash.
4. Management Decisions Relating to Inventory:		
a. Number of Days of Sales in Inventory	$\dfrac{\text{Average Inventory}}{\text{Cost of Goods Sold}} \times 365$	How many days of sales can be made with existing inventory.
b. Inventory Turnover	$\dfrac{\text{Cost of Goods Sold}}{\text{Average Inventory}}$	How many times during the year inventory has been sold and replaced.
5. The Revenue Operating Cycle	Average Number of Days To Turn Over Inventory + Average Number of Days To Collect Receivables.	How long it is between the purchase of inventory and the subsequent collection of cash.

Analysis of Operations Efficiency:

1. Return on Total Assets

$$\frac{\text{Income from Operations}}{\text{Average Total Assets}}$$

How efficiently a company uses its assets as resources to earn net income.

2. Return on Shareholders' Equity

$$\frac{\text{Net Income for the Year}}{\text{Average Shareholders' Equity}}$$

The adequacy of net income as a return on shareholders' equity.

  a. Trading on the Equity
  (This is not a ratio as such but is related to the return on share-holders' equity, which in turn is influenced by the use of long-term financing.)

[See example in section C.]

The use of borrowed money to generate a higher return in the business than the rate being paid on the borrowed money.

  b. Bondholder Protection: Times Interest Earned Ratio.

$$\frac{\text{Income from Operations}}{\text{Interest Expense}}$$

The ability of a company to pay interest to long-term creditors.

3. Return on Each Share: Earnings per Share

$$\frac{\text{Net Income for the Year} - \text{Preferred Dividends}}{\text{Number of Common Shares Outstanding}}$$

The amount of net income that has been earned on each share of common stock.

  a. Price to Earnings Ratio

$$\frac{\text{Market Price per Share}}{\text{Earnings per Share}}$$

The reasonableness of market price in relation to per-share earnings.

  b. Dividend Yield

$$\frac{\text{Dividends per Share}}{\text{Market Price per Share}}$$

The return that can be expected from an investment in a company's shares.

4. Return on Sales
  a. Net Income

$$\frac{\text{Net Income for the Year}}{\text{Net Sales}}$$

  b. Gross Income

$$\frac{\text{Gross Profit}}{\text{Net Sales}}$$

The percentage of sales revenue left in the business after payment of expenses, creditor interest, and government income taxes.

5. Management Decisions Relating to Fixed Assets
  a. Sales to Fixed Assets Ratio

$$\frac{\text{Net Sales}}{\text{Average Net Fixed Assets}}$$

The adequacy of sales in relation to the investment in fixed assets.

  b. Fixed Assets to Shareholders' Equity Ratio.

$$\frac{\text{Average Net Fixed Assets}}{\text{Average Shareholders' Equity}}$$

The amount of shareholders' equity tied up in fixed assets.

APPENDIX: The Impact of Changing Prices

The preceding historical cost financial statements of Bluebeard Computer Corporation were prepared according to the stable dollar assumption. Under this concept, the value of the dollar is assumed to be constant over time. In fact, the Canadian dollar has been unstable recently as a result of inflation, which has, over time, devalued the dollar's purchasing power. The magnitude of this drop is indicated by the Consumer Price Index (CPI), a general price index prepared by Statistics Canada; Figure 15-3 shows the annual percentage change in the CPI during the 1970s and into the 1980s.

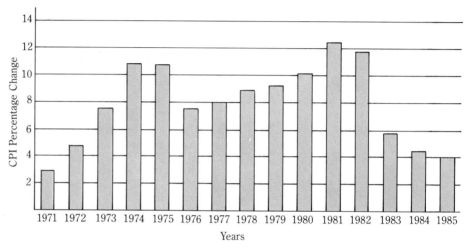

Figure 15-3   Percentage change in CPI

As can be seen, CPI-measured inflation amounted to 2.9 percent in 1971, peaked at 12.5 percent in 1981, and then declined. This annual change accumulates over time with the result that the dollar money unit is effectively devalued. Therefore, as inflation continues, it takes an increasing amount of dollars to make purchases; or, in other words, the dollar loses purchasing power during periods of inflation. This loss in purchasing power is actually hidden in financial statements, which mingle dollars of different purchasing powers. For example, the 1981 12.5-percent change means that, on the average. $112.50 was required to buy what could have been purchased for $100 in 1980; the 4.4-percent 1984 change means that $104.40 was required to purchase what could have been purchased for $100 in 1983. Financial statements prepared at the end of 1985 would therefore include dollars of different purchasing powers.

Constant Dollar Accounting

Constant Dollar Accounting
The conversion of historical costs into a stable unit of measurement over time.

Some accountants propose that all historical cost dollars in financial statements be converted to end-of-the-current-year dollars; this conversion procedure is referred to as **constant dollar accounting**. It includes the construction of a general price index that is used to restate financial statement items from previous years to current year common dollars.

The CPI is a general price index that is available; it can be used to convert previous years' dollars into end-of-the-current year dollars. The following table prepared by

Statistics Canada lists the CPI from 1971 to 1985 and the annual percentage changes in the index.

Year	CPI	Percentage Change	Year	CPI	Percentage Change	Year	CPI	Percentage Change
1971	42.2	2.9	1976	62.9	7.5	1981	100.0	12.5
1972	44.2	4.8	1977	67.9	8.0	1982	110.8	10.8
1973	47.6	7.6	1978	73.9	8.0	1983	117.2	5.8
1974	52.8	10.9	1979	80.7	9.2	1984	122.3	4.4
1975	58.5	10.8	1980	88.9	10.1	1985	127.2	4.0

These CPI numbers are based on a survey of price changes in a fixed shopping basket of hundreds of goods and services. Since the index is a weighted average of prices for a number of different commodities, it is important to note that, while some commodity prices are increasing, others may actually be decreasing. Therefore, while it can be stated that on the average $301 (rounded) ($100 × 127.2 ÷ 42.2) was required to buy what could have been purchased for $100 in 1971, it cannot be claimed that this proportion could be accurately applied to individual assets or services. A specific price index would be required for this purpose. It is, therefore, important to distinguish between general and specific changes because the price of a particular commodity cannot be assumed to increase in the same proportion as a general price increase.

Keeping this in mind, the CPI index can be used to illustrate the adjustment of historical cost financial statements. For example, a building purchased in 1971 for $100,000 would be converted into 1985 dollars by multiplying the $100,000 cost by its 1985 CPI divided by the 1971 CPI as follows:

$$\$100,000 \times \frac{127.2}{42.2} = \$301,422 \text{ (rounded)}.$$

Thus, the constant dollar value of the building is $301,422 in 1985. In actual fact, the building might be worth more or less. The $301,422 simply means that the dollar measurement of the asset is $201,422 more in 1985 than 1971 as a result of a decrease in the purchasing power of the dollar.

The objective of constant dollar accounting is the preparation of financial statements using a stable measuring unit, a constant dollar in terms of purchasing power. This requires the conversion of previous years' dollars with differing purchasing power into end-of-the-current-year purchasing power dollars. A simple balance sheet conversion illustrates the techniques involved. An income statement conversion would also be prepared.

Balance Sheet Conversion

Constant dollar value accounting can be illustrated using the following simple example. Assume that A Corporation was incorporated on January 2, 19X1 when the general price index amounted to 100. On this date, the corporation issued $100,000-worth of common shares for the following assets: Cash, $20,000; Land, $30,000; Building, $50,000. Its balance sheet prepared on this date would appear as follows:

A Corporation
Balance Sheet
At January 2, 19X1

Assets		*Equity*	
Cash	$ 20,000	Common Stock	$100,000
Land	30,000		
Building	50,000		
	$100,000		$100,000

Assume that the corporation was not involved in any other transactions during the year and that the general price index to convert these amounts was 120. A Corporation's balance sheet would be converted into constant dollars as follows:

A Corporation
Balance Sheet
At December 31, 19X1

Assets	*Historical Cost*	*Conversion Factor*	*Constant Dollars*
Cash	$ 20,000	(not converted)	$ 20,000
Land	30,000	120/100	36,000
Building	50,000	120/100	60,000
	$100,000		$116,000
Equity			
Common Stock	$100,000	120/100	$120,000
Purchasing Power Loss	–	$20,000 × 120/100	(4,000)
	$100,000		$116,000

As can be seen, A Corporation suffered a $4,000 purchasing power loss in 19X1, because cash is not converted to constant dollars; it represents $20,000 regardless of changes in the price index. The $4,000 purchasing power loss is converted as follows:

$$\$20,000 \times \frac{120}{100} \text{ (or: } \$20,000 \times 20\%) = \$4,000.$$

Monetary Accounts

The amount of cash was not converted at December 31, 19X1. This is also true of other monetary assets, such as accounts receivable and long-term investments in bonds. They are referred to as monetary assets because their amount of dollars is fixed. Regardless of changes in the price index, only a certain number of dollars will be received. During inflationary periods, holding monetary assets results in purchasing power losses. Monetary liabilities include bank loans, accounts payable, and most liabilities. Because the amount to be paid is also fixed, holding monetary liabilities during inflationary periods results in purchasing power gains, since the purchasing power of the dollars used to repay these debts has been decreasing.

Non-monetary Accounts

Assets that are converted for price index changes are referred to as non-monetary assets. These include inventory, fixed assets, and long-term investments in common stock. Note that this conversion of non-monetary assets into constant dollar amounts is not intended to indicate the current value of any converted items; it simply results in their being reported in dollars with the same purchasing power. In all probability, the land and building of A Corporation could not be sold or purchased for $36,000 and $60,000 respectively.

Therefore, during periods of inflation, monetary assets will result in a purchasing power loss, while monetary liabilities will produce a purchasing power gain. Non-monetary assets will tend to be understated during period of rising prices, unless they are converted to constant dollars.

Income Statement Conversion

The income statement can also be converted to constant dollars. If it is assumed that sales are made and expenses are incurred evenly during the year, they can be converted into common dollars using the average index for the year. Only inventory and depreciation of fixed assets that appeared in the preceding year's balance sheet are converted using the index of the year in which they were purchased.

Assume that Bluebeard Computer Corporation's income statement at December 31, 19X5 included in cost of goods sold $536 of inventory that had been purchased on December 31, 19X4. Assume also that depreciation was calculated on fixed assets that had been purchased on December 31, 19X3. The price index at these different dates was the following:

		Index
19X3	Building purchased	100
19X4	Inventory purchased	120
19X4	December 31, 19X4	120
19X5	Average for 19X5	130
19X5	December 31, 19X5	140

Sales, purchases, and expenses other than depreciation are assumed to have been made evenly throughout the year. They are, therefore, converted to December 31, 1985 purchasing power dollars as follows: $3,200 × 140/130. Since opening inventory is assumed to have been purchased at December 31, 19X4, it is converted to December 31, 19X5 purchasing power dollars by the following calculation: $536 × 140/120. Depreciation expense is converted using the price index existing at the date the fixed asset was purchased; the calculation $75 × 140/100 makes the conversion of these 19X3 dollars into 19X5 purchasing power dollars.

	Historical Cost	Conversion Factor	Constant Dollar
Sales	$3,200	140/130	$3,446*
Cost of Goods Sold	$2,500	(see below)	$2,740
Depreciation	75	140/100	105
Selling & Administrative Expenses	325	140/130	350
Interest	89	140/130	96*
	$2,989		$3,291
Income before Income Tax	$ 211		$ 155
Income Tax	95	140/130	102*
Net Income for the Year	$ 116		$ 53
Cost of Goods Sold:			
Opening Inventory	$ 536	140/120	$ 625*
Purchases	2,764	140/130	2,977*
	$3,300		$3,602
Less: Ending Inventory	800	140/130	862
Total Cost of Goods Sold	$2,500		$2,740

*Rounded to nearest dollar.

As can be seen, net income for 19X5 has been reduced from $116 to $53 as a result of changes in the purchasing power of the dollar. Therefore, during periods of inflation, net income calculated using historical costs will tend to be overstated.

Current Cost Accounting

Current cost accounting focuses on the current cost of replacing assets. It emphasizes the maintenance of operating capability; that is, the entity's capability at the end of an accounting time period should be as great as it was at the beginning of that period. Although the example of constant dollar accounting converts dollars into end-of-the-current-year constant dollars, it does not incorporate into these numbers the current replacement cost of assets. This distinction can be made, using the assets of A Corporation. The following balance sheet illustrates the difference between historical cost of its assets, constant dollar inflation adjusted amounts, and the current cost of these assets.

A Corporation
Partial Balance Sheet
At December 31, 19X1

Assets	Historical Cost	Constant Dollar	Current Costs
Land	$30,000	$36,000	$50,000
Building	50,000	60,000	75,000

As can be seen, the current cost of acquiring similar land and a similar building exceeds both historical cost and historical cost adjusted for a decrease in purchasing power of the dollar. Therefore, only a part of the above increase results from inflation; that is, land has increased $6,000 owing to inflation ($36,000 − $30,000) and the building $10,000 ($60,000 − $50,000). In addition to this, the cost to replace these assets has also increased in excess of inflation; land would cost an additional $14,000 ($50,000 − $36,000) to be replaced, and building an additional $15,000 ($75,000 − $60,000). Therefore, in order to maintain its operating capability, A Corporation is faced not only with an increase resulting from inflation, but also with an additional increase in the current cost of the assets themselves. These amounts are summarized in the following schedule.

	Total Change	Change in Asset Value Because of Inflation	Because of Increase in Asset Cost
Land	$20,000	$ 6,000	$14,000
Building	25,000	10,000	15,000

The *CICA Handbook* does not require the separate disclosure of these two sets of figures. Rather, the information comparing changes that result from inflation and changes that result from asset cost increases are contained in the current cost supplementary disclosure included with financial statements.

In the United States, FASB Statement No. 33 recommends that large public corporations disclose both sets of figures: one to indicate the impact of inflation on historical costs, the other to indicate its impact on current cost changes.

Inventory Replacement

Inventory purchased in a preceding year has to be replaced when sold in a subsequent year. The calculation of current cost data is designed to indicate the impact on the entity of replacing this inventory when current costs have increased.

Impact on the Balance Sheet

The balance sheet impact of inventory replacement, discussed in Chapter 8, includes an analysis prepared for executives of Bluebeard Computer Corporation. This analysis uses current costs to replace year-end inventory; the current cost of ending inventory is $7,000 at the balance sheet date. A comparison of balance sheet amounts shows the following:

	FIFO	
	Historical Cost	*Current Cost*
Ending Inventory	$5,000	$7,000

This comparision illustrates that Bluebeard's ability to maintain its operating capability could be in jeopardy if this difference continues into the future.

Impact on the Income Statement

The analysis also illustrates the impact of current costs on the income statement.

	FIFO	
	Historical Cost	*Current Cost*
Sales	$20,000	$20,000
Cost of Goods Sold:		
Purchases	$15,000	
Ending Inventory	5,000	
Total Cost of Goods Sold	$10,000	$18,000
Gross Profit	$10,000	$ 2,000
Operating Expenses	6,000	6,000
Net Income (Loss) for the Period	$ 4,000	$ (4,000)

These current cost calculations indicate that Bluebeard is losing its operating capability and would eventually be unable to replace inventory without increasing borrowing. In this illustration, the current cost to replace ending inventory is used; this current cost is calculated as $18,000 as shown above.

Fixed Asset Replacement

Fixed assets usually represent a large amount of assets that have to be replaced eventually. The calculation of current cost data is intended to show the effects of increased costs and to draw attention to the entity's ability to maintain its future operating capability.

Impact on the Balance Sheet

The impact of current costs on the balance sheet, introduced in Chapter 9, includes an analysis prepared for executives of Bluebeard Computer Corporation. This analysis illustrated the impact of current cost accounting on fixed assets. Assuming that fixed assets originally cost $20,000, have an estimated useful life of 5 years, and a salvage value of $2,000, straight-line depreciation is calculated as $3,600 ($20,000 − $2,000 = $18,000 ÷ 5 years = $3,600 per year).

	Historical Cost	*Current Cost*
Fixed Assets	$20,000	$28,000
Less: Accumulated Depreciation	3,600(18%)	5,040(18%)
Carrying value	$16,400	$22,960

As can be seen, use of current costs results in different amounts. The current cost of fixed assets amounts to $28,000. The accumulated depreciation is calculated as 18 percent of this $28,000 current cost; this is the same proportion of accumulated depreciation as calculated under historical cost accounting.

A number of different measurement techniques has been suggested to calculate current cost. These techniques include the use of price indices, appraisals, and engineering estimates of the impact of technological change, as well as other factors. Because the calculation of current costs is currently in an experimental stage, further refinements are expected, as experience in their calculation and use develops. For illustrative purposes, the same estimated useful life and straight-line depreciation method was used for current cost as for historical cost calculations.

It should be noted that calculation of current costs is essentially a subjective process; here it was based on management's estimates and assumptions regarding replacement costs, impact of technological changes, and so on.

Impact on the Income Statement

The analysis used to show the impact of current cost calculations on inventory are further developed to illustrate the impact of current cost depreciation expense. The following historical cost and current cost income statements were prepared for executives of Bluebeard Computer Corporation.

	Historical Cost	*Current Cost*
Sales	$20,000	$ 20,000
Cost of Goods Sold	10,000	18,000
Gross Profit	$10,000	$ 2,000
Operating Expenses:		
Depreciation	$ 3,600	$ 5,040
Other Expenses	2,400	2,400
	$ 6,000	$ 7,440
Operating Income (Loss)	$ 4,000	$ (5,440)
Income Tax (50%)	2,000	2,000
Net Income (Loss)	$ 2,000	$ (7,440)

This calculation disclosed a large loss when current costs are used. Under current cost accounting, depreciation expense is viewed as that part of the asset used during the year that has to be replaced eventually to maintain operating capability. On the basis of these calculations, Bluebeard would be unable to replace its fixed assets without additional borrowing; it is losing its ability to operate at the same level in the future.

Even worse, income tax estimated at 50 percent is paid on the historical cost calculation of operating income, while, in fact, an operating loss exists under the current cost net income calculation.

The current cost model, therefore, shows that Bluebeard is losing its operating capacity and will eventually be unable to replace its fixed assets without increased borrowing.

Use of the Historical Cost Concept

A dilemma for the accounting profession centres on its use of historical costs in the preparation of financial statements. Historical costs are used because they are objectively determined, even though the measure used, the stable dollar assumption, is invalid during periods of rapid inflation. Although current cost data are more relevant, their incorporation into financial statements is questioned because the determination of current costs is generally a subjective process, based, in some cases, on management's estimates and assumptions.

Financial Statement Disclosure

Although more relevant, the use of current costs in record-keeping or the incorporation of current costs into the body of financial statements, is not included among *CICA Handbook* recommendations. The AcSC released standards on current cost accounting in December 1982 effective for financial years beginning on or after January 2, 1983; the application of the standards is to be reviewed before 1987. These standards emphasize not only the effects of inflation on historical costs, but also additional increases in the current cost of the assets themselves. The standards recommend use of either the Consumer Price Index or the Gross National Expenditure Implicit Price Deflator to measure the effects of inflation.

The AcSC standards do not require current cost information for all items appearing in financial statements. Rather, this information is required only for the following: (a) inventory and cost of goods sold, and (b) fixed assets and related depreciation expense. Further, it is recommended that current cost data be included with financial statements as supplementary information, rather than be incorporated into financial statements.

In addition to current cost supplementary information, the AcSC standards also require the calculation of a financing adjustment. The financing adjustment may alleviate, at least in part, the operating capability lost by an entity during the year.

A more complete discussion of these topics is beyond the scope of this book; they are usually the subject of advanced accounting courses. It should be noted that the AcSC standards are applicable only to large publicly traded corporations having inventory and fixed assets (before accumulated depreciation) of $50 million and whose total assets exceed $350 million. Financial institutions, however, are exempted from the standards.

Conceptual Issue 15-1

A Case Study on Current Cost Reporting

Under the CICA's standards, financial data show the effect of specific price changes and the impact of general inflation.

Following are some sample — and simplified — current cost financial statements for a typical manufacturing concern.

First, the income statement

For the year ended December 31, 1984
(000s)

Historical cost basis 1984		Current cost basis 1984
$169,000	Sales	$169,000
$116,000	Cost of Goods Sold	$121,190
8,000	Depreciation	13,750
	Selling, General, and	
21,900	Administrative Expenses	21,900
3,900	Interest	3,900
	Gain on Sale of Property,	
(800)	Plant, and Equipment	–
$149,000		$160,740
$ 20,000	Income before Income Taxes	$ 8,260
$ 6,000	Income Taxes — Current	$ 6,000
2,000	— Deferred	2,000
$ 8,000		$ 8,000
$ 12,000	Income	$ 260

As you can see, there are two main differences between the historical cost and current cost figures. First, cost of goods sold is increased from $116 million to $121.9 million because inventory replacement costs at the date of sale were higher than historically recorded. Second, the provision for depreciation is increased from $8 million to $13.75 million because the historical cost provisions do not take into account the increased cost of replacing the company's fixed assets at current prices. As a result, current cost operating income is significantly below the recorded historical cost income.

Current cost profits are lower than the historical cost profits because current cost profits are not reported until provision is made to maintain operating capability by necessary replacement of assets and inventories at today's, not yesterday's, costs. Historical cost profits make provision to replace assets at yesterday's costs.

The common shareholders may also be interested in knowing how their equity in the company has performed. Has common shareholders' equity grown at a rate sufficient to keep pace with inflation? Has it grown at a rate equal to or greater than the specific price changes experienced by the company?

The new accounting standards address these questions by showing three figures:
• the increase in the current costs of assets
• the gain or loss in general purchasing power from holding non-monetary items, and
• a financing adjustment.

The information is disclosed in the following format:

Other supplementary information	1984
Increase in the current cost amounts of inventory and property, plant, and equipment	(000s) $14,740
Effect of general inflation	9,471
Excess of increase in current cost over the effect of general inflation	$ 5,269
Gain in general purchasing power from having net monetary liabilities	$ 2,275
Financing adjustment	$ 3,685

The first three lines of the "Other supplementary information" tell us that the current cost of the inventory and fixed assets owned by the company increased at a rate greater than general inflation. Shareholders' equity increased in real terms by $5,269,000.

This company financed part of its operations with debt. The second item shows that because of inflation the amount of that debt declined in real terms. This resulted in a further 'real' increase in shareholders' equity of $2,275,000, that is, the gain in general purchasing power having net monetary liabilities.

The third item is the financing adjustment of $3,685,000. The company has financed its operations through a combination of shareholders' funds and borrowed funds. If this situation continues, shareholders will not be called on to provide the whole of the increase in capital needed to support the higher current costs of inventory and fixed assets. The $3,685,000 financing adjustment is the increase in the current cost amounts of the portion of inventory and fixed assets financed through debt. It is calculated by multiplying the increase in current cost amounts — $14,740,000 — by the company's debt-to-equity ratio, in this case 1 : 4.

Overall, shareholders' equity has grown by $7,804,000 ($260,000 + $5,269,000 + $2,275,000) more than the amount needed simply to keep pace with inflation and by $3,945,000 ($260,000 + $3,685,000) more than the amount needed to keep pace with the rate of specific price changes experienced by the company.

The three items are not necessarily amounts available for distribution to the shareholders. They are a measure of how price changes have affected in the company's financial position and the shareholders' stake in the company.

It is helpful to note that this supplementary information is based on two different ways of looking at what has been happening to the company's assets and liabilities. In each case, the information presents the impact of both general inflation and of specific price changes:

• The amount recorded as the current cost increases of inventory and fixed assets is a specific price change. The financing adjustment is also based on the specific price changes experienced by this company.

• The impact of inflation, $9,471,000, is, of course, a general figure arrived at by measuring the amount of the increase in inventory and fixed asset costs that would have to take place to keep pace with the Consumer Price Index. Similarly, the gain on net monetary liabilities is a general figure, the result of multiplying the company's net debt by the rate of inflation as measured by the CPI.

Although the income statement had certainly suffered from the rise in the cost of inventories and fixed assets, the news isn't all bad. As the following schedule of assets shows, the balance sheet of the company has been strengthened by the rise in value of the assets.

Schedule of Assets on a Current Cost Basis
At December 31, 1984
(000s)

Historical cost basis 1984		Current cost basis 1984
$34,000	Inventory	$36,000
$36,700	Property, Plant, and Equipment — Net	$56,200
$45,600	Net Assets (Common Shareholders' Equity)	$67,100

The Management Report

Particularly in the early years, perhaps the most important part of the supplementary current cost disclosures will be management's report on where the numbers came from and what they mean. Changing prices affect enterprises in different ways according to their particular circumstances, and annual report readers may not have detailed information about these circumstances. An enterprise's management is in the best position to understand and explain the impact of price changes on its operations. The final test of current cost information will be its usefulness.

The bottom line in current cost accounting is much more informative than the historical cost income figure. Different people who have contributed toward an enterprise have, for their own purposes, different ideas about what current cost income really is and about what the capital invested is supposed to do.

Source   CICA, "Current Cost Reporting" (1983), pp. 10–15.

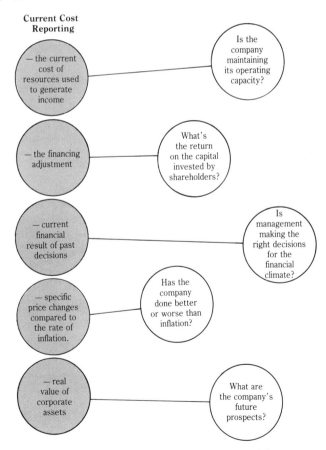

Figure 15-4   Current cost reporting (CICA case study)

Discussion Questions

1. Why are analysts and investors concerned with the financial structure of a particular corporation? How is it possible that the corporation is overfinanced or underfinanced?
2. Is the reliance on creditor financing advisable or inadvisable? Explain its impact on net income.
3. Discuss the advantages and disadvantages of short-term debt financing compared to long-term debt financing.
4. Explain what *solvency* means. When a corporation is insolvent, what are the implications to shareholders? to creditors?
5. How is it possible that a corporation, which is making an acceptable gross profit on operations, can actually be insolvent?
6. What ratios can be calculated to evaluate solvency? Explain what each one indicates.
7. a. Define *working capital*. Distinguish between the current ratio and the acid-test ratio.
   b. ''The current ratio is, by itself, inadequate to measure short-term solvency.'' Discuss this statement.
8. Two firms have the same working capital. Explain how it is possible that one is able to provide its short-term creditors with a guarantee from its current assets, while the other firm cannot.
9. Management decisions relating to accounts receivable and inventory can affect solvency. Explain. What is an acceptable accounts receivable turnover? an acceptable inventory turnover?
10. Discuss the advantages and disadvantages of increasing inventory turnover.
11. Financial analysts compute inventory turnover by dividing cost of goods sold by average inventory. Why is it not theoretically correct to estimate the turnover of inventories by dividing net sales by the average inventory?
12. What is the revenue operating cycle? How is its calculation useful in evaluating solvency?
13. Identify and explain four ratios (and any associated calculations) that evaluate a corporation's efficiency. What does each ratio specify?
14. How is trading on the equity related to the overfinancing or underfinancing of a corporation? Provide an example.
15. ''Leverage is useful but only if you can pay the interest.'' Discuss this statement.
16. The ratio of sales to fixed assets is used to determine adequacy of sales revenue in relation to investment in fixed assets. Discuss what factors may affect the usefulness of this ratio.
17. Comparisons need to be made to determine what is an acceptable or unacceptable ratio. On what basis can comparison be made?
18. Distinguish between a horizontal and a vertical analysis of financial statements.
19. How is the dollar's purchasing power devalued during periods of continuing inflation?
20. What is the CPI and how is it used to convert previous years' dollars into end-of-the-current-year dollars?
21. What are monetary accounts, and why are they not converted?
22. What are non-monetary accounts? Why are they converted into constant dollars?
23. How does current cost accounting emphasize the maintenance of a corporation's operating capability?
24. In what way do changes resulting from inflation differ from changes resulting from asset cost increases?
25. What financial statement disclosure for the impact of changing prices is required by the AcSC?
26. Some accountants have stated that ''the inflation accounting problem will go away as soon as inflation has been brought under control.'' Do you agree or disagree with this statement? Should changing price models only be used during periods of changing prices and then put away when no longer needed? Discuss.

Discussion Cases

Discussion Case 15-1:   Murphy Inc.

The following are condensed comparative financial statements of Murphy Inc. for the three years ended December 31, 19X5, 19X4, and 19X3.

Balance Sheets
At December 31

	19X5	19X4	19X3
CURRENT ASSETS:			
Cash	$ 21	$ 8	$ 17
Accounts Receivable — Trade	38	30	20
Merchandise Inventory	60	40	30
Prepaid Expenses	1	2	3
Total Current Assets	$120	$ 80	$ 70
Fixed Assets (net)	260	150	76
Total Assets	$380	$230	$146
CURRENT LIABILITIES:			
Accounts Payable	$ 98	$ 78	$ 48
Income Tax Payable	2	2	2
Total Current Liabilities	$100	$ 80	$ 50
Bonds Payable	50	50	–
Common Stock	200	80	80
Retained Earnings	30	20	16
Total Liabilities and Equity	$380	$230	$146

Income Statements
For the Years Ended December 31

	19X5	19X4	19X3
Sales	$210	$120	$100
Cost of Goods Sold	158	80	55
Gross Profit	$ 52	$ 40	$ 45
Operating Expenses	42	36	37
Net Income for the Year	$ 10	$ 4	$ 8

Additional information:
a. The company's accounts receivable at December 31, 19X2 totalled $20.
b. The company's merchandise inventory as at December 31, 19X2 was $20.
c. Credit terms are net 60 days from date of invoice.

For Discussion

1. What is your evaluation of:
   a. The financial structure of the corporation?
   b. The proportion of shareholder and creditor claims to its assets?
   c. The structure of its short-term and long-term credit financing?

2. Evaluate the short-term solvency of the corporation.
   a. Calculate appropriate ratios for the three years.
   b. Comment on the significant features in the corporation's balance sheet and income statement that are apparent from the ratios calculated and from the financial statements themselves.

Discussion Case 15-2:   Fitz Inc. and Roy Corp.

The following are comparative financial statements of Fitz Inc. and Roy Corp for the last four years.

Balance Sheets
At December 31
(0,000s)

	Fitz Inc.				Roy Corp.			
	19X5	*19X4*	*19X3*	*19X2*	*19X5*	*19X4*	*19X3*	*19X2*
Current Assets	$185	$165	$155	$140	$480	$450	$410	$381
Current Liabilities	160	135	130	110	272	251	170	180
	$ 25	$ 30	$ 25	$ 30	$208	$199	$240	$201
Fixed Assets (net)	535	397	392	378	599	603	572	601
	$560	$427	$417	$408	$807	$802	$812	$802
Bonds Outstanding								
12% Due in 10 Years	$120	–	–	–				
15% Due in 7 Years					$400	$400	$400	$400
Share Capital								
5% Cumulative Preferred —								
200 Shares	200	$200	$200	$200	200	200	200	200
Common — 100 Shares	100	100	100	100	50	50	50	50
Retained Earnings	140	127	117	108	157	152	162	152
	$560	$427	$417	$408	$807	$802	$812	$802

Income Statements
For the Years Ended December 31
(0,000s)

	19X5	*19X4*	*19X3*	*19X2*	*19X5*	*19X4*	*19X3*	*19X2*
Sales	$600	$540	$528	$516	$330	$220	$320	$270
Cost of Sales	460	430	420	410	105	75	100	90
Gross Profit	$140	$110	$108	$106	$225	$145	$220	$180
Operating Expenses	70	50	50	50	155	155	160	156
Income (Loss) from Operations	$ 70	$ 60	$ 58	$ 56	$ 70	$(10)	$ 60	$ 24
Income Tax	35	30	29	28	30	–	30	12
Net Income (Loss) for the Year	$ 35	$ 30	$ 29	$ 28	$ 40	$(10)	$ 30	$ 12
Dividends Paid —								
Preferred	$ 10	$ 10	$ 10	$ 10	$ 20	–	$ 10	$ 10
Common	12	10	10	10	15	–	10	–

The current stock market quotations for common shares of these corporations are as follows: Fitz Inc. — $2.60; Roy Cor. — $5.00.

For Discussion

1. What is your evaluation of
   a. The financial structure of each corporation?
   b. The proportion of shareholder and creditor claims to their assets?
   c. The structure of their short-term and long-term creditor financing?
2. Evaluate the success with which each corporation is using its assets to earn net income.
   a. Calculate appropriate ratios for each corporation.

b. Comment on the significant features in each corporation's balance sheet and income statement as are apparent from the ratios calculated and from the financial statements themselves.

3. Which corporation would be a better investment if you were planning to purchase common shares in either Fitz or Roy? Support your decision with such calculations as are necessary.

Discussion Case 15-3: Achilles Corporation

The following are condensed comparative financial statements of Achilles Corporation for the three years ended December 31, 19X2, 19X1, and 19X0.

Achilles Corporation
Comparative Balance Sheets
at December 31

	19X2		19X1		19X0	
CURRENT ASSETS:						
Cash		$ 24		$ 9		$ 20
Accounts Receivable	$ 46		$ 37		$ 24	
Less: Allowance for Doubtful Accounts	1	45	1	36	–	24
Merchandise Inventory		72		48		36
Prepaid Expenses		3		3		4
Total Current Assets		$144		$ 96		$84
Fixed Assets	$405		$234		$118	
Less: Accumulated Depreciation	93	312	54	180	27	91
Total Assets		$456		$276		$175
CURRENT LIABILITIES:						
Accounts Payable		$ 90		$ 72		$ 40
Accrued Liabilities		30		24		20
Total Current Liabilities		$120		$ 96		$ 60
Bonds Payable		60		60		–
Total Liabilities		$180		$156		$ 60
SHAREHOLDERS' EQUITY:						
Common Stock (no par-value)		240		96		96
Retained Earnings		36		24		19
Total Liabilities and Shareholders' Equity		$456		$276		$175

Achilles Corporation
Comparative Income Statements
For the Year Ended December 31

	19X2		19X1		19X0	
Sales		$252		$144		$120
Cost of Goods Sold						
Opening Inventory	$ 48		$ 36		$ 24	
Add: Purchases	213		108		78	
	$261		$144		$102	
Less: Ending Inventory	72		48		36	
Total Cost of Goods Sold		189		96		66
Gross Profit		$ 63		$ 48		$ 54
Selling and Administrative Expenses		37		34		30
Income from Operations		$ 26		$ 14		$ 24
Interest Expense		6		6		–
Income before Income Tax		$ 20		$ 8		$ 24
Income Tax		8		3		9
Net Income		$ 12		$ 5		$ 15

Achilles Corporation
Comparative Statements of Retained Earnings
For the Year Ended December 31

	19X2	19X1	19X0
Balance (Jan. 1)	$24	$19	$12
Add: Net Income for the Year	12	5	15
	$36	$24	$27
Less: Dividends	–	–	8
Balance (Dec. 31)	$36	$24	$19

The following additional information is available:
a. All sales are on credit; credit terms are net 60 days after invoice date.
b. Twenty shares of common stock were outstanding in years 19X0 and 19X1. On January 1, 19X2, an additional 30 shares of common stock were sold for $144.
c. Opening balance of accounts receivable on January 2, 19X0 was $19.
d. Net fixed assets on January 1, 19X0 were $91.
e. Total assets on January 1, 19X0 were $165.
f. Total shareholders' equity on January 1, 19X0 was $101.

Required:

1. From this information, calculate for each of the three years:

   a. Short-term solvency:
   Current ratio
   Acid-test ratio
   Accounts receivable
   collection period
   Number of days of sales
   in inventory
   Revenue operating cycle.

   b. Long-term solvency:
   Return on total assets
   Return on shareholders'
   equity
   Times interest earned
   Earnings per share
   Return on sales
   Equity-to-debt ratio
   Sales to fixed assets ratio.

2. Perform a short-term solvency analysis of Achilles Corporation. What conclusion can be drawn from each of the financial ratios calculated in 1, a, above?

3. Perform a long-term solvency analysis of Achilles Corporation. What conclusion can be drawn from each of the financial ratios calculated in 1, b, above? Was Achilles Corporation wise to expand operations?

Discussion Case 15-4:   Bell Canada

The following is the supplementary information from the 1984 annual report of Bell Canada Enterprises Inc. (BCE), dealing with current cost accounting.

Supplementary Information Reporting the Effects of Changing Prices (Unaudited)

The effects of changing prices are not fully and immediately evident in conventional historical cost financial statements. The Canadian Institute of Chartered Accountants (CICA) has adopted recommendations with respect to disclosure of supplementary information to report certain effects of changing prices on an enterprise.

Bell Canada Enterprises Inc. (BCE) recommends caution in interpreting these disclosures for the following reasons:
(i) The CICA's current cost reporting standards are still in an experimental state. To date, no general consensus has emerged on the concepts, interpretation, or usefulness of the information. BCE believes that, while the data may provide insights into the operations of the corporation, they may not be suitable for purposes of valuation of the corporation or its assets, or for reformulation into traditional financial measures or ratios.

(ii) The determination of current costs is a subjective process. It is based on management's estimates and assumptions regarding replacement costs, impacts of technology and price movements. Intercompany comparability, even within an industry, may not be achievable in the near term.

Application of Current Cost Accounting to BCE

The difference between historical cost and current cost accounting, as applied by BCE, relates to the basis on which the consumption of physical assets is measured. With depreciation expense and cost of revenues computed by reference to the estimated current replacement cost of fixed assets and inventory having equivalent operating capability, the measurement of income on a current cost basis provides an indication of the corporation's ability to maintain its level of operating capability.

The financing adjustment is an amount that is added back when determining income applicable to common shareholders on a current cost basis under an operating capability concept of capital. It gives recognition to the corporation's practice of financing its assets in part with borrowed funds, thereby alleviating the need for the common shareholders to be charged with the provision of all funds that may be required to maintain operating capability.

BCE has no reason to expect that the maintenance of its regulated or non-regulated operating capability will become impaired, and considers that the disclosure of income on a current cost basis is appropriate for purposes of complying with the CICA recommendations.

Consolidated Income Applicable to Common Shareholders on a Current Cost Basis under an Operating Capability Concept of Capital (Unaudited)

For the years ended December 31	1984	1983*
	(millions of dollars)	
Net Income applicable to common shares as reported in the historical cost statements	$ 894.2	$ 811.4
Less: extraordinary items	–	(88.3)
Income (before extraordinary items) applicable to common shares on a historical cost basis	$ 894.2	$ 723.1
Add: dividends on first preferred shares	46.1	54.6
Income on a historical cost basis	$ 940.3	$ 777.7
Current cost adjustments		
— depreciation expense (a)	(289.2)	(317.4)
— cost of revenues (b)	27.5	6.1
— net income of associated companies on		
— an equity basis (d)	(8.3)	(11.7)
— minority interest (f)	(6.1)	5.6
Income on a current cost basis	$ 664.2	$ 460.3
Financing adjustment (g)	64.0	88.1
Financing adjustment for associated companies	2.9	4.0
Dividends on first preferred shares	(46.1)	(54.6)
Income (before extraordinary items) applicable to common shareholders on a current cost basis under an operating capability concept of capital	$ 685.0	$497.8

* Restated in average 1984 dollars

Notes and Additional Information

For the years ended December 31	1984	1983
	(millions of dollars)	
(a) Property, plant, and equipment (net of accumulated depreciation) — at December 31		
— on a historical cost basis	$11,655.6	$10,747.3
— on a current cost basis	15,719.9	15,928.1†
(b) Inventories — at December 31		
— on a historical cost basis	$ 1,219.8	$ 705.7
— on a current cost basis	1,227.3	731.5†
(c) Total current cost (decrease) increase in property, plant and equipment and inventories held during the year	$ (284.5)**	$ 604.3*
— Effect of general inflation	608.3	717.4*
— Excess of general inflation over current cost changes	892.8	113.1*

**This decrease results primarily from relatively lower prices for digital technology telecommunications equipment and the introduction of fibre optics as a replacement technology for certain telecommunications property.

	1984	1983
(d) Impact of depreciation expense for associated companies adjusted to current cost	(8.3)	(11.7)*
(e) Under CICA recommendations, no adjustment is made to historical cost income taxes		
— current portion of income taxes	585.3	562.2*
— deferred portion of income taxes	161.9	95.3*
(f) A portion of current cost adjustments is applicable to minority shareholders	(6.1)	5.6*
(g) Financing adjustment based on current cost adjustments to depreciation expense and cost of revenues	64.0	88.1*
— Financing adjustment based on total current cost changes (note (c) above)	(69.6)	171.1*
(h) Net assets — at December 31		
— on a historical cost basis	6,316.9	5,306.9
— on a current cost basis	10,371.4	10,295.6†
(i) General purchasing power gain on net monetary liabilities. This gain does not provide funds to the corporation	157.8	203.4*

* Restated in average 1984 dollars.
† Restated in December 1984 dollars.

Source Bell Canada Enterprises.

Measurement Techniques

A number of measurement techniques has been used to determine the current cost of property, plant, and equipment. The techniques include externally and internally produced price indexes, appraisals, direct and reference pricing techniques, and engineering estimates of the impact of significant technological change. The depreciation rates used reflect the same methods and estimated lives as are used in the historical cost financial statements.

The cost of revenues adjustment reflects the general movement in the costs of manufacturing inputs between the dates of their purchase or application to manufacturing processes and the dates of sale of the related finished products. The calculations are based on indices generated as part of the ongoing management control process.

For Discussion

1. If Bell Canada believes that this information is not suitable for purposes of valuation and traditional measurement, why do you think the corporation includes such information with its financial statements?
2. As a potential investor, how would you use this supplementary information?
3. Calculate several ratios based on these current cost figures. Comment on their usefulness.

Comprehension Problems

Comprehension Problem 15-1

Consider the following financial statement data.

Balance Sheet Data

Cash	$ 20	Current Liabilities	$ 20
Accounts Receivable (net)	20	Bonds Payable (10%)	60
Merchandise Inventory	40	Common Stock (8 shares)	80
Plant (net)	140	Retained Earnings	60
	$220		$220

Income Statement Data

Sales	$100
Cost of Goods Sold	50
Gross Profit	$ 50
Operating Expenses (incl. interest)	20
Net Income before Income Tax	$ 30
Income Tax	10
Net Income	$ 20

Assume that the average of all balance sheet items is equal to the year-end figure and that all sales are on credit.

Required:
1. Calculate the following ratios:
   a. Return on total assets (assume interest has been paid)
   b. Return on shareholders' equity
   c. Times interest earned ratio
   d. Earnings per share
   e. Inventory turnover
   f. Accounts receivable collection period
   g. Sales to fixed assets ratio
   h. Current ratio
   i. Acid-test ratio
   j. Equity-to-debt ratio.
2. Which of these ratios measure short-term solvency?

Note: Solve problems involving changing prices only if the Appendix was studied in your course.

Comprehension Problem 15-2

Here are the balance sheet and income statement of Kong Limited.

Kong Limited
Balance Sheet
At December 31, 19X2

Assets		*Liabilities and Shareholders' Equity*	
Cash	$ 72	Accounts Payable	$ 60
Accounts Receivable (net)	88	Bonds Payable	80
Merchandise Inventory	100	Mortgage Payable	70
Prepaid Expenses	40	Preferred Stock (10%)	60
Land	220	Common Stock	250
Building (net)	100	Retained Earnings	100
Total Assets	$620	Total Liabilities and Shareholders' Equity	$620

Kong Limited
Income Statement
For the Year Ended December 31, 19X2

Sales		$240
Cost of Goods Sold		144
Gross Profit		$ 96
Operating Expenses:		
Salaries	$44	
Depreciation	6	
Interest	8	58
Income before Income Tax		38
Income Tax		18
Net Income		$ 20

Assume that the average of all balance sheet items is equal to the year-end figure, and that all preferred dividends have been paid currently. Number of shares outstanding is 10.

1. The current ratio is (approximately):
   a. 4.33
   b. 2.66
   c. 5
   d. 2.14
   e. None of the above.

2. The return on total assets is (approximately):
   a. 6.1%
   b. 7.4%
   c. 4.8%
   d. 15.4%
   e. None of the above.

3. The inventory turnover is (approximately):
   a. 0.96
   b. 1.44
   c. 2.40
   d. 1.50
   e. None of the above.

4. The acid-test ratio is (approximately):
   a. 4.2
   b. 5
   c. 3.33
   d. 2.66
   e. None of the above.

5. The times interest earned ratio is (approximately):
   a. 5.75
   b. 4.75
   c. 2.5
   d. 7.25
   e. None of the above.

6. The earnings per share of common stock is:
   a. $1.40
   b. $2.00
   c. 3.80
   d. 4.60
   e. None of the above.

7. Eighty percent of sales are on account. The accounts receivable collection period is:
   a. Under 108 days
   b. Over 170 days
   c. Between 150 and 165 days
   d. Between 109 and 148 days
   e. None of the above

8. The return on shareholders' equity is (approximately):
   a. 8%
   b. 9.3%
   c. 6.4%
   d. 4.9%
   e. None of the above.

Comprehension Problem 15-3

Shareholders' equity is $140; total liabilities are $40; non-current assets are $90. The current ratio is 2.5; the acid-test ratio is 1. Total sales are $420; total credit sales are $300.

Required:
1. The current liabilities are:

   a. 40   d. 16
   b. 36   e. None of the above.
   c. 20

2. Prepaid expenses are zero. The inventory is:

   a. 70   d. 50
   b. 54   e. 74.
   c. 90

3. Cash and marketable securities are $6. The accounts receivable turnover is (approximately):

   a. 15   d. 10
   b. 10.5   e. 7.5.
   c. 13.33

4. The gross profit is 30 percent of sales. The inventory turnover is (approximately):

   a. 5.44   d. 6
   b. 2.33   e. 8.4.
   c. 5.55

Comprehension Problem 15-4

Required: Match the following ratios with the appropriate formula.

Ratio or Rate	Formula
_____ Acid-test ratio	a. $\dfrac{\text{Income from Operations}}{\text{Interest Expense}}$
_____ Current ratio	b. $\dfrac{\text{Shareholder's Equity}}{\text{Total Liabilities}}$
_____ Return on shareholders' equity	c. $\dfrac{\text{Net Income for the Year } - \text{ Preferred Dividend}}{\text{Number of Common Shares Outstanding}}$
_____ Times interest earned	d. $\dfrac{\text{Net Sales}}{\text{Average Net Fixed Assets}}$
_____ Earnings per share	e. $\dfrac{\text{Market Price per Share}}{\text{Earnings per Share}}$
_____ Accounts receivable turnover	f. $\dfrac{\text{Current Assets}}{\text{Current Liabilities}}$
_____ Sales to fixed assets	g. $\dfrac{\text{Average Inventory}}{\text{Cost of Goods Sold}} \times 365$
_____ Dividend yield	h. $\dfrac{\text{Net Income for the Year}}{\text{Net Sales}}$
_____ Price-to-earnings ratio	i. $\dfrac{\text{Income from Operations}}{\text{Average Total Assets}}$
_____ Inventory turnover	j. $\dfrac{\text{Net Credit Sales}}{\text{Average Accounts Receivable}}$

_____ Number of days of sales in inventory

_____ Equity-to-debt ratio

_____ Return on sales

_____ Accounts receivable collection period

_____ Return on total assets

k. $\dfrac{\text{Dividends per Share}}{\text{Market Price per Share}}$

l. $\dfrac{\text{Net Income for the Year}}{\text{Average Shareholders' Equity}}$

m. $\dfrac{\text{Quick Current Assets}}{\text{Current Liabilities}}$

n. $\dfrac{\text{Cost of Goods Sold}}{\text{Average Inventory}}$

o. $\dfrac{\text{Average Accounts Receivable}}{\text{Net Credit Sales}} \times 365$

Comprehension Problem 15-5

A company began the month of May with $200,000 of current assets, a 2.5 to 1 current ratio, and a 1.25 to 1 acid-test (quick) ratio. During the month, it completed the following transactions:

	(a) Current Ratio			(b) Working Capital		
	Increase	*Decrease*	*No Change*	*Increase*	*Decrease*	*No Change*

Bought $20,000 of merchandise on account (the company uses a perpetual inventory system)

Sold for $10,000 merchandise that cost $5,000

Collected a $2,500 account receivable

Paid a $10,000 account payable

Wrote off a $1,500 bad debt against the allowance for doubtful accounts

Declared a $1 per-share cash dividend on the 10 000 shares of outstanding common stock

Paid the dividend declared above

Borrowed $10,000 by giving the bank a 60-day, 10-percent note

Borrowed $25,000 by placing a 10-year mortgage on the plant

Used the $25,000 proceeds of the mortgage to buy additional machinery

Required:
1. Indicate the effect on (a) current ratio and (b) working capital of each transaction. (*Working capital* is defined as "current assets minus current liabilities".)
2. At the end of May, what was
   a. The current ratio?
   b. The acid-test ratio?
   c. The working capital?

Problems

Problem 15-1

The following is the balance sheet of the Cosmos Corporation.

Cosmos Corporation
Balance Sheet
At December 31, 19X0

Assets		*Liabilities and Shareholders' Equity*	
CURRENT ASSETS:		CURRENT LIABILITIES:	
Cash	$ 100	Accounts Payable	$ 300
Accounts Receivable	200	Wages Payable	50
Merchandise Inventory	500	Dividends Payable	50
Prepaid Expenses	50	Total Current Liabilities	$ 400
Total Current Assets	$ 850	Bonds Payable	800
Fixed Assets	1,000	Total Liabilities	$1,200
		Common Stock	500
		Retained Earnings	150
		Total Liabilities and	
Total Assets	$1,850	Shareholders' Equity	$1,850

Required: Based on this information, calculate the
1. a. Current ratio
   b. Acid-test ratio
   c. Equity-to-debt ratio.
2. What do these ratios tell you about Cosmos Corporation?
3. What other financial statements are necessary to complete the analysis of Cosmos Corporation?

Problem 15-2

The following information for 19X2 was gathered from the financial statements of the Unicorn Corporation.

Balance Sheet		Income Statement	
Cash	$ 60	Net Credit Sales	$800
Accounts Receivable (net)	140	Cost of Sales	600
Merchandise Inventory	250	Gross Profit	$200
Prepaid Expenses	10	Selling & Administrative Expenses	100
Fixed Assets (net)	330		
Total Assets	$790	Income from Operations	$100
		Interest Expense	20
Accounts Payable	$100	Income before Income Tax	$ 80
Notes Payable (6 months)	20	Income Tax	30
Current Portion of Bonds Payable	60	Net Income	$ 50
Bonds Payable	140		
Preferred Stock, 10% (8 shares)	120		
Common Stock (50 shares)	250		
Retained Earnings	100		
Total Liabilities and Shareholders' Equity	$790		

Additional information from the December 31, 19X1 statements:

Accounts Receivable	$180
Merchandise Inventory	200
Fixed Assets (net)	250
Retained Earnings	80

Required:

1. Compute the following ratios for 19X2:
   a. Equity-to-debt ratio
   b. Current ratio
   c. Acid-test ratio
   d. Accounts receivable collection period
   e. Inventory turnover
   f. Return on shareholders' equity
   g. Earnings per share.
2. Compute dividends per share (common stock) for 19X2.

Problem 15-3

Ajax Corporation's books were destroyed in a fire. The controller of the corporation can only remember a few odd pieces of information (given below) to reconstruct the financial statements:

a. The current ratio was 3.75 to 1.
b. Sales for the year were $73,000.
c. Inventories were $20,000 and were equal to fixed assets and equal to bonds payable.
d. The accounts receivable collection period was 40 days.
e. The bonds payable was 10 times cash.
f. Total current assets were twice common stock.

Required: Using this information, prepare Ajax Corporation's balance sheet at April 30, 19X1.

Problem 15-4

You are an accountant analyzing Zeus Corporation's income statements. The Zeus Corporation has expanded its production facilities by 200 percent since 19X0.

Zeus Corporation
Comparative Income Statements
For the Years Ending December 31

	19X2	19X1	19X0
Sales	$250	$150	$120
Cost of Goods Sold	190	100	60
Gross Profit	$ 60	$ 50	$ 60
Selling and Administrative Expenses	35	34	35
Net Income	$ 25	$ 16	$ 25

Required:
1. Prepare a vertical analysis of Zeus Corporation's income statement for the three years.
2. What important inferences can be drawn from this analysis?

Problem 15-5

The incomplete balance sheet of Alpha Limited is given below.

Alpha Limited
Balance Sheet
At December 31, 19X1
Assets

CURRENT ASSETS:

Cash	$ 30,000	
Accounts Receivable	?	
Merchandise Inventory	?	
Total Current Assets		$?
Fixed Assets	$?	
Less: Accumulated Depreciation	100,000	?
Total Assets		$?

Liabilities and Shareholders' Equity

CURRENT LIABILITIES:

Accounts Payable	$ 50,000	
Accrued Liabilities	?	
Total Current Liabilities		$120,000
8% Bonds Payable		?
Common Stock		?
Retained Earnings		?
Total Liabilities and Shareholders' Equity		$?

Required: Use the following information as of December 31, 19X1 to complete Alpha Limited's balance sheet.

a. The amount of working capital is $150,000.
b. The par value of the stock is $10 per share.
c. Market price per share is $15.
d. Price to earnings ratio is 3.
e. Income before payment of interest and income tax is $80,000.
f. The ratio of shareholder equity to total assets is 0.60 to 1.
g. Income tax equals $30,000.
h. The acid-test ratio is 1.5 to 1.
i. Times interest earned is 8.

Alternate Problems

Alternate Problem 15-1

The Dallas Corporation reported the following information:

Net Income	$61.2
Interest Expense	5.0
Income Tax	20.0

The Dallas Corporation's balance sheet, in the shareholders' equity section, yields the following information: preferred stock (6% cumulative, 10 shares issued and outstanding) — $20; and common stock (15 shares issued and outstanding) — $25. The Dallas Corporation has prided itself on never missing a dividend payment. During 19X1, $5 per-share cash dividends were delcared and paid to the common shareholders. Dividend yield was 27.5 percent.

Required: Determine the
1. Earnings per share
2. Dividends per share
3. Price/earnings ratio.

Alternate Problem 15-2

The following financial statements belong to Banzai Corporation.

Banzai Corporation
Balance Sheet
At December 31, 19X0

Assets		*Liabilities and Shareholders' Equity*	
Cash	$ 20	Accounts Payable	$ 30
Accounts Receivable	60	Wages Payable	10
Merchandise Inventory	90	Total Current Liabilities	40
Total Current Assets	$170	Bonds Payable (8%)	100
		Total Liabilities	$140
Fixed Assets (net)	110		
		Common Stock	100
		Retained Earnings	40
		Total Liabilities and	
Total Assets	$280	Shareholders' Equity	$280

Banzai Corporation
Income Statement
For the Year ended December 31, 19X0

Sales	$300
Cost of Sales	180
Gross Profit	120
Selling and Administrative Expenses	80
Net Income	$ 40

The following additional information is available:
a. Income tax was 50 percent of net income; it is included in selling and administrative expenses.
b. Beginning balances of balance sheet accounts were the same as ending balances.
c. All sales are on credit.

Required: The significance of certain ratios or tests is given below. Give the name of the corresponding ratio or test, and calculate the ratios for the Banzai Corporation.
1. Primary test for solvency
2. A more severe test of immediate solvency
3. Test of efficiency of collection
4. Indication of liquidity of inventory
5. Reflection of financial strength and cushion for creditors
6. Indication of the net productivity of each sales dollar
7. Indication of management's ability to use efficiently the resources provided.

Alternate Problem 15-3

The following financial information is available for Embury Enterprises Limited.

a. The acid-test ratio is 1.5 to 1.
b. Accounts receivable are $3,000 and are half of the quick assets, one-third of the current assets, and twice the fixed assets.
c. Notes payable are long-term liabilities; thus are four times the dollar amount of the marketable securities.
d. Total shareholders' equity is equal to the working capital, and common stock is 150 percent of the dollar amount of the retained earnings.

Required: Using this information, prepare the balance sheet at December 31, 19X8

Alternate Problem 15-4

The following information is taken from the records of P. Jones Corp.

	19X3	19X2
Sales	$1,397	$1,122
Cost of Goods Sold	935	814
Selling Expenses	154	121
General Expenses	88	77
Other Revenue	4	7
Other Expenses	2	9
Income Tax	134	66

Required:
1. Prepare a vertical analysis of the income statement.
2. Indicate the favourable and unfavourable changes.

Alternate Problem 15-5

The following ratios and other data are taken from the financial statements of Delta Company for the year ended December 31, 19X0.

Current Ratio	1.80 to 1
Acid-Test Ratio	1.3 to 1
Net Working Capital	$40,000
Inventory Turnover	5 times
Gross Profit as a Percentage on Sales	50%
Earnings per Share	$0.25
Accounts Receivable Collection Period	73 days
Common Stock Outstanding	50 000 shares
Fixed Assets to Shareholders' Equity Ratio	0.75 to 1
Par-Value on Common Stock	$2.25

The following additional information is available: beginning balance sheet account balances equal ending balance sheet balances.

Required: Using the information given, prepare the balance sheet and income statement.

Supplementary Problems

Supplementary Problem 15-1

Selected financial information of the Moebius Corporation is given below.

Moebius Corporation
Balance Sheet
At December 31

Assets	19X1	19X0
Cash	$ 60	$ 10
Marketable Securities	10	20
Accounts Receivable (net)	60	40
Merchandise Inventories	108	120
Prepaid Expenses	12	10
Total Current Assets	$250	$200
Fixed Assets (net)	100	120
Land	70	60
Total Assets	$420	$380
Liabilities and Shareholders' Equity		
Accounts Payable	$100	$ 80
Accrued Liabilities	20	10
Total Current Liabilties	$120	$ 90
Bonds Payable	50	30
Total Liabilites	$170	$120
Common Stock (10 Shares)	150	150
Retained Earnings	100	110
Total Liabilities and Shareholders' Equity	$420	$380

Required:
1. Prepare a horizontal analysis of Moebius Corporation, showing each individual item.
2. What are readily apparent results of 19X1 operations? Did Moebius make a profit in 19X1?

Supplementary Problem 15-2

Part A

The balance sheet and income statement of Charron Inc. are given below.

Balance Sheet
At December 31, 19X8

Assets		*Liabilities and Shareholders' Equity*	
Cash	$ 60	Accounts Payable	$ 26
Accounts Receivable (net)	120	Notes Payable	66
Merchandise Inventory	240	Accrued Liabilities	10
Prepaid Insurance	6	Common Stock ($10 par-value)	300
Land	40	Retained Earnings	384
Equipment (net)	320		
Total Assets	$786	Total Liabilities and Shareholders' Equity	$786

Income Statement
For the Year Ended December 31, 19X8

Sales			$1,000
Cost of Goods Sold:			
Opening Inventory (Jan. 1)		$200	
Purchases		770	
Cost of Goods Available for Sale		$970	
Ending Inventory (Dec. 31)		240	
Total Cost of Goods Sold			730
Gross Profit			$ 270
Operating Expenses			180
Net Income for the Year			$ 90

Other Information: (a) no shares were issued during the year, and (b) no dividends were paid during the year.

Required: Calculate
a. The current ratio
b. The inventory turnover ratio
c. The earnings per share
d. The return on shareholders' equity ratio

Part B

Assume that the following unrelated transactions occurred in Charron Inc. in 19X9.

Required: Indicate the effect of each transaction on (a) current ratio, and (b) the working capital.

	Current Ratio			Working Capital		
	Increase	*Decrease*	*No Change*	*Increase*	*Decrease*	*No Change*
Additional common stock was sold for cash						
Paid $20,000 of accounts payable						
Purchased $15,000 of inventory on account						
Wrote off $2,000 of accounts receivable as uncollectible.						

Decision Problems

Decision Problem 15-1

The Gazelle Corporation sells merchandise on terms 2/10, n/30. Approximately 40 percent of its sales are for cash. The Accounts Receivable account has an opening balance of $51,780 and a closing balance of $59,200. Total sales for the year were $762,800.

Required:

1. a. Calculate Gazelle's average Accounts Receivable balance.
   b. What is the average collection period?
2. What conclusions about Gazelle's credit policy can be made with this information?

Decision Problem 15-2

You are the bank manager of North Bank. Two companies, A and B, are seeking bank loans. You are given the following financial statements.

Assume that a fair comparison between companies A and B can be made with these data. Ignore income tax.

Balance Sheets
At December 31, 19X1

	Company A	Company B		Company A	Company B
Assets					
Cash	$ 80	$ 165	*Liabilities and Shareholders' Equity*		
Accounts Receivable (net)	125	235	Current Liabilities	$ 240	$ 300
Merchandise Inventory	480	660	Long-Term Liabilities	600	500
Total Current Assets	$ 685	$1,060	Common Stock	250	640
			Retained Earnings	100	160
Fixed Assets (net)	505	540	Total Liabilities and		
Total Assets	$1,190	$1,600	Shareholders' Equity	$1,190	$1,600

Note: Receivables and inventories are not significantly different from the balances at December 31, 19X0.

Income Statements
For the Year Ended December 31, 19X1

	Company A	Company B
Sales (credit)	$1,500	$900
Cost of Goods Sold	1,050	540
Gross Profit	$ 450	$360
Selling and Administrative Expenses	150	200
Income from Operations	$ 300	$160
Interest Expense	60	50
Net Income	$ 240	$110

Required:

1. From this information, calculate for each company
   a. Short-term solvency ratios:
      Current ratio
      Acid-test ratio
      Accounts receivable collection period
      Accounts receivable turnover
      Number of days of sales in inventory
      Inventory turnover.
   b. Long-term solvency ratios:
      Return on total assets
      Times interest earned
      Equity-to-debt ratio.
2. From these ratios, determine to which company you would grant a 6-month, 12-percent loan of $150 without security, and give reasons for your choice. You must choose one company.

Decision Problem 15-3

As controller of Athena Corporation, you have calculated the
following ratios, turnovers, and percentages to enable you to
answer questions the directors are likely to ask at their next
meeting.

	19X2	19X1	19X0
Current Ratio	3.1 : 1	2.6 : 1	2.0 : 1
Acid-Test Ratio	0.8 : 1	1.2 : 1	1.5 : 1
Inventory Turnover	9.5 times	10.0 times	11.2 times
Accounts Receivable Turnover	7.1 times	7.5 times	7.6 times
Return on Shareholders' Equity	12.0%	13.3%	14.1%
Return on Total Assets	12.6%	12.8%	13.3%
Sales Percentage Trend	123.0	118.0	100.0
Selling Expenses to Net Sales Ratio	13.9%	13.9%	14.2%

Required:
Using these statistics, answer each question with a brief explanation to support each answer.

1. Is it becoming easier than in previous years for the company to take advantage of cash discounts?
2. Is the company collecting its accounts receivable more
   rapidly than before?
3. Is the company's investment in accounts receivable
   decreasing?
4. Is the company's investment in inventory increasing?
5. Is the shareholders' investment becoming more profitable?
6. Did the dollar amount of selling expenses decrease during
   the three-year period?

Statement of Changes in Financial Position

The statement of changes in financial position is a financial statement designed to show changes in financial position that occur during a particular accounting time period. Questions asked by readers of financial statements include:

1. How is the corporation financing its activities: internally from operations, externally from other sources, or both?
2. Why did cash decrease even though a net income was earned?
3. Is a decrease in cash a result of good cash management, or does it signal a liquidity problem?
4. Why did working capital decrease even though earnings were favourable?
5. How was an acquisition of a new plant financed?
6. How were the proceeds from sale of an old plant used?
7. What were the proceeds from a bond issue used for?
8. How were the proceeds from an issue of common stock invested?
9. Why were dividends not paid during the year?
10. What exactly do accountants mean by the term *funds*?
11. What are two different definitions of *funds*?
12. How do accountants actually prepare a statement of changes in financial position?

A.   The Function of Financial Statements

As indicated in the opening chapters of this book, the financial activities of a company are reported through four financial statements.

The balance sheet reports the financial position of a company at a particular point in time. Just as a camera takes your snapshot and records for posterity how you look today, a balance sheet records a company's asset, liability, and equity accounts as they are at the date it is prepared. The balance sheet shows the financial results of a company's activities.

The income statement reports the results of a company's operations over a particular time period; for example, a year. This statement can be compared to a movie camera, which records what takes place over a period of time. The income statement provides details of revenues (an inflow of assets or reduction in liabilities) and expenses (an outflow of assets or incurrence of liabilities) incurred to earn these revenues. Those activities of the company that result in a net income or net loss are reported in the income statement.

The statement of retained earnings reports the cause of a change in retained earnings during the time period covered by the income statement. It is not only by a net inflow of assets from net income or a net outflow from net loss that these retained earnings are changed; there are also other causes of change, such as dividends. Such other causes do not belong to the operations of a company and therefore are not shown on the income statement. The statement of retained earnings and the income statement show the change in the balance sheet account Retained Earnings. The statement of retained earnings, in effect, reconciles the beginning and the ending balances of the Retained Earnings account. This reconciliation is shown in Figure 16-1.

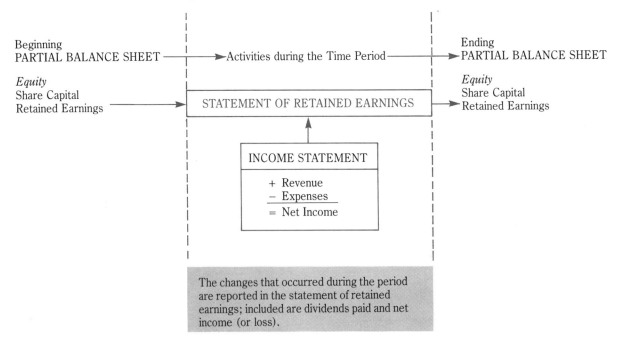

Figure 16-1   The function of the statement of retained earnings

The balance sheet shows the financial results of a company's activities at a particular point in time. Some of these activities, such as operations and dividends, are reported in the income statement and statement of retained earnings. There are other activities, however, that remain unreported.

Financing and investing activities
Those activities of the entity concerned with the raising of capital (financing activities) and with the purchase of non-current assets (investing activities).

These activities are the **financing and investing activities** of a company, which are important to financial statement readers who wish to evaluate the financial position and the results of operations of a particular company. The fourth financial statement, the **statement of changes in financial position** (SCFP) provides information to reveal these otherwise unreported activities. In the same way that the income statement and the statement of retained earnings show the changes that occurred in the balance sheet Retained Earnings acount, the SCFP reports the changes that occurred in asset, liability, and equity accounts. This relationship is shown in Figure 16-2.

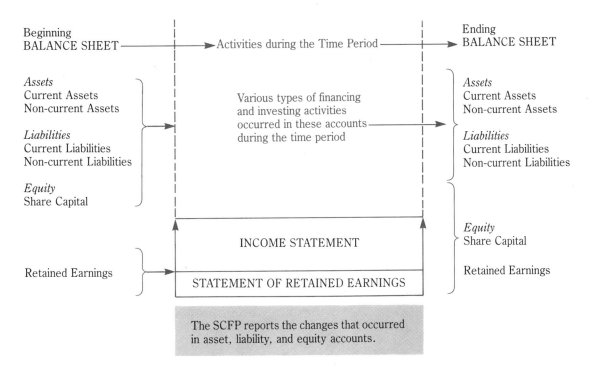

Figure 16-2 The function of the statement of changes in financial position

Statement of changes in financial position (SCFP)
A statement showing the sources and uses of working capital, or resources, or cash during the fiscal year.

The changes in asset, liability, and equity accounts that are reported in the statement of changes in financial position depend on how *funds* are defined.

Definition 1: Funds as Cash Flow
According to this definition, the changes in balance sheet accounts should be shown that have affected a company's Cash account. These changes involve financing and investing activities of a company, where amounts of cash have been received and disbursed during the time period. The cash flow method requires that the financial statements of a company be converted from the accrual basis to a cash basis. The cash definition of *funds* is the narrowest of the three definitions discussed in this chapter. This method is recommended by the CICA.

Real Life Example 16-1

Focus on Cash

"Focus on cash, not working capital, in funds statements."
. . . How are accountants to react to this advice? Is a cash-based statement of changes right for your company? Is a funds statement based on working capital wrong? How companies deal with this issue depends on professional accountants' approach to this financial reporting problem. What are the options?

You can treat the cash vs. working capital dispute as a technical accounting question, but you will be hard pressed to choose between the two fund definitions. The reasons for changing to a cash-based funds statement are not in the *CICA Handbook*. Accounting theory will not settle this controversy.
. . . A statement of changes that hides serious cash-flow problems behind a mask of working capital growth does not benefit business executives or their organizations.

One doesn't have to look far to realize that the funds statement based on working capital has been judged and found wanting. "There are two kinds of funds," quips one critic, "cash and all the rest. Pay me in cash every time." Working capital flows are poor proxies for cash flows; investors want cash-flow information that is not a working capital funds statement.

Some experts believe that a cash definition of funds will restore the statement of changes. Although they are on the right track, a new funds definition is not the whole story. If you really want to improve the funds statement, you also have to upgrade the format used to present cash-flow information.

The Writing on the Wall

. . . The history of the cash vs working capital controversy can be traced back to 1975. The problem is perspective. Busy accountants are aware of the many incidents that created support for a cash-based funds statement; they just have not had the time to put the whole picture together.

The W. T. Grant Controversy

It took a major business failure to trigger serious interest in the cash-based funds statement. The 1975 W. T. Grant bankruptcy shocked investors everywhere. "With all the facts and figures churned out by Grant," declared one bitter shareholder, "where was the truth? Why couldn't we see this coming?" Analysts point an accusing finger at the working-capital-based funds statement.

Figure 1 shows that W. T. Grant's operations were users, not providers, of cash from 1966 to 1975. In the decade preceding the bankruptcy, cash provided by operations was in the black for only two years. Until collapse was imminent, however, Grant's working capital from operations remained positive and fairly stable. Grant's funds statement hid a major liquidity problem.

W. T. Grant finally choked to death on its own inventory. Its failure served notice that there is an important difference between cash flows and working capital flows.

Source Richard S. Clark, "Statement of Changes: In Need of a Change?", *CAMagazine*, February 1983, p. 27.

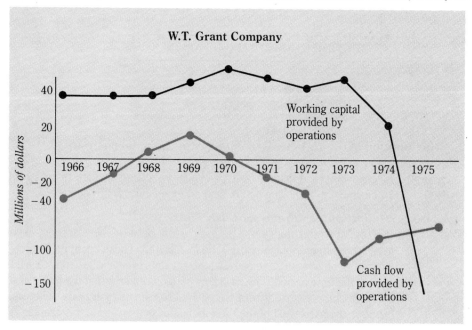

Figure 1

Definition 2: *Funds as Working Capital*

According to this definition, the changes in balance sheet accounts should be shown that have affected a company's sources or uses of working capital. For example, as is explained later, a building acquisition for cash is a change in two balance sheet accounts that would be reported under this definition. Most changes in balance sheet accounts affect working capital.

The importance of cash flow, and the contrast between the concepts of cash and working capital are discussed in Real Life Example 16-1.

Definition of the Term *Funds* in Different Accounting Settings

Funds
Accounting term often used in reference to SCFP. Also used to refer to petty cash fund and bond sinking fund.

The term **funds** is often used in accounting jargon. To the average non-accounting person, ''funds'' is synonymous with ''cash''. What the word means in an accounting environment depends on the context in which it is used. *Funds* as cash flow can be defined as cash only, cash and marketable securities, or cash and marketable securities less short-term debt. For purposes of this chapter, *funds* as cash flow will be defined as ''cash''.

Because of a multitude of possible definitions, the preparation of a statement of changes in financial position requires first a declaration of which definition is to be used in the statement's preparation. The definitions discussed in this chapter are discussed below.

Context for the Term ''Funds''	*Meaning of the Term ''Fund''*
1. When dealing with cash, the term *petty cash fund* is used.	*Fund*, in this case, refers to the amount of cash kept on hand for use in certain, usually well defined, circumstances.
2. When dealing with investments, the term *sinking fund* is used.	*Fund*, in this case, refers to cash and other assets kept separately for use in investment redemption.
3. When dealing with working capital, the term *funds* is often used as a synonym for *working capital*.	*Funds*, in this case, refers to the amount of current assets less current liabilities (working capital). It does *not* mean cash.
4. When dealing with a statement of changes in financial position, reference is made to a **funds statement**.	The term *funds statement* is used in several different ways. For purposes of this text, the term *funds* will be used sparingly to prevent ambiguities. The term is further discussed in the material on working capital.

Funds Statement
When this term is used in describing an SCFP, its exact meaning has to be defined.

The Preparation of the SCFP

There are three steps in the preparation of a statement of changes in financial position, according to the appropriate definitions of funds.

Step 1
Calculate the increase or decrease in funds (as defined) that has occurred during the period.

Step 2
Analyze all appropriate balance sheet accounts to identify the transactions that have resulted in an increase or decrease of funds, according to the definition used.

Step 3
On the basis of the analysis in Step 2, prepare the statement. The net increase or decrease in funds must equal the amount calculated in Step 1.

The preparation of an SCFP according to each of the definitions is illustrated using data from the comparative balance sheets and income statement of Bluebeard Computer Corporation:

Bluebeard Computer Corporation
Comparative Balance Sheets
At December 19X8 and 19X7

(000s)

Assets	19X8	19X7	Liabilities and Shareholders' Equity	19X8	19X7
Current Assets	$1,322	$1,060	Current Liabilities	$ 300	$ 200
Investments (long-term)	$ 140	$ 220	LONG-TERM LIABILITIES:		
			Mortgage Payable	1,000	500
FIXED ASSETS:			Total Liabilities	$1,300	$ 700
Land	70	70			
Buildings	1,200	400	SHAREHOLDERS' EQUITY:		
Machinery	1,000	700	Common Stock	$1,100	$ 800
Accumulated Depreciation	(550)	(300)	Premium on Common Stock	110	-0-
Total Fixed Assets	$1,720	$ 870	Retained Earnings	672	650
			Total Shareholders' Equity	$1,882	$1,450
			Total Liabilities and		
Total Assets	$3,182	$2,150	Shareholders' Equity	$3,182	$2,150

Income Statement
For the Year Ended December 31, 19X8
(000s)

Sales		$1,200
Cost of Goods Sold		674
Gross Profit		$ 526
Operating Expenses:		
Depreciation—Buildings & Machinery	$260	
Other Expenses	200	460
		$ 66
Income from Operations:		
Gain on Sale of Long-Term Investment	$ 24	
Loss on Sale of Machinery	(10)	14
Net Income		$ 80

Ideally, a statement of changes in financial position is prepared from an analysis of transactions recorded in the books of an entity during the accounting period being analyzed. Rarely, however, does the reader of financial statements have access to the entity's accounting records, thereby, to establish the transactions that have occurred. It is therefore necessary to establish what inflows and outflows of funds have occurred. The following summarized transactions from the records of Bluebeard Computer Corporation are the pertinent ones for an SCFP; their effect on working capital is shown, as well as their effect on cash flow. These transactions form the basis of the discussion included in the subsequent discussions of funds as cash flow and as working capital.

Transaction Number	(000s) Description of the Transaction
1	Investments costing $80 were sold for $104
2	A building was purchased for $800 cash
3	Machinery costing $350 was purchased for cash
3	Machinery costing $50 and, having accumulated depreciation of $10, was sold for $30 cash
4	Depreciation expense of $260 was recorded during the year
5	BCC borrowed $500 cash as a mortgage payable during the year
6	Common shares with a par-value of $300 were sold for $410 cash
7	Retained Earnings was reduced by $58-worth of dividends declared and paid during the year
7	Retained Earnings was increased by $80 net income for the year.

B.   Funds as Cash Flow

Cash Flow Definition of Funds

The preparation of an SCFP to show those changes in Balance Sheet accounts that affected the entity's cash account; it is essentially a statement of cash receipts and disbursements categorized into operating, financing, and investing categories.

Under the *cash flow definition of funds*, all operating, financing, and investing activities that involve the receipt and disbursement of cash are reported in the SCFP. According to the *CICA Handbook*, cash flows from financing activities result in the change and composition of the debt and equity capital structure of the entity. These include cash flows from the issue, assumption, redemption, and repayment of debt, and the issue, redemption, and acquisition of share capital (section 1540.15). Although there are different views concerning the disclosure of dividends, dividend outlays are considered as a financing activity for purposes of this chapter. Cash flows from investing activities include outlays for the acquisition of assets, as well as proceeds from their disposal (section 1540.16). Of necessity, therefore, the cash flow definition requires an analysis of cash inflows and cash outflows. This analysis focuses on the Cash account and any transactions that involve both Cash and any other balance sheet account. For a closer look at the debate concerning the use of Cash Flow in the SCFP, see Conceptual Issue 16-1.

The following balance sheet format can be used to visualize this analysis. The bold black line separates the Cash account from all other accounts.

Balance Sheet Format

Assets	*Liabilities and Equity*
Cash	
Non-cash Current Assets	Current Liabilities
Non-current Assets	Non-current Liabilities
	Equity
	+ Revenue
	− Expenses

Any transaction that "crosses the black line" results in either a cash inflow or a cash outflow. Such transactions cause changes within the so-called "cash pool".

Conceptual Issue 16-1

Another Look at Cash Flow

By Cornelius J. Casey, Dartmouth College
and Norman J. Bartczak, Harvard Business School

In recent years, financial analysts and investment advisory services have trumpeted the value of cash flow data in making investment decisions. It is argued that cash flow information is more objective and has greater intuitive appeal than accounting-based earnings as a measure of corporate performance.

Numerous articles in the financial press, as well as statements by the Financial Accounting Standards Board and the CICA, have touted cash flow from operations as an accurate barometer of a company's ability to withstand financial adversity.

Moreover, many analysts believe earnings data have been severely distorted by inflation during the last decade and by the creative accounting practices of some managements. A securities analyst who pierced the earnings veil of the Baldwin-United Corporation and forecast its financial collapse was praised for his studied application of its labyrinthine cash flow problems.

But perhaps surprisingly, investors who rely on cash flow data may find them more of a bane than a boon for their investment performance. A study we recently completed indicates that cash flow data do not predict a company's financial health more accurately than traditional earnings-based numbers. To the contrary, the earnings-based data significantly outperformed the cash flow information.

Our findings should jar advocates of cash flow analysis. We found that cash flow data did not predict bankruptcy as accurately as a combination of profitability, liquidity, leverage and asset turnover indexes. The sad truth is that the cash flow data did not possess even marginal value; predictive accuracy was not improved by combining cash flow with the earnings-based information.

We had expected the study results would favourably reflect the information value of the cash flow numbers. We had been seduced by an armchair theory advanced by proponents of cash flow analysis. This theory — perhaps myth is a better word — holds that businesses that generate lesser amounts of operating cash flow will find it more difficult to satisfy outstanding liabilities and, consequently, face a greater risk of failure. Our instincts proved wrong.

Analysts who accent cash flows are likely to overestimate the chances that financially sound companies will experience economic distress. As it turns out, some of these companies have relatively little debt in their capital structures and/or large reserves of cash and marketable securities. There are many such firms. "Deep pockets" allowed K Mart and Colgate-Palmolive, for example, to stave off financial difficulty during periods when operations were consuming more cash than they were generating.

Consider, too, high-growth companies that have difficulty generating cash flow as they build receivables and invest cash in inventories. This cash-consuming process, however, need not be the kiss of death. Companies such as Digital Equipment and Baxter-Travenol have not only survived but have prospered because of their access to the debt and equity markets. What would early investors in these companies have to show today if they had swallowed the cash flow myth?

Consider, also, companies having "antiques in the barn" that can be sold to cover operating cash flow shortages. For

The Cash Pool

The cash pool is essentially the actual amount of cash available to management. This cash amount is important for financing decisions (Should cash be borrowed?) as well as for dividend payment decisions (Should dividends be paid?) and for investing decisions (Should machinery be purchased?). An analysis is also useful to explain why cash may have decreased, even though net income has been earned.

An SCFP prepared according to the cash flow definition can be labelled several different ways. Among different titles suggested in the *CICA Handbook* are "cash flow statement", "statement of operating, financing, and investing activities", or "statement of cash resources" (section 1540.01). For purposes of this text, an SCFP prepared according to the cash definition is referred to as a "statement of cash flow". It is prepared following three steps:

1. Calculate the amount of Cash increase or decrease.
2. Analyze all balance sheet accounts to identify the transactions that resulted in cash inflows and cash outflows.
3. On the basis of the analysis in Step 2, prepare a statement of cash flow. The net increase or decrease in Cash shown in the statement of cash flow must equal the amount calculated in Step 1.

example, Pan American World Airways raised $1 billion in cash from the sale of its Pan Am Building in central Manhattan and its Intercontinental Hotel subsidiary. Another example is Kaiser Steel, which raised nearly $650 million pretax in 1980 by selling its interests in various investments. This strategy allowed Kaiser to survive long enough to be acquired. Contrast these two companies with Braniff and McLouth Steel; lacking sufficient salable capital assets, they were unable to avoid bankruptcy.

Our findings indicate that those who are surfing the cash flow wave are over-rating its value. Needless to say, we do not suggest that careful study of corporate cash flows is a useless exercise. We believe that cash flow data may provide insight in predicting not only bankruptcy but also other events, such as dividend payouts and corporate acquisitions — but only under certain conditions. Until these conditions are identified, however, cash flow analysis is best viewed as a slippery rock on which to gain a foothold for assessing company prospects, and thus its value in these other uses remains an interesting but untested hypothesis.

One such condition for establishing the value of cash flow data is suggested by a provocative study on the bankruptcy of W. T. Grant, the giant retailer that failed in 1975. That study demonstrated how careful analysis of Grant's sizeable and negative operating cash flows gave a clearer and more timely signal than either Grant's earnings-based financial data or its stock price behaviour. Grant was a mature company in the decade prior to its collapse, but had embarked on a program involving a record number of new stores. To finance this expansion, it should have been generating substantial operating cash flows. As its creditors discovered, this was not the case, and the company eventually went under.

We draw two implications, among others, from our study. First, if there is an alpha and omega for evaluating a company's future prospects, it is not to be found in cash flow data. This is especially important when current developments are enticing financial report users to weigh cash flow data even more heavily. Expanded disclosure requirements for financial reporting and the increased accessibility of computerized financial data bases might encourage analysts to simplify their information search and analysis. Also, financial reports by non–United States companies are becoming an important source of information for a growing number of American investors. Because the quality of earnings data reported by these companies frequently falls short of the standard set by American companies, we expect increased importance to be attached to the foreign concerns' cash flows.

Second, there is a major need for careful research to replace the armchair theories on the relative merits of cash flow analysis. A recent monograph by the FASB notes that surprisingly little research has been done in evaluating the usefulness of historical cash flow data for forecasting business performance.

Financial analysts and academicians owe more than intuitively appealing rules of thumb to their constituencies who engage daily in multi-billion-dollar trading activity. The time has come to devote greater research attention to exploring the value of existing financial measures than to searching for a new "bottom line". We should be able to provide investors with the steak as well as the sizzle.

Given the known limitations of earnings data, the findings of our study beg a more fundamental question. Can the serious investor/ analyst find value in pouring over companies' historical financial reports?

Source   Cornelius J. Casey and Norman J. Bartczak, "Another Look at Cash Flow", *New York Times*, April 8, 1984, p. 3-F.

Analyzing Cash Flow

Step 1   Calculation of the Increase or Decrease in Cash

The change in the Cash account for Bluebeard Computer Corporation is calculated by comparing the end-of-year balance with the beginning-of-year balance.

	19X8	19X7	Change in Cash (000s) Increase	Decrease
Cash	$27	$150	—	$123

Cash has decreased by $123,000 during the year. Rather than cash having been generated during the year, it can be said to have been deployed in this case, because it has decreased.

The amount of available cash is important to financial statement readers. An increase in cash is usually required for growth, since additional sales result in more receivables being financed and in a larger amount of liabilities to be paid for increased purchases. Excess cash is unproductive; however, inadequate cash can affect the entity's liquidity, that is, its ability to pay its debts as they become due. Cash management deals with the optimal amount of cash to be kept on hand.

	Original Journal Entry		(000s)	Effect on Cash		Type of Activity
				Increase	Decrease	
Transaction 1						
Investments costing $80 were sold for $104	Cash	104		104		Financing
	Investments		80			
	Gain on Sale		24			
Transaction 2						
A building was purchased for $800 cash	Building	800				Investing
	Cash		800		800	
Transaction 3						
Machinery costing $350 was purchased for cash	Machinery	350				Investing (net)
	Cash		350		350	
Transaction 3						
Machinery costing $50 and, having accumulated depreciation of $10, was sold for $30 cash	Cash	30		30		Investing (net)
	Accumulated Depreciation	10				
	Loss on Disposal	10				
	Machinery		50			
Transaction 4						
Depreciation expense of $260 was recorded during the year	Depreciation Expense	260		–		Not a cash item (see operating)
	Accumulated Depreciation		260		–	
Transaction 5						
BCC borrowed $500 cash as a mortgage payable during the year.	Cash	500		500		Financing
	Mortgage Payable		500			
Transaction 6						
Common shares with a par-value of $300 were sold for $410 cash	Cash	410		410		Financing
	Common Shares		300			
	Premium on Common Shares		110			
Transaction 7a						
Retained Earnings was reduced by $58-worth of dividends declared and paid during the year	Dividends	58				Financing
	Cash		58		58	
Transaction 7b						
Retained Earnings was increased by $80 net income for the year	[This transaction requires further analysis.]					Operating

In the case of BCC, the reader is faced with the following question. Is the decrease in cash a result of good cash management? Or, does it signal a liquidity problem? Also what are the cash inflows and outflows that resulted in the $123,000 Cash decrease?

Step 2: Analysis of Balance Sheet Accounts

Analyzing Cash Inflows and Outflows   The cash inflows and outflows resulting during the time period are identified by an analysis of financial transactions. As explained, any transaction that affects both Cash and any other balance sheet account results in either an inflow or an outflow. The example introduced in section A continues. The above summarized transactions of Bluebeard indicate whether the Cash account is either debited or credited. The type of activity — operating, financing, or investing — is also indicated.

The transactions that increase or decrease cash are reported in the statement of cash flow, in addition to the calculation of cash provided from operations.

Calculation of Cash Flow from Operations   Does the $80,000 net income in transaction 7b increase or decrease Cash? An income statement analysis is required to calculate cash flow from operations through two steps.
   1. Items that do not affect Cash must be eliminated in the calculation of cash flow from operations. Depreciation expense is one example.
   2. The accrual basis income statement required by GAAP must be converted to a cash basis income statement. A cash basis income statement recognizes revenue only when cash from sales has been received; it recognizes an expense only when a cash payment has been made for inventory and expenses.

Elimination of Non-cash Items from the Income Statement   An analysis of income statement components is necessary to determine if the $80,000 increase in Retained Earnings due to net income for the year increased Cash by $80,000. Study the following comparative income statements.

Income Statements
(000s)

	Basis 1 (Including items that do not affect Cash)		Basis 2 (Excluding items that do not affect Cash)	
Sales		+ $1,200		+ $1,200
Cost of Goods Sold		− 674		− 674
Gross Profit		+ $ 526		+ $ 526
Operating Expenses				
Depreciation	− $260		-0-	
Other Expenses	− 200	− 460	− $200	− 200
		+ $ 66		+ $ 326
Net Income from Operations:				
Gain on Sale of Investment	+ $ 24		-0-	
Loss on Sale of Machinery	− (10)	14	-0-	-0-
Net Income		+ $ 80		+ $ 326

The comparison shows that, while $80,000 net income was calculated during the year, net income amounted to $326,000 when non-cash items are eliminated.

It is customary to provide with the SCFP a detailed reconciliation of net income for the year showing the elimination of non-cash items. The reconciliation is made as shown below.

Calculation of Cash Flow from Operations
(000s)

Net Income		$ 80
Add: Non-Cash Charges against		
Operations		
Deprec. of Building and Machinery	$260	
Loss on Sale of Machinery	10	270
Total		$350
Less: Non-Cash Credits to Operations:		
Gain on Sale of Investments		24
Net Income after Elimination of		
Non-Cash Items		$326

Students sometimes find this calculation a difficult concept, because it works backward from the net income figure. However, it is faster than preparing an income statement as was done in Basis 2.

A summary of the items that do not affect cash and must be eliminated in the preparation of a statement of cash flow is given below. It is a handy reference when making this type of calculation.

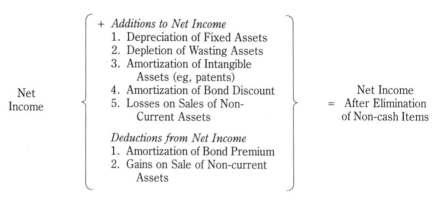

Net Income

+ *Additions to Net Income*
  1. Depreciation of Fixed Assets
  2. Depletion of Wasting Assets
  3. Amortization of Intangible Assets (eg, patents)
  4. Amortization of Bond Discount
  5. Losses on Sales of Non-Current Assets

Deductions from Net Income
  1. Amortization of Bond Premium
  2. Gains on Sale of Non-current Assets

Net Income
= After Elimination of Non-cash Items

Conversion of Net Income from the Accrual Basis to the Cash Basis   The accrual basis net income is then converted to a cash basis net income. Before preparing this conversion, three examples are used to illustrate the difference between the calculation of a cash net income and that of an accrual net income.

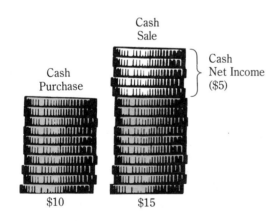

Cash Purchase

Cash Sale

Cash Net Income ($5)

$10 $15

Example 1
- The entity has $10 cash on hand.
- A cash purchase of one inventory unit is made for $10.
- This inventory unit is subsequently sold for $15 cash.
- There is now $15 cash on hand, $5 more cash than before the sale.
- Net income — in this case $5 — is equal to the additional cash on hand $5 ($15 − $10 purchase).

Example 2
- Assume that the entity has no cash on hand.
- A purchase of one inventory unit is made for $10 on account.
- This inventory unit is subsequently sold for $15 on account.
- There is still no cash on hand.
- Net income in this case is also $5 but this amount is equal to the difference between the increase in Accounts Receivable $15 and the increase in Accounts Payable $10 = $5 working capital increase. That is, net income here is equal to the additional accounts receivable on hand.

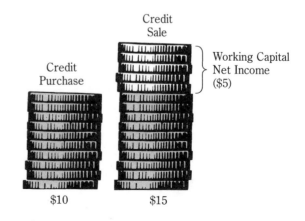

Credit Purchase

Credit Sale

Working Capital Net Income ($5)

$10 $15

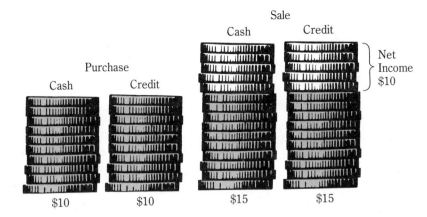

Example 3
- The entity has $10 cash on hand. A cash purchase of inventory unit is made for $10. This inventory unit is sold for $15 cash. Net income is $5 in this case and is equal to the increase of cash on hand ($15 − $10 = $5).
- A purchase of another inventory unit is for $10 on account. This inventory unit is sold for $15 on account. Net income is $5 in this case and is equal to the difference between the increase in Accounts Receivable ($15) and the increase in Accounts Payable ($10) = $5.

An income statement could be prepared at this point for this example, under both the accrual and cash basis.

Accrual Basis Income Statement

Sales ($15 cash sale + $15 credit sale)	$30
Cost of Sales ($10 cash purchase + $10 credit purchase)	20
Net Income (W/C provided)	$10

Cash Basis Income Statement

Sale ($15 cash sale)	$15
Cost of Sales ($10 cash purchase)	10
Net Income (Cash provided)	$ 5

The calculation of net income under the accrual basis results in a working capital provided by operations of $10. This method emphasizes the working capital flow resulting from operations and is in accordance with GAAP.

The calculation of net income under the cash basis results in cash provided by operations of $5. This method emphasizes the cash flow resulting from operations, but is not in accordance with GAAP.

Following GAAP, accountants prepare an income statement according to the accrual basis. The resulting net income incorporates cash inflows, as well as increases and decreases in the following current accounts:

Current Assets:	*Current Liabilities:*
Accounts Receivable (net)	Accounts Payable
Inventory	Accrued Liabilities
Prepaid Expenses (and Supplies)	Income Tax Payable

The preparation of an SCFP according to the cash flow definition requires a conversion of net income calculated on the accrual basis ($10) to net income calculated on the cash basis ($5). This conversion is made by adding and subtracting changes in non-cash current accounts that have accrued during the period. This summary shows how the conversion is prepared.

Add to Net Income:	Deduct from Net Income:
A decrease in any of the following current assets:	An increase in any of the following current assets:
1. Accounts Receivable (net)	1. Accounts Receivable (net)
2. Inventory	2. Inventory
3. Prepaid Expenses (or Supplies)	3. Prepaid Expenses (or Supplies)
An increase in any of the following current liabilities:	A decrease in any of the following current assets:
4. Accounts Payable	4. Accounts Payable
5. Accrued Liabilities	5. Accrued Liabilities
6. Income Tax Payable	6. Income Tax Payable

This summary can be viewed as a short-cut in the conversion of net income calculated on the accrual basis to net income calculated on the cash basis. You can check its applicability by calculating the net income on an accrual basis and comparing the amount with the calculated net income on a cash basis ($5).

Net Income (on the accrual basis)	$10	
Add: Increase in Accounts Payble	10	This amount is the same as that calculated in the cash basis income statement
	$20	
Less: Increase in Accounts Receivable	$15	
Net Income (on a cash basis)	$ 5	

From this calculation, it can be generalized that increases in applicable current liabilities are added to net income and that increases in non-cash current assets are deducted from net income, in calculating net income on a cash basis. Conversely, decreases in applicable current liabilities are deducted from net income, while decreases in non-cash current assets are added to net income.

Changes in current asset accounts (for example, Marketable Securities) and current liability accounts (for example, current portion of Long-Term Liabilities) that do not affect operations, are analyzed and shown separately on the SCFP.

In order to complete the cash flow analysis of Bluebeard Computer Corporation, the $326,000 (Net Income after Elimination of Non-cash Items) must be further converted into cash flow from operations. This analysis is made from an analysis of the balance sheet current accounts that affect the income statement.

(000s)

Current Assets	19X8	19X7	↑ or ↓	Current Liabilities	19X8	19X7	↑ or ↓
Accounts Receivable	$350	$400	↓ $ 50	Accounts Payable	$235	$145	↑ $ 90
Inventory	900	450	↑ 450	Accrued Liabilities	25	30	↓ 5
Prepaid Expenses	20	10	↑ 10	Income Tax Payble	40	25	↑ 15

The $326,000 calculation is then converted into cash flow from operations by adjusting for reported revenues that differed from cash actually received during the year and for reported expenses that differed from cash actually paid during the year.

(000s)

Net Income after Elimination of Non-cash Items		$326
Add: Decrease in Accounts Receivable	$ 50	
Increase in Accounts Payable	90	
Increase in Income Tax Payable	15	155
		$481
Less: Increase in Inventory	$450	
Increase in Prepaid Expenses	10	
Decrease in Accrued Liabilities	5	465
Cash Flow from Operations		$ 16

This analysis of current accounts focused only on those current accounts that affected the income statement. There are, however, other current accounts that do not interact with the income statement. These include the current asset, Marketable Securities, and the current liabilities, Dividends Payable and the current portion of long-term debt. These current accounts must also be analyzed before the statement of cash flow can be prepared.

(000s)

Current Assets	19X8	19X7	↑or↓	*Current Liabilities*	19X8	19X7	↑or↓
Marketable Securities	$25	$50	↓$25	Dividends Payble	–	–	–
				Current Portion of Long-Term Debt	–	–	–

Here, cash flows were increased by the decrease in Marketable Securities and are included in the SCFP. Since dividends declared during the year were also paid, cash was decreased by the amount of these dividends. There is no change to cash flows resulting from dividends declared but unpaid. Dividends declared but unpaid would be excluded from the SCFP prepared, according to the cash definition of funds.

Step 3: Preparation of the Formal Statement of Cash Flow

On the basis of the analysis of balance sheet accounts (including the cash flow from

Bluebeard Computer Corporation
Statement of Cash Flow
For the Year Ended December 31, 19X8

(000s)

CASH FLOW GENERATED (deployed):			
From Operations			$ 16
Financing:			
Increase in Mortgage		$ 500	
Issue of Common Stock		410	
Total		$ 910	
Payment of Dividends		(58)	852
			$ 868
Investing:			
Disposal of Marketable Securities		$ 25	
Sale of Investments		104	
Sale of Machinery		30	
Total		$ 159	
Purchase of Building	$(800)		
Purchase of Machinery	(350)	(1,150)	
			(991)
Net Cash Generated (Deployed)			$(123)

operations, included in Retained Earnings), the formal statement of cash flow can now be prepared as shown on page 725. Note that all cash inflows and outflows are summarized here from financing and investing activities and that the calculation of cash flow from operations is also included.

This statement of cash flow explains what cash inflows and outflows occurred during the period resulting in a cash decrease of $123,000. This cash flow information interpreted in conjunction with other financial statement analysis is useful to assess Bluebeard Computer Corporation's cash management and liquidity.

Non-cash Financing and Investing Activities   Significant financing and investing activities that do not affect cash are also included in the statement of cash flow. For example, assume that in addition to the transactions described earlier, BCC had also purchased additional land (an investing activity) through the issue of common stock (a financing activity). Although no cash was involved and common stock was issued directly to the owners of the land, the transaction must be disclosed as both an investing and financing activity on the statement of cash flow.

C.   Funds as Working Capital

Working capital definition of funds
The preparation of an SCFP to show those changes in non-current balance sheet accounts that affected the entity's sources and uses of working capital.

Although *funds* may be synonymous with cash to the average person, to accountants *funds* may also refer to the difference between current assets and current liabilities, which is also called **working capital**.

$$\text{Current Assets} - \text{Current Liabilities} = \text{Working Capital (funds)}$$

Working Capital from Operations

Every company continuously repeats a particular operating cycle. Inventory is purchased on credit; an accounts receivable is recorded when a sale is made; and cash increases are recorded when the receivable is collected. As long as the company is profitable — that is, more is collected from each sale than was paid for each item purchased — working capital is generated. This cycle and the generation of a "pool" of working capital (the excess of current assets over current liabilities) from operations is illustrated in Figure 16-3.

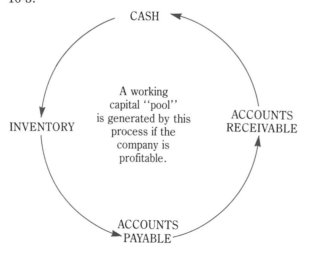

Figure 16-3   The generation of working capital

Note that the balance sheet accounts in the operating cycle are current asset and current liability accounts. Accounts that fall under the headings of current assets and liabilities are listed below.

> *Balance Sheet Accounts Involved in Working Capital:*
> Cash, Accounts Receivable, Inventory, Prepaid Expenses, Accounts Payable, Accruals, Income Tax Payable

Working Capital from Other Activities

Working capital is also injected into the operating cycle by other activities of a company, such as the sale of non-current assets, the issue of long-term debt, and the issue of share capital. Therefore, in addition to working capital generated by operations, other sources may also increase the working capital pool.

How is working capital depleted? Working capital is continuously being depleted by a company's activities; these reductions are referred to as *uses of working capital*. Various activities result in a use of working capital, such as the purchase of non-current assets, retirement of long-term debt, and declaration of dividends. In actual practice, of course, the amount of working capital (the pool) increases and decreases continuously as working capital is injected and depleted. At any particular point in time, accountants need to be able to

1. Measure the amount of working capital that actually exists in a company
2. Calculate whether working capital has increased or decreased over a period of time
3. Analyze what has caused working capital to increase or decrease over this time period
4. Prepare a report showing the detailed increases and decreases of working capital. This report is called a statement of changes in financial position.

Analyzing Funds Flow

Measuring the Amount of Working Capital

At any one point in time, the amount of working capital can be calculated as follows:

(000s)

	19X8
Current Assets	$1,322
− Current Liabilities	300
= Working Capital	$1,022

In this example, Bluebeard's current assets exceed current liabilities and its working capital amounts to $1,022,000. This information is useful to the reader of financial statements because it is one indication of BCC's ability to pay its debts.

Step 1: Calculating Whether Working Capital Has Increased or Decreased

Although the calculation of working capital at a particular point in time is useful, the information is more useful to the reader when it is also indicated whether working capital has increased or decreased over a period of time.

	(000s)	
	19X8	19X7
Current Assets	$1,322	$1,060
− Current Liabilities	300	200
= Working Capital	$1,022	$860

Net increase in working capital = $162,000 ($1,022,000 − 860,000).

In this comparison of working capital from 19X7 to 19X8, the amount of working capital is shown to have increased by $162,000. This information tells the reader that this company's ability to pay its debts from working capital has strengthened during the year.

Step 2: Analyzing the Increase or Decrease in Working Capital

It is important to be able to uncover the transactions that caused working capital to change (increase or decrease) during the year. This analysis is not always easy and, initially, may present some difficulty for students. Essentially, the reasons for a change in working capital are identified through an analysis of transactions recorded in the books of the entity. These transactions may involve: type A — only current accounts; type B — only non-current accounts; or type C — both current and non-current accounts. It is only through the third type of transactions (type C) that increases (from sources) and decreases (though uses) of working capital occur.

Balance Sheet Format

Assets	*Liabilities and Equity*
Current Assets ⟵⟶	Current Liabilities
Non-current Assets	Non-current Liabilities Equity

Type A Transactions

Type A transactions are illustrated in the above balance sheet format. The two-headed arrows represent a transaction involving two accounts. Type A transactions involve two current asset accounts, two current liability accounts, or one of each.

Note that type A transactions do not cross the black line; that is, *they do not cause a change in working capital*. These transactions record changes *within* the working capital pool.

Balance Sheet Format

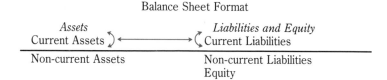

Assets	*Liabilities and Equity*
Current Assets	Current Liabilities
Non-current Assets ⟵⟶	Non-current Liabilities Equity

Type B Transactions

Type B transactions are illustrated in the above balance sheet format. Note that this type of transaction also does not cross the black line, and therefore also does not involve current asset or current liability accounts. Type B transactions involve two accounts from among non-current assets, non-current liabilities, and equity.

Balance Sheet Format

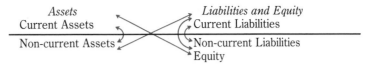

Assets / *Liabilities and Equity*
Current Assets / Current Liabilities
Non-current Assets / Non-current Liabilities / Equity

Type C Transactions

Type C transactions are illustrated in the above balance sheet format. Notice that all possible Type C transactions *do cross* the bold black line; that is, they affect a current account (a working capital account) and a non-current account. If any transaction crosses the black line, working capital is changed; this rule can be used in analyzing transactions.

One other variable has to be explained before proceeding to analyze transactions involving the flow of funds. If a transaction crosses the black line (for example, if a truck — a non-current asset — is purchased for cash — a current asset), is working capital increased or decreased? In the example given, working capital is *decreased* because cash, a working capital account, is decreased.

> 1. If a transaction crosses the black line, working capital is changed by it.
> 2. If a current asset account is decreased, working capital is decreased; if a current asset account is increased, working capital is increased.
> 3. If a current liability account is decreased, working capital is increased; if a current liability account is increased, working capital is decreased.

D. Analyzing Type C Transactions

The following transactions affecting current and non-current balance sheet accounts occurred during the year in Bluebeard Computer Corporation.

Transaction 1

Investments costing $80,000 were sold for $104,000. This transaction increased Cash, a working capital account, and decreased Investments, a non-current account. Here is the journal entry recorded at the time of the sale.

This example shows a change in a non-current account that results in an inflow of working capital.

			Effect on Working Capital	
			Increase	*Decrease*
Cash	104,000		104,000	
Investments		80,000		
Gain on Sale		24,000		

Because Cash, a working capital account, was increased, working capital was increased.

Transaction 2

A building was purchased for $800,000 cash. This transaction reduced Cash, a working capital account, and also increased Building, a non-current account. Here is the journal entry to record the purchase.

This example shows a change in a non-current account that results in an outflow of working capital.

			Effect on Working Capital	
			Increase	*Decrease*
Building	800,000			
Cash		800,000		800,000

Because Cash, a working capital account, was decreased, working capital was decreased.

Transaction 3a and 3b

Machinery costing $350,000 was purchased for cash, and machinery costing $50,000 and having accumulated depreciation of $10,000, was sold for $30,000 credit. These transactions should be analyzed separately to determine their effect on working capital. The purchase of machinery decreased Cash, a working capital account, and increased Machinery, a non-current account. Here is the journal entry recorded at the time of purchase.

> These examples are of change in a non-current account when there is both an outflow and an inflow of working capital.

		Effect on Working Capital	
		Increase	*Decrease*
Machinery	350		
Cash		350	350

The decrease of Cash, a working capital account, also decreased working capital. The sale of machinery increased Accounts Receivable, a working capital account. This transaction was recorded as follows.

		Effect on Working Capital	
		Increase	*Decrease*
Accounts Receivable	30,000	30,000	
Accumulated Depreciation	10,000		
Loss on Disposal	10,000		
Machinery		50,000	

Note that the sale of this machinery resulted in a $10,000 loss, which is discussed later. Working capital was increased by $30,000.

Transaction 4

Depreciation expense of $260,000 was recorded during the year. Here is the journal entry to record this depreciation.

> This example is of a change in a non-current account when there is no inflow or outflow of working capital.

		Effect on Working Capital	
		Increase	*Decrease*
Depreciation Expense	260,000		
Accumulated Depreciation		260,000	–	–

Working capital account was neither increased nor decreased; therefore, the recording of depreciation expense produced no effect on working capital.

Transaction 5

BCC borrowed $500,000 cash as a mortgage payable during the year. This transaction increased Cash, a working capital account, and also increased Mortgage Payable, a non-current liability account. The following journal entry was made.

		Effect on Working Capital	
		Increase	*Decrease*
Cash	500,000	500,000	
Mortgage Payable		500,000	

The increase in cash resulted in a working capital increase.

Transaction 6:

Common shares with a par-value of $300,000 were sold for $410,000 cash. This transaction included a $110,000 premium on common shares, and the following journal entry was made:

			Effect on Working Capital	
			Increase	*Decrease*
Cash	410,000		410,000	
Common Shares		300,000		
Premium on Common Shares		110,000		

A working capital account, Cash, was increased in this transaction, which also increased two non-current equity accounts. Working capital was increased by $410,000.

Transactions 7a and 7b

Retained Earnings were reduced by the declaration of $58,000-worth of dividends during the year, and increased by $80,000 net income for the year. These transactions should be analyzed separately to determine their effect on working capital. The declaration of dividends created a decrease in Cash and decreased the non-current account, Retained Earnings. The dividend declaration was recorded as follows:

			Effect on Working Capital	
			Increase	*Decrease*
Dividends	58,000			
Cash			58,000	58,000

Since a current asset account, Cash, is decreased in this declaration of dividends, working capital is decreased. (The company paid the dividends to shareholders.) The Dividends account is closed to Retained Earnings at year-end, thereby decreasing this non-current equity account.

Does the $80,000 increase in Retained Earnings resulting from net income for the year affect working capital? Study the following balance sheet format, which includes the difference between revenue and expenses for a time period. In actual fact, the net income is part of the balance sheet account Retained Earnings.

Balance Sheet Format

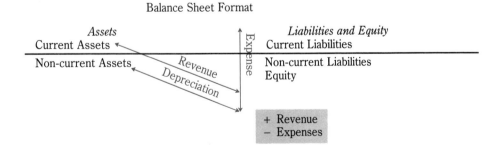

Revenue from sales increases current asset accounts (Accounts Receivable and Cash, for example), which increases working capital. Therefore, revenue from sales increases working capital. Incurring expenses increases Accounts Payable, a current liability account, or decreases Cash, a current asset account; working capital is thereby decreased. There is another category of expense that does not affect any current account — depreciation expense, for example. The recording of depreciation does not cross the black line. There are also other expenses and revenues that are only involved in transactions that do not cross the black line. These items, therefore, do not affect working capital; they are listed below:

Revenues Included in Net Income:	*Expenses Included in Net Income:*
Amortization of Bond Premium	Depreciation of Fixed Assets
Gain on Sale of Non-current Assets	Depletion of Wasting Assets
	Amortization of Intangible Assets (eg, Patents)
	Amortization of Bond Discount
	Losses on Sale of Non-current Assets

For example, a $24,000 gain on the sale of investments was recorded in transaction 1. The following journal entry recording the sale was made:

			Effect on Working Capital	
			Increase	*Decrease*
Cash	104,000		104,000	
Investments		80,000		
Gain on Sale		24,000		

Because Cash, a working capital account, was increased, working capital was increased. Study the following balance sheet format to see how this transaction affected the current (working capital) and non-current accounts.

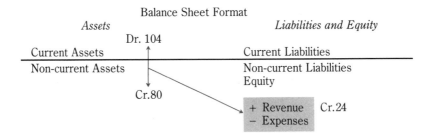

Obviously, a working capital increase of $104,000 results from this transaction. This $104,000 consists of the original costs of the investments and the $24,000 gain on their sale. Since the $24,000 gain is already included in the proceeds from sale of investments, it is excluded when calculating the working capital amount provided by operations.

An analysis of the income statement components is necessary to determine whether the $80,000 increase in Retained Earnings resulting from net income for the year increased working capital by $80,000. Study the following comparative income statements.

Income Statements
(000s)

	Basis 1 (Including items that do not affect working capital)		Basis 2 (Excluding items that do not affect working capital)	
Sales		+ $1,200		+ $1,200
Cost of Goods Sold		− 674		− 674
Gross Profit on Sales		+ $ 526		+ $ 526
Operating Expenses:				
Depreciation	− $260		-0-	
Other Expenses	− 200	− 460	− $200	− 200
Net Income from Operations:		+ $ 66		+ $ 326
Gain on Sale of Investment	+ $ 24		-0-	
Loss on Sale of Machinery	− (10)	14	-0-	-0-
Net Income		+ $ 80		+ $ 326

This comparison shows that, while $80,000 net income resulted during the year, working capital actually increased by $326,000. In other words, the increases and decreases in current asset and current liability accounts during the year resulted in a $326,000 net increase in working capital. This $326,000 increase is a source of funds and is labelled by accountants as "the amount of working capital provided by operations".

It is customary to provide with the SCFP a detailed reconciliation of the net income for the year and the increase in working capital provided by operations. The reconciliation is made as shown below.

(000s)
Calculation of Working Capital Provided by Operations

Net Income		$ 80
Add: Non-working Capital Charges against Operations:		
Deprec. of Building and Machinery	$260	
Loss on Sale of Machinery	10	270
Total		$350
Less: Non-working Capital Credits to Operations:		
Gain on Sale of Investments		24
Working Capital Provided by Operations		$326

> This amount is the working capital generated by operations.

Students sometimes find the calculation of the amount of working capital provided by operations a difficult concept, because it works backward from the net income figure. However, it is faster than preparing an income statement as was done in Basis 2.

A summary of the items that do not affect working capital and must be excluded in calculating the working capital provided by operations is given below. This is a handy reference when making this type of calculation.

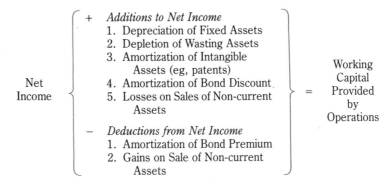

All the preceding items involve transactions in non-current accounts. They do not affect current asset or liability accounts and, therefore, are excluded from the amount of working capital provided by operations.

Step 3: Reporting the Increase or Decrease in Working Capital

A report can now be prepared to indicate the increases and decreases in working capital that occurred during the year. This report is called a statement of changes in financial position. Note that all increases and decreases analyzed in the seven BCC transactions are recorded here.

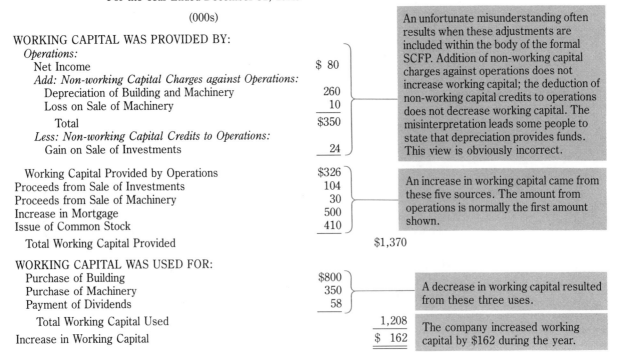

Bluebeard Computer Corporation
Statement of Changes in Financial Position
For the Year Ended December 31, 19X8

(000s)

WORKING CAPITAL WAS PROVIDED BY:
Operations:
Net Income	$ 80
Add: Non-working Capital Charges against Operations:	
Depreciation of Building and Machinery	260
Loss on Sale of Machinery	10
Total	$350
Less: Non-working Capital Credits to Operations:	
Gain on Sale of Investments	24

Working Capital Provided by Operations	$326	
Proceeds from Sale of Investments	104	
Proceeds from Sale of Machinery	30	
Increase in Mortgage	500	
Issue of Common Stock	410	
Total Working Capital Provided		$1,370

WORKING CAPITAL WAS USED FOR:
Purchase of Building	$800	
Purchase of Machinery	350	
Payment of Dividends	58	
Total Working Capital Used		1,208
Increase in Working Capital		$ 162

An unfortunate misunderstanding often results when these adjustments are included within the body of the formal SCFP. Addition of non-working capital charges against operations does not increase working capital; the deduction of non-working capital credits to operations does not decrease working capital. The misinterpretation leads some people to state that depreciation provides funds. This view is obviously incorrect.

An increase in working capital came from these five sources. The amount from operations is normally the first amount shown.

A decrease in working capital resulted from these three uses.

The company increased working capital by $162 during the year.

The preparation of this SCFP follows the usual format of adjusting net income by adding back non-working capital charges against operations and by deducting non-working capital credits to operations. These additions and deductions represent items that did not affect the inflow and outflow of funds from operations of the entity. The resulting amount — working capital provided by operations — represents the actual amount of funds inflow from operations. The inclusion of these additions to and deductions from net income often results in readers of financial statements misinterpreting these adjustments as inflows or outflows of funds. Thus, some people assume that depreciation provides funds. In actual practice, these adjustments should be excluded from the body of the formal SCFP; rather, they should be disclosed in a separate schedule elsewhere. The SCFP should list the amount of working capital provided (or used, in the case of a net loss) from operations with the other items on the statement. Any misunderstanding would then be minimized.

APPENDIX: The T-Account Method of SCFP Preparation

T-account method
The use of T-accounts in analyzing non-current accounts when preparing an SCFP.

Although the statement of changes in financial position can be prepared without a complex methodology in simple situations, the numerous transactions that occur in actual practice necessitate some systematic approach to analysis. The so-called **T-account method** requires that a T-account be set up for each non-current asset, liability, and equity account: the net change that occurred in each of these accounts during the year is entered in the T-account. In this section, the T-account method is explained, using the seven transactions of Bluebeard Computer Corporation that are discussed earlier in the chapter.

Comparative balance sheets for 19X8 and 19X7 are shown below, along with notes. Notice that the net change in each current and non-current account has been already calculated for you. Recalculate the amounts to assure yourself that they are accurate. Notice that the change in working capital is $162.

Bluebeard Computer Corporation
Comparative Balance Sheets
At December 31, 19X8 and 19X7

(000s)

Assets	19X8	19X7	Increase or (Decrease)	
Current Assets	$1,322	$1,060	262	
Investments (long-term)	140	220	(80)	
				Increases in non-current assets are recorded on the debit side of the T-accounts used in Step 2; decreases are recorded on the credit side.
FIXED ASSETS:				
Land	70	70	-0-	
Buildings	1,200	400	800	
Machinery	1,000	700	300[2]	
Accumulated Depreciation	(550)	(300)	(250)[1]	
Total Fixed Assets	1,720	870		
Total Assets	$3,182	$2,150		Working capital increased by $162,000 during the year ($262,000 − $100,000).
Liabilities and Shareholders' Equity				
Current Liabilities	$ 300	$ 200	100	
LONG-TERM LIABILITIES:				
Mortgage Payable	1,000	500	500	
				Increases in liability and equity items are recorded on the credit side of the T-accounts used in Step 2; decreases, if any, are recorded on the debit side.
SHAREHOLDER'S EQUITY:				
Common Stock	1,100	800	300	
Premium on Common Stock	110	-0-	110	
Retained Earnings	672	650	22[3]	
Total Shareholders' Equity	1,882	1,450		
Total Liabilities and Shareholders' Equity	$3,182	$2,150		

Notes:
1. This item represents an increase in an asset contra account, which in turn represents a decrease in an asset account.
2. Machinery costing $50,000 with accumulated depreciation of $10,000 was sold for $30,000 cash.
3. Dividends of $58,000 were declared and paid at the end of 19X8.

Additional information about the company is also provided in the income statement for 19X8.

Income Statement
For the Year Ended December 31, 19X8
(000s)

Sales		$1,200
Cost of Goods Sold		674
Gross Profit		$ 526
Operating Expenses:		
Depreciation — Buildings & Machinery	$260	
Other Expenses	200	460
		$ 66
Income from Operations		
Gain on Sale of Long-Term Investment	$24	
Loss on Sale of Machinery	(10)	14
Net Income		$ 80

The preparation of an SCFP was shown earlier using three steps. The T-account methodology is essentially the same, although six individual steps are identified and used in this section for clarity.

Step 1

Calculate net increase or decrease in working capital during the period.

	19X8	19X7
	(000s)	
Current Assets	$1,322	$1,060
− Current Liabilities	300	200
= Working Capital	$1,022	860

Net Increase in Working Capital: $1,022,000 − $860,000 = $162,000

Step 2

Set up special T-accounts for each non-current (ie, non-working capital) account reported in the comparative balance sheets, and record the net increase or decrease of each non-current account on each T-account. Under the amount draw a line, as illustrated below. The Investments and Mortgage Payable accounts are shown in this example.

T-accounts are opened for:
Investments
Land
Buildings
Machinery
Accumulated Depreciation
Mortgage Payable
Common Stock
Premium on Common Stock
Retained Earnings

Investments

	80,000
Increases in long-term assets are recorded on this side.	Decreases in long-term assets are recorded on this side.

Mortgage Payable

	500,000
Decreases in liability and equity accounts are recorded on this side.	Increases in liability and equity accounts are recorded on this side.

These T-accounts are only used in preparation of the SCFP. They are not part of the general ledger.

Working Capital Summary
An account used in the T-account method of preparing an SCFP; records sources on the debit side and uses on the credit side.

Operations Summary
An account used in the T-account method of preparing an SCFP; used to determine the amount of working capital provided by operations.

Step 3

Set up two additional special T-accounts for **Working Capital Summary** and **Operations Summary**. Then record the net increase or decrease in working capital calculated in Step 1 into the Working Capital Summary account. Under the amount draw a line, as illustrated below.

Working Capital Summary	
162,000	
Increases in working capital are recorded on this side.	Decreases in working capital are recorded on this side.

This account is used in Step 4 to determine which non-current items caused working capital to increase by $162,000.

Operations Summary

No entry is made in this account at this time.

This account is used in Step 4 to determine the amount of working capital provided by operations.

Step 4

Analyze the change in each non-current account in order to identify the transactions that are summarized by the amounts recorded in Steps 2 and 3. The individual transactions summarized by net changes entered above are reconstructed, with journal entries for each transaction. The reconstructed amounts are then entered below the horizontal line of the appropriate T-accounts and must balance with the amount recorded above the line.

Each non-current balance sheet item is analyzed, and a journal entry is prepared and posted to the appropriate T-accounts set up in Steps 2 and 3.

Transaction 1:

The asset account, Investments, is the first non-current account on the balance sheet.

	19X8	19X7	(*Decrease*)
Investments	$140,000	$220,000	$(80,000)

This $80,000 decrease resulted from the sale of investments during the year. The original journal entry is shown again below to help students to understand the T-account entry. This transaction provided funds for the company and, therefore, Working Capital Summary is debited (*a debit to this account records an increase, or source, of working capital*). This accounts for part of the $162,000 increase in working capital in 19X8.

The Investments account is credited because the asset was decreased by the sale, and Operations Summary is credited because the gain appears on the income statement. The T-accounts required in Steps 2 and 3 appear below the journal entries.

Original Journal Entry:			*T-Account Entry:*		
Cash	104,000		Working Capital Summary	104,000	
Investments		80,000	Investments		80,000
Gain on Sale		24,000	Operations Summary		24,000

Working Capital Summary			Investments			Operations Summary	
162,000				80,000			
(1) 104,000			(1) 80,000				(1) 24,000

The increase in working capital from the sale of investments amounted to $104,000.

Since the balance below the line is the same as above the line, it is known that the increase in working capital resulted from this sale of Investments.

The effect on working capital provided by operations is recorded in this account.

It is a good idea to indicate in the Investments T-account that no further analysis is required for this non-current asset. An equals sign (=) written across the vertical line of the T-account (as shown) is a good way to show that all analysis in the Investments account has been completed.

Transaction 2:

The asset account, Land, is the next non-current account on the balance sheet requiring analysis.

	19X8	19X7	*Increase*
Land	$70,000	$70,000	–

As can be seen, there is no change in the amount between 19X7 and 19X8. This does not necessarily mean that no transactions took place during the year; however, since there is no evidence to the contrary, it must be assumed that none did. Therefore, the non-current Building account, is the next to be considered.

	19X8	19X7	*Increase*
Building	$1,200,000	$400,000	$800,000

This $800,000 increase resulted from a purchase made during the year. The purchase represented a use of working capital. The original journal entry is shown again to make it easier for students to understand the T-account entry. The T-account entry for the building purchase is then posted.

Original Journal Entry:			*T-Account Entry:*	
Building	800,000		Building	800,000
Cash		800,000	Working Capital Summary	800,000

Building			Working Capital Summary	
800,000			162,000	
(2) 800,000				(2) 800,000

> Since the balance below the line is the same as that above the line it is known that a decrease in working capital resulted from this purchase of a building.

> The decrease in working capital from the purchase of a building amounted to $800,000.

Transactions 3a and 3b:

Machinery is the next non-current account to be analyzed.

	19X8	19X7	*Increase*
Machinery	$1,000,000	$700,000	$300,000

a. Note 2 to the balance sheets indicated that machinery costing $50,000 and having accumulated depreciation of $10,000 was sold for $30,000 cash. The original recording of this transaction and its reconstruction are shown below.

Original Journal Entry:			*T-Account Entry:*	
Cash	30,000		Working Capital Summary	30,000
Accumulated Depreciation	10,000		Accumulated Depreciation	10,000
Loss on Sale	10,000		Operations Summary	10,000
Machinery		50,000	Machinery	50,000

This sale provided a $30,000 source of funds and, therefore, the Working Capital Summary account is debited. Accumulated Depreciation is also debited, because the accumulated depreciation applicable to the sold machinery has to be removed. Machinery is credited to remove the cost of machinery from the accounts; the loss on sale is debited to Operations Summary because the loss appears on the income statement. The T-accounts required in Steps 2 and 3 are posted.

Working Capital Summary		Accumulated Depreciation		Operations Summary		Machinery	
162,000			250,000	(3) 10,000		300,000	
(3) 30,000		(3) 10,000					(3) 50,000

An increase in working capital is recorded as a debit.	The balance in this account is considered in the next transaction (4).	The effect on working capital provided by operations is recorded in this account.	The balance below the line is not the same as above the line, an additional transaction for $350,000 was recorded.

b. Machinery costing $350,000 was purchased for cash. The original recording of this transaction and its reconstruction are shown below. This $350,000 purchase of machinery represents a use of working capital and, therefore, Working Capital Summary is credited. The T-accounts required in Steps 2 and 3 are then posted.

Original Journal Entry:			*T-Account Entry:*	
Machinery	350,000		Machinery	350,000
Cash		350,000	Working Capital Summary	350,000

Machinery		Working Capital Summary	
300,000		162,000	
	(3) 50,000	(3) 30,000	
(3) 350,000			(3) 350,000
300,000			

The balance above and below are now the same.	A decrease in working capital is recorded as a credit.

Transaction 4:

Accumulated Depreciation is the next non-current account to be analyzed.

	19X8	19X7	*Decrease*
Accumulated Depreciation	$(550,000)	$(300,000)	$(250,000)

According to the Income Statement, depreciation expense amounting to $260,000 was recorded during the year. The original journal entry and its reconstruction are shown below.

Original Journal Entry:			*T-Account Entry:*	
Depreciation Expense	260,000		Operations Summary	260,000
Accumulated Depreciation		260,000	Accumulated Depreciation	260,000

Depreciation expense is an item that appears on the income statement and, therefore, the Operations Summary account is debited. The T-accounts required in Steps 2 and 3 then appear as follows:

Operations Summary		Accumulated Depreciation	
(4) 260,000			250,000
		(3) 10,000	
			(4) 260,000
			250,000

The effect on working capital provided by operations is recorded in this account.

Since the balance below the line agrees with the balance above the line, all transactions in this account have been analyzed.

Transaction 5:

Mortgage Payable is a non-current liability account that is analyzed next.

	19X8	19X7	*Increase*
Mortgage Payable	$1,000,000	$500,000	$500,000

A $500,000 mortgage payment was made during the year. The original journal entry and its reconstruction are shown below. The mortgage increase is a source of funds; therefore, Working Capital Summary is debited. Mortgage Payable is credited to record the liability in the company's records. The T-account entry is posted, as required in steps 2 and 3.

Original Journal Entry:

| Cash | 500,000 | |
| Mortgage Payable | | 500,000 |

T-Account Entry:

| Working Capital Summary | 500,000 | |
| Mortgage Payable | | 500,000 |

Working Capital Summary		Mortgage Payable	
162,000			500,000
(5) 500,000			(5) 500,000

An increase in working capital is recorded by a debit.

Since the balances below and above the line are the same, all transactions in this account have been analyzed.

Transaction 6:

Common Stock and Premium on Common Stock are analyzed next.

	19X8	19X7	*Increase*
Common Stock	$1,100,000	$800,000	$300,000
Premium or Common Stock	110,000	-0-	110,000

Common shares with a par-value of $300,000 were sold for $410,000. The original journal entry and its reconstruction are shown below. The sale of common shares provided a source of funds and, therefore, Working Capital Summary is debited. Common Stock and Premium on Common Stock are credited to record the sale in the company's accounts. As required in Steps 2 and 3, the T-account entry is posted.

	Original Journal Entry			T-Account Entry	
Cash	410,000		Working Capital Summary	410,000	
Common Stock		300,000	Common Stock		300,000
Premium on			Premium on		
Common Stock		110,000	Common Stock		110,000

Working Capital Summary		Common Stock		Premium Common Stock	
162,000			300,000		110,000
(6) 410,000		(6)	300,000	(6)	110,000

> An increase in working capital is recorded by a debit.

> The balances below and above the line are the same; therefore all transactions in these accounts have been analyzed.

Transactions 7a and 7b:

Retained Earnings is the last non-current account on the balance sheet to be analyzed.

	19X8	19X7	Increase
Retained Earnings	$672,000	$650,000	$22,000

a. Note 3 of the balance sheets indicated that dividends of $58,000 were declared and paid at the end of the year. The original journal entry to record this dividend declaration and payment and its reconstruction are reproduced below. The declaration and payment of dividends decreases a current asset and therefore is a use of working capital. The Dividends account is closed to Retained Earnings at year-end, thereby decreasing this non-current equity account. As required in steps 2 and 3, the T-account entry is posted.

	Original Journal Entry:			T-Account Entry:	
Dividends	58,000		Dividends		58,000
Cash		58,000	Working Capital Summary		58,000

Retained Earnings			Working Capital Summary		
	22,000	162,000			
(7) 58,000				(7)	58,000

> The balance below the line is not the same as the balance above the line; an additional transaction remains to be analyzed.

> A decrease in working capital is recorded by a credit

b. Net Income for the year is $80,000. The original entry recording Net Income in Retained Earnings was made by means of a closing entry. The original closing entry and its reconstruction are shown below. Net income is recorded in Operations Summary because it comes from the income statement; Retained Earnings is credited because net income increases this account.

	Original Entry:			T-Account Entry:	
Income Summary	80,000		Operations Summary	80,000	
Retained Earnings		80,000	Retained Earnings		80,000

Operations Summary	
(7) 80,000	

Retained Earnings		
		22,000
(7)	58,000	
	(7)	80,000
		22,000

> The effect on working capital provided by operations is recorded in this account.

> The balances below and above the line are now the same; therefore all transactions affecting this account have been analyzed.

Step 5:

The amounts in the Operations Summary account are recorded in the formal SCFP in adjustments to the reported net income amount in order to calculate the working capital provided by operations. This balance is now transferred to Working Capital Summary by the following journal entry. (This transaction can be numbered 8 for reference.)

Working Capital Summary	326,000	
Operations Summary		326,000

This debit records the increase in working capital that resulted from operations.

When this entry is posted, the Operations Summary account appears as follows:

Operations Summary (000s)

(3) Loss on Sale of		(1) Gain on sale of		
Machinery	10	Investments	24	
(4) Depreciation of Buildings		(8) Working Capital		
and Machinery	260	Provided by Operations	326	
(7) Net Income	80			
	350		350	

Explanations are required.

Following the transfer of the $326,000 working capital provided to operations by Transaction 8, the Working Capital Summary account appears as follows:

Working Capital Summary (000s)

	162		
(1) Sale of Investments	104	(2) Purchase of Building	800
(3) Sale of Machinery	30	(3) Purchase of Machinery	350
(5) Increase in Mortgage	500	(7) Payment of Dividends	58
(6) Issue of Common			
Stock at Premium	410		
(8) Working Capital			
Provided by Operations	326		
	1,370		1,208
Balance	162		

These are sources of working capital.   These are uses of working capital.

Explanations are required.

The details recorded in this account are used to record the sources and uses of working capital on the SCFP.

Following the analysis in Steps 4 and 5, the net change in working capital calculated in Step 3 agrees with the balance in this account.

This account now indicates what caused the working capital to increase by $162,000; notice that the $162,000 net change in working capital entered in Step 3 balances with the $162,000 balance in this account. Therefore, all transactions affecting working capital have been analyzed.

Notice that explanations are provided for each of the entries in the Operations Summary and Working Capital Summary. These explanations in the Working Capital Summary account help prepare the SCFP in Step 6.

Step 6

Prepare the SCFP from details appearing in the Working Capital Summary account, indicating the sources and uses of working capital. Use the details appearing in the Operations Summary account to calculate working capital provided by operations.

Bluebeard Computer Corporation
Statement of Changes in Financial Position
For the Year Ended December 31, 19X8
(000s)

WORKING CAPITAL WAS PROVIDED BY:

Operations:

Net Income	$ 80	
Add: Non-working Capital Charges against Operations:		
Depreciation of Building and Machinery	260	
Loss on Sale of Machinery	10	
Total	$350	
Less: Non-working Capital Credits to Operations:		
Gain on Sale of Investments	24	
Working Capital Provided by Operations	$326	
Proceeds from Sale of Investments	104	
Proceeds from Sale of Machinery	30	
Increase in Mortgage	500	
Issue of Common Stock	410	
Total Working Capital Provided		$1,370

The working capital provided by operations is calculated in this part of this statement.

An increase in working capital came from these five sources.

WORKING CAPITAL WAS USED FOR:

Purchase of Building	$800	
Purchase of Machinery	350	
Payment of Dividends	58	
Total Working Capital Used		1,208
Increase in Working Capital		$ 162

A decrease in working capital resulted from these three uses.

The company increased working capital by $162,000 during the year.

A S S I G N M E N T   M A T E R I A L S

Discussion Questions

1. Using an example, explain in your own words the function of a statement of changes in financial position. Why is it prepared? What does it communicate to the reader of financial statements? What is its advantage over a balance sheet?
2. Why are financing and investing activities of a corporation important to financial statement readers?
3. What is cash flow? How does the cash flow definition of funds differ from the working capital definition?
4. Why is the cash flow from operations usually different from the working capital provided by operations? Which method is required for preparing an SCFP under generally accepted accounting principles?
5. What is the advantage of an SCFP prepared according to the cash flow definition of funds? Why is such a statement usually prepared for management purposes, rather than for readers of financial statements?
6. Explain in your own words how an increase in accounts receivable during the year affects the cash provided by operations? a decrease in accounts receivable?
7. Is a cash flow SCFP really only a summary of cash receipts and disbursements recorded in the corporation's Cash account?
8. What effect does the declaration of a cash dividend have on cash flow? the payment of a dividend declared and paid during the current year? the payment of a dividend declared in the preceding year?
9. Why does an increase or a decrease in the Marketable Securities account not affect the amount of cash provided by operations?
10. Why is it possible that cash may have decreased during the year, even though there has been a substantial net income during the same period?
11. What does the word *funds* mean when used in relation to an SCFP? Explain each of the different definitions of *funds*.
12. Define *working capital*. Why does depreciation not affect working capital? Explain with an example.
13. Operations are said to increase or decrease the so-called working capital pool. How is this pool increased? decreased?
14. Why does the net income for the year usually differ from the increase (decrease) in working capital for the same year? What causes the difference?
15. What causes working capital to be depleted? Give actual examples of items that cause an outflow of working capital.
16. Indicate the main items that use working capital. Explain how balance sheet items are analyzed to identify the uses that have occurred during the year.
17. Why are only non-current balance sheet accounts analyzed in the preparation of an SCFP under the working capital definition of funds?
18. The T-account method is often used for instructional purposes in illustrating the preparation of an SCFP. How does the T-account method work?
19. What is the basic format of an SCFP? Prepare a model format.
20. From your reading of Real Life Example 16-1 and Conceptual Issue 16-1, do you feel that two SCFP's should be prepared: one using cash flow and one using working capital? Discuss.

Discussion Cases

Discussion Case 16-1:   Statement of Cash Flow Decisions

Following are two presentations of cash flows. Comment on the accounting policies and decisions that affect each one.

Statement of Cash Flow
Company A

Operating		
Cash from operations		XX
Financing		
Proceeds from issue of common shares	XX	
Repayment of long-term debt	(XX)	
Borrowing of long-term debt	XX	
Dividends paid	(XX)	
		XX
Investing		
Acquisition of property	(XX)	
Proceeds from sale of plant	XX	
		XX
Net cash generated (deployed)		XX

Statement of Cash Flow
Company B

Operating		
Cash from operations	XX	
Payments for operating, selling, and admin. exp.	(XX)	
Interest paid	(XX)	
Income tax paid	(XX)	
Dividends paid	(XX)	
		XX
Financing		
Proceeds from issue of secured debentures	XX	
Redemption of common shares	(XX)	
		XX
Investing		
Acquisition of property, plant and equipment	(XX)	(XX)
Net cash generated (deployed)		XX

Discussion Case 16-2:   Fry Corporation (SMA adapted)

When Rachel Hardy, the controller of the Fry Corporation, presented the following condensed comparative financial statements to the board of directors at the close of 19X2, the reaction of the board members was very favourable.

Fry Corporation
Comparative Income Statements
(000s)
For Years Ending December 31, 19X2 and 19X1

	19X2	19X1
Sales	$ 990	$ 700
Cost of Goods Sold	610	480
Gross Profit	$ 380	$ 220
Operating Expenses	(190)	(160)
Income Tax	(80)	(25)
Net Income	$ 110	$ 35

Fry Corporation
Comparative Balance Sheets
(000s)
At December 31, 19X2 and 19X1

	19X2	19X1
Current Assets	$ 380	$ 365
Less: Current Liabilities	200	205
Net Working Capital	$ 180	$ 160
Fixed Assets (net)	1,000	660
Total Assets Minus Current Liabilities	$1,180	$ 820
Financed by:		
Long-term Liabilities	$ 250	$ -0-
Common Stock ($50 Par-Value)	500	500
Retained Earnings	430	320
Total Sources of Long-term Capital	$1,180	$ 820

Noting that net income rose from $3.50 per share of common stock to $11 per share, one member of the board proposed that a substantial cash dividend be paid on the company's stock. He said, "Our working capital is up by $20,000, we should be able to make a distribution to shareholders." To this the controller replied that the company's cash position was precarious. "At the end of 19X2 we have a cash balance of only $15,000, a decline from $147,000 at the end of 19X1," Hardy stated. "Remember that we bought $364,000 of new equipment during 19X2." When the board member asked for an explanation of the increase of $20,000 in working capital, Hardy presented the following schedule (in thousands of dollars):

Increases in Working Capital:		
Accounts Receivable Increased by	$ 85	
Inventories Increased by	45	
Prepaid Expenses Increased by	17	
Accounts Payable Reduced by	32	
Accrued Expenses Reduced by	28	
Total Increases		$207
Decrease in Working Capital:		
Cash Decreased by	$132	
Income Tax Liability Increased by	55	187
Net Increase in Working Capital during 19X2		$ 20

After examining this schedule, the board member shook his head and said, "I still don't understand how our cash position can be so tight in the face of an almost tripling of net income and a substantial increase in working capital!"

Additional Information:
1. The company's long-term liabilities consist of a bond issue amounting to $250,000 cash. These bonds were issued at face value.
2. Equipment costing $364,000 was purchased for cash during the year.
3. Depreciation expense amounted to $24,000 for the year.

Required:
1. Prepare an SCFP according to the working capital definition of funds.
2. Prepare a statement of cash flow.
3. Explain to the board member why there is insufficient cash to pay a dividend.
4. Discuss the similarities of the situation faced by Fry Corporation and that faced by W.T. Grant Company as illustrated in Real Life Example 16-1.

Discussion Case 16-3:   Sakalas Corporation

The following statement of changes in financial position was prepared by the controller of Sakalas Corporation at its year-end, for presentation to its board of directors.

Working Capital Was Provided by:		
Operations	$400	
Net Income		
Add: Non-working Capital Charges against Operations		
Depreciation	90	
Amortization of Bond Discount	10	
Working Capital Provided by Operations		$ 500
Sale of Investments		200
Total Working Capital Provided		$ 700
Working Capital was Used for:		
Buildings and Equipment Purchased	$700	
Preferred Shares Redeemed — 1 Share at $106	106	
Bonds Redeemed — 3 at $102	306	
Dividends Paid	300	
Total Working Capital Used		1,412
Decrease in Working Capital		$ 712

The net decrease in working capital was made up as follows:

	December 31	
	19X2	19X1
Current Assets		
Cash	$ 80	$ 130
Accounts Receivable	590	550
Merchandise Inventories	800	1,300
Total Current Assets	$1,470	$1,980
Current Liabilities		
Bank Loan (secured)	$ 50	—
Trade Accounts Payable	1,052	$ 900
Total Current Liabilities	$1,102	$ 900
Working Capital	$ 368	$1,080

Decrease in working capital = $368 − $1080 = $712

For Discussion

1. The working capital and the current ratio have changed between 19X1 and 19X2. What has caused this change?
2. What policies of the corporation are most likely responsible for the change?
3. How do you interpret the decline in inventory and increase in accounts payable as they relate to the continuing operations of the corporation?

Comprehension Problems

Comprehension Problem 16-1

The following transactions were carried out by Zeal Manufacturing Limited.

Required: Indicate into which category each transaction is placed in the statement of cash flow: operating, financing, or investing.

oper	A disbursement of $5,000 was made in payment of the current portion of a long-term loan.
oper	Depreciation expense for equipment was $1,000.
finance	$10,000 worth of common stock was issued for cash.
finance	Cash dividends of $2,500 were declared and paid to shareholders.
finance + invest	Bonds were given in exchange for equipment costing $7,000.
invest	Land was purchased for $25,000 cash.
oper	$750 of accrued salaries were paid.
oper	$5,000 was borrowed by issuing a 60-day note.
oper	$10,000 of accounts receivable were collected.
finance + invest	A building was purchased for $80,000: $30,000 was paid in cash and the rest was in mortgage.
invest	Investment in subsidiary company was sold for $50,000 cash.
oper + invest	Equipment was sold for $6,000. The accumulated depreciation for it was $3,000 with an original cost of $10,000.
oper	$1,200 was paid for a 12-month insurance policy in effect next year.
oper	Patent was amortized for $500.
finance	Bonds were issued for $50,000 cash.

Note: Do not attempt problems that require T-account SCFP preparation unless your course covered the Appendix.

Comprehension Problem 16-2

The following table includes transactions carried out by the McCallum and Lumer Specialist Corporation, and columns for each of the three categories found in the statement of cash flow: Operating, Financing, and Investing.

Required: For each event shown, indicate which category the event falls under. If the event does not appear on the statement of cash flow, do not enter any amount.

	Operating	Financing	Investing
a. Issued $100 worth of bonds for cash.		100	
b. Purchased a building for $90; $60 was on mortgage and the rest was paid in cash.		60	90
c. Declared and paid dividends of $12 during the year.		(12)	
d. Purchased equipment for $20 worth of common stock.		20	(20)
e. Paid long-term debt of $50 in cash.		(50)	
f. Sold land for $30 in cash.			30
g. Earned net income of $75.	75		
h. Purchased equipment costing $15. Of this, $5 was paid in cash and the rest with a 90-day note payable.	10		(15)

i.   Amortized patent by $2.   *2*

j.   Redeemed $100 worth of bonds for
     common stock.   *100 (100)*

k.   Purchased marketable securities
     for $5 cash.   *(5)*

l.   Sold a machine that cost $20
     for $7 cash. The accumulated
     depreciation on it was $10.   *3*   *7*

m.   Depreciation expense for building
     and equipment amounted to $8.   *8*

n.   Paid in cash the note mentioned
     in h above.   *(10)*

o.   Issued $20 of preferred shares
     for cash.   *20*

p.   Purchased a patent for $25 cash.   *(25)*

q.   Paid $1 for the next two months
     of advertising. Recorded as prepaid expense.   *(2)*

r.   Purchased $60 worth of ABC Ltd.
     common stock for cash.   *(60)*

Comprehension Problem 16-3

Required: For each of the following items indicate whether it increases, decreases or has no effect on funds under each of the two definitions, *cash flow* and *working capital*.

Cash Flow			Working Capital			
↑	↓	N.A.	↑	↓	N.A.	
___	___	___	___	___	___	1. Net Income for the year
___	___	___	___	___	___	2. Payment of Bonds Payable
___	___	___	___	___	___	3. Increase in Inventory
___	___	___	___	___	___	4. Issue of Common Stock for Equipment
___	___	___	___	___	___	5. Issue of Bonds Payable for cash
___	___	___	___	___	___	6. Declaration of a cash Dividend for this year
___	___	___	___	___	___	7. Increase in Accounts Receivable
___	___	___	___	___	___	8. Increase in Accounts Payable
___	___	___	___	___	___	9. Purchase of Land for cash
___	___	___	___	___	___	10. Issue of Common Stock for cash
___	___	___	___	___	___	11. Reclassification from long-term liabilities of current portion of Bonds Payable due next year
___	___	___	___	___	___	12. Payment of cash Dividend declared last year
___	___	___	___	___	___	13. Decrease in Marketable Securities
___	___	___	___	___	___	14. Increase in Income Tax Payable

Comprehension Problem 16-4

The following is a draft SCFP for the Ragosta Corporation:

Ragosta Corporation
Statement of Changes in Financial Position
For the Year Ended December 31, 19X1

Working Capital was Provided by:	
Operations:	
Add:	(A)
Total	XXX
Deduct:	(B)
Working Capital Provided by Operations	XXX
Working Capital Provided by Other Sources	(C)
Total Working Capital Provided	XXX
Working Capital Was Used for:	(D)
Increase (Decrease) in Working Capital	XXX

Required: For each of the following items, determine where it appears in the statement of changes in financial position. Designate the position by the letters A, B, C or D as shown in the above statement. Indicate all possible positions if more than one is appropriate. If no position is appropriate, mark the item with the letter E. More than one position may be applicable to an item.

_____ Purchase of land for cash
_____ Declaration of cash dividends
_____ Net income
_____ Sale of long-term investment for cash at a gain
_____ Depreciation of a building
_____ Retirement of long-term bonds payable by issue
_____ of common stock
_____ Gain on the sale of a non-current asset
_____ Amortization of discount on bonds payable
_____ Issue of common stock for cash
_____ Proceeds from the disposal of an asset at a loss
_____ Redemption of long-term bonds for cash
_____ Amortization of goodwill

_____ Payment of a long-term loan
_____ Loss on the sale of an asset
_____ Proceeds from the sale of a building at a gain
_____ Purchase of inventory for cash
_____ Payment of cash dividends, previously declared
_____ Issue of bonds for cash at a discount
_____ Acquisition of a building for a mortgage
_____ Payment in cash of an account payable
_____ Transfer of a portion of long-term bonds payable
_____ to current liabilities
_____ Proceeds from sale of marketable securities
_____ Collection of an accounts receivable — trade.

Comprehension Problem 16-5

The Rosa Maria Corporation had the following balance sheet balances at December 31, 19X2 and 19X1.

	19X2	19X1
Assets		
Current Assets	$55	$50
Fixed Assets	43	35
Less: Accumulated Depreciation	(6)	(5)
	$92	$80
Liabilities and Shareholders' Equity		
Current Liabilities	$19	$ 25
Bonds Payable	10	–
Common Stock	55	50
Retained Earnings	8	5
	$92	$80

Additional information for 19X2: Net Income $7
                                 Dividends $4
No depreciable property was disposed of during 19X2.

Required: Indicate your answer by circling your choice for each of the following questions:
1. The working capital made available from operations is:
   (a) $3   (b) $4   (c) $6   (d) $7   (e) $8
2. The working capital provided by the sale of bonds is:
   (a) $10 (b) $13 (c) $14 (d) $16 (e) $21
3. The increase in working capital is:
   (a) $3   (b) $6   (c) $11 (d) $12 (e) $14

Comprehension Problem 16-6

When using the T-account methodology in preparing an SCFP, Step 3 indicated that an Operations Summary and Working Capital Summary account are set up.

These accounts, used in the analysis of transactions recorded in the books of Boyle Enterprises Corporation for the year ended December 31, 19X3, are reproduced below.

Operations Summary

Loss on Sale of		Gain on Sale of Land	10
Investment	5	Amortization of Bond	
Depreciation Expense	15	Premium	1
Amortization of Patent	1	Working Capital	
Net Income	1	Provided by Operations	11
	22		22

Working Capital Summary

	100		
Sale of Investments	30	Purchase of Building	50
Sale of Land	50	Payment of Dividends	40
Issue of Bonds Payable	70		
Issue of Common Stock	29		
Working Capital			
Provided by Operations	11		
	190		90
Balance	100		

Required:

1. Explain the purpose of the Operations Summary account.
2. Explain the purpose of the Working Capital Summary account.
3. Calculate the amount of Proceeds from Sale of Investments.
4. Calculate the amount of Proceeds from Sale of Land.
5. Prepare an SCFP according to the working capital definition of funds.

Problems

Problem 16-1

The following transactions occurred in the Brennan Corporation during the year ended December 31, 19X8.

a.	Net income for the year (accrual basis) $800	
b.	Depreciation expense	120
c.	Increase in wages payable	20
d.	Increase in accounts receivable	40
e.	Decrease in merchandise inventory	50
f.	Amortization of patents	5
g.	Payment of long-term liabilities	250
h.	Issuance of common stock for cash	500
i.	Amortization of bond premium	6
j.	Declaration of dividends	30

Required:

1. Calculate the cash flow from operations.
2. Prepare in proper form the statement of cash flow, showing the detailed calculation of cash flow from operations on a separate schedule.
3. Does the declaration of dividends affect cash flow? Why or why not?

Problem 16-2

This problem requires the use of the same information contained in Problem 16-1.

Required:
1. Prepare in proper form an SCFP according to the working capital definition of funds.
2. Explain in your own words why there is a difference between the cash definition of funds prepared in Problem 16-1 and the working capital definition.

Problem 16-3

The records of Loyola Corporation showed the following information in the balance sheet accounts at December 31, 19X2 and 19X1.

Debits	19X2	19X1	*Increase (Decrease)*
Cash	$ 11	$ 10	$ 1
Accounts Receivable (net)	24	19	5
Merchandise Inventory	50	52	(2)
Prepaid Expenses	4	3	1
Long-term Investments	–	10	(10)
Fixed Assets (net)	147	95	52
	$236	$189	$ 47
Credits			
Accounts Payable	$ 8	$ 12	$ (4)
Wages Payable	2	3	(1)
Notes Payable — Long-term	48	39	9
Common Stock	150	120	30
Retained Earnings	28	15	13
	$236	$189	$ 47

Additional information for 19X2:
a. Net income was $24.
b. Cash dividends of $11 were paid.
c. Depreciation expense was $3.
d. Common stock was given in exchange for fixed assets costing $30.
e. Fixed assets were purchased for $25; $16 was paid in cash and a long-term note was issued for the difference.

Required:
1. Calculate the cash flow from operations.
2. Prepare in proper form a statement of cash flow; show the detailed calculation of cash flow from operations on a separate schedule.
3. Explain what the statement of cash flow tells you about the Loyola Corporation.
4. Explain why you handled the non-cash acquisition of fixed assets as you did.

Problem 16-4

A student asks your help in the preparation of an SCFP, prepared according to the working capital concept for the year ended December 31, 19X1, for Prairie Company Limited. The student made the necessary calculations of the various items; however, he is unable to put the statement in proper form.

The following are the correct calculations made by the student:

Proceeds from Sale of Equipment	$ 6	Amortization and Depreciation	12
Proceeds from Issue of Common Stock	20	Equipment Purchases	10
Net Income	12	Long-term Note Given for Equipment	26
Purchase of Land	14	Common Stock Issued for Land	30
Long-term Note Paid	8	Cash Dividends Declared	8
Long-term Investments Sold	16		

Required: Prepare in proper form an SCFP according to the working capital definition of funds for the year ended December 31, 19X1.

Problem 16-5

The comparative balance sheets for Alpha Limited, as at December 31, were as follows:

Alpha Limited
Comparative Balance Sheets
At December 31, 19X5 and 19X4

	19X5	19X4
Assets		
Cash	$ 6,000	$ 7,000
Accounts Receivable	4,000	5,000
Allowance for Doubtful Accounts	(1,000)	(500)
Merchandise Inventory	12,000	11,000
Long-term Investment	13,000	10,000
Land	10,000	–
Equipment	40,000	30,000
Accumulated Depreciation	(10,000)	(8,000)
	$ 74,000	$ 54,500
Liabilities and Shareholders' Equity		
Accounts Payable	$ 5,000	$ 7,000
Current Portion — Bonds Payable	6,000	6,000
Bonds Payable	10,000	16,000
Common Shares — No par	8,000	3,000
Retained Earnings — Unrestricted	26,250	22,500
— Restricted	8,750	–
Donated Capital	10,000	–
	$ 74,000	$ 54,500

The 19X5 ledger accounts for non-current items are reproduced below in the format of T-accounts.

Investment		
Bal X4	10,000	
X5 Purchase	3,000	
Bal X5	13,000	

Bonds Payable			
X5 Transferred to current	6,000	Bal. X4	16,000
		Bal X5	10,000

Land

X5 Addition	10,000		

Equipment

Bal. X4	30,000	X5 Disposal	10,000
X5 Acquisition	5,000		
X5 Purchase	15,000		
	50,000		10,000
Bal X5	40,000		

Accumulated Depreciation

		Bal. X4	8,000
X5 Disposal	1,000	X5 Deprec.	3,000
	1,000		11,000
		Bal X5	10,000

Common Stock

	Bal. X4	3,000
	X5 Issued for Equipment	5,000
	Bal X5	8,000

Retained Earnings

		Bal. X4	22,500
X5 Restriction	8,750	X5 Net Income	17,500
X5 Dividends	5,000		
	13,750		40,000
		Bal X5	26,250

Retained Earnings (Restricted)

	X5 Addition	8,750

Donated Capital

	X5 Donation of Land	10,000

Additional Data
There was a $2,000 loss on disposal of equipment.

Required: Prepare in proper form an SCFP according to the working capital definition of funds.

Alternate Problems

Alternate Problem 16-1

During the year ended December 31, 19X3, the Poor Co. Ltd. reported $95,000 of revenues, $70,000 of expenses, and $5,000 of income tax. Following is a list of transactions that occurred during the year.
a. Depreciation expense, $3,000.
b. Increase in wages payable, $500.
c. Increase in accounts receivable, $900.
d. Decrease in merchandise inventory, $1,200.
e. Amortization of patent, $100.
f. Long-term liabilities paid in cash, $5,000.
g. Issue of common stock for cash, $12,500.
h. Amortization of bond discount, $150.
i. Fixed assets, cost $10,000, acquired through issuing 1,000 shares of stock.
j. Just prior to end of the fiscal year, $5,000 cash dividend declared, payable one month later.
k. At the same time that the cash dividend was declared, the company also declared 1,000 shares of common stock as a stock dividend. The fair market value of the stock was $10,000.
l. Old machinery sold for $6,000 cash; it originally cost $15,000 (one-half depreciated). Loss reported on income statement as ordinary item and included in the $70,000 of expenses.
m. Decrease in accounts payable, $1,000.

Required:
1. Calculate the cash flow from operations in a separate schedule.
2. Prepare a statement of cash flow.
3. Explain what this statement of cash flow tells you about the Poor Co. Ltd.

Alternate Problem 16-2

This problem requires the use of the same information contained in Alternate Problem 16-1.

Required:
1. Prepare in proper form an SCFP according to the working capital definition of funds.
2. Explain in your own words the difference between the cash flow definition of funds and the working capital definition as they affect the statement of cash flow prepared in Alternate Problem 16-1.

Alternate Problem 16-3

The comparative balance sheets of Werbin Corporation showed the following information at December 31.

Debits	19X8	19X7
Cash	$ 22	$ 20
Accounts receivable (net)	48	38
Merchandise inventory	100	104
Prepaid expenses	8	6
Land	–	20
Buildings	240	180
Machinery	124	80
Patents	8	10
	$550	$458

Credits		
Accounts payable	$ 16	$ 24
Notes payable	26	18
Wages payable	4	6
Accumulated depreciation	78	80
Notes payable — long term	70	60
Common stock	300	240
Retained earnings	56	30
	$550	$458

Additional Data for 19X8
a. Net income for the year amounted to $48.
b. Amortization of patents amounted to $2.
c. Purchased machinery for $30, paying $10 in cash and gave a five year note for the balance.
d. Purchased $50 of machinery through the issue of common stock.
e. Paid $60 cash for an addition to the building.
f. Paid a $10 long-term note through the issue of common stock.
g. Sold land for $24 (gain or loss is included in the income statement).
h. Paid cash dividends.
i. Depreciation expense for the year amounted to $16.
j. Sold machinery for $14 that had originally cost $36 and was one half depreciated at the time of sale (gain or loss is included in the income statement).

Required:
1. Calculate the cash flow from operations in a separate schedule.
2. Prepare in proper form a statement of cash flow.
3. Explain what the statement of cash flow tells you about Werbin Corporation.
4. Explain why you handled any non-cash investing and financing activities as you did.

Alternate Problem 16-4

The following are financial statements of the John Abbott Corporation.

Balance Sheet
At January 1, 19X2

Assets

Current Assets	$ 32
Land and Buildings	27
Accumulated Depreciation —	
Buildings	(8)
Equipment	33
Accumulated Depreciation —	
Equipment	(4)
	$ 80

Liabilities and Shareholders' Equity

Current Liabilities	$ 12
Common Stock	15
Retained Earnings	53
	$ 80

Statement of Changes in Financial Position
For the Year Ended December 31, 19X2

Working Capital Was Provided by:

Operations		
Net Income	$15	
Add: Non-working Capital Charges against Operations		
Loss on Sale of Equipment	2	
Depreciation of Buildings	2	
Depreciation of Equipment	1	
Working Capital Provided by Operations	$20	
Issue of Stock	5	
Sale of Equipment	7	
Total Working Capital Provided		$32
Working Capital Was Used for:		
Dividends	$ 3	
Purchase of Land	4	
Purchase of Buildings	6	
Purchase of Equipment	11	
Total Working Capital Used		24
Increase in Working Capital		$ 8
Working Capital — Beginning of Year		20
Working Capital — End of Year		$28

Total assets on the December 31, 19X2 balance sheet are $95. The equipment sold had accumulated depreciation of $1.

Required: Choose the best answer for each of the following:
1. The current assets on December 31, 19X2 are:
   (a) $34   (b) $36   (c) $37   (d) $38   (e) $42
2. The common stock on December 31, 19X2 is:
   (a) $10   (b) $13   (c) $15   (d) $18   (e) $20
3. The retained earnings on December 31, 19X2 are:
   (a) $53   (b) $56   (c) $65   (d) $68   (e) $71
4. Net income for 19X2 is:
   (a) $10   (b) $12   (c) $15   (d) $18   (e) $20
5. When the equipment was sold, the Equipment account was credited for:
   (a) $4   (b) $5   (c) $6   (d) $7   (e) $10

Alternate Problem 16-5

The comparative balance sheets of Medicine Hat Corporation showed the following at December 31, 19X2 and 19X1.

	19X2	19X1
Debits		
Cash	$ 10	$ 8
Accounts Receivable (net)	18	10
Merchandise Inventory	24	20
Long-term Investments	10	24
Fixed Assets	94	60
	$156	$122
Credits		
Accumulated Depreciation	$ 14	$ 10
Accounts Payable	16	12
Notes Payable — Long-term	40	32
Common Stock	60	50
Retained Earnings	26	18
	$156	$ 122

The Income Statement for 19X2 appears below:

Medicine Hat Corporation
Income Statement
For the Year Ended December 31, 19X2

Sales		$ 300
Cost of Sales		200
Gross Profit		$ 100
Operating Expenses		
Expenses, including Income Tax	$ 78	
Depreciation	6	84
Income from Operations		$ 16
Other Gains (Losses)		
Gain on Disposal of Fixed Assets		2
Loss on Disposal of Investments		(4)
Net Income		$ 14

Additional data concerning changes in the non-current accounts during 19X2:
a. Cash dividends paid, $6.
b. Issue of shares for cash, $10.
c. Fixed assets disposed during the year cost $6.
d. Ignore income taxes.

Required: Prepare an SCFP according to the working capital definition of funds. Use the T-account method, and show all T-accounts.

Supplementary Problems

Supplementary Problem 16-1

The following trial balance has been prepared from the ledger of Pearson International Corporation at December 31, 19X3, following its first year of operations.

	Account Balances	
	Debit	Credit
Cash	$ 50	
Accounts Receivable — net	100	
Merchandise Inventory,		
December 31, 19X3	60	
Prepaid Rent	10	
Equipment	160	
Accumulated Depreciation —		
Equipment		$ 44
Land	0	
Accounts Payable		50
Dividends Payable		5
Salaries Payable		8
Bonds Payable — due 19X8		80
Premium on Bonds		3
Common Stock		140
Retained Earnings		–
Dividends	10	
Sales		225
Cost of Goods Sold	136	
Selling and Administrative Expenses	42	
Interest Expense	7	
Gain on Sale of Land		20
	$575	$575

Additional Data
a. The company paid $10 cash dividends during the year.
b. Actual interest paid during the year amounted to $8. Amortization of bond premium amounting to $1 was credited to interest expense during the year.
c. Bonds redeemed during the year for $21 cash (par-value, $20, and bond premium $1). The bond premium had been amortized prior to the redemption.
d. Issued common stock for equipment, $40.
e. Land costing $30 was purchased and sold during the year for $50.
f. Issued bonds during the year for $105 cash (par-value $100 and bond premium $5)

Required:
1. Calculate the cash flow from operations during the year on a separate schedule. (Hint: Prepare an income statement before making this calculation.)
2. Prepare in proper form a statement of cash flow.
3. Explain what this statement of cash tells you about Pearson International Corporation at December 31, 19X3.

Supplementary Problem 16-2

The president of the Drana Company Ltd. is concerned about the company's working capital position at the end of 19X2. The following data summarized the financial situation of the company for 19X2 and 19X1:

	19X2	19X1
Debits		
Accounts Receivable	$ 180	$ 220
Building	610	500
Cash	—	50
Merchandise Inventory	110	125
Land	175	90
Long-term Investment	40	100
Machinery	300	170
Prepaid Expenses	5	4
Unamortized Bond Discount	4	5
	$1,424	$1,264
Credits		
Accounts Payable	$ 70	$ 50
Accumulated Depreciation	241	218
Allowance for Doubtful Accounts	10	12
Bank Overdraft	50	—
Bonds Payable	100	50
Common Stock	500	450
Notes Payable — Trade	25	—
Retained Earnings	423	480
Wages Payable	5	4
	$1,424	$1,264

The following additional information is available:
a. A dividend of 15 cents per share was declared and paid on the 500 outstanding shares.
b. Shares have been issued during the year at their par value of $1.
c. Some shares in the long-term investment account were sold during the year to finance a portion of the new building. These shares were carried at a cost of $60 in the books of the company. The selling price was $40.
d. Old machinery that cost $10 was sold for $2. Depreciation on this equipment was $6. The loss was included in expenses for the year.
e. The income statement for the current year is as follows:

Sales		$ 1,350
Cost of Sales		720
Gross Profit		$ 630
Operating Expenses		577
Operating Income		$ 53
Other Gains (Losses)		
Loss on Sale of Investment		(20)
Net Income before Income Tax	$	33
Income Tax		15
Net Income	$	18

Required: Prepare the SCFP according to the working capital definition of funds. Use the T-account method and show all T-accounts.

Supplementary Problem 16-3

The balance sheet data of North-West Limited at December 31 appear below.

North-West Limited
Comparative Balance Sheets
At December 31, 19X2 and 19X1

	19X2	19X1
Debits		
Cash	$ 40	$ 30
Accounts Receivable (net)	38	28
Merchandise Inventory	102	106
Prepaid Expenses	8	6
Long-term Investment	—	20
Buildings	240	180
Machinery	134	80
Patents	8	10
	$570	$460
Credits		
Accounts Payable	$ 18	$ 26
Notes Payable — Short-term	26	18
Wages Payable	4	6
Accumulated Depreciation	76	80
Notes Payable — Long Term	70	60
Common Stock, No par*	310	240
Retained Earnings	66	30
	$570	$460

*Shares outstanding December 31, 19X1 — 15; December 31, 19X2 — 22.

The following additional information is available:
a. Net income for the year was $56.
b. Depreciation recorded on fixed assets was $14.
c. Amortization of patents amounted to $2.
d. Machinery costing $30 was purchased; one-third was paid in cash and a five-year interest-bearing note was given for the balance.
e. Machinery costing $60 was purchased, and was paid for by issuing 6 common shares.
f. Machinery was sold for $14 that originally cost $36 (one-half depreciated); loss or gain reported on the income statement.
g. Addition to building was made costing $60; paid cash.
h. A $10 long-term note was paid by issuing 1 common share.
i. The long-term investment was sold for $24 cash.
j. Cash dividends paid.
k. Sales of $240 made on account.
l. Collection of accounts receivable, $230.

Required:
1. Calculate the change in working capital.
2. Prepare an SCFP according to the working capital definition of funds. Use the T-account method and show all T-accounts.

Supplementary Problem 16-4

RMR Incorporated
Comparative Balance Sheets
At December 31, 19X2 and 19X1

		19X1		19X2
Assets				
Cash		$ 25,000		$48,000
Accounts Receivable (net)		25,000		?
Merchandise Inventory		70,000		?
Marketable Securities		35,000		?
Prepaid Expenses		—		?
Long-term Investment		40,000		?
Unamortized Discount on Bonds		1,200		?
Machinery	$40,000		$?	
Less: Accumulated Depreciation	10,000	30,000	?	?
Building			$?	
Less: Accumulated Depreciation		—	2,000	?
Land		—		?
Other Assets		15,000		?
		$241,200		$?
Liabilities and Shareholders' Equity				
Accounts Payable		$ 20,000		$?
Dividends Payable		—		?
Bonds Payable		50,000		?
Common Stock		100,000		?
Retained Earnings				
— Unrestricted		61,200		?
— Restricted		10,000		20,000
		$241,200		$?

The following additional information is available:
a. $3,000 of marketable securities were sold for cash.
b. Long-term investments were sold for $60,000 cash ($10,000 of expenses related to the disposal were incurred).
c. Land and building were acquired in exchange for $100,000 of par-value bonds. The building is to be depreciated on a 40-year straight-line basis.
d. $10,000 of common stock was issued as a stock dividend.
e. A new piece of machinery was acquired in exchange for an old piece of machinery and $24,000 cash. The old machinery had cost $8,000 and was half depreciated. No loss or gain was incurred.
f. The depreciation charge for machinery in 19X2 was $4,000.
g. The discount on bonds is being amortized on a straight-line basis. The discount will be completely amortized by December 31, 19X7.
h. On March 1, 19X2 the company paid $6,000 of insurance premiums for a period of one year.
i. The net purchases of merchandise for 19X2 were $515,000.
j. Sales for the period amounted to $700,000. The gross profit is 30 percent of sales.
k. Accounts payable increased by 40 percent.
l. Accounts receivable (net) have increased by 52 percent.
m. During 19X2, $10,000 of cash dividends have been declared. Half of these have been paid, the rest will be paid in January of 19X3.
n. Net income for 19X2 is $28,800.
o. Other assets were purchased for $5,000 cash.

Required:
1. Complete the balance sheet for 19X2 based on the above information.
2. Calculate the change in working capital.
3. Prepare an SCFP according to the working capital definition of funds.

Decision Problems

Decision Problem 16-1

Management of the ABC Co. has never prepared an SCFP. It has been recommended to them to include it as part of their financial statements. Management's main problem now is to define the term ''funds''. After much discussion, they have narrowed down the definition to two possible alternatives. One is to define funds as *cash*, the other to define funds as *working capital*.

Required: As the accountant of ABC Co., you are required to present management with an explanation of how each definition would affect the sources and the uses of funds, and present your recommendation with your reasons. You can make use of illustrations to make your point.

Decision Problem 16-2

The year-end of Turner Inc. is December 31, 19X6. The following summarized data are taken from its records.

Cash Sales	$492
Sales on account	168
Cash purchases of merchandise	340
Credit purchases of merchandise	80
Miscellaneous Expenses paid in cash	142
Accounts Receivable:	
Balance January 1, 19X6	46
Balance December 31, 19X6	60
Accounts Payable:	
Balance January 1, 19X6	28
Balance December 31, 19X6	32
Merchandise Inventory account:	
Inventory, January 1, 19X6	100
Inventory, December 31, 19X6	120
Wages Payable at December 31, 19X6 (none at January 1, 19X6)	4
Prepaid Rent at December 31, 19X6 (none at January 1, 19X6)	6
Fixed Assets — Equipment:	
Cost	200
Annual depreciation	20

Required:

1. Using the above information, complete the following income statements on both accrual and cash bases.

Sales		$	Sales		$
Cost of Goods Sold		___	Cost of Goods Sold		___
Gross Profit		$	Gross Profit		$
Operating Expenses			Operating Expenses		
Depreciation	$		Depreciation	$	
Miscellaneous			Miscellaneous		
Rent	___ ___		Rent	___ ___	
Net Income For The Year		$	Net Income For The Year		$

2. Explain in your own words why net income calculated according to the accrual basis results in working capital being provided by operations, while net income calculated according to the cash basis results in cash being provided by operations. Why do the amounts of net income differ?
3. Beginning with the net income calculated according to the accrual basis, calculate the amount of cash provided by operations. Use the method illustrated in this chapter.

Decision Problem 16-3

The January 1, 19X3 balance sheet of Park Limited and an SCFP prepared according to the working capital concept of funds at December 31, 19X3 are reproduced below:

Park Limited
Balance Sheet
At January 1, 19X3

Debits

Cash	$14
Accounts Receivable	36
Buildings	35
Land	10
	$95

Credits

Accounts Payable	$19
Notes Payable — short-term	13
Accumulated Depreciation	5
Bonds Payable	–
Common Stock	50
Retained Earnings	8
	$95

Park Limited
Statement of Changes in Financial Position
For the Year Ended December 31, 19X3

Working Capital Was Provided by:		
Operations		
Net Income	$3	
Add: Non-working Capital Charges		
against Operations:		
Depreciation on Buildings	1	
Working Capital Provided by Operations		$ 4
Issue of bonds		10
Total Working Capital Provided		$14
Working Capital Was Used for:		
Erection of garage		8
Net Increase in Working Capital		$6

Additional Data for 19X3:
An issue of 10-year bonds having a face value of $10 was sold at the beginning of 19X3 at par value. A new garage was erected at a cost of $8. Additional land was obtained in exchange for common stock. By the end of the year, cash had increased by $6 while Accounts Receivable actually decreased by $1. Accounts payable also decreased by $1. There was no change in Notes Payable.

Required: Prepare a balance sheet for Park Limited at December 31, 19X3.

Business Combinations

Numerous publicly owned corporations prepare consolidated financial statements to indicate that all or a controlling interest is owned by one corporation in other corporations.

1. What criterion is used to establish existence of a corporation's interest?
2. What is the distinction in a business combination between a purchase and a pooling of interests?
3. What is the generally accepted method of recording the purchase of a subsidiary's shares?
4. When consolidated financial statements are prepared, does each corporation continue to have its own legal existence as a separate entity?
5. What are the steps used in preparing consolidated financial statements?
6. What are reciprocal amounts? Why are they eliminated in the combination process?
7. Are any entries recorded in the books of either parent corporation or its subsidiary in the preparation of consolidated financial statements?
8. How is goodwill created in the consolidation process?
9. What is minority interest, and how is it accounted for?
10. How is the acquisition of a subsidiary under a pooling of interests accomplished?

A. Business Combinations

Business combination
The acquisition of one corporation by another; also referred to as a *consolidation*.

Purchase
A business combination in which a subsidiary's shares are acquired through the payment of cash or other assets.

Pooling of interests
A business combination in which the subsidiary's shares are acquired only through an exchange of shares.

Often a corporation acquires a controlling interest in another corporation; usually, this control is accomplished through the purchase of voting shares. As mentioned earlier, when the share purchase results in more than 50 percent ownership, the investor controls the voting shares of the other corporation, which is then referred to as a subsidiary of the investing parent. Although there are some exceptions, the individual financial statements of the parent and its subsidiary are combined for the parent's reporting purposes, as if the two were one economic entity, as in accordance with GAAP.

Business combinations can be identified as either a purchase or a pooling of interests. In a **purchase**, either all or more than 50 percent of the subsidiary's shareholders are bought out; the previous owners of the subsidiary no longer continue to have an ownership interest in the subsidiary. In a **pooling of interests**, the parent acquires the subsidiary through an exchange of shares; in this situation the subsidiary's shareholders exchange their shares in the subsidiary for shares of the parent. The original shareholders of the subsidiary then become shareholders in the parent and, thereby, in the group of corporations now controlled by the parent. The distinction between a purchase and pooling of interests is contrasted in Figure 17-1.

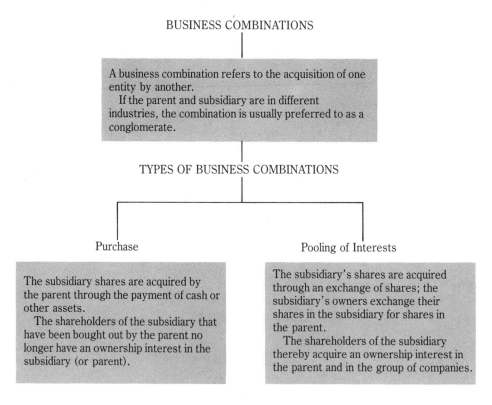

Figure 17-1   **The distinctions between a purchase and a pooling of interests**

The combination process for either a purchase or a pooling of interests is different. Sections B, C, and D of this chapter discuss the combination of financial statements when a purchase occurs. Section E introduces the methodology of combining financial statements when a pooling of interest occurs.

The Accounting Equation Reviewed

Since net assets are the focus of both a purchase and a pooling of interests, it is useful to review the accounting equation at this point. Simply stated, the accounting equation indicates that total assets belonging to an entity must always equal the total claims against those assets. Both creditors and owners contribute these assets and the accounting equation recognizes these contributions.

$$
\begin{array}{ccc}
\text{Assets} & = & \text{Liabilities} & + & \text{Equity} \\
\text{(Resources owned} & & \text{(Creditors' claims} & & \text{(Owners' claims} \\
\text{by the entity)} & & \text{to assets)} & & \text{to assets)}
\end{array}
$$

In addition to recognizing the contribution of both creditors and owners to the assets of the entity, the equation also expresses the equality between assets and total claims by both creditors and owners to these assets.

Business combinations focus on the owners' claim to the net assets of a subsidiary; that is, the amount of net assets left for the owners after all other claims have been taken care of. The accounting equation can therefore be restated in the following manner to emphasize owners' claims to net assets:

$$
\begin{array}{ccc}
\text{Assets} & = & \text{Liabilities} & + & \text{Equity} \\
\text{(Resources owned} & & \text{(Creditors' claims} & & \text{(Owners' claims to} \\
\text{by the entity)} & & \text{to assets)} & & \text{remaining assets)}
\end{array}
$$

Since assets less liabilities is also referred to as net assets, the term *net assets* can be said to be synonymous with owners' equity; that is, the owners' claims to the assets of the entity. The difference between assets and liabilities can therefore be labelled as net assets or as equity. The discussion in business combinations focuses on the net assets of a subsidiary.

Purchase of a Controlling Interest

Controlling interest
The acquisition of more than 50 percent of another corporation's voting shares.

The acquisition of a **controlling interest**, or more than 50 percent of the voting shares of another corporation, was extensively reviewed in an analysis prepared for Bluebeard's management. The parent purchases the controlling interest in voting shares of the subsidiary by a cash payment; this payment is made to the subsidiary's shareholders in exchange for their shares in the subsidiary. In effect, the subsidiary's shareholders are bought out; these previous owners of the subsidiary therefore no longer continue to have any ownership interest in the subsidiary. The purchase results in the parent acquiring ownership claims to the net assets of the subsidiary.

Recording the Acquisition at Cost

Cost is the generally accepted method of recording the purchase of any asset; in this case, the purchase of the subsidiary's shares. Therefore, the share purchase is recorded at acquisition cost. The acquisition cost includes not only the amount paid for the shares, but also brokerage fees and any other costs associated with the purchase. The purchase price is supposed to reflect the fair market value of the subsidiary's net assets.

The analysis prepared for Bluebeard's executives considered the three different alternatives possible in the parent's purchase of its ownership claims to the net assets of the subsidiary. These alternatives are applicable in every similar controlling situation.

Alternative 1	*Alternative 2*	*Alternative 3*
The purchase cost was the same amount as the book value of the subsidiary's net assets now owned by the parent.	The purchase cost was greater than the amount of the book value of the subsidiary's net assets now owned by the parent.	The purchase cost was less than the amount of the book value of the subsidiary's net assets now owned by the parent.
	The difference can result from the existence of unrecorded goodwill applicable to the subsidiary and/or to an undervaluation of the subsidiary's assets.	The difference can result from the existence of so-called negative goodwill and/or to an overevaluation of the subsidiary's assets.

The data used throughout the chapter are taken from the analysis prepared for executives of Bluebeard Computer Corporation. Intrigued by acquisitions occurring within the computer industry, particularly the acquisition of Rolm Corporation by IBM, the analysis was prepared as a working document for understanding business combinations and their financial reporting implications. First, this analysis reviewed the acquisition of a controlling interest in the shares of a subsidiary. This step included both a wholly owned subsidiary and a partially owned subsidiary; the three alternatives that can surface in the acquisition of a subsidiary were considered. Then, the acquisition of a subsidiary through a pooling of interests was evaluated. A different view of the nature of acquisitions is discussed in Real Life Example 17-1. The chapter itself presents BCC's analysis.

For convenience, the investor corporation is referred to as P, the parent and the investee corporation as S, the subsidiary. The assignment material for this chapter continues this approach to facilitate the distinction between a parent and its subsidiary.

B. Wholly Owned Subsidiary

This section of the Bluebeard business combinations analysis deals with the purchase of all voting shares in a subsidiary; in this situation, the parent has in effect acquired ownership claims to 100 percent of the subsidiary's net assets. It is assumed that the acquisition is made on December 31, 19X8.

Recording the Acquisition

The acquisition cost for each alternative discussed in section A is recorded in the journal entries below. In each case, the parent has acquired a 100 percent ownership interest in the subsidiary. Note that the amount paid differs in each case.

Acquisition of 100-Percent Ownership Interest

	Alternative 1		*Alternative 2*		*Alternative 3*	
Investment in Subsidiary	20,000		25,000		16,000	
Cash		20,000		25,000		16,000

Although this purchase is effected in cash, the acquisition can also be made through a payment of other assets. Regardless, the parent purchases a 100-percent ownership interest in the subsidiary's net assets; none of the subsidiary's previous owners then has an ownership interest in the subsidiary.

Real Life Example 17-1

Acquisitions and Takeovers

Acquisition of companies, takeover bids, and defensive tactics by boards of takeover targets have increased dramatically in recent years. Acquisition attempts by corporations or individuals may occur for many different reasons. For example, the takeover of Rolm Corporation by IBM was fuelled because IBM was lagging behind its competitors in a vital technological area. Rather than develop this technology from within the corporation, IBM decided that the acquisition of Rolm would be less expensive and would produce this technology immediately. The management of the Rolm Corporation welcomed this takeover. Their ''independence'' within IBM was guaranteed and the employees and management were retained.

In other instances, acquisitions or takeover attempts are not welcomed by the target companies' managements. Many recent controversial takeover attempts have been viewed as unfriendly; among them is the attempt by Ted Turner, owner of TBS, and Senator Jesse Helms, of North Carolina, to take over CBS. Their actions were prompted by their view that CBS news reporting was politically biased; they wished to control the giant broadcasting company in order to impose their own bias over this medium. The CBS board of directors acted quickly in denouncing the takeover bid and advised shareholders not to accept the Turner proposal. At present, the takeover bid is at a standstill and industry analysts predict that it will never occur.

In Canada, too, the managements of some companies have undertaken defensive tactics in warding off unfriendly takeover attempts. For instance, Yellowknife Bear Resources Inc. of Toronto declared a special dividend of $7.00 per share, a total payout of over $31 million dollars, deliberately making the company less attractive to its suitors. The two acquisitors subsequently withdrew their offers.

Fleet Aerospace Corporation of St. Catharines, Ontario at its annual shareholders meetings, adopted by-laws protecting its board of directors in the event of a takeover. Under its new by-law, if one individual or group acquired 25 percent of the company's common shares and then attempted to change the composition of the board of directors, over 70 percent of the shares outstanding would have to be represented at the meeting called to vote on such changes. This move, in effect, protects the board of directors from being replaced after a takeover. The adoption of these by-laws was challenged by the Ontario Securities Commission.

The rumours of an imminent acquisition can cause a company's share price to rise quickly. A recent rumour of a takeover bid for the shares of Gulf Canada Ltd. sparked a flurry of trading, as over 350 000 shares changed hands. The area of acquisitions and takeovers is one of the most interesting and complicated accounting issues. Many issues occurring during an acquisition must be resolved, involving financing, legal regulations, and restrictions on information that is to be supplied to investors.

Preparation of Consolidated Financial Statements

Although there are some exceptions, the individual financial statements of the parent and its subsidiary are combined for reporting purposes, as if the two were one economic entity and not two separate corporations; this reporting process is in accordance with GAAP. Although accountants prepare this single composite financial report, both parent and subsidiary are, and continue to be, two separate legal entities.

The procedure was explained to the executives of Bluebeard Computer Corporation. At their year-end, December 31, each corporation prepares its own financial statements as usual. These separate statements are then combined to show a financial picture of the whole operation, as if the two were one economic entity. These combined financial statements are then referred to as consolidated financial statements.

The combination of statements consists of two steps. First, the changes that occurred as a result of the acquisition are indicated in the parent's balance sheet; the balances immediately before the purchase and immediately after are shown. Next the balances of both parent and subsidiary are combined and disclosed. Note that liabilities are not listed in the subsidiary's trial balance in the analysis example. This exclusion emphasizes both that the parent is actually purchasing the net assets of the subsidiary and that the assets are the focus of the consolidation. Another example incorporates liabilities; it appears in the illustrative problem in section B.

Alternative 1

In this alternative, the purchase cost is $20,000; the subsidiary's net assets, recorded in the books, are worth $20,000. Since the purchase is made on December 31, 19X8 (after closing entries have been posted), it is easy to compare the change to the parent's financial position immediately after the purchase. Next, the balances of both parent and subsidiary are combined. Note that the combination process involves the elimination of reciprocal amounts (indicated with arrows).

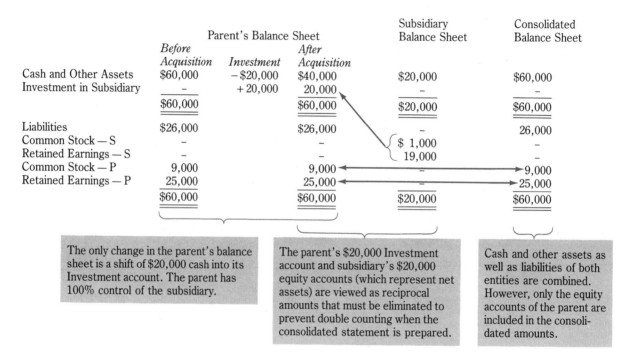

	Parent's Balance Sheet			Subsidiary Balance Sheet	Consolidated Balance Sheet
	Before Acquisition	*Investment*	*After Acquisition*		
Cash and Other Assets	$60,000	− $20,000	$40,000	$20,000	$60,000
Investment in Subsidiary	–	+ 20,000	20,000	–	–
	$60,000		$60,000	$20,000	$60,000
Liabilities	$26,000		$26,000	–	26,000
Common Stock — S	–		–	$ 1,000	–
Retained Earnings — S	–		–	19,000	–
Common Stock — P	9,000		9,000	–	9,000
Retained Earnings — P	25,000		25,000	–	25,000
	$60,000		$60,000	$20,000	$60,000

The only change in the parent's balance sheet is a shift of $20,000 cash into its Investment account. The parent has 100% control of the subsidiary.

The parent's $20,000 Investment account and subsidiary's $20,000 equity accounts (which represent net assets) are viewed as reciprocal amounts that must be eliminated to prevent double counting when the consolidated statement is prepared.

Cash and other assets as well as liabilities of both entities are combined. However, only the equity accounts of the parent are included in the consolidated amounts.

Note that the consolidated column is identical to the parent's column before its investment in the subsidiary. This correlation results because the combined group has the same resources before and after the acquisition in this example.

The important point to note is that the combination process combines only certain amounts. Other amounts, usually referred to as **reciprocal amounts**, are not combined; reciprocal amounts are eliminated in the combination process. The parent investment in Subsidiary account and the subsidiary equity accounts comprise one example of reciprocal amounts that are eliminated for the following reasons.

Reciprocal amounts
Amounts appearing in financial statements of both parent and subsidiary that are not combined in preparing consolidated financial statements; these amounts are eliminated in the consolidation process to prevent double counting.

- The combined entity cannot have an investment in itself, from a consolidation point of view
- The inclusion of the parent's Investment account and the subsidiary's equity accounts would show more assets and equity than actually exist in the combined financial entity. In other words, the inclusion of these reciprocal amounts would result in a double counting of assets and equity in the combined financial statements.

The combination, therefore, eliminates the parent's Investment account and the subsidiary's reciprocal equity accounts. Intercompany transactions, if any, would also be eliminated. Since there have been no intercompany transactions at the acquisition date, no other elimination is required in this example.

Although reciprocal amounts are eliminated in the combination process, it is important to note that no journal entries are actually recorded in the books of either parent or subsidiary. Worksheet entries are prepared and used only toward preparation of consolidated financial statements. (See the illustrative problem in this section.)

Alternative 2

In this alternative, the purchase cost is $25,000; the subsidiary's net assets recorded in its books remain at $20,000 as in Alternative 1. A balance sheet is prepared to show the changes occurring in the parent's balance sheet immediately after the purchase; the balances of both parent and subsidiary are then combined. Note that, this time, the combination process involves not only the elimination of reciprocal amounts but also the creation of **goodwill from consolidation** (discussed briefly in Chapter 7); this goodwill arises because the parent has paid $5,000 in excess of the subsidiary's $20,000 net assets. (It is assumed for this example that the $5,000 payment is for goodwill in the subsidiary. In other examples, the $5,000 excess could counteract an undervaluation of assets in addition to the existence of goodwill.)

Note that the total of the consolidated column ($60,000) is identical to the parent's column total ($60,000) before its investment in the subsidiary. The combined group has the same resources before and after the acquisition, in this alternative. However, the individual components within the asset amounts differ because of the existence of goodwill.

Goodwill (from consolidation)
The amount paid in excess of the fair market value of the net assets of a subsidiary.

	Parent's Balance Sheet			Subsidiary Balance Sheet	Consolidated Balance Sheet
	Before Acquisition	*Investment*	*After Acquisition*		
Cash and Other Assets	$60,000	– $25,000	$35,000	$20,000	$55,000
Investment in Subsidiary	–	+ 25,000	25,000	–	–
Goodwill from consol- dation	–		–	–	5,000
	$60,000		$60,000	$20,000	$60,000
Liabilities	$26,000		$26,000	–	$26,000
Common Stock — S	–		–	$ 1,000	–
Retained Earnings — S	–		–	19,000	–
Common Stock — P	9,000		9,000	–	9,000
Retained Earnings — P	25,000		25,000	–	25,000
	$60,000		$60,000	$20,000	$60,000

The only change in the parent's balance sheet is a shift of $25,000 cash into the Investment account. The parent has 100% ownership of the subsidiary.

The combination process excludes the reciprocal amounts to prevent double counting when the combination is prepared. Note that the combination process also results in the recognition of $5,000 of goodwill arising from the combination in this example.

Assets and liabilities (which exclude inter-company transactions) of both entities are combined.
The $5,000 excess is recognized as goodwill from consolidation. Only the equity accounts of the parent are included in the consolidated amounts.

In this alternative, the parent paid $25,000 to purchase ownership claims to $20,000 of net assets in the subsidiary. The $5,000 excess was paid for goodwill in the subsidiary. Although goodwill is an asset, it is never recorded in the accounts of an entity unless it has been purchased. In this example, the $5,000 excess payment is considered to be recognition of the existence of goodwill in the subsidiary. (If the excess amount was attributable to an undervaluation of the subsidiary's assets, in addition to the existence of goodwill, this situation would be disclosed as in the illustrative problem in this section.)

Alternative 3

In this third alternative, the purchase cost is $16,000; the subsidiary's net assets recorded in its books remain at $20,000, as in the preceding examples. The accounting for this acquisition at a purchase cost that is $4,000 less than the subsidiary's book value is more complex, is seldom seen in Canada, and is more fully explained in an advanced accounting course.[1]

Illustrative Problem: Wholly Owned Subsidiary

This illustrative problem demonstrates the use of a worksheet to prepare a consolidated balance sheet at the date of acquisition. The same problem used in the preceding discussions is used, with the following changes:

1. The amount of the investment is changed to $26,500 to incorporate an example of an amount paid in recognition of an undervaluation of assets in the subsidiary.
2. The assets and liabilities of the subsidiary are altered to include liabilities in the subsidiary's balance sheet. Net assets (assets − liabilities) remain at $20,000.
3. In addition to the previous data, P made a $15,000 loan to S at December 31, 19X8 after the acquisition, as agreed in the acquisition negotiations. P recorded the loan as a receivable; S recorded the amount as a payable. These are reciprocal amounts that must be eliminated on consolidation.

Here are the individual balance sheets of P and S immediately before and after acquisition.

	Parent's Balance Sheet				Subsidiary's Balance Sheet		
	Before Acquisition	*Investment*	*Loan*	*After Acquisition*	*Before Acquisition*	*Loan*	*After Acquisition*
Cash and Other Assets	$60,000	− $26,500	− $15,000	$18,500	$22,000	+ $15,000	$37,000
Loan Receivable — S			+ 15,000	15,000			
Investment in Subsidiary		+ 26,500		26,500			
	$60,000			$60,000	$22,000		$37,000
Liabilities	$26,000			$26,000	$ 2,000		2,000
Loan Payable — P						+ 15,000	15,000
Common Stock — S					1,000		1,000
Retained Earnings — S					19,000		19,000
Common Stock — P	9,000			9,000			
Retained Earnings — P	25,000			25,000			
	$60,000			$60,000	$22,000		$37,000

There are two changes in the parent's balance sheet: (a) $26,500 of cash is used for the investment, and (b) $15,000 of cash is used for the loan. Note that the total assets have not changed.

The only change in the subsidiary's balance sheet is the receipt of $15,000 cash and the creation of loans payable of the same amount. Note that the total assets and total equity have changed, although net assets have not.

These comparisons are included to show the changes resulting from the investment and the loan. The preparation of consolidated financial statements requires the elimination of reciprocal amounts; the elimination of the Investment in Subsidiary account and the subsidiary's equity accounts was considered already. The Loan Receivable and Loan Payable accounts are also reciprocal amounts, since total assets and total liabilities of the combined economic entity did not increase.

Assume that, on December 31, 19X8, P Corporation purchased a 100-percent ownership interest in S Limited by paying $26,500 to the shareholders of S for their shares. Included in the purchase price was an amount in recognition of unrecorded goodwill in S and an undervaluation of an asset of S of $1,500.

On this date, as agreed in the acquisition, P also lent $15,000 to S. Here are the balance sheets prepared immediately after the purchase and recording of the loan.

	P	S	
	Book Value	*Book Value*	*Market Value*
Cash and Other Assets	$18,500	$37,000	$38,500
Loan Receivable — S	15,000	–	
Investment in Subsidiary	26,500	–	
	$60,000	$37,000	
Liabilities	$26,000	$ 2,000	2,000
Loan Payable — P	–	15,000	15,000
Common Stock — S	–	1,000	
Retained Earnings — S	–	19,000	
Common Stock — P	9,000	–	
Retained Earnings — P	25,000	–	
	$60,000	$37,000	

How much was included in the purchase price in recognition of undervalued assets in S?

Market Value of S Assets	(a)	$38,500	
Book Value of S Assets	(b)	37,000	
S Assets Undervalued	(a – b)	$ 1,500	(c)

How much was included in the purchase price in recognition of unrecorded goodwill in S?

Purchase Payment	$26,500	
P Purchased 100% of S	20,000	
Excess	$ 6,500	
Excess Resulting from Asset Undervaluation	1,500	(c)
Balance Is Goodwill	$ 5,000	

Next, the worksheet elimination entries needed to consolidate the individual balance sheets must be prepared.

Worksheet entry (i):   To eliminate intercompany loan.

Loans Payable — P	15,000	
Loans Receivable — S		15,000

Worksheet entry (ii):   To eliminate the Investment in Subsidiary and subsidiary equity accounts and set up undervaluation of S's assets and unrecorded goodwill.

Common Stock — S	1,000	
Retained Earnings — S	19,000	
Assets — S	1,500	
Goodwill from Consolidation	5,000	
Investment in Subsidiary		26,500

A consolidation worksheet is prepared at December 31, 19X8 immediately following the purchase of S's shares and loan of $15,000.

Consolidated Worksheet

| | Book Balances | | Eliminations | | |
	P	S	Debit	Credit	Consolidated
Debits					
Cash and Other Assets	$18,500	$37,000	(b) $1,500		$57,000
Loan Receivable — S	15,000	–		(a) $15,000	–
Investment in Subsidiary	26,500	–		(b) 26,500	–
Goodwill from Consolidation	–	–	(b) 5,000		5,000
	$60,000	$37,000			$62,000
Credits					
Liabilities	$26,000	$ 2,000			$28,000
Loan Payable — P	–	15,000	(a) 15,000		–
Common Stock — S	–	1,000	(b) 1,000		–
Retained Earnings — S	–	19,000	(b) 19,000		–
Common Stock — P	9,000	–			9,000
Retained Earnings — P	25,000	–			25,000
	$60,000	$37,000	$41,500	$41,500	$62,000

A consolidated balance sheet is prepared at December 31, 19X8 immediately following the acquisition of S.

P Corporation and S Limited
Consolidated Balance Sheet
At December 31, 19X8

Assets		*Liabilities and Equity*		
Cash and Other Assets	$57,000	Liabilities		$28,000
Goodwill from Consolidation	5,000	Common Stock	$ 9,000	
		Retained Earnings	25,000	34,000
	$62,000			$62,000

C. Partially Owned Subsidiary

This section of the analysis prepared for Bluebeard's executives considers the possibility of a partially owned subsidiary; the purchase of any amount more than 50 percent of outstanding voting shares of another corporation results in a parent-subsidiary relationship. A 75-percent ownership interest is used in this example, which means that 75 percent of the subsidiary's shareholders were bought out; these previous owners no longer have an ownership interest in the subsidiary. In effect, the 75-percent share purchase results in the parent acquiring a 75-percent ownership claim to the net assets of the subsidiary.

Although the parent is then in a position to control the subsidiary's operations, 25 percent of the subsidiary is still owned by other shareholders. This one-quarter outside ownership is collectively referred to as the **minority interest**; it has a 25-percent ownership claim to the net assets of the subsidiary. This claim must be taken into consideration in the preparation of consolidated financial statements.

Minority interest
The ownership of a subsidiary's shares not owned by the parent corporation.

Recording the Purchase

The acquisition cost for the alternatives discussed in section A is recorded below. The difference in each case this time is that the parent has acquired a 75-percent ownership interest in the subsidiary. Note that the amount paid differs in each case.

Acquisition of 75-Percent Ownership Interest

	Alternative 4	Alternative 5	Alternative 6
Investment in Subsidiary	15,000	18,000	13,000
Cash	15,000	18,000	13,000

Although the purchase involves the payment of cash, the acquisition can also be made through a payment of other assets. Regardless, the parent in effect purchases a 75-percent ownership interest in the subsidiary's net assets; 75 percent of the subsidiary's previous owners no longer have any ownership interest in the subsidiary.

Preparation of Consolidated Financial Statements

The combination of individual parent and subsidiary financial statements is next prepared for the partially owned subsidiary. As before, accountants prepare consolidated financial statements to show a financial picture of the whole operation, as if they were one economic entity; this consolidation is done even though a minority interest exists in the subsidiary.

Alternative 4

In this alternative, the purchase cost is $15,000; this is the amount of the subsidiary's net assets recorded in the books ($20,000 × 75% = $15,000). This December 31, 19X8 purchase changes the parent's balances immediately after the purchase, as shown next. Then, the amounts of both parent and subsidiary are combined. Note that the combination process results in the recognition of the 25-percent minority interest.

	Parent's Balance Sheet Before Acquisition	Investment	Parent's Balance Sheet After Acquisition	Subsidiary Balance Sheet	Consolidated Balance Sheet
Cash and Other Assets	$60,000	−$15,000	$45,000	$20,000	$65,000
Investment in Subsidiary	–	+15,000	15,000	–	–
	$60,000		$60,000	$20,000	$65,000
Liabilities	$26,000		$26,000	–	$26,000
Common Stock — S	–		–	$ 1,000	–
Retained Earnings — S	–		–	19,000	–
Minority Interest	–		–	–	5,000
Common Stock — P	9,000		9,000		9,000
Retained Earnings — P	25,000		25,000		25,000
	$60,000		$60,000	$20,000	$65,000

The only change in the parent's balance sheet is a shift of $15,000 of cash into its Investment account. The parent has 75% ownership of the subsidiary.

The combination process excludes the reciprocal amount up to the $15,000 (75%) purchase. This $15,000 reciprocal amount is eliminated in the consolidation process.

Assets and liabilities of both entities are combined. Only the equity accounts of the parent are shown as equity. However, the $5,000 (25%) of the subsidiary not purchased is shown as a minority interest.

Note that the consolidated column total ($65,000) is $5,000 larger than the parent's column total ($60,000) before its investment in the subsidiary. The consolidated statements include the interests of both the parent and minority interests; therefore, the consolidated statements are increased when minority interests exist in a controlled subsidiary.

In this case, the combination of both entities eliminates the parent's Investment account and 75 percent of the subsidiary's equity accounts; the ownership interest of the subsidiary's remaining shareholders (25 percent) is recognized as a minority interest. The consolidated column, therefore, indicates that both the parent and the minority shareholders of the subsidiary have an ownership interest in the consolidated net assets of the combined group. An important difference between the parent and the minority interest, however, is that the parent is in the position of control of the subsidiary's operations.

Alternative 5

In this fifth alternative, the purchase cost is $18,000; this amount is $3,000 greater than the 75-percent ownership interest in the subsidiary's net assets ($20,000 × 75% = $15,000). The changes occurring in the parent's balances immediately before and after the purchase are prepared; then, the balances of both parent and subsidiary are combined. Note that the combination process results in the recognition of goodwill from consolidation, as well as the recognition of the 25-percent minority interest. The goodwill arises because the parent has paid $3,000 in excess of its 75-percent ownership of the subsidiary's $20,000 net assets (75% × $20,000 = $15,000). In other situations, this $3,000 excess could result from an undervaluation of assets in addition to the existence of goodwill, if any exists in the subsidiary. An example incorporating an asset undervaluation appears in the illustrative problem in section C.

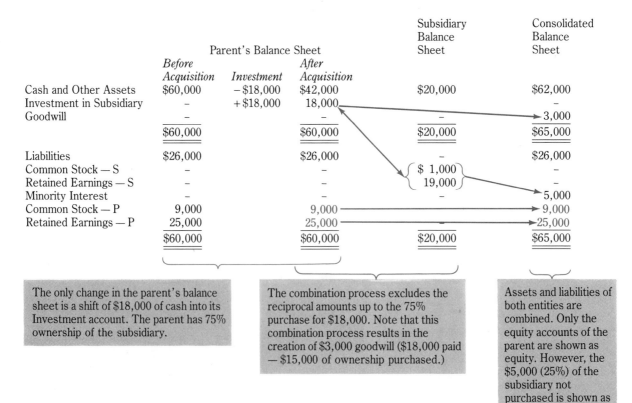

	Parent's Balance Sheet			Subsidiary Balance Sheet	Consolidated Balance Sheet
	Before Acquisition	*Investment*	*After Acquisition*		
Cash and Other Assets	$60,000	− $18,000	$42,000	$20,000	$62,000
Investment in Subsidiary	–	+ $18,000	18,000		–
Goodwill	–		–	–	3,000
	$60,000		$60,000	$20,000	$65,000
Liabilities	$26,000		$26,000	–	$26,000
Common Stock — S	–		–	$ 1,000	–
Retained Earnings — S	–		–	19,000	–
Minority Interest	–		–	–	5,000
Common Stock — P	9,000		9,000		9,000
Retained Earnings — P	25,000		25,000		25,000
	$60,000		$60,000	$20,000	$65,000

The only change in the parent's balance sheet is a shift of $18,000 of cash into its Investment account. The parent has 75% ownership of the subsidiary.

The combination process excludes the reciprocal amounts up to the 75% purchase for $18,000. Note that this combination process results in the creation of $3,000 goodwill ($18,000 paid — $15,000 of ownership purchased.)

Assets and liabilities of both entities are combined. Only the equity accounts of the parent are shown as equity. However, the $5,000 (25%) of the subsidiary not purchased is shown as a minority interest.

Note that the consolidated column ($65,000) is also $5,000 greater than the parent's column ($60,000) before its investment in the subsidiary. This is due to the fact that the consolidated statements include both the parent and minority interests; therefore, the consolidated statements are increased when minority interests exist in a controlled subsidiary.

Alternative 6

In this sixth alternative, the purchase cost is $13,000; the subsidiary's net assets recorded in its books remain at $20,000, as in the preceding examples. The accounting for this acquisition at a purchase cost that is $7,000 less than the subsidiary's book value is more complex, is seldom seen in Canada, and is more fully explained in an advanced accounting course.[2]

Illustrative Problem: Partially Owned Subsidiary

This illustrative problem is identical to the earlier one, with one exception: the parent has purchased only 75% of the subsidiary, paying $19,500 cash. Here are the individual balance sheets of P and S immediately before and after acquisition.

	Parent's Balance Sheet				Subsidiary's Balance Sheet		
	Before Acquisition	*Investment*	*Loan*	*After Acquisition*	*Before Acquisition*	*Loan*	*After Acquisition*
Cash and Other Assets	$60,000	− $19,500	− $15,000	$25,500	$22,000	+ $15,000	$37,000
Loan Receivable — S			+ 15,000	15,000			
Investment in Subsidiary		+ 19,500		19,500			
	$60,000			$60,000	$22,000		$37,000
Liabilities	$26,000			$26,000	$ 2,000		$ 2,000
Loan Payable — P						+ 15,000	15,000
Common Stock — S					1,000		1,000
Retained Earnings — S					19,000		19,000
Common Stock — P	9,000			9,000			
Retained Earnings — P	25,000			25,000			
	$60,000			$60,000	$22,000		$37,000

On December 31, 19X8, P Corporation purchased a 75-percent ownership interest in S Limited by paying $19,500 to 75 percent of the shareholders of S for their shares. Included in the purchase price was an amount in recognition of unrecorded goodwill in S and an undervaluation of an asset. On this date, P also lent $15,000 to S. The balance sheets prepared immediately after the purchase and recording of the loan appeared as follows:

	P	S	
	Book Value	*Book Value*	*Market Value*
Cash and Other Assets	$25,500	$37,000	$38,500
Loan Receivable — S	15,000	–	
Investment in Subsidiary	19,500	–	
	$60,000	$37,000	
Liabilities	$26,000	$ 2,000	$ 2,000
Loan Payable — P	–	15,000	
Common Stock — S	–	1,000	
Retained Earnings — S	–	19,000	
Common Stock — P	9,000	–	
Retained Earnings — P	25,000	–	
	$60,000	$37,000	

How much is included in the purchase price in recognition of undervalued assets in S?

		100%		75%
Market Value of S Assets	(a)	$38,500 × 75% purchased =		$28,875
Book Value of S Assets	(b)	37,000 × 75% purchased =		27,750
S Assets Undervalued	(a − b)	$ 1,500		$ 1,125 (c)

How much is included in the purchase price in recognition of unrecorded goodwill is S?

Purchase Payment	$19,500
P Purchased 75% of S	15,000
Excess	$4,500
Excess Resulting from Asset Undervaluation	1,125 (c)
Balance Is Goodwill	$ 3,375

The amount of minority interest is calculated.

Net Assets of S	$20,000
P purchased 75% of S	15,000
($20,000 × 75%)	
Minority Interest	$ 5,000

The worksheet elimination entries needed to consolidate the individual balance sheets are prepared.

Worksheet entry (i):   To eliminate intercompany loan.

Loans Payable — P	15,000	
Loans Receivable — S		15,000

Worksheet Entry (ii):   To eliminate the Investment in Subsidiary and subsidiary equity accounts and set up the undervaluation of S's assets, the unrecorded goodwill, and the minority interest.

Common Stock — S	1,000	
Retained Earnings — S	19,000	
Assets — S	1,125	
Goodwill from Consolidation	3,375	
Minority Interest		5,000
Investment in Subsidiary		19,500

A consolidation worksheet is prepared for December 31, 19X8 immediately following the purchase of S's shares and the loan of $15,000.

	Book Balances		Eliminations		Consolidated
	P	*S*	*Debit*	*Credit*	
Debits					
Cash and Other Assets	$25,500	$37,000	(b) $ 1,125		$63,625
Loan Receivable — S	15,000	–		(a) $15,000	–
Investment in Subsidiary	19,500	–		(b) 19,500	–
Goodwill from Consolidation	–	–	(b) 3,375		3,375
	$60,000	$37,000			$67,000
Credits					
Liabilities	$26,000	$ 2,000			$28,000
Loan Payable — P	–	15,000	(a) 15,000		–
Common Stock — S	–	1,000	(b) 1,000		–
Retained Earnings — S	–	19,000	(b) 19,000	(b) 5,000	5,000
Common Stock — P	9,000	–			9,000
Retained Earnings — P	25,000	–			25,000
	$60,000	$37,000	$39,500	$39,500	$67,000

Real Life Example 17-2

Shareholders Approve Comterm-Bytec Deal

Shareholders of Comterm Inc. yesterday pinned their hopes on market acceptance of the Hyperion, an IBM-compatible portable personal computer developed by Bytec Management Corp. of Ottawa.

Shareholders at the meeting voted 99.85 percent in favour of an amalgamation between Comterm and Bytec.

Bytec shareholders had accepted the deal — which gives them a 60.5-percent interest in the combined entity on a fully diluted basis — at a morning meeting in Ottawa.

The new company will be known as Bytec-Comterm Inc. and will operate from Comterm's head office in Pointe Claire. A prospectus for a new issue of common shares will be issued within a few weeks, Laurent Nadeau, Comterm's chairman and president, said after the meeting. Terms and conditions of the offering have not yet been revealed.

Nadeau denied an assertion by one shareholder, who later identified himself as Carl Evoniak, that the deal was "a sell-out" of Comterm's shareholders. Nadeau responded by calling the deal "really an amalgamation, a pooling of interests".

Evoniak was nearly alone in his opposition. Only 2993 shares or 0.15 percent of those represented were voted against the deal. The combined entity will rack up sales of more than $100 million in the fiscal year beginning Feb. 1, predicted Micheal Cowpland, a founder of Mitel Corp.

Bytec reported a loss of $14.6 million for the year ended July 31, on sales of $9.2 million.

But the company shipped about 1500 Hyperions in September and showed an unaudited profit during both August and September, Cowpland told reporters after the meeting. The Hyperion is priced between 10 and 15 percent below a comparably equipped IBM Personal Computer, Cowpland said. He said the company expects to be shipping between 3000 and 4000 Hyperions monthly by January.

Source Ian Ravensbergen, "Shareholders approve Comterm-Bytec deal", *The* (Montreal) *Gazette*, October 25, 1983, p. F-1.

A consolidated balance sheet is prepared for December 31, 19X8 immediately following the acquisition of S.

Assets		Liabilities and Equity		
Cash and Other Assets	$63,625	Liabilities		$28,000
Goodwill from Consolidation	3,375	Minority Interest		5,000
		Common Stock	$ 9,000	
		Retained Earnings	25,000	34,000
	$67,000			$67,000

D. Pooling of Interests

The preceding section reviewed the purchase of a controlling interest in the shares of a subsidiary; in this situation, the parent has bought out all or some of the subsidiary's shareholders. The analysis prepared for Bluebeard management also evaluated the method of acquiring a subsidiary commonly referred to as a pooling of interests. The acquisition of the subsidiary under a pooling of interests is accomplished through an exchange of shares; specifically, shareholders of the subsidiary exchange their ownership in the subsidiary for an ownership interest in the parent. These original shareholders of the subsidiary therefore become shareholders in the parent and the group of corporations now controlled by the parent. For an example of a pooling of interests, see Real Life Example 17-2.

Preparation of Consolidated Financial Statements

The combination of individual financial statements of the parent and its subsidiary for a pooling of interests differs from that for the acquisition through a purchase of shares. The different combination process is reflected in the way the acquisition is recorded in the books of the parent. This difference is shown in Figure 17-2.

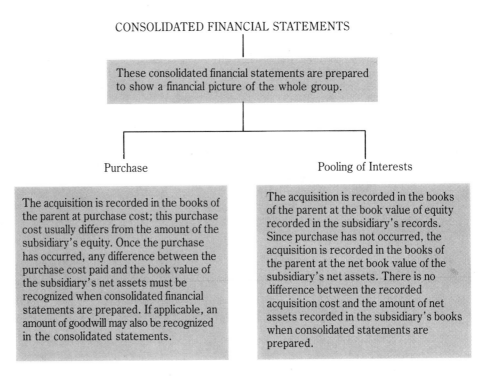

CONSOLIDATED FINANCIAL STATEMENTS

These consolidated financial statements are prepared to show a financial picture of the whole group.

Purchase

The acquisition is recorded in the books of the parent at purchase cost; this purchase cost usually differs from the amount of the subsidiary's equity. Once the purchase has occurred, any difference between the purchase cost paid and the book value of the subsidiary's net assets must be recognized when consolidated financial statements are prepared. If applicable, an amount of goodwill may also be recognized in the consolidated statements.

Pooling of Interests

The acquisition is recorded in the books of the parent at the book value of equity recorded in the subsidiary's records. Since purchase has not occurred, the acquisition is recorded in the books of the parent at the net book value of the subsidiary's net assets. There is no difference between the recorded acquisition cost and the amount of net assets recorded in the subsidiary's books when consolidated statements are prepared.

Figure 17-2   Contrast between a purchase and a pooling of interests as recorded in the consolidated financial statements

The accounting profession has made recommendations for the accounting treatment of business combinations, particularly in the distinction between a purchase and a pooling of interests, even if the acquisition has been made through the exchange of shares. The distinction centres on whether a dominant group emerges from the acquisition. These distinctions are complex and are usually dealt with in advanced accounting courses.

Discussion Questions

1. What is a business combination?
2. What is the distinction between a parent and a subsidiary?
3. Distinguish between a purchase and a pooling of interests.
4. Does a parent corporation acquire the net assets or the equity of a subsidiary? Explain.
5. Why does a subsidiary maintain its own accounting records?
6. Why would the purchase cost of a subsidiary exceed the subsidiary's net assets?
7. Why are reciprocal amounts eliminated in the preparation of consolidated financial statements?
8. How are intercompany transactions handled in a combination? Why?
9. Describe the procedure used in the preparation of consolidated financial statements.
10. How does goodwill arise on consolidation?
11. How does partial ownership of a subsidiary result in a minority interest?
12. How does the preparation of consolidated financial statements differ for a pooling of interests and a purchase?
13. Refer to Real Life Example 17-1. What are the roles of government agencies such as the Ontario Securities Commission in business combinations?

Discussion Cases

Discussion Case 17-1:   The Nordair Merger

Donald Carty admits owning Nordair Inc. will not make CP Air the People Express of the North. The Toronto-born Harvard business graduate spent six years at American Airlines while the United States number two airline was learning to cope with unregulated competition. Yesterday, he mapped out Canadian Pacific Air Lines' strategy for coping with an open skies policy being considered for Canada during the most wide-ranging and frank interview since he joined the Vancouver airline in February.

The goal is to pull in more traffic on both domestic and international routes, simplify the aircraft fleet and cut operating costs 25 to 50 percent over five years.

"Cutting costs is like peeling an onion. Once you take off one layer you find another layer."

Wage costs will be tackled through tough contract talks, work-rule changes, contracting work out, part-time employees and automation, Carty said. But cost chopping must be handled so employees don't feel like leftovers, he admitted.

"An airline that runs on service relies on how people feel. It's a balancing act."

His only great fear about Canadian-style airline deregulation is the ability of government-owned Air Canada to hit Ottawa for a cash injection to buy new planes.

"There is no real evidence they fiscally restrain themselves the way we do," he said of Air Canada management.

Buying Nordair through an exchange of shares amounts to a cheap way to buy used airplanes and broadens CP Air's

| | Net Income | |
| | (000s) | |
Year	CP Air	Nordair
1979	$13,120	$2,053
1980	2,853	$2,742
1981	(22,781)	$1,995
1982	(39,214)	($2,637)
1983	(16,408)	$5,016
1984	13,760	$1,395

ability to pick up feeder traffic from populous Ontario and Quebec.

The total face value of the $17.57 preferred shares offered is $43 million, but they can't be turned in for cash for three years. Nordair's planes, meanwhile, are worth $54 million after debt repayment, Carty guessed.

Meanwhile the Quebec government through wholly owned Quebecair is still in the battle for rival Nordair despite the agreement with CP Air, Canadian Press quoted Transport Minister Guy Tardif as saying yesterday. But Quebec has tried for years for such a merger without being able to interest Nordair in a deal.

Carty, meanwhile, also likes the management at Nordair, an airline known for its champagne breakfasts, clever marketing and the most consistent record of profits among major Canadian airlines.

Although Nordair and CP Air's last acquisition, Eastern Provincial Airways, may operate as separate companies because of different labor contracts, travellers will not notice.

"I'd like the passenger to perceive it's all part of the CP network," he said, referring to CP's existing relationship with Air B.C. and Air Maritime and to Nordair's recently signed deal with Torontair of Markham.

Then CP Air will be better able to break the cycle of travel agents favouring Air Canada when a change of planes is required, Carty argued.

The increased size of CP Air, although still only half that of Air Canada, will provide more bang for the airline's advertising dollar and save on purchases of fuel and insurance.

"Clearly we've got to get costs down in a dramatic way," he said.

One of the major criticisms of Canadian airlines is that they operate too many different types of aircraft. Carty said CP Air is taking steps to remedy that.

"Every time we retire one [jumbo Boeing] 747 pilot, we have to train eight other pilots as they move up the ladder of seniority," Carty said.

Trading the airline's four 409-seat 747s for four McDonnelll Douglas DC10s — as Carty revealed the airline is now negotiating to do — would save on training, repair and parts inventory costs.

Although CP Air has had severe losses in the past five years, Carty said it's a reflection of confidence in the airline that Nordair's main owners agreed to a merger.

The Montreal venture-capital company Innocan Inc. owns 68 percent of Nordair shares. A Quebec-government agency that also owns Quebecair has 22 percent and employees the rest.

A conversion provision offered with the preferred shares could leave Nordair owners holding 13 percent of CP Air, now wholly owned by Canadian Pacific Ltd.

Whether that provision makes the investors more than $17.57 a share will depend on the success the airline has cutting costs and attracting passengers with lower fares.

Source   James Daw, "Nordair merger offers glimpse of CP Air's plans for future", *The Toronto Star*, October 10, 1985, p. E-1.

For Discussion

1. Donald Carty has sought your advice. Would you recommend or disapprove the completion of this merger?
2. How does government regulation of the airline industry affect Carty's company and its operations?

Discussion Case 17-2:   Quebecair to Fight CP Air

Provincially owned Quebecair Inc., having lost the fight to gain control of Nordair Inc. of Montreal to Canadian Pacific Air Lines Ltd., says it will seek to block the merger of the two airlines before the Canadian Transport Commission. In addition, Quebecair said the 22 percent shareholding of the Quebec Government in Nordair will not be tendered to CP Air, which is a unit of Canadian Pacific Ltd. of Montreal.

"We will strongly oppose any transfer of Nordair to CP Air before the CTC, and we will try to block the merger," the airline said.

CP Air, which is based in Vancouver, has obtained 43.7 percent of the 1 070 046 Nordair shares outstanding. It paid $16.25 a share plus one warrant entitling the holder to buy

three CP Air common shares at $7 a share. The Nordair shares were sold to CP Air by 14 institutional holders located in Alberta and Ontario. The same offer is being extended to all other Nordair holders.

For Discussion

1. If CP Air has acquired 43.7 percent of Nordair shares, has a business combination occurred?
2. Assume CP Air gains the approval from the Canadian Transport Commission in its purchase of Nordair. How would you advise Quebecair's management regarding its 22 percent share in Nordair?

Comprehension Problems

Comprehension Problem 17-1

On January 1, 19X2, P Corporation purchased 100 percent of S Limited's shares by paying $300,000 cash to the shareholders of S for their shares. The purchase price included an amount in recognition of an undervaluation in the asset land and also an amount in recognition of goodwill in S. The balance sheet balances of both corporation immediately after the purchase are recorded in this partial consolidation worksheet.

	Book Balances	
	P	*S*
Cash and Other Assets	$350,000	$150,000
Investment in Subsidiary	300,000	–
Land — S	–	200,000
Goodwill	–	–
	$650,000	$350,000
Liabilities	$225,000	$100,000
Common Stock — P	250,000	–
Retained Earnings — P	175,000	–
Common Stock — S	–	200,000
Retained Earnings — S	–	50,000
	$650,000	$350,000

Required:
1. Calculate the amount by which land is undervalued. Assume that the current market value of land is $225,000.
2. Calculate the amount of goodwill included in the purchase price.
3. Prepare the worksheet elimination entry needed to consolidate the individual balance sheets.
4. Complete the consolidation worksheet, using the form in the illustrative problems in the chapter.

Comprehension Problem 17-2

The following consolidation worksheet was prepared on December 31, 19X2 following the purchase of a controlling interest in S Limited by P Corporation. On that date, P also had other transactions with S.

Consolidated Worksheet

| | Book Balances | | Eliminations | | |
	P	S	Debit	Credit	Consolidated
Cash	$ 6,000	$ 2,000			$ 8,000
Accounts Receivable	14,000	11,000		(a) $ 1,000	24,000
Notes Receivable	5,000	–		(b) 5,000	–
Investment in Subsidiary	40,000	–		(c) 40,000	–
Fixed Assets (net)	110,000	43,000			153,000
Goodwill	–	–	(c) $ 5,000		5,000
	$175,000	$56,000			$190,000
Accounts Payable	$ 20,000	$ 1,000	(a) 1,000		$ 20,000
Notes Payable	–	5,000	(b) 5,000		–
Minority Interest	–	–		(c) 15,000	15,000
Common Stock — P	100,000	–			100,000
Retained Earnings — P	55,000	–			55,000
Common Stock — S	–	40,000	(c) 40,000		–
Retained Earnings — S	–	10,000	(c) 10,000		–
	$175,000	$56,000			$190,000

Required:
1. What percentage of S's shares was purchased by P? (*Hint:* Start by calculating the percentage of S owned by minority shareholders.)
2. Was the purchase of S's shares made at book value? Explain.
3. Record the worksheet elimination entries needed to consolidate the individual balance sheets. Explain why each entry is required.
4. Prepare a classified balance sheet at December 31, 19X2.

Comprehension Problem 17-3

On December 31, 19X3, P Corporation purchased two-thirds of S Limited's shares by a cash payment to S's shareholders for their shares. Included in the purchase price was an amount in recognition of unrecorded goodwill in S. On this date, P also made a $5,000 interest-free loan to S; included in P's accounts receivable is $10,000 due from S for an asset sold to S at cost on December 31, 19X3. The balance sheet balances of both corporations immediately after the purchase and the transactions associated with it are recorded below.

Consolidated Worksheet

| | Book Balances | | | Book Balances | |
	P	S		P	S
Cash	$ 10,000	$ 2,000	Accounts Payable	$ 70,000	$ 25,000
Accounts Receivable	65,000	30,000	Accounts Payable — P	–	10,000
Accounts Receivable — S	10,000	–	Loans Payable — P	–	5,000
Loans Receivable — S	5,000	–	Minority Interest	–	–
Investment in Subsidiary	50,000	–	Common Stock — P	20,000	–
Fixed Assets (net)	60,000	68,000	Retained Earnings — P	110,000	–
Goodwill	–	–	Common Stock — S	–	10,000
			Retained Earnings — S	–	50,000
	$200,000	$100,000		$200,000	$100,000

Required:
1. Calculate the amount of goodwill included in the purchase price of shares.
2. Calculate the amount of minority interest.
3. Prepare the worksheet elimination entries needed to consolidate the individual balance sheets.
4. Complete the consolidated worksheet.
5. Prepare a consolidated balance sheet at December 31, 19X3 immediately after the purchase of S's shares.

Comprehension Problem 17-4

On December 31, 19X7, P Corporation purchased an interest in S Limited by paying $250,000 cash to the shareholders of S for their shares. The balance sheets and consolidated balance sheet prepared immediately after the purchase are as follows:

	P	S	Consolidated
Assets			
Cash	$ 20,000	$ 10,000	$ 30,000
Notes Receivable	5,000	–	–
Accounts Receivable	100,000	65,000	150,000
Merchandise Inventory	175,000	160,000	335,000
Investment in Subsidiary	250,000	–	–
Land	150,000	75,000	249,000
Goodwill	–	–	26,000
	$700,000	$310,000	$790,000
Liabilities and Equities			
Accounts Payable	$190,000	$ 55,000	$230,000
Notes Payable	–	5,000	–
Minority Interest	–	–	50,000
Common Stock — P	210,000	–	210,000
Retained Earnings — P	300,000	–	300,000
Common Stock — S	–	200,000	–
Retained Earnings — S	–	50,000	–
	$700,000	$310,000	$790,000

Required:
1. What percentage of S's shares was purchased by P? (*Hint:* Start by calculating the percentage of S owned by minority shareholders.)
2. Was the purchase of S shares made at book value? Explain.
3. Prepare the worksheet elimination entries that were made on the consolidation worksheet to consolidate the balance sheets of P and S.

Problems

Problem 17-1 (CGA adapted)

On December 31, 19X8, P Corporation purchased an interest in S Limited by paying $120,000 cash to the shareholders of S for their shares. Included in this purchase price was an amount in recognition of an undervaluation of the net assets of S. Assume there is no goodwill. Here are some summarized financial data from the balance sheets of both corporations immediately after the purchase.

	P Book Value	S Book Value
Net Assets	$400,000	$90,000
Common Stock	100,000	30,000
Retained Earnings	300,000	60,000

Required: Consider these cases. Case A: P purchased 100 percent of S. Case B: P purchased 70 percent of S. Case C: P purchased 60 percent of S. For each case
1. Calculate the amount of the undervaluation of S's net assets.
2. Prepare the worksheet elimination entry needed to consolidate the individual balance sheets. (The preparation of a consolidation worksheet is not required in this problem.)
3. What amounts would be reported on the consolidated balance sheet for:
   (a) Net assets?
   (b) Common Stock? Retained Earnings?

Problem 17-2

On December 31, 19X1, P Corporation purchased an interest in S Limited by paying cash to the shareholders of S for their shares. S is a newly formed developer of computer micro-chips that was about to begin manufacturing operations. Included in the purchase price was an amount in recognition of the existence of goodwill in S. Immediately before this purchase, the balance sheets of the corporations appeared as follows:

	P Book Value	S Book Value	S Market Value
Cash and other Assets	$450,000	$150,000	$150,000
Liabilities	$ 75,000	$ –	
Common Stock	175,000	$150,000	
Retained Earnings	200,000	–	
	$450,000	$150,000	

Required: Consider these cases. Case A: P purchased 100 percent of S's shares, by paying $175,000 cash. Case B: P purchased 60 percent of S's shares, by paying $100,000 cash. For each case:
1. Calculate the amount of goodwill included in the purchase.
2. Calculate the amount of the minority interest, if applicable.
3. Prepare the entry to record in P's books the purchase of S's shares.
4. Prepare the worksheet elimination entry needed to consolidate the individual balance sheets. (The preparation of a consolidated worksheet is not required in this problem.)
5. Prepare a consolidated balance sheet at December 31, 19X1 immediately following the purchase of S's shares.

Problem 17-3

On June 30, 19X3, P Corporation purchased 70 percent interest in S Limited by paying $225,000 cash to the shareholders of S for their shares. Included in this purchase price was an amount in recognition of an undervaluation in fixed assets of S and also an amount in recognition of goodwill in S. On this date S owed $50,000 to P; this amount is included in the accounts receivable of P and the accounts payable of S. The financial statements of both corporations immediately preceding the purchase are reproduced below:

	P	S	
	Book Value	Book Value	Market Value
Cash	$275,000	$ 30,000	$ 30,000
Accounts Receivable	150,000	20,000	20,000
Inventory	200,000	110,000	110,000
Fixed Assets (net)	335,000	225,000	330,000
	$960,000	$385,000	
Accounts Payable	$ 50,000	$160,000	$160,000
Common Stock	115,000	100,000	
Retained Earnings	795,000	125,000	
	$960,000	$385,000	

Required:
1. Prepare the entry to record in P's books the purchase of S's shares.
2. Calculate the amount of the undervaluation in fixed assets of S.
3. Calculate the amount of goodwill included in the purchase price.
4. Prepare the worksheet elimination entries needed to consolidate the individual balance sheets.
5. Prepare and complete a consolidated worksheet.
6. Prepare a consolidated balance sheet at June 30, 19X3 immediately after the purchase of S's shares.

Problem 17-4

On January 2, 19X3, P purchased an interest in S. The following condensed financial statements of S and P were prepared immediately before the purchase:

	P	S	
	Book Value	Book Value	Market Value
Assets	$150,000	$190,000	
Liabilities	$ 10,000	$ 10,000	
Equity	140,000	?	
	$150,000		

Required: Consider these cases. Case A: P purchased 100 percent of S shares at January 2, 19X3, by paying $210,000 to shareholders of S. Included in the purchase price was an amount in recognition of unrecorded goodwill in S. Case B: P purchased 60 percent of S shares at January 2, 19X3, by paying $125,000 to shareholders of S. Included in the purchase was an amount in recognition of unrecorded goodwill in S. For each case
1. Prepare the entry to record on P's books the purchase of S's shares.
2. Calculate the amount of minority interest to be shown on the consolidated balance sheet immediately after the purchase of S's shares.
3. Calculate the amount of goodwill to be shown on the consolidated balance sheet immediately after the purchase of S's shares.
4. Prepare the worksheet elimination entry needed to remove the Investment in Subsidiary account on P's books and S's equity immediately after the purchase of S's shares.

Problem 17-5

P is an investment company that has assets consisting of cash and investments. On December 31, 19X7, P purchased 70 percent of S's shares by paying $185,000 to shareholders of S. The balance sheet and other financial information of S immediately before the purchase are as follows:

	S			S	
	Book Value	*Market Value*		*Book Value*	*Market Value*
Cash	$ 75,000	$ 75,000	Accounts Payable	$ 55,000	$ 55,000
Land	40,000	85,000	Bonds Payable	80,000	80,000
Building (net)	110,000	190,000	Common Stock	120,000	
Equipment (net)	60,000	20,000	Retained Earnings (Jan. 2, 19X7)	140,000	
Goodwill	50,000	—	Net loss for the year	(60,000)	
	$ 335,000			$335,000	

Required:
1. Included in the purchase price was an amount in recognition of the undervaluation and overvaluation of various balance sheet items. Calculate the amount of the net under- or overvaluation.
2. Was any amount included in the purchase price in recognition of unrecorded goodwill for S? Explain.
3. What amount of assets and liabilities of S would appear on the consolidated balance sheet immediately after the purchase of S's shares by P?
4. Calculate the amount of minority interest that would appear on the consolidated balance sheet immediately after purchase of S's shares by P.

Alternate Problems

Alternate Problem 17-1

On January 2, 19X2, P Corporation purchased an interest in S Limited, by paying cash to the shareholders of S for their shares. The financial statements and other financial information of both corporations immediately before the purchase are as follows:

	P	S	
	Book Value	*Book Value*	*Market Value*
Cash and Other Assets	$205,000	$ 90,000	$90,000
Inventory	95,000	60,000	70,000
Fixed Assets	165,000	50,000	65,000
	$465,000	$200,000	
Liabilities	$ 55,000	$ 45,000	$45,000
Common Stock	260,000	95,000	
Retained Earnings	150,000	60,000	
	$465,000	$200,000	

Required: Consider these cases. Case A: P purchased 100 percent of S's shares for $180,000 cash. Case B: P purchased 60 percent of S's shares for $120,000 cash. For each case:
1. Prepare the entry to record in P's books the purchase of S's shares.
2. Calculate the amount of the minority interest, if any.
3. Was any amount included in the purchase price in recognition of unrecorded goodwill in S? If so, calculate the amount of such goodwill.

4. Calculate the consolidated balances for inventory and goodwill at January 2, 19X2 immediately after the purchase.
5. Prepare the worksheet elimination entry needed to consolidate the individual balance sheets. (The preparation of a consolidated worksheet is not required in this problem.)
6. Prepare a consolidated balance sheet at January 2, 19X2 immediately after the purchase of S's shares.

Alternate Problem 17-2

On January 2, 19X6, P Corporation purchased a 90-percent interest in S Limited by paying $120,000 cash to the shareholders of S for their shares. Included in this purchase price was an amount in recognition of the existence of goodwill in S. Here is selected financial information from the balance sheets of both corporations immediately before the purchase.

	P	S
Common Stock	$120,000	$75,000
Retained Earnings	70,000	25,000

Required: At January 2, 19X6
1. Prepare the entry to record in P's books the purchase of S's shares.
2. Prepare the worksheet elimination entry needed to consolidate the individual balance sheets immediately after the purchase. (Assume that there are no other reciprocal amounts.)
3. Calculate the amount of equity (common stock and retained earnings) that would appear on the consolidated balance sheet.

Alternate Problem 17-3

The following are financial statements and other financial information of P Corporation and S Limited at December 31, 19X6.

	P	S	
	Book Value	Book Value	Market Value
Cash and Other Assets	$160,000	$ 30,000	$ 30,000
Patent	–	75,000	150,000
	$160,000	$105,000	
Liabilities	$ 50,000	$ 45,000	$ 45,000
Common Stock	10,000	15,000	
Retained Earnings	100,000	45,000	
	$160,000	$105,000	

Required: Consider these cases. Case A: P purchased 100 percent of S's shares at December 31, 19X6, by paying $150,000 to shareholders of S. Case B: P purchased 75 percent of S's shares at December 31, 19X6, by paying $135,000 to shareholders of S. Case C: P purchased 75 percent of S's shares at December 31, 19X6, by paying $30,000 to shareholders of S. Assume that the market value of a patent owned by S was $55,000 on this date. For each case
1. Prepare the entry to record in P's books the purchase of S's shares.
2. Included in the purchase price was an amount in recognition of an undervaluation (overvaluation) in the asset patent. Calculate the amount of this undervaluation (or overvaluation).
3. Was any amount included in the purchase price in recognition of unrecorded goodwill in S? If so, calculate the amount of such goodwill.
4. Prepare the worksheet elimination enry needed to consolidate the individual balance sheets. (The preparation of a consolidated worksheet is not required in this problem.)
5. Prepare a consolidated balance sheet at December 31, 19X6 immediately after the purchase of S's shares.

Alternate Problem 17-4

On December 31, 19X2, P Corporation purchased a 70-percent interest in S Limited by paying $200,000 cash to the shareholders of S for their shares. The purchase price included an amount of an undervaluation of Fixed Assets and Bonds Payable and also an amount in recognition of goodwill in S. Here are the balance sheets of both corporations immediately after the purchase.

	P Book Value	S Book Value	S Market Value
Assets			
Current Assets	$ 65,000	$160,000	$160,000
Investment in Subsidiary	200,000	–	
Fixed Assets (net)	585,000	225,000	270,000
Goodwill	110,000	–	
	$960,000	$385,000	
Liabilities and Equities			
Current Liabilities	$ 50,000	$ 60,000	$ 60,000
Bonds Payable (5-year life)	200,000	100,000	115,000
Common Stock	250,000	75,000	
Retained Earnings	460,000	150,000	
	$960,000	$385,000	

Required: At the date of acquisition
1. Calculate the undervaluation of Fixed Assets and Bonds Payable.
2. Calculate the amount of goodwill included in the purchase price.
3. Calculate the amount of minority interest.
4. Prepare the worksheet elimination entry needed to consolidate the individual balance sheets. (The preparation of a consolidation worksheet is not required in this part of the problem.)
5. Prepare a consolidation worksheet at December 31, 19X2.

Alternate Problem 17-5

On December 31, 19X6, P Corporation purchased a 60-percent interest in S Limited, by paying $150,000 cash to shareholders of S for their shares. Included in this purchase price was an excess of cost over book value. At that date, P owed $15,000 to S; the amount is included as an accounts payable in P's books and as an accounts receivable in S's books. Immediately after the purchase, the balance sheets of both corporations appeared as follows:

	P Book Value	S Book Value	S Market Value
Cash and Other Assets	$ 90,000	$105,000	$109,000
Accounts Receivable	160,000	95,000	95,000
Investment in Subsidiary	150,000	–	
	$400,000	$200,000	
Accounts Payable	$ 60,000	$ 25,000	$ 25,000
Common Stock	225,000	100,000	
Retained Earnings	115,000	75,000	
	$400,000	$200,000	

Required:
1. Calculate the excess of cost over book value of the investment in S.
2. Prepare the worksheet elimination entries needed to consolidate the individual balance sheets.
3. Prepare a consolidation worksheet.
4. Prepare a consolidated balance sheet at December 31, 19X6 immediately after the purchase of S's share.

Review Problem

Review Problem 17-1

On December 31, 19X5, P Corporation purchased an interest in S Limited by paying cash to the shareholders of S for their shares. The following financial statements and other financial information are for that date, immediately before the purchase.

	P	S	
	Book Value	*Book Value*	*Market Value*
Cash and Other Assets	$500,000	$200,000	$60,000
Liabilities	$125,000	$ 60,000	
Common Stock	150,000	80,000	
Retained Earnings	225,000	60,000	
	$500,000	$200,000	

Required: Consider these cases. Case A: P purchased 100 percent of S's shares, by paying $140,000 cash. Case B: P purchased 100 percent of S's shares, by paying $180,000 cash. Case C: P purchased 70 percent of S's shares, by paying $98,000 cash. Case D: P purchased 70 percent of S's shares, by paying $110,000 cash. For each case:
1. Prepare the entry to record in P's book the purchase of S's shares.
2. Was any amount included in the purchase price in recognition of overvalued or undervalued assets in S? How can you tell? If applicable, calculate the amount.
3. Was any amount included in the purchase price in recognition of unrecorded goodwill in S? If so, calculate the amount of such goodwill.
4. Prepare the worksheet elimination entry needed to consolidate the individual balance sheets.
5. Prepare a consolidation worksheet for cases B and D only.
6. Prepare a consolidated balance sheet immediately after the purchase of S's shares.

Manufacturing Operations

The nature of a manufacturing business is different from that of a merchandiser. Some cost concepts are unique to a manufacturer. The classified statement of cost of goods manufactured and income statement facilitate the communication of information necessary for decision making.

1. How does the income statement of a manufacturer differ from that of a merchandiser?
2. What accounts are used only by a manufacturer?
3. What is *factory overhead*, and what does it include?
4. What type of inventory accounts are used by a manufacturer?
5. How do product and period costs differ?
6. At what point do product costs become period costs?
7. How does the worksheet for a manufacturer differ from that of a merchandiser?
8. How are opening and ending inventories recorded on a manufacturer's worksheet?
9. What is a Manufacturing Summary account, and why is one used?
10. What is the impact of the perpetual inventory method on manufacturing operations?

A. Manufacturing Cost Concepts

The income statement for a merchandising firm differs from that prepared for an entity involved in manufacturing operations. Merchandising involves the purchase and subsequent resale of goods, while a manufacturer's income statement emphasizes the production of these goods. This difference is indicated in the calculation of cost of goods sold.

Merchandising Operations		*Manufacturing Operations*	
Cost of Goods Sold:		*Cost of Goods Sold:*	
Opening Inventory	$ 4,000	Opening Finished Goods Inventory	$ 4,000
Cost of Goods Purchased	12,000	Cost of Goods Manufactured	12,000
Cost of Goods Available	$16,000	Cost of Goods Available	$16,000
Less: Ending Inventory	6,000	*Less:* Ending Finished Goods Inventory	6,000
Total Cost of Goods Sold	$10,000	Total Cost of Goods Sold	$10,000

The cost of goods purchased calculation for a merchandiser is comparable to the manufacturer's cost of goods manufactured. The merchandiser purchases finished goods for resale, while the manufacturer produces finished goods to be sold.

Manufacturing Costs

The manufacturing process requires several accounts to accumulate the specific costs incurred by manufacturers. These costs are grouped into three categories: (a) raw materials, (b) direct labour, and (c) factory overhead.

Raw Materials

Direct raw materials
The materials used in production that are identifiable in the final product.

Raw materials consist of the goods used in manufacturing the finished product. Usually, more raw materials are purchasd than are actually used during a given time period; the unused amount is the raw materials inventory. Bluebeard Computer Company's manufacturing operations assemble computer terminals from parts purchased from highly specialized manufacturers. Examples of raw materials for BCC's manufacturing include the computer monitor, keyboard, micro chips, cabinet, wiring. These are referred to as **direct raw materials** because they can be easily identified in the final product. Certain raw materials are not easily identified; these are referred to as **indirect raw materials** and are usually accounted for as overhead. Examples of indirect materials for BCC include supplies required for the assembly work, such as screws, nuts and bolts, glue, rivets.

Indirect raw materials
The materials used in production that cannot be easily identified in the final product; included as part of factory overhead.

Direct Labour

Direct labour
Wages paid to employees who are directly involved in manufacturing the product.

Direct labour consists of wage payments for employees directly involved in manufacturing the product. Employees who actually assemble computers are included in direct labour. The wages of employees — such as accountants, supervisors, payroll clerks, cleaners, executive assistants—who are not directly involved in manufacturing the product are referred to as **indirect labour**; their wages are usually accounted for as overhead.

Indirect labour
Wages paid to employees who are not directly involved in manufacturing the product; included as part of factory overhead.

Factory Overhead

Factory overhead
Manufacturing costs, other than direct raw materials and direct labour.

Factory overhead includes indirect materials, indirect labour, and all other costs incurred in the manufacturing process other than direct materials and direct labour. Factory overhead includes:

Plant depreciation and insurance
Heating and other utilities expense
Repairs and maintenance of the factory

Municipal taxes assessed on the factory
Cost of small tools
Employer's shares of payroll taxes

These and similar overhead expenses are only affected by relatively large changes in the level of production; reduced levels of output do not usually have the proportional effect on these expenses as they would on direct materials and direct labour. In other words, reduced output requires fewer direct materials and labour; factory overhead is not as immediately affected by changes in the level of output.

Product and Period Costs

Period costs
Costs identified with the time period in which they are incurred; not included in the cost of the product manufactured.

Product costs
Costs identified with the manufactured item; included in the calculation of the cost of work in process and finished goods inventory.

The manufacturer's income statement distinguishes between period and product costs. **Period costs** include non-manufacturing general and administrative expenses, in addition to selling expenses; these are payments that do not become part of product costs. They are identified with the time period in which they are incurred and are treated as expenses because the resources they represent are assumed to have been used up during the period. Period costs are disclosed on the income statement below the calculation of gross profit.

   Product costs include payments for direct raw materials, direct labour, and factory overhead; they become part of the product manufactured, the asset produced by the manufacturing process. Product costs represent an inventory asset until the manufactured goods are sold; accordingly, the costs of ending inventory are deducted from cost of goods manufactured in the calculation of gross profit. Ending inventory also appears as an asset in the balance sheet.

B. Manufacturing Income Statement

Production is often a continuous process and three different types of inventory usually exist at any given point in time: (a) raw materials, (b) work in process, and (c) finished goods.

Raw Materials Inventory

Raw materials inventory
The balance of raw materials purchased but not yet used in the production process.

Not all raw materials purchased are used immediately in the production process; the unused amount is the **raw materials inventory**. Any materials spoiled or lost during the manufacturing process are automatically included in the cost of materials used, since they do not appear in the ending inventory calculation. The cost of raw materials used during the accounting period is calculated as shown at the top of the next page.

Opening Raw Materials Inventory		$20,000
Purchases	$75,000	
Less: Purchases Returns and Allowances	$3,500	
Purchases Discounts	1,500	5,000
Net Purchases	$70,000	
Add: Transportation in	5,000	
Cost of Goods Purchased		75,000
Cost of Goods Available		$95,000
Less: Ending Raw Materials Inventory		35,000
Total Cost of Raw Materials Used		$60,000

Work in Process Inventory

Work in process inventory
The accumulated production costs during the manufacturing process.

Partially completed products are identified as **work in process inventory** at the end of an accounting period. Work in process inventory includes the amount of direct materials, labour, and factory overhead associated with the stage of completion for the partially completed units. The cost of work in process inventory at the end of the accounting period is calculated as follows:

Raw Materials Used	$ 60,000
Direct Labour	130,000
Factory Overhead	41,720
Total Manufacturing Costs	$231,720
Add: Opening Work in Process Inventory	15,000
Total Goods in Process	$246,720
Less: Ending Work in Process Inventory	25,000
Total Cost of Goods Manufactured	$221,720

Finished Goods Inventory

Finished goods inventory
An accumulation of goods manufactured but not yet sold.

All costs incurred in the manufacture of products completed but not yet sold are included in the **finished goods inventory**. The cost of finished goods inventory at the end of the accounting period is calculated as follows:

Opening Finished Goods Inventory	$ 45,000
Add: Cost of Goods Manufactured	221,720
Goods Available for Sale	$266,720
Less: Ending Finished Goods Inventory	60,000
Total Cost of Goods Sold	$206,720

A physical count of each of the three manufacturing inventories is taken at the end of every accounting time period. This physical count is used to calculate the amount of ending inventory. The periodic inventory system is used when the manufacturer has many different items in stock and when maintenance of detailed records would be expensive. Under the perpetual inventory system, a continuous balance of inventory on hand is calculated in terms of units and, often, also in terms of cost. A physical count of inventory at the end of an accounting period verifies the quantities actually on hand.

The Flow of Production Costs

The flow of production costs through work in process and finished goods inventories is illustrated in Figure 18-1.

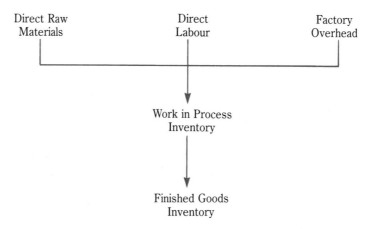

Figure 18-1   The flow of production costs

Calculation of Cost of Goods Manufactured

Cost of goods manufactured
A calculation of the cost of goods manufactured during the accounting time period.

The calculation of **cost of goods manufactured** and the balance sheet disclosure of ending inventories is illustrated below:

Bluebeard Computer Corporation
Cost of Goods Manufactured Statement
For the Year Ended December 31, 19X3

Raw Materials Used:

Opening Raw Materials Inventory	$20,000	
Cost of Goods Purchased (net)	75,000	
Cost of Goods Available	$95,000	
Less: Ending Raw Materials Inventory	35,000	
Total Cost of Raw Materials Used		$ 60,000
Direct Labour		$130,000

Factory Overhead:

Depreciation Expense — Machinery	$ 1,600	
Factory Supplies Used	6,000	
Indirect Labour	25,000	
Maintenance Expense	4,000	
Rent Expense	3,600	
Utilities Expense	1,520	
Total Factory Overhead		41,720
Total Manufacturing Costs		$231,720
Add: Opening Work in Process Inventory		15,000
Total Goods in Process		$246,720
Less: Ending Work in Process Inventory		25,000
Total Cost of Goods Manufactured		$221,720

Partial Balance Sheet
At December 31, 19X3

Assets

Cash		$ 10,800
Accounts Receivable		26,000
Inventories:		
Raw Materials	$35,000	
Work in Process	25,000	
Finished Goods	60,000	120,000

The cost of goods manufactured is added to the amount of opening finished goods inventory in the calculation of goods available for sale. The income statement then appears as follows:

Bluebeard Computer Corporation
Income Statement
For the Year Ended December 31, 19X3

Sales (net)			$300,000
Cost of Goods Sold:			
Opening Finished Goods Inventory		$ 45,000	
Cost of Goods Manufactured		221,720	
Goods Available for Sale		$266,720	
Less: Ending Finished Goods Inventory		60,000	
Total Cost of Goods Sold			206,720
Gross Profit			$ 93,280
OPERATING EXPENSES:			
Selling Expenses:			
Advertising Expense	$10,000		
Commissions Expense	15,000		
Delivery Expense	6,000		
Total Selling Expenses		$ 31,000	
General and Administrative Expenses:			
Insurance Expense	$ 1,200		
Salaries Expense	20,000		
Telephone Expense	1,080		
Total General and Administrative Expenses		22,280	
Total Operating Expenses			53,280
Income from Operations			$ 40,000
Financing Costs:			
Interest Expense			10,000
Income before Income Tax			$ 30,000
Income Tax			15,000
Net Income for the Year			$ 15,000

Note that period costs, consisting of selling, and general and administrative expenses, are classified separately from the product costs included in the cost of goods manufactured and cost of goods sold. Most product costs are readily identified as such and are included in these latter categories; however, some period costs require allocation between product cost and period expense categories. For example, insurance may be allocated to both factory overhead for the factory space and to general and administrative expenses for office space.

In actual practice, estimates are often used in allocating period costs. Sometimes the classification is made on the basis of expediency, particularly if the amounts involved are not material; insurance expenses, for example, which apply to both product cost and period cost categories, have not been allocated by Bluebeard because the amounts are immaterial.

In addition to these categories of period costs, it should be noted that product costs become period costs as finished goods inventory is sold. That is, cost of goods sold represent a period cost that is matched with sales revenue in the calculation of a gross profit amount.

C.   The Transactions Worksheet for a Manufacturer

A manufacturer's worksheet differs from that prepared for a merchandiser in several respects. First, an additional pair of columns labelled "Cost of Goods Manufactured" is used to gather all costs subsequently reported in the cost of goods manufactured statement. All manufacturing costs are extended to these columns. Second, the opening inventory balances for raw materials and work in process are extended to the cost of goods manufactured columns; the opening finished goods inventory is extended to the income statement columns, as is the case for a merchandiser.

The worksheet procedure for raw materials, work in process, and finished goods inventories is as follows:

1. Opening raw materials inventory appears in the trial balance as the opening work in process inventory. These amounts have not changed during the year because Bluebeard follows the periodic inventory system to record the purchase of merchandise for resale.
2. These opening inventory amounts are transferred to the cost of goods manufactured debit columns, because they are used in the calculation of the cost of goods manufactured amount on the income statement.
3. The amounts of ending raw materials and work in process inventories are recorded directly on the worksheet:
   a. as credits in the cost of goods manufactured columns, because they are later used in the calculation of cost of goods manufactured
   b. as debits in the balance sheet columns, because they represent the amount of raw materials and work in process inventories at year-end; assets that appear in the balance sheet require a worksheet debit balance.
4. The beginning finished goods inventory is carried from the adjusted trial balance to the debit income statement column. The ending finished goods inventory is recorded in the income statement credit column and the balance sheet debit column.

The recording of the ending raw materials, work in process, and finished goods inventories amounts into the records is discussed later in this chapter.

Bluebeard Computer Corporation
Manufacturing Worksheet
For the Year Ended December 31, 19X3

Account Title	Trial Balance Dr.	Trial Balance Cr.	Adjustments Dr.	Adjustments Cr.	Cost of Goods Manufactured Dr.	Cost of Goods Manufactured Cr.	Income Statement Dr.	Income Statement Cr.	Balance Sheet Dr.	Balance Sheet Cr.
Cash	10,800								10,800	
Accounts Receivable	26,000								26,000	
Raw Materials Inventory	20,000				20,000	35,000			35,000	
Work in Process										
Inventory	15,000				15,000	25,000			25,000	
Finished Goods										
Inventory	45,000						45,000	60,000	60,000	
Prepaid Insurance	2,400			(a) 1,200					1,200	
Equipment	13,600								13,600	
Accumulated										
Depreciation				(d) 1,600						1,600
Bank Loan—Current		39,000								39,000
Accounts Payable		25,000								25,000
Income Tax Payable				(c)15,000						15,000
Bank Loan—Long-Term		48,500								48,500
Common Stock		10,000								10,000
Retained Earnings		21,750								21,750
Dividends	4,250								4,250	
Sales		308,500						308,500		
Sales Returns and										
Allowances	6,000						6,000			
Sales Discounts	2,500						2,500			
Raw Materials Purchases	75,000				75,000					
Raw Materials Purchases										
Returns and Allowances		3,500				3,500				
Raw Materials Purchases										
Discounts		1,500				1,500				
Transportation In	5,000				5,000					
Direct Labour Expense	130,000				130,000					
Indirect Labour Expense	25,000				25,000					
Factory Supplies Used	6,000				6,000					
Maintenance Expense	4,000				4,000					
Rent Expense	3,600				3,600					
Utilities Expense	1,520				1,520					
Advertising Expense	10,000						10,000			
Commissions Expense	15,000						15,000			
Delivery Expense	6,000						6,000			
Interest Expense	10,000						10,000			
Salaries Expense	20,000						20,000			
Telephone Expense	1,080						1,080			
Totals	457,750	457,750								
Insurance Expenses			(a) 1,200				1,200			
Depreciaton Expense			(b) 1,600		1,600					
Income Tax Expense			(c)15,000				15,000			
Totals			17,800	17,800	286,720	65,000				
Cost of Goods										
Manufactured						221,720	221,720			
					286,720	286,720	353,500	368,500	175,850	160,850
Net Income for the Year							15,000			15,000
Totals							368,500	368,500	175,850	175,850

Real Life Example 18-1
Just in Time

There is no ignoring what has happened over the past two decades concerning the impact that foreign competition has had on the economy.

North American business executives complain that they cannot compete with foreign competition. In the manufacturing sector of the economy it appears as if a greater proportion of goods is coming from overseas.

Who is to blame for this malaise in manufacturing?

The primary reason why our manufacturing has taken a backseat to foreign competition is our attitude toward it. We have been concerned about the marketing and financial aspects of the end product, and have assumed that the manufacturing process would respond. This has been the problem. Manufacturing should be an integral part of the total business planning process. We must better understand the role of manufacturing strategy, trade-offs, and planning and executive techniques if we are to gain and maintain a competitive advantage.

Manufacturing Strategy as a Competitive Weapon

One of the best ways to make manufacturing a competitive weapon is to incorporate the Just-in-Time (JIT) philosophy within the manufacturing plant. JIT means minimal inventory and the elimination of waste in the manufacturing process. When a part is needed in the production process, it arrives at a work center just in time — not before. In essence, the raw material stockroom can be eliminated. This, however, requires precise planning of production schedules — something that the Japanese have perfected, but that American companies have often overlooked.

By making JIT a cornerstone of the manufacturing strategy, and utilizing this approach as a key competitive weapon, the results would be indeed significant. Manufacturers would be able to reduce inventory and production lead times by approximately 75 percent, cut labour costs by 10 percent to 30 percent, reduce set-up times by 75 percent, warehousing by 50 percent, and improve the quality of manufacturing by 75 percent to 90 percent.

How to Get Started

The key priority in eliminating waste under the JIT concept is to reduce the time needed to set up manufacturing tools. If set-up time can be reduced, you do not need to manufacture volume to justify the set-up cost. If the set-up cost can be reduced, and you can produce in one hour what used to take five hours, you can manufacture in smaller lots — 10 to 20 rather than 100 to 1000. What this means is that the production is based upon the demands of the market rather than the economic constraints of the manufacturing process.

Closing Entries

The preparation of year-end closing entries for a manufacturer requires an additional intermediate account called Manufacturing Summary. The debit and credit balances in the cost of goods manufactured columns are closed to the Manufacturing Summary account.

Entry 1: **Closing the Debit Balance Accounts**
The opening Raw Materials Inventory and Work in Process Inventory balances, in addition to other cost of goods manufactured accounts with a debit balance, are closed to Manufacturing Summary.

Entry 2: **Closing the Credit Balance Accounts**
The ending Raw Materials Inventory and ending Work in Process Inventory balances, in addition to other cost of goods manufactured accounts with a credit balance, are next closed to Manufacturing Summary.

The data from the transactions worksheet of BCC's manufacturing operations are used to illustrate preparation of these closing entries.

When set-up time is reduced, and the worker is available to do something else, the traditional linear step-by-step production pattern can be eliminated in favour of manufacturing cells. A manufacturing cell is comprised of machines grouped in a family to perform, in sequence, a variety of operations. With this approach, one machine feeds the work to another, so that products flow through them from start to finish. There are no parts sitting on the floor, waiting to be worked on, and materials no longer have to move from one end of the plant to another. In essence, a plant within a plant is created to minimize manufacturing lead time and excessive waste. This type of manufacturing process can be seen in the figure below.

For example, a client produced medical instruments in lots of 50 units. The normal manufacturing time took six weeks because parts traveled long distances between departments.

Adding sophisticated manufacturing software coupled with factory automation would not have solved the problem. The manufacturing flow had to be addressed as the ultimate cause of the problem. The manufacturing equipment was regrouped into U-shaped cells, with each cell performing a variety of functions in sequence. Now the medical instruments are manufactured in two to three days, because they travel only a few hundred feet in total. The reduction in manufacturing lead time has allowed this company to produce a high quality product at reduced cost, and, more importantly, to be much more responsive to market demand.

Source Manufacturing Strategy as a Key Competitive Weapon, *The CPA Journal*, February 1986, pp. 86–87.

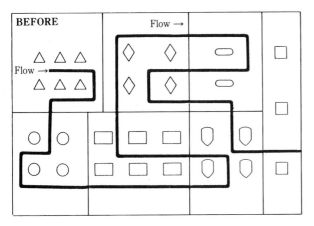

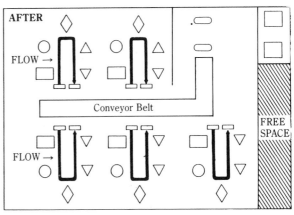

19X3	*Closing Entries*		
Dec. 31	Manufacturing Summary	286,720	
	Raw Materials Inventory (opening)		20,000
	Work in Process Inventory (opening)		15,000
	Raw Materials Purchases		75,000
	Transportation In		5,000
	Direct Labour		130,000
	Indirect Labour		25,000
	Depreciation Expense — Equipment		1,600
	Factory Supplies Used		6,000
	Maintenance Expense		4,000
	Rent Expense		3,600
	Utilities Expense		1,520
	To close opening inventories and cost of goods manufactured accounts with a debit balance.		
31	Raw Materials Inventory (ending)	35,000	
	Work in Process Inventory (ending)	25,000	
	Raw Materials Purchases Returns and Allowances	3,500	
	Raw Materials Purchases Discounts	1,500	
	Manufacturing Summary		65,000
	To record ending inventories and to close manufacturing accounts with a credit balance.		

The income statement columns of the worksheet are next closed. The preparation of these closing entries follows the format for a merchandiser discussed in chapters 4 and 5.

Entry 3:   **Closing the Expense Accounts**
The opening Finished Goods Inventory balance, other accounts with a debit balance, and the Manufacturing Summary account are then closed to Income Summary.

Entry 4:   **Closing the Revenue Accounts**
The ending Finished Goods Inventory balance and other accounts with a credit balance are closed to Income Summary.

Entry 5:   **Closing the Income Summary Account**
The Income Summary account is then closed to Retained Earnings.

Entry 6:   **Closing the Dividend Account**
The Dividend account is closed to Retained Earnings.

Dec. 31	Income Summary	353,500	
	Finished Goods Inventory (opening)		45,000
	Sales Returns and Allowances		6,000
	Sales Discounts		2,500
	Advertising Expense		10,000
	Commissions Expense		15,000
	Delivery Expense		6,000
	Insurance Expense		1,200
	Interest Expense		10,000
	Salaries Expense — Office		20,000
	Salaries Expense — Sales		1,080
	Income Tax Expense		15,000
	Manufacturing Summary		221,720
	To close opening inventory and to close income statement accounts with a debit balance.		
	Finished Goods Inventory (ending)	60,000	
	Sales	308,500	
	Income Summary		368,500
	To record ending inventory and to close income statement accounts with a credit balance.		
	Income Summary	15,000	
	Retained Earnings		15,000
	To close Income Summary account.		
	Retained Earnings	4,250	
	Dividends		4,250
	To close Dividends account.		

Once all six closing entries have been posted, all manufacturing, revenue, expense, and dividends accounts have a zero balance. The accounts with a remaining balance are the opening balances of asset, liability, and equity accounts in the new fiscal year.

D. Cost Accounting Systems and Inventory Valuation

The periodic inventory method is used in this chapter to illustrate accounting for manufacturing operations. This method is useful for small single-product manufacturers, particularly when the cost of maintaining more detailed records would be expensive. Inventories are physically counted whenever financial statements are prepared; a cost of goods sold is then calculated. This method is less useful for large manufacturers that require frequent financial statements in addition to continuous information about production costs for decision making and control. In actual practice, perpetual inventory systems are used to facilitate both inventory costing and financial statement preparation. Cost accounting systems, therefore, incorporate the use of perpetual inventory.

Costing Manufacturers' Inventories

The preceding sections of this chapter introduced the different types of manufacturing inventories, including raw materials, work in process, and finished goods. The cost of raw materials can be easily determined by reference to purchases documents. Calculating the cost of work in process and finished goods is more complex, however, since it includes all or part of each of raw materials, direct labour, and factory overhead components. The amount and cost of raw materials and direct labour in work in process for example, are often estimated as an average quantity, which is then multiplied by an individually calculated cost amount applicable to both raw materials and direct labour. These costs are directly related to the units being manufactured. Factory overhead, however, is **Factory overhead rate** indirectly related to production units. For this reason, a **factory overhead rate** is A predetermined rate established; this rate is used to allocate total factory overhead not only to units still in used to allocate total process at year-end but also to units completed during the year. A relationship is often factory overhead to work established between direct labour costs and factory overhead costs. For example, in in process and finished 19X3 for Bluebeard Computer Corporation, direct labour is $130,000 and factory over-goods. head amounts to $41,720. As calculated, Bluebeard incurred approximately $0.32 of factory overhead for each direct labour dollar. Using these amounts, an overhead rate of 32 percent of the amount of direct labour incurred could be used for overhead cost allocation. The total cost of work in process and finished goods inventories includes an allocated overhead amount, as well as the cost of raw materials and direct labour appropriate to the completion stage of the work in process.

Discussion Questions

1. How do the financial statements of a manufacturing firm and a merchandising firm differ?
2. What accounts are used for a manufacturing firm that are not used for a merchandising or a service firm?
3. What is *factory overhead*, and what does it include?
4. Why are several inventory accounts used by manufacturers?
5. What is the difference between period and product costs?
6. When do product costs become period costs?
7. Explain how the transactions worksheet for a manufacturing firm differs from that for a merchandising firm.
8. How are opening and ending inventories recorded on a manufacturer's worksheet?
9. What is a Manufacturing Summary account, and how is one used?
10. How does a perpetual inventory system affect a manufacturing firm?

Discussion Cases

Discussion Case 18-1:   Software Costing

Quite a few items go into producing a software package: the diskette itself, the labels, and the envelope or sleeve to cover it. Other elements include printed documentation, reference or registration cards, the packaging (such as the vinyl folders in which PC software is often sold), and possibly colour-printed wrap-around or shrink-wrap.

Acceptable quality single-sided diskettes cost $1.30 to $1.70 each. The advertisements in *P.C. Magazine* and other computer magazines are a good place to shop for volume diskette suppliers. You'll find that prices are much lower than you'd pay at retail computer stores—after all, we're talking whole-sale here.

To label your diskettes, you could have custom die-cut labels made. If you don't want to get fancy, you can buy standard ones at a paper supply house or stationery store, for instance, Avery labels number 5523, which cost about $0.01 each. You can have them printed at a neighbourhood quick-printing store for a cost of about $0.01 for each colour print. Let's price labels at $0.03 each.

Envelopes may come free with the diskettes, although bulk-price diskettes without envelopes are often cheaper. If you want customized printed envelopes, a supplier can make them up for you. Expect to pay $0.05 to $0.20 for each envelope.

Copying the diskettes is another element. You may do it yourself at no cost. When you're starting out, in low volume, that can be reasonable.

Another option is to employ a diskette copying service. Copying runs about $0.30 to $0.50 per diskette. That may seem steep, but it can save you time and trouble and give you a technically much higher-quality copy. For the cost estimate we're building, let's take a range of zero (do-it-yourself) to $0.40.

Next let's consider the documentation. The price varies greatly by the size, number of copies, and number of colors printed. Games usually do nicely with just a few pages of documentation. . . . You might expect a range of costs from $0.20 to $1 each, and that's what we'll work with here. You should be able to find local printers that can handle the full job for you—printing, collating, and stapling. Many printers also can arrange typography and layout work for you; or you can use a graphics arts service to produce the camera-ready art that a printer needs. Many services are prepared to set type from files on a PC diskette, which can save you the cost of having a typesetter keyboard your documentation and also avoid the typos that usually come with re-keying.

Packaging is the next major item. Thanks to IBM's lead, two kinds of program packaging have become standards for the PC. One is the slip-case three-ring binder such as ones that encase the DOS and BASIC manuals; the other is a small vinyl folder that holds a diskette and a pamphlet.

We're not really discussing big-league programs here, so the vinyl folder is the sort that we're likely to want. These folders have to be custom-made to your specifications, and most large cities have several companies that specialize in this sort of work. Prices seem to range from $0.80 to $1.20 each. We'll take $1 as a typical price.

To complete your packaging, you may want an eye-catching four-colour, paper cover on one side of the package, similar to the wrapper IBM uses on many of the games it publishes. I'll guess that this small extravagance (which, by the way, makes good marketing sense) will cost $0.10 each. If you shrink-wrap your package in clear plastic, add another $0.10 or $0.20. (A consideration against shrink-wrap is that it prevents potential buyers from being able to browse through the documentation booklet.)

The total production cost of a small software package is about $3.85 per copy.

$1.30 Diskette
 0.30 Copying
 0.15 Envelopes
 0.10 Labels, cards
 0.50 Documentation
 1.00 Vinyl folder
 0.25 Colour card, shrink-wrap
 0.25 Your labour

The figures used to produce this total are based on a reasonably high volume of program sets.

Source Peter Norton, ''The Kitchen Table Software Handbook'', *P.C. Magazine*, June 12, 1984, pp. 119–225.

For Discussion

1. What other issues should you explore before undertaking to manufacture your own software program diskettes?
2. How does the size of a manufacturing operation influence the overhead costs? What are the advantages and disadvantages of a small manufacturer, as opposed to a larger company?

Discussion Case 18-2:   How the U.S. Navy Paid $436 for a $7 Hammer

How did the United States Navy end up paying $436 ($562 in 1984 Canadian dollars) for a hammer that costs $7 (Cdn $9) in a neighbourhood hardware store?

The admirals have given congress the following breakdown of their contract with a defence contractor, identified as Gould Inc., headquartered in suburban Maryland, for: ''hammer, hand, sledge — quality one each''. Cost of the basic hammer is $7. Then add, for each hammer, the following costs (in US$):

— $41 to pay general overhead cost of Gould's engineering staff involved in mapping out the hammer problem. This figure also includes 12 minutes in secretarial time preparing the hammer purchase order, 26 minutes of management time spent on the hammer purchase and 2 hours and 36 minutes the engineers spent mulling over the proper design of the hammer.
— $93 for the 18 minutes it took for ''mechanical sub-assembly'' of the hammer, 4 hours for engineers to map out the hammer assembly process, 90 minutes spent by managers overseeing the hammer manufacturing process, 60 minutes for a project engineer to ensure the hammer was properly assembled, 54 minutes spent by quality control engineers examining the hammer to ensure it didn't have any defects, and 7 hours and 48 minutes devoted to other support activities involved in assembling the hammer.
— $102 went toward ''manufacturing overhead''.
— $37 for 60 minutes Gould's ''spares/repair department'' spent gearing up for either repairing or finding parts, should the hammer ever break.
— $2 for ''material handling overhead'' representing the payroll costs for the people to wrap the hammer and send it out.
— $1 for wrapping paper and a box.

This brought the sub-total of costs for the hammer to $283. This figure was multiplied by a factor of 31.8 percent, representing general administrative costs for Gould, and another $56 was added in a finders' fee given Gould for locating the sort of specific hammer that fitted the navy's needs.

Another $7 was given Gould for the ''capital cost of money'' Gould expended in the hammer purchase.

''How do we explain a system that allows this to happen to our taxpayers?'' protested Rep. Berkley Bedell (Democrat — Iowa), who obtained the navy's explanation for the costly hammer.

A navy official explained that large defence contractors, such as Gould, are permitted to charge off general costs against all contracted items and that, in the case of relatively inexpensive items, these costs may appear disproportionately large.

Source Scripps-Howard News Service, ''How U.S. Navy paid $562 for a $9 hammer'', *The* (Montreal) *Gazette*, May 19, 1984, p. G-8.

For Discussion

1. Calculate the overhead rate for Gould Inc., using data from this article. Do you think Gould uses this rate for all its products? for all its customers? Why?
2. Comment on Congressman Bedell's question.
3. Should the navy purchase a hammer at a neighbourhood hardware store? How can it control the cost of such relatively inexpensive items?

Comprehension Problems

Comprehension Problem 18-1

The Polywog Toy Corporation of Port Hope, Ontario manufactures and distributes to retailers its best-selling toy, "The Polywog". This toy is aimed at the young adult market and is similar to Rubik's Cube. The manufacture and assembly of The Polywog requires plastic, springs, paint, as well as skilled workers. Once assembled, The Polywog is placed in a cardboard box and sealed.

Required: Classify each of the following costs as: Materials, Direct Labour, Factory Overhead, Selling Costs, or Administrative Costs, and state whether each is a period or a product cost.
a. Freight out
b. Sales commissions
c. Accounting fees paid to Clarkson Gordon
d. Port Hope municipal taxes assessed to the factory
e. Lubricants for the machines
f. Plastic to be injected into the moulds
g. Cardboard to make the boxes
h. Overtime paid to workers
i. A wrench to fix the conveyor belt
j. An executive training program.

Comprehension Problem 18-2

Following are manufacturing costs for the Northumberland Boat Works Ltd., of Souris, PEI. Northumberland Boat Works manufactures small fishing and lobster boats. Consider the following data for 19X0.

Grease (used for tools and construction)	$ 2,500	Finished Goods — Beginning (1 boat)	$ 24,100
Rent — Manufacturing Shed	15,000	Finished Goods — Ending (1 boat)	25,200
Direct Labour	110,000	Work in Process — Beginning	28,200
Indirect Materials	1,500	Work in Process — Ending	50,400
Factory Utilities	4,600	General Administrative Expenses	50,000
Insurance — Shed	1,200	Raw Materials — Beginning	21,000
Purchases of Raw Materials	110,000	Raw Materials — Ending	7,400

Required:
1. Prepare a statement of the cost of goods manufactured.
2. Why did the boat built at the beginning of the year cost less than the one being built at the close of the year?

Comprehension Problem 18-3

Jackie Kaiser works as an assembler in the Ford plant in Oakville, Ontario. Last week, she worked 52 hours; during the week, she was idle for 2 hours while there was a back-up in the installation of the rack-and-pinion steering to the main chassis assembly. In the remaining 50 hours, Kaiser spent 49 directly on the manufacture of a new Ford "Taurus". The other hour Kaiser spent in a meeting of the Management-Employee Safety Committee. Kaiser is paid $12.00 per hour for 40 hours a week; she is paid time and a half for work in excess of 40 hours and double time for work in excess of 50 hours per week.

Required: Allocate Jackie Kaiser's wages between direct labour costs and factory overhead.

Comprehension Problem 18-4

The Genero Copier Corporation manufactures its photocopiers for specific orders, which are then sold by several retailers of office equipment under their own brand name. The following information is available about a job that is being prepared under company job number 1067-GHB-376.

Direct Materials issued:
   1000 circuits for assembly: 109.55 per circuit
   1000 photo lens attachments: $153.95 each
   Plastic casing fluid: 10 000 kL at $0.13/kL
   Electric wire: 10 000m at $0.02/m
   Direct labour: 2200 hours at $8/h
   The overhead rate for the factory is $3/h per each direct labour hour.
   Unused material returned: 2000kL of plastic fluid
   Photocopiers started: 1000
   Photocopiers completed: 880
   Photocopiers sold: 240

Required:
   1. Calculate the unit cost of production.
   2. Prepare journal entries to record these transactions.

Problems

Problem 18-1

The following compound closing entry is taken from the records of Nagys Manufacturing Ltd. at December 31, 19X8 its fiscal year-end.

Dec. 31	Raw Materials Inventory	12,000	
	Work in Process Inventory	9,000	
	Raw Materials Purchases Returns and Allowances	5,000	
	Raw Materials Purchases Discounts	1,000	
	Manufacturing Summary	601,000	
	Raw Materials Inventory		10,000
	Work in Process Inventory		15,000
	Raw Materials Purchases		100,000
	Transportation In		3,000
	Direct Labour		300,000
	Indirect Labour		75,000
	Depreciation Expense — Machinery		40,000
	Factory Supplies Used		4,000
	Rent Expense		36,000
	Maintenance Expense		25,000
	Utilities Expense		20,000
	To close manufacturing accounts		
	and set up Manufacturing Summary.		

Required:
   1. Calculate the net cost of materials purchased during 19X8. (Use the form in section B of the chapter.)
   2. Prepare a statement of cost of goods manufactured for 19X8 in proper form. Include the net cost of goods purchased amount calculated in 1 above.
   3. How much factory overhead was incurred in 19X8 for each dollar of direct labour?

Problem 18-2

The following information is extracted from the worksheet of Hobo Corporation at December 31, 19X8, its fiscal year-end.

	Cost of Goods Manufactured		Income Statement	
	Dr.	Cr.	Dr.	Cr.
Raw Materials Inventory	36,000	40,000		
Work in Process Inventory	66,000	90,000		
Finished Goods Inventory			60,000	75,000
Sales				1,171,800
Net Cost of Goods Purchased	300,000			
Direct Labour Expense	360,000			
Indirect Labour Expense	100,000			
Depreciation Expense — Machinery	40,000			
Factory Supplies Used	15,000			
Maintenance Expense	7,000			
Rent Expense	48,000			
Small Tools Used	10,000			
Advertising Expense			48,820	
Commissions Expense			117,180	
Delivery Expense			10,640	
Insurance Expense (office)			8,600	
Salaries Expense (office)			39,000	
Telephone Expense			3,600	
Interest Expense			40,000	
Income Tax Expense			33,480	
Totals	982,000	130,000		
Cost of Goods Manufactured		852,000	852,000	
	982,000	982,000	1,213,320	1,246,800
Net Income for the Year			33,480	
			1,246,800	1,246,800

Required:
1. Prepare a statement of cost of goods manufactured in proper form for the year ended December 31, 19X8.
2. Prepare a classified income statement for the year ended December 31, 19X8.
3. Prepare all necessary closing entries at December 31, 19X8.

Problem 18-3

The trial balance and adjustments columns of Baron Corporation worksheet at December 31, 19X6, its fiscal year-end, are reproduced below.

Account Title	Trial Balance Dr.	Cr.	Adjustments Dr.	Cr.
Cash	12,000			
Raw Materials Inventory	58,300			
Work in Process Inventory	31,725			
Finished Goods Inventory	25,000			
Prepaid Insurance	2,100			(b) 800
Equipment (factory)	16,000			
Accumulated Depreciation		4,000		(a) 2,500
Accounts Payable		27,000		
Common Stock		125,000		
Retained Earnings		24,000		
Dividends	10,000			
Sales		308,625		
Raw Materials Purchases (net)	91,000			
Transportation In	1,000			
Direct Labour Expense	98,000			
Indirect Labour Expense	27,000			
Maintenance Expense	7,000			
Rent Expense (factory)	12,000			
Small Tools Used	2,000			
Advertising Expense	6,000			
Commission Expense	50,000			
Delivery Expense	2,000			
Rent Expense (office)	4,000			
Salaries Expense (office)	29,500			
Telephone Expense (office)	4,000			
Totals	488,625	488,625		
Depreciation Expense			(a) 2,500	
Insurance Expense (factory)			(b) 800	
Income Tax Expense			(c) 4,800	
Income Tax Payable				(c) 4,800
Totals			8,100	8,100

Ending Inventories, December 31, 19X8:

Raw Materials	$69,000
Work in Process	52,000
Finished Goods	50,000

Required:
1. Complete the manufacturing worksheet from the data given.
2. Prepare a cost of goods manufactured statement.
3. Prepare a classified income statement.

Problem 18-4

The following account balances are taken from the records of Fearon Freezing Ltd. at December 31, 19X6, the corporation's fiscal year-end.

	January 1	December 31
Raw Materials Inventory	65,000	52,000
Work in Process Inventory	50,000	120,000
Finished Goods Inventory	120,000	140,000
Raw Materials Purchases (net)		970,000
Transportation In		12,500
Direct Labour		80,000
Indirect Labour		40,000
Depreciation Expense — Factory Machinery		65,500
Factory Supplies Used		60,900
Rent Expense — Factory		120,000
Small Tools Used		16,560
Advertising Expense		20,150
Commissions Expense		185,460
Delivery Expense		46,500
Rent Expense — Office		12,900
Salaries Expense — Office		60,350

Required:

1. Prepare a statement of cost of goods manufactured in proper form for the year ended December 31, 19X6.
2. Prepare the cost of goods sold section of the income statement.
3. Assuming that a relationship between direct labour and factory overhead exists in this corporation, calculate how much factory overhead was incurred for each direct labour dollar.
4. Prepare all necessary closing entries at December 31, 19X6.

Alternate Problems

Alternate Problem 18-1

The following compound closing entry is taken from the records of Yasutis Manufacturing Corp. at December 31, 19X5, the corporation's fiscal year-end.

Dec. 31	Raw Materials Inventory	48,000	
	Work in Process Inventory	36,000	
	Raw Materials Purchases Returns and Allowances	20,000	
	Raw Materials Purchases Discounts	3,200	
	Manufacturing Summary	1,604,800	
	Raw Materials Inventory		40,000
	Work in Process Inventory		60,000
	Raw Materials Purchases		400,000
	Transportation In		12,000
	Direct Labour		800,000
	Indirect Labour		75,000
	Depreciation Expense — Machinery		160,000
	Factory Heating		44,000
	Factory Insurance		50,000
	Factory Supplies Used		46,000
	Maintenance Expense		25,000
	To close manufacturing accounts		
	and set up Manufacturing Summary.		

1. Calculate the net cost of materials purchased during 19X4.
2. Prepare a statement of cost of goods manufactured for 19X4 in proper form. Include the net cost of materials purchased calculated in 1, above.
3. How much factory overhead was incurred in 19X4 for each dollar of direct labour?

Alternate Problem 18-2

The following infomration is extracted from the worksheet of Kitowski Corporation at December 31, 19X8, its fiscal year-end.

	Cost of Goods Manufactured		Income Statement	
	Dr.	Cr.	Dr.	Cr.
Raw Materials Inventory	52,000	65,000		
Work in Process Inventory	110,000	84,000		
Finished Goods Inventory			65,000	67,000
Sales				1,285,600
Raw Materials Purchases (net)	290,000			
Transportation In	6,500			
Direct Labour Expense	450,000			
Indirect Labour Expense	123,000			
Depreciation — Machinery	45,000			
Insurance Expense	5,000			
Maintenance Expense	6,700			
Rent Expense	12,000			
Utilities Expense	8,000			
Advertising Expense			3,000	
Commissions Expense			82,000	
Depreciation Expense — Truck			12,000	
Insurance Expense (truck)			3,000	
Office Supplies Used			9,000	
Salaries Expense (office)			49,000	
Telephone Expense			5,000	
Income Tax Expense			24,870	
Totals	1,108,200	149,000		
Cost of Goods Manufactured		959,200	959,200	
	1,108,200	1,108,200	1,212,070	1,352,600
Net Income for the year			140,530	
			1,352,600	1,352,600

Required:
1. Prepare a statement of cost of goods manufactured in proper format for the year ended December 31, 19X8.
2. Prepare a classified income statement for the year ended December 31, 19X8.
3. Prepare all necessary closing entries at December 31, 19X8.

Alternate Problem 18-3

The trial balance and adjustments columns of Herauf Corporation's worksheet at December 31, 19X9, its fiscal year-end, are reproduced below.

Account Title	Trial Balance Dr.	Trial Balance Cr.	Adjustments Dr.	Adjustments Cr.
Cash	15,800			
Raw Materials Inventory	20,000			
Work in Process Inventory	25,000			
Finished Goods Inventory	85,000			
Prepaid Rent	6,000			(b) 6,000
Equipment (factory)	13,000			
Accumulated Depreciation				(a) 4,000
Accounts Payable		26,000		
Common Stock		35,000		
Retained Earnings		21,000		
Dividends	4,200			
Sales		408,000		
Raw Materials Purchases	83,200			
Transportation	6,000			
Direct Labour	120,000			
Indirect Labour	15,000			
Maintenance Expense	6,000			
Advertising Expense	10,000			
Commissions Expense	36,000			
Delivery Expense	7,000			
Insurance Expense (office)	3,000			
Salaries Expense (office)	27,000			
Telephone Expense (office)	1,800			
Utilities Expense (office)	6,000			
Totals	490,000	490,000		
Depreciation Expense			(a) 4,000	
Rent Expense (factory)			(b) 6,000	
Income Tax Expense			(c) 15,000	
Income Tax Payable				(c) 15,000
Totals			25,000	25,000

Ending Inventories, December 31, 19X8	
Raw Material	$25,000
Work in Process	27,000
Finished Goods	80,000

Required:
1. Complete the manufacturing worksheet.
2. Prepare a cost of goods manufactured statement.
3. Prepare a classified income statement.

Chapter 2

[1] From an *amicus curiae* brief submitted by the American Institute of Certified Public Accountants in a 1968 legal case. Quoted by Howard Ross, *Financial Statements: A Crusade for Current Values* (Toronto, 1969), p. 50.

[2] Ray G. Harris, "A Message from the President", *CA Magazine*, June 1981, p. 5.

[3] FASB, "Scope and Implications of the Conceptual Framework Project" (Stanford, Conn., 1976), p. 1.

Chapter 3

[1] FASB, Statement of Financial Accounting Concept No. 3, *Elements of Financial Statements of Business Enterprises* (December 1980), para. 19, 28, 63, 65, 67, 68.

Chapter 5

[1] Miriam Medom, "News and Notes for the Computing Community", *P.C. World*, May 1984, p. 39.

[2] *Financial Reporting in Canada*, a CICA publication, reports that 171 companies surveyed used the recount form of balance sheet, while 135 used the report form. *FRIC*, 16th ed. (Toronto, 1985), p. 96.

Chapter 8

[1] Henry Rand Hatfield, *Accounting: Its Principles and Problems* (New York, 1927), p. 256.

Chapter 9

[1] Henry Rand Hatfield, *Accounting: Its Principles and Problems* (New York, 1927), p. 130.

Chapter 11

[1] C. A. Barker, "Evaluation of Stock Dividends", *Harvard Business Review*, vol. 36 (July-August 1958), 99–114. Barker's study has been replicated several times in recent years, and his results are still valid — they have withstood the test of time. Another excellent study, using an entirely different methodology yet reaching similar conclusions, is that of E. Fama, L. Fisher, M. C. Jensen, and R. Roll, "The Adjustment of Stock Prices to New Information", *International Economic Review*, February 1969, 1–21.

A follow-up study to Fama, *et al.* that further refines their method is S. Bar-Yosef and L. D. Brown, "A Re-examination of Stock Splits Using Moving Betas)", *Journal of Finance*, September 1977, 1069–1080.

Chapter 17

[1] For a full treatment, refer to: Thomas H. Beechy, *Canadian Advanced Financial Accounting* (Toronto: Holt, Rinehart and Winston of Canada, Limited, 1985), ch. 6–12.

[2] Beechy, p. 196.

INDEX

Those terms with a page reference appearing in boldface indicate where the margin glossary definition will be found.

INDEX OF CASES, CONCEPTUAL ISSUES AND REAL LIFE EXAMPLES BY SUBJECT

To the Owner of this Book

We are interested in your reaction to Henry Dauderis'
**Financial Accounting: An Introduction to Decision
Making**. Through feedback from you, we may be able to
improve this book in future editions.

1. What was your reason for using this book?

_____ college course

_____ university course

_____ continuing education

_____ other (specify)

2. If you used this text for a program, what was the name of that program?

3. Which chapters or sections were omitted from your course?

4. Have you any suggestions for improving this text?

Fold here

- -

**Business
Reply Mail**

No Postage Stamp
Necessary if mailed
in Canada

43652

POSTAGE WILL BE PAID BY

    RICHARD KITOWSKI
      Publisher
College Division
HOLT, RINEHART AND WINSTON
  OF CANADA, LIMITED
55 HORNER AVENUE
TORONTO, ONTARIO
M8Z 9Z9

Tape shut

(Continued from front endpapers)